Law, Governance and Technology Series

Volume 68

The *Law, Governance and Technology Series* is intended to attract manuscripts arising from an interdisciplinary approach in law, artificial intelligence and information technologies. The idea is to bridge the gap between research in IT law and IT-applications for lawyers developing a unifying techno-legal perspective. The series will welcome proposals that have a fairly specific focus on problems or projects that will lead to innovative research charting the course for new interdisciplinary developments in law, legal theory, and law and society research as well as in computer technologies, artificial intelligence and cognitive sciences. In broad strokes, manuscripts for this series may be mainly located in the fields of the Internet law (data protection, intellectual property, Internet rights, etc.), Computational models of the legal contents and legal reasoning, Legal Information Retrieval, Electronic Data Discovery, Collaborative Tools (e.g. Online Dispute Resolution platforms), Metadata and XML Technologies (for Semantic Web Services), Technologies in Courtrooms and Judicial Offices (E-Court), Technologies for Governments and Administrations (E-Government), Legal Multimedia, and Legal Electronic Institutions (Multi-Agent Systems and Artificial Societies).

Nikos Th. Nikolinakos

Adapting the EU Civil Liability Regime to the Digital Age: Artificial Intelligence, Robotics, and Other Emerging Technologies

Springer

Nikos Th. Nikolinakos
Nikolinakos & Partners Law Firm
Athens, Greece

NETMODE Lab
National Technical University of Athens
(NTUA)
Athens, Greece

ISSN 2352-1902 ISSN 2352-1910 (electronic)
Law, Governance and Technology Series
ISBN 978-3-031-67968-1 ISBN 978-3-031-67969-8 (eBook)
https://doi.org/10.1007/978-3-031-67969-8

This Springer imprint is published by the registered company Springer Nature Switzerland AG
The registered company address is: Gewerbestrasse 11, 6330 Cham, Switzerland

"Αὐτόματον γάρ οὐδέν, ἀλλ' ἀπὸ πείρης πάντα ἀνθρώποισι φιλέει γίγνεσθαι".
Ηρόδοτος, Ἱστορίαι, Βιβλίο Η: Πολύμνια, 7.9γ.1.

"Τό δέ ζητούμενον ἁλωτόν, ἐκφεύγει δέ τἀμελούμενον".
Σοφοκλής, Οἰδίπους Τύραννος, στίχοι 110–111.

To Thodoris, Milena, and Dina, for their precious love and understanding.
To my brother, Vangelis, for his unlimited support.

Contents

Part I Introduction—Structure of This Book—The Evolution of EU Policy on Liability for Artificial Intelligence, Robotics and Emerging Digital Technologies—2015 to 2018

1 Introduction—Structure of This Book 3
1.1 Introduction 3
1.2 Structure of this Book 7
Legal/Policy Documents, Studies, Reports, References, and Other Sources 18

2 Major EU Policy Developments on Liability for Artificial Intelligence, Robotics, and Emerging Digital Technologies: 2015 to 2018 21
2.1 Introduction 21
2.2 The Digital Single Market (DSM) Strategy 21
2.3 Mid-Term Review of the Digital Single Market (DSM) Strategy and the "Data Economy" 24
2.4 Artificial Intelligence and the Renewed EU Industrial Policy Strategy 29
2.5 The European Parliament Resolution with Recommendations to the Commission on Civil Law Rules on Robotics 31
2.6 European Commission's Follow up to the 2017 European Parliament Resolution on Civil Law Rules on Robotics 43
2.7 European Parliament: Public Consultation on the Civil-Law Rules for Robotics and AI 46
2.8 The European Council of October 2017 49
2.9 Declaration of Cooperation on Artificial Intelligence 50
2.10 Commission's 2018 Communication on Artificial Intelligence for Europe 52

2.10.1 Introduction 52
2.10.2 Ensuring an Appropriate Ethical and Legal Framework 55
2.10.3 Conclusion 63
2.11 The EU's 2018 Coordinated Plan on Artificial Intelligence . . . 65
2.12 The Council of the European Union of 18 February 2019 68
2.13 Conclusion of Part I: Overview of the European AI Strategy on Liability 69
Legal/Policy Documents, Studies, Reports, and Other Sources 73

Part II Assessing the Key Aspects of the Existing EU Civil Liability Regime for Artificial Intelligence, Robotics and Emerging Digital Technologies: 2018 to 2020

3 The European Commission's Initial Assessment of the Liability Frameworks for Emerging Digital Technologies 79
3.1 Introduction 79
3.2 The Evaluation of the Machinery Directive 82
3.3 The Evaluation of the Product Liability Directive 85
3.4 Commission Staff Working Document on Liability for Emerging Digital Technologies 93
3.4.1 Introduction 93
3.4.2 Extra-Contractual Liability Rules Applicable in the Context of Emerging Digital Technologies 94
3.4.3 The Specific Characteristics of Emerging Digital Technologies 96
3.4.4 Case Studies: Autonomous Drones, Autonomous Cars, and Smart Home Ecosystems 101
3.4.5 Challenges Posed by Emerging Digital Technologies and Questions for Further Analysis 115
3.4.6 Conclusion 123
Legal/Policy Documents, Reports, and Other Sources 124
References 126

4 Assessing the Most Important Safety and Liability Aspects of Artificial Intelligence, Internet of Things and Robotics: 2019 and 2020 129
4.1 Introduction 129
4.2 The European Commission's 2020 White Paper on AI 135
4.2.1 Introduction—Ecosystem of Trust—The Legal/Regulatory Framework for AI 135
4.2.2 Risks for Fundamental Rights, Safety, and Liability . 136
4.2.3 Adjustments to Existing EU Legislative Framework Relating to AI: Issues to Be Addressed 138
4.3 European Commission's 2020 Report on the Safety and Liability Implications of AI, IoT and Robotics 147
4.3.1 Introduction 147

4.3.2 Characteristics of AI, IoT and Robotics Technologies 148
4.3.3 The EU Product Safety Framework 150
4.3.4 The Product Liability Frameworks 170
4.4 Report from the Expert Group on Liability and New Technologies: New Technologies Formation "Liability for Artificial Intelligence and Other Emerging Digital Technologies" 190
4.4.1 Strict Liability of the Operator 190
4.4.2 Responsibility of the Producer 194
4.4.3 Fault Liability by Specifying Further Duties of Care 196
4.4.4 Vicarious Liability for Autonomous Systems 200
4.4.5 Safety Rules: Adapting the Notion of Fault Liability by Shifting the Burden of Proving Causation and Fault 202
4.4.6 Legal Personality 205
4.4.7 Risk-Based Approach 207
4.4.8 Compulsory Liability Insurance 208
4.5 Conclusion 212
Legal/Policy Documents, Studies, Reports and Other Sources 214
References 217

5 The European Parliament's 2020 Legislative Proposal for a Regulation on a Civil Liability Regime for Artificial Intelligence . . 221
5.1 Introduction 221
5.2 Characteristics Shared by AI Systems—Legal Challenges for the Existing Liability Framework—Limitations of Scope of Existing EU Legislation 225
5.3 Liability and Artificial Intelligence: Liability of the Operator . . 232
5.4 Scope of the Parliament's Proposed Regulation 236
5.5 Strict Liability for High-Risk AI Systems and Insurance 236
5.6 Compensation 241
5.7 Fault-Based Liability for Other AI-Systems 242
5.8 Apportionment of Liability 247
5.9 Conclusion 248
Legal/Policy Documents, Studies, and Reports 248
References 250

Part III Reforming the EU Civil Liability Regime Applicable to Artificial Intelligence, Robotics, the Internet of Things, and Other Emerging Digital Technologies

6 Adapting EU Liability Rules to the Digital Age and Artificial Intelligence: The European Commission's 2021 Inception Impact Assessment 253
6.1 Introduction 253

6.2 The Objective of the Liability Framework 256
6.3 The Existing Liability Framework: National Liability Regimes and the Product Liability Directive 257
6.3.1 National Liability Regimes 259
6.3.2 The Product Liability Directive 260
6.4 Main Objectives of the Commission's Initiative 262
6.5 Shortcomings Brought by the Digital Emerging Technologies to the Product Liability Frameworks 263
6.5.1 Liability Rules Not Fit for the Digital Age 265
6.5.2 Significant Obstacles to Getting Compensation and Obstacles in the Internal Market 273
6.6 How the European Commission's Initiative Aims to Address the Challenges Brought by the Digital Emerging Technologies: Proposed Policy Options 281
6.6.1 Options to Adapt Strict Liability Rules to the Digital Age and Circular Economy 282
6.6.2 Other Options to Address Obstacles to Getting Compensation 302
6.7 Conclusion 321
Legal/Policy Documents, Studies, Reports 322
Responses by Organisations, Associations and Corporations to Public Consultations 323
References 324

7 **Adapting EU Liability Rules to the Digital Age and Artificial Intelligence: The 2021–2022 Public Consultation** 327
7.1 Introduction 327
7.2 Commission's Proposed Policy Measures 332
7.2.1 Approaches Regarding the Burden of Proof—Measures to Ease the Victim's Burden of Proof 332
7.2.2 Approaches Regarding Strict Liability for Operating AI-Enabled Products and Providing AI-Enabled Services 335
7.2.3 Approach Regarding Insurance for the Use of AI Systems That Pose a Serious Risk of Injury to the Public 337
7.2.4 Summary of the Proposed Policy Options 339
7.2.5 Other Types of Compensable Harm 340
7.2.6 Admissibility of Contractual Liability Waivers 342
7.3 Summary of the Contributions Made by Stakeholders in the Public Consultation on the Initiative Adapting Civil Liability Rules to the Digital Age and Artificial Intelligence 342
7.3.1 Introduction 342
7.3.2 Views of Respondents on the Product Liability Directive 343

7.3.3 Views of Respondents on the Specific Challenges of AI: Civil Liability Rules for AI 360
7.4 Conclusion 369
Legal/Policy Documents, Studies, Reports 370
Responses by Organisations, Associations and Corporations to Public Consultations 371
References 373

8 Reforming the EU Civil Liability Framework Applicable to Artificial Intelligence and Other Emerging Digital Technologies: The Proposed AI Liability Directive 377
8.1 Introduction 377
8.2 Existing Liability Rules in the EU 385
8.3 Identification of the Problems: Shortcomings in Relation to Digital Technologies and to AI—Reforming the EU Liability Framework Applicable to AI 387
8.3.1 Problem Driver and AI-Specific Problems Regarding Liability 387
8.3.2 Problems Affecting the Product Liability Directive: Need to Adapt the PLD to the Digital Age 395
8.3.3 Two Closely Linked Policy Initiatives: Complementary Proposed Directives—Overview 396
8.4 The Proposed AI Liability Directive 399
8.4.1 Objectives of the Proposed AI Liability Directive—Need for Action at EU Level—Choice of Instrument (Binding v. Non-binding) 399
8.4.2 Minimum (Targeted) Harmonisation Approach 407
8.4.3 Subject Matter, Scope, and Definitions 412
8.4.4 Disclosure of Evidence and Rebuttable Presumption of Non-compliance with a Duty of Care 417
8.4.5 Rebuttable Presumption of a Causal Link in the Case of Fault 423
8.4.6 Evaluation and Targeted Review/Report Clause 432
8.4.7 Discussion and Stakeholders' Views 435
8.5 Conclusion 464
Legal/Policy Documents, Studies, Reports and Other Sources 468
Responses by Organisations, Associations and Corporations to Public Consultations 470
References 471

9 Reforming the EU Civil Liability Framework Applicable to Artificial Intelligence and Other Emerging Digital Technologies: Defective Products—the Revised Product Liability Directive 477
9.1 Introduction 477

9.2 Identification of the Major Problems–Need to Adapt the PLD to the Digital Age–Objectives of the Proposal for a Revised Product Liability Directive 481
9.2.1 Identification of the Major Problems–Reasons for a Revised Product Liability Directive 481
9.2.2 Objectives of the Commission's Proposal for a Revised Product Liability Directive 502
9.3 Need for Action at EU Level—Choice of Instrument 503
9.4 Subject Matter, Scope, Maximum Harmonisation Instrument, Definitions 505
9.4.1 Broader Definition of Product 507
9.4.2 Broader Scope of Liable Parties 517
9.4.3 Removing the Lower and Upper Liability Limits . . . 518
9.4.4 Expanding the Definition of Damage: Harm to Psychological Health and Loss or Corruption of Data—What About Non-Material Damage and Pure Economic Loss? 518
9.5 Right to Compensation 524
9.6 Defectiveness—Safety as Benchmark—Criteria for Determining Whether a Product Is Defective 525
9.7 Economic Operators Liable for Defective Products 530
9.8 Alleviating the Burden of Proof: New Disclosure Obligations—Disclosure of Evidence 538
9.9 Alleviating the Burden of Proof: Rebuttable Legal Presumptions 543
9.9.1 Presumption of Defectiveness 544
9.9.2 Presumption of the Causal Link 545
9.9.3 General Presumption 545
9.10 Exemption from Liability: Defences Available to the Economic Operators 546
9.11 General Provisions on Liability 549
9.11.1 Liability of Multiple Economic Operators 549
9.11.2 Reduction of Liability 550
9.11.3 Mandatory Nature—Exclusion or Limitation of Liability 551
9.11.4 Limitation and Expiry Periods 551
9.12 Final Provisions 553
9.12.1 Transparency 553
9.12.2 Review 553
9.12.3 Repeal and Transitional Provision 554
9.13 The Position of the Council of the EU ("General Approach"): 14 June 2023 554
9.13.1 Scope 555
9.13.2 Damage 556
9.13.3 Defectiveness 557

9.13.4 Liable Operators—Manufacturer's Control—Substantial Modification 558
9.13.5 Burden of Proof—Presumption 560
9.13.6 Technical or Scientific Complexity—Derogation from the Development Risk Defence 561
9.13.7 Court Database: Transparency 562
9.13.8 Time Limitation: Expiry Period 562
9.14 The Position of the European Parliament 563
9.14.1 Draft Joint Report of the Parliament's Co-Leading IMCO and JURI Committees: April 2023 563
9.14.2 The Negotiating Position of the Plenary of the European Parliament: The Parliament's Compromise Text—October 2023 569
9.15 Political Agreement on the Revised Product Liability Directive (December 2023) – Final Text (March 2024) 570
9.15.1 Subject Matter—Objective—Maximum Harmonisation Instrument—Right to Compensation 573
9.15.2 Product—Scope 575
9.15.3 Damage 579
9.15.4 Assessment of Defectiveness 580
9.15.5 Economic Operators Liable for Defective Products 582
9.15.6 Disclosure of Evidence 587
9.15.7 Alleviating the Burden of Proof: Rebuttable Presumptions of Defectiveness and Causal Link 589
9.15.8 Exemption from Liability: Defences Available to the Economic Operators 591
9.15.9 Liability of Multiple Economic Operators and Right of Resource 596
9.15.10 Reduction of Liability 597
9.15.11 Exclusion or Limitation of Liability 598
9.15.12 Limitation Period 598
9.15.13 Expiry Period 599
9.15.14 Transparency—Court Database 600
9.15.15 Evaluation 601
9.15.16 Entry Into Force—Repeal and Transitional Provision—Transposition 601
9.16 Conclusion 602
Legal/Policy Documents, Reports, and Other Sources 612
Responses by Organisations, Associations and Corporations to Public Consultations 615
References 616

10 Conclusions 623
10.1 Identification of the Problem—Liability Rules Are Not Fit for the Digital Age—Shortcomings Brought by AI and Other Digital Emerging Technologies to the Product Liability Frameworks . . 623
10.2 With Regard to the Proposed AI Liability Directive 627
10.3 With Regard to the Revised Product Liability Directive 631
10.4 Concluding Remarks 636

Part I
Introduction—Structure of This Book—The Evolution of EU Policy on Liability for Artificial Intelligence, Robotics and Emerging Digital Technologies—2015 to 2018

Chapter 1
Introduction—Structure of This Book

1.1 Introduction

Policymakers across the world are increasingly focusing on the question of how Artificial Intelligence (AI) systems[1] should be regulated to give people the confidence to embrace AI-enabled technologies while encouraging businesses to innovate and develop them. In the European Union, the European Commission ('Commission'), the European Parliament ('Parliament') and the Council of the European Union ('Council') have repeatedly stressed that Artificial Intelligence is one of the tools for upgrading industry for the digital age, and highlighted the importance of having Europe in a leading position in the development of AI technologies, platforms, and applications. The EU can lead the way in developing and using AI for good and for all, building on its values and its strengths. The European Institutions have underlined the need ("a sense of urgency") to address emerging trends, such as AI, and to develop an approach to artificial intelligence and robotics at European level.[2] The objective is to create a more integrated Single Market, to step up the legislative work and for Member States to implement the relevant EU legislation.

---

[1] "'AI system' means a machine-based system that is designed to operate with varying levels of autonomy and that may exhibit adaptiveness after deployment, and that, for explicit or implicit objectives, infers, from the input it receives, how to generate outputs such as predictions, content, recommendations, or decisions that can influence physical or virtual environments". Regulation (EU) 2024/1689 of the European Parliament and of the Council of 13 June 2024 laying down harmonised rules on artificial intelligence and amending Regulations (EC) No 300/2008, (EU) No 167/2013, (EU) No 168/2013, (EU) 2018/858, (EU) 2018/1139 and (EU) 2019/2144 and Directives 2014/90/EU, (EU) 2016/797 and (EU) 2020/1828 (*EU Artificial Intelligence Act*), OJ L, 12.07.2024, Article 3 ('Definitions'), point 1.

[2] "Like the steam engine or electricity in the past, AI is transforming our world, our society and our industry. Growth in computing power, availability of data and progress in algorithms have turned AI into one of the most strategic technologies of the twenty-first century. The stakes could not be

N. T. Nikolinakos, *Adapting the EU Civil Liability Regime to the Digital Age: Artificial Intelligence, Robotics, and Other Emerging Technologies*, Law, Governance and Technology Series 68, https://doi.org/10.1007/978-3-031-67969-8_1

Liability-related issues are counted amongst the main risks associated with the use of AI. Indeed, liability ranks amongst the top three barriers to the use of AI by European companies and constitutes a major external barrier/challenge for companies that are planning to, but have not yet adopted AI (major obstacles to AI adoption).[3] Therefore, the creation of a clear liability regime for AI and other emerging digital technologies plays a vital role in driving the industry forward, ensuring a level playing field, and reducing the uncertainties for companies considering investing in AI-powered products and services. Creating a stable liability policy and rules is indispensable in order to allow a sound basis for long term planning in the industry and set the environment for commercial initiative and massive investment. In order to make the most of the opportunities offered by AI it is imperative to establish a liability framework that ensures high levels of consumer protection/safety and promotes their trust in AI technologies, while efficiently providing remedies/compensation to affected parties. At the same time, this liability framework must provide businesses with legal certainty, be future-oriented and flexible enough to foster innovation and encourage investment.

---

higher. The way we approach AI will define the world we live in. Amid fierce global competition, a solid European framework is needed". Commission Communication, "Artificial Intelligence for Europe", COM(2018) 237 final, Brussels, 25.4.2018, p. 1.

"Now that humankind stands on the threshold of an era when ever more sophisticated robots, bots, androids and other manifestations of artificial intelligence ("AI") seem to be poised to unleash a new industrial revolution, which is likely to leave no stratum of society untouched, it is vitally important for the legislature to consider its legal and ethical implications and effects, without stifling innovation". European Parliament Resolution of 16 February 2017 with recommendations to the Commission on Civil Law Rules on Robotics (2015/2103(INL)), (2018/C 252/25), OJ C 252, 18.7.2018, pp. 239–257 ("European Parliament Resolution of 16 February 2017"), section "Introduction", recital B, p. 239.

"The hallmarks of this new industrial age are the accelerated pace of economic, societal and environmental transformations as well as technological breakthroughs in areas like robotics, Internet of Things, artificial intelligence, energy systems and bio-economy. Automation, enabled by information technologies, is transforming traditional manufacturing processes and the nature of work". Commission Communication, "Investing in a smart, innovative and sustainable Industry - A renewed EU Industrial Policy Strategy", COM(2017) 479 final, Brussels, 13.9.2017, p. 2.

[3] 'European enterprise survey on the use of technologies based on artificial intelligence', Study prepared for the European Commission, DG Communications Networks, Content & Technology by Ipsos Belgium and iCite (International Centre for Innovation, Technology and Education), 2020, Final report, at pp. 57–60, figures 18–21: "One specific challenge or barrier that seems to stand out is liability for damage caused by AI: while it seems to not be as universally relevant, this barrier seems to pose a major challenge when it is applicable to the business context in which enterprises operate" (at p. 58). . . . "enterprises in the human health sector are consistently in the top three most concerned for all three external barriers, with risks associated with liability for damage caused by AI being rated as a major obstacle by 43% of interviewed enterprises in this sector – the highest proportion across all sectors. Liability for damage caused by AI also stands out as a major obstacle in the transport (39%), accommodation (37%) and other technical and/or scientific (36%) sectors" (at p. 60).

This book does not intend to cover an analysis of the EU ethical and regulatory framework for AI systems.[4] The aim of the book is to examine whether the current EU liability regimes (i.e., the Product Liability Directive and national liability frameworks) are still adequate to facilitate the uptake of the AI and emerging digital technologies (i.e., to promote the rollout of trustworthy AI to harvest the full benefits of AI) by fostering investment stability and users' trust. Indeed, the emergence of new digital technologies like AI, the IoT and robotics raise new challenges in terms of product safety like connectivity, autonomy, data dependency, opacity, complexity of products and systems, software updates and more complex safety management and value chains. In turn, these new safety challenges create challenges in terms of liability. These liability related challenges need to be addressed to ensure that persons having suffered harm caused by AI-enabled systems and services will enjoy equal level of protection as victims of traditional technologies (which operate without AI), while maintaining the balance with the needs of technological innovation. This will help create trust in these new emerging digital technologies and establish investment stability.

Although the primary objective is to prevent/mitigate risks to safety and fundamental rights, it is inevitable that accidents/harm will be caused by hazardous products, including digital products and AI systems. In such cases, it becomes crucial for the liability rules to ascertain the responsible party for the harm caused and establish the circumstances under which the victim can receive compensation. Therefore, the EU liability framework should serve as a safety net, ensuring compensation in the event of damage. Although AI-enabled products/services are (and should be) expected to be safer than traditional ones, accidents/harm will still occur. Indeed, new digital technologies, in particular AI driven products, can develop malfunctions (not necessarily associated with a risk to safety) that may cause a wide range of harm. If/when these risks materialise, specific characteristics of AI technologies may make it difficult to trace back potentially problematic decisions made with the involvement of AI systems. This in turn may make it extremely difficult for persons having suffered harm to obtain compensation under the current EU and national liability legislation.

In particular, national fault-based liability rules are not adapted to handle compensation claims for harm caused by AI-enabled products/services. Under such rules, victims need to prove a wrongful action/omission of a person that caused the damage. The specific characteristics of AI, including autonomy and opacity ("black box" effect) make it difficult or even prohibitively expensive to identify the liable person and prove the requirements for a successful liability claim. Therefore, victims of harm caused by AI could be less protected than victims of traditional technologies. This potential lack of compensation could affect the consumers' trust in AI and ultimately the uptake of AI-enabled products/services.

[4]For such analysis, see Nikos Th. Nikolinakos, EU Policy and Legal Framework for Artificial Intelligence, Robotics, and Related Technologies – The AI Act, Springer, 2023.

At the same time, the current Product Liability Directive (PLD) lays down common EU rules for the strict liability (i.e. liability irrespective of fault or negligence—no-fault liability) of producers for damage caused by defective products. However, certain products, economic actors, and damage in the digital and circular economy are not covered under no-fault (strict) liability. This is because the Product Liability Directive (which dates back to 1985) was conceived long before the digital revolution and, accordingly, is not adapted to the digital age and circular economy. As a result, liability rules are unclear and, thus, should be adapted for products in the digital age. Also, liability rules are unclear for refurbished/remanufactured products. Furthermore, the current rules of the PLD are silent on who should be liable when a product has been directly imported from outside the EU by a consumer. In addition, it is argued that consumers face obstacles to getting compensation, mainly because (i) proving defectiveness and causal link with damage could be very difficult and costly for complex products (such as certain cases involving AI-enabled products) and (ii) liability claims are subject to a number of restrictions.

The emerging digital technologies involve many different layers, e.g. software components, sensors, or data services. The Internet of Things and the advent of robotics can present legal obstacles when it comes to identifying and establishing the defect which caused the damage and in determining liability among the various market players. Legal uncertainty may have a detrimental impact on the development and uptake of AI and emerging digital technologies.

Therefore, the aim is to ensure that damage caused by AI-enabled products and services is remedied efficiently. To this end, alongside a high level of safety and protection for users, it is imperative to provide efficient redress mechanisms for victims in case of damages. An efficient liability framework helps to build user trust and acceptance of AI and other emerging digital technologies, which is a prerequisite for encouraging innovation and technological uptake. The objectives of the EU civil liability rules for AI are to (i) provide legal certainty to industry's market players about the risk they take in the course of their business, (ii) encourage the prevention of damage and (iii) ensure injured parties are compensated. The overarching objective is to strike a balance between protecting citizens and supporting technological innovation. In other words, apart from the issue of safety, the aim is to address unnecessary obstacles to obtaining compensation for damage in order to ensure that injured parties are equally protected throughout the EU, thus leading to consumer uptake of AI and other emerging digital technologies as well as creating trust in innovative products/services and in justice systems.

1.2 Structure of this Book

Part I of this book outlines the structure of the book (this chapter) and traces the evolution of the EU policy on Artificial Intelligence, discussing the main liability-related policy documents and measures which set the tone for strengthening the EU AI ecosystem (Chap. 2).

In particular, Chap. 2 outlines the European Parliament's initial (2017) approach to Artificial Intelligence and Robotics, which covered ethical, legal, and social aspects. The European Parliament paved the way and made wide ranging recommendations to ensure that Europe will have an appropriate ethical and legal framework to deal with AI development and deployment. It also asked the Commission to present a legislative proposal laying down a set of civil law rules and ethical aspects on robotics and artificial intelligence. This part of the book (focusing on liability issues) presents the European AI strategy, which stressed that significant efforts must be made to ensure that Europe is competitive in the AI landscape.

Chapter 2 also presents the Commission's vision of dealing with AI liability issues, offering, *inter alia*, some preliminary insights as to the policy options and what the forthcoming EU liability framework for AI might include. The Commission stressed that there is need for legal certainty as to the allocation of liability in the context of new technologies. In other words, it was underlined that it is imperative to review and assess the adequacy of civil law liability rules in light of new technological developments such as the Internet of Things, advanced robotics and autonomous systems powered by artificial intelligence. AI can benefit the whole of society and the economy but, at the same time, brings with it new challenges and raises legal questions. As it is explained, it is imperative to ensure that AI is developed and applied in an appropriate liability framework which promotes innovation whereas, at the same time, guarantees a high level of consumer protection and ensures that injured parties are remedied/compensated efficiently.

Part II of this book (Chaps. 3–5) covers an initial assessment of the EU liability framework—that took place from 2018 to 2020—in light of AI and emerging digital technologies. In order to fully unlock the digital/data economy, the safety and liability frameworks need to keep up to date with emerging trends and take account of new technological developments. Otherwise, legal uncertainty may hinder the development and uptake of AI-enabled products and services. Part II offers a view of the substantial changes the European Commission and the European Parliament had in mind, and presents the direction in which the AI related liability framework would/should evolve in the near future. It highlights the Commission's and the Parliament's preferred options, with the objective of promoting the development, uptake and use of AI applications and ensuring that the EU liability framework is suitable for emerging digital technologies and innovative products, while also addressing the resulting challenges.

In particular, Chap. 3 focuses on the most important implications for and potential gaps in the liability frameworks for AI, the IoT and robotics. The Commission concluded that the EU's existing product liability legislation contains a number of gaps that need to be addressed. It was recognised that AI is a powerful force for good but, at the same time, it can cause harm, both material (safety and health of individuals, including loss of life, damage to property) and immaterial (loss of privacy, limitations to the right of freedom of expression, human dignity, discrimination). The main risks associated with the use of AI relate to the protection of fundamental rights (e.g. data protection, privacy, non-discrimination), as well as to safety (including cybersecurity, issues concerning AI in critical infrastructure and malicious use of AI) and liability-related issues. If these risks materialise, the lack of clear requirements and the characteristics of AI technologies make it difficult to trace back potentially problematic decisions made with the involvement of AI systems. This in turn may make it extremely difficult for persons having suffered harm to obtain compensation under the current EU and national liability legislation.

Chapter 4 covers the Commission's attempt to examine the applicability of the current Product Liability Directive to new technologies and, in light of an assessment of the existing liability schemes, to develop principles that can serve as guidelines for possible adaptations of applicable laws at EU and national level relating to new technologies. In other words, it is examined whether and to what extent existing liability schemes are adapted to the emerging market realities following the development of the new technologies such as Artificial Intelligence, advanced robotics, the IoT and cybersecurity issues. It is also examined whether the current liability regimes are still adequate to facilitate the uptake of the emerging digital technologies by promoting investment stability and users' trust.

In addition, this chapter examines the most important findings presented in the Report of the Expert Group on Liability and New Technologies "Liability for Artificial Intelligence and Other Emerging Digital Technologies", issued on 21 November 2019. Furthermore, this chapter follows the Commission's 2020 White Paper on AI. This was a significant policy document setting out concrete measures and proposed regulation with the objective of promoting the development, uptake and use of AI applications. The 2020 White provided a clear indication that the EU is seriously considering a formal regulatory regime applicable to AI, it offered a view of the substantial changes the Commission has in mind and presented the direction in which the AI related legal framework might evolve in the near future. With regard to the liability issue, the Commission's 2020 White Paper on AI recognised that the existing EU legislation remains in principle fully applicable despite the involvement of AI. However, it stressed that there is need to be examined whether current legislation is able to address the risks of AI and can be effectively enforced or whether adjustments to specific legal instruments are needed (or, whether new legislation is required). The Commission concluded that the existing laws which are applicable to AI applications are not sufficient to address the risks posed by the development and deployment of AI. Therefore, specific adjustments to and clarifications of existing legislation is required in order to make the EU liability framework fit for the current and forthcoming technological and commercial developments.

Chapter 4 also covers extensively the Commission's 2020 Report on the safety and liability implications of AI, IoT and robotics, which accompanied the

Commission's 2020 White Paper on Artificial Intelligence. This Report provided an overview of the existing rules for liability, focused on key issues and assessed the most important implications for and potential gaps in the liability and safety frameworks for AI, the IoT and robotics. According to the Commission, the safety and liability legal frameworks have two overall goals, namely (i) to ensure that all products and services, including those integrating emerging digital technologies, operate safely, reliably, and consistently and (ii) to ensure that damage caused by the said products is remedied efficiently. Alongside a high level of safety and protection for users it is imperative to provide efficient redress mechanisms for victims in case of damages. An efficient liability framework helps to build user trust and acceptance of these emerging technologies, which is a prerequisite for encouraging innovation and technological uptake.

The Commission's 2020 Report stressed that AI, the IoT and robotics are transforming the characteristics of many products and services and recognised that an assessment of the current liability frameworks should be carried out in light of AI and emerging technologies, i.e. that is imperative to examine whether the existing EU legal framework is adequate and suitable for emerging digital technologies and innovative products. While in principle the existing EU and national liability laws can cope with emerging technologies, the dimension and combined effect of the challenges of AI could make it more difficult to offer victims compensation in all cases where this would be justified. To rectify this and address potential uncertainties in the existing framework, certain adjustments to the current Product Liability Directive and national liability regimes through appropriate EU initiatives should be considered on a targeted, risk-based approach.

Chapter 5 examines the European Parliaments' 2020 Resolution on a civil liability regime for artificial intelligence. With this legislative initiative, the European Parliament urged the Commission to present a future-oriented civil liability framework, laying down rules for the civil liability claims of natural and legal persons against operators of AI-systems. It was stated that a clear legal framework should stimulate innovation by providing businesses with legal certainty, whilst protecting citizens and promoting their trust in AI technologies by deterring activities that might be dangerous. The Parliament considered it necessary to ensure maximum legal certainty throughout the liability chain, including for the producer, operator, injured parties and any other third parties, in order to respond to the new legal challenges created by developments in artificial intelligence (AI) systems.

According to the Parliament, the goal of any liability framework should be to provide legal certainty for all parties. Civil liability rules for AI should strike a balance between protecting potential victims of harm or damage and, at the same time, supporting investment and technological innovation. In brief, the initiative (proposal for a Regulation on liability for the operation of AI systems) called for making those operating high-risk AI systems strictly liable for any resulting damage. The operator in question should not be able to exonerate himself from liability by claiming that he acted with due diligence. Operators of high-risk AI systems should hold liability insurance similar to that used for motor vehicles. This compulsory insurance regime for high-risk AI-systems should cover the amounts and the extent of compensation, as defined in the proposed Regulation. The initiative also stated that the operator of an AI-system that does not constitute a high-risk AI-system should be subject to fault-based liability for any harm or damage that was caused by a physical or virtual activity, device or process driven by the AI-system. Therefore, the operator of a non-high-risk AI system should not be liable if he can prove that the harm or damage was caused without his fault. The Parliament considered that operator liability rules should apply to all types of AI system operations, regardless of the location of the operation and whether it is of a physical or virtual nature.

Part III: Reforming the EU Civil Liability Regime Applicable to Artificial Intelligence, Robotics, the IoT and Other Emerging Digital Technologies (Chaps. 6–10)
Chapter 6 reviews the Commission's 2021 Inception Impact Assessment (IIA) "Adapting liability rules to the digital age and circular economy", which was published on 30 June 2021. According to the Commission, civil liability rules for AI should strike a balance between protecting citizens and promoting technological innovation. It was stressed that, alongside the objective of the EU safety framework to ensure that all products and services, including those integrating emerging digital technologies like AI, robotics and Internet of things (IoT), operate safely and reliably, the objectives of the liability framework are to (i) provide legal certainty to industry's market players about the risk they take in the course of their business, (ii) encourage the prevention of damage and (iii) ensure injured parties are compensated.

The Commission's 2021 Inception Impact Assessment (IIA) was prompted by an evaluation of the Product Liability Directive (PLD) and addressed shortcomings already identified in the evaluation of the PLD and the challenges that the emerging technologies present for the application of liability rules, which were analytically described in the Commission's 2020 White Paper and the accompanying Report on Liability for AI, IoT and Robotics. The Commission examined different policy options to achieve the main two objectives of the initiative, which, alongside the overall objective to ensure the proper functioning of the single market while providing for a high level of consumer/victim protection, are to: (i) modernise and adapt strict liability rules to the digital age and circular economy, taking account of the characteristics and risks of new technologies, including AI-equipped products and services; and (ii) address unnecessary obstacles to getting compensation for damage in order to ensure that injured parties are equally protected throughout the EU, thus leading to consumer uptake of AI and other innovative technologies as well as creating trust in innovative products/services and in justice systems.

Chapter 7 discusses the public consultation (which was open from 18 October 2021 to 10 January 2022) on how to improve the current Product Liability Directive and how to address the challenges that artificial intelligence poses for liability rules. The aim of this public consultation was to confirm the relevance of the issues identified by the 2018 evaluation of the Product Liability Directive (i.e. how to apply the PLD to products in the digital and circular economy), and collect information and opinions on how to improve the PLD (Section I of the consultation). At the same time, Section II of the consultation specifically dealt with AI-related issues, exploring further the major problems connected with certain types of AI, which make it difficult for the victim/injured party to obtain compensation, i.e. to identify the potentially liable person, to prove that person's fault or to prove the defect in the product and the causal link between the defect and the damage. This difficulty becomes even higher as emerging digital technologies and products are becoming increasingly connected and complex.

The Commission put forward proposed policy measures to address those issues related specifically to damage caused by AI systems, covering both the Product Liability Directive and national civil liability rules. The aim is to ensure that victims of damage caused by AI systems are not left with less protection than victims of damage caused by technologies that operate without AI. The Commission's proposed approaches focused on (i) measures to ease the victim's burden of proof as well as (ii) a targeted harmonisation of strict liability and (iii) insurance solutions. In light of the three-pronged objective of the EU liability framework (legal certainty, prevention of damages and efficient compensation to the injured parties), the Commission's proposals (especially those opting for the adoption of 'radical' measures in relation to an expansion of liability as well as for the alleviation or even reversal of the burden of proof) could fundamentally transform the EU liability regime.

Chapter 8 provides a thorough and systematic analysis of the Commission's proposal for a Directive on adapting non-contractual civil liability rules to artificial intelligence (the 'proposed AI Liability Directive').[5] The proposed AI Liability Directive harmonises targeted aspects of the Member States' existing civil liability rules applicable to AI-systems and its aim is to complement and modernise the EU liability framework by introducing new rules specific to damages caused by AI systems.

While the EU Artificial Intelligence Act[6] aims at preventing, monitoring, and addressing/reducing risks to safety and fundamental rights, accidents/harm will still occur. When this happens, the liability rules should be able to determine which party is liable for harm and under which conditions a victim can be compensated. The EU AI Act contains no provisions on liability for the purposes of damages claims and does not compensate the victim for the harm suffered. Currently victims rely on national liability rules and, in certain cases, on the Product Liability Directive (PLD), which is being revised in parallel. However, such national liability rules (in particular fault-based national rules) are not suited to handling compensation claims for harm caused by AI-enabled products and services. Victims need to prove

[5]Proposal for a Directive of the European Parliament and of the Council on adapting non-contractual civil liability rules to artificial intelligence (AI Liability Directive), European Commission, COM(2022) 496 final, Brussels, 28.9.2022 (the 'proposed AI Liability Directive').

[6]Regulation (EU) 2024/1689 of the European Parliament and of the Council of 13 June 2024 laying down harmonised rules on artificial intelligence and amending Regulations (EC) No 300/2008, (EU) No 167/2013, (EU) No 168/2013, (EU) 2018/858, (EU) 2018/1139 and (EU) 2019/2144 and Directives 2014/90/EU, (EU) 2016/797 and (EU) 2020/1828 (*EU Artificial Intelligence Act*), OJ L, 12.07.2024.

a wrongful action or omission of a person that caused the damage, but specific characteristics of AI (including autonomy and opacity, i.e., the so-called "black box" effect) make it difficult or prohibitively expensive to identify the liable person and prove the requirements for a successful liability claim (i.e., to meet the required burden of proof). Accordingly, liability rules are needed to ensure that, in the event that a damage occurs, victims are effectively compensated. A new liability regime should be introduced to ensure greater legal certainty, thereby enhancing consumer trust in AI and facilitating successful investment and innovation across the EU. Thus, while the AI Act aims at preventing damage, the AI Liability Directive introduces a safety-net for compensation in the event of damage.

The objectives of the proposed AI Liability Directive are: (i) to prevent a lack of compensation, by ensuring that victims of AI-enabled products/services are equally protected as victims of traditional technologies (when persons suffer harm caused by AI systems, they should enjoy the same level of protection as those having suffered harm caused by other technologies, because lack of compensation could affect their trust in AI and ultimately the uptake of AI-enabled products/services); (ii) to reduce legal uncertainty regarding the liability exposure of businesses developing or using AI; and (iii) to prevent the emergence of fragmented AI-specific adaptations of national civil liability rules.

The proposed AI Liability Directive attempts to address the AI-specific problems by improving the rights of victims who have suffered any damage—as admissible under national law—due to wrongful use of artificial intelligence. In particular, the proposed AI Liability Directive introduces two key measures: *First*, the 'presumption of causality', which relieves victims from having to explain in detail how a specific fault or omission caused the damage. If victims can show that a party was at fault for not complying with a relevant obligation and that a causal link with the AI performance is reasonably likely, the court can presume that this non-compliance caused the damage. The liable party, however, can rebut this presumption by proving that another cause was responsible for the damage. *Second*, it assists victims in accessing relevant evidence from companies or suppliers when dealing with high-risk AI systems. Victims can request the court to order the disclosure of information about high-risk AI systems, facilitating the identification of the liable party and the understanding of the fault. This disclosure is subject to safeguards to protect sensitive information, including trade secrets.

According to the proposed AI Liability Directive, any type of victim (natural or legal person) can bring a claim for damages against any person for fault that influenced the AI system which caused the harm. The victim can be compensated if harmed by the fault or omission of a provider, developer or user of AI resulting in a damage covered by national law (e.g., health, property, including damage caused by safety issues or resulting from unlawful discrimination or breach of fundamental rights such as privacy). The proposed AI Liability Directive must be reviewed and adopted by the European Parliament and Member States before it comes into effect and, to this end, the Commission's proposal will be discussed by the co-legislators (the main decision-making bodies of the EU), i.e., the European Parliament ("the Parliament") and the Council of the European Union ("the Council"). Once ratified, the AI Liability Directive is expected to strengthen the rights of victims who have suffered damage—as admissible under national law—due to the wrongful use of artificial intelligence. This will enable victims to file successful claims against any party whose fault influenced the AI system causing the damage/harm. Consequently, it will facilitate compensation for victims—whether individuals or businesses—for damages resulting from an AI system's output.

Chapter 9 discusses in detail the European Commission's proposal for a new Directive on liability of defective products, which would revise, repeal, and replace the existing Product Liability Directive (the 'proposal for a revised Product Liability Directive').[7] The chapter compares the Commission's proposal with the "compromise" proposal (general approach) of the Council of the EU, also taking into account the position of the European Parliament. It also covers the provisional (political) agreement reached on 14 December 2023 as well as the final text of the revised Product Liability Directive which was formally endorsed by the European Parliament at the Plenary of 12 March 2024.

The current Product Liability Directive (PLD) establishes common rules at the EU level for the non-fault (strict) liability of producers for damage caused by defective products, regardless of fault or negligence. It provides an avenue for individuals (whether they are the owner or a bystander) who have suffered personal injuries, damage to consumer property, or death due to a defective product to claim financial compensation. However, the evaluation of the Product Liability Directive concluded that the PLD had several shortcomings, such as the lack of legal clarity on how to apply the PLD's definitions to products in the digital and circular economy, difficulties related to the burden of proof in the case of complex products, and limitations on making claims. In particular, it was found that two are the main problems affecting the existing PLD, namely: (i) certain products, economic actors and damage in the digital and circular economy escape (are not covered under) no-fault (strict) liability; (ii) consumers face obstacles to getting compensation. Whereas victims do not have to prove fault (producers bear liability irrespective of fault), proving defectiveness and causal link with damage is very difficult and costly for complex products. Also, liability claims are subject to a number of restrictions (claimants face time limits and thresholds that might disproportionately restrict the number of claims).

Therefore, due to the shortcomings affecting the current PLD, enhancing legal clarity is a crucial objective of the revised PLD. The aim of the revised PLD is to modernise the current EU's product liability regime, based on the strict liability of manufacturers, for the compensation of personal injury, damage to property or data loss caused by unsafe products. The revised PLD is designed to accommodate the latest technological advancements, circular economy business models, and global value chains. This is achieved by ensuring the following: (i) businesses and

[7] Proposal for a Directive of the European Parliament and of the Council on liability for defective products, European Commission, COM(2022) 495 final, Brussels, 28.9.2022 (the 'proposal for a revised Product Liability Directive (PLD)').

consumers/victims are subject to fair and predictable rules; (ii) victims are adequately compensated for any harm caused by hazardous products, including digital products and AI systems; and (iii) a level playing field exists between EU and non-EU manufacturers. To this end, the revised PLD attempts to achieve the following four specific objectives. First, in order to adapt product liability rules to the digital age and circular economy: (i) ensuring liability rules reflect the nature and risks of products in the digital age and circular economy; (ii) ensuring there is always an EU-based business that can be held liable, i.e. it is possible to obtain compensation, when defective products are bought directly from manufacturers/producers outside the EU. Second, in order to reduce disproportionate obstacles to getting compensation: (iii) easing the burden of proof in complex cases (and clarifying liability for undiscoverable defects), while ensuring fair balance between producers/manufacturers and consumers; (iv) easing restrictions on making claims as well as ensuring legal certainty by better aligning the PLD with the new legislative framework created by Decision 768/2008/EC7 and with product safety rules.

The Commission's proposal for a revised Product Liability Directive must be reviewed and adopted by the European Parliament and Member States before it comes into effect and, to this end, the Commission's proposal was discussed by the co-legislators (the main decision-making bodies of the EU), i.e., the European Parliament ("the Parliament") and the Council of the European Union ("the Council").

On 14 June 2023, at the Committee of the Permanent Representatives (COREPER) meeting, the Council of the EU (the Council) adopted its negotiating mandate and formalised its position ("general approach") for a new EU Directive on liability for defective products,[8] extending product liability rules to software and Artificial Intelligence. In general, EU countries have largely maintained the Commission's proposal and have gone further in certain aspects, notably by giving national liability regimes the possibility to cover non-material damages and to hold manufacturers liable for defects that could not be known at the time of the market launch. Coreper also agreed that, on the basis of its 'general approach' text, negotiations could start with the European Parliament in the context of the ordinary legislative procedure.

On the Parliamentary front, the discussions were led by the Committee on Internal Market and Consumer Protection (IMCO) and the Committee on Legal Affairs (JURI) under a joint committee procedure. On 5 April 2023 the European Parliament's co-leading Committees on the proposal for a revised PLD issued their draft Joint Report,[9] which constitutes a significant tone-down of the revised PLD,

---

[8] Council of the European Union, Note: From: General Secretariat of the Council. To: Delegations. Subject: Proposal for a Directive of the European Parliament and of the Council on liability for defective products - Mandate for negotiations with the European Parliament, Brussels, 15 June 2023, Council doc. 10694/23 ("General Secretariat of the Council - General approach on the proposal for a revised PLD, 15 June 2023").

[9] Draft Report of the European Parliament's Committee on Internal Market and Consumer Protection and the Committee on Legal Affairs on the proposal for a directive of the European Parliament

based on the need "to strike the right balance between the interests of injured persons and those of economic operators liable for defective products. Ensuring a fair allocation of risk is essential in [the co-rapporteurs'] view for the revision of the rules of the PLD".[10] On 9 October 2023, following their draft Joint Report of 5 April 2023, the joint committees adopted the final Report[11] and decided to enter into trilogue (i.e. interinstitutional) negotiations with the Council of the EU (and the Commission),[12] with the aim of reaching a political agreement on the legislative text of the amended PLD in the coming months.[13] The European Parliament confirmed the draft mandate at the Plenary session of 16 October 2023.

Following the Interinstitutional negotiations (trilogue), the co-legislators (Council of the EU and the European Parliament) reached a provisional (political) agreement on 14 December 2023. At its meeting on 24 January 2024, the Permanent Representatives Committee of the Council of the EU confirmed the agreement on the compromise text of the revised Product Liability Directive,[14] as it was reached between the negotiating parties on 14 December 2023, and authorised the Presidency to address the habitual offer letter to the European Parliament.

The text of the provisional agreement[15] was submitted to the Committee on the Internal Market and Consumer Protection (IMCO) and the Committee on Legal

---

and of the Council on Liability for defective products (COM(2022)0495 – C9-0322/2022 – 2022/0302(COD)), 05.04.2023, ("Draft Joint Report of the European Parliament's co-leading IMCO and JURI Committees on the proposal for a revised PLD, 5 April 2023").

[10] Draft Joint Report of the European Parliament's co-leading IMCO and JURI Committees on the proposal for a revised PLD, 5 April 2023, Explanatory Statement, p. 37.

[11] Joint Report of the European Parliament's co-leading IMCO and JURI Committees on the proposal for a directive of the European Parliament and of the Council on liability for defective products, A9-0291/2023, 12 October 2023.

[12] On 16.10.2023, the joint committees' decision to enter into interinstitutional negotiations was announced in plenary. On 18.10.2023, the joint committees' decision to enter into interinstitutional negotiations was confirmed by the plenary.

[13] Following the committee vote, JURI Committee co-rapporteur Pascal Arimont stated: "Like its predecessor, the revised Product Liability Directive aims to strike a balance between remaining an effective instrument for victims of defective products, and the legal certainty economic operators deserve in a fast changing market characterised by digitalisation, the circular economy, and global value chains". In the same press release, IMCO Committee co-rapporteur Vlad-Marius Botoş stessed: "In the new Product Liability Directive, we have a balance between the interests of citizens and legal clarity for economic operators regarding software and the loss and corruption of data. In addition, people can get help from consumer protection agencies in building their case to obtain damages". European Parliament, Press Release (IMCO-JURI), "Better protection for consumers against damages by defective products", 09.10.2023.

[14] Council of the European Union, Information Note: From: General Secretariat of the Council. To: Delegations. Subject: Proposal for a Directive of the European Parliament and of the Council on liability for defective products – Letter sent to the European Parliament, Brussels, 24 January 2024, Council doc. 5809/24 ("General Secretariat of the Council – Proposal for a Directive on liability for defective products – Letter sent to the European Parliament, Council doc. 5809/24, 24 January 2024").

[15] European Parliament, Committee on the Internal Market and Consumer Protection (IMCO) and Committee on Legal Affairs (JURI), "Provisional Agreement Resulting from Interinstitutional

Affairs (JURI), which voted on 22 February 2024. The final text of the revised PLD was formally endorsed by the European Parliament at the Plenary of 12 March 2024, which adopted its position at first reading.[16] The revised Product Liability Directive will have to be formally approved by the Council of the EU, too. It will enter into force on the twentieth day following its publication in the EU Official Journal. The new rules will apply to products placed on the market or put into service 24 months after entry into force of the revised PLD.

This chapter argues that, although the revised PLD appears poised to tip the scales further in favor of claimants, particularly in complex cases, thus increasing the likelihood of manufacturers/producers facing considerable litigation risks, including the heightened risk of third-party litigation funding, it ultimately succeeds in establishing an EU product liability framework that: (i) ensures liability rules reflect the nature and risks of products in the digital age and circular economy, (ii) supports businesses bringing safe, AI-enabled and other innovative products to market, (iii) ensures that consumers' health and property are afforded a high level of protection, (iv) reduces disproportionate obstacles to obtaining compensation, and (v) strikes an appropriate balance between the interests of claimants and defendants in Member State courts.

Chapter 10 presents an executive summary of conclusions and provides an assessment of the upcoming/revised EU liability framework for AI and other emerging digital technologies. In particular, it is argued that the proposed AI Liability Directive could (i) prevent a lack of compensation, by ensuring that victims of AI-enabled products/services are equally protected as victims of traditional technologies; (ii) reduce legal uncertainty regarding the liability exposure of businesses developing or using AI; and (iii) prevent the emergence of fragmented AI-specific adaptations of national civil liability rules. It is anticipated that the AI Liability Directive will make it easier for victims—either individuals or businesses—to receive compensation for damages caused by safety issues or for breaches of privacy or when there is unlawful discrimination in a recruitment process involving AI technology.

Furthermore, it is stressed that the revised Product Liability Directive succeeds in striking the right balance between protecting citizens and supporting technological innovation. It adapts product liability rules to the digital age and circular economy

---

Negotiations", Subject: Proposal for a Directive of the European Parliament and of the Council on Liability for defective products (COM(2022)0495 – C9 0322/2022 – 2022/0302(COD)), 31 January 2024.

[16] European Parliament legislative resolution of 12 March 2024 on the proposal for a Directive of the European Parliament and of the Council on liability for defective products (COM(2022)0495 – C9-0322/2022 – 2022/0302(COD)), (Ordinary legislative procedure: first reading) – P9_TC1-COD (2022)0302, Position of the European Parliament adopted at first reading on 12 March 2024 with a view to the adoption of Directive (EU) 2024/... of the European Parliament and of the Council on liability for defective products and repealing Council Directive 85/374/EEC ["Position of the European Parliament of 12 March 2024 for the adoption of a Directive on liability for defective products (revised PLD)"].

and reduces disproportionate obstacles to getting compensation. This is achieved by: (i) guaranteeing that businesses and consumers/victims are subject to fair and predictable rules (i.e., ensuring a fair balance between producers/manufacturers and consumers/victims); (ii) ensuring victims are adequately compensated for any harm caused by hazardous products, including digital products and AI systems; (iii) easing the burden of proof in complex cases (and clarifying liability for undiscoverable defects); (iv) easing restrictions on making claims; (v) a level playing field exists between EU and non-EU manufacturers.

It could be argued that both Directives (the revised PLD and the proposed AI Liability Directive) raise the likelihood of manufacturers/producers/operators and importers operating within the EU facing considerable litigation risks (including the risk of third-party litigation funding), abusive discovery of evidence, and overall higher insurance costs. On the other hand, one of the main objectives of the forthcoming EU liability regime for AI and other emerging digital technologies is to ensure that consumers will have a fair chance of getting compensation, especially in complex cases. To this end, specific measures have been introduced to address unnecessary obstacles to getting compensation for damage, i.e., to ensure that injured/harmed parties are equally protected throughout the EU.

It is expected that the forthcoming EU liability framework for AI and other emerging digital technologies (designed to accommodate the latest technological developments, circular economy business models, and global value chains) will succeed in achieving the EU's overarching objective, namely to strike the right balance between protecting citizens and supporting technological innovation. This can be done by: (i) providing legal certainty to industry's market players about the vast risks they take in the course of their business (in relation to the liability exposure of businesses developing or using AI); (ii) encouraging the prevention of damage; (iii) instilling confidence in the safety and reliability of AI-related products and services; (iv) guaranteeing adequate/fair compensation for victims; (v) fostering innovation and creating stability for AI-enabled technology investment.

It is noted that all major legislative and policy documents are presented in this book in full detail, taking into account the comments delivered by all relevant parties (e.g. the European Commission, the Council of the European Union, the European Parliament, public and governmental organisations, national competent authorities, stakeholders/actors with different interests, such as corporations, business and consumer associations, civil society and other non-profit organisations, academic/research institutions etc.). As a result, readers are provided with an opportunity to comprehend the underlying motives behind the varying approaches of European Institutions, along with the frequently conflicting interests of stakeholders. Consequently, readers can acquire a comprehensive understanding of the forthcoming EU liability framework for artificial intelligence, robotics, the Internet of Things (IoT), and other emerging digital technologies.

Legal/Policy Documents, Studies, Reports, References, and Other Sources

European Commission ('Commission') Communication, "Artificial Intelligence for Europe", COM(2018) 237 final, Brussels, 25.4.2018.

European Parliament Resolution of 16 February 2017 with recommendations to the Commission on Civil Law Rules on Robotics (2015/2103(INL)), (2018/C 252/25), OJ C 252, 18.7.2018, pp. 239-257.

Commission Communication, "Investing in a smart, innovative and sustainable Industry - A renewed EU Industrial Policy Strategy", COM(2017) 479 final, Brussels, 13.9.2017.

'European enterprise survey on the use of technologies based on artificial intelligence', Study prepared for the European Commission, DG Communications Networks, Content & Technology by Ipsos Belgium and iCite (International Centre for Innovation, Technology and Education), 2020, Final report.

Regulation (EU) 2024/1689 of the European Parliament and of the Council of 13 June 2024 laying down harmonised rules on artificial intelligence and amending Regulations (EC) No 300/2008, (EU) No 167/2013, (EU) No 168/2013, (EU) 2018/858, (EU) 2018/1139 and (EU) 2019/2144 and Directives 2014/90/EU, (EU) 2016/797 and (EU) 2020/1828 (*EU Artificial Intelligence Act*), OJ L, 12.07.2024.

Proposal for a Directive of the European Parliament and of the Council on adapting non-contractual civil liability rules to artificial intelligence (AI Liability Directive), European Commission, COM(2022) 496 final, Brussels, 28.9.2022 (the 'proposed AI Liability Directive').

Proposal for a Directive of the European Parliament and of the Council on liability for defective products, European Commission, COM(2022) 495 final, Brussels, 28.9.2022 (the 'proposal for a revised Product Liability Directive (PLD)').

Council of the European Union, Note: From: General Secretariat of the Council. To: Delegations. Subject: Proposal for a Directive of the European Parliament and of the Council on liability for defective products - Mandate for negotiations with the European Parliament, Brussels, 15 June 2023, Council doc. 10694/23 ("General Secretariat of the Council - General approach on the proposal for a revised PLD, 15 June 2023").

Draft Report of the European Parliament's Committee on Internal Market and Consumer Protection and the Committee on Legal Affairs on the proposal for a directive of the European Parliament and of the Council on Liability for defective products (COM(2022)0495 – C9-0322/2022 – 2022/0302(COD)), 05.04.2023, ("Draft Joint Report of the European Parliament's co-leading IMCO and JURI Committees on the proposal for a revised PLD, 5 April 2023").

Joint Report of the European Parliament's co-leading IMCO and JURI Committees on the proposal for a directive of the European Parliament and of the Council on liability for defective products, A9-0291/2023, 12 October 2023.

European Parliament, Press Release (IMCO-JURI), “Better protection for consumers against damages by defective products”, 09.10.2023.

Council of the European Union, Information Note: From: General Secretariat of the Council. To: Delegations. Subject: Proposal for a Directive of the European Parliament and of the Council on liability for defective products – Letter sent to the European Parliament, Brussels, 24 January 2024, Council doc. 5809/24 (“General Secretariat of the Council – Proposal for a Directive on liability for defective products – Letter sent to the European Parliament, Council doc. 5809/ 24, 24 January 2024”).

European Parliament, Committee on the Internal Market and Consumer Protection (IMCO) and Committee on Legal Affairs (JURI), “Provisional Agreement Resulting from Interinstitutional Negotiations”, Subject: Proposal for a Directive of the European Parliament and of the Council on Liability for defective products (COM(2022)0495 – C9 0322/2022 – 2022/0302(COD)), 31 January 2024.

European Parliament legislative resolution of 12 March 2024 on the proposal for a Directive of the European Parliament and of the Council on liability for defective products (COM(2022)0495 – C9-0322/2022 – 2022/0302(COD)), (Ordinary legislative procedure: first reading) – P9_TC1-COD(2022)0302, Position of the European Parliament adopted at first reading on 12 March 2024 with a view to the adoption of Directive (EU) 2024/... of the European Parliament and of the Council on liability for defective products and repealing Council Directive 85/374/EEC [“Position of the European Parliament of 12 March 2024 for the adoption of a Directive on liability for defective products (revised PLD)”].

Nikos Th. Nikolinakos, EU Policy and Legal Framework for Artificial Intelligence, Robotics and Related Technologies – The AI Act, Springer, 2023.

Chapter 2
Major EU Policy Developments on Liability for Artificial Intelligence, Robotics, and Emerging Digital Technologies: 2015 to 2018

2.1 Introduction

This chapter traces the evolution of the EU policy on Artificial Intelligence, discussing the main liability-related policy documents and measures which set the tone for strengthening the EU AI ecosystem. It outlines the European Parliament's initial approach to artificial intelligence and robotics, which asked the European Commission ('Commission') to present a legislative proposal laying down a set of civil law rules and ethical aspects on robotics and artificial intelligence. The chapter also presents the Commission's vision of dealing with AI liability issues, offering, *inter alia*, some preliminary insights as to the policy options and what the forthcoming EU liability framework for AI might include. As it is explained, it is imperative to ensure that AI is developed and applied in an appropriate liability framework which promotes innovation whereas, at the same time, guarantees a high level of consumer protection and ensures that injured parties are remedied/compensated efficiently.

2.2 The Digital Single Market (DSM) Strategy

In 2015 the Commission initiated an ambitious strategy to achieve a Digital Single Market (DSM) in Europe.[1] A key success factor for embracing digital technologies and reaping the full benefits of a DSM is a highly competitive digital industry in Europe and the integration of digital innovations in all sectors.

[1] Commission Communication, "A Digital Single Market Strategy for Europe", COM(2015) 192 final, Brussels, 6.5.2015.

N. T. Nikolinakos, *Adapting the EU Civil Liability Regime to the Digital Age: Artificial Intelligence, Robotics, and Other Emerging Technologies*, Law, Governance and Technology Series 68, https://doi.org/10.1007/978-3-031-67969-8_2

As the Commission put it: "*the global economy is rapidly becoming digital. Information and Communications Technology (ICT) is no longer a specific sector but the foundation of all modern innovative economic systems. The Internet and digital technologies are transforming the lives we lead, the way we work – as individuals, in business, and in our communities as they become more integrated across all sectors of our economy and society. These changes are happening at a scale and speed that bring immense opportunities for innovation, growth and jobs. They also raise challenging policy issues for public authorities which require coordinated EU action. ... For many issues the European level offers the right framework. That is why the European Commission has set the creation of a Digital Single Market as one of its key priorities. A Digital Single Market is one in which the free movement of goods, persons, services and capital is ensured and where individuals and businesses can seamlessly access and exercise online activities under conditions of fair competition, and a high level of consumer and personal data protection, irrespective of their nationality or place of residence. Achieving a Digital Single Market will ensure that Europe maintains its position as a world leader in the digital economy, helping European companies to grow globally*".[2]

According to the Commission, the Digital Single Market Strategy should be built on three pillars: (i) better access for consumers and businesses to online goods and services across Europe—this requires the rapid removal of key differences between the online and offline worlds to break down barriers to cross-border online activity; (ii) creating the right conditions for digital networks and services to flourish—this requires high-speed, secure and trustworthy infrastructures and content services, supported by the right regulatory conditions for innovation, investment, fair competition and a level playing field; (iii) maximising the growth potential of our European Digital Economy—this requires investment in ICT infrastructures and technologies such as Cloud computing and Big Data, and research and innovation to boost industrial competitiveness as well as better public services, inclusiveness and skills.[3]

With regard to the target of creating the right regulatory conditions and establishing a level playing field for advanced digital networks and innovative services, the Commission focused on the necessity to build on trustworthy, high-speed, affordable networks and services in order to safeguard consumers' fundamental rights to privacy and personal data protection while also encouraging innovation. This requires a dynamic and competitive telecoms sector in order to carry out the necessary investments and to exploit innovations such as Cloud computing, Big Data tools or the Internet of Things. The Commission also underlined that the market power of some online platforms could raise major concerns, particularly in relation to the most powerful platforms which are becoming increasingly essential for other market participants.[4]

---

[2] Ibid., at p. 3.

[3] Ibid., at pp. 3–4.

[4] Ibid., at pp. 9–13.

Even before the Communication on a Digital Single Market (DSM) Strategy for Europe, the then Commissioner Jean-Claude Juncker had particularly spoken about the importance of delivering the right conditions for creating a connected single digital market in Europe, and had identified specific legislative steps that should be followed in order to achieve this target and maximise the growth potential of the digital economy.[5]

Artificial intelligence comprises a vital part of the Commission's strategy to digitise industry and to achieve the Digital Single Market (DSM) in Europe.[6] The Commission stated that industry in the EU can build on its strengths in professional digital technologies and on its strong presence in traditional sectors to seize the wide range of opportunities that IoT, big data and AI-based systems offer. The main aim

[5]Source: Jean-Claude Juncker, Extract from the Political Guidelines for the next European Commission – A New Start for Europe: My Agenda for Jobs, Growth, Fairness and Democratic Change (15 July 2014) Priority n°2: A Connected Digital Single Market: "I believe that we must make much better use of the great opportunities offered by digital technologies, which know no borders. To do so, we will need to have the courage to break down national silos in telecoms regulation, in copyright and data protection legislation, in the management of radio waves and in the application of competition law. If we do this, we can ensure that European citizens will soon be able to use their mobile phones across Europe without having to pay roaming charges. We can ensure that consumers can access services, music, movies and sports events on their electronic devices wherever they are in Europe and regardless of borders. We can create a fair level playing field where all companies offering their goods or services in the European Union are subject to the same data protection and consumer rules, regardless of where their server is based. By creating a connected digital single market, we can generate up to EUR 250 billion of additional growth in Europe in the course of the mandate of the next Commission, thereby creating hundreds of thousands of new jobs, notably for younger job-seekers, and a vibrant knowledge-based society. To achieve this, I intend to take, within the first six months of my mandate, ambitious legislative steps towards a connected digital single market, notably by swiftly concluding negotiations on common European data protection rules; by adding more ambition to the ongoing reform of our telecoms rules; by modernising copyright rules in the light of the digital revolution and changed consumer behaviour; and by modernising and simplifying consumer rules for online and digital purchases. This should go hand-in-hand with efforts to boost digital skills and learning across society and to facilitate the creation of innovative start-ups. Enhancing the use of digital technologies and online services should become a horizontal policy, covering all sectors of the economy and of the public sector".

[6]Commission Communication, "Digitising European Industry - Reaping the full benefits of a Digital Single Market", COM(2016) 180 final, Brussels, 19.4.2016, at p. 2: "Progress in digital technologies in combination with other key enabling technologies is changing the way we design, produce, commercialise and generate value from products and related services. Advances in technologies such as the Internet of Things (IoT), 5G, cloud computing, data analytics and robotics are transforming products, processes and business models in all sectors ultimately creating new industrial patterns as global value chains shift. The challenge ahead is for the European industry to seize fully and swiftly these digital opportunities. This is essential to ensure Europe's mid and long term competitiveness with implications for overall welfare. Achieving the Digital Single Market (DSM) in Europe is a prerequisite for attracting investment in digital innovations and for faster business growth in the digital economy. In 2015 the European Commission initiated an ambitious strategy to achieve a DSM. A key success factor for reaping the full benefits of a DSM is a highly competitive digital industry in Europe and the integration of digital innovations in all sectors. Embracing digital technologies will help companies to grow beyond the EU internal market and make the EU an even more attractive location for global investments".

of the Commission is therefore "to reinforce the EU's competitiveness in digital technologies and to ensure that every industry in Europe ... can fully benefit from digital innovations".[7]

The Digital Single Market (DSM) strategy may require, however, a set of coherent policy measures that should be introduced, as part of a DSM technologies and public services modernisation package. Indeed, the fast development and wider use of digital technologies may require further modernisation of the current regulatory framework. It is necessary to provide the appropriate regulatory framework conditions, by clarifying and adjusting the legal framework, in order to establish the required trust and legal certainty for industry in Europe. As the Commission put it, "...digital technologies are developing so fast that the legal framework needs to be monitored constantly to make sure it remains in line with the technological development".[8] To this end, the Commission stated that it will explore the legal frameworks for autonomous systems and IoT applications, and in particular the safety and liability rules as well as the legal conditions to allow large scale testing in real life environments. It also stressed that it will initiate work on the safety of apps and other non-embedded software not covered by sectoral legislation, assessing a possible need for further action at the EU level.[9]

2.3 Mid-Term Review of the Digital Single Market (DSM) Strategy and the "Data Economy"

In May 2017, the Commission published its mid-term Review of the Digital Single Market (DSM) Strategy.[10] It emphasised the significance of building on Europe's scientific and industrial strengths, as well as on its innovative startups, in order to be in a leading position in the development of AI technologies, platforms, and applications. The Communication begun with the then President's Juncker statement in

---

[7] Ibid., at p. 6.

[8] Ibid., at p. 13: "stakeholders expressed a need to examine the regulatory framework for digital innovations with a view to provide further clarity on the following: • Ownership and use of data generated in an industrial context are major areas of concern. When it is personal data, protection is dealt with in the General Data Protection Regulation, together with the ePrivacy Directive. The already foreseen initiative on "free flow of data" under the DSM will examine issues of ownership, interoperability, exploitation and access to data, including industrial data. • Autonomously acting systems such as self-driving cars or drones pose a challenge to current safety and liability rules where a legal person is ultimately responsible. Legal implications of the roll-out of IoT are wider than the allocation of liability as recognised in the DSM strategy and also need to be addressed. • Apps and other non-embedded software (not contained in a tangible medium) might also raise potential safety risks and are currently not fully addressed by the EU legal framework".

[9] Ibid.

[10] Commission Communication on the Mid-Term Review on the implementation of the Digital Single Market Strategy - A Connected Digital Single Market for All, COM(2017) 228 final, Brussels, 10.5.2017.

his State of the European Union speech on 14 September 2016: "Digital technologies and digital communications are permeating every aspect of life. We need to work for a Europe that empowers our citizens and our economy. And today, both have gone digital".[11]

The mid-term Review pointed out that the main goal of the Digital Single Market (DSM) strategy is to create an open market where—through improved access and fair conditions—it is easy for businesses and people to operate as effectively anywhere in Europe as it is at home. It went on to underline that this completion of the EU Single Digital Market requires a clear, transparent and stable legal environment in order "to stimulate innovation, tackle market fragmentation and allow all players to tap into the new market dynamics under fair and balanced conditions. This will provide the bedrock of trust that is essential for business and consumer confidence".[12]

The mid-term Review underlined the Commission's strategy to digitise industry and to achieve the Digital Single Market (DSM) in Europe, stating also that the emerging digital technologies must be based on specific rules in order to provide confidence to consumers and business alike. It recognized that the digital world is a fast-moving environment and that a fair, open and secure digital environment is required. To this end, EU policy needs to adapt to changing circumstances. It pointed out that the Digital Single Market Strategy should be extended to keep up to date with emerging trends and challenges such as those related to online platforms, the data economy and cybersecurity.[13]

With regard to online platforms in particular, one of Commission's targets is to promote online platforms as responsible players of a fair internet ecosystem. Online platforms[14] cover a wide-ranging set of activities including online advertising platforms, search engines, social media and creative content outlets, application distribution platforms, communications services, and payment systems. The Commission acknowledged that online platforms drive innovation and growth in the digital economy, that they play an important role in the development of the online world and create new market opportunities.[15]

---

[11] Ibid., at p. 1. See also at p. 2 of the Communication: "Successive waves of technological change have transformed human societies and economies, with long-term benefits for both economic growth and quality of life. The current digital revolution has the power to do so again".

[12] Ibid., at Section 1.

[13] Ibid., at Section 3.

[14] According to the Commission, a non-exhaustive set of examples is: Google's AdSense, DoubleClick, eBay and Amazon Marketplace, Google and Bing Search, Facebook and YouTube, Google Play and App Store, Facebook Messenger, PayPal, Zalando marketplace and Uber. See Commission Communication, "Online Platforms and the Digital Single Market Opportunities and Challenges for Europe", COM (2016) 288 final, Brussels, 25.05.2016, at p. 2.

[15] "Online platforms share some important and specific characteristics. In particular: - they have the ability to create and shape new markets, to challenge traditional ones, and to organise new forms of participation or conducting business based on collecting, processing, and editing large amounts of data; - they operate in multisided markets but with varying degrees of control over direct interactions between groups of users; - they benefit from 'network effects', where, broadly speaking, the

At the same time, however, the growing importance of the digital economy raises new policy and regulatory challenges. Indeed, platforms have become key gatekeepers of the internet, intermediating access to information, content and online trading. In addition, large online platforms are becoming increasingly dominant in the relevant market due, amongst other reasons, to their ability to track and store personal data. The challenges of managing privacy, cybersecurity as well as avoiding abuses of market power will increase. This creates concerns and, in order to address them, the Commission's policy objective is to safeguard a fair, predictable, sustainable and innovation-friendly business environment in the online economy. It also made the commitment to maintain a balanced and predictable liability regime for online platforms and to pursue a sectoral, problem-driven approach that ensures that illegal content online (e.g. public incitement to violence and hatred, i.e. illegal hate speech, incitement to terrorism or child sexual abuse material) is timely and effectively removed, with proper checks and balances, from online platforms.[16]

Furthermore, as already mentioned, one of the objectives of the Digital Single Market Strategy ("DSM Strategy") was to increase trust in and the security of digital services. The reform of the data protection framework is a key action to this end. The Commission recognised the important role that data economy can play in order to help European businesses to grow, to modernise public services and to empower citizens. For this to happen, data needs to be continuously accessible and able to

---

value of the service increases with the number of users; they often rely on information and communications technologies to reach their users, instantly and effortlessly; - they play a key role in digital value creation, notably by capturing significant value (including through data accumulation), facilitating new business ventures, and creating new strategic dependencies. These features of online platforms have brought a range of important benefits to the digital economy and society. Online platforms facilitate efficiency gains, and act as a magnet for data-driven innovation. They increase consumer choice, thereby contributing to improved competitiveness of industry and enhancing consumer welfare. Online platforms also offer the potential to enhance citizens' participation in society and democracy, as they facilitate access to information, in particular for younger generations and across borders". Commission Communication, "Online Platforms and the Digital Single Market Opportunities and Challenges for Europe", COM (2016) 288 final, Brussels, 25.05.2016, at pp. 2–3.

[16]Commission Communication on the Mid-Term Review on the implementation of the Digital Single Market Strategy—A Connected Digital Single Market for All, COM(2017) 228 final, Brussels, 10.5.2017, at Section 3.1.

See also Commission Communication, "Online Platforms and the Digital Single Market Opportunities and Challenges for Europe", COM (2016) 288 final, Brussels, 25.05.2016, especially pp. 6–14. In this Communication, the Commission stressed that, in order to achieve a balanced regulatory framework for online platforms, the following principles should be taken into account: - a level playing field for comparable digital services; - responsible behaviour of online platforms to protect core values; - transparency and fairness for maintaining user trust and safeguarding innovation; - open and non-discriminatory markets in a data-driven economy.

move freely within the single market, assisted by the necessary high performance computing capability to analyse it.[17]

It should be stressed that the rollout of the Internet of Things brings substantial challenges in terms of the safety of connected systems, products, and services, as well as for businesses' liability. Indeed, faulty sensors, vulnerable software or unstable connectivity may make it difficult to determine who is technically and legally responsible for any ensuing damage. Therefore, in order to fully unlock the data economy, the Commission considered that the current legal framework needs to keep up to date with emerging trends and adapt to changing circumstances in order to take account of new technological developments (including artificial intelligence and robotics), mainly from the angle of civil law liability. As a result, the evaluation of the Directive on liability for defective products (the Product Liability Directive) was considered to be required.[18]

The Commission's Communication on "Building a European Data Economy" also stressed that there is need for legal certainty as to the allocation of liability in the context of the emerging digital technologies, pointing out that new liability issues would arise in light of new technological developments such as the Internet of Things, advanced robotics and autonomous systems powered by artificial intelligence. This is why the Commission acknowledged the need to assess the adequacy of civil law liability rules due to the emergence of the Internet of Things, advanced robotics, and autonomous systems. As it was stated, "other emerging issues concern

[17]According to the Commission, "assuming that an appropriate policy and legislative framework for the data economy is put in place in time, the value of the data economy will increase to EUR 739 billion by 2020, representing 4% of overall EU GDP (more than doubling the situation today), and the number of data professionals will increase from over 6 million in 2016 to over 10 million by 2020, according to the estimates of a high growth scenario". The high growth scenario is characterised by a stronger driving role of digital innovation and higher overall ICT investments as a share of GDP. See Commission Communication on the Mid-Term Review on the implementation of the Digital Single Market Strategy—A Connected Digital Single Market for All, COM (2017) 228 final, Brussels, 10.5.2017, at Section 3.2.

See also European Data Market Study SMART 2013/0063, Final Report, prepared for the European Commission (Directorate-General for Communications Networks, Content and Technology) by IDC and Open Evidence, 1 February 2017.

[18]Commission Communication on the Mid-Term Review on the implementation of the Digital Single Market Strategy—A Connected Digital Single Market for All, COM(2017) 228 final, Brussels, 10.5.2017, at Section 3.2.

See also Commission Communication "Building a European Data Economy", COM(2017) 9 final, Brussels, 10.1.2017, p. 14: "However, it may become difficult or unclear how to apply the provisions of this [Product Liability] Directive in the context of IoT and autonomous connected systems (e.g. robotics), for the following reasons: the characteristics of these systems, for example a complicated product or service value chain, with interdependencies between suppliers, manufacturers and other third parties; uncertainty in relation to the legal nature of IoT devices, i.e. whether they are products, services, or products that come with the sale of a service; and the autonomous nature of these technologies. The Commission has launched a broad evaluation of the Products Liability Directive, to assess its overall functioning and whether its rules, developed for a very different environment, remain appropriate for emerging technologies such as IoT and autonomous connected systems".

the application of the rules on liability for any damages resulting from a fault in a connected device or a robot; and portability and interoperability of the data. In the context of new technologies such as the Internet of Things (IoT) or robotics there are complex and sophisticated interdependencies both within products (based on hardware and software) and across interconnected devices. Moreover, new issues can emerge from autonomous machines, whose unexpected and unintended behaviour could create damages to persons and objects. These phenomena may create legal uncertainty in relation to the application of the existing framework on liability and safety";[19] "another emerging issue concerns the application of the current rules on liability in the data economy in relation to products and services based on emerging technologies such as the Internet of Things (IoT), the factories of the future and autonomous connected systems. IoT is a rapidly growing network of everyday objects, such as watches, vehicles, and thermostats, which are connected to the Internet. Autonomous connected systems, such as self-driving vehicles, act independently of humans and are capable of understanding and interpreting their environments. These emerging technologies use sensors to provide the many types of data that are often required for the product or service to function. All these innovations are likely to contribute to more safety and quality of life, but inevitably there remains the possibility of design errors, malfunctioning or manipulation in every device. This could result from the transmission of erroneous data by a sensor, due to, for instance, software defects, connectivity problems or incorrect operation of the machine. The nature of these systems means that it may be difficult to establish the exact source of a problem that leads to damages, raising the issue of how to ensure that these systems are safe for the users, in order to minimise the occurrence of damage and who should be held liable for damage if it occurs. The issue of how to provide certainty to both users and manufacturers of such devices in relation to their potential liability is therefore of central importance to the emergence of a data economy".[20]

In addition, the Commission highlighted the importance of tackling cybersecurity challenges in order to increase trust in digital technologies and provide confidence to consumers and business alike. It stressed that a connected economy and society is more vulnerable to cyber threats and attacks. Network and information systems and services play a vital role in society and their reliability and security are, therefore, essential for the smooth functioning of the internal market. Due to increased reliance on networks, any vulnerability, such as an unsecured connection or product, can be exploited and cause damage ranging from small-value losses to large-scale breaches of sensitive personal data and terrorism acts.[21] The frequency and impact of security

[19] Commission Communication "Building a European Data Economy", COM(2017) 9 final, Brussels, 10.1.2017, p. 4.

[20] Ibid., pp. 13–14.

[21] Commission Communication on the Mid-Term Review on the implementation of the Digital Single Market Strategy—A Connected Digital Single Market for All, COM(2017) 228 final, Brussels, 10.5.2017, at Section 3.3.

incidents are increasing and represent a major threat to the functioning of network and information systems. Indeed, cyberattacks were already on the increase[22] and tackling them faces the problem that while cyberattacks are often cross-border, law enforcement competences are strictly national. Therefore, in order to ensure cybersecurity and increase trust in digital technologies, an effective EU level response is also required.

2.4 Artificial Intelligence and the Renewed EU Industrial Policy Strategy

Artificial Intelligence is also an essential part of the renewed EU Industrial Policy Strategy.[23] In the age of globalization, technological change is transforming our lives at unprecedented speed and, therefore, more action must be taken to adjust to the challenges posed and reap the benefits of technological advances. As the Commission put it, "the hallmarks of this new industrial age are the accelerated pace of economic, societal and environmental transformations as well as technological breakthroughs in areas like robotics, Internet of Things, artificial intelligence, energy systems and bio-economy. Automation, enabled by information technologies, is transforming traditional manufacturing processes and the nature of work".[24]

The Commission recognises that data are becoming the new competitive factor in our connected world, that Europe's competitors are investing heavily in the upgrade of their industry and that the EU's innovation gap with some countries is increasing.[25] Although Europe is a leader in many manufacturing industries and its companies are often at the forefront of digitisation and automation in key industry sectors,[26] its role in the data and platform economy is limited, the uptake of digital technology by SMEs is low and only a fifth of companies in the EU is highly digitized.[27]

It is therefore imperative to increase EU industry's ability to continuously innovate "by facilitating investment in new technologies and embracing changes brought on by increased digitisation and the transition to a low-carbon and more

[22] Ibid. More than 4000 ransomware attacks have occurred every day since the beginning of 2016, a 300% increase over 2015.

[23] Commission Communication, "Investing in a smart, innovative and sustainable Industry - A renewed EU Industrial Policy Strategy", COM(2017) 479 final, Brussels, 13.9.2017.

[24] Ibid., at p. 2.

[25] Ibid., at pp. 3–4.

[26] Europe has a world market share of 33% in robotics, 30% in embedded systems, 55% of automotive semiconductors, 20% of semiconductor equipment and 20% of photonics components. Commission Communication, "Investing in a smart, innovative and sustainable Industry - A renewed EU Industrial Policy Strategy", COM(2017) 479 final, Brussels, 13.9.2017, at p. 8.

[27] Ibid. See also Europe's Digital Progress Report, SWD(2017) 160, 10 May 2017.

circular economy".[28] This industrial transformation requires substantial investment in advanced manufacturing and "a better functioning Single Market. With technology leading the way, a modern industrial policy can revitalise EU regions and build resilience to adapt to the changing global environment".[29]

In order to cope with the considerable pressure the ongoing industrial transformation[30] is putting on European industry to adapt, the Single Market should be further strengthened and disproportionate regulatory barriers should be tackled. A modern industrial policy is required, one which can upgrade industry for the digital age: "The future of industry will be digital. Digital transformation is at the core of the ongoing industrial revolution. Progress in technologies such as big data, artificial intelligence and robotics, the Internet of Things and high-performance computing is impacting the very nature of work and society as a whole. With the advent of digital technologies, the service component of industry is becoming ever more important. Boosting the uptake of smart technologies along and across industrial value chains and promoting firm growth is therefore key to Europe's growth and competitiveness".[31]

The Commission underlined the importance of having a comprehensive strategy on Digitising European Industry,[32] it stressed that the key for embracing the emerging digital technologies is the creation of a Digital Single—and competitive—Market and stated that, in order to maximise the growth potential of European Digital Economy, investment in ICT infrastructures and technologies is required, accompanied by the right legal/regulatory conditions for innovation, fair competition and a level playing field.[33]

---

[28] Commission Communication, "Investing in a smart, innovative and sustainable Industry - A renewed EU Industrial Policy Strategy", COM(2017) 479 final, Brussels, 13.9.2017, at p. 4.

[29] Ibid.

[30] "We are still in the early phase of the transformation where digitalisation, robots, artificial intelligence, the internet of things, 3D printing will revolutionise how we produce, work, move and consume. ... Virtually all sectors will be changed, such as: • transport with e.g. driverless and connected cars, drones or car-sharing, • energy with e.g. smart grids, renewable energy, distributed generation, • agri-food with e.g. climate friendly farming, applications to reduce food waste, • telecommunication with e.g. more powerful networks, virtual reality, virtual workspace, • distribution with the growing importance of e-commerce, • financial services with e.g. virtual banks and insurance, or crowdfunding, • factory production with automation, or • health care, with e.g. online diagnosis, increased cross border mobility of medical professionals". Commission Communication, "Reflection Paper on Harnessing Globalisation", COM (2017) 240 final, Brussels, 10.5.2017, p. 11.

[31] Commission Communication, "Investing in a smart, innovative and sustainable Industry - A renewed EU Industrial Policy Strategy", COM(2017) 479 final, Brussels, 13.9.2017, at p. 8.

[32] Commission Communication, "Digitising European Industry - Reaping the full benefits of a Digital Single Market", COM(2016) 180 final, Brussels, 19.4.2016.

[33] Commission Communication, "Investing in a smart, innovative and sustainable Industry - A renewed EU Industrial Policy Strategy", COM(2017) 479 final, Brussels, 13.9.2017, at pp. 8–9: "Digital industrial platforms (e.g. industrial internet and industrial data platforms) will help to bring together different technologies and applications, facilitating the development of new products, processes, and in particular as well new business and service models. ... Many other initiatives under the Digital Single Market Strategy are pushing the digitisation of industry and modernisation

2.5 The European Parliament Resolution with Recommendations to the Commission on Civil Law Rules on Robotics

In January 2017, and based on the "Ethical Aspects of Cyber-Physical Systems (CPS)"[34] and "European Civil Rules in Robotics"[35] studies, the European Parliament's Legal Affairs (JURI) Committee took the initiative to draft a report tabling a motion for a Resolution of a legislative character and including recommendations to the Commission on the civil-law and ethical aspects of robotics.[36] While the European Commission was expected to present one or more legislative proposals related to robotics and artificial intelligence, the European Parliament decided to pave the way for such initiatives using its rights under Article 225 of the Treaty on the Functioning of the European Union and Rule 46 of its Rules of Procedure.

After a hot debate, the European Parliament adopted, on 16 February 2017, a Resolution containing recommendations to the Commission on Civil Law Rules on

---

of public services, including through actions on ICT standardisation, public administration, high-speed connectivity (including 5G) and the Internet of Things. But the mid-term review of the Strategy shows that Europe needs to go further. The Commission will put forward under this mandate a number of further ambitious initiatives to give European industry the Digital Single Market it needs. These initiatives address issues like the development of the data economy, artificial intelligence and high performance computing, which are critical for smart industrial eco-systems and big-data applications. The comprehensive cyber-security package adopted today is an important contribution to address cyber-threats and further reinforces Europe's strength in data security and data protection. State of the art digital infrastructure and harnessing appropriate spectrum resources are also essential both for the development of ground-breaking digital innovations such as additive manufacturing or automated driving, as well as for a wide roll-out of digitisation to all parts of our economies and to citizens. The EU and its Member States must provide the right framework conditions for such infrastructures to develop. ... Next-generation connectivity – especially 5G – is the foundation on which future business models will be built. Autonomous vehicles, the Internet of Things and countless other applications that future industrial strength will hinge on simply cannot be realised without faster and seamless internet speed. The efforts to expedite 5G adoption are formidable, but so are the potential rewards which can give European industry a first-mover advantage and global competitive edge".

[34] Scientific Foresight Study "Ethical Aspects of Cyber-Physical Systems"—Science and Technology Options Assessment—European Parliamentary Research Service (EPRS)—Scientific Foresight Unit (STOA)—PE563.501, June 2016. The study was requested by the Science and Technology Options Assessment Panel (STOA). The main part of the study was conducted by Technopolis Group and managed by the Scientific Foresight Unit within the Directorate-General for Parliamentary Research Services (DG EPRS) of the European Parliament.

[35] Study "European Civil Rules in Robotics"—Directorate General for Internal Policies—Policy Department C: Citizens' Rights and Constitutional Affairs—Legal Affairs—Study for the JURI Committee, October 2016.

[36] Report of the Committee on Legal Affairs of the European Parliament with recommendations to the Commission on Civil Law Rules on Robotics—Motion for a European Parliament Resolution (2015/2103(INL)), 27.1.2017, A8-0005/2017.

Robotics (the 'Resolution').[37] The Resolution made wide ranging recommendations and asked the Commission to present a legislative proposal laying down a set of civil law rules on robotics and artificial intelligence. It is reminded that the Resolution is not in itself a legislative initiative but rather a set of recommendations destined for the European Commission, asking the executive body to draw up a legal framework for the civilian use of robots.

The Parliament's Resolution was set out in several sections on the development of robotics and artificial intelligence solely for civil use, namely: ethical principles such as transparency, and the well-established bioethical principles of beneficence, non-maleficence, autonomy and justice; the creation of a European agency to provide technical, ethical and regulatory expertise and guidelines on best practice; intellectual property rights and the flow of data; standardisation, safety and security; autonomous vehicles; care robots; medical robots; human repair and enhancement; drones; education and employment impact forecast; liability and international aspects thereof; as well as a code for research ethics committees. The Resolution called for EU legislation introducing a register of robots, setting up an EU Agency for Robotics and laying down principles of civil liability for damages caused by robots. Such legislation should be complemented by ethical codes of conduct.

The Resolution recognised that artificial intelligence has become an area of strategic importance and a key driver of economic development. In order to make the most of the opportunities offered by AI it is necessary to establish a legal framework which ensures high levels of protection and safety, while, at the same time, it is future-oriented and flexible enough to promote innovation: "now that humankind stands on the threshold of an era when ever more sophisticated robots, bots, androids and other manifestations of artificial intelligence ("AI") seem to be poised to unleash a new industrial revolution, which is likely to leave no stratum of society untouched, it is vitally important for the legislature to consider its legal and ethical implications and effects, without stifling innovation";[38] "a gradualist, pragmatic and cautious approach should be adopted for the Union with regard to future initiatives on robotics and AI so as to ensure that we do not stifle innovation".[39]

It was also underlined that, in order to properly address the development of robotics and AI for civil use, a common definition of smart autonomous[40] robots is fundamental: "there is a need to create a generally accepted definition of robot and

[37] European Parliament Resolution of 16 February 2017 with recommendations to the Commission on Civil Law Rules on Robotics (2015/2103(INL)), (2018/C 252/25), OJ C 252, 18.7.2018, pp. 239–257 ("European Parliament Resolution of 16 February 2017 on Civil Law Rules on Robotics").

[38] European Parliament Resolution of 16 February 2017 on Civil Law Rules on Robotics, section "Introduction", recital B, p. 239.

[39] ibid., section "Introduction", recital X, p. 241.

[40] Ibid., section "Liability", recital AA, p. 242. "A robot's autonomy can be defined as the ability to take decisions and implement them in the outside world, independently of external control or influence; this autonomy is of a purely technological nature and its degree depends on how sophisticated a robot's interaction with its environment has been designed to be".

AI that is flexible and is not hindering innovation".[41] The Parliament's Resolution called on the Commission to propose EU legislation defining a 'smart robot' as one which has autonomy through the use of sensors and/or interconnectivity with the environment, which has at least a minor physical support, which adapts its behaviour and actions to the environment and which cannot be defined as having 'life' in the biological sense. The exact text of the Resolution, which did not propose a straightforward definition, reads as follows: "Calls on the Commission to propose common Union definitions of cyber physical systems, autonomous systems, smart autonomous robots and their subcategories by taking into consideration the following characteristics of a smart robot: the acquisition of autonomy through sensors and/or by exchanging data with its environment (inter-connectivity) and the trading and analysing of those data; self-learning from experience and by interaction (optional criterion); at least a minor physical support; the adaptation of its behaviour and actions to the environment; absence of life in the biological sense".[42]

The Parliament's Resolution proposed that a system of registration of advanced robots should be introduced that would be managed by an EU Agency for Robotics and Artificial Intelligence.[43] Specific criteria should be established for the classification of those advanced robots that would need to be registered. As it was stated, "registration of smart robots: For the purposes of traceability and in order to facilitate the implementation of further recommendations, a system of registration of advanced robots should be introduced, based on the criteria established for the classification of robots. The system of registration and the register should be Union-wide, covering the internal market, and could be managed by a designated EU Agency for Robotics and Artificial Intelligence in case such an Agency is created".[44] This proposed Agency was considered to be necessary in order to guarantee coherent cross-border rules in the EU, to allow the deployment of robots which are consistent with the required levels of safety and security and to provide technical, ethical and regulatory expertise on robotics to public authorities.[45]

As regards liability for damage caused by robots, the Resolution pointed out that robots increasingly operate in close proximity to humans and, therefore, the

---

[41] Ibid., section "Introduction", recital C, p. 239.

[42] Ibid., section "General principles concerning the development of robotics and artificial intelligence for civil use", point 1, p. 243.

[43] Ibid., section "General principles concerning the development of robotics and artificial intelligence for civil use", point 2, p. 243.

[44] Annex to the European Parliament Resolution of 16 February 2017 on Civil Law Rules on Robotics: Recommendations as to the content of the proposal requested ("Annex to the European Parliament Resolution of 16 February 2017 on Civil Law Rules on Robotics"), at p. 252.

[45] European Parliament Resolution of 16 February 2017 on Civil Law Rules on Robotics, section "A European Agency", points 15–17, pp. 244–245. At point 16 the Commission was asked "to consider the designation of a European Agency for Robotics and Artificial Intelligence in order to provide the technical, ethical and regulatory expertise needed to support the relevant public actors, at both Union and Member State level, in their efforts to ensure a timely, ethical and well-informed response to the new opportunities and challenges, in particular those of a cross-border nature, arising from technological developments in robotics, such as in the transport sector".

behaviour of robots could potentially have civil law implications, both in terms of contractual and of non-contractual liability. The Resolution underlined the fact that "thanks to the impressive technological advances of the last decade, not only are today's robots able to perform activities which used to be typically and exclusively human, but the development of certain autonomous and cognitive features – e.g. the ability to learn from experience and take quasi-independent decisions – has made them more and more similar to agents that interact with their environment and are able to alter it significantly; . . .in such a context, the legal responsibility arising through a robot's harmful action becomes a crucial issue".[46]

Thus clarification of responsibility for the actions of robots and eventually of the legal capacity and the status of robots and AI is essential in order to ensure transparency and legal certainty for both producers and consumers. According to the Resolution, "the more autonomous robots are, the less they can be considered to be simple tools in the hands of other actors (such as the manufacturer, the operator, the owner, the user, etc.); this, in turn, questions whether the ordinary rules on liability are sufficient or whether it calls for new principles and rules to provide clarity on the legal liability of various actors concerning responsibility for the acts and omissions of robots where the cause cannot be traced back to a specific human actor and whether the acts or omissions of robots which have caused harm could have been avoided".[47]

---

[46] Ibid., section "Liability", recital Z, p. 242.

[47] Ibid., section "Liability", recital AB, p. 242.

See also some important issues underlined by the Parliament's Resolution, at section "Liability", recitals AD-AI, pp. 242–243: "AD. whereas under the current legal framework robots cannot be held liable per se for acts or omissions that cause damage to third parties; whereas the existing rules on liability cover cases where the cause of the robot's act or omission can be traced back to a specific human agent such as the manufacturer, the operator, the owner or the user and where that agent could have foreseen and avoided the robot's harmful behaviour; whereas, in addition, manufacturers, operators, owners or users could be held strictly liable for acts or omissions of a robot; AE. whereas according to the current legal framework product liability (where the producer of a product is liable for a malfunction) and rules governing liability for harmful actions (where the user of a product is liable for a behaviour that leads to harm) apply to damages caused by robots or AI; AF. whereas in the scenario where a robot can take autonomous decisions, the traditional rules will not suffice to give rise to legal liability for damage caused by a robot, since they would not make it possible to identify the party responsible for providing compensation and to require that party to make good the damage it has caused; AG. whereas the shortcomings of the current legal framework are also apparent in the area of contractual liability insofar as machines designed to choose their counterparts, negotiate contractual terms, conclude contracts and decide whether and how to implement them make the traditional rules inapplicable, which highlights the need for new, efficient and up-to-date ones, which should comply with the technological development and the innovations recently arisen and used on the market; AH. whereas, as regards non-contractual liability, Council Directive 85/374/EEC can cover only damage caused by a robot's manufacturing defects and on condition that the injured person is able to prove the actual damage, the defect in the product and the causal relationship between damage and defect, therefore strict liability or liability without fault framework may not be sufficient; AI. whereas, notwithstanding the scope of the Directive 85/374/EEC, the current legal framework would not be sufficient to cover the damage caused by the new generation of robots, insofar as they can be equipped with adaptive and learning

The Parliament suggested that liability could either be based on strict liability (no fault required) or on a risk-management approach (liability of a person who was able to minimise the risks).[48] Strict liability requires only proof that damage has occurred and the establishment of a causal link between the harmful functioning of the robot and the damage suffered by the injured party. On the other hand, the risk management approach does not focus on the person who acted negligently as individually liable but on the person who is able, under certain circumstances, to minimise risks and deal with negative impacts.[49] Liability should be proportionate to the actual level of instructions given to the robot and to its degree of autonomy, "so that the greater a robot's learning capability or autonomy, and the longer a robot's training, the greater the responsibility of its trainer should be"; "... skills resulting from 'training' given to a robot should be not confused with skills depending strictly on its self-learning abilities when seeking to identify the person to whom the robot's harmful behaviour is actually attributable; ... at least at the present stage the responsibility must lie with a human and not a robot.[50]

The Parliament's Resolution stressed that, similarly to what already happens with motor vehicles, rules on liability could be complemented by a compulsory insurance scheme for robot users, as a possible solution to the complexity of allocating responsibility for damage caused by increasingly autonomous robots: "An obligatory insurance scheme, which could be based on the obligation of the producer to take out insurance for the autonomous robots it produces, should be established".[51]

---

abilities entailing a certain degree of unpredictability in their behaviour, since those robots would autonomously learn from their own variable experience and interact with their environment in a unique and unforeseeable manner".

[48] It was pointed out that whatever legal solution it applies to the civil liability for damage caused by robots and artificial intelligence in cases other than those of damage to property, the future legislative instrument should in no way restrict the type or the extent of the damages which may be recovered, nor should it limit the forms of compensation which may be offered to the aggrieved party, on the sole grounds that damage is caused by a non-human agent. See European Parliament Resolution of 16 February 2017 on Civil Law Rules on Robotics, section "Liability", point 52, p. 249. See also the Annex to the European Parliament Resolution of 16 February 2017 on Civil Law Rules on Robotics, section "Civil law liability", p. 252.

According to Rapporteur Mady Delvaux (S&D, LU), "we have two options. According to the principle of strict liability it should be the manufacturer who is liable, because he is best placed to limit the damage and deal with providers. The other option is a risk assessment approach according to which tests have to be carried out beforehand [to assess the risks] and compensation has to be shared by all stakeholders. We also propose there should be compulsory insurance, at least for the big robots". See "Rise of the robots: Mady Delvaux on why their use should be regulated", News - European Parliament, 15.02.2017, https://www.europarl.europa.eu/news/en/headlines/economy/20170109STO57505/rise-of-the-robots-mady-delvaux-on-why-their-use-should-be-regulated.

[49] European Parliament Resolution of 16 February 2017 on Civil Law Rules on Robotics, section "Liability", points 54-55, p. 249.

[50] Ibid., section "Liability", point 56, p. 249.

[51] Annex to the European Parliament Resolution of 16 February 2017 on Civil Law Rules on Robotics, section "Civil law liability", p. 252.

Under this scenario "producers, or owners of robots would be required to take out insurance cover for the damage potentially caused by their robots".[52]

Furthermore, the Parliament underlined that this obligatory insurance system should be supplemented by a compensation fund[53] to ensure victims are fully compensated in those cases where accidents were caused by a robot or a driverless car and no insurance policy covered the risk: "the insurance system should be supplemented by a fund in order to ensure that damages can be compensated for in cases where no insurance cover exists".[54]

Thus the Parliament's Resolution stressed that the Commission's future legislative instrument should be based on an in-depth evaluation determining the implications of all possible legal solutions, namely "a) establishing a compulsory insurance scheme where relevant and necessary for specific categories of robots whereby, similarly to what already happens with cars, producers, or owners of robots would be required to take out insurance cover for the damage potentially caused by their robots; b) ensuring that a compensation fund would not only serve the purpose of guaranteeing compensation if the damage caused by a robot was not covered by insurance; c) allowing the manufacturer, the programmer, the owner or the user to benefit from limited liability if they contribute to a compensation fund, as well as if they jointly take out insurance to guarantee compensation where damage is caused by a robot; d) deciding whether to create a general fund for all smart autonomous robots or to create an individual fund for each and every robot category, and whether a contribution should be paid as a one-off fee when placing the robot on the market or whether periodic contributions should be paid during the lifetime of the robot; e) ensuring that the link between a robot and its fund would be made visible by an individual registration number appearing in a specific Union register, which would allow anyone interacting with the robot to be informed about the nature of the fund, the limits of its liability in case of damage to property, the names and the functions of the contributors and all other relevant details".[55]

According to the Resolution, "the autonomy of robots raises the question of their nature in the light of the existing legal categories or whether a new category should be created, with its own specific features and implications".[56] Thus, according to the Parliament, the possibility of creating a specific legal status of "electronic persons" for the most sophisticated autonomous robots, so as to clarify responsibility in cases of damage, should be considered by the Commission, at least in the long-term:

[52] European Parliament Resolution of 16 February 2017 on Civil Law Rules on Robotics, section "Liability", points 57 and 59(a), pp. 249-250. It was pointed out, however, that unlike the insurance system for road traffic, where the insurance covers human acts and failures, an insurance system for robotics should take into account all potential responsibilities in the chain.

[53] Ibid., section "Liability", point 58, p. 250.

[54] Annex to the European Parliament Resolution of 16 February 2017 on Civil Law Rules on Robotics, section "Civil law liability", p. 252.

[55] European Parliament Resolution of 16 February 2017 on Civil Law Rules on Robotics, section "Liability", point 59, p. 250.

[56] Ibid., section "Liability", recital AC, p. 242.

"creating a specific legal status for robots in the long run, so that at least the most sophisticated autonomous robots could be established as having the status of electronic persons responsible for making good any damage they may cause, and possibly applying electronic personality to cases where robots make autonomous decisions or otherwise interact with third parties independently".[57]

This approach of the European Parliament, namely to leave open to discussion the possibility to create a special legal status for sufficiently advanced autonomous robots that would amount to electronic personhood, was publicly criticized by a group of experts in AI, robotics, commerce, law, and ethics, who signed an open letter to the European Commission, stating that they are concerned by the European Parliament Resolution on Civil Law Rules of Robotics and its recommendation to the European Commission.[58] This open letter, addressed to the then Commission's president Jean-Claude Juncker among others, denounced the European Parliament's proposal to grant personhood status to intelligent machines, suggesting that current robots do not have moral standing and should not be considered capable of having rights. The letter called upon the European Commission to ignore the Parliament's move and reject 'electronic personality', as it would be inappropriate, ideological, nonsensical, and non-pragmatic to introduce such a legal status.

The letter pointed to a lack of understanding of how AI works or what an autonomous machine is truly capable of, as an erroneous starting point for this suggestion of electronic personhood. In particular, it was argued that "the creation of a Legal Status of an 'electronic person' for 'autonomous', 'unpredictable' and 'self-learning' robots is justified by the incorrect affirmation that damage liability would be impossible to prove".[59] It was also stressed that, from a technical perspective, the European Parliament's proposal was based on "an overvaluation of the actual capabilities of even the most advanced robots, a superficial understanding of unpredictability and self-learning capacities and, a robot perception distorted by science fiction and a few recent sensational press announcements".[60] Furthermore it was stated that the creation of a legal status of an electronic person for autonomous robots is inappropriate also from an legal and ethical perspective.[61] In addition, the

[57] Ibid., section "Liability", point 59(f), p. 250.

[58] Open Letter to the European Commission – Artificial Intelligence and Robotics, 2018, http://www.robotics-openletter.eu/.

[59] Ibid.

[60] Ibid.

[61] Ibid.: "a. A legal status for a robot can't derive from the Natural Person model, since the robot would then hold human rights, such as the right to dignity, the right to its integrity, the right to remuneration or the right to citizenship, thus directly confronting the Human rights. This would be in contradiction with the Charter of Fundamental Rights of the European Union and the Convention for the Protection of Human Rights and Fundamental Freedoms. b. The legal status for a robot can't derive from the Legal Entity model, since it implies the existence of human persons behind the legal person to represent and direct it. And this is not the case for a robot. c. The legal status for a robot can't derive from the Anglo-Saxon Trust model also called Fiducie or Treuhand in Germany. Indeed, this regime is extremely complex, requires very specialized competences and would not solve the liability issue. More importantly, it would still imply the existence of a human being as a

opponents to the creation of a legal status of an electronic person for self-learning robots argued that, by adopting legal personhood for robots, responsibility of manufacturers for the actions of their machines would be erased.[62]

On the other hand, it was argued that the creation of a legal status of an electronic person for self-learning and autonomous machines could allow robots to be insured individually and be held liable for damages if they hurt people or damage property. Those pushing for such a legal change, including some manufacturers and their affiliates, argued that the European Parliament's proposal is common sense. Legal personhood would not make robots virtual people who can benefit from human rights; it would simply put them on par with corporations, which already have status as 'legal persons', and are treated as such by courts.

The proponents for the creation of a legal status of an electronic person for self-learning robots (AGI—Artificial General Intelligence or singularity, i.e. a system capable of human-level thinking) underlined that current state-of-the-art technology (complex, intelligent and self-learning) allows computers to learn and make their own decisions by mimicking and proliferating human brain patterns. This could make it difficult to determine who is technically and legally responsible for any ensuing damage. The legal responsibility arising through an autonomous robot's harmful action becomes, therefore, a crucial issue. They are concerned that such complex processes could turn machines into "black boxes" whose decision-making processes are almost impossible to understand and, therefore, impenetrable for litigators seeking to attribute legal responsibility. This is the reason why, they argued, Europe should grant 'legal status' to the robots themselves, rather than burden their manufacturers or owners. The current model, in which either the manufacturer, the owner, or both are liable, would become defunct in an age of fully autonomous robots, and the EU should give robots some sort of legal personality. This is the only way, the argument goes, to hold robots responsible, if/when they malfunction, by setting up a compulsory insurance scheme that could be fed by the wealth a robot is accumulating over the time of its 'existence'. It was pointed out that the idea behind coming up with an electronic personality was not about giving human rights to robots—but to make sure that a robot is and will remain a machine with a human backing it. The proposed legal status for robots would be analogous to corporate personhood, which allows firms to take part in legal cases both as the plaintiff and respondent. As Rapporteur Mady Delvaux (S&D, LU) stated: "When self-learning robots arise, different solutions will become necessary and we are

---

last resort – the trustee or fiduciary – responsible for managing the robot granted with a Trust or a Fiducie".

[62] Janosch Delcker, "Europe divided over robot 'personhood', Politico, 13.04.2018, https://www.politico.eu/article/europe-divided-over-robot-ai-artificial-intelligence-personhood/.

Noel Sharkey, Emeritus Professor of artificial intelligence and robotics at the University of Sheffield, stated that "this [European Parliament position] was what I'd call a slimy way of manufacturers getting out of their responsibility". Whereas Nathalie Navejans, an Associate Professor at the Université d'Artois, pointed out that "by adopting legal personhood, we are going to erase the responsibility of manufacturers".

asking the Commission to study options. One could be to give robots a limited "e-personality" [comparable to "corporate personality", a legal status which enables firms to sue or be sued] at least where compensation is concerned. It is similar to what we now have for companies, but it is not for tomorrow. What we need now is to create a legal framework for the robots that are currently on the market or will become available over the next 10 to 15 years".[63]

Apart from its aforementioned recommendations concerning liability for damage caused by robots and AI systems, the Parliament's Resolution proposed, as an annex, two draft codes of conduct—a Code of Ethical Conduct for Robotics Engineers and a Code for Research Ethics Committees. The first code put forward four ethical principles in robotics engineering: (i) beneficence (robots should act in the best interests of humans); (ii) non-maleficence (robots should not harm humans); (iii) autonomy (human interaction with robots should be voluntary—the capacity to make an informed, un-coerced decision about the terms of interaction with robots;); (iv) justice (the benefits of robotics should be distributed fairly—also, affordability of homecare and healthcare robots in particular).[64]

Robots and AI increase their interaction with humans in very diverse fields and the risks posed by these new interactions should be properly tackled, ensuring that a set of fundamental values is translated into every stage of contact between robots, AI and humans. In this process, the aim of the ethical conduct code is to ensure that robots and AI operate in accordance with legal safety and ethical standards. Special emphasis should be given to human safety, privacy, integrity, dignity and autonomy.[65]

---

[63] "Rise of the robots: Mady Delvaux on why their use should be regulated", News - European Parliament, 15.02.2017, https://www.europarl.europa.eu/news/en/headlines/economy/20170109STO57505/rise-of-the-robots-mady-delvaux-on-why-their-use-should-be-regulated.

[64] Annex to the European Parliament Resolution of 16 February 2017 on Civil Law Rules on Robotics, p. 253.

See also the European Parliament Resolution of 16 February 2017 on Civil Law Rules on Robotics, section "Ethical principles", points 13 and 14, p. 244: "(13) ... the guiding ethical framework should be based on the principles of beneficence, non-maleficence, autonomy and justice, on the principles and values enshrined in Article 2 of the Treaty on European Union and in the Charter of Fundamental Rights, such as human dignity, equality, justice and equity, non-discrimination, informed consent, private and family life and data protection, as well as on other underlying principles and values of the Union law, such as non-stigmatisation, transparency, autonomy, individual responsibility and social responsibility, and on existing ethical practices and codes"; "(14) ... special attention should be paid to robots that represent a significant threat to confidentiality owing to their placement in traditionally protected and private spheres and because they are able to extract and send personal and sensitive data".

[65] European Parliament Resolution of 16 February 2017 on Civil Law Rules on Robotics, section "Ethical principles", point 10, p. 244: "the potential for empowerment through the use of robotics is nuanced by a set of tensions or risks and should be seriously assessed from the point of view of human safety, health and security; freedom, privacy, integrity and dignity; self-determination and non-discrimination, and personal data protection". See also recital O and point 13 of the Resolution.

See also the Annex to the European Parliament Resolution of 16 February 2017 on Civil Law Rules on Robotics, p. 254: "Robotics research activities should respect fundamental rights and be

The Resolution considered it essential to guarantee that humans have control over intelligent machines at all times,[66] that robotics engineers and designers should be accountable for the social, environmental and human health impacts that robotics may impose (accountability),[67] that they should respect human well-being, health and rights, guarantee transparency and inclusiveness,[68] and disclose promptly factors that might endanger the public or the environment (safety).[69]

The Resolution stressed that concerns over safety and security related to the use of robots and AI need to be addressed.[70] As the proposed text for a licence for designers put it, "you should safeguard the safety and health of those interacting and coming in touch with robotics, given that robots as products should be designed using processes which ensure their safety and security. A robotics engineer must preserve human well-being while also respecting human rights and may not deploy a

---

conducted in the interests of the well-being and self-determination of the individual and society at large in their design, implementation, dissemination and use. Human dignity and autonomy – both physical and psychological – is always to be respected".

[66] European Parliament Resolution of 16 February 2017 on Civil Law Rules on Robotics, section "General principles concerning the development of robotics and artificial intelligence for civil use", point 3, p. 243.

[67] Ibid., section "Introduction", recital M, p. 240: "the trend towards automation requires that those involved in the development and commercialisation of AI applications build in security and ethics at the outset, thereby recognizing that they must be prepared to accept legal liability for the quality of the technology they produce". See also recital U.

See also the Annex to the European Parliament Resolution of 16 February 2017 on Civil Law Rules on Robotics, p. 254: "Accountability: Robotics engineers should remain accountable for the social, environmental and human health impacts that robotics may impose on present and future generations".

[68] Annex to the European Parliament Resolution of 16 February 2017 on Civil Law Rules on Robotics, p. 254: "Inclusiveness allows for participation in decision-making processes by all stakeholders involved in or concerned by robotics research activities".

[69] Ibid.: "Robot designers should consider and respect people's physical wellbeing, safety, health and rights. A robotics engineer must preserve human wellbeing, while also respecting human rights, and disclose promptly factors that might endanger the public or the environment"; "Precaution: Robotics research activities should be conducted in accordance with the precautionary principle, anticipating potential safety impacts of outcomes and taking due precautions, proportional to the level of protection, while encouraging progress for the benefit of society and the environment".

[70] European Parliament Resolution of 16 February 2017 on Civil Law Rules on Robotics, section "Standardisation, safety and security", point 23, p. 246: "Emphasises that testing robots in real-life scenarios is essential for the identification and assessment of the risks they might entail, as well as of their technological development beyond a pure experimental laboratory phase; underlines, in this regard, that testing of robots in real-life scenarios, in particular in cities and on roads, raises a large number of issues, including barriers that slow down the development of those testing phases and requires an effective strategy and monitoring mechanism; calls on the Commission to draw up uniform criteria across all Member States which individual Member States should use in order to identify areas where experiments with robots are permitted, in compliance with the precautionary principle".

robot without safeguarding the safety, efficacy and reversibility of the operation of the system".[71]

In addition, the Parliament reiterated that the right to the protection of private life and the right to the protection of personal data apply to all areas of robotics and artificial intelligence and that the EU legal framework for data protection must be fully complied with. It specifically pointed out that the right to privacy must always be respected. This is why the Resolution made specific reference to "robots that represent a significant threat to confidentiality owing to their placement in traditionally protected and private spheres and because they are able to extract and send personal and sensitive data".[72] The Parliament underlined the responsibility of designers of robotics and artificial intelligence to develop products which follow procedures for data processing compliant with existing legislation and respect principles such as confidentiality and anonymity. Robotics engineers must guarantee that private information is kept secure and only used appropriately and that individuals cannot be identifiable, unless a clear and unambiguous informed consent is obtained. According to the Parliament's Resolution, "the right to privacy must always be respected. A robotics engineer should ensure that private information is kept secure and only used appropriately. Moreover, a robotics engineer should guarantee that individuals are not personally identifiable, aside from exceptional circumstances and then only with clear, unambiguous informed consent. human informed consent should be pursued and obtained prior to any man-machine interaction. As such, robotics designers have a responsibility to develop and follow procedures for valid consent, confidentiality, anonymity, fair treatment and due process. Designers will comply with any requests that any related data be destroyed, and removed from any datasets".[73] Also, according to the proposed text of a licence for designers, "you should introduce privacy by design features so as to ensure that private information is kept secure and only used appropriately. You should introduce trustworthy system design principles across all aspects of a robot's operation, for both hardware and software design, and for any data processing on or off the platform for security purposes".[74]

A robotics engineer should not deploy a robot without safeguarding the reversibility of the operation of the system. Reversibility, which is a necessary condition of controllability, is an essential concept when programming robots to behave in a safe and reliable manner. The reversibility model informs the robot which actions are reversible and how to reverse them. This ability to undo the last action or a sequence

[71] Annex to the European Parliament Resolution of 16 February 2017 on Civil Law Rules on Robotics, p. 256. Also, at p. 256: "You should introduce trustworthy system design principles across all aspects of a robot's operation, for both hardware and software design, and for any data processing on or off the platform for security purposes".

[72] European Parliament Resolution of 16 February 2017 on Civil Law Rules on Robotics, section "Ethical principles", point 14, p. 244.

[73] Annex to the European Parliament Resolution of 16 February 2017 on Civil Law Rules on Robotics, p. 254.

[74] Ibid., p. 256.

of actions provides users with the opportunity to undo undesired actions and "get back to the 'good' stage of their work".[75] Also, robot designers should include obvious opt-out mechanisms ("kill" switches) so that robots can be turned off in case of emergencies.[76]

The Parliament's Resolution stressed the importance of the principle of transparency, namely that the logic behind any decision taken with the aid of AI (especially when the said decision can have a substantive impact on one or more persons' lives) should always be provided.[77] It highlighted that advanced robots should be equipped with a 'black box' which records data on every transaction carried out by the machine, including the rationale that contributed to its decisions (understandability in decision making). It also stated that it should always be possible to reduce the AI system's computations to a form which is easily comprehensible by humans.[78] As the Resolution (in its proposed text for a licence for designers) put it, "you should ensure that the robot's decision-making steps are amenable to reconstruction and traceability. You should ensure that maximal transparency is required in the programming of robotic systems, as well as predictability of robotic behaviour. ... You should develop tracing tools at the robot's design stage. These tools will facilitate accounting and explanation of robotic behaviour, even if limited, at the various levels intended for experts, operators and users".[79]

Furthermore, it was underlined that interoperability of network-connected autonomous robots, based on security and privacy by design, should be guaranteed. This is crucial for real time data flows enabling robots and artificial intelligence to become more flexible and autonomous and ensuring that robots can communicate with each other. It also safeguards their continued operation, availability, reliability, and security. Interoperability between systems, devices and cloud services is also a key factor for future competition in the field of artificial intelligence and robotics technologies. The Resolution pointed out that testing, certification and market approval should only be required in a single Member State and that this approach should be accompanied by effective market surveillance report. It also stressed the importance of setting harmonized and forward-looking technical standards for robotics and artificial intelligence in order to avoid discrepancies between Member States, to foster innovation, to guarantee a high level of product safety and consumer protection, and to avoid lock-in in proprietary systems that restrain interoperability.[80]

---

[75] Ibid., p. 254.

[76] Ibid., p. 256.

[77] European Parliament Resolution of 16 February 2017 on Civil Law Rules on Robotics, section "Ethical principles", point 12, p. 244.

[78] Ibid.

[79] Annex to the European Parliament Resolution of 16 February 2017 on Civil Law Rules on Robotics, p. 256.

[80] European Parliament Resolution of 16 February 2017 on Civil Law Rules on Robotics, points 9 and 22, pp. 244–245.

See also Annex to the European Parliament Resolution of 16 February 2017 on Civil Law Rules on Robotics, p. 252.

The Parliament's Resolution pointed out that, in order to protect and foster innovation in the area of robotics and AI, the Commission should propose a "balanced approach" to intellectual property rights when applied to hardware and software standards and codes. This approach should be horizontal and technologically neutral, applicable to the various sectors in which robotics could be employed.[81]

Due to the increasing use of robots and AI technologies, and in order to avoid discrepancies between Member States, it was pointed out that specific provisions should be applied to specific types of robots. According to the Resolution, individual rules should be adopted for autonomous vehicles, care robots, medical robots, human repair and enhancement, as well as drones (RPAS).[82]

The Parliament also pointed out that the development of robotics and AI technologies could result in big societal changes, including the creation and loss of jobs in certain fields. As it was stated, "despite the undeniable advantages afforded by robotics, its implementation may entail a transformation of the labour market"[83] and "the widespread use of robots might not automatically lead to job replacement, but lower skilled jobs in labour-intensive sectors are likely to be more vulnerable to automation".[84] The Resolution stressed the need to prepare for those changes and assess their impact on employment, education and social policies. To this end, it urged the Commission to follow these issues closely, including new employment models and the viability of the current tax and social system for robotics: "calls on the Commission to start analysing and monitoring medium- and long-term job trends more closely, with a special focus on the creation, displacement and loss of jobs in the different fields/areas of qualification in order to know in which fields jobs are being created and those in which jobs are being lost as a result of the increased use of robots".[85]

2.6 European Commission's Follow up to the 2017 European Parliament Resolution on Civil Law Rules on Robotics

In May 2017, in its follow-up to the European Parliament's Resolution, the European Commission published a preliminary response[86] to some of Parliament's basic recommendations.

[81] European Parliament Resolution of 16 February 2017 on Civil Law Rules on Robotics, section "Intellectual property rights and the flow of data", point 18, p. 245.

[82] Ibid., points 24–40, pp. 246–248.

[83] Ibid., section "Introduction", recital I, p. 240.

[84] Ibid., section "Introduction", recital J, p. 240.

[85] Ibid., section "Education and employment", point 43, p. 248.

[86] Commission's follow up to the European Parliament resolution of 16 February 2017 on civil law rules on robotics 2015/2103 (INL), 16 May 2017.

The Commission agreed with some of Parliament's suggestions, mainly that there is a "need for legal certainty as to the allocation of liability"[87] in the context of new technologies. In particular, the Commission stressed that the need to review and assess the adequacy of civil law liability rules in light of new technological developments such as the Internet of Things, advanced robotics and autonomous systems powered by artificial intelligence has already been demonstrated in various Commission's papers, such as the Digital Single Market Strategy,[88] the Commission Communication on Digitising the European Industry,[89] the Communication on Building a European Data Economy,[90] and the mid-term review of the Digital Single Market Strategy.[91] It pointed out that these emerging digital technologies and the rollout of the Internet of Things brings substantial challenges in terms of the safety of connected systems, products and services, as well as for businesses' liability. Many different layers are involved in these technologies and, therefore, vulnerable software, faulty sensors, or unstable connectivity may make it difficult to determine who is technically and legally responsible for any ensuing damage.[92] Thus the Commission, in order to fully unlock the digital/data economy, considered that the current legal framework needs to keep up to date with emerging trends and take account of new technological developments; otherwise, legal uncertainty "may affect negatively the development and uptake of robots and data-driven products and services". To this end, the Commission "intends to work with the European Parliament and the Member States on an EU response to this challenge".[93]

However, the Commission was of the opinion that the ordinary liability rules are not sufficient to provide clarity and expressed its intention to explore different scenarios and solutions (compared to the options proposed by the European Parliament) with a view to dealing with the issue of liability. In particular, the Commission considered that a review and evaluation of Directive 85/374/EEC on liability for defective products is required. This Directive lays down common rules of strict (non-contractual) liability for producers at EU level, which allows the injured party to claim financial compensation for death or personal injuries and also for damage caused to an item or property intended and used for private purposes. The evaluation of Directive 85/374/EEC should attempt to assess to what extent it applies to new

[87] Ibid., p. 1.

[88] Commission Communication, "A Digital Single Market Strategy for Europe", COM(2015) 192 final, Brussels, 6.5.2015.

[89] Commission Communication, "Digitising European Industry - Reaping the full benefits of a Digital Single Market", COM(2016) 180 final, Brussels, 19.4.2016.

[90] Commission Communication "Building a European Data Economy", COM(2017) 9 final, Brussels, 10.1.2017.

[91] Commission Communication on the Mid-Term Review on the implementation of the Digital Single Market Strategy - A Connected Digital Single Market for All, COM(2017) 228 final, Brussels, 10.5.2017.

[92] Commission's follow up to the European Parliament resolution of 16 February 2017 on civil law rules on robotics 2015/2103 (INL), 16 May 2017, at p. 1.

[93] Ibid., at p. 2.

technological developments (i.e. Internet of Things, software, advanced robots, automated and autonomous systems, cloud computing), whether it covers, for instance, cases of malfunctioning apps and non-embedded software, and whether it complies with the technological development and takes sufficiently into account the complexity of new technological products. The Commission stressed that the current legal framework would not be sufficient to cover the damage caused by the new generation of robots, since those robots could be equipped with adaptive and learning abilities entailing a certain degree of unpredictability in their behaviour. As a result, those robots would autonomously learn from their own experience and interact with their environment in a unique and unforeseeable/unpredictable manner. As the Commission put it, "advanced robots involve, in addition to the machinery part, complex software systems and suppose the provision of services, data transmission and possibly internet connectivity and, depending on the category of robot, a degree of artificial intelligence. All these elements taken together trigger difficulties for determining who should be held liable (and to what extent) for damages arising in the context of an autonomous behaviour of a robot. The specific features which an autonomous robot may display, such as self-learning capacities and ability to interact to, and impact, in unpredictable ways, upon its surrounding environment, raise therefore important questions as to the suitability of current EU and national rules".[94]

The Commission expressed its intention to explore different solutions with a view to dealing with the issue of liability. In particular, alongside the review of Directive 85/374/EEC, the Commission pointed out that it could develop risk-based liability regimes, based on a risk-opening approach (for instance, allocating liability to market players generating a major risk for the others and benefiting from the relevant device/ product/ service) or a risk management approach where liability is assigned to the market player best placed to minimize risks or avoid their realization. The Commission agreed with the European Parliament that an insurance system for robotics would be "instrumental" in the context of both risk-based solutions or a review of the current Directive 85/374/EEC and, thus, it needs to be carefully examined.[95]

The Commission noted that it anticipates the response of the European Parliament's public consultation on robotics, that it will conduct its own public consultation and stakeholder dialogue on the issues and that it will assess whether future policy and legislative action is necessary once the two parallel stakeholder consultation exercises (namely, the consultations on product liability challenges in the context of the Internet of Things and autonomous systems and the consultation on the evaluation of Directive 85/374/EEC) will have been concluded.[96]

Furthermore, the Commission seemed to speculate as to whether a definition of robots was necessary, acknowledging that it is difficult to clearly make a distinction between what constitutes artificial intelligence/robotics and what does not. Further

---

[94] Ibid.

[95] Ibid.

[96] Ibid., p. 3.

analysis is required to decide about suitable definitions and criteria, in particular when it comes to their use for regulation purposes. According to the Commission, "thorough examination of the existing robotics technologies and assessment of their potential development is necessary before being able to decide whether the definition of cyber physical systems, autonomous systems, smart autonomous robots and of their subcategories is necessary for regulatory purposes. Such a preliminary clarification would also help identify technologies for which a comprehensive Union system of registration could be relevant".[97]

The Commission fully agreed with the European Parliament on the need to ensure the highest level possible of protection of fundamental rights and ethics as robotics and artificial intelligence are being deployed. According to the Commission, this can be achieved through the Better Regulation Package in order to assess the impact on fundamental rights of policy measures and legislative proposals.[98] Finally, it is reminded that the European Parliament proposed that an EU Agency for Robotics and Artificial Intelligence should be introduced. The Parliament believed that this proposed Agency could facilitate the deployment of robots which are consistent with the required levels of safety and security and provide expertise on robotics to public authorities. On the other hand, however, the Commission stated that it is not necessary to designate a new European Agency for robotics and artificial intelligence. The Commission took the view that, in addition to the evaluation and potential review of Machinery Directive 2006/42/EC (this Directive deals with the safety of robots, it provides CE marking requirements for their placing on the EU market and could be revised in order to adapt its health and safety requirements to autonomous robots and Artificial Intelligence), it is necessary to establish a high-level advisory body on robotics and artificial intelligence which could provide knowledge and technical, ethical and regulatory expertise to the Commission.[99]

2.7 European Parliament: Public Consultation on the Civil-Law Rules for Robotics and AI

As already mentioned, a public consultation on the civil-law rules for robotics was requested and coordinated by the Committee on Legal Affairs of the European Parliament (prepared by the European Added Value Unit of EPRS). The public consultation was open to all EU citizens and consisted of one general public survey and one survey targeted to a "specialised" audience ("experts"). The aim of the consultation was to stimulate a broad debate with a wide range of stakeholders and to seek views on how to address the challenging ethical, legal, social, and economic

[97] Ibid.

[98] Ibid., p. 7.

[99] Ibid., p. 8.

issues related to robotics and artificial intelligence developments. The preliminary results of the Parliament's public consultation were released on 6 October 2017.

The vast majority of individual respondents declared to have a positive or very positive view on robotics (79%) and AI (68%) while only 3% (robotics) and 7% (AI) had a negative or strongly negative perception. At the same time, a large majority of the respondents considered that technology would require careful management (92%), that robotics would be particularly helpful for hard and dangerous jobs (92%), and that it would ensure efficient methods of transport and delivery (71%). On the other hand, some respondents were concerned that robotics would eliminate jobs (34%) or would create inequalities in society (18%). Privacy was identified as the most prominent concern regarding artificial intelligence (52% of the respondents) while 29% considered that AI could pose a threat to humanity, and 16% considered AI a threat to fundamental human rights.[100]

In addition, 90% of individual respondents supported the need for public regulation of robotics and AI with only 6% against regulation and 4% noted as 'other'. The reasons provided in support of public regulation and taking legislative action included the need to address concerns about ethics, human rights, data protection and privacy; the importance of avoiding abuse by the industry; the need to set common standards for industry to have certainty; and, to achieve high levels of consumer protection.[101]

Amongst those individuals favouring a regulatory intervention, an overwhelming majority (96%) favored action at EU or international level rather than at Member State level (4%). The arguments supporting regulatory action at EU level were, among others, the need to protect EU values (especially data protection, privacy and ethical values), to ensure the EU's global competitiveness and to safeguard more efficient enforcement (including liability issues) of adopted regulation. Respondents stated that an EU-wide regulation of AI and robotics was most urgent in specific sectors across different areas, equally covering autonomous vehicles, medical robots, care robots, drones, and human repair and enhancement. Those individual respondents opposing legislative action stressed the difficulties of regulating emerging technologies and claimed that regulating too early could hinder innovation, creativity, investment, and competition.[102]

As regards the survey targeted to a "specialised" audience, organisations and companies were asked to evaluate the potential impacts of robotics and AI in their working environment and they identified changes in the nature of work (20%) and the possibility of generating new products/services (20%) as the most immediate consequences, alongside changes in organisational structures and business models (14%). Some of the respondents (15%) expressed the opinion that robotics and AI would create new opportunities for entrepreneurs. Human resources, i.e. employee

[100] "Summary of the public consultation on the future of robotics and artificial intelligence (AI) with an emphasis on civil law rules", October 2017, pp. 4–5.

[101] Ibid., p. 5.

[102] Ibid.

skills and training (20%), public attitude and acceptance (14%), technical issues related to testing and application of technology (13%), and technical issues related to development of technology (12%) were identified as the most prominent concerns and barriers that could prevent a full development of robotics and AI.[103]

However, national (10%) and EU (8%) legal frameworks were also identified as obstacles. If the EU were to take action to encourage innovation, productivity and global competitiveness in robotics and AI, 21% of the respondents considered that a better regulatory framework (21 %) would certainly be helpful. To this end, it was argued by many respondents that the EU should avoid unnecessary bureaucracy and be flexible (namely, the regulatory framework should be designed around specific technological applications, rather than an all-encompassing generic regulation covering all AI/robotics). Also, the respondents considered that action at EU level should take place in order to add value to actions taken at national level. In particular, it was stressed that action at EU level helps to avoid divergent national standards (17%), to enhance protection of fundamental rights and ethical rules (14%), and to facilitate cross-border business opportunities (11%). Some respondents expressed concerns about the potential negative effects that the development of robotic and AI would have on privacy (6%), and fundamental rights (6%), as well as the shortage of the necessary, highly skilled workforce (4%).[104]

The organisations and companies that participated in the survey identified logistics and transport (19%), healthcare (14%), manufacturing (13%), consumer robots such as used in domestic appliances, education (13%), and financial services (10%) as those sectors that could experience the fastest economic growth during the next five years. They expressed the opinion that, within these sectors, the key policy areas that would require most urgent EU regulatory/legal intervention would be autonomous vehicles (29%), medical robots (16%), drones (13%), and technologies for human repair and enhancement (13%). Finally, liability rules (21%), connectivity, intellectual property and flow of data (20%), and ethics (19%) were amongst those matters identified as the most prominent concerns and thus would urgently need to be addressed.[105]

As regards the responses given by both individuals and organisations, liability was indicated as by far the most urgent concern (81%), while 19% are either neutral or not concerned. Furthermore, when invited to evaluate the current EU regulatory framework on liability, the views of both individuals and organisations were mixed. Some respondents (38%) argued that no modifications are necessary; others (18%) mentioned that major modifications to the current framework are required; 21% took the view that some modifications are required in both contractual and non-contractual liability; and 14% of the respondents were in favour of a non-legislative instrument in addition to the existing legal regime.

[103] Ibid., p. 6.

[104] Ibid.

[105] Ibid., pp. 6–7.

The proposal of the European Parliament to leave open to discussion the possibility to create a special legal status for sufficiently advanced autonomous robots that would amount to electronic personhood, was opposed by the majority of the respondents (approximately 60%). Furthermore stakeholders did not agree with the view that rules on liability could be complemented by a compulsory insurance scheme for robot users, as a possible solution to the complexity of allocating responsibility for damage caused by increasingly autonomous robots. Also, the respondents were against the idea that this obligatory insurance system should be supplemented by a compensation fund to ensure victims are fully compensated in those cases where accidents were caused by a robot and no insurance policy covered the risk.[106]

Amongst those favouring a regulatory approach and action at EU level, it was argued that, as a matter of priority, the EU should address the issues of free movement of data, interconnected robots and AI network security, protection of personal data, and privacy in communication between humans, robots and AI.[107]

Finally, respondents were invited to identify those ethical principles which should be observed and complement the existing EU legal framework, in case a guiding ethical framework or a code of conduct for robotic engineers is to be established at EU level. According to the answers received, non-maleficence (the doctrine of 'first, do not harm', namely that robots should not harm humans) is the most crucial principle, followed by safety and the principle of accountability, i.e. that robotics engineers and designers should be accountable for the social, environmental and human health impacts that robotics may impose on present and future generations.[108]

2.8 The European Council of October 2017

The European Council of October 2017[109] underlined the need for a stronger and more coherent Digital Europe, it pointed out that digitalisation offers immense opportunities for innovation, growth and jobs, and acknowledged that the challenges posed by the digital transformation need to be tackled. In addition, it stressed that the EU needs to complete the Digital Single Market Strategy by reviewing policies affected by digitalization and by establishing a future-oriented regulatory framework.[110] The determination of the European Council to speed up this process was clear: "the European Council is ready to do what it takes for Europe to go digital".[111]

[106] Ibid., p. 7.

[107] Ibid., pp. 7–8.

[108] ibid., p. 7.

[109] General Secretariat of the Council, Subject: European Council meeting (19 October 2017) – Conclusions, Brussels, 19 October 2017 (OR. en), EUCO 14/17, at Section II – Digital Europe.

[110] Ibid., p. 5.

[111] Ibid., p. 6.

It was stated that, in order to successfully build a Digital Europe, the EU has to prioritize the work on the Digital Single Market and to create a future-oriented regulatory framework); to achieve first rate and very high-speed fixed and mobile networks (5G) all across the EU; to develop a common approach to cybersecurity (with a more proactive security by design in all digital policies, adequate security certification of products and services, and increased capacity to prevent, deter, detect and respond to cyberattacks); to combat terrorism and online crime; to increase R&D and investment effort; and, perhaps more importantly, to cope with the ongoing digital transformation, to adjust to the challenges posed, and to accelerate the process of addressing technological breakthroughs in areas like artificial intelligence.[112]

The European Council stressed that immediate action must be taken in order to reap the benefits of technological advances—"a sense of urgency to address emerging trends: this includes issues such as artificial intelligence and blockchain technologies, while at the same time ensuring a high level of data protection, digital rights and ethical standards".[113] This is why it invited the Commission "to put forward a European approach to artificial intelligence by early 2018".[114] Furthermore it reaffirmed that the objective is to create a more integrated Single Market, and it highlighted the necessity for the institutions to step up the legislative work and for Member States to implement the relevant EU legislation and to take all the required measures in order to "shape the new digital era".[115]

2.9 Declaration of Cooperation on Artificial Intelligence

On 10 April 2018, twenty-four Member States and Norway signed a Declaration of cooperation on Artificial Intelligence.[116] In May and July 2018 four other EU Member States countries joined the initiative.[117] Technology has become a key driver for economic growth through the digitisation of industry and for society as a whole. This Declaration built further on the achievements and investments of the European research and business community in AI, aiming at facilitating the progress towards the creation of a Digital Single Market.

Whereas a number of Member States had already announced national initiatives on Artificial Intelligence, these European countries decided to declare a strong will

[112] Ibid., pp. 5–7.

[113] Ibid., p. 7.

[114] Ibid.

[115] Ibid., p. 8.

[116] EU Declaration of cooperation on Artificial Intelligence, Brussels, 10 April 2018. The signatory countries of Declaration were: Austria, Belgium, Bulgaria, Czech Republic, Denmark, Estonia, Finland, France, Germany, Hungary, Ireland, Italy, Latvia, Lithuania, Luxembourg, Malta, Netherlands, Poland, Portugal, Slovakia, Slovenia, Spain, Sweden, United Kingdom and Norway.

[117] Greece, Cyprus, Romania, and Croatia.

to join forces and engage in a European approach to deal with the many and varied issues raised. By teaming up, the opportunities of AI for Europe can be more fully explored and ensured, while the challenges can be dealt with collectively. Indeed, the emergence of AI also brings challenges which need to be addressed. An anticipatory approach is needed to deal with AI's transformation of the labour market. In addition, it is necessary to modernise Europe's education and training systems, including upskilling and reskilling European citizens. New legal and ethical questions should also be considered. An environment of trust and accountability around the development and use of AI is needed to fully profit from the opportunities it brings.

Therefore, it was agreed to exchange views on ethical and legal frameworks related to AI in order to ensure responsible AI deployment. The signatory countries also stressed the need to contribute to the sustainability and trustworthiness of AI-based solutions, for instance by enhancing information security, promoting safety and vigilance in the design and implementation, and increasing accountability of AI systems. To this end, the signatories of the Declaration committed to a regular assessment of the progress made and to the adoption of the appropriated measures in order to react to the emerging evolution of AI.[118]

---

[118]EU Declaration of cooperation on Artificial Intelligence, Brussels, 10 April 2018, at pp. 3–5. In particular, the participating Member States agreed to cooperate on: "- Boosting Europe's technology and industrial capacity in AI and its uptake, including better access to public sector data; these are essential conditions to influence AI development, fueling innovative business models and creating economic growth and new qualified jobs. - Addressing socio-economic challenges, such as the transformation of the labour markets and modernising Europe's education and training systems, including upskilling & reskilling EU citizens. - Ensuring an adequate legal and ethical framework, building on EU fundamental rights and values, including privacy and protection of personal data, as well as principles such as transparency and accountability".

"In particular, the participating Member States agreed to work towards a comprehensive and integrated European approach on AI to increase the EU's competitiveness, attractiveness and excellence in R&D in AI, and where needed review and modernise national policies to ensure that the opportunities arising from AI are seized and the emerging challenges are addressed; encourage discussions with stakeholders on AI and support the development of a broad and diverse community of stakeholders in a "European AI Alliance"; consider the allocation of R&D&I funding to the further development and deployment of AI; exchange views with other Member States and the Commission on AI research agendas and strategies to create synergies in relevant R&D&I funding schemes across Europe; cooperate on reinforcing AI research centres and supporting their pan-European dimension; contribute to the establishment of a dense network of Digital Innovation Hubs at European level; contribute to efforts to make AI available and beneficial to government administrations and to all companies, in particular SMEs and companies from non-technological sectors; exchange best practices on procuring and using AI in government administrations of any size and at any level, and in the public sector more generally; contribute to efforts to make more public sector data available, support private businesses to follow this example, and improve the re-usability of scientific research data resulting from public funding, without prejudice to existing rights, regulations and contractual freedom; exchange views on ethical and legal frameworks related to AI in order to ensure responsible AI deployment; contribute to the sustainability and trustworthiness of AI-based solutions, for instance by working towards improved information security, promoting safety and vigilance in the design and implementation, and increasing accountability of AI systems; ensure that humans remain at the centre of the development, deployment and decision-

Thus the European countries agreed to work together on the most important issues raised by Artificial Intelligence, from ensuring Europe's competitiveness in the research and deployment of AI (including better access to the public sector data), to dealing with social and economic challenges. Furthermore the twenty-nine signing European countries agreed to cooperate on "ensuring an adequate legal and ethical framework, building on EU fundamental rights and values, including privacy and protection of personal data, as well as principles such as transparency and accountability".[119]

The EU Declaration demonstrated an obvious concern for the ethical issues arising out of current and future AI-system's development and deployment. Following this concern, it committed its signatories to cooperating in order "to ensure that humans remain at the centre of the development, deployment and decision-making of AI", "to prevent the harmful creation and use of AI applications" and "to advance public understanding of AI". Despite its non-binding nature, the Declaration should be considered as a serious manifestation of commitment of the Member States to collaborate on AI and to strengthen EU leadership. This commitment was taken up from the European Commission's 'Communication on Artificial Intelligence for Europe' and further sustained by the subsequent 'Coordinated Plan on AI'.

2.10 Commission's 2018 Communication on Artificial Intelligence for Europe

2.10.1 Introduction

On 25 April 2018, the Commission published its Communication on "Artificial Intelligence for Europe",[120] in response to the European Council's

---

making of AI, prevent the harmful creation and use of AI applications, and advance public understanding of AI; exchange views on the impact of AI on labour markets and discuss best practices on how to mitigate such impacts, including on the adoption of measures in education and practical training on skills to be acquired to allow citizens to benefit from AI and ensure social stability; engage in a continuous dialogue with the Commission on AI".

[119] Ibid., at p. 3.

Welcoming the signatories, Andrus Ansip, Vice-President for the Digital Single Market, and Mariya Gabriel, Commissioner for Digital Economy and Society, stated: "In Europe, any successful strategy dealing with AI needs to be cross-border. A large number of Member States agreed to work together on the opportunities and challenges brought by AI. That is excellent news. Cooperation will focus on reinforcing European AI research centres, creating synergies in R&D&I funding schemes across Europe, and exchanging views on the impact of AI on society and the economy. Member States will engage in a continuous dialogue with the Commission, which will act as a facilitator". Shaping Europe's digital future - EU Member States sign up to cooperate on Artificial Intelligence, DIGIBYTE, 10 April 2018.

[120] Commission Communication "Artificial Intelligence for Europe", COM (2018) 237 final, Brussels, 25.4.2018.

call[121] to put forward a European approach to AI. The Communication laid the groundwork for the 'Coordinated Plan on AI' and outlined the steps required to achieve a more committed alignment of resources and goals between Member States.

Building on the strong political endorsement granted by the Declaration of cooperation on Artificial Intelligence (which was signed by all Member States), the Communication recognised that it is time to make significant efforts to ensure that Europe is competitive in the AI landscape. Furthermore, it was underlined that modernisation of education should be a priority and that specific measures in education and training should be adopted so that all Europeans can have every opportunity to acquire the skills they need and thus benefit from AI and digital innovations. It was also stated that it is imperative to ensure that AI is developed and applied in an appropriate regulatory framework which promotes innovation and, at the same time, respects the Union's values and fundamental rights as well as ethical principles such as transparency and accountability.

As the Communication stated, "the European Union (EU) should have a coordinated approach to make the most of the opportunities offered by AI and to address the new challenges that it brings. The EU can lead the way in developing and using AI for good and for all, building on its values and its strengths".[122] The Communication outlined a European approach to Artificial Intelligence and Robotics and dealt with technological, ethical, legal and socio-economic aspects in order to increase the EU's research and industrial capacity and to put AI at the service of European citizens. According to the Communication, "Like the steam engine or electricity in the past, AI is transforming our world, our society and our industry. Growth in computing power, availability of data and progress in algorithms have turned AI into one of the most strategic technologies of the 21st century. The stakes could not be higher. The way we approach AI will define the world we live in. Amid fierce global competition, a solid European framework is needed".[123]

The 'AI for Europe' Communication reminded that its mid-term review of the Digital Single Market strategy,[124] which was published in May 2017, highlighted the importance of building on Europe's scientific and industrial strengths in order to be in a leading position in the development of AI technologies, platforms, and applications. It also stressed that the European Parliament made wide ranging recommendations on the civil-law and ethical aspects of robotics[125] and that the

---

[121] General Secretariat of the Council, Subject: European Council meeting (19 October 2017) – Conclusions, Brussels, 19 October 2017 (OR. en), EUCO 14/17, at Section II – Digital Europe.

[122] Commission Communication "Artificial Intelligence for Europe", COM (2018) 237 final, Brussels, 25.4.2018, p. 2.

[123] Ibid., p. 1.

[124] Commission Communication "On the Mid-Term Review on the implementation of the Digital Single Market Strategy - A Connected Digital Single Market for All", COM(2017) 228 final, Brussels, 10.5.2017.

[125] European Parliament Resolution of 16 February 2017 with recommendations to the Commission on Civil Law Rules on Robotics (2015/2103(INL)), (2018/C 252/25), OJ C 252, 18.7.2018, pp. 239-257 ("European Parliament Resolution of 16 February 2017").

Commission's Communication of 13 September 2017 on Investing in a smart, innovative and sustainable Industry—A renewed EU Industrial Policy Strategy,[126] highlighted Artificial Intelligence as one of the tools for upgrading industry for the digital age. Furthermore, the 'AI for Europe' Communication reminded the conclusions adopted by the European Council at its meeting on 19 October 2017, which highlighted the need ("a sense of urgency") to address emerging trends, such as AI, and to develop an approach to Artificial Intelligence at European level, while on the other hand "ensuring a high level of data protection, digital rights and ethical standards". This is why it invited the Commission "to put forward a European approach to artificial intelligence by early 2018".[127]

In response of the above mentioned clear political commitment, the Commission put forward the European approach to artificial intelligence, which is based on three major pillars: (a) to boost the EU's technological and industrial capacity (and thus ensuring competitiveness and staying at the forefront of this technological evolution) and encourage AI uptake across the economy both by the public and private sectors; (b) to prepare Europe for socio-economic changes associated with AI and to ensure that no one is left behind in the digital transformation. This can be achieved "by encouraging the modernisation of education and training systems, nurturing talent, anticipating changes in the labour market, supporting labour market transitions and adaptation of social protection systems";[128] (c) to ensure that Europe will have an appropriate ethical and legal framework to deal with AI development and deployment, based on the Union's values and in line with the Charter of Fundamental Rights of the EU.[129] According to the Commission, "this includes guidance on existing product liability rules, a detailed analysis of emerging challenges, and cooperation with stakeholders, through a European AI Alliance, for the development of AI ethics guidelines".[130] One of the Commission's main target is to follow an approach to AI "that benefits people and society as a whole" and that "can place the power of AI at the service of human progress".[131]

[126] Commission Communication, "Investing in a smart, innovative and sustainable Industry - A renewed EU Industrial Policy Strategy", COM(2017) 479 final, Brussels, 13.9.2017.

[127] General Secretariat of the Council, Subject: European Council meeting (19 October 2017) – Conclusions, Brussels, 19 October 2017 (OR. en), EUCO 14/17, at Section II – Digital Europe, at p. 7.

[128] Commission Communication "Artificial Intelligence for Europe", COM (2018) 237 final, Brussels, 25.4.2018, p. 3.

[129] Article 2 of the Treaty on EU reads: "The Union is founded on the values of respect for human dignity, freedom, democracy, equality, the rule of law and respect for human rights, including the rights of persons belonging to minorities". The Member States share a "society in which pluralism, non-discrimination, tolerance, justice, solidarity and equality between women and men prevail".

[130] Commission Communication "Artificial Intelligence for Europe", COM (2018) 237 final, Brussels, 25.4.2018, p. 3.

[131] Ibid., at pp. 2 and 19.

2.10.2 *Ensuring an Appropriate Ethical and Legal Framework*

The Communication noted the importance of trust and accountability, as well as a predictable legal environment, in order to ensure that the EU remains competitive and innovative in relation to AI, based on the Union's values and in line with the EU Charter of Fundamental Rights. The Commission stated that the EU has set high standards in terms of safety, product liability, network/information systems security and protection of personal data and that it has "a strong and balanced regulatory framework to build on, which can set the global standard for a sustainable approach to this technology".[132]

To this end, the Commission stressed the importance of a series of proposals—put forward under the Digital Single Market strategy—such as the Regulation on the free flow of non-personal data, the ePrivacy Regulation and the Cybersecurity Act, which could facilitate the development of AI, enhance trust in the online world, and create a predictable legal environment. It also pointed out that the General Data Protection Regulation (GDPR)[133] guarantees the free flow of personal data within the Union and ensures a high standard of personal data protection, including the principles of data protection by design and by default. The Commission underlined that the GDPR has provisions on decision-making based solely on automated processing, including profiling (AI-based systems). In such cases, data subjects have the right to be provided with meaningful information about the logic involved in the decision. The GDPR also grants individuals the right not to be subject solely to automated decision-making (except in certain situations) such as automatic refusal of an online credit application or e-recruiting practices without any human intervention. Such processing includes profiling which consists of any form of automated processing of personal data evaluating the personal aspects relating to a natural person (AI-based systems), in particular to analyse or predict aspects concerning the data subject's performance at work, economic situation, health, personal preferences or interests, reliability or behaviour, location or movements, where it produces legal effects concerning the individual or similarly significantly affects him.[134]

The Commission also noted that attention should be paid to the interaction between AI and intellectual property rights. In particular, it pointed out that using AI to create works could have implications on intellectual property, with questions arising for instance on patentability, copyright and right ownership. According to the Commission, a balanced approach should be reached, namely one which can foster

---

[132] Ibid., p. 14.

[133] Regulation (EU) 2016/679 of the European Parliament and of the Council of 27 April 2016 on the protection of natural persons with regard to the processing of personal data and on the free movement of such data, and repealing Directive 95/46/EC (General Data Protection Regulation) (OJ L 119, 4.5.2016, pp. 1–88).

[134] Commission Communication, "Artificial Intelligence for Europe", COM(2018) 237 final, Brussels, 25.4.2018, p. 14.

both innovation and legal certainty.[135] For instance, innovation has been the result of direct human intervention that creates a technical solution to a practical problem. However, as technology continues to develop and AI becomes more advanced, it is likely that innovators will become more reliant on AI to help develop new inventions. Therefore, the question of whether patent protections can be extended to inventions developed by AI technology—i.e. how to handle applications for inventions created by AI machines—will be high on the agenda in the forthcoming years. How do we afford patent protection when novel ideas are created by artificial intelligence or when AI is contributing to inventions? The problem with AI inventorship is its link with ownership. Machines are not legal or natural persons and cannot own property; AI cannot hold ownership rights in intellectual property. As the Commission mentioned, a balanced solution is required. If the ideas generated by such machines are not assigned patent protection, this could ultimately stifle innovation, research and development in various industries. On the other hand, it could be argued that crediting AI with the invention may deter developers from creating the AI itself.

2.10.2.1 Safety and Liability

Alongside its decision to address ethical concerns,[136] the Commission stressed the need to review and assess the adequacy and suitability of some established rules on

---

[135] Ibid.

[136] As a first step to address ethical concerns, the Commission proposed the establishment of a European AI Alliance by July 2018. The AI Alliance is a multi-stakeholder forum launched in June 2018 within the framework of the European Strategy on Artificial Intelligence. The forum's initial scope was the provision of feedback to the High-Level Expert Group on Artificial Intelligence (AI HLEG), which was appointed by the Commission to assist with policy development. Over time, the AI Alliance has become a point of reference in stakeholder-driven discussions on AI policy.

The aim is to bring together relevant stakeholders to draft guidelines on AI ethics and new safety and technical interoperability standards by the end of 2018, in cooperation with the European Group on Ethics in Science and New Technologies. Due to the scale of the challenges associated with AI, the Commission considered the full participation of all actors, including businesses, academics, consumer organisations, trade unions, policy makers and representatives of civil society, to be essential. This is why the Commission brought together a broad community of stakeholders around AI-relevant questions under the European AI Alliance. The European AI Alliance will provide broader input for the work of the High-Level Expert Group on Artificial Intelligence, a group comprising fifty-two experts from academia, civil society, as well as industry. The High-Level Expert Group on AI (which serves as the steering group for the European AI Alliance's work) was appointed by the Commission in June 2018 in order to support the implementation of the European strategy on artificial intelligence, including the elaboration of recommendations on future AI-related policy development and on ethical, legal and societal issues related to AI.

These AI ethics guidelines address a range of issues, including safety, security, privacy, algorithmic transparency, fairness, social inclusion, future of work, dignity, non-discrimination and consumer protection, helping to ensure that key values (such as democratic principles and respect for fundamental rights of the EU) are embedded into both the development and use of AI solutions. Although it was pointed out that self-regulation can offer a first set of benchmarks against

safety and civil law liability rules in light of new technological developments such as the Internet of Things, advanced robotics and autonomous systems powered by artificial intelligence. Indeed, "the complex enabling ecosystem and the feature of autonomous decision-making" as well as the rollout of the Internet of Things bring substantial challenges in terms of the safety of connected systems, products, and services, as well as for businesses' liability. Many different layers are involved in these emerging digital technologies and, therefore, it could be difficult to determine who is technically and legally responsible for any ensuing damage. Also, products empowered by AI may act in ways that were not envisaged at the time when the system was first put into the market. Thus, according to the Commission, "given AI's widespread uses, both horizontal and sectoral rules may need to be reviewed".[137]

The Commission was quick to note that the Innovation Principle should apply for any new regulatory proposals required to address emerging issues resulting from AI and related technologies.[138] The Innovation Principle is a set of tools and guidelines that was developed to ensure that all Commission's initiatives, all new EU policy or regulations support innovation and that the regulatory framework in Europe is innovation-friendly. It is a tool to help achieve EU policy objectives by safeguarding that legislation is designed in a way that generates the best possible conditions for innovation to thrive. To put it simply, the principle means that when the Commission develops new initiatives it will take into account the effect on innovation.[139] According to DG RTD, the Innovation Principle could be summarized as follows:

---

which emerging applications and outcomes can be assessed, the Commission noted that public authorities should be in a position to step in and provide the required safety net in order to ensure that the regulatory frameworks for developing and using of AI technologies are in line with these EU fundamental rights. The Commission, at the same time, will monitor new technological and market developments and, if necessary, review existing legal frameworks to better adapt them to specific challenges, aiming at ensuring the respect of the Union's fundamental principles. See Commission Communication "Artificial Intelligence for Europe", COM (2018) 237 final, Brussels, 25.4.2018, at pp. 14–15.

For analysis of the Commission's ethical guidelines, see Dr. Nikos Th. Nikolinakos, EU Policy and Legal Framework for Artificial Intelligence, Robotics, and Related Technologies – The AI Act, Springer, 2023, especially Part II (The EU Ethical Framework for Trustworthy Artificial Intelligence), chapters 3 (Ethical Principles for Trustworthy AI) and 4 (Realising Trustworthy AI).

[137] Commission Communication "Artificial Intelligence for Europe", COM (2018) 237 final, Brussels, 25.4.2018, section 3.3 ("Ensuring an appropriate ethical and legal framework"), p. 15.

[138] Ibid.

[139] The Innovation Principle covers the entire three phases of the policy-making cycle, i.e.: (a) 1st phase, agenda-setting: the possible effects of emerging technologies on EU rules should be scrutinised early in the legislative process as part of the Innovation Principle. Examples of this include artificial intelligence or block chain, where the new technologies are likely to introduce changes to legislation. (b) 2nd phase, legislation: new EU legislative initiatives should respond to the needs of innovative companies. This means providing data and evidence for impact assessments, consulting innovators and taking their suggestions for drafting legislation into account. (c) 3rd phase, implementation: the Commission offers Innovation Deals to deal with existing EU rules. These identify if an EU rule or regulation is an obstacle to innovation and if so, help to find solutions.

"EU policy and legislation should be developed, implemented and assessed in view of encouraging innovations that help realise the EU's environmental, social and economic objectives, and to anticipate and harness future technological advances".[140] The main objectives of the innovation principle are "to i) improve the design of existing and future EU regulations with regard to their impact on encouraging beneficial innovation; ii) steer the development of innovative solutions addressing new and complex challenges in a way that embeds EU values and protects Europeans; and iii) achieve an optimal balance between predictability of the regulatory environment and adaptability to scientific and technological progress".[141]

According to the Commission, the EU safety framework (mainly the Machinery Directive,[142] the Radio Equipment Directive,[143] which applies to all products, including embedded software, using the radio frequency spectrum, the General Product Safety Directive,[144] which aims to ensure that only safe consumer products are placed on the market and acts as a safety net role for products and risks not covered by the harmonisation safety legislation, as well as specific safety rules such as those for medical devices or toys)[145] addresses the intended use and foreseeable (mis)use of products when placed on the market. As a result, a solid body of standards in the area of AI-enabled devices has been developed. This body of standards is continuously being adapted in line with technological progress. Consumers and European businesses will benefit from the further development and promotion of such safety and interoperability standards, especially if those standards are supported by EU and international standardisation organisations.[146]

However, the Commission recognised that, in order to fully unlock the digital/data economy, the current safety and liability frameworks need to keep up to date with emerging trends and take account of new technological developments. Otherwise, legal uncertainty may hinder the development and uptake of AI-enabled

---

[140] "The Innovation Principle", European Commission, Research and Innovation, 13.12.2019, at p. 1.

[141] Ibid.

[142] Directive 2006/42/EC of the European Parliament and of the Council of 17 May 2006 on machinery, and amending Directive 95/16/EC (recast) (OJ L 157, 9.6.2006, pp. 24–86) (the Machinery Directive).

[143] Directive 2014/53/EU of the European Parliament and of the Council of 16 April 2014 on the harmonisation of the laws of the Member States relating to the making available on the market of radio equipment and repealing Directive 1999/5/EC (OJ L 153, 22.5.2014, pp. 62–106).

[144] Directive 2001/95/EC of the European Parliament and the Council of 3 December 2001 on general product safety.

[145] See for instance: Council Directive 90/385/EEC on Active Implantable Medical Devices (AIMDD); the Council Directive 93/42/EEC on Medical Devices (MDD); Council Directive 98/79/EC on In Vitro Diagnostic Medical Devices (IVDMD); Council Directive 89/391/EEC on the introduction of measures to encourage improvements in the safety and health of workers at work.

[146] Commission Communication "Artificial Intelligence for Europe", COM (2018) 237 final, Brussels, 25.4.2018, at p. 15.

products and services. This is why "a high level of safety and an efficient redress mechanism for victims in case of damages helps to build user trust and social acceptance of these technologies".[147] The Commission stressed that evaluations of both the Machinery Directive and the Product Liability Directive have taken place. As it will be shown analytically below, both evaluations were parts of the Commission's target to ensure that EU legal framework is suitable for emerging digital technologies and innovative products. An initial assessment was also carried out on the current liability frameworks in light of AI and emerging technologies.[148]

To this end, the Commission would be supported by an Expert Group on Liability and New Technologies[149] to further analyse crucial liability questions.[150] In particular, the Expert Group would be invited to provide the Commission with expertise on the applicability of the Product Liability Directive to traditional products, new technologies and new societal challenges ('the Product Liability Directive formation')[151] and, in light of an assessment of the existing liability schemes, support the Commission in developing principles that can serve as guidelines for possible adaptations of applicable laws at EU and national level relating to new technologies ('the New Technologies formation').[152] In the call for applications, the New

---

[147] Ibid., at p. 16.

[148] Commission Staff Working Document on "Liability for emerging digital technologies - Accompanying the document Commission Communication 'Artificial intelligence for Europe'", SWD (2018) 137 final, Brussels, 25.4.2018.

[149] It was decided that the Expert Group on Liability and New Technologies (which was set up by the Commission in March 2018) would work in two formations: a Product Liability Directive formation managed by DG Internal Market, Industry, Entrepreneurship and SMEs (GROW) and a New Technologies formation managed by DG GROW, DG Communications Networks, Content and Technology (CNECT) and DG Justice and Consumers (JUST).

[150] Commission Communication "Artificial Intelligence for Europe", COM (2018) 237 final, Brussels, 25.4.2018, at p. 16.

[151] The aim of the Product Liability Directive formation was to provide advice and expertise on the implementation of the Directive. In particular, it shall help to interpret the provisions of the Product Liability Directive and assess the extent to which the provisions of the Directive are adequate to solve questions of liability in relation to traditional products, new technologies and new societal challenges (e.g. pharmaceutical products and medical devices, environmental damages and refurbished products). The Product Liability Directive formation would also provide assistance to the Commission on the implementation of the Directive, also with a particular view to the developments of the jurisprudence of the Court of Justice and national courts, new and emerging technologies (e.g. 3D printing, IoT, AI, robotics and cybersecurity) and any other development in the field of product liability. See: Call for Applications for the Selection of Members of the Expert Group on Liability and New Technologies, at p. 4.

[152] The aim of the New Technologies formation was to assess whether and to what extent existing liability schemes are adapted to the emerging market realities following the development of the new technologies such as Artificial Intelligence, advanced robotics, the IoT and cybersecurity issues. It shall identify the shortcomings and assess whether the overall liability regime is adequate to facilitate the uptake of the above-mentioned new technologies by fostering investment stability and users' trust. In case the existing overall liability regime is deemed not to be adequate, the New Technologies formation shall provide recommendations on how it should be designed. The regulatory framework to be considered for analysis should include national tort law as well as

Technologies formation in particular was asked to assess "whether and to what extent existing liability schemes are adapted to the emerging market realities following the development of the new technologies such as Artificial Intelligence, advanced robotics, the IoT and cybersecurity issues".[153] The experts were asked to examine whether the current liability regimes are still "adequate to facilitate the uptake of the above-mentioned new technologies by fostering investment stability and users' trust".[154] If there are shortcomings, the New Technologies formation should make recommendations for amendments, without being limited to existing national and EU legal instruments. However, recommendations should be limited to matters of extracontractual liability, leaving aside in particular corresponding (and complementary) rules on safety and other technical standards.

2.10.2.2 Summary of Key Actions to be Taken by the Commission to Ensure an Appropriate Legal Framework for AI

Developments in AI require a legal/regulatory framework that is flexible enough to promote innovation while ensuring high levels of consumer protection and safety. In order to enhance the development of AI in Europe and create an appropriate ethical and legal framework, the Commission decided to pursue a comprehensive approach including a number of steps to be implemented.

In particular, as a first step, the Commission proposed the establishment (by July 2018) of a framework for stakeholders and experts—the European AI Alliance—in order to develop draft guidelines on AI ethics and new safety and technical

any possible specific national liability regimes, the rationale or contents of which may be relevant. Questions of liability should be analysed holistically looking at various actors (e.g. liability of owners/operators, insurers) and legal relationships (e.g. questions of redress in the technology value chain). The assessment should not be constrained by existing legal instruments or concepts in EU or national law and can propose new concepts. The New Technologies formation shall also assist the Commission in developing EU-wide principles which can serve as guidelines for possible adaptations of applicable laws at EU and national level as regards the new technologies following the development of the new technologies such as Artificial Intelligence, advanced robotics, the IoT and cybersecurity issues. The principles should address among others key issues in connection with damages caused by the above-mentioned new technologies, such as the assignment of liability (e.g. liable person, exclusive/joint liability, the role of mandatory or voluntary insurance to cover the liability risk), the nature of liability (fault/non-fault based), whether it is necessary for the victim to establish a defect, who should bear the burden of proof and which redress possibilities insurance providers would have to recover compensated damage. The assessment of existing liability schemes and development of principles should be completed by June 2019 at the latest. Following the assessment, the New Technologies formation of the Expert Group may be asked to assist the Commission with expert advice in the discussion on and possible implementation of these principles.

See: Call for Applications for the Selection of Members of the Expert Group on Liability and New Technologies, at pp. 4–5.

[153] Ibid., at p. 4.

[154] Ibid.

interoperability standards by the end of 2018,[155] in cooperation with the European Group on Ethics in Science and New Technologies. These guidelines will address a range of issues, including safety, security, algorithmic transparency and consumer protection, helping to ensure that key values (such as democratic principles and respect for fundamental rights) are embedded into the development and use of AI solutions. The European AI Alliance will also provide broader input for the work of the High-Level Expert Group on Artificial Intelligence,[156] a group comprising fifty-two experts from academia, civil society, as well as industry. The High-Level Expert Group on AI (which serves as the steering group for the European AI Alliance's work) was appointed by the Commission in June 2018, following an open selection process. The general objective of the group is to support the implementation of the European strategy on artificial intelligence, including the elaboration of

[155] Ibid.

[156] For further information on the High-Level Expert Group on Artificial Intelligence, see the Call for Applications for the Selection on Members of the High-Level Group of Experts on Artificial Intelligence, especially at pp. 1–4: The Commission's Directorate-General for Communications Networks, Content and Technology ('DG CNECT') has set up a High-Level group of experts on Artificial Intelligence ('the group'). The general objective of the group shall be to support the implementation of the European initiative on AI. This will include the elaboration of recommendations on future AI-related policy development and on ethical, legal and societal issues related to AI, including socio-economic challenges (at p. 1). The group shall steer the AI Alliance's work, interact with other initiatives and help stimulate a multi-stakeholder dialogue, gather participants' views and reflect them in its analysis and reports (at p. 1). The group will be tasked to: 1. Advise the Commission on next steps addressing AI-related mid to long-term challenges and opportunities through recommendations which will feed into the policy development process, the legislative evaluation process and the development of a next-generation digital strategy. 2. Support the Commission on further engagement and outreach mechanisms to interact with a broader set of stakeholders in the context of the AI Alliance, share information and gather their input on the group's and the Commission's work. 3. Propose to the Commission AI ethics guidelines, covering issues such as fairness, safety, transparency, the future of work, democracy and more broadly the impact on the application of the Charter of Fundamental Rights, including privacy and personal data protection, dignity, consumer protection and non-discrimination. These guidelines will build on the work of the European Group on Ethics in Science and New Technologies and of the EU Fundamental Rights Agency in this area (at p. 2). Timetable for the deliverables of the group: - Spring 2018: Kick-off of the work with the stakeholders joining the AI Alliance through the online platform; roadmap for the group's engagements and workshops. - Summer 2018: Draft AI ethics guidelines. - Autumn 2018: Consultation with members of the AI Alliance through a dedicated platform and workshops; consolidation of comments and proposal of AI ethics guidelines to the Commission. - Beginning 2019: Presentation of the AI ethics guidelines during the first annual assembly of the AI Alliance and gathering commitments from members of the AI Alliance. - Spring 2019: Draft recommendations for next steps addressing AI-related mid to long-term challenges and opportunities, including input to inform post-2020 activities; consultations with the other members of the AI Alliance on the draft recommendations. - Summer 2019: Final recommendations for next steps (at p. 2). The group will build on existing evidence on the topics discussed and on scientific insights. It will be supported by information streams and engagement opportunities framed by studies and projects commissioned by the Commission, as well as stakeholder workshops, engagement events and other relevant data sources and studies, identified by the experts (at p. 4).

recommendations on future AI-related policy development and on ethical, legal and societal issues related to AI, including socio-economic challenges.

Furthermore, the Commission's Communication on AI for Europe decided to issue a guidance document on the interpretation of the Product Liability Directive in light of technological developments by mid-2019 in order to facilitate a common understanding between EU countries, to ensure legal safety and clarity for consumers and producers in case of defective products and to further clarify to what extent it applies to emerging technologies.[157] To the same regard, as another step for building trust and in order to move a step forward on ensuring legal clarity in AI-based applications, the Commission proposed to issue by mid-2019 a report on the broader implications for, potential gaps in and orientations for, the safety and liability frameworks for AI, Internet of Things and robotics.[158] The Expert Group on liability and new technologies was invited to analyse the challenges brought about by AI and, in light of an assessment of the existing liability schemes, to assist the Commission in developing principles that can serve as guidelines for possible adaptations of applicable laws at EU and national level relating to emerging digital technologies.[159]

Moreover, following a proposal of the European Parliament, the Commission will support research in the development of "explainable AI" and implement a pilot project on Building Algorithmic Awareness.[160] In particular, the Commission will carry out an analysis of both opportunities and challenges brought by algorithmic decision-making (automated decision making), including biases and discrimination (2018–2019).[161] To this end, the Commission intends to raise public awareness on emerging issues raised by the use of algorithms, establish a solid evidence-base about the main issues in algorithmic decision-making, and draft the policy responses as well as propose solutions to those challenges. From various AI applications to ranking results in search engines, algorithms play an important role in the way we can access information online. This has significant implications for consumers and

[157] Commission Communication "Artificial Intelligence for Europe", COM (2018) 237 final, Brussels, 25.4.2018, final, at p. 16.

[158] Ibid.

[159] "We will issue guidance on the (Product Liability) Directive as well as a report on the broader implications for, and potential gaps in and orientations for, the liability and safety frameworks for AI, Internet of Things and robotics in mid-2019. If necessary, the Commission will update certain aspects of the Directive, such as the concepts of 'defect', 'damage', 'product' and 'producer'. However, the overall principle of strict liability will remain intact. A coherent, technology-neutral safety framework should prevent accidents as far as possible. However, when accidents do happen, our liability framework should ensure that those who suffer injury are compensated". Report from the Commission on the Application of the Council Directive on the approximation of the laws, regulations, and administrative provisions of the Member States concerning liability for defective products (85/374/EEC) {SWD(2018) 157 final} - {SWD(2018) 158 final}, COM(2018) 246 final, Brussels, 7.5.2018, at p. 10.

[160] Commission Communication "Artificial Intelligence for Europe", COM (2018) 237 final, Brussels, 25.4.2018, at p. 16.

[161] Ibid.

businesses in areas such as online platforms. Therefore, algorithmic transparency/ explainability in an in-depth manner is key for informed policy-making and an important safety net for accountability and fairness in decision-making. As the Commission put it, "to further strengthen trust, people also need to understand how the technology works, hence the importance of research into the explainability of AI systems. Indeed, in order to increase transparency and minimise the risk of bias or error, AI systems should be developed in a manner which allows humans to understand (the basis of) their actions".[162]

Finally, the Commission stated that it aims at ensuring a high standard of personal data protection across the EU and that it will closely follow the application of the General Data Protection Regulation (GDPR) in the context of AI. It is reminded that the GDPR contains provisions on decision-making based solely on automated processing, including profiling. In such cases, data subjects have the right to be provided with meaningful information about the logic involved in the decision. They are also given the right not to be subject solely to automated decision-making, except in certain situations. The Commission is determined to support national and EU-level consumer organisations and data protection regulatory authorities in developing an understanding of AI-powered applications with the input of the European Consumer Consultative Group and of the European Data Protection Board.[163]

2.10.3 Conclusion

The Commission's Communication on Artificial Intelligence for Europe proposed a European approach to strengthen the EU AI ecosystem and make the most out of the opportunities offered by artificial intelligence, while addressing the new challenges AI brings. To this end, the Commission presented a series of measures to put artificial intelligence at the service of Europeans and boost Europe's competitiveness in this field.

In particular, building on European values, the Commission set out a European initiative on AI and proposed a three-core steps approach, in order to: (i) enhance Europe's technological and industrial capacity as well as AI uptake and increase both public and private investments; (ii) prepare Europe for socio-economic changes associated with AI; (iii) ensure that Europe has an appropriate ethical and legal framework to cope with AI development and deployment. This includes guidance on existing product liability rules, a detailed analysis of emerging challenges, suitability of some established rules on safety and civil law liability rules in light of new technological developments, and drafting of AI ethics guidelines through the High-Level Expert Group on AI and the European AI Alliance.

[162] Ibid.

[163] Ibid.

It should be noted that the Communication on AI for Europe set out the Commission's ambitious vision of advancing as well as regulating artificial intelligence, offering, *inter alia*, some preliminary insights as to the policy options and what the forthcoming new framework for AI might include. More importantly, it put forward trust as a prerequisite to ensure a human-centric approach to AI—i.e. an approach that places people at the centre of the development of AI—and this is the reason why the Commission has repeatedly stated that the proper regulatory framework for AI should be based on the Union's values and in line with the EU Charter of Fundamental Rights. AI should serve people, aiming at increasing human well-being and benefiting people and society as a whole. The power of AI should be placed at the service of human progress, human dignity, freedom, pluralism, justice, and equality.

As the Commission put it, "trust is a prerequisite to ensure a human-centric approach to AI: AI is not an end in itself, but a tool that has to serve people with the ultimate aim of increasing human well-being";[164] "an environment of trust and accountability around the development and use of AI is needed";[165] "citizens and businesses alike need to be able to trust the technology they interact with, have a predictable legal environment and rely on effective safeguards protecting fundamental rights and freedoms";[166] "to achieve this, the trustworthiness of AI should be ensured. The values on which our societies are based need to be fully integrated in the way AI develops. The Union is founded on the values of respect for human dignity, freedom, democracy, equality, the rule of law and respect for human rights, including the rights of persons belonging to minorities. These values are common to the societies of all Member States in which pluralism, non-discrimination, tolerance, justice, solidarity and equality prevail. In addition, the EU Charter of Fundamental Rights brings together—in a single text—the personal, civic, political, economic and social rights enjoyed by people within the EU";[167] "the EU can lead the way in developing and using AI for good and for all, building on its values and its strengths";[168] "this is how the EU can make a difference – and be the champion of an approach to AI that benefits people and society as a whole";[169] "the EU has a

---

[164] Commission Communication, "Building Trust in Human-Centric Artificial Intelligence", COM (2019) 168 final, Brussels, 8.4.2019, at pp. 1–2.

[165] Commission Communication, "Artificial Intelligence for Europe", COM(2018) 237 final, Brussels, 25.4.2018, at p. 13.

[166] Ibid., at p. 14.

[167] Commission Communication, "Building Trust in Human-Centric Artificial Intelligence", COM (2019) 168 final, Brussels, 8.4.2019, at p. 2.

[168] Commission Communication "Artificial Intelligence for Europe", COM (2018) 237 final, Brussels, 25.4.2018, at p. 2.

Article 2 of the Treaty on EU reads: "The Union is founded on the values of respect for human dignity, freedom, democracy, equality, the rule of law and respect for human rights, including the rights of persons belonging to minorities". The Member States share a "society in which pluralism, non-discrimination, tolerance, justice, solidarity and equality between women and men prevail."

[169] Commission Communication "Artificial Intelligence for Europe", COM (2018) 237 final, Brussels, 25.4.2018, at p. 2.

strong scientific and industrial base to build on, with leading research labs and universities, recognised leadership in robotics as well as innovative startups. It has a comprehensive legal framework which protects consumers while promoting innovation and it is making progress in creating a Digital Single Market. The main ingredients are there for the EU to become a leader in the AI revolution, in its own way and based on its values. The approach to AI described in this document shows the way forward and highlights the need to join forces at European level, to ensure that all Europeans are part of the digital transformation, that adequate resources are devoted to AI and that the Union's values and fundamental rights are at the forefront of the AI landscape. Together, we can place the power of AI at the service of human progress".[170]

2.11 The EU's 2018 Coordinated Plan on Artificial Intelligence

It is recalled that the Commission's Communication "Artificial Intelligence for Europe", which was published on 25 April 2018, underlined that the EU should have a coordinated approach to take advantage of the opportunities offered by AI and to address the new challenges that it brings.[171]

According to the Communication, the Commission is committed to cooperate with Member States on a coordinated plan on AI. "The discussion will take place in the framework of the existing European platform of national initiatives to digitise industry, with the view to agree this plan by the end of 2018. The main aims will be to maximise the impact of investments at EU and national levels, encourage synergies and cooperation across the EU, exchange best practices and collectively define the way forward to ensure that the EU as a whole can compete globally".[172] The Commission will facilitate the dialogue with Member States in order to agree a coordinated plan on AI by the end of 2018 to prepare Europeans for the AI transformation and address legal and ethical considerations.[173]

This proposal for a coordinated plan on AI was endorsed by the European Council which, at its meeting on 28 June 2018, invited the Commission to work with Member States on a coordinated plan on Artificial Intelligence,[174] building on its Communication "Artificial Intelligence for Europe".

[170] Ibid., at pp. 18–19.

[171] Ibid., at p. 2.

[172] Ibid., at p. 3.

[173] Ibid., at pp. 17 and 18.

[174] See European Council conclusions, 28 June 2018, European Council Press Release, 29 June 2018: https://www.consilium.europa.eu/en/press/press-releases/2018/06/29/20180628-euco-conclusions-final/, at conclusion 20 (section IV, Innovation and digital): "20. It is vital to deliver on the remaining legislative proposals concerning the Digital Single Market before the end of the

As a result, on 7 December 2018, the Commission submitted the Communication "Coordinated Plan on Artificial Intelligence",[175] accompanied by its Annex entitled "Coordinated Plan on the Development and Use of Artificial Intelligence Made in Europe – 2018"[176] prepared by the Member States, Norway, Switzerland and the Commission in the context of the work of the Member States' Group on Digitising European Industry and Artificial Intelligence.

Delivering on the Commission's EU strategy on artificial intelligence, the coordinated plan on AI proposed joint actions for closer and more efficient cooperation between Member States, Norway, Switzerland and the Commission in four key areas: increasing investment, making more data available, fostering talent and ensuring trust. According to the Commission, stronger coordination at European level is essential in order to ensure the success of the EU strategy on AI and fulfill the ambition of Europe becoming the world-leading region for developing and deploying cutting-edge, ethical and secure AI as well as promoting a human-centric approach in the global context.[177] This coordination extends to "investment, excellence in and diffusion of AI, data availability, societal challenges, ethics and the regulatory framework".[178] Only if Member States and the Commission work together will Europe be able to turn vision into reality;[179] "by working together the Union can maximise its impact to compete globally".[180]

The Member States' Group on Digitising European Industry and AI and the Commission discussed between June and November 2018 possible issues and actions for cooperation. In particular, in order to accommodate the fast pace of the AI-induced change in societies and economies, the Commission, Member States, Norway and Switzerland agreed to put in place a rolling coordinated plan that is to be monitored and reviewed annually, so as to ensure it remains up to date. The plan was prepared during several meetings between June and November 2018, whereas

current legislative cycle. To build a European data economy, further action is needed to improve the efficient use of data across the EU and foster trust through high data protection standards and full implementation and proportionate enforcement of the General Data Protection Regulation in respect of all economic actors doing business in our single market. High-quality data are essential for the development of Artificial Intelligence. The European Council invites the co-legislators to swiftly examine the latest data package. It invites the Commission to work with Member States on a coordinated plan on Artificial Intelligence, building on its recent communication".

[175] Commission Communication "Coordinated Plan on Artificial Intelligence", COM(2018) 795 final, Brussels, 7.12.2018.

[176] Annex to the Commission Communication 'Coordinated Plan on Artificial Intelligence', COM (2018) 795 final, Brussels, 7.12.2018—Coordinated Plan on the Development and Use of Artificial Intelligence Made in Europe—2018.

[177] Ibid., at p. 1. See also Commission Communication "Coordinated Plan on Artificial Intelligence", COM(2018) 795 final, Brussels, 7.12.2018, at p. 1.

[178] Annex to the Commission Communication 'Coordinated Plan on Artificial Intelligence', COM (2018) 795 final, Brussels, 7.12.2018 - Coordinated Plan on the Development and Use of Artificial Intelligence Made in Europe – 2018, at p. 2.

[179] Ibid., at p. 1.

[180] Ibid., at p. 2.

exchanges also took place during Competitiveness Council meetings under the Austrian Presidency of the EU, which included AI as a priority in the context of the transformation of the industry.[181] During these meetings, Member States and the Commission identified a series of common actions to increase investments, pool data, foster talent and ensure trust. They also prioritised areas of public interest, such as healthcare, transport and mobility, safety, security and energy, as well as important economic sectors such as manufacturing and financial services.[182]

The result of this joint work, i.e. the coordinated plan (its first edition), was the Annex to the Communication "Coordinated Plan on Artificial Intelligence" ("Coordinated Plan on the Development and Use of Artificial Intelligence Made in Europe – 2018"), which mainly details actions for 2019 and 2020 and prepares the ground for activities in the following years. The plan is expected to run possibly until 2027 and will be reviewed and updated annually.

The key objectives of this 'AI made in Europe' coordinated plan—meeting citizens' aspirations, responding to societal needs, and boosting competitiveness—were highlighted by the Annex to the Commission's Communication as essential to: (i) boost investment and promote excellence in AI applications that are trustworthy and "ethical and secure by design"; (ii) develop and implement agendas for collaboration on research, development, and innovation shared between industry and academia; (iii) adopt learning and training programmes and systems to prepare Europe's society and its future generations for AI; (iv) ensure that public administrations in Europe are global leaders ("frontrunners") in the use of AI; (v) implement, *inter alia* with the guidance of the High-Level Expert Group on AI, ethics guidelines on the development and use of AI technology, in order to set global ethical standards and position Europe as a global leader in "ethical, trusted AI"; (vi) where required, review the current national and European legal framework to better adapt them to technological challenges.[183]

As an important step for building trust on and ensuring legal clarity in AI-based applications, the Commission stated that it will issue guidance on the broader implications for, and potential gaps in and orientations for, the liability and safety frameworks for AI, Internet of Things and robotics by mid-2019. In particular, the Expert Group on liability and new technologies was invited to analyse the challenges brought about by AI and, in light of an assessment of the existing liability schemes, to assist the Commission in developing principles that can serve as guidelines for possible adaptations of applicable laws at EU and national level relating to emerging digital technologies. Also, the Commission stated that it has tasked the Expert Group on Liability and New Technologies to assist in drawing up further guidance on the

[181] Council of the EU, Presidency note 11972/18 of 14 September 2018.

[182] Commission Communication "Coordinated Plan on Artificial Intelligence", COM(2018) 795 final, Brussels, 7.12.2018, at p. 2.

[183] Annex to the Commission Communication 'Coordinated Plan on Artificial Intelligence', COM (2018) 795 final, Brussels, 7.12.2018 - Coordinated Plan on the Development and Use of Artificial Intelligence Made in Europe – 2018, at pp. 2–3.

interpretation of the Product Liability Directive in the light of technological developments in order to ensure trust and legal clarity for consumers and producers in the event of defective products.[184]

2.12 The Council of the European Union of 18 February 2019

The Council of the European Union ("Council") discussed the coordinated plan during the course of January 2019, and on 18 February 2019 adopted conclusions on the Coordinated Plan on the development and use of Artificial Intelligence "made in Europe".[185] With its conclusions, it stressed that the Council, on the basis of the work carried out by the Member States' Group on Digitising European Industry and Artificial Intelligence, should play a key role in monitoring the implementation and annual updating of the Coordinated Plan on AI.[186] The Council called for stronger deployment of AI applications in all economic sectors, "with the aim of making Europe a global leader in Artificial Intelligence".[187] It underlined the crucial importance of facilitating the development and use of AI in Europe by increasing investment, reinforcing excellence in AI technologies and applications, and strengthening research and innovation collaboration between industry and academia in this field.[188] The Council of the EU strongly supported the broad diffusion of and access to AI capacity in each Member State through the AI-on-demand platform, the network of digital innovation hubs and clusters, as well as the network of centres of excellence.[189]

With regard to the required legal/regulatory regime, the Council of the EU stressed that it is imperative to analyse the challenges brought about by AI and called the Commission, in light of an assessment of the existing liability and security regimes, to develop principles that can serve as guidelines for possible adaptations of applicable laws at EU and national level relating to emerging digital technologies. As the Council of the EU put it: "Underlines that all EU legislation should be fit for purpose and encourage the cross-border development and application of Artificial Intelligence-based technologies, and invites the Commission to take this objective into account when evaluating existing or considering new legislation; calls for

[184] Ibid., at p. 17. See also Commission Communication "Coordinated Plan on Artificial Intelligence", COM(2018) 795 final, Brussels, 7.12.2018, at p. 8.

[185] Council of the European Union, Brussels, 11 February 2019, Subject: Artificial intelligence - Conclusions on the coordinated plan on artificial intelligence – Draft Council Conclusions on the Coordinated Plan on the Development and Use of Artificial Intelligence Made in Europe.

[186] Ibid., Conclusion 15, at p. 9.

[187] Ibid., Conclusion 1, at p. 4.

[188] Ibid., Conclusion 2, at p. 5.

[189] Ibid., Conclusion 5, at p. 6.

reviewing, where appropriate, the existing relevant legislation in line with the principles of Better Regulation with a view to ensuring that it is fit for purpose to the new opportunities and challenges raised by Artificial Intelligence including on issues such as safety, privacy and liability and decisions and actions taken without human interaction".[190] To promote the development and use of AI, it is crucial that legislation offers a framework capable of addressing possible risks raised by the use of, and interactions with the technology, including cybersecurity concerns. The Council supported the development of standards in order to make AI-based systems, including connected objects, more cyber-secure. This is why the Council of the EU stressed the significance of tackling cybersecurity challenges, "the need for establishing appropriate cyber security requirements for Artificial Intelligence", and underlined the importance of "ensuring accountability and the protection of fundamental rights".[191] An environment of trust and accountability around the development and use of AI is needed to fully benefit from the opportunities it brings.

Finally, the Council encouraged Member States to develop their national AI strategy by mid-2019 and strongly supported the proposed actions for closer and more efficient cooperation between Member States, extending this cooperation to increasing investment, diffusion of AI, fostering talent, making more and high-quality data available, dealing with societal challenges, and creating a secured and predictable regulatory framework, *inter alia* by following a human-centric approach and implementing ethics-by-design principles.[192]

2.13 Conclusion of Part I: Overview of the European AI Strategy on Liability

Part I of this book traced the evolution of the EU policy on Artificial Intelligence, especially in 2017 and 2018, discussing the main policy documents which set the tone for the European strategy on AI liability. As it was explained, AI can benefit the whole of society and the economy but, at the same time, also brings with it new challenges and raises legal and ethical questions.

It is imperative, therefore, to ensure that AI is developed and applied in an appropriate legal framework which promotes innovation and, at the same time, respects the EU's values and guarantees a high level of safety/security, data protection, and ethical standards. The EU strategy proposed a three-pronged approach, namely: (i) to boost the EU's technological/industrial capacity and competitiveness; (ii) to prepare for socio-economic changes associated with AI (ensuring that no one is left behind in the digital transformation); (iii) to ensure that Europe will have an appropriate ethical and legal framework to deal with AI development and

[190] Ibid., Conclusion 12, at p. 8.

[191] Ibid.

[192] Ibid., Conclusions 13 and 14, at p. 9.

deployment, based on the Union's values and in line with the Charter of Fundamental Rights of the EU.

The EU strategy on AI set out the ambitious vision of advancing as well as regulating artificial intelligence, offering, *inter alia*, some solid preliminary insights as to the policy options and what the forthcoming EU liability framework for AI might include. It put forward trust/safety/security as a prerequisite to ensure a human-centric approach to AI. Artificial Intelligence should serve people, aiming at increasing human well-being and benefiting people and society as a whole. The power of AI should be placed at the service of human progress, human dignity, freedom, pluralism, justice, and equality.

Policymakers across the world are increasingly focusing on the question of how to tackle the risks associated with the development of AI-enabled technologies and their impact on society. It is reminded that, in January 2017, the European Parliament's Legal Affairs (JURI) Committee took the initiative to draft a report tabling a motion for a Resolution of a legislative character and including recommendations to the Commission on the civil-law and ethical aspects of robotics.[193] The European Parliament adopted, on 16 February 2017, a Resolution containing recommendations to the Commission on Civil Law Rules on Robotics.[194] The Resolution made wide ranging recommendations and asked the Commission to assess the impact of AI and present a legislative proposal laying down a set of civil law rules on robotics and artificial intelligence. The Parliament's Resolution called for EU legislation introducing a register of robots, setting up an EU Agency for Robotics and AI (tasked with providing the technical, ethical and regulatory expertise needed in an AI-driven environment) and laying down principles of civil liability for damages caused by robots. Such legislation should be complemented by ethical codes of conduct.

In particular, the Resolution proposed, as an annex, two draft codes of conduct—a Code of Ethical Conduct for Robotics Engineers and a Code for Research Ethics Committees. The first code, which could update and complement the existing EU legal framework, put forward four ethical principles in robotics engineering: (i) beneficence (robots should act in the best interests of humans); (ii) non-maleficence (robots should not harm humans); (iii) autonomy (human interaction with robots should be voluntary—the capacity to make an informed, un-coerced decision about the terms of interaction with robots;); (iv) justice (the benefits of robotics should be distributed fairly—also, affordability of homecare and

[193] Report of the Committee on Legal Affairs of the European Parliament with recommendations to the Commission on Civil Law Rules on Robotics – Motion for a European Parliament Resolution (2015/2103(INL)), 27.1.2017, A8-0005/2017.

[194] European Parliament Resolution of 16 February 2017 with recommendations to the Commission on Civil Law Rules on Robotics (2015/2103(INL)), (2018/C 252/25), OJ C 252, 18.7.2018, pp. 239-257 ("European Parliament Resolution of 16 February 2017 on Civil Law Rules on Robotics").

healthcare robots in particular).[195] AI and robots increase their interaction with humans in very diverse fields and the risks posed by these new interactions should be properly tackled, ensuring that a set of fundamental values is translated into every stage of contact between robots, AI and humans. In this process, the aim of the ethical conduct code is to ensure that robots and AI operate in accordance with legal safety and ethical standards. Special emphasis should be given to human safety, privacy, integrity, dignity and autonomy.[196] The European Parliament considered it essential to guarantee that humans have control over intelligent machines at all times,[197] that robotics engineers and designers should be accountable for the social, environmental and human health impacts that robotics may impose (accountability),[198] that they should respect human well-being, health and rights, guarantee

---

[195] Annex to the European Parliament Resolution of 16 February 2017 on Civil Law Rules on Robotics, p. 253.

See also European Parliament Resolution of 16 February 2017 on Civil Law Rules on Robotics, section "Ethical principles", points 13 and 14, p. 244: "(13) ... the guiding ethical framework should be based on the principles of beneficence, non-maleficence, autonomy and justice, on the principles and values enshrined in Article 2 of the Treaty on European Union and in the Charter of Fundamental Rights, such as human dignity, equality, justice and equity, non-discrimination, informed consent, private and family life and data protection, as well as on other underlying principles and values of the Union law, such as non-stigmatisation, transparency, autonomy, individual responsibility and social responsibility, and on existing ethical practices and codes"; "(14) ... special attention should be paid to robots that represent a significant threat to confidentiality owing to their placement in traditionally protected and private spheres and because they are able to extract and send personal and sensitive data".

[196] European Parliament Resolution of 16 February 2017 on Civil Law Rules on Robotics, section "Ethical principles", point 10, p. 244: "the potential for empowerment through the use of robotics is nuanced by a set of tensions or risks and should be seriously assessed from the point of view of human safety, health and security; freedom, privacy, integrity and dignity; self-determination and non-discrimination, and personal data protection". See also: recital O and point 13.

See also the Annex to the European Parliament Resolution of 16 February 2017 on Civil Law Rules on Robotics, at pp. 253 and 254: "Robotics research activities should respect fundamental rights and be conducted in the interests of the well-being and self-determination of the individual and society at large in their design, implementation, dissemination and use. Human dignity and autonomy – both physical and psychological – is always to be respected".

[197] European Parliament Resolution of 16 February 2017 on Civil Law Rules on Robotics, section "General principles concerning the development of robotics and artificial intelligence for civil use", point 3, p. 243.

[198] Annex to the European Parliament Resolution of 16 February 2017 on Civil Law Rules on Robotics, p. 255.

See also European Parliament Resolution of 16 February 2017 on Civil Law Rules on Robotics, recital M, p. 240: "the trend towards automation requires that those involved in the development and commercialisation of AI applications build in security and ethics at the outset, thereby recognizing that they must be prepared to accept legal liability for the quality of the technology they produce".

transparency and inclusiveness,[199] and disclose promptly factors that might endanger the public or the environment (safety).[200]

Against this background, i.e. the European Parliament's Resolution of 16 February 2017 containing recommendations to the Commission on Civil Law Rules on Robotics, and in response to the European Council's call[201] to put forward a European approach to AI, the Commission published, on 25 April 2018, its Communication on "Artificial Intelligence for Europe".[202] This "AI for Europe" Communication presented the European AI strategy, recognising that AI can benefit the whole of society and the economy but, at the same time, also brings with it new challenges and raises legal and ethical questions. This EU strategy placed people at the centre of the development of AI, i.e. human-centric AI, and proposed a three-pronged approach, namely to boost the EU's technological and industrial capacity and AI uptake across the economy, prepare for socio-economic changes, and ensure an appropriate ethical and legal framework. The "AI for Europe" Communication laid the groundwork for the 'Coordinated Plan on AI' and outlined the steps required to achieve a more committed alignment of resources and goals between Member States in order to take advantage of the opportunities offered by AI and to address the new challenges that it brings.

The proposal for a coordinated plan on AI was endorsed by the European Council[203] which, at its meeting on 28 June 2018, invited the Commission to work with Member States on a coordinated plan on Artificial Intelligence, building on its Communication "Artificial Intelligence for Europe", to create synergies, pool data and increase joint investments. As a result, and in order to coordinate the EU Member States' national AI strategies, the Commission submitted on 7 December 2018 the Communication "Coordinated Plan on Artificial Intelligence",[204] accompanied by its Annex entitled "Coordinated Plan on the Development and Use of

[199] "Inclusiveness allows for participation in decision-making processes by all stakeholders involved in or concerned by robotics research activities". Annex to the European Parliament Resolution of 16 February 2017 on Civil Law Rules on Robotics, p. 254.

[200] "Robot designers should consider and respect people's physical wellbeing, safety, health and rights. A robotics engineer must preserve human wellbeing, while also respecting human rights, and disclose promptly factors that might endanger the public or the environment"; "Precaution: Robotics research activities should be conducted in accordance with the precautionary principle, anticipating potential safety impacts of outcomes and taking due precautions, proportional to the level of protection, while encouraging progress for the benefit of society and the environment". Annex to the European Parliament Resolution of 16 February 2017 on Civil Law Rules on Robotics, p. 254.

[201] General Secretariat of the Council, Subject: European Council meeting (19 October 2017) – Conclusions, Brussels, 19 October 2017 (OR. en), EUCO 14/17, at Section II – Digital Europe.

[202] Commission Communication "Artificial Intelligence for Europe", COM(2018) 237 final, Brussels, 25.4.2018.

[203] European Council conclusions, 28 June 2018, European Council Press Release, 29 June 2018: https://www.consilium.europa.eu/en/press/press-releases/2018/06/29/20180628-euco-conclusions-final/.

[204] Commission Communication "Coordinated Plan on Artificial Intelligence", COM(2018) 795 final, Brussels, 7.12.2018.

Artificial Intelligence Made in Europe – 2018"[205] prepared by the Member States, Norway, Switzerland and the Commission in the context of the work of the Member States' Group on Digitising European Industry and Artificial Intelligence.

Legal/Policy Documents, Studies, Reports, and Other Sources

European Commission ('Commission') Communication, "A Digital Single Market Strategy for Europe", COM(2015) 192 final, Brussels, 6.5.2015.

Jean-Claude Juncker, Extract from the Political Guidelines for the next European Commission—A New Start for Europe: My Agenda for Jobs, Growth, Fairness and Democratic Change (15 July 2014) Priority n°2: A Connected Digital Single Market.

Commission Communication, "Digitising European Industry - Reaping the full benefits of a Digital Single Market", COM(2016) 180 final, Brussels, 19.4.2016.

Commission Communication, "Online Platforms and the Digital Single Market Opportunities and Challenges for Europe", COM (2016) 288 final, Brussels, 25.05.2016.

Commission Communication "Building a European Data Economy", COM(2017) 9 final, Brussels, 10.1.2017.

Commission Communication "On the Mid-Term Review on the implementation of the Digital Single Market Strategy - A Connected Digital Single Market for All", COM(2017) 228 final, Brussels, 10.5.2017.

European Data Market Study SMART 2013/0063, Final Report, prepared for the European Commission (Directorate-General for Communications Networks, Content and Technology) by IDC and Open Evidence, 1 February 2017.

Commission Communication, "Investing in a smart, innovative and sustainable Industry - A renewed EU Industrial Policy Strategy", COM(2017) 479 final, Brussels, 13.9.2017.

Commission Communication, "Reflection Paper on Harnessing Globalisation", COM (2017) 240 final, Brussels, 10.5.2017.

Europe's Digital Progress Report, SWD(2017) 160, 10 May 2017.

Scientific Foresight Study "Ethical Aspects of Cyber-Physical Systems"—Science and Technology Options Assessment—European Parliamentary Research Service (EPRS)—Scientific Foresight Unit (STOA)—PE563.501, June 2016. The main part of the study was conducted by Technopolis Group and managed by the Scientific Foresight Unit within the Directorate-General for Parliamentary Research Services (DG EPRS) of the European Parliament.

[205] Annex to the Commission Communication 'Coordinated Plan on Artificial Intelligence', COM (2018) 795 final, Brussels, 7.12.2018—Coordinated Plan on the Development and Use of Artificial Intelligence Made in Europe – 2018.

Study "European Civil Rules in Robotics"—Directorate General for Internal Policies—Policy Department C: Citizens' Rights and Constitutional Affairs—Legal Affairs—Study for the JURI Committee, October 2016.

Report of the Committee on Legal Affairs of the European Parliament with recommendations to the Commission on Civil Law Rules on Robotics—Motion for a European Parliament Resolution (2015/2103(INL)), 27.1.2017, A8-0005/2017.

European Parliament Resolution of 16 February 2017 with recommendations to the Commission on Civil Law Rules on Robotics (2015/2103(INL)), (2018/C 252/25), OJ C 252, 18.7.2018, pp. 239–257 ("European Parliament Resolution of 16 February 2017 on Civil Law Rules on Robotics").

"Rise of the robots: Mady Delvaux on why their use should be regulated", News - European Parliament, 15.02.2017.

"Open Letter to the European Commission – Artificial Intelligence and Robotics, 2018, http://www.robotics-openletter.eu/

Janosch Delcker, "Europe divided over robot 'personhood', Politico, 13.04.2018, https://www.politico.eu/article/europe-divided-over-robot-ai-artificial-intelligence-personhood/

Commission's follow up to the European Parliament resolution of 16 February 2017 on civil law rules on robotics 2015/2103 (INL), 16 May 2017.

"Summary of the public consultation on the future of robotics and artificial intelligence (AI) with an emphasis on civil law rules", October 2017.

General Secretariat of the Council, Subject: European Council meeting (19 October 2017)—Conclusions, Brussels, 19 October 2017 (OR. en), EUCO 14/17, at Section II—Digital Europe.

EU Declaration of cooperation on Artificial Intelligence, Brussels, 10 April 2018.

Shaping Europe's digital future—EU Member States sign up to cooperate on Artificial Intelligence, DIGIBYTE, 10 April 2018.

Commission Communication "Artificial Intelligence for Europe", COM (2018) 237 final, Brussels, 25.4.2018.

Regulation (EU) 2016/679 of the European Parliament and of the Council of 27 April 2016 on the protection of natural persons with regard to the processing of personal data and on the free movement of such data, and repealing Directive 95/46/EC (General Data Protection Regulation) (OJ L 119, 4.5.2016, pp. 1–88).

"The Innovation Principle", European Commission, Research and Innovation, 13.12.2019.

Directive 2006/42/EC of the European Parliament and of the Council of 17 May 2006 on machinery, and amending Directive 95/16/EC (recast) (OJ L 157, 9.6.2006, pp. 24–86) (the Machinery Directive).

Directive 2014/53/EU of the European Parliament and of the Council of 16 April 2014 on the harmonisation of the laws of the Member States relating to the making available on the market of radio equipment and repealing Directive 1999/5/EC (OJ L 153, 22.5.2014, pp. 62–106).

Directive 2001/95/EC of the European Parliament and the Council of 3 December 2001 on general product safety.

Council Directive 90/385/EEC on Active Implantable Medical Devices (AIMDD).

Council Directive 93/42/EEC on Medical Devices (MDD).
Council Directive 98/79/EC on In Vitro Diagnostic Medical Devices (IVDMD).
Council Directive 89/391/EEC on the introduction of measures to encourage improvements in the safety and health of workers at work.
Commission Staff Working Document on "Liability for emerging digital technologies - Accompanying the document Commission Communication 'Artificial intelligence for Europe'", SWD(2018) 137 final, Brussels, 25.4.2018.
Report from the Commission on the Application of the Council Directive on the approximation of the laws, regulations, and administrative provisions of the Member States concerning liability for defective products (85/374/EEC) {SWD (2018) 157 final} - {SWD(2018) 158 final}, COM(2018) 246 final, Brussels, 7.5.2018.
Commission Communication, "Building Trust in Human-Centric Artificial Intelligence", COM(2019) 168 final, Brussels, 8.4.2019.
European Council conclusions, 28 June 2018, European Council Press Release, 29 June 2018: https://www.consilium.europa.eu/en/press/press-releases/2018/06/29/20180628-euco-conclusions-final/
Commission Communication "Coordinated Plan on Artificial Intelligence", COM (2018) 795 final, Brussels, 7.12.2018.
Annex to the Commission Communication 'Coordinated Plan on Artificial Intelligence', COM(2018) 795 final, Brussels, 7.12.2018 - Coordinated Plan on the Development and Use of Artificial Intelligence Made in Europe – 2018.
Council of the EU, Presidency note 11972/18 of 14 September 2018.
Council of the European Union, Brussels, 11 February 2019, Subject: Artificial intelligence - Conclusions on the coordinated plan on artificial intelligence – Draft Council Conclusions on the Coordinated Plan on the Development and Use of Artificial Intelligence Made in Europe.
Nikos Th. Nikolinakos, EU Policy and Legal Framework for Artificial Intelligence, Robotics, and Related Technologies – The AI Act, Springer, 2023.

Part II
Assessing the Key Aspects of the Existing EU Civil Liability Regime for Artificial Intelligence, Robotics and Emerging Digital Technologies: 2018 to 2020

Chapter 3
The European Commission's Initial Assessment of the Liability Frameworks for Emerging Digital Technologies

3.1 Introduction

AI is a powerful force for good but, at the same time, it can cause harm, both material (safety and health of individuals, including loss of life, damage to property) and immaterial (loss of privacy, limitations to the right of freedom of expression, human dignity, discrimination). The main risks associated with the use of AI relate to the protection of fundamental rights (e.g. data protection, privacy, non-discrimination), as well as to safety (including cybersecurity, issues concerning AI in critical infrastructure and malicious use of AI) and liability-related issues. In order to fully unlock the digital/data economy, the liability (and safety) frameworks need to keep up to date with emerging trends and take account of new technological developments. Otherwise, legal uncertainty may hinder the development and uptake of AI-enabled products and services. Evaluations of both the Machinery Directive and the Product Liability Directive were parts of the European Commission's aim to ensure that the EU liability framework is suitable for emerging digital technologies and innovative products.

This chapter focuses on the most important implications for and potential gaps in the liability frameworks for artificial intelligence, the Internet of Things (IoT), and robotics. In particular, the Commission's Staff Working Document on liability for emerging digital technologies[1] attempted to identify the legal challenges that technologies, such as Artificial Intelligence (AI), advanced robotics, autonomous systems, and the Internet of Things (IoT), can pose to the existing EU and Member States legislation due to their novel technical and operational characteristics.

[1]Commission Staff Working Document on "Liability for emerging digital technologies" - Accompanying the document Commission Communication "Artificial intelligence for Europe", SWD (2018) 137 final, Brussels, 25.4.2018.

N. T. Nikolinakos, *Adapting the EU Civil Liability Regime to the Digital Age: Artificial Intelligence, Robotics, and Other Emerging Technologies*, Law, Governance and Technology Series 68, https://doi.org/10.1007/978-3-031-67969-8_3

According to the Commission's initial (2018) assessment on liability for emerging digital technologies, the EU's existing product liability legislation contains a number of gaps that need to be addressed. If the safety risks materialise, the specific characteristics of those technologies could make it difficult to trace back potentially problematic decisions made with the involvement of AI systems. This in turn may make it extremely difficult for persons having suffered harm to obtain compensation under the current EU and national liability legislation. Therefore, in the context of emerging digital technologies, it is imperative to offer an adequate level of legal certainty for businesses, to ensure that appropriate redress mechanisms for consumers of these emerging AI-enabled products and services are in place, and to avoid any potential disparities and fragmentation in the Digital Single Market.[2]

---

[2]For interesting reading, analysis, and useful academic commentary on the legal challenges that technologies, such as artificial intelligence, advanced robotics, autonomous systems, and the Internet of Things (IoT) could pose to the existing EU and Member States legislation due to their novel technical and operational characteristics, see the following:

D. Fairgrieve and Eleonora Rajneri, 'Is Software a Product under the Product Liability Directive?', Zeitschrift für Internationales Wirtschaftsrecht, January 2019, Volume 1/2019, pp. 24–28.

Charlotte de Meeus, 'The Product Liability Directive at the Age of the Digital Industrial Revolution: Fit for Innovation?', (2019), Vol. 8, Journal of European Consumer and Market Law, Issue 4, pp. 149–154.

Timan, T., R. Snijders, M. Kirova, S. Suardi, M. v. Lieshout, M. Chen, P. Costenco, E. Palmerini, A. Bertolini, A. Tejada, S. v. Montfort, M. Bolchi, S. Alberti, R. Brouwer, K. Karanilokova, F. Episcopo and S. Jansen (2019). Study on safety of non-embedded software. Service, data access, and legal issues of advanced robots, autonomous, connected, and AI-based vehicles and systems: final study report regarding CAD/CCAM and industrial robots. Brussel, European Commission.

Borghetti J-S, 'How can artificial intelligence be defective'. In: Lohsse S, Schulze R, Staudenmayer D (eds) Liability for artificial intelligence and the Internet of Things. Nomos, Baden-Baden (2019), pp. 63–76.

Gerald Spindler, 'User Liability and Strict Liability in the Internet of Things and for Robots' in Sebastian Lohsse, Reiner Schulze and Dirk Staudenmayer (eds), Liability for Artificial Intelligence and the Internet of Things. Nomos, Baden-Baden (2019), pp. 125–145.

Miquel Martín-Casals, 'Causation and Scope of Liability in the Internet of Things (IoT)' in Sebastian Lohsse/Reiner Schulze/Dirk Staudenmayer (ed), Liability for Artificial Intelligence and the Internet of Things. Nomos, Baden-Baden (2019), pp. 201–228.

Lohsse, S., Schulze, R., & Staudenmayer, D., 'Liability for Artificial Intelligence', In S. Lohsse, R. Schulze, & D. Staudenmayer (eds.), Liability for Artificial Intelligence and the Internet of Things. Nomos, Baden-Baden (2019), pp. 99–116.

Gerhard Wagner, 'Robot Liability' in S.Lohsse/R.Schulze/D.Staudenmayer (eds), Liability for Artificial Intelligence and the Internet of Things. Nomos, Baden-Baden (2019), pp. 27–62.

Tatjana Evas, A common EU approach to liability rules and insurance for connected and autonomous vehicles, Study. European Added Value Assessment - Accompanying the European Parliament's legislative own-initiative report (Rapporteur: Mady Delvaux). Study, European Parliamentary Research Service (EPRS), February 2018.

Boom, Willem H van, Borghetti, Jean-Sébastien, Ehlers, Andreas Bloch, Karner, Ernst, Nolan, Donal, Oliphant, Ken, Scarso, Alessandro, Ulfbeck, Vibe and Wagner, Gerhard. "Product Liability in Europe". Product Liability: Fundamental Questions in a Comparative Perspective, edited by Helmut Koziol, Michael D. Green, Mark Lunney, Ken Oliphant and Lixin Yang, Berlin, Boston: De Gruyter, 2018, pp. 255–356.

Yavar Bathaee, "The artificial intelligence black box and the failure of intent and causation", Harvard Journal of Law & Technology, Volume 31, Number 2, 889–938, (2018).

Thomas Verheyen, "Full Harmonization, Consumer Protection and Products Liability: A Fresh Reading of the Case Law of the ECJ", 26 (1) European Review of Private Law, 119–140, (2018).

Maurice Schellekens, 'No-Fault Compensation Schemes for Self-Driving Vehicles', Law, Innovation and Technology, 2018, 10:2, 314–333.

Andrea Bertolini, Artificial Intelligence and civil law - Liability rules for drones, Study requested by the European Parliament's Committee on Legal Affairs, Policy Department for Citizens' Rights and Constitutional Affairs, November 2018.

Leenes, R., E. Palmerini, B.-J. Koops, A. Bertolini, P. Salvini and F. Lucivero (2017). "Regulatory challenges of robotics: Some guidelines for addressing legal and ethical issues." Law Innovation and Technology 9: 1–44.

Stefan Grundmann and Philipp Hacker, "Digital Technology as a Challenge to European Contract Law – From the Existing to the Future Architecture", 13 European Review of Contract Law, 255–293, 2017.

Howells, G., Twigg-Flesner, C., and Willett, C., Product Liability and Digital Products. In T-E. Synodinou, P. Jougleux, C. Markou, & T. Prastitou (eds.), EU Internet Law: Regulation and Enforcement. 2017, Springer Nature, 183–195.

Aída Ponce del Castillo, 'A Law on Robotics and Artificial Intelligence in the EU?', (October 3, 2017). Foresight Brief, European Trade Union Institute (ETUI) Research Paper - Foresight Brief #02-September 2017.

Palmerini, E., A. Bertolini, F. Battaglia, B.-J. Koops, A. Carnevale and P. Salvini (2016). "RoboLaw: Towards a European framework for robotics regulation", Robotics and Autonomous Systems 86: 78–85.

Nathalie Nevejans, 'European Civil Law Rules in Robotics', Study requested by the European Parliament's Committee on Legal Affairs (JURI Committee), 2016.

D. Fairgrieve, G. Howells, P. Møgelvang-Hansen et al., Product Liability Directive. In: P. Machnikowski (ed), European Product Liability: An Analysis of the State of the Art in the Era of New Technologies. Principles of European Tort Law. Intersentia; 2016:17–108.

Piotr Machnikowski, Conclusions, in: P Machnikowski (ed), European Product Liability: An Analysis of the State of the Art in the Era of New Technologies. Principles of European Tort Law. Intersentia; 2016:669–705.

Melinda Florina Lohmann, "Liability issues concerning self-driving vehicles", European Journal of Risk Regulation, 7(2), 335–340, (2016).

Roeland de Bruin, "Autonomous Intelligent Cars on the European Intersection of Liability and Privacy: Regulatory Challenges and the Road Ahead", European Journal of Risk Regulation, 2016, 7(3):485–501.

Konstantinos Christidis and Michael Devetsikiotis, "Blockchains and Smart Contracts for the Internet of Things", (2016) IEEE Access, vol. 4, pp. 2292–2303.

Susanne Beck, 'The problem of ascribing legal responsibility in the case of robotics', AI & Society, 2016, vol 31, n°4, pp. 473–481.

Mihalis Kritikos, 'Legal and ethical reflections concerning robotics', Scientific Foresight Unit (STOA) Policy Briefing, European Parliament Research Service (EPRS), PE 563.501, June 2016.

Daily Wuyts, "The Product Liability Directive – More than two Decades of Defective Products in Europe" Journal of European Tort Law, vol. 5, no. 1, 2014, pp. 1–34.

Andrea Bertolini, 'Robots as Products: The Case for a Realistic Analysis of Robotic Applications and Liability Rules', Law Innovation and Technology, 2013, vol. 5, pp. 214–247.

3.2 The Evaluation of the Machinery Directive

The Machinery Directive 2006/42/EC,[3] which is a key piece of legislation and the EU's central safety framework for AI robots, has two overall objectives, namely (i) ensuring a high level of safety and protection for users of machinery and other people exposed to it; and (ii) securing the free movement of machinery in the internal market. The Directive sets general health and safety requirements for products. This means that it is left to manufacturers to decide which are the technical solutions that should be deployed to meet the required high safety level. For this reason, the Directive functions like an umbrella framework leaving space for products to be innovated. Certain aspects of emerging technologies which are not explicitly addressed by the Directive should be examined, such as issues arising from human-machine collaboration.

The evaluation of the Machinery Directive[4] indicated that, although the Machinery Directive allows for technological developments in a digital era, further analysis is required as regards its effectiveness and fitness for purpose going forward, with respect to developments in digitalisation, such as IoT, AI and the new generation of autonomous robots;[5] "there are questions raised with respect to its effectiveness with

[3]Directive 2006/42/EC of the European Parliament and of the Council of 17 May 2006 on machinery, and amending Directive 95/16/EC (recast) (OJ L 157, 9.6.2006, pp. 24–86) (the Machinery Directive).

[4]Commission Staff Working Document, Evaluation of the Machinery Directive, SWD(2018) 160, final, Brussels, 7.5.2018.

It was concluded that the Machinery Directive has successfully contributed towards its overarching objectives by facilitating the free movement of machinery across the Union and protecting the health and safety of consumers and users. Therefore, the evaluation indicated that the Directive has maintained its relevance related to both its objectives, despite changes in technology and the business environment.

However, the Machinery Directive was widely perceived as being less able to deal with coming emerging digital innovations than it was so far. In particular, doubts were raised on the relevance of the Directive to cover future digital innovation. While the majority of stakeholders (mainly manufacturers) are of the opinion that the Directive is still a suitable framework, the analysis carried out in the context of the evaluation indicated that some characteristics of the emerging digital technologies, such as Artificial Intelligence and Internet of Things, may test the suitability of the Directive. This may reduce its effectiveness going forward.

The overall conclusion was that the Machinery Directive is generally relevant, effective, efficient, coherent and has EU added value. However, a need for greater legal clarity of some of its provisions and better coherence with other legislation was identified. In addition, the evaluation indicated that shortcomings in monitoring and enforcement of the Directive have affected its effectiveness. It further detected some administrative requirements that affect the efficiency of the directive and could be simplified. The evaluation showed that the Directive is sufficiently flexible to allow technological developments in a digital era. Yet, new innovations in digitisation may test Directive's effectiveness and fitness for purpose going forward.

[5]See Inception Impact Assessment - Revision of the Machinery Directive, Ref. Ares(2019)132242 - 10/01/2019.

the advent of emerging digital technologies",[6] "it is quite possible that some characteristics of the emerging digital technologies may come to test the limits of the existing product safety framework... over time and in view of emerging technologies the Directive will no longer be able to deal with innovations in the same way as it did in the past".[7]

Certain essential health and safety requirements that relate to emerging digital technologies, such as AI, IoT and advanced autonomous robots, should be addressed. According to the Commission, "AI-powered advanced robots and autonomous self-learning systems alike must meet the essential health and safety requirements (EHSR) laid down in the Machinery Directive, additional to any other applicable legislation. Manufacturers must ensure that products meet the applicable EHSR identified through the risk assessment. In choosing the most appropriate methods for ensuring compliance with the EHSR, the manufacturer must apply the so called 'principles of safety integration' by eliminating or reducing risks as far as possible at the design phase. The manufacturer should also take the necessary protective measures in relation to risks that cannot be eliminated and inform users of the residual risks by means of warnings or manual of instruction. Manufacturers should keep the technical documentation about the products that they place on the market".[8]

Consideration should also be given to the autonomous behaviour of AI systems and robots. Indeed, robots, while continuing to be products, may display an increasingly autonomous and self-learning behaviour. As the Commission put it: "In contrast to purely software based AI systems that depend on software designed for a specific problem to guide its response, robots enabled by AI have increased capabilities to interpret the environment, interact with humans, learn new behaviours and execute actions autonomously without human intervention. Such systems are increasingly penetrating all aspects of our lives. In human-machine collaboration, AI robots are posing much higher risks than purely software AI systems, due to their mechanical moving parts. This gives a new safety edge to the interaction between humans and technology. These emerging digital technologies may not be inherently less safe than more traditional products whose risks are well addressed by the Machinery Directive, but their evolutionary and self-learning capabilities require attention in terms of safety".[9]

It was also underlined that consideration should be given to cyber threats. Cybersecurity requirements could be addressed by specific revised legislation on machinery or through cross-cutting measures. Also, the interaction of any new

---

[6] Commission Staff Working Document, Evaluation of the Machinery Directive, SWD(2018) 160, final, Brussels, 7.5.2018, at p. 28.

[7] Ibid., at p. 30.

[8] Ibid., at p. 29.

[9] Ibid., at p. 29. Also, various questions are emerging, such as to which extent the existing EHSR for the safety and reliability of control systems are exhaustively reflecting the potential risks related to control systems in an IoT ecosystem, at p. 30.

solution on cybersecurity with the existing legal framework, in particular the Radio Equipment Directive, should be evaluated. As the Commission characteristically pointed out, "In a digital market driven by the Internet of Things and AI powered systems, vulnerability to cyberattacks of factories and critical infrastructures is a de facto concern and a growing threat. For example, some industrial processes nowadays are conveniently managed through mobile apps. While such remote controls might increase production's efficiency, they also create targets for cyber-attacks. This means that cybersecurity has a direct impact on workplace safety, and that the cybersecurity of industrial control systems and networks has therefore become a prerequisite".[10]

It was concluded, therefore, that the Machinery Directive needs updating to improve safety levels further, to take into account the need for greater legal clarity and simplification, and adapt to the latest technological innovations. To this end, the Commission adopted a proposal for a Regulation on machinery products, aiming to tackle some of the issues identified by the evaluation.[11] By converting the Machinery Directive into a Regulation, which would be directly applicable in the Member States, the Commission anticipates that matters for stakeholders and national administrations will be simplified. The new Machinery Regulation will represent a common and directly applicable reference, unlike the different national legislative acts for different stages of transposing a Directive. The proposed revision aligns the Directive with EU harmonised legislation on product health and safety and tackles the challenges that may arise from technical progress in digitization. Its aim is to adapt the Machinery Directive's scope and definitions as well as the essential health and safety requirements, so as to explicitly address aspects relating to emerging digital technologies, e.g. AI, cybersecurity, IoT.[12]

[10] Ibid., at p. 30.

[11] The Commission presented its proposal for a new Machinery Regulation, revising the relevant Directive, in April 2021, as part of the bigger AI package. See the Commission's Proposal for a Regulation of the European Parliament and of the Council on machinery products, COM(2021) 202 final, Brussels, 21.4.2021.

The final text of the new Machinery Regulation was adopted on 14 June 2023 and published in the Official Journal on 29 June 2023: Regulation (EU) 2023/1230 of the European Parliament and of the Council of 14 June 2023 on machinery and repealing Directive 2006/42/EC of the European Parliament and of the Council and Council Directive 73/361/EEC, OJ L165/1, 29.06.2023.

[12] European Commission, Press Release, "Commission welcomes political agreement on new rules to ensure the safety of machinery and robots", Brussels, 15.12.2022.

According to Margrethe Vestager, Executive Vice-President for a Europe Fit for the Digital Age, "the new Machinery Regulation will make sure that advanced machines, such as autonomous machines or collaborative robots can be safely placed in the EU market. Also, the regulation will boost innovation and ensure the competitiveness of machinery in which the EU industry is a world leader".

Also, according to Thierry Breton, Commissioner for Internal Market, "the new Machinery Regulation will increase trust in digital technologies including AI, human/robot collaboration, connected and self-learning machinery and hence increase their uptake. The rules will ensure that Europe's machinery industry can continue to innovate, set standards and strengthen the

3.3 The Evaluation of the Product Liability Directive

The Product Liability Directive[13] was one of the first pieces of EU legislation that explicitly aimed to protect consumers. It applies to all movable products, even if integrated into another movable product, and specifically includes electricity. The Directive introduced the concept of strict liability of producers,[14] according to which if a defective product causes death, personal injury or material damage (above EUR 500) to consumers or their private property (in the EU), the producer is liable to provide compensation irrespectively of whether there is negligence or fault on the consumers' part.[15] To put it simply, producers are responsible for defective products, regardless of whether the defect is their fault. A product is considered defective if it does not provide the safety a person is entitled to expect.[16] The Product Liability Directive does not cover contractual liability, which is imposed on an entity by the terms of a contract; it provides the injured person with an extra-contractual regime of liability.[17]

---

competitiveness of the sector. A strong machinery sector plays a crucial role in delivering the digital and green transition of the European industry".

[13] Council Directive 85/374/EEC of 25 July 1985 on the approximation of the laws, regulations and administrative provisions of the Member States concerning liability for defective products, as modified by Directive 1999/34/EC of the European Parliament and of the Council of 10 May 1999 (OJ L 210/29, 7.8.1985, and OJ L 141/20, 4.6.1999, the 'Product Liability Directive' – 'PLD').

[14] The notion of "producer" includes the manufacturer of a finished product, the producer of any raw material or the manufacturer of a component part and any person who, by putting his name, trade mark or other distinguishing feature on the product presents himself as its producer (Article 3 of the Product Liability Directive).

[15] Strict liability represents a strong tool for the protection of injured persons. However, there are a number of circumstances where the Directive allows producers to take certain calculated risks when placing innovative products on the market. The producer is not liable if he can prove that: (i) the defect did not exist when the product was put into circulation; (ii) the defect is due to compliance with regulations issued by public authorities; or (iii) the state of technical knowledge at the time of putting the product on the market made it impossible to discover the defect. Member States may obtain a derogation from this last exemption.

From the day that they become aware of the defect, injured persons have three (3) years to claim damages. Claims are no longer possible ten (10) years after the product was put in circulation. To sustain their claim, those who have suffered injury must prove the damage, the defect and the causal link between the defect and the damage.

[16] This takes all circumstances into account, including the presentation of the product, the use to which it could reasonably be expected the product would be put, and the time the product was put into circulation. Article 6 of the Product Liability Directive states that a product must not be considered defective for the sole reason that a better product is subsequently put into circulation.

[17] Extra-contractual liability is set outside of a contract, for example directly in imposed pieces of legislation or through common law as types of: a) Liability arising from an offense: The person who committed the offense will be liable in front of the injured party or responsible for the damage he/she caused to the party without any contractual agreement between them. An offense can be an intentional act or negligence; b) Liability in the absence of an offense: In liability without an offense, a person may be liable notwithstanding that the damage caused was unforeseeable. For

Given that the Product Liability Directive was never evaluated since its entry into force, and in the light of the recent technological developments, the Commission carried out an evaluation of the Directive to assess its performance. The Commission's evaluation of the Product Liability Directive was based on an external study whose findings were presented in the Commission's Staff Working Document.[18]

The evaluation examined whether the Product Liability Directive (i) continues to be effective in meeting its original objectives; (ii) is efficient; (iii) is consistent with the relevant EU rules; (iv) remains relevant by embracing recent technological changes; and (v) whether EU product liability legislation continues to provide added value to businesses and injured persons. Facing the challenges of digital transformation and in particular to facilitate the investment into and the development of the digital economy, questions arose concerning the clarity of the legal framework, in particular the scope of the Product Liability Directive to deal with liability issues for IoT devices and complex autonomous systems. The Commission had already recognised that the uptake of the Internet of Things, robotics and automated systems (such as robots, highly automated cars, distribution intelligence as part of the smart grids) would create challenges with respect to liability for damages of the economic players as well as to the allocation of liability.[19]

Focusing on the recent technological developments, the evaluation examined whether the Product Liability Directive "remains fit-for-purpose vis-à-vis emerging digital technologies such as the Internet of Things and autonomous systems. For this purpose, the evaluation examines to what extent it has been used in Member States when it comes to damage caused by advanced robots, autonomous systems, Internet of Things, defective applications or other non-embedded software. In this context,

example, the occupier of a building shall be liable for any damage caused by objects falling from it. Sometimes, not only one party should be held liable. For example, where two motor vehicles have a collision and each of the vehicles shall be deemed to have contributed equally to the accident, the owner of each vehicle shall bear half of the total amount of the damage resulting from the accident. c) Liability for the action of others: if a person is liable for another person by law he/she is bound to compensate the injured party (e.g. a parent is liable under law if his child incurs liability).

[18] Commission Staff Working Document, Evaluation of Council Directive 85/374/EEC of 25 July 1985 on the approximation of the laws, regulations and administrative provisions of the Member States concerning liability for defective products – Accompanying the Evaluation Report – SWD (2018) 157 final, Brussels, 7.5.2018 ['Commission Staff Working Document, 'Evaluation of Product Liability Directive', SWD(2018) 157 final, Brussels, 07.05.2018'].

[19] Commission Communication "Digitising European Industry - Reaping the full benefits of a Digital Single Market", COM(2016) 180 final, 19 April 2016.

Also: Commission Staff Working Document "Advancing the Internet of Things in Europe" (accompanying the Commission Communication "Digitising European Industry - Reaping the full benefits of a Digital Single Market", COM(2016) 180 final, 19 April 2016), Brussels, SWD(2016) 110 final, 19.4.2016.

this evaluation also assesses whether the objectives and requirements of the Directive are still fit for purpose in light of these technologies".[20]

The Evaluation Report[21] stated that the Product Liability Directive continues to strike a good balance[22] between consumer protection, harmonising and delivering a

---

[20]Commission Staff Working Document, 'Evaluation of Product Liability Directive', SWD(2018) 157 final, Brussels, 07.05.2018, at p. 3.

The Commission identified, inter alia, the following questions: "... has technical and technological progress and, in particular the development of connected objects, affected the effectiveness of the Directive? To what extent do the initial objectives correspond to the current needs, including new needs created by innovative products? To what extent is there a need to clarify or modify the concept of product, producer, defective, damage or the category of exemptions in the Directive? How well is the term "defective" in the Directive adapted to new technological or scientific advances such as apps and non-embedded software, advanced robots and autonomous/intelligent systems? How well adapted is the intervention to the changing market environment: often blurred distinction between private and professional use of products and the servitisation of products when products and services are often sold and consumed together? How has the strict liability been allocated in case of damage caused by a product which is interconnected with other products or services in the IoT? Why? How has the strict liability been allocated when the damage comes from the unintended behaviour of an autonomous system or an advanced robot? Why?" (at pp. 15 and 16).

[21]Report from the Commission on the Application of the Council Directive on the approximation of the laws, regulations, and administrative provisions of the Member States concerning liability for defective products (85/374/EEC) {SWD(2018) 157 final} - {SWD(2018) 158 final}, COM(2018) 246 final, Brussels, 7.5.2018, ['Commission Report on the Application of the Product Liability Directive, COM(2018) 246 final, Brussels, 07.05.2018'].

[22]The Product Liability Directive is about striking a balance between injured persons' and producers' interests. Its costs are a direct trade-off: what is to the benefit of the injured persons is the producers' cost and vice versa. The main cost for producers is the strict liability. For consumers, costs are related to the burden of proof, the EUR 500 threshold and time limitations. The concepts are simple, but their application may not always be. See Commission Report on the Application of the Product Liability Directive, COM(2018) 246 final, Brussels, 07.05.2018, at p. 6.

Also, differing opinions have been expressed on the effectiveness of specific provisions of the Product Liability Directive, notably about the burden of proof, the defence of regulatory compliance, the development of risk defence and the EUR 500 threshold for property damage. Organisations representing consumers, for instance, claimed to be unfairly disadvantaged by the burden of proof in product liability claims and stressed the difficulties to investigate claims properly or to gain access to essential information especially in case of technical products. Moreover, consumer organisations asked for more protection at a lower cost, which would imply removing the threshold of EUR 500. On the side of the producers and insurers, however, the arguments raised focused on the risk that any relaxation of the rules on the burden of proof or on the threshold for property damages would lead to more claims for minor damages. See Commission Staff Working Document, 'Evaluation of Product Liability Directive', SWD(2018) 157 final, Brussels, 07.05.2018, at p. 5.

See also at p. 31 where it is pointed out that, for most consumer associations, the Directive is not fully effective, as they consider producer's interests to be better protected than those of consumers. Similarly, consumers believe that the Directive is not always effective in protecting consumers mainly because: • claimants have to prove the defect, the damage and their link, which can be burdensome in some fields, as for instance pharmaceutical or complex products, (these arguments have also been raised with regards to new technological developments), • the EUR 500 threshold aims to avoiding litigation for small claims, • compensation of the damage only if the item of property was intended and used for private purpose and not when the defective product was used for

stable legal framework as well as encouraging innovation and fair competition in the EU. It was also stressed that the Directive continues to be an adequate tool, even though products are much more complex today than in 1985. In particular, τhe Commission stated: "2018 is not 1985. The EU and its rules on product safety have evolved, as have the economy and technologies. Many products available today have characteristics that were considered science fiction in the 1980s. The challenges we are facing now and even more acutely in the future - to name but a few - relate to digitisation, the Internet of Things, artificial intelligence and cybersecurity. Exponential growth in computing power, the availability of data and progress in algorithms turn are making especially artificial intelligence (AI) in particular into one of the most important technologies of the 21st century. Exponential growth in computing power, the availability of data and progress in algorithms turn are making especially artificial intelligence (AI) in particular into one of the most important technologies of the 21st century. ... Product safety and liability - should there be damage - are one essential aspect in finding of a policy response that enables European societies, businesses and consumers to benefit from artificial intelligence".[23]

Furthermore, it was underlined that some of the Directive's concepts require guidance and clarification as they hinder its effectiveness. In particular, a better common understanding of what is meant by the terms 'product',[24] 'damage' and 'defect' as well as clarifications on the burden of proof[25] would render the

professional purposes; • the time limit of 3 and 10 years to obtain compensation is too short in cases of complex products that require more expertise; • the exceptions to liability in favour of the producers are too advantageous (such as the development risk clause). Conversely, producers deem the Directive as effective in protecting consumers because: • claimants may request compensation without need to prove the fault or negligence of the producer, • clear identification of the operator (s) to be held liable.

[23] Commission Report on the Application of the Product Liability Directive, COM(2018) 246 final, Brussels, 07.05.2018, at pp. 1 and 8.

[24] The Product Liability Directive does not make any reference to the concept of service nor does it provide for the distinction between products and services. It solely provides for the definition of product, according to Article 2. The notion of product mainly refers to movables even though incorporated into another movable or into an immovable. Services do not fall into the definition of product. According to the Commission, the products that could be found in the European market in 1985 where the Directive was adopted may not present the same technical complexity or characteristics as they do today, but they continue to be covered by the notion of product set out in the Directive. However, it was recognized that the distinction between products and services for the purpose of the Directive is becoming increasingly blurred with regards to new technological developments. A clarification of the concept "product", e.g. with regards to software, may therefore contribute to improving effectiveness. Therefore, it was stated that this requires further assessment. See Commission Staff Working Document, 'Evaluation of Product Liability Directive', SWD (2018) 157 final, Brussels, 07.05.2018, at pp. 23–24.

[25] It appeared that the main difficulty for the injured party to obtain compensation was the burden of proof, namely, to prove the defect in the product and the link between the defect and the damage. Issues related to the burden of proof raise significant concerns mostly among consumers. Claimants find it particularly difficult to prove the defect and the link between defect and damage in court. The burden of proof is the central component of the Directive that triggers the right for compensation.

Directive's application more effective. It was stressed that specific questions exist with regard to what separates a product from a service (e.g. for the Internet of Things, where products and services interact), the scope of damage covered (currently limited to material damage), the notion of what constitutes a defect or the concept of the burden of proof, which is becoming complex, as may be the case with some emerging digital technologies.[26]

For instance, the Commission stated that it is burdensome to distinguish a product from a service when they are bundled together in the context of new technological developments, especially when dealing with cloud technologies and IoT: "Today, embedded software or other specific technical features are already an integral component of many products. In terms of EU product safety legislation, the producer is responsible for the safety of the final product as a whole. Therefore, for products which include software at the moment they were put into circulation by the producer, the Directive could address liability claims for damages caused by defects in this software. The more open nature of new products, where the producer is no longer able to control software or other technical features subsequently installed in or learned by the product may however pose a challenge for establishing claims under the Directive".[27] Therefore, since the distinction between products and services may in the future no longer be pertinent, it was recognized that there is a need to clarify what products and features are covered by the Product Liability Directive.[28] For instance, providing data through an IoT system could be considered a service, and thus fall, as such, outside the product liability and safety regimes.

The most frequent reasons to reject claims relate to the proof of the defect and its link with the damage, which together account for 53% of the cases of rejection. Difficulties in applying the definition of defective product and subsequently in proving the link between damage and defect seem to be particularly relevant in cases of complex products, such as pharmaceuticals. For those products, the injured party need to gather expertise to be able to prove the lack of safety of the product and the link to the damage suffered. According to victims of medicines (Stevens-Johnson Syndrome, Valproate or Distilben) the definition of "defect" is not suitable for pharmaceutical products because the leaflet's information about the risk of serious adverse effects exonerates the producer for these effects. Therefore, it is extremely difficult for such an injured party to demonstrate the causality and the defect of a medicine in connection with the damage. Either the adverse effect of the medicine is unknown and it is therefore hard to provide sufficient scientific elements to establish the link (causality) and the development risk clause may be invoked, or it is known and was therefore published in the leaflet, which means that the medicine was not defective. Injured persons potentially find themselves in a Catch-22 situation where they have to bear the full cost of damages without access to compensation. In this respect, while the definition of defect, damage and their link seem to be effective for tangible products in general, the distinction between a known risk and an unexpected risk—particularly for pharmaceutical products—may be less clear. See Commission Staff Working Document, 'Evaluation of Product Liability Directive', SWD(2018) 157 final, Brussels, 07.05.2018, at pp. 25–26.

[26]Commission Report on the Application of the Product Liability Directive, COM(2018) 246 final, Brussels, 07.05.2018, at pp. 2, 6 and 8.

[27]Commission Staff Working Document, 'Evaluation of Product Liability Directive', SWD(2018) 157 final, Brussels, 07.05.2018, at p. 52.

[28]ibid.

One of the main questions in relation to new technological developments was how to classify the devices/products resulting from these technologies. The definition of "product" as per article 2 of the Product Liability Directive is related to the concept of "movable". This was interpreted as meaning that only tangible goods can be considered products, due to the fact that when the Directive was adopted, no clear examples of non-tangible goods were widespread in the market. It is anticipated that the services relating to tangible products will become more prominent in the near future and thus the balance between products and services may shift towards services, and products will increasingly come with the provision of services. As the Commission put it, "the non-tangible nature of some new technological developments (software, applications, Internet of Things, Artificial Intelligence systems) makes it difficult to classify them as products rather than services".[29] It was argued by some stakeholders that there is a need for an interpretation of the concept of product or an enlargement of the concept of product, including some new technological developments such as Artificial intelligence or cloud technologies, as well as applications. According to the Commission, this is particularly relevant "in the context of the Directive where the nontangible element is not included in the product put into circulation by the producer but installed subsequently as a stand-alone feature".[30] In the light of new technological developments, the definition of product appears to no longer be as clear-cut as it may have been when the Directive was adopted and, "given that the Directive applies to products, a clarification of its scope could therefore be envisaged".[31]

The notion of producer provided for in Article 3 of the Product Liability Directive reflects the definition of product for the purpose of the Directive.[32] According to the Commission, the new technological developments involve different actors in the value chain, including product manufacturers, software producers, the connectivity

[29] Ibid., at pp. 53–54.

[30] Ibid., at p. 54.

[31] Ibid., at p. 61.

[32] 'Producer' (Article 3 of the Product Liability Directive) means the manufacturer of a finished product, the producer of any raw material or the manufacturer of a component part and any person who, by putting his name, trade mark or other distinguishing feature on the product presents himself as its producer, as well as any person who imports into the European Union a product for sale, hire, leasing or any form of distribution in the course of his business. The producer defined as such shall be liable for damage caused to consumers by a defect in his product. Where the producer cannot be identified, each supplier of the product shall be treated as its producer unless he informs the injured party, within a reasonable time of the identity of the producer or of the person who supplied him with the product. The term "producer" is deliberately broad so that an injured person easily find a liable person. In case of an anonymous product, the supplier will be held liable unless he discloses the identity of the producer. The Directive does not define the term "supplier", but according to the case-law of the Court of Justice, the supplier must be regarded as any intermediary involved in the marketing or distribution chain of the product (see, for instance, CJEU, Judgement of 21 December 2011, Case C-495/11, Dutrueux and Caisse primaire d'assurance maladie du Jura). The Directive foresees that where two or more persons are liable for the same damage, they shall be liable jointly and severally, without prejudice to the provisions of national law concerning the rights of contribution or recourse (Article 5 of the Product Liability Directive).

service providers, sensor manufacturers, owners of the object, service providers. Furthermore, some of these technological developments have a very open ecosystem, (e.g. Internet of Things applications), as new features could be added by the user or even third parties to create a new one. The Commission made reference to the European Parliament's Resolution of 16 February 2017 on Civil Law Rules on Robotics[33] and raised the question of whether the concept of 'producer', as defined in the context of Product Liability Directive, fits with the type of responsibilities that may arise in systems encompassing software, Artificial Intelligence systems, data services and other emerging technologies. It concluded that, although the concept of the producer as responsible for his products is still relevant, "it is imperative to assess the impact of changing product (and/or product/service) configurations on this concept to see whether it should be clarified".[34] As the Commission put it, "as products are more easily, altered adapted and combined with services, the definition of the producer may become less clear particularly in the context of emerging digital technologies and the circular economy. The definition of the producer, while continuing to be valuable as it ensures strict liability, may therefore no longer be fully relevant in its current form".[35]

The notion of what constitutes a defect may also need to be re-examined in order to provide certainty regarding new technological developments such as apps and non-embedded software, advanced robots, and autonomous/intelligent systems. For instance, the Commission raised the question whether software vulnerability—e.g. a cyber-attack or a failure to update security software or a misuse of information—could be considered to be a defect. In the field of robotics in particular, it was still open whether an unintended autonomous behaviour of an advanced robot is a defect or not. According to the Commission, "robots are meant to perform autonomous behaviours, they are programmed to do so. Given their self-learning capacities, one could in consequence argue that not all unforeseen autonomous behaviour is a defect. On the other hand, these robots will be employed to perform certain tasks, which will inevitably be linked to safety expectations".[36] The Commission concluded that the definition of defect "may require being updated to new types of problems such as infringements of privacy or how to link the notion of defect with the types of autonomous behaviours leading to damages. Extending the scope of the

---

[33] For robotics, according to European Parliament Resolution of 16 February 2017 with recommendations to the Commission on Civil Law Rules on Robotics, "the concepts of product, producer, damage or the category of exemptions as defined in the Directive [. . .] could not be apt anymore when dealing with the emerging field of robotics: "[. . .] in the scenario where a robot can take autonomous decisions, the traditional rules will not suffice to activate a robot's liability, since they would not make it possible to identify the party responsible for providing compensation and to require this party to make good the damage it has caused". Commission Staff Working Document, 'Evaluation of Product Liability Directive', SWD(2018) 157 final, Brussels, 07.05.2018, at p. 54.

[34] Commission Staff Working Document, 'Evaluation of Product Liability Directive', SWD(2018) 157 final, Brussels, 07.05.2018, at p. 54.

[35] Ibid., at p. 61.

[36] Ibid., at pp. 56–57.

Directive in this direction is, however, a political decision that will have to be carefully assessed".[37]

The feedback received from stakeholders on the application of the Product Liability Directive to new technological developments was divergent. Representatives from public authorities, civil society and consumer associations agreed that there are major issues which are not adequately covered by the Directive with regard to new technological developments, while businesses were more reluctant to amending the Directive.[38]

The overall conclusion of the Commission was that the application of the Product Liability Directive to new technological developments—such as Artificial Intelligence systems, advanced robots and Internet of Things—is not straightforward and that the characteristics of the emerging technologies (particularly their complexity and autonomy) "may challenge whether the existing product liability framework is appropriate to ensure effective redress for consumers and investment stability for businesses".[39] "To remain relevant for the future, the Directive would benefit from clarification to address such issues. ... Guidance can help to make these concepts more effective and highlight their continued relevance";[40] "a detailed assessment of the effects of such changes within the existing framework needs to be carried out. There may be a need for guidance, clarification and if necessary adaptation of certain aspects in light of technological developments to ensure that the Directive continues to meet its objectives to the extent possible. The roll out of these technologies should be closely monitored and observed".[41]

---

[37] Ibid., at p. 61.

[38] Many producers, some consumers, insurers and public authorities/civil society representatives argued that there is no need to update the Directive vis-à-vis new technological developments. Others from all consulted categories found it difficult to apply the Directive to these items, given their intangible nature and increasing complexity. For almost half of the public authorities and civil society representatives and almost all consumers, the scope of the Directive should be broadened to new technological developments and balance consumers' safety and innovation, considering the distinction between products and services and the concept of "defect" as not adequate for these developments. Most businesses consider apps, non-embedded software and IoT components to be "products" pursuant to the Directive, while they have diverging views as to whether the liability is adequately allocated among the different operators. Furthermore, for them defect is adequately defined as to damages caused by an advanced robot or an autonomous system. For a large majority of businesses the exemptions under the Product Liability Directive are adequate for new technological developments and the Directive already applies to them. They consider the Directive to be fit-for-purpose and neutral to different technologies. Similarly, for a large majority of insurer associations there is no need to adapt the Directive to new technological developments. See Commission Staff Working Document, 'Evaluation of Product Liability Directive', SWD(2018) 157 final, Brussels, 07.05.2018, at pp. 66–67.

[39] Commission Report on the Application of the Product Liability Directive, COM(2018) 246 final, Brussels, 07.05.2018, at p. 6.

[40] ibid., at p. 9.

[41] Commission Staff Working Document, 'Evaluation of Product Liability Directive', SWD(2018) 157 final, Brussels, 07.05.2018, at p. 61.

3.4 Commission Staff Working Document on Liability for Emerging Digital Technologies

3.4.1 Introduction

In parallel with the Commission's 2018 Communication on AI for Europe,[42] an initial assessment of the liability[43] frameworks in light of AI and emerging technologies was conducted in April of 2018. The European Commission Staff Working Document on liability for emerging digital technologies[44] attempted to identify the legal challenges that emerging technologies, such as Artificial Intelligence (AI), advanced robotics, autonomous systems and the Internet of Things (IoT), can pose to the existing EU and Member States legislation due to their novel technical and operational characteristics.

The objective of this Staff Working Document was to present "a first mapping of liability challenges" that occur in the context of emerging digital technologies in order to achieve legal clarity and to ensure that adequate redress mechanisms are in place. In particular, the Working Document asked whether the current EU legal framework can provide an adequate level of legal certainty for businesses and appropriate redress mechanisms for consumers of these emerging AI-enabled products and services. It reflected on future developments regarding liability, in order to ensure equitable remedies and compensation to consumers, to offer legal clarity for producers, as well as to identify and avoid any potential disparities and fragmentation in the Digital Single Market: "In certain cases, when digital technology products or services cause a damage, the allocation of liability may be complex due to their specific characteristics. In addition, ensuring their safety over their lifetime is important, as it can prevent or reduce potential damages and liability issues. It is therefore necessary to examine whether existing rules at EU and national level for safety and for the allocation of liability and the conditions, under which a victim is entitled to obtain compensation for damages caused by products and services stemming from emerging digital technologies, are appropriate and whether, for the producers and services providers, the framework continues to deliver an adequate level of legal certainty".[45]

---

[42] Commission Communication "Artificial Intelligence for Europe", COM (2018) 237 final, Brussels, 25.4.2018.

[43] 'Liability' means the responsibility of one party for harm or damage caused to another party, which may be a cause for compensation, financially or otherwise, by the former to the latter. See Commission Staff Working Document on "Liability for emerging digital technologies" - Accompanying the document Commission Communication "Artificial intelligence for Europe", SWD (2018) 137 final, Brussels, 25.4.2018, at p. 2.

[44] Commission Staff Working Document on "Liability for emerging digital technologies" - Accompanying the document Commission Communication "Artificial intelligence for Europe", SWD (2018) 137 final, Brussels, 25.4.2018.

[45] Ibid., at p. 2.

The Commission stated that, in order to fully benefit from the opportunities presented by these new products and services, it is critical to achieve legal certainty and investment stability in emerging digital technologies. It also stressed that these new products and services should not be considered as inherently less safe than traditional products. "Consumers' trust and the uptake of these technologies will depend on whether they are perceived to be safe and on whether the legal framework is considered clear and effective to provide remedies to victims. Clearly, the way in which technologies and tools are used is important for safety and liability aspects".[46]

It was pointed out that the current liability framework in the European Union "is a stable framework that incites investment, innovation and risk-taking". At the same time, however, it was recognized that there is a need to consider possible adaptations of the current framework, in order to achieve clarity that would help stimulate investment in emerging digital technologies and to ensure that adequate redress mechanisms are in place in case of damages caused by such products and services. As the Commission put it, "a reflection on future needs and developments is required, not only from the perspective of the victim i.e. in order to ensure equitable remedies, compensation and allocation of responsibility, but also from the perspective of the innovators and companies operating in the EU as legal certainty is a key element for good business development".[47]

3.4.2 Extra-Contractual Liability Rules Applicable in the Context of Emerging Digital Technologies

Since product liability and product safety are complementary legal frameworks aiming to provide trust and safety to consumers, the Commission's Working Document outlined the existing safety and liability frameworks. It mentioned that EU product safety legislation is based on common safety rules and aims at ensuring that only safe products can be placed on the EU market, while the EU product liability framework (the Product Liability Directive) provides for liability of producers of defective products that cause damage to natural persons or their property.

In addition, various national liability regimes may apply if damage occurs. Thus, at national level, the rules implementing the Product Liability Directive coexist[48] with other extra-contractual[49] liability rules that could also be invoked by victims of

---

[46] Ibid.

[47] Ibid.

[48] According to Article 13 of the Product Liability Directive, the "Directive shall not affect any rights which an injured person may have according to the rules of the law of contractual or non-contractual liability or a special liability system existing at the moment when this Directive is notified".

[49] Extra-contractual liability relates to the civil law responsibility for damage caused outside the context of a contract (the damage being caused by a violation of a right or legitimate interest protected by law). Extra-contractual liability can be imposed by general civil law rules or specific

damages. Those national extra-contractual liability rules could be classified into two broad categories, depending on whether the compensation of the victim requires a fault of the person considered liable by the law or not, namely fault-based extra-contractual liability regimes on the one hand and special regimes of strict liability (extra-contractual) on the other.

In particular, in most EU member jurisdictions, extra-contractual liability regimes are fault-based. Therefore, the fault of the author of the wrongful behaviour leading to a damage—which could be an act or an omission whether intentional or by negligence—is a necessary element to be proven for the liability claim to be successful. The victim submitting a claim needs to provide the evidence required to support his liability claim.[50]

Furthermore, as already mentioned, strict liability is defined as a liability that does not depend on a fault and the claimant needs only to prove the damage and the causal link.[51] Special regimes of strict liability may apply to a diverse set of situations

---

legislation. Product liability is a form of statutory extracontractual liability referring to the civil liability of manufacturers. See Commission Staff Working Document on "Liability for emerging digital technologies" - Accompanying the document Commission Communication "Artificial intelligence for Europe", SWD(2018) 137 final, Brussels, 25.4.2018, at p. 6.

[50] There are situations, however, where national law introduces variations in order to facilitate the burden of proof of the victim so as to increase the possibility of compensation for the victim. Such variations may consist in a presumption of fault by the wrongdoer (or a reversal of the burden of proof), whereby the wrongdoer is liable unless he proves that he was not in fault—for instance, the responsibility of parents/tutors/guardians/teachers for damages caused by a minor, pupil, student/apprentice or mentally impaired person (unless they can prove that they were not able to prevent the damages from happening); or the responsibility of the owner/possessor of the building in case of damages causes by his/her building (unless he/she proves that he/she observed appropriate care for the purpose of avoiding the damage); or the responsibility of a person carrying a dangerous activity (unless he/she proves that all appropriate measures to avoid the damage have been taken). Examples of those variations are cited in Commission Staff Working Document on "Liability for emerging digital technologies" - Accompanying the document Commission Communication "Artificial intelligence for Europe", SWD(2018) 137 final, Brussels, 25.4.2018, at pp. 7–8.

[51] The reversal of the burden of proof in the context of a fault-based extra-contractual liability and the principle of strict liability typically respond to a common rationale. They both aim overall at facilitating the compensation of the victim of damages in situations where the legislator considers it too burdensome or unbalanced to apply the general fault-based liability rule. Some forms of strict liability may go even a step further by linking liability simply to the materialization of a risk and/or making the discharge of liability either impossible or possible only under the proof that the damaging event was caused by an exceptional/unforeseen circumstance that could not be avoided. There may be also other cases where the risk of damage is linked to the unpredictability of behaviour of specific risk groups, like animals or certain persons: in these cases liability may be attributed to the persons that are considered responsible to supervise the animal or the person, because it is them who should normally be in the condition to adopt measures to prevent or reduce the risk of damages. Finally, when the risk of damages is linked to dangerous activities, some jurisdictions may attribute liability to the person that carries out the activity (e.g. the operator of a nuclear power plant or of an aircraft or the driver of a car) or is ultimately responsible for the dangerous activity to happen (e.g. the owner of a vehicle). The rationale typically is that this person has created a risk, which materialises in a damage and at the same time also derives an economic benefit from this activity. See Commission Staff Working Document on "Liability for emerging

which generate different types of risks and damages, especially when the risk of damages is linked to specific (e.g. dangerous) activities "such as the liability of the owners of animals for the damages caused by the animals under their custody; the strict liability of the person responsible for carrying out an unspecified or specified dangerous activity (for example the operation of nuclear power plants, aircrafts or motor vehicles) or other cases linked to a legal or factual relationship between two persons or a person and an object, such as when the damages are caused by someone executing a task in the interest of someone else (employee/employer) or by an object that is under his/her custody".[52]

Although none of the above-mentioned national law provisions are specifically applicable to damages that could be caused by emerging digital technologies, they may constitute helpful points of reference, especially since several Member States analysed the liability implications of emerging digital technologies, primarily in the area of autonomous vehicles, and proceeded with the introduction of sector-specific legislative measures.[53]

3.4.3 The Specific Characteristics of Emerging Digital Technologies

The Commission Staff Working Document described in a more analytical way the specific characteristics of the Internet of Things and Artificial Intelligence, explaining that their characteristics are equally shared, at least to a certain degree, by other emerging digital technologies like blockchain, 3D printing and cloud computing. It summarized the specific characteristics of emerging digital technologies as follows: increasing level of complexity and variety of ecosystems, actors and value chains (high interdependency); autonomy in decision making, self-learning and actuating; generation, processing of and reliance on big volumes of data; and openness to software extensions, updates and patches after the products have been put into circulation.

---

digital technologies" - Accompanying the document Commission Communication "Artificial intelligence for Europe", SWD(2018) 137 final, Brussels, 25.4.2018, at p. 8.

[52] Commission Staff Working Document on "Liability for emerging digital technologies" - Accompanying the document Commission Communication "Artificial intelligence for Europe", SWD (2018) 137 final, Brussels, 25.4.2018, at pp. 8–9.

[53] For example, Germany amended its Street Traffic Act to allow autonomous cars to operate on the streets, provided that a human driver is present to take over control at all times. Sweden introduced a law which allows the testing of autonomous vehicles. In the UK, the Government proposed legislation which would amend insurance legislation in connection with the possible roll-out of autonomous vehicles. See Commission Staff Working Document on "Liability for emerging digital technologies" - Accompanying the document Commission Communication "Artificial intelligence for Europe", SWD(2018) 137 final, Brussels, 25.4.2018, at p. 9. See also House of Commons Library, Briefing Paper, Automated and Electric Vehicles Bill 2017-19, 28 November 2017. Available at: http://researchbriefings.files.parliament.uk/documents/CBP-8118/CBP8118.pdf.

In light of these characteristics, it was concluded that both AI and IoT encompass all of the main specificities that revolve around the emerging digital technologies. Indeed, IoT combines the following specific characteristics: (i) complexity, due to the numerous interdependencies in the value chain and the variety of actors;[54] (ii) autonomous behaviour, as many of the operations provided through and by an IoT system can be fully autonomous;[55] (iii) data driven, because IoT systems entail data generation, data gathering, data processing and data analysis;[56] (iv) openness due to IoT's digital dimension encompassing tangible and intangible elements (software and data).[57] Equally, AI demonstrates the following specific

[54]The Internet of Things (IoT) is about setting up new ecosystems that cut across vertical areas, and create new markets for hardware (connected devices), software (IoT platforms and systems) and services (IoT applications). IoT has a horizontal and cross-cutting character. It should be understood as an ecosystem where areas that have been developed as vertical silos (manufacturing, transport, healthcare, devices, etc.) relate to each other, thanks to common platforms and cross-cutting innovation. IoT ecosystems are, therefore, based on bringing together multiple sectors and a variety of stakeholders to cover an increasingly complex value chain. IoT is based on various disciplines and technologies like sensors, embedded systems, various communications technologies. It requires a specific configuration for object identification and search, open/closed data sharing, lightweight communication protocols, trade-off between local and networked based information processing, and back-end integration. It also requires specific considerations of data security (e.g. location-based profiling), liability (many service providers involved), seamless identification and authentication mechanisms (including those of persons/entities needed for managing contractual relations, attribution and liability) and trust. All this increases the complexity of the IoT ecosystem. See Commission Staff Working Document on "Liability for emerging digital technologies" - Accompanying the document Commission Communication "Artificial intelligence for Europe", SWD (2018) 137 final, Brussels, 25.4.2018, at p. 22.

[55]The data provided by connected sensors and objects allow single and networked objects to take decisions based on the data and actuate or perform specific functions derived from sensing, analysis and intelligence gathered. This takes place normally within the boundaries of given applications but it is expected, with increasing computing power and sophistication, to gain high levels of autonomy in their behaviour and "life". Examples include factory automation, logistics and robotics. See Commission Staff Working Document on "Liability for emerging digital technologies" - Accompanying the document Commission Communication "Artificial intelligence for Europe", SWD (2018) 137 final, Brussels, 25.4.2018, at p. 22.

[56]Connected sensors in private, business or city environments collect data from objects (e.g. a car, a phone, etc.) and these data are analysed either through embedded systems or through cloud-based and Internet systems enabling the creation of new services based on big data analytics. See Commission Staff Working Document on "Liability for emerging digital technologies" - Accompanying the document Commission Communication "Artificial intelligence for Europe", SWD (2018) 137 final, Brussels, 25.4.2018, at p. 22.

[57]Sensors and smart connected objects are not only designed and optimised to perform certain functions on the basis of vertical business models. They become part of a bigger connectivity network which creates new opportunities to combine more intelligence and actuation across vertical markets and to provide a whole new set of services. Technical and semantic interoperability are the key factor of success. It enables the programming of complex systems to integrate a number of device- and service-providers to deliver complete IoT solutions e.g. at home, in cities, between industries. See Commission Staff Working Document on "Liability for emerging digital technologies" - Accompanying the document Commission Communication "Artificial intelligence for Europe", SWD(2018) 137 final, Brussels, 25.4.2018, at p. 22.

characteristics: (i) complexity: with machine learning, AI can learn from other AI;[58] (ii) autonomous behaviour, because, depending on the application, AI software can reason, gather knowledge, plan intelligently, learn, communicate, perceive, and manipulate objects;[59] (iii) data driven, because AI entails data gathering, data processing and data analysis;[60] (iv) openness, due to the fact that AI, combined with hardware, can create new tangible products and/or deliver services.[61]

The Commission Staff Working Document underlined that the emerging digital technologies display certain levels of complexity due to the interdependency between different components. For instance, the IoT and AI-enabled products and services comprise tangible parts/devices (sensors, actuators, hardware), different software components and applications, data, data services (i.e. collection, processing, curating, analysing), and connectivity features. Since many different layers are involved in these technologies, vulnerable software, faulty sensors, or unstable connectivity may make it difficult to determine who is technically and legally responsible for any ensuing damage or how to identify the root cause of the problem. However, it was pointed out that "as far as they constitute 'movable' items, IoT devices and any other items containing intangible elements or presenting

[58] AI is used in a variety of ways and can be found across a large number of sectors, from assembly line robots to advanced toys, and from speech recognition systems to medical research. Its most common application is to find patterns in data, which is why it is commonly applied in online search engines and recommendation sites. Another common application is advanced robotics. See Commission Staff Working Document on "Liability for emerging digital technologies" - Accompanying the document Commission Communication "Artificial intelligence for Europe", SWD(2018) 137 final, Brussels, 25.4.2018, at p. 23.

[59] Artificial intelligence aims to study and develop intelligent machines and software. The associated ICT research includes the development of software that can reason, gather knowledge, plan intelligently, learn, communicate, perceive, and manipulate objects. See Commission Staff Working Document on "Liability for emerging digital technologies" - Accompanying the document Commission Communication "Artificial intelligence for Europe", SWD(2018) 137 final, Brussels, 25.4.2018, at p. 23.

[60] AI can allow users of big data to automate and enhance complex descriptive and predictive analytical tasks that would be extremely labour intensive and time consuming, if performed by humans. Unleashing AI on big data can have a significant impact on the role data plays in deciding how we work, how we travel and how we conduct business. More and more aspects of our lives can become predictable, from travel time to customer satisfaction to how long it will take an abled bodied worker to complete a given task. Also, AI can provide this type of information ahead of time, allowing for improved planning, scheduling, and decision making, providing users with critical information at the right time to make the best opportunities when they present themselves. See Commission Staff Working Document on "Liability for emerging digital technologies" - Accompanying the document Commission Communication "Artificial intelligence for Europe", SWD (2018) 137 final, Brussels, 25.4.2018, at p. 23.

[61] Tying the use of artificial intelligence on big data to responsively designed user applications allows for improved user experience that benefits from receiving the required information based on interaction context, without swiping, pinching, scrolling or clicking. See Commission Staff Working Document on "Liability for emerging digital technologies" - Accompanying the document Commission Communication "Artificial intelligence for Europe", SWD(2018) 137 final, Brussels, 25.4.2018, at p. 23.

connectivity features qualify as 'products' and defects in these products are covered by the Product Liability Directive".[62]

Irrespective of whether third party components are included or not in those emerging technologies, the producers still have to ensure the safety of the final product, and in turn, producers and sellers should be liable for any damage arising from the products placed on the market or sold to customers. According to the Commission, the crucial question relates to whether effective redress mechanisms for victims and adequate level of legal certainty for producers are ensured, especially since IoT and AI-enabled products and services are increasingly connected and complex both in the design and the system integration.[63]

It was also pointed out that sensor technologies are becoming widely available and, consequently, the emerging digital technologies will acquire the feature of autonomy through sensors and/or by exchanging data with their environment (inter-connectivity). Those AI and IoT-enabled devices will have the ability to trade and analyse data as well as to adapt their behaviours and actions to their environment. It is anticipated that they will have the capacity to learn through experience and interaction (self-learning). As the Commission put it, "advanced robots or devices empowered by AI and IoT will have increased capabilities to interpret the environment (via sensing, actuating, cognitive vision, machine learning, etc.), to interact with humans, to cooperate with other artefacts, to learn new behaviours and execute actions autonomously without human intervention. The more autonomous systems are, the less they depend on other actors (i.e. the manufacturer, the owner, the user, etc.) and the greater is their impact on their environment and on third parties".[64] "The potential of AI and IoT powered systems is immense and not yet fully known or predictable at this stage. It is already clear, however, that AI applications and systems can generate autonomous decision-making and autonomous behaviour in the physical environment in which they operate including physical contact with humans and their property. This inevitably carries an inherent risk of causing damage to a third party's physical integrity or property. Damages may also be caused by AI systems that are not embedded in a hardware structure, for example economic damage caused by an autonomous trading algorithm at the stock exchange".[65]

The built-in autonomy and self-learning ability are characteristics of "advanced" robots and AI-enabled products and their degree depends on how sophisticated a system's interaction with its environment has been designed to be. The capacity of those technologies to acquire autonomy, to learn through their own variable experience and interaction and to adapt their behaviour and actions to the environment

---

[62] Commission Staff Working Document on "Liability for emerging digital technologies" - Accompanying the document Commission Communication "Artificial intelligence for Europe", SWD (2018) 137 final, Brussels, 25.4.2018, at p. 9.

[63] Ibid., at p. 10.

[64] Ibid.

[65] Ibid., at p. 11.

could raise questions regarding liability. Indeed, it was considered that the current legal framework would not be sufficient to cover the damage caused by those advanced robots and AI-systems, mainly because they could be equipped with adaptive and learning abilities entailing a certain degree of unpredictability in their behaviour. They could generate autonomous decision-making and interact with their environment in an unforeseeable manner. This unpredictability in behaviour of those autonomous applications and systems inevitably raises serious liability questions, as it could be difficult to determine who is technically and legally responsible for any ensuing damage. The legal responsibility arising through an autonomous system's harmful action becomes, therefore, a crucial issue. This is why the Commission stated that "combined with self-learning and autonomy, the behaviour of these technologies may be difficult to predict. This could raise questions regarding liability, in situations where the damage caused by a machine operating with a certain degree of autonomy cannot be linked to a defect or a human wrongdoing (e.g. of the driver; the car manufacturer, etc.), but also in the wider context of safeguards to be introduced to ensure the safety of such technologies (e.g. should machines be allowed to freely learn from their context or should they be prevented from learning inadequate/dangerous behaviours). As a consequence, the question of how to attribute liability where the expected outcome of the technology was not identified either before the market launch or after that launch needs to be examined".[66]

Moreover, the Commission pointed out that digital technology products and services generate (e.g. via sensors) and/or process data (e.g. through actuators, algorithms). Due to their reliance on quality data, any vulnerability, such as an unsecured connection, vulnerable software and faulty or corrupted data, can cause damage ranging from small-value losses to large-scale breaches of sensitive personal data and security incidents. In those cases, faulty or corrupted data could render the systems malfunctioning. Furthermore, it was stressed that providing data through an IoT system could be considered a service, and thus fall outside the product liability and safety frameworks.[67] Therefore, it is critical to answer who should be held responsible if IoT and AI-enabled systems fail due to the supply of erroneous data or by a failure to supply data. Finding the main cause and attributing liability will prove very difficult. For instance, is it the developer or producer of the systems or the software programmer? This also raises the question of who is responsible for ensuring that the data collected is being kept safe.[68]

Furthermore, it was stressed that digital technology products are open to software extensions, updates and patches after the products in question were put in circulation. Any change to the software of the system may affect the behaviour of the entire system or of individual components (and thus making it more difficult to allocate liability) or may extend its functionality. In addition, software can be updated or revised by the producer of the system or of individual system components or by third

[66] ibid., at p. 10.

[67] Ibid.

[68] Ibid.

parties, in a way that can affect the safety of these technologies. Updates usually close safety holes through patches, but new codes also add or remove features in ways that change the risk profile of these technologies. Again, the open nature of new products may pose a serious challenge for allocating liability and establishing claims, since the producer could be no longer able to control software or other technical features subsequently installed in or learned by the products in question.[69]

Failure of a software provider to comply with his contractual obligations, such as providing a certain level of safety and cybersecurity as well as updates for a certain period of time, may trigger contractual liability claims. Such claims will aim at remedies in case of non-conformity with the contract, e.g. bringing it into conformity, price reduction or termination of the contract, or at damages for breach of contract. The contractual liability of a software provider could be limited to the extent its customer contributed to the actual damage, for instance because he did not install an available update. It could also be limited according to the terms of the contract, provided that such contractual limitation is permitted by the applicable law. The extent to which extra-contractual liability claims can be raised in parallel with possible contractual liability depends on national law.[70]

3.4.4 Case Studies: Autonomous Drones, Autonomous Cars, and Smart Home Ecosystems

The Commission Working Document also featured a number of specific technology use case studies (i.e. autonomous drones, autonomous cars and smart home ecosystems) in order to offer a preliminary description of civil liability questions and examined whether (and how) existing EU rules for safety and for the allocation of liability can adequately cover and apply to the innovative IoT and AI-enabled products and services. Although it recognized that fully autonomous systems or IoT devices are not yet part of everyday life for the vast majority of people, it argued that "it is possible to anticipate likely realistic scenarios raising civil liability questions based on the current state of technological development and of known testing and pilot projects. ... the analysis that follows cannot yet rely on specific liability cases or court decisions and therefore works with some inevitable assumptions and theoretical considerations. ... The primary goal of the use cases is to prepare the ground for further reflection".[71] Those case studies covered AI powered

[69]Ibid.

[70]Ibid., at pp. 10–11. See also the case decided by the Court of Appeal in Ghent (Belgium) in December 2016. De Redactie, Geldboetes voor UZ Gent en 3 bedrijven voor foute hersenbestraling, 7 September 2015. Available at: http://deredactie.be/cm/vrtnieuws/regio/oostvlaanderen/1.243450 5.

[71]Commission Staff Working Document on "Liability for emerging digital technologies" - Accompanying the document Commission Communication "Artificial intelligence for Europe", SWD (2018) 137 final, Brussels, 25.4.2018, at p. 11.

devices and systems (autonomous drones and autonomous cars) and IoT (smart home ecosystem and cyber-attacks).

3.4.4.1 AI Powered Devices and Systems: Autonomous Unmanned Aircraft (Autonomous Drones)

Unmanned aircrafts (drones) represent a rapidly developing sector of aviation.[72] While the level of automation may vary depending on the specific application, fully autonomous drones already exist for instance for the delivery of packages. Drones can be used for various purposes such as package delivery, surveillance and monitoring, data collection, inspection, search and rescue. They comprise tangible parts/devices (sensors, actuators, hardware) and different software components and applications, which enable the drone's operation.

The Commission Staff Working Document discussed possible liability claims scenarios in the context of a parcel delivery drone that attempted to fly autonomously (from take-off to selection of the route, avoidance of obstacles, landing) from the seller's warehouse to the customer's dwelling. In case of an accident (for instance, it unexpectedly fell to the ground or collided in-air with another flying vessel) and damage caused by an automated drone (e.g. it dropped the package resulting in property damage or personal injury), it could be argued that autonomous drones are "aircrafts"[73] and, therefore, the key components of the liability regime for autonomous drones—without prejudice to any possible national legislation addressing specific liability—are the national liability laws and international conventions applicable to aircrafts.[74]

In that case, aircrafts are subject to a strict liability regime and the party liable for damage is considered to be the operator: "In the majority of EU Member States, but

[72] Ibid. The Commission predicted that, by 2035, the European drone sector will directly employ more than 100,000 people and have an economic impact exceeding €10 billion per year, mainly in services.

[73] "Aircraft" is defined as "any machine that can derive support in the atmosphere from the reactions of the air other than the reactions of the air against the earth's surface". "Autonomous aircraft" is defined as "an unmanned aircraft that does not allow pilot intervention in the management of the flight". "Drone" is defined as "a remote-controlled pilotless aircraft". "Remotely Piloted Aircraft" is defined as "an aircraft where the flying pilot is not on board the aircraft". "Remotely Piloted Aircraft System (RPAS)" is defined as a set of configurable elements consisting of a remotely-piloted aircraft, its associated remote pilot station(s), the required command and control links and any other system elements as may be required, at any point during flight operation. Other features may include, inter alia, software, health monitoring, ATC communications equipment, a flight termination system, and launch and recovery elements". Steer Davies Gleeve, Study on the Third-Party Liability and Insurance Requirements of Remotely Piloted Aircraft Systems, Final Report, November 2014, at p. i (Glossary).

[74] Commission Staff Working Document on "Liability for emerging digital technologies" - Accompanying the document Commission Communication "Artificial intelligence for Europe", SWD (2018) 137 final, Brussels, 25.4.2018, at p. 12.

not all, national law defines that the liability regime for RPAS is strict (meaning that the defined party is automatically liable for damage, without there being any need to attribute fault)". ... "We have also established that in Member States with a strict liability regime, the party liable for damage is generally the operator. As RPAS are aircraft, operators are required by Regulation 785/2004 to have insurance for third-party liability, which as a minimum must be at the levels defined in the Regulation. Failing this, their assets would be liquidated to compensate the victims".[75] According to the Commission, in the case of autonomous drones, the operator would be the person or entity that, although not remotely or manually steering it, has control on the overall use of the drone. Therefore, if the national law stipulating the liability for aircraft accidents also covers drones, the victim would have a strict liability claim against the operator without the need to attribute fault; the claimant needs only to prove the damage and the causal link: "autonomous features of the drones should not have an impact on the likelihood of success of the victim's claim against the drone operator under strict liability air traffic legislation. The victim should only prove that the damage was caused by the drone without having to substantiate what made the drone fall down or drop the package".[76]

The victim may also sue the operator under general national tort law provisions which would require a fault of the operator. The fault of the operator leading to a damage is a necessary element to be proven for the liability claim to be successful. The victim submitting such a claim needs to provide the evidence required to support his liability claim—for instance, such a fault could be proven if the drone was operated under hazardous weather conditions or if the operator did not perform the required maintenance.[77] If the drone relies on third party service providers, then the operator could also be held responsible if the accident—and the subsequent damage—was caused by malfunctioning of the services provided by third parties, such as the provider of GPS mapping and the provider of weather data.

Alternatively, the victim could also have a claim against the manufacturer under the national law rules implementing the Product Liability Directive. In this case, however, the claimant would need to demonstrate a defect of the drone and the casual link, namely that the damage was caused by that defect. Due to the characteristics of drones, such as increasing level of complexity and variety of ecosystems, actors and value chains (high interdependency), and since IoT and AI-enabled products are increasingly connected and complex both in the design and the system

---

[75] Steer Davies Gleeve, Study on the Third-Party Liability and Insurance Requirements of Remotely Piloted Aircraft Systems, Final Report, November 2014, at p. 1 (paras 7 and 8).

[76] Commission Staff Working Document on "Liability for emerging digital technologies" - Accompanying the document Commission Communication "Artificial intelligence for Europe", SWD (2018) 137 final, Brussels, 25.4.2018, at p. 12. However, this might not be the case in jurisdictions where a fault-based liability regime applies. In those jurisdictions, the fault of the author of the wrongful behaviour leading to a damage is a necessary element to be proven for the liability claim to be successful. The victim submitting a claim needs to provide the evidence required to support his liability claim.

[77] ibid.

integration, it is recognized that the accident of a drone may be a result of a large set of unknown circumstances (for instance a defect of the device, exceptional weather conditions or other circumstances such as a cyber-attacker). It will be difficult, therefore, for the victim to prove the substantial elements of a liability claim.[78]

It seems that the Working Document prefers the option of a strict liability claim against the operator, since most national regimes stipulating the liability for aircraft accidents are considered as covering drones, and "this appears to be an efficient way for the victim to achieve compensation".[79] Indeed, in that case the victim should only prove that the damage was caused by the drone without the need to attribute fault.

The importance of having an efficient redress mechanism for victims in case of damages should be pointed out. If the operator has compensated the victim and it is demonstrated that the accident was caused by a defect of the drone or a breach of the obligations of a service provider (for instance, the provider of GPS mapping or the provider of weather data) the operator could seek redress against the manufacturer or the service provider. If the operation of the parcel delivery drone is subject to mandatory insurance coverage, any such redress claim could under statutory law be transferred to the insurance.[80]

3.4.4.2 AI Powered Devices and Systems: Autonomous Cars

Autonomous cars represent a rapidly developing sector and are, at present, one of the most important AI applications. Core systems include Electronic Stability Control (ESC), Intelligent Speed Adaptation (ISA), Collision Avoidance System (CAS), lateral control/support, blind spot detection, side collision avoidance, driver monitoring, Adaptive Cruise Control (ACC), route guidance and navigation, vision

---

[78] Ibid.

[79] Ibid., at pp. 12–13.

[80] Ibid., at p. 13.

The Commission's Working Document referred to an accident involving an autonomous drone which crashed into a crane in the UK in June 2017. The data programmed into the drone did not include information about the crane which was erected after the programming. In particular, the unmanned aircraft (UA) was surveying a foreshore close to a construction site using a flight plan of pre-programmed waypoints. During the flight, the UA was affected by a change in the wind that resulted in it flying larger than normal turns. This caused the UA to overshoot its downwind waypoints and fly over the construction site. During one such overshoot the UA began to descend, as programmed, and collided with a crane on the construction site about 250 m inland. The pilot commented that the main cause of the accident was poor flight planning. The overshoot and collision could have been prevented by aligning the flight legs east/west instead of north/south and maintaining 400 ft near the construction site. The pilot did not do this because optimum imaging uses crosswind legs, in this case north/south. Also the position of the tower cranes, outside the planned flight area, were not fully considered during the planning stage due to their more remote location. Additionally, the pilot did not intervene and initiate a climb before the collision because the distance and height of the cranes were difficult to perceive. See also at: https://assets.publishing.service.gov.uk/media/5a0ac567ed915d0ade60db62/Quest_Q-200_UAS_None_12-17.pdf.

enhancement, Anti Blocking System (ABS), alcohol interlocks, seat belt reminder and post-crash systems (black box and eCall).[81]

The level of automation may vary depending on the specific application. Although many new cars feature technology that partially assists with driving, we still do not have fully self-driving cars available for purchase. Autonomous cars are motor vehicles equipped with AI systems that allow operating the vehicle without human intervention either partially, or completely (full automation). With increasing levels of vehicle autonomy being a priority for car manufacturers, accurate, robust and affordable sensor technologies are becoming widely available. These are necessary to fully detect the environment around the vehicle, contributing to safety and to the reduction of congestion and the ensuing pollution. Indeed, the benefits of autonomous cars range from a remarkable decrease in the number of road accidents[82] to reduced travelling time, improved traffic flow and environmental benefits.[83]

---

[81] Advanced emergency braking systems, intelligent speed assistance, emergency lane-keeping systems, driver drowsiness and attention warning, advanced driver distraction warning and reversing detection are safety systems that have a high potential to reduce casualty numbers considerably. In addition, some of those safety systems form the basis of technologies which will also be used for the deployment of automated vehicles. Any such safety systems should function without the use of any kind of biometric information of drivers or passengers, including facial recognition. Therefore, harmonised rules and test procedures for the type-approval of vehicles as regards those systems and for the type-approval of those systems as separate technical units should be established at Union level. The technological progress of those systems should be taken into account in every evaluation of the existing legislation, in order to be future-proof, whilst strictly adhering to the principles of privacy and data protection, and to reduce or eliminate accidents and injuries in road transport. It is also necessary to ensure that those systems can be used safely throughout the life cycle of the vehicle. See Regulation (EU) 2019/2144 of the European Parliament and of the Council of 27 November 2019 on type-approval requirements for motor vehicles and their trailers, and systems, components and separate technical units intended for such vehicles, as regards their general safety and the protection of vehicle occupants and vulnerable road users, at Recital 10.

[82] According to the World Health Organization, every year approximately 1.35 million people die as a result of car accidents. It is considered that 90% of accidents each year are caused by human error. Also, between 20 and 50 million more people suffer non-fatal injuries, with many incurring a disability as a result of their injury. Road traffic injuries cause considerable economic losses to individuals, their families, and to nations as a whole. These losses arise from the cost of treatment as well as lost productivity for those killed or disabled by their injuries, and for family members who need to take time off work or school to care for the injured. Road traffic crashes cost most countries 3% of their gross domestic product. See World Health Organization (WHO) at: https://www.who.int/news-room/fact-sheets/detail/road-traffic-injuries.

See also Regulation (EU) 2019/2144 of the European Parliament and of the Council of 27 November 2019 on type-approval requirements for motor vehicles and their trailers, and systems, components and separate technical units intended for such vehicles, as regards their general safety and the protection of vehicle occupants and vulnerable road users, at Recital 23: "Automated vehicles have the potential to make a huge contribution to reducing road fatalities, given that more than 90% of road accidents are estimated to result from some level of human error".

[83] Commission Staff Working Document on "Liability for emerging digital technologies" - Accompanying the document Commission Communication "Artificial intelligence for Europe", SWD (2018) 137 final, Brussels, 25.4.2018, at p. 13.

In the case of partial, conditional automation, the vehicle operates under the supervision of the driver, but without human input under specific conditions only (for example, on certain road types or in specific geographic areas). Outside these limited environments, the car requires the control by a human driver or, if the driver does not take control, it may enter into a safe fall-back mode (for instance, park the vehicle). In these cases, the driver has the responsibility to supervise the vehicle and be prepared to regain control if needed or upon notice. In case of higher levels of automation, the car can operate without any human intervention and with full automation also on any road and in any conditions. There might not even be a human person inside the car and the vehicle might not even be equipped with a steering wheel or pedals.[84]

The Commission's Working Document pointed out that, currently, only few Member States have adopted rules specifically targeting highly automated or fully automated vehicles. As a result, the key components of the liability regime for automated vehicles are the national civil liability rules applicable to motor vehicles. However, under the Motor Insurance Directive,[85] all Member States are obliged to ensure that civil liability for the use of vehicles is covered by insurance and that victims of an accident caused by a vehicle enjoy a direct claim against the insurer covering the person responsible against civil liability. Although the Motor Insurance Directive does not harmonise issues of civil liability, it provides an effective safety net for victims irrespective of the allocation of liability according to the different national civil liability regimes.[86]

[84] To help define how sophisticated the automated technology actually is, the Society of Automotive Engineers (SAE) classified these systems using five levels. Level 1 is driver assistance, where the vehicle is able to control steering or braking, but not both simultaneously. Level 2 is partial automation, where the car can assist with both steering and braking simultaneously, but your attention is required on the road at all times. Both Tesla's Autopilot and General Motors' Super Cruise are examples of this. Level 3 is conditional automation, where certain circumstances allow the car to handle most aspects of driving and the driver has the ability to temporarily take their eyes off the road. Level 4 is high automation, where, in the right conditions, the car can take full control, giving the driver a chance to focus on other tasks. And Level 5 is full automation. In this hypothetical situation, the car drives you, and there is not even a steering wheel. See: SAE International's On-Road Automated Vehicle Standards Committee published the SAE Information Report: (J3016) "Taxonomy and Definitions for Terms Related to On-Road Motor Vehicle Automated Driving Systems", issued on 16.01.2014 (revised: 30.04.2021). The SAE table, summarizing the different levels of driving automation, defines "conditional automation" (level 3) the situation in which the automated driving system performs all aspects of the dynamic driving task with the expectation that the human driver responds adequately to a request to intervene ("fallback performance").

[85] Directive 2009/103/EC of the European Parliament and of the Council of 16 September 2009 relating to insurance against civil liability in respect of the use of motor vehicles, and the enforcement of the obligation to insure against such liability ("the Motor Insurance Directive"). This is a minimum harmonisation Directive, so Member States may apply higher levels of protection such as obligatory amounts of insurance cover.

[86] Commission Staff Working Document on "Liability for emerging digital technologies" - Accompanying the document Commission Communication "Artificial intelligence for Europe", SWD (2018) 137 final, Brussels, 25.4.2018, at pp. 13–14.

According to the Commission's Working Document, in case of an accident caused by a fully automated vehicle, liability for a damage may be allocated to the driver/holder of the vehicle under civil law liability rules. In practice, all Member States attribute liability for damages caused by motor vehicles to the holder or the driver of the vehicle. Liability is either fault-based, including cases where the fault can be presumed unless the holder/driver proves the opposite, or risk-based, where the holder/driver is strictly liable for having opened the risk associated with the circulation of a motor vehicle on public streets. Under the fault-based liability scenario, the victim may sue the holder/driver of the vehicle, which would require a fault of the holder/driver. Such a fault could be envisaged for example when the vehicle was driven under dangerous weather conditions or when the required maintenance was not performed. Depending on the provisions of national law that is applicable and to the extent the operation of the vehicle relies on third party service providers (for instance, the provider of GPS mapping) the holder could under certain conditions also be responsible if the accident was caused by malfunctioning of the services provided by the third party. It should be stressed, however, that in most national regimes a strict liability claim against the holder/driver of the vehicle exists, i.e. the liability of the holder of the car is typically risk-based: the victim would have a strict liability claim against the holder/driver without the need to attribute fault; the claimant needs only to prove the damage and the causal link. Strict liability requires only proof that damage has occurred and the establishment of a causal link between the harmful functioning of the vehicle and the damage suffered by the injured party: "If the victim claims damages against the holder of a motor vehicle based on strict liability rules, normally there is no need to demonstrate whether the accident was caused by a wrongdoing of the car driver or another person or by any deficiency of the car".[87]

Alternatively, in case of an accident caused by a fully automated vehicle, liability for a damage may be allocated to the manufacturer of the automated vehicle under the rules implementing the Product Liability Directive. In that case, the victim could have a claim against the manufacturer of the car; however, the claimant would need to demonstrate a defect of the vehicle and the casual link, namely that the damage was caused by that defect.[88] Nevertheless, due to the increasing level of complexity and variety of ecosystems, actors and value chains (high interdependency), and since IoT and AI-enabled products are becoming increasingly connected and complex, it was pointed out that an accident caused by a fully automated vehicle may be the result of a large set of unknown circumstances (for instance the defect or malfunctioning of the devices or services provided by third parties or other circumstances such as a cyber-attack). It will be difficult, therefore, for the victim to prove the substantial elements of a liability claim.[89]

---

[87] Ibid., at p. 14.

[88] Ibid.

[89] Ibid.

The Commission's Working Document stressed the importance of having an efficient redress mechanism for victims in case of damages. In particular, all Member States are obliged, under the Motor Insurance Directive, to ensure that civil liability for the use of vehicles is covered by insurance and that victims of an accident caused by a vehicle enjoy a direct claim against the insurer covering the person responsible against civil liability. In those cases, victims of accidents with insured vehicles will approach insurers directly to receive compensation and the damages will usually be paid by the insurer. Also, liability for a damage may be allocated to the manufacturer/producer of the automated vehicle under the rules implementing the Product Liability Directive if the accident occurred due to a defect of the fully automated vehicle. In this case, as already mentioned, the claimant would need to demonstrate a defect of the vehicle and the casual link, namely that the damage was caused by that defect. In this context, national law could provide for redress possibilities of the insurer who compensated the victim against the producer of the defective vehicle.[90]

Finally, the Working Document referred to several accidents (some of them fatal) that occurred when the drivers were operating the vehicle (Tesla, Google, Uber) in autopilot mode. For instance, on May 7, 2016, a semi-automated Tesla Model S struck and passed beneath a truck. At the time of the collision, the truck was making a left turn and impact with the right side of the semitrailer sheared off the roof of the Tesla. The driver of the Tesla died in the crash. System performance data downloaded from the Tesla revealed that the driver was operating the car using automated vehicle control systems: Traffic-Aware Cruise Control and Autosteer lane keeping systems.[91] The use of Tesla's Autopilot software has been implicated in several crashes. For instance, a Tesla vehicle involved in a fatal crash in California in 2018 was in Autopilot mode, raising further questions about the safety of self-

[90] Ibid.

[91] The investigations revealed that, although the autopilot functioned as designed, it did not detect the truck. The truck was cutting across the car's path instead of driving directly in front of it, which the radar is better at detecting, and the camera-based system was not trained to recognize the flat slab of a truck's side as a threat. The Tesla driver's lack of responsiveness indicated overreliance on automation and the monitoring steering wheel torque was not an effective method of ensuring driver engagement. The competent authority concluded that the crash was not the result of any specific defect in the autopilot system, thus Tesla was not found responsible for the accident. The competent authority noted that Tesla did an adequate job warning its customers that the autopilot system demands their supervision that their hands should remain on the wheel and their eyes on the road. The Terms of Services of the Tesla car included in cause provisions which were clarifying the semi-autonomous nature of the autopilot and were requiring the driver to take over the control of the car in 4 seconds, if the driver noticed things were not going in the right direction. Since that accident, Tesla introduced new safety measures. For instance, it has changed the Autopilot system so that, if a driver repeatedly ignores the Autopilot warnings, the system will stop functioning and will be prevented from restarting for the duration of the trip. If the driver never responds, the car will gradually slow down until it stops and the flashing hazard lights will come on. See Commission Staff Working Document on "Liability for emerging digital technologies" - Accompanying the document Commission Communication "Artificial intelligence for Europe", SWD(2018) 137 final, Brussels, 25.4.2018, at pp. 14–15.

driving technology.[92] On February 14, 2016, a Google self-driving car attempted to pass a municipal bus in Mountain View, California. The bus did not behave as the autonomous car predicted, and the self-driving car crashed into it, while attempting to move back into its lane. The Google car was traveling at the stately speed of 2 mph, and there were no injuries. Google released a statement accepting fault and announcing that it was tweaking its software to avoid this type of collision in the future. This crash was the first in which Google has acknowledged its car made a mistake that led to a collision.[93] With regard to the issues of civil liability and

---

[92] In particular, one of the company's Model X cars crashed into a roadside barrier and caught fire on 23 March 2018. Autopilot was engaged at the time of the accident involving the driver, who died soon afterwards. According to the National Transportation Safety Board (NTSB): i) The Tesla driver had not taken control of the car because he had been distracted by a smartphone video game; ii) The Tesla's collision avoidance system was "not designed to detect the crash [barrier]"; iii) Tesla's Autopilot system did not "provide an effective means of monitoring the driver's engagement". The system lets the car operate semi-autonomously, changing lanes and adjusting its speed. But critics argue that the "Autopilot" branding makes some drivers think the car is driving fully autonomously. The National Transportation Safety Board (NTSB) stated that the driver had been "over-reliant" on the software. It is true that Tesla does instruct drivers to keep their hands on the wheel when using Autopilot, and an audible warning sounds if they fail to do so. But the NTSB underlined that "monitoring of driver-applied steering wheel torque is an ineffective surrogate measure of driver engagement... If Tesla does not incorporate system safeguards that limit the use of the Autopilot system to those conditions for which it was designed, continued use of the system beyond its operational design domain is foreseeable and the risk for future crashes will remain".

The NTSB ended its report with several recommendations including: i) improving collision avoidance systems to include common obstacles such as traffic barriers; ii) evaluating Tesla's Autopilot to determine whether the ability to operate it "outside the intended operational design" posed an unreasonable risk to safety; iii) preventing automation complacency in drivers; iv) requiring all new passenger vehicles with semi-autonomous features to be equipped with a driver monitoring system that meets new standards. It also suggested smartphone manufacturers should develop a "distracted driving lockout mechanism" to "disable any driver-distracting functions when a vehicle is in motion but that allows the device to be used in an emergency". Furthermore, it urged Apple to "implement a company policy that bans the non-emergency use of portable electronic devices while driving by all employees and contractors". See: https://www.bbc.com/news/technology-51645566.

The US National Transportation Safety Board (NTSB) published the results of its investigation, following the crash in March 2018. See: https://www.ntsb.gov/news/events/Documents/2020-HWY18FH011-BMG-abstract.pdf.

[93] Commission Staff Working Document on "Liability for emerging digital technologies" - Accompanying the document Commission Communication "Artificial intelligence for Europe", SWD (2018) 137 final, Brussels, 25.4.2018, at p. 15.

Google wrote that its car was trying to get around some sandbags on a street when its left front struck the right side of the bus. The car's test driver, who under state law must be in the front seat to grab the wheel when needed, thought the bus would yield and did not have control when the collision happened, according to Google's report. In a detailed statement from its monthly report on its self-driving car project, Google said that the incident happened on El Camino Real, a busy six-lane boulevard with hundreds on intersections. The car was following a recent change to its programming, following "the spirit of the road" as well as the traffic code by hugging the far side of the right-turn lane to allow other cars to pass on the left. "It then detected sandbags near a storm drain blocking its path, so it needed to come to a stop. After waiting for some other vehicles to pass, our vehicle, still in autonomous mode, began angling back toward the center of the lane at around

insurance, it was mentioned that this particular case is an example of the increasing level of complexity that will soon be common: "here, the software didn't avoid the accident, but the human could have taken over. ... Who's at fault – the driver, the bus driver, or the software? ... in real world situations, both the driver and injured party will actually be incentivized to blame the software which, if found to be guilty, will leave the driver's record clear and likely have a higher payout for the injured party. ... Everybody's going to be blaming the software all the time". It was also stressed that autonomous car insurance would be cheaper than human-driven car insurance because humans are not (in comparison with machines) very good drivers. "At a very visceral level, people will accept a higher chance of being maimed or killed by a human being than they will by being maimed or killed by software. ... The self-driving car will likely be able to make better risk calculations".[94]

On 19 March 2018 a woman in the street in Arizona died when hit by an autonomous Uber car, in what appeared to be the first reported fatal crash involving a self-driving vehicle and a pedestrian in the US. Local police reported the self-driving car was in autonomous mode at the time of the crash and that the vehicle hit a woman, who was walking outside of the crosswalk and later died at a hospital. There was a vehicle operator inside the car at the time of the crash.[95]

2mph – and made contact with the side of a passing bus traveling at 15mph. Our car had detected the approaching bus, but predicted that it would yield to us because we were ahead of it," Google stated. "Our test driver, who had been watching the bus in the mirror, also expected the bus to slow or stop. And we can imagine the bus driver assumed we were going to stay put. Unfortunately, all these assumptions led us to the same spot in the lane at the same time. This type of misunderstanding happens between human drivers on the road every day." Google pointed out that it has refined its software following the incident, acknowledging that buses and other large vehicles are less likely to yield. "In this case we clearly bear some responsibility because if our car hadn't moved there wouldn't have been a collision. ... We hope to handle situations like this more gracefully in the future." See *The Guardian*, "Google self-driving car collides with bus in California, accident report says", by Nellie Bowles, 1 March 2016, https://www.theguardian.com/technology/2016/feb/29/google-self-driving-car-accident-california.

[94] Hilary Rowen, partner at Sedgwick LLP. See *The Guardian*, "Google self-driving car collides with bus in California, accident report says", by Nellie Bowles, 1 March 2016, https://www.theguardian.com/technology/2016/feb/29/google-self-driving-car-accident-california.

[95] Commission Staff Working Document on "Liability for emerging digital technologies" - Accompanying the document Commission Communication "Artificial intelligence for Europe", SWD (2018) 137 final, Brussels, 25.4.2018, at p. 15.

According to the report of the National Transportation Safety Board (NTSB) "although the [Automatic Driving System] sensed the pedestrian nearly six seconds before the impact, the system never classified her as a pedestrian — or predicted correctly her goal as a jaywalking pedestrian or a cyclist — because she was crossing ... at a location without a crosswalk". "The system design did not include a consideration for jaywalking pedestrians". The vehicle's software also kept changing its classification of the victim as a vehicle, a bicycle, and an unknown object, preventing the car from braking or steering away, the report confirmed. "As the ADS changed the classification of the pedestrian several times ... the system was unable to correctly predict the path of the detected object," the report pointed out.

Among the investigation's findings were the following: i) the Uber ATG automated driving system detected the pedestrian 5.6 seconds before impact. Although the system continued to track

3.4.4.3 AI Powered Devices and Systems: Internet of Things

3.4.4.3.1 Smart Home Ecosystem

Smart home ecosystems are based on various disciplines and technologies like sensors, embedded systems, and various communications technologies. They include appliances, such as smart smoke detectors, smart thermostats, smart fridges, which are connected to the internet and to each other and have the ability to collect information and communicate with each other and with other systems and humans. These ecosystems are, therefore, based on bringing together multiple sectors and a variety of stakeholders to cover an increasingly complex value chain. Their operation relies on various sources of data, such as embedded sensors that automatically measure e.g. environmental parameters or monitor activity and transfer data to databases in an autonomous way, without human intervention. The data are accessed, processed and analysed by applications, which transfer commands to the physical devices in the smart home ecosystem. It is expected that those smart home

---

the pedestrian until the crash, it never accurately identified the object crossing the road as a pedestrian—or predicted its path; ii) had the vehicle operator been attentive, the operator would likely have had enough time to detect and react to the crossing pedestrian to avoid the crash or mitigate the impact; iii) while Uber ATG managers had the ability to retroactively monitor the behavior of vehicle operators, they rarely did so. The company's ineffective oversight was exacerbated by its decision to remove a second operator from the vehicle during testing of the automated driving system; iv) Uber ATG made several changes to address the deficiencies identified, including implementation of a safety management system. See the National Transportation Safety Board (NTSB) News Release (11.19.2019), https://www.ntsb.gov/news/press-releases/Pages/NR20191119c.aspx.

The National Transportation Safety Board determined that the probable cause of the crash in Tempe, Arizona, was the failure of the vehicle operator to monitor the driving environment and the operation of the automated driving system because she was visually distracted throughout the trip by her personal cell phone. Contributing to the crash were the Uber Advanced Technologies Group's (1) inadequate safety risk assessment procedures, (2) ineffective oversight of vehicle operators, and (3) lack of adequate mechanisms for addressing operators' automation complacency—all a consequence of its inadequate safety culture. Further factors contributing to the crash were (1) the impaired pedestrian's crossing of N. Mill Avenue outside a crosswalk, and (2) the Arizona Department of Transportation's insufficient oversight of automated vehicle testing. See https://www.ntsb.gov/news/events/Documents/2019-HWY18MH010-BMG-abstract.pdf.

Uber has since put two drivers in its piloted vehicles, increased training on defensive and distracted driving, improved tracking and detection of pedestrians and cyclists, and enabled automatic emergency stops.

According to Matt Henshon, a Boston lawyer who has written on artificial intelligence and self-driving cars, while a civil suit would be fairly straightforward, the question of potential criminal liability is much more complicated. Could the human driver have intervened? Were developers negligent in their design and rollout of the software? Was a nonworking sensor missed by inspectors? The analogy is autopilot, in the airline case, where you put it on autopilot but the pilot still remains legally responsible. Who had ultimate responsibility, the human driver or the car itself? See The Washington Post, "Self-driving Uber vehicle strikes and kills pedestrian", by Faiz Siddiqui and Michael Laris, 19.04.2018, https://www.washingtonpost.com/news/dr-gridlock/wp/2018/03/19/uber-halts-autonomous-vehicle-testing-after-a-pedestrian-is-struck/.

ecosystems will gain higher levels of autonomy in their behaviour, especially due to increasing computing power and sophistication.

The various components in this ecosystem (devices, sensors, applications, etc.) are being provided by different suppliers in order to cover an increasingly complex value chain.[96] In addition, the data provided by connected sensors, applications and devices allow the smart home ecosystem to take decisions based on the data and perform specific functions derived from sensing, analysis and intelligence gathered. This increases the complexity of the IoT ecosystem and requires specific considerations of, among others attribution of liability. It is stated, for instance, that for most technological ecosystems (i.e. systems with interacting devices or programs), no specific liability regimes exist. Therefore, product liability, general tort law rules (fault-based liability, tort of negligence, breach of statutory duty), and contractual liability, occupy centre stage. It is acknowledged that the more complex and sophisticated an ecosystem becomes due to the emerging digital technologies, the more increasingly challenging it may be for the home owner to trace back any upcoming problem to its origin.[97]

According to the Commission's Working Document, in case of a fire, not sending an alert to the fire department may result in the destruction of the house and/or damage of a neighbour's house. This may be the result of a malfunctioning of the smoke detector, a faulty data processing by the application, a failure of the electronic communication services or an autonomous decision to switch off the smoke detector, e.g. because of high energy consumption levels of the smoke detector.[98]

Thus the home owner could raise a contractual claim for damages against the seller of the thermostat or the seller of the smoke detector, provided that the thermostat or the smoke detector in question were not in conformity with the sales contract. Moreover, if the decision to switch off the smoke detector was taken by the application autonomously, a contractual liability of the seller of the smoke detector could be established on the basis that the device had to be designed in a way not to allow a third-party application to switch it off. Therefore, the application provider would, in general, be contractually liable for the application's erroneous decision.[99]

---

[96] As the Commission's Working Document put it: "For example, a smart smoke detector can be produced by manufacturer A and sold to the homeowner by seller B, a smart thermostat can be produced by manufacturer C and sold to the homeowner by seller D, the data analysis application could be provided by provider E or by one of the manufacturers of the smart appliances and the connectivity dimension is provided by internet provider F. The smart smoke detector can detect a source of fire and alert the homeowner or the fire department. In addition, the smoke detector can also communicate with other smart home appliances in the ecosystem, such as smart doors, instructing them to unlock in order to allow access to the fire fighters". See Commission Staff Working Document on "Liability for emerging digital technologies" - Accompanying the document Commission Communication "Artificial intelligence for Europe", SWD(2018) 137 final, Brussels, 25.4.2018, at p. 15.

[97] Ibid., at p. 15.

[98] Ibid., at pp. 15–16.

[99] Ibid., at p. 16.

Furthermore, the home owner or the neighbour, who suffered damages from the fire, could have a claim against the manufacturer of the smoke detector or the thermostat under the rules implementing the Product Liability Directive. The claimant would need to demonstrate a defect of the device—which part of the smart home ecosystem was not working properly—and the required causal link, namely that the damage was caused by that defect. Again, since IoT products are becoming increasingly connected and complex (high interdependency), it could become difficult for the home owner to identify the defect and prove the substantial elements of a liability claim against the manufacturer.[100]

In addition, the neighbour could raise a claim for damages against the home owner under national tort law, provided that a wrongdoing of the home owner can be demonstrated. Finally, it is pointed out that, if the home owner's insurance covered the damage caused by the fire, then any claim for damages which the home owner might have against the person responsible for the fire will be transferred to the insurance. It was stressed that, due to the increasing level of complexity of smart home ecosystems, it will not be easy for the insurance to prove the substantial elements of a liability claim and identify the cause for the fire and the responsible actor.[101]

3.4.4.3.2 Cyber-Attacks

Due to the complexity of smart home ecosystems, the Commission's Working Document underlined the fact that Internet of Things (IoT) devices may constitute targets of cyber-attacks. In particular, it was pointed out that vulnerability to cyberattacks is a de facto concern and a growing threat. For example, it was described that many smart home devices and processes nowadays are conveniently managed through mobile applications. While such remote controls could increase efficiency and make life easier, they also create potential targets for cyber-attacks and are affected by an increasing number of security incidents. Indeed, in the case of smart home devices, poor security measures at design, manufacturing or operation stage may allow cyber-attackers to take control of the device and modify its functioning or the functioning of other smart devices in the same ecosystem. Due to increased reliance on networks, any vulnerability, such as an unsecured connection or product, can be exploited and cause damage. Therefore, apart from the importance of preventing outsiders from hacking and infiltrating these devices and systems for nefarious purposes—in order to increase trust in digital technologies and provide confidence to consumers—, poor security measures require specific considerations of attribution of liability.[102]

[100] Ibid.

[101] Ibid.

[102] Ibid.

In particular, in the absence of a contractual relationship to cater for cyber-attack damages, courts could impose tort liabilities on businesses (e.g. manufacturers, vendors, etc.) for the harm that a cyber-attack causes to third parties. On the other hand, if we decide to apply product liability rules to cyber-attack examples, allocating liability may become unclear and claims potentially difficult to enforce. For instance, according to the Commission, "the notions of defect, the level of safety that users are generally "entitled to expect" and the impact of software updates and functionality revisions on the safety of the product are difficult to define. Is a product defective simply because it has no update capabilities? Should the notion of defect include also a security objective, on top of the safety one?".[103] It is reminded that the Product Liability Directive exempts the producer from liabilities if he can prove that the defect did not exist when the product was put into circulation or that the state of technical knowledge at the time of putting the product on the market made it impossible to discover the defect. This exemption could be triggered by the manufacturer in a cyber-attack context in order to demonstrate that, at the time of putting the product into circulation, no software vulnerability was discovered.[104]

[103] Ibid.

[104] Ibid., at p. 17. The Working Document cited as an example the WannaCry ransomware which spread throughout the Internet and affected Windows-based computer systems that were running on outdated software. In addition, the Mirai virus botnet leading to Distributed-Denial-of-Service attacks (on 21 October) remained under sustained assault for most of the day, bringing down sites including Twitter, the Guardian, Netflix, Reddit, CNN and many others in Europe and the US. These attacks caused disruptions in various places, including hospitals, businesses, and universities resulting in multiple types of damages from destruction (or loss) of data, system downtime, lost productivity, disruption to the normal course of business, forensic investigation, restoration and deletion of hostage data and systems, reputational harm, etc. A stream of (potential) extra-contractual and contractual liability could flow from the attack with various parties to blame for it: the programmers of the malware and the attackers' group; potentially the users who failed to install the Windows security patch as the vulnerability was discovered and the patch announced, and the software vendor, which supplied the insecure code in the first place. It is unclear how liability would be allocated (if at all) between such parties in the absence of a specific regime (e.g. the duty to ensure the protection of personal data; the duty to ensure a specific level of safety or (cyber) security resilience.) Most evidently, the attacker would be liable, but most of such cyberattacks are anonymous and it is difficult if not impossible for the victim to identify the attacker(s) and obtain any compensation from them. Particular users (including businesses) that failed to install the Windows security patch could also potentially face legal actions (not limited to civil actions) for the negligent failure to deliver services following the attack. In addition, contractual liability may not apply since standard terms of service frequently do not contain any promise of (cyber) security resilience. On the contrary, vendors, and especially software vendors, typically attempt to minimize or even exclude their civil liability by inserting warranty disclaimers and limitations of liability in their terms of service. That said, it is questionable whether such limitations of liability would be upheld in case of litigation in the event of a cyber-attack, since liability limitations may be deemed null and void in the case of gross negligence.

For further information, see:

CSO online, What is WannaCry ransomware, how does it infect, and who was responsible?, 27 September. Available at: http://www.csoonline.com/article/3227906/ransomware/what-is-wannacryransomware-how-does-it-infect-and-who-was-responsible.html.

3.4.5 *Challenges Posed by Emerging Digital Technologies and Questions for Further Analysis*

As already mentioned, the Commission carried out an evaluation of the Product Liability Directive to assess its performance. The Commission's evaluation of the Product Liability Directive was based on an external study whose findings were presented in the Commission's relevant Staff Working Document and Evaluation Report.[105] Focusing on the recent technological developments, the evaluation examined whether the Product Liability Directive remains fit-for-purpose vis-à-vis emerging digital technologies such as the Internet of Things and autonomous systems. The Commission also examined whether technological progress and, in particular the development of connected objects, has affected the effectiveness of the Directive.

The Evaluation Report stated that the Product Liability Directive continues to strike a good balance between consumer protection, harmonising and delivering a stable legal framework as well as encouraging innovation and fair competition in the EU. It was also stressed that the Directive continues to be an adequate tool, even though products are much more complex today than in 1985: "Since its adoption, it has accompanied many technological evolutions remaining a relevant and useful liability framework ensuring legal certainty for all parties involved. In particular, products today already include features relevant to emerging digital technologies, such as embedded software as a component of the product or connectivity elements, and have so far been adequately covered by the Product Liability Directive ... the Directive continues - to some extent - to be adequate for the current state of technological developments".[106]

However, it was underlined that some of the Product Liability Directive's concepts require guidance and clarification as they could hinder its effectiveness. The evaluation process included a preliminary assessment of the continued relevance of concepts, such as product, producer, defect, damage and the burden of proof, in light of the emerging digital technologies. It concluded that a better common understanding of what is meant by the terms 'product', 'damage' and 'defect' as well as clarifications on the burden of proof and the concept of 'producer' would render the Directive's application more effective.

The Guardian, DDoS attack that disrupted internet was largest of its kind in history, experts say, 26 October 2016. Available at: http://www.theguardian.com/technology/2016/oct/26/ddos-attack-dyn-miraibotnet.

Studer, Evelyne and de Werra, Jacques, Regulating Cybersecurity - What Civil Liability in Case of Cyber-Attacks?, 19 August 2017. Expert Focus 8/2017, 511–517. Available at: https://papers.ssrn.com/sol3/papers.cfm?abstract_id=3022522.

[105] Commission Staff Working Document, 'Evaluation of Product Liability Directive', SWD(2018) 157 final, Brussels, 07.05.2018. Also: Commission Report on the Application of the Product Liability Directive, COM(2018) 246 final, Brussels, 07.05.2018.

[106] Commission Staff Working Document on "Liability for emerging digital technologies" - Accompanying the document Commission Communication "Artificial intelligence for Europe", SWD(2018) 137 final, Brussels, 25.4.2018, at pp. 17–18.

In particular, the Product Liability Directive does not make any reference to the concept of service nor does it provide for the distinction between products and services. It solely provides for the definition of product, according to Article 2. The notion of product mainly refers to movables even though incorporated into another movable or into an immovable. Services do not fall into the definition of product. However, it was recognized that the distinction between products and services for the purpose of the Directive is becoming increasingly blurred with regards to new technological developments. So, a number of open questions were identified related to software be it embedded or non-embedded and, therefore, a clarification of the concept "product", e.g. with regards to software, requires further assessment.[107]

The notion of producer provided for in Article 3 of the Product Liability Directive reflects the definition of product for the purpose of the Directive. 'Producer' means the manufacturer of a finished product, the producer of any raw material or the manufacturer of a component part and any person who, by putting his name, trade mark or other distinguishing feature on the product presents himself as its producer, as well as any person who imports into the European Union a product for sale, hire, leasing or any form of distribution in the course of his business. According to the Commission, the new technological developments involve different actors in the value chain, including product manufacturers, software producers, the connectivity service providers, sensor manufacturers, owners of the object, service providers. Furthermore, new features could be added by the user or even third parties to create a new system. Thus the Commission raised the question to what extent the producer maintains control over the features of a product in the context of emerging digital technologies and can therefore be held liable for them. It concluded that there might be cases where it would not be possible to identify the final product and producer and, thus, the party responsible for providing compensation.[108]

The burden of proof and the notion of defectiveness are central components of the Product Liability Directive that trigger the right for compensation. In particular, the injured party can obtain compensation only if he can prove the defect in the product and the link between the defect and the damage. Claimants often find it difficult to prove the defect and the link between defect and damage in court. This difficulty could become even higher in cases of complex products. This is why it was argued that the term "defective" in the Product Liability Directive should probably be adapted to new technological or scientific advances such as apps and non-embedded software, advanced robots and autonomous/intelligent systems. Therefore, the notion of what constitutes a defect may need to be re-examined in order to provide certainty regarding new technological developments such as apps and non-embedded software, advanced robots and autonomous/intelligent systems. Also, since emerging digital technologies and products are becoming increasingly connected and complex, it could become challenging for a claimant to identify the defect and prove the substantial elements of a liability claim. The injured party needs

---

[107] Ibid., at p. 18.

[108] Ibid.

to gather expertise in order to be able to prove the lack of safety of the product and the link to the damage suffered. In addition, the injured party could face major difficulties when attempting to gain access to essential information, especially in the case of complex digital technology products.

This is why the Commission stated that, "the notions of defectiveness and burden of proof of the Directive are fairly wide and refer to the safety levels that a consumer is entitled to expect. The defectiveness must be assessed based on an objective analysis of the expectations of an average consumer rather than on subjective expectations or predisposition of one person. The defectiveness of a product is assessed on a case-by-case basis, considering all the relevant circumstances, on the basis of objective criteria, including especially product safety legislation, and all other circumstances, including the presentation of the product, the reasonably expected use and the time when the product was put into circulation. In the context of the emerging digital technologies, it may be difficult to identify whether the damage has been caused by the product itself or by other elements interconnected to it in a digital ecosystem. In this respect, it will be necessary to provide for adequate safety levels for all types of products, taking also account of any new risks that may be posed regarding the emerging digital technologies";[109] "it is also important to assess the issue of the burden of proof. National regimes including fault-based liability schemes or different forms of strict liability regimes often include provisions, whereby the burden of proof for a possible fault, defect or other condition is not placed on the victim. Thus, the person held liable by law would need to prove to be discharged from liability, for instance, that the damage was caused as a result of force majeure or an act/behaviour of a third party. Whether the burden of proof should be on the claimant or reversed, what substantive conditions the claimant should demonstrate as well as the impact on the ability of the claimant to obtain compensation are important elements to assess".[110]

Furthermore, the Product Liability Directive stipulates an obligation of producers to compensate natural persons for damages caused by defective products resulting from death, personal injury or damage to or destruction of an item of property. According to the Product Liability Directive, damages are limited to either physical or material damages to property that is intended for private use. The Directive is without prejudice to national provisions relating to non-material damage. This distinction between private and professional use for the purpose of the Directive could become increasingly blurred with regards to new technological developments and, therefore, further assessment is required. Also, the type of damage should be further explored.

As the Commission put it: "Which type of damage caused by these technologies should be compensated; death, bodily harm, harm to property or also consequential damages in form of purely economic damage? Non-material damage? Especially for the latter, one would also need to consider whether the damage of only natural or also

---

[109] ibid.

[110] Ibid., at p. 20.

of legal persons should be compensated. In this context, it would also need to be considered whether the liability for the use of AI powered devices should have a threshold and/or be capped, which amount(s) should be chosen and whether they should differ according to sectors. In the context of this set of questions, it would be helpful to consider the damages including non-material damages that could typically materialize in light of the risks connected with the use of AI powered systems taking into account that these technologies may create new types of risks or accentuate existing risks".[111]

Moreover, the exemption of the EUR 500 threshold for property damages was contested[112] by some stakeholders, such as organisations representing consumers, which claimed to be unfairly disadvantaged and asked for more protection at a lower cost, which would result in removing the threshold of EUR 500. On the other hand, it could be argued that any relaxation on the threshold for property damages would lead to more claims for minor damages, which would contradict one of the main purposes of the threshold, namely to avoid litigation for small claims.

Some stakeholders raised questions related to the infringement of privacy and cybersecurity as well as how to link the notion of defect with the types of cyber-attacks leading to damages. Information systems and databases are affected by an increasing number of security incidents and cybersecurity attacks. Those incidents can range from technical failures and unintentional mistakes to malicious attacks. Due to increased reliance on networks, a connected economy and society are more vulnerable to cyber threats and attacks. Therefore, any vulnerability can be exploited and cause serious damages (e.g. large-scale breaches of sensitive personal data and terrorism acts). The frequency and impact of security incidents are increasing and represent a major threat to the functioning of network and information systems. Due to the characteristics of emerging digital products, such as increasing level of complexity and variety of ecosystems, actors and value chains, and especially since IoT and AI-enabled products are increasingly connected and complex both in the design and the system integration, it is recognized that in the case of a cyber-attack it would be extremely difficult for the victim/claimant to identify the defect and the actual wrong-doer and prove the substantial elements of a liability claim. Thus, if we decide to apply product liability rules to cyber-attack incidents, allocating liability may become unclear and claims potentially difficult to enforce.

This is why the Commission stated: "Security breaches, in particular through cybersecurity attacks, are certainly among the most serious risks posed by these technologies. In most cases, it is likely very difficult, if not impossible, for the victim to identify the attackers and bring a claim for damages against them, meaning that, absent holding someone else liable vis-à-vis the victim, this would likely remain without compensation. If one considers the possibility of holding the operator/owner of the device or the producer liable, such liability would be however of a very different nature. Although the risk inherent in the emerging digital technologies

[111] Ibid.

[112] Ibid., at p. 19.

would have been materialised, the existence of an actual wrong-doer at the origin of the damage would have been known, but not his/her identity. If therefore such liability were to be created at all, one would have to consider – at least in such cases – to grant the operator or producer a defence if the operator/owner of the device had used all applicable standards of care and diligence for the use and maintenance/ production of the device and yet the cyberattack was successful".[113]

As already mentioned, the extra-contractual liability regimes of most EU member jurisdictions are fault-based. Therefore, the fault of the author of the wrongful behaviour leading to a damage—which could be an act or an omission whether intentional or by negligence—is a necessary element to be proven for the liability claim to be successful. Fault-based liability is justified by the reasoning that a wrongdoer did not respect certain requirements, for instance the reasonable standard of care. On the other hand, strict liability is defined as a liability which does not depend on a fault and, consequently, the claimant needs only to prove the damage and the causal link. Strict liability builds on the concept that a person who created a risk for his own benefit should be responsible for any damage materialised in connection to that risk.

However, special regimes may apply where the reversal of the burden of proof in the context of a fault-based extra-contractual liability and the principle of strict liability aim at facilitating the compensation of the victim. Such variations may consist in a presumption of fault by the wrongdoer (or a reversal of the burden of proof), whereby the wrongdoer is liable unless he can prove that he was not in fault—for instance, the responsibility of parents/tutors/guardians/teachers for damages caused by a minor, pupil, student/apprentice or mentally impaired person or the responsibility of the owner/possessor of a building in case of damages caused by his building (unless, of course, he proves that he observed appropriate care for the purpose of avoiding the damage). Some forms of strict liability may go even a step further by linking liability to a particular person who has generated a risk, which materialises in a damage, and at the same time he derives an economic benefit from this activity—making the discharge of liability possible only under the proof that the damaging event was caused by an exceptional/unforeseen circumstance that could not be avoided. When the risk of damages is linked to dangerous activities, liability may be attributed to the person that carries out the activity (e.g. the operator of a nuclear power plant or of an aircraft or the driver of a car) or is ultimately responsible for the dangerous activity to happen (e.g. the owner of a vehicle). There may be also other cases where the risk of damage is linked to the unpredictability of behaviour of specific risk groups, like animals: in these cases liability may be attributed to the persons who are responsible to supervise the animal, because it is them who should normally be in the condition to adopt measures to prevent or reduce the risk of damages.

---

[113] Commission Staff Working Document on "Liability for emerging digital technologies" - Accompanying the document Commission Communication "Artificial intelligence for Europe", SWD(2018) 137 final, Brussels, 25.4.2018, at p. 20.

Based on the above, the Commission stated that a detailed assessment needs to be carried out as to whether—and to what extent—concepts like the liability of a guardian are appropriate to technologies like AI. As the Commission pointed out: "While AI cannot of course be assimilated to humans or animals, the autonomy element is an intrinsic feature that is relevant and very prominent in both cases. Within the limits set by relevant safety frameworks, an AI powered robot can, and actually is supposed to, act autonomously and independently, i.e. without any supervision. The approach to liability for animals is linked to the concept of lack of predictability and therefore interesting to that extent in the context of autonomous behaviour. Safety legislation will have an important role to play in reducing this unpredictability to a socially accepted minimum".[114] Furthermore, the Commission stressed the need to assess whether liability should be fault-based or strict for AI systems and concluded that existing strict liability provisions could apply to the use of certain AI powered devices, in particular, in the case of automated vehicles.

The Commission also underlined that an assessment should be conducted as to whether (and to what extent) it matters for determining liability—in addition to the damage suffered by the victim—if the damage could have been avoided or not.[115] It was reminded that, according to specific national liability schemes, in the case of collapse or ruin of buildings, a presumption of fault by the wrongdoer (or a reversal of the burden of proof) exists, whereby the wrongdoer is liable in case of damages caused by his building unless he can prove that he was not in fault. Therefore, in this case, any person held liable by law could avoid liability by proving that he did everything possible for the purpose of avoiding the damage or that he observed reasonable/appropriate care considering similar circumstances: "... if the owner of a building shows that he used reasonable care in the maintenance of the building, and therefore the damage was not caused by poor maintenance, he can avoid liability".[116] The same concept could apply, by analogy, to the owner of an advanced robot, meaning that the owner of an advanced robot could avoid liability by proving that "he had used and maintained the robot properly, respecting the instructions of the producers and updating the software when required".[117] However, the built-in autonomy and self-learning ability—which are essential characteristics of "advanced" robots and AI-enabled technologies/products—could generate autonomous decision-making, entailing a certain degree of unpredictability in the behaviour of those systems. Since an AI powered robot can, and actually is supposed to, act autonomously and without any human supervision, a damage might occur even if both the use and maintenance of the robot were impeccable. This unpredictability in behaviour and the autonomy aspect of those applications and systems inevitably raises the question of "what actions a person held liable could possibly put in place in order to avoid the damage caused by the autonomous behaviour of emerging digital

[114] Ibid., at p. 19.

[115] Ibid.

[116] Ibid.

[117] Ibid.

technologies".[118] In other words, and in order to avoid liability, how a person can prove that the damage caused by his advanced robot was not his fault, that he used reasonable and appropriate care, and that he did everything possible for the purpose of preventing the occurred damage.

The importance of having an efficient redress mechanism for victims in case of damages was stressed, especially since IoT and AI-enabled products and services are increasingly connected and complex both in the design and the system integration. Indeed, IoT and AI ecosystems are based on bringing together multiple sectors and a variety of stakeholders to cover an increasingly complex value chain. They are also based on various disciplines and technologies like sensors, embedded systems, and various communications technologies. Furthermore, some of these emerging digital technologies have a very open ecosystem, as new features could be added by the user or even third parties to create a new system. As the Commission put it, "While it is not necessarily relevant for the purpose of ensuring that the victim obtains compensation for the damages suffered - which may happen satisfactorily - the question of redress has to be considered from an overall policy standpoint, particularly in situations where a complex ecosystem of market operators enables the roll-out and functioning of the emerging digital technologies".[119]

Therefore, due to specific characteristics of emerging digital technologies, such as increasing level of complexity and variety of ecosystems, actors and value chains (high interdependency), the issue of redress between actors in the value chain—including product manufacturers, service operators, software producers and providers, traders, connectivity service providers, conformity assessment bodies, sensor manufacturers, infrastructure providers—is crucial and should be assessed. Otherwise, legal uncertainty may hinder the development and uptake of AI-enabled products and services: "The redress is indeed crucial for the roll-out emerging digital technologies as the value chain of these technologies present a degree of complexity that is higher than that of other value chains and it will answer the question of who ultimately bears the cost for possible damages".[120] If, for instance, the owner or operator of an AI system is held strictly liable by law, even if he is not in a position to control the behaviour of the advanced robot or the AI-enabled system (*inter alia*, due to their built-in autonomy and self-learning characteristics) or prevent any associated risks with the adoption of precautionary measures (i.e. proper use and maintenance of the AI system), he should be able to seek redress for the damages occurred, provided that the wrongful or undesirable behaviour of the AI system may be attributable to someone else, e.g. the producer. However, although the person held strictly liable under national law does not have to prove the fault of the producer under the Product Liability Directive, this person would still need to demonstrate a

[118] Ibid., at pp. 19–20.

[119] Ibid., at pp. 20–21.

[120] Commission Staff Working Document on "Liability for emerging digital technologies" - Accompanying the document Commission Communication "Artificial intelligence for Europe", SWD(2018) 137 final, Brussels, 25.4.2018, at p. 21.

defect of the AI system and the casual link, namely that the damage was caused by that defect. Therefore, since claimants find it particularly difficult to prove the defect and the link between defect and damage in court, especially in complex cases involving emerging digital technologies where the occurred damage may be a result of a large set of unknown circumstances or due to the difficultly to gain access to essential information, it might be challenging to prove the substantial elements of a liability claim.[121]

A strict liability approach to AI powered devices would ensure that potential victims are compensated by the liable person, regardless of any wrongdoing. In this context, law could provide for redress possibilities of the insurer who compensated the victim against the producer of the defective AI system. Furthermore, it was stressed that, similarly to what already happens with motor vehicles, rules on liability could be complemented by a compulsory insurance scheme for various actors, as a possible solution to the complexity of allocating responsibility for damage caused by increasingly autonomous robots. According to the Commission "in order to facilitate the victim's compensation and protecting the victim from the risk of insolvency of the liable person, it could be discussed, among other solutions, whether various actors in the value chain should be required to take out insurance coverage as it is the case today for cars. In case of an accident, the victim would be compensated by the insurance".[122] Besides, insurance companies—despite the difficulties stemming from the complexity of the emerging digital technologies—would be in a better position to investigate claims properly and gain access to essential information in order to "assess whether a redress claim against the manufacturer of the AI powered device or any other person can be enforced".[123]

All the above mentioned questions posed by the Commission were more closely examined with the assistance of the Expert Group on liability,[124] consisting of two formations: the Product Liability Directive formation and the New Technologies formation. The approaches put forward by the Commission's "Building a European

[121] Ibid.

[122] Ibid.

[123] Ibid.

[124] The Expert Group on Liability and New Technologies (set up by the Commission in March 2018) worked in two formations: a Product Liability Directive (PLD) formation managed by DG Internal Market, Industry, Entrepreneurship and SMEs (GROW) and a New Technologies formation managed by DG GROW, DG Communications Networks, Content and Technology (CNECT) and DG Justice and Consumers (JUST).

The aim of the Product Liability Directive formation was to provide advice on the implementation of the PLD, *inter alia* assessing the extent to which the provisions of the PLD are adequate to solve questions of liability in relation to traditional products, new technologies and new societal challenges. In parallel, the aim of the New Technologies formation was to assess whether and to what extent existing liability schemes are adapted to the emerging market realities following the development of the new technologies such as AI, advanced robotics, the IoT and cybersecurity issues.

Data Economy" Communication[125]—in light of new technological developments and based on input from stakeholders—would also be considered. It is indicated that several legislative actions will be proposed to ensure an appropriate technical and legal framework for AI, in line with the Commission's vision of advancing as well as regulating AI. It could be argued that some initial insights were offered as to what the forthcoming new framework might comprise. Indeed, the Commission was quick to note that, in the context of the analysis of the overall liability regimes and approaches that could be relevant to the goal of facilitating the uptake of emerging digital technologies by fostering innovation, investment and protecting consumers, the type and form of regulatory intervention should be discussed: "if a regulatory intervention on these technologies appears appropriate and necessary (in terms of new rules or an amendment to existing rules), it should be discussed whether that intervention should be developed in a horizontal or sectorial way and whether new legislation should be enacted at EU level".[126]

3.4.6 Conclusion

This chapter focused on the most important implications for and potential gaps in the liability frameworks for AI, the IoT and robotics. In particular, the European Commission's Staff Working Document on liability for emerging digital technologies attempted to identify the legal challenges that technologies, such as artificial intelligence (AI), advanced robotics, autonomous systems and the Internet of Things (IoT), can pose to the existing EU and Member States legislation due to their novel technical and operational characteristics.

According to the Commission's initial (2018) assessment on liability for emerging digital technologies, the EU's existing product liability legislation contains a number of gaps that need to be addressed. If the safety risks materialise, the specific characteristics of those technologies could make it difficult to trace back potentially problematic decisions made with the involvement of AI systems. This in turn may make it extremely difficult for persons having suffered harm to obtain compensation under the current EU and national liability legislation. Therefore, in the context of emerging digital technologies, it is imperative to offer an adequate level of legal certainty for businesses, to ensure that appropriate redress mechanisms for consumers of these emerging AI-enabled products and services are in place, and to avoid any potential disparities and fragmentation in the Digital Single Market.

[125] Commission Communication "Building a European Data Economy", COM(2017) 9 final, Brussels, 10.1.2017.

[126] Commission Staff Working Document on "Liability for emerging digital technologies" - Accompanying the document Commission Communication "Artificial intelligence for Europe", SWD(2018) 137 final, Brussels, 25.4.2018, at p. 21.

Legal/Policy Documents, Reports, and Other Sources

European Commission ('Commission') Communication "Digitising European Industry - Reaping the full benefits of a Digital Single Market", COM(2016) 180 final, 19 April 2016.

Commission Staff Working Document "Advancing the Internet of Things in Europe" (accompanying the Commission Communication "Digitising European Industry - Reaping the full benefits of a Digital Single Market", COM(2016) 180 final, 19 April 2016), Brussels, SWD(2016) 110 final, 19.4.2016.

Commission Communication "Building a European Data Economy", COM(2017) 9 final, Brussels, 10.1.2017.

Commission Communication "Artificial Intelligence for Europe", COM (2018) 237 final, Brussels, 25.4.2018.

Commission Staff Working Document on "Liability for emerging digital technologies" - Accompanying the document Commission Communication "Artificial intelligence for Europe", SWD(2018) 137 final, Brussels, 25.4.2018.

Commission Staff Working Document, Evaluation of Council Directive 85/374/EEC of 25 July 1985 on the approximation of the laws, regulations and administrative provisions of the Member States concerning liability for defective products – Accompanying the Evaluation Report – SWD(2018) 157 final, Brussels, 7.5.2018 ('Commission Staff Working Document, 'Evaluation of Product Liability Directive', SWD(2018) 157 final, Brussels, 07.05.2018').

Report from the Commission on the Application of the Council Directive on the approximation of the laws, regulations, and administrative provisions of the Member States concerning liability for defective products (85/374/EEC) {SWD (2018) 157 final} - {SWD(2018) 158 final}, COM(2018) 246 final, Brussels, 7.5.2018 ('Commission Report on the Application of the Product Liability Directive, COM(2018) 246 final, Brussels, 07.05.2018').

Directive 2006/42/EC of the European Parliament and of the Council of 17 May 2006 on machinery, and amending Directive 95/16/EC (recast) (OJ L 157, 9.6.2006, pp. 24–86) (the Machinery Directive).

Commission Staff Working Document, Evaluation of the Machinery Directive, SWD(2018) 160, final, Brussels, 7.5.2018.

Inception Impact Assessment - Revision of the Machinery Directive, Ref. Ares (2019)132242 - 10/01/2019.

Commission's Proposal for a Regulation of the European Parliament and of the Council on machinery products, COM(2021) 202 final, Brussels, 21.4.2021.

Regulation (EU) 2023/1230 of the European Parliament and of the Council of 14 June 2023 on machinery and repealing Directive 2006/42/EC of the European Parliament and of the Council and Council Directive 73/361/EEC, OJ L165/1, 29.06.2023.

European Commission, Press Release, "Commission welcomes political agreement on new rules to ensure the safety of machinery and robots", Brussels, 15.12.2022.

Council Directive 85/374/EEC of 25 July 1985 on the approximation of the laws, regulations and administrative provisions of the Member States concerning liability for defective products, as modified by Directive 1999/34/EC of the European Parliament and of the Council of 10 May 1999 (OJ L 210/29, 7.8.1985, and OJ L 141/20, 4.6.1999).

Regulation (EU) 2019/2144 of the European Parliament and of the Council of 27 November 2019 on type-approval requirements for motor vehicles and their trailers, and systems, components and separate technical units intended for such vehicles, as regards their general safety and the protection of vehicle occupants and vulnerable road users.

SAE International's On-Road Automated Vehicle Standards Committee published the SAE Information Report: (J3016) "Taxonomy and Definitions for Terms Related to On-Road Motor Vehicle Automated Driving Systems", issued on 16.01.2014 (revised: 30.04.2021).

Directive 2009/103/EC of the European Parliament and of the Council of 16 September 2009 relating to insurance against civil liability in respect of the use of motor vehicles, and the enforcement of the obligation to insure against such liability ("the Motor Insurance Directive").

The Guardian, "Google self-driving car collides with bus in California, accident report says", by Nellie Bowles, 1 March 2016, https://www.theguardian.com/technology/2016/feb/29/google-self-driving-car-accident-california

National Transportation Safety Board (NTSB) News Release (11.19.2019), https://www.ntsb.gov/news/press-releases/Pages/NR20191119c.aspx https://www.ntsb.gov/news/events/Documents/2019-HWY18MH010-BMG-abstract.pdf

The Washington Post, "Self-driving Uber vehicle strikes and kills pedestrian", by Faiz Siddiqui and Michael Laris, 19.04.2018, https://www.washingtonpost.com/news/dr-gridlock/wp/2018/03/19/uber-halts-autonomous-vehicle-testing-after-a-pedestrian-is-struck/

CSO online, What is WannaCry ransomware, how does it infect, and who was responsible?, 27 September. Available at: http://www.csoonline.com/article/3227906/ransomware/what-is-wannacryransomware-how-does-it-infect-and-who-was-responsible.html.

The Guardian, DDoS attack that disrupted internet was largest of its kind in history, experts say, 26 October 2016. Available at: http://www.theguardian.com/technology/2016/oct/26/ddos-attack-dyn-miraibotnet.

Studer, Evelyne and de Werra, Jacques, Regulating Cybersecurity - What Civil Liability in Case of Cyber-Attacks?, 19 August 2017. Expert Focus 8/2017, 511-517. Available at: https://papers.ssrn.com/sol3/papers.cfm?abstract_id=3022522.

References

Bathaee Y (2018) The artificial intelligence black box and the failure of intent and causation. Harv J Law Technol 31(2):889–938

Beck S (2016) The problem of ascribing legal responsibility in the case of robotics. AI Soc 31(4): 473–481

Bertolini A (2013) Robots as products: the case for a realistic analysis of robotic applications and liability rules. Law Innov Technol 5:214–247

Bertolini A (2018) Artificial intelligence and civil law - liability rules for drones, Study requested by the European Parliament's Committee on Legal Affairs, Policy Department for Citizens' Rights and Constitutional Affairs, November 2018

Borghetti J-S (2019) How can artificial intelligence be defective. In: Lohsse S, Schulze R, Staudenmayer D (eds) Liability for artificial intelligence and the internet of things. Nomos, Baden-Baden, pp 63–76

Christidis K, Devetsikiotis M (2016) Blockchains and smart contracts for the internet of things. IEEE Access 4:2292–2303

de Bruin R (2016) Autonomous intelligent cars on the European intersection of liability and privacy: regulatory challenges and the road ahead. Eur J Risk Regul 7(3):485–501

de Meeus C (2019) The Product Liability Directive at the age of the digital industrial revolution: fit for innovation? J Eur Consum Market Law 8(4):149–154

Evas T (2018) A common EU approach to liability rules and insurance for connected and autonomous vehicles, Study. European Added Value Assessment - Accompanying the European Parliament's legislative own-initiative report (Rapporteur: Mady Delvaux). Study, European Parliamentary Research Service (EPRS), February 2018

Fairgrieve D, Rajneri E (2019) Is software a product under the Product Liability Directive? Zeitschrift für Internationales Wirtschaftsrecht 1:24–28

Fairgrieve D, Howells G, Møgelvang-Hansen P et al (2016) Product Liability Directive. In: Machnikowski P (ed) European product liability: an analysis of the state of the art in the era of new technologies. Principles of European tort law. Intersentia, pp 17–108

Grundmann S, Hacker P (2017) Digital technology as a challenge to European contract law – from the existing to the future architecture. Eur Rev Contract Law 13:255–293

Howells G, Twigg-Flesner C, Willett C (2017) Product liability and digital products. In: Synodinou T-E, Jougleux P, Markou C, Prastitou T (eds) EU internet law: regulation and enforcement. Springer Nature, pp 183–195

Kritikos M (2016) Legal and ethical reflections concerning robotics. Scientific Foresight Unit (STOA) Policy Briefing, European Parliament Research Service (EPRS), PE 563.501, June 2016

Leenes R, Palmerini E, Koops B-J, Bertolini A, Salvini P, Lucivero F (2017) Regulatory challenges of robotics: some guidelines for addressing legal and ethical issues. Law Innov Technol 9:1–44

Lohmann MF (2016) Liability issues concerning self-driving vehicles. Eur J Risk Regul 7(2): 335–340

Lohsse S, Schulze R, Staudenmayer D (2019) Liability for artificial intelligence. In: Lohsse S, Schulze R, Staudenmayer D (eds) Liability for artificial intelligence and the internet of things. Nomos, Baden-Baden, pp 99–116

Machnikowski P (2016) Conclusions. In: Machnikowski P (ed) European product liability: an analysis of the state of the art in the era of new technologies. Principles of European tort law. Intersentia, pp 669–705

Martín-Casals M (2019) Causation and scope of liability in the internet of things (IoT). In: Lohsse S, Schulze R, Staudenmayer D (eds) Liability for artificial intelligence and the internet of things. Nomos, Baden-Baden, pp 201–228

Nevejans N (2016) European civil law rules in robotics. Study requested by the European Parliament's Committee on Legal Affairs (JURI Committee)

Palmerini E, Bertolini A, Battaglia F, Koops B-J, Carnevale A, Salvini P (2016) RoboLaw: towards a European framework for robotics regulation. Rob Auton Syst 86:78–85

Ponce del Castillo A (2017) A law on robotics and artificial intelligence in the EU? (October 3, 2017). Foresight Brief, European Trade Union Institute (ETUI) Research Paper - Foresight Brief #02-September 2017

Schellekens M (2018) No-fault compensation schemes for self-driving vehicles. Law Innov Technol 10(2):314–333

Spindler G (2019) User liability and strict liability in the internet of things and for robots. In: Lohsse S, Schulze R, Staudenmayer D (eds) Liability for artificial intelligence and the internet of things. Nomos, Baden-Baden, pp 125–145

Timan T, Snijders R, Kirova M, Suardi S, Lieshout MV, Chen M, Costenco P, Palmerini E, Bertolini A, Tejada A, Montfort SV, Bolchi M, Alberti S, Brouwer R, Karanilokova K, Episcopo F, Jansen S (2019) Study on safety of non-embedded software. Service, data access, and legal issues of advanced robots, autonomous, connected, and AI-based vehicles and systems: final study report regarding CAD/CCAM and industrial robots. European Commission, Brussel

van Boom WH, Borghetti J-S, Ehlers AB, Karner E, Nolan D, Oliphant K, Scarso A, Ulfbeck V, Wagner G (2018) Product liability in Europe. In: Koziol H, Green MD, Lunney M, Oliphant K, Yang L (eds) Product liability: fundamental questions in a comparative perspective. De Gruyter, Berlin, Boston, pp 255–356

Verheyen T (2018) Full harmonization, consumer protection and products liability: a fresh reading of the case law of the ECJ. Eur Rev Priv Law 26(1):119–140

Wagner G (2019) Robot liability. In: Lohsse S, Schulze R, Staudenmayer D (eds) Liability for artificial intelligence and the internet of things. Nomos, Baden-Baden, pp 27–62

Wuyts D (2014) The Product Liability Directive – more than two decades of defective products in Europe. J Eur Tort Law 5(1):1–34

Chapter 4
Assessing the Most Important Safety and Liability Aspects of Artificial Intelligence, Internet of Things and Robotics: 2019 and 2020

4.1 Introduction

This chapter follows the European Commission's attempt to examine the applicability of the existing Product Liability Directive to new technologies and, in light of an assessment of the existing liability schemes, to develop principles that can serve as guidelines for possible adaptations of applicable laws at EU and national level relating to new technologies. In other words, it reviews whether and to what extent existing liability schemes are adapted to the emerging market realities following the development of the new technologies such as Artificial Intelligence, advanced robotics, the IoT and cybersecurity issues. It is also examined whether the current EU liability regimes are still adequate to facilitate the uptake of the emerging digital technologies by promoting investment stability and users' trust.

In particular, this chapter covers the Commission's 2020 White Paper on AI, which concluded that the existing liability laws which are applicable to AI applications are not sufficient to address the risks posed by the development and deployment of AI. Therefore, specific adjustments to and clarifications of existing legislation is required in order to make the EU liability framework fit for the current and forthcoming technological and commercial developments.

This chapter also covers extensively the Commission's 2020 Report on the safety and liability implications of AI, IoT and robotics, which accompanied the Commission's 2020 White Paper on Artificial Intelligence. This Report provided an overview of the existing rules for liability, focused on key issues, and assessed the most important implications for and potential gaps in the liability and safety frameworks for AI, the IoT and robotics. While in principle the existing EU and national liability laws could cope with emerging technologies, the combined effect of the challenges of AI could make it more difficult to offer victims compensation in all cases where this would be justified. To rectify this and address potential uncertainties in the existing framework, certain adjustments to the current Product Liability Directive

N. T. Nikolinakos, *Adapting the EU Civil Liability Regime to the Digital Age: Artificial Intelligence, Robotics, and Other Emerging Technologies*, Law, Governance and Technology Series 68, https://doi.org/10.1007/978-3-031-67969-8_4

and national liability regimes through appropriate EU initiatives should be considered on a targeted, risk-based approach.

Also, this chapter examines the most important findings presented in the Report of the Expert Group on Liability and New Technologies, titled "Liability for Artificial Intelligence and Other Emerging Digital Technologies", issued on 21 November 2019.

It is reminded that, in its 2018 Communication on AI for Europe, the Commission stated that it would issue (as a step for building trust and ensuring legal clarity in AI-based applications) by mid-2019 a report on the broader implications for, potential gaps in and orientations for, the safety and liability frameworks for AI, Internet of Things and robotics.[1] To this end, as already discussed, an initial assessment on the current liability frameworks in light of AI and emerging technologies was issued in April 2018 (Commission Staff Working Document on "Liability for emerging digital technologies"),[2] accompanying the Commission's Communication "Artificial Intelligence for Europe".

Furthermore, the Expert Group on Liability and New Technologies[3] (which was set up by the Commission in March 2018) was invited to analyse crucial liability questions and the challenges brought about by AI.[4] In particular, the Expert Group was invited to provide the Commission with expertise on the applicability of the Product Liability Directive to traditional products, new technologies and new soci-

[1]Commission Communication, "Artificial Intelligence for Europe", COM(2018) 237 final, Brussels, 25.4.2018, p. 16.

[2]Commission Staff Working Document on "Liability for emerging digital technologies" - Accompanying the document Commission Communication "Artificial intelligence for Europe", SWD (2018) 137 final, Brussels, 25.4.2018.

[3]It was decided that the Expert Group on Liability and New Technologies (which was set up by the Commission in March 2018) would work in two formations: a Product Liability Directive formation managed by DG Internal Market, Industry, Entrepreneurship and SMEs (GROW) and a New Technologies formation managed by DG GROW, DG Communications Networks, Content and Technology (CNECT) and DG Justice and Consumers (JUST).

[4]Commission Communication, "Artificial Intelligence for Europe", COM(2018) 237 final, Brussels, 25.4.2018, at p. 16.

See also Report from the Commission on the Application of the Council Directive on the approximation of the laws, regulations, and administrative provisions of the Member States concerning liability for defective products (85/374/EEC) {SWD(2018) 157 final} - {SWD(2018) 158 final}, COM(2018) 246 final, Brussels, 7.5.2018, ['Commission Report on the Application of the Product Liability Directive, COM(2018) 246 final, Brussels, 07.05.2018'] at p. 10: "We will issue guidance on the (Product Liability) Directive as well as a report on the broader implications for, and potential gaps in and orientations for, the liability and safety frameworks for AI, Internet of Things and robotics in mid-2019. If necessary, the Commission will update certain aspects of the Directive, such as the concepts of 'defect', 'damage', 'product' and 'producer'. However, the overall principle of strict liability will remain intact. A coherent, technology-neutral safety framework should prevent accidents as far as possible. However, when accidents do happen, our liability framework should ensure that those who suffer injury are compensated".

etal challenges ('the Product Liability Directive formation')[5] and, in light of an assessment of the existing liability schemes, support the Commission in developing principles that can serve as guidelines for possible adaptations of applicable laws at EU and national level relating to new technologies ('the New Technologies formation').[6] In the call for applications,[7] the New Technologies formation was asked to assess "whether and to what extent existing liability schemes are adapted to the emerging market realities following the development of the new technologies such as Artificial Intelligence, advanced robotics, the IoT and cybersecurity issues".[8] It

[5]The aim of the Product Liability Directive formation was to provide advice and expertise on the implementation of the Directive. In particular, it shall help to interpret the provisions of the Product Liability Directive and assess the extent to which the provisions of the Directive are adequate to solve questions of liability in relation to traditional products, new technologies and new societal challenges (e.g. pharmaceutical products and medical devices, environmental damages and refurbished products). The Product Liability Directive formation would also provide assistance to the Commission on the implementation of the Directive, also with a particular view to the developments of the jurisprudence of the Court of Justice and national courts, new and emerging technologies (e.g. 3D printing, IoT, AI, robotics and cybersecurity) and any other development in the field of product liability. See: Call for Applications for the Selection of Members of the Expert Group on Liability and New Technologies, at p. 4.

[6]The aim of the New Technologies formation was to assess whether and to what extent existing liability schemes are adapted to the emerging market realities following the development of the new technologies such as Artificial Intelligence, advanced robotics, the IoT and cybersecurity issues. It shall identify the shortcomings and assess whether the overall liability regime is adequate to facilitate the uptake of the above-mentioned new technologies by fostering investment stability and users' trust. In case the existing overall liability regime is deemed not to be adequate, the New Technologies formation shall provide recommendations on how it should be designed. The regulatory framework to be considered for analysis should include national tort law as well as any possible specific national liability regimes, the rationale or contents of which may be relevant. Questions of liability should be analysed holistically looking at various actors (e.g. liability of owners/operators, insurers) and legal relationships (e.g. questions of redress in the technology value chain). The assessment should not be constrained by existing legal instruments or concepts in EU or national law and can propose new concepts. The New Technologies formation shall also assist the Commission in developing EU-wide principles which can serve as guidelines for possible adaptations of applicable laws at EU and national level as regards the new technologies following the development of the new technologies such as Artificial Intelligence, advanced robotics, the IoT and cybersecurity issues. The principles should address among others key issues in connection with damages caused by the above-mentioned new technologies, such as the assignment of liability (e.g. liable person, exclusive/joint liability, the role of mandatory or voluntary insurance to cover the liability risk), the nature of liability (fault/non-fault based), whether it is necessary for the victim to establish a defect, who should bear the burden of proof and which redress possibilities insurance providers would have to recover compensated damage. The assessment of existing liability schemes and development of principles should be completed by June 2019 at the latest. Following the assessment, the New Technologies formation of the Expert Group may be asked to assist the Commission with expert advice in the discussion on and possible implementation of these principles. See: Call for Applications for the Selection of Members of the Expert Group on Liability and New Technologies, at pp. 4–5.

[7]Call for Applications for the Selection of Members of the Expert Group on Liability and New Technologies. Available at: http://ec.europa.eu/transparency/regexpert/index.cfm?do=news.open_doc&id=12065.

[8]Ibid., at p. 4.

was also asked to examine whether the current liability regimes are still “adequate to facilitate the uptake of the above-mentioned new technologies by fostering investment stability and users’ trust”.[9] If shortcomings were identified, the New Technologies formation should make recommendations for amendments, leaving aside rules on safety and other technical standards.

As a result, the New Technologies formation (which was first convened in June 2018 and held nine further meetings up to May 2019) analysed the relevant national laws, examined specific use cases (such as autonomous cars, smart home, blockchain, autonomous healthcare applications, algorithmic decision making in the financial and other sectors, drones), and compared various aspects of existing liability regimes. The findings of the New Technologies formation were presented in the Report “Liability for Artificial Intelligence and Other Emerging Digital Technologies”, issued on 21 November 2019.[10]

Furthermore, the Commission issued in February 2020 its Report on the safety and liability implications of AI, IoT and robotics.[11] The Commission’s Report (which accompanied the 2020 White Paper on Artificial Intelligence) provided an overview of the existing rules for safety and liability, focused on key issues, and assessed the most important implications for and potential gaps in the liability and safety frameworks for AI, the IoT and robotics.[12]

---

[9] Ibid.

[10] Report from the Expert Group on Liability and New Technologies – New Technologies Formation “Liability for Artificial Intelligence and Other Emerging Digital Technologies”, 21 November 2019.

[11] Commission Communication “Report on the safety and liability implications of Artificial Intelligence, the Internet of Things and robotics”, Brussels, COM (2020) 64 final, 19.2.2020.

[12] For interesting reading, analysis, and useful academic commentary on the applicability of the current Product Liability Directive to new technologies, as well as on assessing the most important implications and potential gaps in the liability and safety frameworks for AI, the IoT and robotics (including whether existing national liability laws are sufficient to address the risks posed by AI-powered systems), see the following:

Ernst Karner, Bernhard A. Koch, Mark A. Geistfeld, ‘Comparative Law Study on Civil Liability for Artificial Intelligence’, European Commission, Directorate-General for Justice and Consumers, 2021.

Christian Twigg-Flesner, ‘Guiding Principles for Updating the Product Liability Directive for the Digital Age’ (Pilot ELI Innovation Paper), European Law Institute (January 2021).

Michael Chatzipanagiotis and George Leloudas, ‘Automated Vehicles and Third-Party Liability: A European Perspective’, University of Illinois Journal of Law, Technology & Policy 2020(1), pp. 109–199.

Christiane Wendehorst, “Strict liability for AI and other emerging technologies”, Journal of European Tort Law (JETL) 2020, 11(2): 150–180.

Tiago Sérgio Cabral, “Liability and artificial intelligence in the EU: Assessing the adequacy of the current Product Liability Directive”, Maastricht Journal of European and Comparative Law, 27(5), 615–635, (2020).

Tatjana Evas, Civil liability regime for artificial intelligence, Study, European Parliamentary Research Service (EPRS), September 2020.

Joasia Luzak, “A Broken Notion: Impact of Modern Technologies on Product Liability”, European Journal of Risk Regulation, 11(3):630–649, (2020).

Steven Shavell, "On the Redesign of Accident Liability for the World of Autonomous Vehicles", (2020) 49 The Journal of Legal Studies, 243–285.

Andrea Bertolini, Artificial intelligence and civil liability, Study requested by the European Parliament's Committee on Legal Affairs, Policy Department for Citizens' Rights and Constitutional Affairs – Directorate-General for Internal Policies, PE 621.926, July 2020.

Tambiama Madiega, 'Reform of the EU Liability Regime for Online Intermediaries: Background on the Forthcoming Digital Services Act: In Depth Analysis', European Parliamentary Research Service (EPRS), May 2020.

Martin Ebers and Susanna Navas (eds.), Algorithms and Law, Cambridge University Press, 2020.

Susanna Navas, 'Robot Machines and Civil Liability'. In M. Ebers & S. Navas (eds.), Algorithms and Law. Cambridge University Press, 2020, 157–173.

Herbert Zech: "Liability for autonomous systems: tackling specific risks of modern IT". In: Lohsse, S., Schulze, R., Staudenmeyer, D. (eds.), Liability for Artificial Intelligence and the Internet of Things. Nomos, Baden-Baden (2019), pp. 187–200.

Borghetti J-S, 'How can artificial intelligence be defective'. In: Lohsse S, Schulze R, Staudenmayer D (eds) Liability for artificial intelligence and the Internet of Things. Nomos, Baden-Baden (2019), pp. 63–76.

Gerald Spindler, 'User Liability and Strict Liability in the Internet of Things and for Robots' in Sebastian Lohsse, Reiner Schulze and Dirk Staudenmayer (eds), Liability for Artificial Intelligence and the Internet of Things. Nomos, Baden-Baden (2019), pp. 125–145.

Miquel Martín-Casals, 'Causation and Scope of Liability in the Internet of Things (IoT)' in Sebastian Lohsse/Reiner Schulze/Dirk Staudenmayer (ed), Liability for Artificial Intelligence and the Internet of Things. Nomos, Baden-Baden (2019), pp. 201–228.

Lohsse, S., Schulze, R., & Staudenmayer, D., 'Liability for Artificial Intelligence', In S. Lohsse, R. Schulze, & D. Staudenmayer (eds.), Liability for Artificial Intelligence and the Internet of Things. Nomos, Baden-Baden (2019), 99–116.

Gerhard Wagner, 'Robot Liability' in S. Lohsse/R. Schulze/D. Staudenmayer (eds), Liability for Artificial Intelligence and the Internet of Things. Nomos, Baden-Baden (2019), pp. 27–62.

Gerhard Wagner, "Robot, Inc.: Personhood for Autonomous Systems?", 88 Fordham Law Review, 591 (2019).

D. Fairgrieve and Eleonora Rajneri, 'Is Software a Product under the Product Liability Directive?', Zeitschrift für Internationales Wirtschaftsrecht, January 2019, Volume 1/2019, pp. 24–28.

Timan, T., R. Snijders, M. Kirova, S. Suardi, M. v. Lieshout, M. Chen, P. Costenco, E. Palmerini, A. Bertolini, A. Tejada, S. v. Montfort, M. Bolchi, S. Alberti, R. Brouwer, K. Karanilokova, F. Episcopo and S. Jansen (2019). Study on safety of non-embedded software. Service, data access, and legal issues of advanced robots, autonomous, connected, and AI-based vehicles and systems: final study report regarding CAD/CCAM and industrial robots. Brussel, European Commission.

Mihalis Kritikos, 'Artificial Intelligence ante portas: Legal & ethical reflections', European Parliamentary Research Service (EPRS), Scientific Foresight Unit (STOA), March 2019.

Francesco Mezzanotte, 'Liability for Digital Products', in: A De Franceschi/R Schulze (eds), Digital Revolution – New Challenges for Law, 169–188. Nomos, (2019).

Charlotte de Meeus, 'The Product Liability Directive at the Age of the Digital Industrial Revolution: Fit for Innovation?', (2019), Vol. 8, Journal of European Consumer and Market Law, Issue 4, pp. 149–154.

Francesco Paolo Patti, "The European Road to Autonomous Vehicles", 43 Fordham Int'l L.J. 125 (2019).

Maurice Schellekens, 'No-Fault Compensation Schemes for Self-Driving Vehicles', Law, Innovation and Technology, 2018, 10:2, 314–333.

Boom, Willem H van, Borghetti, Jean-Sébastien, Ehlers, Andreas Bloch, Karner, Ernst, Nolan, Donal, Oliphant, Ken, Scarso, Alessandro, Ulfbeck, Vibe and Wagner, Gerhard. "Product Liability in Europe". Product Liability: Fundamental Questions in a Comparative Perspective, edited by Helmut Koziol, Michael D. Green, Mark Lunney, Ken Oliphant and Lixin Yang, Berlin, Boston: De Gruyter, 2018, pp. 255–356.

Yavar Bathaee, "The artificial intelligence black box and the failure of intent and causation", Harvard Journal of Law & Technology, Volume 31, Number 2, 889–938, (2018).

Tatjana Evas, A common EU approach to liability rules and insurance for connected and autonomous vehicles, Study. European Added Value Assessment - Accompanying the European Parliament's legislative own-initiative report (Rapporteur: Mady Delvaux). Study, European Parliamentary Research Service (EPRS), February 2018.

Andrea Bertolini, Artificial Intelligence and civil law - Liability rules for drones, Study requested by the European Parliament's Committee on Legal Affairs, Policy Department for Citizens' Rights and Constitutional Affairs, November 2018.

Thomas Verheyen, "Full Harmonization, Consumer Protection and Products Liability: A Fresh Reading of the Case Law of the ECJ", 26 (1) European Review of Private Law, 119–140, (2018).

Leenes, R., E. Palmerini, B.-J. Koops, A. Bertolini, P. Salvini and F. Lucivero (2017). "Regulatory challenges of robotics: Some guidelines for addressing legal and ethical issues." Law Innovation and Technology 9: 1–44.

Howells, G., Twigg-Flesner, C., and Willett, C., Product Liability and Digital Products. In T-E. Synodinou, P. Jougleux, C. Markou, & T. Prastitou (eds.), EU Internet Law: Regulation and Enforcement. 2017, Springer Nature, 183–195.

Stefan Grundmann and Philipp Hacker, "Digital Technology as a Challenge to European Contract Law – From the Existing to the Future Architecture", 13 European Review of Contract Law, 255–293, 2017.

Aída Ponce del Castillo, 'A Law on Robotics and Artificial Intelligence in the EU?', (October 3, 2017). Foresight Brief, European Trade Union Institute (ETUI) Research Paper - Foresight Brief #02-September 2017.

Melinda Florina Lohmann, "Liability issues concerning self-driving vehicles", European Journal of Risk Regulation, 7(2), 335–340, (2016).

Roeland de Bruin, "Autonomous Intelligent Cars on the European Intersection of Liability and Privacy: Regulatory Challenges and the Road Ahead", European Journal of Risk Regulation, 2016, 7(3):485–501.

Nathalie Nevejans, 'European Civil Law Rules in Robotics', Study requested by the European Parliament's Committee on Legal Affairs (JURI Committee), 2016.

Susanne Beck, 'The problem of ascribing legal responsibility in the case of robotics', AI & Society, 2016, vol 31, n°4, pp. 473–481.

Mihalis Kritikos, 'Legal and ethical reflections concerning robotics', Scientific Foresight Unit (STOA) Policy Briefing, European Parliament Research Service (EPRS), PE 563.501, June 2016.

D. Fairgrieve, G. Howells, P. Møgelvang-Hansen et al., Product Liability Directive. In: P. Machnikowski (ed), European Product Liability: An Analysis of the State of the Art in the Era of New Technologies. Principles of European Tort Law. Intersentia; 2016:17–108.

Piotr Machnikowski, Conclusions, in: P Machnikowski (ed), European Product Liability: An Analysis of the State of the Art in the Era of New Technologies. Principles of European Tort Law. Intersentia; 2016:669–705.

Konstantinos Christidis and Michael Devetsikiotis, "Blockchains and Smart Contracts for the Internet of Things", (2016) IEEE Access, vol. 4, pp. 2292–2303.

Palmerini, E., A. Bertolini, F. Battaglia, B.-J. Koops, A. Carnevale and P. Salvini (2016). "RoboLaw: Towards a European framework for robotics regulation", Robotics and Autonomous Systems 86: 78–85.

Daily Wuyts, "The Product Liability Directive – More than two Decades of Defective Products in Europe" Journal of European Tort Law, vol. 5, no. 1, 2014, pp. 1–34.

Andrea Bertolini, 'Robots as Products: The Case for a Realistic Analysis of Robotic Applications and Liability Rules', Law Innovation and Technology, 2013, vol. 5, pp. 214–247.

4.2 The European Commission's 2020 White Paper on AI

4.2.1 Introduction—Ecosystem of Trust—The Legal/Regulatory Framework for AI

On 19 February 2020, the European Commission ('Commission') published for consultation its much-anticipated White Paper on Artificial Intelligence – A European Approach to Excellence and Trust ("White Paper on AI"),[13] a policy document setting out concrete measures and proposed regulation with the objective of promoting the development, uptake and use of AI applications, while also addressing the resulting fundamental rights challenges. The White Paper on AI set out ambitious objectives, it provided a clear indication that the EU is seriously considering a formal regulatory regime applicable to AI, it offered a view of the substantial changes the Commission has in mind and presented the direction in which the AI related legal framework might evolve in the near future. The White Paper on AI recognised the opportunities and benefits AI presents to individuals, to the society and Europe's digital economy.[14] At the same time, it recognised that there are disadvantages and potential risks, "such as opaque decision-making, gender-based or other kinds of discrimination, intrusion in our private lives or being used for criminal purposes".[15] It presented an approach aiming at promoting the use of AI on one hand and reducing the risks associated with the technology on the other.

The guiding principles of the White Paper on AI are the creation of ecosystems of excellence ("the Policy Framework") and of trust ("the Regulatory Framework"). In order to promote the adoption of AI while addressing risks associated with certain AI applications, the Commission proposed creating a policy framework that will mobilize resources across Europe to achieve an "ecosystem of excellence" along the entire AI value chain, and a legal/regulatory framework that will create a unique "ecosystem of trust".[16]

---

[13] Commission Communication "White Paper On Artificial Intelligence - A European approach to excellence and trust", COM(2020) 65 final, Brussels, 19.2.2020.

[14] Ibid., at p. 1: "Artificial Intelligence is developing fast. It will change our lives by improving healthcare (e.g. making diagnosis more precise, enabling better prevention of diseases), increasing the efficiency of farming, contributing to climate change mitigation and adaptation, improving the efficiency of production systems through predictive maintenance, increasing the security of Europeans, and in many other ways that we can only begin to imagine".

[15] Ibid.

[16] Ibid., at pp. 2–3: "This White Paper presents policy options to enable a trustworthy and secure development of AI in Europe, in full respect of the values and rights of EU citizens. The main building blocks of this White Paper are: i) The policy framework setting out measures to align efforts at European, national and regional level. In partnership between the private and the public sector, the aim of the framework is to mobilise resources to achieve an 'ecosystem of excellence' along the entire value chain, starting in research and innovation, and to create the right incentives to accelerate the adoption of solutions based on AI, including by small and medium-sized enterprises (SMEs). ii) The key elements of a future regulatory framework for AI in Europe that will create a unique 'ecosystem of trust'. To do so, it must ensure compliance with EU rules, including the rules protecting fundamental

4.2.2 Risks for Fundamental Rights, Safety, and Liability

The Commission recognised that AI is a powerful force for good but, at the same time, it can also cause harm, both material (safety and health of individuals, including loss of life, damage to property) and immaterial (loss of privacy, limitations to the right of freedom of expression, human dignity, discrimination for instance in access to employment).[17] According to the Commission, the main risks associated with the use of AI relate to the protection of fundamental rights (e.g. data protection, privacy, non-discrimination),[18] as well as to safety (including

rights and consumers' rights, in particular for AI systems operated in the EU that pose a high risk. Building an ecosystem of trust is a policy objective in itself, and should give citizens the confidence to take up AI applications and give companies and public organisations the legal certainty to innovate using AI. The Commission strongly supports a human-centric approach based on the Communication on Building Trust in Human-Centric AI and will also take into account the input obtained during the piloting phase of the Ethics Guidelines prepared by the High-Level Expert Group on AI".

[17] Ibid., p. 10.

According to the "Summary Report on the open public consultation on the White Paper on Artificial Intelligence" (at p. 3), the main concerns of the participants "were related to the possibility of AI breaching fundamental rights and the use of AI that may lead to discriminatory outcomes - respectively 90% and 87% of respondents find these concerns important or very important. The possibility that AI endangers safety or takes actions that cannot be explained were also considered as (very) important by respectively 82% and 78% of respondents. Concerns over AI's possible lack of accuracy (70%) and lack of compensations following harm caused by AI (68%) follow".

See also the Commission's "Final Report - Public consultation on the AI White Paper", November 2020, at p. 7.

Also, the Commission's Inception Impact Assessment, Title of the Initiative "Proposal for a legal act of the European Parliament and the Council laying down requirements for Artificial Intelligence", 23.07.2020, Ref. Ares(2020)3896535, at p. 2: "Material harm might relate to the safety and health of individuals and their property (for instance in case of accidents linked to autonomous vehicles or AI-driven robotic applications in general). Immaterial harm can relate to, for instance, loss of privacy or limitations to the right of freedom of expression (possibly caused by intrusive surveillance or monitoring systems) or unlawful discrimination (such as in the case of recruitment tools that display a bias against certain groups of the population) or discrimination in the access to products and services such as lack of accessibility for persons with disabilities, to name but a few. Harm caused by the use of AI may be the consequence of multiple causes, such as flaws in the overall design of the AI system, the use of poor quality or biased data, or machine learning related characteristics, such as the probabilistic nature of the system or the ability of certain AI systems to continue learning when in use".

[18] "The use of AI can affect the values on which the EU is founded and lead to breaches of fundamental rights, including the rights to freedom of expression, freedom of assembly, human dignity, nondiscrimination based on sex, racial or ethnic origin, religion or belief, disability, age or sexual orientation, as applicable in certain domains, protection of personal data and private life, or the right to an effective judicial remedy and a fair trial, as well as consumer protection. These risks might result from flaws in the overall design of AI systems (including as regards human oversight) or from the use of data without correcting possible bias (e.g. the system is trained using only or mainly data from men leading to suboptimal results in relation to women). AI can perform many functions that previously could only be done by humans. As a result, citizens and legal entities will increasingly be subject to actions and decisions taken by or with the assistance of AI systems, which may sometimes be difficult to understand and to effectively challenge where necessary. Moreover, AI increases the

cybersecurity, issues concerning AI in critical infrastructure and malicious use of AI) and liability-related issues.[19]

If the safety risks materialise, the specific characteristics of AI technologies create challenges in identifying potentially problematic decisions made with the assistance of AI systems. Consequently, individuals who have suffered harm may encounter

---

possibilities to track and analyse the daily habits of people. For example, there is a potential risk that AI may be used, in breach of EU data protection and other rules, by state authorities or other entities for mass surveillance and by employers to observe how their employees behave. By analysing large amounts of data and identifying links among them, AI may also be used to retrace and de-anonymise data about persons, creating new personal data protection risks even in respect to datasets that per se do not include personal data. AI is also used by online intermediaries to prioritise information for their users and to perform content moderation. The processed data, the way applications are designed and the scope for human intervention can affect the rights to free expression, personal data protection, privacy, and political freedoms. Bias and discrimination are inherent risks of any societal or economic activity. Human decision-making is not immune to mistakes and biases. However, the same bias when present in AI could have a much larger effect, affecting and discriminating many people without the social control mechanisms that govern human behaviour. This can also happen when the AI system 'learns' while in operation. In such cases, where the outcome could not have been prevented or anticipated at the design phase, the risks will not stem from a flaw in the original design of the system but rather from the practical impacts of the correlations or patterns that the system identifies in a large dataset. The specific characteristics of many AI technologies, including opacity ('black box-effect'), complexity, unpredictability and partially autonomous behaviour, may make it hard to verify compliance with, and may hamper the effective enforcement of, rules of existing EU law meant to protect fundamental rights. Enforcement authorities and affected persons might lack the means to verify how a given decision made with the involvement of AI was taken and, therefore, whether the relevant rules were respected. Individuals and legal entities may face difficulties with effective access to justice in situations where such decisions may negatively affect them". Commission Communication "White Paper On Artificial Intelligence - A European approach to excellence and trust", COM(2020) 65 final, Brussels, 19.2.2020, pp. 11–12.

[19]"AI technologies may present new safety risks for users when they are embedded in products and services. For example, as result of a flaw in the object recognition technology, an autonomous car can wrongly identify an object on the road and cause an accident involving injuries and material damage. As with the risks to fundamental rights, these risks can be caused by flaws in the design of the AI technology, be related to problems with the availability and quality of data or to other problems stemming from machine learning. While some of these risks are not limited to products and services that rely on AI, the use of AI may increase or aggravate the risks. A lack of clear safety provisions tackling these risks may, in addition to risks for the individuals concerned, create legal uncertainty for businesses that are marketing their products involving AI in the EU. Market surveillance and enforcement authorities may find themselves in a situation where they are unclear as to whether they can intervene, because they may not be empowered to act and/or don't have the appropriate technical capabilities for inspecting systems [An example may be the smart watch for children. This product may cause no direct harm to the child wearing it, but lacking a minimum level of security, it can be easily used as a tool to have access to the child. Market surveillance authorities may find it difficult to intervene in cases where the risk is not linked to the product as such]. Legal uncertainty may therefore reduce overall levels of safety and undermine the competitiveness of European companies". Commission Communication "White Paper On Artificial Intelligence - A European approach to excellence and trust", COM(2020) 65 final, Brussels, 19.2.2020, p. 12.

See also Commission's Inception Impact Assessment, Title of the Initiative "Proposal for a legal act of the European Parliament and the Council laying down requirements for Artificial Intelligence", 23.07.2020, Ref. Ares(2020)3896535, p. 2.

difficulties in seeking and obtaining compensation under the existing EU and national liability laws. As the Commission stated, in order to demonstrate the potential risks: "Under the Product Liability Directive, a manufacturer is liable for damage caused by a defective product. However, in the case of an AI based system such as autonomous cars, it may be difficult to prove that there is a defect in the product, the damage that has occurred and the causal link between the two. In addition, there is some uncertainty about how and to what extent the Product Liability Directive applies in the case of certain types of defects, for example if these result from weaknesses in the cybersecurity of the product. ... Thus, the difficulty of tracing back potentially problematic decisions taken by AI systems ... applies ... to safety and liability-related issues. Persons having suffered harm may not have effective access to the evidence that is necessary to build a case in court, for instance, and may have less effective redress possibilities compared to situations where the damage is caused by traditional technologies. These risks will increase as the use of AI becomes more widespread".[20]

4.2.3 Adjustments to Existing EU Legislative Framework Relating to AI: Issues to Be Addressed

The Commission's 2020 White Paper referred to the extensive body of existing EU product safety and liability legislation, which is potentially applicable to various emerging AI applications,[21] and provided an overview of the relevant EU legislative

[20] Commission Communication "White Paper On Artificial Intelligence - A European approach to excellence and trust", COM(2020) 65 final, Brussels, 19.2.2020, p. 13.

[21] For a detailed description and analysis of the existing EU product safety and liability legislation, see the Commission Communication "Report on the safety and liability implications of Artificial Intelligence, the Internet of Things and robotics", COM (2020) 64 final, Brussels, 19.2.2020, which accompanied the Commission's 2020 White Paper on Artificial Intelligence. The Commission's Report provided an overview of the existing rules for safety and liability, focused on key issues, and assessed the most important implications for and potential gaps in the liability and safety frameworks for AI, the IoT and robotics. See also the Report from the Expert Group on Liability and New Technologies – New Technologies Formation "Liability for Artificial Intelligence and Other Emerging Digital Technologies", 21 November 2019.

It is reminded that, in its 2018 Communication on AI in Europe (Commission Communication, "Artificial Intelligence for Europe", COM(2018) 237 final, Brussels, 25.4.2018), the Commission stated that it would issue (as a step for building trust and ensuring legal clarity in AI-based applications) by mid-2019 a report on the broader implications for, potential gaps in and orientations for, the safety and liability frameworks for AI, Internet of Things and robotics. To this end, an initial assessment on the current liability frameworks in light of AI and emerging technologies was issued in April 2018, see the Commission's Staff Working Document on "Liability for emerging digital technologies" - Accompanying the document Commission Communication "Artificial intelligence for Europe", SWD(2018) 137 final, Brussels, 25.4.2018. Furthermore, the Expert Group on Liability and New Technologies (which was set up by the Commission in March 2018) was invited to analyse crucial liability questions and the challenges brought about by AI. In

framework in relation to the protection of fundamental and consumer rights. The Commission recognised that the existing EU legislation remains in principle fully applicable despite the involvement of AI. However, it stressed that there is need to be examined whether current legislation is able to address the risks of AI and can be effectively enforced or whether adjustments to specific legal instruments are needed (or, whether new legislation is required).

The Commission concluded that the existing laws which are applicable to AI applications are not sufficient to address the risks posed by the development and deployment of AI and, therefore, specific adjustments to and clarifications of existing legislation are required in order to make the EU liability framework fit for the current and forthcoming technological and commercial developments.[22]

---

particular, the Expert Group was invited to provide the Commission with expertise on the applicability of the Product Liability Directive to traditional products, new technologies and new societal challenges ('the Product Liability Directive formation') and, in light of an assessment of the existing liability schemes, support the Commission in developing principles that can serve as guidelines for possible adaptations of applicable laws at EU and national level relating to new technologies ('the New Technologies formation'). In the "Call for Applications for the Selection of Members of the Expert Group on Liability and New Technologies" (at p. 4), the New Technologies formation was asked to assess "whether and to what extent existing liability schemes are adapted to the emerging market realities following the development of the new technologies such as Artificial Intelligence, advanced robotics, the IoT and cybersecurity issues". It was also asked to examine whether the current liability regimes are still "adequate to facilitate the uptake of the above-mentioned new technologies by fostering investment stability and users' trust". If shortcomings were identified, the New Technologies formation should make recommendations for amendments, leaving aside rules on safety and other technical standards. As a result, the New Technologies formation analysed the relevant national laws, examined specific use cases (such as autonomous cars, smart home, blockchain, autonomous healthcare applications, algorithmic decision making in the financial and other sectors, drones), and compared various aspects of existing liability regimes. The findings of the New Technologies formation were presented in the Report "Liability for Artificial Intelligence and Other Emerging Digital Technologies", issued on 21 November 2019 (Report from the Expert Group on Liability and New Technologies – New Technologies Formation "Liability for Artificial Intelligence and Other Emerging Digital Technologies", 21 November 2019).

[22]The 2020 White Paper on AI referred to the following Reports: Commission Communication "Report on the safety and liability implications of Artificial Intelligence, the Internet of Things and robotics", COM (2020) 64 final, Brussels, 19.2.2020; Report from the Expert Group on Liability and New Technologies – New Technologies Formation "Liability for Artificial Intelligence and Other Emerging Digital Technologies", 21 November 2019.

In summary, according to the Commission's 2020 White Paper on AI, the Report on the safety and liability implications of AI identified specific uncertainties as to the application of the current framework with respect to the specific risks posed by AI systems and other digital technologies and concluded the following: "the current product safety legislation already supports an extended concept of safety protecting against all kind of risks arising from the product according to its use. However, provisions explicitly covering new risks presented by the emerging digital technologies could be introduced to provide more legal certainty. • The autonomous behaviour of certain AI systems during its life cycle may entail important product changes having an impact on safety, which may require a new risk assessment. In addition, human oversight from the product design and throughout the lifecycle of the AI products and systems may be needed as a safeguard. • Explicit obligations for producers could be considered also in respect of mental safety risks of users when appropriate (ex. collaboration with humanoid robots). • Union product safety legislation could

According to the 2020 White Paper on AI, the current liability framework could be improved by adjusting or clarifying existing legislation, aiming at addressing, *inter alia*, the following issues and risks:

4.2.3.1 Effective Application and Enforcement of Existing EU and National Liability Legislation

The Commission has repeatedly stated that AI-based products and systems are characterised by various degrees of opacity (the internal complexity of the algorithms involved), resulting to a decision-making process of the AI system that can be extremely difficult to trace ('black box-effect'). It was acknowledged that, due to the autonomy aspect and the opacity issue (black-box effect) of AI systems, getting compensation could become hard for damage caused by autonomous AI-applications.[23]

Indeed, it could be difficult to trace the damage back to a specific human behaviour and, at the same time, extremely costly to understand (and get access to) the algorithm and the data used by the AI system. Finding the main cause of damage and attributing liability becomes complicated. Therefore, the allocation of liability may be unfair or inefficient, whereas liability claims may be difficult or overly costly to be made and/or to be proven. As a result, victims may not be

---

provide for specific requirements addressing the risks to safety of faulty data at the design stage as well as mechanisms to ensure that quality of data is maintained throughout the use of the AI products and systems. • The opacity of systems based on algorithms could be addressed through transparency requirements. • Existing rules may need to be adapted and clarified in the case of a stand-alone software placed as it is on the market or downloaded into a product after its placing on the market, when having an impact on safety. • Given the increasing complexity of supply chains as regards new technologies, provisions specifically requesting cooperation between the economic operators in the supply chain and the users could provide legal certainty.

The characteristics of emerging digital technologies like AI, the IoT and robotics may challenge aspects of the liability frameworks and could reduce their effectiveness. Some of these characteristics could make it hard to trace the damage back to a person, which would be necessary for a fault-based claim in accordance with most national rules. This could significantly increase the costs for victims and means that liability claims against others than producers may be difficult to make or prove. • Persons having suffered harm caused with the involvement of AI systems need to enjoy the same level of protection as persons having suffered harm caused by other technologies, whilst technological innovation should be allowed to continue to develop. • All options to ensure this objective should be carefully assessed, including possible amendments to the Product Liability Directive and possible further targeted harmonisation of national liability rules. For example, the Commission is seeking views whether and to what extent it may be needed to mitigate the consequences of complexity by adapting the burden of proof required by national liability rules for damage caused by the operation of AI applications". Commission Communication "White Paper On Artificial Intelligence - A European approach to excellence and trust", COM(2020) 65, final, Brussels, 19.2.2020, at p. 15.

[23] See, for instance, the Commission Communication "Report on the safety and liability implications of Artificial Intelligence, the Internet of Things and robotics", Brussels, COM (2020) 64 final, 19.2.2020, at p. 15.

adequately compensated.[24] The White Paper referred to the Commission's Report on the safety and liability implications of AI and stated: "The lack of transparency (opaqueness of AI) makes it difficult to identify and prove possible breaches of laws, including legal provisions that protect fundamental rights, attribute liability and meet the conditions to claim compensation. Therefore, in order to ensure an effective application and enforcement, it may be necessary to adjust or clarify existing legislation in certain areas, for example on liability as further detailed in the Report, which accompanies this White Paper".[25]

4.2.3.2 Limitations of Scope of Existing EU Legislation

The Product Liability Directive does not make any reference to the concept of service nor does it provide for the distinction between products and services. It solely provides for the definition of product, according to Article 2 of the Directive. Services do not fall into the definition of product. However, it is recognized that the distinction between products and services for the purpose of the Product Liability Directive is becoming increasingly blurred with regards to new technological developments. Therefore, the definition of product appears to no longer be as clear-cut as it may have been when the Product Liability Directive was adopted. It is also questionable whether software is covered by the legal concept of product or product component.[26]

---

[24] As the Commission stated, "the need to understand the algorithm and the data used by the AI requires analytical capacity and technical expertise that victims could find prohibitively costly. In addition, access to the algorithm and the data could be impossible without the cooperation of the potentially liable party. In practice, victims may thus not be able to make a liability claim. In addition, it would be unclear, how to demonstrate the fault of an AI acting autonomously, or what would be considered the fault of a person relying on the use of AI". Commission Communication "Report on the safety and liability implications of Artificial Intelligence, the Internet of Things and robotics", Brussels, COM (2020) 64 final, 19.2.2020, at p. 15.

See also the Report from the Expert Group on Liability and New Technologies – New Technologies Formation "Liability for Artificial Intelligence and Other Emerging Digital Technologies", 21 November 2019, at p. 24: "Generally, the victim has to prove that the defendant (or someone whose conduct is attributable to them) was at fault. The victim therefore not only needs to identify which duties of care the defendant should have discharged, but also to prove to the court that these duties were breached. Proving the defendant is at fault entails providing the court with evidence that may lead it to believe what the applicable standard of care was and that it has not been met. The second part of this is to provide evidence of how the event giving rise to the damage occurred. The more complex the circumstances leading to the victim's harm are, the harder it is to identify relevant evidence. For example, it can be difficult and costly to identify a bug in a long and complicated software code. In the case of AI, examining the process leading to a specific result (how the input data led to the output data) may be difficult, very time-consuming and expensive".

[25] Commission Communication "White Paper On Artificial Intelligence - A European approach to excellence and trust", COM(2020) 65 final, Brussels, 19.2.2020, p. 14.

[26] "Technology and industry have evolved drastically over the last decades. Especially the dividing line between products and services may no longer be as clear-cut as it was. Products and the provision of services are increasingly intertwined". See Commission Communication "Report on

The Commission has taken the view that applications and other non-embedded software (i.e. not contained in a tangible medium) could raise serious liability issues which are currently not fully addressed by the EU legal framework. AI, combined with hardware, can create new tangible products and/or deliver services. Since the distinction between products and services is becoming less relevant, there is a need to clarify what products and features are covered by the Product Liability Directive.

For instance, providing data through an IoT system could be considered a service, and thus fall, as such, outside the product liability (and safety) regime. Therefore, an interpretation of the concept of product or an enlargement of the concept of product might be needed, especially where the non-tangible element is not included in the product put into circulation by the producer but installed subsequently as a stand-alone feature. This is particularly true with regards to software; a clarification of the concept 'product' would contribute to improving effectiveness and, therefore, further assessment and clarification is needed.[27] As the White Paper put it, "an essential focus of EU product safety legislation is on the placing of products on the market.

---

the safety and liability implications of Artificial Intelligence, the Internet of Things and robotics", Brussels, COM (2020) 64 final, 19.2.2020, p. 13.

See also the Report from the Expert Group on Liability and New Technologies – New Technologies Formation "Liability for Artificial Intelligence and Other Emerging Digital Technologies", 21 November 2019, at p. 28: "The scope of the product liability regime rests on the concept of product. For the purposes of the Product Liability Directive, products are defined as movable objects, even when incorporated into another movable or immovable object, and include electricity. So far, the distinction of products and services has not encountered insurmountable difficulties. However, emerging digital technologies, especially AI systems, challenge that clear distinction and raise open questions. In AI systems, products and services permanently interact and a sharp separation between them is unfeasible. It is also questionable whether software is covered by the legal concept of product or product component. It is particularly discussed whether the answer should be different for embedded and non-embedded software, including over-the-air software updates or other data feeds. In any case, where such updates or other data feeds are provided from outside the EEA, the victim may not have anybody to turn to within the EEA, as there will typically not be an intermediary importer domiciled within the EEA in the case of direct downloads".

[27] "Software and also AI merit specific attention in respect of product liability. Software is essential to the functioning of a large number of products and may affect their safety. It is integrated into products but it may also be supplied separately to enable the use of the product as intended. Neither a computer nor a smartphone would be of particular use without software. This means that software can make a tangible product defective and lead to physical damage. This could eventually result in the liability of the producer of the product under the Product Liability Directive. However, as software comes in many types and forms, answers related to the classification of software as a service or as a product may not always be straightforward. Thus while software steering the operations of a tangible product could be considered part or component of that product, some forms of stand-alone software could be more difficult to classify". Commission Communication "Report on the safety and liability implications of Artificial Intelligence, the Internet of Things and robotics", COM (2020) 64 final, Brussels, 19.2.2020, pp. 13–14.

See also Commission Staff Working Document, Evaluation of Council Directive 85/374/EEC of 25 July 1985 on the approximation of the laws, regulations and administrative provisions of the Member States concerning liability for defective products – Accompanying the Evaluation Report – SWD(2018) 157 final, Brussels, 7.5.2018 ['Commission Staff Working Document, 'Evaluation of Product Liability Directive', SWD(2018) 157 final, Brussels, 07.05.2018'], at pp. 52, 53–54, 61.

While in EU product safety legislation software, when is part of the final product, must comply with the relevant product safety rules, it is an open question whether stand-alone software is covered by EU product safety legislation, outside some sectors with explicit rules. General EU safety legislation currently in force applies to products and not to services, and therefore in principle not to services based on AI technology either (e.g. health services, financial services, transport services)".[28]

4.2.3.3 Changing Functionality of AI Systems

The Commission has focused on those cases where the software is not included in the product put into circulation by the producer but installed subsequently as a stand-alone feature. It is argued that the EU product safety legislation does not adequately address the issue of stand-alone software and pointed out that existing rules may need to be adapted and clarified in the case of a stand-alone software placed as it is on the market or downloaded into a product after its placing on the market, when having an impact on safety.[29] In line with the analysis detailed in the Commission Report on the safety and liability implications of AI, which accompanied the White Paper, it was stressed: "the integration of software, including AI, into products can modify the functioning of such products and systems during their lifecycle. This is particularly true for systems that require frequent software updates or which rely on machine learning. These features can give rise to new risks that were not present when the system was placed on the market. These risks are not adequately addressed in the existing legislation which predominantly focuses on safety risks present at the time of placing on the market".[30]

Also: Commission Staff Working Document on "Liability for emerging digital technologies" - Accompanying the document Commission Communication "Artificial intelligence for Europe", SWD(2018) 137 final, Brussels, 25.4.2018, at pp. 9–11.

[28]Commission Communication "White Paper On Artificial Intelligence - A European approach to excellence and trust", COM(2020) 65 final, Brussels, 19.2.2020, p. 14.

[29]"While the Union product safety legislation takes into account the safety risks stemming from software integrated in a product at the time of its placing on the market and, potentially subsequent updates foreseen by the manufacturer, specific and/or explicit requirements on standalone software could be needed (e.g. an 'app' that would be downloaded). Particular considerations should be given to the stand-alone software ensuring safety functions in the AI products and systems. Additional obligations may be needed for manufacturers to ensure that they provide features to prevent the upload of software having an impact on safety during the lifetime of the AI products". Commission Communication "Report on the safety and liability implications of Artificial Intelligence, the Internet of Things and robotics", COM (2020) 64 final, Brussels, 19.2.2020, p. 11.

[30]Commission Communication "White Paper On Artificial Intelligence - A European approach to excellence and trust", COM(2020) 65 final, Brussels, 19.2.2020, p. 14.

4.2.3.4 Uncertainty as Regards the Allocation of Responsibilities Between Different Economic Operators in the Supply Chain

The Commission also raised the question of whether the concept of 'producer', as defined in the context of Product Liability Directive, fits with the type of responsibilities that may arise in systems encompassing software, AI systems, data services and other emerging technologies.[31] An assessment should take account that AI products can change during their life cycle: "in close coordination with corresponding changes in the Union safety framework, the notion of 'putting into circulation' that is currently used by the Product Liability Directive could be revisited to take into account that products may change and be altered. This could also help to clarify who is liable for any changes that are made to the product".[32] As it was stated in the Commission's

---

[31] Commission Communication "Report on the safety and liability implications of Artificial Intelligence, the Internet of Things and robotics", COM (2020) 64 final, Brussels, 19.2.2020, at p. 14: "Although the Product Liability Directive's definition of product is broad, its scope could be further clarified to better reflect the complexity of emerging technologies and ensure that compensation is always available for damage caused by products that are defective because of software or other digital features. This would better enable economic actors, such as software developers, to assess whether they could be considered producers according to the Product Liability Directive".

Furthermore, see Commission Staff Working Document, 'Evaluation of Product Liability Directive', SWD(2018) 157 final, Brussels, 07.05.2018, at pp. 52, 54, 61. For instance, it was examined whether the concept of 'producer', as defined in the context of Product Liability Directive, fits with the type of responsibilities that may arise in systems encompassing software, Artificial Intelligence systems, data services and other emerging technologies. It was concluded that, although the concept of the producer as responsible for his products is still relevant, "it is imperative to assess the impact of changing product (and/or product/service) configurations on this concept to see whether it should be clarified"; "as products are more easily, altered adapted and combined with services, the definition of the producer may become less clear particularly in the context of emerging digital technologies and the circular economy. The definition of the producer, while continuing to be valuable as it ensures strict liability, may therefore no longer be fully relevant in its current form".

See also the European Parliament Resolution of 16 February 2017 with recommendations to the Commission on Civil Law Rules on Robotics (2015/2103(INL)), (OJ C 252, 18.7.2018, pp. 239–257), which stated that the concepts of product, producer, damage or the category of exemptions as defined in the Product Liability Directive could not be apt anymore when dealing with the emerging field of robotics: "[...] in the scenario where a robot can take autonomous decisions, the traditional rules will not suffice to activate a robot's liability, since they would not make it possible to identify the party responsible for providing compensation and to require this party to make good the damage it has caused" (AF, at p. 242).

[32] Commission Communication "Report on the safety and liability implications of Artificial Intelligence, the Internet of Things and robotics", COM (2020) 64 final, Brussels, 19.2.2020, p. 15.

See also the Report from the Expert Group on Liability and New Technologies – New Technologies Formation "Liability for Artificial Intelligence and Other Emerging Digital Technologies", 21 November 2019, at pp. 28–29: "As the PLD focuses on the moment when the product was put into circulation as the key turning point for the producer's liability, this cuts off claims for anything the producer may subsequently add via some update or upgrade. In addition, the PLD does not provide for any duties to monitor the products after putting them into circulation. Highly sophisticated AI systems may not be finished products that are put on the market in a traditional way. The producer may retain some degree of control over the product's further development in the

White Paper, "in general, EU legislation on product safety allocates the responsibility to the producer of the product placed on the market, including all components e.g. AI systems. But the rules can for example become unclear if AI is added after the product is placed on the market by a party that is not the producer. In addition, EU product liability legislation provides for liability of producers and leaves national liability rules to govern liability of others in the supply chain".[33]

4.2.3.5 Changes to the Concept of Safety

According to the Commission's 2020 White Paper on AI, the main characteristics shared by the emerging digital technologies could lead to risk of harm and potentially create challenges to the existing EU product safety framework. The essential characteristics of AI-based products and systems include connectivity between an AI-system and other AI-systems and non-AI-systems, autonomy (increasingly autonomous AI-systems using, inter alia, machine-learning and deep-learning techniques), dependency on external data, vulnerability to cybersecurity breaches, complexity, and complex value chain (including a multitude of actors involved in AI systems' lifecycle). Therefore, the use of AI in services and products could create risks that EU legislation currently does not explicitly address, mainly linked to cyber threats, security risks—associated with new applications of AI such as home appliances—or risks that result from loss of connectivity. These risks could arise at the time of placing products on the market or appear as a result of software updates or self-learning when the product is being used.[34]

AI systems display certain levels of complexity due to the interdependency between different components. For instance, the IoT and AI-enabled products and services comprise tangible parts/devices (sensors, actuators, hardware), different software components and applications, data, data services (i.e. collection, processing, curating, analysing), and connectivity features: "various components, devices and products can be integrated and have influence on each other's functioning (e.g. products part of a smart home ecosystem)".[35] Therefore, risks stemming from

form of additions or updates after circulation. At the same time, the producer's control may be limited and nonexclusive if the product's operation requires data provided by third parties or collected from the environment, and depends on self-learning processes and personalising settings chosen by the user. This dilutes the traditional role of a producer, when a multitude of actors contribute to the design, functioning and use of the AI product/system. This is related to another limitation of liability – most Member States adopted the so-called development risk defence, which allows the producer to avoid liability if the state of scientific and technical knowledge at the time when he put the product into circulation was not such as to enable the existence of the defect to be discovered (Article 7 lit e PLD). The defence may become much more important practically with regard to sophisticated AI-based products".

[33]Commission Communication "White Paper On Artificial Intelligence - A European approach to excellence and trust", COM(2020) 65 final, Brussels, 19.2.2020, p. 14.

[34]ibid.

[35]Commission Communication "Report on the safety and liability implications of Artificial Intelligence, the Internet of Things and robotics", COM (2020) 64 final, Brussels, 19.2.2020, p. 9.

the complexity of the products and systems might have an impact on safety. Connectivity[36] is a central feature in an ever-growing number of products and services, and the risk of loss of connectivity of emerging digital technologies may lead to new challenges concerning both safety and security. Indeed, the connectivity feature—if combined with poor security measures at design, manufacturing or operation stage—could compromise the safety of the product and result in serious security breaches. Corrupted data (e.g. due to connectivity problems or when hacked) may affect the behaviour of the entire system or of individual components or it may render the system malfunctioning.[37] In order to address these issues, the Commission stated that provisions explicitly covering new risks presented by these emerging digital technologies could be introduced: "explicit provisions in this respect could be considered for the scope of the relevant Union pieces of legislation"[38] and that "the EU should make full use of the tools at its disposal to enhance its evidence base on potential risks linked to AI applications, including using the experience of the EU Cybersecurity Agency (ENISA) for assessing the AI threat landscape".[39]

[36] "Sensors and smart connected objects are not only designed and optimised to perform certain functions on the basis of vertical business models. They become part of a bigger connectivity network which creates new opportunities to combine more intelligence and actuation across vertical markets and to provide a whole new set of services. Technical and semantic interoperability are the key factor of success. It enables the programming of complex systems to integrate a number of device- and service-providers to deliver complete IoT solutions e.g. at home, in cities, between industries". See, for instance, the Commission Staff Working Document on "Liability for emerging digital technologies" - Accompanying the document Commission Communication "Artificial intelligence for Europe", SWD(2018) 137 final, Brussels, 25.4.2018, p. 22.

[37] For instance, if a connected fire alarm loses connectivity it may not alert the user in case of a fire. Also, cyber-attackers could have the opportunity to take control of the said system and modify its functioning or the functioning of other smart devices in the same ecosystem. As the Commission put it, connectivity "is challenging the traditional concept of safety, as connectivity may directly compromise the safety of the product and indirectly when it can be hacked leading to security threats and affecting the safety of users. . . . Industrial applications may also be exposed to cyber threats affecting the safety of persons at larger scale when such applications lack the necessary levels of security. This can be the case for example of cyber-attacks on a critical control system of an industrial plant intended to trigger an explosion that might cost lives". See Commission Communication "Report on the safety and liability implications of Artificial Intelligence, the Internet of Things and robotics", COM (2020) 64 final, Brussels, 19.2.2020, at p. 5. Some examples of safety/security risks posed by these technologies are provided by the Commission: "An example is given by an EU Rapid Alert System notification from Iceland concerning a smart watch for children. This product would not cause a direct harm to the child wearing it, but lacking a minimum level of security, it can be easily used as a tool to have access to the child. As one of the product's intended function is to keep children safe through localisation, a consumer would expect that it would not pose security threats to children that may affect their safety by potentially being tracked and/or contacted by anyone. Another example is indicated in a notification submitted by Germany regarding a passenger car. The radio in the vehicle may have certain software security gaps allowing unauthorised third-party access to the interconnected control systems in the vehicle. If these software security gaps were exploited by a third party for malicious purposes, a road accident could occur".

[38] Commission Communication "Report on the safety and liability implications of Artificial Intelligence, the Internet of Things and robotics", COM (2020) 64 final, Brussels, 19.2.2020, p. 6.

[39] Commission Communication, "White Paper On Artificial Intelligence - A European approach to excellence and trust", COM(2020) 65 final, Brussels, 19.2.2020, pp. 14–15.

4.3 European Commission's 2020 Report on the Safety and Liability Implications of AI, IoT and Robotics

4.3.1 Introduction

As already mentioned, the European Commission's 2020 Report on the safety and liability implications of AI, the IoT and robotics[40] (which accompanied the 2020 White Paper on Artificial Intelligence)[41] provided an overview of the existing rules for safety and liability, focused on key issues, and assessed the most important implications for and potential gaps in the liability and safety frameworks for AI, the IoT and robotics.

According to the Commission, in order to fully unlock the digital/data economy and achieve the goal of making Europe a world-leader in AI, IoT and robotics, a clear and predictable legal framework addressing the technological challenges is required: "a clear safety and liability framework is particularly important when new technologies like AI, the IoT and robotics emerge, both with a view to ensure consumer protection and legal certainty for businesses".[42]

To this end, the Commission's Report stated that the current safety and liability frameworks need to keep up to date with emerging trends as well as take account of and create trust in these emerging digital technological developments. Otherwise, legal uncertainty may hinder the development and uptake of AI-enabled products and services. According to the Commission, the safety and liability legal frameworks have two overall goals, namely (i) to ensure that all products and services, including those integrating emerging digital technologies, operate safely, reliably, and consistently and (ii) to ensure that damage caused by the said products is remedied efficiently. Safeguarding a high level of safety and protection for users of machinery and other people exposed to it in conjunction with providing efficient redress mechanisms for victims in case of damages helps to build user trust and acceptance of these emerging technologies. "High levels of safety for products and systems integrating new digital technologies and robust mechanisms remedying occurred damage (i.e. the liability framework) contribute to better protect consumers" and create trust in these emerging technologies, which is a prerequisite for encouraging innovation and technological uptake.[43]

---

[40]Commission Communication, "Report on the safety and liability implications of Artificial Intelligence, the Internet of Things and robotics", COM (2020) 64 final, Brussels, 19.2.2020.

[41]Commission Communication, "White Paper On Artificial Intelligence - A European approach to excellence and trust", COM(2020) 65 final, Brussels, 19.2.2020.

[42]Commission Communication "Report on the safety and liability implications of Artificial Intelligence, the Internet of Things and robotics", COM (2020) 64 final, Brussels, 19.2.2020, p. 1.

[43]Ibid. See also the Commission Report on the Application of the Product Liability Directive, COM (2018) 246 final, Brussels, 07.05.2018, at p. 1: "Product safety and liability - should there be damage - are one essential aspect in finding of a policy response that enables European societies, businesses and consumers to benefit from artificial intelligence".

The Commission's Report stressed that the current EU safety and product liability frameworks, complemented by national (non-harmonised) liability legislation, are 'robust and reliable', ensuring the well-being of European citizens, fostering investment and facilitating the uptake of the emerging digital technologies.[44] However, it was quick to note that "AI, the IoT and robotics are transforming the characteristics of many products and services" and recognised that an assessment of the current safety and liability frameworks should be carried out in light of AI and emerging technologies, i.e. that is imperative to examine whether the existing EU legal framework is adequate and suitable for emerging digital technologies and innovative products.[45]

4.3.2 Characteristics of AI, IoT and Robotics Technologies

According to the Commission's Report, AI, IoT and robotics share many characteristics. They can combine increasing level of complexity, connectivity and interdependency, variety of ecosystems, actors and value chains ("plurality of economic operators involved in the supply chain and the multiplicity of components, parts, software, systems or services, which together form the new technological ecosystems"); autonomy in decision making, self-learning and actuating (learning from experience); generation, processing of and reliance on big volumes of data (data dependency); and openness to software extensions, updates and patches after the products have been placed on the market.[46] The analysis of the Commission's Report follows the view taken by the Commission's 2018 Staff Working Document on "Liability for emerging digital technologies", which had stated that AI demonstrates the following specific characteristics: (i) complexity (with machine learning, AI can learn from other AI; also, there are numerous interdependencies in the value chain and a variety of actors;[47] (ii) autonomous behaviour (depending on the application, AI software can reason, gather knowledge, plan intelligently, learn,

[44] Commission Communication "Report on the safety and liability implications of Artificial Intelligence, the Internet of Things and robotics", COM (2020) 64 final, Brussels, 19.2.2020, p. 1.

[45] Ibid.

[46] Ibid., at p. 2: "AI, IoT and robotics share many characteristics. They can combine connectivity, autonomy and data dependency to perform tasks with little or no human control or supervision. AI equipped systems can also improve their own performance by learning from experience. Their complexity is reflected in both the plurality of economic operators involved in the supply chain and the multiplicity of components, parts, software, systems or services, which together form the new technological ecosystems. Added to this is the openness to updates and upgrades after their placement on the market".

[47] AI is used in a variety of ways and can be found across a large number of sectors, from assembly line robots to advanced toys, and from speech recognition systems to medical research. Its most common application is to find patterns in data, which is why it is commonly applied in online search engines and recommendation sites. Another common application is advanced robotics. See Commission Staff Working Document on "Liability for emerging digital technologies" - Accompanying

communicate, and manipulate objects); (iii) data driven (AI entails data gathering, data processing and data analysis);[48] (iv) openness (AI, combined with hardware, can create new tangible products and/or deliver services).[49]

Apart from the opportunities and benefits that AI, IoT and robotics can bring to the economy and our societies,[50] it is precisely their above-mentioned characteristics that could create a risk of harm: "The vast amounts of data involved, the reliance on algorithms and the opacity of AI decision-making, make it more difficult to predict

---

the document Commission Communication "Artificial intelligence for Europe", SWD(2018) 137 final, Brussels, 25.4.2018, at p. 23.

[48] AI can allow users of big data to automate and enhance complex descriptive and predictive analytical tasks that would be extremely labour intensive and time consuming, if performed by humans. Unleashing AI on big data can have a significant impact on the role data plays in deciding how we work, how we travel and how we conduct business. More and more aspects of our lives can become predictable, from travel time to customer satisfaction to how long it will take an abled bodied worker to complete a given task. Also, AI can provide this type of information ahead of time, allowing for improved planning, scheduling, and decision making, providing users with critical information at the right time to make the best opportunities when they present themselves. See Commission Staff Working Document on "Liability for emerging digital technologies" - Accompanying the document Commission Communication "Artificial intelligence for Europe", SWD (2018) 137 final, Brussels, 25.4.2018, at p. 23.

[49] Tying the use of artificial intelligence on big data to responsively designed user applications allows for improved user experience that benefits from receiving the required information based on interaction context, without swiping, pinching, scrolling or clicking. See Commission Staff Working Document on "Liability for emerging digital technologies" - Accompanying the document Commission Communication "Artificial intelligence for Europe", SWD(2018) 137 final, Brussels, 25.4.2018, at p. 23.

[50] Commission Communication "Report on the safety and liability implications of Artificial Intelligence, the Internet of Things and robotics", COM (2020) 64 final, Brussels, 19.2.2020, at pp. 2–3: "Increasing users' trust and social acceptance in emerging technologies, improving products, processes and business models and helping European manufacturers to become more efficient are only some of the opportunities created by AI, IoT and robotics. Beyond productivity and efficiency gains, AI also promises to enable humans to develop intelligence not yet reached, opening the door to new discoveries and helping to solve some of the world's biggest challenges: from treating chronic diseases, predicting disease outbreaks or reducing fatality rates in traffic accidents to fighting climate change or anticipating cybersecurity threats. These technologies can bring many benefits by improving the safety of products, making them less prone to certain risks. For instance, connected and automated vehicles could improve road safety, as most road accidents are currently caused by human errors. Moreover, IoT systems are designed to receive and process vast amounts of data from different sources. This increased level of information might be used so that products can self-adapt and consequently become safer. New technologies can contribute to better effectiveness of product recalls as for example products could warn the users to avoid a safety problem. If a safety issue arises during the use of a connected product, producers can directly communicate with users, on the one hand to warn the users about the risks and on the other hand, if possible, to directly fix the problem by providing, for example, a safety update. For instance, during the recall of one of its devices in 2017, a smartphone producer carried out a software update to reduce to zero the battery capacity of the recalled phones so that users would stop using the dangerous devices. Furthermore, new technologies can contribute to improve the traceability of products. For instance, IoT connectivity features can enable businesses and market surveillance authorities to track dangerous products and identify risks across supply chains".

the behaviour of an AI-enabled product and to understand the potential causes of a damage. ... connectivity and openness can also expose AI and IoT products to cyber-threats".[51] According to the Commission, the risks and harm brought by the digital emerging technologies will inevitably increase as the field of applications expands and, therefore, it is imperative to examine whether and to what extent the current legal frameworks on safety and liability are still adequate to protect users.[52]

4.3.3 The EU Product Safety Framework

4.3.3.1 Overview

According to the Commission's Communication "Building Trust in Human-Centric Artificial Intelligence", "AI systems should integrate safety and security-by-design mechanisms to ensure that they are verifiably safe at every step, taking at heart the physical and mental safety of all concerned".[53] In line with this statement, the Commission's Report provides an overview of the EU product safety legislation, presents the main challenges that can be brought by the digital emerging technologies to the EU product safety framework, and assesses whether the existing EU framework can ensure that AI systems integrate safety and security-by-design, fostering both innovation and users' trust.

The EU product safety framework aims to ensure that products placed on the European market meet high health, safety and environmental requirements and that such products can circulate freely throughout the internal market of the Union. In particular, the current EU product safety legislation includes the following main legal instruments: (i) the General Product Safety Directive,[54] which aims to ensure that only safe consumer products are placed on the market; (ii) the Machinery Directive,[55] which ensures a high level of safety and protection for users of machinery and other people exposed to it and secures the free movement of machinery in the internal market. The Machinery Directive also sets general health and safety requirements for products, leaving it to manufacturers to decide which are the technical solutions that should be deployed to meet the required high safety level; (iii) the

---

[51] Ibid., p. 2.

[52] Ibid., p. 3.

[53] Commission Communication "Building Trust in Human-Centric Artificial Intelligence", COM (2019) 168 final, Brussels, 8.4.2019, p. 5.

[54] Directive 2001/95/EC of the European Parliament and the Council of 3 December 2001 on general product safety (The General Product Safety Directive), (OJ L 11, 15.1.2002, pp. 4–17).

[55] Directive 2006/42/EC of the European Parliament and of the Council of 17 May 2006 on machinery, and amending Directive 95/16/EC (OJ L 157, 9.6.2006, pp. 24–86) (the Machinery Directive).

so-called New Legislative Framework;[56] (iv) the Radio Equipment Directive (RED),[57] which applies to all products, including embedded software, using the radio frequency spectrum; (v) specific safety rules such as those for medical devices or toys, i.e. the Regulation on Medical Devices,[58] the Medical Devices Directives,[59] the Toys Safety Directive,[60] and the Directive on measuring

---

[56]In order to improve the internal market for goods and strengthen the conditions for placing a wide range of products on the EU market, the "new legislative framework" was adopted in 2008. It is a package of measures that aim to improve market surveillance and boost the quality of conformity assessments. It also clarifies the use of CE marking and creates a toolbox of measures for use in product legislation. The new legislative framework consists of: i) Regulation (EC) 765/2008 setting out the requirements for accreditation and the market surveillance of products; ii) Decision 768/2008 on a common framework for the marketing of products, which includes reference provisions to be incorporated whenever product legislation is revised. In effect, it is a template for future product harmonisation legislation; iii) Regulation (EU) 2019/1020 on market surveillance and compliance of products.

The new legislative framework reinforces the application and enforcement of internal market legislation. It: • improves market surveillance rules to better protect both consumers and professionals from unsafe products, including those imported from outside the EU. In particular, this applies to procedures for products which can pose danger to health or the environment; • sets clear and transparent rules for the accreditation of conformity assessment bodies; • boosts the quality of and confidence in the conformity assessment of products through stronger and clearer rules on the requirements for the notification of conformity assessment bodies; • clarifies the meaning of CE marking and enhances its credibility; • establishes a common legal framework for industrial products in the form of a toolbox of measures for use in future legislation. This includes definitions of terms commonly used in product legislation, and procedures to allow future sectorial legislation to become more consistent and easier to implement.

[57]Directive 2014/53/EU of the European Parliament and of the Council of 16 April 2014 on the harmonisation of the laws of the Member States relating to the making available on the market of radio equipment and repealing Directive 1999/5/EC (OJ L 153, 22.5.2014, pp. 62–106). The Radio Equipment Directive (RED) establishes a regulatory framework for placing radio equipment on the market. It ensures a single market for radio equipment by setting essential requirements for safety and health, electromagnetic compatibility, and the efficient use of the radio spectrum. It also provides the basis for further regulation governing some additional aspects. These include technical features for the protection of privacy, personal data and against fraud. Furthermore, additional aspects cover interoperability, access to emergency services, and compliance regarding the combination of radio equipment and software.

[58]Regulation (EU) 2017/745 of the European Parliament and of the Council of 5 April 2017 on medical devices, amending Directive 2001/83/EC, Regulation (EC) No 178/2002 and Regulation (EC) No 1223/2009 and repealing Council Directives 90/385/EEC and 93/42/EEC, OJ L 117, 5.5.2017, pp. 1–175.

[59]See for instance: Council Directive 90/385/EEC on Active Implantable Medical Devices (AIMDD); the Council Directive 93/42/EEC on Medical Devices (MDD) [both Directives were repealed by Regulation (EU) 2017/745]; Council Directive 98/79/EC on In Vitro Diagnostic Medical Devices (IVDMD); Council Directive 89/391/EEC on the introduction of measures to encourage improvements in the safety and health of workers at work.

[60]Directive 2009/48/EC of the European Parliament and of the Council of 18 June 2009 on the safety of toys (The Toys Safety Directive), OJ L 170, 30.6.2009, pp. 1–37.

instruments;[61] (vi) the Cybersecurity Act,[62] which sets up voluntary cybersecurity certification framework for information and communications technology (ICT) products, services and processes; (vii) safety rules are complemented with market surveillance and the powers conferred to national authorities under the Market Surveillance Regulation[63] and the General Product Safety Directive; (viii) the vehicle-type approval legislation, where additional rules apply for placing a motor vehicle,[64] an aircraft or a ship in service. These rules govern safety during operation, including tasks for operators as well surveillance tasks for authorities; (ix) European standardisation is also an essential element of the EU product safety legislation. A solid body of standards and essential safety requirements in the area of AI-enabled devices has been developed and is continuously being adapted in line with technological progress. Given the global nature of digitisation and emerging digital technologies, consumers and businesses will benefit from the development of such safety and interoperability standards, especially when those standards are supported by international standardisation organisations.[65]

[61] Directive 2014/32/EU of the European Parliament and of the Council of 26 February 2014 on the harmonisation of the laws of the Member States relating to the making available on the market of measuring instruments, OJ L 96, 29.3.2014, pp. 149–250.

[62] Regulation (EU) 2019/881 of the European Parliament and of the Council of 17 April 2019 on ENISA (the European Union Agency for Cybersecurity) and on information and communications technology cybersecurity certification and repealing Regulation (EU) No 526/2013 (the Cybersecurity Act), OJ L 151, 7.6.2019, pp. 15–69.

Certification plays a critical role in increasing trust and security in products and services that are crucial for the Digital Single Market. Without a common framework for EU-wide valid cybersecurity certificates, there is an increasing risk of fragmentation and barriers in the European Single Market. This is why the Cybersecurity Act established an EU certification framework for ICT digital products, services and processes. The EU cybersecurity certification framework enables the creation of tailored and risk-based EU certification schemes.

[63] Regulation (EU) 2019/1020 of the European Parliament and of the Council of 20 June 2019 on market surveillance and compliance of products and amending Directive 2004/42/EC and Regulations (EC) No 765/2008 and (EU) No 305/2011 (OJ L 169, 25.6.2019, pp. 1–44). Regulation (EC) No 765/2008 of the European Parliament and of the Council of 9 July 2008 setting out the requirements for accreditation and market surveillance relating to the marketing of products and repealing Regulation (EEC) No 339/93, OJ L 218, 13.8.2008, pp. 30–47.

[64] Regulation (EU) 2018/858 of the European Parliament and of the Council of 30 May 2018 on the approval of motor vehicles and their trailers, and of systems, components and separate technical units intended for such vehicles, amending Regulations (EC) No 715/2007 and (EC) No 595/2009 and repealing Directive 2007/46/EC (OJ L 151, 14.6.2018, pp. 1–218). This Regulation (with effect from 1 September 2020) repealed and replaced Directive 2007/46/EC—approval of motor vehicles and their trailers, and of systems, components and separate technical units intended for such vehicles.

[65] Commission Communication "Report on the safety and liability implications of Artificial Intelligence, the Internet of Things and robotics", COM (2020) 64 final, Brussels, 19.2.2020, p. 4.

See also the Commission Staff Working Document on "Liability for emerging digital technologies" - Accompanying the document Commission Communication "Artificial intelligence for Europe", SWD(2018) 137 final, Brussels, 25.4.2018, at p. 5: "The production of European harmonised standards for IoT, AI-powered advanced robots and autonomous systems is ongoing. European Standardization Organisations draw up these standards in order to offer a level playing

According to the Commission's Report, a significant part of the EU's product safety framework was drafted prior to the emergence of digital technologies such as AI, the IoT or robotics and, therefore, it does not always explicitly address aspects relating to these technologies.[66] The products that could be found in the market when this legislation was adopted may not presented the same technical complexity or characteristics as they do today. However, it was stressed that the existing product safety framework is technology neutral and, therefore, it could still cover the products incorporating these technologies. Indeed, AI systems, IoT devices and any other items containing intangible elements or presenting connectivity features—as far as they constitute 'movable' items—qualify as 'products' and, therefore, defects in these products are covered by the Product Liability Directive. Moreover, other legislative acts, such as in the medical devices or cars sectors, have already taken account of new technological developments and explicitly dealt with aspects of emerging digital technologies, e.g. automated decisions, software as a separate product and connectivity.[67]

4.3.3.2 The Challenges Brought by the Digital Emerging Technologies to the EU Product Safety Framework

As already mentioned, the main characteristics shared by the emerging digital technologies could lead to risk of harm and potentially create challenges to the existing EU product safety framework. The essential characteristics of AI-based products and systems (and the challenges brought by them) can be summarized as follows: connectivity between an AI-system and other AI-systems and non-AI-systems, autonomy (increasingly autonomous AI-systems using, inter alia, machine-learning and deep-learning techniques), dependency on external data, vulnerability to cybersecurity breaches, opacity ("black box" element), complexity, and complex value chain (including a multitude of actors involved in AI systems' lifecycle).

---

field and a competitive advantage to European manufacturers. These standards would offer presumption of conformity with the European safety legislation, under which they are developed, in particular under the Machinery Directive 2006/42/EC and the Radio Equipment Directive 2014/53/EU. The European Standardization Organizations are also working on standards for "combined" products, i.e. where several pieces of EU safety legislation apply".

[66] Commission Communication "Report on the safety and liability implications of Artificial Intelligence, the Internet of Things and robotics", COM (2020) 64 final, Brussels, 19.2.2020, p. 4.

[67] Ibid.

4.3.3.2.1 Connectivity

There is increasing connectivity[68] between an AI-system and other AI-systems and non-AI-systems. Connectivity is a central feature in an ever-growing number of products and services, which, however, could lead to additional new challenges concerning both safety and security. The risk of loss of connectivity of emerging digital technologies may entail risks related to safety and security. Indeed, the connectivity feature—if combined with poor security measures at design, manufacturing or operation stage—could compromise the safety of the product and result in serious security breaches. Corrupted data (e.g. due to connectivity problems or when hacked) may affect the behaviour of the entire system or of individual components or it may render the system malfunctioning. For instance, if a connected fire alarm loses connectivity, it may not alert the user in case of a fire. Also, cyber-attackers could have the opportunity to take control of the said system and modify its functioning or the functioning of other smart devices in the same ecosystem. As the Commission put it, connectivity "is challenging the traditional concept of safety, as connectivity may directly compromise the safety of the product and indirectly when it can be hacked leading to security threats and affecting the safety of users. ... Industrial applications may also be exposed to cyber threats affecting the safety of persons at larger scale when such applications lack the necessary levels of security. This can be the case for example of cyber-attacks on a critical control system of an industrial plant intended to trigger an explosion that might cost lives".[69]

---

[68] "Sensors and smart connected objects are not only designed and optimised to perform certain functions on the basis of vertical business models. They become part of a bigger connectivity network which creates new opportunities to combine more intelligence and actuation across vertical markets and to provide a whole new set of services. Technical and semantic interoperability are the key factor of success. It enables the programming of complex systems to integrate a number of device- and service-providers to deliver complete IoT solutions e.g. at home, in cities, between industries". See the Commission Staff Working Document on "Liability for emerging digital technologies" - Accompanying the document Commission Communication "Artificial intelligence for Europe", SWD(2018) 137 final, Brussels, 25.4.2018, at p. 22.

[69] Commission Communication "Report on the safety and liability implications of Artificial Intelligence, the Internet of Things and robotics", COM (2020) 64 final, Brussels, 19.2.2020, at p. 5. Examples of safety/security risks posed by these technologies are provided by the Commission: "An example is given by an EU Rapid Alert System notification from Iceland concerning a smart watch for children. This product would not cause a direct harm to the child wearing it, but lacking a minimum level of security, it can be easily used as a tool to have access to the child. As one of the product's intended function is to keep children safe through localisation, a consumer would expect that it would not pose security threats to children that may affect their safety by potentially being tracked and/or contacted by anyone. Another example is indicated in a notification submitted by Germany regarding a passenger car. The radio in the vehicle may have certain software security gaps allowing unauthorised third party access to the interconnected control systems in the vehicle. If these software security gaps were exploited by a third party for malicious purposes, a road accident could occur".

The Commission states that, although provisions related to security aspects could be found in various legal instruments (such as in the Regulation on Medical Devices, the Directive on measuring instruments, the Radio Equipment Directive, the vehicle-type approval legislation, and the Cybersecurity Act), EU product safety legislation does not generally provide for specific mandatory essential requirements against cyber-threats affecting the safety of users.[70] It then goes to stress that the existing product safety legislation already supports an extended concept of safety protecting against all kind of risks arising from the product according to its use. In other words, the concept of product safety includes protection against all kinds of risks arising from the product, including not only mechanical, chemical, electrical risks but also cyber risks and risks related to the loss of connectivity of devices.[71]

Therefore, the use of AI in services and products could create risks that EU legislation currently does not explicitly address. These risks are mainly linked to cyber threats, security risks—associated with new applications of AI such as home appliances—or risks that result from loss of connectivity. To address these issues, and in order to increase legal certainty and user protection, the Commission stated that provisions explicitly covering new risks presented by these emerging digital technologies could be introduced: "explicit provisions in this respect could be considered for the scope of the relevant Union pieces of legislation".[72]

4.3.3.2.2 Autonomy

The emerging digital technologies are increasingly acquiring the feature of autonomy[73] through sensors and/or by exchanging data with their environment. These AI and IoT-enabled devices will have the ability (without human intervention) to trade and analyse data, to adapt their behaviours and actions to their environment, and to learn through experience and interaction (self-learning). The built-in autonomy and self-learning ability are characteristics of "advanced" robots and AI-enabled products and their degree depends on how sophisticated a system's interaction with its environment has been designed to be.

However, the capacity of those technologies to acquire autonomy, to learn through their own variable experience and interaction and to adapt their behaviour and actions to the environment could raise critical questions regarding safety. Indeed, on the one hand it was stated that, as far as the behaviour of AI products can be determined in advance by the risk assessment carried out by the manufacturer

---

[70] Commission Communication "Report on the safety and liability implications of Artificial Intelligence, the Internet of Things and robotics", COM (2020) 64 final, Brussels, 19.2.2020, p. 6.

[71] Ibid.

[72] Ibid.

[73] Ibid. However, the Commission notes that "while AI based products can act autonomously by perceiving their environment and without following a set of pre-determined set of instructions, their behaviour is constrained by the goal they are given and other relevant design choices made by their developers".

before the products in question are placed on the market, the existing EU product safety framework already sets several obligations for producers to take into account in the risk assessment the "use" of the products throughout their lifetime.[74] It is reminded that producers are obliged to make the required risk assessment based on the intended use of the product, the foreseeable use and/or the reasonably foreseeable misuse. In addition, the existing EU product safety framework stipulates that manufacturers must provide for instructions and safety information for users or warnings.[75] On the other hand, however, it was acknowledged that the autonomous behaviour of an AI system during its life cycle may entail important product changes having an impact on safety, which could require a new risk assessment. Indeed, there could be cases where the future behaviour of AI products cannot be determined in advance by the initial risk assessment carried out by the manufacturer before the said products are placed on the market: "in these cases, insofar as the intended use, initially foreseen by the manufacturer, is modified due to the autonomous behaviour and the compliance with the safety requirements is affected, it could be considered to require a new re-assessment of the self-learning product".[76] Since an AI powered system can, and actually is supposed to, act autonomously and without any human supervision, a damage might occur even if both the use and maintenance of the system were impeccable. This unpredictability in behaviour and the autonomy aspect of those applications and systems inevitably raises serious safety concerns. As a result, provisions of the current framework (for instance, if producers become aware that a product, throughout its lifecycle, poses risks having an impact on safety, they are required to immediately inform the competent authorities and take actions to prevent the risks for users)[77] are not considered to be sufficient to tackle the

---

[74] Ibid.

[75] See, for instance, Decision No 768/2008/EC of the European Parliament and of the Council of 9 July 2008 on a common framework for the marketing of products, and repealing Council Decision 93/465/EEC, OJ L 218, 13.8.2008, pp. 82–128. Annex I, Article R2.7 reads: "Manufacturers shall ensure that the product is accompanied by instructions and safety information in a language which can be easily understood by consumers and other end-users, as determined by the Member State concerned". In addition, the Radio Equipment Directive (RED) [Directive 2014/53/EU of the European Parliament and of the Council of 16 April 2014 on the harmonisation of the laws of the Member States relating to the making available on the market of radio equipment and repealing Directive 1999/5/EC (OJ L 153, 22.5.2014, pp. 62–106)] establishes a regulatory framework for placing radio equipment on the market. It ensures a single market for radio equipment by setting essential requirements for safety and health, electromagnetic compatibility, and the efficient use of the radio spectrum. It requires the manufacturer to include instructions with information about how to use the radio equipment in accordance with its intended use. For instance, Article 10 (8) of the Radio Equipment Directive refers to the instructions for the end user and Annex VI refers to the EU Declaration of Conformity.

[76] Commission Communication "Report on the safety and liability implications of Artificial Intelligence, the Internet of Things and robotics", COM (2020) 64 final, Brussels, 19.2.2020, p. 7.

[77] See, for instance, Article 5 of Directive 2001/95/EC of the European Parliament and of the Council of 3 December 2001 on general product safety (the General Product Safety Directive), (OJ L 11, 15.1.2002, pp. 4–17).

"unpredictability in behaviour" and the "autonomy aspect" issues. Therefore, an additional (updated) risk assessment is considered to be indispensable, especially when the AI system is, during its life cycle, subject to important changes (not possibly foreseen by the manufacturer) which could have an impact on safety. As the Commission stated, "besides the risk assessment performed before placing a product on the market, a new risk assessment procedure could be put in place where the product is subject to important changes during its lifetime, e.g. different product function, not foreseen by the manufacturer in the initial risk assessment. This should focus on the safety impact caused by the autonomous behaviour throughout the product lifetime. The risk assessment should be performed by the appropriate economic operator. In addition, the relevant Union pieces of legislation could include reinforced requirements for manufacturers on instructions and warnings for users".[78]

Furthermore, the Commission pointed out that AI applications and systems can generate autonomous decision-making and autonomous behaviour in the physical environment in which they operate including physical contact with humans and their property. This self-learning ability of the AI systems "may enable the machine to take decisions that deviate from what was initially intended by the producers and consequently what is expected by the users"[79] and thus it inevitably carries an inherent risk of causing damage to a third party's physical integrity or property. It also raised questions about human control, so that humans should always have the option to choose when and how to delegate decisions and actions to AI products and systems, to accomplish human-chosen objectives. It acknowledged that the existing EU product safety legislation does not explicitly address the human oversight in the context of AI self-learning systems and, therefore, it stated that human oversight from the product design and throughout the lifecycle of the AI products and systems may be needed as a safeguard: "the relevant Union pieces of legislation may foresee specific requirements for human oversight, as a safeguard, from the product design and throughout the lifecycle of the AI products and systems".[80]

[78] Commission Communication "Report on the safety and liability implications of Artificial Intelligence, the Internet of Things and robotics", COM (2020) 64 final, Brussels, 19.2.2020, p. 7. The Commission stresses that similar risk assessments are already used and required in transport legislation where, if a railway vehicle is modified after its certification, clear criteria determine whether the relevant authority needs to be involved or not. In particular, in case of any change to the railway system that may have an impact on safety (e.g. technical, operational change or also organisational change which could impact the operational or maintenance process), the process to follow is described in Annex I to COM Implementing regulation (EU) 2015/1136 (OJ L 185, 14.7.2015, p. 6). In case of 'significant change' a safety assessment report should be provided to the proposer of the change by an independent 'assessment body' (could be the national safety authority or another technically competent). Following the risk analysis process, the proposer of the change should apply the appropriate measures to mitigate risks.

[79] Commission Communication "Report on the safety and liability implications of Artificial Intelligence, the Internet of Things and robotics", COM (2020) 64 final, Brussels, 19.2.2020, p. 7.

[80] Ibid., pp. 7–8.

In addition, the Commission reminded that AI products and systems could affect people's both physical and mental wellbeing. The effects of these systems must therefore be carefully monitored and addressed. To this end, the Commission underlined the importance of tackling the mental health risks for users deriving from the collaboration with humanoid AI robots and systems.[81] Indeed, if the mental

[81] Ibid., p. 8. See also the World Health Organization (WHO) Constitution, first bullet point: "Health is a state of complete physical, mental and social well-being and not merely the absence of disease or infirmity." (https://www.who.int/about/who-we-are/constitution)

With regard to issues of mental health that could derive from human-robot interaction and the fact that robot technology might have long-term harmful impacts on the human psyche, see: "Oh, Dignity too?" Said the Robot: Human Dignity as the Basis for the Governance of Robotics, Lexo Zardiashvili and Eduard Fosch-Villaronga, Minds and Machines, 2020, Springer, pp. 30:121–143; "Social Robots: Technological, Societal and Ethical Aspects of Human-Robot Interaction", pp. 237–264, Research, Neziha// Akalin, Annica Kristoffersson and Amy Loutfi, July 2019; Bicchi, A., Peshkin, M. A., & Colgate, J. E. (2008), "Safety for physical human–robot interaction", in B. Siciliano & O. Khatib (Eds.), Springer Handbook of Robotics (pp. 1335–1348), Springer, Berlin, Heidelberg; Birnbaum, G. E., Mizrahi, M., Hoffman, G., Reis, H. T., Finkel, E. J., & Sass, O. (2016), "What robots can teach us about intimacy: The reassuring effects of robot responsiveness to human disclosure". Computers in Human Behavior, 63, 416–423; Boholm, M., Möller, N., & Hansson, S. O. (2016), "The concepts of risk, safety, and security: applications in everyday language", Risk Analysis, 36(2), 320–338; Boström, M., Ernsth Bravell, M., Björklund, A., & Sandberg, J. (2016), "How older people perceive and experience sense of security when moving into and living in a nursing home: a case study", European Journal of Social Work, 20(5), 1–14; Charalambous, G., Fletcher, S., & Webb, P. (2016), "The development of a scale to evaluate trust in industrial human-robot collaboration", International Journal of Social Robotics, 8(2), 193–209; Fischinger, D., Einramhof, P., Papoutsakis, K., Wohlkinger, W., Mayer, P., Panek, P., Hofmann, S., Koertner, T., Weiss, A., Argyros, A., & Vincze, M. (2016), "Hobbit, a care robot supporting independent living at home: First prototype and lessons learned", Robotics and Autonomous Systems, 75(A), 60–78; Pandey, K. A. & Gelin, R. (2018), "A mass-produced sociable humanoid robot: Pepper: The first machine of its kind", IEEE Robotics & Automation Magazine, 25(3), 40–48; Salem, M., Lakatos, G., Amirabdollahian, F., & Dautenhahn, K. (2015), "Towards safe and trustworthy social robots: Ethical challenges and practical issues", in ICSR, (pp. 584–593); Vandemeulebroucke, T., de Casterle, B. D., & Gastmans, C. (2018), "How do older adults experience and perceive socially assistive robots in aged care: a systematic review of qualitative evidence", Aging & Mental Health, 22(2), 149–167.

Also, in relation to considerations of ethics, regulation of robotics and human dignity, see: E. Hilgendorf, Problem Areas in the Dignity Debate and the Ensemble Theory of Human Dignity, in: D. Grimm, A. Kemmerer, C. Möllers (eds.), Human Dignity in Context. Explorations of a Contested Concept, 2018, pp. 325 ff; E. Fosch-Villaronga & J. Albo-Canals, "'I'll take care of you', said the robot", Paladyn, Journal of Behavioral Robotics, 2019, 10(1), pp. 77–93; E. Fosch-Villaronga & A. Golia, "Robots, standards and the law: Rivalries between private standards and public policymaking for robot governance", 2019, Computer Law & Security Review, 35(2), pp. 129–144; E. Fosch-Villaronga & M. Heldeweg, "'Regulation, I presume?" said the robot—Towards an iterative regulatory process for robot governance", 2018, Computer law & security review, 34(6), pp. 1258–1277; D. Schroeder & A. H. Bani-Sadr, Dignity in the 21st century: Middle east and west, 2017, Berlin, Springer International Publishing; M. Guihot, A. F. Matthew, & N. P. Suzor, "Nudging robots: Innovative solutions to regulate artificial intelligence", 2017, Vanderbilt Journal of Entertainment & Technology Law, 20, 385; A. Sharkey, Robots and human dignity: A consideration of the effects of robot care on the dignity of older people, 2014, Ethics and Information Technology, 16(1), pp. 63–75; L. Floridi, "Soft Ethics and the Governance of the

health risks are not addressed, the violation of human dignity and long-term harmful impact on the human psyche seem inevitable. This is why the Commission had already identified that "AI systems should integrate safety and security-by-design mechanisms to ensure that they are verifiably safe at every step, taking at heart the physical and mental safety of all concerned".[82] Although the Commission pointed out that the definition of health should include both physical and mental wellbeing, it stressed that explicit obligations for producers should be considered in respect of mental safety risks of users when appropriate: "mental health risks should be explicitly covered within the concept of product safety in the legislative framework";[83] "explicit obligations for producers of, among others, AI humanoid robots to explicitly consider the immaterial harm their products could cause to users, in particular vulnerable users such as elderly persons in care environments, could be considered for the scope of relevant EU legislation".[84]

Digital, Philosophy & Technology", March 2018, Volume 31, Issue 1, pp. 1–8; L. Floridi, "On human dignity as a foundation for the right to privacy", Philosophy & Technology, 2016, 29(4), pp. 307–312; L. Floridi, The fourth revolution. How the infosphere is reshaping human reality, 2014, Oxford, Oxford University Press; F. Grodzinsky, K. W. Miller and M.J. Wolf, "The ethics of designing artificial agents", Ethics and Information Technology, 2008, 10 (2–3), pp. 115–121; M. Kritikos, "Legal and ethical reflections concerning robotics", STOA Policy Briefing, June 2016 – PE 563.501, Brussels, European Parliament Research Service; A. Fiske, P. Henningsen, and A. Buyx, "Your robot therapist will see you now: Ethical implications of embodied artificial intelligence in psychiatry, psychology, and psychotherapy", Journal of medical Internet research, 2019, 21(5), e13216; C. Cath, Governing artificial intelligence: ethical, legal and technical opportunities and challenges, 2018, Philosophical Transactions Royal Society A, 376, 2133; K. Dautenhahn, B. Ogden and T. Quick, From embodied to socially embedded agents—implications for interaction-aware robots. Cognitive Systems Research, 3(3), 397–428, 2002; E. Di Nucci (2017). Sexual rights, disability, and sex robots. In J. Danaher & N. McArthur (Eds.), Robot sex: Social and ethical implications (pp. 73–88). Cambridge: MIT Press; C. O'Mahony, "There is no such thing as a right to dignity", 2012, International Journal of Constitutional Law, 10(2), pp. 551–574; T. Tzimas, Legal and Ethical Challenges of Artificial Intelligence from an International Law Perspective; Springer: Cham, Switzerland, 2021; pp. 9–32; A. F. Winfield and M. Jirotka, "Ethical governance is essential to building trust in robotics and artificial intelligence systems". Philosophical Transactions of the Royal Society A: Mathematical, Physical and Engineering Sciences, 2018, 376(2133), 20180085.

[82]Commission Communication, "Building Trust in Human-Centric Artificial Intelligence", COM (2019) 168 final, Brussels, 8.4.2019, p. 5.

[83]Commission Communication "Report on the safety and liability implications of Artificial Intelligence, the Internet of Things and robotics", COM (2020) 64 final, Brussels, 19.2.2020, p. 8.

[84]ibid. According to the Commission, "the autonomy should not cause excessive stress and discomfort for extended periods and harm mental health. In this regard, the factors that positively affect the sense of safety for older people are considered to be: having secure relationships with health care service staff, having control over daily routines, and being informed about them. Producers of robots interacting with older people should take these factors into consideration to prevent mental health risks".

4.3.3.2.3 Data Dependency

The Commission's Report stated that reliance on big volumes of data (data dependency) is an essential characteristic of AI-based products and systems and, therefore, data accuracy and relevance is vital to ensure that AI based systems take the decisions as intended by the producer.[85] Indeed, in order to prevent critical and damaging consequences, the decisions of AI systems should be accurate, and the data used to develop the AI system in question should be up-to-date, of high quality, complete and to reflect the environment the system is going to be deployed in. Accuracy is related to an AI system's ability to make correct judgements, for example to correctly classify information into the proper categories, or its ability to make correct decisions and predictions.

The Commission pointed out that the current EU product safety legislation, although it supports an extended concept of safety protecting against all kind of risks arising from the product according to its use, it does not explicitly address the risks to safety derived from faulty data: "according to the 'use' of the product, producers should anticipate during the design and testing phases the data accuracy and its relevance for safety functions".[86] Therefore, provisions explicitly covering these new risks could be introduced to provide more legal certainty. To this end, the Commission's Report stated that the EU product safety legislation should provide for specific requirements addressing the risks to safety of faulty data at the design stage as well as mechanisms to ensure that quality of data is maintained throughout the use of the AI products and systems.[87]

4.3.3.2.4 Opacity

The Commission's Report stressed that opacity[88] is another main characteristic of some of the AI based products and systems. In particular, it underlined that AI-based products and systems can be characterised by various degrees of opacity (the internal

---

[85] Ibid.

[86] Ibid. The Commission's Report provided the following examples. An AI-based system designed to detect specific objects may face difficulties recognising items, especially under poor lighting conditions. To address this challenge, designers should include data coming from product tests in both typical and poorly lit environments. Another example relates to agricultural robots such as fruit-picking robots aimed at detecting and locating ripe fruits on trees or on the ground. While the algorithms involved already show success rates for classification of over 90%, a shortcoming in the datasets fuelling those algorithms could lead those robots to take a poor decision and, as a consequence, injure an animal or a person (at pp. 8–9).

[87] Ibid., p. 9.

[88] "Opacity: The more complex emerging digital technologies become, the less those taking advantage of their functions or being exposed to them can comprehend the processes that may have caused harm to themselves or to others. Algorithms often no longer come as more or less easily readable code, but as a black-box that has evolved through self-learning and which we may be able to test as to its effects, but not so much to understand". See Report from the Expert Group on

complexity of the algorithms involved), leading to a decision-making process of the system which can be extremely difficult to trace ('black box-effect').[89] Due to the number and complexity of stages involved in these deep learning systems, it is almost impossible to provide an explanation as to why an AI system has produced a particular output or decision; even the developers of these systems cannot always be certain about the factors that led a system to decide one thing over another.

The Commission acknowledged that humans may not need to understand every single step of this decision-making process but, as AI algorithms grow more advanced, it highlighted the importance of making AI understandable to developers, users and regulators ("it is decisive that humans can be able to understand how the algorithmic decisions of the system have been reached").[90] When the decision-making processes and the actual decisions made by an AI system are transparent, they can be understood and thus traced and contested by humans, facilitating the work of ex-post enforcement mechanisms (i.e. allowing the enforcement authorities to trace the responsibility of AI systems behaviours and choices).[91]

Once more it stated that the EU product safety legislation does not explicitly address the risks derived from the opacity of systems based on algorithms and, in line with the key requirements proposed by the High-Level Expert Group in the Ethics guidelines for trustworthy AI[92] (and the subsequent assessment list for self-

Liability and New Technologies – New Technologies Formation "Liability for Artificial Intelligence and Other Emerging Digital Technologies", 21 November 2019, at p. 33.

[89] Commission Communication "Report on the safety and liability implications of Artificial Intelligence, the Internet of Things and robotics", COM (2020) 64 final, Brussels, 19.2.2020, p. 9.

[90] Ibid.

[91] Ibid. See also Commission Communication "Building Trust in Human-Centric Artificial Intelligence", COM(2019) 168 final, Brussels, 8.4.2019: "Accountability Mechanisms should be put in place to ensure responsibility and accountability for AI systems and their outcomes, both before and after their implementation. Auditability of AI systems is key in this regard, as the assessment of AI systems by internal and external auditors, and the availability of such evaluation reports, strongly contributes to the trustworthiness of the technology. External auditability should especially be ensured in applications affecting fundamental rights, including safety-critical applications", at p. 6. ... "The traceability of AI systems should be ensured; it is important to log and document both the decisions made by the systems, as well as the entire process (including a description of data gathering and labelling, and a description of the algorithm used) that yielded the decisions. Linked to this, explainability of the algorithmic decision-making process, adapted to the persons involved, should be provided to the extent possible. Ongoing research to develop explainability mechanisms should be pursued. In addition, explanations of the degree to which an AI system influences and shapes the organisational decision-making process, design choices of the system, as well as the rationale for deploying it, should be available (hence ensuring not just data and system transparency, but also business model transparency)", at p. 5.

[92] "Ethics Guidelines for Trustworthy AI", High-Level Expert Group on Artificial Intelligence, 8 April 2019, at p. 18: "Traceability: The data sets and the processes that yield the AI system's decision, including those of data gathering and data labelling as well as the algorithms used, should be documented to the best possible standard to allow for traceability and an increase in transparency. This also applies to the decisions made by the AI system. This enables identification of the reasons why an AI-decision was erroneous which, in turn, could help prevent future mistakes. Traceability facilitates auditability as well as explainability". ... "The requirement of accountability

assessment),[93] it stressed that explicability measures such as traceability, auditability and transparent communication on system capabilities are required, and that clear principles and specific obligations related to transparency, accountability and intelligibility need to be established and imposed. As the Commission's Report put it, "the Union product safety legislation does not explicitly address the increasing risks derived from the opacity of systems based on algorithms. It is therefore necessary to consider requirements for transparency of algorithms, as well as for robustness, accountability and when relevant, human oversight and unbiased outcomes, particularly important for the ex-post mechanism of enforcement and to build trust in the use of those technologies. One way of tackling this challenge would be imposing obligations on developers of the algorithms to disclose the design parameters and metadata of datasets in case accidents occur".[94]

. . . necessitates that mechanisms be put in place to ensure responsibility and accountability for AI systems and their outcomes, both before and after their development, deployment and use. Auditability entails the enablement of the assessment of algorithms, data and design processes. This does not necessarily imply that information about business models and intellectual property related to the AI system must always be openly available. Evaluation by internal and external auditors, and the availability of such evaluation reports, can contribute to the trustworthiness of the technology. In applications affecting fundamental rights, including safety-critical applications, AI systems should be able to be independently audited", at pp. 19–20.

[93] "The Assessment List for Trustworthy Artificial Intelligence (ALTAI) for self-assessment", High-Level Expert Group on AI (AI HLEG), 17 July 2020, at p. 21: "Accountability – Auditability: The possibility to conduct evaluations as well as to access records on said evaluations can contribute to Trustworthy AI. In applications affecting fundamental rights, including safety-critical applications, AI systems should be able to be independently audited. This does not necessarily imply that information about business models and intellectual property related to the AI system must always be openly available. • Did you establish mechanisms that facilitate the AI system's auditability (e.g. traceability of the development process, the sourcing of training data and the logging of the AI system's processes, outcomes, positive and negative impact)? • Did you ensure that the AI system can be audited by independent third parties?". . . . "Explainability is crucial for building and maintaining users' trust in AI systems. AI driven decisions – to the extent possible – must be explained to and understood by those directly and indirectly affected, in order to allow for contesting of such decisions. An explanation as to why a model has generated a particular output or decision (and what combination of input factors contributed to that) is not always possible. These cases are referred to as 'blackboxes' and require special attention. In those circumstances, other explainability measures (e.g. traceability, auditability and transparent communication on the AI system's capabilities) may be required, provided that the AI system as a whole respects fundamental rights. The degree to which explainability is needed depends on the context and the severity of the consequences of erroneous or otherwise inaccurate output to human life. • Did you explain the decision(s) of the AI system to the users? • Do you continuously survey the users if they understand the decision(s) of the AI system?", at pp. 14–15.

[94] Commission Communication "Report on the safety and liability implications of Artificial Intelligence, the Internet of Things and robotics", COM (2020) 64 final, Brussels, 19.2.2020, p. 9.

4.3.3.2.5 Complexity of the Products and Systems

The Report underlined that AI systems display certain levels of complexity due to the interdependency between different components. For instance, the IoT and AI-enabled products and services comprise tangible parts/devices (sensors, actuators, hardware), different software components and applications, data, data services (i.e. collection, processing, curating, analysing), and connectivity features: "various components, devices and products can be integrated and have influence on each other's functioning (e.g. products part of a smart home ecosystem)".[95] Therefore, risks stemming from the complexity of the products and systems might have an impact on safety.

However, according to the Commission, it appears that the current EU product safety legislation already explicitly addresses the risks that could be derived from the complexity of the products and systems: "The Union product safety legislation, including transport legislation, already takes into account to a certain extent the complexity of products or systems to tackle the risks that may have an impact on the safety of users".[96] Indeed, the existing EU product safety framework already sets several obligations for producers to carry out the required risk assessment[97] taking into account not only the intended use[98] of the product but also the foreseeable use

[95] Ibid.

[96] Ibid., p. 10.

[97] See Directive 2006/42/EC of the European Parliament and of the Council of 17 May 2006 on machinery, and amending Directive 95/16/EC (OJ L 157, 9.6.2006, pp. 24–86) (the Machinery Directive), at Annex I, Essential health and safety requirements relating to the design and construction of machinery, General Principles: "1. The manufacturer of machinery or his authorised representative must ensure that a risk assessment is carried out in order to determine the health and safety requirements which apply to the machinery. The machinery must then be designed and constructed taking into account the results of the risk assessment. By the iterative process of risk assessment and risk reduction referred to above, the manufacturer or his authorised representative shall: — determine the limits of the machinery, which include the intended use and any reasonably foreseeable misuse thereof, — identify the hazards that can be generated by the machinery and the associated hazardous situations, — estimate the risks, taking into account the severity of the possible injury or damage to health and the probability of its occurrence, — evaluate the risks, with a view to determining whether risk reduction is required, in accordance with the objective of this Directive, — eliminate the hazards or reduce the risks associated with these hazards by application of protective measures, in the order of priority established in section 1.1.2(b). 2. The obligations laid down by the essential health and safety requirements only apply when the corresponding hazard exists for the machinery in question when it is used under the conditions foreseen by the manufacturer or his authorised representative or in foreseeable abnormal situations. In any event, the principles of safety integration referred to in section 1.1.2 and the obligations concerning marking of machinery and instructions referred to in sections 1.7.3 and 1.7.4 apply. 3. The essential health and safety requirements laid down in this Annex are mandatory; however, taking into account the state of the art, it may not be possible to meet the objectives set by them. In that event, the machinery must, as far as possible, be designed and constructed with the purpose of approaching these objectives".

[98] 'Intended use' means the use of machinery in accordance with the information provided in the manufacturer's instructions for use. See Directive 2006/42/EC of the European Parliament and of

and/or the reasonably foreseeable misuse.[99] Therefore, in line with this obligation, when carrying out the required risk assessment, the producer should consider the possibility that the device in question will be interconnected with other devices. Use or misuses should be determined on the basis of experience of past use of the same type of product, accident investigations or human behaviour.[100] In addition,

---

the Council of 17 May 2006 on machinery, and amending Directive 95/16/EC (OJ L 157, 9.6.2006, pp. 24–86) (the Machinery Directive), at Annex I, 1.1.1. (h).

See also "Guide to application of the Machinery Directive 2006/42/EC", Edition 2.2 – October 2019 (Update of 2nd Edition), European Commission, Directorate-General for Internal Market, Industry, Entrepreneurship and SMEs: "The first step of the risk assessment process is to determine the limits of the machinery, which include the intended use of the machinery. Machinery is not necessarily safe for all possible uses: for example, the manufacturer of machinery intended for working metal has usually not designed the machinery for safely working wood and vice versa; for example, the manufacturer of a mobile elevating work platform usually has not designed the machine to be safely used as a crane. The manufacturer's risk assessment and the design and construction of the machinery must therefore be based on specified use or uses. The specification of the intended use of the machinery must cover, where appropriate, the different operating modes and phases of use of the machinery. In particular, the parameters on which the safe use of the machinery depends and their limits must be precisely specified. Such parameters include, for example, the maximum load for lifting machinery; the maximum slope on which mobile machinery can be used without loss of stability; the maximum wind-speed in which machinery can be safely used outdoors; the maximum dimensions of workpieces and the type of material that can be safely processed by a machine tool" (para. 171, pp. 162–163). ... "The description of the intended use of the machinery must include a precise indication of the purposes for which the machinery is intended. The description of the intended use of the machinery must specify the limits on the conditions of use taken into account in the manufacturer's risk assessment and in the design and construction the machinery. The description of the intended use of the machinery must cover all the different operating modes and phases of use of the machinery and specify safe values for the parameters on which the safe use of the machinery depends. Such parameters may include, inter alia: – the maximum load for lifting machinery; – the maximum slope on which mobile machinery can be used without loss of stability; – the maximum wind-speed in which machinery can be safely used outdoors; – the maximum dimensions of workpieces; – the maximum speed for rotating tools where break-up due to overspeed is a hazard; – the type of materials that can be safely processed by the machinery" (para. 263, p. 259).

[99] 'Reasonably foreseeable misuse' means the use of machinery in a way not intended in the instructions for use, but which may result from readily predictable human behaviour. See Directive 2006/42/EC of the European Parliament and of the Council of 17 May 2006 on machinery, and amending Directive 95/16/EC (OJ L 157, 9.6.2006, pp. 24–86) (the Machinery Directive), at Annex I, 1.1.1. (i).

[100] Commission Communication "Report on the safety and liability implications of Artificial Intelligence, the Internet of Things and robotics", COM (2020) 64 final, Brussels, 19.2.2020, p. 10.

See also "Guide to application of the Machinery Directive 2006/42/EC", Edition 2.2 – October 2019 (Update of 2nd Edition), European Commission, Directorate-General for Internal Market, Industry, Entrepreneurship and SMEs, para. 172, pp. 163–164: "The first step of the risk assessment process ... also requires the manufacturer to take account of reasonably foreseeable misuse of machinery. The machinery manufacturer cannot be expected to take account of all possible misuse of the machinery. However, certain kinds of misuse, whether intentional or unintentional, are predictable on the basis of experience of past use of the same type of machinery or of similar machinery, accident investigations and knowledge about human behaviour. The "A" type standard EN ISO 12100:2010 gives the following examples of the kinds of misuse or readily predictable

transport legislation and sectorial safety legislation (such as the Medical Devices Regulation)[101] address this complexity at system level. Furthermore, Article 2 para. (b) (ii) of the General Product Safety Directive provides that a safe product should take into account "the effect on other products, where it is reasonably foreseeable that it will be used with other products"[102] and, as a result, it is anticipated that the

human behaviour that may have to be taken into account: – loss of control of the machine by the operator; – reflex behaviour of a person in case of malfunction, incident or failure during the use of the machine; – behaviour resulting from lack of concentration or carelessness; – behaviour resulting from taking the line of least resistance in carrying out a task; – behaviour resulting from pressures to keep machinery running in all circumstances; – the behaviour of certain persons such as children. Such behaviour can result in a range of misuse situations, such as, for example, using a crane or a MEWP without deploying the stabilisers; leaving the door open on an earth-moving truck in hot weather thereby defeating the air filtering and noise control equipment; two people operating a press designed for use by a single person".

[101] Regulation (EU) 2017/745 of the European Parliament and of the Council of 5 April 2017 on medical devices, amending Directive 2001/83/EC, Regulation (EC) No 178/2002 and Regulation (EC) No 1223/2009 and repealing Council Directives 90/385/EEC and 93/42/EEC, OJ L 117, 5.5.2017, pp. 1–175. See, for instance, Article 2: "... (10) 'procedure pack' means a combination of products packaged together and placed on the market with the purpose of being used for a specific medical purpose; (11) 'system' means a combination of products, either packaged together or not, which are intended to be interconnected or combined to achieve a specific medical purpose". Also, Article 22: "Systems and procedure packs: 1. Natural or legal persons shall draw up a statement if they combine devices bearing a CE marking with the following other devices or products, in a manner that is compatible with the intended purpose of the devices or other products and within the limits of use specified by their manufacturers, in order to place them on the market as a system or procedure pack: (a) other devices bearing the CE marking; (b) in vitro diagnostic medical devices bearing the CE marking in conformity with Regulation (EU) 2017/746; (c) other products which are in conformity with legislation that applies to those products only where they are used within a medical procedure or their presence in the system or procedure pack is otherwise justified. 2. In the statement made pursuant to paragraph 1, the natural or legal person concerned shall declare that: (a) they verified the mutual compatibility of the devices and, if applicable other products, in accordance with the manufacturers' instructions and have carried out their activities in accordance with those instructions; (b) they packaged the system or procedure pack and supplied relevant information to users incorporating the information to be supplied by the manufacturers of the devices or other products which have been put together; (c) the activity of combining devices and, if applicable, other products as a system or procedure pack was subject to appropriate methods of internal monitoring, verification and validation".

[102] See Directive 2001/95/EC of the European Parliament and the Council of 3 December 2001 on general product safety (the General Product Safety Directive), (OJ L 11, 15.1.2002, pp. 4–17), at Article 2 para. (b): "'safe product' shall mean any product which, under normal or reasonably foreseeable conditions of use including duration and, where applicable, putting into service, installation and maintenance requirements, does not present any risk or only the minimum risks compatible with the product's use, considered to be acceptable and consistent with a high level of protection for the safety and health of persons, taking into account the following points in particular: (i) the characteristics of the product, including its composition, packaging, instructions for assembly and, where applicable, for installation and maintenance; (ii) the effect on other products, where it is reasonably foreseeable that it will be used with other products; (iii) the presentation of the product, the labelling, any warnings and instructions for its use and disposal and any other indication or information regarding the product; (iv) the categories of consumers at risk when using the product, in particular children and the elderly. The feasibility of obtaining higher levels of safety or the

producer of a connected AI device, intended to be part of a smart home ecosystem, should be in a position to reasonably foresee that the product in question will have an impact on the safety of other products.[103]

4.3.3.2.6 Software

As already stated, the complexity of AI products is reflected, amongst others, in the multiplicity of components, parts, software, systems or services, which together form the new complex technological ecosystems. Software is an essential component of an AI based system and parts of the EU product safety legislation already refer explicitly to the software integrated in a product. For instance, it is stipulated that a fault in the software of the control system should not lead to hazardous situations.[104] In addition, the manufacturer of the final product, when carrying out the required risk assessment, is obliged to foresee the risks of software integrated in that product at the time of its placing on the market.[105]

According to the Commission, software updates could be assimilated to maintenance operations for safety reasons, provided that they do not significantly modify a product already placed on the market and they do not introduce risks not foreseen in the initial risk assessment.[106] However, if the software update substantially modifies

---

availability of other products presenting a lesser degree of risk shall not constitute grounds for considering a product to be 'dangerous'".

[103] Commission Communication "Report on the safety and liability implications of Artificial Intelligence, the Internet of Things and robotics", COM (2020) 64 final, Brussels, 19.2.2020, p. 10.

[104] See Directive 2006/42/EC of the European Parliament and of the Council of 17 May 2006 on machinery, and amending Directive 95/16/EC (OJ L 157, 9.6.2006, pp. 24–86) (the Machinery Directive), at Section 1.2.1 of Annex I: "1.2. Control Systems: 1.2.1. Safety and reliability of control systems: Control systems must be designed and constructed in such a way as to prevent hazardous situations from arising. Above all, they must be designed and constructed in such a way that: … – a fault in the hardware or the software of the control system does not lead to hazardous situations".

[105] See Directive 2006/42/EC of the European Parliament and of the Council of 17 May 2006 on machinery, and amending Directive 95/16/EC (OJ L 157, 9.6.2006, pp. 24–86) (the Machinery Directive), at Annex I, Essential health and safety requirements relating to the design and construction of machinery, General Principles.

[106] Commission Communication "Report on the safety and liability implications of Artificial Intelligence, the Internet of Things and robotics", COM (2020) 64 final, Brussels, 19.2.2020, p. 10.

See also: European Commission Notice "The 'Blue Guide' on the implementation of EU products rules 2016", (2016/C 272/01, 26.7.2016), at p. 17: "Products which have been repaired or exchanged (for example following a defect), without changing the original performance, purpose or type, are not to be considered as new products according to Union harmonisation legislation. Thus, such products do not need to undergo conformity assessment again, whether or not the original product was placed on the market before or after the legislation entered into force. … Software updates or repairs could be assimilated to maintenance operations provided that they do not modify a product already placed on the market in such a way that compliance with the applicable requirements may be affected".

the product in which it is downloaded (and the required risk assessment leads to the conclusion that the nature of the hazard has changed) the entire product might be considered as a new product[107] and compliance with the relevant safety product legislation must be reassessed at the time the modification is performed. The person who carries out the changes becomes the manufacturer with the corresponding obligations, i.e. compliance of the modified product with the applicable essential requirements has to be reassessed.

It appears that the Commission focuses on the cases where the software is not included in the product put into circulation by the producer but installed subsequently as a stand-alone feature. It argued that, apart from certain pieces of legislation,[108] the EU product safety legislation does not adequately address the issue of

---

[107] Commission Communication "Report on the safety and liability implications of Artificial Intelligence, the Internet of Things and robotics", COM (2020) 64 final, Brussels, 19.2.2020, p. 10.

See also: European Commission Notice "The 'Blue Guide' on the implementation of EU products rules 2016", (2016/C 272/01, 26.7.2016), at pp. 15–17: "A product which has been subject to important changes or overhauls aiming to modify its original performance, purpose or type may be considered as a new product. The person who carries out the changes becomes then the manufacturer with the corresponding obligations. ... A product, which has been subject to important changes or overhaul aiming to modify its original performance, purpose or type after it has been put into service, having a significant impact on its compliance with Union harmonisation legislation, must be considered as a new product. This has to be assessed on a case-by-case basis and, in particular, in view of the objective of the legislation and the type of products covered by the legislation in question. Where a rebuilt or modified product is considered as a new product, it must comply with the provisions of the applicable legislation when it is made available or put into service. This has to be verified by applying the appropriate conformity assessment procedure laid down by the legislation in question. In particular, if the risk assessment leads to the conclusion that the nature of the hazard has changed or the level of risk has increased, then the modified product has to be considered as a new product, i.e. compliance of the modified product with the applicable essential requirements has to be reassessed and the person carrying out the modification has to fulfil the same requirements as an original manufacturer, for example preparation of the technical documentation, drawing up a EU declaration of conformity and affixing the CE marking on the product".

[108] For instance, see Directive 2014/53/EU of the European Parliament and of the Council of 16 April 2014 on the harmonisation of the laws of the Member States relating to the making available on the market of radio equipment and repealing Directive 1999/5/EC (OJ L 153, 22.5.2014, pp. 62–106) (the Radio Equipment Directive – RED):

Recital 16: "The compliance of some categories of radio equipment with the essential requirements set out in this Directive may be affected by the inclusion of software or modification of its existing software. The user, the radio equipment or a third party should only be able to load software into the radio equipment where this does not compromise the subsequent compliance of that radio equipment with the applicable essential requirements". Recital 30: "The manufacturer should provide sufficient information on the intended use of the radio equipment so as to allow its use in compliance with the essential requirements. Such information may need to include a description of accessories such as antennas and of components such as software, and specifications of the installation process of the radio equipment". Article 3 (3) (i) of the Radio Equipment Directive requires that specific classes or categories of radio equipment support features ensuring that the compliance of that equipment is not compromised when software is uploaded: "Radio equipment within certain categories or classes shall be so constructed that it complies with the following essential requirements: ... (3)(i) radio equipment supports certain features in order to ensure that

stand-alone software and pointed out that existing rules may need to be adapted and clarified in the case of a stand-alone software placed as it is on the market or

---

software can only be loaded into the radio equipment where the compliance of the combination of the radio equipment and software has been demonstrated". Also, Article 4 (1) reads: "Provision of information on the compliance of combinations of radio equipment and software 1. Manufacturers of radio equipment and of software allowing radio equipment to be used as intended shall provide the Member States and the Commission with information on the compliance of intended combinations of radio equipment and software with the essential requirements set out in Article 3. Such information shall result from a conformity assessment carried out in accordance with Article 17, and shall be given in the form of a statement of compliance which includes the elements set out in Annex VI. Depending on the specific combinations of radio equipment and software, the information shall precisely identify the radio equipment and the software which have been assessed, and it shall be continuously updated". Article 10 (8): "Manufacturers shall ensure that the radio equipment is accompanied by instructions and safety information in a language which can be easily understood by consumers and other end-users, as determined by the Member State concerned. Instructions shall include the information required to use radio equipment in accordance with its intended use. Such information shall include, where applicable, a description of accessories and components, including software, which allow the radio equipment to operate as intended. Such instructions and safety information, as well as any labelling, shall be clear, understandable and intelligible".

See also the Regulation on Medical Devices [Regulation (EU) 2017/745 of the European Parliament and of the Council of 5 April 2017 on medical devices, amending Directive 2001/83/EC, Regulation (EC) No 178/2002 and Regulation (EC) No 1223/2009 and repealing Council Directives 90/385/EEC and 93/42/EEC, OJ L 117, 5.5.2017, pp. 1–175]: Recital 19: "It is necessary to clarify that software in its own right, when specifically intended by the manufacturer to be used for one or more of the medical purposes set out in the definition of a medical device, qualifies as a medical device, while software for general purposes, even when used in a healthcare setting, or software intended for life-style and well-being purposes is not a medical device. The qualification of software, either as a device or an accessory, is independent of the software's location or the type of interconnection between the software and a device". 'Software' is included in the definitions of medical and active devices (see Article 2(1) and (4) and Article 2 (25) and (26) – concerning compatibility and interoperability). Furthermore, see Annex I, Chapter 1, 14.2: "Devices shall be designed and manufactured in such a way as to remove or reduce as far as possible: . . . (d) the risks associated with the possible negative interaction between software and the IT environment within which it operates and interacts". Also: Annex I, Chapter 1, 17.1: "Devices that incorporate electronic programmable systems, including software, or software that are devices in themselves, shall be designed to ensure repeatability, reliability and performance in line with their intended use. In the event of a single fault condition, appropriate means shall be adopted to eliminate or reduce as far as possible consequent risks or impairment of performance. 17.2. For devices that incorporate software or for software that are devices in themselves, the software shall be developed and manufactured in accordance with the state of the art taking into account the principles of development life cycle, risk management, including information security, verification and validation. 17.3. Software referred to in this Section that is intended to be used in combination with mobile computing platforms shall be designed and manufactured taking into account the specific features of the mobile platform (e.g. size and contrast ratio of the screen) and the external factors related to their use (varying environment as regards level of light or noise). 17.4. Manufacturers shall set out minimum requirements concerning hardware, IT networks characteristics and IT security measures, including protection against unauthorised access, necessary to run the software as intended". And Annex I, Chapter 1, 23.4: "Information in the instructions for use - (ab) for devices that incorporate electronic programmable systems, including software, or software that are devices in themselves, minimum requirements concerning hardware, IT networks characteristics and IT security measures, including protection against unauthorised access, necessary to run the software as intended".

downloaded into a product after its placing on the market, when having an impact on safety: "while the Union product safety legislation takes into account the safety risks stemming from software integrated in a product at the time of its placing on the market and, potentially subsequent updates foreseen by the manufacturer, specific and/or explicit requirements on standalone software could be needed (e.g. an 'app' that would be downloaded). Particular considerations should be given to the stand-alone software ensuring safety functions in the AI products and systems. Additional obligations may be needed for manufacturers to ensure that they provide features to prevent the upload of software having an impact on safety during the lifetime of the AI products".[109]

4.3.3.2.7 Complex Value Chains

The Commission's Report emphasised that progress in digital technologies is transforming products, processes and business models in all sectors, eventually creating new industrial patterns. The advances in technologies set up new ecosystems that cut across areas and create new markets for hardware, software and services. AI is used in a variety of ways and can be found across a large number of sectors, from assembly line robots to advanced toys, and from speech recognition systems to medical research. As the Commission put it, the complexity of AI equipped systems "is reflected in both the plurality of economic operators involved in the supply chain and the multiplicity of components, parts, software, systems or services, which together form the new technological ecosystems".[110]

These new ecosystems are based on bringing together multiple sectors and a variety of stakeholders to cover an increasingly complex value chain. However, the Commission stressed that this complexity "is not new, nor exclusively an issue brought by new emerging digital technologies such as AI or the IoT".[111] Indeed, under the existing EU product safety framework, regardless the complexity of the value chain, the responsibility for the safety of the product stays with the producer that has placed the final product (including the parts integrated in the product, e.g. the software of a computer) on the market. However, apart from certain pieces of legislation that explicitly refer to situations in which economic operators intervene on a product before the latter is being placed on the market,[112] the Commission

[109] Commission Communication "Report on the safety and liability implications of Artificial Intelligence, the Internet of Things and robotics", COM (2020) 64 final, Brussels, 19.2.2020, p. 11.

[110] Ibid., p. 2.

[111] Ibid., p. 11.

[112] For instance, Annex I, Article 1.7.4.2 of Directive 2006/42/EC of the European Parliament and of the Council of 17 May 2006 on machinery, and amending Directive 95/16/EC (OJ L 157, 9.6.2006, pp. 24–86) (the Machinery Directive), requires manufacturers of equipment to provide information to the operator on how to assembly that equipment with another machinery: "Each instruction manual must contain, where applicable, at least the following information: ... (i) assembly, installation and connection instructions, including drawings, diagrams and the means

acknowledged that the existing EU product safety legislation cannot adequately address the increasing complexity of supply chains. As a result, it was underlined that, given the increasing complexity of supply chains as regards new technologies, the introduction of provisions specifically requesting cooperation between the economic operators in the supply chain and the users could provide more legal certainty: "The Union product safety legislation takes into account the complexity of the value chains, imposing obligations to several economic operators following the principle of 'shared responsibility'. While the producer's responsibility on the final product safety has been proved adequate for current complex value chains, explicit provisions specifically requesting cooperation between the economic operators in the supply chain and the users could provide legal certainty in perhaps even more complex value chains. In particular, each actor in the value chain having an impact on the product safety (e.g. software producers) and users (by modifying the product) would assume their responsibility and provide the next actor in the chain with the necessary information and measures".[113]

4.3.4 The Product Liability Frameworks

4.3.4.1 Overview

Product liability and product safety are complementary legal frameworks aiming to provide trust and safety to consumers. The EU product safety legislation ensures that only safe products can be placed on the EU market, while the EU product liability framework provides for liability of producers of defective products that cause damage to natural persons or their property. Indeed, the safety framework aims at preventing accidents; however, when accidents do happen, the liability framework should ensure that those who suffered damage or injury are properly compensated. As the Commission put it, "while optimising Union safety rules for AI can help avoiding accidents, they may nevertheless happen. This is when civil liability intervenes".[114] Civil liability rules always attempt to strike a careful balance between

---

of attachment and the designation of the chassis or installation on which the machinery is to be mounted".

Also, Article 16(2) of Directive 2014/33/EU of the European Parliament and of the Council of 26 February 2014 on the harmonisation of the laws of the Member States relating to lifts and safety components for lifts (the Lifts Directive), OJ L 96, 29.3.2014, pp. 251–308, requires the economic operator, i.e. the person who is responsible for the design and manufacture of the lift, to provide the installer (i.e. the person who is responsible for the installation and testing of the lift) with "all the necessary documents and information to enable the latter to ensure correct and safe installation and testing of the lift".

[113] Commission Communication "Report on the safety and liability implications of Artificial Intelligence, the Internet of Things and robotics", COM (2020) 64 final, Brussels, 19.2.2020, p. 11.

[114] Ibid., p. 12. Also: "At Union level, product safety and product liability provisions are two complementary mechanisms to pursue the same policy goal of a functioning single market for

protecting consumers on the one hand and encouraging businesses to introduce innovative products on the other.[115]

According to the Commission, the current liability framework in the EU is a stable and adequate framework ("liability frameworks in the Union have functioned well"),[116] relying on both the Product Liability Directive[117] (which harmonised the liability of the producer of defective products) and other non-harmonised national liability regimes. Therefore, at national level, the rules implementing the Product Liability Directive coexist with other extra-contractual liability rules that could also be invoked by victims of damages.[118]

In particular, the Product Liability Directive was one of the first pieces of EU legislation that explicitly aimed to protect consumers, offering a layer of protection that national fault-based liability alone cannot provide. It applies to all movable products, even if integrated into another movable product, Thus, if AI is integrated into a product and a defect can be proven in a product that caused material damage to a person, the producer will be liable to pay compensation. The actual cause of events

goods that ensures high levels of safety, i.e. minimise the risk of harm to users and provides for compensation for damages resulting from defective goods. At national level, non-harmonised civil liability frameworks complement these Union rules by ensuring compensation for damages from various causes (such as products and services) and by addressing different liable persons (such as owners, operators or service providers)".

[115] Ibid.: "Civil liability rules play a double role in our society: on the one hand, they ensure that victims of a damage caused by others get compensation and, on the other hand, they provide economic incentives for the liable party to avoid causing such damage. Liability rules always have to strike a balance between protecting citizens from harm while enabling businesses to innovate".

[116] Ibid. See also Commission Staff Working Document on "Liability for emerging digital technologies" - Accompanying the document Commission Communication "Artificial intelligence for Europe", SWD(2018) 137 final, Brussels, 25.4.2018, at p. 2.

[117] Council Directive 85/374/EEC of 25 July 1985 on the approximation of the laws, regulations and administrative provisions of the Member States concerning liability for defective products, as modified by Directive 1999/34/EC of the European Parliament and of the Council of 10 May 1999 (OJ L 210/29, 7.8.1985, and OJ L 141/20, 4.6.1999) (the Product Liability Directive).

[118] Commission Communication "Report on the safety and liability implications of Artificial Intelligence, the Internet of Things and robotics", COM (2020) 64 final, Brussels, 19.2.2020, p. 12.

See also the Report from the Expert Group on Liability and New Technologies – New Technologies Formation "Liability for Artificial Intelligence and Other Emerging Digital Technologies", 21 November 2019, at p. 3: "Artificial intelligence and other emerging digital technologies, such as the Internet of Things or distributed ledger technologies, have the potential to transform our societies and economies for the better. However, their rollout must come with sufficient safeguards, to minimise the risk of harm these technologies may cause, such as bodily injury or other harm. In the EU, product safety regulations ensure this is the case. However, such regulations cannot completely exclude the possibility of damage resulting from the operation of these technologies. If this happens, victims will seek compensation. They typically do so on the basis of liability regimes under private law, in particular tort law, possibly in combination with insurance. Only the strict liability of producers for defective products, which constitutes a small part of this kind of liability regimes, is harmonised at EU level by the Product Liability Directive, while all other regimes – apart from some exceptions in specific sectors or under special legislation – are regulated by the Member States themselves".

that lead to damage or incident is decisive for the attribution of liability. The Directive introduced the concept of strict liability of producers,[119] according to which if a defective product causes death, personal injury or material damage (above EUR 500) to consumers or their private property, the producer is liable to provide compensation irrespectively of whether there is negligence or fault on the consumers' part.[120] Therefore, producers are responsible for defective products, regardless of whether the defect of the product is their fault. A product is considered defective if it does not provide the safety a person is entitled to expect.[121] To sustain their claim, those who have suffered injury or material damage must prove the damage, the defect and the causal link between the defect and the damage: "in case of a physical or material damage, the injured party is entitled to compensation if he or she proves the damage, the defect in the product (i.e. that it did not provide the safety that the public is entitled to expect) and the causal link between the defective product and the damage".[122] The Product Liability Directive does not cover

[119] According to Article 3 of the Product Liability Directive, the notion of "producer" includes the manufacturer of a finished product, the producer of any raw material or the manufacturer of a component part and any person who, by putting his name, trademark or other distinguishing feature on the product presents himself as its producer.

[120] Strict liability represents a strong tool for the protection of persons who have suffered injury or material damage. However, there are a number of circumstances where the Directive allows producers to take certain calculated risks when placing innovative products on the market. The producer is not liable if he can prove that: (i) the defect did not exist when the product was put into circulation; (ii) the defect is due to compliance with regulations issued by public authorities; or (iii) the state of technical knowledge at the time of putting the product on the market made it impossible to discover the defect. Member States may obtain a derogation from this last exemption. From the day that they become aware of the defect, injured persons have three (3) years to claim damages. Claims are no longer possible ten (10) years after the product was put in circulation. To sustain their claim, those who have suffered injury must prove the damage, the defect and the causal link between the defect and the damage.

[121] "Safety which a person is entitled to expect" (Article 6 para. 1 of the Product Liability Directive). This takes all circumstances into account, including the presentation of the product, the use to which it could reasonably be expected the product would be put, and the time the product was put into circulation. Article 6 of the Product Liability Directive states that a product must not be considered defective for the sole reason that a better product is subsequently put into circulation.

See also the Report from the Expert Group on Liability and New Technologies – New Technologies Formation "Liability for Artificial Intelligence and Other Emerging Digital Technologies", 21 November 2019, at p. 28: "The second key element of the product liability regime is the notion of defect. Defectiveness is assessed on the basis of the safety expectations of an average consumer, 79F 80 taking into account all relevant circumstances. The interconnectivity of products and systems makes it hard to identify defectiveness. Sophisticated AI autonomous systems with self-learning capabilities also raise the question of whether unpredictable deviations in the decision-making path can be treated as defects. Even if they constitute a defect, the state-of-the-art defence may apply. Additionally, the complexity and the opacity of emerging digital technologies complicate chances for the victim to discover and prove the defect and prove causation".

[122] Commission Communication "Report on the safety and liability implications of Artificial Intelligence, the Internet of Things and robotics", COM (2020) 64 final, Brussels, 19.2.2020, p. 12.

contractual liability, which is imposed on an entity by the terms of a contract; it provides the injured person with an extra-contractual regime of liability.[123]

As already mentioned, co-existing with the rules implementing the Product Liability Directive, various national liability regimes apply and could be invoked by victims of damages. Depending on whether the compensation of the victim requires a fault of the person considered liable by the law or not, these national extra-contractual liability rules are classified into two broad categories, namely fault-based extra-contractual liability regimes on the one hand and special regimes of strict liability (extra-contractual) on the other. In most EU member states, extra-contractual liability regimes are fault-based. Therefore, the fault of the author of the wrongful behaviour leading to a damage—which could be an act or an omission whether intentional or by negligence—is a necessary element to be proven for the liability claim to be successful. The victim submitting a claim needs to provide the evidence required to support his liability claim: "National non-harmonised regimes provide fault-based liability rules, according to which victims of damage need to prove the fault of the liable person, the damage and causality between the fault and the damage in order to establish a successful liability claim".[124] Furthermore, national non-harmonised regimes also provide strict liability rules, where liability does not depend on a fault and the claimant needs only to prove the damage and the

[123]Extra-contractual liability is set outside of a contract, for example directly in imposed pieces of legislation or through common law as types of: i) Liability arising from an offense: The person who committed the offense will be liable in front of the injured party or responsible for the damage he/she caused to the party without any contractual agreement between them. An offense can be an intentional act or negligence; ii) Liability in the absence of an offense: In liability without an offense, a person may be liable notwithstanding that the damage caused was unforeseeable. For example, the occupier of a building shall be liable for any damage caused by objects falling from it. Sometimes, not only one party should be held liable. Also, if two motor vehicles have a collision and each of the vehicles is deemed to have contributed equally to the accident, the owner of each vehicle shall bear half of the total amount of the damage resulting from the accident. iii) Liability for the action of others: if a person is liable for another person by law, then he/she is bound to compensate the injured party (e.g. a parent is liable under law if his child incurs liability).

[124]Commission Communication "Report on the safety and liability implications of Artificial Intelligence, the Internet of Things and robotics", COM (2020) 64 final, Brussels, 19.2.2020, p. 12.

There are situations, however, where national law introduces variations in order to facilitate the burden of proof of the victim so as to increase the possibility of compensation for the victim. Such variations may consist in a presumption of fault by the wrongdoer (or a reversal of the burden of proof), whereby the wrongdoer is liable unless he proves that he was not in fault – for instance, the responsibility of parents/tutors/guardians/teachers for damages caused by a minor, pupil, student/ apprentice or mentally impaired person (unless they can prove that they were not able to prevent the damages from happening); or the responsibility of the owner/possessor of the building in case of damages causes by his/her building (unless he/she proves that he/she observed appropriate care for the purpose of avoiding the damage); or the responsibility of a person carrying a dangerous activity (unless he/she proves that all appropriate measures to avoid the damage have been taken). Examples of those variations are cited in Commission Staff Working Document on "Liability for emerging digital technologies" - Accompanying the document Commission Communication "Artificial intelligence for Europe", SWD(2018) 137 final, Brussels, 25.4.2018, at pp. 7–8.

causal link.[125] These regimes of strict liability may apply to a diverse set of situations which generate different types of risks and damages, especially when the risk of damage is linked to specific (e.g. dangerous) activities. National non-harmonised regimes provide strict liability rules "where the national legislator has attributed liability for a risk to a specific person, without the need for a victim to prove fault/ defect or causality between fault/defect and the damage".[126]

Depending on whether the compensation of the victim requires a fault of the person considered liable by the law or not, national non-harmonised liability regimes provide victims with several parallel compensation claims, which are based on fault or strict liability. These claims could be directed against different liable persons and apply under different conditions. In practice, all Member States attribute liability for damages caused by motor vehicles to the owner/holder or the driver of the vehicle. Thus, for instance, in case of an accident caused by a car, the victim could have—under national civil law—the following options. First, a strict-liability claim against the owner of the car, i.e. the person who takes out motor vehicle liability insurance and is strictly liable for having opened the risk associated with the circulation of a motor vehicle on public streets. In most national regimes a strict liability claim

[125] The reversal of the burden of proof in the context of a fault-based extra-contractual liability and the principle of strict liability typically respond to a common rationale. They both aim at facilitating the compensation of the victim of damages in situations where the legislator considers it too burdensome or unbalanced to apply the general fault-based liability rule. Some forms of strict liability may go even a step further by linking liability simply to the materialization of a risk and/or making the discharge of liability either impossible or possible only under the proof that the damaging event was caused by an exceptional/unforeseen circumstance that could not be avoided. There may be also other cases where the risk of damage is linked to the unpredictability of behaviour of specific risk groups, like animals or certain persons: in these cases liability may be attributed to the persons that are considered responsible to supervise the animal or the person, because it is them who should normally be in the condition to adopt measures to prevent or reduce the risk of damages. Finally, when the risk of damages is linked to dangerous activities, some jurisdictions may attribute liability to the person that carries out the activity (e.g. the operator of a nuclear power plant or of an aircraft or the driver of a car) or is ultimately responsible for the dangerous activity to happen (e.g. the owner of a vehicle). The rationale typically is that this person has created a risk, which materialises in a damage and at the same time also derives an economic benefit from this activity. See Commission Staff Working Document on "Liability for emerging digital technologies" - Accompanying the document Commission Communication "Artificial intelligence for Europe", SWD(2018) 137 final, Brussels, 25.4.2018, at p. 8.

[126] Commission Communication "Report on the safety and liability implications of Artificial Intelligence, the Internet of Things and robotics", COM (2020) 64 final, Brussels, 19.2.2020, p. 12.

Examples of cases where the risk of damage is linked to specific (e.g. dangerous) activities include: the liability of the owners of animals for the damages caused by the animals under their custody; the strict liability of the person responsible for carrying out an unspecified or specified dangerous activity (for example the operation of nuclear power plants, aircrafts or motor vehicles) or other cases linked to a legal or factual relationship between two persons or a person and an object, such as when the damages are caused by someone executing a task in the interest of someone else (employee/employer) or by an object that is under his/her custody. See Commission Staff Working Document on "Liability for emerging digital technologies" - Accompanying the document Commission Communication "Artificial intelligence for Europe", SWD(2018) 137 final, Brussels, 25.4.2018, at pp. 8–9.

against the owner of the vehicle exists ("strict liability is applied for the person in whose name the motor vehicle is registered"), i.e. the liability of the holder of the car is typically risk-based. The victim would have a strict liability claim against the owner without the need to attribute fault. The claimant needs only to prove the damage and the causal link. Strict liability requires only proof that damage has occurred and the establishment of a causal link between the harmful functioning of the vehicle and the damage suffered by the injured party.[127] Second, a fault-based liability claim against the driver of the vehicle. In this case, a fault of the driver is required and such a fault could be envisaged for instance when the accident was caused by human error of the driver or the vehicle was driven under dangerous weather conditions or if the required maintenance was not performed.[128] At the same time, the victim has—under the Product Liability Directive—a claim against the producer/manufacturer if the vehicle had a defect.[129] Indeed, liability for a damage may be allocated to the manufacturer of the car under the rules implementing the Product Liability Directive. In that case, the victim could have a claim against the manufacturer of the car; however, the claimant would need to demonstrate a defect of the vehicle and the casual link, namely that the damage was caused by that specific defect.[130]

Under the Motor Insurance Directive,[131] all Member States are obliged to ensure that civil liability for the use of vehicles is covered by insurance and that victims of an accident caused by a vehicle enjoy a direct claim against the insurer covering the person responsible against civil liability. Although the Motor Insurance Directive does not harmonise issues of civil liability, it provides an effective safety net for victims irrespective of the allocation of liability according to the different national

[127] Commission Communication "Report on the safety and liability implications of Artificial Intelligence, the Internet of Things and robotics", COM (2020) 64 final, Brussels, 19.2.2020, p. 12.

See also the Commission Staff Working Document on "Liability for emerging digital technologies" - Accompanying the document Commission Communication "Artificial intelligence for Europe", SWD(2018) 137 final, Brussels, 25.4.2018, at p. 14: "If the victim claims damages against the holder of a motor vehicle based on strict liability rules, normally there is no need to demonstrate whether the accident was caused by a wrongdoing of the car driver or another person or by any deficiency of the car".

[128] Commission Communication "Report on the safety and liability implications of Artificial Intelligence, the Internet of Things and robotics", COM (2020) 64 final, Brussels, 19.2.2020, p. 12.

[129] Ibid.

[130] Commission Staff Working Document on "Liability for emerging digital technologies" - Accompanying the document Commission Communication "Artificial intelligence for Europe", SWD(2018) 137 final, Brussels, 25.4.2018, at p. 14.

[131] Directive 2009/103/EC of the European Parliament and of the Council of 16 September 2009 relating to insurance against civil liability in respect of the use of motor vehicles, and the enforcement of the obligation to insure against such liability ("the Motor Insurance Directive"). This is a minimum harmonisation Directive, so Member States may apply higher levels of protection such as obligatory amounts of insurance cover.

civil liability regimes.[132] As the Commission's Report put it, "in accordance with the harmonised rules on motor vehicle insurance, the use of the vehicle must be insured and the insurer is always in practice the first point of claim for compensation for personal injury or material damage. According to these rules, the obligatory insurance compensates the victim and protects the insured person who is liable under national civil law rules to pay financial damages for the accident involving the motor vehicle".[133]

It is pointed out that producers are not subject to mandatory insurance under the Product Liability Directive. At the same time, the key components of the liability regime for automated vehicles are the national civil liability rules applicable to motor vehicles. The Commission's Report stressed the importance of having an efficient redress mechanism for victims in case of damages. In particular, since Member States are obliged, under the Motor Insurance Directive, to ensure that civil liability for the use of vehicles is covered by insurance and that victims of an accident caused by a vehicle enjoy a direct claim against the insurer covering the person responsible against civil liability, victims of accidents with insured vehicles will approach insurers directly to receive compensation and the damages will usually be paid by the insurer. The same could apply in cases of accidents caused by automated vehicles. As the Commission stated, "autonomous vehicles are not treated in Union legislation any differently from non-autonomous vehicles as regards motor insurance. Such vehicles, like all vehicles, must be covered by the third party motor liability insurance, which is the easiest way for the injured party to get compensation".[134]

---

[132] Commission Staff Working Document on "Liability for emerging digital technologies" - Accompanying the document Commission Communication "Artificial intelligence for Europe", SWD(2018) 137 final, Brussels, 25.4.2018, pp. 13–14.

[133] Commission Communication "Report on the safety and liability implications of Artificial Intelligence, the Internet of Things and robotics", COM (2020) 64 final, Brussels, 19.2.2020, p. 12.

[134] Ibid., p. 13. "Taking out proper insurance can mitigate the negative consequences of accidents by providing for a smooth compensation for the victim. Clear liability rules help insurance companies to calculate their risks and to claim reimbursement from the party ultimately liable for the damage. For example, if an accident is caused by a defect, the motor insurer can claim reimbursement from the manufacturer after compensating the victim".

See also the Commission Staff Working Document on "Liability for emerging digital technologies" - Accompanying the document Commission Communication "Artificial intelligence for Europe", SWD(2018) 137 final, Brussels, 25.4.2018, at p. 21: similarly to what already happens with motor vehicles, rules on liability could be complemented by a compulsory insurance scheme for various actors, as a possible solution to the complexity of allocating responsibility for damage caused by increasingly autonomous robots. "In order to facilitate the victim's compensation and protecting the victim from the risk of insolvency of the liable person, it could be discussed, among other solutions, whether various actors in the value chain should be required to take out insurance coverage as it is the case today for cars. In case of an accident, the victim would be compensated by the insurance". Besides, insurance companies – despite the difficulties stemming from the complexity of the emerging digital technologies – would be in a better position to investigate claims properly and gain access to essential information in order to "assess whether a redress claim against the manufacturer of the AI powered device or any other person can be enforced".

4.3.4.2 The Challenges Brought by the Digital Emerging Technologies to the Product Liability Frameworks

This section attempts to explain how the main characteristics shared by the emerging digital technologies could challenge the existing product liability frameworks and how these challenged could be addressed. According to the Commission, the increasing level of complexity and variety of ecosystems, actors and value chains (high interdependency), in conjunction with the fact that IoT, AI-enabled products and robotics are becoming more connected and complex, could challenge aspects of both the EU and national liability frameworks, cause legal uncertainty as to how existing laws would apply and thus reduce the frameworks' effectiveness. It could also discourage investment, reduce user trust and social acceptance of these technologies, and lead to discrepancies between Member States and further fragmentation of the European Union internal market.

In particular, the Commission underlined that a damage caused by those emerging digital technologies may be the result of a large set of unknown circumstances (for instance the defect or malfunctioning of the devices or services provided by third parties or other circumstances such as a cyber-attack), making it extremely difficult for the victim to identify the damage caused by a specific human fault and thus to prove the substantial elements of a liability claim. Also, persons having suffered harm caused by of AI systems should enjoy equal level of protection as persons having suffered harm caused by other technologies. As the Commission stated, "the characteristics of emerging digital technologies like AI, the IoT and robotics challenge aspects of Union and national liability frameworks and could reduce their effectiveness. Some of these characteristics could make it hard to trace the damage back to a human behaviour, which could give grounds for a fault-based claim in accordance with national rules. This means that liability claims based on national tort laws may be difficult or overly costly to prove and consequently victims may not be adequately compensated. It is important that victims of accidents of products and services including emerging digital technologies like AI do not enjoy a lower level of protection compared to similar other products and services, for which they would get compensation under national tort law. This could reduce societal acceptance of those emerging technologies and lead to hesitance to use them".[135]

---

[135] Commission Communication "Report on the safety and liability implications of Artificial Intelligence, the Internet of Things and robotics", COM (2020) 64 final, Brussels, 19.2.2020, p. 13. Also, according to the Commission, "it will need to be assessed whether challenges of the new technologies to the existing frameworks could also cause legal uncertainty as to how existing laws would apply (e.g. how the concept of fault would apply to damage caused by AI). These could in turn discourage investment as well as increase information and insurance costs for producers and other businesses in the supply chain, especially European SMEs. In addition, should Member States eventually address the challenges to national liability frameworks, it could lead to further fragmentation, thereby increasing the costs of putting innovative AI-solutions and reducing cross-border trade in the Single Market. It is important that companies know their liability risks throughout the value chain and can reduce or prevent them and insure themselves effectively against these risks".

4.3.4.2.1 Complexity of Products, Services, and the Value-Chain

It is reminded that the Product Liability Directive does not make any reference to the concept of service nor does it provide for the distinction between products and services. It solely provides for the definition of product, according to Article 2. Services do not fall into the definition of product. However, it was recognized by the Commission that the distinction between products and services for the purpose of the Product Liability Directive is becoming increasingly blurred with regards to new technological developments. Therefore, the definition of product appears to no longer be as clear-cut as it may have been when the Product Liability Directive was adopted. As the Commission put it, "technology and industry have evolved drastically over the last decades. Especially the dividing line between products and services may no longer be as clear-cut as it was. Products and the provision of services are increasingly intertwined".[136]

See also the Report from the Expert Group on Liability and New Technologies – New Technologies Formation "Liability for Artificial Intelligence and Other Emerging Digital Technologies", 21 November 2019, at p. 3: "In its assessment of existing liability regimes in the wake of emerging digital technologies, the New Technologies Formation of the Expert Group has concluded that the liability regimes in force in the Member States ensure at least basic protection of victims whose damage is caused by the operation of such new technologies. However, the specific characteristics of these technologies and their applications – including complexity, modification through updates or self-learning during operation, limited predictability, and vulnerability to cybersecurity threats – may make it more difficult to offer these victims a claim for compensation in all cases where this seems justified. It may also be the case that the allocation of liability is unfair or inefficient. To rectify this, certain adjustments need to be made to EU and national liability regimes". Also, at pp. 5 and 34, Key Finding [3]: "While existing rules on liability offer solutions with regard to the risks created by emerging digital technologies, the outcomes may not always seem appropriate, given the failure to achieve: (a) a fair and efficient allocation of loss, in particular because it could not be attributed to those: • whose objectionable behaviour caused the damage; or • who benefitted from the activity that caused the damage; or • who were in control of the risk that materialised; or • who were cheapest cost avoiders or cheapest takers of insurance. (b) a coherent and appropriate response of the legal system to threats to the interests of individuals, in particular because victims of harm caused by the operation of emerging digital technologies receive less or no compensation compared to victims in a functionally equivalent situation involving human conduct and conventional technology; (c) effective access to justice, in particular because litigation for victims becomes unduly burdensome or expensive".

[136]Commission Communication "Report on the safety and liability implications of Artificial Intelligence, the Internet of Things and robotics", COM (2020) 64 final, Brussels, 19.2.2020, p. 13.

See also the Report from the Expert Group on Liability and New Technologies – New Technologies Formation "Liability for Artificial Intelligence and Other Emerging Digital Technologies", 21 November 2019, at p. 28: "The scope of the product liability regime rests on the concept of product. For the purposes of the Product Liability Directive, products are defined as movable objects, even when incorporated into another movable or immovable object, and include electricity. So far, the distinction of products and services has not encountered insurmountable difficulties. However, emerging digital technologies, especially AI systems, challenge that clear distinction and raise open questions. In AI systems, products and services permanently interact and a sharp separation between them is unfeasible. It is also questionable whether software is covered by the legal concept of product or product component. It is particularly discussed whether the answer should be different for embedded and non-embedded software, including over-the-air software

Furthermore, it was pointed out that the notion of product mainly refers to movables even though incorporated into another movable or into an immovable. It is pointed out that insofar as they constitute 'movable' items, AI and IoT devices as well as any other items containing intangible elements or presenting connectivity features could be qualified as 'products' and, therefore, defects appeared in these products could be covered by the Product Liability Directive. According to the Commission, an interpretation of the concept of product or an enlargement of the concept of product might be needed, especially where the non-tangible element is not included in the product put into circulation by the producer but installed subsequently as a stand-alone feature. This is particularly true with regards to software; a clarification of the concept 'product' could contribute to improving effectiveness and, therefore, further assessment is needed. As the Commission stated, "software and also AI merit specific attention in respect of product liability. Software is essential to the functioning of a large number of products and may affect their safety. It is integrated into products but it may also be supplied separately to enable the use of the product as intended. Neither a computer nor a smartphone would be of particular use without software. This means that software can make a tangible product defective and lead to physical damage. This could eventually result in the liability of the producer of the product under the Product Liability Directive. However, as software comes in many types and forms, answers related to the classification of software as a service or as a product may not always be straightforward. Thus while software steering the operations of a tangible product could be considered part or component of that product, some forms of stand-alone software could be more difficult to classify".[137]

The Commission concluded that applications and other non-embedded software (i.e. not contained in a tangible medium) might raise serious liability issues which are currently not fully addressed by the EU legal framework. AI, combined with hardware, can create new tangible products and/or deliver services. Since the distinction between products and services may become less relevant in the near future, it was recognized that there is a need to clarify what products and features are covered by the Product Liability Directive. For instance, providing data through an

updates or other data feeds. In any case, where such updates or other data feeds are provided from outside the EEA, the victim may not have anybody to turn to within the EEA, as there will typically not be an intermediary importer domiciled within the EEA in the case of direct downloads".

[137] Commission Communication "Report on the safety and liability implications of Artificial Intelligence, the Internet of Things and robotics", COM (2020) 64 final, Brussels, 19.2.2020, pp. 13–14.

See also Commission Staff Working Document, 'Evaluation of Product Liability Directive', SWD(2018) 157 final, Brussels, 07.05.2018, at pp. 52, 53–54, 61. For instance: "the non-tangible nature of some new technological developments (software, applications, Internet of Things, Artificial Intelligence systems) makes it difficult to classify them as products rather than services".

Also: Commission Staff Working Document on "Liability for emerging digital technologies" - Accompanying the document Commission Communication "Artificial intelligence for Europe", SWD(2018) 137 final, Brussels, 25.4.2018, at pp. 9–11.

IoT system could be considered a service, and thus fall, as such, outside the product liability (and safety) regime.

Furthermore, the Commission raised the question of whether the concept of 'producer', as defined in the context of Product Liability Directive, fits with the type of responsibilities that may arise in systems encompassing software, AI systems, data services and other emerging technologies. As it was stated, "although the Product Liability Directive's definition of product is broad, its scope could be further clarified to better reflect the complexity of emerging technologies and ensure that compensation is always available for damage caused by products that are defective because of software or other digital features. This would better enable economic actors, such as software developers, to assess whether they could be considered producers according to the Product Liability Directive".[138]

4.3.4.2.2 Complex IoT Environments

The Commission's Report underlined that the emerging digital technologies display certain levels of complexity due to the interdependency between different components. For instance, AI applications are usually integrated in complex IoT environments[139] where many different connected devices and services interact. The IoT and

---

[138] Commission Communication "Report on the safety and liability implications of Artificial Intelligence, the Internet of Things and robotics", COM (2020) 64 final, Brussels, 19.2.2020, p. 14.

See also Commission Staff Working Document, 'Evaluation of Product Liability Directive', SWD(2018) 157 final, Brussels, 07.05.2018, at pp. 52, 54, 61. For instance, it was examined whether the concept of 'producer', as defined in the context of Product Liability Directive, fits with the type of responsibilities that may arise in systems encompassing software, Artificial Intelligence systems, data services and other emerging technologies. It was concluded that, although the concept of the producer as responsible for his products is still relevant, "it is imperative to assess the impact of changing product (and/or product/service) configurations on this concept to see whether it should be clarified"; "as products are more easily, altered adapted and combined with services, the definition of the producer may become less clear particularly in the context of emerging digital technologies and the circular economy. The definition of the producer, while continuing to be valuable as it ensures strict liability, may therefore no longer be fully relevant in its current form".

See also the European Parliament Resolution of 16 February 2017 with recommendations to the Commission on Civil Law Rules on Robotics (2015/2103(INL)), (OJ C 252, 18.7.2018, pp. 239–257), which stated that the concepts of product, producer, damage or the category of exemptions as defined in the Product Liability Directive could not be apt anymore when dealing with the emerging field of robotics: "[...] in the scenario where a robot can take autonomous decisions, the traditional rules will not suffice to activate a robot's liability, since they would not make it possible to identify the party responsible for providing compensation and to require this party to make good the damage it has caused" (AF, at p. 242).

[139] See, for instance, the Commission Staff Working Document on "Liability for emerging digital technologies" - Accompanying the document Commission Communication "Artificial intelligence for Europe", SWD(2018) 137 final, Brussels, 25.4.2018, at p. 22: "The Internet of Things (IoT) is about setting up new ecosystems that cut across vertical areas, and create new markets for hardware (connected devices), software (IoT platforms and systems) and services (IoT applications). IoT has a horizontal and cross-cutting character. It should be understood as an ecosystem where areas that

AI-enabled products and services comprise tangible parts/devices (sensors, actuators, hardware), different software components and applications, data, data services (i.e. collection, processing, curating, analysing), and connectivity features. Furthermore, AI-related products and services are increasingly interacting with traditional technologies, leading to added complexity when it comes to liability.[140]

Since many different layers are involved in these technologies, vulnerable software, faulty sensors, or unstable connectivity may make it difficult to determine who is technically and legally responsible for any ensuing damage or how to identify the root cause of the problem. As the Commission put it, "combining different digital components in a complex ecosystem and the plurality of actors involved can make it difficult to assess where a potential damage originates and which person is liable for it. Due to the complexity of these technologies, it can be very difficult for victims to identify the liable person and prove all necessary conditions for a successful claim, as required under national law. The costs for this expertise may be economically prohibitive and discourage victims from claiming compensation".[141]

It is reminded that, in most EU member jurisdictions, extra-contractual liability regimes are fault-based. The fault of the author of the wrongful behaviour leading to a damage—which could be an act or an omission whether intentional or by negligence—is a necessary element to be proven for the liability claim to be successful. The victim submitting a claim needs to provide the evidence required to support his liability claim. Therefore, the burden of proof is the central component of the Product Liability Directive that triggers the right for compensation.

However, it is noted that, at least in specific cases, consumers could be disadvantaged by the burden of proof in product liability claims, facing difficulties to investigate claims properly or to gain access to essential information. Indeed, it is acknowledged that the main difficulty for the victim/injured party to obtain compensation is the burden of proof, namely, to prove the defect in the product and the

---

have been developed as vertical silos (manufacturing, transport, healthcare, devices, etc.) relate to each other, thanks to common platforms and cross-cutting innovation. IoT ecosystems are, therefore, based on bringing together multiple sectors and a variety of stakeholders to cover an increasingly complex value chain. IoT is based on various disciplines and technologies like sensors, embedded systems, various communications technologies. It requires a specific configuration for object identification and search, open/closed data sharing, lightweight communication protocols, trade-off between local and networked based information processing, and back-end integration. It also requires specific considerations of data security (e.g. location-based profiling), liability (many service providers involved), seamless identification and authentication mechanisms (including those of persons/entities needed for managing contractual relations, attribution and liability) and trust. All this increases the complexity of the IoT ecosystem".

[140] For example, autonomous cars will share the road with traditional ones for a certain time. Similar complexity of interacting actors will arise in some services sectors (such as traffic management and healthcare) where partially automated AI systems will support human decision-making. See Commission Communication "Report on the safety and liability implications of Artificial Intelligence, the Internet of Things and robotics", COM (2020) 64 final, Brussels, 19.2.2020, p. 14.

[141] Commission Communication "Report on the safety and liability implications of Artificial Intelligence, the Internet of Things and robotics", COM (2020) 64 final, Brussels, 19.2.2020, p. 14.

causal link between the defect and the damage.[142] This difficulty could become even higher in cases where complex technical products are involved. Indeed, since emerging digital technologies and products are becoming increasingly connected and complex, it could be extremely challenging for a claimant to identify the defect and prove the substantial elements of a liability claim. As already mentioned, the injured party needs to gather expertise in order to be able to prove the lack of safety of the product and the link to the damage suffered. In addition, the victim would face major difficulties when attempting to gain access to essential information, especially in the case of complex AI related products.

To tackle the issue of the burden of proof in product liability claims, and as a possible solution to the complexity of allocating responsibility for damage caused by increasingly autonomous systems, the Commission examined whether, and under what circumstance, a relaxation of the rules on the burden of proof should be decided: "The Commission is seeking views whether and to what extent it may be needed to mitigate the consequences of complexity by alleviating/reversing the burden of proof required by national liability rules for damage caused by the operation of AI applications, through an appropriate EU initiative".[143] It is noted that, under specific circumstances, EU member jurisdictions appear to facilitate the burden of proof of the victim so as to increase the possibility of compensation. For instance, there are cases where a presumption of fault by the wrongdoer exists, i.e. the wrongdoer is considered to be liable unless he can prove that he was not in fault. This is linked, inter alia, to the responsibility of parents/tutors/guardians/teachers for damages (unless they can prove that they were not able to prevent the

[142] See, for instance Commission Staff Working Document, 'Evaluation of Product Liability Directive', SWD(2018) 157 final, Brussels, 07.05.2018, at pp. 25–26. The most frequent reasons to reject claims relate to the proof of the defect and its link with the damage, which together account for 53% of the cases of rejection. Difficulties in applying the definition of defective product and subsequently in proving the link between damage and defect seem to be particularly relevant in cases of complex products, such as pharmaceuticals. For those products, the injured party need to gather expertise to be able to prove the lack of safety of the product and the link to the damage suffered. According to victims of medicines (Stevens-Johnson Syndrome, Valproate or Distilben) the definition of "defect" is not suitable for pharmaceutical products because the leaflet's information about the risk of serious adverse effects exonerates the producer for these effects. Therefore, it is extremely difficult for such an injured party to demonstrate the causality and the defect of a medicine in connection with the damage. Either the adverse effect of the medicine is unknown and it is therefore hard to provide sufficient scientific elements to establish the link (causality) and the development risk clause may be invoked, or it is known and was therefore published in the leaflet, which means that the medicine was not defective. Injured persons potentially find themselves in a Catch-22 situation where they have to bear the full cost of damages without access to compensation. In this respect, while the definition of defect, damage and their link seem to be effective for tangible products in general, the distinction between a known risk and an unexpected risk—particularly for pharmaceutical products—may be less clear.

See also: Commission Report on the Application of the Product Liability Directive, COM(2018) 246 final, Brussels, 07.05.2018, at pp. 2, 6 and 8.

[143] Commission Communication "Report on the safety and liability implications of Artificial Intelligence, the Internet of Things and robotics", COM (2020) 64 final, Brussels, 19.2.2020, p. 14.

damages from happening) caused by a minor, pupil, student/apprentice or mentally impaired person. Other examples where national law introduces variations in order to facilitate the burden of proof include the responsibility of the owner/possessor of a building in case of damages caused by that building (unless he/she proves that he/she observed appropriate care for the purpose of avoiding the damage); or the responsibility of a person carrying a dangerous activity (unless he can prove that all appropriate measures to avoid the damage have been taken).[144]

The reversal of the burden of proof in the context of a fault-based extra-contractual liability attempts to respond to the need to facilitate the compensation of the victim of damages in situations where the legislator considers it too burdensome or unbalanced to apply the general fault-based liability rule. While none of the above-mentioned examples of national law provisions facilitating the burden of proof are specifically linked to damages that may potentially be caused by emerging digital technologies, nonetheless they could become helpful precedents when examining how to best address elements of risks and damages caused by the emerging digital technologies. This is the reason why the Commission stated that "adaptations of national laws to facilitate the burden of proof for the victims of AI-related damage could be considered. For example, the burden of proof could be linked to the compliance (by a relevant operator) with specific cyber-security or other safety obligations set by law: if one does not comply with these rules, a change to the burden of proof as regards fault and causation could apply".[145]

---

[144] Examples of those variations are cited in the Commission Staff Working Document on "Liability for emerging digital technologies" - Accompanying the document Commission Communication "Artificial intelligence for Europe", SWD(2018) 137 final, Brussels, 25.4.2018, at pp. 7–9. Furthermore, as already mentioned, national legal systems may provide for special regimes of strict liability, i.e. a liability that does not depend on a fault and the claimant needs only to prove the damage and the causal link. "Special regimes of strict liability may apply to a diverse set of factual situations generating different types of risks and damages, such as the liability of the owners of animals for the damages caused by the animals under their custody; the strict liability of the person responsible for carrying out an unspecified or specified dangerous activity (for example the operation of nuclear power plants, aircrafts or motor vehicles) or other cases linked to a legal or factual relationship between two persons or a person and an object, such as when the damages are caused by someone executing a task in the interest of someone else (employee/employer) or by an object that is under his/her custody".

[145] Commission Communication "Report on the safety and liability implications of Artificial Intelligence, the Internet of Things and robotics", COM (2020) 64 final, Brussels, 19.2.2020, p. 14. "As regards Union legislation, according to the Product Liability Directive, a product that does not meet mandatory safety rules would be considered defective, regardless of the producers' fault. There may, however, also be reasons to contemplate ways on how to facilitate the burden of proof for victims under the Directive: the Directive relies on national rules on the evidence and the establishment of causation".

Back in 2018, the Commission had already identified this specific issue: "it is also important to assess the issue of the burden of proof. National regimes including fault-based liability schemes or different forms of strict liability regimes often include provisions, whereby the burden of proof for a possible fault, defect or other condition is not placed on the victim. Thus, the person held liable by law would need to prove to be discharged from liability, for instance, that the damage was caused as a result of force majeure or an act/behaviour of a third party. Whether the burden of proof should be

This conclusion is in line with the findings of the New Technologies formation which were presented in the Report "Liability for Artificial Intelligence and Other Emerging Digital Technologies", issued on 21 November 2019.[146] In particular, the Report from the Expert Group on Liability and New Technologies underlined that adaptations and amendments to existing liability regimes should be considered in order to facilitate the burden of proof for the victims of AI-related damage. As a general rule, the burden of proof for both causation and damage should remain with the victim, as is the case under existing liability frameworks ("the victim should continue to be required to prove what caused her harm").[147] In certain circumstances, however, it appears to be appropriate to reverse or lower this burden, especially when it is disproportionately high. For instance, the burden of proof should be reversed if damage was caused by a breach of some other set of rules (such as safety/security rules, including cybersecurity). As the Report from the Expert Group on Liability and New Technologies has specifically recommended: "A person operating a permissible technology that nevertheless carries an increased risk of harm to others, for example AI-driven robots in public spaces, should be subject to strict liability for damage resulting from its operation";[148] "where a particular technology increases the difficulties of proving the existence of an element of liability beyond what can be reasonably expected, victims should be entitled to facilitation of proof";[149] "emerging digital technologies should come with logging features, where appropriate in the circumstances, and failure to log, or to provide

---

on the claimant or reversed, what substantive conditions the claimant should demonstrate as well as the impact on the ability of the claimant to obtain compensation are important elements to assess". Commission Staff Working Document on "Liability for emerging digital technologies" - Accompanying the document Commission Communication "Artificial intelligence for Europe", SWD (2018) 137 final, Brussels, 25.4.2018, p. 20.

[146] Report from the Expert Group on Liability and New Technologies – New Technologies Formation "Liability for Artificial Intelligence and Other Emerging Digital Technologies", 21 November 2019. It is reminded that, in the call for applications, the 'New Technologies formation' was asked to assess "whether and to what extent existing liability schemes are adapted to the emerging market realities following the development of the new technologies such as Artificial Intelligence, advanced robotics, the IoT and cybersecurity issues". It was also asked to examine whether the current liability regimes are still "adequate to facilitate the uptake of the above-mentioned new technologies by fostering investment stability and users' trust". If shortcomings were identified, the New Technologies formation should make recommendations for amendments, leaving aside rules on safety and other technical standards. The 'New Technologies formation' analysed the relevant national laws, examined specific use cases (such as autonomous cars, smart home, blockchain, autonomous healthcare applications, drones, algorithmic decision making in the financial and other sectors), and compared various aspects of existing liability regimes. The findings of the New Technologies formation were presented in its Report "Liability for Artificial Intelligence and Other Emerging Digital Technologies", issued on 21 November 2019.

[147] Report from the Expert Group on Liability and New Technologies – New Technologies Formation "Liability for Artificial Intelligence and Other Emerging Digital Technologies", 21 November 2019, Key Finding (25), at p. 8.

[148] Ibid., at p. 3.

[149] Ibid., at p. 4.

reasonable access to logged data, should result in a reversal of the burden of proof in order not be to the detriment of the victim";[150] "if it is proven that an emerging digital technology has caused harm, the burden of proving defect should be reversed if there are disproportionate difficulties or costs pertaining to establishing the relevant level of safety or proving that this level of safety has not been met";[151] "the absence of logged information or failure to give the victim reasonable access to the information should trigger a rebuttable presumption that the condition of liability to be proven by the missing information is fulfilled";[152] "where the damage is of a kind that safety rules were meant to avoid, failure to comply with such safety rules, including rules on cybersecurity, should lead to a reversal of the burden of proving (a) causation, and/or (b) fault, and/or (c) the existence of a defect";[153] "without prejudice to the reversal of the burden of proof proposed . . ., the burden of proving causation may be alleviated in light of the challenges of emerging digital technologies if a balancing of the following factors warrants doing so: (a) the likelihood that the technology at least contributed to the harm; (b) the likelihood that the harm was caused either by the technology or by some other cause within the same sphere; (c) the risk of a known defect within the technology, even though its actual causal impact is not self-evident; (d) the degree of ex-post traceability and intelligibility of processes within the technology that may have contributed to the cause (informational asymmetry); (e) the degree of ex-post accessibility and comprehensibility of data collected and generated by the technology (f) the kind and degree of harm potentially and actually caused";[154] "if it is proven that an emerging digital technology caused harm, and liability therefor is conditional upon a person's intent or negligence, the burden of proving fault should be reversed if disproportionate difficulties and costs of establishing the relevant standard of care and of proving their violation justify it. This is without prejudice to the reversal of the (proposed) burden of proof".[155]

[150] Ibid.

[151] Ibid., Key Finding (15), at p. 6.

[152] Ibid., Key Finding (22), at p. 7.

[153] Ibid., Key Finding (24), at p. 7.

[154] Ibid., Key Finding (26), at p. 8.

[155] Ibid., Key Finding (27), at p. 8.

4.3.4.2.3 Connectivity and Openness

The increasing complexity, connectivity, openness[156] and vulnerability[157] of the emerging digital technologies can expose AI and IoT products to cyber-threats and have a considerable impact on product liability. In addition, new and possibly more advanced safety rules may be introduced. Indeed, "traditional" product safety differs from "digital" product safety in various ways, including the issue of cybersecurity. For instance, cybersecurity gaps and weaknesses may exist from the beginning, i.e. when a product was initially put into circulation, but they may also appear at a later stage, i.e. after the product was put into circulation.

In fault-based liability frameworks, the establishment of specific cyber-security obligations provides the operators with the opportunity to determine what needs to be done in advance to avoid becoming liable. Under the Product Liability Directive, a product that does not meet mandatory safety rules would be considered defective, regardless of the producers' fault. Indeed, it is assumed that failing to meet a safety standard means that the product does not provide the level of safety that the consumer is entitled to expect. However, the notion of foreseeable reasonable use[158] and questions of contributory negligence[159] could appear more often in practice, potentially reducing a producer's liability and thus making it more difficult for injured persons to receive compensation for damages caused by a defect in a product. This is why the Commission stated that "it is currently not entirely clear

[156] "Openness: Emerging digital technologies are not completed once put into circulation, but by their nature depend upon subsequent input, in particular more or less frequent updates or upgrades. Often they need to interact with other systems or data sources in order to function properly. They therefore need to remain open by design, i.e. permit external input either via some hardware plug or through some wireless connection, and come as hybrid combinations of hardware, software, continuous software updates, and various continuous services. This shift from the classic notion of a product completed at a certain point in time to a merger of products and ongoing services has a considerable impact on, among other things, product liability". Report from the Expert Group on Liability and New Technologies – New Technologies Formation "Liability for Artificial Intelligence and Other Emerging Digital Technologies", 21 November 2019, at p. 33.

[157] "Vulnerability: Emerging digital technologies are typically subject to more or less frequent updates and operate in more or less constant interaction with outside information. The built-in features granting access to such input make these technologies particularly vulnerable to cybersecurity breaches. These may cause the system itself to malfunction and/or modify its features in a way more likely to cause harm". Report from the Expert Group on Liability and New Technologies – New Technologies Formation "Liability for Artificial Intelligence and Other Emerging Digital Technologies", 21 November 2019, at pp. 33–34.

[158] According to the 'later defect defence', a producer is not liable if the defect did not exist at the time the product was put into circulation. Also, according to the 'development risk defence', the state-of-the-art knowledge at the time could not have foreseen the defect (i.e. the state of technical knowledge at the time of putting the product on the market made it impossible to discover the defect).

[159] An example of contributory negligence is when the injured party has failed to perform/download safety relevant updates and, therefore, liability of the producer could be reduced. In other words, liability of the producer could be limited to the extent the injured party has contributed to the actual damage.

what safety expectations may be with regard to damage that results from cybersecurity breaches in the product and whether such damage would be adequately compensated under the Product Liability Directive".[160]

As already stated, however, there might be appropriate to reverse or lower the burden of proof, especially when it is considered to be disproportionately high, as in cases where damages were caused by a breach of safety and cybersecurity rules. The reversal of the burden of proof is essential in the area of fault-based liability. In particular, according to the recommendations of the Report from the Expert Group on Liability and New Technologies, failing to comply with safety rules could lead to a reversal of the burden of proof concerning key elements of liability, including causation and fault: "where the damage is of a kind that safety rules were meant to avoid, failure to comply with such safety rules, including rules on cybersecurity, should lead to a reversal of the burden of proving (a) causation, and/or (b) fault, and/or (c) the existence of a defect".[161]

4.3.4.2.4 Autonomy and Opacity

It has been already mentioned that AI and IoT-enabled devices are increasingly having the ability (without human intervention) to analyse data, to adapt their behaviours and actions to their environment, and to learn through experience and interaction (autonomy and self-learning ability): "where AI applications are able to act autonomously, they perform a task without every step being pre-defined and with less or eventually entirely without immediate human control or supervision".[162] This built-in autonomy and self-learning ability may entail important product changes during the life cycle of an AI system and, therefore, could have an impact on safety.

[160] Commission Communication "Report on the safety and liability implications of Artificial Intelligence, the Internet of Things and robotics", COM (2020) 64 final, Brussels, 19.2.2020, p. 14.

[161] Report from the Expert Group on Liability and New Technologies – New Technologies Formation "Liability for Artificial Intelligence and Other Emerging Digital Technologies", 21 November 2019, Key Finding (24), at pp. 7 and 48. The Report provides the following example/illustration (No 18): "Imagine there is a new rule on cybersecurity of IoT household equipment, designed to prevent hacking and the resulting harm. The victim's private Wi-Fi is hacked in a way typical of cybersecurity gaps in IoT equipment. Where the victim can show that a water kettle produced by P failed to comply with the standard of safety under adopted safety rules, the victim could sue P, and the onus would be on P to prove that the damage had been caused by a different device", at p. 49.

[162] Commission Communication "Report on the safety and liability implications of Artificial Intelligence, the Internet of Things and robotics", COM (2020) 64 final, Brussels, 19.2.2020, p. 15.

See also the Report from the Expert Group on Liability and New Technologies – New Technologies Formation "Liability for Artificial Intelligence and Other Emerging Digital Technologies", 21 November 2019, at p. 33: "Autonomy: Emerging new technologies increasingly perform tasks with less, or entirely without, human control or supervision. They are themselves capable of altering the initial algorithms due to self-learning capabilities that process external data collected in the course of the operation. The choice of such data and the degree of impact it has on the outcome is constantly adjusted by the evolving algorithms themselves".

Indeed, this unpredictability[163] in behaviour and the autonomy aspect of AI applications and systems could raise serious safety issues which could not be initially foreseen by the manufacturer of the product. This is why the Commission underlined that "autonomy can affect the safety of the product, because it may alter a product's characteristics substantially, including its safety features" and raised the critical question "under what conditions self-learning features prolong liability of the producer and to what extent should the producer have foreseen certain changes".[164] Further concerns are arisen since AI-based products and systems can be characterised by various degrees of opacity (the internal complexity of the algorithms involved), resulting to a decision-making process of the AI system that can be extremely difficult to trace ('black box-effect'): "algorithms based on machine-learning can be difficult, if not impossible, to understand (the so-called 'black-box effect').[165]

The Commission acknowledged that, due to the autonomy aspect and the opacity issue (black-box effect) of AI systems, "getting compensation could become difficult for damage caused by autonomous AI-applications".[166] Indeed, it could be hard to trace the damage back to a specific human behaviour and, at the same time, extremely costly to understand (and get access to) the algorithm and the data used by the AI system. Finding the main cause of damage and attributing liability becomes complicated. Therefore, the allocation of liability may be unfair or inefficient, whereas liability claims may be difficult or overly costly to be made and/or to be proven (especially when a victim has to prove that the damage suffered was caused by a conduct attributable to an AI system and, in order to achieve this, an analysis of complex underlying code should take place, which could be beyond the—financial and technical—ability of the majority of victims). As a result, victims may not be adequately compensated. As the Commission stated, "the need to understand the algorithm and the data used by the AI requires analytical capacity

[163] Report from the Expert Group on Liability and New Technologies – New Technologies Formation "Liability for Artificial Intelligence and Other Emerging Digital Technologies", 21 November 2019, at p. 33: "Predictability: Many systems are designed to not only respond to pre-defined stimuli, but to identify and classify new ones and link them to a self-chosen corresponding reaction that has not been pre-programmed as such. The more external data systems are capable of processing, and the more they are equipped with increasingly sophisticated AI, the more difficult it is to foresee the precise impact they will have once in operation".

[164] Commission Communication "Report on the safety and liability implications of Artificial Intelligence, the Internet of Things and robotics", COM (2020) 64 final, Brussels, 19.2.2020, p. 15.

[165] Ibid. See also the Report from the Expert Group on Liability and New Technologies – New Technologies Formation "Liability for Artificial Intelligence and Other Emerging Digital Technologies", 21 November 2019, at p. 33: "Opacity: The more complex emerging digital technologies become, the less those taking advantage of their functions or being exposed to them can comprehend the processes that may have caused harm to themselves or to others. Algorithms often no longer come as more or less easily readable code, but as a black-box that has evolved through self-learning and which we may be able to test as to its effects, but not so much to understand".

[166] Commission Communication "Report on the safety and liability implications of Artificial Intelligence, the Internet of Things and robotics", COM (2020) 64 final, Brussels, 19.2.2020, p. 15.

and technical expertise that victims could find prohibitively costly. In addition, access to the algorithm and the data could be impossible without the cooperation of the potentially liable party. In practice, victims may thus not be able to make a liability claim. In addition, it would be unclear, how to demonstrate the fault of an AI acting autonomously, or what would be considered the fault of a person relying on the use of AI".[167]

The Commission noted that national laws have already developed various solutions to lower the burden of proof for victims in similar situations whereas it stressed that, as a guiding principle for the EU product safety and product liability, producers are obliged to ensure that the products put into circulation should be safe during their lifecycle as well as for the use of the product that can reasonably be expected. "This means that a manufacturer would have to make sure that a product using AI respects certain safety parameters. The features of AI do not preclude that there is an entitlement to safety expectations for products, whether they are automatic lawnmowers or surgery robots".[168] The Commission reminded that the EU product safety legislation does not explicitly address the increasing risks derived from the autonomy and opacity of AI systems and it stated that, alongside the need to introduce safety requirements for transparency of algorithms, intelligibility, explicability, accountability, human oversight and unbiased outcomes, the Product Liability Directive should be re-assessed in order to take into account that AI products can change during their life cycle: "in close coordination with corresponding changes in the Union safety framework, the notion of 'putting into circulation' that is currently used by the Product Liability Directive could be revisited to take into account that products may change and be altered. This could also help to clarify who is liable for any changes that are made to the product".[169]

---

[167] Ibid. See also Report from the Expert Group on Liability and New Technologies – New Technologies Formation "Liability for Artificial Intelligence and Other Emerging Digital Technologies", 21 November 2019, at p. 24: "In addition to the difficulties of determining what constitutes fault in the case of damage caused by an emerging digital technology, there may also be problems with proving fault. Generally, the victim has to prove that the defendant (or someone whose conduct is attributable to them) was at fault. The victim therefore not only needs to identify which duties of care the defendant should have discharged, but also to prove to the court that these duties were breached. Proving the defendant is at fault entails providing the court with evidence that may lead it to believe what the applicable standard of care was and that it has not been met. The second part of this is to provide evidence of how the event giving rise to the damage occurred. The more complex the circumstances leading to the victim's harm are, the harder it is to identify relevant evidence. For example, it can be difficult and costly to identify a bug in a long and complicated software code. In the case of AI, examining the process leading to a specific result (how the input data led to the output data) may be difficult, very time-consuming and expensive".

[168] Commission Communication "Report on the safety and liability implications of Artificial Intelligence, the Internet of Things and robotics", COM (2020) 64 final, Brussels, 19.2.2020, p. 15.

[169] Ibid. See also the Report from the Expert Group on Liability and New Technologies – New Technologies Formation "Liability for Artificial Intelligence and Other Emerging Digital Technologies", 21 November 2019, at pp. 28–29: "As the PLD focuses on the moment when the product was put into circulation as the key turning point for the producer's liability, this cuts off claims for anything the producer may subsequently add via some update or upgrade. In addition, the PLD does

4.4 Report from the Expert Group on Liability and New Technologies: New Technologies Formation "Liability for Artificial Intelligence and Other Emerging Digital Technologies"

This section examines the recommendations of the Report from the Expert Group on Liability and New Technologies on how existing liability concepts might be applied, with adjustments, to emerging digital technologies.

4.4.1 Strict Liability of the Operator

One of the most important recommendations of the Expert Group's Report (alongside the recommendation to facilitate the burden of proof for victims of AI-related damage, i.e. reversing or lowering the burden of proof if it is proven that an emerging digital technology has caused harm and it is too burdensome or unbalanced to apply the general fault-based liability rule) was that, under certain circumstances, and in order to achieve effective compensation of victims, it might be appropriate to impose strict liability for damage caused by emerging technologies.[170] In line with the

not provide for any duties to monitor the products after putting them into circulation. Highly sophisticated AI systems may not be finished products that are put on the market in a traditional way. The producer may retain some degree of control over the product's further development in the form of additions or updates after circulation. At the same time, the producer's control may be limited and nonexclusive if the product's operation requires data provided by third parties or collected from the environment, and depends on self-learning processes and personalising settings chosen by the user. This dilutes the traditional role of a producer, when a multitude of actors contribute to the design, functioning and use of the AI product/system. This is related to another limitation of liability – most Member States adopted the so-called development risk defence, which allows the producer to avoid liability if the state of scientific and technical knowledge at the time when he put the product into circulation was not such as to enable the existence of the defect to be discovered (Article 7 lit e PLD). The defence may become much more important practically with regard to sophisticated AI-based products".

[170] "The advantage of strict liability for the victim[s] is obvious, as it exempts them from having to prove any wrongdoing within the defendant's sphere, let alone the causal link between such wrongdoing and the victim's loss, allowing the victim to focus instead only on whether the risk brought about by the technology materialised by causing them harm. However, one has to bear in mind that often strict liabilities are coupled with liability caps or other restrictions in order to counterbalance the increased risk of liability of those benefiting from the technology. Such caps are often further justified as contributing to making the risk insurable, as strict liability statutes often require adequate insurance cover for the liability risks. A factor which any legislator considering the introduction of strict liability will have to take into account is the effect that such introduction may have on the advancement of the technology, as some may be more hesitant to actively promote technological research if the risk of liability is considered a deterrent. On the other hand, this allegedly chilling effect of tort law is even stronger as long as the question of liability is entirely unresolved and therefore unpredictable, whereas the introduction of a specific statutory solution at

principle of proportionality, the application of strict liability should be limited to situations where the emerging technologies may create specific risks (which are likely to arise in circumstances where digital technologies move in public spaces, e.g., drones, autonomous cars, traffic management services), expose the public at large to risks, and cause significant harm to life, health, and property. The Commission cited the Report from the Expert Group on Liability and New Technologies by stating that "the operation of some autonomous AI devices and services could have a specific risk profile in terms of liability, because they may cause significant harm to important legal interests like life, health and property, and expose the public at large to risks. This could mainly concern AI devices that move in public spaces (e.g. fully autonomous vehicles, drones and package delivery robots) or AI-based services with similar risks (e.g. traffic management services guiding or controlling vehicles or management of power distribution). The challenges of autonomy and opacity to national tort laws could be addressed following a risk-based approach. Strict liability schemes could ensure that whenever that risk materialises, the victim is compensated regardless of fault. The impact of choosing who should be strictly liable for such operations on the development and uptake of AI would need to be carefully assessed and a risk-based approach be considered".[171]

In particular, the Report from the Expert Group on Liability and New Technologies[172] pointed out—when considering adaptations and amendments to existing rules of liability due to the risks created by emerging digital technologies—that "emerging digital technologies make it difficult to apply fault-based liability rules, due to the lack of well-established models of proper functioning of these technologies and the possibility of their developing as a result of learning without direct

---

least more or less clearly delimits the risks and contributes to making them insurable". Report from the Expert Group on Liability and New Technologies – New Technologies Formation "Liability for Artificial Intelligence and Other Emerging Digital Technologies", 21 November 2019, at pp. 26–27.

[171] Commission Communication "Report on the safety and liability implications of Artificial Intelligence, the Internet of Things and robotics", COM (2020) 64 final, Brussels, 19.2.2020, p. 16.

[172] The following paragraph comprises an executive summary of the main recommendations of the Report from the Expert Group on Liability and New Technologies (in brackets, the number of the recommendations/key findings): "... strict liability of the operator of some emerging digital technology may be justified, given the competing interests of said operator and of the victim, as well as the victim's alternatives to getting compensation ([9]-[12]). In the case of a product defect, the manufacturer of that product may be the appropriate addressee of claims arising out of such defects ([13]-[15]). However, adapting the notion of fault liability by specifying further duties of care ([16]-[17]), or by shifting the burden of proving fault ([22](b), [24](b), [27]), for example, may already resolve disruptive effects of emerging digital technologies in the field of tort law, if necessary and appropriate at all. Remaining gaps may often be filled by extending vicarious liability to the use of autonomous technology in lieu of human auxiliaries ([18]). If there are systemic practical difficulties in proving causation and other factors, it may be necessary to make some adjustments in this respect ([22], [24], [25]- [26], [29]-[30]). An insurance requirement may be necessary in some cases, to ensure that victims will get compensation ([33]). Compensation funds can also play a complementary role ([34])". See the Report from the Expert Group on Liability and New Technologies – New Technologies Formation "Liability for Artificial Intelligence and Other Emerging Digital Technologies", 21 November 2019, at p. 36.

human control".[173] This is the reason why the Report stated that strict liability of the operator of some emerging digital technology may be justified: "a person operating a permissible technology that nevertheless carries an increased risk of harm to others, for example AI-driven robots in public spaces, should be subject to strict liability for damage resulting from its operation";[174] "strict liability is an appropriate response to the risks posed by emerging digital technologies, if, for example, they are operated in non-private environments and may typically cause significant harm".[175] According to the Report from the Expert Group on Liability and New Technologies, the introduction of strict liability for emerging digital technologies could grant victims easier access to compensation, retaining a parallel fault liability claim if its requirements are satisfied. Furthermore, while strict liability will typically direct liability to the liable person (for example, the operator of the technology), this person will maintain the right to seek recourse from others who also contributed to the risk, such as the producer.[176]

It was also examined whether strict liability for emerging digital technologies should lie with the traditional concepts of owner/user/keeper of the technology (these concepts are not considered helpful in the context of emerging digital technologies)[177] or with the producer ("if strict liability for operating the technology—

[173] Report from the Expert Group on Liability and New Technologies – New Technologies Formation "Liability for Artificial Intelligence and Other Emerging Digital Technologies", 21 November 2019, at p. 23.

[174] Ibid., at p. 3. One of the examples (Illustration 6) used by the Report is the following: "The sensors controlling the path of an AI-driven robot transporting heavy component parts in Factory F malfunction, causing the robot to leave its intended path, exit the factory and run into passer-by P on the street. Even if existing rules of strict motor vehicle liability may not apply in this case, P should still be able to seek compensation from F without having to prove that F or of one of its staff is at fault". See Report from the Expert Group on Liability and New Technologies – New Technologies Formation "Liability for Artificial Intelligence and Other Emerging Digital Technologies", 21 November 2019, at p. 40.

[175] Ibid., Key Finding [9], at pp. 6 and 39. According to the Expert Group's Report, the term 'significance' is determined by the interplay of the potential frequency and the severity of possible harm. Also, at p. 40: "The mere fact that technology is new is not justification enough for introducing strict liability. Nevertheless, emerging digital technologies that may typically cause significant harm comparable to the risks already subject to strict liability should also be subject to strict liability. This is because victims should be treated alike if they are exposed to and ultimately harmed by similar dangers. For the time being, this applies primarily to emerging digital technologies which move in public spaces, such as vehicles, drones, or the like. Smart home appliances will typically not be proper candidates for strict liability. It is in particular objects of a certain minimum weight, moved at a certain minimum speed, that are candidates for additional bases of strict liability, such as AI-driven delivery or cleaning robots, at least if they are operated in areas where others may be exposed to risk. Strict liability may not be appropriate for merely stationary robots (e.g. surgical or industrial robots), even if AI-driven, which are exclusively employed in a confined environment, with a narrow range of people exposed to risk, who in addition are protected by a different – including contractual – regime".

[176] Ibid., at p. 40.

[177] Ibid., at pp. 40–41: "It has been pointed out, in particular in the context of autonomous cars, that while the vast majority of accidents used to be caused by human error in the past, most accidents

besides product liability—were on the producer, the cost of insurance would be passed on to the owners anyway through the price mechanism").[178] Instead, the Report of the Expert Group opted for the more neutral and flexible concept of 'operator': "strict liability should lie with the person who is in control[179] of the risk connected with the operation of emerging digital technologies and who benefits from their operation (operator)".[180] In addition, it was stated that existing national schemes of strict liability (reflecting a focus on continuous control by humans) include a range of defences and exceptions that cannot be considered to be appropriate in the case of emerging digital technologies.[181] As a result, the Report recommended the following: "Existing defences and statutory exceptions from strict liability may have to be reconsidered in the light of emerging digital technologies, in particular if these defences and exceptions are tailored primarily to traditional notions of control by humans".[182]

Furthermore, it was recognised that, with emerging digital technologies, there are often two or more operators, i.e. the owner/user/keeper who operates the technology on the frontend and, at the same time, a central backend provider who, on an ongoing basis, provides essential backend support services.[183] In those cases, the Report

---

will be caused by the malfunctioning of technology in the future (though not necessarily of the autonomous car itself). This in turn could mean that it would not be appropriate to hold the owner/user/keeper strictly liable in the first place, because it is the producer who is the cheapest cost avoider and who is primarily in a position to control the risk of accidents. On the other hand, it is still the owner/user/keeper who decides when, where and for which purposes the technology is used, and who directly benefits from its use".

[178] Report from the Expert Group on Liability and New Technologies – New Technologies Formation "Liability for Artificial Intelligence and Other Emerging Digital Technologies", 21 November 2019, at p. 41.

[179] Ibid.: "'Control' is a variable concept, though, ranging from merely activating the technology, thus exposing third parties to its potential risks, to determining the output or result (such as entering the destination of a vehicle or defining the next tasks of a robot), and may include further steps in between, which affect the details of the operation from start to stop. However, the more sophisticated and more autonomous a system, the less someone exercises actual 'control' over the details of the operation, and defining and influencing the algorithms, for example by continuous updates, may have a greater impact than just starting the system".

[180] Ibid., Key Finding [10], at pp. 6, 39, 41.

[181] Ibid., at p. 42. According to the example (Illustration 8) used by the Report, "several national traffic liability schemes focus on the existence of a driver or allow for a defence in case of an unavoidable event or similar notions. These concepts do not translate properly into risk scenarios involving emerging digital technologies because the driver of an AV more resembles a passenger and because liability (or the exclusion of it) can no longer be linked to human control, which is typically missing entirely, at least with level 5 AVs".

[182] Ibid., Key Finding [12], at p. 39.

[183] Ibid., at p. 41. The illustration (No 7) provided by the Report is the following: "An AV may be privately owned by an individual who decides whether to use the AV for shopping or for going on a business trip, and how often, when and where. This individual is the frontend operator. The producer of the AV or another service provider is likewise controlling the AV on a continuous basis, e.g. by continuously providing cloud navigation services, continuously updating map data or the AV software as a result of supervised fleet machine learning, and deciding when the AV needs

proposed the following: "If there are two or more operators, in particular (a) the person primarily deciding on and benefitting from the use of the relevant technology (frontend operator) and (b) the person continuously defining the features of the relevant technology and providing essential and ongoing backend support (backend operator), strict liability should lie with the one who has more control over the risks of the operation".[184]

4.4.2 *Responsibility of the Producer*

In addition, the Report of the Expert Group on Liability and New Technologies argued that, apart from the operator's strict liability, the principle of producer responsibility should also apply to emerging digital technologies. In particular, the Report stated: "Strict liability of the producer should play a key role in indemnifying damage caused by defective products and their components, irrespective of whether they take a tangible or a digital form";[185] "the producer should be strictly liable for

---

what kind of maintenance. This person is the backend operator. Of course frontend and backend operator may also be the same person, such as in a 'mobility as a service' scheme (MaaS), where an AV is operated by a fleet operator who is also the backend operator".

[184]Report from the Expert Group on Liability and New Technologies – New Technologies Formation "Liability for Artificial Intelligence and Other Emerging Digital Technologies", 21 November 2019, Key Finding [11], at p. 39. See also at pp. 41–42: "This backend operator may have a high degree of control over the operational risks others are exposed to. From an economic point of view, the backend operator also benefits from the operation, because that operator profits from data generated by the operation, or that operator's remuneration is directly calculated on the basis of the duration, continuous nature or intensity of the operation, or because a one-off payment this backend operator has received reflects the estimated overall duration, continuous nature and intensity of the operation. ... While both control and benefit are decisive for qualifying a person as operator, the benefit is often very difficult to quantify, so relying only on benefit as the decisive factor for deciding who, out of two operators, should be liable, would lead to uncertainty. ... Very often, the frontend operator will have more control, but where emerging digital technologies become more backend-focused, there may be cases where so much continuous control over the technology remains with the backend operator that – despite the fact that the technology is sold to individual owners – it is more convincing to hold the backend operator liable as the person primarily in a position to control, reduce and insure the risks associated with the use of the technology. ... Ideally, in order to avoid uncertainty, the legislator should define which operator is liable under which circumstances, and all other matters that need to be regulated (concerning insurance for example). For instance, the legislator could decide that for AVs with a level of automation of 4 or 5, it is the provider running the system and who enters the AV in the national registry who is liable. This provider would therefore also take out insurance and could pass on the premiums through the fees paid for its services. Where several providers fulfil the function of backend operators, one of them would have to be designated as responsible operator for every AV".

[185]Ibid., Key Finding [13], at p. 42. According to the Report (at p. 43), "it is in line with the principle of functional equivalence, that damage caused by defective digital content should trigger the producer's liability because digital content fulfils many of the functions tangible movable items used to fulfil when the PLD was drafted and passed. This is all the more true for defective digital elements of other products, some of which come separately from the tangible item (for example, as a

defects in emerging digital technologies even if said defects appear after the product was put into circulation, as long as the producer was still in control of updates to, or upgrades on, the technology. A development risk defence should not apply";[186] "if it is proven that an emerging digital technology has caused harm, the burden of proving defect should be reversed if there are disproportionate difficulties or costs pertaining to establishing the relevant level of safety or proving that this level of safety has not been met".[187]

---

control app to be downloaded onto the user's smartphone), or as over-the-air updates after the product has been put into circulation (security updates for example), or as digital services provided on a continuous basis during the time the product is being used (for example, navigation cloud services)".

[186] Ibid., Key Finding [14], at p. 42. It is reminded that the so-called development risk defence allows the producer to avoid liability if the state of scientific and technical knowledge at the time when he put the product into circulation was not such as to enable the existence of the defect to be discovered (Article 7(e) of the Product Liability Directive - PLD). This defence may become increasingly important and result in limitation of liability when AI-based products are involved. As the Report put it (at p. 28), "As the PLD focuses on the moment when the product was put into circulation as the key turning point for the producer's liability, this cuts off claims for anything the producer may subsequently add via some update or upgrade. In addition, the PLD does not provide for any duties to monitor the products after putting them into circulation. Highly sophisticated AI systems may not be finished products that are put on the market in a traditional way. The producer may retain some degree of control over the product's further development in the form of additions or updates after circulation. At the same time, the producer's control may be limited and nonexclusive if the product's operation requires data provided by third parties or collected from the environment, and depends on self-learning processes and personalising settings chosen by the user. This dilutes the traditional role of a producer, when a multitude of actors contribute to the design, functioning and use of the AI product/system".

See also, at p. 43: "emerging digital technologies are characterised by limited predictability. This phenomenon will intensify with the dissemination of machine learning. The interconnectedness of devices, as well as threats to cyber security, also contribute to difficulties in predicting the product's performance. A defect in digital content or in a product with digital elements may therefore result from the impact of the environment in which the product operates or from the product's evolution, for which the manufacturer only created a general framework but which they did not design in detail. In view of the need to share benefits and risks efficiently and fairly, the development risk defence, which allows the producer to avoid liability for unforeseeable defects, should not be available in cases where it was predictable that unforeseen developments might occur". ... "When the defect came into being as a result of the producer's interference with the product already put into circulation (by way of a software update for example), or the producer's failure to interfere, it should be regarded as a defect in the product for which the producer is liable. The point in time at which a product is placed on the market should not set a strict limit on the producer's liability for defects where, after that point in time, the producer or a third party acting on behalf of the producer remains in charge of providing updates or digital services. The producer should therefore remain liable where the defect has its origin (i) in a defective digital component or digital ancillary part or in other digital content or services provided for the product with the producer's assent after the product has been put into circulation; or (ii) in the absence of an update of digital content, or of the provision of a digital service which would have been required to maintain the expected level of safety within the time period for which the producer is obliged to provide such updates".

[187] Ibid., Key Finding [15], at p. 42. See also at pp. 43–44 of the Report: "Features of emerging digital technologies, such as opacity, openness, autonomy and limited predictability, may often result in unreasonable difficulties or costs for the victim to establish both what safety an average

4.4.3 Fault Liability by Specifying Further Duties of Care

Furthermore, the Report of the Expert Group on Liability and New Technologies stressed that adapting the notion of fault liability by specifying further duties of care or by shifting the burden of proving fault may tackle disruptive effects of emerging digital technologies.

In particular, the Report pointed out that operators' strict liability should be supplemented with fault-based liability. As a result, operators of emerging digital technologies should comply with a range of duties of care, including the choice of technology in light of the tasks to be performed, the framework provided with regard to proper monitoring, and other issues in relation to maintenance, safety checks and repair. As the Report stated: "Fault liability and duties of care: Operators of emerging digital technologies should have to comply with an adapted range of duties of care, including with regard to (a) choosing the right system for the right task and skills; (b) monitoring the system; and (c) maintaining the system".[188] It should be underlined that failure of the operator of the AI system to comply with such duties could trigger fault liability irrespective of whether the operator may also be strictly liable for the risk created by the said technology. Indeed, operators may not only be strictly liable for the risks inherent in operating emerging digital technologies (which are operated in non-private environments and may cause significant harm), but also for their failure to comply with specific duties of care.[189]

The same approach should also apply to producers, i.e. producers' strict liability for defective products should be supplemented with fault-based liability for failure to

---

user is entitled to expect, and the failure to achieve this level of safety. At the same time, it may be significantly easier for the producer to prove relevant facts. This asymmetry justifies the reversal of the burden of proof".

[188] Report from the Expert Group on Liability and New Technologies – New Technologies Formation "Liability for Artificial Intelligence and Other Emerging Digital Technologies", 21 November 2019, Key Finding [16], at p. 44.

[189] Ibid. The Report provided the following relevant example (illustration 9): "Despite adverse weather conditions due to a heavy storm, which were entirely foreseeable, retailer (R) continues to employ drones to deliver goods to customers. One of the drones is hit by a strong wind, falls to the ground and severely injures a passerby. R may not only be strictly liable for the risks inherent in operating drones, but also for its failure to interrupt the use of such drones during the storm" (at p. 44).

Furthermore, the Report underlined that, with emerging digital technologies, such duties of care—despite all new opportunities and safety-enhancing technologies these systems may feature—are often raised and magnified to a point where it is difficult to draw the line between fault liability and strict liability. In order to demonstrate this point, the Report used the following illustration (number 10): "Airline A buys a plane from producer P. A new AI element of the auto pilot may, under very exceptional circumstances, cause the plane to crash if the software is not manually disabled by the pilot. Airline A has a duty of care to make itself familiar with the new feature, to monitor the plane and to make sure pilots receive appropriate training and exchange information about and experience of dealing with the new software. If A breaches this duty, A may be liable under fault liability (without prejudice to existing international legal instruments that may limit A's liability)" (at p. 45).

discharge specific duties. Indeed, it is critical for producers to comply with a range of monitoring duties of care, especially in the light of the characteristics of emerging digital technologies, such as openness[190] and dependency on the general digital environment, including the emergence of new malware. Furthermore, it was recognised that the emerging digital technologies are becoming increasingly advanced and, therefore, it becomes complicated for operators to develop the right skills and comply will all duties. As the Report of the Expert Group on Liability and New Technologies stressed, "while the risk of insufficient skills should still be borne by the operators, it would be unfair to leave producers entirely out of the equation. Rather, producers have to design, describe and market products in a way effectively enabling operators to discharge their duties".[191] As a result, the Report recommended the following: "Producers, whether or not they incidentally also act as operators ..., should have to: (a) design, describe and market products in a way effectively enabling operators to comply with the [following] duties [i.e. choosing the right system for the right task and skills; monitoring the system; and maintaining the system]; and (b) adequately monitor the product after putting it into circulation".[192]

In addition, the Report of the Expert Group on Liability and New Technologies argued that further duties should apply to producers, especially the obligation to equip technology with means of recording information related to the operation of the technology ('logging by design'). The importance of introducing an obligation to provide appropriate and proportionate logging and to disclose the necessary data to the victim in readable format is highlighted by the Report, when it states that "emerging digital technologies ... offer unprecedented possibilities of reliable and detailed documentation of events that may enable the identification inter alia of what has caused an accident. This can usually be done by using log files. ... Any requirements must definitely be suitable for the goals to be achieved and proportionate, taking into account, in particular, the technical feasibility and costs of logging, the values at stake, the magnitude of the risk, and any adverse implications for the rights of others. Logging would have to be done in such a way that no

[190] Ibid., at p. 33. "Openness: Emerging digital technologies are not completed once put into circulation, but by their nature depend upon subsequent input, in particular more or less frequent updates or upgrades. Often they need to interact with other systems or data sources in order to function properly. They therefore need to remain open by design, i.e. permit external input either via some hardware plug or through some wireless connection, and come as hybrid combinations of hardware, software, continuous software updates, and various continuous services. This shift from the classic notion of a product completed at a certain point in time to a merger of products and ongoing services has a considerable impact on, among other things, product liability".

[191] Report from the Expert Group on Liability and New Technologies – New Technologies Formation "Liability for Artificial Intelligence and Other Emerging Digital Technologies", 21 November 2019, at p. 45. The Report underlined (see illustration 11, at p. 45) that in illustration 10 (already described above), "it is primarily P who has to alert its customer (A) to the particular features and risks of the software in question, and possibly to offer the necessary training courses, and to monitor the system once it is on the market".

[192] Ibid., Key Finding [17], at p. 44.

interested party could manipulate the data and that the victim and/or the person who compensates the victim in the first place, for example an insurance provider, has access to it. Furthermore, it goes without saying that logging must be done in accordance with otherwise applicable law, notably on data protection and the protection of trade secrets".[193] 'Logging by design' is vital and this is why it was also highlighted by the High-Level Expert Group on AI (AI HLEG) in its assessment list (which, *inter alia*, provides guidance on self-assessing whether the data and processes that yield the AI system's decisions are properly logged and well documented to allow for traceability and auditability of the algorithmic decision-making process),[194] and emphasized by the Commission's Report on the safety and liability implications of AI, IoT and robotics.[195] Therefore, the Report from the Expert Group on Liability and New Technologies underlined that emerging digital technologies should come with logging features, and failure to comply with a logging and disclosure (providing reasonable access to logged data) duty should result in a reversal of the burden of proof: "failure to comply with a logging and disclosure duty should lead to a rebuttable presumption that the information would, if logged and disclosed, have revealed that the relevant element of liability is fulfilled".[196] As a result, the relevant recommendation of the Report reads as follows: "Logging by design: There should be a duty on producers to equip technology with means of recording information about the operation of the technology (logging by design), if such information is typically essential for establishing whether a risk of the technology materialised, and if logging is appropriate and proportionate, taking into account, in particular, the technical feasibility and the costs of logging, the availability of alternative means of gathering such information, the type and magnitude of the risks posed by the technology, and any adverse

---

[193] Ibid., at p. 47.

[194] "The Assessment List for Trustworthy Artificial Intelligence (ALTAI) for self-assessment", High-Level Expert Group on AI (AI HLEG), 17 July 2020. See, for instance: "Reliability, Fall-back plans and Reproducibility: Did you put in place verification and validation methods and documentation (e.g. logging) to evaluate and ensure different aspects of the AI system's reliability and reproducibility? (at p. 11); "Traceability: Did you put adequate logging practices in place to record the decision(s) or recommendation(s) of the AI system? (at p. 14); "Accountability – Auditability: Did you establish mechanisms that facilitate the AI system's auditability (e.g. traceability of the development process, the sourcing of training data and the logging of the AI system's processes, outcomes, positive and negative impact)?", at p. 21.

[195] Commission Communication "Report on the safety and liability implications of Artificial Intelligence, the Internet of Things and robotics", COM (2020) 64 final, Brussels, 19.2.2020, p. 16: "one of the issues flagged by the Report from the New Technologies formation of the Expert Group on Liability and New Technologies is the situation when the potentially liable party has not logged the data relevant for assessing liability or is not willing to share them with the victim".

[196] Report from the Expert Group on Liability and New Technologies – New Technologies Formation "Liability for Artificial Intelligence and Other Emerging Digital Technologies", 21 November 2019, at p. 48.

implications logging may have on the rights of others".[197] "Logging must be done in accordance with otherwise applicable law, in particular data protection law and the rules concerning the protection of trade secrets".[198] "The absence of logged information or failure to give the victim reasonable access to the information should trigger a rebuttable presumption that the condition of liability to be proven by the missing information is fulfilled".[199] "If and to the extent that, as a result of the presumption under [22], the operator were obliged to compensate the damage, the operator should have a recourse claim against the producer who failed to equip the technology with logging facilities".[200]

---

[197] Ibid., Key Finding [20], at p. 47. The benefits derived from logging should substantially exceed the anticipated individual risks, adequate measures should be taken to mitigate these risks, and the final decision should be compatible with the principle of proportionality: "Any requirements must definitely be suitable for the goals to be achieved and proportionate, taking into account, in particular, the technical feasibility and costs of logging, the values at stake, the magnitude of the risk, and any adverse implications for the rights of others" (at p. 47).

The relevant illustration (No 14) provided by the Report (at p. 47) refers to autonomous vehicles (AVs), and concludes—following a risk assessment carried out by the Expert Group—as follows: "There would be a logging duty in the case of AVs. Traffic accidents occur rather frequently and often cause severe harm to the life and health of humans. Motor vehicles are very sophisticated and expensive anyway, so adding logging technology should not significantly increase the costs of production. There is a lot of data that can reasonably be logged and will serve to reconstruct events and causal chains that are both essential for allocating liability (for example by finding out which AV has caused the crash by not replying to a signal sent by the other AV) and could hardly be reconstructed otherwise".

On the other hand, when examining whether logging could be imposed as a duty in the case of an AI-equipped doll for children, the Report understandably reached the opposite conclusion (Illustration 15, at p. 48): "Logging would not be advisable, however, in the case of an AI-equipped doll for children. The risks associated with the doll are not of a kind where logging would be a suitable response. With regard to the risk of hidden merchandising, meaning that the doll manipulates the child's mind by mentioning and repeating certain product brands, the negative implications of logging (which would have to include, to a certain extent, the recording of conversations) for data protection would outweigh any possible benefit. With regard to the risk of a stranger hacking into the doll, the proper response is more cybersecurity to prevent this, not a duty to log".

[198] Report from the Expert Group on Liability and New Technologies – New Technologies Formation "Liability for Artificial Intelligence and Other Emerging Digital Technologies", 21 November 2019, Key Finding [21], at p. 47.

[199] Ibid., Key Finding [22], at p. 47. The example provided by the Report [Illustration 16] is the following (at p. 48): "Failure to comply with a logging and disclosure duty should lead to a rebuttable presumption that the information would, if logged and disclosed, have revealed that the relevant element of liability is fulfilled. . . . Take the example of a crash between A's AV and B's AV, injuring B. The traffic situation was one where, normally, the two AVs would exchange data and "negotiate" which AV enters the lane first. When sued by B, A refuses to disclose the data logged in her AV's recordings. It is therefore presumed that her AV sent a signal telling B's AV to enter the lane first, but nevertheless went first itself".

[200] Ibid., Key Finding [23], at p. 47. According to the Report, if a product used by the operator did not contain a logging option and the operator is, for this particular reason, exposed to liability, the operator should have a resource claim against the producer. Therefore, the operator should be able to pass on the loss (resulting from not complying with the duty of disclosing logged data to the victim) to the producer. The example used by the Report is the following (Illustration 17): "Imagine

4.4.4 Vicarious Liability for Autonomous Systems

According to the Report of the Expert Group on Liability and New Technologies, a person using a technology which has a certain degree of autonomy should not be less accountable for ensuing harm than if said harm had been caused by a human auxiliary. The Report recommended, therefore, to extend vicarious liability to the use of autonomous technology in lieu of human auxiliaries.[201] As it was stated: "If harm is caused by autonomous technology used in a way functionally equivalent to the employment of human auxiliaries, the operator's liability for making use of the technology should correspond to the otherwise existing vicarious liability regime of a principal for such auxiliaries".[202]

---

that, in Illustration 16, it is not that A refused to disclose the data, but that A's AV failed to log the kind of data in question. If A had to pay damages to B for this reason only, she should also be able to sue the producer".

[201] Ibid., at pp. 24–25: "Existing tort laws in Europe differ substantially in their approach to holding someone (the principal) liable for the conduct of another (the auxiliary). Some attribute an auxiliary's conduct to the principal without further requirements, other than that the auxiliary acted under the direction of the principal and for the benefit of the principal. Others hold the principal liable in tort law only under very exceptional circumstances, such as known dangerousness of the auxiliary or the auxiliary's complete unsuitability for the assigned task, or if the defendant was at fault in selecting or supervising the auxiliary. There are also jurisdictions which use both approaches. ... Irrespective of such differences, the concept of vicarious liability is considered by some as a possible catalyst for arguing that operators of machines, computers, robots or similar technologies should also be strictly liable for their operations, based on an analogy to the basis of vicarious liability. If someone can be held liable for the wrongdoing of some human helper, why should the beneficiary of such support not be equally liable if they outsource their duties to a non-human helper instead, considering that they equally benefit from such delegation? The policy argument is quite convincing that using the assistance of a self-learning and autonomous machine should not be treated differently from employing a human auxiliary, if such assistance leads to harm of a third party ('principle of functional equivalence'). However, at least in those jurisdictions which consider vicarious liability a variant of fault liability, holding the principal liable for the wrongdoing of another, it may be challenging to identify the benchmark against which the operations of non-human helpers will be assessed in order to mirror the misconduct element of human auxiliaries. The potential benchmark should take into account that in many areas of application non-human auxiliaries are safer, that is less likely to cause damage to others than human actors, and the law should at least not discourage their use".

[202] Report from the Expert Group on Liability and New Technologies – New Technologies Formation "Liability for Artificial Intelligence and Other Emerging Digital Technologies", 21 November 2019, Key Finding [18], at p. 45. According to the Report, "one option proposed for addressing the risks of emerging digital technology is the potential expansion of the notion of vicarious liability, leaving the respective national regime of liability for others intact, but expanding it (either directly or by way of analogy) to functionally equivalent situations where use is made of autonomous technology instead of using a human auxiliary. This may complement strict liability and fault liability based on the notion of enhanced duties of care" (at pp. 45–46). The example used by the Report (Illustration 12, p. 46) is the following: "A hospital uses an AI-driven surgical robot. Despite the fact that the hospital has complied with all possible duties of care, a patient is harmed because the robot malfunctions in a way nobody could have foreseen. The hospital should be liable, in any case, under the principle outlined in Key Finding [18]".

Due to the development of emerging digital technologies, especially of systems with a high degree of decision-making autonomy, the requirements of equivalence should be respected in order to ensure the same level of protection compared to victims of traditional technologies. Indeed, the requirements of equivalence can prevent the emergence of unsatisfactory results, such as when compensation is denied in a situation involving emerging digital technologies whereas there would be compensation in a functionally equivalent situation involving human conduct and conventional technology.[203] As the Report stated, "where the use of a human auxiliary would give rise to the liability of a principal, the use of a digital technology tool instead should not allow the principal to avoid liability. Rather, it should give rise to such liability to the same extent".[204]

However, it was stressed that, in various national jurisdictions, the notion of vicarious liability requires the auxiliary to have misbehaved and, therefore, the question in relation to the benchmark for assessing performance/conduct by autonomous technology becomes critical. According to the Report, this benchmark "should primarily be the benchmark accepted for human auxiliaries, but once autonomous technology outperforms human auxiliaries in terms of preventing harm, the benchmark should be determined by the performance of comparable technology that is available on the market. As there is usually a broad range of technologies available, which may feature very different safety benchmarks, in choosing the appropriate point of comparison, the same principles should apply as with traditional technologies (such as x-ray machines or other equipment), i.e. reference should be made to the operator's duty of care with regard to the choice of system".[205] Based on the above analysis, the Report reached the following recommendation: "The benchmark for assessing performance by autonomous technology in the context of vicarious liability is primarily the one accepted for human auxiliaries. However, once autonomous technology outperforms human auxiliaries, this will be determined by the performance of comparable available technology

---

[203] Ibid., at p. 35. The example provided by the Report (Illustration 3) is as follows: "Hospital H uses an AI-based surgical robot. Despite the fact that H and its staff have discharged all possible duties of care, damage is caused to patient P by way of some malfunctioning of the robot nobody could have foreseen, and which is unrelated to the condition in which the robot was shipped. If P were not indemnified for the ensuing harm, this would be inconsistent with the outcome in the functionally equivalent situation in which H has employed a human doctor and is liable for that doctor's comparable misconduct under national rules of vicarious liability".

[204] Report from the Expert Group on Liability and New Technologies – New Technologies Formation "Liability for Artificial Intelligence and Other Emerging Digital Technologies", 21 November 2019, at p. 46.

[205] Ibid. The example provided by the Report (Illustration 13, p. 46) is the following: "In the example of the surgical robot (Illustration 12), it is not difficult to establish relevant misconduct where, for example, the cut made by the robot is twice as long as one a human surgeon would have made. If the cut is longer than the best robots on the market would have made, but still shorter than that of a human surgeon, the question of whether the hospital should have bought a better robot must be answered according to the same principles as the question of whether a hospital should have bought a better X-ray machine or employed extra doctors".

which the operator could be expected to use, taking into account the operator's duties of care".[206]

4.4.5 *Safety Rules: Adapting the Notion of Fault Liability by Shifting the Burden of Proving Causation and Fault*

When examining how to best address elements of risks and damages caused by the emerging digital technologies, the Report of the Expert Group on Liability and New Technologies stressed that the burden of proof should be linked to the compliance with specific cyber-security or other safety obligations set by law. Failure to comply with safety rules (including cybersecurity) should lead to a change of the burden of proof as regards fault and causation (i.e. shifting the burden of proving causation, fault, and the existence of a defect). As the Report stated, "Where the damage is of a kind that safety rules were meant to avoid, failure to comply with such safety rules, including rules on cybersecurity, should lead to a reversal of the burden of proving (a) causation, and/or (b) fault, and/or (c) the existence of a defect".[207]

4.4.5.1 Burden of Proving Causation

As a general rule, the burden of proof should remain with the victim, as is the case under existing liability frameworks ("as a general rule, the victim should continue to be required to prove what caused her harm").[208] In certain circumstances, however, it appears to be appropriate to reverse or lower this burden,[209] especially when it is

---

[206] Ibid., Key Finding [19], at p. 45.

[207] Ibid., Key Finding [24], at p. 48. The example used by the Report (Illustration 18, at p. 49) is as follows: "Imagine there is a new rule on cybersecurity of IoT household equipment, designed to prevent hacking and the resulting harm. The victim's private Wi-Fi is hacked in a way typical of cybersecurity gaps in IoT equipment. Where the victim can show that a water kettle produced by P failed to comply with the standard of safety under adopted safety rules, the victim could sue P, and the onus would be on P to prove that the damage had been caused by a different device".

[208] Report from the Expert Group on Liability and New Technologies – New Technologies Formation "Liability for Artificial Intelligence and Other Emerging Digital Technologies", 21 November 2019, Key Finding (25), at p. 49. "As is already the standard rule in all jurisdictions, whoever demands compensation from another should in general prove all necessary requirements for such a claim, including in particular the causal link between the harm to be indemnified on the one hand and the activities or risks within the sphere of the addressee of the claim may trigger the latter's liability on the other. This general principle is supported inter alia by concerns of fairness and results from the need to consider and balance the interests of both sides", at p. 50.

[209] "Lowering the bar for the claimant to prove causation may be advisable for victims of emerging digital technologies if the following factors are at play: • First, the technology itself may be known to have certain potentially harmful features, which could be taken into account even though it is not (yet) proven that such risks have indeed materialised. If the claimant can prove that there was a

disproportionately high: "given the practical implications of the complexity and opacity of emerging digital technologies in particular, victims may be in a weaker position to establish causation than in other tort cases, where the events leading to the harm can be more easily analysed in retrospect, even from the victim's point of view".[210] As a result, the Report of the Expert Group on Liability and New Technologies stated: "Without prejudice to the reversal of the burden of proof proposed in [22] and [24](a), the burden of proving causation may be alleviated in light of the challenges of emerging digital technologies if a balancing of the following factors warrants doing so: (a) the likelihood that the technology at least contributed to the harm; (b) the likelihood that the harm was caused either by the technology or by some other cause within the same sphere; (c) the risk of a known

---

defect in a product incorporating emerging digital technologies, thereby creating an extraordinary risk in addition to the ones commonly associated with flawless products, but – again – the harm caused cannot be (fully) traced to said defect, this might still be considered in the overall assessment of how to implement the burden of proving causation. • If there are multiple possible causes and it remains unclear what exactly triggered the harm (or which combination of potential causes at which percentage of probability), but if the likelihood of all possible causes combined, that are attributable to one party (e.g. the operator) exceeds a certain threshold (e.g. 50% or more), this may also contribute to placing the burden of producing evidence rebutting such first-hand impressions onto that party".

The example used by the Report (Illustration 19) is the following: "A small delivery robot operated by retailer R injures a pedestrian on the street. It remains unclear which of the following possible causes triggered the accident: the robot may have been defective from the start; R may have failed to install a necessary update that would have prevented the accident; R's employee E may have overloaded the robot; hacker H may have intentionally manipulated the robot; some teenagers may have jumped onto the robot for fun; a roof tile may have fallen off a nearby building, and so on. If the likelihood of all possible causes that are attributable to R significantly exceeds the likelihood of all other possible causes, the onus should be on R to prove that none of the causes within its own sphere triggered the accident". See the Report from the Expert Group on Liability and New Technologies – New Technologies Formation "Liability for Artificial Intelligence and Other Emerging Digital Technologies", 21 November 2019, p. 51.

Further aspects relating to the analysis of the causal events and who is predominantly in control of the expertise and evidence contributing to such analysis, include the following: "the informational asymmetry found between those developing and producing emerging digital technologies on the one hand and third-party victims on the other hand as another argument in the overall assessment of who should bear the burden of proving causation and to what extent. This includes the technology itself, but also potential evidence generated by such technology on the occasion of the harmful event. The latter not only considers who can retrieve such data, but also who can read and interpret it (particularly if it is encrypted or only intelligible with specific expert knowledge). One specific aspect in this context is if an item that was involved in the harmful event did (or according to industry standards should) have some logging device installed, which could have collected information that is capable of shedding light on what actually happened". Also, the type and extent of harm may affect whether – and to what extent – it should still be the victim who should prove the cause of his damage. See the Report from the Expert Group on Liability and New Technologies – New Technologies Formation "Liability for Artificial Intelligence and Other Emerging Digital Technologies", 21 November 2019, pp. 51–52.

[210] Report from the Expert Group on Liability and New Technologies – New Technologies Formation "Liability for Artificial Intelligence and Other Emerging Digital Technologies", 21 November 2019, p. 50.

defect within the technology, even though its actual causal impact is not self-evident; (d) the degree of ex-post traceability and intelligibility of processes within the technology that may have contributed to the cause (informational asymmetry); (e) the degree of ex-post accessibility and comprehensibility of data collected and generated by the technology; (f) the kind and degree of harm potentially and actually caused".[211]

4.4.5.2 Burden of Proving Fault

Again, the Report pointed out that, due to the characteristics of emerging digital technologies (such as complexity, opacity, openness, autonomy, and limited predictability), victims may be in a weaker position to prove fault than in other tort cases. In those cases, it appears to be appropriate to reverse the burden of proving fault: "When the damage results from an activity in which emerging digital technologies play a role, the victim may face significant difficulties in proving facts that substantiate her damages claim based on negligence or fault. This justifies rethinking the traditional approach to proving these conditions of liability".[212] The analysis of the Report led to the following recommendation: "Burden of proving fault: If it is proven that an emerging digital technology caused harm, and liability therefor is conditional upon a person's intent or negligence, the burden of proving fault should be reversed if disproportionate difficulties and costs of establishing the relevant

[211] Ibid., Key Finding [26], pp. 49–50.

[212] Ibid., at p. 52. Also, at p. 55: "Features of emerging digital technologies such as opacity, openness, autonomy and limited predictability may often result in unreasonable difficulties or costs for the plaintiff to prove facts necessary for the establishment of fault. At the same time, the proof of relevant facts may be much easier for the defendant (producer or operator of the technology). This asymmetry justifies the reversal of the burden of proof".

Also (at p. 54): "In theory, the claimant has to prove that the defendant breached an applicable standard (level) of care and did so intentionally or negligently. In practice, however, if the standard of care has not been normatively prescribed (by a statute or otherwise), the claimant's burden extends to proving (or persuading) what level of care should apply to the defendant's behaviour. The lack of a clear standard therefore puts the party with the burden of proving the existence of the standard, or its breach, at a disadvantage. The question is thus whether all these evidentiary difficulties should remain with the victim or all or some of them, in all or in specific circumstances, should affect the defendant. Items of proof, the burden for which normally is on the claimant, but could be allocated to the defendant are: • breach of a duty of care by the defendant (the producer, with regard to designing, manufacturing, monitoring, etc., and the user with regard to the choice of technology and operating/ monitoring it), • intention or negligence of the defendant, • substandard qualities of the technology, • incorrect functioning of the technology. In various legal systems, various factors are recognised as justifying modification of the burden of proof in favour of the claimant, in particular: a) high likelihood of fault, b) the parties' practical ability to prove fault, c) violation of statutory obligation by the defendant, d) particular dangerousness of the defendant's activity that resulted in damage, e) nature and scope of the damage".

standard of care and of proving their violation justify it. This is without prejudice to the reversal of the burden of proof proposed in [22] and [24](b)".[213]

4.4.5.3 Damage Caused to Data

It is reminded that the Product Liability Directive protects life and health as well as consumer property. With regard to the latter, it is not entirely clear whether it covers damage to data, as data may not be an 'item of property' within the meaning of Article 9 (b) of the Product Liability Directive. Indeed, the Report of the Expert Group on Liability and New Technologies pointed out that, while there is consensus that injuries to a person or to physical property can trigger tortious liability, it is not universally accepted that damage to or the destruction of data constitutes a property loss, because, according to some legal systems, the notion of 'property' is limited to corporeal objects and excludes intangibles.

The Report underlined that "with much of our lives and our 'property' becoming digital, it is no longer appropriate to limit liability to the tangible world. However, neither is it appropriate to simply equate data with tangible property for the purposes of liability".[214] This is why the Report argued that, under specific conditions, the destruction of the victim's data should be regarded as compensable damage, and laid down the following recommendation: "Damage caused to data may lead to liability where (a) liability arises from contract; or (b) liability arises from interference with a property right in the medium on which the data was stored or with another interest protected as a property right under the applicable law; or (c) the damage was caused by conduct infringing criminal law or other legally binding rules whose purpose is to avoid such damage; or (d) there was an intention to cause harm".[215]

4.4.6 Legal Personality

The Report of the Expert Group on Liability and New Technologies reminded that, according to the European Parliament Resolution of 16 February 2017 with recommendations to the Commission on Civil Law Rules on Robotics, "the autonomy of robots raises the question of their nature in the light of the existing legal categories or whether a new category should be created, with its own specific features and

[213] Report from the Expert Group on Liability and New Technologies – New Technologies Formation "Liability for Artificial Intelligence and Other Emerging Digital Technologies", 21 November 2019, Key Finding [27], at p. 52.

[214] Ibid., at p. 59.

[215] Ibid., Key Finding [32], at p. 59.

implications".[216] Indeed, according to the European Parliament's 2017 Resolution, the possibility of creating a specific legal status of "electronic persons" for the most sophisticated autonomous robots, so as to clarify responsibility in cases of damage, should be considered by the Commission, at least in the long-term: "creating a specific legal status for robots in the long run, so that at least the most sophisticated autonomous robots could be established as having the status of electronic persons responsible for making good any damage they may cause, and possibly applying electronic personality to cases where robots make autonomous decisions or otherwise interact with third parties independently".[217]

However, this proposal of the European Parliament, namely to leave open to discussion the possibility to create a special legal status for sufficiently advanced autonomous robots that would amount to electronic personhood, was publicly criticized by, amongst others, a group of experts in AI, robotics, commerce, law, and ethics, who signed an open letter to the Commission, stating that they are concerned by the European Parliament Resolution on Civil Law Rules of Robotics and its recommendation to the European Commission.[218]

On the other hand, it was argued that legal personhood would not make robots virtual people who can benefit from human rights; it would simply put them on par with corporations, which already have status as 'legal persons', and are treated as such by courts. Indeed, the proposed legal status for robots would be analogous to corporate personhood, which allows firms to take part in legal cases both as the plaintiff and respondent. As Rapporteur Mady Delvaux (S&D, LU) pointed out: "When self-learning robots arise, different solutions will become necessary, and we are asking the Commission to study options. One could be to give robots a limited "e-personality" [comparable to "corporate personality", a legal status which enables firms to sue or be sued] at least where compensation is concerned. It is similar to what we now have for companies, but it is not for tomorrow. What we need now is to

[216] European Parliament Resolution of 16 February 2017 with recommendations to the Commission on Civil Law Rules on Robotics (2015/2103(INL)), OJ C 252, 18.7.2018, pp. 239–257, point AC, at p. 242.

[217] Ibid., point 59(f), at p. 250.

[218] Open Letter to the European Commission – Artificial Intelligence and Robotics, http://www.robotics-openletter.eu/.

This open letter, addressed to the then Commission's president Jean-Claude Juncker amongst others, denounced the European Parliament's proposal to grant personhood status to intelligent machines, suggesting that current robots do not have moral standing and should not be considered capable of having rights. The letter called upon the Commission to ignore the Parliament's move and reject 'electronic personality', as it would be inappropriate, ideological, nonsensical, and non-pragmatic to introduce such a legal status. There were also arguments stating that, in case of adopting legal personhood for robots, responsibility of manufacturers for the actions of their machines would be erased.

create a legal framework for the robots that are currently on the market or will become available over the next 10 to 15 years".[219]

The Report of the Expert Group on Liability and New Technologies stated that there is no need to grant a legal personality to emerging digital technologies: "Harm caused by even fully autonomous technologies is generally reducible to risks attributable to natural persons or existing categories of legal persons, and where this is not the case, new laws directed at individuals are a better response than creating a new category of legal person".[220] The recommendation of the Report, therefore, was that "for the purposes of liability, it is not necessary to give autonomous systems a legal personality".[221]

4.4.7 Risk-Based Approach

According to the Commission, not every use of AI systems and services necessarily creates significant risks and causes significant harm. Therefore, a risk-based approach should be followed, considering the fact that different AI applications pose different risks. As a result, the Commission, based on the recommendations of the Expert Group's Report, identified two major categories of AI applications, namely AI applications with a specific risk profile in terms of liability (it asked

[219] "Rise of the robots: Mady Delvaux on why their use should be regulated", News - European Parliament, 15.02.2017, https://www.europarl.europa.eu/news/en/headlines/economy/20170109STO57505/rise-of-the-robots-mady-delvaux-on-why-their-use-should-be-regulated.

[220] Report from the Expert Group on Liability and New Technologies – New Technologies Formation "Liability for Artificial Intelligence and Other Emerging Digital Technologies", 21 November 2019, at p. 38. "Any sort of legal personality for emerging digital technologies may raise a number of ethical issues. More importantly, it would only make sense to go down that road if it helps legal systems to tackle the challenges of emerging digital technologies. Any additional personality should go hand-in-hand with funds assigned to such electronic persons, so that claims can be effectively brought against them. This would amount to putting a cap on liability and – as experience with corporations has shown – subsequent attempts to circumvent such restrictions by pursuing claims against natural or legal persons to whom electronic persons can be attributed, effectively 'piercing the electronic veil'. In addition, in order to give a real dimension to liability, electronic agents would have to be able to acquire assets on their own. This would require the resolution of several legislative problems related to their legal capacity and how they act when performing legal transactions".

[221] Ibid., Key Finding [8], at p. 37. The example used by the Report (Illustration 5, at pp. 38–39) is the following: "Imagine liability for a fully autonomous car were on the car instead of its operator. Victims of accidents would receive compensation only if insurance is taken out for the car and someone (who?) pays the premiums, or if someone (who?) provides the car with assets from which damages could be paid. If such assets did not suffice to fully compensate the victims of an accident, said victims would have a strong incentive to seek compensation from the person benefiting from the operation of the car instead. If the car's assets were sufficient to pay the same level of compensation as under existing liability and insurance regimes, there would not be any cause for discussion, but in that case, giving the car a legal personality would be a mere formality and not really change the situation".

whether and to what extent strict liability is required) and the rest AI applications (it asked whether the burden of proof concerning causation and fault should be adapted).

As the Commission stated: "For the operation of AI applications with a specific risk profile, the Commission is seeking views on whether and to what extent strict liability, as it exists in national laws for similar risks to which the public is exposed (for instance for operating motor vehicles, airplanes or nuclear power plants), may be needed in order to achieve effective compensation of possible victims. … For the operation of all other AI applications, which would constitute the large majority of AI applications, the Commission is reflecting whether the burden of proof concerning causation and fault needs to be adapted. In this respect, one of the issues flagged by the Report from the New Technologies formation of the Expert Group on Liability and New Technologies is the situation when the potentially liable party has not logged the data relevant for assessing liability or is not willing to share them with the victim".[222]

4.4.8 *Compulsory Liability Insurance*

The Commission's Report on the safety and liability implications of AI, the IoT of and robotics stated that "the Commission is also seeking views on coupling strict liability with a possible obligation to conclude available insurance, following the example of the Motor Insurance Directive, in order to ensure compensation irrespective of the liable person's solvency and to help reducing the costs of damage".[223] This also follows the findings of the Report from the Expert Group on Liability and New Technologies where it was stated that "for situations exposing third parties to an increased risk of harm, compulsory liability insurance could give victims better access to compensation and protect potential tortfeasors against the

[222]Commission Communication "Report on the safety and liability implications of Artificial Intelligence, the Internet of Things and robotics", COM (2020) 64 final, Brussels, 19.2.2020, p. 16.

See also the Report from the Expert Group on Liability and New Technologies – New Technologies Formation "Liability for Artificial Intelligence and Other Emerging Digital Technologies", 21 November 2019, at p. 4: "Emerging digital technologies should come with logging features, where appropriate in the circumstances, and failure to log, or to provide reasonable access to logged data, should result in a reversal of the burden of proof in order not be to the detriment of the victim". Also: "Where a particular technology increases the difficulties of proving the existence of an element of liability beyond what can be reasonably expected, victims should be entitled to facilitation of proof". Also (at p. 3): "a person using a technology that does not pose an increased risk of harm to others should still be required to abide by duties to properly select, operate, monitor and maintain the technology in use and – failing that – should be liable for breach of such duties if at fault".

[223]Commission Communication "Report on the safety and liability implications of Artificial Intelligence, the Internet of Things and robotics", COM (2020) 64 final, Brussels, 19.2.2020, p. 16.

risk of liability";[224] "the more frequent or severe potential harm resulting from emerging digital technology, and the less likely the operator is able to indemnify victims individually, the more suitable mandatory liability insurance for such risks may be".[225]

---

[224]Report from the Expert Group on Liability and New Technologies – New Technologies Formation "Liability for Artificial Intelligence and Other Emerging Digital Technologies", 21 November 2019, at p. 4.

In 2017, the European Parliament had already identified the necessity for a compulsory liability insurance. In particular, the European Parliament Resolution of 16 February 2017 with recommendations to the Commission on Civil Law Rules on Robotics (2015/2103(INL)), (2018/C 252/25) stressed that, similarly to what happens with motor vehicles, rules on liability could be complemented by a compulsory insurance scheme for robot users, as a possible solution to the complexity of allocating responsibility for damage caused by increasingly autonomous robots: "An obligatory insurance scheme, which could be based on the obligation of the producer to take out insurance for the autonomous robots it produces, should be established". Under this scenario "producers, or owners of robots would be required to take out insurance cover for the damage potentially caused by their robots". It pointed out, however, that unlike the insurance system for road traffic, where the insurance covers human acts and failures, an insurance system for robotics should take into account all potential responsibilities in the chain. See Annex to the Motion for a Resolution: Detailed Recommendations as to the content of the Proposal Requested, at p. 20; Annex to the Resolution: Recommendations as to the content of the proposal requested, at p. 252; Report – Motion for a European Parliament Resolution with recommendations to the Commission on Civil Law Rules on Robotics - (2015/2103(INL)) - 27.1.2017, points 57 and 59, at p. 17. (Resolution, point 57, at p. 249).

[225]Report from the Expert Group on Liability and New Technologies – New Technologies Formation "Liability for Artificial Intelligence and Other Emerging Digital Technologies", 21 November 2019, Key Finding [33], at pp. 9 and 61.

See also at p. 30: "An obligatory insurance scheme for certain categories of AI/robots has been proposed as a possible solution to the problem of allocating liability for damage caused by such systems (sometimes combined with compensation funds for damage not covered by mandatory insurance policies). However, an obligatory insurance scheme cannot be considered the only answer to the problem of how to allocate liability and cannot completely replace clear and fair liability rules. Insurance companies form a part of the whole social ecosystem and need liability rules to protect their own interests in relation to other entities (redress rights). Moreover, in order to keep emerging digital technologies as safe as possible and, therefore, trustworthy, a duty of care should be affected by insurance as little as possible. Yet, at the same time, cases of very high or catastrophic risks need to be insured in order to secure compensation for potentially serious damage. Hence, the question relates to whether first-party or third-party insurance, or a combination of both, should be required or at least recommended and in which cases. Currently, EU law requires obligatory liability (third-party) insurance e.g. for the use of motor vehicles, air carriers and aircraft operators, or carriers of passengers by sea. Laws of the Member States require obligatory liability insurance in various other cases, mostly coupled with strict liability schemes, or for practising certain professions".

"Compulsory liability insurance should not be introduced without a careful analysis of whether it is really needed, rather than automatically linked to a certain activity. After all, the tortfeasor may be able to compensate victims of her activities out of her own funds if the overall losses to be expected can be covered even without insurance. Also, the market may simply not offer insurance cover for a certain risk, particularly if it is difficult to calculate due to missing experience, which is quite likely with new technologies (and may therefore also be a problem with emerging digital technologies). Requiring insurance in the latter situation may effectively prevent the deployment of the

According to the Report of the Expert Group on Liability and New Technologies, compensation funds for damage not covered by mandatory insurance policies can also play a complementary role and be used to protect victims who are entitled to compensation, but whose claims cannot be satisfied.[226] This is why the Report

---

technology, if this requires proof of insurance despite the fact that no-one on the market is willing to underwrite such yet unknown risks. This may in part be remedied by capping liability for certain risks at a pre-determined (though regularly adjusted) amount, as is often the case with statutory strict liability regimes. One could also imagine a less specific requirement to provide cover (so not necessarily by taking out insurance, but also other financial securities). Nevertheless, as experience in at least some fields (mostly motorised traffic) has shown, mandatory liability insurance can work well and is indeed appropriate under certain conditions. From an insurance perspective, certain sectors are the most suited to compulsory insurance schemes, including transportation, industries with a high potential for personal injury and/or environmental harm, hazardous activities and certain professional sectors. Therefore, it may indeed be advisable to make liability insurance cover compulsory for certain emerging digital technologies. This is particularly true for highly significant risks (which may either lead to substantial harm and/or cause frequent losses), where it seems unlikely that potential injurers will be capable of compensating all victims themselves (either out of their own funds, with the help of alternative financial securities, or through voluntary self-insurance)". See the Report from the Expert Group on Liability and New Technologies – New Technologies Formation "Liability for Artificial Intelligence and Other Emerging Digital Technologies", 21 November 2019, at pp. 61–62.

[226]Report from the Expert Group on Liability and New Technologies – New Technologies Formation "Liability for Artificial Intelligence and Other Emerging Digital Technologies", 21 November 2019, Key Finding [34], at p. 62.

This was also highlighted in the European Parliament Resolution of 16 February 2017 with recommendations to the Commission on Civil Law Rules on Robotics (2015/2103(INL)), (2018/C 252/25), OJ C 252, 18.7.2018, pp. 239–257 ("European Parliament Resolution of 16 February 2017 on Civil Law Rules on Robotics"). In particular, it was underlined that an obligatory insurance system should be supplemented by a compensation fund to ensure victims are fully compensated in those cases where accidents were caused by a robot or a driverless car and no insurance policy covered the risk: "the insurance system should be supplemented by a fund in order to ensure that damages can be compensated for in cases where no insurance cover exists". European Parliament Resolution of 16 February 2017 on Civil Law Rules on Robotics, section "Liability", point 58, p. 250; Annex to the European Parliament Resolution of 16 February 2017 on Civil Law Rules on Robotics, section "Civil law liability", p. 252.

Furthermore, the European Parliament Resolution of 16 February 2017 stressed that the Commission's future legislative instrument should be based on an in-depth evaluation determining the implications of all possible legal solutions, namely "a) establishing a compulsory insurance scheme where relevant and necessary for specific categories of robots whereby, similarly to what already happens with cars, producers, or owners of robots would be required to take out insurance cover for the damage potentially caused by their robots; b) ensuring that a compensation fund would not only serve the purpose of guaranteeing compensation if the damage caused by a robot was not covered by insurance; c) allowing the manufacturer, the programmer, the owner or the user to benefit from limited liability if they contribute to a compensation fund, as well as if they jointly take out insurance to guarantee compensation where damage is caused by a robot; d) deciding whether to create a general fund for all smart autonomous robots or to create an individual fund for each and every robot category, and whether a contribution should be paid as a one-off fee when placing the robot on the market or whether periodic contributions should be paid during the lifetime of the robot; e) ensuring that the link between a robot and its fund would be made visible by an individual registration number appearing in a specific Union register, which would allow anyone interacting

proposed that, at least in those areas where compulsory liability insurance is introduced, a compensation fund should be established to redress damage caused by an unidentified or uninsured technology: "As hacking is a serious threat to users of software-based technologies and traditional tort law rules may often prove insufficient because of the victim's inability to identify the tortfeasor, it may be advisable to introduce a non-fault compensation scheme equivalent to that applicable to victims of violent crimes, if and to the extent that a cybercrime constitutes an offence equivalent to the latter. Persons who have suffered serious personal injuries as a result of cybercrime could therefore be treated the same way as victims of violent crime".[227]

with the robot to be informed about the nature of the fund, the limits of its liability in case of damage to property, the names and the functions of the contributors and all other relevant details". European Parliament Resolution of 16 February 2017 on Civil Law Rules on Robotics, section "Liability", point 59, p. 250.

[227] Report from the Expert Group on Liability and New Technologies – New Technologies Formation "Liability for Artificial Intelligence and Other Emerging Digital Technologies", 21 November 2019, at pp. 62–63. According to the Report, such a scheme could be based on the model described in Article 10 of the Motor Insurance Directive, which reads as follows: "Article 10 - Body responsible for compensation: 1. Each Member State shall set up or authorise a body with the task of providing compensation, at least up to the limits of the insurance obligation for damage to property or personal injuries caused by an unidentified vehicle or a vehicle for which the insurance obligation provided for in Article 3 has not been satisfied. The first subparagraph shall be without prejudice to the right of the Member States to regard compensation by the body as subsidiary or non-subsidiary and the right to make provision for the settlement of claims between the body and the person or persons responsible for the accident and other insurers or social security bodies required to compensate the victim in respect of the same accident. However, Member States may not allow the body to make the payment of compensation conditional on the victim establishing in any way that the person liable is unable or refuses to pay. 2. The victim may in any event apply directly to the body which, on the basis of information provided at its request by the victim, shall be obliged to give him a reasoned reply regarding the payment of any compensation. Member States may, however, exclude the payment of compensation by that body in respect of persons who voluntarily entered the vehicle which caused the damage or injury when the body can prove that they knew it was uninsured. 3. Member States may limit or exclude the payment of compensation by the body in the event of damage to property by an unidentified vehicle. However, where the body has paid compensation for significant personal injuries to any victim of the same accident in which damage to property was caused by an unidentified vehicle, Member States may not exclude the payment of compensation for damage to property on the basis that the vehicle is unidentified. Nevertheless, Member States may provide for an excess of not more than EUR 500 to be borne by the victim of such damage to property. The conditions in which personal injuries are to be regarded as significant shall be determined in accordance with the legislation or administrative provisions of the Member State in which the accident takes place. In this regard, Member States may take into account, inter alia, whether the injury required hospital care. 4. Each Member State shall apply its laws, regulations and administrative provisions to the payment of compensation by the body, without prejudice to any other practice which is more favourable to the victim".

4.5 Conclusion

This chapter followed the European Commission's attempt to examine the applicability of the current Product Liability Directive to new technologies and, in light of an assessment of the existing liability schemes, to develop principles that can serve as guidelines for possible adaptations of applicable laws at EU and national level relating to new technologies.

It reviewed whether and to what extent existing liability schemes are adapted to the emerging market realities following the development of the new technologies such as Artificial Intelligence, advanced robotics, the IoT and cybersecurity issues. It also examined whether the current EU liability regimes are still adequate to facilitate the uptake of the emerging digital technologies by promoting investment stability and users' trust.

In particular, this chapter examined the most important findings presented in the Report of the Expert Group on Liability and New Technologies "Liability for Artificial Intelligence and Other Emerging Digital Technologies", issued on 21 November 2019. Furthermore, this chapter covered the Commission's 2020 White Paper on AI, which concluded that the existing liability laws which are applicable to AI applications are not sufficient to address the risks posed by the development and deployment of AI. As a result, specific adjustments to and clarifications of existing legislation are required to make the EU liability framework fit for the current and forthcoming technological and commercial developments. In addition, it covered extensively the Commission's 2020 Report on the safety and liability implications of AI, IoT and robotics, which accompanied the Commission's 2020 White Paper on Artificial Intelligence.

While in principle the existing EU and national liability laws can cope with emerging technologies, the dimension and combined effect of the challenges of AI could make it more difficult to offer victims compensation in all cases where this would be justified. Thus, the allocation of the cost when damage occurs may be unfair or inefficient under the current rules. To rectify this and address potential uncertainties in the existing framework, certain adjustments to the Product Liability Directive and national liability regimes through appropriate EU initiatives could be considered on a targeted, risk-based approach, i.e. taking into account that different AI applications pose different risks.[228] As the Commission stated, the main objective

[228] In relation to how liability regimes should be designed to meet the challenges brought by emerging digital technologies, see also the summary of the major findings of the Report from the Expert Group on Liability and New Technologies – New Technologies Formation "Liability for Artificial Intelligence and Other Emerging Digital Technologies", 21 November 2019, at pp. 3–4 (Executive Summary): "• A person operating a permissible technology that nevertheless carries an increased risk of harm to others, for example AI-driven robots in public spaces, should be subject to strict liability for damage resulting from its operation. • In situations where a service provider ensuring the necessary technical framework has a higher degree of control than the owner or user of an actual product or service equipped with AI, this should be taken into account in determining who primarily operates the technology. • A person using a technology that does not pose an increased

is to ensure that individuals who have suffered harm resulting from the use of AI systems should receive an equivalent level of protection as those harmed by other technologies. At the same time, technological innovation should be allowed to continue to progress. To this end, "all options to ensure this objective should be carefully assessed, including possible amendments to the Product Liability Directive and possible further targeted harmonisation of national liability rules. For example, the Commission is seeking views whether and to what extent it may be needed to mitigate the consequences of complexity by adapting the burden of proof required by national liability rules for damage caused by the operation of AI applications".[229]

---

risk of harm to others should still be required to abide by duties to properly select, operate, monitor and maintain the technology in use and – failing that – should be liable for breach of such duties if at fault. • A person using a technology which has a certain degree of autonomy should not be less accountable for ensuing harm than if said harm had been caused by a human auxiliary. • Manufacturers of products or digital content incorporating emerging digital technology should be liable for damage caused by defects in their products, even if the defect was caused by changes made to the product under the producer's control after it had been placed on the market. • For situations exposing third parties to an increased risk of harm, compulsory liability insurance could give victims better access to compensation and protect potential tortfeasors against the risk of liability. • Where a particular technology increases the difficulties of proving the existence of an element of liability beyond what can be reasonably expected, victims should be entitled to facilitation of proof. • Emerging digital technologies should come with logging features, where appropriate in the circumstances, and failure to log, or to provide reasonable access to logged data, should result in a reversal of the burden of proof in order not be to the detriment of the victim. • The destruction of the victim's data should be regarded as damage, compensable under specific conditions. • It is not necessary to give devices or autonomous systems a legal personality, as the harm these may cause can and should be attributable to existing persons or bodies".

[229] Commission Communication, "White Paper On Artificial Intelligence - A European approach to excellence and trust", COM(2020) 65 final, Brussels, 19.2.2020, p. 15.

See also the "Summary Report on the open public consultation on the White Paper on Artificial Intelligence", 2020 (at p. 5), where it was stated that "the overall objective of the safety and liability legal frameworks is to ensure that all products and services, including those integrating emerging digital technologies, operate safely, reliably and consistently, and that damage that has already occurred is remedied efficiently. 60.7% of respondents supported a revision of the existing Product Liability directive to cover particular risks engendered by certain AI applications. 47% of respondents supported that national liability rules should also be adapted for all AI applications and 16% for specific AI applications to better ensure proper compensation in case of damage and a fair allocation of liability".

See also the Commission's "Final Report - Public consultation on the AI White Paper", November 2020, at pp. 13–14: "• *Do you think that the current EU legislative framework for liability (Product Liability Directive) should be amended to better cover the risks engendered by certain AI applications?* – 61% of respondents supported a revision of the existing EU legislative framework for liability, the Product Liability Directive, to cover particular risks engendered by certain AI applications. Civil society was mostly in favour: 74% argued for amending the Product Liability Directive. 65% of academia supported the revision of the EU framework for liability. Business and industry was divided. Overall, 38% supported a revision of the Product Liability Directive, 30% were opposed. While the largest share of SMEs was in favour of revising the EU framework for liability (62%), only 32% of large companies agreed. • *Do you think that the current national liability rules should be adapted for the operation of AI to better ensure proper compensation for damage and a fair allocation of liability?* – On a national level, the public consultation

Legal/Policy Documents, Studies, Reports and Other Sources

European Commission ('Commission') Communication, "Artificial Intelligence for Europe", COM(2018) 237 final, Brussels, 25.4.2018.

Commission Staff Working Document on "Liability for emerging digital technologies" - Accompanying the document Commission Communication "Artificial intelligence for Europe", SWD(2018) 137 final, Brussels, 25.4.2018.

Report from the Commission on the Application of the Council Directive on the approximation of the laws, regulations, and administrative provisions of the Member States concerning liability for defective products (85/374/EEC) {SWD (2018) 157 final} - {SWD(2018) 158 final}, COM(2018) 246 final, Brussels, 7.5.2018, ['Commission Report on the Application of the Product Liability Directive, COM(2018) 246 final, Brussels, 07.05.2018'].

Commission Staff Working Document, Evaluation of Council Directive 85/374/EEC of 25 July 1985 on the approximation of the laws, regulations and administrative provisions of the Member States concerning liability for defective products – Accompanying the Evaluation Report – SWD(2018) 157 final, Brussels, 7.5.2018 ['Commission Staff Working Document, 'Evaluation of Product Liability Directive', SWD(2018) 157 final, Brussels, 07.05.2018'].

Commission Communication "Building Trust in Human-Centric Artificial Intelligence", COM(2019) 168 final, Brussels, 8.4.2019.

Report from the Expert Group on Liability and New Technologies – New Technologies Formation "Liability for Artificial Intelligence and Other Emerging Digital Technologies", 21 November 2019.

Commission Communication "Report on the safety and liability implications of Artificial Intelligence, the Internet of Things and robotics", COM (2020) 64 final, Brussels, 19.2.2020.

Commission Communication "White Paper On Artificial Intelligence - A European approach to excellence and trust", COM(2020) 65 final, Brussels, 19.2.2020.

Commission's "Final Report - Public consultation on the AI White Paper", November 2020.

Commission's Inception Impact Assessment, Title of the Initiative "Proposal for a legal act of the European Parliament and the Council laying down requirements for Artificial Intelligence", 23.07.2020, Ref. Ares(2020)3896535.

European Parliament Resolution of 16 February 2017 with recommendations to the Commission on Civil Law Rules on Robotics (2015/2103(INL)), (OJ C 252, 18.7.2018, pp. 239–257).

asked whether national liability rules need to be adapted to ensure proper compensation in case of damage and a fair allocation of liability. 47% of respondents saw a need to adapt this for all AI applications. A further 16% argued that specific AI applications require an adaptation of national liability rules. Share of respondents by stakeholder type that want an adaptation for all AI applications: Civil society (59%); Citizens (64%), Academia (50%), Business and Industry (21%)".

Directive 2001/95/EC of the European Parliament and the Council of 3 December 2001 on general product safety (The General Product Safety Directive), (OJ L 11, 15.1.2002, pp. 4–17).
Directive 2006/42/EC of the European Parliament and of the Council of 17 May 2006 on machinery, and amending Directive 95/16/EC (OJ L 157, 9.6.2006, pp. 24–86) (the Machinery Directive).
Regulation (EC) 765/2008 setting out the requirements for accreditation and the market surveillance of products.
Decision 768/2008 on a common framework for the marketing of products, which includes reference provisions to be incorporated whenever product legislation is revised. In effect, it is a template for future product harmonisation legislation.
Regulation (EU) 2019/1020 on market surveillance and compliance of products.
Directive 2014/53/EU of the European Parliament and of the Council of 16 April 2014 on the harmonisation of the laws of the Member States relating to the making available on the market of radio equipment and repealing Directive 1999/5/EC [Radio Equipment Directive (RED), OJ L 153, 22.5.2014, pp. 62–106].
Regulation (EU) 2017/745 of the European Parliament and of the Council of 5 April 2017 on medical devices, amending Directive 2001/83/EC, Regulation (EC) No 178/2002 and Regulation (EC) No 1223/2009 and repealing Council Directives 90/385/EEC and 93/42/EEC, OJ L 117, 5.5.2017, pp. 1–175.
Council Directive 90/385/EEC on Active Implantable Medical Devices (AIMDD) and Council Directive 93/42/EEC on Medical Devices (MDD) [both Directives were repealed by Regulation (EU) 2017/745].
Council Directive 98/79/EC on In Vitro Diagnostic Medical Devices (IVDMD); Council Directive 89/391/EEC on the introduction of measures to encourage improvements in the safety and health of workers at work.
Directive 2009/48/EC of the European Parliament and of the Council of 18 June 2009 on the safety of toys (The Toys Safety Directive), OJ L 170, 30.6.2009, pp. 1–37.
Directive 2014/32/EU of the European Parliament and of the Council of 26 February 2014 on the harmonisation of the laws of the Member States relating to the making available on the market of measuring instruments, OJ L 96, 29.3.2014, pp. 149–250.
Regulation (EU) 2019/881 of the European Parliament and of the Council of 17 April 2019 on ENISA (the European Union Agency for Cybersecurity) and on information and communications technology cybersecurity certification and repealing Regulation (EU) No 526/2013 (the Cybersecurity Act), OJ L 151, 7.6.2019, pp. 15–69.
Regulation (EU) 2019/1020 of the European Parliament and of the Council of 20 June 2019 on market surveillance and compliance of products and amending Directive 2004/42/EC and Regulations (EC) No 765/2008 and (EU) No 305/2011 (OJ L 169, 25.6.2019, pp. 1–44).
Regulation (EC) No 765/2008 of the European Parliament and of the Council of 9 July 2008 setting out the requirements for accreditation and market surveillance

relating to the marketing of products and repealing Regulation (EEC) No 339/93, OJ L 218, 13.8.2008, pp. 30–47.

Regulation (EU) 2018/858 of the European Parliament and of the Council of 30 May 2018 on the approval of motor vehicles and their trailers, and of systems, components and separate technical units intended for such vehicles, amending Regulations (EC) No 715/2007 and (EC) No 595/2009 and repealing Directive 2007/46/EC (OJ L 151, 14.6.2018, pp. 1–218).

Decision No 768/2008/EC of the European Parliament and of the Council of 9 July 2008 on a common framework for the marketing of products, and repealing Council Decision 93/465/EEC, OJ L 218, 13.8.2008, pp. 82–128.

Directive 2001/95/EC of the European Parliament and of the Council of 3 December 2001 on general product safety (the General Product Safety Directive), (OJ L 11, 15.1.2002, pp. 4–17).

Regulation (EU) 2015/1136 of 13 July 2015 amending Implementing Regulation (EU) No 402/2013 on the common safety method for risk evaluation and assessment, OJ L 185/6, 14.7.2015.

"Ethics Guidelines for Trustworthy AI", High-Level Expert Group on Artificial Intelligence, 8 April 2019.

"The Assessment List for Trustworthy Artificial Intelligence (ALTAI) for self-assessment", High-Level Expert Group on AI (AI HLEG), 17 July 2020.

Directive 2006/42/EC of the European Parliament and of the Council of 17 May 2006 on machinery, and amending Directive 95/16/EC (OJ L 157, 9.6.2006, pp. 24–86) (the Machinery Directive).

"Guide to application of the Machinery Directive 2006/42/EC", Edition 2.2 – October 2019 (Update of 2nd Edition), European Commission, Directorate-General for Internal Market, Industry, Entrepreneurship and SMEs.

Regulation (EU) 2017/745 of the European Parliament and of the Council of 5 April 2017 on medical devices, amending Directive 2001/83/EC, Regulation (EC) No 178/2002 and Regulation (EC) No 1223/2009 and repealing Council Directives 90/385/EEC and 93/42/EEC, OJ L 117, 5.5.2017, pp. 1–175.

Directive 2001/95/EC of the European Parliament and the Council of 3 December 2001 on general product safety (the General Product Safety Directive), (OJ L 11, 15.1.2002, pp. 4–17).

European Commission Notice "The 'Blue Guide' on the implementation of EU products rules 2016", (2016/C 272/01, 26.7.2016).

Regulation on Medical Devices [Regulation (EU) 2017/745 of the European Parliament and of the Council of 5 April 2017 on medical devices, amending Directive 2001/83/EC, Regulation (EC) No 178/2002 and Regulation (EC) No 1223/2009 and repealing Council Directives 90/385/EEC and 93/42/EEC, OJ L 117, 5.5.2017, pp. 1–175].

Directive 2014/33/EU of the European Parliament and of the Council of 26 February 2014 on the harmonisation of the laws of the Member States relating to lifts and safety components for lifts (the Lifts Directive), OJ L 96, 29.3.2014, pp. 251–308.

Council Directive 85/374/EEC of 25 July 1985 on the approximation of the laws, regulations and administrative provisions of the Member States concerning liability for defective products, as modified by Directive 1999/34/EC of the European Parliament and of the Council of 10 May 1999 (OJ L 210/29, 7.8.1985, and OJ L 141/20, 4.6.1999) (the Product Liability Directive).

Directive 2009/103/EC of the European Parliament and of the Council of 16 September 2009 relating to insurance against civil liability in respect of the use of motor vehicles, and the enforcement of the obligation to insure against such liability ("the Motor Insurance Directive").

"Summary Report on the open public consultation on the White Paper on Artificial Intelligence", 2020.

Commission's "Final Report - Public consultation on the AI White Paper", November 2020.

References

Akalin N, Kristoffersson A, Loutfi A (2019) Social robots: technological, societal and ethical aspects of human-robot interaction, pp 237–264, Research, July 2019

Bathaee Y (2018) The artificial intelligence black box and the failure of intent and causation. Harv J Law Technol 31(2):889–938

Beck S (2016) The problem of ascribing legal responsibility in the case of robotics. AI Soc 31(4): 473–481

Bertolini A (2013) Robots as products: the case for a realistic analysis of robotic applications and liability rules. Law Innov Technol 5:214–247

Bertolini A (2018) Artificial intelligence and civil law - liability rules for drones, Study requested by the European Parliament's Committee on Legal Affairs, Policy Department for Citizens' Rights and Constitutional Affairs, November 2018

Bertolini A (2020) Artificial intelligence and civil liability, Study requested by the European Parliament's Committee on Legal Affairs, Policy Department for Citizens' Rights and Constitutional Affairs – Directorate-General for Internal Policies, PE 621.926, July 2020

Bicchi A, Peshkin MA, Colgate JE (2008) Safety for physical human–robot interaction. In: Siciliano B, Khatib O (eds) Springer handbook of robotics. Springer, Berlin, Heidelberg, pp 1335–1348

Birnbaum GE, Mizrahi M, Hoffman G, Reis HT, Finkel EJ, Sass O (2016) What robots can teach us about intimacy: the reassuring effects of robot responsiveness to human disclosure. Comput Hum Behav 63:416–423

Boholm M, Möller N, Hansson SO (2016) The concepts of risk, safety, and security: applications in everyday language. Risk Anal 36(2):320–338

Borghetti J-S (2019) How can artificial intelligence be defective. In: Lohsse S, Schulze R, Staudenmayer D (eds) Liability for artificial intelligence and the internet of things. Nomos, Baden-Baden, pp 63–76

Boström M, Ernsth Bravell M, Björklund A, Sandberg J (2016) How older people perceive and experience sense of security when moving into and living in a nursing home: a case study. Eur J Soc Work 20(5):1–14

Cabral TS (2020) Liability and artificial intelligence in the EU: assessing the adequacy of the current Product Liability Directive. Maastricht J Eur Comp Law 27(5):615–635

Cath C (2018) Governing artificial intelligence: ethical, legal and technical opportunities and challenges. Philos Trans R Soc A 376:2133

Charalambous G, Fletcher S, Webb P (2016) The development of a scale to evaluate trust in industrial human-robot collaboration. Int J Soc Robot 8(2):193–209

Chatzipanagiotis M, Leloudas G (2020) Automated vehicles and third-party liability: a European perspective. Univ Ill J Law Technol Policy 1:109–199

Christidis K, Devetsikiotis M (2016) Blockchains and smart contracts for the internet of things. IEEE Access 4:2292–2303

Dautenhahn K, Ogden B, Quick T (2002) From embodied to socially embedded agents—implications for interaction-aware robots. Cogn Syst Res 3(3):397–428

de Bruin R (2016) Autonomous intelligent cars on the European intersection of liability and privacy: regulatory challenges and the road ahead. Eur J Risk Regul 7(3):485–501

de Meeus C (2019) The Product Liability Directive at the age of the digital industrial revolution: fit for innovation? J Eur Consum Market Law 8(4):149–154

del Castillo AP (2017) A law on robotics and artificial intelligence in the EU? (October 3, 2017). Foresight Brief, European Trade Union Institute (ETUI) Research Paper - Foresight Brief #02-September 2017

Di Nucci E (2017) Sexual rights, disability, and sex robots. In: Danaher J, McArthur N (eds) Robot sex: social and ethical implications. MIT Press, Cambridge, pp 73–88

Ebers M, Navas S (eds) (2020) Algorithms and law. Cambridge University Press

Evas T (2018) A common EU approach to liability rules and insurance for connected and autonomous vehicles, Study. European Added Value Assessment - Accompanying the European Parliament's legislative own-initiative report (Rapporteur: Mady Delvaux). Study, European Parliamentary Research Service (EPRS), February 2018

Evas T (2020) Civil liability regime for artificial intelligence, Study, European Parliamentary Research Service (EPRS), September 2020

Fairgrieve D, Rajneri E (2019) Is software a product under the Product Liability Directive? Zeitschrift für Internationales Wirtschaftsrecht 1:24–28

Fairgrieve D, Howells G, Møgelvang-Hansen P et al (2016) Product Liability Directive. In: Machnikowski P (ed) European product liability: an analysis of the state of the art in the era of new technologies. Principles of European tort law. Intersentia, pp 17–108

Fischinger D, Einramhof P, Papoutsakis K, Wohlkinger W, Mayer P, Panek P, Hofmann S, Koertner T, Weiss A, Argyros A, Vincze M (2016) Hobbit, a care robot supporting independent living at home: first prototype and lessons learned. Robot Auton Syst 75(A):60–78

Fiske A, Henningsen P, Buyx A (2019) Your robot therapist will see you now: ethical implications of embodied artificial intelligence in psychiatry, psychology, and psychotherapy. J Med Internet Res 21(5):e13216

Floridi L (2014) The fourth revolution. How the infosphere is reshaping human reality. Oxford University Press, Oxford

Floridi L (2016) On human dignity as a foundation for the right to privacy. Philos Technol 29(4): 307–312

Floridi L (2018) Soft ethics and the governance of the digital. Philos Technol 31(1):1–8

Fosch-Villaronga E, Albo-Canals J (2019) 'I'll take care of you', said the robot. Paladyn J Behav Robot 10(1):77–93

Fosch-Villaronga E, Golia A (2019) Robots, standards and the law: rivalries between private standards and public policymaking for robot governance. Comput Law Secur Rev 35(2): 129–144

Fosch-Villaronga E, Heldeweg M (2018) "Regulation, I presume?" said the robot—towards an iterative regulatory process for robot governance. Comput Law Secur Rev 34(6):1258–1277

Grodzinsky F, Miller KW, Wolf MJ (2008) The ethics of designing artificial agents. Ethics Inf Technol 10(2–3):115–121

Grundmann S, Hacker P (2017) Digital technology as a challenge to European contract law – from the existing to the future architecture. Eur Rev Contract Law 13:255–293

Guihot M, Matthew AF, Suzor NP (2017) Nudging robots: innovative solutions to regulate artificial intelligence. Vanderbilt J Ent Technol Law 20:385

Hilgendorf E (2018) Problem areas in the dignity debate and the ensemble theory of human dignity. In: Grimm D, Kemmerer A, Möllers C (eds) Human dignity in context. Explorations of a contested concept, pp 325 ff
Howells G, Twigg-Flesner C, Willett C (2017) Product liability and digital products. In: Synodinou T-E, Jougleux P, Markou C, Prastitou T (eds) EU internet law: regulation and enforcement. Springer Nature, pp 183–195
Karner E, Koch BA, Geistfeld MA (2021) Comparative law study on civil liability for artificial intelligence. European Commission, Directorate-General for Justice and Consumers
Kritikos M (2016) Legal and ethical reflections concerning robotics. Scientific Foresight Unit (STOA) Policy Briefing, European Parliament Research Service (EPRS), PE 563.501, June 2016
Kritikos M (2019) Artificial intelligence ante portas: legal & ethical reflections. European Parliamentary Research Service (EPRS), Scientific Foresight Unit (STOA), March 2019
Leenes R, Palmerini E, Koops B-J, Bertolini A, Salvini P, Lucivero F (2017) Regulatory challenges of robotics: some guidelines for addressing legal and ethical issues. Law Innov Technol 9:1–44
Lohmann MF (2016) Liability issues concerning self-driving vehicles. Eur J Risk Regul 7(2): 335–340
Lohsse S, Schulze R, Staudenmayer D (2019) Liability for artificial intelligence. In: Lohsse S, Schulze R, Staudenmayer D (eds) Liability for artificial intelligence and the internet of things. Nomos, Baden-Baden, pp 99–116
Luzak J (2020) A broken notion: impact of modern technologies on product liability. Eur J Risk Regul 11(3):630–649
Machnikowski P (2016) Conclusions. In: Machnikowski P (ed) European product liability: an analysis of the state of the art in the era of new technologies. Principles of European tort law. Intersentia, pp 669–705
Madiega T (2020) Reform of the EU Liability Regime for Online Intermediaries: Background on the Forthcoming Digital Services Act: In Depth Analysis. European Parliamentary Research Service (EPRS), May 2020
Martín-Casals M (2019) Causation and scope of liability in the internet of things (IoT). In: Lohsse S, Schulze R, Staudenmayer D (eds) Liability for artificial intelligence and the internet of things. Nomos, Baden-Baden, pp 201–228
Mezzanotte F (2019) Liability for digital products. In: A De Franceschi/R Schulze (eds), Digital revolution – new challenges for law, 169-188. Nomos,
Navas S (2020) Robot machines and civil liability. In: Ebers M, Navas S (eds) Algorithms and law. Cambridge University Press, pp 157–173
Nevejans N (2016) European civil law rules in robotics. Study requested by the European Parliament's Committee on Legal Affairs (JURI Committee)
O'Mahony C (2012) There is no such thing as a right to dignity. Int J Const Law 10(2):551–574
Palmerini E, Bertolini A, Battaglia F, Koops B-J, Carnevale A, Salvini P (2016) RoboLaw: towards a European framework for robotics regulation. Robot Auton Syst 86:78–85
Pandey KA, Gelin R (2018) A mass-produced sociable humanoid robot: Pepper: the first machine of its kind. IEEE Robot Autom Mag 25(3):40–48
Patti FP (2019) The European road to autonomous vehicles. Fordham Int Law J 43:125
Salem M, Lakatos G, Amirabdollahian F, Dautenhahn K (2015) Towards safe and trustworthy social robots: ethical challenges and practical issues. In: ICSR, pp 584–593
Schellekens M (2018) No-fault compensation schemes for self-driving vehicles. Law Innov Technol 10(2):314–333
Schroeder D, Bani-Sadr AH (2017) Dignity in the 21st century: Middle east and west. Springer International Publishing, Berlin
Sharkey A (2014) Robots and human dignity: a consideration of the effects of robot care on the dignity of older people. Ethics Inf Technol 16(1):63–75
Shavell S (2020) On the redesign of accident liability for the world of autonomous vehicles. J Leg Stud 49:243–285

Spindler G (2019) User liability and strict liability in the internet of things and for robots. In: Lohsse S, Schulze R, Staudenmayer D (eds) Liability for artificial intelligence and the internet of things. Nomos, Baden-Baden, pp 125–145

Timan T, Snijders R, Kirova M, Suardi S, Lieshout MV, Chen M, Costenco P, Palmerini E, Bertolini A, Tejada A, Montfort SV, Bolchi M, Alberti S, Brouwer R, Karanilokova K, Episcopo F, Jansen S (2019) Study on safety of non-embedded software. Service, data access, and legal issues of advanced robots, autonomous, connected, and AI-based vehicles and systems: final study report regarding CAD/CCAM and industrial robots. European Commission, Brussel

Twigg-Flesner C (2021) 'Guiding Principles for Updating the Product Liability Directive for the Digital Age' (Pilot ELI Innovation Paper). European Law Institute, January 2021

Tzimas T (2021) Legal and ethical challenges of artificial intelligence from an international law perspective. Springer, Cham, Switzerland, pp 9–32

van Boom WH, Borghetti J-S, Ehlers AB, Karner E, Nolan D, Oliphant K, Scarso A, Ulfbeck V, Wagner G (2018) Product liability in Europe. In: Koziol H, Green MD, Lunney M, Oliphant K, Yang L (eds) Product liability: fundamental questions in a comparative perspective. De Gruyter, Berlin, Boston, pp 255–356

Vandemeulebroucke T, de Casterle BD, Gastmans C (2018) How do older adults experience and perceive socially assistive robots in aged care: a systematic review of qualitative evidence. Aging Mental Health 22(2):149–167

Verheyen T (2018) Full harmonization, consumer protection and products liability: a fresh reading of the case law of the ECJ. Eur Rev Priv Law 26(1):119–140

Wagner G (2019a) Robot liability. In: Lohsse S, Schulze R, Staudenmayer D (eds) Liability for artificial intelligence and the internet of things. Nomos, Baden-Baden, pp 27–62

Wagner G (2019b) Robot, Inc.: personhood for autonomous systems? Fordham Law Rev 88:591

Wendehorst C (2020) Strict liability for AI and other emerging technologies. J Eur Tort Law (JETL) 11(2):150–180

Winfield AF, Jirotka M (2018) Ethical governance is essential to building trust in robotics and artificial intelligence systems. Philos Trans R Soc A: Math Phys Eng Sci 376(2133):20180085

Wuyts D (2014) The Product Liability Directive – more than two decades of defective products in Europe. J Eur Tort Law 5(1):1–34

Zardiashvili L, Fosch-Villaronga E (2020) "Oh, Dignity too?" Said the Robot: human dignity as the basis for the governance of robotics. Minds Mach 30:121–143

Zech H (2019) Liability for autonomous systems: tackling specific risks of modern IT. In: Lohsse S, Schulze R, Staudenmeyer D (eds) Liability for artificial intelligence and the internet of things. Nomos, Baden-Baden, pp 187–200

Chapter 5
The European Parliament's 2020 Legislative Proposal for a Regulation on a Civil Liability Regime for Artificial Intelligence

5.1 Introduction

This chapter examines the European Parliaments' 2020 Resolution on a civil liability regime for artificial intelligence.[1] With this legislative initiative, the European Parliament ("Parliament") urged the European Commission ("Commission") to present a future-oriented civil liability framework, laying down rules for the civil liability claims of natural and legal persons against operators of AI-systems. It was stated that a clear legal framework should stimulate innovation by providing businesses with legal certainty, whilst protecting citizens and promoting their trust in AI technologies by deterring activities that might be dangerous. The Parliament considered it necessary to ensure maximum legal certainty throughout the liability chain, including for the producer, operator, injured parties and any other third parties, in order to respond to the new legal challenges created by developments in AI systems. According to the Parliament, civil liability rules for AI should strike a balance between protecting potential victims of harm or damage and, at the same time, supporting investment and technological innovation.

---

[1] European Parliament Resolution of 20 October 2020 with recommendations to the Commission on a civil liability regime for artificial intelligence (2020/2014(INL)) P9_TA(2020)0276 (hereafter: European Parliament's Resolution of 20 October 2020 on a civil liability regime for AI).

Also: Annex to the Resolution: detailed recommendations for drawing up a Regulation on liability for the operation of artificial intelligence-systems, A. Principles and Aims of the Proposal. B. Text of the Proposal Requested—Proposal for a Regulation on liability for the operation of Artificial Intelligence-systems (hereafter: Annex to the European Parliament's Resolution of 20 October 2020 on a civil liability regime for AI).

N. T. Nikolinakos, *Adapting the EU Civil Liability Regime to the Digital Age: Artificial Intelligence, Robotics, and Other Emerging Technologies*, Law, Governance and Technology Series 68, https://doi.org/10.1007/978-3-031-67969-8_5

In particular, following the Commission's 2020 White Paper on AI,[2] the European Parliament set up (on 18 June 2020) a special committee to analyse the impact of artificial intelligence on the EU economy and to ensure that the EU develops "a holistic approach providing a common, long-term position that highlights the EU's key values and objectives relating to artificial intelligence in the digital age". This approach should be common (to avoid the fragmentation of the single market), human-centric, and in line with the Union's core principles, values and fundamental rights.[3]

In April 2020, the European Parliament's Legal Affairs Committee ("JURI") published three draft reports to the Commission providing recommendations on a framework for: (i) AI ethics and human-centric AI, urging the Commission to present a new legal framework outlining the ethical principles and legal obligations to be followed when developing, deploying and using AI, robotics and related technologies in the EU (i.e., the AI Act); (ii) AI liability, calling for a future-oriented civil liability framework, making those operating high-risk AI strictly liable for any resulting damage; iii) copyright protection for AI assisted human creations and safeguards within the EU's patent system to protect the innovation of AI developers, but not at the expense of human creators' interests nor the European Union's ethical principles. The subsequent three legal initiatives, summarised in final reports and recommendations, were adopted by the plenary of the Parliament on 20 October 2020.[4] As the Parliament stated: "The European Parliament is among the

[2]Commission Communication, "White Paper On Artificial Intelligence - A European approach to excellence and trust", COM(2020) 65 final, Brussels, 19.2.2020.

[3]European Parliament Decision of 18 June 2020 on setting up a special committee on artificial intelligence in a digital age, and defining its responsibilities, numerical strength and term of office, 18 June 2020, (2020/2684(RSO)).

The European Parliament "decides to set up a special committee on artificial intelligence in a digital age, vested with the following strictly defined responsibilities: (a) to analyse the future impact of artificial intelligence in the digital age on the EU economy, in particular on skills, employment, fintech, education, health, transport, tourism, agriculture, environment, defence, industry, energy and e-government; (b) to further investigate the challenge of deploying artificial intelligence and its contribution to business value and economic growth; (c) to analyse the approach of third countries and their contribution to complementing EU actions; (d) to submit to Parliament's responsible standing committees an evaluation defining common EU objectives in the medium- and long-term and include the major steps needed to reach them, using as a starting point the following Commission communications published on 19 February 2020: - Shaping Europe's digital future (COM(2020)0067), - A European Strategy for Data (COM(2020)0066), White Paper on Artificial Intelligence - a European approach to excellence and trust (COM(2020)0065), Report on the safety and liability implications of Artificial Intelligence, the Internet of Things and robotics (COM(2020) 0064), including a roadmap on 'A Europe fit for the digital age', which shall provide the EU with a strategic plan defining its common objectives in the medium- and long-term and the major steps needed to reach them".

[4]European Parliament Resolution of 20 October 2020 with recommendations to the Commission on a framework of ethical aspects of artificial intelligence, robotics and related technologies (2020/2012 (INL)), P9_TA(2020)0275.

European Parliament Resolution of 20 October 2020 with recommendations to the Commission on a civil liability regime for artificial intelligence (2020/2014(INL)), P9_TA(2020)0276.

first institutions to put forward recommendations on what AI rules should include with regards to ethics, liability and intellectual property rights. These recommendations will pave the way for the EU to become a global leader in the development of AI. The Commission legislative proposal is expected early next year".[5]

This chapter examines the European Parliaments' 2020 Resolution on a civil liability regime for artificial intelligence.[6] As already mentioned, with this legislative

European Parliament Resolution of 20 October 2020 on intellectual property rights for the development of artificial intelligence technologies (2020/2015(INI)), P9_TA(2020)0277.

[5]European Parliament, Press Release, "Parliament leads the way on first set of EU rules for Artificial Intelligence", 20.10.2020, at p. 2.

[6]For interesting reading, analysis, and useful academic commentary, see the following:

Gerhard Wagner, Liability for Artificial Intelligence: A Proposal by the European Parliament, in: H. Eidenmüller/G. Wagner, Law by Algorithm (2021) 127.

Ernst Karner, Bernhard A. Koch, Mark A. Geistfeld, 'Comparative Law Study on Civil Liability for Artificial Intelligence', European Commission, Directorate-General for Justice and Consumers, 2021.

Martin Ebers, "Liability For Artificial Intelligence And EU Consumer Law", 12 (2021) JIPITEC 204-220.

Emiliano Marchisio, "In support of "no-fault" civil liability rules for artificial intelligence" (2021) 1 SN Social Sciences 1, 54 (2021).

Anna Beckers, Gunther Teubner, "Three Liability Regimes for Artificial Intelligence: Algorithmic Actants, Hybrids, Crowds", Bloomsbury Publishing, 2021.

Henrique Sousa Antunes, Civil Liability Applicable to Artificial Intelligence: A Preliminary Critique of the European Parliament Resolution of 2020 (December 5, 2020). Available at SSRN: https://ssrn.com/abstract=3743242 or https://doi.org/10.2139/ssrn.3743242.

Tatjana Evas, Civil liability regime for artificial intelligence, Study, European Parliamentary Research Service (EPRS), September 2020.

Christiane Wendehorst, "Strict liability for AI and other emerging technologies", Journal of European Tort Law (JETL) 2020, 11(2): 150–180.

Andrea Bertolini, Artificial intelligence and civil liability, Study requested by the European Parliament's Committee on Legal Affairs, Policy Department for Citizens' Rights and Constitutional Affairs – Directorate-General for Internal Policies, PE 621.926, July 2020.

Borges, G.: New Liability Concepts: the potential of insurance and compensation funds. In: Lohsse, S., Schulze, R., Staudenmeyer, D. (eds.) Liability for Artificial Intelligence and the Internet of Things. Nomos, Baden-Baden (2019), pp. 145–163.

Borghetti J-S, 'How can artificial intelligence be defective'. In: Lohsse S, Schulze R, Staudenmayer D (eds) Liability for artificial intelligence and the Internet of Things. Nomos, Baden-Baden (2019), pp. 63–76.

Gerald Spindler, 'User Liability and Strict Liability in the Internet of Things and for Robots' in Sebastian Lohsse, Reiner Schulze and Dirk Staudenmayer (eds), Liability for Artificial Intelligence and the Internet of Things. Nomos, Baden-Baden (2019), pp. 125–145.

Miquel Martín-Casals, 'Causation and Scope of Liability in the Internet of Things (IoT)' in Sebastian Lohsse/Reiner Schulze/Dirk Staudenmayer (ed), Liability for Artificial Intelligence and the Internet of Things. Nomos, Baden-Baden (2019), pp. 201–228.

Lohsse, S., Schulze, R., & Staudenmayer, D., 'Liability for Artificial Intelligence', In S. Lohsse, R. Schulze, & D. Staudenmayer (eds.), Liability for Artificial Intelligence and the Internet of Things. Nomos, Baden-Baden (2019), 99–116.

Gerhard Wagner, 'Robot Liability' in S.Lohsse/R.Schulze/D.Staudenmayer (eds), Liability for Artificial Intelligence and the Internet of Things. Nomos, Baden-Baden (2019), pp. 27–62.

initiative,[7] the European Parliament urged the Commission to present a future-oriented civil liability framework, laying down rules for the civil liability claims of natural and legal persons against operators of AI-systems.[8] It was stated that a clear legal framework should stimulate innovation by providing businesses with legal certainty, whilst protecting citizens and promoting their trust in AI technologies by deterring activities that might be dangerous. The Parliament considered it necessary to ensure maximum legal certainty[9] throughout the liability chain, including for the producer, operator, injured parties and any other third parties, in order to respond to the new legal challenges created by developments in artificial intelligence (AI) systems.

Civil liability rules for AI should strike a balance between protecting citizens and supporting technological innovation. As it was stated: "whereas any future-oriented civil liability legal framework has to instill confidence in the safety, reliability and consistency of products and services, including in digital technology, in order to strike a balance between efficiently and fairly protecting potential victims of harm or damage and, at the same time, providing enough leeway to make it possible for enterprises, and particularly small and medium-sized enterprises, to develop new technologies, products or services; whereas this will help build confidence and create stability for investment; whereas ultimately, the goal of any liability framework should be to provide legal certainty for all parties, whether it be the producer, the operator, the affected person or any other third party".[10]

In brief, the Parliament's initiative recognised that the type of AI-system the operator is exercising control over should be a determining factor regarding liability. In this regard, it stressed that an AI-system that entails an inherent high risk and acts autonomously potentially endangers the user or the general public to a much higher degree and in a manner that is random and goes beyond what can reasonably be

---

Andrea Bertolini, Artificial Intelligence and civil law - Liability rules for drones, Study requested by the European Parliament's Committee on Legal Affairs, Policy Department for Citizens' Rights and Constitutional Affairs, November 2018.

Tatjana Evas, A common EU approach to liability rules and insurance for connected and autonomous vehicles, Study. European Added Value Assessment - Accompanying the European Parliament's legislative own-initiative report (Rapporteur: Mady Delvaux). Study, European Parliamentary Research Service (EPRS), February 2018.

Nathalie Nevejans, 'European Civil Law Rules in Robotics', Study requested by the European Parliament's Committee on Legal Affairs (JURI Committee), 2016.

[7]European Parliament Report with recommendations to the Commission on a civil liability regime for artificial intelligence (2020/2014(INL)), Committee on Legal Affairs, A9-0178/2020, 05.10.2020.

European Parliament Resolution of 20 October 2020 with recommendations to the Commission on a civil liability regime for artificial intelligence (2020/2014(INL)) P9_TA(2020)0276.

[8]Annex to the European Parliament's Resolution of 20 October 2020 on a civil liability regime for AI – Text of the Proposal for a Regulation on liability for the operation of AI systems, Article 1.

[9]European Parliament's Resolution of 20 October 2020 on a civil liability regime for AI, recital K: "Legal certainty is also an essential condition for the dynamic development and innovation of AI-based technology".

[10]Ibid., recital B.

expected. Therefore, different liability rules should apply for different risks, following a risk-based approach. As a result, the Parliament's proposed Regulation on liability for AI systems stressed that a strict liability regime for high-risk AI systems should apply, i.e. the operator of a high-risk AI-system should be strictly liable for any harm or damage that was caused by a physical or virtual activity, device or process driven by that AI-system. According to the Parliament's Resolution, operators of high-risk AI systems should hold liability insurance similar to that used for motor vehicles. This compulsory insurance regime for high-risk AI-systems should cover the amounts and the extent of compensation, as defined in the proposed Regulation. The initiative also stated that the operator of an AI-system that does not constitute a high-risk AI-system should be subject to fault-based liability for any harm or damage that was caused by a physical or virtual activity, device or process driven by the AI-system. Therefore, the operator of a non-high-risk AI system should not be liable if he can prove that the harm or damage was caused without his fault. The Parliament considered that operator liability rules should apply to all types of AI system operations, regardless of the location of the operation and whether it is of a physical or virtual nature.

More analytically:

5.2 Characteristics Shared by AI Systems—Legal Challenges for the Existing Liability Framework—Limitations of Scope of Existing EU Legislation

The European Parliament repeated that the emergence of new digital technologies like AI systems raise new challenges in terms of product safety and liability like connectivity, autonomy, data dependency, opacity, complexity of products and systems, software updates and more complex safety management and value chains.[11]

[11] "The rise of AI, however, presents a significant challenge for the existing liability frameworks. Using AI-systems in our daily life will lead to situations in which their opacity ("black box" element) and the multitude of actors who intervene in their lifecycle make it extremely expensive or even impossible to identify who was in control of the risk of using the AI-system in question or which code or input caused the harmful operation. That difficulty is compounded by the connectivity between an AI-system and other AI-systems and non-AI-systems, by its dependency on external data, by its vulnerability to cybersecurity breaches, as well as by the increasing autonomy of AI-systems triggered by machine-learning and deep-learning capabilities. In addition to these complex features and potential vulnerabilities, AI-systems could also be used to cause severe harm, such as compromising human dignity and European values and freedoms, by tracking individuals against their will, by introducing social credit systems, by taking biased decisions in matters of health insurance, credit provision, court orders, recruitment or employment or by constructing lethal autonomous weapon systems". Annex to the European Parliament's Resolution of 20 October 2020 on a civil liability regime for AI—Text of the Proposal for a Regulation on liability for the operation of AI systems, recital 3.

It is recalled that AI systems display certain levels of complexity due to the interdependency between different components. For instance, the IoT and AI-enabled products and services comprise tangible parts/devices (sensors, actuators, hardware), different software components and applications, data, data services (i.e. collection, processing, curating, analysing), and connectivity features.[12] Therefore, risks stemming from the complexity of the products and systems might have a serious impact on safety. Connectivity[13] is a central feature in an ever-growing number of products and services, and the risk of loss of connectivity of emerging digital technologies may lead to new challenges concerning both safety and security.[14] Furthermore, AI-based products and systems are characterised by various

It is reminded that, according to the Commission's White Paper, the main characteristics shared by the emerging digital technologies could lead to risk of harm and potentially create challenges to the existing EU product safety framework. The essential characteristics of AI-based products and systems include connectivity between an AI-system and other AI-systems and non-AI-systems, autonomy (increasingly autonomous AI-systems using, inter alia, machine-learning and deep-learning techniques), dependency on external data, vulnerability to cybersecurity breaches, complexity, and complex value chain (including a multitude of actors involved in AI systems' lifecycle). Therefore, the use of AI in services and products could create risks that EU legislation currently does not explicitly address, mainly linked to cyber threats, security risks—associated with new applications of AI such as home appliances—or risks that result from loss of connectivity. These risks could arise at the time of placing products on the market or appear as a result of software updates or self-learning when the product is being used. See Commission Communication "White Paper On Artificial Intelligence - A European approach to excellence and trust", COM(2020) 65 final, Brussels, 19.2.2020, p. 14.

[12] "Various components, devices and products can be integrated and have influence on each other's functioning (e.g. products part of a smart home ecosystem)". Commission Communication, "Report on the safety and liability implications of Artificial Intelligence, the Internet of Things and robotics", Brussels, COM (2020) 64 final, 19.2.2020, p. 9.

[13] "Sensors and smart connected objects are not only designed and optimised to perform certain functions on the basis of vertical business models. They become part of a bigger connectivity network which creates new opportunities to combine more intelligence and actuation across vertical markets and to provide a whole new set of services. Technical and semantic interoperability are the key factor of success. It enables the programming of complex systems to integrate a number of device- and service-providers to deliver complete IoT solutions e.g. at home, in cities, between industries". See, for instance, the Commission Staff Working Document on "Liability for emerging digital technologies" - Accompanying the document Commission Communication "Artificial intelligence for Europe", SWD(2018) 137 final, Brussels, 25.4.2018, at p. 22.

[14] Indeed, the connectivity feature—if combined with poor security measures at design, manufacturing or operation stage—could compromise the safety of the product and result in serious security breaches. Corrupted data (e.g. due to connectivity problems or when hacked) may affect the behaviour of the entire system or of individual components or it may render the system malfunctioning. For instance, if a connected fire alarm loses connectivity it may not alert the user in case of a fire. Also, cyber-attackers could have the opportunity to take control of the said system and modify its functioning or the functioning of other smart devices in the same ecosystem. As the Commission has put it, connectivity "is challenging the traditional concept of safety, as connectivity may directly compromise the safety of the product and indirectly when it can be hacked leading to security threats and affecting the safety of users. ... Industrial applications may also be exposed to cyber threats affecting the safety of persons at larger scale when such applications lack the necessary levels of security. This can be the case for example of cyber-attacks on a critical control

degrees of opacity (the internal complexity of the algorithms involved), resulting to a decision-making process of the AI system that can be extremely difficult to trace. Due to the autonomy aspect and the opacity issue (black-box effect) of AI systems, getting fair compensation[15] could become difficult for harm caused by certain AI-applications. Indeed, it could be hard to trace the damage back to a specific human behaviour and, at the same time, extremely costly to understand (and get

system of an industrial plant intended to trigger an explosion that might cost lives". See Commission Communication "Report on the safety and liability implications of Artificial Intelligence, the Internet of Things and robotics", Brussels, COM (2020) 64 final, 19.2.2020, at p. 5. The Commission provided specific examples of safety/security risks posed by these technologies: "An example is given by an EU Rapid Alert System notification from Iceland concerning a smart watch for children. This product would not cause a direct harm to the child wearing it, but lacking a minimum level of security, it can be easily used as a tool to have access to the child. As one of the product's intended function is to keep children safe through localisation, a consumer would expect that it would not pose security threats to children that may affect their safety by potentially being tracked and/or contacted by anyone. Another example is indicated in a notification submitted by Germany regarding a passenger car. The radio in the vehicle may have certain software security gaps allowing unauthorised third-party access to the interconnected control systems in the vehicle. If these software security gaps were exploited by a third party for malicious purposes, a road accident could occur".

The use of AI in services and products could create risks that EU legislation currently does not explicitly address, mainly linked to cyber threats, security risks or risks that result from loss of connectivity. These risks could arise at the time of placing products on the market or appear as a result of software updates or self-learning when the product is being used It is reminded that similar risks could arise where the software is not included in the product put into circulation by the producer but installed subsequently as a stand-alone feature. "While the Union product safety legislation takes into account the safety risks stemming from software integrated in a product at the time of its placing on the market and, potentially subsequent updates foreseen by the manufacturer, specific and/or explicit requirements on standalone software could be needed (e.g. an 'app' that would be downloaded). Particular considerations should be given to the stand-alone software ensuring safety functions in the AI products and systems. Additional obligations may be needed for manufacturers to ensure that they provide features to prevent the upload of software having an impact on safety during the lifetime of the AI products". See Commission "Report on the safety and liability implications of Artificial Intelligence, the Internet of Things and robotics", Brussels, COM (2020) 64 final, 19.2.2020, at p. 11.

Also, as it has been stated by the Commission in the White Paper on AI: "the integration of software, including AI, into products can modify the functioning of such products and systems during their lifecycle. This is particularly true for systems that require frequent software updates or which rely on machine learning. These features can give rise to new risks that were not present when the system was placed on the market. These risks are not adequately addressed in the existing legislation which predominantly focuses on safety risks present at the time of placing on the market". See Commission Communication "White Paper On Artificial Intelligence - A European approach to excellence and trust", Brussels, 19.2.2020, COM(2020) 65 final, at p. 14.

[15] According to the European Parliament, "fair compensation procedures mean that each person who suffers harm caused by AI-systems or whose property damage is caused by AI-systems should have the same level of protection compared to cases without involvement of an AI-system; the user needs to be sure that potential damage caused by systems using AI is covered by adequate insurance and that there is a defined legal route for redress". European Parliament's Resolution of 20 October 2020 on a civil liability regime for AI, recital J.

access to) the algorithm and the data used by the AI system.[16] This was also underlined by the Commission's White Paper on AI: "The lack of transparency (opaqueness of AI) makes it difficult to identify and prove possible breaches of laws, including legal provisions that protect fundamental rights, attribute liability and meet the conditions to claim compensation. Therefore, in order to ensure an effective application and enforcement, it may be necessary to adjust or clarify existing legislation in certain areas, for example on liability".[17]

[16]Finding the main cause of damage and attributing liability becomes complex. Therefore, the allocation of liability could be unfair or inefficient, whereas liability claims may be difficult or overly costly to be made and/or to be proven. As a result, victims may not be adequately compensated. See, for instance, the Commission's "Report on the safety and liability implications of Artificial Intelligence, the Internet of Things and robotics", Brussels, COM (2020) 64 final, 19.2.2020, at p. 15: "the need to understand the algorithm and the data used by the AI requires analytical capacity and technical expertise that victims could find prohibitively costly. In addition, access to the algorithm and the data could be impossible without the cooperation of the potentially liable party. In practice, victims may thus not be able to make a liability claim. In addition, it would be unclear, how to demonstrate the fault of an AI acting autonomously, or what would be considered the fault of a person relying on the use of AI".

See also the Report from the Expert Group on Liability and New Technologies – New Technologies Formation "Liability for Artificial Intelligence and Other Emerging Digital Technologies", 21 November 2019, at p. 24: "Generally, the victim has to prove that the defendant (or someone whose conduct is attributable to them) was at fault. The victim therefore not only needs to identify which duties of care the defendant should have discharged, but also to prove to the court that these duties were breached. Proving the defendant is at fault entails providing the court with evidence that may lead it to believe what the applicable standard of care was and that it has not been met. The second part of this is to provide evidence of how the event giving rise to the damage occurred. The more complex the circumstances leading to the victim's harm are, the harder it is to identify relevant evidence. For example, it can be difficult and costly to identify a bug in a long and complicated software code. In the case of AI, examining the process leading to a specific result (how the input data led to the output data) may be difficult, very time-consuming and expensive".

[17]Commission Communication "White Paper On Artificial Intelligence - A European approach to excellence and trust", Brussels, 19.2.2020, COM(2020) 65 final, at p. 14. See also: "The specific characteristics of many AI technologies, including opacity ('black box-effect'), complexity, unpredictability and partially autonomous behaviour, may make it hard to verify compliance with, and may hamper the effective enforcement of, rules of existing EU law meant to protect fundamental rights. Enforcement authorities and affected persons might lack the means to verify how a given decision made with the involvement of AI was taken and, therefore, whether the relevant rules were respected. Individuals and legal entities may face difficulties with effective access to justice in situations where such decisions may negatively affect them" (at pp. 11–12). "If the safety risks materialise, the lack of clear requirements and the characteristics of AI technologies mentioned above make it difficult to trace back potentially problematic decisions made with the involvement of AI systems. This in turn may make it difficult for persons having suffered harm to obtain compensation under the current EU and national liability legislation. Under the Product Liability Directive, a manufacturer is liable for damage caused by a defective product. However, in the case of an AI based system such as autonomous cars, it may be difficult to prove that there is a defect in the product, the damage that has occurred and the causal link between the two. In addition, there is some uncertainty about how and to what extent the Product Liability Directive applies in the case of certain types of defects, for example if these result from weaknesses in the cybersecurity of the product. Thus, the difficulty of tracing back potentially problematic decisions taken by AI systems and referred to above in relation to fundamental rights applies equally to safety and

In line with the Commission's analysis, the Parliament stated that "there is no need for a complete revision of the well-functioning liability regimes, but that the complexity, connectivity, opacity, vulnerability, the capacity of being modified through updates, the capacity for self-learning and the potential autonomy of AI-systems, as well as the multitude of actors involved represent nevertheless a significant challenge to the effectiveness of Union and national liability framework provisions; considers that specific and coordinated adjustments to the liability regimes are necessary to avoid a situation in which persons who suffer harm or whose property is damaged end up without compensation";[18] "the opacity, connectivity and autonomy of AI-systems could make it in practice very difficult or even impossible to trace back specific harmful actions of AI-systems to specific human input or to decisions in the design";[19] "certain AI-systems present significant legal challenges for the existing liability framework and could lead to situations in which their opacity could make it extremely expensive or even impossible to identify who was in control of the risk associated with the AI-system, or which code, input or data have ultimately caused the harmful operation; ... this factor could make it harder to identify the link between harm or damage and the behaviour causing it, with the result that victims might not receive adequate compensation; ... the legal challenges also result from the connectivity between an AI-system and other AI-systems and non-AI-systems, their dependency on external data, their vulnerability to cybersecurity breaches as well as from the design of increasingly autonomous AI-systems using, inter alia, machine-learning and deep-learning techniques".[20]

With regard to the issue of limitations of scope of existing EU legislation, it is recalled that the Product Liability Directive does not make any reference to the concept of service nor does it provide for the distinction between products and

liability-related issues. Persons having suffered harm may not have effective access to the evidence that is necessary to build a case in court, for instance, and may have less effective redress possibilities compared to situations where the damage is caused by traditional technologies. These risks will increase as the use of AI becomes more widespread" (at pp. 12–13).

[18] European Parliament's Resolution of 20 October 2020 on a civil liability regime for AI, section "Liability and Artificial Intelligence", point 6.

[19] Ibid., point 7.

[20] Ibid., recitals H and I.

See also the Annex to the European Parliament's Resolution of 20 October 2020 on a civil liability regime for AI – Text of the Proposal for a Regulation on liability for the operation of AI systems, recital 7: "There are however also AI-systems that are developed and deployed in a critical manner and are based on technologies such as neuronal networks and deep-learning processes. Their opacity and autonomy could make it very difficult to trace back specific actions to specific human decisions in their design or in their operation. An operator of such an AI-system might, for instance, argue that the physical or virtual activity, device or process causing the harm or damage was outside of his or her control because it was caused by an autonomous operation of his or her AI-system. Moreover, the mere operation of an autonomous AI-system should not be a sufficient ground for admitting the liability claim. As a result, there might be liability cases in which the allocation of liability could be unfair or inefficient, or in which a person who suffers harm or damage caused by an AI-system cannot prove the fault of the producer, of an interfering third party or of the operator and ends up without compensation".

services. It solely provides for the definition of product, according to Article 2 of the Directive. Services do not fall into the definition of product. It is recognized that the distinction between products and services for the purpose of the Product Liability Directive is becoming increasingly blurred with regards to new technological developments. Therefore, the definition of product appears to no longer be as clear-cut as it may have been when the Product Liability Directive was adopted. It is also questionable whether software is covered by the legal concept of product or product component.[21] Applications and other non-embedded software (i.e. not contained in a tangible medium) could raise serious liability issues which are currently not fully addressed by the EU legal framework. AI, combined with hardware, can create new tangible products and/or deliver services. Since the distinction between products and services becomes less relevant, there is need to clarify what products and features are covered by the Product Liability Directive. For instance, providing data through an IoT system could be considered a service, and thus fall, as such, outside the product liability (and safety) regime.[22] Furthermore, a question relates to whether the

---

[21] "Technology and industry have evolved drastically over the last decades. Especially the dividing line between products and services may no longer be as clear-cut as it was. Products and the provision of services are increasingly intertwined". Commission Communication "Report on the safety and liability implications of Artificial Intelligence, the Internet of Things and robotics", COM (2020) 64 final, Brussels, 19.2.2020, p. 13.

See also the Report from the Expert Group on Liability and New Technologies—New Technologies Formation "Liability for Artificial Intelligence and Other Emerging Digital Technologies", 21 November 2019, at p. 28: "The scope of the product liability regime rests on the concept of product. For the purposes of the Product Liability Directive, products are defined as movable objects, even when incorporated into another movable or immovable object, and include electricity. So far, the distinction of products and services has not encountered insurmountable difficulties. However, emerging digital technologies, especially AI systems, challenge that clear distinction and raise open questions. In AI systems, products and services permanently interact and a sharp separation between them is unfeasible. It is also questionable whether software is covered by the legal concept of product or product component. It is particularly discussed whether the answer should be different for embedded and non-embedded software, including over-the-air software updates or other data feeds. In any case, where such updates or other data feeds are provided from outside the EEA, the victim may not have anybody to turn to within the EEA, as there will typically not be an intermediary importer domiciled within the EEA in the case of direct downloads".

[22] Therefore, an interpretation of the concept of product or an enlargement of the concept of product might be needed, especially where the non-tangible element is not included in the product put into circulation by the producer but installed subsequently as a stand-alone feature. This is particularly true with regards to software; a clarification of the concept 'product' would contribute to improving effectiveness and, therefore, further assessment and clarification is needed. "Software and also AI merit specific attention in respect of product liability. Software is essential to the functioning of a large number of products and may affect their safety. It is integrated into products but it may also be supplied separately to enable the use of the product as intended. Neither a computer nor a smartphone would be of particular use without software. This means that software can make a tangible product defective and lead to physical damage. This could eventually result in the liability of the producer of the product under the Product Liability Directive. However, as software comes in many types and forms, answers related to the classification of software as a service or as a product may not always be straightforward. Thus while software steering the operations of a tangible product could be considered part or component of that product, some forms of stand-alone software

concept of 'producer', as defined in the context of Product Liability Directive, fits with the type of responsibilities that may arise in systems encompassing software, AI systems, data services and other emerging technologies.[23] An assessment should

---

could be more difficult to classify". Commission Communication "Report on the safety and liability implications of Artificial Intelligence, the Internet of Things and robotics", COM (2020) 64 final, Brussels, 19.2.2020, pp. 13–14.

Furthermore, see Commission Staff Working Document, Evaluation of Council Directive 85/374/EEC of 25 July 1985 on the approximation of the laws, regulations and administrative provisions of the Member States concerning liability for defective products – Accompanying the Evaluation Report – SWD(2018) 157 final, Brussels, 7.5.2018, at pp. 52, 53-54, 61. Also: Commission Staff Working Document on "Liability for emerging digital technologies" - Accompanying the document Commission Communication "Artificial intelligence for Europe", SWD(2018) 137 final, Brussels, 25.4.2018, pp. 9–11.

See also Commission Communication "White Paper On Artificial Intelligence - A European approach to excellence and trust", COM(2020) 65 final, Brussels, 19.2.2020, p. 14: "an essential focus of EU product safety legislation is on the placing of products on the market. While in EU product safety legislation software, when is part of the final product, must comply with the relevant product safety rules, it is an open question whether stand-alone software is covered by EU product safety legislation, outside some sectors with explicit rules. General EU safety legislation currently in force applies to products and not to services, and therefore in principle not to services based on AI technology either (e.g. health services, financial services, transport services)".

[23] See, for instance, Commission Communication "Report on the safety and liability implications of Artificial Intelligence, the Internet of Things and robotics", Brussels, COM (2020) 64 final, 19.2.2020, p. 14: "Although the Product Liability Directive's definition of product is broad, its scope could be further clarified to better reflect the complexity of emerging technologies and ensure that compensation is always available for damage caused by products that are defective because of software or other digital features. This would better enable economic actors, such as software developers, to assess whether they could be considered producers according to the Product Liability Directive".

In addition, see Commission Staff Working Document, Evaluation of Council Directive 85/374/EEC of 25 July 1985 on the approximation of the laws, regulations and administrative provisions of the Member States concerning liability for defective products – Accompanying the Evaluation Report – SWD(2018) 157 final, Brussels, 7.5.2018, at pp. 52, 54, 61. For instance, it was examined whether the concept of 'producer', as defined in the context of Product Liability Directive, fits with the type of responsibilities that may arise in systems encompassing software, Artificial Intelligence systems, data services and other emerging technologies. It was concluded that, although the concept of the producer as responsible for his products is still relevant, "it is imperative to assess the impact of changing product (and/or product/service) configurations on this concept to see whether it should be clarified"; "as products are more easily, altered adapted and combined with services, the definition of the producer may become less clear particularly in the context of emerging digital technologies and the circular economy. The definition of the producer, while continuing to be valuable as it ensures strict liability, may therefore no longer be fully relevant in its current form".

See also the European Parliament Resolution of 16 February 2017 with recommendations to the Commission on Civil Law Rules on Robotics (2015/2103(INL)), (OJ C 252, 18.7.2018, pp. 239–257), which stated that the concepts of product, producer, damage or the category of exemptions as defined in the Product Liability Directive could not be apt anymore when dealing with the emerging digital technologies: "[...] in the scenario where a robot can take autonomous decisions, the traditional rules will not suffice to activate a robot's liability, since they would not make it possible to identify the party responsible for providing compensation and to require this party to make good the damage it has caused" (AF, at p. 242).

take account that AI products can change during their life cycle: "in close coordination with corresponding changes in the Union safety framework, the notion of 'putting into circulation' that is currently used by the Product Liability Directive could be revisited to take into account that products may change and be altered. This could also help to clarify who is liable for any changes that are made to the product".[24]

5.3 Liability and Artificial Intelligence: Liability of the Operator

The Parliament concluded that the emergence of AI-systems "does not pose a need for a complete revision of liability rules throughout the Union. Specific adjustments to the existing legislation and the introduction of well-accessed and targeted new provisions would be sufficient to accommodate the AI-related challenges, with a view to preventing regulatory fragmentation and ensuring the harmonisation of civil liability legislation throughout the Union in connection with AI".[25]

---

[24] Commission Communication "Report on the safety and liability implications of Artificial Intelligence, the Internet of Things and robotics", COM (2020) 64 final, Brussels, 19.2.2020, p. 15.

Furthermore, see the Report from the Expert Group on Liability and New Technologies – New Technologies Formation "Liability for Artificial Intelligence and Other Emerging Digital Technologies", 21 November 2019, at pp. 28–29: "As the PLD focuses on the moment when the product was put into circulation as the key turning point for the producer's liability, this cuts off claims for anything the producer may subsequently add via some update or upgrade. In addition, the PLD does not provide for any duties to monitor the products after putting them into circulation. Highly sophisticated AI systems may not be finished products that are put on the market in a traditional way. The producer may retain some degree of control over the product's further development in the form of additions or updates after circulation. At the same time, the producer's control may be limited and nonexclusive if the product's operation requires data provided by third parties or collected from the environment, and depends on self-learning processes and personalising settings chosen by the user. This dilutes the traditional role of a producer, when a multitude of actors contribute to the design, functioning and use of the AI product/system. This is related to another limitation of liability—most Member States adopted the so-called development risk defence, which allows the producer to avoid liability if the state of scientific and technical knowledge at the time when he put the product into circulation was not such as to enable the existence of the defect to be discovered (Article 7 lit e PLD). The defence may become much more important practically with regard to sophisticated AI-based products".

See also Commission Communication "White Paper On Artificial Intelligence - A European approach to excellence and trust", COM(2020) 65 final, Brussels, 19.2.2020, p. 14: "in general, EU legislation on product safety allocates the responsibility to the producer of the product placed on the market, including all components e.g. AI systems. But the rules can for example become unclear if AI is added after the product is placed on the market by a party that is not the producer. In addition, EU product liability legislation provides for liability of producers and leaves national liability rules to govern liability of others in the supply chain".

[25] Annex to the European Parliament's Resolution of 20 October 2020 on a civil liability regime for AI – Text of the Proposal for a Regulation on liability for the operation of AI systems, recital 8.

The Parliament stated that the Product Liability Directive (PLD) has proven its effectiveness as a tool to obtain compensation for damage triggered by a defective product for more than thirty years and, therefore, it should continue to be used with regard to civil liability claims against the producer of a defective AI-system, when the AI-system qualifies as a product under that Directive. However, the PLD should be revised to make it better adapted to the digital world and able to meet the challenges posed by emerging digital technologies[26] ("any necessary legislative adjustments should be considered during the necessary review of that Directive").[27] This is why the Parliament urged the Commission "to assess whether the PLD should be transformed into a regulation, to clarify the definition of 'products' by determining whether digital content and digital services fall under its scope and to consider adapting concepts such as 'damage', 'defect' and 'producer'".[28] The Parliament believes that the concept of 'producer' should include manufacturers, developers, programmers, service providers as well as backend operators.[29]

Furthermore, the Parliament called on the Commission to consider reversing the rules governing the burden of proof for harm caused by emerging digital technologies in clearly defined cases,[30] and stressed that any update of the product liability framework should go in parallel with the update of Directive 2001/95/EC on general product safety in order to ensure that AI systems integrate safety and security by design principles.[31] In addition, the Parliament expressed the view that the existing fault-based law of the Member States offers in most cases a sufficient level of protection for persons that suffer harm caused by an interfering third party like a

[26] European Parliament's Resolution of 20 October 2020 on a civil liability regime for AI, section "Liability and Artificial Intelligence", at point 8.

[27] Annex to the European Parliament's Resolution of 20 October 2020 on a civil liability regime for AI – Text of the Proposal for a Regulation on liability for the operation of AI systems, recital 9. See also recital 23: "It is of utmost importance that any future changes to this Regulation go hand in hand with the necessary review of the Product Liability Directive, in order to revise it in a comprehensive and consistent manner and to guarantee the rights and obligations of all parties concerned throughout the liability chain. The introduction of a new liability regime for the operator of AI-systems requires that the provisions of this Regulation and the review of the Product Liability Directive be closely coordinated in terms of substance as well as approach so that they together constitute a consistent liability framework for AI-systems, balancing the interests of producer, operator, consumer and the affected person, as regards the liability risk and the relevant compensation arrangements. Adapting and streamlining the definitions of AI-system, frontend and backend operator, producer, defect, product and service throughout all pieces of legislation is therefore necessary and should be envisaged in parallel".

[28] European Parliament's Resolution of 20 October 2020 on a civil liability regime for AI, section "Liability and Artificial Intelligence", at point 8.

[29] Ibid.

[30] Ibid. See also the Annex to the European Parliament's Resolution of 20 October 2020 on a civil liability regime for AI – Text of the Proposal for a Regulation on liability for the operation of AI systems, recital 9.

[31] European Parliament's Resolution of 20 October 2020 on a civil liability regime for AI, section "Liability and Artificial Intelligence", at point 8.

hacker or for persons whose property is damaged by such a third party, as the interference regularly constitutes a fault-based action.[32]

The Parliament considered the following principles and aims which should serve as guidance for the proposed Regulation on liability for AI systems: "1. A genuine Digital Single Market requires full harmonisation by means of a Regulation. 2. New legal challenges posed by the development of Artificial Intelligence (AI) systems have to be addressed by establishing maximal legal certainty throughout the liability chain, including for the producer, the operator, the affected person and any other third party. 3. There should be no over-regulation and red tape must be prevented as this would hamper European innovation in AI, especially in the case of technology, products or services developed by SMEs or start-ups. 4. Civil liability rules for AI should seek to strike a balance between the protection of the public, on the one hand, and business incentives to invest in innovation, especially AI systems, on the other. 5. Instead of replacing the well-functioning existing liability regimes, a few necessary adjustments should be made by introducing new and future-oriented ideas. 6. The future proposal for a Regulation and the Product Liability Directive are two pillars of a common liability framework for AI-systems and require close coordination and alignment between all political actors, at Union and national levels. 7. Citizens should be entitled to the same level of protection and rights, irrespective of whether the harm is caused by an AI-system or not, or if it takes place physically or virtually, so that their confidence in the new technology is strengthened. 8. Both material and immaterial harm should be taken into account in the future proposal for a Regulation".[33]

Based on the above-mentioned conclusions, the Parliament took the view that the proposed Regulation should focus on civil liability claims against the operator[34] of

[32] Ibid., at point 9. "Only for specific cases, including those where the third party is untraceable or impecunious, does the addition of liability rules to complement existing national tort law seem necessary".

See also the Annex to the European Parliament's Resolution of 20 October 2020 on a civil liability regime for AI – Text of the Proposal for a Regulation on liability for the operation of AI systems, recital 9.

[33] Annex to the European Parliament's Resolution of 20 October 2020 on a civil liability regime for AI – A. Principles and Aims of the Proposal, p. 115.

[34] "Considers it appropriate to understand 'operator' to cover both the frontend and backend operator, as long as the latter is not covered by the PLD; notes that the frontend operator should be defined as the natural or legal person who exercises a degree of control over a risk connected with the operation and functioning of the AI-system and benefits from its operation; states that the backend operator should be defined as the natural or legal person who, on a continuous basis, defines the features of the technology, provides data and essential backend support service and therefore also exercises a degree of control over the risk connected with the operation and functioning of the AI-system; considers that exercising control means any action of the operator that influences the operation of the AI-system and thus the extent to which it exposes third parties to its potential risks". European Parliament's Resolution of 20 October 2020 on a civil liability regime for AI, section "Liability of the operator", at point 12.

See also the Annex to the European Parliament's Resolution of 20 October 2020 on a civil liability regime for AI – Text of the Proposal for a Regulation on liability for the operation of AI

an AI-system.[35] As it was stated: "This Regulation sets out rules for the civil liability claims of natural and legal persons against operators of AI-systems".[36] This is justified by the fact that the operator exercises a degree of control over a risk associated with the AI-system, which is comparable to that of an owner of a car. Besides, due to the AI-system's characteristics of complexity and connectivity, the operator will be very often the first visible contact point for the affected person.[37] It was also stated that civil liability rules involving the operator should cover all

---

systems, recital 10: "The liability of the operator under this Regulation is based on the fact that he or she exercises a degree of control over a risk connected with the operation and functioning of an AI-system, which is comparable to that of an owner of a car. The more sophisticated and more autonomous a system is, the greater the impact of defining and influencing the algorithms, for example by continuous updates, becomes. As there is often more than one person who could, in a meaningful way, be considered as 'operating' the AI-system, under this Regulation 'operator' should be understood to cover both the frontend and the backend operator. Although in general, the frontend operator appears as the person who 'primarily' decides on the use of the AI-system, the backend operator could in fact have a higher degree of control over the operational risks. If the backend operator also qualifies as 'producer' as defined in Article 3 of the Product Liability Directive, that Directive should apply to him or her. If there is only one operator and that operator is also the producer of the AI-system, this Regulation should prevail over the Product Liability Directive".

See also the Annex to the European Parliament's Resolution of 20 October 2020 on a civil liability regime for AI – Text of the Proposal for a Regulation on liability for the operation of AI systems, Article 3 (d)-(g): "(d)'operator' means both the frontend and the backend operator as long as the latter's liability is not already covered by Directive 85/374/EEC; (e) 'frontend operator' means any natural or legal person who exercises a degree of control over a risk connected with the operation and functioning of the AI-system and benefits from its operation; (f) 'backend operator' means any natural or legal person who, on a continuous basis, defines the features of the technology and provides data and an essential backend support service and therefore also exercises a degree of control over the risk connected with the operation and functioning of the AI-system; (g) 'control' means any action of an operator that influences the operation of an AI-system and thus the extent to which the operator exposes third parties to the potential risks associated with the operation and functioning of the AI-system; such actions can impact the operation at any stage by determining the input, output or results, or can change specific functions or processes within the AI-system; the degree to which those aspects of the operation of the AI-system are determined by the action depends on the level of influence the operator has over the risk connected with the operation and functioning of the AI-system".

[35] European Parliament's Resolution of 20 October 2020 on a civil liability regime for AI, section "Liability and Artificial Intelligence", at point 10.

See also the Annex to the European Parliament's Resolution of 20 October 2020 on a civil liability regime for AI – Text of the Proposal for a Regulation on liability for the operation of AI systems, recital 9.

[36] Annex to the European Parliament's Resolution of 20 October 2020 on a civil liability regime for AI – Text of the Proposal for a Regulation on liability for the operation of AI systems, Article 1.

[37] European Parliament's Resolution of 20 October 2020 on a civil liability regime for AI, section "Liability and Artificial Intelligence", at point 10.

See also the Annex to the European Parliament's Resolution of 20 October 2020 on a civil liability regime for AI – Text of the Proposal for a Regulation on liability for the operation of AI systems, recital 10.

AI-systems, irrespective of where the operation takes place and whether it happens physically or virtually.[38]

5.4 Scope of the Parliament's Proposed Regulation

The requested proposal for a Regulation should apply on the territory of the EU where a physical or virtual activity, device or process driven by an AI-system has caused harm or damage to the life, health, physical integrity of a natural person, to the property of a natural or legal person or has caused significant immaterial harm resulting in a verifiable economic loss.[39] It was stated that any agreement between an operator of an AI-system and a natural or legal person who suffers harm or damage caused by an AI-system will be deemed null and void if the said agreement circumvents or limits the rights and obligations set out in the proposed Regulation.[40] Furthermore, the proposed Regulation is without prejudice to any additional liability claims resulting from contractual relationships between the operator and the natural or legal person who suffered harm or damage caused by an AI-system.[41]

5.5 Strict Liability for High-Risk AI Systems and Insurance

The proposed Regulation recognised that the type of AI-system the operator is exercising control over should be a determining factor regarding liability. In this regard, it stressed that an AI-system that entails an inherent high risk and acts autonomously potentially endangers the user or the general public to a much higher

---

[38] European Parliament's Resolution of 20 October 2020 on a civil liability regime for AI, section "Liability of the operator", at point 11.

See also the Annex to the European Parliament's Resolution of 20 October 2020 on a civil liability regime for AI – Text of the Proposal for a Regulation on liability for the operation of AI systems, recital 12: "This Regulation should enable the affected person to bring forward liability claims throughout the liability chain and throughout the lifecycle of an AI-system. It should also cover in principle all AI-systems, no matter where they are operating and whether the operations take place physically or virtually. The majority of liability claims under this Regulation should, however, address cases of third-party liability, where an AI-system operates in a public space and exposes many persons to a risk. In that situation, the affected persons will often not be aware of the operating AI-system and will not have any contractual or legal relationship towards the operator. Consequently, the operation of the AI-system puts them into a situation in which, in the event of harm or damage being caused, they only have fault-based liability claims against the operator of the AI-system, while facing severe difficulties to prove fault on the part of the operator".

[39] Annex to the European Parliament's Resolution of 20 October 2020 on a civil liability regime for AI – Text of the Proposal for a Regulation on liability for the operation of AI systems, Article 2(1).

[40] Ibid., Article 2(2).

[41] Ibid., Article 2(3).

degree and in a manner that is random and goes beyond what can reasonably be expected.[42] Therefore, different liability rules should apply for different risks, following a risk-based approach.[43]

As a result, and in line with the Report from the Expert Group on Liability and New Technologies[44] and the Commission's view,[45] the Parliament stated that "an AI-system that entails an inherent high risk and acts autonomously potentially endangers the general public to a much higher degree. ... [B]ased on the legal challenges that AI-systems pose to the existing civil liability regimes, it seems

[42]European Parliament's Resolution of 20 October 2020 on a civil liability regime for AI, section "Different liability rules for different risks", at point 15.

See also the Annex to the European Parliament's Resolution of 20 October 2020 on a civil liability regime for AI – Text of the Proposal for a Regulation on liability for the operation of AI systems, recital 13: "This means that at the start of the autonomous operation of the AI-system, the majority of the potentially affected persons are unknown and not identifiable, for example persons on a public square or in a neighbouring house, compared to the operation of an AI-system that involves specific persons, who have regularly consented to its deployment before, for example surgery in a hospital or a sales demonstration in a small shop".

[43]European Parliament's Resolution of 20 October 2020 on a civil liability regime for AI, section "Different liability rules for different risks", at point 14.

[44]Report from the Expert Group on Liability and New Technologies – New Technologies Formation "Liability for Artificial Intelligence and Other Emerging Digital Technologies", 21 November 2019. For instance, the Report stated that "emerging digital technologies make it difficult to apply fault-based liability rules, due to the lack of well-established models of proper functioning of these technologies and the possibility of their developing as a result of learning without direct human control" (at p. 23). This is why the Report underlined that strict liability of the operator of some emerging digital technology may be justified: "a person operating a permissible technology that nevertheless carries an increased risk of harm to others, for example AI-driven robots in public spaces, should be subject to strict liability for damage resulting from its operation" (at p. 40); "strict liability is an appropriate response to the risks posed by emerging digital technologies, if, for example, they are operated in non-private environments and may typically cause significant harm" (at p. 39).

[45]According to the Commission's thinking—which is based on the analysis of the Report from the Expert Group on Liability and New Technologies –, the application of strict liability should be limited to situations where the emerging technologies may create specific risks (which are likely to arise in circumstances where digital technologies move in public spaces, e.g., drones, autonomous cars, traffic management services), expose the public at large to risks, and cause significant harm to life, health, and property. As the Commission stated, "the operation of some autonomous AI devices and services could have a specific risk profile in terms of liability, because they may cause significant harm to important legal interests like life, health and property, and expose the public at large to risks. This could mainly concern AI devices that move in public spaces (e.g. fully autonomous vehicles, drones and package delivery robots) or AI-based services with similar risks (e.g. traffic management services guiding or controlling vehicles or management of power distribution). The challenges of autonomy and opacity to national tort laws could be addressed following a risk-based approach. Strict liability schemes could ensure that whenever that risk materialises, the victim is compensated regardless of fault. The impact of choosing who should be strictly liable for such operations on the development and uptake of AI would need to be carefully assessed and a risk-based approach be considered". Commission Communication "Report on the safety and liability implications of Artificial Intelligence, the Internet of Things and robotics", COM (2020) 64 final, Brussels, 19.2.2020, p. 16.

reasonable to set up a common strict liability regime for those high-risk autonomous AI-systems";[46] "the victims of harm or damage caused by AI-systems need to have a right to redress and to full compensation for the harm or damage that they have suffered".[47] So, the Parliament's proposed Regulation on liability for AI systems stressed that a strict liability regime for high-risk AI systems[48] should apply, i.e. the operator of a high-risk AI-system should be strictly liable for any harm or damage that was caused by a physical or virtual activity, device or process driven by that AI-system.[49] According to the Parliament's initiative, all high-risk AI-systems and

---

[46] European Parliament's Resolution of 20 October 2020 on a civil liability regime for AI, section "Different liability rules for different risks", at point 14.

[47] Annex to the European Parliament's Resolution of 20 October 2020 on a civil liability regime for AI – Text of the Proposal for a Regulation on liability for the operation of AI systems, recital 5.

[48] According to the European Parliament, for the purposes of this (proposed) Regulation, the definitions of 'AI-system', 'autonomous' and 'high risk' are the following:

"(a) 'AI-system' means a system that is either software-based or embedded in hardware devices, and that displays behaviour simulating intelligence by, inter alia, collecting and processing data, analysing and interpreting its environment, and by taking action, with some degree of autonomy, to achieve specific goals; (b) 'autonomous' means an AI-system that operates by interpreting certain input and by using a set of pre-determined instructions, without being limited to such instructions, despite the system's behaviour being constrained by, and targeted at, fulfilling the goal it was given and other relevant design choices made by its developer; (c) 'high risk' means a significant potential in an autonomously operating AI-system to cause harm or damage to one or more persons in a manner that is random and goes beyond what can reasonably be expected; the significance of the potential depends on the interplay between the severity of possible harm or damage, the degree of autonomy of decision-making, the likelihood that the risk materializes and the manner and the context in which the AI-system is being used". Annex to the European Parliament's Resolution of 20 October 2020 on a civil liability regime for AI – Text of the Proposal for a Regulation on liability for the operation of AI systems, Article 3 (Definitions).

According to the European Parliament, determining whether an AI-system is high-risk (i.e. how significant the potential is of a high-risk AI-system to cause harm or damage) depends "on the interplay between the purpose of use for which the AI system is put on the market, the manner in which the AI-system is being used, the severity of the potential harm or damage, the degree of autonomy of decision-making that can result in harm and the likelihood that the risk materialises. The degree of severity should be determined based on relevant factors such as the extent of the potential harm resulting from the operation on affected persons, including in particular effects on fundamental rights, the number of affected persons, the total value for the potential damage, as well as the harm to society as a whole. The likelihood for the harm or damage to occur should be determined based on relevant factors such as the role of the algorithmic calculations in the decision-making process, the complexity of the decision and the reversibility of the effects. Ultimately, the manner of usage should depend on relevant factors such as the context and sector in which the AI-system operates, if it could have legal or factual effects on important legally protected rights of the affected person, and whether the effects can reasonably be avoided". Annex to the European Parliament's Resolution of 20 October 2020 on a civil liability regime for AI – Text of the Proposal for a Regulation on liability for the operation of AI systems, at recital 13.

[49] Annex to the European Parliament's Resolution of 20 October 2020 on a civil liability regime for AI – Text of the Proposal for a Regulation on liability for the operation of AI systems, Article 4(1).

See also the Report of the Expert Group on Liability and New Technologies which stated that "strict liability should lie with the person who is in control of the risk connected with the operation of emerging digital technologies and who benefits from their operation (operator)". Report from the

critical sectors where they are used must be exhaustively listed in the Annex to the Regulation. Given the rapid technological developments and the required technical expertise, the Commission must review the Annex without undue delay (at least every six months) and, if necessary, will have the power to amend this exhaustive list through a delegated act.[50]

Unless the harm or damage was caused by force majeure, operators of high-risk AI-systems should not be able to exonerate themselves from liability by claiming that they acted with due diligence or that the harm or damage was caused by an autonomous activity, device or process driven by their AI-system.[51]

As already mentioned, the Parliament took the view that very often more than one person could be considered as operating an AI-system[52] and, therefore, the term 'operator' should cover both the frontend and the backend operator, as long as the latter is not already covered by the Product Liability Directive. Currently, it is the frontend operator who appears to be the person that primarily decides on the use of the AI-system", defined as the natural or legal person who exercises a degree of control over a risk connected with the operation and functioning of the AI-system and benefits from its operation.[53] Also, the backend operator—who could in fact have a higher degree of control over the operational risks as emerging digital technologies are becoming more backend-focused[54]—is any natural or legal person

---

Expert Group on Liability and New Technologies – New Technologies Formation "Liability for Artificial Intelligence and Other Emerging Digital Technologies", 21 November 2019, Key Finding [10], at pp. 6, 39, 41.

[50] Annex to the European Parliament's Resolution of 20 October 2020 on a civil liability regime for AI – Text of the Proposal for a Regulation on liability for the operation of AI systems, Article 4(2).

[51] Ibid., Article 4(3).

[52] This also follows the approach of the Report from the Expert Group on Liability and New Technologies where it was recognised that, with emerging digital technologies, there are often two or more operators, i.e. the owner/user/keeper who operates the technology on the frontend and, at the same time, a central backend provider who, on an ongoing basis, provides essential backend support services. In those cases, the Report proposed the following: "If there are two or more operators, in particular (a) the person primarily deciding on and benefitting from the use of the relevant technology (frontend operator) and (b) the person continuously defining the features of the relevant technology and providing essential and ongoing backend support (backend operator), strict liability should lie with the one who has more control over the risks of the operation". Report from the Expert Group on Liability and New Technologies – New Technologies Formation "Liability for Artificial Intelligence and Other Emerging Digital Technologies", 21 November 2019, Key Finding [11], at p. 39.

[53] Annex to the European Parliament's Resolution of 20 October 2020 on a civil liability regime for AI – Text of the Proposal for a Regulation on liability for the operation of AI systems, Article 3 (e). See also recital 10.

See also: European Parliament's Resolution of 20 October 2020 on a civil liability regime for AI, section "Liability of the operator", at point 12.

[54] See, for instance, the Report from the Expert Group on Liability and New Technologies – New Technologies Formation "Liability for Artificial Intelligence and Other Emerging Digital Technologies", 21 November 2019, at pp. 41–42: "This backend operator may have a high degree of control over the operational risks others are exposed to. From an economic point of view, the backend operator also benefits from the operation, because that operator profits from data generated by the

who, on a continuous basis, defines the features of the technology and provides data and an essential backend support service and therefore also exercises a degree of control over the risk connected with the operation and functioning of the AI-system.[55] The term 'exercising control' means any action of the operator that influences the operation of the AI-system and thus the extent to which it exposes third parties to its potential risks.[56]

According to the Parliament's proposed Regulation on liability for AI systems, the users need to be sure that potential damage caused by AI-systems is covered by

---

operation, or that operator's remuneration is directly calculated on the basis of the duration, continuous nature or intensity of the operation, or because a one-off payment this backend operator has received reflects the estimated overall duration, continuous nature and intensity of the operation. ... While both control and benefit are decisive for qualifying a person as operator, the benefit is often very difficult to quantify, so relying only on benefit as the decisive factor for deciding who, out of two operators, should be liable, would lead to uncertainty. ... Very often, the frontend operator will have more control, but where emerging digital technologies become more backend-focused, there may be cases where so much continuous control over the technology remains with the backend operator that – despite the fact that the technology is sold to individual owners – it is more convincing to hold the backend operator liable as the person primarily in a position to control, reduce and insure the risks associated with the use of the technology. ... Ideally, in order to avoid uncertainty, the legislator should define which operator is liable under which circumstances, and all other matters that need to be regulated (concerning insurance for example). For instance, the legislator could decide that for AVs with a level of automation of 4 or 5, it is the provider running the system and who enters the AV in the national registry who is liable. This provider would therefore also take out insurance and could pass on the premiums through the fees paid for its services. Where several providers fulfil the function of backend operators, one of them would have to be designated as responsible operator for every AV".

[55] Annex to the European Parliament's Resolution of 20 October 2020 on a civil liability regime for AI – Text of the Proposal for a Regulation on liability for the operation of AI systems, Article 3 (f). See also recital 10.

See also: European Parliament's Resolution of 20 October 2020 on a civil liability regime for AI, section "Liability of the operator", at point 12.

[56] Annex to the European Parliament's Resolution of 20 October 2020 on a civil liability regime for AI – Text of the Proposal for a Regulation on liability for the operation of AI systems, Article 3 (g): "'control' means any action of an operator that influences the operation of an AI-system and thus the extent to which the operator exposes third parties to the potential risks associated with the operation and functioning of the AI-system; such actions can impact the operation at any stage by determining the input, output or results, or can change specific functions or processes within the AI-system; the degree to which those aspects of the operation of the AI-system are determined by the action depends on the level of influence the operator has over the risk connected with the operation and functioning of the AI-system".

See also the Report from the Expert Group on Liability and New Technologies – New Technologies Formation "Liability for Artificial Intelligence and Other Emerging Digital Technologies", 21 November 2019, at p. 41:"'Control' is a variable concept, though, ranging from merely activating the technology, thus exposing third parties to its potential risks, to determining the output or result (such as entering the destination of a vehicle or defining the next tasks of a robot), and may include further steps in between, which affect the details of the operation from start to stop. However, the more sophisticated and more autonomous a system, the less someone exercises actual 'control' over the details of the operation, and defining and influencing the algorithms, for example by continuous updates, may have a greater impact than just starting the system".

adequate insurance and that there is a defined legal route for redress. This is why proper liability coverage is considered as "one of the key factors that defines the success of new technologies, products and services" and as "essential for assuring the public that it can trust the new technology despite the potential for suffering harm or for facing legal claims by affected persons";[57] "insurance can help guarantee that victims receive effective compensation and pool the risks of all insured persons".[58] Therefore, all operators of high-risk AI systems should hold liability insurance similar to that used for motor vehicles.[59] This compulsory insurance regime for high-risk AI-systems should cover the amounts and the extent of compensation laid down by the proposed Regulation. In particular, both the frontend and backend operators of a high-risk AI-system should ensure that operations of the AI-system (in the case of the frontend operator) and its services (in the case of the backend operator) are covered by liability insurance and by business liability or product liability insurance respectively that is adequate in relation to the amounts and extent of compensation provided for in the proposed Regulation.[60]

5.6 Compensation

According to the Parliament, the proposed Regulation on liability for AI systems should cover violations (harm or damage)[61] of the important legally protected rights to life, health, physical integrity, property as well as significant immaterial harm[62] that results in a verifiable economic loss above a specific threshold.

In particular, an operator of a high-risk AI-system that has been held liable for harm or damage under the proposed Regulation should compensate to a maximum of

[57] European Parliament's Resolution of 20 October 2020 on a civil liability regime for AI, section "Insurances and AI-systems", at point 23.

[58] Annex to the European Parliament's Resolution of 20 October 2020 on a civil liability regime for AI – Text of the Proposal for a Regulation on liability for the operation of AI systems, at recital 21.

[59] European Parliament's Resolution of 20 October 2020 on a civil liability regime for AI, section "Insurances and AI-systems", at point 24.

[60] Annex to the European Parliament's Resolution of 20 October 2020 on a civil liability regime for AI – Text of the Proposal for a Regulation on liability for the operation of AI systems, Article 4(4).

[61] "'Harm or damage' means an adverse impact affecting the life, health, physical integrity of a natural person, the property of a natural or legal person or causing significant immaterial harm that results in a verifiable economic loss". Annex to the European Parliament's Resolution of 20 October 2020 on a civil liability regime for AI – Text of the Proposal for a Regulation on liability for the operation of AI systems, Article 3(i).

[62] "Significant immaterial harm should be understood as meaning harm as a result of which the affected person suffers considerable detriment, an objective and demonstrable impairment of his or her personal interests and an economic loss calculated having regard, for example, to annual average figures of past revenues and other relevant circumstances". Annex to the European Parliament's Resolution of 20 October 2020 on a civil liability regime for AI – Text of the Proposal for a Regulation on liability for the operation of AI systems, recital 16.

two million euros in the event of death of, or harm caused to the health or physical integrity of, an affected person.[63] Furthermore, the operator of a high-risk AI-system should compensate to a maximum of one million euros in the event of significant immaterial harm that results in a verifiable economic loss or of damage caused to property.[64] If the affected person also holds a contractual liability claim against the operator of a high-risk AI-system, no compensation should be paid under the proposed Regulation, if the total amount of the damage to property or the significant immaterial harm falls below five hundred euros.[65]

The Parliament's proposed Regulation on liability for AI systems determined the extent of compensation[66] as well as the limitation period for bringing forward liability claims. In particular, with regard to civil liability claims concerning harm to life, health or physical integrity, compensation should be claimable within thirty years from the date on which the harm occurred.[67] With regard to civil liability claims concerning damage to property or significant immaterial harm that resulted in a verifiable economic loss, compensation should be claimable (i) within ten years from the date when the property damage occurred or the verifiable economic loss resulting from the significant immaterial harm, respectively, occurred, or (ii) thirty years from the date on which the operation of the high-risk AI-system that subsequently caused the property damage or the immaterial harm took place.[68]

5.7 Fault-Based Liability for Other AI-Systems

It is recalled that the Report of the Expert Group on Liability and New Technologies[69] stressed that operators' strict liability should be supplemented with fault-based liability. As a result, operators of emerging digital technologies should comply with a range of duties of care, including the choice of technology in light of the tasks to be

---

[63] Annex to the European Parliament's Resolution of 20 October 2020 on a civil liability regime for AI – Text of the Proposal for a Regulation on liability for the operation of AI systems, Article 5(1)(a).

The term 'affected person' means "any person who suffers harm or damage caused by a physical or virtual activity, device or process driven by an AI-system, and who is not its operator". Annex to the European Parliament's Resolution of 20 October 2020 on a civil liability regime for AI – Text of the Proposal for a Regulation on liability for the operation of AI systems, Article 3(h).

[64] Annex to the European Parliament's Resolution of 20 October 2020 on a civil liability regime for AI – Text of the Proposal for a Regulation on liability for the operation of AI systems, Article 5(1)(b).

[65] Ibid.

[66] Ibid., Article 6 ("Extent of compensation").

[67] Ibid., Article 7(1).

[68] Ibid., Article 7(2).

[69] Report from the Expert Group on Liability and New Technologies – New Technologies Formation "Liability for Artificial Intelligence and Other Emerging Digital Technologies", 21 November 2019.

performed, the framework provided with regard to proper monitoring, and other issues in relation to maintenance, safety checks and repair.

Following the same approach, the proposed Regulation on liability for the operation of AI systems stated that, alongside the strict liability regime for high-risk AI systems, a fault-based liability regime for AI systems that do not constitute "high-risk AI systems" should apply. In particular, it stressed that the operator of all physical or virtual activities, devices or processes driven by AI-systems that cause harm or damage but are not listed as high-risk AI-systems in the Annex to the proposed Regulation should remain subject to fault-based liability,[70] unless stricter national laws and consumer protection legislation is in force.[71]

The Parliament took the view that the affected person should benefit from a presumption of fault on the part of the operator,[72] and the latter should be able to

---

[70] Annex to the European Parliament's Resolution of 20 October 2020 on a civil liability regime for AI – Text of the Proposal for a Regulation on liability for the operation of AI systems, Article 8(1).

However, it was pointed out that an AI system that has not been assessed by the Commission and, thus, is not yet classified as high-risk and not included in the list set out in the Annex to the proposed Regulation, should nevertheless be subject to strict liability if it caused repeated incidents resulting in serious harm or damage. In such cases, the Parliament urged the Commission to assess, without undue delay, the need to revise the Annex in order to add the AI-system in question to the relevant list. The Parliament went on to underline that, if the Commission, following its assessment, decides to include that AI-system on the high-risk list, that inclusion should have retroactive effect from the time of the first proven incident caused by that AI-system, which resulted in serious harm or damage. See European Parliament's Resolution of 20 October 2020 on a civil liability regime for AI, section "Different liability rules for different risks", at point 21.

[71] Annex to the European Parliament's Resolution of 20 October 2020 on a civil liability regime for AI – Text of the Proposal for a Regulation on liability for the operation of AI systems, recital 17.

[72] Ibid. See also: European Parliament's Resolution of 20 October 2020 on a civil liability regime for AI, section "Different liability rules for different risks", at point 20.

It is recalled that the Report of the Expert Group on Liability and New Technologies, when examining how to best address elements of risks and damages caused by the emerging digital technologies, stressed that the burden of proof should be linked to the compliance with specific cyber-security or other safety obligations set by law. Failure to comply with safety rules (including cybersecurity) should lead to a change of the burden of proof as regards fault and causation (i.e. shifting the burden of proving causation, fault, and the existence of a defect). As the Report stated, "Where the damage is of a kind that safety rules were meant to avoid, failure to comply with such safety rules, including rules on cybersecurity, should lead to a reversal of the burden of proving (a) causation, and/or (b) fault, and/or (c) the existence of a defect". See Report from the Expert Group on Liability and New Technologies – New Technologies Formation "Liability for Artificial Intelligence and Other Emerging Digital Technologies", 21 November 2019, Key Finding [24], at p. 48. The example used by the Report (at p. 49) was the following: "Imagine there is a new rule on cybersecurity of IoT household equipment, designed to prevent hacking and the resulting harm. The victim's private Wi-Fi is hacked in a way typical of cybersecurity gaps in IoT equipment. Where the victim can show that a water kettle produced by P failed to comply with the standard of safety under adopted safety rules, the victim could sue P, and the onus would be on P to prove that the damage had been caused by a different device". Furthermore, it is noted that the analysis of the Report of the Expert Group on Liability and New Technologies led to the following additional recommendation: "Burden of proving fault: If it is proven that an emerging digital technology caused harm, and liability therefor is conditional upon a person's intent or negligence, the burden of proving fault should be reversed if disproportionate difficulties and costs of establishing the relevant standard of

exculpate himself by proving he has abided by his duty of care. In particular, the degree of diligence that can be expected from an operator should be linked to the nature of the AI system, the legally-protected right potentially affected, the potential harm or damage that could be caused by the AI-system, and the likelihood of such damage.[73]

Relying on the recommendations of the Report of the Expert Group on Liability and New Technologies, the Parliament stated that an operator of a non-high-risk AI system will not be liable if he can prove that the harm or damage was caused without his fault, by relying on a lack of knowledge that the AI system was activated or by demonstrating that due diligence was observed.[74] In particular, it should be presumed that the operator has observed the due care that can reasonably be expected from him (and thus will not be liable), if he can prove that the harm or damage was caused without his fault because the AI-system in question was activated without his knowledge and, at the same time, all reasonable and necessary measures to prevent such activation outside of the operator's control were taken.[75] Furthermore, it should be presumed that the operator has observed the due care that can reasonably be expected from him if he has performed all the following actions: (i) selecting a

---

care and of proving their violation justify it". See Report from the Expert Group on Liability and New Technologies – New Technologies Formation "Liability for Artificial Intelligence and Other Emerging Digital Technologies", 21 November 2019, Key Finding [27], at p. 52.

See also Commission Communication "Report on the safety and liability implications of Artificial Intelligence, the Internet of Things and robotics", COM (2020) 64 final, Brussels, 19.2.2020, p. 14: "adaptations of national laws to facilitate the burden of proof for the victims of AI-related damage could be considered. For example, the burden of proof could be linked to the compliance (by a relevant operator) with specific cyber-security or other safety obligations set by law: if one does not comply with these rules, a change to the burden of proof as regards fault and causation could apply".

[73] Annex to the European Parliament's Resolution of 20 October 2020 on a civil liability regime for AI – Text of the Proposal for a Regulation on liability for the operation of AI systems, recital 18.

[74] As the Report of the Expert Group on Liability and New Technologies stated: "Fault liability and duties of care: Operators of emerging digital technologies should have to comply with an adapted range of duties of care, including with regard to (a) choosing the right system for the right task and skills; (b) monitoring the system; and (c) maintaining the system". See Report from the Expert Group on Liability and New Technologies – New Technologies Formation "Liability for Artificial Intelligence and Other Emerging Digital Technologies", 21 November 2019, Key Finding [16], at p. 44. It should be underlined that, according to the Report of the Expert Group on Liability and New Technologies (at p. 44), failure of the operator of the AI system to comply with such duties could trigger fault liability irrespective of whether the operator may also be strictly liable for the risk created by the said technology. Indeed, operators may not only be strictly liable for the risks inherent in operating emerging digital technologies (which are operated in non-private environments and may cause significant harm), but also for their failure to comply with specific duties of care.

[75] Annex to the European Parliament's Resolution of 20 October 2020 on a civil liability regime for AI – Text of the Proposal for a Regulation on liability for the operation of AI systems, Article 8(2)(a).

suitable AI-system for the right task and skills;[76] (ii) putting the AI-system duly into operation and monitoring properly the activities of the system, i.e. the operator is in a position to prove that he actually and regularly monitored the AI-system during its operation and that he informed the manufacturer about potential irregularities during the operation of the AI-system under examination;[77] (iii) maintaining the operational reliability by regularly installing all available updates provided by the producer of the AI-system.[78] Depending on the degree of sophistication of operators, i.e. whether the operator is consumer or professional, the aforementioned duties of care are expected to be adapted accordingly.[79]

Moreover, it was explicitly stated that, unless the harm or damage was caused by force majeure, the operator should not be able to exculpate himself by arguing that the harm or damage was caused by an autonomous activity, device or process driven by his AI-system.[80] The Parliament believes that the existing fault-based liability law of the Member States offers in most cases a sufficient level of protection for persons that suffer harm or damage caused by an interfering third party (such as a hacker who interferes with the AI-system by modifying its functioning or its effects in order to cause harm) as the interference regularly constitutes a fault-based action.[81] Nevertheless, it was underlined that, for specific cases, including those where the third (interfering) party is 'untraceable' or 'impecunious', additional liability rules to complement existing national tort law seem necessary and, therefore, the operator should be liable for the payment of compensation.[82]

The Parliament's proposed Regulation on liability for AI systems also stressed that, in order to facilitate the operator to prove that he was not at fault, or to enable the affected person to prove the existence of fault (and thus to allow for the identification of the liabilities), producers of AI-systems should have the duty to cooperate with both parties concerned (i.e. at the request of the operator and the affected person), including by providing well-documented information, to the extent

[76] Ibid., Article 8(2)(b). According to the European Parliament, the operator could rely on the ground that he selected an AI-system which has been certified under a scheme similar to the voluntary certification scheme envisaged by the Commission's 2020 White Paper on AI. See the Annex to the European Parliament's Resolution of 20 October 2020 on a civil liability regime for AI – Text of the Proposal for a Regulation on liability for the operation of AI systems, recital 18.

[77] Annex to the European Parliament's Resolution of 20 October 2020 on a civil liability regime for AI – Text of the Proposal for a Regulation on liability for the operation of AI systems, Article 8(2)(b) and recital 18.

[78] Ibid.

[79] Ibid., recital 18.

[80] Ibid., Article 8(2).

[81] Ibid., recital 9. Also: European Parliament's Resolution of 20 October 2020 on a civil liability regime for AI, section "Liability and Artificial Intelligence", point 9.

[82] Annex to the European Parliament's Resolution of 20 October 2020 on a civil liability regime for AI – Text of the Proposal for a Regulation on liability for the operation of AI systems, Article 8(3) and recital 9.

See also European Parliament's Resolution of 20 October 2020 on a civil liability regime for AI, section "Liability and Artificial Intelligence", point 9.

justified by the significance of the claim.[83] This proposal follows in principle the approach taken by the Report of the Expert Group on Liability and New Technologies, where it was recommended that an obligations should be imposed on producers to equip technology with means of recording information related to the operation of the technology ('logging by design'). In other words, producers should have the duty to provide appropriate and proportionate logging and to disclose the necessary data to the victim and/or the person who compensates the victim in readable format.[84] Thus emerging digital technologies should come with logging features, and failure to comply with a logging and disclosure (providing reasonable access to logged data) duty should result in a reversal of the burden of proof.[85]

---

[83] Annex to the European Parliament's Resolution of 20 October 2020 on a civil liability regime for AI – Text of the Proposal for a Regulation on liability for the operation of AI systems, Article 8(4) and recital 19. Furthermore, it was stressed that producers established within and outside the EU should have the duty to designate an AI-liability representative within the EU as a contact point for replying to all requests from operators, in a manner similar to the Data Protection Officers (DPOs) as set out in Article 37 of the General Data Protection Regulation (GDPR).

[84] Report from the Expert Group on Liability and New Technologies – New Technologies Formation "Liability for Artificial Intelligence and Other Emerging Digital Technologies", 21 November 2019, at pp. 47–48.

See also Commission Communication "Report on the safety and liability implications of Artificial Intelligence, the Internet of Things and robotics", COM (2020) 64 final, Brussels, 19.2.2020, at p. 16: "one of the issues flagged by the Report from the New Technologies formation of the Expert Group on Liability and New Technologies is the situation when the potentially liable party has not logged the data relevant for assessing liability or is not willing to share them with the victim".

'Logging by design' was also highlighted by the High-Level Expert Group on AI (AI HLEG) in its assessment list (which, inter alia, provides guidance on self-assessing whether the data and processes that yield the AI system's decisions are properly logged and well documented to allow for traceability and auditability of the algorithmic decision-making process). In particular, see "The Assessment List for Trustworthy Artificial Intelligence (ALTAI) for self-assessment", High-Level Expert Group on AI (AI HLEG), 17 July 2020: "Reliability, Fall-back plans and Reproducibility: Did you put in place verification and validation methods and documentation (e.g. logging) to evaluate and ensure different aspects of the AI system's reliability and reproducibility? (at p. 11); "Traceability: Did you put adequate logging practices in place to record the decision(s) or recommendation(s) of the AI system? (at p. 14); "Accountability – Auditability: Did you establish mechanisms that facilitate the AI system's auditability (e.g. traceability of the development process, the sourcing of training data and the logging of the AI system's processes, outcomes, positive and negative impact)?", at p. 21.

[85] Report from the Expert Group on Liability and New Technologies – New Technologies Formation "Liability for Artificial Intelligence and Other Emerging Digital Technologies", 21 November 2019. The relevant recommendations of the Report read as follows: "Logging by design: There should be a duty on producers to equip technology with means of recording information about the operation of the technology (logging by design), if such information is typically essential for establishing whether a risk of the technology materialised, and if logging is appropriate and proportionate, taking into account, in particular, the technical feasibility and the costs of logging, the availability of alternative means of gathering such information, the type and magnitude of the risks posed by the technology, and any adverse implications logging may have on the rights of others" (Key Finding [20], at p. 47); "Logging must be done in accordance with otherwise applicable law, in particular data protection law and the rules concerning the protection of trade

5.8 Apportionment of Liability

The European Parliament stated that, if a harmful event is caused by a physical or virtual activity, device or process driven by an AI-system and, at the same time, by the actions of an affected person or of any person for whom the affected person is responsible (i.e., negligent or intentional contribution to the risk), the extent of liability of the operator under the proposed Regulation should be reduced accordingly. Consequently, the operator of the AI-system should not be liable if the affected person or the person for whom he is responsible is solely to blame for the harm or damage caused.[86] Both the operator and the affected person may use the data generated by the AI-system in order to prove contributory negligence on the part of the affected person on the one hand and to prove or clarify the liability claim on the other.[87] In situations in which more than one operator are involved, for instance a backend and frontend operator, all operators should be jointly and severally liable[88] and should have the right to recourse proportionately against each other.[89]

---

secrets" (Key Finding [21], at p. 47); "The absence of logged information or failure to give the victim reasonable access to the information should trigger a rebuttable presumption that the condition of liability to be proven by the missing information is fulfilled" (Key Finding [22], at p. 47); "If ... the operator was obliged to compensate the damage, the operator should have a recourse claim against the producer who failed to equip the technology with logging facilities" (Key Finding [23], at p. 47).

[86] Annex to the European Parliament's Resolution of 20 October 2020 on a civil liability regime for AI – Text of the Proposal for a Regulation on liability for the operation of AI systems, Article 10(1).

[87] Ibid., Article 10(2).

[88] Ibid., Article 11: "If there is more than one operator of an AI-system, they shall be jointly and severally liable. If a frontend operator is also the producer of the AI-system, this Regulation shall prevail over the Product Liability Directive. If the backend operator also qualifies as a producer as defined in Article 3 of the Product Liability Directive, that Directive should apply to him or her. If there is only one operator and that operator is also the producer of the AI-system, this Regulation should prevail over the Product Liability Directive".

[89] Ibid., Article 12: "1. The operator shall not be entitled to pursue a recourse action unless the affected person has been paid in full any compensation which that person is entitled to receive under this Regulation. 2. In the event that the operator is held jointly and severally liable with other operators in respect of an affected person and has fully compensated that affected person, in accordance with Article 4(1) or 8(1), that operator may recover part of the compensation from the other operators, in proportion to his or her liability. The proportions of liability shall be based on the respective degrees of control the operators had over the risk connected with the operation and functioning of the AI-system. If the contribution attributable to a jointly and severally liable operator cannot be obtained from him or her, the shortfall shall be borne by the other operators. To the extent that a jointly and severally liable operator compensates the affected person and demands adjustment of advance payments from the other liable operators, the claim of the affected person against the other operators shall be subrogated to the operator. The subrogation of claims shall not be asserted to the disadvantage of the original claim. 3. In the event that the operator of a defective AI-system fully indemnifies the affected person for harm or damages in accordance with Article 4(1) or 8(1) of this Regulation, he or she may take action for redress against the producer of the defective AI-system in accordance with Directive 85/374/EEC and with national provisions concerning liability for defective products. 4. In the event that the insurer of the operator

5.9 Conclusion

This chapter examined the European Parliaments' 2020 Resolution on a civil liability regime for artificial intelligence. The Parliament urged the Commission to present a future-oriented civil liability framework, laying down rules for the civil liability claims of natural and legal persons against operators of AI-systems. It was stated that the goal of any liability framework should be to provide legal certainty for all parties. Civil liability rules for AI should strike a balance between protecting potential victims of harm or damage and, at the same time, supporting investment and technological innovation.

In brief, the Parliament's initiative (proposal for a Regulation on liability for the operation of AI systems) called for making those operating high-risk AI systems strictly liable for any resulting damage. The operator in question should not be able to exonerate himself from liability by claiming that he acted with due diligence. Operators of high-risk AI systems should hold liability insurance similar to that used for motor vehicles. This compulsory insurance regime for high-risk AI-systems should cover the amounts and the extent of compensation, as defined in the proposed Regulation. The initiative also stated that the operator of an AI-system that does not constitute a high-risk AI-system should be subject to fault-based liability for any harm or damage that was caused by a physical or virtual activity, device or process driven by the AI-system. Therefore, the operator of a non-high-risk AI system should not be liable if he can prove that the harm or damage was caused without his fault. The Parliament considered that operator liability rules should apply to all types of AI system operations, irrespective of the operation's location or whether it is physical or virtual in nature.

Legal/Policy Documents, Studies, and Reports

European Parliament Resolution of 20 October 2020 with recommendations to the Commission on a civil liability regime for artificial intelligence (2020/2014 (INL)) P9_TA(2020)0276.

Annex to the European Parliament Resolution: detailed recommendations for drawing up a Regulation on liability for the operation of artificial intelligence-systems, A. Principles and Aims of the Proposal. B. Text of the Proposal Requested—Proposal for a Regulation on liability for the operation of Artificial Intelligence-systems (Annex to the European Parliament's Resolution of 20 October 2020 on a civil liability regime for AI).

---

indemnifies the affected person for harm or damage in accordance with Article 4(1) or 8(1), any civil liability claim of the affected person against another person for the same damage shall be subrogated to the insurer of the operator to the extent of the amount the insurer of the operator has compensated the affected person".

European Parliament Report with recommendations to the Commission on a civil liability regime for artificial intelligence (2020/2014(INL)), Committee on Legal Affairs, A9-0178/2020, 05.10.2020.

European Parliament Resolution of 20 October 2020 with recommendations to the Commission on a framework of ethical aspects of artificial intelligence, robotics and related technologies (2020/2012 (INL)), P9_TA(2020)0275.

European Parliament Resolution of 20 October 2020 on intellectual property rights for the development of artificial intelligence technologies (2020/2015(INI)), P9_TA(2020)0277.

European Parliament Decision of 18 June 2020 on setting up a special committee on artificial intelligence in a digital age, and defining its responsibilities, numerical strength and term of office, 18 June 2020, (2020/2684(RSO)).

European Parliament, Press Release, "Parliament leads the way on first set of EU rules for Artificial Intelligence", 20.10.2020.

European Parliament Resolution of 16 February 2017 with recommendations to the Commission on Civil Law Rules on Robotics (2015/2103(INL)), (OJ C 252, 18.7.2018, pp. 239–257).

European Commission ('Commission') Communication, "White Paper On Artificial Intelligence - A European approach to excellence and trust", COM (2020) 65 final, Brussels, 19.2.2020.

Commission Communication, "Report on the safety and liability implications of Artificial Intelligence, the Internet of Things and robotics", COM (2020) 64 final, Brussels, 19.2.2020.

Commission Communication, "A European Strategy for Data", COM (2020) 66 final, Brussels, 19.2.2020.

Commission Communication, "Shaping Europe's digital future", COM (2020) 67 final, Brussels, 19.2.2020.

Commission Communication "Artificial Intelligence for Europe", COM (2018) 237 final, Brussels, 25.4.2018.

Commission Staff Working Document on "Liability for emerging digital technologies" - Accompanying the document Commission Communication "Artificial intelligence for Europe", SWD(2018) 137 final, Brussels, 25.4.2018.

Commission Staff Working Document, Evaluation of Council Directive 85/374/EEC of 25 July 1985 on the approximation of the laws, regulations and administrative provisions of the Member States concerning liability for defective products – Accompanying the Evaluation Report – SWD(2018) 157 final, Brussels, 7.5.2018.

"The Assessment List for Trustworthy Artificial Intelligence (ALTAI) for self-assessment", High-Level Expert Group on AI (AI HLEG), 17 July 2020.

Report from the Expert Group on Liability and New Technologies – New Technologies Formation "Liability for Artificial Intelligence and Other Emerging Digital Technologies", 21 November 2019.

References

Beckers A, Teubner G (2021) Three liability regimes for artificial intelligence: algorithmic actants, hybrids, crowds. Bloomsbury Publishing

Bertolini A (2018) Artificial intelligence and civil law - liability rules for drones. Study requested by the European Parliament's Committee on Legal Affairs, Policy Department for Citizens' Rights and Constitutional Affairs, November

Bertolini A (2020) Artificial intelligence and civil liability, Study requested by the European Parliament's committee on legal affairs, policy department for citizens' rights and constitutional affairs – directorate-general for internal policies. PE 621:926

Borges G (2019) New liability concepts: the potential of insurance and compensation funds. In: Lohsse S, Schulze R, Staudenmeyer D (eds) Liability for artificial intelligence and the internet of things. Nomos, Baden-Baden, pp 145–163

Borghetti J-S (2019) How can artificial intelligence be defective. In: Lohsse S, Schulze R, Staudenmayer D (eds) Liability for artificial intelligence and the internet of things. Nomos, Baden-Baden, pp 63–76

Ebers M (2021) Liability for artificial intelligence and EU consumer law, JIPITEC 12:204–220

Evas T (2018) A common EU approach to liability rules and insurance for connected and autonomous vehicles, Study. European Added Value Assessment - Accompanying the European Parliament's legislative own-initiative report (Rapporteur: Mady Delvaux). Study, European Parliamentary Research Service (EPRS), February

Evas T (2020) Civil liability regime for artificial intelligence, Study. European Parliamentary Research Service (EPRS)

Henrique Sousa Antunes (2020) Civil Liability Applicable to Artificial Intelligence: A Preliminary Critique of the European Parliament Resolution of 2020 (December 5, 2020). Available at SSRN: https://ssrn.com/abstract=3743242 or https://doi.org/10.2139/ssrn.3743242

Karner E, Koch BA, Geistfeld MA (2021) Comparative law study on civil liability for artificial intelligence. European Commission, Directorate-General for Justice and Consumers

Lohsse S, Schulze R, Staudenmayer D (2019) Liability for artificial intelligence. In: Lohsse S, Schulze R, Staudenmayer D (eds) Liability for artificial intelligence and the internet of things. Nomos, Baden-Baden, pp 99–116

Marchisio E (2021) In support of "no-fault" civil liability rules for artificial intelligence. SN Soc Sci 1:54

Martín-Casals M (2019) Causation and scope of liability in the internet of things (IoT). In: Lohsse S, Schulze R, Staudenmayer D (eds) Liability for artificial intelligence and the internet of things. Nomos, Baden-Baden, pp 201–228

Nevejans N (2016) European Civil Law Rules in Robotics. Study requested by the European Parliament's Committee on Legal Affairs (JURI Committee)

Spindler G (2019) User liability and strict liability in the internet of things and for robots. In: Lohsse S, Schulze R, Staudenmayer D (eds) Liability for artificial intelligence and the internet of things. Nomos, Baden-Baden, pp 125–145

Wagner G, Robot liability. In: S. Lohsse/R. Schulze/D. Staudenmayer (eds) Liability for artificial intelligence and the internet of things, Nomos, Baden-Baden (2019), pp. 27–62.

Wagner G (2021) Liability for artificial intelligence: a proposal by the European Parliament. In: Eidenmüller H, Wagner G (eds) Law by Algorithm, p 127

Wendehorst C (2020) Strict liability for AI and other emerging technologies. J Eur Tort Law (JETL) 11(2):150–180

Part III
Reforming the EU Civil Liability Regime Applicable to Artificial Intelligence, Robotics, the Internet of Things, and Other Emerging Digital Technologies

Chapter 6
Adapting EU Liability Rules to the Digital Age and Artificial Intelligence: The European Commission's 2021 Inception Impact Assessment

6.1 Introduction

This chapter examines the European Commission's 2021 Inception Impact Assessment (IIA) "Adapting liability rules to the digital age and circular economy", which was published on 30 June 2021.[1] The Commission's 2021 IIA was prompted by an evaluation of the Product Liability Directive (PLD) and addressed shortcomings already identified in the evaluation of the PLD and the challenges that the emerging technologies present for the application of liability rules, which were described in detail in the Commission's 2020 White Paper and the accompanying Report on Liability for AI, IoT and Robotics.

According to the Commission, civil liability rules for AI should strike a balance between protecting citizens and promoting technological innovation. The Commission examined different policy options to achieve the initiative's primary objectives. These objectives, alongside the overall goal of ensuring the proper functioning of the single market while providing for a high level of consumer/victim protection, are: (i) to modernise and adapt strict liability rules to the digital age and circular economy, taking account of the characteristics and risks of new technologies, including AI-equipped products and services; and (ii) to address unnecessary obstacles to obtaining compensation for damage, ensuring that injured parties are equally protected throughout the EU. This approach aims to foster consumer uptake of AI

[1]Commission's Inception Impact Assessment "Adapting liability rules to the digital age and circular economy", Ref. Ares(2021)4266516, 30.06.2021.

N. T. Nikolinakos, *Adapting the EU Civil Liability Regime to the Digital Age: Artificial Intelligence, Robotics, and Other Emerging Technologies*, Law, Governance and Technology Series 68, https://doi.org/10.1007/978-3-031-67969-8_6

and other innovative technologies, build trust in innovative products and services, and strengthen confidence in justice systems.[2]

[2]For interesting reading, analysis, and useful academic commentary, see the following:

Koch, Bernhard A, Borghetti, Jean-Sébastien, Machnikowski, Piotr, Pichonnaz, Pascal, Rodríguez de las Heras Ballell, Teresa, Twigg-Flesner, Christian and Wendehorst, Christiane, "Response of the European Law Institute to the Public Consultation on Civil Liability – Adapting Liability Rules to the Digital Age and Artificial Intelligence", Journal of European Tort Law, vol. 13, no. 1, 2022, pp. 25–63.

Nikos Th. Nikolinakos, 'Adapting the EU Liability Regime to Artificial Intelligence (AI): The European Commission's Proposed Policy Options', (2022) 28 Computer & Telecommunications Law Review (C.T.L.R.), Issue 3, pp. 66–83.

Susanna Tenhunen, 'Aligning the Product Liability Directive with the circular economy and emerging technologies: Revision of Directive 85/374/EEC', Implementation Appraisal Briefing, European Parliamentary Research Service (EPRS), October 2022.

Gerhard Wagner, 'Software as a Product' in: S. Lohsse/R. Schulze/D. Staudenmayer (eds.), Smart Products, 157, (2022), Hart, Nomos.

Gerhard Wagner, "Liability Rules for the Digital Age – Aiming for the Brussels Effect", Journal of European Tort Law (JETL) 2022, vol. 13, no. 3, pp. 191–243.

Ernst Karner, Bernhard A. Koch, Mark A. Geistfeld, 'Comparative Law Study on Civil Liability for Artificial Intelligence', European Commission, Directorate-General for Justice and Consumers, 2021.

Gerhard Wagner, Liability for Artificial Intelligence: A Proposal by the European Parliament, in: H. Eidenmüller/G. Wagner, Law by Algorithm (2021) 127

Christian Twigg-Flesner, 'Guiding Principles for Updating the Product Liability Directive for the Digital Age' (Pilot ELI Innovation Paper), European Law Institute (January 2021).

Herbert Zech, 'Liability for AI: public policy considerations', Academy of European Law (ERA) Forum, Volume 22, 147–158, Springer, 2021.

Christiane Wendehorst, 'Safety and Liability Related Aspects of Software', Study commissioned by the European Commission, 2021.

Michael Chatzipanagiotis and George Leloudas, 'Automated Vehicles and Third-Party Liability: A European Perspective', University of Illinois Journal of Law, Technology & Policy 2020(1), pp. 109–199.

Tiago Sérgio Cabral, "Liability and artificial intelligence in the EU: Assessing the adequacy of the current Product Liability Directive", Maastricht Journal of European and Comparative Law, 27(5), 615–635, (2020).

Christiane Wendehorst, "Strict liability for AI and other emerging technologies", Journal of European Tort Law (JETL) 2020, 11(2): 150–180.

Tatjana Evas, Civil liability regime for artificial intelligence, Study, European Parliamentary Research Service (EPRS), September 2020.

Tambiama Madiega, 'Reform of the EU Liability Regime for Online Intermediaries: Background on the Forthcoming Digital Services Act: In Depth Analysis', European Parliamentary Research Service (EPRS), May 2020.

Martin Ebers and Susanna Navas (eds.), Algorithms and Law, Cambridge University Press, 2020.

Susanna Navas, 'Robot Machines and Civil Liability'. In M. Ebers & S. Navas (eds.), Algorithms and Law. Cambridge University Press, 2020, 157–173.

Joasia Luzak, "A Broken Notion: Impact of Modern Technologies on Product Liability", European Journal of Risk Regulation, 11(3):630–649, (2020).

Steven Shavell, "On the Redesign of Accident Liability for the World of Autonomous Vehicles", (2020) 49 The Journal of Legal Studies, 243–285.

Andrea Bertolini, Artificial intelligence and civil liability, Study requested by the European Parliament's Committee on Legal Affairs, Policy Department for Citizens' Rights and Constitutional Affairs – Directorate-General for Internal Policies, PE 621.926, July 2020.

Gerhard Wagner, 'Robot Liability' in S.Lohsse/R.Schulze/D.Staudenmayer (eds), Liability for Artificial Intelligence and the Internet of Things. Nomos, Baden-Baden (2019), pp. 27–62.

Gerhard Wagner, "Robot, Inc.: Personhood for Autonomous Systems?", 88 Fordham Law Review, 591 (2019).

D. Fairgrieve and Eleonora Rajneri, 'Is Software a Product under the Product Liability Directive?', Zeitschrift für Internationales Wirtschaftsrecht, January 2019, Volume 1/2019, pp. 24–28.

Timan, T., R. Snijders, M. Kirova, S. Suardi, M. v. Lieshout, M. Chen, P. Costenco, E. Palmerini, A. Bertolini, A. Tejada, S. v. Montfort, M. Bolchi, S. Alberti, R. Brouwer, K. Karanilokova, F. Episcopo and S. Jansen (2019). Study on safety of non-embedded software. Service, data access, and legal issues of advanced robots, autonomous, connected, and AI-based vehicles and systems: final study report regarding CAD/CCAM and industrial robots. Brussel, European Commission.

Francesco Paolo Patti, "The European Road to Autonomous Vehicles", 43 Fordham Int'l L.J. 125 (2019).

Mihalis Kritikos, 'Artificial Intelligence ante portas: Legal & ethical reflections', European Parliamentary Research Service (EPRS), Scientific Foresight Unit (STOA), March 2019.

Herbert Zech: "Liability for autonomous systems: tackling specific risks of modern IT". In: Lohsse, S., Schulze, R., Staudenmeyer, D. (eds.), Liability for Artificial Intelligence and the Internet of Things. Nomos, Baden-Baden (2019), pp. 187–200.

Borghetti J-S, 'How can artificial intelligence be defective'. In: Lohsse S, Schulze R, Staudenmayer D (eds) Liability for artificial intelligence and the Internet of Things. Nomos, Baden-Baden (2019), pp. 63–76.

Gerald Spindler, 'User Liability and Strict Liability in the Internet of Things and for Robots' in Sebastian Lohsse, Reiner Schulze and Dirk Staudenmayer (eds), Liability for Artificial Intelligence and the Internet of Things. Nomos, Baden-Baden (2019), pp. 125–145.

Miquel Martín-Casals, 'Causation and Scope of Liability in the Internet of Things (IoT)' in Sebastian Lohsse/Reiner Schulze/Dirk Staudenmayer (ed), Liability for Artificial Intelligence and the Internet of Things. Nomos, Baden-Baden (2019), pp. 201–228.

Lohsse, S., Schulze, R., & Staudenmayer, D., 'Liability for Artificial Intelligence', In S. Lohsse, R. Schulze, & D. Staudenmayer (eds.), Liability for Artificial Intelligence and the Internet of Things. Nomos, Baden-Baden (2019), 99–116.

Francesco Mezzanotte, 'Liability for Digital Products', in: A De Franceschi/R Schulze (eds), Digital Revolution – New Challenges for Law, 169–188. Nomos, (2019).

Charlotte de Meeus, 'The Product Liability Directive at the Age of the Digital Industrial Revolution: Fit for Innovation?', (2019), Vol. 8, Journal of European Consumer and Market Law, Issue 4, pp. 149–154.

Tatjana Evas, A common EU approach to liability rules and insurance for connected and autonomous vehicles, Study. European Added Value Assessment - Accompanying the European Parliament's legislative own-initiative report (Rapporteur: Mady Delvaux). Study, European Parliamentary Research Service (EPRS), February 2018.

Andrea Bertolini, Artificial Intelligence and civil law - Liability rules for drones, Study requested by the European Parliament's Committee on Legal Affairs, Policy Department for Citizens' Rights and Constitutional Affairs, November 2018.

Boom, Willem H van, Borghetti, Jean-Sébastien, Ehlers, Andreas Bloch, Karner, Ernst, Nolan, Donal, Oliphant, Ken, Scarso, Alessandro, Ulfbeck, Vibe and Wagner, Gerhard. "Product Liability in Europe". Product Liability: Fundamental Questions in a Comparative Perspective, edited by Helmut Koziol, Michael D. Green, Mark Lunney, Ken Oliphant and Lixin Yang, Berlin, Boston: De Gruyter, 2018, pp. 255–356.

Yavar Bathaee, "The artificial intelligence black box and the failure of intent and causation", Harvard Journal of Law & Technology, Volume 31, Number 2, 889-938, (2018).

Thomas Verheyen, "Full Harmonization, Consumer Protection and Products Liability: A Fresh Reading of the Case Law of the ECJ", 26 (1) European Review of Private Law, 119–140, (2018).

6.2 The Objective of the Liability Framework

It is reminded that the European Parliament (the "Parliament") urged the Commission to present a future-oriented civil liability framework, laying down rules for the civil liability claims of natural and legal persons against operators of AI-systems.[3]

Maurice Schellekens, 'No-Fault Compensation Schemes for Self-Driving Vehicles', Law, Innovation and Technology, 2018, 10:2, 314–333.

Stefan Grundmann and Philipp Hacker, "Digital Technology as a Challenge to European Contract Law – From the Existing to the Future Architecture", 13 European Review of Contract Law, 255–293, 2017.

Leenes, R., E. Palmerini, B.-J. Koops, A. Bertolini, P. Salvini and F. Lucivero (2017). "Regulatory challenges of robotics: Some guidelines for addressing legal and ethical issues." Law Innovation and Technology 9: 1–44.

Howells, G., Twigg-Flesner, C., and Willett, C., Product Liability and Digital Products. In T-E. Synodinou, P. Jougleux, C. Markou, & T. Prastitou (eds.), EU Internet Law: Regulation and Enforcement. 2017, Springer Nature, 183–195.

Aída Ponce del Castillo, 'A Law on Robotics and Artificial Intelligence in the EU?', (October 3, 2017). Foresight Brief, European Trade Union Institute (ETUI) Research Paper - Foresight Brief #02-September 2017.

D. Fairgrieve, G. Howells, P. Møgelvang-Hansen et al., Product Liability Directive. In: P. Machnikowski (ed), European Product Liability: An Analysis of the State of the Art in the Era of New Technologies. Principles of European Tort Law. Intersentia; 2016:17–108.

Piotr Machnikowski, Conclusions, in: P Machnikowski (ed), European Product Liability: An Analysis of the State of the Art in the Era of New Technologies. Principles of European Tort Law. Intersentia; 2016:669–705.

Roeland de Bruin, "Autonomous Intelligent Cars on the European Intersection of Liability and Privacy: Regulatory Challenges and the Road Ahead", European Journal of Risk Regulation, 2016, 7(3):485–501.

Konstantinos Christidis and Michael Devetsikiotis, "Blockchains and Smart Contracts for the Internet of Things", (2016) IEEE Access, vol. 4, pp. 2292–2303.

Susanne Beck, 'The problem of ascribing legal responsibility in the case of robotics', AI & Society, 2016, vol 31, n°4, pp. 473–481.

Melinda Florina Lohmann, "Liability issues concerning self-driving vehicles", European Journal of Risk Regulation, 7(2), 335–340, (2016).

Palmerini, E., A. Bertolini, F. Battaglia, B.-J. Koops, A. Carnevale and P. Salvini (2016). "RoboLaw: Towards a European framework for robotics regulation", Robotics and Autonomous Systems 86: 78–85.

Mihalis Kritikos, 'Legal and ethical reflections concerning robotics', Scientific Foresight Unit (STOA) Policy Briefing, European Parliament Research Service (EPRS), PE 563.501, June 2016.

Nathalie Nevejans, 'European Civil Law Rules in Robotics', Study requested by the European Parliament's Committee on Legal Affairs (JURI Committee), 2016.

Daily Wuyts, "The Product Liability Directive – More than two Decades of Defective Products in Europe" Journal of European Tort Law, vol. 5, no. 1, 2014, pp. 1–34.

Andrea Bertolini, 'Robots as Products: The Case for a Realistic Analysis of Robotic Applications and Liability Rules', Law Innovation and Technology, 2013, vol. 5, p. 214–247.

[3]Annex to the European Parliament Resolution of 20 October 2020 with recommendations to the Commission on a civil liability regime for artificial intelligence: detailed recommendations for drawing up a Regulation on liability for the operation of artificial intelligence systems, A. Principles and Aims of the Proposal. B. Text of the Proposal Requested—Proposal for a Regulation on liability for the operation of Artificial Intelligence-systems (hereafter: Annex to the European

According to the Parliament, a clear legal framework is required to accelerate innovation by providing businesses with legal certainty, whilst protecting citizens and promoting their trust in AI technologies by preventing activities that might be dangerous. The Parliament considered it necessary to ensure maximum legal certainty throughout the liability chain (producer, operator, injured parties and any other third parties) to respond to the new legal challenges created by developments in AI systems. Therefore, as it was stated, civil liability rules for AI should strike a balance between protecting citizens and supporting technological innovation.[4]

Similarly, the Commission's 2021 Inception Impact Assessment (IIA) "Adapting liability rules to the digital age and circular economy" stressed that, alongside the objective of the EU safety framework to ensure that all products and services, including those integrating emerging digital technologies like AI, robotics and Internet of things (IoT), operate safely and reliably, "the objectives of the liability framework are to (i) provide legal certainty to industry about the risk they take in the course of their business, (ii) encourage the prevention of damage and (iii) ensure injured parties are compensated. Liability rules must strike a delicate balance between these objectives and promoting innovation".[5]

6.3 The Existing Liability Framework: National Liability Regimes and the Product Liability Directive

The existing liability framework in the EU relies on both the Product Liability Directive[6] (which harmonised the liability of the producer of defective products) and other non-harmonised national liability regimes. Therefore, at national level, the

---

Parliament's Resolution of 20 October 2020 on a civil liability regime for AI – Text of the Proposal for a Regulation on liability for the operation of AI systems), Article 1.

[4]European Parliament Resolution of 20 October 2020 with recommendations to the Commission on a civil liability regime for artificial intelligence (2020/2014(INL)) P9_TA(2020)0276 (hereafter: European Parliament's Resolution of 20 October 2020 on a civil liability regime for AI), recital B: "whereas any future-oriented civil liability legal framework has to instill confidence in the safety, reliability and consistency of products and services, including in digital technology, in order to strike a balance between efficiently and fairly protecting potential victims of harm or damage and, at the same time, providing enough leeway to make it possible for enterprises, and particularly small and medium-sized enterprises, to develop new technologies, products or services; whereas this will help build confidence and create stability for investment; whereas ultimately, the goal of any liability framework should be to provide legal certainty for all parties, whether it be the producer, the operator, the affected person or any other third party". See also recital K: "Legal certainty is also an essential condition for the dynamic development and innovation of AI-based technology".

[5]Commission's Inception Impact Assessment "Adapting liability rules to the digital age and circular economy", Ref. Ares(2021)4266516, 30.06.2021, p. 1.

[6]Council Directive 85/374/EEC of 25 July 1985 on the approximation of the laws, regulations and administrative provisions of the Member States concerning liability for defective products, as

rules implementing the Product Liability Directive coexist with other extra-contractual liability rules that could also be invoked by victims of damages.[7]

modified by Directive 1999/34/EC of the European Parliament and of the Council of 10 May 1999 (OJ L 210/29, 7.8.1985, and OJ L 141/20, 4.6.1999) (the Product Liability Directive).

[7]Commission's Inception Impact Assessment "Adapting liability rules to the digital age and circular economy", Ref. Ares(2021)4266516, 30.06.2021, p. 1.

See also Commission "Report on the safety and liability implications of Artificial Intelligence, the Internet of Things and robotics", Brussels, COM (2020) 64 final, 19.2.2020, at p. 12.

Also, the Report from the Expert Group on Liability and New Technologies—New Technologies Formation "Liability for Artificial Intelligence and Other Emerging Digital Technologies", 21 November 2019, at p. 3: "Artificial intelligence and other emerging digital technologies, such as the Internet of Things or distributed ledger technologies, have the potential to transform our societies and economies for the better. However, their rollout must come with sufficient safeguards, to minimise the risk of harm these technologies may cause, such as bodily injury or other harm. In the EU, product safety regulations ensure this is the case. However, such regulations cannot completely exclude the possibility of damage resulting from the operation of these technologies. If this happens, victims will seek compensation. They typically do so on the basis of liability regimes under private law, in particular tort law, possibly in combination with insurance. Only the strict liability of producers for defective products, which constitutes a small part of this kind of liability regimes, is harmonised at EU level by the Product Liability Directive, while all other regimes—apart from some exceptions in specific sectors or under special legislation—are regulated by the Member States themselves".

It should be stressed that, depending on whether the compensation of the victim requires a fault of the person considered liable by the law or not, national non-harmonised liability regimes provide victims with several parallel compensation claims, which are based on fault or strict liability. These claims could be directed against different liable persons and apply under have different conditions. For instance, in practice all Member States attribute liability for damages caused by motor vehicles to the owner/holder or the driver of the vehicle. Thus, for instance, in case of an accident caused by car, the victim could have—under national civil law—the following options. First, a strict-liability claim against the owner of the car, i.e. the person who takes out motor vehicle liability insurance and is strictly liable for having opened the risk associated with the circulation of a motor vehicle on public streets. In most national regimes a strict liability claim against the owner of the vehicle exists ("strict liability is applied for the person in whose name the motor vehicle is registered"), i.e. the liability of the holder of the car is typically risk-based. The victim would have a strict liability claim against the owner without the need to attribute fault. The claimant needs only to prove the damage and the causal link. Strict liability requires only proof that damage has occurred and the establishment of a causal link between the harmful functioning of the vehicle and the damage suffered by the injured party. Second, a fault-based liability claim against the driver of the vehicle. In this case, a fault of the driver is required and such a fault could be envisaged for instance when the accident was caused by human error of the driver or the vehicle was driven under dangerous weather conditions or if the required maintenance was not performed. At the same time, the victim has—under the Product Liability Directive—a claim against the producer/manufacturer if the vehicle had a defect. Indeed, liability for a damage may be allocated to the manufacturer of the car under the rules implementing the Product Liability Directive. In that case, the victim could have a claim against the manufacturer of the car; however, the claimant would need to demonstrate a defect of the vehicle and the casual link, namely that the damage was caused by that specific defect. For further analysis, see: Commission "Report on the safety and liability implications of Artificial Intelligence, the Internet of Things and robotics", Brussels, COM (2020) 64 final, 19.2.2020, at p. 12; and the Commission Staff Working Document on "Liability for emerging digital technologies"—Accompanying the document Commission Communication "Artificial intelligence for Europe", SWD (2018) 137 final, Brussels, 25.4.2018, at p. 14.

6.3.1 *National Liability Regimes*

As already explained, depending on whether the compensation of the victim requires a fault of the person considered liable by the law or not, these national extra-contractual liability rules are classified into two broad categories, namely fault-based liability regimes on the one hand and special regimes of strict liability on the other.

In most EU member states, extra-contractual liability regimes are fault-based. Therefore, the fault of the author of the wrongful behaviour leading to a damage—which could be an act or an omission whether intentional or by negligence—is a necessary element to be proven for the liability claim to be successful. The victim submitting a claim needs to provide the evidence required to support his liability claim: “National non-harmonised regimes provide fault-based liability rules, according to which victims of damage need to prove the fault of the liable person, the damage and causality between the fault and the damage in order to establish a successful liability claim”.[8]

Furthermore, national non-harmonised regimes also provide strict liability rules, where liability does not depend on a fault and the claimant needs only to prove the damage and the causal link.[9] These regimes of strict liability may apply to a diverse

[8]Commission Communication “Report on the safety and liability implications of Artificial Intelligence, the Internet of Things and robotics”, COM (2020) 64 final, Brussels, 19.2.2020, p. 12. There are situations, however, where national law introduces variations in order to facilitate the burden of proof of the victim so as to increase the possibility of compensation for the victim. Such variations may consist in a presumption of fault by the wrongdoer (or a reversal of the burden of proof), whereby the wrongdoer is liable unless he proves that he was not in fault—for instance, the responsibility of parents/tutors/guardians/teachers for damages caused by a minor, pupil, student/apprentice or mentally impaired person (unless they can prove that they were not able to prevent the damages from happening); or the responsibility of the owner/possessor of the building in case of damages causes by his/her building (unless he/she proves that he/she observed appropriate care for the purpose of avoiding the damage); or the responsibility of a person carrying a dangerous activity (unless he/she proves that all appropriate measures to avoid the damage have been taken). Examples of those variations are cited in Commission Staff Working Document on “Liability for emerging digital technologies”—Accompanying the document Commission Communication “Artificial intelligence for Europe”, SWD(2018) 137 final, Brussels, 25.4.2018, at pp. 7–8.

[9]The reversal of the burden of proof in the context of a fault-based extra-contractual liability and the principle of strict liability typically respond to a common rationale. They both aim at facilitating the compensation of the victim of damages in situations where the legislator considers it too burdensome or unbalanced to apply the general fault-based liability rule. Some forms of strict liability may go even a step further by linking liability simply to the materialization of a risk and/or making the discharge of liability either impossible or possible only under the proof that the damaging event was caused by an exceptional/unforeseen circumstance that could not be avoided. There may be also other cases where the risk of damage is linked to the unpredictability of behaviour of specific risk groups, like animals or certain persons: in these cases liability may be attributed to the persons that are considered responsible to supervise the animal or the person, because it is them who should normally be in the condition to adopt measures to prevent or reduce the risk of damages. Finally, when the risk of damages is linked to dangerous activities, some jurisdictions may attribute liability to the person that carries out the activity (e.g. the operator of a nuclear power plant or of an aircraft

set of situations which generate different types of risks and damages, especially when the risk of damage is linked to specific (e.g. dangerous) activities. National non-harmonised regimes provide strict liability rules "where the national legislator has attributed liability for a risk to a specific person, without the need for a victim to prove fault/defect or causality between fault/defect and the damage".[10]

In line with the above, the Commission's 2021 Inception Impact Assessment (IIA) stated that "national liability regimes regulate various liability claims for damages caused by products and services. Many claims are based on a liable person's conduct ('fault-based liability'), for example, a producer, service provider or individual user of a product. For various other claims, a person identified by law (usually the operator, user or owner, who benefits from an activity that exposes the public to a risk) is held liable independently of fault ('strict liability')".[11]

6.3.2 The Product Liability Directive

Alongside the national liability regimes, the Product Liability Directive harmonised the liability of the producer of defective products, offering a layer of consumer protection that national fault-based liability alone cannot provide. The Directive applies to all movable products, even if integrated into another movable product. Thus, if Artificial Intelligence is integrated into a product and a defect can be proven in a product that caused material damage to a person, the producer will be liable to pay compensation. The actual cause of events that lead to damage or incident is decisive for the attribution of liability.

---

or the driver of a car) or is ultimately responsible for the dangerous activity to happen (e.g. the owner of a vehicle). The rationale typically is that this person has created a risk, which materialises in a damage and at the same time also derives an economic benefit from this activity. See Commission Staff Working Document on "Liability for emerging digital technologies"—Accompanying the document Commission Communication "Artificial intelligence for Europe", SWD (2018) 137 final, Brussels, 25.4.2018, p. 8.

[10]Commission Communication "Report on the safety and liability implications of Artificial Intelligence, the Internet of Things and robotics", COM (2020) 64 final, Brussels, 19.2.2020, p. 12.

Examples of cases where the risk of damage is linked to specific (e.g. dangerous) activities include: the liability of the owners of animals for the damages caused by the animals under their custody; the strict liability of the person responsible for carrying out an unspecified or specified dangerous activity (for example the operation of nuclear power plants, aircrafts or motor vehicles) or other cases linked to a legal or factual relationship between two persons or a person and an object, such as when the damages are caused by someone executing a task in the interest of someone else (employee/employer) or by an object that is under his/her custody. See Commission Staff Working Document on "Liability for emerging digital technologies"—Accompanying the document Commission Communication "Artificial intelligence for Europe", SWD(2018) 137 final, Brussels, 25.4.2018, pp. 8–9.

[11]Commission's Inception Impact Assessment "Adapting liability rules to the digital age and circular economy", Ref. Ares(2021)4266516, 30.06.2021, p. 1.

The Product Liability Directive introduced the concept of strict liability of producers,[12] according to which if a defective product causes death, personal injury or material damage (above EUR 500) to consumers or their private property, the producer is liable to provide compensation irrespectively of whether there is negligence or fault on the consumers' part.[13] Therefore, producers are responsible for defective products, regardless of whether the defect of the product is their fault. A product is considered defective if it does not provide the safety a person is entitled to expect.[14]

To sustain their claim, those who have suffered injury or material damage must prove the damage, the defect and the causal link between the defect and the damage: "in case of a physical or material damage, the injured party is entitled to compensation if he or she proves the damage, the defect in the product (i.e. that it did not provide the safety that the public is entitled to expect) and the causal link between the defective product and the damage".[15] The Product Liability Directive does not cover

[12]According to Article 3 of the Product Liability Directive, the notion of "producer" includes the manufacturer of a finished product, the producer of any raw material or the manufacturer of a component part and any person who, by putting his name, trademark or other distinguishing feature on the product presents himself as its producer.

[13]Strict liability represents a strong tool for the protection of persons who have suffered injury or material damage. However, there are a number of circumstances where the Directive allows producers to take certain calculated risks when placing innovative products on the market. The producer is not liable if he can prove that: (i) the defect did not exist when the product was put into circulation; (ii) the defect is due to compliance with regulations issued by public authorities; or (iii) the state of technical knowledge at the time of putting the product on the market made it impossible to discover the defect. Member States may obtain a derogation from this last exemption. From the day that they become aware of the defect, injured persons have three (3) years to claim damages. Claims are no longer possible ten (10) years after the product was put in circulation. To sustain their claim, those who have suffered injury must prove the damage, the defect and the causal link between the defect and the damage.

[14]"Safety which a person is entitled to expect" (Article 6 para. 1 of the Product Liability Directive). This takes all circumstances into account, including the presentation of the product, the use to which it could reasonably be expected the product would be put, and the time the product was put into circulation. Article 6 of the Product Liability Directive states that a product must not be considered defective for the sole reason that a better product is subsequently put into circulation.

See also the Report from the Expert Group on Liability and New Technologies—New Technologies Formation "Liability for Artificial Intelligence and Other Emerging Digital Technologies", 21 November 2019, at p. 28: "The second key element of the product liability regime is the notion of defect. Defectiveness is assessed on the basis of the safety expectations of an average consumer, taking into account all relevant circumstances. The interconnectivity of products and systems makes it hard to identify defectiveness. Sophisticated AI autonomous systems with self-learning capabilities also raise the question of whether unpredictable deviations in the decision-making path can be treated as defects. Even if they constitute a defect, the state-of-the-art defence may apply. Additionally, the complexity and the opacity of emerging digital technologies complicate chances for the victim to discover and prove the defect and prove causation".

[15]Commission Communication "Report on the safety and liability implications of Artificial Intelligence, the Internet of Things and robotics", COM (2020) 64 final, Brussels, 19.2.2020, p. 12.

contractual liability, which is imposed on an entity by the terms of a contract; it provides the injured person with an extra-contractual regime of liability.[16]

As the Commission's 2021 Inception Impact Assessment (IIA) put it, "the Product Liability Directive harmonises one group of claims at EU level: claims against the producer for damage caused to a consumer due to the defectiveness of a product. The producer is strictly liable for damage caused by a defect in their product, provided that the injured party proves the damage, the defect and the causal link between the two. The Directive lays down one set of rules for a vast range of products, from raw materials to complex AI-driven devices. The Directive's implementation is dependent on national rules, for example, rules on evidence and causation".[17]

6.4 Main Objectives of the Commission's Initiative

The Commission's 2021 Inception Impact Assessment (IIA) was prompted by an evaluation of the Product Liability Directive (PLD) 85/374/EEC and addressed shortcomings already identified in the evaluation of the PLD and the challenges that the emerging technologies present for the application of liability rules, which were analytically described in the Commission's 2020 White Paper and the accompanying Report on Liability for AI, IoT and Robotics.

The Commission examined different policy options to achieve the main two objectives of the initiative, which, alongside the overall objective to ensure the proper functioning of the single market while providing for a high level of consumer/victim protection,[18] are to: (i) modernise and adapt strict liability rules to the digital age and circular economy, taking account of the characteristics and risks of

[16] Extra-contractual liability is set outside of a contract, for example directly in imposed pieces of legislation or through common law as types of: (i) Liability arising from an offense: The person who committed the offense will be liable in front of the injured party or responsible for the damage he/she caused to the party without any contractual agreement between them. An offense can be an intentional act or negligence; (ii) Liability in the absence of an offense: In liability without an offense, a person may be liable notwithstanding that the damage caused was unforeseeable. For example, the occupier of a building shall be liable for any damage caused by objects falling from it. Sometimes, not only one party should be held liable. Also, if two motor vehicles have a collision and each of the vehicles is deemed to have contributed equally to the accident, the owner of each vehicle shall bear half of the total amount of the damage resulting from the accident. (iii) Liability for the action of others: if a person is liable for another person by law, then he/she is bound to compensate the injured party (e.g. a parent is liable under law if his child incurs liability).

[17] Commission's Inception Impact Assessment "Adapting liability rules to the digital age and circular economy", Ref. Ares(2021)4266516, 30.06.2021, p. 1.

[18] Ibid., p. 3: "Member States acting individually would not be able to ensure the same objectives in a consistent manner. EU liability rules harmonise only what is necessary and will continue to rely on national legal systems for many aspects of their functioning, such as rules on establishing proof. Any further harmonisation of national liability rules on AI would be carried out in a targeted manner, focusing only on those aspects that are challenged by the AI's characteristics of

new technologies, including AI-equipped products and services (Objective 1);[19] and (ii) address unnecessary obstacles to getting compensation for damage in order to ensure that injured parties are equally protected throughout the EU, thus leading to consumer uptake of AI and other innovative technologies as well as creating trust in innovative products/services and in justice systems (Objective 2).[20]

With regard to AI in particular, the Commission noted that this initiative will complement the proposed Artificial Intelligence Act and revised safety legislation such as the Machinery Regulation and General Product Safety Directive. To this end, the initiative should "take into account the proposed AI Act, including, in particular, (i) the definition of AI, (ii) the requirements of the AI Act and (iii) risk-related considerations, as well as other EU safety legislation to ensure consistency and complementarity, while providing effective and proportionate solutions for liability".[21]

6.5 Shortcomings Brought by the Digital Emerging Technologies to the Product Liability Frameworks

This section attempts to explain how the main characteristics shared by the emerging digital technologies could challenge the existing product liability frameworks.

The Commission repeated that the emergence of new digital technologies like AI systems raise new challenges in terms of product safety and liability like connectivity, autonomy, data dependency, opacity, complexity of products and systems, software updates and more complex safety management and value chains.[22]

---

autonomous behaviour, limited predictability, continuous adaptation and opacity. The measures would therefore respect the principle of subsidiarity".

[19] Ibid. According to the Commission's thinking, "this is so businesses will have the legal clarity they need to plan their investment, assess their liability exposure, insure themselves and place safe, innovative and sustainable products on the market".

[20] Ibid.

[21] Ibid.

[22] Commission's Inception Impact Assessment "Adapting liability rules to the digital age and circular economy", Ref. Ares(2021)4266516, 30.06.2021, p. 2: "Certain features of digital technologies such as the intangibility of digital products, their dependence on data, their complexity, and connectivity, present challenges in applying liability rules. So do features specific to AI, such as autonomous behaviour, continuous adaptation, limited predictability and opacity. This creates legal uncertainty for businesses and may make it difficult for consumers and other injured parties to get compensation for damage caused by products and services that use these technologies".

See also the Commission Staff Working Document on "Liability for emerging digital technologies" - Accompanying the document Commission Communication "Artificial intelligence for Europe", SWD(2018) 137 final, Brussels, 25.4.2018, especially at pp. 22–23. In particular, the Commission Staff Working Document described in an analytical way the specific characteristics of the Internet of Things and Artificial Intelligence, explaining that their characteristics are equally shared, at least to a certain degree, by other emerging digital technologies like blockchain, 3D

The Commission pointed to the 2018 Evaluation of the Product Liability Directive. In particular, it is recalled that the Commission carried out an evaluation of the Product Liability Directive to assess its performance. The Commission's evaluation of the Product Liability Directive was based on an external study whose findings were presented and analysed in the Commission's 2018 Report and in the Staff Working Document "Evaluation of Council Directive 85/374/EEC - Accompanying the Evaluation Report".[23]

The 2018 Evaluation of the Product Liability Directive identified several shortcomings in relation to digital technologies and stressed that some of the Directive's concepts require guidance and clarification as they can hinder its effectiveness. In particular, a better common understanding of what is meant by the terms 'product',

---

printing and cloud computing. It summarised the specific characteristics of emerging digital technologies as follows: increasing level of complexity and variety of ecosystems, actors and value chains (high interdependency); autonomy in decision making, self-learning and actuating; generation, processing of and reliance on big volumes of data; and openness to software extensions, updates and patches after the products have been put into circulation. In light of these characteristics, it was concluded that both AI and IoT encompass all of the main specificities that revolve around the emerging digital technologies. Indeed, IoT combines the following specific characteristics: (i) complexity, due to the numerous interdependencies in the value chain and the variety of actors; (ii) autonomous behaviour, as many of the operations provided through and by an IoT system can be fully autonomous; (iii) data driven, because IoT systems entail data generation, data gathering, data processing and data analysis; (iv) openness due to IoT's digital dimension encompassing tangible and intangible elements (software and data). Equally, AI demonstrates the following specific characteristics: (i) complexity: with machine learning, AI can learn from other AI; (ii) autonomous behaviour, because, depending on the application, AI software can reason, gather knowledge, plan intelligently, learn, communicate, perceive, and manipulate objects; (iii) data driven, because AI entails data gathering, data processing and data analysis; (iv) openness, due to the fact that AI, combined with hardware, can create new tangible products and/or deliver services.

See also Commission Communication "White Paper On Artificial Intelligence - A European approach to excellence and trust", COM(2020) 65 final, Brussels, 19.2.2020, p. 14, where it was stated that the essential characteristics of AI-based products and systems include connectivity between an AI-system and other AI-systems and non-AI-systems, autonomy (increasingly autonomous AI-systems using, inter alia, machine-learning and deep-learning techniques), dependency on external data, vulnerability to cybersecurity breaches, complexity, and complex value chain (including a multitude of actors involved in AI systems' lifecycle). Therefore, the use of AI in services and products could create risks that EU legislation currently does not explicitly address, mainly linked to cyber threats, security risks—associated with new applications of AI such as home appliances—or risks that result from loss of connectivity. These risks could arise at the time of placing products on the market or appear as a result of software updates or self-learning when the product is being used.

[23] Commission Staff Working Document, Evaluation of Council Directive 85/374/EEC of 25 July 1985 on the approximation of the laws, regulations and administrative provisions of the Member States concerning liability for defective products—Accompanying the Evaluation Report—SWD (2018) 157 final, Brussels, 7.5.2018.

See also: Report from the Commission on the Application of the Council Directive on the approximation of the laws, regulations, and administrative provisions of the Member States concerning liability for defective products (85/374/EEC) {SWD(2018) 157 final} - {SWD(2018) 158 final}, COM(2018) 246 final, Brussels, 7.5.2018.

'damage' and 'defect' as well as clarifications on the burden of proof would render the Directive's application more effective. It was stressed that specific questions exist with regard to what separates a product from a service (e.g. for the Internet of Things, where products and services interact), the scope of damage covered (currently limited to material damage), the notion of what constitutes a defect or the concept of the burden of proof, which is becoming complex, as may be the case with some emerging digital technologies.[24] More analytically:

6.5.1 Liability Rules Not Fit for the Digital Age

6.5.1.1 Digital Technologies: Shortcomings

The Commission's 2021 Inception Impact Assessment identified the following shortcomings in relation to digital technologies:

6.5.1.1.1 Intangibility of Digital Products

"Digital content, software and data play a crucial role in the safe functioning of many products but it is not clear to what extent such intangible elements can be classified as products under the Directive. It is therefore unclear whether injured parties can always be compensated for damage caused by software, including software updates, and who will be liable for such damage".[25]

It is pointed out that the Product Liability Directive does not make any reference to the concept of service nor does it provide for the distinction between products and services. It solely provides, at Article 2, for the definition of product. Services do not fall into the definition of product. It is recognised that the distinction between products and services for the purpose of the Product Liability Directive is becoming increasingly blurred with regards to new technological developments and, therefore, the definition of product appears to no longer be as clear-cut as it may have been when the Product Liability Directive was adopted. Since the Directive applies to products, a clarification of its scope could be required. It is also questionable whether software is covered by the legal concept of product or product component.[26]

[24] Report from the Commission on the Application of the Council Directive on the approximation of the laws, regulations, and administrative provisions of the Member States concerning liability for defective products (85/374/EEC) {SWD(2018) 157 final} - {SWD(2018) 158 final}, COM(2018) 246 final, Brussels, 7.5.2018, at pp. 2, 6 and 8.

[25] Commission's Inception Impact Assessment "Adapting liability rules to the digital age and circular economy", Ref. Ares(2021)4266516, 30.06.2021, p. 2.

[26] "Technology and industry have evolved drastically over the last decades. Especially the dividing line between products and services may no longer be as clear-cut as it was. Products and the provision of services are increasingly intertwined". Commission Communication "Report on the

Applications and other non-embedded software (i.e. not contained in a tangible medium) could raise serious liability issues which are currently not fully addressed by the EU legal framework. AI, combined with hardware, can create new tangible products and/or deliver services. Since the distinction between products and services becomes less relevant, there is need to clarify what products and features are covered by the Product Liability Directive. For instance, providing data through an IoT system could be considered a service, and thus fall, as such, outside the product liability (and safety) regime.[27]

---

safety and liability implications of Artificial Intelligence, the Internet of Things and robotics", COM (2020) 64 final, Brussels, 19.2.2020, p. 13.

See also the Report from the Expert Group on Liability and New Technologies—New Technologies Formation "Liability for Artificial Intelligence and Other Emerging Digital Technologies", 21 November 2019, at p. 28: "The scope of the product liability regime rests on the concept of product. For the purposes of the Product Liability Directive, products are defined as movable objects, even when incorporated into another movable or immovable object, and include electricity. So far, the distinction of products and services has not encountered insurmountable difficulties. However, emerging digital technologies, especially AI systems, challenge that clear distinction and raise open questions. In AI systems, products and services permanently interact and a sharp separation between them is unfeasible. It is also questionable whether software is covered by the legal concept of product or product component. It is particularly discussed whether the answer should be different for embedded and non-embedded software, including over-the-air software updates or other data feeds. In any case, where such updates or other data feeds are provided from outside the EEA, the victim may not have anybody to turn to within the EEA, as there will typically not be an intermediary importer domiciled within the EEA in the case of direct downloads".

[27] Therefore, an interpretation of the concept of product or an enlargement of the concept of product might be needed, especially where the non-tangible element is not included in the product put into circulation by the producer but installed subsequently as a stand-alone feature. This is particularly true with regards to software; a clarification of the concept 'product' would contribute to improving effectiveness and, therefore, further assessment and clarification is needed. "Software and also AI merit specific attention in respect of product liability. Software is essential to the functioning of a large number of products and may affect their safety. It is integrated into products but it may also be supplied separately to enable the use of the product as intended. Neither a computer nor a smartphone would be of particular use without software. This means that software can make a tangible product defective and lead to physical damage. This could eventually result in the liability of the producer of the product under the Product Liability Directive. However, as software comes in many types and forms, answers related to the classification of software as a service or as a product may not always be straightforward. Thus while software steering the operations of a tangible product could be considered part or component of that product, some forms of stand-alone software could be more difficult to classify". Commission Communication "Report on the safety and liability implications of Artificial Intelligence, the Internet of Things and robotics", COM (2020) 64 final, Brussels, 19.2.2020, pp. 13–14.

Furthermore, see Commission Staff Working Document, Evaluation of Council Directive 85/374/EEC of 25 July 1985 on the approximation of the laws, regulations and administrative provisions of the Member States concerning liability for defective products—Accompanying the Evaluation Report—SWD(2018) 157 final, Brussels, 7.5.2018, especially at pp. 53-54, 61. One of the main questions in relation to new technological developments was how to classify the devices/ products resulting from these technologies. The definition of "product" as per article 2 of the Product Liability Directive is related to the concept of "movable". This was interpreted as meaning that only tangible goods can be considered products, due to the fact that when the Directive was adopted, no clear examples of non-tangible goods were widespread in the market. It is anticipated

6.5.1.1.2 Connectivity and Cybersecurity

The Commission has also recognised that connectivity[28] is a central feature in an ever-growing number of products and services, and the risk of loss of connectivity of emerging digital technologies may lead to new challenges concerning both safety and security.[29] The increasing complexity, connectivity,

---

that the services relating to tangible products will become more prominent in the near future and thus the balance between products and services may shift towards services, and products will increasingly come with the provision of services. As the Commission put it, "the non-tangible nature of some new technological developments (software, applications, Internet of Things, Artificial Intelligence systems) makes it difficult to classify them as products rather than services". It was argued by some stakeholders that there is a need for an interpretation of the concept of product or an enlargement of the concept of product, including some new technological developments such as Artificial intelligence or cloud technologies, as well as applications. According to the Commission, this is particularly relevant "in the context of the Directive where the nontangible element is not included in the product put into circulation by the producer but installed subsequently as a standalone feature". In the light of new technological developments, the definition of product appears to no longer be as clear-cut as it may have been when the Directive was adopted and, "given that the Directive applies to products, a clarification of its scope could therefore be envisaged".

In addition, see Commission Staff Working Document on "Liability for emerging digital technologies"—Accompanying the document Commission Communication "Artificial intelligence for Europe", SWD(2018) 137 final, Brussels, 25.4.2018, at pp. 9–11.

See also Commission Communication "White Paper On Artificial Intelligence - A European approach to excellence and trust", COM(2020) 65 final, Brussels, 19.2.2020, p. 14: "an essential focus of EU product safety legislation is on the placing of products on the market. While in EU product safety legislation software, when is part of the final product, must comply with the relevant product safety rules, it is an open question whether stand-alone software is covered by EU product safety legislation, outside some sectors with explicit rules. General EU safety legislation currently in force applies to products and not to services, and therefore in principle not to services based on AI technology either (e.g. health services, financial services, transport services)".

[28] "Sensors and smart connected objects ... become part of a bigger connectivity network which creates new opportunities to combine more intelligence and actuation across vertical markets and to provide a whole new set of services. Technical and semantic interoperability are the key factor of success. It enables the programming of complex systems to integrate a number of device- and service-providers to deliver complete IoT solutions e.g. at home, in cities, between industries". See, for instance, the Commission Staff Working Document on "Liability for emerging digital technologies" - Accompanying the document Commission Communication "Artificial intelligence for Europe", SWD(2018) 137 final, Brussels, 25.4.2018, at p. 22.

[29] Indeed, the connectivity feature—if combined with poor security measures at design, manufacturing or operation stage—could compromise the safety of the product and result in serious security breaches. Corrupted data (e.g. due to connectivity problems or when hacked) may affect the behaviour of the entire system or of individual components or it may render the system malfunctioning. For instance, if a connected fire alarm loses connectivity it may not alert the user in case of a fire. Also, cyber-attackers could have the opportunity to take control of the said system and modify its functioning or the functioning of other smart devices in the same ecosystem. As the Commission put it, connectivity "is challenging the traditional concept of safety, as connectivity may directly compromise the safety of the product and indirectly when it can be hacked leading to security threats and affecting the safety of users. ... Industrial applications may also be exposed to cyber threats affecting the safety of persons at larger scale when such applications lack the necessary levels of security. This can be the case for example of cyber-attacks on a critical control

openness[30] and vulnerability[31] of the emerging digital technologies can expose AI and IoT products to cyber-threats and have a considerable impact on product

---

system of an industrial plant intended to trigger an explosion that might cost lives". Commission Communication "Report on the safety and liability implications of Artificial Intelligence, the Internet of Things and robotics", COM (2020) 64 final, Brussels, 19.2.2020, p. 5. The Commission provided specific examples of safety/security risks posed by these technologies: "An example is given by an EU Rapid Alert System notification from Iceland concerning a smart watch for children. This product would not cause a direct harm to the child wearing it, but lacking a minimum level of security, it can be easily used as a tool to have access to the child. As one of the product's intended function is to keep children safe through localisation, a consumer would expect that it would not pose security threats to children that may affect their safety by potentially being tracked and/or contacted by anyone. Another example is indicated in a notification submitted by Germany regarding a passenger car. The radio in the vehicle may have certain software security gaps allowing unauthorised third-party access to the interconnected control systems in the vehicle. If these software security gaps were exploited by a third party for malicious purposes, a road accident could occur".

The use of AI in services and products could create risks that EU legislation currently does not explicitly address, mainly linked to cyber threats, security risks or risks that result from loss of connectivity. These risks could arise at the time of placing products on the market or appear as a result of software updates or self-learning when the product is being used It is reminded that similar risks could arise where the software is not included in the product put into circulation by the producer but installed subsequently as a stand-alone feature. "While the Union product safety legislation takes into account the safety risks stemming from software integrated in a product at the time of its placing on the market and, potentially subsequent updates foreseen by the manufacturer, specific and/or explicit requirements on standalone software could be needed (e.g. an 'app' that would be downloaded). Particular considerations should be given to the stand-alone software ensuring safety functions in the AI products and systems. Additional obligations may be needed for manufacturers to ensure that they provide features to prevent the upload of software having an impact on safety during the lifetime of the AI products". Commission Communication "Report on the safety and liability implications of Artificial Intelligence, the Internet of Things and robotics", COM (2020) 64 final, Brussels, 19.2.2020, p. 11.

Also, as it has been stated by the Commission in the White Paper on AI: "the integration of software, including AI, into products can modify the functioning of such products and systems during their lifecycle. This is particularly true for systems that require frequent software updates or which rely on machine learning. These features can give rise to new risks that were not present when the system was placed on the market. These risks are not adequately addressed in the existing legislation which predominantly focuses on safety risks present at the time of placing on the market". Commission Communication "White Paper On Artificial Intelligence - A European approach to excellence and trust", COM(2020) 65 final, Brussels, 19.2.2020, p. 14.

[30] "Openness: Emerging digital technologies are not completed once put into circulation, but by their nature depend upon subsequent input, in particular more or less frequent updates or upgrades. Often they need to interact with other systems or data sources in order to function properly. They therefore need to remain open by design, i.e. permit external input either via some hardware plug or through some wireless connection, and come as hybrid combinations of hardware, software, continuous software updates, and various continuous services. This shift from the classic notion of a product completed at a certain point in time to a merger of products and ongoing services has a considerable impact on, among other things, product liability". See Report from the Expert Group on Liability and New Technologies – New Technologies Formation "Liability for Artificial Intelligence and Other Emerging Digital Technologies", 21 November 2019, at p. 33.

[31] "Vulnerability: Emerging digital technologies are typically subject to more or less frequent updates and operate in more or less constant interaction with outside information. The built-in

liability. In addition, new and possibly more advanced safety rules may be introduced. Indeed, "traditional" product safety differs from "digital" product safety in various ways, including the issue of cybersecurity. For instance, cybersecurity gaps and weaknesses may exist from the beginning, i.e. when a product was initially put into circulation, but they may also appear at a later stage, i.e. after the product was put into circulation. Therefore, the notion of what constitutes a defect may need to be re-examined to provide certainty regarding new technological developments such as apps and non-embedded software, advanced robots and autonomous/intelligent systems. For instance, the Commission raised the question whether software vulnerability—e.g. a cyber-attack or a failure to update security software or a misuse of information—could be considered to be a defect.[32]

As the Commission's 2021 Inception Impact Assessment put it, "new technologies bring with them new risks, such as openness to data inputs that affect safety, cybersecurity risks, risks of damage to digital assets or privacy infringements. But the Directive provides for compensation only for physical or material damage and it is unclear if the notion of defect covers cyber vulnerabilities".[33]

6.5.1.1.3 Complexity

The Commission has repeatedly emphasised that AI systems display certain levels of complexity due to the interdependency between different components. For instance, AI applications are usually integrated in complex IoT environments[34] where many

---

features granting access to such input make these technologies particularly vulnerable to cybersecurity breaches. These may cause the system itself to malfunction and/or modify its features in a way more likely to cause harm". See the Report from the Expert Group on Liability and New Technologies—New Technologies Formation "Liability for Artificial Intelligence and Other Emerging Digital Technologies", 21 November 2019, at pp. 33–34.

[32] In the field of robotics, it is still open whether an unintended autonomous behaviour of an advanced robot is a defect or not. According to the Commission, "robots are meant to perform autonomous behaviours, they are programmed to do so. Given their self-learning capacities, one could in consequence argue that not all unforeseen autonomous behaviour is a defect. On the other hand, these robots will be employed to perform certain tasks, which will inevitably be linked to safety expectations". The Commission concluded that the definition of defect "may require being updated to new types of problems such as infringements of privacy or how to link the notion of defect with the types of autonomous behaviours leading to damages. Extending the scope of the Directive in this direction is, however, a political decision that will have to be carefully assessed". Commission Staff Working Document, Evaluation of Council Directive 85/374/EEC of 25 July 1985 on the approximation of the laws, regulations and administrative provisions of the Member States concerning liability for defective products—Accompanying the Evaluation Report—SWD (2018) 157 final, Brussels, 7.5.2018, pp. 56–57, 61.

[33] Commission's Inception Impact Assessment "Adapting liability rules to the digital age and circular economy", Ref. Ares(2021)4266516, 30.06.2021, p. 2.

[34] Commission Staff Working Document on "Liability for emerging digital technologies"—Accompanying the document Commission Communication "Artificial intelligence for Europe", SWD (2018) 137 final, Brussels, 25.4.2018, at p. 22: "The Internet of Things (IoT) is about setting up

different connected devices and services interact. The IoT and AI-enabled products and services comprise tangible parts/devices (sensors, actuators, hardware), different software components and applications, data, data services (i.e. collection, processing, curating, analysing), and connectivity features. Furthermore, AI-related products and services are increasingly interacting with traditional technologies, leading to added complexity when it comes to liability.[35]

Therefore, risks stemming from the complexity of the products and systems might have a serious impact on safety and, at the same time, could make it very difficult for victims to identify the liable person.[36] Indeed, since many different layers are involved in these digital technologies, vulnerable software, faulty sensors, or unstable connectivity may make it difficult to determine who is technically and legally responsible for any ensuing damage or how to identify the root cause of the problem. As the Commission has pointed out "combining different digital components in a complex ecosystem and the plurality of actors involved can make it difficult to assess where a potential damage originates and which person is liable for it. Due to the complexity of these technologies, it can be very difficult for victims to identify the liable person and prove all necessary conditions for a successful claim, as required

new ecosystems that cut across vertical areas, and create new markets for hardware (connected devices), software (IoT platforms and systems) and services (IoT applications). IoT has a horizontal and cross-cutting character. It should be understood as an ecosystem where areas that have been developed as vertical silos (manufacturing, transport, healthcare, devices, etc.) relate to each other, thanks to common platforms and cross-cutting innovation. IoT ecosystems are, therefore, based on bringing together multiple sectors and a variety of stakeholders to cover an increasingly complex value chain. IoT is based on various disciplines and technologies like sensors, embedded systems, various communications technologies. It requires a specific configuration for object identification and search, open/closed data sharing, lightweight communication protocols, trade-off between local and networked based information processing, and back-end integration. It also requires specific considerations of data security (e.g. location-based profiling), liability (many service providers involved), seamless identification and authentication mechanisms (including those of persons/ entities needed for managing contractual relations, attribution and liability) and trust. All this increases the complexity of the IoT ecosystem".

[35] For example, autonomous cars will share the road with traditional ones for a certain time. Similar complexity of interacting actors will arise in some services sectors (such as traffic management and healthcare) where partially automated AI systems will support human decision-making. See Commission Communication "Report on the safety and liability implications of Artificial Intelligence, the Internet of Things and robotics", COM (2020) 64 final, Brussels, 19.2.2020, p. 14.

[36] Commission's Inception Impact Assessment "Adapting liability rules to the digital age and circular economy", Ref. Ares(2021)4266516, 30.06.2021, p. 2: "The complexity of digital technologies (e.g. within IoT systems) could make it very challenging for injured parties to identify the producer responsible".

See also Commission Communication "Report on the safety and liability implications of Artificial Intelligence, the Internet of Things and robotics", COM (2020) 64 final, Brussels, 19.2.2020, p. 9: "Various components, devices and products can be integrated and have influence on each other's functioning (e.g. products part of a smart home ecosystem)".

under national law. The costs for this expertise may be economically prohibitive and discourage victims from claiming compensation".[37]

6.5.1.2 The Notion of Producer

The notion of producer provided for in Article 3 of the Product Liability Directive reflects the definition of product for the purpose of the Directive.[38] According to the Commission, the new technological developments involve different actors in the value chain, including product manufacturers, software producers, the connectivity service providers, sensor manufacturers, owners of the object, service providers. Furthermore, some of these technological developments have a very open ecosystem, (e.g. Internet of Things applications), as new features could be added by the user or even third parties to create a new one.

The Commission raised the question of whether the concept of 'producer', as defined in the context of Product Liability Directive, fits with the type of responsibilities that may arise in systems encompassing software, Artificial Intelligence systems, data services and other emerging technologies. It concluded that, "as products are more easily altered, adapted and combined with services, the definition of the producer may become less clear particularly in the context of emerging digital technologies and the circular economy. The definition of the producer, while continuing to be valuable as it ensures strict liability, may therefore no longer be fully relevant in its current form".[39] Similarly, the Commission's 2021 Inception Impact Assessment stated that, under the Product Liability Directive, "importers are treated

---

[37] Commission Communication "Report on the safety and liability implications of Artificial Intelligence, the Internet of Things and robotics", COM (2020) 64 final, Brussels, 19.2.2020, p. 14.

[38] 'Producer' (Article 3 of the Product Liability Directive) means the manufacturer of a finished product, the producer of any raw material or the manufacturer of a component part and any person who, by putting his name, trade mark or other distinguishing feature on the product presents himself as its producer, as well as any person who imports into the European Union a product for sale, hire, leasing or any form of distribution in the course of his business. The producer defined as such shall be liable for damage caused to consumers by a defect in his product. Where the producer cannot be identified, each supplier of the product shall be treated as its producer unless he informs the injured party, within a reasonable time of the identity of the producer or of the person who supplied him with the product. The term "producer" is deliberately broad so that an injured person easily find a liable person. In case of an anonymous product, the supplier will be held liable unless he discloses the identity of the producer. The Directive does not define the term "supplier", but according to the case-law of the Court of Justice, the supplier must be regarded as any intermediary involved in the marketing or distribution chain of the product (see, for instance, CJEU, Judgement of 21 December 2011, Case C-495/11, Dutrueux and Caisse primaire d'assurance maladie du Jura). The Product Liability Directive foresees (at article 5) that where two or more persons are liable for the same damage, they shall be liable jointly and severally, without prejudice to the provisions of national law concerning the rights of contribution or recourse.

[39] Commission Staff Working Document, Evaluation of Council Directive 85/374/EEC of 25 July 1985 on the approximation of the laws, regulations and administrative provisions of the Member States concerning liability for defective products—Accompanying the Evaluation Report—SWD

as producers for product liability purposes. However, the digital age has brought changes to value chains too. The rise of online marketplaces has enabled consumers to buy products from outside the EU without there being an importer, leaving consumers with no liable person from whom to seek compensation under the Directive in the event of damage".[40]

6.5.1.3 Difficulties to Get Compensation for Damages

Furthermore, the Commission's 2021 Inception Impact Assessment (IAA) stated that, as will be shown more analytically below, the specific characteristics of AI make it especially difficult to get compensation for damages under the Product Liability Directive and national civil liability rules. According to the Commission, it is also uncertain whether and to what extent certain national 'strict liability' rules are applied to products using AI.[41]

6.5.1.4 Circular Economy

Lastly, the IAA dealt with challenges posed by circular business models in which products are repaired, recycled, refurbished or upgraded. Such business models are central to the EU's efforts to achieve specific sustainability and waste-reduction goals. However, under the Product Liability Directive the defectiveness of a product is determined at the moment it is put into circulation. The 2018 Evaluation found the PLD to be unclear about who should be held liable for defects resulting from changes to products after they are put into circulation. According to the Commission, further analysis of the extent of this problem is needed. It was also stressed that environmental damage cannot yet be compensated under the Product Liability Directive.[42]

(2018) 157 final, Brussels, 7.5.2018 ['Commission Staff Working Document, 'Evaluation of Product Liability Directive', SWD(2018) 157 final, Brussels, 07.05.2018'], p. 61.

See also Commission Communication "Report on the safety and liability implications of Artificial Intelligence, the Internet of Things and robotics", COM (2020) 64 final, Brussels, 19.2.2020, p. 14: "although the Product Liability Directive's definition of product is broad, its scope could be further clarified to better reflect the complexity of emerging technologies and ensure that compensation is always available for damage caused by products that are defective because of software or other digital features. This would better enable economic actors, such as software developers, to assess whether they could be considered producers according to the Product Liability Directive".

[40] Commission's Inception Impact Assessment "Adapting liability rules to the digital age and circular economy", Ref. Ares(2021)4266516, 30.06.2021, p. 2.

[41] Ibid.

[42] Ibid.

6.5.2 *Significant Obstacles to Getting Compensation and Obstacles in the Internal Market*

6.5.2.1 Specific Characteristics of AI Make It Difficult for Injured Parties to Receive Compensation–Heavy Burden of Proof

It is recalled that the 2018 Evaluation of the Product Liability Directive concluded that the complexity of certain products (such as pharmaceuticals and products that use emerging digital technologies) makes it especially difficult for injured parties to prove that a defect caused the damage they suffered and therefore to get compensation.[43]

The built-in autonomy and self-learning ability are characteristics of "advanced" robots and AI-enabled products, and their degree depends on how sophisticated a system's interaction with its environment has been designed to be. The capacity of those technologies to acquire autonomy, to learn through their own variable experience and interaction and to adapt their behaviour and actions to the environment raise serious questions regarding liability. Indeed, those advanced robots and AI-systems are equipped with adaptive and learning abilities entailing a certain degree of unpredictability in their behaviour. They could generate autonomous decision-making and interact with their environment in an unforeseeable manner. This unpredictability in the behaviour of those autonomous applications and systems inevitably raises serious liability questions, as it could be difficult to determine who is technically and legally responsible for any ensuing damage. The legal responsibility arising through an autonomous system's harmful action has become, therefore, a crucial issue.[44]

---

[43] Ibid.

[44] Commission Staff Working Document on "Liability for emerging digital technologies"—Accompanying the document Commission Communication "Artificial intelligence for Europe", SWD (2018) 137 final, Brussels, 25.4.2018, at p. 10: "combined with self-learning and autonomy, the behaviour of these technologies may be difficult to predict. This could raise questions regarding liability, in situations where the damage caused by a machine operating with a certain degree of autonomy cannot be linked to a defect or a human wrongdoing (e.g. of the driver; the car manufacturer, etc.), but also in the wider context of safeguards to be introduced to ensure the safety of such technologies (e.g. should machines be allowed to freely learn from their context or should they be prevented from learning inadequate/dangerous behaviours). As a consequence, the question of how to attribute liability where the expected outcome of the technology was not identified either before the market launch or after that launch needs to be examined". ... "It is critical to answer who should be held responsible if IoT and AI-enabled systems fail duc to the supply of erroneous data or by a failure to supply data. Finding the main cause and attributing liability will prove very difficult. For instance, is it the developer or producer of the systems or the software programmer? This also raises the question of who is responsible for ensuring that the data collected is being kept safe".

The European Parliament also stressed that the emergence of new digital technologies like AI systems raise new challenges in terms of product safety and liability like connectivity, autonomy, data dependency, opacity, complexity of products and systems, software updates and more complex safety management and value chains: "The rise of AI, however, presents a significant challenge for the existing liability frameworks. Using AI-systems in our daily life will lead to situations in which

Furthermore, it has been already described that AI-based products and systems are characterised by various degrees of opacity (the internal complexity of the algorithms involved), resulting to a decision-making process of the AI system that can be extremely difficult to trace. Due to the autonomy and self-learning ability aspects as well as the opacity issue (black-box effect) of AI systems, getting fair compensation[45] could become difficult for harm caused by certain AI-applications. Indeed, it could be hard to trace the damage back to a specific human behaviour and,

their opacity ("black box" element) and the multitude of actors who intervene in their lifecycle make it extremely expensive or even impossible to identify who was in control of the risk of using the AI-system in question or which code or input caused the harmful operation. That difficulty is compounded by the connectivity between an AI-system and other AI-systems and non-AI-systems, by its dependency on external data, by its vulnerability to cybersecurity breaches, as well as by the increasing autonomy of AI-systems triggered by machine-learning and deep-learning capabilities. In addition to these complex features and potential vulnerabilities, AI-systems could also be used to cause severe harm, such as compromising human dignity and European values and freedoms, by tracking individuals against their will, by introducing social credit systems, by taking biased decisions in matters of health insurance, credit provision, court orders, recruitment or employment or by constructing lethal autonomous weapon systems". Annex to the European Parliament's Resolution of 20 October 2020 on a civil liability regime for AI—Text of the Proposal for a Regulation on liability for the operation of AI systems, recital 3.

[45] According to the European Parliament, "fair compensation procedures mean that each person who suffers harm caused by AI-systems or whose property damage is caused by AI-systems should have the same level of protection compared to cases without involvement of an AI-system; the user needs to be sure that potential damage caused by systems using AI is covered by adequate insurance

at the same time, extremely costly to understand (and get access to) the algorithm and the data used by the AI system.[46]

and that there is a defined legal route for redress". European Parliament's Resolution of 20 October 2020 on a civil liability regime for AI, recital J.

[46]Finding the main cause of damage and attributing liability becomes complex. Therefore, the allocation of liability could be unfair or inefficient, whereas liability claims may be difficult or overly costly to be made and/or to be proven. As a result, victims may not be adequately compensated. Therefore, the allocation of liability may be unfair or inefficient, whereas liability claims may be difficult or overly costly to be made and/or to be proven (especially when a victim has to prove that the damage suffered was caused by a conduct attributable to an AI system and, in order to achieve this, an analysis of complex underlying code should take place, which could be beyond the—financial and technical—ability of the majority of victims). As a result, victims may not be adequately compensated.

See, for instance, Commission Communication "Report on the safety and liability implications of Artificial Intelligence, the Internet of Things and robotics", COM (2020) 64 final, Brussels, 19.2.2020, p. 15: "the need to understand the algorithm and the data used by the AI requires analytical capacity and technical expertise that victims could find prohibitively costly. In addition, access to the algorithm and the data could be impossible without the cooperation of the potentially liable party. In practice, victims may thus not be able to make a liability claim. In addition, it would be unclear, how to demonstrate the fault of an AI acting autonomously, or what would be considered the fault of a person relying on the use of AI". The Commission underlined that a damage caused by those emerging digital technologies may be the result of a large set of unknown circumstances (for instance the defect or malfunctioning of the devices or services provided by third parties or other circumstances such as a cyber-attack), making it extremely difficult for the victim to identify the damage caused by a specific human fault and thus to prove the substantial elements of a liability claim. Also, persons having suffered harm caused by of AI systems should enjoy equal level of protection as persons having suffered harm caused by other technologies. As the Commission stated, "the characteristics of emerging digital technologies like AI, the IoT and robotics challenge aspects of Union and national liability frameworks and could reduce their effectiveness. Some of these characteristics could make it hard to trace the damage back to a human behaviour, which could give grounds for a fault-based claim in accordance with national rules. This means that liability claims based on national tort laws may be difficult or overly costly to prove and consequently victims may not be adequately compensated. It is important that victims of accidents of products and services including emerging digital technologies like AI do not enjoy a lower level of protection compared to similar other products and services, for which they would get compensation under national tort law. This could reduce societal acceptance of those emerging technologies and lead to hesitance to use them" (at p. 13). ... Since many different layers are involved in the emerging digital technologies, vulnerable software, faulty sensors, or unstable connectivity may make it difficult to determine who is technically and legally responsible for any ensuing damage or how to identify the root cause of the problem. As the Commission put it, "combining different digital components in a complex ecosystem and the plurality of actors involved can make it difficult to assess where a potential damage originates and which person is liable for it. Due to the complexity of these technologies, it can be very difficult for victims to identify the liable person and prove all necessary conditions for a successful claim, as required under national law. The costs for this expertise may be economically prohibitive and discourage victims from claiming compensation" (at p. 14).

See also the Report from the Expert Group on Liability and New Technologies—New Technologies Formation "Liability for Artificial Intelligence and Other Emerging Digital Technologies", 21 November 2019, at p. 24: "In addition to the difficulties of determining what constitutes fault in the case of damage caused by an emerging digital technology, there may also be problems with proving fault. Generally, the victim has to prove that the defendant (or someone whose conduct is attributable to them) was at fault. The victim therefore not only needs to identify which duties of care the defendant should have discharged, but also to prove to the court that these duties were breached. Proving the defendant is at fault entails providing the court with evidence that may lead it to believe what the applicable standard of care was and that it has not been met. The second part of this is to provide evidence of how the event giving rise to the damage occurred. The more complex the circumstances leading to the victim's harm are, the harder it is to identify relevant evidence. For example, it can be difficult and costly to identify a bug in a long and complicated software code. In the case of AI, examining the process leading to a specific result (how the input data led to the output data) may be difficult, very time-consuming and expensive".

Furthermore, see Commission Communication "White Paper On Artificial Intelligence - A European approach to excellence and trust", COM(2020) 65 final, Brussels,19.2.2020: "The lack of transparency (opaqueness of AI) makes it difficult to identify and prove possible breaches of laws, including legal provisions that protect fundamental rights, attribute liability and meet the conditions to claim compensation. Therefore, in order to ensure an effective application and enforcement, it may be necessary to adjust or clarify existing legislation in certain areas, for example on liability" (at p. 14). . . . "The specific characteristics of many AI technologies, including opacity ('black box-effect'), complexity, unpredictability and partially autonomous behaviour, may make it hard to verify compliance with, and may hamper the effective enforcement of, rules of existing EU law meant to protect fundamental rights. Enforcement authorities and affected persons might lack the means to verify how a given decision made with the involvement of AI was taken and, therefore, whether the relevant rules were respected. Individuals and legal entities may face difficulties with effective access to justice in situations where such decisions may negatively affect them" (at pp. 11–12). . . . "If the safety risks materialise, the lack of clear requirements and the characteristics of AI technologies mentioned above make it difficult to trace back potentially problematic decisions made with the involvement of AI systems. This in turn may make it difficult for persons having suffered harm to obtain compensation under the current EU and national liability legislation. Under the Product Liability Directive, a manufacturer is liable for damage caused by a defective product. However, in the case of an AI based system such as autonomous cars, it may be difficult to prove that there is a defect in the product, the damage that has occurred and the causal link between the two. In addition, there is some uncertainty about how and to what extent the Product Liability Directive applies in the case of certain types of defects, for example if these result from weaknesses in the cybersecurity of the product. Thus, the difficulty of tracing back potentially problematic decisions taken by AI systems and referred to above in relation to fundamental rights applies equally to safety and liability-related issues. Persons having suffered harm may not have effective access to the evidence that is necessary to build a case in court, for instance, and may have less effective redress possibilities compared to situations where the damage is caused by traditional technologies. These risks will increase as the use of AI becomes more widespread" (at pp. 12–13).

See also European Parliament's Resolution of 20 October 2020 on a civil liability regime for AI, (section "Liability and Artificial Intelligence", points 6 and 7, and recitals H and I). In particular, in line with the Commission's analysis, the European Parliament stated that "there is no need for a complete revision of the well-functioning liability regimes, but that the complexity, connectivity, opacity, vulnerability, the capacity of being modified through updates, the capacity for self-learning and the potential autonomy of AI-systems, as well as the multitude of actors involved represent nevertheless a significant challenge to the effectiveness of Union and national liability framework provisions; considers that specific and coordinated adjustments to the liability regimes are necessary to avoid a situation in which persons who suffer harm or whose property is damaged end up without compensation"; (at point 6) . . . "the opacity, connectivity and autonomy of AI-systems could make it in practice very difficult or even impossible to trace back specific harmful actions of AI-systems to specific human input or to decisions in the design"; (at point 7) . . . "certain AI-systems present significant legal challenges for the existing liability framework and could lead to situations in which their opacity could make it extremely expensive or even impossible to identify who was in control of the risk associated with the AI-system, or which code, input or data have ultimately caused the harmful operation; . . . this factor could make it harder to identify the link between harm or damage

As the Commission stated, "several specific characteristics of AI (autonomous[47] behaviour, continuous adaptation, limited predictability[48] and opacity[49]) also make it difficult for injured parties to get compensation, both under the Directive and under national civil liability rules. AI systems can perform tasks with increasingly less human intervention and are in certain cases able to learn autonomously while in use. With certain opaque AI systems it is possible only to a limited extent to understand

---

and the behaviour causing it, with the result that victims might not receive adequate compensation; ... the legal challenges also result from the connectivity between an AI-system and other AI-systems and non-AI-systems, their dependency on external data, their vulnerability to cybersecurity breaches as well as from the design of increasingly autonomous AI-systems using, inter alia, machine-learning and deep-learning techniques" (recitals H and I).

Furthermore, see the Annex to the European Parliament's Resolution of 20 October 2020 on a civil liability regime for AI—Text of the Proposal for a Regulation on liability for the operation of AI systems, recital 7: "There are however also AI-systems that are developed and deployed in a critical manner and are based on technologies such as neuronal networks and deep-learning processes. Their opacity and autonomy could make it very difficult to trace back specific actions to specific human decisions in their design or in their operation. An operator of such an AI-system might, for instance, argue that the physical or virtual activity, device or process causing the harm or damage was outside of his or her control because it was caused by an autonomous operation of his or her AI-system. Moreover, the mere operation of an autonomous AI-system should not be a sufficient ground for admitting the liability claim. As a result, there might be liability cases in which the allocation of liability could be unfair or inefficient, or in which a person who suffers harm or damage caused by an AI-system cannot prove the fault of the producer, of an interfering third party or of the operator and ends up without compensation".

[47] "Autonomy: Emerging new technologies increasingly perform tasks with less, or entirely without, human control or supervision. They are themselves capable of altering the initial algorithms due to self-learning capabilities that process external data collected in the course of the operation. The choice of such data and the degree of impact it has on the outcome is constantly adjusted by the evolving algorithms themselves". Report from the Expert Group on Liability and New Technologies—New Technologies Formation "Liability for Artificial Intelligence and Other Emerging Digital Technologies", 21 November 2019, at p. 33.

See also Commission Communication "Report on the safety and liability implications of Artificial Intelligence, the Internet of Things and robotics", COM (2020) 64 final, Brussels, 19.2.2020, p. 15: "where AI applications are able to act autonomously, they perform a task without every step being pre-defined and with less or eventually entirely without immediate human control or supervision".

[48] "Predictability: Many systems are designed to not only respond to pre-defined stimuli, but to identify and classify new ones and link them to a self-chosen corresponding reaction that has not been pre-programmed as such. The more external data systems are capable of processing, and the more they are equipped with increasingly sophisticated AI, the more difficult it is to foresee the precise impact they will have once in operation". Report from the Expert Group on Liability and New Technologies—New Technologies Formation "Liability for Artificial Intelligence and Other Emerging Digital Technologies", 21 November 2019, at p. 33.

[49] "Opacity: The more complex emerging digital technologies become, the less those taking advantage of their functions or being exposed to them can comprehend the processes that may have caused harm to themselves or to others. Algorithms often no longer come as more or less easily readable code, but as a black-box that has evolved through self-learning and which we may be able to test as to its effects, but not so much to understand". Report from the Expert Group on Liability and New Technologies—New Technologies Formation "Liability for Artificial Intelligence and Other Emerging Digital Technologies", 21 November 2019, at p. 33.

how they produce a certain output. These features could make it very difficult and costly for injured parties to identify and prove the fault of a potentially liable person or a defect and the causal link between that fault/defect and the damage suffered. This heavy burden of proof is compounded by the fact that injured parties may not have sufficient technical information about AI products and services, therefore placing them at a considerable disadvantage. National courts may apply diverging ad hoc solutions, e.g. by alleviating the burden of proof or developing extensive interpretations of strict liability regimes under national law. If Member States attempt to address the resulting legal uncertainty at national level, this could lead to further fragmentation of liability rules across the EU for damage caused by AI. Taking into account the specific features and the economic importance of AI as a crucial enabling technology, a lack of harmonised rules in this area could therefore lead to obstacles in the internal market".[50]

6.5.2.2 The Notion of 'Defect'

It is reminded that, according to the Product Liability Directive, a product is considered defective if it does not provide the safety a person is entitled to expect.[51] The self-learning ability of advanced AI-equipped products, i.e. their capacity to learn through their own variable experience and interaction and to adapt their behaviour and actions to the environment, entails a certain degree of unpredictability in their behaviour. Indeed, those systems/products could generate autonomous decision-making and interact with their environment in an unforeseeable manner. This unpredictability in behaviour of those autonomous applications and systems could lead to unpredictable outcomes (and subsequent damages) making it unclear whether those outcomes could/should be treated as 'defects' under the Product Liability Directive. Therefore, the notion of what constitutes a 'defect' should be re-examined.[52] This is why the Commission stated that "in respect of AI-equipped

[50] Commission's Inception Impact Assessment "Adapting liability rules to the digital age and circular economy", Ref. Ares(2021)4266516, 30.06.2021, pp. 2–3.

[51] According to Article 6 para. 1 of the Product Liability Directive, this takes all circumstances into account, such as the presentation of the product, the use to which it could reasonably be expected the product would be put, and the time the product was put into circulation. Article 6 para. 2 of the Product Liability Directive states that a product must not be considered defective for the sole reason that a better product is subsequently put into circulation.

[52] Commission Staff Working Document, 'Evaluation of Product Liability Directive', SWD(2018) 157 final, Brussels, 07.05.2018. For instance, the Commission raised the question whether software vulnerability—e.g. a cyber-attack or a failure to update security software or a misuse of information—could constitute a defect. Also, it stated that it is still open whether an unintended autonomous behaviour of an advanced robot is a defect or not. According to the Commission, "robots are meant to perform autonomous behaviours, they are programmed to do so. Given their self-learning capacities, one could in consequence argue that not all unforeseen autonomous behaviour is a defect. On the other hand, these robots will be employed to perform certain tasks, which will inevitably be linked to safety expectations" (at pp. 56–57). This is why the Commission

products that continuously learn and adapt while in operation, it is not clear whether unpredictable outcomes that lead to damage can be treated as 'defects' under the Directive".[53]

6.5.2.3 The 'Development Risk' and 'Later Defect' Defence

However, according to the Commission, even if unpredictable outcomes can be treated as 'defects' under the Product Liability Directive, the 'development risk defence' exempts producers from liability for defects that did not exist or were undiscoverable when the product was put into circulation.[54] Therefore, the 'development risk defence' could make it difficult for injured parties to get compensation.[55]

Indeed, it is reminded that, although strict liability represents a strong tool for the protection of victims, there are specific circumstances where the Product Liability Directive allows producers to take calculated risks when placing innovative products on the market. In particular, according to article 7 of the Product Liability Directive, the producer is not liable if, *inter alia*, he can prove that the defect in question did not exist when the product was put into circulation or the state of technical knowledge at the time of putting the product on the market made it impossible to discover the defect. Therefore, the notion of foreseeable reasonable use (alongside questions of contributory negligence)[56] could appear more often in practice, potentially reducing a producer's liability and thus making it more difficult for injured persons to receive compensation for damages caused by a defect in a product. This is why the Commission stated that an assessment of the Product Liability Directive should consider the

---

concluded that the definition of defect "may require being updated to new types of problems such as infringements of privacy or how to link the notion of defect with the types of autonomous behaviours leading to damages. Extending the scope of the Directive in this direction is, however, a political decision that will have to be carefully assessed" (at p. 61).

See also Report from the Commission on the Application of the Council Directive on the approximation of the laws, regulations, and administrative provisions of the Member States concerning liability for defective products (85/374/EEC) {SWD(2018) 157 final}–{SWD(2018) 158 final}, COM(2018) 246 final, Brussels, 7.5.2018, ['Commission Report on the Application of the Product Liability Directive, COM(2018) 246 final, Brussels, 07.05.2018'], pp. 2, 6, 8, 9.

[53] Commission's Inception Impact Assessment "Adapting liability rules to the digital age and circular economy", Ref. Ares(2021)4266516, 30.06.2021, p. 3.

[54] According to the 'development risk defence', the state-of-the-art knowledge at the time could not have foreseen the defect (i.e. the state of technical knowledge at the time of putting the product on the market made it impossible to discover the defect). Also, according to the 'later defect defence', a producer is not liable if the defect did not exist at the time the product was put into circulation.

[55] Commission's Inception Impact Assessment "Adapting liability rules to the digital age and circular economy", Ref. Ares(2021)4266516, 30.06.2021, p. 3.

[56] An example of contributory negligence is when the injured party has failed to perform/download safety relevant updates and, therefore, liability of the producer could be reduced. In other words, liability of the producer could be limited to the extent the injured party has contributed to the actual damage.

fact that AI products can change during their life cycle: "the notion of 'putting into circulation' that is currently used by the Product Liability Directive could be revisited to take into account that products may change and be altered. This could also help to clarify who is liable for any changes that are made to the product".[57]

6.5.2.4 Time Limits and Minimum Threshold

It is recalled that, according to Article 9 of the Product Liability Directive, if a product is defective and causes personal injury or material damage above EUR 500 to an item of property mainly for private use or consumption, producers are liable regardless of whether or not they are at fault. Furthermore, the Product Liability Directive establishes two deadlines. In particular, according to Article 10 of the PLD a limitation period of three years applies to proceedings for the recovery of damages. Therefore, the PLD does not apply three (3) years after the injured party knew or could have become aware of the relevant facts (i.e. the damage, the defect, and the identity of the producer). Article 11 of the PLD releases the producer from liability ten (10) years after the product causing the damage was put into circulation (unless the injured person has in the meantime instituted proceedings against the producer).

---

[57] Commission Communication "Report on the safety and liability implications of Artificial Intelligence, the Internet of Things and robotics", COM (2020) 64 final, Brussels, 19.2.2020, p. 15.

See also the Report from the Expert Group on Liability and New Technologies—New Technologies Formation "Liability for Artificial Intelligence and Other Emerging Digital Technologies", 21 November 2019, pp. 28–29: "As the PLD focuses on the moment when the product was put into circulation as the key turning point for the producer's liability, this cuts off claims for anything the producer may subsequently add via some update or upgrade. In addition, the PLD does not provide for any duties to monitor the products after putting them into circulation. Highly sophisticated AI systems may not be finished products that are put on the market in a traditional way. The producer may retain some degree of control over the product's further development in the form of additions or updates after circulation. At the same time, the producer's control may be limited and nonexclusive if the product's operation requires data provided by third parties or collected from the environment, and depends on self-learning processes and personalising settings chosen by the user. This dilutes the traditional role of a producer, when a multitude of actors contribute to the design, functioning and use of the AI product/system. This is related to another limitation of liability—most Member States adopted the so-called development risk defence, which allows the producer to avoid liability if the state of scientific and technical knowledge at the time when he put the product into circulation was not such as to enable the existence of the defect to be discovered (Article 7 lit e PLD). The defence may become much more important practically with regard to sophisticated AI-based products".

See also Commission Communication "White Paper On Artificial Intelligence - A European approach to excellence and trust", COM(2020) 65 final, Brussels, 19.2.2020, p. 14: "in general, EU legislation on product safety allocates the responsibility to the producer of the product placed on the market, including all components e.g. AI systems. But the rules can for example become unclear if AI is added after the product is placed on the market by a party that is not the producer. In addition, EU product liability legislation provides for liability of producers and leaves national liability rules to govern liability of others in the supply chain".

The Commission is of the opinion that, apart from the obstacles to getting compensation once a claim has been submitted, victims seeking compensation under the Product Liability Directive face additional limitations on making claims in the first place due to the time limits and the minimum threshold for property damage of EUR 500 imposed by the Directive.[58]

6.6 How the European Commission's Initiative Aims to Address the Challenges Brought by the Digital Emerging Technologies: Proposed Policy Options

This section attempts to explain how the aforementioned challenges brought by the digital emerging technologies to the product liability frameworks could be efficiently addressed. The options put forward by the Commission's Inception Impact Assessment followed, as expected, a "gradual intervention logic", ranging from the baseline position of enacting no legislation, i.e. no changes to current liability rules (baseline scenario—Option 0) to policy options of different degrees of regulatory intervention.

Clearly against the baseline scenario, the Commission stated that, in the absence of EU action, the risks would remain unaddressed. There could also be a lack of clarity of how liability rules will be applied in respect of AI, whereas serious obstacles to getting compensation for damage will remain. Moreover, no EU policy change could lead to increased fragmentation due to interventions at Member States level.[59]

In general, the Commission put forward policy options of different degrees of regulatory intervention for how to achieve its main objectives (namely to modernise liability rules and to reduce obstacles to getting compensation for damage),

[58] Commission's Inception Impact Assessment "Adapting liability rules to the digital age and circular economy", Ref. Ares(2021)4266516, 30.06.2021, p. 3.

See also Commission Report on the Application of the Product Liability Directive, COM(2018) 246 final, Brussels, 07.05.2018, at p. 6: "The EUR 500 threshold and time limitations for claims (especially for certain products such as pharmaceuticals) also limit the number of cases for which consumers can claim compensation".

[59] The rationale used by the Commission for not supporting the baseline scenario is the following: "Baseline scenario: No changes to current liability rules. Legal uncertainty persists for businesses in respect of how liability rules will be applied in the digital age, including in respect of AI, and how they will be applied to the circular economy. Difficulties for injured parties to get compensation persist. Risk of fragmentation of the internal market because of emergence of diverging national rules". See Commission's Inception Impact Assessment "Adapting liability rules to the digital age and circular economy", Ref. Ares(2021)4266516, 30.06.2021, p. 4.

With regard to the risk of fragmentation of the internal market, the European Parliament had also stated that "specific adjustments to the existing legislation and the introduction of well-accessed and targeted new provisions would be sufficient to accommodate the AI-related challenges, with a view to preventing regulatory fragmentation and ensuring the harmonisation of civil liability legislation throughout the Union in connection with AI". See the Annex to the European Parliament's Resolution of 20 October 2020 on a civil liability regime for AI – Text of the Proposal for a Regulation on liability for the operation of AI systems, at recital 8.

including by extending the current strict liability rules to cover intangible products and online marketplaces, and by reversing or amending the burden of proof in some circumstances. It was stated that the Commission's preferred policy option is a combination of options and sub-options under two specific headings, namely options to adapt strict liability rules to the digital age and circular economy and options to address obstacles to getting compensation.

It should be stressed that, in light of the three-pronged objective of the EU liability framework (legal certainty, prevention of damages and efficient compensation to the injured parties), the Commission's proposals (especially those opting for the adoption of 'radical' measures in relation to an expansion of liability) could fundamentally change the EU liability regime. In this regard, the proposed measures include the following options: expansion to include digital products and inclusion of non-material damages (option 1.b); burden of proof reversal (option 2.1.b); removal of the development risk defence (option 2.1.c); easing conditions for making claims (option 2.1.d); harmonisation of claims involving operator's fault and its burden of proof reversal (option 2.2.d). More analytically:

6.6.1 *Options to Adapt Strict Liability Rules to the Digital Age and Circular Economy*

6.6.1.1 Extending Existing Strict Liability Rules to Cover Intangible Products: Compensating for Non-Material Damages

Option 1.a of the Commission's 2021 Inception Impact Assessment (IAA) proposed the revision of the Product Liability Directive to extend existing strict liability rules to cover intangible products (e.g. digital content and stand-alone software) that cause physical/material damage, and to address connectivity and cybersecurity risks as well as defects resulting from interactions with other products and services (e.g. IoT) or from changes to products after they have been put into circulation (e.g. software updates or circular economy activities like product refurbishments).[60]

---

[60] Commission's Inception Impact Assessment "Adapting liability rules to the digital age and circular economy", Ref. Ares(2021)4266516, 30.06.2021, p. 4.

This option (1.a) also proposed to extend strict liability to online marketplaces where they fail to identify the producer. For an interesting analysis, where it is stressed that online marketplaces should be included within the scope of the PLD, see BEUC's (the European Consumer Organisation) feedback on the European Commission's Inception Impact Assessment on "Civil liability – adapting liability rules to the digital age and artificial intelligence", submitted on 28.07.2021: "online marketplaces have been responsible for the circulation of millions of defective products potentially causing harm to millions of consumers. In February 2021, six members of the BEUC and the International Consumer Research and Testing (ICRT) – Test Achats/Test Aankoop, Altroconsumo, Consumentenbond, Forbrugerrådet Tænk, Stiftung Warentest and Which? - published the results of a testing showing that, out of 250 products bought on online marketplaces, 66% of them did not meet the EU safety standards. In November 2020, our Swedish member

Option 1.a of the IAA was supported by a broad range of stakeholders, mainly consumer, civil society and other non-profit organisations, who asked for an extension of the definition of "products" as provided in Article 3 of the Product Liability Directive to ensure that it covers damages caused by digital contents and software. In other words, they stated that the Product Liability Directive should apply to all tangible and non-tangible goods. Those organisations also argued that, in order to address connectivity and cybersecurity risks/vulnerabilities as well as defects resulting from changes to products after they have been put into circulation (e.g. software updates), the notion of "defect" should be broadened and no longer limited to users' safety expectations.[61]

---

organisation Sveriges Konsumenter published the results of a study on unsafe direct imports via online marketplaces and found that, out of the 28 products investigated, 26 of them (i.e., 93%) turn out to be dangerous for consumers. In parallel, consumers today expect marketplaces to ensure that the products that they sell are safe. In November 2020, a study published by our German member organisation vzbv found that 93% of respondents expect rather online marketplaces to make sure that EU safety rules are respected. In parallel, online marketplaces are often in the best position to minimize the harm arising out from the circulation of defective products. Finally, whereas online platforms have the capacity to prevent the circulation of defective products, in practice, in many situations, they are still not incentivized to do it on a regular basis. A 2020 report from Which? highlighted that online marketplaces have been failing to remove banned products even after consumers report them. As a consequence, online marketplaces must be fully liable for the products that they sell on their platforms when they have a predominant role in the supply of goods. This is also in line with other developments happening in other parts of the world, which also aim at including online marketplaces within the scope of product liability rules. BEUC considers therefore that online marketplaces should be included explicitly in the scope of the PLD. There are several options to do this: • First, online marketplaces may be held liable as "suppliers" under the PLD. This means that online marketplaces would be liable in the event the producer is not known. Although this would already represent a significant improvement compared to the existing situation, it may not entirely solve the problem as, in many cases, the producer may be known but located in a third country (e.g., in China). In such a situation, it remains very complex (if not impossible) for the harmed individuals to claim and obtain compensation. If the lability of online marketplaces as "suppliers" is ultimately retained, BEUC takes the view that it should be accompanied by a "fall-back plan" where online marketplaces may be held liable in situations where the producer is known but fails to take action to remedy the harm. • Alternatively, online marketplaces may be held liable as "importers" under the PLD. This would allow harmed individuals to directly turn to the online marketplaces in case of harm to obtain compensation. All actors involved in the supply chain would be jointly and severally liable. The online marketplaces and the producer would apportion liability as they wish via contractual arrangements. – BEUC calls on the European Commission to carefully consider these two options to include online marketplaces in the scope of the PLD" (at pp. 3–4).

[61] For instance, contributions in favour of the Commission's proposal include the following:

Contribution by The Future Society (TFS), "Liability rules for Trust in Excellence & Excellence in Trust - Inception Impact Assessment - Adapting liability rules to the digital age and circular economy", Belgium, 28 July 2021: "While not tangible in the eye of the users and perhaps of the operators, software is in fact embodied ("saved") in tangible chemical layouts on tangible semiconductors. The use of the software also results in tangible changes (through electronic activation of the chemical layout), which may occasionally result in damage through a complicated but explainable chain of cause and effects. Even without considering the chemical substrate, software can be considered a pattern of electric signals to be interpreted by a computer. This would also reasonably fall within the scope of the Product Liability Directive (PLD), as it states that the definition of

On the other hand, corporations and organisations representing businesses stressed that option 1.a of the IIA would disproportionately extend the Product

---

product "includes electricity". ... The liability uncertainty arising from these issues could be resolved more succinctly by the proper inclusion of software in the existing regime. We therefore think that it is appropriate to include digital content and software that cause damage in the strict liability rules, the same way other tangible products are covered" (at pp. 2–3).

BEUC (the European Consumer Organisation), "Product Liability 2.0 - How to make EU rules fit for consumers in the digital age", submitted on 07.05.2020: "The PLD should apply to all tangible and non-tangible goods, including digital services and digital content" (at p. 1). ... "It is usually accepted that a 'product' can also include digital content if they are embedded into a tangible media. This covers the hardware/software bundle that characterises many IoT products, such as smart meters or connected household appliances. A problem with the embedded software renders the final 'hard' product defective, which ultimately triggers the liability of the producer. However, it is open to debate whether digital content itself qualifies as a 'product' within the meaning of the PLD. The question is particularly acute for unbundled 'standalone' software that can be downloaded separately and added to existing hardware. In the near future, it can also be expected that hardware and software will no longer come as a bundle but will be purchased separately. Consumers may also have the possibility to change or modify pre-installed software. In this context, there is uncertainty as to whether software should be considered as a product or a service, and whether the PLD is ultimately applicable. It is essential to revise the notion of a product to consider its full 'digitalised dimension' in which tangible items, digital services and digital content continuously interact and cannot be differentiated. All of them should be covered under the definition of a 'product'. BEUC recommendation: • The PLD should apply to all tangible and non-tangible goods, including digital services and digital content" (at pp. 12-13). ... "The notion of "defect" should be broadened and no longer limited to users' safety expectations: • The PLD should build on an extended notion of 'defect' no longer only limited to users' safety expectations. A product should be considered 'defective' when it deviates from the reasonable expectations that users may have, which include: the product should be safe, it should be free from cybersecurity failures and other personal security risks and should be GDPR-compliant. In addition, a product using self-learning capacities and taking autonomous decisions should be deemed defective when its unintended behaviour has caused harm to the user. • A lack of post-marketing updates by producers should be considered as a defect in case of harm to the user" (at pp. 1–2 and 13–15).

ACEA (The European Automobile Manufacturers' Association) response to the European Commission's inception impact assessment on civil liability—Adapting liability rules to the digital age and circular economy, 28.07.2021: "ACEA believes that the definition of "products" as provided in Article 3 of the Directive should be adapted to ensure that it covers damages caused by digital contents and software. We believe that developers, manufacturers and providers of digital content, software, applications, and algorithms that are embedded in the product and that serve to use the product as it was intended should be held liable for damages caused by defects in these intangible products. This reflects the reality of today's interconnected products the safe functioning of which can be affected by such intangible elements" (at p. 1). ... "The Directive should cover defects resulting from changes to products after they have been put into circulation. Companies that remanufacture or refurbish products should be held liable for damages caused by defects resulting from these changes. To the extent that the remanufacture or refurbishment results in a substantial modification of the initial product, they should be considered producers for the purpose of this Directive and be subject to all obligations it imposes on producers. Similarly, developers, manufacturers and providers of digital content, software, applications, and algorithms that are installed in a product after it has been put on the market and that serve to use the product as it was intended should be held liable for damages caused by defects in these intangible products. This also follows from the inclusion of intangible products in the scope of the Directive as suggested above" (at pp. 1–2).

Liability Directive's strict liability rules to cover 'intangible products (e.g., digital content/software)', failing to recognise fundamental differences between physical products and services/software processes. Moreover, expanding legal exposure to software developers and others playing an intermediate role in the value chain would hinder innovation and the roll-out and uptake of AI-based technologies and negatively affect European industry and corporations. This is why they asked the Commission to maintain the Product Liability Directive's focus on tangible products (which is sufficiently flexible so that it may include products that include embedded software) and avoid extending the Directive's strict liability regime to either stand-alone software or to services. Furthermore, they argued that product liability for intangible products should also not be extended to defects resulting from interaction with other products and services (e.g. IoT). This is because the producer of digital content or software can hardly foresee or control which other intangible products the operator/user will combine with this digital content or software.[62]

[62] Contributions opposing the Commission's proposed option 1.a included the following:

Microsoft comments on the Inception Impact Assessment "Adapting liability rules to the digital age and circular economy", 28 July 2021: "Option 1.a of the IIA would extend the PLD's strict liability rules to cover 'intangible products (e.g., digital content/software)'. This fails to recognize fundamental differences between products and services. Whereas tangible products typically have a discrete set of uses, and therefore a foreseeable range of risks, the digital services—standing alone–that are the focus of the IIA may be deployed in an almost unlimited number of scenarios and for a wide range of uses. How services function, and the risks they present, will therefore often depend on how the user deploys the service. By way of example, it is far easier to foresee the potential uses and risks of a tangible product such as hedge clippers than, for instance, a speech recognition system, which can be used in an almost infinite range of scenarios. It is virtually impossible, as a practical matter, for service providers to anticipate every conceivable use of the service, or its associated risks. Targeting the PLD's strict liability regime at software and services could deter suppliers from offering them on the EU market, or could lead to increased prices for EU consumers. To avoid this outcome, we urge the Commission to maintain the PLD's current focus on tangible products (which is sufficiently flexible so that it may include products that include embedded software) and avoid extending the Directive's strict liability regime to either stand-alone software or to services (at p. 3).

See also Google's views on the European Commission's inception impact assessment on civil liability - adapting liability rules to the digital age and AI, 28 July 2021: "we have yet to see real-world evidence of problems that warrant altering such a fundamental underpinning of European law and running the risk of severe unintended consequences. In particular, a strict liability regime is unnecessary and ill-suited to the properties of software and AI systems, and would have a profound chilling effect on innovation and digitization in Europe, disproportionately impacting European SMEs. In addition, any potential changes to liability rules should take into account the effects of the recently proposed AI Act (AIA). ... Rather than prematurely adding new rules on liability that could create redundant or conflicting requirements and add additional complexity, the Commission should, at a minimum, evaluate the impact of the AIA on the gaps identified in the evaluation before introducing any changes to liability frameworks" (at p. 1). "Any initiative to introduce "strict liability" for AI systems/digital content/software should be approached with great caution. Globally, strict liability frameworks are reserved for abnormally hazardous situations, as they preclude any consideration of intent or negligence. Introducing strict liability would mean that anyone involved in developing or operating an AI system could be held liable for problems they had no awareness of or influence over. This could lead to misplaced responsibility if the AI system was simply a conduit rather than the source of harm (such as if an operator used an automatic translation system to mistranslate medical advice even though the system clearly stated it is not intended to be used for medical purposes). Furthermore, while software providers do extensive testing and debugging before releasing software, bugs almost always become apparent over time and are fixed by updates or in later releases. This includes bugs that create cyber vulnerabilities in software that can be exploited by malicious actors. Despite decades of effort, it has proven impossible to entirely eradicate bugs from software due to the complexity of writing code, and this is generally accepted as an inherent feature of software development" (at p. 2).

The Information Technology Industry Council (ITI), "Comments to European Commission's Inception Impact Assessment on the Revision of EU Liability Rule", 28.07.2021: "Option 1a of the IIA lays out the possibility to update the PLD to extend strict liability rules to cover intangible elements (such as all software) which can cause material damage. First, it is important to consider here that physical products differ from software processes. The latter can be deployed in a variety of ways and depend strongly on how they are being used. The existing PLD recognises the characteristics of software processes in their environments by providing safeguards against defective software but refraining from liability provisions for stand-alone software which a user downloads and puts into use. More generally, expanding legal exposure to software developers and others playing an intermediate role in the value chain would be disproportionate. It would also have a significant chilling effect on innovation and competition, and most likely negatively affect European SMEs. If Europe were to become the first global player to apply strict liability to services and software, as mentioned in the IIA, the roll-out and uptake of AI-based technologies would also be hindered, hitting businesses and start-ups operating in Europe and opposing the stated goals of the Commission to encourage innovation and create an ecosystem of excellence in Europe. Strict liability is a powerful tool which should only be used for a very limited number of cases. Introducing strict liability for software and AI-based technologies would disproportionately spread liability throughout the supply chain, exposing to liability also actors that could not reasonably be expected to bear responsibility for situations beyond their control. In the case of AI, this becomes especially critical if AI technology is purposefully misused, e.g., by bad actors for illegitimate surveillance, or for consciously discriminating in hiring processes. While AI systems can be well developed, bad actors might abuse these tools for their own agendas, and if liability rules are not carefully designed, they could unjustly expose developers, even when the cause of harm was not the AI system, but its misuse. The IIA also proposes the extension of strict liability to software to address cybersecurity risk. Cyber vulnerabilities should not per se be classified as defects, as these are dynamic risks that can in most instances be mitigated through responsible system configuration to enable remote updates and responsible cyber hygiene practices by consumers. In particular, discovered vulnerabilities in software products can be patched after they have been placed on the market via patches developed in a timely manner by the manufacturer. However, software producers do not fully control in all instances whether updates are installed—oftentimes, it falls to the user to install or accept these updates and in such cases vulnerabilities can either go unnoticed or are not fixed, with users maintaining some level of responsibility for mitigation. The imperative of user responsibility also underscores a particular challenge in the use of existing product testing and certification regimes, which are largely geared toward the assessment of static product safety risks, to fully assess dynamic risks such as cyber vulnerabilities. It is important to educate consumers regarding responsible cyber hygiene practices, so they are aware of the importance of updating systems in those instances where automated remote updates are unavailable" (at p. 2).

Fujitsu, "Response to the European Commission's inception impact assessment on civil liability - adapting liability rules to the digital age and artificial intelligence, submitted on 28.07.2021: "the allocation of responsibility and risks made by the existing legal framework should also be maintained for products using AI. It is not evident why something different should apply to products using artificial intelligence than to products without using this technology. Definition of "product": Extending the strict product liability based on the Product Liability Directive 85/374/EEC (the Directive) to intangible products (e.g. digital content/software) as such ("stand-alone") does not seem necessary, as such intangible products can only cause physical/material damage to a person or physical object in combination with a tangible product. Product liability for intangible products should also not be extended to defects resulting from interaction with other products and services (e.g. IoT). This is because the producer of digital content or software can hardly foresee or control which other intangible products the user will combine with this digital content or software".

Response of the Center for Data Innovation to the European Commission's inception impact assessment on civil liability—adapting liability rules to the digital age and AI, submitted on 28.07.2021: "the Commission has not presented evidence that the PLD is inadequate for products with software components. It is thus not clear why the PLD needs to be proactively amended. Article 1 of the PLD states simply, 'the producer shall be liable for damage caused by a defect in his product.' Expanding this definition to include non-tangible product categories like software and services is a major expansion of the PLD and will have far-reaching consequences for the IT industry and the insurance market. It fundamentally changes the purpose of the PLD, which is to maintain an EU-wide framework for liability in the context of physical damage incurred by a manufactured product with discrete sets of uses. To the extent that such products contain software, the PLD already applies to them (at p. 1). ... "The lack of clarity and legal precedent around the applicability of newly expanded "product" definitions will deter innovation as companies will be wary of assuming potential legal liabilities in areas previously regulated by member states' consumer protection laws. Expanding the PLD into non-tangible products requires concrete evidence that the existing liability framework doesn't adequately cover the risks caused by products featuring AI. Only once gaps in the current framework are clearly established should PLD reforms be undertaken so that any changes address specific needs" (at p. 2).

Input from ZVEI—German Electrical and Electronic Manufacturers' Association on "Civil liability – adapting liability rules to the digital age and artificial intelligence", submitted on 28.07.2021: "The question of whether liability under the PLD should be extended to intangible products such as digital content and stand-alone software (1.a) should be considered cautiously and very carefully. We reject a deviation from the principle that the defect must be inherent in the product at the time it is put into circulation (1.a.i). Not every update should lead to a new putting into circulation, especially not if, for example, it only serves to correct a defect. Such a renewed putting into circulation would have to be reserved for updates that create new functionalities and change the characteristics of the product in a relevant way. It does not seem sensible to cast this in a rigid legal provision but should be left to court rulings. We have not yet conclusively assessed the extent to which an amendment of the concept of defect is necessary to include risks arising from the interaction of products and services (1.a.ii), but we advocate great caution here, as well as on the question of the inclusion of connectivity and cybersecurity risks (1.a.iii)" (at pp. 1–2).

Bitkom Bundesverband Informationswirtschaft, Telekommunikation und neue Medien e.V. (Federal Association for Information Technology, Telecommunications and New Media), "Position Paper - Inception Impact Assessment: Adapting liability rules to the digital age and artificial intelligence", 27.07.2021: "Extension of the product definition: One argument against extending the established concept of product to software, especially if it includes artificial intelligence, is that there have not been any liability gaps in the deployment and use of such systems to date and that the applicable product liability law has proven its effectiveness. It is already recognized by case law that a manufacturer is liable under the applicable principles of product liability if the damage was caused by the malfunction of control software (embedded software) integrated into the product. An argument against the qualification of stand-alone software as a product is that significant dangers, e.g. security vulnerabilities, depend not only on the original

Option 1.b of the Commission's Inception Impact Assessment suggested extending the range of damages for which compensation could be claimed under the Product Liability Directive, on top of option 1.a., to non-material damages

manufacturer of the stand-alone software, but also substantially on the user/operator. In particular, the manufacturer of the software can hardly foresee or control with which other software components the operator/user will connect the software. Furthermore, applying product liability to stand-alone software would impose unacceptable liability risks on the creators of open source software, which would lead to this type of software no longer being offered. Finally, the requirement to include services in the concept of product and thus in the scope of application of product liability law has so far not been sufficiently substantiated and jeopardizes the necessary balance of interests which the Commission aims to protect. In particular, it is not clear how damage to uninvolved third parties can occur outside the contractual relationship for a service. If the customer of a service is harmed, he can already obtain sufficient compensation for this under current contract law" (at p. 3).

BSA—The Software Alliance, "Comments on the Initial Impact Assessment on adapting liability rules to the digital age", 28.07.2021: "Recognize the difference between physical products and software: Each of the Commission's proposed reforms in Option 1 would extend the existing liability regime beyond physical products, to encompass software (including, but not limited to, AI). In contrast to physical products, which are generally used for a foreseeable range of purposes, however, software often can be deployed in an almost unlimited number of ways across a wide range of devices for many different purposes; further, software's functioning often depends heavily on the person using the service and the context in which it is used. The PLD recognizes this distinction. It imposes no-fault liability on defective products. Where software is embedded in a product before it is put into circulation, the PLD provides a remedy. But it does not extend liability to stand-alone software that a user subsequently downloads onto a device. Other EU laws also recognize the distinction between products and services, e.g. the recently adopted Digital Content Directive versus the Sales of Goods Directive. We thus encourage the Commission to keep the focus of the PLD on products. To the extent the Commission believes there is a need for a liability framework for software, we encourage the Commission to identify real and demonstrable gaps in the existing protections available to consumers (including via consumer protection laws, cybersecurity rules, the recently adopted Digital Content Directive, and various national rules) and to target any changes narrowly and precisely" (at p. 3).

COCIR (the European Coordination Committee of the Radiological, Electromedical and Healthcare IT Industry) feedback on the European Commission's inception impact assessment—Civil Liability—adapting liability rules to the digital age and artificial intelligence, submitted on 28.07.2021: "In the case of artificial intelligence, health technology manufacturers are already subject to provisions under the Medical Device Regulation, the In-vitro Diagnostics Regulation, the General Data Protection Regulation and potentially might also have to face additional burden under the proposed Artificial Intelligence Act. The introduction of new liability rules—or possible extension of damages, statute of limitations or reversal of the burden of proof - would also disregard and undermine both the legal and practical reality of responsibility and accountability at sector-specific level. Within healthcare, in particular when it comes to cybersecurity and the use of AI-based systems, there is a shared responsibility between different actors. The Medical Device Regulation also defines rules for distance sales that include online marketplaces. Next to that, the MDR specifies how refurbishing affects liability. The MDR/IVDR already explicitly identify the responsible persons among various stakeholders" (pp. 1–2).

(e.g. data loss, privacy infringements or environmental damage).[63] This follows the European Parliament's recommendation that "both material and immaterial harm should be taken into account in the future proposal for a Regulation".[64]

Again, this option was supported by consumer, civil society and other non-profit organisations, which favoured the extension of the Product Liability Directive to non-material damages. They argued that non-material damages should be included in the range of damages for which compensation can be claimed. They stressed that this option addresses the challenges posed by digital products, including the fact that these products can be updated after being put in circulation, the complex interactions between different products and services, and the cybersecurity risks. The Product Liability Directive protects life and health as well as consumer property, but it is not certain whether it covers damage to data (as data may not be an 'item of property' within the meaning of Article 9 (b) of the Directive). Since it appears that data loss does not fall within the scope of the Product Liability Directive (or it is at least uncertain whether damage to or the destruction of data is a property loss) in conjunction with the fact that digital products increasingly trigger significant changes in the types of harm likely to impair the consumers' wellbeing (e.g. loss of data, identify theft, privacy), it was stressed that the Directive should extend the

---

[63] Commission's Inception Impact Assessment "Adapting liability rules to the digital age and circular economy", Ref. Ares(2021)4266516, 30.06.2021, p. 4.

It is reminded that the Product Liability Directive protects life and health as well as consumer property. With regard to the latter, it is not entirely clear whether it covers damage to data, as data may not be an 'item of property' within the meaning of Article 9 (b) of the Product Liability Directive. Indeed, the Report of the Expert Group on Liability and New Technologies pointed out that, while there is consensus that injuries to a person or to physical property can trigger tortious liability, it is not universally accepted that damage to or the destruction of data constitutes a property loss, because, according to some legal systems, the notion of 'property' is limited to corporeal objects and excludes intangibles. The Report underlined that "with much of our lives and our 'property' becoming digital, it is no longer appropriate to limit liability to the tangible world. However, neither is it appropriate to simply equate data with tangible property for the purposes of liability". This is why the Report argued that, under specific conditions, the destruction of the victim's data should be regarded as compensable damage, and laid down the following recommendation: "Damage caused to data may lead to liability where (a) liability arises from contract; or (b) liability arises from interference with a property right in the medium on which the data was stored or with another interest protected as a property right under the applicable law; or (c) the damage was caused by conduct infringing criminal law or other legally binding rules whose purpose is to avoid such damage; or (d) there was an intention to cause harm". Report from the Expert Group on Liability and New Technologies – New Technologies Formation "Liability for Artificial Intelligence and Other Emerging Digital Technologies", 21 November 2019, at p. 59.

[64] Annex to the European Parliament's Resolution of 20 October 2020 on a civil liability regime for AI – A. Principles and Aims of the Proposal, principle 8.

See also European Parliament's Resolution of 20 October 2020 on a civil liability regime for AI, section "Different liability rules for different tasks", at point 19.

scope of compensable damage to also cover damage to digital assets, including privacy infringements, consumers' data loss, as well as environmental damage.[65]

On the other hand, corporations and organisations representing businesses stressed that liability should be limited to physical/material damage to consumers and urged the Commission not to adopt option 1.b of the Commission's Inception Impact Assessment. In particular, they rejected an extension of liability under the Project Liability Directive to non-material damage as not necessary, since non-material damage can be compensated under data protection law, anti-discrimination law and tort law. For instance, they argued that existing EU legislation already provides redress mechanisms for consumers for many types of

[65] For comments supporting the Commission's proposal see, for instance, the following:

Contribution by The Future Society (TFS), "Liability rules for Trust in Excellence & Excellence in Trust - Inception Impact Assessment - Adapting liability rules to the digital age and circular economy", Belgium, 28 July 2021: "the boundary between material and non-material damages evolves: some non-material damages (notably environmental or related to data loss) have an increasingly material interpretation as they are increasingly assigned a monetary value. This gives rise to uncertainty. The PLD's recital does not clear this uncertainty, by stipulating that the Directive should not prejudice compensation for pain and 'other non-material damages'. As these damages could be interpreted as material and as consumers would naturally expect defective software producers to be held liable for non-material damage the software causes -as is the case with other products they use day-to-day-, we believe non-material damages should be included in the range of damages for which compensation can be claimed. This would reduce uncertainty for both producers and consumers, incentivize the prevention of these newly recognised damages and facilitate compensation. Option 1.b therefore seems to us to be the most in line with the objectives of the liability framework" (at p. 3).

The Future of Life Institute (FLI) comments on the Commission's Inception Impact Assessment on "Civil liability – adapting liability rules to the digital age and artificial intelligence", submitted on 28 July 2021:

> FLI supports a revision of the Product Liability Directive as described in 1.a. and its extension to non-material damages (option 1.b.). We believe this option addresses most of the specific challenges posed by digital products today such as the fact that they can be updated after being put in circulation, the complex interactions between different products and services, and the cybersecurity risks. We note that including non-material damages is especially important for digital products, as was explained thoughtfully by the Commission in its prior White Paper. Non-material damages include privacy infringements, consumers' data loss, environmental damage, and loss of chance (e.g. if an algorithmic decision-making system deprived someone of a job opportunity) (at p. 3).

BEUC (the European Consumer Organisation), "Product Liability 2.0 - How to make EU rules fit for consumers in the digital age", submitted on 07.05.2020: "Revise the scope of compensable damage: the PLD should extend the scope of compensable damage to also cover damage to digital assets, including data" (at p.2). ... "The PLD leaves aside compensation for pure economic losses. Yet with the life of consumers being increasingly virtualised, digital products have triggered significant changes in the types of harm likely to impair their wellbeing (e.g. loss of data, identify theft, privacy, etc). In this context, it is unclear whether data loss falls within the scope of the PLD. As the Expert Group has noted, it is "not universally accepted throughout Europe that damage to or the destruction of data is a property loss since in some legal systems the notion of property is limited to corporeal objects and excludes intangibles". In line with the recommendation of the Expert Group, damage to data should be regarded as a damage compensable under the PLD (at p. 15).

non-material damages (Articles 79(1) and 82(1) of the GDPR). Also, they pointed out that damages for privacy infringements are difficult to quantify and the procedural burdens for all parties involved would be disproportionate. Financial liability associated with non-material damages is less predictable, and thus more difficult for providers to foresee and adequately address, than is the case with material damages. Furthermore, environmental damages could raise complex issues of causation that would be difficult to address under a strict liability regime. Indeed, environmental damages appear unfit to be included in the scope of the Product Liability Directive since they are associated with harm done to society rather than to an individual consumer.[66]

---

[66] Contributions opposing option 1.b of the Commission's Inception Impact Assessment include the following:

Microsoft argued that liability should be limited to physical / material damage to consumers: "Option 1.b of the IIA proposes to 'extend the range of damages for which compensation can be claimed under the [PLD] to non-material damages (e.g., data loss, privacy infringements or environmental damage)'. We urge the Commission not to adopt this proposal. First, existing EU legislation already provides redress mechanisms for consumers for many types of non-material damages. For example, Article 79(1) of the GDPR gives data subjects the right to an effective judicial remedy for any infringement of their rights under the Regulation, and Article 82(1) gives them the right to obtain compensation for both material and non-material damage. Providing a separate, potentially overlapping basis for compensation will cause confusion, could lead to forum shopping, and could lead to double claims for a single harm. Second, the potential financial liability associated with non-material damages is less predictable, and thus more difficult for providers to accurately foresee and adequately address, than is the case with material damages". See Microsoft comments on the Inception Impact Assessment "Adapting liability rules to the digital age and circular economy", 28 July 2021, at p. 3.

Google's response to the Commission's 2021 Inception Impact Assessment: "There are also fundamental issues with the notion of extending the types of damage for which losses are recoverable via strict liability to non-material damages. Doing so would put a disproportionate burden on software developers". ... "Furthermore, many of the specific types of non-material damages referenced in the IIA raise their own challenges. For example, damages for privacy infringements are notoriously difficult to quantify and the procedural burdens for all parties involved would be disproportionate. These risks to consumers are also already covered by the GDPR, which imposes severe penalties, providing a strong incentive for producers to protect their customers' privacy and personal data. Environmental damages, as another example, would raise particularly complex issues of causation and remoteness that would be difficult to address under a strict liability regime. It is also hard to imagine how environmental damage could be associated with an individual consumer in a way that would be appropriate to a consumer protection framework like the Directive". See Google's views on the European Commission's inception impact assessment on civil liability—adapting liability rules to the digital age and AI, 28 July 2021, at p. 3.

See also Input from ZVEI – German Electrical and Electronic Manufacturers' Association on "Civil liability – adapting liability rules to the digital age and artificial intelligence", submitted on28.07.2021: "We reject an extension of liability under the PLD to non-material damage (1.b). Such an extension is not necessary, as non-material damage can be compensated, for example, under data protection law, anti-discrimination law and tort law" (at p. 2).

ACEA (The European Automobile Manufacturers' Association) response to the European Commission's inception impact assessment on civil liability—Adapting liability rules to the digital age and circular economy, 28.07.2021: "ACEA does not believe that the range of damages covered under the Directive needs to be extended to cover non-material damages. The automobile industry

6.6.1.2 Imposing Strict Liability on the Provider, Operator, and Users of AI-Based Services

The Commission stated that the extent of harmonisation of strict liability could vary, following a 'risk-based' approach and possibly taking into consideration whether the

---

believes that compensation for such damages can already be sought by injured parties under the Directive (e.g., psychological harm) or under other EU instruments (e.g. GDPR). Environmental damages appear particularly unfit to be included in the scope of the Directive since they relate to harm done to society rather than to an individual" (at p. 2).

Response of the App Association (ACT) to the European Commission's inception impact assessment on civil liability—Adapting liability rules to the digital age and circular economy, 28.07.2021: "Option 1 proposes the adaptation of strict liability rules to the digital age and circular economy. This could be done as option 1.a. proposes under which strict liability rules would cover intangible products that cause physical or material damages, e.g., software updates, refurbishments, defects resulting from interaction with other devices (IoT), cybersecurity risks and online market-places where the producer cannot be identified. Option 1.b. suggests extending the range of damages on top of 1.a. to non-material damages, including loss of privacy or data or environmental damage. The App Association opposes options 1.a. and 1.b. as neither of them take a risk-based approach or balance risk-mitigation and liability" (at p. 5.)

Bitkom Bundesverband Informationswirtschaft, Telekommunikation und neue Medien e.V. (Federal Association for Information Technology, Telecommunications and New Media), "Position Paper - Inception Impact Assessment: Adapting liability rules to the digital age and artificial intelligence", 27.07.2021: "Product liability is subject to comparatively low requirements in order to provide adequate protection primarily for consumers, irrespective of existing contracts. To compensate for this, damages can only be claimed in the event of infringements of particularly important legal interests. This balance must not be eliminated by an unrestricted expansion of the protected legal interests. Infringements of data privacy and personal rights with the aid of digital tools are already sanctioned outside of product liability in data privacy law, anti-discrimination law and tort liability. There are therefore no gaps in protection in this respect. It would not make sense to double the already severe sanctions for companies. A necessary risk-oriented approach to liability also means that there should not be multiple liability for any damage under the same conditions. It must therefore remain the case that data loss only leads to product liability if the data loss can also be seen as material damage to the data carrier" (at p. 5).

The Information Technology Industry Council (ITI), "Comments to European Commission's Inception Impact Assessment on the Revision of EU Liability Rule", 28.07.2021: "Option 1b proposes to extend the range of damages for which compensation can be claimed to non-material damages. The PLD currently defines damage as death, personal injury, or damage to the product in questions or other products. We suggest avoiding references to immaterial damages as they could potentially lead to waves of compensation claims for producers on illegitimate grounds and lead to a backlog in assessing cases all while mostly being covered already by existing legislation in the fields of data protection, non-discrimination and freedom of expression" (at p. 3).

Fujitsu, "Response to the European Commission's inception impact assessment on civil liability - adapting liability rules to the digital age and artificial intelligence, submitted on 28.07.2021: "Extending the range of damages for which compensation can be claimed based on the Directive to include non-material damages (e.g. loss of data or privacy infringements) would not correspond to the original purpose of the Directive. The original goal is providing consumers with compensation, even without a contract and regardless of fault, under low prerequisites if they have been harmed by a defective product. This low prerequisites for a claim are balanced by the fact that the claim must refer to injury to the person or damage to an object for private use, i.e. damage to high legal interests. This balance would be affected by an extension to immaterial damage".

AI-systems in question have a specific risk profile (such as those endangering the lives, health and property of members of the public).[67] This is in line with the Report

---

[67] "The extent of harmonisation of strict liability can vary: (i) Recommendation to Member States of a targeted and risk-based harmonisation of the strict liability of operators/users of AI-systems that enable products and services with a specific risk profile (such as those endangering the lives, health and property of members of the public), possibly coupled with an insurance obligation. (ii) Targeted and risk-based harmonising legislative measure covering the same elements as 1.c (i). This option would create for those AI-systems with a specific risk profile a liability framework at EU level similar to what happens in almost all Member States' legal systems as regards motor vehicle liability: strict liability of the producer for defects under the Directive as well as strict liability of the owner/operator. (iii) Risk-based, but broader harmonisation of the operator's/user's strict liability, similar to 1.c (ii) but including additional aspects such as statutory limitation periods for lodging a claim and rules for joint liability, as envisaged by European Parliament (EP) Resolution 2020/2014(INL). (iv) Strict liability of the operators/users of AI-systems in general (irrespective of their risk profile). Commission's Inception Impact Assessment "Adapting liability rules to the digital age and circular economy", Ref. Ares(2021)4266516, 30.06.2021, p. 4.

See Microsoft comments on the Inception Impact Assessment "Adapting liability rules to the digital age and circular economy", 28 July 2021, at p. 4: "Reserve strict liability for AI systems presenting high risks of severe harm: For the reasons set out above, the need to impose strict liability on products or services that incorporate AI (Option 1.c), or to alter the burdens of proof in cases involving such products or services (Option 2.2) is not evident. If the Commission nonetheless moves forward, we urge it to proceed incrementally and focus in the first instance on AI systems presenting unique particularly severe risks. For instance, the Commission might consider limiting strict liability to some specifically defined AI systems within the "high risk" AI systems under the proposed AI Act (so long as compliance with its requirements, as well as other recognized defenses to strict liability, such as contributory negligence, product misuse or assumption of risk would constitute a defense). Imposing strict liability on all products and services that incorporate AI—irrespective of whether the product or services presents a unique and severe risk of harm, or whether the AI component is a contributing factor to that risk—makes little sense from a policy perspective".

Similarly, see BSA—The Software Alliance, "Comments on the Initial Impact Assessment on adapting liability rules to the digital age", 28.07.2021: "Ensure any new rules are technology neutral: the IIA proposes a range of specific reforms to the EU liability regime that would target AI systems and the products that integrate them (see Options 1(c), 2.1(c), 2.2(b)-(d)). Products and services shouldn't be subject to unique or heightened liability rules simply because they integrate AI. That approach will deter providers from offering AI-driven products that may in fact make consumers safer, out of fear that doing so could expose them to increased liability. Further, because AI is deployed in a virtually limitless set of scenarios — from AI-powered tangible products and fully autonomous systems to AI software that merely assists or informs human action and decision-making, and including systems that evolve through machine learning and / or can be personalized — a one-sized-fits-all liability regime (as proposed in Option 1(c)(iv) of the IIA) would be all but impossible to implement. In effect, such a regime would impose the same liability rules on both driverless cars and, for example, AI systems that retailers use to predict what color of paint a particular customer might prefer" (at p. 3).

On the other hand, see BEUC (the European Consumer Organisation) feedback on the European Commission's Inception Impact Assessment on "Civil liability – adapting liability rules to the digital age and artificial intelligence", submitted on 28.07.2021: "BEUC believes that many of the problems relating to digital and AI may be addressed via an ambitious revision of the PLD. However, the European Commission seems willing to develop a separate and complementary instrument on civil liability for AI. We called on the Commission to carefully consider the need to build new liability rules based on the risk profile of AI systems. This is because a risk-based approach is not in the interest of consumers without a solid safety net provided by the PLD. From

from the Expert Group on Liability and New Technologies[68] and the Commission's earlier view in 2020.[69] Furthermore, it follows the thinking of the European Parliament's Resolution of 20 October 2020 on a civil liability regime for AI which underlined that the type of AI-system the operator is exercising control over should be a determining factor regarding liability. In this regard, the European Parliament stressed that an AI-system that entails an inherent high risk and acts autonomously potentially endangers the user or the general public to a much higher degree and in a

the perspective of consumers, it does not matter whether the AI system causing the harm has been classified as low or high risk, what matters for consumers is a fair compensation for the damage suffered, regardless of what type of risk ultimately materialized. BEUC also believes that a very limited number of AI systems may ultimately fall within the "high-risk" category leaving thus the bulk of products as "low risks" with the risk of having different set of rules at national levels, which could ultimately contribute to fragmenting the EU Single Market. That is why we urge the Commission to ensure consistency between the revised PLD and this additional instrument on civil liability for AI" (at p. 4).

[68] Report from the Expert Group on Liability and New Technologies – New Technologies Formation "Liability for Artificial Intelligence and Other Emerging Digital Technologies", 21 November 2019, which stated that "emerging digital technologies make it difficult to apply fault-based liability rules, due to the lack of well-established models of proper functioning of these technologies and the possibility of their developing as a result of learning without direct human control" (at p. 23). This is why the Report pointed out that strict liability of the operator of some emerging digital technology may be justified: "a person operating a permissible technology that nevertheless carries an increased risk of harm to others, for example AI-driven robots in public spaces, should be subject to strict liability for damage resulting from its operation" (at pp. 3 and 40); "strict liability is an appropriate response to the risks posed by emerging digital technologies, if, for example, they are operated in non-private environments and may typically cause significant harm" (at p. 39).

[69] According to the Commission's thinking—based on the analysis of the Report from the Expert Group on Liability and New Technologies –, the application of strict liability should be limited to situations where the emerging technologies may create specific risks (which are likely to arise in circumstances where digital technologies move in public spaces, e.g., drones, autonomous cars, traffic management services), expose the public at large to risks, and cause significant harm to life, health, and property: "the operation of some autonomous AI devices and services could have a specific risk profile in terms of liability, because they may cause significant harm to important legal interests like life, health and property, and expose the public at large to risks. This could mainly concern AI devices that move in public spaces (e.g. fully autonomous vehicles, drones and package delivery robots) or AI-based services with similar risks (e.g. traffic management services guiding or controlling vehicles or management of power distribution). The challenges of autonomy and opacity to national tort laws could be addressed following a risk-based approach. Strict liability schemes could ensure that whenever that risk materialises, the victim is compensated regardless of fault. The impact of choosing who should be strictly liable for such operations on the development and uptake of AI would need to be carefully assessed and a risk-based approach be considered". Commission "Report on the safety and liability implications of Artificial Intelligence, the Internet of Things and robotics", Brussels, COM (2020) 64 final, 19.2.2020, at p. 16.

manner that is random and goes beyond what can reasonably be expected.[70] Therefore, according to the European Parliament, different liability rules should apply for different risks, following a risk-based approach, and, to this end, it stated that "it seems reasonable to set up a common strict liability regime for those high-risk autonomous AI-systems".[71]

Option 1.c of the Commission's 2021 Inception Impact Assessment (IAA) proposed to impose strict liability on the "provider" of AI-based services, the "operators/users" of such services, or both, and, therefore, injured parties would only have to prove that the damage emanates from the sphere of the operator of the AI-system.[72] On the other hand, various corporations and organisations representing

---

[70] European Parliament's Resolution of 20 October 2020 on a civil liability regime for AI, section "Liability of the operator", at point 15.

See also the Annex to the European Parliament's Resolution of 20 October 2020 on a civil liability regime for AI – Text of the Proposal for a Regulation on liability for the operation of AI systems, at recital 13: "This means that at the start of the autonomous operation of the AI-system, the majority of the potentially affected persons are unknown and not identifiable, for example persons on a public square or in a neighbouring house, compared to the operation of an AI-system that involves specific persons, who have regularly consented to its deployment before, for example surgery in a hospital or a sales demonstration in a small shop".

[71] European Parliament's Resolution of 20 October 2020 on a civil liability regime for AI, section "Liability of the operator", at point 14.

[72] Commission's Inception Impact Assessment "Adapting liability rules to the digital age and circular economy", Ref. Ares(2021)4266516, 30.06.2021, p. 4.

See also: BEUC (the European Consumer Organisation), "Product Liability 2.0 - How to make EU rules fit for consumers in the digital age", submitted on 07.05.2020: "Under the PLD (Art.3), liability rests on the 'producer,' which covers: - The manufacturer of the finished product. - The producer of any raw material or the manufacturer of any component part. - Any person, who, by putting their name or other distinguishing feature on the product, presents themself as a producer. The following persons may also be held liable under the PLD: - The person who imports a product into the EU. - The person supplying a product where the producer or the importer cannot be identified and where the supplier fails to inform, within a reasonable time, the injured person of the identity of the producer or of the person who supplied them with the product. Why this is problematic: Current EU product liability rules do not apply to all parties involved in the supply chain. Many actors who come to be in contact with the product still fall outside the scope of the PLD. Yet in practice, digital goods require the intervention of many different parties (e.g. manufacturers, software developers, creators of digital content etc.) It is, for example, unclear whether stand-alone software developers fall within the scope of the PLD. If the PLD is revised to also cover digital content and digital services, those providing digital input should also be considered as "manufacturers of any component part", and thus be held liable as well. In any case, all professionals involved in the production of digital goods should be held jointly liable if their activities have affected the reasonable expectations which users may have about their product. Consumers' options for recourse should not be prevented by problems in identifying the relevant liable party in situations where different parties are involved in the production chain" (at p. 18). . . . "Clarify the scope of liable persons (including online marketplaces): • All professionals involved in the production of digital goods should be held jointly liable if their activities have affected the reasonable expectations which users may have about their products. • Online marketplaces should bear subsidiary liability as 'suppliers' under the PLD. Online marketplaces should be held liable provided that at least one of the following conditions is fulfilled: (1) The producer cannot be identified; (2) The marketplace fails to inform the consumer in due time of the identity of the

businesses opposed this option and stressed that "if software developers are subject to strict liability for any bug in their code, it could effectively forestall the deployment of virtually all software in Europe, and disproportionately impact European SMEs. Applying strict liability to software updates and refurbishments would further disincentivize software development and maintenance by effectively removing any time-limitation on strict liability, making harder for producers to extend the useful lives of digital products and address bugs and vulnerabilities in software. Such a drastic change would destroy the current well-functioning balance struck between business innovation and consumer protection, and is unnecessary. ... In addition, software providers have limited control over security updates actually being accepted by end users, meaning this approach could make software providers directly liable for the omissions of other market participants".[73]

---

producer and does not enable communication between the consumer and the producer by providing relevant contact details; (3) The marketplace received clear evidence about non-compliant products on its platforms; (4) The producer is identified but does not take measures to remedy the harm, or if; (5) The marketplace has a predominant influence or control in the transaction chain" (at pp. 2, 9 and 19).

[73] Google's views on the European Commission's inception impact assessment on civil liability—adapting liability rules to the digital age and AI, 28.07.2021, at p. 2.

Furthermore, see the following comments received by various corporations and business associations/organisations:

Microsoft comments on the Inception Impact Assessment "Adapting liability rules to the digital age and circular economy", 28 July 2021, at pp. 3-4: "Option 1.c of the IIA proposes to impose strict liability on the "provider" of AI-based services, the "operators/users" of such services, or both. ... We believe that imposing any form of new liability rules, including strict liability, on products or services merely because they incorporate AI is not needed. If the Commission nonetheless moves forward on these proposals, we believe these rules will be most effective if they impose liability on the entity that is in the best position to foresee and mitigate risk. In many cases, this will be the entity that controls how and whether the final product or service incorporating the AI features is deployed or otherwise put into service (e.g., a retailer that deploys a facial recognition system; a bank that uses an AI tool to generate consumer credit ratings). This entity can then contractually allocate indemnification for any defects in the system's components to relevant suppliers, through indemnity clauses and the like. This is a common practice for other complex products that involve multiple suppliers and ensures that parties address financial responsibility for any harms based on the unique attributes and characteristics of the product or service at issue". ... "Any change to the EU's product liability framework should align with and complement the EU's broader consumer protection and product safety regimes. ... The Commission's proposed AI Act, once adopted, will also impose a comprehensive EU-wide safety regime on AI systems. The Commission should allow those rules to take effect before deciding whether amendment of the EU's liability regime is also needed. If the Commission does move ahead with changes before then, it will be important to ensure alignment between all these regimes. For instance, any AI system that complies with the AI Act's requirements, including with any standards or common specifications adopted under the Act, enjoys a presumption that it is not defective in that regard, and therefore cannot form the basis of a strict liability claim" (at pp. 2–3).

BSA—The Software Alliance, "Comments on the Initial Impact Assessment on adapting liability rules to the digital age", 28.07.2021: "Impose liability on the party best able to mitigate risk. As the proposed AI Act recognizes, many AI systems are developed by multiple entities working in collaboration, and they have the potential to operate in a wide range of different settings, with the involvement of a number of actors. Some parties create "enabling technologies" for AI —

As the Commission stressed, option 1.c "harmonise[s] the existing strict liability schemes of operators/users that apply to AI-equipped products and providers of AI-based services (where injured parties only have to prove that the damage emanates from the sphere of the operator of the AI-system). Following existing

such as database hosting capabilities, template tools and AI models. Other parties may customize these tools for specific use cases. And these parties may be separate from the party that actually deploys the AI in the real world. A key goal of any reform to the EU product liability regime should be to ensure that liability for harm falls on the entity best positioned to foresee and mitigate risk — generally the user, as suggested in IIA Option 1(c). This would be similar to the GDPR's concept of controller. Article 29 Working Party guidance on controllers and processors (WP 169) describes this party as the "determining body" that decides the "how" and the "why" of a processing operation. Applying this concept in the context of AI, the "AI controller" will generally be the deployer of an AI system (e.g., a vehicle manufacturer that integrates an AI-driven language recognition system into an automobile, or a bank that uses an AI tool to score consumers for loans)" (at pp. 3-4). ... "Apply strict liability only in narrow circumstances, to the highest risk AI. The type of strict liability seemingly contemplated in Option 1(c) — i.e. liability that is imposed regardless of the producer's fault or whether a product is defective — is generally reserved for extreme circumstances involving abnormally dangerous activities that present substantial risks to others. In effect, the "condition" of allowing this substantial risk is that the party imposing it must take responsibility for harms that result from it, irrespective of any fault or product defect. Strict liability should only be imposed on AI systems in similarly narrow circumstances. Given the current state of AI development and deployment, subjecting today's AI systems to strict liability of the sort contemplated in IIA Option 1(c) is unwarranted. When considering future AI-driven products, strict liability would be appropriate only when a product operates in public spaces and poses a substantial risk of physical harm to "innocent bystanders" (i.e. individuals that did not willingly engage with the AI enabled product in some way)" (at p. 4).

Bitkom Bundesverband Informationswirtschaft, Telekommunikation und neue Medien e.V. (Federal Association for Information Technology, Telecommunications and New Media), "Position Paper - Inception Impact Assessment: Adapting liability rules to the digital age and artificial intelligence", 27.07.2021: "the maintenance of software requires considerable effort on the part of the manufacturer. The more complex and specific the software is, the greater is the effort needed. For this reason, software maintenance services are regularly provided in business transactions between companies only on the basis of special contractual arrangements and in return for payment. Within the scope of software maintenance, the specific operating environment of a software product, the interaction with other hardware and software components, and current technical progress as well as current cyber security threats can be taken into account appropriately and on a customer-specific basis. A similar update obligation based on product liability would not only deprive manufacturers of an important business segment, but such an obligation would simply not be feasible for them in terms of the necessary customer individualization. A legal obligation to guarantee that updates are free of errors that goes even further would further increase costs and would no longer be calculable for manufacturers. Ultimately, the manufacturer of software, and in particular of AI systems, can only be expected to accept strict liability to the extent that he has direct and immediate influence on the course of events. However, such controllability of the course of events is only given on the basis of a contract or until a product is placed on the market" (at p. 4).

Response of the Center for Data Innovation to the European Commission's inception impact assessment on civil liability—adapting liability rules to the digital age and AI, submitted on 28.07.2021, at p. 3: "Not all products containing AI will incur novel product liability risks, and the inclusion of AI in a product should not a priori force strict liability because of the aforementioned costs to insurance and innovation. The concept of strict liability only makes sense where the risk profile of the product in question is appropriate, a topic that insurers (as well as producers and consumers) will be able to comment further on".

national models, the operator could be defined as a person, other than the producer, who is able to exercise a degree of control over the risks associated with the operation (such as owners and service providers). Alternatively, the strictly liable person could be identified by reference to the 'user' as defined in the proposed AI Act".[74]

The Commission's view follows the European Parliament's approach which stated that its 2020 proposal for a Regulation on liability for the operation of AI systems should focus on civil liability claims against the operator of an AI-system.[75] According to the European Parliament's proposal, a strict liability regime for high-risk[76] AI systems should apply, i.e. the operator of a high-risk AI-system should be

---

[74] Commission's Inception Impact Assessment "Adapting liability rules to the digital age and circular economy", Ref. Ares(2021)4266516, 30.06.2021, p. 4.

[75] European Parliament's Resolution of 20 October 2020 on a civil liability regime for AI, section "Liability and Artificial Intelligence", at point 10.

See also the Annex to the European Parliament's Resolution of 20 October 2020 on a civil liability regime for AI—Text of the Proposal for a Regulation on liability for the operation of AI systems, at recital 9. As it was stated: "This Regulation sets out rules for the civil liability claims of natural and legal persons against operators of AI-systems" (Article 1).

The Parliament also stated that civil liability rules involving the operator should cover all AI-systems, irrespective of where the operation takes place and whether it happens physically or virtually: "This Regulation should enable the affected person to bring forward liability claims throughout the liability chain and throughout the lifecycle of an AI-system. It should also cover in principle all AI-systems, no matter where they are operating and whether the operations take place physically or virtually. The majority of liability claims under this Regulation should, however, address cases of third-party liability, where an AI-system operates in a public space and exposes many persons to a risk. In that situation, the affected persons will often not be aware of the operating AI-system and will not have any contractual or legal relationship towards the operator. Consequently, the operation of the AI-system puts them into a situation in which, in the event of harm or damage being caused, they only have fault-based liability claims against the operator of the AI-system, while facing severe difficulties to prove fault on the part of the operator". Annex to the European Parliament's Resolution of 20 October 2020 on a civil liability regime for AI – Text of the Proposal for a Regulation on liability for the operation of AI systems, at recital 12.

[76] According to the European Parliament, for the purposes of the proposal for a Regulation on liability for the operation of AI systems, the definition of 'high risk' is the following: "... (c) 'high risk' means a significant potential in an autonomously operating AI-system to cause harm or damage to one or more persons in a manner that is random and goes beyond what can reasonably be expected; the significance of the potential depends on the interplay between the severity of possible harm or damage, the degree of autonomy of decision-making, the likelihood that the risk materializes and the manner and the context in which the AI-system is being used". Annex to the European Parliament's Resolution of 20 October 2020 on a civil liability regime for AI – Text of the Proposal for a Regulation on liability for the operation of AI systems, Article 3 (Definitions).

According to the European Parliament, determining whether an AI-system is high-risk (i.e. how significant the potential is of a high-risk AI-system to cause harm or damage) depends "on the interplay between the purpose of use for which the AI system is put on the market, the manner in which the AI-system is being used, the severity of the potential harm or damage, the degree of autonomy of decision-making that can result in harm and the likelihood that the risk materialises. The degree of severity should be determined based on relevant factors such as the extent of the potential harm resulting from the operation on affected persons, including in particular effects on fundamental rights, the number of affected persons, the total value for the potential damage, as well

strictly liable for any harm or damage that was caused by a physical or virtual activity, device or process driven by that AI-system.[77] Therefore, unless the harm or

---

as the harm to society as a whole. The likelihood for the harm or damage to occur should be determined based on relevant factors such as the role of the algorithmic calculations in the decision-making process, the complexity of the decision and the reversibility of the effects. Ultimately, the manner of usage should depend on relevant factors such as the context and sector in which the AI-system operates, if it could have legal or factual effects on important legally protected rights of the affected person, and whether the effects can reasonably be avoided". Annex to the European Parliament's Resolution of 20 October 2020 on a civil liability regime for AI—Text of the Proposal for a Regulation on liability for the operation of AI systems, at recital 13.

See also the European Parliament's proposal for a Regulation on ethical principles for AI, robotics and related technologies, which defined the term 'high risk' as follows: "'High risk' means a significant risk entailed by the development, deployment and use of artificial intelligence, robotics and related technologies to cause injury or harm to individuals or society in breach of fundamental rights and safety rules as laid down in Union law, considering their specific use or purpose, the sector where they are developed, deployed or used and the severity of injury or harm that can be expected to occur". European Parliament Resolution of 20 October 2020 with recommendations to the Commission on a framework of ethical aspects of artificial intelligence, robotics and related technologies (2020/2012 (INL)), P9_TA(2020)0275 – Annex to the Resolution: detailed recommendations as to the content of the proposal requested, B. Text of the Legislative Proposal Requested - Proposal for a Regulation of the European Parliament and of the Council on ethical principles for the development, deployment and use of artificial intelligence, robotics and related technologies ("European Parliament's Proposal for a Regulation on ethical principles for the development, deployment and use of artificial intelligence, robotics and related technologies"), at Article 4(e). See also at ground 11: "Artificial intelligence, robotics and related technologies whose development, deployment and use entail a significant risk of causing injury or harm to individuals or society in breach of fundamental rights and safety rules as laid down in Union law, should be considered as high-risk technologies. For the purposes of assessing them as such, the sector where they are developed, deployed or used, their specific use or purpose and the severity of the injury or harm that can be expected to occur should be considered. The degree of severity should be determined based on the extent of the potential injury or harm, the number of affected persons, the total value of damage caused and the harm to society as a whole. Severe types of injury and harm are, for instance, violations of children's, consumers' or workers' rights that, due to their extent, the number of children, consumers or workers affected or their impact on society as a whole entail a significant risk to breach fundamental rights and safety rules as laid down in Union law. This Regulation should provide an exhaustive and cumulative list of high-risk sectors, and high-risk uses and purposes".

In line with the approach followed by the Commission's 2020 White Paper on AI, the Annex to the European Parliament's proposal for a Regulation on ethical principles for AI, robotics and related technologies, provided an exhaustive and cumulative list of high-risk sectors and high-risk uses and purposes that entail a risk of breach of fundamental rights and safety rules. "*High-risk sectors*: • Employment • Education • Healthcare • Transport • Energy • Public sector (asylum, migration, border controls, judiciary and social security services) • Defence and security • Finance, banking, insurance". "*High-risk uses or purposes*: • Recruitment • Grading and assessment of students • Allocation of public funds • Granting loans • Trading, brokering, taxation, etc. • Medical treatments and procedures • Electoral processes and political campaigns • Public sector decisions that have a significant and direct impact on the rights and obligations of natural or legal persons • Automated driving • Traffic management • Autonomous military systems • Energy production and distribution • Waste management • Emissions control".

[77] Annex to the European Parliament's Resolution of 20 October 2020 on a civil liability regime for AI—Text of the Proposal for a Regulation on liability for the operation of AI systems, Article 4(1).

damage was caused by force majeure, operators of high-risk AI-systems should not be able to exonerate themselves from liability by claiming that they acted with due diligence or that the harm or damage was caused by an autonomous activity, device or process driven by their AI-system.[78] This is also in line with the Report of the Expert Group on Liability and New Technologies which stated that "strict liability should lie with the person who is in control of the risk connected with the operation of emerging digital technologies and who benefits from their operation (operator)".[79]

This is justified by the fact that the operator exercises a degree of control over a risk associated with the AI-system, which is comparable to that of an owner of a car. Besides, due to the AI-system's characteristics of complexity and connectivity, the operator will be very often the first visible contact point for the affected person.[80] According to the European Parliament, in line with the Report from the Expert Group on Liability and New Technologies,[81] more than one person could be considered as operating an AI-system and, therefore, the term 'operator' should cover both the frontend and the backend operator, as long as the latter is not covered by the Product Liability Directive.[82] Currently, it is the frontend operator who

---

All high-risk AI-systems and critical sectors where those systems are used must be exhaustively listed in the Annex to the proposed Regulation on liability for the operation of AI systems, whereas the Commission must review the Annex at least every six months and, if necessary, will have the power to amend this exhaustive list through a delegated act. See Annex to the European Parliament's Resolution of 20 October 2020 on a civil liability regime for AI—Text of the Proposal for a Regulation on liability for the operation of AI systems, Article 4(2)).

[78] Annex to the European Parliament's Resolution of 20 October 2020 on a civil liability regime for AI—Text of the Proposal for a Regulation on liability for the operation of AI systems, Article 4(3).

[79] Report from the Expert Group on Liability and New Technologies—New Technologies Formation "Liability for Artificial Intelligence and Other Emerging Digital Technologies", 21 November 2019, Key Finding [10], at pp. 6, 39, 41.

[80] European Parliament's Resolution of 20 October 2020 on a civil liability regime for AI, section "Liability and Artificial Intelligence", at point 10.

See also the Annex to the European Parliament's Resolution of 20 October 2020 on a civil liability regime for AI—Text of the Proposal for a Regulation on liability for the operation of AI systems, at recital 10.

[81] The Report from the Expert Group on Liability and New Technologies pointed out that, with emerging digital technologies, there are often two or more operators, i.e. the owner/user/keeper who operates the technology on the frontend and, at the same time, a central backend provider who, on an ongoing basis, provides essential backend support services. In those cases, the Report proposed the following: "If there are two or more operators, in particular (a) the person primarily deciding on and benefitting from the use of the relevant technology (frontend operator) and (b) the person continuously defining the features of the relevant technology and providing essential and ongoing backend support (backend operator), strict liability should lie with the one who has more control over the risks of the operation". Report from the Expert Group on Liability and New Technologies – New Technologies Formation "Liability for Artificial Intelligence and Other Emerging Digital Technologies", 21 November 2019, Key Finding [11], at p. 39.

[82] Annex to the European Parliament's Resolution of 20 October 2020 on a civil liability regime for AI—Text of the Proposal for a Regulation on liability for the operation of AI systems, recital 10: "As there is often more than one person who could, in a meaningful way, be considered as 'operating' the AI-system, under this Regulation 'operator' should be understood to cover both

appears to be the person that primarily decides on the use of the AI-system; however, the backend operator is expected to have a higher degree of control over the operational risks as emerging digital technologies are becoming more backend-focused.[83] The term 'exercising control' means any action of the operator that

---

the frontend and the backend operator. Although in general, the frontend operator appears as the person who 'primarily' decides on the use of the AI-system, the backend operator could in fact have a higher degree of control over the operational risks. If the backend operator also qualifies as 'producer' as defined in Article 3 of the Product Liability Directive, that Directive should apply to him or her. If there is only one operator and that operator is also the producer of the AI-system, this Regulation should prevail over the Product Liability Directive".

See also Annex to the European Parliament's Resolution of 20 October 2020 on a civil liability regime for AI—Text of the Proposal for a Regulation on liability for the operation of AI systems, Article 3 (d)-(f): "(d)'operator' means both the frontend and the backend operator as long as the latter's liability is not already covered by Directive 85/374/EEC; (e) 'frontend operator' means any natural or legal person who exercises a degree of control over a risk connected with the operation and functioning of the AI-system and benefits from its operation; (f) 'backend operator' means any natural or legal person who, on a continuous basis, defines the features of the technology and provides data and an essential backend support service and therefore also exercises a degree of control over the risk connected with the operation and functioning of the AI-system".

"Considers it appropriate to understand 'operator' to cover both the frontend and backend operator, as long as the latter is not covered by the PLD; notes that the frontend operator should be defined as the natural or legal person who exercises a degree of control over a risk connected with the operation and functioning of the AI-system and benefits from its operation; states that the backend operator should be defined as the natural or legal person who, on a continuous basis, defines the features of the technology, provides data and essential backend support service and therefore also exercises a degree of control over the risk connected with the operation and functioning of the AI-system; considers that exercising control means any action of the operator that influences the operation of the AI-system and thus the extent to which it exposes third parties to its potential risks". See European Parliament Resolution of 20 October 2020 with recommendations to the Commission on a civil liability regime for artificial intelligence (2020/2014(INL)) P9_TA (2020)0276, (section "Liability of the operator"), at point 12.

[83] Annex to the European Parliament's Resolution of 20 October 2020 on a civil liability regime for AI—Text of the Proposal for a Regulation on liability for the operation of AI systems, at recital 10.

See also European Parliament's Resolution of 20 October 2020 on a civil liability regime for AI, section "Liability of the operator", at point 12.

See also the Report from the Expert Group on Liability and New Technologies—New Technologies Formation "Liability for Artificial Intelligence and Other Emerging Digital Technologies", 21 November 2019, at pp. 41–42: "This backend operator may have a high degree of control over the operational risks others are exposed to. From an economic point of view, the backend operator also benefits from the operation, because that operator profits from data generated by the operation, or that operator's remuneration is directly calculated on the basis of the duration, continuous nature or intensity of the operation, or because a one-off payment this backend operator has received reflects the estimated overall duration, continuous nature and intensity of the operation. . . . While both control and benefit are decisive for qualifying a person as operator, the benefit is often very difficult to quantify, so relying only on benefit as the decisive factor for deciding who, out of two operators, should be liable, would lead to uncertainty. . . . Very often, the frontend operator will have more control, but where emerging digital technologies become more backend-focused, there may be cases where so much continuous control over the technology remains with the backend operator that—despite the fact that the technology is sold to individual owners—it is more convincing to hold the backend operator liable as the person primarily in a position to control, influences the operation of the AI-system and thus the extent to which it exposes third parties to its potential risks.[84]

6.6.2 *Other Options to Address Obstacles to Getting Compensation*

6.6.2.1 Options to Reduce Obstacles to Getting Compensation Under the Product Liability Directive

6.6.2.1.1 Alleviating the Burden of Proof

Option 2.1.a of the Commission's 2021 Inception Impact Assessment (IAA) proposed to alleviate the burden of proof by (i) obliging the producer to disclose technical information to the injured party and (ii) allowing courts to infer that a product is defective or caused the damage under certain circumstances, e.g. when other products in the same production series have already been proven to be defective or when a product clearly malfunctions.[85]

---

reduce and insure the risks associated with the use of the technology. ... Ideally, in order to avoid uncertainty, the legislator should define which operator is liable under which circumstances, and all other matters that need to be regulated (concerning insurance for example). For instance, the legislator could decide that for AVs with a level of automation of 4 or 5, it is the provider running the system and who enters the AV in the national registry who is liable. This provider would therefore also take out insurance and could pass on the premiums through the fees paid for its services. Where several providers fulfil the function of backend operators, one of them would have to be designated as responsible operator for every AV".

[84] Annex to the European Parliament's Resolution of 20 October 2020 on a civil liability regime for AI—Text of the Proposal for a Regulation on liability for the operation of AI systems, Article 3 (g): "'control' means any action of an operator that influences the operation of an AI-system and thus the extent to which the operator exposes third parties to the potential risks associated with the operation and functioning of the AI-system; such actions can impact the operation at any stage by determining the input, output or results, or can change specific functions or processes within the AI-system; the degree to which those aspects of the operation of the AI-system are determined by the action depends on the level of influence the operator has over the risk connected with the operation and functioning of the AI-system".

See also the Report from the Expert Group on Liability and New Technologies—New Technologies Formation "Liability for Artificial Intelligence and Other Emerging Digital Technologies", 21 November 2019, at p. 41:"'Control' is a variable concept, though, ranging from merely activating the technology, thus exposing third parties to its potential risks, to determining the output or result (such as entering the destination of a vehicle or defining the next tasks of a robot), and may include further steps in between, which affect the details of the operation from start to stop. However, the more sophisticated and more autonomous a system, the less someone exercises actual 'control' over the details of the operation, and defining and influencing the algorithms, for example by continuous updates, may have a greater impact than just starting the system".

[85] Commission's Inception Impact Assessment "Adapting liability rules to the digital age and circular economy", Ref. Ares(2021)4266516, 30.06.2021, p. 4.

It is recalled that the Report of the Expert Group on Liability and New Technologies stressed that "where a particular technology increases the difficulties of proving the existence of an element of liability beyond what can be reasonably expected, victims should be entitled to facilitation of proof".[86] In addition, the Report stated that "without prejudice to the reversal of the burden of proof proposed . . . , the burden of proving causation may be alleviated in light of the challenges of emerging digital technologies if a balancing of the following factors warrants doing so: (a) the likelihood that the technology at least contributed to the harm; (b) the likelihood that the harm was caused either by the technology or by some other cause within the same sphere; (c) the risk of a known defect within the technology, even though its actual causal impact is not self-evident; (d) the degree of ex-post traceability and intelligibility of processes within the technology that may have contributed to the cause (informational asymmetry); (e) the degree of ex-post accessibility and comprehensibility of data collected and generated by the technology (f) the kind and degree of harm potentially and actually caused".[87] Furthermore, the Report pointed out that the obligation to equip technology with means of recording information related to the operation of the technology ('logging by design')[88] should apply to producers. The Report highlighted the importance of

According to the response of the Center for Data Innovation to the European Commission's inception impact assessment on civil liability—adapting liability rules to the digital age and AI, submitted on 28.07.2021, "this option is a reasonable adjustment to the PLD that strengthens plaintiffs' discovery rights, holds producers accountable, and encourages the maintenance of proper development documentation. It does create a "guilty until proven innocent" standard for software-powered products" (at p. 3).

[86]Report from the Expert Group on Liability and New Technologies – New Technologies Formation "Liability for Artificial Intelligence and Other Emerging Digital Technologies", 21 November 2019, at p. 4.

[87]Ibid., Key Finding (26), at p. 8.

[88]'Logging by design' was also highlighted by the High-Level Expert Group on AI (AI HLEG) in its assessment list (which, inter alia, provides guidance on self-assessing whether the data and processes that yield the AI system's decisions are properly logged and well documented to allow for traceability and auditability of the algorithmic decision-making process). See "The Assessment List for Trustworthy Artificial Intelligence (ALTAI) for self-assessment", High-Level Expert Group on AI (AI HLEG), 17 July 2020: "Reliability, Fall-back plans and Reproducibility: Did you put in place verification and validation methods and documentation (e.g. logging) to evaluate and ensure different aspects of the AI system's reliability and reproducibility? (at p. 11); "Traceability: Did you put adequate logging practices in place to record the decision(s) or recommendation(s) of the AI system? (at p. 14); "Accountability – Auditability: Did you establish mechanisms that facilitate the AI system's auditability (e.g. traceability of the development process, the sourcing of training data and the logging of the AI system's processes, outcomes, positive and negative impact)?", at p. 21.

The importance of 'Logging by design' was also emphasised by the Commission's Report on the safety and liability implications of AI, IoT and robotics. See Commission "Report on the safety and liability implications of Artificial Intelligence, the Internet of Things and robotics", Brussels, COM (2020) 64 final, 19.2.2020, at p. 16: "one of the issues flagged by the Report from the New Technologies formation of the Expert Group on Liability and New Technologies is the situation when the potentially liable party has not logged the data relevant for assessing liability or is not willing to share them with the victim".

introducing an obligation to provide appropriate and proportionate logging and to disclose the necessary data to the victim and/or the person who compensates the victim in readable format.[89] Therefore, the Report from the Expert Group on Liability and New Technologies underlined that emerging digital technologies should come with logging features, and failure to comply with a logging and disclosure (providing reasonable access to logged data) duty should result in a reversal of the burden of proof: "failure to comply with a logging and disclosure duty should lead to a rebuttable presumption that the information would, if logged and disclosed, have revealed that the relevant element of liability is fulfilled".[90]

This obligation was also recommended by the European Parliament's proposal for a Regulation on liability for the operation of AI systems, which stressed that, in order to facilitate the operator to prove that he was not at fault, or to enable the affected person to prove the existence of fault (and thus to allow for the identification of the liabilities), producers of AI-systems should have the duty to cooperate with both parties concerned (i.e. at the request of the operator and the affected person), including by providing well-documented information, to the extent justified by the significance of the claim.[91]

6.6.2.1.2 Reversing the Burden of Proof

Option 2.1.b of the Commission's 2021 Inception Impact Assessment (IAA) went even further and proposed to reverse the burden of proof so that, in case a damage occurred, the producer would have to prove that the product was not defective.[92]

---

[89] Report from the Expert Group on Liability and New Technologies—New Technologies Formation "Liability for Artificial Intelligence and Other Emerging Digital Technologies", 21 November 2019, at pp. 47–48.

[90] Ibid., at p. 48. The relevant recommendations of the Report read as follows: "Logging by design: There should be a duty on producers to equip technology with means of recording information about the operation of the technology (logging by design), if such information is typically essential for establishing whether a risk of the technology materialised, and if logging is appropriate and proportionate, taking into account, in particular, the technical feasibility and the costs of logging, the availability of alternative means of gathering such information, the type and magnitude of the risks posed by the technology, and any adverse implications logging may have on the rights of others" (Key Finding [20], at p. 47); "Logging must be done in accordance with otherwise applicable law, in particular data protection law and the rules concerning the protection of trade secrets" (Key Finding [21], at p. 47); "The absence of logged information or failure to give the victim reasonable access to the information should trigger a rebuttable presumption that the condition of liability to be proven by the missing information is fulfilled" (Key Finding [22], at p. 47); "If … the operator was obliged to compensate the damage, the operator should have a recourse claim against the producer who failed to equip the technology with logging facilities" (Key Finding [23], at p. 47).

[91] Annex to the European Parliament's Resolution of 20 October 2020 on a civil liability regime for AI—Text of the Proposal for a Regulation on liability for the operation of AI systems, Article 8(4) and recital 19.

[92] Commission's Inception Impact Assessment "Adapting liability rules to the digital age and circular economy", Ref. Ares(2021)4266516, 30.06.2021, p. 4.

Option 2.1.c of the IIA, in addition to the aforementioned options 2.1.a or 2.1.b of the IIA, proposed to adapt the notion of 'defect' and the alleviation/reversal of burden of proof to the specific case of AI.

Option 2.1.b (reversing the burden of proof) was mainly supported by consumer, civil society and other non-profit organisations, which stated that, given how opaque AI systems can be, it would be almost impossible for consumers to prove a manufacturing or design defect. Even if consumers were given access to the model itself, they would still be missing required information on the outcome on others. Therefore, according to their comments, the burden of the proof concerning defect and causation should be reversed. It should be enough for the injured party to prove the existence of damage resulting from a product.[93]

---

[93]For comments supporting Option 2.1.b (reversing the burden of proof) of the Commission's 2021 Inception Impact Assessment, see, for instance, the following:

The Future of Life Institute (FLI) comments on the Commission's Inception Impact Assessment on "Civil liability – adapting liability rules to the digital age and artificial intelligence", submitted on 28 July 2021: "Three types of defects in products have generally been identified: manufacturing defect (when a single item is different from the rest of the batch), information defect (when the risks have not been adequately communicated), and design defect (if the design of the product is not safe enough). Given how opaque AI systems can be, it would be nearly impossible for a consumer to prove a manufacturing or design defect. And even if given access to the model itself, they would still be missing required information on the outcome on others. Taking the example of an algorithmic decision-making tool, a single individual would not be able to prove they were discriminated against if they did not have access to aggregated data concerning other impacted individuals from the same category. We thus believe it is especially important to reverse the burden of proof (option 2.1.b.). As consumer organisation BEUC has pointed out in its public response, this would help make EU liability rules more relevant to European consumers. After all and under current rules only 798 claims based on EU product liability rules had been identified between 2000 and 2016" (at p. 3).

BEUC (the European Consumer Organisation), "Product Liability 2.0 - How to make EU rules fit for consumers in the digital age", submitted on 07.05.2020: "The burden of the proof concerning defect and causation should be reversed. It should be enough for the injured party to prove the existence of damage resulting from a product" (at pp. 2 and 18). . . . "The injured party must prove the damage, the defect and the causal relationship between the damage and the defect (Art.4). If proving the damage is often relatively simple, this however does not constitute the proof that the product is defective. The claimant must still prove the defect and the causal link. In many cases, consumers cannot provide proof and therefore their rights cannot be enforced. The burden of proof is clearly the pivotal element upon which rests the right to compensation" (at pp. 16-17). . . . "New technologies have exacerbated evidentiary difficulties for consumers who must bear the burden of proof. In practice, this means that their rights cannot be enforced and that they are denied access to justice. This view is also supported by academics stressing that the burden of proof "will weigh even more heavily upon the person injured by digital goods that the one injured by traditional products". - Proving the defect: defects in digital goods can be multi-faceted and multi-centred. As the Expert Group pointed out in November 2019, "the interconnectivity of products and systems makes it hard to identify defectiveness". In addition, traditional methods for evaluating defects may no longer be adapted when it comes to complex algorithms. - Establishing the causal link: problems resulting from digital goods can have a multitude of complex concurring causes. As the Expert Group noted, "it will become much more of an issue in the future, given the interconnectedness of emerging digital technologies and their increased dependency on external input and data, making it increasingly doubtful whether the damage at stake was triggered by a single original cause or the interplay of multiple (actual or potential) causes" (at p. 17). . . . "For reasons of fairness, and to mitigate the informational asymmetries impairing the situation of injured parties, we call for a reversal of the burden of proof concerning defect and causation. It should be enough for the injured party to prove the existence of damage resulting from a product. It should then be up to the producer to provide the

On the other hand, corporations and business organisations/associations opposed this option, stressed that a reversal of the burden of proof does not appear necessary to protect the interests of the injured party, and cautioned against reversing the burden of proof in the Product Liability Directive. They stated that complainants should remain

---

proof that the product was free of defects where a damage occurred. It should be the responsibility of the company with access to relevant information and technical means to investigate the cause of the damage" (at p. 18).

Contribution by The Future Society (TFS), "Liability rules for Trust in Excellence & Excellence in Trust - Inception Impact Assessment - Adapting liability rules to the digital age and circular economy", Belgium, 28 July 2021: "The reversal of the burden of proof in 2.1.b is a more radical change than the measures outlined in 2.1.a. Yet, we believe 2.1.b is superior to fulfill the objectives of the liability framework and prevent long-term degradations in the EU market for AI systems. As the obligation to disclose technical information suggested in 2.1.a makes clear, information is key to determine efficiently whether there is a defect. Moreover, there is a recognition that the producer has more information available. AI being a field of advanced technologies progressing quickly, consumers cannot realistically educate themselves to the point of having the same level of information as the producers, even when organised in and protected by consumer associations. The same applies to business customers in other industries than AI production. Moreover, the dissemination of technical information from producers to consumers, while desirable in general, would not suffice to educate consumers about whether the AI system is defective in their case. Indeed, many AI-related defects will likely depend on broad patterns in the decisions concerning many other consumers. This means that, despite technical information being disclosed, society would incur an additional coordination cost (exacerbated by the need to comply with privacy regulations while obtaining and cross-referencing the data of all these other potentially affected consumers). While it can have millions of users, a given AI system has generally a single legally recognised producer, who does not face these coordination costs and additional privacy concerns. These "socialised" education and coordination costs would only disappear if the producer itself bore the burden of proof. This means we should prefer option 2.1.b for efficiency. The concern that such a reversal reduces the incentives to innovate is common (and warranted), but market forces will ensure that margins on AI systems in the EU will be high enough and match the consumers' greater willingness to pay arising from this additional protective legal certainty. An additional argument in favor of option 2.1.b comes from the incentives faced by producers and consumers. In a scenario where consumers have to educate themselves, coordinate among themselves and then prove the defect, while the AI systems prices would surely be lower, the market might wither out of the consumers' distrust. To offset this, providers will have stronger incentives to invest in "educating" consumers and society through more marketing, good PR crisis management in case of scandals, and a good legal team if some cases do reach courts. Many producers would behave ethically in the face of these incentives, but in a competitive market we should expect some would be pressured by shareholders to invest in more aggressive marketing/PR. On the other hand, if the producers carried the burden of proof -making producers effectively more easily threatened by defects, not by whether defects are proved- the shareholders' incentives would be to invest more in preventing defects than in marketing and PR. Finally, a third argument in favor of option 2.1.b comes from the longer-term impact of the asymmetry of information. If the producers do not bear the burden of proof, they have more incentives to hide defects from consumers, as explained in the paragraph above. Consumers cannot easily detect defects (and sometimes the associated non-material damages, such as loss of opportunity). This implies a certain distrust and therefore a lower willingness to pay on average. If it is costlier for the producers to prevent defects rather than to make consumers believe there is no defect, then the "ethical" producers actually investing in the trustworthiness of their AI systems will be weeded out of the markets in the long-term. Their products, despite being objectively better, are too expensive compared to the deflated willingness to pay from consumers and indistinguishable from defective products because the consumers cannot make the difference. This is an example of a "market for lemons" described by economist and Nobel Prize winner George A. Akerlof. Reversing the burden of proof and placing it onto producers -as per 2.1.b- would prevent this by rewarding ethical producers for defect-prevention, while offsetting the incentives for "misleading" consumers" (at pp. 3–4).

responsible to substantiate their demand by establishing a credible and reasoned causality link between the product failure and the damage caused. Besides, as they pointed out, it has already been confirmed by the case law on existing product liability law that the injured party is entitled to relief in the burden of proof (i.e. the injured party already benefits from simplifications of proof such as prima facie evidence and presumption of fault/defect). The injured party does not have to name the specific type of defect or explain the technical background of the defect. Thus, a product defect is regularly assumed if the product in question has caused personal injury or property damage despite proper use. It was also argued that a reversal of the burden of proof would have severe consequences for all EU industries (significantly hindering innovation and affecting the rollout and take up of AI technologies), since it would create an assumption that AI products placed on the market are defective until proven otherwise. In other words, it would create an assumption that all damages suffered due to the use of an AI product was caused by a defect in that product, thus severely impacting consumer trust. This could also lead to frivolous and/or fraudulent legal action—with manufacturers facing groundless claims based on suspicions and assumptions that would prevent them from conducting accurate analysis of every single submitted case –, mainly at the disadvantage of SMEs that do not have the required resources to defend themselves through prolonged court proceedings.[94]

[94]For comments opposing Option 2.1.b (reversing the burden of proof), see the following:

Google's response: "As a general rule, we believe that alleged victims should continue to be required to prove what caused them harm under the liability framework. The strict liability regime of the Directive is designed to protect consumers, not to provide a simple route for consumers to obtain judicial remedies, beyond the strict liability itself. Any proposals to reduce obstacles should consider the advantageous rights and remedies claimants already have under the Directive. The burden of proving causation should only be altered if, given the properties of a specific AI system, establishing proof would create an unreasonable obstacle for the alleged victim. In making this determination, factors to take into account include the likelihood that the technology contributed to the harm (e.g., if there are known defects), the nature and scale of the harm claimed, and the degree of ex-post traceability of contributing processes within the technology. ... Any changes to the liability framework should reflect a rigorous analysis of real-world problems that persist after the AI Act is in place". See Google's response to the European Commission's inception impact assessment on civil liability - adapting liability rules to the digital age and AI, 28.07.2021, at p. 4.

Response of the Center for Data Innovation to the European Commission's inception impact assessment on civil liability—adapting liability rules to the digital age and AI, submitted on 28.07.2021: "The idea of reversing the burden of proof in the context of AI-powered products is another substantial change to the status quo. Currently, plaintiffs must prove that defects in a product caused them damage. Turning this model on its head creates an implied assumption that AI products placed on the market are defective until proven otherwise. This would spark a chilling effect on AI adoption in Europe" (at p. 2).

Fujitsu, "Response to the European Commission's inception impact assessment on civil liability - adapting liability rules to the digital age and artificial intelligence, submitted on 28.07.2021: "The necessary proof that a product is defective can be difficult for an injured party to provide, especially in the case of complex products. However, also in this respect it is not evident why something different should apply to products that use AI than to products that do not use AI. A reversal of the burden of proof does not appear necessary to protect the interests of the injured party. The case law on existing product liability law has already confirmed that the injured party is entitled to relief in the burden of proof (e.g. prima facie evidence, presumption of defect). Thus, a product defect is regularly already assumed if a product has led to personal injury or property damage despite proper use. If the product does not comply with the relevant technical standards or statutory safety regulations, this also gives rise to a rebuttable presumption of defectiveness".

Bitkom Bundesverband Informationswirtschaft, Telekommunikation und neue Medien e.V. (Federal Association for Information Technology, Telecommunications and New Media), "Position Paper - Inception Impact Assessment: Adapting liability rules to the digital age and artificial intelligence", 27.07.2021: "Change of the burden of proof: First of all, it should be pointed out that difficulties in proving justified claims for damages can arise not only with software and AI systems, but with any type of product. Potentially existing difficulties of proof are not increased by the fact that software/AI systems are integrated in a product. Also, according to the case law of the applicable law, the injured party already benefits from simplifications of proof such as prima facie evidence and presumption of fault. The injured party does not have to name the specific type of defect or explain the technical background of the defect. Thus, a product defect is regularly assumed if a product has caused personal injury or property damage despite proper use. If the product does not comply with the relevant statutory safety regulations or technical standards, this also gives rise to a rebuttable presumption of defectiveness. The sometimes criticized opacity of machine learning processes is therefore primarily to the disadvantage of the manufacturer, as he has to prove that no fault in the system he placed on the market was responsible for any damage that occurred. For this reason, manufacturers have been working for a long time and in their own interest to develop methods and test procedures to increase transparency" (at pp. 5–6).

ACEA (The European Automobile Manufacturers' Association) response to the European Commission's inception impact assessment on civil liability—Adapting liability rules to the digital age and circular economy, 28.07.2021: ACEA strongly cautions against reversing the burden of proof in the Product Liability Directive. The principle that a plaintiff must prove their claim is common to all Member States and exceptions to that principle, whether at national or European level, are few and far between. Such a reversal would have severe and far-reaching consequences for all industries in the EU, as it would create an assumption that all damages suffered due to the use of a product was caused by a defect in that product. This could quickly turn into an assumption that all products put on the market can be assumed to be defective, until proven otherwise. This would severely impact consumer trust. It would also very likely lead to a dramatic surge in the number of lawsuits brought against producers in the EU, many of which will likely be frivolous, which would not only financially burden the industry, but also courts in all Member States" (at p. 3).

Response of the App Association (ACT) to the European Commission's inception impact assessment on civil liability—Adapting liability rules to the digital age and circular economy, 28.07.2021: "The App Association does not support lowering the burden of proof or reducing obstacles to receive compensation under the Directive. An EU liability framework addressing AI should prevent frivolous and/or fraudulent claims. We especially oppose the proposal 2.1.b to reverse the burden of proof on to the producer, as this could invite frivolous legal action and cause disproportionate harm for small businesses that don't have the resources to defend themselves, even if they are fully in the right, through prolonged court proceedings" (at p. 5).

DJI—the global leading manufacturer of small drones, "Response to the European Commission's inception impact assessment on civil liability - adapting liability rules to the digital age and AI", 28.07.2021: "inverting the burden of proof for damages allegedly committed by AI products would pose an overwhelming burden on authorities and manufacturers to properly analyze every single suspicion of malfunctioning reported by a user. Complainants should remain responsible to substantiate its demand by establishing a credible and reasoned causality link between the product failure and the damage caused. Otherwise, manufacturers could face a cascade of groundless claims based on suspicions and assumptions that would prevent them from conducting accurate and timely analysis of every single submitted case. This approach would irremediably become unsustainable for every manufacturer and subsequent administrative costs could end up discouraging the development of cutting-edge technologies in Europe" (at p. 1).

The Information Technology Industry Council (ITI), "Comments to European Commission's Inception Impact Assessment on the Revision of EU Liability Rule", 28.07.2021: "We urge the Commission to carefully consider any blanket reversal of the burden of proof as proposed in option 2.1(b). This tool should only be considered for very specific cases and motivated by the profile of harm of a particular product. For the case of AI, a one-size-fits-all measure applying to all AI applications would become an excessive burden on AI developers and users, significantly hampering innovation in the field and affecting the rollout and take up of AI technologies in the EU" (at p. 3).

It should be stressed that the European Parliament had already called on the Commission to consider reversing the rules governing the burden of proof for harm caused by emerging digital technologies in clearly defined cases.[95] In particular, the European Parliament put forward the view that, alongside the strict liability regime for high-risk AI systems, a fault-based liability regime for AI systems that are not listed as "high-risk AI systems" should apply. Therefore, the operator of all physical or virtual activities, devices or processes driven by AI-systems that cause harm or damage but are not listed as high-risk AI-systems should remain subject to fault-based liability.[96] The Parliament took the view that the affected person should benefit from a presumption of fault on the part of the operator,[97] and the latter should be able to exculpate himself by proving he has abided by his duty of care.[98] Therefore, the operator of the non-high-risk AI system in question should not be liable if he can prove that the harm or damage was caused without his fault.

It is reminded that the burden of proof and the notion of defectiveness refer to the safety levels that a consumer is entitled to expect and are central components of the

---

[95] European Parliament's Resolution of 20 October 2020 on a civil liability regime for AI, section "Liability and Artificial Intelligence", at point 8.

See also the Annex to the European Parliament's Resolution of 20 October 2020 on a civil liability regime for AI—Text of the Proposal for a Regulation on liability for the operation of AI systems, at recital 9.

[96] Annex to the European Parliament's Resolution of 20 October 2020 on a civil liability regime for AI—Text of the Proposal for a Regulation on liability for the operation of AI systems, Article 8(1).

However, it was pointed out that an AI system that has not been assessed by the Commission and, thus, is not yet classified as high-risk and not included in the list set out in the Annex to the proposed Regulation, should nevertheless be subject to strict liability if it caused repeated incidents resulting in serious harm or damage. In such cases, the Parliament urged the Commission to assess, without undue delay, the need to revise the Annex in order to add the AI-system in question to the relevant list. The Parliament went on to underline that, if the Commission, following its assessment, decides to include that AI-system on the high-risk list, that inclusion should have retroactive effect from the time of the first proven incident caused by that AI-system, which resulted in serious harm or damage. See European Parliament's Resolution of 20 October 2020 on a civil liability regime for AI, section "Different liability rules for different risks", at point 21.

[97] Annex to the European Parliament's Resolution of 20 October 2020 on a civil liability regime for AI—Text of the Proposal for a Regulation on liability for the operation of AI systems, recital 17.

Also: European Parliament's Resolution of 20 October 2020 on a civil liability regime for AI, section "Different liability rules for different risks", at point 20.

See also Commission Communication "Report on the safety and liability implications of Artificial Intelligence, the Internet of Things and robotics", COM (2020) 64 final, Brussels, 19.2.2020, at p. 14: "adaptations of national laws to facilitate the burden of proof for the victims of AI-related damage could be considered. For example, the burden of proof could be linked to the compliance (by a relevant operator) with specific cyber-security or other safety obligations set by law: if one does not comply with these rules, a change to the burden of proof as regards fault and causation could apply".

[98] The degree of diligence that can be expected from an operator should be linked to the nature of the AI system, the legally-protected right potentially affected, the potential harm or damage that could be caused by the AI-system, and the likelihood of such damage. See the Annex to the European Parliament's Resolution of 20 October 2020 on a civil liability regime for AI—Text of the Proposal for a Regulation on liability for the operation of AI systems, recital 18.

Product Liability Directive that trigger the right for compensation. In particular, the injured party can obtain compensation only if he can prove the defect in the product and the link between the defect and the damage. Therefore, the burden of proof is the key element of the Product Liability Directive that triggers the right for compensation.

However, at least in specific cases, consumers could be disadvantaged by the burden of proof in product liability claims, facing difficulties to investigate claims properly or to gain access to essential information. It is acknowledged that the main difficulty for the victim/injured party to obtain compensation is the burden of proof, namely, to prove the defect in the product and the causal link between the defect and the damage. Indeed, claimants often find it difficult to prove the defect and the link between defect and damage in court.[99]

This difficulty could become even higher in cases of complex products. Since emerging digital technologies and products are becoming increasingly connected and complex, it can become challenging for a claimant to identify the defect and prove the substantial elements of a liability claim. The injured party needs to gather expertise to be able to prove the lack of safety of the product and the link to the damage suffered. In addition, the injured party could face major difficulties when attempting to gain access to essential information, especially in the case of complex digital technology products.[100]

---

[99] See, for instance, the Commission Staff Working Document, Evaluation of Council Directive 85/374/EEC of 25 July 1985 on the approximation of the laws, regulations and administrative provisions of the Member States concerning liability for defective products—Accompanying the Evaluation Report—SWD(2018) 157 final, Brussels, 7.5.2018, at pp. 25-26. The most frequent reasons to reject claims relate to the proof of the defect and its link with the damage, which together account for 53% of the cases of rejection. Difficulties in applying the definition of defective product and subsequently in proving the link between damage and defect seem to be particularly relevant in cases of complex products, such as pharmaceuticals. For those products, the injured party need to gather expertise to be able to prove the lack of safety of the product and the link to the damage suffered.

See also Report from the Commission on the Application of the Council Directive on the approximation of the laws, regulations, and administrative provisions of the Member States concerning liability for defective products (85/374/EEC) {SWD(2018) 157 final} - {SWD(2018) 158 final}, COM(2018) 246 final, Brussels, 7.5.2018, at pp. 2, 6 and 8.

[100] See, e.g., Commission Staff Working Document on "Liability for emerging digital technologies"—Accompanying the document Commission Communication "Artificial intelligence for Europe", SWD(2018) 137 final, Brussels, 25.4.2018: "the notions of defectiveness and burden of proof of the Directive are fairly wide and refer to the safety levels that a consumer is entitled to expect. The defectiveness must be assessed based on an objective analysis of the expectations of an average consumer rather than on subjective expectations or predisposition of one person. The defectiveness of a product is assessed on a case-by-case basis, considering all the relevant circumstances, on the basis of objective criteria, including especially product safety legislation, and all other circumstances, including the presentation of the product, the reasonably expected use and the time when the product was put into circulation. In the context of the emerging digital technologies, it may be difficult to identify whether the damage has been caused by the product itself or by other elements interconnected to it in a digital ecosystem. In this respect, it will be necessary to provide for adequate safety levels for all types of products, taking also account of any

In order to tackle the issue of the burden of proof in product liability claims—due to the complexity of allocating responsibility for damage caused by increasingly autonomous systems—the Commission decided to examine whether a relaxation of the rules on the burden of proof should be decided.[101] The reversal of the burden of proof in the context of a fault-based liability attempts to respond to the need to facilitate the compensation of the victim of damages in situations where the legislator considers it too burdensome or unbalanced to apply the general fault-based liability rule. This is why the Commission stated that "adaptations of national laws to facilitate the burden of proof for the victims of AI-related damage could be considered. For example, the burden of proof could be linked to the compliance (by a

new risks that may be posed regarding the emerging digital technologies" (at p. 18). . . . "It is also important to assess the issue of the burden of proof. National regimes including fault-based liability schemes or different forms of strict liability regimes often include provisions, whereby the burden of proof for a possible fault, defect or other condition is not placed on the victim. Thus, the person held liable by law would need to prove to be discharged from liability, for instance, that the damage was caused as a result of force majeure or an act/behaviour of a third party. Whether the burden of proof should be on the claimant or reversed, what substantive conditions the claimant should demonstrate as well as the impact on the ability of the claimant to obtain compensation are important elements to assess" (at p. 20).

[101] "The Commission is seeking views whether and to what extent it may be needed to mitigate the consequences of complexity by alleviating/reversing the burden of proof required by national liability rules for damage caused by the operation of AI applications, through an appropriate EU initiative". Commission Communication "Report on the safety and liability implications of Artificial Intelligence, the Internet of Things and robotics", COM (2020) 64 final, Brussels, 19.2.2020, at p. 14.

It should be noted that, under specific circumstances, EU member jurisdictions appear to facilitate the burden of proof of the victim to increase the possibility of compensation. For instance, there are cases where a presumption of fault by the wrongdoer exists, i.e. the wrongdoer is considered to be liable unless he can prove that he was not in fault. This is linked, inter alia, to the responsibility of parents/tutors/guardians/teachers for damages (unless they can prove that they were not able to prevent the damages from happening) caused by a minor, pupil, student/apprentice or mentally impaired person. Other examples where national law introduces variations to facilitate the burden of proof include the responsibility of the owner/possessor of a building in case of damages caused by that building (unless he/she proves that he/she observed appropriate care for the purpose of avoiding the damage); or the responsibility of a person carrying a dangerous activity (unless he can prove that all appropriate measures to avoid the damage have been taken). Examples of those variations are cited in the Commission Staff Working Document on "Liability for emerging digital technologies"—Accompanying the document Commission Communication "Artificial intelligence for Europe", SWD(2018) 137 final, Brussels, 25.4.2018, at pp. 7–9. Furthermore, as already mentioned, national legal systems may provide for special regimes of strict liability, i.e. a liability that does not depend on a fault and the claimant needs only to prove the damage and the causal link. "Special regimes of strict liability may apply to a diverse set of factual situations generating different types of risks and damages, such as the liability of the owners of animals for the damages caused by the animals under their custody; the strict liability of the person responsible for carrying out an unspecified or specified dangerous activity (for example the operation of nuclear power plants, aircrafts or motor vehicles) or other cases linked to a legal or factual relationship between two persons or a person and an object, such as when the damages are caused by someone executing a task in the interest of someone else (employee/employer) or by an object that is under his/her custody".

relevant operator) with specific cyber-security or other safety obligations set by law: if one does not comply with these rules, a change to the burden of proof as regards fault and causation could apply".[102]

This conclusion is in line with the findings of the Report from the Expert Group on Liability and New Technologies, which—although it stated that, as a general rule, the burden of proof for both causation and damage should remain with the victim, as is the case under existing liability frameworks ("the victim should continue to be required to prove what caused her harm")[103]—it nevertheless underlined that, in certain circumstances, it appears to be appropriate to reverse or lower this burden, especially when it is disproportionately high.[104] For instance, the burden of proof could be reversed if damage was caused by a breach of some other set of rules (such as safety/security rules, including cybersecurity). In particular, according to the recommendations of the Report from the Expert Group on Liability and New Technologies, failing to comply with safety rules could lead to a reversal of the burden of proof concerning key elements of liability, including causation and fault: "where the damage is of a kind that safety rules were meant to avoid, failure to comply with such safety rules, including rules on cybersecurity, should lead to a reversal of the burden of proving (a) causation, and/or (b) fault, and/or (c) the existence of a defect";[105] "if it is proven that an emerging digital technology has caused harm, the burden of proving defect should be reversed if there are disproportionate difficulties or costs pertaining to establishing the relevant level of safety or proving that this level of safety has not

[102] Commission Communication "Report on the safety and liability implications of Artificial Intelligence, the Internet of Things and robotics", COM (2020) 64 final, Brussels, 19.2.2020, at p. 14. "As regards Union legislation, according to the Product Liability Directive, a product that does not meet mandatory safety rules would be considered defective, regardless of the producers' fault. There may, however, also be reasons to contemplate ways on how to facilitate the burden of proof for victims under the Directive: the Directive relies on national rules on the evidence and the establishment of causation".

[103] Report from the Expert Group on Liability and New Technologies—New Technologies Formation "Liability for Artificial Intelligence and Other Emerging Digital Technologies", 21 November 2019, Key Finding (25), at pp. 8 and 49. "As is already the standard rule in all jurisdictions, whoever demands compensation from another should in general prove all necessary requirements for such a claim, including in particular the causal link between the harm to be indemnified on the one hand and the activities or risks within the sphere of the addressee of the claim may trigger the latter's liability on the other. This general principle is supported inter alia by concerns of fairness and results from the need to consider and balance the interests of both sides", at p. 50.

[104] Ibid., at pp. 43–44: "Features of emerging digital technologies, such as opacity, openness, autonomy and limited predictability, may often result in unreasonable difficulties or costs for the victim to establish both what safety an average user is entitled to expect, and the failure to achieve this level of safety. At the same time, it may be significantly easier for the producer to prove relevant facts. This asymmetry justifies the reversal of the burden of proof".

[105] Ibid., Key Finding (24), at pp. 7 and 48. The Report provides the following example/illustration (No 18): "Imagine there is a new rule on cybersecurity of IoT household equipment, designed to prevent hacking and the resulting harm. The victim's private Wi-Fi is hacked in a way typical of cybersecurity gaps in IoT equipment. Where the victim can show that a water kettle produced by P failed to comply with the standard of safety under adopted safety rules, the victim could sue P, and the onus would be on P to prove that the damage had been caused by a different device", at p. 49.

been met";[106] "if it is proven that an emerging digital technology caused harm, and liability therefor is conditional upon a person's intent or negligence, the burden of proving fault should be reversed if disproportionate difficulties and costs of establishing the relevant standard of care and of proving their violation justify it. This is without prejudice to the reversal of the burden of proof".[107]

6.6.2.1.3 Removing the 'Development Risk Defence'

Option 2.1.c of the Commission's 2021 Inception Impact Assessment (IAA) suggested, in addition to the aforementioned options 2.1.a or 2.1.b of the IIA and alongside the proposal to adapt the notion of 'defect' and the alleviation/reversal of burden of proof to the specific case of AI, removing the 'development risk defence' in order to ensure producers of AI-related products that continuously learn and adapt while in operation remain strictly liable for damage.[108]

Option 2.1.c is in line with the proposals put forward by the Report of the Expert Group on Liability and New Technologies, which underlined that, apart from the operator's strict liability, the principle of producer responsibility should also apply to emerging digital technologies. As the Report stated: "Strict liability of the producer should play a key role in indemnifying damage caused by defective products and their components, irrespective of whether they take a tangible or a digital form";[109] "the producer should be strictly liable for defects in emerging digital technologies even if said defects appear after the product was put into circulation, as long as the producer was still in control of updates to, or upgrades on, the technology. A development risk defence should not apply".[110]

---

[106] Ibid., Key Finding (15), at p. 6.

[107] Ibid., Key Finding (27), at pp. 8 and 52.

[108] Commission's Inception Impact Assessment "Adapting liability rules to the digital age and circular economy", Ref. Ares(2021)4266516, 30.06.2021, p. 4.

[109] Report from the Expert Group on Liability and New Technologies—New Technologies Formation "Liability for Artificial Intelligence and Other Emerging Digital Technologies", 21 November 2019, Key Finding [13], at p. 42. According to the Report (at p. 43), "it is in line with the principle of functional equivalence, that damage caused by defective digital content should trigger the producer's liability because digital content fulfils many of the functions tangible movable items used to fulfil when the PLD was drafted and passed. This is all the more true for defective digital elements of other products, some of which come separately from the tangible item (for example, as a control app to be downloaded onto the user's smartphone), or as over-the-air updates after the product has been put into circulation (security updates for example), or as digital services provided on a continuous basis during the time the product is being used (for example, navigation cloud services)".

[110] Ibid., Key Finding [14], at p. 42. It is reminded that the so-called development risk defence allows the producer to avoid liability if the state of scientific and technical knowledge at the time when he put the product into circulation was not such as to enable the existence of the defect to be discovered (Article 7(e) of the Product Liability Directive—PLD). This defence may become increasingly important and result in limitation of liability when AI-based products are involved. As the Report put it (at p. 28), "As the PLD focuses on the moment when the product was put into

Option 2.1.c of the Commission's 2021 Inception Impact Assessment was supported by consumer, civil society and other non-profit organisations. For instance, the European Consumer Organisation (BEUC) stated that "the time at which the product was placed on the market should no longer be relevant when assessing defects. ... When it is established that a product is defective, the PLD provides the defendant with several defences to escape liability. Two are particularly controversial in the context of new technologies, namely the so-called 'development-risk defence' and the 'regulatory compliance' defence. The development risk defence (Art. 7e) provides that the producer shall not be liable if the state of scientific and technical knowledge at the time when the product was put into circulation was not such as to enable the existence of the defect to be discovered. ... Many digital goods may change after they have been put onto the market. It is therefore essential that an injured person who suffers damage be always compensated regardless of whether the defect was detectable or not. ... BEUC recommendation: the development risk-defence should be abolished".[111]

Similarly, the Future of Life Institute (FLI) stressed that "some digital products present unique features, including continuous learning, which can raise unique

circulation as the key turning point for the producer's liability, this cuts off claims for anything the producer may subsequently add via some update or upgrade. In addition, the PLD does not provide for any duties to monitor the products after putting them into circulation. Highly sophisticated AI systems may not be finished products that are put on the market in a traditional way. The producer may retain some degree of control over the product's further development in the form of additions or updates after circulation. At the same time, the producer's control may be limited and nonexclusive if the product's operation requires data provided by third parties or collected from the environment, and depends on self-learning processes and personalising settings chosen by the user. This dilutes the traditional role of a producer, when a multitude of actors contribute to the design, functioning and use of the AI product/system".

See also, at p. 43: "emerging digital technologies are characterised by limited predictability. This phenomenon will intensify with the dissemination of machine learning. The interconnectedness of devices, as well as threats to cyber security, also contribute to difficulties in predicting the product's performance. A defect in digital content or in a product with digital elements may therefore result from the impact of the environment in which the product operates or from the product's evolution, for which the manufacturer only created a general framework but which they did not design in detail. In view of the need to share benefits and risks efficiently and fairly, the development risk defence, which allows the producer to avoid liability for unforeseeable defects, should not be available in cases where it was predictable that unforeseen developments might occur". ... "When the defect came into being as a result of the producer's interference with the product already put into circulation (by way of a software update for example), or the producer's failure to interfere, it should be regarded as a defect in the product for which the producer is liable. The point in time at which a product is placed on the market should not set a strict limit on the producer's liability for defects where, after that point in time, the producer or a third party acting on behalf of the producer remains in charge of providing updates or digital services. The producer should therefore remain liable where the defect has its origin (i) in a defective digital component or digital ancillary part or in other digital content or services provided for the product with the producer's assent after the product has been put into circulation; or (ii) in the absence of an update of digital content, or of the provision of a digital service which would have been required to maintain the expected level of safety within the time period for which the producer is obliged to provide such updates".

[111] BEUC (the European Consumer Organisation), "Product Liability 2.0 - How to make EU rules fit for consumers in the digital age", submitted on 07.05.2020, at pp. 2, 19-20.

issues. For that reason, we believe it is necessary to revise the notion of defect, as well as remove the development risk defence (option 2.1.c.). The development risk defence states that companies can avoid liability if the state of scientific and technical knowledge at the time the product was put into circulation was not such as to enable the defect to be discovered. We believe this doctrine could create a significant loophole in the liability of self-learning and continuous AI systems, and should thus be removed. ... FLI believes that the defect of continual self-learning AI systems should not be classified as later defect if the defect is tied directly to the fact that the learning done by the system in the product lifecycle produced unanticipated harm. The fact that a system can self-learn while being used by a customer is not a 'later' defect, as self-learning is at the very core of the market value of the product that is known to have possible unintended negative consequences. In addition, it is important to avoid the unpredictability of the behavior of autonomous machines breaking the chain of causation. If a company is building a system with great autonomy, it must acknowledge and accept the risk that their system will perform in ways that are unpredictable, which should not be considered as an unanticipated, later defect".[112]

[112] The Future of Life Institute (FLI) comments on the Commission's Inception Impact Assessment on "Civil liability – adapting liability rules to the digital age and artificial intelligence", submitted on 28 July 2021, at pp. 3–4.

For similar comments, see the Contribution by The Future Society (TFS), "Liability rules for Trust in Excellence & Excellence in Trust - Inception Impact Assessment - Adapting liability rules to the digital age and circular economy", Belgium, 28 July 2021: "Products that continuously learn and adapt while in operation present a novel challenge to liability rules and in particular to the "development risk defence". Our belief is that the costs of the "development risk defence" outweigh the benefits, and its removal is therefore warranted (2.1.c). ... information is key to determine whether the removal of the "development risk defence" is efficient. ... the producer has significantly more technical information available about the AI system than the consumer. However, the nuance with the "development risk defence" is that it applies specifically to information that the producer does not have at the time of putting the system in circulation. ... the software is embedded and tangible. The initial parameters enabling "continuous learning" in some AI systems are therefore likewise embedded in that tangible substrate and known to the producers. Their interactions with the environment, regardless of continuous learning, are reasonably foreseeable ..., i.e. the producers are increasingly able to address the "known unknowns" ex ante, thanks to the ease with which one can simulate or synthesize a digital environment. What can be done for the "unknowns" rendering an AI system defective and that remain unknown until after deployment (e.g. discovery that a mathematical estimation method used in the model systematically causes bias or undermines robustness)? The ability of many AI systems to be updated over-the-air reduces the likelihood that a defect discovered post-deployment cannot be fixed, mitigated or at least flagged to the consumer. The benefits of the development risk defence, in a world of pre-deployment digital simulations, over-the-air updating and continuous learning, are therefore limited to few special cases where both digital simulation/data synthesis and over-the-air update or notification are impossible. Its costs however, can be significant. Indeed, the liberal use of the development risk defence would disincentivize exploration of the defects that would fall within its scope (e.g. "unknown unknowns"). For example, fundamental and applied research in the control of AI systems, efficient but thorough testing techniques and prevention/mitigation of "unpredictable outcomes" would wither. Over the medium term, the market would moreover structurally disincentivize academic research and innovation in fundamental aspects of the trustworthiness of

6.6.2.1.4 Time Limits and Minimum Threshold for Property Damage

It has already been stated that, according to the Commission, victims seeking compensation under the Product Liability Directive face additional limitations on making claims in the first place due to the time limits and the minimum threshold for property damage of EUR 500 imposed by the Directive.[113]

Option 2.1.d of the Commission's 2021 Inception Impact Assessment (IAA) proposed to ease the conditions for making claims under the Product Liability Directive (i.e. the time limits and the EUR 500 minimum threshold for property damage).[114] This proposal is in line with the view of consumer organisations, which

---

AI systems—a field where the EU would otherwise excel thanks to its strong consumer protection, its AI Act and high performance in academic research. Moreover, when maintaining the "development risk defence" and given the asymmetry of information between the consumers and the producers, the EU market for AI would risk withering into a "lemons market", similar to the argument elaborated upon in the section on 2.1.b above. As described there, the increased "costs" of production from having to carry out more thorough tests would simply be reflected in the price of AI systems in the EU. The advantage would come from the fact that consumers could confidently buy these products, knowing full well that the producers' interests are aligned with consumers' (i.e. EU citizens and businesses') interests and that the best efforts have indeed been made to prevent "unknown unknowns" to the greatest extent possible. These consumers' willingness to pay would therefore be higher, leaving margins for producers to innovate and invest in higher quality products. The net economic gains to society will be from avoiding the so-called "deadweight loss" from the asymmetric information and the asymmetric control over the design of the system. We therefore support the option 2.1.c" (at pp. 5-6).

For the opposite view, see, e.g.: Input from ZVEI – German Electrical and Electronic Manufacturers' Association on "Civil liability – adapting liability rules to the digital age and artificial intelligence", submitted on 28.07.2021: "We are opposed to an AI-specific concept of defect and a removal of the development risk defence for AI (2.1.c). The development risk defence is an expression of the balance between the interests of the injured parties and the producers, serves to maintain innovation incentives for the producers and must be retained in order not to unduly inhibit product development in the promising AI market. Moreover, the development risk defence does not mean that the producer is not liable because of damage caused by a defect that was not known at the time the product was put into circulation. If he culpably breached his duty to observe the product after it was put into circulation, he is still liable, but only on a fault-based approach via tort law" (at p. 2).

[113] Commission's Inception Impact Assessment "Adapting liability rules to the digital age and circular economy", Ref. Ares(2021)4266516, 30.06.2021, p. 3.

See also Report from the Commission on the Application of the Council Directive on the approximation of the laws, regulations, and administrative provisions of the Member States concerning liability for defective products (85/374/EEC) -{SWD(2018) 157 final} - {SWD(2018) 158 final}, COM(2018) 246 final, Brussels, 7.5.2018, at p. 6: "The EUR 500 threshold and time limitations for claims (especially for certain products such as pharmaceuticals) also limit the number of cases for which consumers can claim compensation".

[114] Commission's Inception Impact Assessment "Adapting liability rules to the digital age and circular economy", Ref. Ares(2021)4266516, 30.06.2021, p. 4.

asked for an extension of the 10-year limitation period,[115] contested the exemption of the EUR 500 threshold for property damages (claiming to be unfairly disadvantaged) and asked for more protection at a lower cost, which could result in removing the threshold of EUR 500.[116] On the other hand, it could be argued that any

[115] See, for instance, BEUC (the European Consumer Organisation), "Product Liability 2.0 - How to make EU rules fit for consumers in the digital age", submitted on 07.05.2020: "Review timelines and prescription periods: The 10-year limitation period should be extended to 20 years" (at p. 2). ... "Timelines and prescription periods: What is the situation? The PLD establishes two deadlines: the PLD no longer applies three years after the injured party knew or could have become aware of the relevant facts (i.e. the damage, the defect and the identity of the producer) (Art. 10), and it ends ten years after the date the product was put onto the market (Art. 11). Why this is problematic: The PLD introduced these time limits to counterbalance the strict liability regime and to avoid hindering innovations. However, these timelines are no longer appropriate. First, when it comes to digital goods, producers keep significant control over their products even after they have been put onto the market. When digital contents are provided on a continuous basis, it is essential that consumers be protected during the entire lifespan of the product. Second, the time limits are not appropriate for certain types of products such as foodstuffs or pharmaceutical products where damage is likely to occur long after the product has been put into circulation. ... Third, these time limits should be regarded as a violation of the right of access to justice. ... Fourth, BEUC calls for a more sustainable consumption where products have a longer lifespan. This preoccupation is in line with the European Green Deal, and goes hand-in-hand with the right to have products repaired. Therefore, liability rules must ensure that the time limits in which producers shall be held liable match consumer expectations on long-lasting products. Furthermore, spare parts can also have an impact on product safety, so it is important that in the event of harm stemming from the replacement of parts and components, consumers have a right to recourse against the parts producer. Ultimately, it is important that the PLD strikes a balance between the need for flexible prescription periods adapted to the dynamic features of digital goods and the need to provide legal certainty for all stakeholders. Moreover, the need for harmonisation is needed to avoid the risk of patchy national legislations that would set different timelines. ... BEUC recommendation: • The limitation period should be extended to 20 years" (at pp. 21–22).

[116] Commission Staff Working Document, Evaluation of Council Directive 85/374/EEC of 25 July 1985 on the approximation of the laws, regulations and administrative provisions of the Member States concerning liability for defective products—Accompanying the Evaluation Report—SWD (2018) 157 final, Brussels, 7.5.2018: "Organisations representing consumers, for instance, claimed to be unfairly disadvantaged by the burden of proof in product liability claims and stressed the difficulties to investigate claims properly or to gain access to essential information especially in case of technical products. Moreover, consumer organisations asked for more protection at a lower cost, which would imply removing the threshold of EUR 500" (at p. 5). ..." For most consumer associations, the Directive is not fully effective, as they consider producer's interests to be better protected than those of consumers. Similarly, consumers believe that the Directive is not always effective in protecting consumers mainly because, *inter alia*, the EUR 500 threshold aims to avoiding litigation for small claims, • compensation of the damage only if the item of property was intended and used for private purpose and not when the defective product was used for professional purposes; • the time limit of 3 and 10 years to obtain compensation is too short in cases of complex products that require more expertise (at p. 31).

For comments supporting this option see, for instance, the following:

The Future of Life Institute (FLI) comments on the Commission's Inception Impact Assessment on "Civil liability – adapting liability rules to the digital age and artificial intelligence", submitted on 28 July 2021: "we support easing the conditions for making liability claims (option 2.1.d.). We believe there are multiple reasons to lower the 500 euros threshold. Some of the non-material damages caused by digital products can be hard to quantify (e.g. data loss, environmental damage). In addition, a defective AI system could impose a small loss to all the individuals subject to its use, which would amount to a large loss for society at large" (at p. 4).

BEUC (the European Consumer Organisation), "Product Liability 2.0 - How to make EU rules fit for consumers in the digital age", submitted on 07.05.2020: "Consumers have long indicated that the €500 threshold unduly restrains the number of cases for which consumers can claim compensation. First, the threshold was initially adopted to avoid a flood of small cases against producers. However, in practice, this concern has been more hypothetical than real. Conversely, this threshold has contributed to impairing consumers' access to justice and limiting their compensation. As the Commission noted in 2018, "according to the information obtained, in four out of five cases a compensation is not claimed as the damage is below the threshold". Second, the threshold has given rise to diverging national interpretations. In some Member States, the threshold is regarded as a deductible (i.e. the amount of damages awarded to the claimant is reduced by this amount in case of success) while in others this amount is a minimum, below which no damages can be recovered. Consumers may therefore suffer from different levels of protection across the EU, which is not acceptable from a Single Market perspective. Third, should a loss or destruction of data eventually be regarded as a compensable harm, quantifying such a loss may lead to different results in Member States. For example, some Member States may take the view that a loss of data is below the threshold. This would create the risk of unequal treatment between consumers. Fourth, there is a contradiction between, on the one hand, current EU efforts to facilitate law enforcement and compensation for small-value claims (see for example the proposal for a Directive on representative actions for consumers) and, on the other hand, the €500 threshold, which precisely hinders such claims from being brought" (at pp. 15–16). … "The maximum ceiling of €70m creates an unfair distribution of risks for product liability in the case of damage to persons caused by identical items with the same defect. This cap should be removed as well in order to respect the fundamental right of redress for damage suffered. Damage should always be fully compensated" (at p. 16). "BEUC recommendations: • The PLD should also cover damage to digital assets, including data. • The €500 threshold should be removed. • The maximum cap of €70m should be removed" (at p. 16).

Contribution by The Future Society (TFS), "Liability rules for Trust in Excellence & Excellence in Trust - Inception Impact Assessment - Adapting liability rules to the digital age and circular economy", Belgium, 28 July 2021: "while material compensation is often assumed to be the primary driver, consumers also value non-material compensation such as the peace of mind associated with justice and fairness, whether at the individual level or in society at large. Focusing solely on a financial threshold to determine whether to pursue a case assumes a narrow view of society - especially if non-material damages are likely to occur. While the time limit can be justified by the fact that case-relevant information or evidence degrades over time and increases the cost of efficient adjudication, the financial threshold seems arbitrary. Even if focusing on quantifiable material damages out of practicality, it is unclear why a threshold would be needed at all: given the costs in time and energy to the consumers, a presumably injured consumer anyway has to decide for himself whether it is worthwhile to take action. That consumer surely knows best whether the damages suffered justify taking action, without having to quantify them financially and officially - and the consumer can even factor in non-material factors much more efficiently. The threshold therefore only adds burdensome quantification and fees to an already complex procedure to obtain fair compensation for damages due to defects. This extra step reduces the efficiency of the liability system and introduces inequality in access to non-material compensation such as justice - especially for the least wealthy citizens of the EU for whom <500€ is a significant share of yearly income. While we are concerned about frivolous civil liability claims or, in the longer term, a form of "trolling" (in a way similar to Intellectual Property trolls), we do not think the threshold prevents such behaviors and another, more nuanced legal test will very probably be more appropriate if these abuses do start to occur. Therefore, we would recommend withdrawing the financial threshold for damage to property - as per 2.1.d" (at pp. 6–7).

relaxation on the threshold for property damages would lead to more claims for minor damages, thus contradicting one of the main purposes of the threshold, namely to avoid litigation for small claims.[117]

6.6.2.2 Options to Address Proof-Related Challenges Posed by AI to National Liability Rules

The extent of harmonisation of national liability rules to address proof-related challenges can vary. Indeed, the options put forward by the Commission's 2021 Inception Impact Assessment (IAA) followed a "gradual intervention logic", ranging from enacting 'soft law', i.e. non-legislative approach (Option 2.2.a—Recommendation to Member States of targeted adaptations to the burden of proof)[118] to

---

[117] Commission Staff Working Document, Evaluation of Council Directive 85/374/EEC of 25 July 1985 on the approximation of the laws, regulations and administrative provisions of the Member States concerning liability for defective products – Accompanying the Evaluation Report – SWD (2018) 157 final, Brussels, 7.5.2018, at p. 5: "On the side of the producers and insurers, however, the arguments raised focused on the risk that any relaxation of the rules on the burden of proof or on the threshold for property damages would lead to more claims for minor damages (at p. 5).

According to Google's response, "changing the conditions under which claims can be made under the [Product Liability] directive is unnecessary and carries substantial risks. The rationale for a minimum damage threshold in the Directive was to avoid overburdening the courts with frivolous litigation. This risk is arguably greater for software-related claims, given that a defect in a single line of code (out of millions) that was used in millions of devices could (under this proposal) be the basis for a strict liability claim from each individual user. It is also unnecessary, since nothing would prevent consumers from bringing actions in the national courts for lower value claims, they just cannot rely on strict liability under the Directive when doing so. Similarly, the Directive stresses that it is in the interests of both the injured person and of the producer to have a uniform period of limitation for bringing a claim. The limitation period provides an incentive to diligently pursue damages claims and provides legal certainty to all parties involved". See Google's views on the European Commission's inception impact assessment on civil liability - adapting liability rules to the digital age and AI, 28.07.2021, at pp. 4-5.

Response of the App Association (ACT) to the European Commission's inception impact assessment on civil liability - Adapting liability rules to the digital age and circular economy, 28.07.2021: "As for the impact on fundamental rights, we stress again that lightening the burden of proof and lowering the €500 threshold could lead to frivolous claims and put businesses at an unnecessary disadvantage" (at p. 6).

Bitkom Bundesverband Informationswirtschaft, Telekommunikation und neue Medien e.V. (Federal Association for Information Technology, Telecommunications and New Media), "Position Paper - Inception Impact Assessment: Adapting liability rules to the digital age and artificial intelligence", 27.07.2021: "The minimum threshold for making claims for damage of property under the Product Liability Directive should remain at EUR 500 in order to avoid litigation in an excessive number of cases, as stated in Recital 9 of the Product Liability Directive. In accordance with the applicable fault-based law, an injured party can always pursue any claim for lesser damages under the applicable fault-based law, so that there is no gap in legal protection" (at p. 6).

[118] Commission's Inception Impact Assessment "Adapting liability rules to the digital age and circular economy", Ref. Ares(2021)4266516, 30.06.2021, p. 5.

introducing specific legislative measures mainly in relation to a harmonised reversal or alleviation of burden of proof: "2.2.b - Legislative measure providing for a harmonised reversal of or other ways of alleviating burden of proof linked to non-compliance with AI-specific obligations in EU safety legislation (e.g. documentation or human oversight obligations under the proposed AI Act), in order to better enforce these obligations through civil liability claims and further promote compliance.[119] 2.2.c - Legislative measure adapting the burden of proof where the claimant would otherwise be required to demonstrate how an opaque AI system produced a certain output that caused the damage. 2.2.d - Harmonisation of claims involving fault of the operator of AI systems without a specific risk profile, by introducing a reversed burden of proof regarding fault, as well as harmonisation of additional aspects such as the types of compensable harm, limitation periods and joint liability, as envisaged by EP resolution 2020/2014(INL)".[120]

According to the response of the Center for Data Innovation to the European Commission's inception impact assessment on civil liability - adapting liability rules to the digital age and AI, submitted on 28.07.2021, "this option allows for evidence-driven policy adjustments instead of top-down ex ante decisions that could seriously disrupt the normal flow or proceedings in liability cases and negatively impact the provision of AI-powered goods in Europe (in terms of insurance availability, cost, or both)" (at p. 3).

See also ACEA (The European Automobile Manufacturers' Association) response to the European Commission's inception impact assessment on civil liability - Adapting liability rules to the digital age and circular economy, 28.07.2021: "European institutions should issue recommendations and guidance with a view to ensuring that Member States put in place clear rules regarding extra-contractual liability applicable to damages caused by AI, and to avoid any wide and irresolvable discrepancies between the rules applicable in various European jurisdictions, thus averting the emergence of legal fragmentation or legal uncertainty. ACEA therefore believes that the adoption of such non-binding initiatives should be given priority, and that any legally binding initiative should only be envisaged after careful consideration, should such non-binding measures prove ineffective in preventing the emergence of legal fragmentation and legal uncertainty" (at p. 4).

Also: Response of the App Association (ACT) to the European Commission's inception impact assessment on civil liability - Adapting liability rules to the digital age and circular economy, 28.07.2021: "In order to address proof-related challenges posed by AI to national liability rules, we strongly urge the Commission to adapt a risk-based approach here and encourage Member States to do so, as suggested in option 2.2.a." (at p. 5).

[119] According to the Information Technology Industry Council (ITI), "Comments to European Commission's Inception Impact Assessment on the Revision of EU Liability Rule", 28.07.2021: "Further EU-level harmonisation of proof-related measures in national liability rules would be welcome, as it would increase legal certainty for companies operating in the Single Market and increase consumer trust in AI technologies. However, as regards for instance option 2.2 (b), more clarity would be needed regarding the stated purpose of the legislative measure to "better enforce these obligations through civil liability claims and further promote compliance". Given that the AI Act is still under discussion with the co-legislators, and it is far from entering into force, it may be too early to plan legislative instruments in support of its enforcement through liability rules. It would be useful to have the first evaluations of the impact of the AI Act before planning such instrument" (at p. 3).

[120] Commission's Inception Impact Assessment "Adapting liability rules to the digital age and circular economy", Ref. Ares(2021)4266516, 30.06.2021, p. 5.

According to the Contribution by The Future Society (TFS), "Liability rules for Trust in Excellence & Excellence in Trust - Inception Impact Assessment - Adapting liability rules to the

6.7 Conclusion

This chapter examined the Commission's 2021 Inception Impact Assessment (IIA) "Adapting liability rules to the digital age and circular economy", which was prompted by an evaluation of the Product Liability Directive (PLD). It addressed shortcomings already identified in the evaluation of the PLD and the challenges that the emerging technologies present for the application of liability rules, which were analytically described in the Commission's 2020 White Paper and the accompanying Report on Liability for AI, IoT and Robotics.

According to the Commission, civil liability rules for AI should strike a balance between protecting citizens and promoting technological innovation. It was stressed that, alongside the objective of the EU safety framework to ensure that all products and services, including those integrating emerging digital technologies like AI, robotics and Internet of things (IoT), operate safely and reliably, the objectives of the liability framework are to (i) provide legal certainty to industry's market players about the risk they take in the course of their business, (ii) encourage the prevention of damage and (iii) ensure injured parties are compensated.

The Commission examined different policy options to achieve the initiative's primary objectives. These objectives, alongside the overall goal of ensuring the proper functioning of the single market while providing for a high level of consumer/victim protection, are: (i) to modernise and adapt strict liability rules to the digital age and circular economy, taking account of the characteristics and risks of new technologies, including AI-equipped products and services; and (ii) to address unnecessary obstacles to obtaining compensation for damage, ensuring that injured parties are equally protected throughout the EU. This approach aims to foster

digital age and circular economy", Belgium, 28 July 2021, "the first part of 2.2.d is explicit enough: "harmonisation of claims involving fault of the operator of AI systems without a specific risk profile, by introducing a reversed burden of proof regarding fault". This is desirable, based on the same reasoning as for option 2.1.b. The major difference comes from introducing the operator as an intermediary between the producer and the consumer. For the reversal of the fault-based burden of proof onto the operator to be efficient, a crucial assumption is that the operator has more information than the end user and the producer about the way the operator prevents fault. This assumption is very likely to be true and therefore this reversal is very probably efficient. Similar to the reasoning for 2.1.b, this will incentivize a greater level of care for decisions and behavior within the operator's scope of effective control. It will also lead in the long term to greater investment in R&D for better safeguards to limit operator-induced damages, translating in novel approaches and greater innovation (e.g. better human-computer interfacing technologies, better processes for understanding AI systems' outcomes, etc.). Option 2.2.d therefore seems preferable" (at p. 7).

Similarly, see The Future of Life Institute (FLI) comments on the Commission's Inception Impact Assessment on "Civil liability – adapting liability rules to the digital age and artificial intelligence", submitted on 28 July 2021: "In addition to updating the Directive, FLI believes it is important to harmonise current domestic liability framework in relation to the operators and users of AI systems (option 2.2.d.). A fault-based regime incentivises companies to make the right decision and prioritise safety over other considerations. FLI therefore supports harmonising domestic laws and reversing the burden of proof given how difficult it could be for consumers to have the necessary information to prove damage from digital products" (at p. 4).

consumer uptake of AI and other innovative technologies, build trust in innovative products and services, and strengthen confidence in justice systems.

Legal/Policy Documents, Studies, Reports

Council Directive 85/374/EEC of 25 July 1985 on the approximation of the laws, regulations and administrative provisions of the Member States concerning liability for defective products, as modified by Directive 1999/34/EC of the European Parliament and of the Council of 10 May 1999 (OJ L 210/29, 7.8.1985, and OJ L 141/20, 4.6.1999) (the Product Liability Directive).

European Commission's ('Commission') Inception Impact Assessment "Adapting liability rules to the digital age and circular economy", Ref. Ares(2021)4266516, 30.06.2021.

Commission Staff Working Document on "Liability for emerging digital technologies" - Accompanying the document Commission Communication "Artificial intelligence for Europe", SWD(2018) 137 final, Brussels, 25.4.2018.

Report from the Commission on the Application of the Council Directive on the approximation of the laws, regulations, and administrative provisions of the Member States concerning liability for defective products (85/374/EEC) {SWD (2018) 157 final} - {SWD(2018) 158 final}, COM(2018) 246 final, Brussels, 7.5.2018, ['Commission Report on the Application of the Product Liability Directive, COM(2018) 246 final, Brussels, 07.05.2018'].

Commission Staff Working Document, Evaluation of Council Directive 85/374/ EEC of 25 July 1985 on the approximation of the laws, regulations and administrative provisions of the Member States concerning liability for defective products – Accompanying the Evaluation Report – SWD(2018) 157 final, Brussels, 7.5.2018 ['Commission Staff Working Document, 'Evaluation of Product Liability Directive', SWD(2018) 157 final, Brussels, 07.05.2018'].

Commission Communication "Report on the safety and liability implications of Artificial Intelligence, the Internet of Things and robotics", COM (2020) 64 final, Brussels, 19.2.2020.

Commission Communication "White Paper On Artificial Intelligence - A European approach to excellence and trust", COM(2020) 65 final, Brussels, 19.2.2020.

European Parliament Resolution of 20 October 2020 with recommendations to the Commission on a civil liability regime for artificial intelligence (2020/2014 (INL)) P9_TA(2020)0276 ('European Parliament's Resolution of 20 October 2020 on a civil liability regime for AI').

Annex to the European Parliament Resolution of 20 October 2020 with recommendations to the Commission on a civil liability regime for artificial intelligence: detailed recommendations for drawing up a Regulation on liability for the operation of artificial intelligence systems, A. Principles and Aims of the Proposal. B. Text of the Proposal Requested—Proposal for a Regulation on liability for the operation of Artificial Intelligence-systems ('Annex to the

European Parliament's Resolution of 20 October 2020 on a civil liability regime for AI').

Report from the Expert Group on Liability and New Technologies – New Technologies Formation "Liability for Artificial Intelligence and Other Emerging Digital Technologies", 21 November 2019.

"The Assessment List for Trustworthy Artificial Intelligence (ALTAI) for self-assessment", High-Level Expert Group on AI (AI HLEG), 17 July 2020.

Responses by Organisations, Associations and Corporations to Public Consultations

BEUC (the European Consumer Organisation), feedback on the European Commission's Inception Impact Assessment on "Civil liability – adapting liability rules to the digital age and artificial intelligence", submitted on 28.07.2021.

BEUC (the European Consumer Organisation), "Product Liability 2.0 - How to make EU rules fit for consumers in the digital age", submitted on 07.05.2020.

The Future Society (TFS), "Liability rules for Trust in Excellence & Excellence in Trust - Inception Impact Assessment - Adapting liability rules to the digital age and circular economy", Belgium, 28 July 2021.

ACEA (The European Automobile Manufacturers' Association), Response to the European Commission's inception impact assessment on civil liability - Adapting liability rules to the digital age and circular economy, 28.07.2021.

Microsoft, Comments on the Inception Impact Assessment "Adapting liability rules to the digital age and circular economy", 28 July 2021.

Google, Views on the European Commission's inception impact assessment on civil liability - adapting liability rules to the digital age and AI, 28 July 2021.

The Information Technology Industry Council (ITI), "Comments to European Commission's Inception Impact Assessment on the Revision of EU Liability Rule", 28.07.2021.

Fujitsu, "Response to the European Commission's inception impact assessment on civil liability - adapting liability rules to the digital age and artificial intelligence, submitted on 28.07.2021.

Center for Data Innovation, Response to the European Commission's inception impact assessment on civil liability - adapting liability rules to the digital age and AI, submitted on 28.07.2021.

Input from ZVEI – German Electrical and Electronic Manufacturers' Association on "Civil liability – adapting liability rules to the digital age and artificial intelligence", submitted on 28.07.2021.

Bitkom Bundesverband Informationswirtschaft, Telekommunikation und neue Medien e.V. (Federal Association for Information Technology, Telecommunications and New Media), "Position Paper - Inception Impact Assessment: Adapting liability rules to the digital age and artificial intelligence", 27.07.2021.

BSA – The Software Alliance, "Comments on the Initial Impact Assessment on adapting liability rules to the digital age", 28.07.2021.

COCIR (the European Coordination Committee of the Radiological, Electromedical and Healthcare IT Industry) feedback on the European Commission's inception impact assessment - Civil Liability – adapting liability rules to the digital age and artificial intelligence, submitted on 28.07.2021.

App Association (ACT), Response to the European Commission's inception impact assessment on civil liability - Adapting liability rules to the digital age and circular economy, 28.07.2021.

The Information Technology Industry Council (ITI), "Comments to European Commission's Inception Impact Assessment on the Revision of EU Liability Rule", 28.07.2021.

DJI - the global leading manufacturer of small drones, "Response to the European Commission's inception impact assessment on civil liability - adapting liability rules to the digital age and AI", 28.07.2021.

References

Bathaee Y (2018) The artificial intelligence black box and the failure of intent and causation. Harv J Law Technol 31(2):889–938

Beck S (2016) The problem of ascribing legal responsibility in the case of robotics. AI Soc 31(4): 473–481

Bertolini A (2018) Artificial Intelligence and civil law - Liability rules for drones, Study requested by the European Parliament's Committee on Legal Affairs, Policy Department for Citizens' Rights and Constitutional Affairs, November 2018

Bertolini A (2020) Artificial intelligence and civil liability, Study requested by the European Parliament's Committee on Legal Affairs, Policy Department for Citizens' Rights and Constitutional Affairs – Directorate-General for Internal Policies, PE 621.926, July 2020

Bertolini A (2013) Robots as products: the case for a realistic analysis of robotic applications and liability rules. Law Innov Technol 5:214–247

Boom WH v, Borghetti J-S, Ehlers AB, Karner E, Nolan D, Oliphant K, Scarso A, Ulfbeck V, Wagner G (2018) Product liability in Europe. In: Koziol H, Green MD, Lunney M, Oliphant K, Yang L (eds) Product liability: fundamental questions in a comparative perspective. De Gruyter, Berlin, pp 255–356

Borghetti J-S (2019) How can artificial intelligence be defective. In: Lohsse S, Schulze R, Staudenmayer D (eds) Liability for artificial intelligence and the internet of things. Nomos, Baden-Baden, pp 63–76

Chatzipanagiotis M, Leloudas G (2020) Automated vehicles and third-party liability: a European perspective. Univ Ill J Law Technol Policy 1:109–199

Christidis K, Devetsikiotis M (2016) Blockchains and smart contracts for the internet of things. IEEE Access 4:2292–2303

de Bruin R (2016) Autonomous intelligent cars on the European intersection of liability and privacy: regulatory challenges and the road ahead. Eur J Risk Regul 7(3):485–501

de Meeus C (2019) The product liability directive at the age of the digital industrial revolution: fit for innovation? J Eur Consum Mark Law 8(4):149–154

Ebers M, Navas S (eds) (2020) Algorithms and law. Cambridge University Press

Evas T (2018) A common EU approach to liability rules and insurance for connected and autonomous vehicles, Study. European Added Value Assessment - Accompanying the

European Parliament's legislative own-initiative report (Rapporteur: Mady Delvaux). Study, European Parliamentary Research Service (EPRS), February 2018
Evas T (2020) Civil liability regime for artificial intelligence, study. European Parliamentary Research Service (EPRS), September 2020
Fairgrieve D, Rajneri E (2019) Is software a product under the product liability directive? Zeitschrift für Internationales Wirtschaftsrecht 1:24–28
Fairgrieve D, Howells G, Møgelvang-Hansen P et al (2016) Product liability directive. In: Machnikowski P (ed) European product liability: an analysis of the state of the art in the era of new technologies. Principles of European Tort Law, Intersentia, pp 17–108
Florina Lohmann M (2016) Liability issues concerning self-driving vehicles. Eur J Risk Regul 7(2): 335–340
Grundmann S, Hacker P (2017) Digital technology as a challenge to European contract law – from the existing to the future architecture. Eur Rev Contr Law 13:255–293
Howells G, Twigg-Flesner C, Willett C (2017) Product liability and digital products. In: Synodinou T-E, Jougleux P, Markou C, Prastitou T (eds) EU internet law: regulation and enforcement. Springer Nature, pp 183–195
Karner E, Koch BA, Geistfeld MA (2021) Comparative law study on civil liability for artificial intelligence. European Commission, Directorate-General for Justice and Consumers
Koch BA, Borghetti J-S, Machnikowski P, Pichonnaz P, Rodríguez de las Heras Ballell T, Twigg-Flesner C, Wendehorst C (2022) Response of the European law institute to the public consultation on civil liability – adapting liability rules to the digital age and artificial intelligence. J Eur Tort Law 13(1):25–63
Kritikos M (2016) Legal and ethical reflections concerning robotics. Scientific Foresight Unit (STOA) Policy Briefing, European Parliament Research Service (EPRS), PE 563.501, June 2016
Kritikos M (2019) Artificial Intelligence ante Portas: legal & ethical reflections. European Parliamentary Research Service (EPRS), Scientific Foresight Unit (STOA), March 2019
Leenes R, Palmerini E, Koops B-J, Bertolini A, Salvini P, Lucivero F (2017) Regulatory challenges of robotics: some guidelines for addressing legal and ethical issues. Law Innov Technol 9:1–44
Lohsse S, Schulze R, Staudenmayer D (2019) Liability for artificial intelligence. In: Lohsse S, Schulze R, Staudenmayer D (eds) Liability for artificial intelligence and the internet of things. Nomos, Baden-Baden, pp 99–116
Luzak J (2020) A broken notion: impact of modern technologies on product liability. Eur J Risk Regulat 11(3):630–649
Machnikowski P (2016) Conclusions. In: Machnikowski P (ed) European product liability: an analysis of the state of the art in the era of new technologies. Principles of European Tort Law, Intersentia, pp 669–705
Madiega T (2020) Reform of the EU liability regime for online intermediaries: background on the forthcoming digital services act: in depth analysis. European Parliamentary Research Service (EPRS), May 2020
Martín-Casals M (2019) Causation and scope of liability in the internet of things (IoT). In: Lohsse S, Schulze R, Staudenmayer D (eds) Liability for artificial intelligence and the internet of things. Nomos, Baden-Baden, pp 201–228
Francesco Mezzanotte (2019) Liability for digital products. In: De Franceschi A, Schulze R (eds) Digital revolution – new challenges for law. Nomos, 169-188.
Navas S (2020) Robot machines and civil liability. In: Ebers M, Navas S (eds) Algorithms and law. Cambridge University Press, pp 157–173
Nevejans N (2016) European civil law rules in robotics. Study requested by the European Parliament's Committee on Legal Affairs (JURI Committee)
Nikolinakos NT (2022) Adapting the EU liability regime to artificial intelligence (AI): the European Commission's proposed policy options. Comput Telecommun Law Rev (C.T.L.R.) 28(3):66–83
Palmerini E, Bertolini A, Battaglia F, Koops B-J, Carnevale A, Salvini P (2016) RoboLaw: towards a European framework for robotics regulation. Rob Auton Syst 86:78–85

Paolo Patti F (2019) The European road to autonomous vehicles. Fordham Int Law J 43:125
Ponce del Castillo A (2017) A law on robotics and artificial intelligence in the EU? (October 3, 2017). Foresight Brief, European Trade Union Institute (ETUI) Research Paper - Foresight Brief #02-September 2017
Schellekens M (2018) No-fault compensation schemes for self-driving vehicles. Law Innov Technol 10(2):314–333
Sérgio Cabral T (2020) Liability and artificial intelligence in the EU: assessing the adequacy of the current product liability directive. Maastricht J Eur Comp Law 27(5):615–635
Shavell S (2020) On the redesign of accident liability for the world of autonomous vehicles. J Legal Stud 49:243–285
Spindler G (2019) User liability and strict liability in the internet of things and for robots. In: Lohsse S, Schulze R, Staudenmayer D (eds) Liability for artificial intelligence and the internet of things. Nomos, Baden-Baden, pp 125–145
Tenhunen S (2022) Aligning the Product Liability Directive with the circular economy and emerging technologies: Revision of Directive 85/374/EEC. Implementation Appraisal Briefing, European Parliamentary Research Service (EPRS), October 2022
Timan T, Snijders R, Kirova M, Suardi S, van Lieshout M, Chen M, Costenco P, Palmerini E, Bertolini A, Tejada A, van Montfort S, Bolchi M, Alberti S, Brouwer R, Karanilokova K, Episcopo F, Jansen S (2019) Study on safety of non-embedded software. Service, data access, and legal issues of advanced robots, autonomous, connected, and AI-based vehicles and systems: final study report regarding CAD/CCAM and industrial robots. European Commission, Brussel
Twigg-Flesner C (2021) Guiding principles for updating the product liability directive for the digital age. (Pilot ELI Innovation Paper), European Law Institute (January 2021)
Verheyen T (2018) Full harmonization, consumer protection and products liability: a fresh reading of the case law of the ECJ. Eur Rev Priv Law 26(1):119–140
Wagner G (2019a) Robot liability. In: Lohsse S, Schulze R, Staudenmayer D (eds) Liability for artificial intelligence and the internet of things. Nomos, Baden-Baden, pp 27–62
Wagner G (2019b) Robot, Inc.: personhood for autonomous systems? Fordham Law Rev 88:591
Wagner G (2021) Liability for artificial intelligence: a proposal by the European Parliament. In: Eidenmüller H, Wagner G (eds) Law by Algorithm, p 127
Wagner G (2022a) Software as a product. In: Lohsse S, Schulze R, Staudenmayer D (eds) Smart products. Hart, Nomos, p 157
Wagner G (2022b) Liability rules for the digital age – aiming for the Brussels effect. J Eur Tort Law (JETL) 13(3):191–243
Wendehorst C (2020) Strict liability for AI and other emerging technologies. J Eur Tort Law (JETL) 11(2):150–180
Wendehorst C (2021) Safety and liability related aspects of Software. Study Commissioned by the European Commission.
Wuyts D (2014) The product liability directive – more than two decades of defective products in Europe. J Eur Tort Law 5(1):1–34
Zech H (2021) Liability for AI: public policy considerations. Academy of European Law (ERA) Forum 22:147-158, Springer.
Zech H (2019) Liability for autonomous systems: tackling specific risks of modern IT. In: Lohsse S, Schulze R, Staudenmeyer D (eds) Liability for artificial intelligence and the internet of things. Nomos, Baden-Baden, pp 187–200

Chapter 7
Adapting EU Liability Rules to the Digital Age and Artificial Intelligence: The 2021–2022 Public Consultation

7.1 Introduction

This chapter discusses the public consultation (which was open from 18 October 2021 to 10 January 2022) on how to improve the Product Liability Directive (PLD) and how to address the challenges that artificial intelligence poses for liability rules.[1]

---

[1] For interesting reading, analysis, and useful academic commentary, see the following:

Gerhard Wagner, 'Software as a Product' in: S. Lohsse/R. Schulze/D. Staudenmayer (eds.), Smart Products, 157, (2022), Hart, Nomos.

Gerhard Wagner, "Liability Rules for the Digital Age – Aiming for the Brussels Effect", Journal of European Tort Law (JETL) 2022, vol. 13, no. 3, pp. 191–243.

Nikos Th. Nikolinakos, 'Adapting the EU Liability Regime to Artificial Intelligence (AI): The European Commission's Proposed Policy Options', (2022) 28 Computer & Telecommunications Law Review (C.T.L.R.), Issue 3, pp. 66–83.

Susanna Tenhunen, 'Aligning the Product Liability Directive with the circular economy and emerging technologies: Revision of Directive 85/374/EEC', Implementation Appraisal Briefing, European Parliamentary Research Service (EPRS), October 2022.

Koch, Bernhard A, Borghetti, Jean-Sébastien, Machnikowski, Piotr, Pichonnaz, Pascal, Rodríguez de las Heras Ballell, Teresa, Twigg-Flesner, Christian and Wendehorst, Christiane, "Response of the European Law Institute to the Public Consultation on Civil Liability – Adapting Liability Rules to the Digital Age and Artificial Intelligence", Journal of European Tort Law, vol. 13, no. 1, 2022, pp. 25–63.

Philipp Hacker and Jan-Hendrik Passoth, "Varieties of AI Explanations under the Law. From the GDPR to the AIA, and Beyond", in: Holzinger, Goebel, Fong, Moon, Müller and Samek (eds.), Lecture Notes on Artificial Intelligence 13200: xxAI - beyond explainable AI, Springer, 2022.

Gerhard Wagner, Liability for Artificial Intelligence: A Proposal by the European Parliament, in: H. Eidenmüller/G. Wagner, Law by Algorithm (2021) 127.

Ernst Karner, Bernhard A. Koch, Mark A. Geistfeld, 'Comparative Law Study on Civil Liability for Artificial Intelligence', European Commission, Directorate-General for Justice and Consumers, 2021.

N. T. Nikolinakos, *Adapting the EU Civil Liability Regime to the Digital Age: Artificial Intelligence, Robotics, and Other Emerging Technologies*, Law, Governance and Technology Series 68, https://doi.org/10.1007/978-3-031-67969-8_7

Christiane Wendehorst, 'Safety and Liability Related Aspects of Software', Study commissioned by the European Commission, 2021.

Thomas Verheyen, "On Behavioural Asymmetry in Product Liability Law: How Privatising Nudging Will Get European Product Liability Theory Back on Track", Journal of European Tort Law, vol. 12, no. 1, 2021, pp. 40–64.

Herbert Zech, 'Liability for AI: public policy considerations', Academy of European Law (ERA) Forum, Volume 22, 147–158, Springer, 2021.

Christian Twigg-Flesner, 'Guiding Principles for Updating the Product Liability Directive for the Digital Age' (Pilot ELI Innovation Paper), European Law Institute (January 2021).

Christiane Wendehorst, "Strict liability for AI and other emerging technologies", Journal of European Tort Law (JETL) 2020, 11(2): 150–180.

Tiago Sérgio Cabral, "Liability and artificial intelligence in the EU: Assessing the adequacy of the current Product Liability Directive", Maastricht Journal of European and Comparative Law, 27(5), 615–635, (2020).

Tatjana Evas, Civil liability regime for artificial intelligence, Study, European Parliamentary Research Service (EPRS), September 2020.

Joasia Luzak, "A Broken Notion: Impact of Modern Technologies on Product Liability", European Journal of Risk Regulation, 11(3):630–649, (2020).

Steven Shavell, "On the Redesign of Accident Liability for the World of Autonomous Vehicles", (2020) 49 The Journal of Legal Studies, 243–285.

Tambiama Madiega, 'Reform of the EU Liability Regime for Online Intermediaries: Background on the Forthcoming Digital Services Act: In Depth Analysis', European Parliamentary Research Service (EPRS), May 2020.

Michael Chatzipanagiotis and George Leloudas, 'Automated Vehicles and Third-Party Liability: A European Perspective', University of Illinois Journal of Law, Technology & Policy 2020(1), pp. 109–199.

Andrea Bertolini, Artificial intelligence and civil liability, Study requested by the European Parliament's Committee on Legal Affairs, Policy Department for Citizens' Rights and Constitutional Affairs – Directorate-General for Internal Policies, PE 621.926, July 2020.

Susanna Navas, 'Robot Machines and Civil Liability'. In M. Ebers & S. Navas (eds.), Algorithms and Law. Cambridge University Press, 2020, 157–173.

Gerhard Wagner, 'Robot Liability' in S.Lohsse/R.Schulze/D.Staudenmayer (eds), Liability for Artificial Intelligence and the Internet of Things. Nomos, Baden-Baden (2019), pp. 27–62.

Gerhard Wagner, "Robot, Inc.: Personhood for Autonomous Systems?", 88 Fordham Law Review, 591 (2019).

Mihalis Kritikos, 'Artificial Intelligence ante portas: Legal & ethical reflections', European Parliamentary Research Service (EPRS), Scientific Foresight Unit (STOA), March 2019.

Francesco Mezzanotte, 'Liability for Digital Products', in: A De Franceschi/R Schulze (eds), Digital Revolution – New Challenges for Law, 169–188. Nomos, (2019).

Herbert Zech: "Liability for autonomous systems: tackling specific risks of modern IT". In: Lohsse, S., Schulze, R., Staudenmeyer, D. (eds.), Liability for Artificial Intelligence and the Internet of Things. Nomos, Baden-Baden (2019), pp. 187–200.

Borghetti J-S, 'How can artificial intelligence be defective'. In: Lohsse S, Schulze R, Staudenmayer D (eds) Liability for artificial intelligence and the Internet of Things. Nomos, Baden-Baden (2019), pp. 63–76.

Gerald Spindler, 'User Liability and Strict Liability in the Internet of Things and for Robots' in Sebastian Lohsse, Reiner Schulze and Dirk Staudenmayer (eds), Liability for Artificial Intelligence and the Internet of Things. Nomos, Baden-Baden (2019), pp. 125–145.

Miquel Martín-Casals, 'Causation and Scope of Liability in the Internet of Things (IoT)' in Sebastian Lohsse/Reiner Schulze/Dirk Staudenmayer (ed), Liability for Artificial Intelligence and the Internet of Things. Nomos, Baden-Baden (2019), pp. 201–228.

Lohsse, S., Schulze, R., & Staudenmayer, D., 'Liability for Artificial Intelligence', In S. Lohsse, R. Schulze, & D. Staudenmayer (eds.), Liability for Artificial Intelligence and the Internet of Things. Nomos, Baden-Baden (2019), 99–116.

D. Fairgrieve and Eleonora Rajneri, 'Is Software a Product under the Product Liability Directive?', Zeitschrift für Internationales Wirtschaftsrecht, January 2019, Volume 1/2019, pp. 24–28.

Francesco Paolo Patti, "The European Road to Autonomous Vehicles", 43 Fordham Int'l L.J. 125 (2019).

Charlotte de Meeus, 'The Product Liability Directive at the Age of the Digital Industrial Revolution: Fit for Innovation?', (2019), Vol. 8, Journal of European Consumer and Market Law, Issue 4, pp. 149–154.

Timan, T., R. Snijders, M. Kirova, S. Suardi, M. v. Lieshout, M. Chen, P. Costenco, E. Palmerini, A. Bertolini, A. Tejada, S. v. Montfort, M. Bolchi, S. Alberti, R. Brouwer, K. Karanilokova, F. Episcopo and S. Jansen (2019). Study on safety of non-embedded software. Service, data access, and legal issues of advanced robots, autonomous, connected, and AI-based vehicles and systems: final study report regarding CAD/CCAM and industrial robots. Brussel, European Commission.

Thomas Verheyen, "Full Harmonization, Consumer Protection and Products Liability: A Fresh Reading of the Case Law of the ECJ", 26 (1) European Review of Private Law, 119–140, (2018).

Tatjana Evas, A common EU approach to liability rules and insurance for connected and autonomous vehicles, Study. European Added Value Assessment - Accompanying the European Parliament's legislative own-initiative report (Rapporteur: Mady Delvaux). Study, European Parliamentary Research Service (EPRS), February 2018.

Andrea Bertolini, Artificial Intelligence and civil law - Liability rules for drones, Study requested by the European Parliament's Committee on Legal Affairs, Policy Department for Citizens' Rights and Constitutional Affairs, November 2018.

Boom, Willem H van, Borghetti, Jean-Sébastien, Ehlers, Andreas Bloch, Karner, Ernst, Nolan, Donal, Oliphant, Ken, Scarso, Alessandro, Ulfbeck, Vibe and Wagner, Gerhard. "Product Liability in Europe". Product Liability: Fundamental Questions in a Comparative Perspective, edited by Helmut Koziol, Michael D. Green, Mark Lunney, Ken Oliphant and Lixin Yang, Berlin, Boston: De Gruyter, 2018, pp. 255–356.

Yavar Bathaee, "The artificial intelligence black box and the failure of intent and causation", Harvard Journal of Law & Technology, Volume 31, Number 2, 889-938, (2018).

Maurice Schellekens, 'No-Fault Compensation Schemes for Self-Driving Vehicles', Law, Innovation and Technology, 2018, 10:2, 314-333.

Howells, G., Twigg-Flesner, C., and Willett, C., Product Liability and Digital Products. In T-E. Synodinou, P. Jougleux, C. Markou, & T. Prastitou (eds.), EU Internet Law: Regulation and Enforcement. 2017, Springer Nature, 183–195.

D. Fairgrieve, G. Howells, P. Møgelvang-Hansen et al., Product Liability Directive. In: P. Machnikowski (ed), European Product Liability: An Analysis of the State of the Art in the Era of New Technologies. Principles of European Tort Law. Intersentia; 2016:17–108.

Piotr Machnikowski, Conclusions, in: P Machnikowski (ed), European Product Liability: An Analysis of the State of the Art in the Era of New Technologies. Principles of European Tort Law. Intersentia; 2016:669–705.

Daily Wuyts, "The Product Liability Directive – More than two Decades of Defective Products in Europe" Journal of European Tort Law, vol. 5, no. 1, 2014, pp. 1–34.

In particular, following the European Commission's 2021 Inception Impact Assessment (IIA) "Adapting liability rules to the digital age and circular economy",[2] further input was gathered and more comments were received from a wide variety of stakeholders (including consumers and civil society organisations, industry associations, businesses, and public authorities) during a 12-week public consultation period, starting on 18 October 2021 and ending on 10 January 2022. The aim of this public consultation was to confirm the relevance of the issues identified by the 2018 evaluation of the Product Liability Directive (i.e. how to apply the Directive to products in the digital and circular economy), and collect information and opinions on how to improve the PLD (Section I of the consultation).[3] At the same time, Section II of the consultation specifically dealt with AI-related issues, exploring further the major problems connected with certain types of AI, which make it difficult for the victim/injured party to obtain compensation, i.e. to identify the potentially liable person, to prove that person's fault or to prove the defect in the product and the causal link between the defect and the damage.[4] This difficulty becomes even higher as emerging digital technologies and products are becoming increasingly connected and complex.

The Commission expected to receive, in the course of the three months consultation period, information on the need and possible recommendations to address those issues related specifically to damage caused by AI systems, which concerns both the Product Liability Directive and national civil liability rules. In relation to Section II of the consultation, the Commission repeated that its aim is to provide the legal certainty required for innovation and investment and to ensure that persons having suffered harm caused by of AI systems should enjoy equal level of protection as persons having suffered harm caused by other technologies that operate without AI.[5]

Section II of the consultation covered all three pillars of the existing liability framework, namely (i) the Product Liability Directive, which deals with consumer claims against producers of defective products, and it is up to the injured party to prove the product was defective and the causal link between that defect and the damage; (ii) National fault-based liability rules, where the injured party has to prove the defendant's fault, i.e. negligence or intent to harm, and a causal link between that fault and the damage; (iii) National strict liability regimes which are set by member states for technologies or activities considered to pose an increased risk to society. Strict liability lies with the person who, irrespective of fault, exercises a degree of

[2] Commission's Inception Impact Assessment "Adapting liability rules to the digital age and circular economy", Ref. Ares(2021)4266516, 30.06.2021.

[3] Commission's Public Consultation, "Adapting liability rules to the digital age and Artificial Intelligence", 18 October 2021, p. 1.

[4] Ibid.

[5] Ibid., p. 29.

control over a risk connected with the operation of a technology/activity and benefits from exposing the public to a risk.[6]

Once again, the Commission stated that specific characteristics of AI—high degree of autonomous behaviour, continuous adaptation and limited predictability, limited explainability (complexity/'black box effect') and limited transparency (opacity)—could make it difficult for injured parties to get compensation, both under the Product Liability Directive and under national civil liability rules, since, in certain situations, it could become difficult for injured parties to identify and prove the fault of a potentially liable person or that a product is defective as well as the causal link between that fault/defect and the damage suffered.[7] It was also stated that a lack of harmonised rules in this area could hinder the development and deployment of AI-enabled products and services. Member States could attempt to address the resulting legal uncertainty at national level, and national courts could apply diverging ad hoc solutions, leading to further fragmentation of liability rules across the EU for damage caused by AI products and services. As the Commission put it, "it may also be uncertain whether and to what extent national strict liability regimes (e.g. for dangerous activities) will apply to the use of AI-enabled products or services. National laws may change, and courts may adapt their interpretation of the law, to address these potential challenges";[8] "with the growing number of AI-enabled products and services on the market, Member States may adapt their respective liability regimes to the specific challenges of AI, which could lead to increasing differences between national liability rules. The Product Liability Directive could also be interpreted in different ways by national courts for damage caused by AI".[9]

The Commission put forward the following general statements, expecting to receive specific comments by the participants in the course of the public consultation: "(i) There is uncertainty as to how the Product Liability Directive (i.e. liability for defective products) applies to damage caused by AI. (ii) There is uncertainty as to whether and how liability rules under national law apply to damage caused by AI. (iii) When AI operates with a high degree of autonomy, it could be difficult to link the damage it caused to the actions or omissions of a human actor. (iv) In the case of AI that lacks transparency (opacity) and explainability (complexity), it could be difficult for injured parties to prove that the conditions of liability (such as fault, a defect, or causation) are fulfilled. (v) Because of AI's specific characteristics, victims of damage caused by AI may in certain cases be less protected than victims of damage that did not involve AI. (vi) It is uncertain how national courts will address possible difficulties of proof and liability gaps in relation to AI. (vii) The lack of

---

[6]Ibid.

[7]Ibid., pp. 29 and 33.

[8]Ibid., p. 29.

[9]Commission's Public Consultation, "Adapting liability rules to the digital age and Artificial Intelligence", 18 October 2021, p. 32.

adaptation of the current liability framework to AI may negatively affect trust in AI ... and may negatively affect the uptake of AI-enabled products and services".[10]

7.2 Commission's Proposed Policy Measures

Based on the abovementioned general statements, the Commission put forward proposed policy measures to ensure that victims of damage caused by AI systems are not left with less protection than victims of damage caused by technologies that operate without AI. Those proposed measures, which "aim to help the victim recover damage more easily",[11] are based on existing approaches in national liability regimes (e.g. alleviating the burden of proof for the injured party or strict liability for the producer). They could also complement the Commission's relevant policy initiatives, such as the proposed AI Act. As explained in detail below, the Commission's proposed approaches focused on (i) measures to ease the victim's burden of proof as well as (ii) a targeted harmonisation of strict liability and (iii) insurance solutions.[12]

7.2.1 Approaches Regarding the Burden of Proof—Measures to Ease the Victim's Burden of Proof

The Commission put forward specific approaches (alongside the option that EU action to ease the victim's burden of proof is not necessary or justified) regarding the burden of proof in order to assist the victim recover damage more easily.

Amongst the Commission's proposals appears the obligation of the defendant (e.g. producer, user, service provider, operator) to disclose necessary technical information (e.g. log data) to the injured party to enable the latter to prove the conditions of the claim. However, if the defendant refuses to disclose such necessary technical information, courts should infer that the conditions to be proven by that information are fulfilled.[13]

---

[10] Ibid., pp. 30–31.

[11] Ibid., p. 34.

[12] Ibid.

[13] Ibid. See also Option 2.1.a of the Commission's 2021 Inception Impact Assessment (IAA), which proposed to alleviate the burden of proof by (i) obliging the producer to disclose technical information to the injured party and (ii) allowing courts to infer that a product is defective or caused the damage under certain circumstances, e.g. when other products in the same production series have already been proven to be defective or when a product clearly malfunctions. Commission's Inception Impact Assessment "Adapting liability rules to the digital age and circular economy", Ref. Ares(2021)4266516, 30.06.2021, at p. 4.

Furthermore, with regard to claims raised under the Product Liability Directive, the Commission put forward the statement that, in case an AI-enabled product clearly malfunctioned (e.g. driverless vehicle swerving off the road despite no obstacles), courts should infer that the said AI-enabled product was defective and caused the damage.[14]

The Commission also put forward the statement that, if the provider or the user of an AI system failed to comply with their safety or other legal obligations to prevent harm (such as those proposed under the draft AI Act), courts should infer that the damage was caused due to that person's fault or that, for claims against the provider under the Product Liability Directive, the AI system was defective.[15]

It was also underlined that, in case it is necessary to establish how a complex and/or opaque AI system (i.e. an AI system with limited transparency and explainability) operates in order to substantiate a claim, the burden of proof should

---

Furthermore, it is reminded that the Expert Group on Liability and New Technologies stressed the importance of introducing an obligation to provide appropriate and proportionate logging and to disclose the necessary data to the victim and/or the person who compensates the victim in readable format. It pointed out that failure to comply with a logging and disclosure (providing reasonable access to logged data) duty should result in "a rebuttable presumption that the information would, if logged and disclosed, have revealed that the relevant element of liability is fulfilled". See Report from the Expert Group on Liability and New Technologies – New Technologies Formation "Liability for Artificial Intelligence and Other Emerging Digital Technologies", 21 November 2019, at pp. 47 and 48, Key Finding [22].

[14] Commission's Public Consultation, "Adapting liability rules to the digital age and Artificial Intelligence", 18 October 2021, p. 34.

[15] Ibid., pp. 34–35. It is reminded that, according to the Commission, "the burden of proof could be linked to the compliance (by a relevant operator) with specific cyber-security or other safety obligations set by law: if one does not comply with these rules, a change to the burden of proof as regards fault and causation could apply". See Commission "Report on the safety and liability implications of Artificial Intelligence, the Internet of Things and robotics", Brussels, COM (2020) 64 final, 19.2.2020, at p. 14.

This is also in line with the findings of the Report from the Expert Group on Liability and New Technologies, which underlined that, in certain circumstances, it could be appropriate to reverse or lower the burden of proof if damage was caused by a breach of some other set of rules (such as safety/security rules, including cybersecurity). Failing to comply with safety rules could lead to a reversal of the burden of proof concerning key elements of liability, including causation and fault: "where the damage is of a kind that safety rules were meant to avoid, failure to comply with such safety rules, including rules on cybersecurity, should lead to a reversal of the burden of proving (a) causation, and/or (b) fault, and/or (c) the existence of a defect". See Report from the Expert Group on Liability and New Technologies – New Technologies Formation "Liability for Artificial Intelligence and Other Emerging Digital Technologies", 21 November 2019, Key Finding (24), at pp. 7 and 48. Furthermore, according to the findings of the Report from the Expert Group on Liability and New Technologies, "if it is proven that an emerging digital technology has caused harm, the burden of proving defect should be reversed if there are disproportionate difficulties or costs pertaining to establishing the relevant level of safety or proving that this level of safety has not been met". See Report from the Expert Group on Liability and New Technologies – New Technologies Formation "Liability for Artificial Intelligence and Other Emerging Digital Technologies", 21 November 2019, Key Finding (15), at p. 6.

be shifted from the victim to the defendant in that respect.[16] Indeed, it is argued that, given how opaque AI systems can become, it would be extremely difficult, if not impossible, for consumers to prove a manufacturing or design defect. Therefore, the burden of proof concerning defect and causation could be reversed and the injured party would just need to prove the existence of damage resulting from a product. This is in line with Option 2.1.b of the Commission's 2021 Inception Impact Assessment (IAA), which proposed to reverse the burden of proof so that, in case a damage occurred, the producer would have to prove that the product was not defective.[17] The Commission also put forward the alternative option that specific types of opaque or highly autonomous AI systems could be defined for which the burden of proof regarding fault and causation should always be on the person responsible for that AI system (i.e., reversal of burden of proof).[18]

Furthermore, regarding claims raised under the Product Liability Directive, the Commission stated that, if a product integrating an AI system that continuously learns and adapts while in operation causes damage, the producer should be liable irrespective of defectiveness. In this case, the victim will have to prove only that the damage was caused by this particular product.[19] This is in line with Option 2.1.c of the Commission's 2021 Inception Impact Assessment (IAA), which suggested removing the 'development risk defence' in order to ensure producers of AI-related products that continuously learn and adapt while in operation remain strictly liable for damage.[20] It is reminded that, according to Article 7(e) of the Product Liability Directive, the 'development risk defence' allows the producer to

---

[16] Commission's Public Consultation, "Adapting liability rules to the digital age and Artificial Intelligence", 18 October 2021, p. 35.

[17] Commission's Inception Impact Assessment "Adapting liability rules to the digital age and circular economy", Ref. Ares(2021)4266516, 30.06.2021, p. 4.

See also the approach followed by the Report of the Expert Group on Liability and New Technologies, which stated, *inter alia*, that "if it is proven that an emerging digital technology caused harm, and liability therefor is conditional upon a person's intent or negligence, the burden of proving fault should be reversed if disproportionate difficulties and costs of establishing the relevant standard of care and of proving their violation justify it. This is without prejudice to the reversal of the burden of proof". See Report from the Expert Group on Liability and New Technologies – New Technologies Formation "Liability for Artificial Intelligence and Other Emerging Digital Technologies", 21 November 2019, Key Finding (27), at pp. 8 and 52.

[18] Commission's Public Consultation, "Adapting liability rules to the digital age and Artificial Intelligence", 18 October 2021, p. 35.

[19] Ibid.

[20] Commission's Inception Impact Assessment "Adapting liability rules to the digital age and circular economy", Ref. Ares(2021)4266516, 30.06.2021, p. 4.

This also follows the proposal put forward by the Report of the Expert Group on Liability and New Technologies, which stated that "the producer should be strictly liable for defects in emerging digital technologies even if said defects appear after the product was put into circulation, as long as the producer was still in control of updates to, or upgrades on, the technology. A development risk defence should not apply". Report from the Expert Group on Liability and New Technologies – New Technologies Formation "Liability for Artificial Intelligence and Other Emerging Digital Technologies", 21 November 2019, Key Finding [14], at p. 42.

avoid liability if the state of scientific and technical knowledge at the time when he put the product into circulation was not such as to enable the existence of the defect to be discovered.

7.2.2 *Approaches Regarding Strict Liability for Operating AI-Enabled Products and Providing AI-Enabled Services*

Separately from the strict liability of producers under the Product Liability Directive, the Commission appears to favour ("a possible policy option at EU level") the extension of harmonisation of strict liability based on a 'risk-based' approach, i.e. taking into consideration whether the AI-systems have a specific risk profile (such as those endangering the lives, health and property of members of the public). This proposal looks to harmonise the existing national strict liability schemes of operators/users that apply to AI-equipped products and providers of AI-based services (where injured parties only have to prove that the damage emanates from the sphere of the operator of the AI-system). This would be similar to what exists in almost all Member States' legal systems as regards motor vehicle liability, namely strict liability of the producer for defects under the Product Liability Directive as well as strict liability of the owner/operator. Therefore, the Commission seems willing to develop a separate and complementary (to the Product Liability Directive) instrument (a Directive) on strict civil liability (for the owner/user/operator) for AI based on the risk profile of AI systems, i.e., depending on whether the AI system causing the harm has been classified as low or high risk. In other words, the Commission appears to reserve strict liability for AI systems presenting high risks, i.e., it considers limiting strict liability to some specifically defined AI systems (possibly to the "high risk" AI systems defined as such under the proposed AI Act). Such an option is in line with the principle of proportionality, as products and services should not be subject to increased liability rules simply because they integrate AI (i.e., irrespective of whether the product or service presents a unique and severe risk of harm, or whether the AI component is a contributing factor to that risk).

As the Commission put it, "strict liability means that a certain risk of damage is assigned to a person irrespective of fault. A possible policy option at EU level could be to harmonise strict liability (full or minimum), separately from the Product Liability Directive, for damage caused by the operation of certain AI-enabled products or the provision of certain AI-enabled services. This could notably be considered in cases where the use of AI (e.g. in autonomous vehicles and autonomous drones) exposes the public to the risk of damage to important values like life, health and property. Where strict liability rules already exist in a Member State, e.g. for cars, the EU harmonisation would not lead to an additional strict liability regime".[21]

[21] Commission's Public Consultation, "Adapting liability rules to the digital age and Artificial Intelligence", 18 October 2021, p. 36.

See also the Commission's Inception Impact Assessment "Adapting liability rules to the digital age and circular economy", Ref. Ares(2021)4266516, 30.06.2021, p. 4.

This is also in line with the Report from the Expert Group on Liability and New Technologies, which stated that "a person operating a permissible technology that nevertheless carries an increased risk of harm to others, for example AI-driven robots in public spaces, should be subject to strict liability for damage resulting from its operation"; "strict liability is an appropriate response to the risks posed by emerging digital technologies, if, for example, they are operated in non-private environments and may typically cause significant harm". See Report from the Expert Group on Liability and New Technologies – New Technologies Formation "Liability for Artificial Intelligence and Other Emerging Digital Technologies", 21 November 2019, at pp. 3, 39 and 40.

In 2020, based on the analysis of the Report from the Expert Group on Liability and New Technologies, the Commission stated that the application of strict liability should be limited to situations where the emerging technologies may create specific risks (which are likely to arise in circumstances where digital technologies move in public spaces, e.g., drones, autonomous cars, traffic management services), expose the public at large to risks, and cause significant harm to life, health, and property: "the operation of some autonomous AI devices and services could have a specific risk profile in terms of liability, because they may cause significant harm to important legal interests like life, health and property, and expose the public at large to risks. This could mainly concern AI devices that move in public spaces (e.g. fully autonomous vehicles, drones and package delivery robots) or AI-based services with similar risks (e.g. traffic management services guiding or controlling vehicles or management of power distribution). The challenges of autonomy and opacity to national tort laws could be addressed following a risk-based approach. Strict liability schemes could ensure that whenever that risk materialises, the victim is compensated regardless of fault. The impact of choosing who should be strictly liable for such operations on the development and uptake of AI would need to be carefully assessed and a risk-based approach be considered". See Commission "Report on the safety and liability implications of Artificial Intelligence, the Internet of Things and robotics", Brussels, COM (2020) 64 final, 19.2.2020, at p. 16.

The Commission also follows the recommendation put forward by the European Parliament's proposal for a Regulation on liability for the operation of AI systems, which stated that the type of AI-system the operator is exercising control over should be a determining factor regarding liability. The European Parliament underlined that an AI-system that entails an inherent high risk and acts autonomously potentially endangers the user or the general public to a much higher degree and in a manner that is random and goes beyond what can reasonably be expected. See European Parliament Resolution of 20 October 2020 with recommendations to the Commission on a civil liability regime for artificial intelligence (2020/2014(INL)) P9_TA(2020)0276, (section "Liability of the operator"), at point 15. See also the European Parliament's Proposal for a Regulation on liability for the operation of AI systems, at recital 13: "This means that at the start of the autonomous operation of the AI-system, the majority of the potentially affected persons are unknown and not identifiable, for example persons on a public square or in a neighbouring house, compared to the operation of an AI-system that involves specific persons, who have regularly consented to its deployment before, for example surgery in a hospital or a sales demonstration in a small shop". As the European Parliament put it, different liability rules should apply for different risks, following a risk-based approach and, as a result "it seems reasonable to set up a common strict liability regime for those high-risk autonomous AI-systems". See European Parliament Resolution of 20 October 2020 with recommendations to the Commission on a civil liability regime for artificial intelligence (2020/2014 (INL)) P9_TA(2020)0276, (section "Liability of the operator"), at point 14.

Based on the above, the Commission followed a gradual intervention policy logic, ranging from the position of enacting no legislation ("strict liability for operating AI-enabled products and providing of AI-enabled services should not be harmonised at EU level")[22] to policy options of different degrees of regulatory intervention. The Commission invited interested parties to express their views on whether full harmonisation of strict liability for operating AI-enabled products and providing AI-enabled services, limited to cases where these activities create serious injury risks (e.g. life, health, property) for the public, is required.[23] This option could be further extended by allowing Member States to maintain broader and/or more far-reaching national strict liability schemes applicable to other (e.g. non high-risk) AI-enabled products and services.[24]

7.2.3 Approach Regarding Insurance for the Use of AI Systems That Pose a Serious Risk of Injury to the Public

Under many Member States' strict liability schemes, the person liable is required by law to take out insurance. The Commission examined whether a similar solution could be selected at EU level for damage caused by certain types of AI systems that create serious injury risks (e.g. life, health, property) for the public.

In particular, the Commission put forward specific statements[25] and asked interested parties to express their views on whether there should be harmonisation of mandatory insurance coverage for using certain (high-risk) AI products and providing certain AI-based services: "A harmonised insurance obligation should be laid down at EU level, where it does not exist yet, for using AI products and providing AI-based services that pose a serious injury risk (e.g. life, health, property) to the public".[26] This approach seems to follow the findings of the Report from the Expert

---

[22]Commission's Public Consultation, "Adapting liability rules to the digital age and Artificial Intelligence", 18 October 2021, p. 36.

[23]Ibid.

[24]Ibid.

[25]Ibid., p. 37: "Parties subject to possible harmonised strict liability rules ... would likely be covered by (voluntary or mandatory) insurance". "In cases where possible facilitations of the burden of proof would apply ..., the potentially liable party would likely be covered by (voluntary or mandatory) liability insurance". "Insurance solutions (be they voluntary or mandatory) could limit the costs of potential damage for the liable person to the insurance premium ... and "could ensure that the injured person receives compensation".

[26]Ibid., p. 38. According to the Commission, reasons supporting the introduction of a harmonised insurance obligation at EU level are the following: "Mandatory insurance coverage ensures that the injured party receives due compensation; mandatory insurance makes potential liability costs more predictable by limiting them to the insurance premiums, which facilitates business planning and lowers market entry barriers, especially across borders; mandatory insurance coverage ultimately spreads the liability costs over everyone taking out insurance, avoiding very high and burdensome one-off costs for the liable party" (at p. 39).

Group on Liability and New Technologies, which stated that "for situations exposing third parties to an increased risk of harm, compulsory liability insurance could give victims better access to compensation and protect potential tortfeasors against the risk of liability";[27] "the more frequent or severe potential harm resulting from emerging digital technology, and the less likely the operator is able to indemnify victims individually, the more suitable mandatory liability insurance for such risks may be".[28] It is also in line with the European Parliament's proposal for a Regulation on liability for the operation of AI systems, which stressed that users need to be sure that potential damage caused by AI-systems is covered by adequate insurance and that there is a defined legal route for redress. Proper liability coverage was considered as "one of the key factors that defines the success of new technologies, products and services" and as "essential for assuring the public that it can trust the new technology despite the potential for suffering harm or for facing legal claims by affected persons";[29] "insurance can help guarantee that victims receive effective compensation and pool the risks of all insured persons".[30] Therefore, according to the European Parliament's proposal, all operators of high-risk AI systems should hold liability insurance similar to that used for motor vehicles.[31]

---

[27] Report from the Expert Group on Liability and New Technologies – New Technologies Formation "Liability for Artificial Intelligence and Other Emerging Digital Technologies", 21 November 2019, at p. 4.

[28] Ibid., Key Finding [33], at pp. 9 and 61. See also at pp. 61–62: "As experience in at least some fields (mostly motorised traffic) has shown, mandatory liability insurance can work well and is indeed appropriate under certain conditions. From an insurance perspective, certain sectors are the most suited to compulsory insurance schemes, including transportation, industries with a high potential for personal injury and/or environmental harm, hazardous activities and certain professional sectors. Therefore, it may indeed be advisable to make liability insurance cover compulsory for certain emerging digital technologies. This is particularly true for highly significant risks (which may either lead to substantial harm and/or cause frequent losses), where it seems unlikely that potential injurers will be capable of compensating all victims themselves (either out of their own funds, with the help of alternative financial securities, or through voluntary self-insurance)".

See also: Commission Staff Working Document on "Liability for emerging digital technologies" - Accompanying the document Commission Communication "Artificial intelligence for Europe", SWD(2018) 137 final, Brussels, 25.4.2018, at pp. 13–14 and 21; Commission "Report on the safety and liability implications of Artificial Intelligence, the Internet of Things and robotics", Brussels, COM (2020) 64 final, 19.2.2020, at pp. 12 and 13.

[29] European Parliament's Resolution of 20 October 2020 on a civil liability regime for AI, (section "Insurances and AI-systems"), at point 23.

[30] Annex to the European Parliament's Resolution of 20 October 2020 on a civil liability regime for AI – B. Text of the Proposal for a Regulation on liability for the operation of AI systems, at recital 21.

[31] European Parliament's Resolution of 20 October 2020 on a civil liability regime for AI, (section "Insurances and AI-systems"), at point 24.

This compulsory insurance regime for high-risk AI-systems should cover the amounts and the extent of compensation laid down by the Parliament's proposed Regulation. Both the frontend and backend operators of a high-risk AI-system should ensure that operations of the AI-system (in the case of the frontend operator) and its services (in the case of the backend operator) are covered by liability insurance and by business liability or product liability insurance respectively that is

7.2.4 *Summary of the Proposed Policy Options*

Based on the above, the Commission summarised the options presented in the public consultation document, ranging from the position of enacting no legislation ("Option 8: No EU action. Outside the existing scope of the Product Liability Directive, each Member State would be free to adapt liability rules for AI if and as they see fit")[32] to policy options of different degrees of regulatory intervention: "Option 1: Amending the Product Liability Directive to ease the burden on victims when proving an AI-enabled product was defective and caused the damage. Option 2: Targeted harmonisation of national rules on proof, e.g. by reversing the burden of proof under certain conditions, to ensure that it is not excessively difficult for victims to prove, as appropriate, fault and/or causation for damage caused by certain AI-enabled products and services. Option 3: Harmonisation of liability irrespective of fault ('strict liability') for operators of AI technologies that pose a serious injury risk (e.g. life, health, property) to the public. Option 4: option 3 + mandatory liability insurance for operators subject to strict liability. Option 5: option 1 + option 2. Option 6: option 1 + option 2 + option 3. Option 7: option 1 + option 2 + option 4".[33]

Therefore, if option 7 is to be selected, the proposal would include the following: (i) amendment of the Product Liability Directive to ease the victim's burden of proof when an AI-enabled product was defective and caused the damage; (ii) harmonisation of national rules on proof, e.g. by reversing the burden of proof under certain conditions, to ensure that it is not excessively difficult for victims to prove fault and/or causation for damage caused by certain AI-enabled products and services; (iii) harmonisation of strict liability for operators of AI technologies that pose a serious injury risk; and (iv) mandatory liability insurance for operators subject to strict liability.[34]

---

adequate in relation to the amounts and extent of compensation provided for in the Parliament's proposed Regulation. See the Annex to the European Parliament's Resolution of 20 October 2020 on a civil liability regime for AI – B. Text of the Proposal for a Regulation on liability for the operation of AI systems, Article 4(4).

[32] Commission's Public Consultation, "Adapting liability rules to the digital age and Artificial Intelligence", 18 October 2021, p. 40.

[33] Ibid., pp. 39–40.

[34] According to the Commission, the proposed policy options of regulatory intervention could have the following beneficial impacts (compared to the position of enacting no EU legislation): "Victims would be equally well protected when AI causes damage as in cases where AI is not involved; positive impact on trust in AI-enabled products and services; increased legal certainty regarding liability for AI; increased uptake of AI-driven products and services; . . . reduced legal information costs; reduced insurance costs; economies of scale due to a reduced need for technological adaptations when providing AI-based products or services cross-border; cost savings due to a reduced need to adapt business models in light of diverging national liability rules; companies may choose to bring forward or pursue certain cross-border business activities involving AI technologies that they would otherwise have reduced, deferred or abandoned; companies may extend across borders certain business activities involving AI that they would otherwise have limited to a single

7.2.5 *Other Types of Compensable Harm*

It is reminded that the Product Liability Directive protects life and health as well as consumer property. However, it is not entirely clear whether 'consumer property' covers damage to data, since data may not be an 'item of property' within the meaning of Article 9 (b) of the Product Liability Directive. Indeed, it is not universally acknowledged that damage to or the destruction of data constitutes a property loss, because, according to various legal systems, the notion of 'property' excludes intangibles and, therefore, tortious liability cannot be triggered.

However, the Commission explicitly stated that, aside from bodily injury and property damage, some of the uses of AI may also cause immaterial harm and affect people's mental wellbeing.[35] The effects of AI systems must be carefully monitored and addressed and, therefore, the fact that coverage for such harm differs widely in Member States led the Commission examine the option of harmonising compensation for certain types of immaterial harm, specifically for cases where using AI leads to harm.[36] According to the Commission, the types of immaterial harm could include (i) pure economic loss (e.g. loss of profit); (ii) loss of or damage to data (not covered by the GDPR) resulting in a verifiable economic loss; (iii) loss of or damage to data (not covered by the GDPR) not resulting in a verifiable economic loss; (iv) immaterial harm like pain and suffering, reputational damage or psychological harm.[37]

This approach is in line with the Commission's view in 2020, when it was stated that "immaterial harm can relate to, for instance, loss of privacy or limitations to the right of freedom of expression (possibly caused by intrusive surveillance or monitoring systems) or unlawful discrimination (such as in the case of recruitment tools that display a bias against certain groups of the population) or discrimination in the access to products and services such as lack of accessibility for persons with disabilities, to name but a few. Harm caused by the use of AI may be the consequence of multiple causes, such as flaws in the overall design of the AI system, the use of poor quality or biased data, or machine learning related characteristics, such as the probabilistic nature of the system or the ability of certain AI systems to continue

---

Member State or a smaller number of Member States; positive impact on the development, roll-out and uptake of AI technologies in the internal market; higher costs due to increased insurance premiums and compensation claims; companies will pass on to consumers /customers cost increases linked to liability; negative impact on the development, roll-out and uptake of AI technologies in the internal market". Commission's Public Consultation, "Adapting liability rules to the digital age and Artificial Intelligence", 18 October 2021, pp. 40–41.

[35] Commission's Public Consultation, "Adapting liability rules to the digital age and Artificial Intelligence", 18 October 2021, p. 40.

[36] Ibid., p. 42.

[37] Ibid.

learning when in use".[38] It also follows the Commission's 2021 Inception Impact Assessment, which suggested extending the range of damages for which compensation could be claimed under the Product Liability Directive to non-material damages (i.e. data loss, privacy infringements or environmental damage),[39] the European Parliament's recommendation that "both material and immaterial harm should be taken into account in the future proposal for a Regulation",[40] as well as the Report of the Expert Group on Liability and New Technologies which pointed out that, under specific conditions, the destruction of the victim's data should be regarded as compensable damage.[41] In addition, it is reminded that the Commission has underlined the importance of tackling the mental health risks for users deriving from the collaboration with humanoid AI robots and systems and pointed out that the definition of health should include both physical and mental wellbeing.[42]

---

[38] Commission's Inception Impact Assessment, Title of the Initiative "Proposal for a legal act of the European Parliament and the Council laying down requirements for Artificial Intelligence", 23.07.2020, Ref. Ares(2020)3896535, at p. 2.

[39] Commission's Inception Impact Assessment "Adapting liability rules to the digital age and circular economy", Ref. Ares(2021)4266516, 30.06.2021, Option 1.b, p. 4.

[40] European Parliament's Resolution of 20 October 2020 on a civil liability regime for AI, section "Different liability rules for different tasks", at point 19.

See also the Annex to the European Parliament's Resolution of 20 October 2020 on a civil liability regime for AI – A. Principles and Aims of the Proposal, principle 8.

[41] The Report of the Expert Group on Liability and New Technologies stressed that "with much of our lives and our 'property' becoming digital, it is no longer appropriate to limit liability to the tangible world. However, neither is it appropriate to simply equate data with tangible property for the purposes of liability". . . . "Damage caused to data may lead to liability where (a) liability arises from contract; or (b) liability arises from interference with a property right in the medium on which the data was stored or with another interest protected as a property right under the applicable law; or (c) the damage was caused by conduct infringing criminal law or other legally binding rules whose purpose is to avoid such damage; or (d) there was an intention to cause harm". Report from the Expert Group on Liability and New Technologies – New Technologies Formation "Liability for Artificial Intelligence and Other Emerging Digital Technologies", 21 November 2019, at p. 59.

[42] Commission Communication "Report on the safety and liability implications of Artificial Intelligence, the Internet of Things and robotics", COM (2020) 64 final, Brussels, 19.2.2020, p. 8.

See also the World Health Organization (WHO) Constitution, first bullet point: "Health is a state of complete physical, mental and social well-being and not merely the absence of disease or infirmity." (https://www.who.int/about/who-we-are/constitution). If the mental health risks are not addressed, the violation of human dignity and long-term harmful impact on the human psyche seem inevitable. This is why the Commission identified that "AI systems should integrate safety and security-by-design mechanisms to ensure that they are verifiably safe at every step, taking at heart the physical and mental safety of all concerned". See Commission Communication, "Building Trust in Human-Centric Artificial Intelligence", COM(2019) 168 final, Brussels, 8.4.2019, p. 5.

Furthermore, the Commission stressed that explicit obligations for producers should be considered in respect of mental safety risks of users when appropriate: "mental health risks should be explicitly covered within the concept of product safety in the legislative framework"; "explicit obligations for producers of, among others, AI humanoid robots to explicitly consider the immaterial harm their products could cause to users, in particular vulnerable users such as elderly persons in care environments, could be considered for the scope of relevant EU legislation". See

7.2.6 *Admissibility of Contractual Liability Waivers*

Lastly, the Commission pointed out that contractual liability provisions may exclude (or place limits on) the right to compensation. For instance, software vendors typically attempt to minimise or even exclude their civil liability by inserting warranty disclaimers and limitations of liability in their terms of service. It is common to agree to waive the right to recover indirect, consequential, and punitive damages, or to limit liability for direct damages even those caused by the negligence of the vendor. According to some Member States, all or certain such clauses should be prohibited or restricted. It is also recalled that the Product Liability Directive does not allow producers limit or exclude their liability towards the injured person by contract.[43]

Based on the above, and in case it is chosen to harmonise at EU level the liability of operators/users for damage caused by AI, the Commission asked interested parties to express their views on specific approaches that could be followed regarding contractual clauses excluding or limiting in advance the victim's right to compensation. In particular, the Commission put forward the following policy options of regulatory intervention: (i) no action is required, i.e., the admissibility of contractual liability waivers should not be addressed at all; (ii) contractual liability waivers should be prohibited vis-à-vis consumers; (iii) contractual liability waivers should be prohibited vis-à-vis consumers and between businesses; (iv) the contractual exclusion or limitation of liability should be prohibited only for certain types of harm (e.g. to life, body or health) and/or for harm arising from gross negligence or intent.[44]

7.3 Summary of the Contributions Made by Stakeholders in the Public Consultation on the Initiative Adapting Civil Liability Rules to the Digital Age and Artificial Intelligence

7.3.1 *Introduction*

An extensive consultation strategy was implemented by the Commission in order to ensure a wide participation of stakeholders. As a result, the online public consultation, which was open from 18 October 2021 to 10 January 2022, gathered views from a wide variety of stakeholders, including consumer and civil society

Commission Communication "Report on the safety and liability implications of Artificial Intelligence, the Internet of Things and robotics", COM (2020) 64 final, Brussels, 19.2.2020, p. 8.

[43] Commission's Public Consultation, "Adapting liability rules to the digital age and Artificial Intelligence", 18 October 2021, p. 42.

[44] Ibid., p. 43.

organisations, industry associations, businesses, and public authorities. After analysing the responses received, the Commission published a summary of the public consultation results, i.e. an outcome of the contributions made by stakeholders on how to improve the Product Liability Directive and how to address the challenges that artificial intelligence poses for liability rules.[45]

7.3.2 Views of Respondents on the Product Liability Directive

7.3.2.1 Adapting the Product Liability Directive to the Digital Age and Circular Economy

7.3.2.1.1 Intangible Items: Software and Digital Services

This section of the public consultation focused on the need to adapt the Product Liability Directive to the digital age and, in particular, on the crucial role that digital content, software, algorithms, digital services and data should play in the safe functioning of many products.[46]

It is reminded that the Product Liability Directive does not make any reference to the concept of service nor does it provide for the distinction between products and services. It solely provides for the definition of product. Services do not fall into the definition of product. It was recognised, therefore, that the distinction between products and services for the purpose of the Product Liability Directive is becoming increasingly blurred with regards to new technological developments. As a result, the definition of product appears to no longer be as clear-cut and, therefore, a clarification of its scope (e.g., whether software is covered by the legal concept of product or product component) should be required.

---

[45] "Section I of the consultation was on the Product Liability Directive (PLD) and concerned the difficulties of applying the Directive to products in the digital and circular economy and the difficulties for consumers of getting compensation and making claims. Section II of the consultation concerned problems linked to certain types of AI that make it possibly difficult to identify the potentially liable person, to prove that person's fault and/or the defect of a product and the causal link with the damage". Commission, DG GROW and DG JUST, "Factual summary report of the open public consultation on Adapting Civil Liability Rules to the Digital Age and AI", Ref. Ares (2022)2620305, 06.04.2022, p. 2.

[46] Commission, DG GROW and DG JUST, "Factual summary report of the open public consultation on Adapting Civil Liability Rules to the Digital Age and AI", Ref. Ares(2022)2620305, 06.04.2022, p. 2.

See also the Commission's Inception Impact Assessment "Adapting liability rules to the digital age and circular economy", Ref. Ares(2021)4266516, 30.06.2021, p. 2: "Digital content, software and data play a crucial role in the safe functioning of many products but it is not clear to what extent such intangible elements can be classified as products under the Directive. It is therefore unclear whether injured parties can always be compensated for damage caused by software, including software updates, and who will be liable for such damage".

The Commission asked whether the EU's existing product liability regime should be extended beyond physical products to encompass software, "digital services" and "digital content". According to the Commission, all respondents agreed that consumers should get compensation under the Product Liability Directive when intangible products are defective and cause physical/property damage, although less than half of the respondents were in favour of including data or information per se.[47]

---

[47]Commission, DG GROW and DG JUST, "Factual summary report of the open public consultation on Adapting Civil Liability Rules to the Digital Age and AI", Ref. Ares(2022)2620305, 06.04.2022, p. 3: "In particular in the case of: software that controls how a product works (78% or 122 out of 155); software upgrades and updates (66% or 102 out of 154); software supplied separately to use on a product (56% or 87 out of 155); digital services that controls how a product work (55% or 85 out of 154). . . . Individual members of the public (122), on the other hand, showed even stronger agreement, with 96%, on average, agreeing or strongly agreeing that consumers should get compensation if damaged by defective software or digital services that control how a product works and software upgrades/updates".

According to the Irish Council for Civil Liberties (ICCL) ("ICCL - Submission to the consultation on adapting liability rules to the digital age and artificial intelligence", 7 January 2022, p. 2), the definition of 'product' in Article 2 of the Product Liability Directive should be updated to include software: "the definition of a product should be updated. Article 2 of PLD . . . should be updated to clearly state that software is a product".

Similarly, according to Eurosmart ("Eurosmart on the Product Liability Directive", 12.01.2022, p. 1), "Software as a product: Software solutions are fully part of our daily lives and their malfunctioning can lead to significant damage. Such damage should be covered by the Product Liability Directive. Therefore, the definition of a product should be revised to encompass software, including artificial intelligence systems. Thus, Article 2 of the Directive could be extended as follows: For the purpose of this Directive, "product means all movables, even if incorporated into another movable or into an immovable. "Product" includes electricity and software".

See also the view submitted by the European Law Institute ("Response of the European Law Institute (ELI) - Public Consultation on Civil Liability Adapting liability rules to the digital age and artificial intelligence", Bernhard A Koch, Jean-Sébastien Borghetti, Piotr Machnikowski et al., 12.01.2022, p. 9), which stated that "the definition of 'product' currently used in the PLD should be updated to cover: (i) the combination of goods with digital elements; and (ii) digital content and certain digital services supplied as 'digital products'". For an interesting analysis, see pp. 9–14 of the European Law Institute's response.

For an opposite view, see for instance the following:

The response submitted by BSA – The Software Alliance, "Response to the European Commission's consultation on civil liability – adapting liability rules to the digital age and artificial intelligence", 10.01.2022, pp. 3–4: "If the Commission chooses to proceed with reform of the civil liability regime to accommodate software and AI systems despite the concerns expressed above, we recommend it consider the following when drafting any new rules: 1. Any reforms to the civil liability regime should recognize the difference between physical products and software: The consultation queries whether the EU's existing product liability regime should be extended beyond physical products to encompass software, "digital services" and "digital content" (it is unclear what specific technologies are included in these categories or how they differ). In contrast to physical products, however, which are typically used for a specific and foreseeable range of purposes, software often can be deployed in an almost unlimited number of ways, across a wide range of products, and for many different purposes. In addition, software's functioning, and in turn its ultimate deployment, is often heavily dependent on the user of the software and the context in which it is used—rendering it much more like a service than a product. The Directive recognizes these differences and imposes no-fault liability only on defective products. Where the software is embedded in a product before being put into circulation, the Directive provides a means of redress for consumers. However, it does not extend liability to stand-alone software or to digital services (indeed, the Directive does not apply to any services). We encourage the Commission to take this distinction into account and keep the focus of any reforms to the Directive on products.

See also the response submitted by BusinessEurope, "Comments – Adapting liability rules to the digital age and Artificial Intelligence", 10.01.2022, pp. 1-2: "Physical products should remain the basis for the application of the Directive and clarity on the coverage of embedded software could be enhanced through clearer guidance. . . . Only physical and property damage should continue to be covered under the Product Liability framework. . . . The application of the PLD to technologies that operate more as a service than as products, such as the online use of software, should mainly be addressable under the existing framework and be consistent with the Artificial Intelligence Act. A better understanding of the existing possibilities under the PLD is needed in order to provide clarity on the concept of "product" – this could happen for example by continuation of the existing expert group on the PLD. More clarity on the coverage of embedded software could also be enhanced through clearer guidance, including the incoming update to the Commission Blue Guide for product safety. In all cases, software or data should not be defined as a 'product' as understood in the Product Liability Directive. This would broaden the scope of the Directive and change its logic. Not only would it raise many practical issues related to other concepts in the Directive, most notably that of 'defect', what is key is that the consumer can effectively address the producer of the tangible product, who in turn will have recourse to other parts of the supply chain. Very little evidence has been established of cases where standalone software would have caused bodily harm or property damage. Potential problems in high-risk areas should be addressed by the relevant sector-specific framework. . . . Therefore, we recommend that physical products remain the basis for the application of the Directive and that any possible initiatives do not explicitly define services as a product".

In addition, see the Computer & Communications Industry Association (CCIA Europe), "A product liability regime fit for the digital age", 20.12.2021, at p. 2: "It should be carefully evaluated whether the definition of 'product' should be expanded to include intangible products, such as stand-alone software, digital content and other AI/automated-decision making processes, even services. A strict liability regime is ill-suited to the properties of software and AI systems. Due to the complexity of writing code, it is not realistic to expect a software that is 100% free of errors. If software developers are subject to strict liability for any error in their code, it would deter software development in Europe, and disproportionately impact European companies".

Furthermore, according to Google's comments "Public consultation: Civil liability – adapting liability rules to the digital age and artificial intelligence", 7 January 2022, pp. 1-2: "Google believes that Europe's current liability framework remains fit for purpose; there is no need for legislative change at this time. It is effective and technology neutral. Despite hypothetical edge cases that have been proposed to justify changes to the EU's liability framework, in practice the existing framework continues to provide effective protections for consumers while enabling innovation and competition. We have seen no evidence of widespread challenges in real cases that would warrant altering such a fundamental underpinning. We would caution against introducing sweeping changes to the current liability framework. In particular, it seems unnecessary and ill-suited to apply a strict liability regime directly to software and AI systems. . . . In Google's view the existing product liability framework remains effective and fit for purpose. Strict liability is a concept that deviates from the legal norm that liability should prerequisite fault. It is reserved for situations that are especially hazardous and bear a risk of damage to other persons or property, although they are legally allowed, such as operating a vehicle, disposing hazardous waste (cf. Environmental Damages Directive), operating a nuclear power plant or, as seen in product liability, placing a product on the market. It should therefore be applied with great caution. So far, there is no real-world evidence of problems that would warrant fundamental change. Far-reaching legislative change should not be initiated without proof that there actually is a problem that needs to be solved, and without exact knowledge of which issues need to be addressed. The liability regime needs to balance the goal of ensuring that consumers can receive compensation for grave injuries caused by products, with maintaining incentives for developers and producers to pursue development and innovation. In fact, amending the framework for software-enabled products could create additional burdens on consumers. Existing rules under the Product Liability Directive are already applicable to tangible products with embedded software or otherwise containing software. This ensures that the manufacturer is the responsible party and consumers can seek remedies with them directly. . . . Imposing strict liability for software bugs could also lead to significant harms to consumers, and create a severe chilling effect on digitization and innovation in the EU. While software providers do extensive testing and debugging before releasing software, bugs almost always become apparent over time and are fixed by updates or in later releases. Despite decades of effort, it has proven impossible to entirely eradicate bugs from software due to the complexity of writing code, and this is generally accepted as an inherent feature of software development. Strict liability for software bugs would effectively discourage developers from developing and releasing any software, with a severe impact on European consumers and the EU's digital strategy, and a disproportionate impact on European SMEs. This would be a problem in particular for open source software developers, because they have less control over how the software will be used and/or further developed and could not control any safety risks".

Also, according to the position submitted by Siemens ("Siemens – Executive summary on EU (civil) tort liability framework", 07.01.2022, p. 1), "stand-alone software needs to be carefully excluded from the scope of the PLD. We, however, support clarification – preferably via a Guidance of the European Commission - that embedded software as part of a tangible product has been included in the strict liability regime of the PLD, even if such embedded software has been updated after the physical product has been put on the market. This position relies on the current liability regime which balances strict liability with appropriate liability restrictions (e.g. liable producer is the entity which puts the physical product on the market) and defences (e.g. for component suppliers like the provider of embedded software). These defences consider the individual split of controls and responsibilities in the course of development and production cycle of physical products and should remain in place. The scope of the PLD should continue to focus on the physical products and embedded software since stand-alone software or data is hardly to cause bodily injury or property damage on its own, while potential high-risk areas can be addressed more appropriately by the relevant sector-specific framework and AI Act".

Similarly, the Software & Information Industry Association (SIIA) stated ("Comments of the Software & Information Industry Association (SIIA) on the Public Consultation regarding Adapting liability rules to the digital age and Artificial Intelligence", 10.01.2022, at pp. 1–3) that "extending the strict liability rules in the Product Liability Directive to software and other intangible, digital products is ill-advised, and will lead to numerous negative consequences for innovators and consumers alike. The rationale underlying the Product Liability Directive, that producers should be held liable for defective products that cause damage to persons or property, regardless of intent, cannot apply to software and other intangible digital products due to their unique characteristics. . . . Software is by its nature in a regular state of development. Even after software is introduced to the marketplace, it is regularly updated to make improvements (often to respond to consumer demands), patch cybersecurity vulnerabilities (which typically are not known at the time of development), and for other reasons. Moreover, not all software is sold directly to consumers, and it is common for software created by one company to be combined with software products created by another company. In other words, the very factors that lead the EC to consider software to be "intangible" make the translation of product liability rules designed for "tangible" products inappropriate for these digital products or services. The movement of much software to the cloud has further widened this gap. . . . Imposition of a strict liability regime on software will harm innovation, development, and consumer welfare. The mere specter of liability for product defects will lead many developers to hold on releasing products to the public. Rather than creating certainty, the possibility of legal liability for "imperfect" or "defective" products will generate significant uncertainty. . . . From the consumer safety perspective, application of product liability to software would create perverse incentives. The notion that a software update could itself be grounds for liability could lead developers to withhold critical updates to fix bugs and cyber vulnerabilities and chill innovation. . . . Ultimately, it is the consumer that is likely to bear the costs and inconveniences that a strict liability regime will generate".

7.3.2.1.2 Online Marketplaces and Products Coming from Outside the EU

Online marketplaces have enabled consumers to buy products from outside the EU without there being an importer, leaving consumers with no liable person from whom to seek compensation under the Product Liability Directive if damage has occurred.[48] This is why the majority (64%) of all respondents agreed that the PLD needs to ensure consumer protection if defective products cause damage bought through online marketplaces where there is no EU-based producer or importer. However, of those, 83% were non-business respondents (i.e., consumer, civil society and other non-profit organisations), while only 17% were corporations and business organisations/associations.[49]

---

[48] Commission, DG GROW and DG JUST, "Factual summary report of the open public consultation on Adapting Civil Liability Rules to the Digital Age and AI", Ref. Ares(2022)2620305, 06.04.2022, pp. 3-4.

See also the Commission's Inception Impact Assessment "Adapting liability rules to the digital age and circular economy", Ref. Ares(2021)4266516, 30.06.2021, p. 2.

[49] Commission, DG GROW and DG JUST, "Factual summary report of the open public consultation on Adapting Civil Liability Rules to the Digital Age and AI", Ref. Ares(2022)2620305, 06.04.2022, p. 4. Among respondents, 45% disagreed on whether the proposed draft Digital Services Act (DSA) and draft General Product Safety Regulation (GPSR) were sufficient to ensure consumer protection as regards online marketplaces, while only 29% were favourable. Out of 45%, 66% were consumer organisations, NGOs and citizens and only 22% were business associations and industries. Out of 29%, 63% were business associations and industries and 31% were consumer organisations, NGOs and citizens.

With regard to the view supported by non-business stakeholders, see for instance the response submitted by BEUC (the European Consumer Organisation) to the European Commission's public consultation on Civil liability – adapting liability rules to the digital age and artificial intelligence, 23.12.2021, at pp. 5–6: "Online marketplaces must fully become part of the supply chain and be subsidiarily liable under the PLD. . . . Experience shows that online marketplaces are today the main gateway to the European market for non-EU defective products. Hence, relying on the authorized representatives will not solve the problem of access to compensation for consumers when things go wrong. This is because the mandate of the authorized representative can be ended from the side of the manufacturer at any time and there is not even a period for which such a representative must be available after the product has been sold. It is therefore likely that there will be no longer an authorized representative available to answer questions to the authorities about product compliance if a problem arises several years after the product has been put on the market. . . . Online marketplaces have a very important responsibility when it comes to selling and distributing defective products. Our member organisations have found a wealth of evidence showing that defective products are circulating on online marketplaces. Hence online marketplaces must minimize the risk of harm and only strong liability rules can perform that role. . . . It is wrong to believe that the proposal for a General Product Safety Regulation (GPSR) and the proposal for a Digital Services Act (DSA) alone can solve this issue. Both the GPSR and the DSA intend to add new obligations for online marketplaces. However, they do not solve the issue of liability of online marketplaces in case of harms caused to consumers or their property by products purchased through these platforms. There is thus a gap that the PLD should bridge and only a consistent reform of all relevant pieces of legislation can ensure that consumers will be kept safe, and markets are fair. . . . The European Commission should consider the developments happening in other parts of the world which tend to recognize online marketplaces as important actors in the field of product liability. . . . Addressing the issue of liability for online marketplaces does not require to create new legal

7.3.2.1.3 New Categories of Risks and New Kinds of Damage

Overall, the majority (70%) of respondents supported the view that producers should be liable for failing to provide security updates. Of those, consumer organisations, NGOs and EU citizens overwhelmingly (93%) confirmed this view, while the majority (69%) of corporations and business organisations/associations opposed this statement.[50] Furthermore, the majority (60%) of respondents agreed with the

---

categories within the PLD. The existing categories, such as the one of "suppliers", could be adapted and applied to online marketplaces. We therefore strongly encourage the European Commission to consider holding online marketplaces as "suppliers" under the PLD and to adapt the conditions under which suppliers can be held liable. Under the existing rules, "suppliers" bear a subsidiary liability, meaning that they can be held liable if the producer is unknown. We think that online marketplaces must be subject to similar subsidiary liability but that the conditions should be reviewed".

For an opposite view, see the argument submitted by BusinessEurope, "Comments – Adapting liability rules to the digital age and Artificial Intelligence", 10.01.2022, at p. 2: "The role of online marketplaces and their responsibilities is well established under the current and proposed EU legal framework, in particular the Digital Services Act, the General Product Safety Regulation, the Market Surveillance Regulation, and the Platform to Business Regulation. In our opinion, these (proposals for) regulations are sufficient to ensure consumer protection as regards products bought through online marketplaces. Furthermore, new provisions under the proposed Digital Services Act (Art. 14 and 22) and the General Product Safety Regulation (Art. 20) provide for strict due dilligence and traceability obligations on online marketplaces. These requirements are completed by the new obligation for economic operators to appoint an EU representative for high-risk products sold in the EU where there is no EU-based producer or importer, recently applicable in the framework of the Market Surveillance Regulation, which is sufficient to ensure the same level of protection for the purchases of products online. Holding online marketplaces strictly liable for products of which they are not the producer, seller or importer would make them liable for products which are not under their control. We should be careful not to impose large barriers for new intermediaries to enter the market. Therefore, the impact of these new regulations should be carefully assessed before considering any further change to the EU liability framework to ensure that it remains consistent".

[50]Commission, DG GROW and DG JUST, "Factual summary report of the open public consultation on Adapting Civil Liability Rules to the Digital Age and AI", Ref. Ares(2022)2620305, 06.04.2022, p. 4.

See for instance the view put forward by BusinessEurope, "Comments – Adapting liability rules to the digital age and Artificial Intelligence", 10.01.2022, at pp. 2–3: "BusinessEurope recommends that only physical and property damage should continue to be covered under the Product Liability framework. We stress that the EU product safety legal framework provides sound safety and cybersecurity obligations ex-ante that will be complemented with stricter horizontal requirements in the framework of the announced EU Cyber Resilience Act, based on the principles of the New Legislative Framework for products. To the extent that safety legislation ensures the safety of products on the market, it will reduce the need for consumers to seek for compensation under product liability rules. While issues with cybersecurity may indeed result eventually in a 'defect' as understood by the Directive, the consumer can find recourse with the producer of the physical product, who can then in turn recover the costs further up in the supply chain through contractual relations. Therefore, we do not see the need to explicitly widen the concept of 'defect' to include cybersecurity. In addition, cyberattacks usually involve economic damages, which are not and should not be covered by strict liability. If software is used to control safety critical applications, the relevant safety standards should be addressed by special legislation. Furthermore, it is difficult to

statement that producers should be liable for damage to data. Again, consumer organisations, NGOs and EU citizens overwhelmingly (87%) supported this view, with only 18% of business and industry stakeholders agreeing with this statement.[51]

---

quantify to what type of damages it would lead, and how harmful the impact is for consumers. It is important to ensure legal certainty for businesses and to balance strict liability for damages linked to poor cyber-hygiene practices by users. Since infringements of data privacy and personal rights are already sanctioned in data privacy law, anti-discrimination law and tort liability, we see no gaps in legal protection. In addition, a risk-oriented approach to liability also means that there should not be multiple liability for any damage under the same conditions. We should be cautious not to limit innovation because manufacturers are potentially exposed to unlimited damage claims that go beyond property damage/physical injury".

See also the response submitted by the Computer & Communications Industry Association (CCIA Europe), "A product liability regime fit for the digital age", 20.12.2021, at pp. 2–3: "Applying strict liability to software updates and refurbishments is unnecessary and would further disincentive software development and maintenance by making it harder for producers to extend the lives of digital products and address software errors. This would ultimately undermine innovation and efforts to encourage sustainability in the circular economy, for example, by discouraging producers from providing spare parts. ...Software providers have limited control over security updates - often accepted by the users themselves- however, they would still be strictly liable for omissions of other market participants. In this line, it is important to bear in mind that the AI ecosystem and value chain are highly complex. Expanding responsibilities for defective products beyond the producer to, for example, the engineer, deployer, developer, or whoever is in charge of the updated software would need to consider the different life cycles of AI products, and who is responsible for what at each stage".

Also, see a slightly different response submitted by the GSMA ("GSMA response to the EC public consultation on Adapting Liability Rules to the Digital Age and AI", 22.12.2021, p. 1): "The Tangible Goods Directive, Digital Content Directive and Consumer Sales Directive already provides a baseline framework regarding software updates. For example, Directive (EU) 2019/771 introduces the obligation for sellers and traders to install software. Therefore, consumers can rely on EU wide rules on liabilities based on their contractual rights. The PLD should be more precise about IT-security vulnerabilities, particularly with regard to networked products to close IT-security gaps quickly and to provide updates throughout the entire lifecycle. In this sense, the concept of damage should be expanded to include IT-security vulnerabilities".

With regard to the issue of IT-security vulnerabilities, see the response submitted by Eurosmart ("Eurosmart on the Product Liability Directive", 12.01.2022, p. 1): "Robustness against attacks: New technologies, hardware and software, require a new definition of the conditions under which a product is considered defective. Currently, Article 5 of the Product Liability Directive stipulates that "[a] product is defective when it does not provide the safety which a person is entitled to expect [...]". As safety and security become more and more intertwined, Eurosmart believes that security is part of the features that consumers are entitled to expect from a product. However, cybersecurity is a moving target, hence consumers should be entitled to expect a certain level of robustness against attacks, but it cannot be expected from a product to provide absolute security. The Product Liability Directive should be complemented by a document drawing a classification of cyber-risks per functionality. There are different levels of security according to the risk evaluation and having a harmonised risk classification is key to ensure legal certainty".

[51] Commission, DG GROW and DG JUST, "Factual summary report of the open public consultation on Adapting Civil Liability Rules to the Digital Age and AI", Ref. Ares(2022)2620305, 06.04.2022, p. 4.

For instance, as it was stated by Eurosmart ("Eurosmart on the Product Liability Directive", 12.01.2022, p. 2): "Enlarging the definition of "damage": The current definition of "damage" does not encompass new types of damage that were not foreseen when the directive was first drafted. For

In addition, the majority (59%) of respondents agreed with the statement that producers should be liable for data protection infringements. There were significant variations in the perspectives of businesses and consumers, with only 18% of business and industry stakeholders agreeing with the abovementioned statement, compared to 86% of consumer associations, and citizens.[52]

---

instance, a loss of data is a form of damage to property which is not recognised as such across the entire EU. This is particularly important for companies whose business model is based on data management, where raw or anonymised data represents a large part of the companies' assets. For instance, if the legislator wants to support the deployment of Europe-based data and AI solutions, a certain level of "safeguard" must be granted. A modernisation of the concept of "damage", as defined by Article 9, should align approaches on this issue".

Also, as it was stated by the European Law Institute ("Response of the European Law Institute (ELI) - Public Consultation on Civil Liability Adapting liability rules to the digital age and artificial intelligence", Bernhard A Koch, Jean-Sébastien Borghetti, Piotr Machnikowski et al., 12.01.2022, pp. 16–17): " Revisions to the Notion of 'Damage': At present, the PLD covers two types of damage: (i) death or personal injury; and (ii) damage or destruction to an 'item of property' if that item was intended, and actually used, for private use/ consumption. While we recommend maintaining this limitation in principle and to leave it to the Member States to provide for the indemnification of pure economic loss or standalone emotional harm, for example, certain adjustments to the delimitations of compensable harm under the PLD may nevertheless be necessary. . . . *Damage to digital elements and data*: the notion of damage might be reviewed to include damage to digital elements and data. To-day, damage might not only be caused to individuals and physical property, but also to digital items and data created by an individual, whether stored on a physical device or on a digital service (cloud). The growth of digital assets and tokens adds a further dimension. A revision to the notion of 'damage' is required to ensure that a reformed product liability regime adequately covers the novel features of the digital era. In particular, loss of data should be brought within the scope of 'damage', as should damage to other digital content. This requires a careful definition of what exactly is recoverable for such damage, as this may be a loss of a mere copy of a still existing master copy or damage to the latter, in which case intellectual property issues as well as questions regarding the compensability of emotional harm (e.g., in the case of lost digital pictures) may arise. At least the latter should not be addressed by the PLD, however, but left to the Member States, similar to other instances of non-pecuniary loss".

[52] Commission, DG GROW and DG JUST, "Factual summary report of the open public consultation on Adapting Civil Liability Rules to the Digital Age and AI", Ref. Ares(2022)2620305, 06.04.2022, p. 4.

See for instance the response submitted by the Computer & Communications Industry Association (CCIA Europe), "A product liability regime fit for the digital age", 20.12.2021, at p. 3: "Extending the range of damages to non-material damages (e.g. privacy infringements, psychological harm) would increase legal uncertainty over other pieces of legislation that already cover non-material damages, for example, damages for privacy infringements can be compensated under the General Data Protection Regulation (GDPR). On the other hand, other types of damages such as emotional damage are already covered by national legal rules. Applying strict liability is unnecessary and would put a disproportionate burden to providers as non-material damages are less predictable and difficult to measure than in the case of material damages".

For a similar view, see the response submitted by the GSMA ("GSMA response to the EC public consultation on Adapting Liability Rules to the Digital Age and AI", 22.12.2021, p. 2): "The GDPR and national tort law and anti-discrimination laws already sanction and foresee a compensation for immaterial damages in case of data protection infringements. An expansion of the scope to include immaterial harm is not recommended as not every economic loss is immaterial harm and would impose excessive burdens and risks on industry. Furthermore, harm cannot be defined in an isolated

7.3.2.1.4 Adapting the PLD to the Circular Economy

Under the Product Liability Directive the defectiveness of a product is determined at the moment it is put into circulation. However, in the context of circular economy business models, changes to products after they have been put into circulation (e.g. software updates) are increasingly common. Therefore, respondents were asked about who should be held liable for defects resulting from changes to products after they are placed on the market (i.e., when repaired, recycled, refurbished, remanufactured or upgraded products were defective and caused damage).[53] Over

---

way. Data loss does not constitute per se a damage, as the quantity and quality of personal data needs to be taken into account. An extension (e.g. in the direction of psychological and environmental damage) of the absolute legal interests (life, limb etc.) would be a paradigm shift with unclear consequences, which would cause the legal text to lose clarity and precision".

[53] As it was stated by BusinessEurope, "Comments – Adapting liability rules to the digital age and Artificial Intelligence", 10.01.2022, at p. 3: "BusinessEurope agrees that when substantial modifications are made to a product after they are placed on the market, new risks may occur. We therefore support the concept of "substantial modification", in which case the responsibility for the safety of the product or part of a product, shifts to the economic operator making the modification (in this case the repairer, or refurbisher). The definition of "substantial modification" must be clearly defined, based on robust criteria, and be consistent with the proposed Machinery Regulation, the Artificial Intelligence Act and the General Product Safety Regulation".

See also the response submitted by the European Games Developer Federation e.f. (EGDF) on the adapting liability rules to the digital age and artificial intelligence (Civil liability) consultation, 10.01.2022, p. 3: "When a third party refurbishes or remanufactures a product or a spare part and places it on the market as a new product, they should also be liable for defects causing damage".

In addition, the Irish Council for Civil Liberties (ICCL) ("ICCL - Submission to the consultation on adapting liability rules to the digital age and artificial intelligence", 7 January 2022, pp. 2–3) stated: "Remove the reference to the time when software is first put into circulation: Article 6(1) of PLD is problematic. It states: A product is defective when it does not provide the safety which a person is entitled to expect, taking all circumstances into account, including: (a) the presentation of the product; (b) the use to which it could reasonably be expected that the product would be put; (c) the time when the product was put into circulation. This should not apply to software. The time when the product was put into circulation is irrelevant for software, because it can be regularly updated after that time by the provider/producer. For this reason, Directive 2019/770 (Supply of Digital Content and Digital Services) included software updates as a requirement for conformity. This change to Article 6(1) is particularly relevant for AI systems, because not only can the software code be updated but also the AI model can be updated after the product has been placed in the market".

Furthermore, according to Eurosmart ("Eurosmart on the Product Liability Directive", 12.01.2022, p. 2), "the definition of a producer, laid down in Article 4, is quite restrictive in relation to new technologies. Software developers play an important role in terms of safety and security: they should be considered producers pursuant to the Product Liability Directive. Therefore, the term "producer" in the meaning of the Article 3 of the Directive should include developers. ... New technologies make the identification of responsibilities more complicated. In this respect, Article 5 on joint liability is more accurate than ever as it provides the possibility to hold several persons liable for the same damage. However, as a general rule, Eurosmart believes that liability should lie within the person who is most responsible for the defective features of a product. For instance, failure of a software due to an intrinsic vulnerability at the development stage triggers the developer's liability".

60% of all respondents supported the view that the PLD should also cover defective refurbished or remanufactured products and defective spare parts that cause damage. Whereas just more than half of business stakeholders (55%) agreed with the statement, 89% of consumer organisations, NGOs, academic institutes, and citizens supported this view.[54]

7.3.2.1.5 Policy Options for Adapting the PLD to the Digital and Circular Economy

Concerning the need (or not) for legislative change, there were significant variations in the perspectives of businesses and consumers, with academic/research institutions, consumer organisations and NGOs supporting it, while business associations and industry stakeholders opposing it.[55] Overall, more than half of respondents

---

[54] Commission, DG GROW and DG JUST, "Factual summary report of the open public consultation on Adapting Civil Liability Rules to the Digital Age and AI", Ref. Ares(2022)2620305, 06.04.2022, p. 4.

For instance, as it was stated by the European Law Institute ("Response of the European Law Institute (ELI) - Public Consultation on Civil Liability Adapting liability rules to the digital age and artificial intelligence", Bernhard A Koch, Jean-Sébastien Borghetti, Piotr Machnikowski et al., 12.01.2022, p. 16): "the notion of 'defect' should be amended to reflect the particular features of digital products and products with digital elements. Currently, a product is defective under the PLD if it did not 'provide the safety which a person is entitled to expect, taking all circumstances into account'. Circumstances mentioned expressly in the PLD are: the presentation of the product, the uses to which the product could reasonably be expected to be put, and the time when the product was put into circulation (with the proviso that the mere fact that a 'better product' is subsequently put into circulation does not render earlier products defective). These factors work well with tangible products, as is the case under the PLD, and those which are supplied at a single, fixed point in time. However, both products which rely on digital elements to perform their functionalities and purely digital products do not fit this model. In particular, such products will require regular updates (whether to improve functionality, fix bugs or deal with security issues). This might make the proviso regarding the later availability of 'better products' as not being relevant no longer workable. Furthermore, the PLD repeatedly points to a product being 'put into circulation'. This made sense when the PLD was adopted and when it was possible to identify a single moment when this occurred. In the case of products with digital elements and digital products, this no longer holds. Continuous monitoring and updating, particularly of digital elements, mean that the responsibility of the producer can extend well beyond the point when the product was initially put into circulation".

[55] Amongst the industry stakeholders who opposed the need for legislative change, see for instance the following:

Amazon's response to the public consultation on Adapting liability rules to the digital age and Artificial Intelligence (10 January 2022, p. 1): "The current PLD is effective, striking a fair balance in protecting consumers and supporting product innovation. Its simplicity and product neutrality ensured its effectiveness. PLD still seems to be very effective. ... Available evidence does not indicate a problem with the current PLD. The policy options are based on the assumption that change is required and that unacceptable "obstacles" to compensation exist. ... If any changes are considered, they should be evidence-based and should not follow assumptions that are merely based on theoretical/academic reasoning. Changes to the current text of the PLD or the introduction of separate new liability rules such as for AI may result in stifling product innovation. Investment in consumer products that include IoT or more advanced AI technology are only starting to take up by now. For example, one of the stated goals of the EU AI Act is to 'ensure legal certainty to facilitate investment and innovation in AI'. Burdensome new rules that also risk to not address real problems could undermine the development and provisioning of new technologies in the EU and it would be important to keep industry as a key discussion partner".

See also the response of the American Chamber of Commerce to the European Union (AmCham EU) to the consultation Civil liability – adapting liability rules to the digital age and artificial intelligence (12.01.2022, p. 2), which stated that "no additional measures are needed to adapt the Product Liability Directive (PLD) to the digital and circular economy. The Directive's adaptability comes from its simplicity, which guarantees product neutrality. As there also seems to be no demonstrated obstacle in the Directive's implementation, for instance, relative to compensation, we consider that no legislative change is needed. If the European Commission believes that new initiatives are needed to meet the challenges posed by the digital and circular economy, issuing guidance on how to interpret the current rules of the Directive would be more helpful for stakeholders than changing the existing norms. Further, AmCham EU believes that it would not be appropriate to amend the scope of the PLD to encompass standalone software, as its inclusion would fail to take into account the specific characteristics of software, which differ from physical products".

Similarly, see BSA – The Software Alliance, "Response to the European Commission's consultation on civil liability – adapting liability rules to the digital age and artificial intelligence", 10.01.2022, pp. 1–2: "We thus agree that it makes sense to regularly revisit the EU's civil liability regime to ensure that consumer protections are not weakened as the digital economy evolves and as the use of AI-enabled products becomes more common. At the same time, it is important that any reforms to the EU's civil liability regime respond to actual, clearly identified barriers to consumer redress for defective products. Currently, however, many of the potential barriers identified in the consultation seem speculative; others will likely be impacted (and potentially resolved) by pending legislative proposals on AI and digital services. For these reasons, we encourage the Commission to take more time before legislating, in order to ensure that we are not seeking to fix a problem that does not exist. ... *Reforms to the existing civil liability regime should be driven by a clear and demonstrable need to fix actual, identified problems*: The Product Liability Directive ("Directive") has worked well for over 35 years in a wide variety of contexts and during a period of significant technological change. It sets out clear, easy-to-understand, and time-tested rules, which are technology neutral and are able to adapt as digital technologies emerge and evolve. In addition, the Directive is complemented by national civil liability regimes in EU Member States, reflecting Member State legal traditions and principles, including on evidentiary rules and damages. Together, these regimes provide a high standard of consumer protection when seeking redress for defective products, including products that are software-enabled. Before upending this robust regime, further empirical evidence is needed to clearly identify actual real-world problems that need fixing, rather than problems that might occur. At present, however, many of the problems identified in the consultation appear to be speculative or unsubstantiated".

In addition, see the position paper submitted by the European Association of Automotive Suppliers (CLEPA), "Artificial Intelligence - For a coherent regulatory framework that ensures safety and trust", 12.01.2022, at p. 11: "The existing liability framework can already address AI: Even though AI systems and applications are posing new legal challenges to the existing liability regime, they are not so different to other technologies, which are sometimes based on even more complex software. This means that these new legal challenges do not require major changes to be made to the liability framework. From our point of view, the current EU legislation on security, liability, and responsibility is effective and does not need to be fundamentally altered for artificial intelligence. The Product Liability Directive (PLD), in particular, already provides a sound legal basis to address consumer protection and may therefore serve as a foundation for discussions and evaluations with respect to effective consumer protection and compensation for AI products. Furthermore, there has not been any concrete evidence so far that harm caused by AI applications cannot be compensated for using the existing framework".

(56%) were in favour of legislative change, proposing the revision of the Product Liability Directive to cover intangible products (e.g. digital content and stand-alone software) that cause physical/material damage. It is questionable whether software is covered by the legal concept of product or product component. Amongst the respondents who supported a legislative change, 62% were in favour of treating digital content/software as a product in its own right, whereas 38% were in favour of only covering digital content as a component of a tangible product.[56]

7.3.2.2 Reducing Obstacles to Making Claims and Getting Compensation

According to the Evaluation of the Product Liability Directive consumers could face significant difficulties in claiming and getting compensation for damage caused by defective products. In particular:

7.3.2.2.1 Reducing Obstacles to Getting Compensation

Respondents argued that, due to the technical complexity of specific products, it could become difficult for the victim/injured party to obtain compensation, i.e. to identify the potentially liable person, to prove the defect in the product and the causal link between the defect and the damage. This difficulty becomes even higher as emerging digital technologies/products are becoming increasingly connected and complex. As it was stated, "respondents point to difficulties in proving defectiveness and causality in the event of damage due to the technical complexity of certain products. In particular, they pointed to moderate, large and very large difficulties in case of: AI-enabled products (77%), technically complex products (77%), IoT products (72%) and pharmaceuticals (65%)".[57]

---

[56] Commission, DG GROW and DG JUST, "Factual summary report of the open public consultation on Adapting Civil Liability Rules to the Digital Age and AI", Ref. Ares(2022)2620305, 06.04.2022, p. 4.

[57] Ibid., p. 5. Amongst consumer organisations, non-governmental organisations and citizens, 95% underlined the difficulties/challenges for each of these items.

On the other hand, only 38% amongst business respondents acknowledged such challenges in demonstrating defectiveness and causality. See, for instance, the response submitted by BSA – The Software Alliance, "Response to the European Commission's consultation on civil liability – adapting liability rules to the digital age and artificial intelligence, 10.01.2022, p. 2, where it was argued that "many of the problems identified in the consultation appear to be speculative or unsubstantiated. For example, the consultation states that "the technical complexity of certain products (e.g., emerging digital technologies) could make it especially difficult and costly for consumers to actually prove they were defective and that they caused the damage". However, the consultation fails to cite any substantial empirical evidence that consumers, on the rare occasions that they are harmed by such technologies, are unable to obtain compensation for those harms, or have struggled to prove a causal link between the damage suffered and the defective product. The

7.3.2.2.2 The Development Risk Defence

It is reminded that, according to the so-called development risk defence, the producer is allowed to avoid liability if the state of scientific and technical knowledge at the time when he put the product into circulation was not such as to enable the existence of the defect to be discovered (Article 7(e) of the Product Liability Directive).

Overall 56% of all respondents argued that there should be no change in the development risk defence. However, there were differing opinions in the perspectives of businesses and consumers on the effectiveness of keeping the development risk defence unchanged. For instance, amongst business stakeholders 81% agreed with this statement, while 73% of consumer organisations and NGOs disagreed that there should be no change.[58]

Furthermore, 68% of all respondents disagreed with the possibility of removing the development risk defence from the PLD. Again, there were significant variations in the perspectives of businesses and consumers on a disaggregated level. Amongst business respondents, 78% disagreed that the defence should be removed, compared to 44% of non-business respondents who agreed with its removal.[59] Of the suggested

---

consultation points to the evaluation of the Directive, which found that failure to prove the product in question caused damage to the consumer "accounted for 53% of rejected compensation claims". However, it is unclear that such claims concern AI or other software-enabled products—and indeed, the evaluation report suggests this problem may be centered around medical devices and pharmaceutical products. We therefore encourage the Commission, as a first step, to compile real-world case studies in order to determine whether the existing civil liability rules are in fact inadequate and impose significant obstacles to consumers obtaining compensation for damage caused by defective software-enabled products".

See also the view put forward by the Computer & Communications Industry Association (CCIA Europe): "A product liability regime fit for the digital age", 20.12.2021, at p. 1, which stated that "the Commission has not provided real-world evidence showing that the Product Liability Directive prevents consumers from seeking redress and obtaining compensation from injuries or other harms caused by a digital product. Strict liability and burden shifting should be based on solid evidence of proven flaws in the current liability framework. For this reason, the current review is not justified and the problems that the Commission's initiative aims to tackle are purely speculative. Adapting the current liability framework will not provide additional protection to consumers, nor solve problems for the production, distribution, trust or uptake of AI-enabled products and services, in fact, it may create additional issues to many businesses by increasing legal and financial burden on companies".

Furthermore, according to Google's comments "Public consultation: Civil liability – adapting liability rules to the digital age and artificial intelligence", 7 January 2022, p. 4: "... we are not aware of any real-world evidence that confirms the hypothesis that claimants in the EU are systematically disadvantaged when making claims related to damages caused by AI-enabled products and services and thus cause a lack of trust in AI. It follows that we do not think that introducing such legislative measures will have significant measurable effects in the market".

[58] Commission, DG GROW and DG JUST, "Factual summary report of the open public consultation on Adapting Civil Liability Rules to the Digital Age and AI", Ref. Ares(2022)2620305, 06.04.2022, p. 5.

[59] See for instance the response submitted by BEUC (the European Consumer Organisation) to the European Commission's public consultation on Civil liability – adapting liability rules to the digital age and artificial intelligence, 23.12.2021, at p. 7: "The PLD should be adapted to the dynamic

changes in the questionnaire, the one that received most support (39% of respondents) was denying the defence for AI products that continue to learn and adapt while in operation.[60]

---

nature of digital products: More and more digital products are dynamic in the sense that they evolve during their lifespan. In parallel, professionals also collect on an ongoing basis data from consumers about the use of their products. Professionals know how their tools are used and may detect problems quickly when they arise. In other words, producers keep a much higher degree of control over their products even after they have been placed on the market. Liability rules must follow and be adapted to this evolution. The risk-development defence or the late defect defence are clearly incompatible with the dynamic nature of digital goods".

Also, according to the Irish Council for Civil Liberties (ICCL) ("ICCL - Submission to the consultation on adapting liability rules to the digital age and artificial intelligence", 7 January 2022, pp. 3–4): "'Development risk defence' should be removed for all AI systems so that producers remain strictly liable for damage. Under Article 7(e) of PLD, 'development risk defence' exempts producers from liability if they can prove "that the state of scientific and technical knowledge at the time when he put the product into circulation was not such as to enable the existence of the defect to be discovered". This exemption is inappropriate for AI for the following reasons: a) PLD assumes "material objects placed on the market by a one-time action of the producer, after which the producer does not maintain control over the product". As we note above, and as Directive 2019/770 recognises, this is not applicable to software that can be updated. b) In addition, the producers should be held liable if they do not update software when new information about a defect is known, in scientific literature or elsewhere. Whether the scientific and technical knowledge was available when the software was initially placed on the market should not be considered. c) 'Development risk defence' creates a perverse incentive for producers to deploy products without adequate safety research, or to delay safety related research and/or the publication of research results until the product is placed on the market".

Similarly, as it was stated by Eurosmart ("Eurosmart on the Product Liability Directive", 12.01.2022, p. 3), "Artificial intelligence challenges Article 7 of the Product Liability Directive, which states that a producer shall not be liable if he proves "that having regard to the circumstances, it is probable that the defect which caused the damage did not exist at the time when the product was put into circulation by him or that this defect came into being afterwards". Artificial intelligence systems evolve over time, and vulnerabilities might arise in the course of such an evolution. The concept of liability would be meaningless if producers were not liable for such vulnerabilities arising after placing on the market as they still designed the systems in the first place".

For an opposite view, see the argument put forward by BusinessEurope, "Comments – Adapting liability rules to the digital age and Artificial Intelligence", 10.01.2022, at p. 4, which stated that "the use of the development risk defence should remain available without any change. BusinessEurope is concerned that discussions seem to be driven by concerns which are misconceived and based on an overvaluation of the capabilities of AI systems. None of the case studies from the Commission's Staff Working Document on liability for emerging digital technologies for example demonstrates that existing safeguards were insufficient to deal with the scenarios outlined. We should allow leeway for innovation and not impose a de facto indefinite liability for the producer in case of systems that operate with a degree of autonomy. Instead, the defences should be interpreted in such a way that they also apply for such systems, where it may be equally possible that the defect did not exist or could not be discovered when the product was put into circulation".

[60] Commission, DG GROW and DG JUST, "Factual summary report of the open public consultation on Adapting Civil Liability Rules to the Digital Age and AI", Ref. Ares(2022)2620305, 06.04.2022, p. 5.

For instance, as it was stated by the Confederation of European Security Services (CoESS) ("Confederation of European Security Services (CoESS) - Position Paper on the European Commission Consultation on adapting liability rules to the digital age and AI", 20 December 2021, p. 4):

7.3.2.2.3 Reducing Obstacles to Making Claims

Respondents were asked to assess whether the following features of the PLD (and to what extent) can create obstacles to consumers making compensation claims: (i) consumers can claim compensation only for damage to property intended and used for private purposes; (ii) consumers can claim compensation only for damage to property worth more than EUR 500; (iii) consumers have to start legal proceedings within 3 years of becoming aware of the damage; (iv) producers are released from liability for property damage and death/personal injury 10 years after placing the product on the market.[61]

55% of all respondents argued that the EUR 500 thresholds for damage to property creates obstacles to consumers making compensation claims. Out of this 55%, 89% were consumer organisations and NGOs (i.e., non-business respondents), asking for more protection at a lower cost,[62] while only 11% were business respondents (who argued that any relaxation on the threshold for property damages would lead to more claims for minor damages).[63]

Furthermore, just more than half (51%) of all respondents indicated that the 10-year time limit for death/personal injury creates obstacles to consumers making compensation claims. Out of this 51%, while consumer organisations and NGOs accounted for 89%, corporations and business organisations/associations represented the remaining 11%.[64]

"As regards 'development risk defence' of providers, we believe that the concept should be evaluated in the face of emerging technologies. Notably, we believe that the defence should not be available for products designed to be influenced by other interconnected products or services (e.g. complex IoT systems), and for AI products that continue to learn and adapt while in operation".

[61] Commission, DG GROW and DG JUST, "Factual summary report of the open public consultation on Adapting Civil Liability Rules to the Digital Age and AI", Ref. Ares(2022)2620305, 06.04.2022, p. 6.

[62] See, for instance, the response submitted by BEUC (the European Consumer Organisation) to the European Commission's public consultation on Civil liability – adapting liability rules to the digital age and artificial intelligence, 23.12.2021, at p. 8: "All harm should be compensated: Currently, the PLD only covers physical injuries and damage to property arising out in non-professional activities with a lower threshold of €500. This is problematic for several reasons. First, the PLD excludes immaterial damage although IoT products may cause a much wider range of harm than traditional products, including data destruction or losses. Second, the 500€ threshold is arbitrary and in practice has been impairing access to justice for consumers in too many cases. As the European Commission already noted in its 2018 report, 'in four out of five cases, a compensation is not claimed as the damage is below the threshold'. It is essential that all consumers have access to compensation regardless of the value and the type of their harm".

[63] Commission, DG GROW and DG JUST, "Factual summary report of the open public consultation on Adapting Civil Liability Rules to the Digital Age and AI", Ref. Ares(2022)2620305, 06.04.2022, p. 6.

[64] Ibid. See for instance: BusinessEurope, "Comments – Adapting liability rules to the digital age and Artificial Intelligence", 10.01.2022, at p. 4, which argued that "the 10-year time limit also provides important certainty about producers' claims risk and is important for insurance purposes. It

In contrast, there was greater disagreement among respondents who stated that the requirement to start legal proceedings within three years of becoming aware of damage is the least significant obstacle to making claims (only 37% of the respondents argued that this constitutes an obstacle).[65]

7.3.2.2.4 Policy Options for Reducing Obstacles to Making Claims and Getting Compensation

There were significant variations in the perspectives of businesses and consumers concerning the support for legislative change to reduce obstacles to making claims and getting compensation. Overall, more than half of respondents (53%) were in favour of legislative change.[66] Furthermore, 75% of all respondents agreed with alleviating the burden of proof[67] for technically complex products by obliging the

---

provides legal certainty for industry and other stakeholders as well (e.g., healthcare professionals). Additionally, providing an expiry period of 10 is five times as long as most warranties, which are typically around 2 years".

[65] Commission, DG GROW and DG JUST, "Factual summary report of the open public consultation on Adapting Civil Liability Rules to the Digital Age and AI", Ref. Ares(2022)2620305, 06.04.2022, p. 6.

[66] Ibid. Out of 53%, 93% were business respondents while only 7% were non-business respondents.

See, for instance, the Comments of the Association for Computing Machinery Europe Technology Policy Committee (ACM-ETPC) in the Commission Consultation on Civil Liability: Adapting Liability Rules to the Digital Age & Artificial Intelligence, 10.01.2022, at p. 1: "Europe TPC favors all options for legal reform presented in this section other than 'no legislative action'".

[67] Some non-business respondents argued that "merely alleviating the burden of proof will not solve this problem" and, therefore, "a reversal of the burden of proof should be introduced, especially for complex products". See for instance the response submitted by BEUC (the European Consumer Organisation) to the European Commission's public consultation on Civil liability – adapting liability rules to the digital age and artificial intelligence, 23.12.2021, at pp. 6–7: "The burden of proof must be shifted: A reversal of the burden of proof should be introduced, especially for complex products. Experience with the PLD shows that the burden of proof has been a major obstacle for getting compensation. In its 2018 report, the European Commission already noted that the impossibility to prove a defect and the link with the damage accounted for 53% of the cases of rejection. The Expert Group set up by the European Commission on liability and new technologies also highlighted that the digital context has exacerbated evidentiary difficulties and widened the information asymmetries between claimants and defendants. Merely alleviating the burden of proof will not solve this problem. Although consumers may in certain cases benefit from presumptions (as cleared by the CJEU case law), they still may have difficulties to substantiate their claims. Moreover, requesting professionals to disclose the technical information will not help as consumers may not have the expertise and the sufficient skills to interpret the data and traders may be willing to avoid complying with this obligation by pretexting trade secrets. In turn this will significantly contribute to extend the costs and the length of the proceedings. Shifting the burden of proof is therefore clearly justified on the ground of both fairness and access to justice".

On the other hand, as it was argued by BusinessEurope, "Comments – Adapting liability rules to the digital age and Artificial Intelligence", 10.01.2022, at pp. 3–4, "complexity of products from the consumer perspective is not a valid reason to reverse the burden of proof and causality on manufacturers. In addition, national judiciary systems have proved to facilitate the burden of

producer to disclose technical information to the injured party and by allowing courts to infer that a product is defective or caused the damage under certain circumstances (for instance, when other products in the same production series have already been proven to be defective or when a product clearly malfunctions).[68]

---

proving defectiveness and causality when consumers lack technical expertise. Any mechanism to reverse the burden of proof should be carefully assessed and focus on potential high-risk areas aligned with the relevant sector-specific framework and the Artificial Intelligence Act. A blanket approach is not consistent with a risk-based approach and would greatly undermine the uptake of new technologies in the EU".

See also the response of the Computer & Communications Industry Association (CCIA Europe): "A product liability regime fit for the digital age", 20.12.2021, at pp. 3–4: "There is no evidence showing that the burden of proof of the Directive places consumers at a disadvantage. Changing the burden of proof does not appear necessary and carries substantial risks. Moreover, it is not evident why products that use AI should go through different procedures than products that do not use AI. Just because a product is AI-enabled does not mean that is more likely to cause injury for which the customer is unable to seek redress or compensation. Such an assumption risks overbroad and inflexible liability rules which may ultimately discourage innovation and investment in AI technologies in the EU. In this regard, alleged victims should continue to be required to prove the causation and the damage in order to prevent frivolous and fraudulent claims and cause disproportionate harm to businesses with extensive liability claims".

[68] Commission, DG GROW and DG JUST, "Factual summary report of the open public consultation on Adapting Civil Liability Rules to the Digital Age and AI", Ref. Ares(2022)2620305, 06.04.2022, p. 6. Out of 75%, 75% were business respondents while only 25% were non-business respondents.

See also the Commission's Inception Impact Assessment "Adapting liability rules to the digital age and circular economy", Ref. Ares(2021)4266516, 30.06.2021, p. 4.

Furthermore, according to the response of the Center for Data Innovation to the Commission's inception impact assessment on civil liability - adapting liability rules to the digital age and AI, submitted on 28.07.2021 (at p. 3), "this option is a reasonable adjustment to the PLD that strengthens plaintiffs' discovery rights, holds producers accountable, and encourages the maintenance of proper development documentation. It does create a "guilty until proven innocent" standard for software-powered products".

Also, see the comments of the Association for Computing Machinery Europe Technology Policy Committee (ACM-ETPC) in the Commission Consultation on Civil Liability: Adapting Liability Rules to the Digital Age & Artificial Intelligence, 10.01.2022, at p. 1: "Europe TPC most endorses Option 4: 'a) adapt the notion of 'defect' and the alleviation/reversal of burden of proof to the specific case of AI; and b) remove the 'development risk defence' to ensure producers of products that continuously learn and adapt while in operation remain strictly liable for damage'. Such changes, the Committee believes, will lead to less burden for the injured party in that the manufacturer will have to prove that it was not at fault and that it was not objectively negligent".

7.3.3 Views of Respondents on the Specific Challenges of AI: Civil Liability Rules for AI

7.3.3.1 Overview of Responses on the Existence of Specific Problem Drivers as Regards AI Liability

7.3.3.1.1 Problem Driver 1: The Specific Characteristics of AI Make It Difficult to Meet the Burden of Proof–Difficulties in Proving the Conditions of Liability

The majority of respondents argued that the specific characteristics of AI (such as high degree of autonomous behaviour, continuous adaptation, limited predictability and explainability, complexity/'black box effect', limited transparency/opacity) could make it difficult for injured parties to identify and prove the fault of a potentially liable person or that a product is defective as well as the causal link between that fault/defect and the damage suffered: "67% of respondents agreed that it could be difficult to link damage caused by highly autonomous AI to the actions or omissions of a human actor";[69] "74% of overall respondents agreed that it could be difficult for victims to prove that the conditions of liability (fault, defect or causation) are fulfilled in the case of opaque and complex AI";[70] "61% of overall respondents agreed that victims of damage involving AI may in certain cases be less protected than victims of damage involving AI due to AI's specific characteristics".[71]

7.3.3.1.2 Problem Driver 2: The Lack of Adaptation of the Current Liability Framework to AI May Negatively Affect Trust in AI

The majority (60%) of all respondents confirmed the link between a lack of compensation and a lack of trust while only 25% disagreed. Also, 56% confirmed the link between lack of compensation and a reduced uptake of AI, whereas only 27% did not confirm it. On a disaggregated level, among non-business respondents (NGOs, consumer organisations, academic/research institutions) 89% and 78%

[69] Commission, DG GROW and DG JUST, "Factual summary report of the open public consultation on Adapting Civil Liability Rules to the Digital Age and AI", Ref. Ares(2022)2620305, 06.04.2022, p. 7. An almost unanimous agreement (94%) was reached amongst responding consumer organisations, national ministries and academic/research associations. On the other hand, amongst business stakeholders, more disagreed (45%) than agreed (36%).

[70] Ibid. A unanimous agreement was reached amongst responding consumer organisations, national ministries and academic/research institutions. On the other hand, business stakeholders expressed more differentiated opinions and they were relatively evenly split ("amongst business stakeholders, the majority in agreement is relative"): 41% agreed, while 28% disagreed with this problem driver.

[71] Ibid. There was 84% agreement amongst responding consumer organisations, national ministries, NGOs and academic/research institutions. On the other hand, as concerns business stakeholders, there was an absolute majority which disagreed (54%) with this problem driver, while 26% agreed.

respectively agreed that the lack of adaptation of existing liability rules to AI may negatively affect i) trust in AI and ii) the uptake of AI-enabled products and services.[72] On the other hand, among non-business respondents the majority (58%) disagreed with the aforementioned statements.[73]

7.3.3.1.3 Problem Driver 3: Legal Uncertainty

The majority (63%) of all respondents identified legal uncertainty as an additional problem driver, whereas 22% disagreed. There were significant variations in the perspectives of businesses and consumers on the issue of legal uncertainty. For instance, amongst non-business stakeholders (NGOs, consumer organisations and academic/research institutions) 84% and 81% respectively agreed with the statements that (i) it is uncertain whether and how liability rules under national law apply to damage caused by AI and that (ii) it is uncertain how national courts will address possible difficulties of proof and liability gaps in relation to AI.[74] On the other hand, more than half of business respondents (52%) did not confirm the existence of such uncertainty.[75]

7.3.3.1.4 Problem Driver 4: Legal Fragmentation

It is reminded that both the Commission and the Parliament stressed that if Member States attempt to address the resulting legal uncertainty at national level, and national courts apply diverging ad hoc solutions, this could lead to further fragmentation of

[72] Commission, DG GROW and DG JUST, "Factual summary report of the open public consultation on Adapting Civil Liability Rules to the Digital Age and AI", Ref. Ares(2022)2620305, 06.04.2022, p. 8.

[73] Ibid. However, amongst those business respondents who considered that AI can make it difficult to claim compensation, 64% confirmed the link between lack of compensation and a lack of trust in AI, and 59% agreed that the lack of compensation leads to reduced uptake of AI.

[74] Ibid.

[75] Ibid.: "Just more than half of business stakeholders (52% or 44 out of 85) disagreed with the statement about uncertainty pertaining to "whether" and "how" national law applies to AI-related damages, while around one third (32% or 27 out of 85) expressed uncertainty in this respect. As regards national courts addressing the challenges of AI, views of business stakeholders were similar: 34% (29 out of 85) confirmed uncertainty, while 43% (36 out of 85) did not. In addition, 27% of business stakeholders (23 out of 85) expect additional costs for companies, like legal information and insurance costs, while 20% (17 out of 85) agree that companies may defer or abandon certain investments in AI technologies if the current liability framework is not adapted. 21% (18 out of 85) agree that companies may refrain from using AI when automating certain processes. The percentages for each negative consequence are well over 60% amongst those business stakeholders who confirmed the perception of legal uncertainty".

liability rules across the EU for damage caused by AI products and services.[76] In line with this view, the majority of all respondents (approximately 70%) stated that legal fragmentation (i.e., in case Member States adapt liability rules for AI in a divergent way, or national courts follow diverging interpretations of existing liability rules in the case of damage caused by AI) can cause additional costs for companies when producing, distributing or using AI-enabled products or services and can also result to limitations to cross-border AI-related activities.[77]

7.3.3.2 Need for EU Action: Overview of Responses Regarding Policy Options on AI Liability

Overall 75% of all respondents (and 51% of business respondents) expressed clear support for EU action to introduce AI-specific harmonised measures, commenting on the proposed different policy options.[78]

---

[76] For instance, according to the Commission, no EU policy change could lead to increased fragmentation due to interventions at Member States level. See Commission's Inception Impact Assessment "Adapting liability rules to the digital age and circular economy", Ref. Ares(2021) 4266516, 30.06.2021, p. 4.

See also the Commission's Public Consultation, "Adapting liability rules to the digital age and Artificial Intelligence", 18 October 2021, at pp. 29 and 32. "It may also be uncertain whether and to what extent national strict liability regimes (e.g. for dangerous activities) will apply to the use of AI-enabled products or services. National laws may change, and courts may adapt their interpretation of the law, to address these potential challenges" (p. 29); ... "with the growing number of AI-enabled products and services on the market, Member States may adapt their respective liability regimes to the specific challenges of AI, which could lead to increasing differences between national liability rules. The Product Liability Directive could also be interpreted in different ways by national courts for damage caused by AI" (p. 32).

Furthermore, with regard to the risk of fragmentation of the internal market, the European Parliament stated that "specific adjustments to the existing legislation and the introduction of well-accessed and targeted new provisions would be sufficient to accommodate the AI-related challenges, with a view to preventing regulatory fragmentation and ensuring the harmonisation of civil liability legislation throughout the Union in connection with AI". See the Annex to the European Parliament's Resolution of 20 October 2020 on a civil liability regime for AI – B. Text of the Proposal for a Regulation on liability for the operation of AI systems, at recital 8.

[77] Commission, DG GROW and DG JUST, "Factual summary report of the open public consultation on Adapting Civil Liability Rules to the Digital Age and AI", Ref. Ares(2022)2620305, 06.04.2022, p. 9. "Business stakeholders expressed similar views as overall respondents when it comes to the impacts of legal fragmentation: 54% (46 out of 85) expect additional costs (while 15% or 13 out of 85 do not), 36% (31 out of 85) expect reduced cross-border AI-related activities (while 28% or 24 out of 85 disagree), and 39% (33 out of 85) expect a negative impact on AI technologies roll-out (while 29% or 25 out of 85 do not expect such an impact). In addition, 46% (39 out of 85) also expect (but 18% or 15 out of 85 do not) that legal fragmentation will result in a need to adapt AI technologies, distribution models and cost management models. 38% (32 out of 85) think that legal fragmentation regarding liability for AI will lead to higher prices for AI-enabled products and services, while 25% (21 out of 85) do not".

[78] On the other hand, amongst those who opposed the need for EU action, see the response of the American Chamber of Commerce to the European Union (AmCham EU) to the consultation Civil

7.3.3.2.1 AI-Specific Measures to Ease the Burden of Proof Under Civil Liability Rules

Representatives of consumer organisations and NGOs argued that victims should not bear the burden of proof and that there is a need for an alleviation,[79] compared to

---

liability – adapting liability rules to the digital age and artificial intelligence (12.01.2022, p. 2), which stated that "in regard to artificial intelligence (AI), AmCham EU does not believe legislative change is required on liability for AI, whether in a revised PLD or a new legislative instrument. The PLD already covers any product, including any embedded AI technology if essential for the functioning of the product. Moreover, new safeguards – such as those included in the proposed AI Act – are designed to mitigate any potential risk of consumer harm and will reduce the likelihood of such risks emerging. The European Commission should await the adoption and implementation of the AI Act before considering if further legislative initiatives are warranted in this area. AmCham EU does not see evidence to suggest that new legislation on AI liability is necessary to foster uptake of, and trust in, AI technology. Indeed, new far-reaching AI liability provisions, whether on EU or national levels, could harm the development, deployment and use of AI across the EU. Additionally, we are not aware of other countries, regions or EU Member States considering changes to liability laws to take account of AI. The European Commission should adopt a cautious approach to AI liability initiatives and base any future action on a thorough analysis of the evidence. If the Commission does launch new AI liability legislation, it should ensure harmonisation and avoid overlap and inconsistency with other relevant legislation. It should focus narrowly on serious health and safety risks to consumers from physical products and exclude other, more speculative, immaterial harms. Finally, it should not be extended to business-to-business relationships, as companies have well-established practices for contractual allocation of liability for potential harms as appropriate to the risk, context and applicable laws".

See also the position paper submitted by the European Association of Automotive Suppliers (CLEPA), "Artificial Intelligence - For a coherent regulatory framework that ensures safety and trust", 12.01.2022, at p. 11: "The Product Liability Directive (PLD) already provides a sound legal basis to address consumer protection and may therefore serve as a foundation for discussions and evaluations with respect to effective consumer protection and compensation for AI products. Furthermore, there has not been any concrete evidence so far that harm caused by AI applications cannot be compensated for using the existing framework. The PLD covers compensation for damages resulting from defective products, irrespective of whether the product comes with or without AI technology. This makes perfect sense since, from a product liability perspective, the decisive point is whether a product provides the safety a person is entitled to expect, and it is not necessary to distinguish between technologies used within the product in question. Therefore, it should not make a difference whether a product comes with AI or not. Both scenarios are already well covered by the PLD as it stands today".

[79] See for instance the response submitted by BEUC (the European Consumer Organisation) to the European Commission's public consultation on Civil liability – adapting liability rules to the digital age and artificial intelligence, 23.12.2021, at p. 9: "The burden of proof should be alleviated: The burden of proof will be the central issue upon which will depend injured parties' access to compensation. Considering the characteristics of AI systems, and in particular their opacity, complexity and autonomy, consumers will not be able to substantiate their claims in practice. While the disclosure of technical information by professionals can to some extent contribute to alleviate the burden of proof, it cannot alone solve this problem as consumers may not have the sufficient skills to use and interpret the data. For this reason, additional measures are necessary including a reversal of the burden of proof to ensure a levelled playing field. In all liability cases involving automated decision-making or machine-learning, the burden of proving should lie with the professional".

business respondents who were not in favour of a shift of the burden of proof and stated that sufficient alleviations can be granted by courts under existing national regimes and procedural laws.[80]

Since it was widely accepted that the specific characteristics of AI make it difficult to meet the burden of proof under civil liability rules, the majority of non-business respondents overwhelmingly supported the following measures: (i) measures regarding the disclosure of information (94%), e.g., obliging the producer to disclose technical information to the injured party; (ii) inferring facts from the refusal to disclose information (68%), e.g., allowing courts to infer that a product is defective or caused the damage under certain circumstances; (iii) presuming causality in the case of non-compliance by AI providers (81%) and users (65%) with their safety obligations (such as those proposed under the AI Act); (iv) alleviation of the burden of proof regarding the functioning of AI systems (91%).[81]

Also, according to the Irish Council for Civil Liberties (ICCL) ("ICCL - Submission to the consultation on adapting liability rules to the digital age and artificial intelligence", 7 January 2022, pp. 4–5): "Reversing the burden of proof: The burden of proof should be on the defendant when harm is caused by AI systems. For natural persons harmed by AI systems, gathering evidence is disproportionately difficult. There is little transparency about how AI systems operate, or how and whether they are used by companies and public bodies. Indeed, it can be difficult for a person to know whether a private company or a public authority is using AI systems. For example, without making an access request under Regulation 2016/679 (GDPR), one may not know whether their claim for welfare benefit was evaluated and unfairly dismissed by an AI system. ... Information asymmetry between the producers of AI systems and the public is significant. AI systems, and the different techniques and the trade-offs between them, are unlikely to be understood by the public. Even if they were, updates and self-learning may make it impossible for people to remain so. It is therefore the producer, and not the injured party, who has the means to gather evidence".

[80] As it was stated by Google ("Google's comments - Public consultation: Civil liability – adapting liability rules to the digital age and artificial intelligence", 7 January 2022, pp. 5–6): "In litigation, the burden of proof should only be alleviated or shifted in cases where establishing proof would create an unreasonable obstacle for one party. For such cases, national procedural laws already provide for a reversal of the burden of proof and for legal assumptions aiding the claimant. There is no need to create a special set of rules just for certain product categories. As a general rule, we believe that alleged victims should continue to be required to prove what caused them harm under the liability framework. The burden of proving causation should only be altered if, given the properties of a specific AI system, establishing proof would create an unreasonable obstacle for the alleged victim. In making this determination, factors to take into account include the likelihood that the technology contributed to the harm (e.g. if there are known defects), the nature and scale of the harm claimed, and the degree of ex-post traceability of contributing processes within the technology. They should not be based on the nature of the product (e.g. AI-enabled software) as such".

[81] Commission, DG GROW and DG JUST, "Factual summary report of the open public consultation on Adapting Civil Liability Rules to the Digital Age and AI", Ref. Ares(2022)2620305, 06.04.2022, p. 9.

On the other hand, business respondents were evenly split on the measure regarding the disclosure of information, while the majority disagreed with inferring facts from the refusal to disclose information (63%), shifting the burden of proof (63%), or presuming causality (41%, with 30% supporting such a presumption).[82]

---

[82]Commission, DG GROW and DG JUST, "Factual summary report of the open public consultation on Adapting Civil Liability Rules to the Digital Age and AI", Ref. Ares(2022)2620305, 06.04.2022, p. 9.

As it was stated, for instance, by Siemens Healthineers ("Siemens Healthineers contribution to the public consultation on Adapting liability rules to the digital age and Artificial Intelligence", 10.01.2022, pp. 4–5): "Before amending the rules on the burden of proof involving AI/IoT-enabled devices, it should be borne in mind that AI and IoT are still in development stages. There has not been an overwhelming body of evidence demonstrating that current liability regime fails to protect injured parties with respect to damages caused by such products. Any regulatory intervention should not be based on assumptions or expectations, especially when it comes to liability. Singling out AI and IoT among all the products may be harmful as this approach ignores other types of products or services with complex features. Any modifications of liability rules linked to specific types of AI or IoT technology applied in a given product or service should be carefully assessed against a potential risk of damage: not all AI or IoT applications bear the same level of potential risk. Similarly, not all AI technology (a set of various techniques) poses obstacle to effective functioning of the PLD. Thus, there is no need to create another layer of rules simply because a product is using a certain technology. Liability rules – similarly to PLD, should be technology-neutral. ... In certain cases, involving AI/IoT, we may support an ease of the burden of proof through disclosing of necessary technical information. However, to avoid disclosing any and all information which may contain sensitive data, it would be justified if only a specific part of technical documentation (e.g., clinical evaluation report) is requested when and if it is relevant for assessment/detection of a defect in a product claimed to have caused damage. ... The request for disclosure of relevant technical information should also be justified by the claimant. ... There should be utmost caution to introducing any rules allowing to quasi-automatic inference on defectiveness of a product based on one-sided information, such as compliance with safety regulations or malfunctioning of a product. When assessing defectiveness, it should be accounted for an ability of a customer/consumer to influence product's functioning with the input data (contributing to a system "learning" to function differently or altering originally programmed settings), leading to malfunctioning which caused damage. Manufacturer should not be liable for damage only because it placed an AI/IOT-enabled product on the market. Other relevant factors and circumstantial evidence should be factored in. Inference as regards product's defectiveness should take into account compliance with safety or other legal obligations but should not solely rely on that. The compliance itself should be a contestable condition in the relevant court proceeding to ensure the balance of parties' rights, including the assessment of the relation between compliance and the occurred damage, and if there is any causal link between the two. ... Autonomy, opacity, and complexity are not AI-specific. It is therefore not justified to apply a stricter burden of proof to products or services that are AI-enabled. In case of new rules for AI, the burden of proof should be the same as in the current PLD, to ensure alignment".

Also, as it was underlined by the Confederation of European Security Services (CoESS) ("Confederation of European Security Services (CoESS) - Position Paper on the European Commission Consultation on adapting liability rules to the digital age and AI", 20 December 2021, p. 2): "Technological neutrality and burden of proof: Persons suffering material harm from the malfunctioning of an AI system should have the same level of protection compared to cases without involvement of an AI system, following an approach of technological neutrality. CoESS agrees that in certain situations, the lack of transparency (opacity) and explainability (complexity) of AI systems could make it difficult for injured parties to prove that a product is defective or to prove fault. Therefore, it should be assessed how to ease the burden of proof for injured parties. CoESS

7.3.3.2.2 Strict Liability / Mandatory Insurance for AI Use-Cases with a Specific Risk Profile

Amongst NGOs, academic/research institutions, and consumer organisations there was clear support for either full or minimum harmonization of strict liability for operating AI-enabled products and providing AI-enabled services, where these activities create serious injury risks (e.g. life, health, property) for the public.[83] These organisations also supported the harmonisation of mandatory insurance coverage for using certain (high-risk) AI products and providing certain AI-based services (i.e., mandatory liability insurance for operators subject to strict liability): "A tendency to favour a harmonised insurance obligation to cover such a strict liability regime, where it does not exist yet, was also identified".[84]

---

thereby agrees that the defendant (any actor along the liability chain) should be obliged to disclose necessary technical information (e.g. log data) to the injured party to enable the latter to prove the conditions of the claim. It is, however, of outmost importance to define "necessary technical information" in an appropriate way to ensure that the defendant's intellectual property rights are adequately protected. For example, the defendant should not be required to disclose the source code or the operating model of the AI system – but rather information on the input data and output data used by the AI system. CoESS believes that, as a baseline, when any operator along the liability chain of an AI system failed to comply with their legal obligations as laid down in the EU AI Act, courts should infer that the damage was caused due to that operator's fault. A prerequisite should, however, be that the injured party can prove a causal link between that fault and the damage. In cases of complex and/or opaque and/or highly autonomous AI systems, we however stress that it would be inappropriate to shift the burden of proof from the injured party to the defendant – not even if it, in a given case, is necessary to establish how such an AI system operates in order to substantiate a claim".

[83] Commission, DG GROW and DG JUST, "Factual summary report of the open public consultation on Adapting Civil Liability Rules to the Digital Age and AI", Ref. Ares(2022)2620305, 06.04.2022, p. 10. "In particular, 73% of NGOs and research institutions (19 out of 26) favoured the minimum harmonisation of strict liability, while 69% (18 out of 26) favoured the full harmonisation approach. The corresponding percentages for EU citizens were 54% (47 out of 88) and 77% (68 out of 88) respectively. The 7 responding consumer organisations supported only the minimum harmonisation approach".

[84] Ibid.

See for instance the response submitted by BEUC (the European Consumer Organisation) to the European Commission's public consultation on Civil liability – adapting liability rules to the digital age and artificial intelligence, 23.12.2021, at p. 9: "Mandatory insurance can be a positive step to facilitate compensation: It is positive that the European Commission is considering mandatory insurance as this can contribute to facilitate claimants' compensation. However, this would require drawing a list of products/systems to which this requirement would apply. Mandatory insurance should come in addition of the harmonised rules".

On the other hand, business stakeholders did not support a harmonised insurance obligation to cover a strict liability regime. See for instance Amazon's response to the public consultation on Adapting liability rules to the digital age and Artificial Intelligence, 10th January 2022, p. 2: "We do not have evidence that insurances are particularly important for cross-border business activities".

On the other hand, concerning business stakeholders, there was an overwhelming majority that disagreed with the harmonisation of strict liability. Amongst business respondents, opposition was stronger regarding a minimum harmonisation (70% disagreement versus 14% agreement) than a full harmonisation approach (42% opposition versus 30% support). Of the few business stakeholders who supported the harmonisation of strict liability, it was stated that this harmonisation should be limited to a few high-risk cases.[85]

[85] Commission, DG GROW and DG JUST, "Factual summary report of the open public consultation on Adapting Civil Liability Rules to the Digital Age and AI", Ref. Ares(2022)2620305, 06.04.2022, p. 10.

See for instance the response submitted by BSA – The Software Alliance, "Response to the European Commission's consultation on civil liability – adapting liability rules to the digital age and artificial intelligence", 10.01.2022, p. 5: "Apply "strict liability" only to the highest risk AI: The consultation identifies a range of situations involving AI systems in which it might be appropriate to impose liability regardless of the producer's fault or whether a product is defective—e.g., products that continuously learn and adapt, malfunctioning products, or scenarios where the producer failed to comply with its obligations under the AI Act. This sort of strict liability, however, is generally reserved only for circumstances involving dangerous activities that pose substantial risks to third parties having no contractual relationship to the supplier (e.g., pedestrians harmed by autonomous driving). In effect, the "condition" of allowing the substantial risk is that the party carrying out activities that may lead to substantial risks to others takes responsibility for harms that result from it, irrespective of any fault or product defect. Strict liability should only be imposed on AI-enabled products in similarly narrow circumstances. Given the burgeoning state of AI development and deployment in the EU, subjecting all AI systems that, for example, continuously learn and adapt, is unwarranted. If the Commission chooses to proceed, it might, for example, limit the application of strict liability to those high-risk AI systems that pose inherent and unavoidable risks to the public (e.g., AI systems used in critical infrastructure). The need to consider which AI systems (if any) are sufficiently high-risk to merit strict liability is yet another reason to delay legislating for liability until the AI Act has been adopted and enters into force".

See also the response submitted by BusinessEurope, "Comments – Adapting liability rules to the digital age and Artificial Intelligence", 10.01.2022, pp. 1 and 4: "The need to introduce separate and new liability rules for AI should rely on solid evidence, and, in any case, be limited to specific and high-risk use-cases not covered yet, to avoid creating unnecessary overlaps and stifling innovation".

In addition, see Google's position ("Google's comments - Public consultation: Civil liability – adapting liability rules to the digital age and artificial intelligence", 7 January 2022, p. 4): "Clarity around scope is necessary. The high risk definition in the AIA would not be suitable for the liability framework, since the assessment of liability by nature requires a narrower, compensation-oriented framing. However, it would not be ideal to have different definitions of "high risk" in legislation on the same issue. A possible approach could be to provide an exhaustive list of "high risk" AI applications which play a significant role in situations where strict liability already applies (e.g., nuclear power plants, aviation). Adherence to existing safety standards that mitigate the increased risk could provide exemptions on a case by case basis, similar to the approach taken in the AIA. However, in these high risk areas strict liability will almost always already exist at member state level. This would make additional AI liability unnecessary".

Furthermore, as it was put by the Confederation of European Security Services (CoESS) ("Confederation of European Security Services (CoESS) - Position Paper on the European Commission Consultation on adapting liability rules to the digital age and AI", 20 December 2021, pp. 1-2), "any liability regime would need to be carefully examined and evaluated in order to avoid negative effects, e.g. on innovation and AI uptake. Strict liability rules for AI should be reserved for a limited number of AI-enabled products and services which impose a high material risk (e.g. life,

7.3.3.2.3 Types of Compensable Harm

Representatives of consumer organisations, research institutions and NGOs favoured the extension of the range of damages for which compensation could be claimed (i.e., life, health, and consumer property) to non-material damages (e.g., loss of profit, loss of or damage to data, privacy infringements, reputational damage or psychological harm, environmental damage).[86]

On the other hand, business stakeholders stressed that liability should be limited to physical / material damage to consumers and urged the Commission not to extend the scope of compensable harm. In particular, they rejected an extension of liability to non-material damage as not necessary, arguing that damages for privacy infringements are difficult to quantify, that financial liability associated with non-material damages is less predictable, that environmental damages could raise complex issues of causation that would be difficult to address under a strict liability regime, and that existing EU legislation already provides redress mechanisms for consumers for many types of non-material damages (e.g., non-material damage can be compensated under data protection law, anti-discrimination law and tort law).[87]

---

health, property) for the public, following a risk-based and use-case focused approach. All AI-systems with a high-risk, including their use-cases, should be exhaustively listed in an Annex of the liability regime. Systems that are not listed in the Annex should remain subject to fault-based liability. Due to the rapid technological developments in AI, such a list should be able to be amended by means of Delegated Acts".

[86] Commission, DG GROW and DG JUST, "Factual summary report of the open public consultation on Adapting Civil Liability Rules to the Digital Age and AI", Ref. Ares(2022)2620305, 06.04.2022, p. 10.

See for instance the response submitted by BEUC (the European Consumer Organisation) to the European Commission's public consultation on Civil liability – adapting liability rules to the digital age and artificial intelligence, 23.12.2021, at p. 9: "All harm should be compensated: AI systems may cause a wide range of harm, including immaterial damage. It is essential that all type of harm be compensated. If not, this instrument will remain a limited relevance as a large part of consumer harm will not be compensated. While Member States follow different traditions in this field of law, we consider that harmonisation of the damages victims could be entitled to ask for is necessary to ensure a high-level of consumer protection across the Union. In this regard, material and immaterial damages (such as data loss) should be part of the upcoming rules".

[87] Commission, DG GROW and DG JUST, "Factual summary report of the open public consultation on Adapting Civil Liability Rules to the Digital Age and AI", Ref. Ares(2022)2620305, 06.04.2022, p. 10. "… business stakeholders were mainly opposed to such rules. Their opposition was strongest regarding the compensability of immaterial harm (63% disagreement (52 out of 83) v. 23% support (19 out of 83) and of data loss/damage not resulting in a verifiable economic loss (75% opposition (63 out of 84) v. 12% support (10 out of 84)). The written contributions submitted by business stakeholders emphasised the very diverse approaches under existing national rules and the concern that harmonisation for AI-related damage would create inconsistent outcomes compared to cases not involving AI".

For instance, according to Google ("Google's comments - Public consultation: Civil liability – adapting liability rules to the digital age and artificial intelligence", 7 January 2022, p. 5), "there are also fundamental issues with extending strict liability to non-material damages. Doing so would put a disproportionate burden on software developers. For example, if a student failed to submit a paper due to a software crash and failed their class, they could sue the developer for compensation of all

7.4 Conclusion

This chapter discussed the Commission's public consultation (which was open from 18 October 2021 to 10 January 2022) on how to improve the Product Liability Directive and how to address the challenges that artificial intelligence poses for liability rules.

In particular, the aim of the 2021–2022 public consultation (following the Commission's 2021 Inception Impact Assessment (IIA) "Adapting liability rules to the digital age and circular economy") was to confirm the relevance of the issues identified by the 2018 evaluation of the Product Liability Directive (i.e. how to apply the PLD to products in the digital and circular economy), and collect information and opinions on how to improve the PLD (Section I of the consultation). At the same time, Section II of the consultation specifically dealt with AI-related issues, exploring further the major problems connected with certain types of AI, which make it difficult for the victim/injured party to obtain compensation, i.e. to identify the potentially liable person, to prove that person's fault or to prove the defect in the product and the causal link between the defect and the damage. This difficulty becomes even higher as emerging digital technologies and products are becoming increasingly connected and complex.

the consequential damages, e.g. an additional year of studies and lost income. Where non-material damages are claimed under a fault-based or breach of contract claim, they are only recoverable if the claimant can prove that the losses were caused by the relevant failure of standard of care or breach of contract, and were not too remote (amongst other factors). Applying strict liability equitably to these less proximate forms of damage will be effectively impossible without the kind of detailed analysis (factual and legal) of the relationship between cause and effect that occurs in a fault-based or contract claim. Strict liability is only appropriate in the clearer cut cases of personal injury and damage to property that have direct and severe consequences for consumers. The procedural burdens for all parties involved in case of non-material damages would be disproportionate. Furthermore, many of the non-material damages referenced in the public consultation questionnaire are notoriously difficult to quantify. This is the case, for example, of damages for privacy infringements. Risks for consumers in this area are already covered by the GDPR, whose severe penalties are a powerful incentive for producers to protect their customers' privacy. Environmental damages, as another example, would raise particularly complex issues of causation and remoteness that would be difficult to address under a strict liability regime. It is also hard to imagine how environmental damage could be associated with an individual consumer in a way that would be appropriate to a consumer protection framework".

See also the argument submitted by Siemens ("Siemens – Executive summary on EU (civil) tort liability framework", 07.01.2022, p. 5): "No additional types of harm due to use of technology (immaterial harm e.g. pain and suffering, reputational damage or psychological harm). Since infringements of data privacy and personal rights are already sanctioned in data privacy law, anti-discrimination law and tort liability, we see no gaps in legal protection. In addition, a risk-oriented approach to liability also means that there should not be multiple liability for any damage under the same conditions".

The Commission put forward proposed policy measures to address those issues related specifically to damage caused by AI systems, covering both the Product Liability Directive and national civil liability rules. The aim is to ensure that victims of damage caused by AI systems are not left with less protection than victims of damage caused by technologies that operate without AI. The Commission's proposed approaches focused on (i) measures to ease the victim's burden of proof as well as (ii) a targeted harmonisation of strict liability and (iii) insurance solutions.

In light of the three-pronged objective of the EU liability framework (legal certainty, prevention of damages and efficient compensation to the injured parties), the Commission's proposals (especially those opting for the adoption of 'radical' measures in relation to an expansion of liability as well as for the alleviation or even reversal of the burden of proof) could fundamentally transform the EU liability regime for AI, IoT and other emerging digital technologies. The Commission believes that investment in and societal acceptance of emerging technologies require legal certainty and trust. A clear legal framework is essential to accelerate innovation by providing businesses with legal certainty for the development and innovation of AI-based technology, whilst protecting citizens (potential victims of harm or damage) and promoting their trust in AI technologies. Therefore, if the EU proceeds with the revision of the Product Liability Directive and the enactment of a specific Directive on AI liability, as detailed in Chapters 8 and 9 of this book, it should address the specific challenges posed by artificial intelligence, provide legal certainty for all parties involved, instill confidence in the safety and reliability of AI-related products and services, and foster stability for AI-based technology investment.

Legal/Policy Documents, Studies, Reports

European Commission's ('Commission) Inception Impact Assessment "Adapting liability rules to the digital age and circular economy", Ref. Ares(2021)4266516, 30.06.2021.

Commission's Inception Impact Assessment, Title of the Initiative "Proposal for a legal act of the European Parliament and the Council laying down requirements for Artificial Intelligence", 23.07.2020, Ref. Ares(2020)3896535.

Commission's Public Consultation, "Adapting liability rules to the digital age and Artificial Intelligence", 18 October 2021.

Commission, DG GROW and DG JUST, "Factual summary report of the open public consultation on Adapting Civil Liability Rules to the Digital Age and AI", Ref. Ares(2022)2620305, 06.04.2022.

Commission Staff Working Document on "Liability for emerging digital technologies" - Accompanying the document Commission Communication "Artificial intelligence for Europe", SWD(2018) 137 final, Brussels, 25.4.2018.

Commission Communication, "Building Trust in Human-Centric Artificial Intelligence", COM(2019) 168 final, Brussels, 8.4.2019.

Commission Communication "Report on the safety and liability implications of Artificial Intelligence, the Internet of Things and robotics", COM (2020) 64 final, Brussels, 19.2.2020.

European Parliament Resolution of 20 October 2020 with recommendations to the Commission on a civil liability regime for artificial intelligence (2020/2014 (INL)) P9_TA(2020)0276 ('European Parliament's Resolution of 20 October 2020 on a civil liability regime for AI').

Annex to the European Parliament Resolution of 20 October 2020 with recommendations to the Commission on a civil liability regime for artificial intelligence: detailed recommendations for drawing up a Regulation on liability for the operation of artificial intelligence systems, A. Principles and Aims of the Proposal. B. Text of the Proposal Requested—Proposal for a Regulation on liability for the operation of Artificial Intelligence-systems ('Annex to the European Parliament's Resolution of 20 October 2020 on a civil liability regime for AI').

Report from the Expert Group on Liability and New Technologies – New Technologies Formation "Liability for Artificial Intelligence and Other Emerging Digital Technologies", 21 November 2019.

Responses by Organisations, Associations and Corporations to Public Consultations

BEUC (the European Consumer Organisation), Comments to the European Commission's public consultation on Civil liability – adapting liability rules to the digital age and artificial intelligence, 23.12.2021.

European Law Institute, "Response of the European Law Institute (ELI) - Public Consultation on Civil Liability Adapting liability rules to the digital age and artificial intelligence", Bernhard A Koch, Jean-Sébastien Borghetti, Piotr Machnikowski et al., 12.01.2022.

BSA – The Software Alliance, "Response to the European Commission's consultation on civil liability – adapting liability rules to the digital age and artificial intelligence", 10.01.2022.

BusinessEurope, "Comments – Adapting liability rules to the digital age and Artificial Intelligence", 10.01.2022.
Computer & Communications Industry Association (CCIA Europe), "A product liability regime fit for the digital age", 20.12.2021.
Google, "Public consultation: Civil liability – adapting liability rules to the digital age and artificial intelligence", 7 January 2022.
Irish Council for Civil Liberties (ICCL) – "Submission to the consultation on adapting liability rules to the digital age and artificial intelligence", 7 January 2022.
Siemens, "Executive summary on EU (civil) tort liability framework", 07.01.2022.
Siemens Healthineers, "Contribution to the public consultation on Adapting liability rules to the digital age and Artificial Intelligence", 10.01.2022.
Software & Information Industry Association (SIIA) – "Comments of the Software & Information Industry Association (SIIA) on the Public Consultation regarding Adapting liability rules to the digital age and Artificial Intelligence", 10.01.2022.
GSMA, "GSMA response to the EC public consultation on Adapting Liability Rules to the Digital Age and AI", 22.12.2021.
European Games Developer Federation e.f. (EGDF) on the adapting liability rules to the digital age and artificial intelligence (Civil liability) consultation, 10.01.2022.
Eurosmart, "On the Product Liability Directive", 12.01.2022.
Amazon, Response to the public consultation on Adapting liability rules to the digital age and Artificial Intelligence, 10 January 2022.
The American Chamber of Commerce to the European Union (AmCham EU), Response to the consultation Civil liability – adapting liability rules to the digital age and artificial intelligence, 12.01.2022.
European Association of Automotive Suppliers (CLEPA), Position Paper, "Artificial Intelligence - For a coherent regulatory framework that ensures safety and trust", 12.01.2022.
Confederation of European Security Services (CoESS) ("Confederation of European Security Services (CoESS) - Position Paper on the European Commission Consultation on adapting liability rules to the digital age and AI", 20 December 2021.
Association for Computing Machinery Europe Technology Policy Committee (ACM-ETPC), Response to the Commission Consultation on Civil Liability: Adapting Liability Rules to the Digital Age & Artificial Intelligence, 10.01.2022.
Center for Data Innovation, Response to the Commission's inception impact assessment on civil liability - adapting liability rules to the digital age and AI, submitted on 28.07.2021.

References

Bathaee Y (2018) The artificial intelligence black box and the failure of intent and causation. Harv J Law Technol 31(2):889–938

Bertolini A (2018) Artificial intelligence and civil law - liability rules for drones. Study requested by the European Parliament's Committee on Legal Affairs, Policy Department for Citizens' Rights and Constitutional Affairs, November 2018

Bertolini A (2020) Artificial intelligence and civil liability. Study requested by the European Parliament's Committee on Legal Affairs, Policy Department for Citizens' Rights and Constitutional Affairs – Directorate-General for Internal Policies, PE 621.926, July 2020

Borghetti J-S (2019) How can artificial intelligence be defective. In: Lohsse S, Schulze R, Staudenmayer D (eds) Liability for artificial intelligence and the Internet of Things. Nomos, Baden-Baden, pp 63–76

Chatzipanagiotis M, Leloudas G (2020) Automated vehicles and third-party liability: a European perspective. Univ Ill J Law Technol Policy 1:109–199

de Meeus C (2019) The product liability directive at the age of the digital industrial revolution: fit for innovation? J Eur Consum Mark Law 8(4):149–154

Evas T (2018) A common EU approach to liability rules and insurance for connected and autonomous vehicles, Study. European Added Value Assessment - Accompanying the European Parliament's legislative own-initiative report (Rapporteur: Mady Delvaux). Study, European Parliamentary Research Service (EPRS), February 2018

Evas T (2020) Civil liability regime for artificial intelligence. Study, European Parliamentary Research Service (EPRS), September 2020

Fairgrieve D, Rajneri E (2019) Is software a product under the product liability directive? Zeitschrift für Internationales Wirtschaftsrecht 1:24–28

Fairgrieve D, Howells G, Møgelvang-Hansen P et al (2016) Product liability directive. In: Machnikowski P (ed) European product liability: an analysis of the state of the art in the era of new technologies. Principles of European tort law. Intersentia, pp 17–108

Hacker P, Passoth J-H (2022) Varieties of AI explanations under the law. From the GDPR to the AIA, and beyond. In: Holzinger A, Goebel R, Fong R, Moon T, Müller KR, Samek W (eds) Lecture Notes on Artificial Intelligence 13200: xxAI - beyond explainable AI. Springer

Howells G, Twigg-Flesner C, Willett C (2017) Product liability and digital products. In: Synodinou T-E, Jougleux P, Markou C, Prastitou T (eds) EU internet law: regulation and enforcement. Springer Nature, pp 183–195

Karner E, Koch BA, Geistfeld MA (2021) Comparative law study on civil liability for artificial intelligence. European Commission, Directorate-General for Justice and Consumers

Koch BA, Borghetti J-S, Machnikowski P, Pichonnaz P, Rodríguez de las Heras Ballell T, Twigg-Flesner C, Wendehorst C (2022) Response of the European Law Institute to the public consultation on civil liability – adapting liability rules to the digital age and artificial intelligence. J Eur Tort Law 13(1):25–63

Kritikos M (2019) Artificial intelligence ante portas: legal & ethical reflections. European Parliamentary Research Service (EPRS). Scientific Foresight Unit (STOA), March 2019

Lohsse S, Schulze R, Staudenmayer D (2019) Liability for artificial intelligence. In: Lohsse S, Schulze R, Staudenmayer D (eds) Liability for artificial intelligence and the internet of things. Nomos, Baden-Baden, pp 99–116

Luzak J (2020) A broken notion: impact of modern technologies on product liability. Eur J Risk Regul 11(3):630–649

Machnikowski P (2016) Conclusions. In: Machnikowski P (ed) European product liability: an analysis of the state of the art in the era of new technologies. Principles of European tort law. Intersentia, pp 669–705

Madiega T (2020) Reform of the EU liability regime for online intermediaries: background on the forthcoming digital services act: in depth analysis. European Parliamentary Research Service (EPRS), May 2020

Martín-Casals M (2019) Causation and scope of liability in the internet of things (IoT). In: Lohsse S, Schulze R, Staudenmayer D (eds) Liability for artificial intelligence and the internet of things. Nomos, Baden-Baden, pp 201–228

Mezzanotte F (2019) Liability for digital products. In: De Franceschi A, Schulze R (eds) Digital revolution – new challenges for law. Nomos, pp 169–188

Navas S (2020) Robot machines and civil liability. In: Ebers M, Navas S (eds) Algorithms and law. Cambridge University Press, pp 157–173

Nikolinakos NT (2022) Adapting the EU liability regime to artificial intelligence (AI): the European Commission's proposed policy options. Comput Telecommun Law Rev (C.T.L.R.) 28(3):66–83

Paolo Patti F (2019) The European road to autonomous vehicles. Fordham Int Law J 43:125

Schellekens M (2018) No-fault compensation schemes for self-driving vehicles. Law, Innov Technol 10(2):314–333

Sérgio Cabral T (2020) Liability and artificial intelligence in the EU: assessing the adequacy of the current product liability directive. Maastricht J Eur Comp Law 27(5):615–635

Shavell S (2020) On the redesign of accident liability for the world of autonomous vehicles. J Legal Stud 49:243–285

Spindler G (2019) User liability and strict liability in the internet of things and for robots. In: Lohsse S, Schulze R, Staudenmayer D (eds) Liability for artificial intelligence and the internet of things. Nomos, Baden-Baden, pp 125–145

Tenhunen S (2022) Aligning the Product Liability Directive with the circular economy and emerging technologies: Revision of Directive 85/374/EEC. Implementation Appraisal Briefing, European Parliamentary Research Service (EPRS)

Timan T, Snijders R, Kirova M, Suardi S, Lieshout MV, Chen M, Costenco P, Palmerini E, Bertolini A, Tejada A, Montfort SV, Bolchi M, Alberti S, Brouwer R, Karanilokova K, Episcopo F, Jansen S (2019) Study on safety of non-embedded software. Service, data access, and legal issues of advanced robots, autonomous, connected, and AI-based vehicles and systems: final study report regarding CAD/CCAM and industrial robots. European Commission, Brussel

Twigg-Flesner C (2021) Guiding principles for updating the product liability directive for the digital age (Pilot ELI Innovation Paper), European Law Institute (January 2021)

van Boom WH, Borghetti J-S, Ehlers AB, Karner E, Nolan D, Oliphant K, Scarso A, Ulfbeck V, Wagner G (2018) Product liability in Europe. In: Koziol H, Green MD, Lunney M, Oliphant K, Yang L (eds) Product liability: fundamental questions in a comparative perspective. De Gruyter, Berlin, Boston, pp 255–356

Verheyen T (2018) Full harmonization, consumer protection and products liability: a fresh reading of the case law of the ECJ. Eur Rev Priv Law 26(1):119–140

Verheyen T (2021) On behavioural asymmetry in product liability law: how privatising nudging will get European product liability theory back on track. J Eur Tort Law 12(1):40–64

Wagner G (2019) Robot, Inc.: personhood for autonomous systems? Fordham Law Rev 88:591

Wagner G (2021) Liability for artificial intelligence: a proposal by the European Parliament. In: Eidenmüller H, Wagner G (eds) Law by Algorithm 127

Wagner G (2019) Robot liability. In: Lohsse S, Schulze R, Staudenmayer D (eds) Liability for artificial intelligence and the internet of things. Nomos, Baden-Baden, pp 27–62

Wagner G (2022) Software as a product. In: Lohsse S, Schulze R, Staudenmayer D (eds) Smart products, vol 157. Hart, Nomos

Wagner G (2022) Liability rules for the digital age – aiming for the Brussels effect. J Eur Tort Law (JETL) 13(3):191–243

Wendehorst C (2020) Strict liability for AI and other emerging technologies. J Eur Tort Law (JETL) 11(2):150–180

Wendehorst C (2021) Safety and liability related aspects of software. Study commissioned by the European Commission

Wuyts D (2014) The product liability directive – more than two decades of defective products in Europe. J Eur Tort Law 5(1):1–34

Zech H (2019) Liability for autonomous systems: tackling specific risks of modern IT. In: Lohsse S, Schulze R, Staudenmeyer D (eds) Liability for artificial intelligence and the internet of things. Nomos, Baden-Baden, pp 187–200
Zech H (2021) Liability for AI: public policy considerations. Acad Eur Law (ERA) Forum 22:147–158, Springer

Chapter 8
Reforming the EU Civil Liability Framework Applicable to Artificial Intelligence and Other Emerging Digital Technologies: The Proposed AI Liability Directive

8.1 Introduction

This chapter provides a thorough and systematic analysis of the European Commission's proposal for a Directive on adapting non-contractual civil liability rules to artificial intelligence (the 'proposed AI Liability Directive').[1] The proposed AI Liability Directive harmonises targeted aspects of the Member States' existing civil liability rules applicable to AI-systems and its aim is to complement and modernise the EU liability framework by introducing new rules specific to damages caused by AI systems.

While the EU AI Act[2] aims at preventing, monitoring, and addressing/reducing risks to safety and fundamental rights, harm will still occur. When this happens, the liability rules should be able to determine which party is liable for harm and under which conditions a victim can be compensated. The EU AI Act contains no provisions on liability for the purposes of damages claims and does not compensate the victim for the harm suffered.

Currently victims rely on national liability rules and, in certain cases, on the Product Liability Directive (PLD), which is being revised in parallel. However, such national liability rules (in particular fault-based national rules) are not suited to handling compensation claims for harm caused by AI-enabled products and services.

[1] Proposal for a Directive of the European Parliament and of the Council on adapting non-contractual civil liability rules to artificial intelligence (AI Liability Directive), European Commission, COM(2022) 496 final, Brussels, 28.9.2022 (the 'proposed AI Liability Directive').

[2] Regulation (EU) 2024/1689 of the European Parliament and of the Council of 13 June 2024 laying down harmonised rules on artificial intelligence and amending Regulations (EC) No 300/2008, (EU) No 167/2013, (EU) No 168/2013, (EU) 2018/858, (EU) 2018/1139 and (EU) 2019/2144 and Directives 2014/90/EU, (EU) 2016/797 and (EU) 2020/1828 (*EU Artificial Intelligence Act*), OJ L, 12.07.2024.

N. T. Nikolinakos, *Adapting the EU Civil Liability Regime to the Digital Age: Artificial Intelligence, Robotics, and Other Emerging Technologies*, Law, Governance and Technology Series 68, https://doi.org/10.1007/978-3-031-67969-8_8

Indeed, under such rules, victims need to prove a wrongful action/omission of a person that caused the damage. In other words, the burden is on the victim to identify the responsible person and to prove the fault (action or omission), damage, and causal link. However, in the absence of targeted measures to ease the burden of proof, the specific characteristics of AI (including autonomy and opacity, i.e., the so-called "black box" effect) make it difficult or prohibitively expensive for victims to identify the liable person and prove the requirements for a successful liability claim (i.e., to meet the required burden of proof). Tracing the victim's loss back to the defendant may be challenging if the suspected cause of that loss is related to the operation of an AI system, due to the increasingly autonomous nature of some AI systems and their peculiar characteristics. Accordingly, liability rules need to ensure that, if damage occurs, victims are effectively compensated. A new liability regime should be introduced to ensure greater legal certainty, thereby enhancing consumer trust in AI and facilitating successful investment and innovation across the EU. Thus, while the AI Act aims at preventing damage, the proposed AI Liability Directive introduces a safety-net for compensation in the event of damage.

The objectives of the proposed AI Liability Directive are: (i) to prevent a lack of compensation, by ensuring that victims of AI-enabled products/services are equally protected as victims of traditional technologies (when persons suffer harm caused by AI systems, they should enjoy the same level of protection as those having suffered harm caused by other technologies, because lack of compensation could affect their trust in AI and ultimately the uptake of AI-enabled products/services); (ii) to reduce legal uncertainty regarding the liability exposure of businesses developing or using AI; and (iii) to prevent the emergence of fragmented AI-specific adaptations of national civil liability rules. Together, these problems cause internal market obstacles.

The proposed AI Liability Directive attempts to address the AI-specific problems by improving the rights of victims who have suffered any damage—as admissible under national law—due to wrongful use of artificial intelligence. In particular, the proposed AI Liability Directive introduces two key measures: *First*, the 'presumption of causality', which relieves victims from having to explain in detail how a specific fault or omission caused the damage. If victims can show that a party was at fault for not complying with a relevant obligation and that a causal link with the AI performance is reasonably likely, the court can presume that this non-compliance caused the damage. The liable party, however, can rebut this presumption by proving that another cause was responsible for the damage. *Second*, it assists victims in accessing relevant evidence from companies or suppliers when dealing with high-risk AI systems. Victims can request the court to order the disclosure of information about high-risk AI systems, facilitating the identification of the liable party and the understanding of the fault. This disclosure is subject to safeguards to protect sensitive information, including trade secrets.

Any type of victim (natural or legal person) can bring a claim for damages against any person for fault that influenced the AI system which caused the damage. The victim can be compensated if harmed by the fault or omission of a provider, developer or user of AI resulting in a damage covered by national law (e.g., health, property, including damage caused by safety issues or resulting from unlawful discrimination or breach of fundamental rights like privacy etc.). It is expected that the AI Liability Directive, once ratified, will facilitate compensation for victims—whether individuals or businesses—for damages caused by an AI system's output (certain faults or omissions), by enhancing the victims' ability to file successful claims against any party whose fault influenced the AI system causing the damage.[3]

---

[3]This chapter focuses on the views expressed by stakeholders/actors with different and, sometimes, conflicting interests who have been actively involved in the relevant public consultations. These stakeholders include governmental organisations and national competent authorities, industry representatives (corporations, business associations, software developers, manufacturers/producers etc.), consumer associations, civil society and other non-profit organisations, and academic/research institutions.

For interesting reading, analysis, and useful academic commentary, see the following:

Dieter Frizberg with Petra Porubčanová, 'Adapting liability rules to artificial intelligence', Briefing, Initial Appraisal of a European Commission Impact Assessment, European Parliamentary Research Service (EPRS), March 2024.

Miriam C. Buiten, 'Product liability for defective AI', European Journal of Law and Economics 57, 239–273 (2024).

Nynke E. Vellinga, (2024). 'Rethinking compensation in light of the development of AI'. International Review of Law, Computers & Technology, 1–22.

Stefano De Luca, 'New Product Liability Directive', In "A Europe Fit for the Digital Age", Legislative Train Schedule, European Parliamentary Research Service (EPRS), 20 April 2024.

Eldakak, A., Alremeithi, A., Dahiyat, E. et al. Civil liability for the actions of autonomous AI in healthcare: an invitation to further contemplation. Humanit Soc Sci Commun 11, 305 (2024).

Jan De Bruyne, Orian Dheu, Charlotte Ducuing, 'The European Commission's approach to extra-contractual liability and AI – An evaluation of the AI Liability Directive and the Revised Product Liability Directive', Computer Law & Security Review, Volume 51, November 2023, 105894.

Orian Dheu and Jan De Bruyne, 'Artificial Intelligence and Tort Law: A 'Multi-faceted' Reality', (2023), European Review of Private Law, Volume 31, Issue 2, pp. 261–298.

Marta Ziosi, Jakob Mökander, Claudio Novelli, Federico Casolari, Mariarosaria Taddeo, Luciano Floridi, "The EU AI Liability Directive (AILD): Bridging Information Gaps", European Journal of Law and Technology, Vol. 14 No. 3 (2023).

Ioana Bratu, "A First Critical Analysis of the European Approach to Damage Caused by Artificial Intelligence Enabled by Global Navigation Satellite Systems. A Bridge to Nowhere or a Cloud with a Silver Lining?", 2023, International Review of Law, Computers & Technology, 37 (2): 147–165.

Mindy Nunez Duffourc and Sara Gerke, 'The proposed EU Directives for AI liability leave worrying gaps likely to impact medical AI', npj Digit. Med. 6, 77 (2023).

Geistfeld, Mark A., Karner, Ernst, Koch, Bernhard A. and Wendehorst, Christiane. Civil Liability for Artificial Intelligence and Software, Berlin, Boston: De Gruyter, 2023.

E. Karner, B. A. Koch, Comparative Study on Civil Liability for Artificial Intelligence, in: M. A. Geistfeld/E. Karner/B. A. Koch/C. Wendehorst, Civil Liability for Artificial Intelligence (2023).

Baris Soyer and Andrew Tettenborn, "Artificial intelligence and civil liability—do we need a new regime?", International Journal of Law and Information Technology, 30(4), pp. 385–397, February 2023.

Philipp Hacker, "The European liability directives - Critique of a half-hearted approach and lessons for the future", Computer Law & Security Review 51 (2023) 105871.

Philipp Hacker, "Manipulation by algorithms. Exploring the triangle of unfair commercial practice, data protection, and privacy law. European Law Journal, 29(1–2), 142–175, (2023).

Josh Cowls, Andreas Tsamados, Mariarosaria Taddeo & Luciano Floridi, "The AI gambit: leveraging artificial intelligence to combat climate change—opportunities, challenges, and recommendations", AI & Society 38, 283–307, (2023).

Rebecca Crootof, Margot E. Kaminski, W. Nicholson Price II, "Humans in the Loop" (2023) 76 Vanderbilt Law Review 429–510.

Stefano De Luca, 'New Product Liability Directive', In "A Europe Fit for the Digital Age", Legislative Train Schedule, European Parliamentary Research Service (EPRS), 15 December 2023.

Esther Kramer with Arianna Cantarelli, 'Updating liability rules for defective products', Briefing, European Parliamentary Research Service (EPRS), January 2023.

Tambiama Madiega, 'Artificial intelligence liability directive', Briefing, European Parliamentary Research Service (EPRS), February 2023.

Orian Dheu, Jan De Bruyne, Charlotte Ducuing, 'The European Commission's Approach To Extra Contractual Liability and AI – A First Analysis and Evaluation of the Two Proposals', CiTiP Working Paper Series, 6 October 2022.

Koch, Bernhard A, Borghetti, Jean-Sébastien, Machnikowski, Piotr, Pichonnaz, Pascal, Rodríguez de las Heras Ballell, Teresa, Twigg-Flesner, Christian and Wendehorst, Christiane, "Response of the European Law Institute to the Public Consultation on Civil Liability – Adapting Liability Rules to the Digital Age and Artificial Intelligence", Journal of European Tort Law, vol. 13, no. 1, 2022, pp. 25–63.

Ugo Pagallo, 'The way ahead on AI liability issues - Will the developing EU liability framework for regulating AI prove sufficient?', The Ada Lovelace Institute, 20 October 2022.

Christiane Wendehorst, "AI liability in Europe: anticipating the EU AI Liability Directive", Ada Lovelace Institute, 2022.

Alexandre Lodie, Stephanie Celis Juarez, Theodoros Karathanasis. Towards a New Regime of Civil Liability for AI Systems: Comment on the European Commission's Proposals. 2022. hal-04130851.

Nikos Th. Nikolinakos, 'Adapting the EU Liability Regime to Artificial Intelligence (AI): The European Commission's Proposed Policy Options', (2022) 28 Computer & Telecommunications Law Review (C.T.L.R.), Issue 3, pp. 66–83.

Philipp Hacker and Jan-Hendrik Passoth, "Varieties of AI Explanations under the Law. From the GDPR to the AIA, and Beyond", in: Holzinger, Goebel, Fong, Moon, Müller and Samek (eds.), Lecture Notes on Artificial Intelligence 13200: xxAI - beyond explainable AI, Springer, 2022.

Susanna Tenhunen, 'Aligning the Product Liability Directive with the circular economy and emerging technologies: Revision of Directive 85/374/EEC', Implementation Appraisal Briefing, European Parliamentary Research Service (EPRS), October 2022.

Mosoreanu, Marius; Ulicna, Daniela; Paetz, Stephan; Podobea, Vlad; Schubert, Manuel; Stauf, Julia; Renda, Andrea; Sipiczki, Agnes, 'Behavioural Study on the link between challenges of artificial intelligence for Member States' civil liability rules and consumer attitudes towards AI-enabled products and services', Report, European Commission, Directorate-General for Justice and Consumers, Publications Office of the European Union, 2022.

Gerhard Wagner, "Liability Rules for the Digital Age – Aiming for the Brussels Effect", Journal of European Tort Law (JETL) 2022, vol. 13, no. 3, pp. 191–243.

Gerhard Wagner, 'Software as a Product' in: S. Lohsse/R. Schulze/D. Staudenmayer (eds.), Smart Products, 157, (2022), Hart, Nomos.

Samar Abbas Nawaz, The Proposed EU AI Liability Rules: Ease or Burden? (2022), European Law Blog.

Bart Custers and Eduard Fosch-Villaronga, 'Law and Artificial Intelligence – Regulating AI and Applying AI in Legal Practice', Information Technology and Law Series (ITLS), volume 35, 2022, Springer.

N. Helberger, M. Sax, J. Strycharz et al., "Choice Architectures in the Digital Economy: Towards a New Understanding of Digital Vulnerability", Journal of Consumer Policy 45, 175–200 (2022).

Christian Twigg-Flesner, 'Guiding Principles for Updating the Product Liability Directive for the Digital Age' (Pilot ELI Innovation Paper), European Law Institute (January 2021).

Martin Ebers, "Liability For Artificial Intelligence And EU Consumer Law", 12 (2021) JIPITEC 204–220.

Ernst Karner, Bernhard A. Koch, Mark A. Geistfeld, 'Comparative Law Study on Civil Liability for Artificial Intelligence', European Commission, Directorate-General for Justice and Consumers, 2021.

Herbert Zech, 'Liability for AI: public policy considerations', Academy of European Law (ERA) Forum, Volume 22, 147–158, Springer, 2021.

Christiane Wendehorst, 'Safety and Liability Related Aspects of Software', Study commissioned by the European Commission, 2021.

Gerhard Wagner, Liability for Artificial Intelligence: A Proposal by the European Parliament, in: H. Eidenmüller/G. Wagner, Law by Algorithm (2021) 127.

Anna Beckers, Gunther Teubner, "Three Liability Regimes for Artificial Intelligence: Algorithmic Actants, Hybrids, Crowds", Bloomsbury Publishing, 2021.

Miriam Buiten, Alexandre de Streel, Martin Peitz 'EU Liability Rules for the Age of Artificial Intelligence', Centre on Regulation in Europe (CERRE), March 2021.

Emiliano Marchisio, "In support of "no-fault" civil liability rules for artificial intelligence" (2021) 1 SN Social Sciences 1, 54 (2021).

Thomas Verheyen, "On Behavioural Asymmetry in Product Liability Law: How Privatising Nudging Will Get European Product Liability Theory Back on Track", Journal of European Tort Law, vol. 12, no. 1, 2021, pp. 40–64.

Stefan Strauß, "Deep Automation Bias: How to Tackle a Wicked Problem of AI?", Big Data and Cognitive Computing, 5, 18 (2021).

Christian Twigg-Flesner, 'Guiding Principles for Updating the Product Liability Directive for the Digital Age', European Law Institute (ELI) Innovation Paper Series, 2021.

Steven Van Uytsel, 'Different Liability Regimes for Autonomous Vehicles: One Preferable Above the Other?', in Steven Van Uytsel and Danilo Vasconcellos Vargas (eds), Autonomous Vehicles – Business, Technology and Law. Part of the book series: Perspectives in Law, Business and Innovation (PLBI), Springer 2021, pp. 67–92.

Jan De Bruyne, Elias Van Gool, Thomas Gils, 'Tort Law and Damage Caused by AI Systems', in J. De Bruyne and C. Vanleenhove, Artificial Intelligence and the Law, 359–404, Intersentia, 2021.

Beatrice Schütte, Lotta Majewski, Katri Havu, 'Damages Liability for Harm Caused by Artificial Intelligence – EU Law in Flux', Helsinki Legal Studies Research Paper No. 69, August 2021.

Micaela Del Monte and Stephanie Brenda Smialowski, "Understanding trilogue – Informal tripartite meetings to reach provisional agreement on legislative files", European Parliamentary Research Service (EPRS), May 2021.

Roger Brown, 'Property Ownership and the Legal Personhood of Artificial Intelligence', (2021) Information & Communications Technology Law, 30(2), 208–234.

Tiago Sérgio Cabral, "Liability and artificial intelligence in the EU: Assessing the adequacy of the current Product Liability Directive", Maastricht Journal of European and Comparative Law, 27(5), 615–635, (2020).

Tatjana Evas, Civil liability regime for artificial intelligence, Study, European Parliamentary Research Service (EPRS), September 2020.

Christiane Wendehorst, "Strict liability for AI and other emerging technologies", Journal of European Tort Law (JETL) 2020, 11(2): 150–180.

Christiane Wendehorst, Liability for Pure Data Loss, in: E Karner/U Magnus/J Spier/P Widmer (eds), Essays in Honor of Helmut Koziol (2020) 225–242.

Tambiama Madiega, 'Reform of the EU Liability Regime for Online Intermediaries: Background on the Forthcoming Digital Services Act: In Depth Analysis', European Parliamentary Research Service (EPRS), May 2020.

Philipp Hacker, Ralf Krestel, Stefan Grundmann, Felix Naumann, "Explainable AI under contract and tort law: legal incentives and technical challenges", 28 Artificial Intelligence and Law 415, (2020).

Andrea Bertolini, Artificial intelligence and civil liability, Study requested by the European Parliament's Committee on Legal Affairs, Policy Department for Citizens' Rights and Constitutional Affairs – Directorate-General for Internal Policies, PE 621.926, July 2020.

Joasia Luzak, "A Broken Notion: Impact of Modern Technologies on Product Liability", European Journal of Risk Regulation, 11(3):630–649, (2020).

Susanna Navas, 'Robot Machines and Civil Liability'. In M. Ebers & S. Navas (eds.), Algorithms and Law. Cambridge University Press, 2020, 157–173.

Eirini Ntoutsi, P. Fafalios, U. Gadiraju and others, 'Bias in data-driven artificial intelligence systems—An introductory survey' (2020) 10 Wiley Interdisciplinary Reviews: Data Mining and Knowledge Discovery e1356.

Steven Shavell, "On the Redesign of Accident Liability for the World of Autonomous Vehicles", (2020) 49 The Journal of Legal Studies, 243–285.

Kim Watts, 'Potential of No-Fault Comprehensive Compensation Funds to Deal with Automation and Other 21st Century Transport Developments', European Journal of Commercial Contract Law, 2020, vol. 12, 1–21.

David Levy, 'Intelligent No-Fault Insurance for Robots', Journal of Future Robot Life, 2020, vol. 1, 1–23.

Omri Rachum-Twaig, 'Whose robot is it anyway?: Liability for artificial intelligence-based products', University of Illinois Law Review, Vol. 2020, No. 4, pp. 1141–1175.

Michael Chatzipanagiotis and George Leloudas, 'Automated Vehicles and Third-Party Liability: A European Perspective', University of Illinois Journal of Law, Technology & Policy 2020(1), pp. 109–199.

Francesco Paolo Patti, "The European Road to Autonomous Vehicles", 43 Fordham Int'l L.J. 125 (2019).

Herbert Zech: "Liability for autonomous systems: tackling specific risks of modern IT". In: Lohsse, S., Schulze, R., Staudenmeyer, D. (eds.), Liability for Artificial Intelligence and the Internet of Things. Nomos, Baden-Baden (2019), pp. 187–200.

Borges, G.: New Liability Concepts: the potential of insurance and compensation funds. In: Lohsse, S., Schulze, R., Staudenmeyer, D. (eds.) Liability for Artificial Intelligence and the Internet of Things. Nomos, Baden-Baden (2019), pp. 145–163.

Borghetti J-S, 'How can artificial intelligence be defective'. In: Lohsse S, Schulze R, Staudenmayer D (eds) Liability for artificial intelligence and the Internet of Things. Nomos, Baden-Baden (2019), pp. 63–76.

Gerald Spindler, 'User Liability and Strict Liability in the Internet of Things and for Robots' in Sebastian Lohsse, Reiner Schulze and Dirk Staudenmayer (eds), Liability for Artificial Intelligence and the Internet of Things. Nomos, Baden-Baden (2019), pp. 125–145.

Miquel Martín-Casals, 'Causation and Scope of Liability in the Internet of Things (IoT)' in Sebastian Lohsse/Reiner Schulze/Dirk Staudenmayer (ed), Liability for Artificial Intelligence and the Internet of Things. Nomos, Baden-Baden (2019), pp. 201–228.

Jeremias Adams-Prassl, "What if Your Boss Was an Algorithm? The Rise of Artificial Intelligence at Work", (2019) 41(1) Comparative Labor Law & Policy Journal 123.

A. Michael Froomkin, Ian Kerr and Joelle Pineau, "When AIs Outperform Doctors: Confronting the Challenges of a Tort-Induced Over-Reliance on Machine Learning (February 20, 2019). 61 Ariz. L. Rev. 33–99, (2019), University of Miami Legal Studies Research Paper No. 18-3.

Philipp Maume, "Reducing Legal Uncertainty and Regulatory Arbitrage for Robo-Advice", European Company and Financial Law Review 2019, 622–651.

Lohsse, S., Schulze, R., & Staudenmayer, D., 'Liability for Artificial Intelligence', In S. Lohsse, R. Schulze, & D. Staudenmayer (eds.), Liability for Artificial Intelligence and the Internet of Things. Nomos, Baden-Baden (2019), 99–116.

Gerhard Wagner, 'Robot Liability' in S. Lohsse/R. Schulze/D. Staudenmayer (eds), Liability for Artificial Intelligence and the Internet of Things. Nomos, Baden-Baden (2019), pp. 27–62.

Timan, T., R. Snijders, M. Kirova, S. Suardi, M. v. Lieshout, M. Chen, P. Costenco, E. Palmerini, A. Bertolini, A. Tejada, S. v. Montfort, M. Bolchi, S. Alberti, R. Brouwer, K. Karanilokova, F. Episcopo and S. Jansen (2019). Study on safety of non-embedded software. Service, data access, and legal issues of advanced robots, autonomous, connected, and AI-based vehicles and systems: final study report regarding CAD/CCAM and industrial robots. Brussel, European Commission.

Gabriele Mazzini, "A System of Governance for Artificial Intelligence through the Lens of Emerging Intersections between AI and EU Law" in A. De Franceschi/ R. Schulze (ed), Digital Revolution – New challenges for Law (2019).

Gerhard Wagner, "Robot, Inc.: Personhood for Autonomous Systems?", 88 Fordham Law Review, 591 (2019).

Charlotte de Meeus, 'The Product Liability Directive at the Age of the Digital Industrial Revolution: Fit for Innovation?', (2019), Vol. 8, Journal of European Consumer and Market Law, Issue 4, pp. 149–154.

Mihalis Kritikos, 'Artificial Intelligence ante portas: Legal & ethical reflections', European Parliamentary Research Service (EPRS), Scientific Foresight Unit (STOA), March 2019.

Francesco Mezzanotte, 'Liability for Digital Products', in: A De Franceschi/R Schulze (eds), Digital Revolution – New Challenges for Law, 169–188. Nomos, (2019).

D. Fairgrieve and Eleonora Rajneri, 'Is Software a Product under the Product Liability Directive?', Zeitschrift für Internationales Wirtschaftsrecht, January 2019, Volume 1/2019, pp. 24–28.

Tolan S., Miron M., Gomez E. and Castillo C. "Why Machine Learning May Lead to Unfairness: Evidence from Risk Assessment for Juvenile Justice in Catalonia", Best Paper Award, International Conference on AI and Law, 2019.

Tatjana Evas, A common EU approach to liability rules and insurance for connected and autonomous vehicles, Study. European Added Value Assessment - Accompanying the European Parliament's legislative own-initiative report (Rapporteur: Mady Delvaux). Study, European Parliamentary Research Service (EPRS), February 2018.

Andrea Bertolini, Artificial Intelligence and civil law - Liability rules for drones, Study requested by the European Parliament's Committee on Legal Affairs, Policy Department for Citizens' Rights and Constitutional Affairs, November 2018.

Maurice Schellekens, 'No-Fault Compensation Schemes for Self-Driving Vehicles', Law, Innovation and Technology, 2018, 10:2, 314–333.

Boom, Willem H van, Borghetti, Jean-Sébastien, Ehlers, Andreas Bloch, Karner, Ernst, Nolan, Donal, Oliphant, Ken, Scarso, Alessandro, Ulfbeck, Vibe and Wagner, Gerhard. "Product Liability in Europe". Product Liability: Fundamental Questions in a Comparative Perspective, edited by Helmut Koziol, Michael D. Green, Mark Lunney, Ken Oliphant and Lixin Yang, Berlin, Boston: De Gruyter, 2018, pp. 255–356.

Yavar Bathaee, "The artificial intelligence black box and the failure of intent and causation", Harvard Journal of Law & Technology, Volume 31, Number 2, 889–938, (2018).

Thomas Verheyen, "Full Harmonization, Consumer Protection and Products Liability: A Fresh Reading of the Case Law of the ECJ", 26 (1) European Review of Private Law, 119–140, (2018).

Jian-hua Li, "Cyber security meets artificial intelligence: a survey", Frontiers of Information Technology & Electronic Engineering 19, 1462–1474 (2018).

Naveed Akhtar and Ajmal Mian, "Threat of adversarial attacks on deep learning in computer vision: A survey" (2018) 6 IEEE Access 14410.

Joy Buolamwini, Timnit Gebru, 'Proceedings of the 1st Conference on Fairness, Accountability and Transparency', PMLR 81:77–91, 2018.

Howells, G., Twigg-Flesner, C., and Willett, C., Product Liability and Digital Products. In T-E. Synodinou, P. Jougleux, C. Markou, & T. Prastitou (eds.), EU Internet Law: Regulation and Enforcement. 2017, Springer Nature, 183–195.

Leenes, R., E. Palmerini, B.-J. Koops, A. Bertolini, P. Salvini and F. Lucivero (2017). "Regulatory challenges of robotics: Some guidelines for addressing legal and ethical issues." Law Innovation and Technology 9: 1–44.

Stefan Grundmann and Philipp Hacker, "Digital Technology as a Challenge to European Contract Law – From the Existing to the Future Architecture", 13 European Review of Contract Law, 255–293, 2017.

Aída Ponce del Castillo, 'A Law on Robotics and Artificial Intelligence in the EU?', (October 3, 2017). Foresight Brief, European Trade Union Institute (ETUI) Research Paper - Foresight Brief #02-September 2017.

Nathalie Nevejans, 'European Civil Law Rules in Robotics', Study requested by the European Parliament's Committee on Legal Affairs (JURI Committee), 2016.

D. Fairgrieve, G. Howells, P. Møgelvang-Hansen et al., Product Liability Directive. In: P. Machnikowski (ed), European Product Liability: An Analysis of the State of the Art in the Era of New Technologies. Principles of European Tort Law. Intersentia; 2016:17–108.

Piotr Machnikowski, Conclusions, in: P Machnikowski (ed), European Product Liability: An Analysis of the State of the Art in the Era of New Technologies. Principles of European Tort Law. Intersentia; 2016:669–705.

Melinda Florina Lohmann, "Liability issues concerning self-driving vehicles", European Journal of Risk Regulation, 7(2), 335–340, (2016).

Roeland de Bruin, "Autonomous Intelligent Cars on the European Intersection of Liability and Privacy: Regulatory Challenges and the Road Ahead", European Journal of Risk Regulation, 2016, 7(3):485–501.

Susanne Beck, 'The problem of ascribing legal responsibility in the case of robotics', AI & Society, 2016, vol 31, n°4, pp. 473–481.

Konstantinos Christidis and Michael Devetsikiotis, "Blockchains and Smart Contracts for the Internet of Things", (2016) IEEE Access, vol. 4, pp. 2292–2303.

Mihalis Kritikos, 'Legal and ethical reflections concerning robotics', Scientific Foresight Unit (STOA) Policy Briefing, European Parliament Research Service (EPRS), PE 563.501, June 2016.

Palmerini, E., A. Bertolini, F. Battaglia, B.-J. Koops, A. Carnevale and P. Salvini (2016). "RoboLaw: Towards a European framework for robotics regulation." Robotics and Autonomous Systems 86: 78–85.

Daily Wuyts, "The Product Liability Directive – More than two Decades of Defective Products in Europe" Journal of European Tort Law, vol. 5, no. 1, 2014, pp. 1–34.

Andrea Bertolini, 'Robots as Products: The Case for a Realistic Analysis of Robotic Applications and Liability Rules', Law Innovation and Technology, 2013, vol. 5, pp. 214–247.

8.2 Existing Liability Rules in the EU

It is recalled that the existing liability framework in the EU relies on both (a) the Product Liability Directive[4] (which harmonised the liability of the producer of defective products) and (b) other non-harmonised national liability regimes that apply in parallel. Therefore, at the national level, the rules implementing the Product Liability Directive coexist with other extra-contractual liability rules that could also be invoked by victims of damages. As a result, in relation to liability claims in the EU, the victim currently has three avenues available for claiming compensation (complementary pillars of liability), i.e., it can seek compensation based on a fault-based liability claim, on a strict liability claim, or on a claim against the producer of a defective product.[5] In particular:

(a) The *existing Product Liability Directive (PLD)* harmonises no-fault based (i.e., strict) liability regimes for claims for damage caused to a consumer due to the defectiveness of a (movable) product at EU level. The Product Liability Directive harmonises the liability of the producer (i.e., deals with consumer claims against producers) of defective products, laying down common rules under which the producer is held liable for damage caused by a defect in his product. The actual cause of events that lead to damage or incident is decisive for the attribution of liability. The Product Liability Directive introduced the concept of strict liability of producers, according to which if a defective product causes death, personal injury or material damage (above EUR 500) to consumers or their private property, the producer is liable to provide compensation irrespectively of whether there is negligence or fault on the consumers' part. Therefore, producers are responsible for defective products, regardless of whether the defect of the product is their fault. A product is considered defective if it does not provide the safety a person is entitled to expect. To sustain their claim, those who have suffered injury (physical damage) or material damage

[4]Council Directive 85/374/EEC of 25 July 1985 on the approximation of the laws, regulations and administrative provisions of the Member States concerning liability for defective products, as modified by Directive 1999/34/EC of the European Parliament and of the Council of 10 May 1999 (OJ L 210/29, 7.8.1985, and OJ L 141/20, 4.6.1999) (the 'Product Liability Directive', 'PLD').

[5]Commission Staff Working Document, "Impact Assessment Report – Accompanying the document Proposal for a Directive of the European Parliament and of the Council on adapting non-contractual civil liability rules to artificial intelligence", SWD(2022) 319 final, Brussels, 28.9.2022, p. 3: "A victim currently relies on national liability rules and in certain cases on the Product Liability Directive (PLD) to claim compensation for damage arising from AI-enabled products and services. Depending on each case, a victim has several avenues available for claiming compensation. Various persons could be held liable in parallel under different conditions and for different reasons. Neither of these rules contains specific provisions for AI. Example: A traffic accident victim may have in parallel a fault-based liability claim against the driver whose fault caused the accident, a 'PLD' claim against the producer if the vehicle had a defect, and a strict liability claim against the vehicle's owner".

must prove the defect in the product (i.e. that the product did not provide the safety that the public is entitled to expect), the damage, and the causal link between the defect and the damage.[6]

(b) *National liability rules* offer different paths to victims to claim compensation. Depending on whether the compensation of the victim requires a fault of the person considered liable by the law or not, these national extra-contractual liability rules are classified into two broad categories, namely fault-based liability regimes on the one hand and special regimes of strict liability on the other. In particular: (i) *National (non-harmonised) fault-based liability regimes*, where a victim can make a claim for damages caused by products and services based on a person's conduct. According to national fault-based liability rules, the victim of damage has to prove the defendant's fault, i.e. negligence or intent to harm, the damage, and a causal link (causality) between that fault and the damage. Therefore, the fault of the author of the wrongful behaviour leading to a damage—which could be an act or an omission whether intentional or by negligence—is a necessary element to be proven for the liability claim to be successful. The victim submitting a claim needs to provide the evidence required to support his liability claim.[7] (ii) *National (non-harmonised) strict (non-fault) liability regimes*, which are set by member states for technologies or activities considered to pose an increased risk to society. Strict liability lies with the person who, irrespective of fault, exercises a degree of control over a risk connected with the operation of a technology/activity and benefits from exposing the public to a risk (i.e., a certain risk of damage is assigned to a person irrespective of fault). In national strict liability regimes, liability does not depend on a fault and there is no need for a victim to prove fault or causality between fault and the damage. The claimant usually needs only to prove that the risk stemming from the liable person identified by law materialised.[8]

[6]ibid., p. 4: "Victims may have, under the PLD, a claim against the producer of a defective product for a defect present when the product was put on the market. The victim must prove that the product was defective and the causal link between that defect and the damage. Under the PLD, the victim can claim compensation for personal injury or damage to consumer property. The PLD does not cover damage caused to property intended for professional use, damage caused during the provision of a service, damage to victims other than natural persons or claims based on the wrongful use of a product".

[7]Ibid., p. 3: "The victim could have a fault-based liability claim based on another person's wrongful behaviour, i.e. fault. A fault-based claim usually requires proving the existence of: - a damage, - a fault of the liable person, and - causality between that fault and the damage. ... As a matter of principle, it is the victim that needs to prove these three elements. Such claims apply irrespective of the technology/activity involved in causing harm and can be addressed against any type of wrongdoer (e.g. businesses, including service providers, or private persons) by any type of victim (e.g. business, private individual, public entity). They can compensate any type of harm protected by national law, e.g. physical injury, property damage, damage to or loss of data, economic loss like lost profit, non-economic loss like pain/ suffering or harm caused by discrimination".

[8]Ibid., pp. 3–4: "In addition to fault-based claims, victims could rely on liability independent of fault - so-called strict liability, with different scopes and conditions set by national laws. Strict liability rules assign liability for the relevant risk to a person, irrespective of fault. This is usually

8.3 Identification of the Problems: Shortcomings in Relation to Digital Technologies and to AI—Reforming the EU Liability Framework Applicable to AI

8.3.1 Problem Driver and AI-Specific Problems Regarding Liability

Liability-related issues are counted amongst the main risks associated with the use of AI. Indeed, liability ranks amongst the top three barriers to the use of AI by European companies and constitutes a major external barrier/challenge for companies that are planning to, but have not yet adopted AI (major obstacles to AI adoption).[9]

---

justified by the fact that this person draws a benefit from exposing the public to that risk. Normally, for that person to be found liable, the victim has only to prove that the risk stemming from the sphere of the liable person materialized".

See also Ernst Karner, Bernhard A. Koch, Mark A. Geistfeld, 'Comparative Law Study on Civil Liability for Artificial Intelligence', European Commission, Directorate-General for Justice and Consumers, 2021, at p. 31: "When it comes to strict liability, ... it depends upon how its trigger is defined in the legislation. Typically, liability irrespective of fault is linked to the materialisation of a certain risk either as such or one linked to a certain object or activity. If it is the latter, the claimant merely needs to prove that the activity or the operation of the object caused her loss without going further into explaining why she was harmed. If the keeper of an animal is strictly liable for any harm it causes, the victim only needs to prove that she was injured by the animal, but not that the keeper did anything wrong (such as failed to keep it under control). The hurdle for proving causation is therefore much lower than in a fault liability setting. Similarly, if it is the operation of a motor vehicle that triggers strict liability, again the victim only needs to submit evidence that she suffered loss in the course of the vehicle's operation, but neither that it was defective nor that it was improperly conducted, maintained or controlled. If there were strict liability for some AI-driven system, presumably proof of harm resulting from its mere operation would already trigger its keeper's (or operator's) duty to indemnify the victim (unless some defence applies). The victim would therefore not have to explain to the court what exactly went wrong within the AI system and why, and how this can be traced back to the operator, developer, or programmer, and she also need not show that it was the software rather than the hardware that was flawed".

[9] 'European enterprise survey on the use of technologies based on artificial intelligence', Study prepared for the European Commission, DG Communications Networks, Content & Technology by Ipsos Belgium and iCite (International Centre for Innovation, Technology and Education), 2020, Final report, at pp. 57–60, figures 18–21: "One specific challenge or barrier that seems to stand out is liability for damage caused by AI: while it seems to not be as universally relevant, this barrier seems to pose a major challenge when it is applicable to the business context in which enterprises operate" (at p. 58). ... "enterprises in the human health sector are consistently in the top three most concerned for all three external barriers, with risks associated with liability for damage caused by AI being rated as a major obstacle by 43% of interviewed enterprises in this sector – the highest proportion across all sectors. Liability for damage caused by AI also stands out as a major obstacle in the transport (39%), accommodation (37%) and other technical and/or scientific (36%) sectors" (at p. 60).

8.3.1.1 Problem Driver: The Specific Characteristics of AI Make It Difficult to Meet the Burden of Proof

Current fault-based national liability rules are not fit to deal with compensation claims for harm caused by AI-enabled products/services. Indeed, under such rules, victims need to prove a wrongful action/omission of a person that caused the damage. Thus, in the absence of targeted measures to ease the burden of proof, the specific characteristics[10] of certain AI-systems could make it extremely difficult and/or prohibitively expensive for victims to identify and prove the fault of a potentially liable person (i.e., uncertainty as regards the allocation of responsibilities) as well as the causal link between that fault and the damage suffered. Tracing the victim's loss back to the defendant may be challenging if the suspected cause of that loss is related to the operation of an AI system, due to the increasingly autonomous nature of some AI systems and their peculiar characteristics. In other words, the specific characteristics of AI make it difficult to meet the burden of proof and causation and thus prove the requirements for a successful liability claim.[11]

In particular, it is difficult to link damage caused by a highly autonomous AI system to the actions and/or omissions of a human actor (e.g., between the human

[10] "Certain AI systems may include only some of the relevant characteristics and may include mitigating mechanisms to reduce negative effects of some of these characteristics. As a rule, the more specific characteristics a given AI system has, the higher the probability that it becomes a 'black box'". Commission Staff Working Document, "Impact Assessment Report – Accompanying the document Proposal for a Directive of the European Parliament and of the Council on adapting non-contractual civil liability rules to artificial intelligence", SWD(2022) 319 final, Brussels, 28.9.2022, p. 120.

[11] Ernst Karner/Bernhard Koch/Mark Geistfeld, 'Comparative Law Study on Civil Liability for Artificial Intelligence', European Commission, Directorate-General for Justice and Consumers, 2021, pp. 30–31: "the likelihood of success in establishing causation obviously primarily depends upon what exactly the claimant needs to prove, ie which (and what kind of) cause she claims to have triggered liability. ... It is primarily human conduct and aspects related thereto that stand at the centre of the court's and therefore also of the claimant's attention. While the latter need not prove fault as such (which is a legal assessment by the court), she still needs to come forward with evidence of con-duct attributable to the defendant that can be qualified as faulty. If she needs to trace back the cause of her loss to some conduct influencing or at least initiating the operation of some AI-driven system, she will typically also need to prove how exactly the conduct at the beginning of the chain of causation impacted upon the operation in a way that led to her harm. Unless courts are willing to accept prima facie evidence (which will be tricky at least initially where there is no experience yet with what 'typically' results from AI operations), the claimant will not only have to prove the conduct of (or attributable to) the defendant as such, but also how exactly such conduct subsequently led the AI system to inflict harm upon the claimant, which appears to be a major challenge in such a black box situation. While human conduct is literally visible and can be witnessed (even the abstention from action), identifying the processes within an AI system and convincing the court thereof seems much more challenging, even if the defendant's conduct relating to the AI system can be traced back with convincing evidence. Even if a claimant can prove, for example, that someone entered false data into an AI system, this typically does not yet suffice in and of itself to prove that this error led the AI system to ultimately cause the harm at stake if such data is only part of the overall collection of information on which the 'behaviour' of the system is based, particularly if the system includes methods to validate individual information with big data".

actor related to the AI system and the damage caused by this AI system to a victim, the AI-system takes an autonomous action which is not pre-determined by a human), whereas in the case of opaque and complex AI it could be difficult for injured parties to prove that the conditions of liability are fulfilled (e.g., the way the AI action is performed cannot be understood, mainly due to the opacity and complexity of certain forms of AI).[12] As a result, because of AI's specific characteristics, victims

[12]In order to provide an illustration of the AI-specific difficulties in claiming compensation and to demonstrate the shortcomings of fault-based national regimes (and those of the Product Liability Directive) when it comes to specific AI systems, the Commission used the following example/case scenario (concerning autonomous cleaning robots):

"*Example*: A company deploys a fleet of autonomous cleaning robots to provide cleaning services throughout a city. It tasks one of its employees with the remote supervision of the fleet. One of the cleaning robots fails to recognise a colourful baby stroller, which is parked in front of a similarly patterned advertising banner. Because of the collision, the baby is injured and the stroller is damaged. The father witnessing the accident suffers psychological trauma. The accident could be due to a variety of possible causes, e.g. an image segmentation error of the robot's AI-based perception system, a failure by the provider of the AI vision component to provide an available software update or a failure by the user (the cleaning company) to install it, a failure by the human remote operator to appropriately monitor the operation of the fleet (possibly due to a malfunction of the human-robot interface) or also a deliberate attack on the robot's sensors by a third party (jamming, spoofing, sabotage through adversarial machine learning etc.). ... *Fault*: Given the cleaning robot's highly autonomous mode of operation, as well as the opacity and complexity of the different AI components, it is highly uncertain that the victim could ascertain relevant actions or omissions of, for instance, the employee charged with providing the cleaning instructions or monitoring the fleet of robots remotely. This would however be necessary to make a successful claim against the company. ... *Causality*: Assuming a wrongdoer's fault can be established, it is uncertain whether and how the victim can prove the causal link between such faulty behaviour and the damage. If an expert has access to logged information on inputs, outputs and internal states of the AI subsystems, she may be able to discard certain causes of the accident (e.g. jamming or spoofing of sensors) and to suppose certain correlations between, for instance, a detection failure and a control decision to move forward until colliding with the stroller. But due to the high degree of autonomy, complexity and the lack of explainability of the AI systems involved (not only the perception module but also e.g. the trajectory planning system and low-level controllers), it will likely be impossible to infer a clear causal link between any specific input and the harmful output. In view of AI specificities, to prove the necessary degree of likelihood is highly uncertain. ... *Product Liability Directive (PLD)*: When claiming compensation under the PLD, the victim does not have to prove the producer's fault, but that the cleaning robot was defective (i.e. it failed to provide the level of safety the public at large is entitled to expect) and the causal link between the defect and the harm. The victim would not have to prove how the cleaning robot became defective; whether it was a mechanical or software flaw is irrelevant. However, the PLD has shortcomings when it comes to digital products: producers are not liable for defects that emerge after the product was put into circulation (e.g. if the defect was due to a subsequently downloaded software module) and software producers themselves, including AI-system providers, cannot be pursued. These issues are dealt with in the PLD impact assessment, as they concern not only AI technologies. The PLD does not help the victim for any claims against other parties than the producer (e.g. the cleaning company), claims based on other grounds than defect (e.g. a failure to appropriately supervise the robot fleet), and claims for the compensation of damage not covered by the PLD (e.g. the psychological harm suffered by the baby's father)".

See Commission Staff Working Document, "Impact Assessment Report – Accompanying the document Proposal for a Directive of the European Parliament and of the Council on adapting

may in certain cases be less protected compared to victims of damage that did not involve AI.

As already explained in this book, the specific characteristics of certain AI-systems that may make it unduly difficult for victims to meet the burden of proof and challenge existing liability rules are the following: (i) high degree of autonomous behaviour (AI systems perform tasks with less, or entirely without, direct human intervention, and this characteristic makes it difficult to prove the link between a damaging output of the AI system and the action or omission of a potentially liable person, as required under fault-based liability rules);[13] (ii) limited transparency/opacity and explainability (due to the opacity of certain AI systems, it may not be possible to explain how the output is exactly derived from its input in a given context, thus making it extremely difficult for victims to prove the link between the harmful AI output and a human action or omission);[14] (iii) complexity

---

non-contractual civil liability rules to artificial intelligence", SWD(2022) 319 final, Brussels, 28.9.2022, pp. 8–9. For further analysis, see Annex 13, especially pp. 233–237. See also the case scenario 2 (socially assistive robots in education), pp. 237–242.

[13] Commission Staff Working Document, "Impact Assessment Report – Accompanying the document Proposal for a Directive of the European Parliament and of the Council on adapting non-contractual civil liability rules to artificial intelligence", SWD(2022) 319 final, Brussels, 28.9.2022, p. 120: "AI systems can increasingly perform tasks with less, or entirely without, direct human intervention. The level of autonomy of AI systems is a continuum, ranging from fully supervised and controlled systems to more independent ones that combine environmental feedback with an analysis of their current situation and can perform tasks without direct human intervention, even when operating in a complex environment. While the high-level objectives of AI systems are always defined by humans, for a number of AI systems their outputs and the mechanisms to reach these objectives are not concretely specified, enabling automated decision-making, within pre-set boundaries, without the involvement of a human operator. An increasing degree of autonomy of the system is one of the key aspects sought by the users of certain AI systems. While it is in some cases technically necessary for the automation of a certain task, and commercially desirable, this characteristic makes it difficult to prove the link between a damaging output of the AI system and the action or omission of a potentially liable person, as required under fault-based liability rules. It is very difficult to attribute directly the damaging output to an action/omission of a human liable person if between the human act of deploying the AI system and the damage caused by the AI system to a victim, the AI-system takes a highly autonomous action which is not pre-determined by a human. To prove such a link is however a necessary condition for a successful liability claim".

[14] Ibid., pp. 120–121: "Some AI systems lack transparency because the rules followed, which lead from input to output, are not fully pre-determined by a human. Due to the opacity of certain AI systems, it may not be possible to explain how the output is exactly derived from its input in a given context. An AI system can namely be opaque with respect to how exactly it functions as a whole, how the algorithm was realised in code and how the programme actually runs in a particular case, including the hardware and input data. As a result, some AI systems are opaque in a way ('black box effect') that other digital systems are not. Where damage happens, the opacity of an AI system can make it very challenging to establish which input data lead to a specific output creating a damage, and how. In the absence of a targeted alleviation of the burden of proof, and targeted rules on the disclosure of information on AI-systems in the context of civil proceedings, this can make it very hard or even impossible for victims to prove the link between the harmful AI output and a human action or omission. These difficulties are compounded by the fact that any human behaviour in developing or using an AI system will be accompanied and followed by built-in processes of the AI

(AI systems display certain levels of complexity due to the interdependency between different components. Combining different digital components in a complex eco-system and the plurality of actors involved can make it difficult for victims to identify the liable person and assess where a potential damage originates. This characteristic can contribute to a lack of explainability and, in the absence of a targeted alleviation of the burden of proof, it can make it difficult to establish that a certain wrongful human behaviour triggered the AI output that caused the relevant damage);[15] (iv) continuous adaptation and limited predictability (continuous adaptation renders an AI-system more unpredictable, which could make it impossible to prove the link between the damaging AI output and a specific cause, in particular the fault of a person).[16]

---

system that in turn depend upon a variety of internal and external factors independent from such conduct, for instance input data collected by sensors, which makes it again more difficult to link a harmful output to a human action or omission".

[15]For instance, AI applications are usually integrated in complex IoT environments where many different connected devices and services interact. The IoT and AI-enabled products and services comprise tangible parts/devices (sensors, actuators, hardware), different software components and applications, data, data services (i.e. collection, processing, curating, analysing), and connectivity features. Furthermore, AI-related products and services are increasingly interacting with traditional technologies, leading to added complexity when it comes to liability. Therefore, risks stemming from the complexity of the products and systems (apart from serious impact on safety) could make it very difficult for victims to identify the liable person and prove all necessary conditions for a successful claim. Indeed, since many different layers are involved in these digital technologies, vulnerable software, faulty sensors, or unstable connectivity may make it difficult to determine who is technically and legally responsible for any ensuing damage or how to identify the root cause of the problem.

See also Commission Staff Working Document, "Impact Assessment Report – Accompanying the document Proposal for a Directive of the European Parliament and of the Council on adapting non-contractual civil liability rules to artificial intelligence", SWD(2022) 319 final, Brussels, 28.9.2022, p. 121: "Advanced AI models frequently have more than a billion parameters and process very large amounts of data. In addition, AI systems are usually combined together in complex systems in real-world scenarios (e.g. in a robot many AI systems for perception, navigation, control, can be integrated). Due to this multiplicity of elements constituting such AI systems, they may not be understandable in practice for humans. While some AI systems can be comprehensible from an ex-post perspective despite their complexity (e.g. complex rule-based systems), complexity can contribute to a lack of explainability of outputs in other cases. In the absence of a targeted alleviation of the burden of proof, e.g. in the form of targeted presumptions easing the burden of proof, this can make it difficult to establish that a certain wrongful human behaviour triggered the AI output that caused the relevant damage".

[16]Commission Staff Working Document, "Impact Assessment Report – Accompanying the document Proposal for a Directive of the European Parliament and of the Council on adapting non-contractual civil liability rules to artificial intelligence", SWD(2022) 319 final, Brussels, 28.9.2022, p. 121: "Some AI systems can 'learn' while in use. In these cases, the rules being followed by the system adapt based on the input it receives while in use. Such continuous adaptation will render an AI-system more unpredictable. Machine learning based on continuous adaptation may therefore make it impossible to prove the link between the damaging AI output and a specific cause, in particular the fault of a person. But limited predictability concerns not only AI systems that continuously adapt while in use. Learning-based/data driven AI systems in general have a probabilistic behaviour as they are based on data that usually does not represent all possible scenarios.

8.3.1.2 AI-Specific Problems Regarding Liability

According to the Commission, there are three AI-specific problems regarding liability: (i) lack of compensation for victims contributing to the lack of societal trust in AI use; (ii) legal uncertainty, and (iii) increased legal fragmentation, which in their combination cause internal market obstacles.

These three problems are driven by the fact that, under existing liability rules, victims normally have to prove the necessary conditions for a successful claim, i.e., they have to identify the possibly liable person(s), the action/omission of that person which could be characterised as fault, and the causal link between that action/omission and the damage. However, there are neither targeted provisions for AI to ease the victim's burden of proof under fault-based claims, nor AI-specific strict liability regimes that would exempt the victim from making this proof. Therefore, these three major problems are primarily linked to the difficulty of the victim to prove the necessary facts due to the specific characteristics of certain AI systems, which make it very difficult to attribute directly the damaging output of the AI to an action/omission of a liable person.

(i) Lack of compensation diminishing consumer trust

As a result of the AI-specific characteristics that challenge liability rules, victims may not have effective access to the evidence necessary to build a case in courts (the cost for this expertise may be prohibitive and discourage victims from claiming compensation) and economic operators may face high uncertainty as regards the allocation of responsibilities. This leads to a lack of compensation for victims, thus contributing to the lack of societal trust in AI use.[17]

Outputs of these systems have a high input sensitivity and even a small change in the inputs can lead to an unpredictable behaviour of the system, and thus a lack of predictability. Moreover, while recurrent systems that depend on the internal state of an AI system are not necessarily designed for continuous adaptation, they nevertheless produce different outputs for the same inputs at different times, even when exposed to the same input. The challenges regarding the attribution of AI output for the purposes of liability claims hence apply more broadly than in the context of continuous adaptation".

[17] Ibid., pp. 12–14: "Victims are likely to incur significantly higher up-front costs and face significantly longer legal proceedings, when claiming compensation for damage caused by AI-enabled products or services, compared to cases not involving AI applications. Substantial burdens on victims are anticipated, due to the specific challenges of AI, for almost all national legal systems covered by the analysis commissioned for this impact assessment, often going beyond a 100% increase of fees paid for legal and technical expertise. This could deter victims from claiming compensation. Ultimately victims may be left under- or even uncompensated. AI-specific barriers are therefore likely to impinge on the right to an effective judicial remedy. As a consequence, the compensation function of liability law would fail. This would undermine the fundamental concept of justice as fairness ('distributive justice') that underpins our legal order and citizens' trust in the justice system. If victims are left without compensation when AI is involved, they would find themselves at a disadvantage compared to a situation where traditional technology would have caused the damage. Such an AI-induced lack of compensation would be particularly problematic if future autonomous technologies would create a significant risk of harm to life, health

(ii) Legal uncertainty

Because current fault-based national liability rules do not address the AI-specific difficulties of proof, the general burden of proof conditions apply. This creates legal uncertainty. Indeed, it is uncertain whether and how liability rules under national regimes would be interpreted (especially due to the AI-specific difficulties of meeting the burden of proving fault and causation)[18] and apply to damage caused by AI as well as to how national courts will address possible difficulties of proof and liability gaps in relation to AI. This would lead to the result that victims may decide to not even claim compensation.[19]

---

and significant property values, due to the important legal interests at stake. ... The expected lower likelihood of receiving compensation if AI applications cause damage is amongst the reasons for low levels of consumer trust in such applications. ... A lower level of trust in AI applications and the perception that persons suffering damage caused by AI-enabled products and services are less likely to obtain compensation correlate with a lower willingness to take up such products and services. Businesses also consider that the lack of citizens' trust is one of the most relevant obstacles to the take-up of AI-technologies in Europe. Other factors, such as the perceived risk of accidents, were also shown to have a significant effect on the level of societal trust and consumer uptake".

See also the Report from the Expert Group on Liability and New Technologies – New Technologies Formation "Liability for Artificial Intelligence and Other Emerging Digital Technologies", 21 November 2019, p. 35: "Existing rules on liability may also lead to inappropriate results for reasons related more to coherence and consistency, in particular taking into account the principle of functional equivalence, such as where compensation is denied in a situation involving emerging digital technologies when there would be compensation in a functionally equivalent situation involving human conduct and conventional technology. *Illustration:* Hospital H uses an AI-based surgical robot. Despite the fact that H and its staff have discharged all possible duties of care, damage is caused to patient P by way of some malfunctioning of the robot nobody could have foreseen, and which is unrelated to the condition in which the robot was shipped. If P were not indemnified for the ensuing harm, this would be inconsistent with the outcome in the functionally equivalent situation in which H has employed a human doctor and is liable for that doctor's comparable misconduct under national rules of vicarious liability. ... The application of traditional liability rules may also lead to unsatisfactory results because, while the victim might theoretically receive compensation, litigation would be unduly burdensome and expensive, leaving them without effective access to justice. This may be the case if the liability requirements they would have to prove either are entirely unsuitable for the risk posed by emerging digital technologies or too difficult to establish. Leaving the victim uncompensated or undercompensated in such cases may be undesirable, as it may effectively deprive the victim of basic protection with regard to significant legally protected interests of theirs (such as life, health, bodily integrity and property, or other important rights)".

[18] Ernst Karner/Bernhard Koch/Mark Geistfeld, 'Comparative Law Study on Civil Liability for Artificial Intelligence', European Commission, Directorate-General for Justice and Consumers, 2021, especially pp. 32–51.

See also the Report from the Expert Group on Liability and New Technologies – New Technologies Formation "Liability for Artificial Intelligence and Other Emerging Digital Technologies", 21 November 2019, pp. 50–55.

[19] Commission Staff Working Document, "Impact Assessment Report – Accompanying the document Proposal for a Directive of the European Parliament and of the Council on adapting non-contractual civil liability rules to artificial intelligence", SWD(2022) 319 final, Brussels, 28.9.2022, pp. 10–11: "The victim and the possible liable person wanting to check liability risks, as well as the judges having to decide a liability claim, will be confronted with cases where they

(iii) Legal fragmentation

If Member States attempt to address the resulting legal uncertainty at national level, and national courts apply diverging ad hoc solutions, this would lead (apart from legal uncertainty) to further fragmentation of liability rules across the EU for damage caused by AI products and services. Legal fragmentation (i.e., in case Member States adapt liability rules for AI in a divergent way, or national courts follow diverging interpretations of existing liability rules in the case of damage caused by AI) can cause additional costs for companies when producing, distributing or using AI-enabled products or services and can also result to limitations to cross-border AI-related activities.[20]

The aforementioned three problems, namely potential lack of compensation for victims, legal uncertainty and legal fragmentation, could lead to the lack of societal trust in AI use and ultimately create major market obstacles and affect the uptake of AI-enabled products and services.[21]

---

would need to interpret general rules which were not designed with AI in mind. They would have to apply them to AI-technologies that are qualitatively different from previous technologies, because of their specific characteristics. It is quite uncertain how existing liability rules would be interpreted in light of the AI-specific difficulties of meeting the burden of proving fault and causation. Such difficulties would lead in all likelihood to the result that the victim would not be able to meet this burden of proof. Victims may therefore decide to not even claim compensation. As an economic consequence, they would have to bear the burden of the damage. If the case goes to court nevertheless, national courts may decide - on an ad-hoc basis - to stick to the traditional allocation of the burden of proof on the victim. This would lead in all likelihood to the result that the victim would lose the case, not obtain compensation and bear the economic burden of the damage. If such a result is not considered as equitable, national courts may decide - again on an ad-hoc basis - to adapt to the specificities of AI and alleviate the burden of proof of the victim, in order to achieve a fair outcome in each single case. These uncertainties surrounding AI liability are especially relevant in a cross-border context, because MS' existing burden of proof rules are already very diverse".

[20] Ibid., pp. 11–12: "In a cross-border context, the law applicable to a liability claim is by default the law of the country in which the damage occurs. This means that different liability regimes and burden of proof rules could be applied to the same kind of AI-enabled product/service deployed in several MS which causes the same kind of damage. Consequently, a company disseminating/operating the same AI- enabled product/service in various MS (Member States) could face different liability exposures if that product or service causes, for the same reason, the same type of damage in several MS. Aside from the general burden of proof rules, there are also different rules about information disclosures in liability claims. This means that victims face greater information asymmetries in some MS. In addition, national AI strategies show that several MS are considering, or even concretely planning, legislative action on civil liability for AI. The fact that in the public consultation on the AI White Paper, more than 63% of respondents were in favour of adapting national liability rules for all or for specific AI applications suggests that MS are likely to face pressure to address the issue of liability for damage caused by AI".

[21] Ibid., p. 8: "The three problems (uncertainty, fragmentation and lack of compensation) are driven by the fact that, under existing liability rules, victims normally have to prove the necessary conditions for a successful claim. Under current rules, victims generally have to identify the possibly liable person(s), the action/omission of that person which could be characterised as fault, and the causal link between that action/omission and the damage. There are neither targeted provisions for AI to ease the victim's burden of proof under fault-based claims, nor AI-specific strict liability regimes that would exempt the victim from making this proof. However, certain

8.3.2 Problems Affecting the Product Liability Directive: Need to Adapt the PLD to the Digital Age

In addition, it is reminded that under the Product Liability Directive the burden of proof is less onerous on victims than under national fault-based liability rules, mainly because the victim does not have to prove fault. Nevertheless, proving that a product is defective (i.e. that it does not provide the level of safety a person is entitled to expect) is still (occasionally, extremely) challenging for complex products, such as AI-enabled products, even if the victim does not have to prove how the product became unsafe.

The PLD evaluation found that it was difficult to apply its rules to digital technologies in general, including AI-enabled products. It found also that the rules made it difficult to prove liability in the case of complex products, including AI-enabled products, but also others such as pharmaceuticals. The main two problems affecting the existing PLD are the following: (i) Certain products, economic actors and damage in the digital and circular economy escape (are not covered under) no-fault (strict) liability. For instance, the current PLD does not cover categories of products emerging from new digital technologies, like smart products and AI. This is because the Product Liability Directive (which dates back to 1985) was conceived long before the digital revolution and, accordingly, has not adapted to the digital age and circular economy. (ii) Consumers face obstacles to getting compensation. Indeed, whereas victims do not have to prove fault (producers bear liability irrespective of fault), proving defectiveness and causal link with damage is very difficult and costly for complex products. Also, liability claims are subject to a number of restrictions (claimants face time limits and thresholds).[22]

AI-systems have characteristics that make it prohibitively difficult or even impossible for victims to provide that proof. The specific characteristics that challenge current liability rules are: increasingly autonomous behaviour, opacity/lack of transparency and explainability, complexity, continuous adaptation and lack of predictability. These characteristics make it very difficult to attribute directly the damaging output of the AI to an action/omission of a liable person, i.e. to identify: - the person who could possibly have done something wrong, - the action or omission of that person which might not comply with the relevant standard of care, and - the causal link between that action or omission and the victim's damage. This is linked to two situations that can occur due to the use of AI systems: - between the human actor(s) related to the AI system and the damage caused by this AI system to a victim, the AI-system takes an autonomous action which is not pre-determined by a human and/or - the way the AI action is performed cannot be understood (mainly due to the opacity and complexity of certain forms of AI)".

[22]For analysis of the problems affecting the current Product Liability Directive, the need to adapt it to the digital age, as well as a detailed review of the revised PLD, see Chap. 9 of this book.

8.3.3 *Two Closely Linked Policy Initiatives: Complementary Proposed Directives—Overview*

This is why on 28 September 2022 the Commission published two complementary[23] draft Directives to adapt the existing liability rules to new digital technologies,

[23] Proposal for a Directive of the European Parliament and of the Council on adapting non-contractual civil liability rules to artificial intelligence (AI Liability Directive), European Commission, COM(2022) 496 final, Brussels, 28.9.2022 (the 'proposed AI Liability Directive'), Explanatory Memorandum, at p. 3: "The Commission takes a holistic approach in its AI policy to liability by proposing adaptations to the producer's liability for defective products under the Product Liability Directive as well as the targeted harmonisation under this [the AI Liability Directive] proposal. These two policy initiatives are closely linked and form a package, as claims falling within their scope deal with different types of liability. The Product Liability Directive covers producer's no-fault liability for defective products, leading to compensation for certain types of damages, mainly suffered by individuals. This [the AI Liability Directive] proposal covers national liability claims mainly based on the fault of any person with a view of compensating any type of damage and any type of victim. They complement one another to form an overall effective civil liability system. Together these rules will promote trust in AI (and other digital technologies) by ensuring that victims are effectively compensated if damage occurs despite the preventive requirements of the AI Act and other safety rules".

See also Commission Staff Working Document, "Impact Assessment Report – Accompanying the document Proposal for a Directive of the European Parliament and of the Council on adapting non-contractual civil liability rules to artificial intelligence", SWD(2022) 319 final, Brussels, 28.9.2022, at pp. 5–6, 26, and 50: "the PLD review is about adapting it to the digital age, preserving its technology-neutral nature and coverage. It also helps victims of damage caused by AI-enabled products to have a more effective compensation claim against the producer. The AI liability proposal tackles the AI-specific problems regarding other liability rules. Together, they will contribute to guaranteeing the effective functioning of the internal market in AI-enabled products/services and ensure that victims of harm caused by AI have the same level of protection as victims of harm caused by other technologies" (at p. 5). ... "Interaction with the pending revision of the PLD: The Commission takes a holistic approach in its AI policy to liability by considering adaptations to the producer's liability for defective products under the PLD as well as a targeted harmonisation of specific aspects of the other liability rules. These two policy initiatives are closely linked and form a package, as the claims within their scope deal with different types of liability. They complement one another to form an overall effective civil liability system. For AI, they achieve the AI White Paper objective that persons having suffered harm caused by AI systems enjoy the same level of protection as persons having suffered harm caused by other technologies" (at p. 6). ... "The measures for AI-induced damage looked at in the present impact assessment would complement the PLD for those liability claims not covered by the PLD, in particular for: - claims based on the fault of a person that led the AI to cause harm (not on product defect); - claims against other entities than producers (e.g. users, operators, service providers, cyber attackers); - claims for damage caused by AI-enabled services; - claims to compensate damage suffered by businesses' - claims to compensate types of damage not covered under the PLD (e.g. immaterial damage not resulting from personal injury or damage to consumer property, damage caused by discrimination, etc.)" (at p. 26). ... The measures proposed by the AI liability initiative "would be coherent with the measures envisaged in the framework of the PLD review. These instruments are complementary as they address challenges posed by emerging digital technologies with respect to claims based on different grounds, directed against different liable persons and covering compensation for different victims and types of harm. The respective instruments use a consistent approach and similar tools (access to information, alleviations of the burden of proof) to ensure in their combination that

including AI, and the circular economy as well as to tackle the AI-specific problems regarding other liability rules. In particular:

(A) Building on five years of analysis and in order to address the findings/recommendations of specific reports/studies[24] (taking also into account the positions

---

products or services using AI or other digital technologies do not make it more difficult under any of the existing pillars of liability to get compensation compared to traditional products. The envisaged measures will together contribute to creating a more consistent and adequate liability framework, without upsetting the balance established by the existing rules" (at p. 50).

[24]It is reminded that the preparatory work started in 2018. In particular:

In its 2018 Communication on AI in Europe [Commission Communication, "Artificial Intelligence for Europe", COM(2018) 237 final, 25.4.2018], the Commission stated that it would issue (as a step for building trust and ensuring legal clarity in AI-based applications) by mid-2019 a report on the broader implications for, potential gaps in and orientations for, the safety and liability frameworks for AI, Internet of Things and robotics.

To this end, as already discussed, an initial assessment on the current liability frameworks in light of AI and emerging technologies was issued in April 2018 [Commission Staff Working Document on "Liability for emerging digital technologies" - Accompanying the document Commission Communication "Artificial intelligence for Europe", SWD(2018) 137 final, 25.4.2018].

Furthermore, the Expert Group on Liability and New Technologies (which was set up by the Commission in March 2018) was invited to analyse crucial liability questions and the challenges brought about by AI. In particular, the Expert Group was invited to provide the Commission with expertise on the applicability of the Product Liability Directive to traditional products, new technologies and new societal challenges ('the Product Liability Directive formation') and, in light of an assessment of the existing liability schemes, support the Commission in developing principles that can serve as guidelines for possible adaptations of applicable laws at EU and national level relating to new technologies ('the New Technologies formation'). In the call for applications, the New Technologies formation was asked to assess "whether and to what extent existing liability schemes are adapted to the emerging market realities following the development of the new technologies such as Artificial Intelligence, advanced robotics, the IoT and cybersecurity issues". It was also asked to examine whether the current liability regimes are still "adequate to facilitate the uptake of the above-mentioned new technologies by fostering investment stability and users' trust". If shortcomings were identified, the New Technologies formation should make recommendations for amendments, leaving aside rules on safety and other technical standards. As a result, the New Technologies formation (which was first convened in June 2018) analysed the relevant national laws, examined specific use cases (such as autonomous cars, smart home, blockchain, autonomous healthcare applications, algorithmic decision making in the financial and other sectors, drones), and compared various aspects of existing liability regimes.

The findings of the New Technologies formation were presented in the Report "Liability for Artificial Intelligence and Other Emerging Digital Technologies", issued on 21 November 2019 [Report from the Expert Group on Liability and New Technologies – New Technologies Formation "Liability for Artificial Intelligence and Other Emerging Digital Technologies", 21 November 2019].

Furthermore, the Commission issued in February 2020 its Report on the safety and liability implications of AI, IoT and robotics. [Commission "Report on the safety and liability implications of Artificial Intelligence, the Internet of Things and robotics", COM (2020) 64 final, 19.2.2020].

The Commission's Report (which accompanied the 2020 White Paper on Artificial Intelligence [Commission's "White Paper On Artificial Intelligence - A European approach to excellence and trust", COM(2020) 65 final Brussels, 19.2.2020] provided an overview of the existing rules for safety and liability, focused on key issues and assessed the most important implications for and potential gaps in the liability and safety frameworks for AI, the IoT and robotics.

submitted during this long consultation period by relevant stakeholders—academics, businesses, consumer associations, Member States, NGOs etc.), the Commission published a proposal for a Directive on adapting non-contractual civil liability rules to artificial intelligence (the 'proposed AI Liability Directive').[25] The proposed AI Liability Directive harmonises targeted aspects of the Member States' existing civil liability rules applicable to AI-systems and its aim is to complement and modernise the EU liability framework by introducing new rules specific to damages caused by AI systems. According to the Commission's proposal, the AI Liability Directive will make it easier for victims—either individuals or businesses—to receive compensation for damages caused by safety issues or for breaches of privacy or when there is unlawful discrimination in a recruitment process involving AI technology.

The proposed AI Liability Directive harmonises how the information recorded/documented according to the product safety rules of the AI Act can be disclosed in court proceedings so that the victim can prove which action or omission led to the damage suffered. It provides national courts with the power to order disclosure of evidence (right of access to evidence) about high-risk AI systems suspected of having caused damage. Also, if the defendant fails to comply with an order by a national court in a claim for damages to disclose or to preserve evidence at its disposal, national courts will presume the defendant's non-compliance with a relevant duty of care. Furthermore, it creates a rebuttable 'presumption of causality' in order to address the need to ease the burden of proof for victims seeking to establish damage caused by an AI system. If the victim demonstrates that the liable person did not comply with AI Act safety requirements (or with a duty of care laid down in EU or national law) designed to prevent damage, the national courts could presume that this non-compliance caused the damage (and the potentially liable person would have the opportunity to rebut such a presumption). Moreover, the Commission's proposal introduces a review mechanism to re-assess the need for harmonisation of strict liability (for high-risk AI systems) and mandatory insurance at a later point in time when all the information for that decision will be available.

The input from the Expert Group Report [Report from the Expert Group on Liability and New Technologies – New Technologies Formation "Liability for Artificial Intelligence and Other Emerging Digital Technologies", 21 November 2019] was complemented by three external studies:

- a comparative law study [Ernst Karner/Bernhard Koch/Mark Geistfeld, 'Comparative Law Study on Civil Liability for Artificial Intelligence', European Commission, Directorate-General for Justice and Consumers, 2021]
- a behavioural economics study [Kantar, 'Behavioural Study on the link between challenges of Artificial Intelligence for Member States' civil liability rules and consumer attitudes towards AI-enabled products and services', JUST/2020/RCON/FW/CIVI/0065 Final Report 2021]; and
- an economic study [Deloitte, Study to support the Commission's Impact Assessment on liability for artificial intelligence, 2021].

[25] Proposal for a Directive of the European Parliament and of the Council on adapting non-contractual civil liability rules to artificial intelligence (AI Liability Directive), European Commission, COM(2022) 496 final, Brussels, 28.9.2022 (the 'proposed AI Liability Directive').

(B) In addition, the Commission published a proposal for a new Directive on liability of defective products, which would revise, repeal and replace the existing Product Liability Directive (the 'proposal for a revised Product Liability Directive'/ the 'proposed new Product Liability Directive').[26] The aim of the proposal for a revised Product Liability Directive is to modernise the current EU's product liability regime, based on the strict liability of manufacturers, for the compensation of personal injury, damage to property or data loss caused by unsafe products.

The proposal introduces provisions to address liability for products such as software (including AI systems) and digital services that affect how the product works (e.g. navigation services in autonomous vehicles). Also, the proposal clarifies the liability rules for companies that substantially modify products before resale. According to the Commission's proposal, the notion of "defect" is broadened and allows compensation for damage when products like robots, drones or IoT smart-home systems become unsafe by software updates, AI or digital services that are needed to operate the product, as well as when manufacturers fail to address connectivity and cybersecurity risks/vulnerabilities. Under certain circumstances, the proposal alleviates the burden of proof for victims (consumers) seeking compensation for damages suffered because of defective products, and obliges manufacturers to disclose information where plausible claims for compensation are made.

These two complementary Directives, which aim to adapt the existing liability rules to new digital technologies and to AI, are discussed in the following sections of this chapter (AI Liability Directive) and in Chap. 9 of this book (revised Product Liability Directive).

8.4 The Proposed AI Liability Directive

8.4.1 Objectives of the Proposed AI Liability Directive—Need for Action at EU Level—Choice of Instrument (Binding v. Non-binding)

8.4.1.1 Objectives of the Proposed AI Liability Directive

While the EU AI Act[27] aims at preventing, monitoring, and addressing/reducing risks to safety and fundamental rights (therefore AI-enabled products/services are

[26] Proposal for a Directive of the European Parliament and of the Council on liability for defective products, European Commission, COM(2022) 495 final, Brussels, 28.9.2022 (the 'proposal for a revised Product Liability Directive (PLD)'/the 'proposed new Product Liability Directive (PLD)').

[27] Regulation (EU) 2024/1689 of the European Parliament and of the Council of 13 June 2024 laying down harmonised rules on artificial intelligence and amending Regulations (EC) No 300/2008, (EU) No 167/2013, (EU) No 168/2013, (EU) 2018/858, (EU) 2018/1139 and (EU) 2019/2144 and Directives 2014/90/EU, (EU) 2016/797 and (EU) 2020/1828 (*EU Artificial Intelligence Act*), OJ L, 12.07.2024.

expected to be safer than traditional ones), accidents will still occur. When this happens, the liability rules should be able to determine which party is liable for harm and under which conditions a victim can be compensated.

The EU AI Act contains no provisions on liability for the purposes of damages claims and does not compensate the victim for the harm suffered.[28] Also, as already discussed, currently victims rely on national liability rules and, in certain cases, on the Product Liability Directive (PLD), which is being revised in parallel. However, such liability rules (in particular fault-based national rules) are not suited to handling compensation claims for harm caused by AI-enabled products and services. Victims need to prove a wrongful action or omission of a person that caused the damage, but the specific characteristics of AI (including autonomy and opacity, i.e., the so-called "black box" effect) make it difficult or prohibitively expensive to identify the liable person and prove the requirements for a successful liability claim (i.e., to meet the required burden of proof).[29]

Accordingly, liability rules are needed to ensure that, in the event that a damage occurs, victims are effectively compensated. A new liability regime should be introduced to ensure greater legal certainty, thereby enhancing consumer trust in AI and facilitating successful investment and innovation across the EU. Thus, while the EU AI Act aims at preventing damage, the AI Liability Directive introduces a safety-net for compensation in the event of damage. As it is stated, "in the AI Act proposal, the Commission has proposed rules that seek to reduce risks for safety and protect fundamental rights. Safety and liability are two sides of the same coin: they

[28] Proposed AI Liability Directive, Recital 2: "While such requirements [laid down in the AI Act] intended to reduce risks to safety and fundamental rights are meant to prevent, monitor and address risks and thus address societal concerns, they do not provide individual relief to those that have suffered damage caused by AI. Existing requirements provide in particular for authorisations, checks, monitoring and administrative sanctions in relation to AI systems in order to prevent damage. They do not provide for compensation of the injured person for damage caused by an output or the failure to produce an output by an AI system".

[29] Ibid., Recital 3: "When an injured person seeks compensation for damage suffered, Member States' general fault-based liability rules usually require that person to prove a negligent or intentionally damaging act or omission ('fault') by the person potentially liable for that damage, as well as a causal link between that fault and the relevant damage. However, when AI is interposed between the act or omission of a person and the damage, the specific characteristics of certain AI systems, such as opacity, autonomous behaviour and complexity, may make it excessively difficult, if not impossible, for the injured person to meet this burden of proof. In particular, it may be excessively difficult to prove that a specific input for which the potentially liable person is responsible had caused a specific AI system output that led to the damage at stake".

See also Proposed AI Liability Directive, Explanatory Memorandum, at pp. 1 and 2: "The specific characteristics of AI, including complexity, autonomy and opacity (the so-called "black box" effect), may make it difficult or prohibitively expensive for victims to identify the liable person and prove the requirements for a successful liability claim. In particular, when claiming compensation, victims could incur very high up-front costs and face significantly longer legal proceedings, compared to cases not involving AI. Victims may therefore be deterred from claiming compensation altogether" (p. 1) ... "The 'black box' effect can make it difficult for the victim to prove fault and causality and there may be uncertainty as to how the courts will interpret and apply existing national liability rules in cases involving AI" (p. 2).

apply at different moments and reinforce each other. While rules to ensure safety and protect fundamental rights will reduce risks, they do not eliminate those risks entirely. Where such a risk materialises, damage may still occur. In such instances, the liability rules of this proposal will apply".[30]

The specific objectives of the proposed AI Liability Directive are: (i) to prevent a lack of compensation, by ensuring that victims of AI-enabled products/services are equally protected as victims of traditional technologies (when persons suffer harm caused by AI systems, they should enjoy the same level of protection as those having suffered harm caused by other technologies, because lack of compensation could affect their trust in AI and ultimately the uptake of AI-enabled products/services); (ii) to reduce legal uncertainty regarding the liability exposure of businesses developing or using AI; and (iii) to prevent the emergence of fragmented AI-specific adaptations of national civil liability rules.[31]

The overarching objective of the Commission's proposed AI Liability Directive is to promote the rollout of trustworthy AI in Europe ("the primary general objective of this initiative is to contribute to the roll-out of AI in order to reap its benefits as a set of enabling technologies for the growth of the digital economy and its societal advantages")[32] by reducing legal uncertainty, by preventing the emergence of fragmented AI-specific adaptations of national civil liability rules, and by ensuring victims (e.g., citizens, businesses) of damage caused by AI obtain equivalent protection to victims of damage caused by other products in general or traditional technologies.[33]

---

[30]Proposed AI Liability Directive, Explanatory Memorandum, at p. 2.

See also the Commission Staff Working Document, "Impact Assessment Report – Accompanying the document Proposal for a Directive of the European Parliament and of the Council on adapting non-contractual civil liability rules to artificial intelligence", SWD(2022) 319 final, Brussels, 28.9.2022, at p. 6.

[31]Commission Staff Working Document, "Impact Assessment Report – Accompanying the document Proposal for a Directive of the European Parliament and of the Council on adapting non-contractual civil liability rules to artificial intelligence", SWD(2022) 319 final, Brussels, 28.9.2022, at pp. 23–25.

[32]Ibid., at p. 23: "The contribution of this initiative to this objective is twofold. Firstly, it would improve the conditions for the functioning of the internal market: reducing existing obstacles and preventing the emergence of new obstacles to the cross-border trade in AI-enabled products and services. This would have beneficial effects for the European economy and the competitiveness of the European AI-sector. Secondly, in line with the Commission human-centric approach and the White Paper on AI, this initiative contributes to the 'ecosystem of trust' in AI by ensuring that persons having suffered harm caused with the involvement of AI systems enjoy the same level of protection as persons having suffered harm caused by other technologies and that efficient redress mechanisms fairly distribute loss. Increased trust will lead to increased uptake of AI".

[33]Proposed AI Liability Directive, Recitals 4 and 5: "(4) In such cases, the level of redress afforded by national civil liability rules may be lower than in cases where technologies other than AI are involved in causing damage. Such compensation gaps may contribute to a lower level of societal acceptance of AI and trust in AI-enabled products and services. (5) To reap the economic and societal benefits of AI and promote the transition to the digital economy, it is necessary to adapt in a targeted manner certain national civil liability rules to those specific characteristics of certain AI

8.4.1.2 Need for Action at EU Level

The Commission's initiative cites fragmentation of national rules as one of the main justifications for the need to act at EU level. In particular, it is stated that it is uncertain how national liability rules can be applied to the specificities of AI. The Commission stressed that the existing tort liability regimes differ significantly across Member States, that their adaptation to deal with AI-liability cases is likely to increase such differences,[34] and that emerging divergent national rules (i.e., relying on separate AI-specific measures on liability at the level of each Member State) would increase legal uncertainty and fragmentation, creating obstacles to the rollout of AI-enabled products and services across the EU market. It is expected that, in the absence of EU action, Member States will adapt their own (divergent) national liability rules to the challenges of AI, resulting in further fragmentation and increased costs for businesses active across borders.[35] Also, there is uncertainty as

---

systems. Such adaptations should contribute to societal and consumer trust and thereby promote the roll-out of AI. Such adaptations should also maintain trust in the judicial system, by ensuring that victims of damage caused with the involvement of AI have the same effective compensation as victims of damage caused by other technologies".

See also proposed AI Liability Directive, Explanatory Memorandum, at p. 2.

Also, Commission Staff Working Document, "Executive Summary of the Impact Assessment Report – Accompanying the document Proposal for a Directive of the European Parliament and of the Council on adapting non-contractual civil liability rules to artificial intelligence", SWD(2022) 320 final, Brussels, 28.9.2022, at p. 1: "The AI initiative will: - Ensure that victims of AI-enabled products/services are equally protected as victims of traditional technologies. - Reduce legal uncertainty regarding the liability exposure of businesses developing or using AI. - Prevent the emergence of fragmented AI-specific adaptations of national civil liability rules".

[34] Commission Staff Working Document, "AI Subsidiarity Grid – Accompanying the document Proposal for a Directive of the European Parliament and of the Council on adapting non contractual civil liability rules to artificial intelligence (AI Liability Directive)", SWD(2022) 318 final, Brussels, 28.9.2022, at p. 4: "Tort law traditions differ significantly across Member States and their adaptation to deal with AI-liability cases is likely to increase such differences. The latter concern for instance the standard of proof for causation, procedural alleviations of the burden of proof, administrative law measures assisting those charged with the burden of proof, the basis for liability, different approaches to causal uncertainty etc. In addition, while fault-based liabilities are the liability regimes by default in Europe and are framed very differently across Member States, some Member States also have strict liability regimes in place".

[35] Proposed AI Liability Directive, Recital 6: "In the absence of Union action, at least some Member States are likely to adapt their civil liability rules to address compensation gaps and legal uncertainty linked to the specific characteristics of certain AI systems. This would create legal fragmentation and internal market barriers for businesses that develop or provide innovative AI-enabled products or services. Small and medium-sized enterprises would be particularly affected".

See also proposed AI Liability Directive, Explanatory Memorandum, at pp. 2 and 5: "National AI strategies show that several Member States are considering, or even concretely planning, legislative action on civil liability for AI. Therefore, it is expected that, if the EU does not act, Member States will adapt their national liability rules to the challenges of AI. This will result in further fragmentation and increased costs for businesses active throughout the EU" (at p. 2). ... "There are concrete signs that a number of Member States are considering unilateral legislative measures to address the specific challenges posed by AI with respect to liability. For example, AI

to how national courts could interpret and apply existing liability rules in AI-related cases. For instance, when faced with the specific challenges of AI, national courts might adapt the way in which they apply the existing liability rules on an ad hoc basis, thus increasing fragmentation and legal uncertainty.[36]

Therefore, as it was stated, "in the absence of EU harmonised rules for compensating damage caused by AI systems, providers, operators and users of AI systems on the one hand and injured persons on the other hand would be faced with 27 different liability regimes, leading to different levels of protection and distorted competition among businesses from different Member States",[37] which contradicts "the core objective of the Treaty to establish a well-functioning internal market. At the same time, the fact that victims of harm caused by AI systems would not benefit of the same level of protection as victims of harm caused by other technologies is

strategies adopted in Czechia, Italy, Malta, Poland and Portugal mention initiatives to clarify liability. Given the large divergence between Member States' existing civil liability rules, it is likely that any national AI-specific measure on liability would follow existing different national approaches and therefore increase fragmentation. Therefore, adaptations of liability rules taken on a purely national basis would increase the barriers to the rollout of AI-enabled products and services across the internal market and contribute further to fragmentation" (at p. 5).

See also Commission Staff Working Document, "AI Subsidiarity Grid – Accompanying the document Proposal for a Directive of the European Parliament and of the Council on adapting non contractual civil liability rules to artificial intelligence (AI Liability Directive)", SWD(2022) 318 final, Brussels, 28.9.2022, at p. 3: "Given the existing differences between tort liability regimes across Member States and the likelihood that those differences would only increase if measures were adopted at national level to adapt such liability regimes to AI risks, the objectives of the proposed action (such as ensuring legal certainty on a cross-border basis and consistently preventing compensation gaps in cases where AI systems are involved) cannot be sufficiently achieved by Member States acting alone. In absence of EU action, the identified obstacles to a well-functioning internal market for safe AI-enabled products and services would still persist. ... In the area covered by this proposal, emerging divergent national rules would increase legal uncertainty and fragmentation, creating obstacles to the rollout of AI-enabled products and services across the internal market. Legal uncertainty would particularly affect companies active cross-borders by imposing the need for additional legal information/representation, risk management costs and foregone revenue. At the same time, differing national rules on compensation claims for damage caused by AI would increase transaction costs for businesses, especially for cross-border trade, entailing significant internal market barriers".

[36]Proposed AI Liability Directive, Recital 6: "Interested stakeholders – injured persons suffering damage, potentially liable persons, insurers – face legal uncertainty as to how national courts, when confronted with the specific challenges of AI, might apply the existing liability rules in individual cases in order to achieve just results".

See also proposed AI Liability Directive, Explanatory Memorandum, at p. 2: "If a victim brings a claim, national courts, faced with the specific characteristics of AI, may adapt the way in which they apply existing rules on an ad hoc basis to come to a just result for the victim. This will cause legal uncertainty. Businesses will have difficulties to predict how the existing liability rules will be applied, and thus to assess and insure their liability exposure. The effect will be magnified for businesses trading across borders, as the uncertainty will cover different jurisdictions. It will particularly affect small and medium-sized enterprises (SMEs), which cannot rely on in-house legal expertise or capital reserves".

[37]Ibid., Explanatory Memorandum, at p. 6.

against the principle of equal access to justice, hampering the trust in AI and ultimately the uptake of AI-enabled products/services across the EU Member States";[38] "adaptations of liability rules taken on a purely national basis would increase the barriers to the rollout of AI-enabled products and services across the internal market and contribute further to fragmentation";[39] "the objectives of this proposal cannot be adequately achieved at national level because emerging divergent national rules would increase legal uncertainty and fragmentation, creating obstacles to the rollout of AI-enabled products and services across the internal market. Legal uncertainty would particularly affect companies active cross-borders by imposing the need for additional legal information/representation, risk management costs and foregone revenue. At the same time, differing national rules on compensation claims for damage caused by AI would increase transaction costs for businesses, especially for cross-border trade, entailing significant internal market barriers. Further, legal uncertainty and fragmentation disproportionately affect start-ups and SMEs, which account for most companies and the major share of investments in the relevant markets".[40]

As a result, relying only on possible measures at national level would increase legal fragmentation across the EU and create obstacles to cross-border activities, hindering the conditions for the roll-out and development of AI-technologies. On the contrary, compared to possible adaptations of liability rules at national level, the aim to ensure legal certainty and prevent fragmentation and compensation gaps in cases where AI-enabled systems are involved, thus significantly improving the conditions for the deployment of AI-technologies in the internal market, can be better achieved through harmonised measures at EU level (i.e., by replacing different national policies and rules with a more homogenous policy approach, thus ensuring a minimum level of harmonisation).[41]

---

[38] Commission Staff Working Document, "AI Subsidiarity Grid – Accompanying the document Proposal for a Directive of the European Parliament and of the Council on adapting non contractual civil liability rules to artificial intelligence (AI Liability Directive)", SWD(2022) 318 final, Brussels, 28.9.2022, at p. 3.

[39] Proposed AI Liability Directive, Explanatory Memorandum, at p. 5.

[40] Ibid., at pp. 5–6.

See also Commission Staff Working Document, "AI Subsidiarity Grid – Accompanying the document Proposal for a Directive of the European Parliament and of the Council on adapting non contractual civil liability rules to artificial intelligence (AI Liability Directive)", SWD(2022) 318 final, Brussels, 28.9.2022, at p. 2.

[41] Proposed AI Liability Directive, Explanatory Memorandum, at p. 6: "Harmonised measures at EU level would significantly improve conditions for the rollout and development of AI-technologies in the internal market by preventing fragmentation and increasing legal certainty. This added value would be generated notably through reduced fragmentation and increased legal certainty regarding stakeholders' liability exposure. Moreover, only EU action can consistently achieve the desired effect of promoting consumer trust in AI-enabled products and services by preventing liability gaps linked to the specific characteristics of AI across the internal market. This would ensure a consistent (minimum) level of protection for all victims (individuals and companies) and consistent incentives to prevent damage and ensure accountability".

8.4.1.3 Considerations Regarding the Choice of Instrument (Binding Versus Non-binding)

According to the Commission, although a non-binding instrument (soft law), such as a recommendation, presents a less intrusive approach and allows Member States maximum flexibility in assessing whether and how to adjust their national rules, it is not suitable to address the identified problems in an effective manner and to ensure a consistent implementation of the proposed measures. Soft law has been discarded since it does not provide for the right level of legal certainty. Indeed, the desired harmonisation effect and legal certainty is unlikely to be delivered by a non-binding instrument. In addition, a non-binding instrument cannot be coherent with the EU's overall AI policy, which aims at creating an ecosystem of trust and promoting the roll-out of AI in the internal market through a reliable and harmonised legal framework.

As it was stated, "while a non-binding instrument would be less intrusive, it is unlikely to address the identified problems in an effective manner. The implementation rate of non-binding instruments is difficult to predict and there is insufficient indication that the persuasive effect of a recommendation would be strong enough to produce consistent adaptation of national laws. This effect is even more unlikely for measures concerning private law, of which non contractual liability rules form part. This area is characterised by long-standing legal traditions, which makes Member States reluctant to pursue coordinated reform unless driven by the clear prospect of internal market benefits under a binding EU instrument or the need to adapt to new technologies in the digital economy. The existing significant divergences between

---

See also Commission Staff Working Document, "AI Subsidiarity Grid – Accompanying the document Proposal for a Directive of the European Parliament and of the Council on adapting non contractual civil liability rules to artificial intelligence (AI Liability Directive)", SWD(2022) 318 final, Brussels, 28.9.2022, at pp. 4 and 5: "The objectives of the proposed action, to ensure legal certainty and consistently prevent compensation gaps in cases where AI systems are involved, thus creating the conditions for the deployment of AI-technologies in the internal market, can be better achieved at Union level, by ensuring a minimum level of harmonisation. This will increase public trust and the uptake of AI-enabled products and services, enabling companies (in particular SMEs, which are among the most active in the AI sector) to expand their activities across borders. On the contrary, relying only on possible measures at national level would increase legal fragmentation across the EU and will create obstacles to cross-border activities" (p. 4). . . . "The conditions for the roll-out and development of AI-technologies in the internal market can be significantly improved by preventing fragmentation and increasing legal certainty through harmonised measures at EU level, compared to possible adaptations of liability rules at national level" (p. 5). . . . "Harmonising at EU level the relevant liability rules to respond to the risks posed by AI systems would significantly improve the conditions for the roll-out and development of AI-technologies in the internal market. Such more homogenous approach is needed to prevent legal fragmentation (which may result from possible adaptations of liability rules at national level) and increase legal certainty for consumers and businesses, while preventing liability gaps and ensuring that victims of harm caused by AI systems are duly compensated, including in cases with cross-border dimensions" (at p. 5).

Member States' liability frameworks are another reason why a recommendation is unlikely to be implemented in a consistent manner".[42]

On the contrary, a mandatory instrument is able to prevent protection gaps stemming from partial or no implementation and, among the binding instruments, a Directive seems to be the most appropriate/adequate legislative tool. This is because a Directive can achieve the set policy objectives and provide the desired harmonisation effect and legal certainty, while giving the Member States the needed flexibility (in contrast to a Regulation which would not have allowed for such flexibility) to integrate the harmonised measures into their traditional national liability regimes without creating frictions, i.e., allowing Member States to preserve their national approaches and long-established legal traditions in the politically sensitive field of civil law. In other words, compared to a Regulation (which would have been too stringent), a Directive leaves some margin of manoeuvre to Member States on the implementation, i.e., leaves sufficient margin to Member

[42] Proposed AI Liability Directive, Explanatory Memorandum, at p. 7.

The same paragraph was also used in the Commission Staff Working Document, "Impact Assessment Report – Accompanying the document Proposal for a Directive of the European Parliament and of the Council on adapting non-contractual civil liability rules to artificial intelligence", SWD(2022) 319 final, Brussels, 28.9.2022, at p. 51. It was also added that "divergences and reduced legal certainty in cross-border cases would thus persist even to the – likely very limited – extent that Member States choose to implement a recommendation. A selective and inconsistent implementation would solve neither the problem of legal uncertainty nor that of impending fragmentation and it would not ensure consistent victim protection throughout the EU. The economic study confirmed that a non-binding initiative would not address the identified internal market obstacles effectively, as the underpinning problems will likely be perpetuated to a substantial extent. It concluded that a non-binding instrument would not achieve any increase in cross-border trade. Due to this likely lack of effectiveness, choosing a non-binding instrument would not be in line with the principle of proportionality, which requires the choice of the least burdensome PO, which is still suitable to achieve the policy purpose" (at p. 51). … "The implementation rate of non-binding instruments is difficult to predict and there is no sufficient indication that the persuasive effect of a recommendation would be strong enough to produce consistent adaptations of national laws. Therefore, the desired harmonisation effect and legal certainty is unlikely to be delivered by a recommendation. This applies to a special degree to measures concerning the private law of obligations, of which extra-contractual liability rules form part. This area is characterised by long-standing legal traditions, which traditionally makes Member States reluctant to pursue harmonised reform unless driven by the clear prospect of internal market benefits under a binding EU instrument. Moreover, the significant existing divergences between Member States' civil liability frameworks are another reason why a recommendation is unlikely to be implemented in a consistent manner. While the expected slight increase in insurance premiums might be even lower if PO1 were implemented by a non-binding instrument, divergences and reduced legal certainty in cross-border cases would persist (even to the – likely very limited – extent that Member States choose to implement a recommendation). Likewise, compensation gaps are likely to persist to a large extent and the expected cost savings for victims linked to the alleviations of the burden of proof would mostly not materialise. The economic study confirmed that a non-binding initiative would not address the identified internal market obstacles effectively, as the underlying problems will likely be perpetuated to a substantial extent. It concluded that a non-binding instrument would not achieve any increase in cross-border trade" (at pp. 201–202).

States to adapt to national constraints.[43] On the other hand, it could be argued that, even after the adoption of a Directive, there could be further delays and inconsistencies in relation to its transposition into national law and its implementation. In contrast, a Regulation serves exactly the aim to take immediate action. It is binding in its entirety and requires no transposition by the Member States.

8.4.2 *Minimum (Targeted) Harmonisation Approach*

The objectives of the proposed AI Liability Directive, namely to ensure legal certainty and to prevent fragmentation, thus creating the right conditions for the rollout and development of AI-enabled products and services across the internal market, can be better achieved at EU level by ensuring a minimum level of harmonisation of the relevant liability rules to respond to the risks posed by AI systems. This approach, which is based on "a realistic assessment of political feasibility",[44] was also recommended by the European Parliament's Resolution of 20 October 2020 on a civil liability regime for artificial intelligence[45] which opted for a minimum harmonisation approach.[46]

---

[43]Commission Staff Working Document, "AI Subsidiarity Grid – Accompanying the document Proposal for a Directive of the European Parliament and of the Council on adapting non contractual civil liability rules to artificial intelligence (AI Liability Directive)", SWD(2022) 318 final, Brussels, 28.9.2022, at pp. 7–8.

See also Commission Staff Working Document, "Impact Assessment Report – Accompanying the document Proposal for a Directive of the European Parliament and of the Council on adapting non-contractual civil liability rules to artificial intelligence", SWD(2022) 319 final, Brussels, 28.9.2022, at p. 51.

[44]Commission Staff Working Document, "Impact Assessment Report – Accompanying the document Proposal for a Directive of the European Parliament and of the Council on adapting non-contractual civil liability rules to artificial intelligence", SWD(2022) 319 final, Brussels, 28.9.2022, at p. 40.

[45]European Parliament Resolution of 20 October 2020 with recommendations to the Commission on a civil liability regime for artificial intelligence (2020/2014(INL)) P9_TA(2020)0276 ('-European Parliament's Resolution of 20 October 2020 on a civil liability regime for AI') – Annex to the European Parliament Resolution: detailed recommendations for drawing up a Regulation on liability for the operation of artificial intelligence-systems, A. Principles and Aims of the Proposal. B. Text of the Proposal Requested—Proposal for a Regulation on liability for the operation of Artificial Intelligence-systems ('Annex to the European Parliament's Resolution of 20 October 2020 on a civil liability regime for AI').

[46]The European Parliament:

"believes that there is no need for a complete revision of the well-functioning liability regimes, but that the complexity, connectivity, opacity, vulnerability, the capacity of being modified through updates, the capacity for self-learning and the potential autonomy of AI-systems, as well as the multitude of actors involved represent nevertheless a significant challenge to the effectiveness of Union and national liability framework provisions; considers that specific and coordinated adjustments to the liability regimes are necessary to avoid a situation in which persons who suffer harm or whose property is damaged end up without compensation". European Parliament's Resolution of

The proposed AI Liability Directive follows a minimum harmonisation approach, based on a minimum intervention at EU level, putting forward a balanced approach regarding liability for damage caused by AI. It focuses on the alleviation of the burden of proof, ensures that victims of AI-enabled products/services are not less (but also not more) protected victims of traditional technologies, and respects to the maximum extent possible Member States' well-established liability systems. The approach followed by the proposed AI Liability Directive does not go beyond what is necessary, since it takes into account the different levels of regulatory intervention of Member States as regards the tort liability for damages caused by AI systems. As a result, this minimum harmonisation approach—contrary to full harmonisation[47]—ensures that the new rules can be integrated without frictions into the existing legal civil liability framework within each Member State: "Member States could fit the envisaged alleviations of the burden of proof into their national liability regimes without disrupting their respective legal traditions. [This approach] allows for sufficient flexibility and is based on tools that are already well-known in Member States' civil liability systems".[48]

---

20 October 2020 on a civil liability regime for AI, section "Liability and Artificial Intelligence", at point 6.

"Considers that the existing fault-based tort law of the Member States offers in most cases a sufficient level of protection for persons that suffer harm caused by an interfering third party like a hacker or for persons whose property is damaged by such a third party, as the interference regularly constitutes a fault-based action; notes that only for specific cases, including those where the third party is untraceable or impecunious, does the addition of liability rules to complement existing national tort law seem necessary". European Parliament's Resolution of 20 October 2020 on a civil liability regime for AI, section "Liability and Artificial Intelligence", at point 9.

"Instead of replacing the well-functioning existing liability regimes, a few necessary adjustments should be made by introducing new and future-oriented ideas". Annex to the European Parliament's Resolution of 20 October 2020 on a civil liability regime for AI – A. Principles and Aims of the Proposal, principle 5, p. 115.

"The rise of AI-systems does not pose a need for a complete revision of liability rules throughout the Union. Specific adjustments to the existing legislation and the introduction of well-accessed and targeted new provisions would be sufficient to accommodate the AI-related challenges, with a view to preventing regulatory fragmentation and ensuring the harmonisation of civil liability legislation throughout the Union in connection with AI". Annex to the European Parliament's Resolution of 20 October 2020 on a civil liability regime for AI – B. Text of the Proposal for a Regulation on liability for the operation of AI systems, at recital 8, p. 117.

[47] Commission Staff Working Document, "Impact Assessment Report – Accompanying the document Proposal for a Directive of the European Parliament and of the Council on adapting non-contractual civil liability rules to artificial intelligence", SWD(2022) 319 final, Brussels, 28.9.2022, at p. 40: "In contrast, full harmonisation could lead to a lower level of protection compared to situations where Member States provide already for a more general strict liability regimes in their national law which could also apply to AI technology. In the light of the long-standing and entrenched divergences between national tort law traditions, an attempt of a full harmonisation blocking maintaining existing further-reaching national rules would meet with strong opposition from Member States. It would also be opposed by certain stakeholders as the position of consumer associations participating in the public consultation shows".

[48] Ibid., at p. 50. See also at p. 40.

In particular, the proposed AI Liability Directive is limited to the measures strictly necessary (proportional) to address the AI-specific problems identified. Thus its intervention is targeted because it will only alleviate the burden of proof for victims. Indeed, it focuses on targeted proof-related measures (disclosure of information and alleviation of the burden of proof through establishment of causality rebuttable presumptions subject to strict conditions).[49] From the various tools[50] available in national legal regimes for easing the burden of proof, the approach followed by the proposed AI Liability Directive is to use rebuttable presumptions (they are commonly found in national liability systems and they balance the interests of claimants and defendants) as the least interventionist tool ("the least interfering way of alleviating the burden of proof".[51] As a result, the proposal does not lead to a

---

[49] Commission Staff Working Document, "AI Subsidiarity Grid – Accompanying the document Proposal for a Directive of the European Parliament and of the Council on adapting non contractual civil liability rules to artificial intelligence (AI Liability Directive)", SWD(2022) 318 final, Brussels, 28.9.2022, at p. 5.

[50] Commission Staff Working Document, "Impact Assessment Report – Accompanying the document Proposal for a Directive of the European Parliament and of the Council on adapting non-contractual civil liability rules to artificial intelligence", SWD(2022) 319 final, Brussels, 28.9.2022, at pp. 32–33: "The existing legal framework offers a limited set of alternative tools to help victims overcome these proof-related difficulties:

- Rebuttable presumptions: If the victim meets a reduced burden of proof, e.g. by demonstrating the plausibility or likelihood of certain facts, it is presumed that those facts occurred. In order to avoid having to pay compensation, it is then for the liable party to demonstrate that these facts did in reality not occur or that other facts, for which the liable party is not responsible, occurred. This tool leaves the basic distribution of the burden of proof intact, but makes it easier for the victim to discharge that burden.
- Shifts/reversals of the burden of proof: This tool departs from the general principle that the party invoking a legal provision has to prove that the conditions for the application of that provision are fulfilled. The victim hence no longer bears the burden of proof, but it is for the liable person to prove that one or all conditions of liability are not fulfilled. Such a solution was proposed by the European Parliament for fault-based liability. According to that resolution, the operator of an AI system would by default be liable for harm or damage caused by that system, unless they can prove that the harm or damage was caused without his or her fault.
- Irrebuttable presumptions: This tool goes even further than a reversal of the burden of proof, as it posits certain conditions or facts as given, without allowing for the possibility to proof that this presumption is wrong".

[51] Commission Staff Working Document, "AI Subsidiarity Grid – Accompanying the document Proposal for a Directive of the European Parliament and of the Council on adapting non contractual civil liability rules to artificial intelligence (AI Liability Directive)", SWD(2022) 318 final, Brussels, 28.9.2022, at pp. 6 and 7.

See also Commission Staff Working Document, "Impact Assessment Report – Accompanying the document Proposal for a Directive of the European Parliament and of the Council on adapting non-contractual civil liability rules to artificial intelligence", SWD(2022) 319 final, Brussels, 28.9.2022, at p. 33: "For the following reasons, only the tool of a rebuttable presumption has been retained in the PO for detailed assessment: - MS' civil laws are based on the principle that the victim has to prove all the facts necessary to support their claim. A rebuttable presumption would leave this fundamental principle in place. This approach would make it easier for MS to integrate the harmonised AI-specific adaptations of liability rules into their respective legal systems without

reversal of the burden of proof, in order to avoid exposing providers, operators and users of AI systems to higher liability risks, which may hinder innovation and prevent the rollout of AI-enabled products and services.[52]

Moreover, since the proposed AI Liability Directive follows an approach of a minimum intervention at EU level (minimum harmonisation), i.e., focuses on disclosure of information and alleviation of the burden of proof through establishment of causality presumption subject to strict conditions, victims of damage caused by AI systems are allowed to invoke more favourable rules of national law. Thus, Member States remain free to use in their national legal regimes more invasive tools/ extensive measures if they deem it appropriate, such as reversals of the burden of proof under fault-based regimes, irrebuttable presumptions, national no-fault liability (strict liability) regimes of which there are already a large variety in national laws, etc.[53] The minimum harmonisation approach means that Member States could maintain or—outside of the scope of the Product Liability Directive—introduce national liability rules that are more favourable for victims: "for example, Member States could have more general reversals of the burden of proof regarding fault or causation. They could also maintain general strict liability regimes (e.g. for 'dangerous things or activities') applicable also to damage caused with the involvement of AI systems".[54]

friction. It also preserves a maximum of consistency between the rules applicable in cases involving AI and the general rules applying in other cases. - The AI liability initiative seeks to help victims meet their burden in the most targeted, i.e. proportionate manner possible. A rebuttable presumption is the least interfering way of alleviating the burden of proof".

[52] Commission Staff Working Document, "AI Subsidiarity Grid – Accompanying the document Proposal for a Directive of the European Parliament and of the Council on adapting non contractual civil liability rules to artificial intelligence (AI Liability Directive)", SWD(2022) 318 final, Brussels, 28.9.2022, at pp. 6 and 7.

See also Commission Staff Working Document, "Impact Assessment Report – Accompanying the document Proposal for a Directive of the European Parliament and of the Council on adapting non-contractual civil liability rules to artificial intelligence", SWD(2022) 319 final, Brussels, 28.9.2022, at p. 33: "- A reversal of the burden of proof regarding fault and causation, as suggested by the European Parliament, or, to an even greater extent, an irrebuttable presumption represent a more far-reaching exception from MS' general civil liability rules, which puts into doubt their political feasibility. - Such approaches would create a situation where victims of damage caused with the involvement of AI would systematically be in a more favourable situation than victims of damage caused by other technologies. They would thus overshoot the Commission's policy objective defined in the AI White Paper, and risk dis-incentivising the uptake of AI".

[53] Commission Staff Working Document, "AI Subsidiarity Grid – Accompanying the document Proposal for a Directive of the European Parliament and of the Council on adapting non contractual civil liability rules to artificial intelligence (AI Liability Directive)", SWD(2022) 318 final, Brussels, 28.9.2022, at pp. 5 and 7.

[54] Commission Staff Working Document, "Impact Assessment Report – Accompanying the document Proposal for a Directive of the European Parliament and of the Council on adapting non-contractual civil liability rules to artificial intelligence", SWD(2022) 319 final, Brussels, 28.9.2022, at p. 40.

On the other hand, for a critique, see the response submitted by the Ada Lovelace Institute, which stated that the minimal harmonisation approach could also lead to fragmented liability regimes in

Furthermore, the proposed AI Liability Directive will only harmonise elements of liability that are challenged by AI, leaving other elements like the determination of fault and causality to the existing national laws. It does not touch upon the substantive conditions of liability like fault or causality (which remain in the remit of national law), but focus on targeted proof-related measures.[55] Indeed, it builds on the substantive conditions of liability currently existing in national rules, such as fault or causality, but focuses on targeted proof-related measures, ensuring that victims have the same level of protection as in cases not involving AI systems.

Also, the assessment of the need to harmonise strict liability has been postponed to a later stage, when more information about the AI and its uses can be gathered. Indeed, under the review clause, the proposed Directive provides for re-assessing the need for more stringent or more extensive measures (including situations where no-fault/strict liability would be more appropriate, as requested by the European Parliament's 2020 Resolution on a civil liability regime for AI), at a later stage (five years later), without committing to specific outcomes of such review.

Therefore, the proposed AI Liability Directive attempts to achieve the set objectives with a minimally invasive approach through a staged approach. In particular:

(a) In the first stage, the proposal introduces the following three measures to alleviate the victims' burden to prove their liability claim: (i) Harmonising how the information recorded/documented according to the product safety rules of the AI Act can be disclosed in court proceedings so that the victim can identify and prove which action/omission led to the damage suffered. (ii) If the victim shows that the liable person did not comply with AI Act safety requirements designed to prevent damage, the courts could presume that this non-compliance caused the damage. The potentially liable person would have the opportunity to rebut such a presumption, e.g. by proving than another cause led to the damage. (iii) In case the only way for the victim to prove the liability claim is to demonstrate what happened inside the AI, such burden on the victim would be alleviated. The potentially liable person would have the opportunity to prove that they did not act negligently.
(b) In the second stage, on the basis of a review clause, the proposed AI Liability Directive introduces a review mechanism to re-assess (five years later, once a

the EU: "given that the AILD is a Directive with a minimal harmonisation approach, the application will likely be very different across different Member States. This means harmed persons will have much stronger protections in some Member States than in others. Liability law would thus be fragmented in the EU single market. In our view, a more holistic approach based on offering an equal level of protection for all people in the EU would be preferable and offer more legal certainty". The Ada Lovelace Institute, "Feedback to the European Commission on its proposal for a Directive on adapting non-contractual civil liability rules to artificial intelligence", November 2022, at p. 1.

[55] Commission Staff Working Document, "AI Subsidiarity Grid – Accompanying the document Proposal for a Directive of the European Parliament and of the Council on adapting non contractual civil liability rules to artificial intelligence (AI Liability Directive)", SWD(2022) 318 final, Brussels, 28.9.2022, at p. 7.

more robust evidence base that could justify more ambitious action is in place) the need (in addition to the measures alleviating the burden of proof) for a higher level of regulatory intervention, i.e., the need for harmonising strict liability for AI use cases with a particular risk profile, possibly coupled with a mandatory insurance. As it was stated, this targeted review mechanism takes a "forward-looking perspective", it provides for additional substantial steps to be taken by the Commission and, although it would not (yet) implement all elements suggested by the European Parliament's legislative own-initiative Resolution, it "would nevertheless reflect the approach suggested by the Parliament, that is to say a combination of measures to ease the burden of proof for fault-based claims with a harmonised strict liability regime for certain specific AI applications. It would also demonstrate that the Commission is ready to act on the opinions expressed by non-business stakeholders in the public consultation, who showed clear support for strict liability. The targeted review provides a framework and prepares the ground for the Commission to take a policy decision specifically on the harmonisation of strict liability and mandatory insurance, at a later point in time when all the information for that decision will be available".[56]

8.4.3 Subject Matter, Scope, and Definitions

Article 1 specifies the subject matter and scope of the proposed AI Liability Directive, which applies to non-contractual civil law claims for damages caused with the involvement of AI systems, where such claims are brought under fault-based liability regimes (i.e., national regimes that provide for a statutory responsibility to compensate for damage caused intentionally or by a negligent act or omission).[57]

[56] Commission Staff Working Document, "Impact Assessment Report – Accompanying the document Proposal for a Directive of the European Parliament and of the Council on adapting non-contractual civil liability rules to artificial intelligence", SWD(2022) 319 final, Brussels, 28.9.2022, at p. 39. See also at pp. 57–58: "The following factors will improve the efficiency of the measures potentially taken at the second stage: - By ensuring that the assessment of a possible strict liability regime for the use of AI-enabled technologies can rely on a more developed factual basis, the staged approach minimises the risk of creating an uneven playing field for AI-enabled technologies. - The staged approach allows the development of tailored market-driven insurance solutions, which can be taken into account at the second stage when assessing the need for and effects of a mandatory insurance regime. Moreover, AI-technologies potentially subject to such a regime will be rolled out over the coming years and statistical accident data will be accumulated. Therefore the lack of actuarial data as main potential cost-driver of AI-specific liability insurance will have become considerably less relevant by the time of the targeted review under PO3. - As relevant safety standards for the AI-enabled technologies will be available by the time of the targeted review, the conditions for assessing liability risks will have improved for both insurers and liable users/operators".

[57] Proposed AI Liability Directive, Article 1(2).

The proposed AI Liability Directive eases the burden of proof in a proportionate manner by introducing two main measures, namely the use of disclosure and rebuttable presumptions. In particular, it establishes for those seeking compensation for damage a possibility to obtain information on high-risk AI systems and provides national courts with the power to order disclosure of evidence (right of access to evidence) about high-risk AI systems suspected of having caused damage. Furthermore, it creates a rebuttable 'presumption of causality' in order to address the need to ease the burden of proof for victims seeking to establish damage caused by an AI system. As it is stated, the proposed Directive "lays down common rules on: a) the disclosure of evidence on high-risk artificial intelligence (AI) systems to enable a claimant to substantiate a non-contractual fault-based civil law claim for damages;[58] b) the burden of proof in the case of non-contractual fault-based civil law claims brought before national courts for damages caused by an AI system".[59]

The purpose of the proposed AI Liability Directive is to harmonise in a targeted and proportionate manner certain aspects of fault-based liability rules at EU level in order to increase legal certainty and create a level playing field for AI systems. The focus is on targeted proof-related measures and, therefore, the measures provided in the proposed AI Liability Directive were chosen as pragmatic, and proportionate: "targeted measures to ease the burden of proof in form of rebuttable presumptions were chosen as pragmatic and appropriate ways to help victims meet their burden of proof in the most targeted and proportionate manner possible";[60] "such tools are not new; they can be found in national legislative systems. Hence, these national tools constitute helpful reference points on how to address the issues raised by AI for existing liability rules in a way which interferes as little as possible with the different national legal regimes".[61]

Apart from the presumptions it establishes, the proposed AI Liability Directive does not affect EU or national rules determining, for instance, which party has the burden of proof, what degree of certainty is required as regards the standard of proof or how fault is defined. As it was underlined, "the measures provided in this Directive can fit without friction in existing civil liability systems, since they reflect an approach that does not touch on the definition of fundamental concepts like 'fault' or 'damage', given that the meaning of those concepts varies considerably across the Member States".[62] In order to respect the principle of proportionality, the proposed Directive harmonises only those fault-based liability rules that govern the burden of proof for persons claiming compensation for any damage (as it is defined and covered by national law) caused with the involvement of AI systems: "This Directive should not harmonise general aspects of civil liability which are regulated in different ways by national civil liability rules, such as the definition of fault or

[58] Ibid., Article 1(1)(a).

[59] Ibid., Article 1(1)(b).

[60] Ibid., Explanatory Memorandum, at p. 11.

[61] Ibid.

[62] Ibid.

causality, the different types of damage that give rise to claims for damages, the distribution of liability over multiple tortfeasors, contributory conduct, the calculation of damages or limitation periods".[63] Therefore, it is stated that the proposed AI Liability Directive does not affect "national rules determining which party has the burden of proof, which degree of certainty is required as regards the standard of proof, or how fault is defined, other than in respect of what is provided for in Articles 3 and 4".[64]

Furthermore, the proposed AI Liability Directive does not affect existing rules regulating the conditions of liability in the field of transport[65] or any rights which an injured person may have under national rules implementing the Product Liability Directive[66] or the exemptions from liability and the due diligence obligations set by the Digital Services Act (DSA).[67] Also, while it does not apply with respect to criminal liability,[68] it may be applicable with respect to state liability[69] due to the fact that state authorities are subject of the obligations in the AI Act.

The proposed Directive does not apply retroactively, but only to claims for compensation of damages that occur after the end of its transposition period.[70] Furthermore, it complements the proposal for a revised Product Liability Directive, as both the Commission's proposals were adopted "in a package aiming to adapt

[63] Ibid., Recital 10.

[64] Proposed AI Liability Directive, Article 1(3), point (d). See also Recital 13: "Other than in respect of the presumptions it lays down, this Directive does not harmonise national laws regarding which party has the burden of proof or which degree of certainty is required as regards the standard of proof".

[65] Ibid., Article 1(3), point (a). See also Recital 11: "in the field of transport, Union law regulating the liability of transport operators should remain unaffected by this Directive".

[66] Ibid., Article 1(3), point (b). See also Recital 11: "The laws of the Member States concerning the liability of producers for damage caused by the defectiveness of their products are already harmonised at Union level by Council Directive 85/374/EEC. Those laws do not, however, affect Member States' rules of contractual or non-contractual liability, such as warranty, fault or strict liability, based on other grounds than the defect of the product. While at the same time the revision of Council Directive 85/374/EEC seeks to clarify and ensure that injured person can claim compensation for damages caused by defective AI-enabled products, it should therefore be clarified that the provisions of this Directive do not affect any rights which an injured person may have under national rules implementing Directive 85/374/EEC".

[67] Ibid., Article 1(3), point (c). See also Recital 12: "[The Digital Services Act (DSA)] fully harmonises the rules applicable to providers of intermediary services in the internal market, covering the societal risks stemming from the services offered by those providers, including as regards the AI systems they use. This Directive does not affect the provisions of [the Digital Services Act (DSA)] that provide a comprehensive and fully harmonised framework for due diligence obligations for algorithmic decision-making by hosting service providers, including the exemption from liability for the dissemination of illegal content uploaded by recipients of their services where the conditions of that Regulation are met".

[68] Ibid., Article 1(2), second subparagraph.

[69] Ibid., Explanatory Memorandum, at p. 11.

[70] Ibid., Article 1(2), first subparagraph. See also the Explanatory Memorandum, at p. 11.

liability rules to the digital age and AI, ensuring the necessary alignment between these two complementary legal instruments".[71]

In addition, it is stressed that the proposed AI Liability Directive follows a minimum harmonisation approach, thus allowing claimants in cases of damage caused by AI systems to invoke more favourable national rules: "national laws could, for example, maintain reversals of the burden of proof under national fault-based regimes, or national no-fault liability (referred to as 'strict liability') regimes of which there are already a large variety in national laws, possibly applying to damage caused by AI systems".[72] As a result, it is explicitly stated that "Member States may adopt or maintain national rules that are more favourable for claimants to substantiate a non-contractual civil law claim for damages caused by an AI system, provided such rules are compatible with Union law".[73]

The proposed AI Liability Directive does not define AI, but instead, in order to ensure consistency,[74] relies on the same concept of AI used in the EU AI Act and particularly its definition of 'AI systems'.[75] The rules of the proposed Directive will apply to damage caused by AI systems, irrespective of whether they are defined as high-risk[76] or not under the AI Act: "The Directive is focused on providing victims with the same standards of protection when harmed by AI systems as they would be if harmed under any other circumstances. The AI Liability proposal thus applies to damage caused by any type of AI systems: both high-risk and not high-risk. . . . The Directive will apply to damage caused by AI systems, irrespective if they are high-risk or not according to AI Act".[77]

---

[71] Proposed AI Liability Directive, Explanatory Memorandum, at p. 11.

[72] Ibid., Recital 14.

[73] Ibid., Article 1(4).

[74] Ibid., Recital 15: "Consistency with [the AI Act] should also be ensured. It is therefore appropriate for this Directive to use the same definitions in respect of AI systems, providers and users".

[75] Ibid., Article 2, point (1): "'AI system' means an AI system as defined in [Article 3 (1) of the AI Act]". In the (final) text of the EU AI Act, "'AI system' means a machine-based system that is designed to operate with varying levels of autonomy and that may exhibit adaptiveness after deployment, and that, for explicit or implicit objectives, infers, from the input it receives, how to generate outputs such as predictions, content, recommendations, or decisions that can influence physical or virtual environments". Regulation (EU) 2024/1689 of the European Parliament and of the Council of 13 June 2024 laying down harmonised rules on artificial intelligence and amending Regulations (EC) No 300/2008, (EU) No 167/2013, (EU) No 168/2013, (EU) 2018/858, (EU) 2018/1139 and (EU) 2019/2144 and Directives 2014/90/EU, (EU) 2016/797 and (EU) 2020/1828 (*EU Artificial Intelligence Act*), OJ L, 12.07.2024. Article 3 ('Definitions'), point 1.

[76] Proposed AI Liability Directive, Article 2, point (2).

[77] European Commission, Questions & Answers: AI Liability Directive, Brussels, 28 September 2022, p. 2.

According to the proposed AI Liability Directive, any type of victim (natural or legal person)[78] can bring a claim for damages[79] and can be compensated if they are harmed by the fault or omission of a provider, developer or user of AI resulting in a damage covered by national law (e.g., health, property, privacy etc.).[80] In relation to the definition of 'claimant',[81] the proposed AI Liability Directive stipulates that claims for damages can be brought not only by the injured person but also by persons that have succeeded in or have been subrogated into the rights of the injured person.[82] Furthermore, it is stated that an action for damages can also be brought by someone acting on behalf of one or more injured parties, in accordance with EU or national law.[83]

---

[78] Proposed AI Liability Directive, Article 2, point (7). See also Explanatory Memorandum, at p. 9: "The preferred policy option would ensure that victims of AI-enabled products and services (natural persons, businesses and any other public or private entities) are no less protected than victims of traditional technologies".

[79] Ibid., Article 2, point (5): "'claim for damages' means a non-contractual fault-based civil law claim for compensation of the damage caused by an output of an AI system or the failure of such a system to produce an output where such an output should have been produced".

See also Recital 15: "this Directive should only cover claims for damages when the damage is caused by an output or the failure to produce an output by an AI system through the fault of a person, for example the provider or the user under [the AI Act]. There is no need to cover liability claims when the damage is caused by a human assessment followed by a human act or omission, while the AI system only provided information or advice which was taken into account by the relevant human actor. In the latter case, it is possible to trace back the damage to a human act or omission, as the AI system output is not interposed between the human act or omission and the damage, and thereby establishing causality is not more difficult than in situations where an AI system is not involved".

[80] European Commission, Questions & Answers: AI Liability Directive, Brussels, 28 September 2022, pp. 1–2: "The new rules cover national liability claims based on the fault or omission of any person (providers, developers, users), for the compensation of any type of damage covered by national law (life, health, property, privacy, etc.) and for any type of victim (individuals, companies, organisations, etc.). (at p. 1); ... "The new AI Liability Directive makes a targeted reform of national fault-based liability regimes and will apply to claims against any person for fault that influenced the AI system which caused the damage; any type of damage covered under national law (including resulting from discrimination or breach of fundamental rights like privacy); and claims made by any natural or legal person" (at p. 2).

[81] Proposed AI Liability Directive, Article 2, points (6) and(7): "(6) 'claimant' means a person bringing a claim for damages that: (a) has been injured by an output of an AI system or by the failure of such a system to produce an output where such an output should have been produced; (b) has succeeded to or has been subrogated to the right of an injured person by virtue of law or contract; or (c) is acting on behalf of one or more injured persons, in accordance with Union or national law. . . . (7) 'potential claimant' means a natural or legal person who is considering but has not yet brought a claim for damages".

[82] Ibid., Explanatory Memorandum, at p. 12: "Subrogation is the assumption by a third party (such as an insurance company) of another party's legal right to collect a debt or damages. Thus one person is entitled to enforce the rights of another for their own benefit. Subrogation would also cover heirs of a deceased victim".

[83] Ibid.: "This provision aims to give more possibilities to persons injured by an AI system to have their claims assessed by a court, even in cases where individual actions may seem too costly or too

8.4.4 *Disclosure of Evidence and Rebuttable Presumption of Non-compliance with a Duty of Care*

8.4.4.1 Disclosure of Evidence/Information

Article 3 of the proposed AI Liability Directive contains several provisions on the disclosure of evidence concerning a specific high-risk AI system that is suspected of having caused damage. In particular, it is stated that at least in specific cases (high risk AI systems), victims could be disadvantaged by the burden of proof in product liability claims, facing difficulties to investigate claims properly and to gain access to essential information. Plaintiffs need to gather specific information/evidence to be able to prove the conditions for a claim for damages, i.e., to prove the defendant's fault and/or the defect of a product and the causal link with the damage suffered. Therefore, in order to substantiate a damages claim and establish liability, it is crucial to introduce rules on the disclosure of specific evidence by those that have it at their disposal.[84] As the Commission put it, "access to information about specific high-risk AI systems that are suspected of having caused damage is an important factor to ascertain whether to claim compensation and to substantiate claims for compensation. … [F]or high risk AI systems, [the AI Act] provides for specific documentation, information and logging requirements, but does not provide a right to the injured person to access that information. It is therefore appropriate to lay down rules on the disclosure of relevant evidence by those that have it at their disposal, for the purposes of establishing liability. This should also provide an additional incentive to comply with the relevant requirements laid down in [the AI Act] to document or record the relevant information".[85]

---

cumbersome to bring, or where joint actions may entail a benefit of scale. To enable victims of damage caused by AI systems to enforce their rights in relation to this Directive through representative actions, Article 6 amends Annex I to Directive (EU) 2020/1828".

[84] Similar approaches have been successfully implemented at EU level e.g. in the 'Damages Directive' (2014/104/EU) facilitating the private enforcement of EU competition law, and the 'Enforcement Directive' (2004/48/EC) ensuring a homogeneous level of protection in the internal market and the effective civil enforcement of harmonised intellectual property rights (see e.g., Articles 5 and 6 of the 'Enforcement Directive').

[85] Proposed AI Liability Directive, Recital 16.

See also Commission Staff Working Document, "Impact Assessment Report – Accompanying the document Proposal for a Directive of the European Parliament and of the Council on adapting non-contractual civil liability rules to artificial intelligence", SWD(2022) 319 final, Brussels, 28.9.2022, at p. 30: "Obtaining information recorded or documented pursuant to the AI Act could help the victim to make a successful liability claim. For instance, it could help to provide evidence for demonstrating fault as one of the conditions of liability to be proven by the victim. This could be done for example by proving that the liable person did not comply with their obligations under the AI Act".

The example provided by the Commission (at p. 30) is the following: "Example: A highly autonomous cleaning robot causes harm. … The victim claims compensation from the company operating the cleaning robot. For the purpose of the AI Act, this company is the 'user' of the robot's AI systems. Access to relevant parts of the technical documentation (Annex IV of the AI Act),

Furthermore, it is stressed that in a system with multiple stakeholders and decisions being made by AI, it is of paramount importance to identify who is responsible—and liable—in the event of failure/damage. Due to the characteristics of AI and other emerging digital technologies (such as complexity, opacity, openness, autonomy, and limited predictability), victims are in a weaker position (compared to other tort cases) to identify the liable person and prove all necessary conditions/facts that substantiate their damages claim. Also, the many different layers involved in the emerging digital technologies (e.g., vulnerable software, faulty sensors, or unstable connectivity) as well as the large number of people involved in the design, development, deployment and operation of high-risk AI systems can make it extremely hard for victims to determine who is technically and legally responsible for any ensuing damage or how to identify the root cause of the problem ("makes it difficult for injured persons to identify the person potentially liable for damage caused and to prove the conditions for a claim for damages").[86]

To remedy this, the proposed AI Liability Directive aims at providing "persons seeking compensation for damage caused by high-risk AI systems with effective means to identify potentially liable persons and relevant evidence for a claim. ... Such means serve to exclude falsely identified potential defendants, saving time and costs for the parties involved and reducing the case load for courts".[87] As a result, the proposed AI Liability Directive underlines that, in order to allow injured persons to determine whether a claim for damages is well-founded, it is appropriate to grant claimants a right to access essential/critical information and, thus, a right to request a court to order the disclosure of specific evidence (in relation to a specific high-risk AI system that is suspected of having caused damage). According to the Commission, the proposed rules, i.e., the victims' right to ask the court to order disclosure of information about high-risk AI systems, would allow victims to access relevant evidence in order to identify the person that could be held liable and to detect the root cause of the problem, for instance when damage is caused because an operator of drones delivering packages does not respect the instructions for use or because a provider does not follow specific requirements when using AI-enabled recruitment services.[88]

---

e.g. the instructions of use, would show the victim what the user was required to do to prevent such accidents. For example, the user may be required to ensure human oversight. The user might also be required to ensure that the AI systems are only used in certain operational environments (e.g. geographical and meteorological conditions, etc.). This information can help the victim to establish that the liable person has not complied with such requirements and therefore committed a fault".

[86] Proposed AI Liability Directive, Recital 17.

[87] Ibid., Explanatory Memorandum, at p. 12.

See also Recital 17: "Ordering disclosure should lead to a reduction of unnecessary litigation and avoid costs for the possible litigants caused by claims which are unjustified or likely to be unsuccessful".

[88] European Commission, Questions & Answers: AI Liability Directive, Brussels, 28 September 2022, p. 1.

It is explicitly stated that requests for evidence cannot be addressed to parties that bear no obligations under the AI Act and, therefore, have no access to the evidence. Therefore, requests could be addressed to the provider of AI system, a person who is subject to the provider's obligations laid down in the AI Act or a user pursuant to the AI Act, either as defendants or third parties to the claim for damages.[89] Indeed, it is recognised that, under specific circumstances, the claimant could also request the disclosure of evidence held by entities (providers or users) that are not defendants,[90] but only if all proportionate attempts made to obtain the evidence from the defendant were unsuccessful.[91]

Article 3 of the proposed AI Liability Directive provides that national courts may order the disclosure of relevant evidence about specific high-risk[92] AI systems that are suspected of having caused damage, provided that the requested evidence/ information is at the addressees' disposal. These requests for evidence could be submitted by claimants or potential claimants and be addressed to the provider of an

---

See also Commission Staff Working Document, "Impact Assessment Report – Accompanying the document Proposal for a Directive of the European Parliament and of the Council on adapting non-contractual civil liability rules to artificial intelligence", SWD(2022) 319 final, Brussels, 28.9.2022, at p. 154: "The envisaged rules on the disclosure of information to be documented/ logged under the AI Act will help victims of damage to meet the burden of proof. The logging and documentation obligations of the AI Act apply, in the context of pending civil proceedings, with respect to 'high risk' AI systems. This includes uses of AI posing a high risk of fundamental rights breaches, in particular regarding the rights to equality and non-discrimination (e.g. AI systems used for the purposes of recruitment and staff matters, access to education, access to essential services through credit scoring, etc.). The proposal on civil liability for AI would enable victims of discrimination to leverage that information to substantiate their compensation claims".

[89] Proposed AI Liability Directive, Recital 19: "National courts should be able, in the course of civil proceedings, to order the disclosure or preservation of relevant evidence related to the damage caused by high-risk AI systems from persons who are already under an obligation to document or record information pursuant to [the AI Act], be they providers, persons under the same obligations as providers, or users of an AI system, either as defendants or third parties to the claim".

[90] Ibid.: "There could be situations where the evidence relevant for the case is held by entities that would not be parties to the claim for damages but which are under an obligation to document or record such evidence pursuant to [the AI Act]. It is thus necessary to provide for the conditions under which such third parties to the claim can be ordered to disclose the relevant evidence".

[91] Ibid., Explanatory Memorandum, at p. 12: "the claimant can request the disclosure of evidence from providers or users that are not defendants only in case all proportionate attempts were unsuccessfully made to gather the evidence from the defendant". See also at Recital 20: "to ensure a proportionate application of a disclosure measure towards third parties in claims for damages, the national courts should order disclosure from third parties only if the evidence cannot be obtained from the defendant.

[92] Ibid., Recital 18. The proposed AI Liability Directive, by limiting the obligation to disclose evidence to high-risk AI systems only, aims to ensure proportionality in disclosing evidence and ensure consistency with the AI Act: "The limitation of disclosure of evidence as regards high-risk AI systems is consistent with [the AI Act], which provides certain specific documentation, record keeping and information obligations for operators involved in the design, development and deployment of high-risk AI systems. Such consistency also ensures the necessary proportionality by avoiding that operators of AI systems posing lower or no risk would be expected to document information to a level similar to that required for high-risk AI systems under [the AI Act]".

AI system, a person who is subject to the provider's obligations laid down by Articles 24 or 28(1) of the proposed AI Act or a user pursuant to the AI Act. It is underlined that with regard to the 'potential claimant' (who is differentiated from the actual 'claimant') additional requirements apply before the court can order the disclosure of evidence. Indeed, such disclosure could only be ordered where the potential claimant (i) presents facts/evidence/information sufficient to support the plausibility of the contemplated claim for damages and (ii) has submitted a prior request (to the provider, the person subject to the obligations of a provider or the user) to disclose such evidence, which (the prior request) has been refused.[93] Therefore, the potential claimant can only benefit from the disclosure of evidence when his request (supported by facts and evidence sufficient to establish the plausibility of the contemplated claim) has been refused. By contrast, in the context of a claim for damages, the claimant can request the disclosure of relevant evidence (and then the national court can order the disclosure of the evidence) only if he has made proportionate effort to obtain the evidence from the defendant.[94]

In addition, for the judicial means to be effective, the proposed AI Liability Directive provides that, upon request of the claimant, national courts may also order the preservation of evidence supporting a claim for damages.[95] Furthermore, the national courts may order the disclosure of evidence, only to the extent necessary to support the claim, i.e., the disclosure of evidence must be necessary and proportionate. In other words, national courts must limit the disclosure (and the preservation) of evidence to what is necessary and proportionate for sustaining a potential claim or a claim for damages.[96] As it was put by the Commission, "disclosure should only concern evidence that is necessary for a decision on the respective claim for damages, for example only the parts of the relevant records or data sets required to prove non-compliance with a requirement laid down by [the AI Act]".[97] The aim of limiting the obligation to disclose or preserve to necessary and proportionate evidence is "to ensure proportionality in disclosing evidence, i.e. to limit the disclosure to the necessary minimum and prevent blanket requests".[98] To this end, in determining whether an order for the disclosure or preservation of evidence is

[93] Ibid., Article 3(1): "- Member States shall ensure that national courts are empowered, either upon the request of a potential claimant who has previously asked a provider, a person subject to the obligations of a provider pursuant to [Article 24 or Article 28(1) of the AI Act] or a user to disclose relevant evidence at its disposal about a specific high-risk AI system that is suspected of having caused damage, but was refused, or a claimant, to order the disclosure of such evidence from those persons. - In support of that request, the potential claimant must present facts and evidence sufficient to support the plausibility of a claim for damages".

[94] Ibid., Article 3(2): "In the context of a claim for damages, the national court shall only order the disclosure of the evidence by one of the persons listed in paragraph 1, if the claimant has undertaken all proportionate attempts at gathering the relevant evidence from the defendant".

[95] Ibid., Article 3(3).

[96] Ibid., Article 3(4), first subparagraph.

[97] Ibid., Recital 20.

[98] Ibid., Explanatory Memorandum, at p. 12.

proportionate, national courts will be required to achieve a balance between the claimant's rights and the need to ensure that such disclosure would be subject to specific safeguards to protect the legitimate interests of all parties (providers, users, and third parties) concerned, such as the protection of trade secrets and of confidential information (e.g., information in relation to public or national security).[99] Furthermore, where the disclosure of a confidential trade secret is ordered, national courts may take specific measures necessary to preserve confidentiality of disclosed evidence when that evidence is used or referred to in legal proceedings.[100] In the same context, Member States also need to ensure that the person ordered to disclose or to preserve the relevant evidence has at its disposal appropriate procedural remedies against the order of disclosure or preservation.[101]

8.4.4.2 Rebuttable Presumption of Non-compliance with a Duty of Care

The problem, according to the Commission, is that "while national courts have the means of enforcing their orders for disclosure through various measures, any such enforcement measures could delay claims for damages and thus potentially create additional expenses for the litigants. For injured persons, such delays and additional expenses may make their recourse to an effective judicial remedy more difficult".[102]

---

[99] Ibid., Article 3(4), second subparagraph.

See also Commission Staff Working Document, "Impact Assessment Report – Accompanying the document Proposal for a Directive of the European Parliament and of the Council on adapting non-contractual civil liability rules to artificial intelligence", SWD(2022) 319 final, Brussels, 28.9.2022, at p. 30: "According to this measure, the victim could request from the possibly liable party the disclosure of such information concerning the victim's claim. The competent national court could order that such disclosure would be subject to stringent safeguards to ensure proportionality and protect the legitimate interests of all parties concerned, for instance confidential information, intellectual property rights and trade secrets".

[100] Proposed AI Liability Directive, Article 3(4), third subparagraph.

See also at Recital 20: "In respect of trade secrets or alleged trade secrets which the court has identified as confidential within the meaning of Directive (EU) 2016/943, national courts should be empowered to take specific measures to ensure the confidentiality of trade secrets during and after the proceedings, while achieving a fair and proportionate balance between the trade-secret holder's interest in maintaining secrecy and the interest of the injured person. This should include measures to restrict access to documents containing trade secrets and access to hearings or documents and transcripts thereof to a limited number of people. When deciding on such measures, national courts should take into account the need to ensure the right to an effective remedy and to a fair trial, the legitimate interests of the parties and, where appropriate, of third parties, and any potential harm to either party or, where appropriate, to third parties, resulting from the granting or rejection of such measures".

[101] Ibid., Article 3(4), fourth subparagraph.

[102] Ibid., Recital 21.

This is the reason why the proposed AI Liability Directive introduces a rebuttable presumption of non-compliance with a duty of care.[103] In particular, where a defendant in a claim for damages fails to disclose or preserve evidence at his disposal as ordered by a national court, the proposed Directive lays down a presumption of non-compliance with those duties of care which that evidence was intended to prove. In other words, if the defendant fails to comply with an order by a national court to disclose or to preserve evidence at its disposal, the court in question will presume the evidence requested was intended to prove non-compliance with a relevant duty of care obligation.[104] However, it is noted that the defendant may rebut that presumption by submitting evidence to the contrary.[105]

[103] Ibid., Article 2, point (9): "(9) 'duty of care' means a required standard of conduct, set by national or Union law, in order to avoid damage to legal interests recognised at national or Union law level, including life, physical integrity, property and the protection of fundamental rights".

[104] Ibid., Article 3(5), first subparagraph.

See also Commission Staff Working Document, "Impact Assessment Report – Accompanying the document Proposal for a Directive of the European Parliament and of the Council on adapting non-contractual civil liability rules to artificial intelligence", SWD(2022) 319 final, Brussels, 28.9.2022, at pp. 30 and 154: "If the possibly liable person does not disclose the information, the victim would benefit from a presumption that the facts, which the withheld information might have proven actually, did occur. Such presumption would facilitate the burden of proof of the victim" (at p. 30). . . . "If the defendant refuses without just motivation to disclose information, the facts that might have been proven (e.g. the application of criteria correlating with criteria protected by the right to non-discrimination, or unequal treatment) would be presumed. This rebuttable presumption will for instance help victims of discrimination to meet the prima facie threshold under the existing non-discrimination/equal treatment Directives" (at p. 154).

[105] Proposed AI Liability Directive, Article 3(5), second subparagraph.

See also Commission Staff Working Document, "Impact Assessment Report – Accompanying the document Proposal for a Directive of the European Parliament and of the Council on adapting non-contractual civil liability rules to artificial intelligence", SWD(2022) 319 final, Brussels, 28.9.2022, at pp. 30–31: "The liable person would have the opportunity to rebut the presumption. This means that the liable person would have the opportunity to prove that the presumed facts did in reality not occur. That person could also avoid liability by refuting any of the liability conditions set by the applicable liability rules, for instance demonstrate that the relevant AI system was carefully selected and used, taking into account the requirements of the AI Act".

The example given by the Commission (at pp. 30–31) is the following: "Example: In the cleaning robot example, the victim requests access to the data recorded during the operation of the cleaning robot in order to prove that the robot's sensors were not properly cleaned at the time of the accident. The competent court can order necessary safeguard measures to ensure that all legitimate confidentiality interests are protected. If the company responsible for operating the cleaning robot (= the possibly liable party) nevertheless does not disclose this information, the victim could claim and the court would presume for the purposes of the victim's liability claim that the sensors were not properly cleaned. This may constitute a fault of the liable party. However, the liable party could rebut the presumption by showing that the sensors were actually clean. It could also avoid liability in other ways, e.g. by showing that there is no causal link between the presumed failure to clean the sensors and the damage".

The measure set out in Article 3(5) of the proposed AI Liability Directive is a "procedural tool", where "the actual defendant in a claim for damages . . . bears the consequences of not complying with a request to disclose or preserve evidence".[106] According to the Commission, this rebuttable presumption "will reduce the duration of litigation and facilitate more efficient court proceedings",[107] it "aims to promote disclosure but also to expedite court proceedings",[108] and, as already mentioned, it provides "an additional incentive to comply with the relevant requirements laid down in [the AI Act] to document or record the relevant information".[109]

Finally, it is noted that the refusal of the provider or the user—prior to the request to the court—to disclose evidence should not trigger the presumption of non-compliance with relevant duties of care by the person who refused such disclosure.[110] Such presumption can be triggered only when the defendant has failed to comply with an order issued by the court.

8.4.5 Rebuttable Presumption of a Causal Link in the Case of Fault

The Commission stated that, with regard to damage caused by AI systems, the aim of the proposed AI Liability Directive is to provide an effective basis for claiming compensation in connection with the fault consisting in the lack of compliance with a duty of care under EU or national law.[111] This is because, as it is reminded, it can be challenging for claimants to establish a causal link between such non-compliance and the output produced by the AI system or the failure of the AI system to produce an output that gave rise to the relevant damage.[112] This is why a targeted rebuttable presumption of causality (which is "the least burdensome measure to address the

[106] Proposed AI Liability Directive, Explanatory Memorandum, at p. 13.

[107] Ibid., Recital 21.

[108] Ibid., Explanatory Memorandum, at p. 13.

[109] Ibid., Recital 16.

See also Commission Staff Working Document, "Impact Assessment Report – Accompanying the document Proposal for a Directive of the European Parliament and of the Council on adapting non-contractual civil liability rules to artificial intelligence", SWD(2022) 319 final, Brussels, 28.9.2022, at p. 31: "This measure would not only help the victim. Providers and users of AI systems would be given an additional incentive to comply with the documentation/logging requirements of the AI Act. If they had complied, they could disclose the information (subject to necessary confidentiality safeguards) and would be able to demonstrate that they acted in accordance with legal requirements. This additional incentive would support the compliance with the AI Act. Thereby this measure would achieve synergies with the AI Act".

[110] Proposed AI Liability Directive, Recital 17.

[111] Ibid., Explanatory Memorandum, at p. 13.

[112] Ibid.

need for fair compensation of the victim")[113] has been introduced regarding this causal link. As it was stated by the Commission, "in order to address the difficulties to prove that a specific input for which the potentially liable person is responsible had caused a specific AI system output that led to the damage at stake, it is appropriate to provide, under certain conditions, for a presumption of causality".[114]

---

[113] Ibid.

[114] Ibid., Recital 22.

See also Commission Staff Working Document, "Impact Assessment Report – Accompanying the document Proposal for a Directive of the European Parliament and of the Council on adapting non-contractual civil liability rules to artificial intelligence", SWD(2022) 319 final, Brussels, 28.9.2022, at pp. 31–32 and 154: "(ii) If the victim shows that the liable person did not comply with AI Act requirements designed to prevent damage, the second measure could establish a rebuttable presumption that this non-compliance caused the damage. This measure would further facilitate the exercise of the burden of proof as regards the causality link between fault and damage for the victim. The victim could demonstrate that the liable person did not comply with AI Act requirements. In that case the victim could claim and the court would presume for the purposes of the victim's liability claim that such non-compliance would have caused the harm. Again, such presumption would be rebuttable. This means that the possibly liable person could avoid liability by proving that their non-compliance with the AI Act requirements did not cause the damage. ... In line with the AI Act, this measure would be primarily relevant for claims against providers and users of high-risk AI-systems. It would give them an additional incentive to comply with the AI Act, because in case of non-compliance it would be presumed that their behaviour caused the damage" (pp. 31–32). ... "Presumption of causality: If the victim establishes (where necessary using information to be disclosed in accordance with the first measure described above) that the defendant did not comply with their obligations under the AI Act, it would be presumed that harm of a type the relevant obligations were intended to prevent (e.g. discrimination) was caused by that non-compliance. For example, where the victim shows that the defendant did not comply with their obligation to minimize the risk of discrimination by ensuring high quality training, validation and testing data, it would be presumed that this failure to comply with the AI Act entailed the discrimination for which compensation is sought. This rebuttable presumption could thus help victims to overcome the AI-specific difficulty of establishing a link between specific input parameters and a harmful output, linked to the probabilistic nature and complexity of certain AI systems" (at p. 154).

The example provided by the Commission is the following (at p. 31): "Example: Under the AI Act the user of a high-risk AI system, like the company operating an AI-enabled highly autonomous cleaning robot, is obliged to use such systems in accordance with the instructions of use accompanying the system. These instructions of use could specify, for instance: - the type of input data the system should be exposed to, e.g. meteorological or lighting conditions perceived through the cleaning robot's sensors; - circumstances which may lead to risks to health, safety or fundamental rights, e.g. the type of terrain or surface the cleaning robot is capable to move on safely without causing harm. The victim may be able to prove that the company operating the AI-enabled highly autonomous cleaning robot (= the possibly liable party) did not comply with such instruction, e.g. that the robot's AI-enabled perception system was used in an environment where it was exposed to inadequate input data (e.g. poor lighting conditions) or under circumstances which may lead to health risks (e.g. on uneven terrain frequented by many human passers-by). Access to information in accordance with measure (i) could help the victim to prove such facts. The competent court would presume that it was the non–compliance of the liable party with its obligations that caused the damage. The possibly liable party could rebut this presumption by demonstrating that there is no causal link between the non-compliance and the damage, e.g. by showing that someone pushed the cleaning robot, causing the accident. That party could also avoid liability by showing that they

As it will be seen below, Article 4 of the proposed AI Liability Directive differentiates between (i) the 'fault of the defendants' in general, which consists in the non-compliance with a duty of care laid down in EU or national law directly intended to protect against the damage that occurred (Article 4 para. 1); (ii) the 'fault of defendants who are providers of high-risk AI systems regulated under the proposed AI Act', where the fault can only consist in the non-compliance with certain listed requirements laid down in the proposed AI Act (Article 4 para. 2); (iii) the 'fault of defendants who are users of high-risk AI systems subject to the proposed AI Act', where the fault can consist not only in the non-compliance with certain listed requirements laid down in the proposed AI Act but also in the non-compliance with other duties of care laid down in EU or national law, in light of Article 29 (2) of the proposed AI Act.

8.4.5.1 The Presumption of Causality in the Case of Fault of the Defendants

In particular, the proposed AI Liability Directive lays down a rebuttable presumption of causality establishing a causal link between non-compliance with a duty of care under EU or national law (i.e. the fault of the defendant) and the output produced by the AI system or the failure of the AI system to produce an output that gave rise to the relevant damage.[115] As it was explained by the Commission, "for the presumption of causality under this Directive to apply, the fault of the defendant should be established as a human act or omission which does not meet a duty of care under Union law or national law that is directly intended to protect against the damage that occurred. Thus, this presumption can apply, for example, in a claim for damages for physical injury when the court establishes the fault of the defendant for non-complying with the instructions of use which are meant to prevent harm to natural persons".[116]

However, such presumption of causality only applies when the cumulative following conditions are met: (a) the fault of the defendant (which can be established for non-compliance with a duty of care) has been proven by the claimant; (b) the given fault has influenced the relevant AI system output or lack thereof that gave rise to the relevant damage; (c) the claimant has proved that the AI system (i.e. its output or failure to produce one) gave rise to the damage.[117] In particular: First, the fault of the defendant (or of a person for whose behaviour the defendant is responsible) has to be proven by the claimant according to the applicable EU law or national rules, or presumed by the national court pursuant to Article 3(5) of the proposed AI Liability

applied all the care that could reasonably be expected of them under the relevant circumstances, which means that they were not at fault".

[115] Proposed AI Liability Directive, Article 4(1).

[116] Ibid., Recital 22.

[117] Ibid., Article 4(1)(a)-(c).

Directive ('rebuttable presumption of non-compliance with a duty of care'). Such a fault can be established for non-compliance with a duty of care directly intended to protect against the damage that occurred.[118] Such fault, according to the Commission, "can be established, for example, for non-compliance with a duty of care pursuant to the AI Act or pursuant to other rules set at Union level, such as those regulating the use of automated monitoring and decision-making for platform work or those regulating the operation of unmanned aircraft. Such fault can also be presumed by the court on the basis of a non-compliance with a court order for disclosure or preservation of evidence under Article 3(5)".[119] On the other hand, it is expressly stated that the presumption of causality will not apply if the non-compliance refers to duties of care that were not directly intended to protect against the damage that occurred. For instance, "a provider's failure to file required documentation with competent authorities would not lead to the application of the presumption in claims for damages due to physical injury".[120] Second, for the presumption of causality under the proposed AI Liability Directive to apply, it should be considered reasonably likely, based on the circumstances of the case, that the fault has influenced the output produced by the AI system or the failure of the AI system to produce an output.[121] Third, the claimant needs to prove that the output

[118] Ibid., Article 4(1)(a): "(a) the claimant has demonstrated or the court has presumed pursuant to Article 3(5), the fault of the defendant, or of a person for whose behaviour the defendant is responsible, consisting in the non-compliance with a duty of care laid down in Union or national law directly intended to protect against the damage that occurred".

[119] Ibid., Explanatory Memorandum, at p. 13.

See also Recitals 23 and 24: "Such a fault can be established in respect of non-compliance with Union rules which specifically regulate high-risk AI systems like the requirements introduced for certain high-risk AI systems by [the AI Act], requirements which may be introduced by future sectoral legislation for other high-risk AI systems according to [Article 2(2) of the AI Act], or duties of care which are linked to certain activities and which are applicable irrespective whether AI is used for that activity. (Recital 23). . . . In areas not harmonised by Union law, national law continues to apply and fault is established under the applicable national law. All national liability regimes have duties of care, taking as a standard of conduct different expressions of the principle how a reasonable person should act, which also ensure the safe operation of AI systems in order to prevent damage to recognised legal interests. Such duties of care could for instance require users of AI systems to choose for certain tasks a particular AI system with concrete characteristics or to exclude certain segments of a population from being exposed to a particular AI system. National law can also introduce specific obligations meant to prevent risks for certain activities, which are applicable irrespective whether AI is used for that activity, for example traffic rules or obligations specifically designed for AI systems, such as additional national requirements for users of high-risk AI systems pursuant to Article 29 (2) of [the AI Act]" (Recital 24).

[120] Ibid., Recital 22.

[121] Ibid., Article 4(1)(b) and Recital 22.

See also the Explanatory Memorandum, at p. 13: "It is only appropriate to introduce a presumption of causality when it can be considered likely that the given fault has influenced the relevant AI system output or lack thereof, which can be assessed on the basis of the overall circumstances of the case".

The Commission stressed that not every fault should lead to the application of the rebuttable presumption linking it to the output of the AI, even when fault consisting of a non-compliance with

produced by the AI system or the failure of the AI system to produce an output gave rise to the damage.[122]

8.4.5.2 The Presumption of Causality in the Case of Fault of Providers and Users of a High-Risk AI System

The above-mentioned Article 4(1) of the proposed AI Liability Directive covers and deals with defendants in general. However, paragraphs 2 and 3 of Article 4 make a further distinction and differentiate between (i) claims brought against the *provider* of a high-risk AI system or against a person subject to the provider's obligations under the AI Act and (ii) claims brought against the *user* of such high-risk AI systems. In consistency with the logic of the proposed AI Act, these provisions refer to several obligations of those parties (providers and users of high-risk AI systems) under the AI Act, following the respective provisions and relevant conditions of the AI Act. Thus claims for damages involving providers and users of high-risk AI systems are subject to conditions related to the non-compliance of provisions applicable under the AI Act including the requirements regarding data training, transparency, human oversight, accuracy, robustness and cybersecurity. As it was stated, "this Directive covers the fault constituting non-compliance with certain listed requirements laid down in Chapters 2 and 3 of [the AI Act] for providers and users of high-risk AI systems, the non-compliance with which can lead, under certain conditions, to a presumption of causality".[123]

Thus, with regard to claims for damages against a *provider* of a high-risk AI system or a person subject to the provider's obligations, the requirement of fault (i.e., the condition of Article 4(1)(a)) is only met when the complainant has demonstrated that those actors failed to comply with specific requirements in the AI Liability Directive which are laid down in the Commission's proposed AI Act.[124] Therefore, in the case of a claim for damages against a provider of a high-risk AI system,

---

a duty of care directly intended to protect against the damage that occurred is established. As it was stated, "it can be for example considered reasonably likely that the fault has influenced the output or failure to produce an output, when that fault consists in breaching a duty of care in respect of limiting the perimeter of operation of the AI system and the damage occurred outside the perimeter of operation. On the contrary, a breach of a requirement to file certain documents or to register with a given authority, even though this might be foreseen for that particular activity or even be applicable expressly to the operation of an AI system, could not be considered as reasonably likely to have influenced the output produced by the AI system or the failure of the AI system to produce an output" (recital 25).

[122] Ibid., Article 4(1)(c).

[123] Proposed AI Liability Directive, Recital 26.

[124] Ibid., Article 4(2).

See also Recital 26: "The AI Act provides for full harmonisation of requirements for AI systems, unless otherwise explicitly laid down therein. It harmonises the specific requirements for high-risk AI systems. Hence, for the purposes of claims for damages in which a presumption of causality according to this Directive is applied, the potential fault of providers or persons subject to the

national courts must presume the causal link between the non-compliance of these requirements and the output produced by the AI system, or the failure of the AI system to produce an output that gave rise to a relevant damage. Furthermore, it is recognised that, in practice, it may be difficult for the claimant to prove such non-compliance when the defendant is a provider of the AI system and, as a result, it is stated that in the case of claims based on Article 4(2), the defendants' compliance with the obligations listed in that paragraph should be assessed in the light of the established risk management system and its results, i.e. risk management measures, under the AI Act.[125] According to Article 4(2) of the proposed AI Liability Directive, a provider is considered to have committed a fault if he failed to comply with any of the following requirements: the AI system is a system which makes use of techniques involving the training of models with data and which was not developed on the basis of training, validation and testing data sets that meet the quality criteria referred to in Article 10(2) to 10(4) of the proposed AI Act;[126] the AI system was not designed and developed in a way that meets the transparency requirements laid down in Article 13 of the proposed AI Act;[127] the AI system was not designed and developed in a way that allows for an effective oversight by natural persons during the period in which the AI system is in use' pursuant to Article 14 of the proposed AI Act;[128] the AI system 'was not designed and developed so as to achieve, in the light of its intended purpose, an appropriate level of accuracy, robustness and cybersecurity' pursuant to Article 15 and Article 16 (a) of the proposed AI Act;[129] the necessary corrective actions were not immediately taken to bring the AI system in conformity with the obligations laid down in Title III, Chapter 2 of the proposed AI Act or to withdraw or recall the system, as appropriate, pursuant to Article 16, point (g), and Article 21 of the proposed AI Act.[130]

With regard to claims for damages against a *user* of a high-risk AI system, the requirement of a fault (i.e., the condition of Article 4(1)(a)) is met when the claimant

---

obligations of a provider pursuant to [the AI Act] is established only through a non-compliance with such requirements".

[125] Ibid., Article 4(2).

See also Recital 26: "Given that in practice it may be difficult for the claimant to prove such non-compliance when the defendant is a provider of the AI system, and in full consistency with the logic of [the AI Act], this Directive should also provide that the steps undertaken by the provider within the risk management system and the results of the risk management system, i.e. the decision to adopt or not to adopt certain risk management measures, should be taken into account in the determination of whether the provider has complied with the relevant requirements under the AI Act referred to in this Directive. The risk management system put in place by the provider pursuant to [the AI Act] is a continuous iterative process run throughout the lifecycle of the high-risk AI system, whereby the provider ensures compliance with mandatory requirements meant to mitigate risks and can, therefore, be a useful element for the purpose of the assessment of this compliance".

[126] Proposed AI Liability Directive, Article 4(2)(a).

[127] Ibid., Article 4(2)(b).

[128] Ibid., Article 4(2)(c).

[129] Ibid., Article 4(2)(d).

[130] Ibid., Article 4(2)(e).

has demonstrated that the user of the high-risk AI system (i) failed to comply with his obligations to use or monitor the AI system in accordance with the accompanying instructions of use or, where appropriate, suspend or interrupt its use pursuant to Article 29 of the proposed AI Act; or (ii) exposed the AI system to input data under his control which is not relevant in view of the system's intended purpose' pursuant to Article 29(3) of the proposed AI Act.[131] It should be underlined that, apart from the case of non-compliance with certain specific requirements set by the Commission's proposed AI Act, the fault of users of high-risk AI systems could also consist in the non-compliance with other duties of care laid down in EU or national law.[132]

8.4.5.3 Exception from the Presumption of Causality Where the Defendant Demonstrates That the Claimant Could Reasonably Access Sufficient Evidence and Expertise to Prove the Causal Link in the Case of High-Risk AI Systems

Article 4(4) of the proposed AI Liability Directive establishes an exception to the presumption of causality specifically for high-risk AI systems. In particular, in the case of a claim for damages concerning a high-risk AI system, national courts should not apply the presumption of causality (laid down in Article 4(1)) if the defendant demonstrates that the claimant could reasonably access sufficient evidence and expertise (for instance, through documentation and logging requirements pursuant to the AI Act)[133] to prove the causal link between the fault of the defendant and the output produced by the AI system or the failure of the AI system to produce an output that gave rise to a relevant damage.[134] According to the Commission's thinking, this possibility for an exception to the presumption of causality facilitates compliance and contributes to the enforcement of the requirements for high-risk AI systems imposed by the AI Act, as it provides defendants with an additional incentive to respect their obligations regarding their expected conduct and to comply

[131] Ibid., Article 4(3).

[132] Ibid., Recital 26: "This Directive also covers the cases of users' fault, when this fault consists in non-compliance with certain specific requirements set by [the AI Act]. In addition, the fault of users of high-risk AI systems may be established following non-compliance with other duties of care laid down in Union or national law, in light of Article 29 (2) of [the AI Act]".

[133] Ibid., Recital 27: "While the specific characteristics of certain AI systems, like autonomy and opacity, could make it excessively difficult for the claimant to meet the burden of proof, there could be situations where such difficulties do not exist because there could be sufficient evidence and expertise available to the complainant to prove the causal link. This could be the case, for example, in respect of high-risk AI systems where the claimant could reasonably access sufficient evidence and expertise through documentation and logging requirements pursuant to [the AI Act]. In such situations, the court should not apply the presumption".

[134] ibid., Article 4(4).

with the relevant requirements laid down in the proposed AI Act to document or record the relevant information.[135]

8.4.5.4 Targeted Alleviation of the Burden of Proof: Condition for the Applicability of the Presumption of Causality in the Case of Non-high Risk AI Systems Where the Court Considers It Excessively Difficult for the Claimant to Prove the Causal Link

The proposed AI Liability Directive introduces an additional measure to alleviate the victims' burden to prove their liability claim. In particular, where the only way for the victim to prove the liability claim is to demonstrate what happened inside the AI, such burden on the victim would be alleviated, and the potentially liable person would have the opportunity/onus to prove that he did not act negligently. Indeed, the specific characteristics of the AI-system could make the victim's burden of proof excessively difficult or even impossible to meet. There will be cases when the victim will not be able to identify or explain how something that the liable person did (or failed to do) was 'translated' by the AI into the output that caused the damage. In that case, a targeted alleviation of the exercise of the burden of proof could apply, so that the victim would not have to prove how or why an AI-system arrived at the relevant (harmful) output, as this could be excessively difficult due to the specific characteristics of AI (i.e., the victim does not have to explain the inner workings of the AI).[136] This measure would apply irrespective of whether the relevant AI-system is qualified as 'high-risk' by the AI Act. Therefore, this presumption of causality could also apply to non-high risk AI systems because there could be excessive difficulties of proof for the claimant.

---

[135] Ibid., Explanatory Memorandum, at p. 13: "This possibility can incentivise defendants to comply with their disclosure obligations, with measures set by the AI Act to ensure a high level of transparency of the AI or with documenting and recording requirements".

[136] See, for instance, the example provided by the Commission Staff Working Document, "Impact Assessment Report – Accompanying the document Proposal for a Directive of the European Parliament and of the Council on adapting non-contractual civil liability rules to artificial intelligence", SWD(2022) 319 final, Brussels, 28.9.2022, at p. 32: "Example: In the cleaning robot example, several potentially liable persons are responsible for different input parameters. Such alternative causes for the harm caused to the victim could lie, for example, in a failure by a human supervisor to react to a distress signal, flawed training or testing data, exposure to input data not in conformity with the instructions of use, failure to provide or install a necessary update or an external attack (e.g. jamming, spoofing, adversarial machine learning). Each of these inputs could be the reason of the damage caused by the highly autonomous AI system. However, the opacity of that system can make it prohibitively difficult or even impossible for the victim to prove which of these persons effectively caused the damage. The victim may be able to establish facts such as that the liable party used the AI system in circumstances or conditions that were inappropriate or failed to take instructions of use into account. If the victim can prove such facts, the court can relieve the victim from the obligation to prove that these facts led the AI system to arrive at the specific output that caused the damage. As with the other measures, the potentially liable persons could prove an alternative cause for the damage or show that they acted diligently and thus avoid liability".

This is why Article 4(5) of the proposed AI Liability Directive establishes a condition for the applicability of the presumption of causality specifically for non-high risk AI systems. In particular, in the case of a claim for damages concerning a non-high risk AI system, the presumption of causality would only apply where the national court considers it excessively difficult for the claimant to prove the causal link.[137] As it is explained by the Commission, such difficulties of proof for the claimant "could be assessed in light of the characteristics of certain AI systems, such as autonomy and opacity, which render the explanation of the inner functioning of the AI system very difficult in practice, negatively affecting the ability of the claimant to prove the causal link between the fault of the defendant and the AI output".[138] ... "A national court should apply the presumption where the claimant is in an excessively difficult position to prove causation, since it is required to explain how the AI system was led by the human act or omission that constitutes fault to produce the output or the failure to produce an output which gave rise to the damage. However, the claimant should neither be required to explain the characteristics of the AI system concerned nor how these characteristics make it harder to establish the causal link".[139]

8.4.5.5 Condition for the Applicability of the Presumption of Causality for AI Systems Used in the Course of a Personal, Non-professional, Activity

Article 4(6) of the proposed AI Liability Directive establishes a further differentiated regime for situations where the AI system from which the alleged damage arose was used in the course of a personal, non-professional, activity. It is argued that alleviating the burden of proving causation is not always appropriate where the defendant is not a professional user but rather a person using the AI system for its private activities. Therefore, in the case of a claim for damages against a defendant who used the AI system in the course of a personal, non-professional activity, the presumption of causality should only apply (when all the other conditions are also fulfilled) if the defendant has materially interfered with the conditions of the operation of the AI system or if the defendant was required and able to determine the conditions of operation of the AI system and failed to do so.[140] According to the Commission, this condition is justified by the need to balance the interests of injured persons and non-professional users, by excluding from the application of the presumption of

[137] Proposed AI Liability Directive, Article 4(5).

[138] Ibid., Explanatory Memorandum, at pp. 13–14. See also Recital 28.

[139] Ibid., Recital 28.

[140] Ibid., Article 4(6). See also Explanatory Memorandum, at p. 14, and Recital 29.

causality the cases in which non-professional users do not add to the risk of an AI system causing damage through their behaviour.[141]

8.4.5.6 The Defendant's Right to Rebut the Presumption of Causality

As the proposed AI Liability Directive introduces a rebuttable presumption (namely that, under specific conditions, national courts will presume the causal link between the fault of the defendant and the output produced by the AI system or the failure of the AI system to produce an output), it is expressly stated that the defendant will have the right to rebut the presumption of causality laid down in Article 4(1).[142] Therefore, the defendant should be able to rebut it by submitting evidence to the contrary, for instance by demonstrating that their fault could not have caused the damage.[143]

8.4.6 Evaluation and Targeted Review/Report Clause

As already discussed, the Commission's proposal did not introduce a strict liability regime for high-risk systems. Instead, it opted for a targeted harmonisation of specific aspects of fault-based liability rules in the EU. In particular, the proposed AI Liability Directive harmonises only those fault-based liability rules that govern the burden of proof for persons claiming compensation for damage caused by AI systems. According to the Commission, this view took into account the differences between long-standing national civil law systems and legal traditions (which makes Member States reluctant to pursue coordinated reform), the current state of

---

[141] Ibid., Explanatory Memorandum, at p. 14, and Recital 29: "If the provider of an AI system has complied with all its obligations and, in consequence, that system was deemed sufficiently safe to be put on the market for a given use by non-professional users and it is then used for that task, a presumption of causality should not apply for the simple launch of the operation of such a system by such non-professional users. A non-professional user that buys an AI system and simply launches it according to its purpose, without interfering materially with the conditions of operations, should not be covered by the causality presumption laid down by this Directive. However, if a national court determines that a non-professional user materially interfered with the conditions of operation of an AI system or was required and able to determine the conditions of operation of the AI system and failed to do so, then the presumption of causality should apply, where all the other conditions are fulfilled. This could be the case, for example, when the non-professional user does not comply with the instructions of use or with other applicable duties of care when choosing the area of operation or when setting performance conditions of the AI system. This is without prejudice to the fact that the provider should determine the intended purpose of an AI system, including the specific context and conditions of use, and eliminate or minimise the risks of that system as appropriate at the time of the design and development, taking into account the knowledge and expertise of the intended user".

[142] Ibid., Article 4(7).

[143] Ibid., Recital 30.

technological development, the potential impact on the roll-out and uptake of AI-enabled products and services, and potential risks involving damage to significant legal rights (life, health and property) through the operation of AI-enabled products or services. As it was stated, "the proposal takes into account the differences between national legal traditions and the fact that the kind of products and services equipped with AI systems that could affect the public at large and put at risk important legal rights, such as the right to life, health and property, and therefore could be subject to a strict liability regime, are not yet widely available on the market".[144]

At the same time, however, the Commission decided to leave the door open for future legislative development, in order to assess whether additional measures would be needed, such as introducing a strict liability regime and/or mandatory insurance for the operation of certain AI systems, as suggested by the European Parliament's Resolution of 20 October 2020 on a civil liability regime for artificial intelligence (which supported a limited strict liability regime for high-risk AI systems and a facilitated/reversed burden of proof under fault-based liability rules for non-high risk AI systems). To this end, it was proposed that five years after the end of the transposition period,[145] the Commission must review the application of the AI Liability Directive and present a report to the European Parliament and to the Council of the EU, accompanied, if appropriate, by a specific legislative proposal.[146]

[144] Ibid., Explanatory Memorandum, at p. 14.

See also the Commission Staff Working Document, "Impact Assessment Report – Accompanying the document Proposal for a Directive of the European Parliament and of the Council on adapting non-contractual civil liability rules to artificial intelligence", SWD(2022) 319 final, Brussels, 28.9.2022, at p. 6: "As AI is only gradually being rolled-out, there are not yet many documented cases of harm as the relevant products/services are not yet on the market".

[145] Article 7(1) of the proposed AI Liability Directive sets a deadline of not later than two years after the entry into force of the AI Liability Directive for Member States to adopt the necessary transposition measures: "Member States shall bring into force the laws, regulations and administrative provisions necessary to comply with this Directive by [two years after the entry into force] at the latest". This is justified by the Commission "given the need to make adaptations to national civil liability and procedural rules to foster the rolling-out of AI-enabled products and services under beneficial internal market conditions, societal acceptance and consumer trust in AI technology and the justice system" (Recital 32).

See also the Explanatory Memorandum, at p. 14: "When notifying the Commission of national transposition measures to comply with this Directive, Member States should also provide explanatory documents which give sufficiently clear and precise information and state, for each provision of this Directive, the national provision(s) ensuring its transposition. This is necessary to enable the Commission to identify, for each provision of the Directive requiring transposition, the relevant part of national transposition measures creating the corresponding legal obligation in the national legal order, whatever the form chosen by the Member States".

[146] Proposed AI Liability Directive, Article 5(1).

See also Commission Staff Working Document, "AI Subsidiarity Grid – Accompanying the document Proposal for a Directive of the European Parliament and of the Council on adapting non contractual civil liability rules to artificial intelligence (AI Liability Directive)", SWD(2022) 318 final, Brussels, 28.9.2022, at p. 6: "The second stage included in the proposal ensures that future technological, regulatory and jurisprudential developments will be taken into account when

In its report the Commission will analyse the effectiveness of Articles 3 and 4 of the AI Liability Directive (i.e., whether they achieved the objectives pursued by the Directive). It will evaluate the appropriateness of those provisions and examine whether there is a need to create no-fault (strict) liability rules for claims against the operator, combined with a mandatory insurance for the operation of certain AI systems, taking also into account the effect and impact on the production and dissemination of AI-enabled products and services.[147] In order to ensure the availability of the information necessary to conduct such a review, it is vital to collect and analyse data and other evidence covering the relevant matters. To this end, a monitoring programme will be established to provide the Commission with information on incidents involving AI systems.[148]

---

re-assessing the need to harmonise other elements of the claims for compensation, including situations where no-fault liability would be more appropriate, as requested by the European Parliament. Such assessment would also likely consider whether such a harmonisation would need to be coupled with mandatory insurance to ensure effectiveness".

See also the Commission Staff Working Document, "Impact Assessment Report – Accompanying the document Proposal for a Directive of the European Parliament and of the Council on adapting non-contractual civil liability rules to artificial intelligence", SWD(2022) 319 final, Brussels, 28.9.2022, at p. 57: "The second stage, i.e. the targeted review mechanism, would systematically re-assess the need for the strict liability and mandatory insurance elements. [It] would ensure that the necessary information for this re-assessment is available. The review would assess if the technological and market developments as well as empirical evidence on AI liability cases confirm the need for such measures. This mechanism does not pre-empt the necessary future policy decision on the harmonisation of strict liability and mandatory insurance. But if there were a policy decision to that effect, the targeted review mechanism would have prepared the groundwork. . . . The second stage would also gain more certainty about the technological and regulatory context defining the risk-profile and conditions of deployment of the AI-enabled technologies with a potential strict liability profile. This would thus allow to specify the material and personal scope of a possible strict liability regime with greater precision. It would therefore be conducive to ensuring legal certainty and uniform implementation".

147 Proposed AI Liability Directive, Article 5(2).

Also, as it was stated, the following points could be included in the targeted review and re-assessment: "- the market developments regarding the rollout of products and services enabled by AI-systems with the characteristics that challenge existing (primarily fault-based) liability rules: a high degree of behavioural autonomy, opacity (complexity + lack of transparency), continuous adaptation and limited predictability; - the risk-profile and operating environment of the products and services, in particular whether they can cause harm to high-ranking legal interests of the public at large; - the incidence rate of accidents caused by AI systems, in particular those involving harm to high-ranking legal interests of unwitting third parties in the course of the operation of the relevant products or provision of the relevant services; - any AI-specific liability gaps regarding damage caused by the identified products and services, despite the alleviations of the burden of proof implemented under PO1". See Commission Staff Working Document, "Impact Assessment Report – Accompanying the document Proposal for a Directive of the European Parliament and of the Council on adapting non-contractual civil liability rules to artificial intelligence", SWD(2022) 319 final, Brussels, 28.9.2022, at p. 40.

148 Proposed AI Liability Directive, Article 5(3), and Explanatory Memorandum, at p. 10.

See also the Commission Staff Working Document, "Impact Assessment Report – Accompanying the document Proposal for a Directive of the European Parliament and of the Council on adapting non-contractual civil liability rules to artificial intelligence", SWD(2022) 319 final,

8.4.7 *Discussion and Stakeholders' Views*

The Commission's proposal should be welcomed, as it attempts to address the AI-specific problems by improving the rights of victims who have suffered any damage—as admissible under national law—due to wrongful use of artificial intelligence. As already stated, the proposed AI Liability Directive attempts to achieve the set objectives with a minimally invasive approach through a stated approach.

In particular, it follows a minimum harmonisation approach, based on a minimum intervention at EU level (i.e., it takes into account the different levels of regulatory intervention of Member States as regards the tort liability for damages caused by AI systems). It respects to the maximum extent possible Member States' well-established liability systems and introduces three main measures to alleviate the victims' burden to prove their liability claim. Indeed, it focuses on targeted proof-related measures, namely disclosure of information and alleviation of the burden of proof through rebuttable presumptions (as the least interventionist tool). Therefore, it does not introduce new grounds of liability and keeps the basic allocation of the burden of proof intact. It does not involve a general reversal of the burden of proof, but only targeted adjustments to counter-balance the specific challenges of AI. Furthermore, in the second stage, on the basis of a review clause, the proposed AI Liability Directive introduces a review mechanism to re-assess (five years later) the need for a higher level of regulatory intervention, i.e., the need for harmonising strict liability for high-risk AI use cases, possibly coupled with a mandatory insurance.

Brussels, 28.9.2022, at pp. 62–63 and p. 231 (Annex 12, 'Monitoring and evaluation'), where it is stressed that, in order to ensure that the targeted review mechanism can rely on a sufficient evidentiary basis, this monitoring mechanism could/should cover the following types of data and evidence: "- provide for reporting and information sharing by Member States regarding the application of the measures (under PO 1) in national judicial or out-of-court settlement procedures; - use information collected by the Commission or market surveillance authorities under the AI Act (in particular Article 62) or other relevant instruments; - use information and analyses supporting the evaluation of the AI Act and the reports to be prepared by the Commission on the implementation of that act; - take into account any information and analyses supporting the assessment of relevant future policy measures under the 'old approach' safety legislation; - rely on the information and analyses supporting the Commission's report on the application of the Motor Insurance Directive with regard to technological developments (in particular autonomous and semi-autonomous vehicles) pursuant to its Article 28c(2)(a) MID".

See also the Commission Staff Working Document, "Executive Summary of the Impact Assessment Report – Accompanying the document Proposal for a Directive of the European Parliament and of the Council on adapting non-contractual civil liability rules to artificial intelligence", SWD (2022) 320 final, Brussels, 28.9.2022, at p. 4, where it is stated that no significant impacts on national budgets and administrations are expected. "Member States will have to report on the implementation of the initiative and provide certain information for the Commission's targeted review. However, these reporting requirements will be limited to information available through Member States' existing databases and information reported under other legal instruments (e.g. the AI Act or the Motor Insurance Directive), which will achieve synergies and ensure the coherence of future policy measures across various policy areas".

8.4.7.1 Calls for Introducing a Strict Liability Regime for High-Risk AI Systems and Establishing a Fault-Based Liability Regime with a Reversal of the Burden of Proof for Fault and Causation for Other (Non-high Risk) AI Systems

(i) Civil society, consumer organisations and academic/research institutions

Representatives from NGOs, civil society and consumer associations, as well as various academic/research institutes, although they welcomed the proposed new EU liability rules, warned that there are major issues which are not adequately covered by the proposed AI Liability Directive.[149]

In particular, they criticised the Commission's proposal for placing the responsibility on consumers to prove that the fault lies with the operator. Taking into account how opaque and complex AI systems are, they argued that it will be extremely difficult or even impossible for consumers to use their right to compensation for damages. The burden on victims remains too high. As the European Consumer Organisation (BEUC) stated, "contrary to traditional product liability rules, if a consumer gets harmed by an AI service operator, they will need to prove the fault lies with the operator. Considering how opaque and complex AI systems are, these conditions will make it de facto impossible for consumers to use their right to compensation for damages".[150]

[149] The Future of Life Institute (FLI), "FLI Position Paper on AI Liability – FLI position on the proposal for a Directive on adapting non-contractual civil liability rules to artificial intelligence (AI Liability Directive)", November 2022, at p. 3: "FLI welcomes the adoption of the new proposal to update liability rules to the digital age. . . . The proposal for an AI liability Directive (AILD) applies to non-contractual fault-based civil law claims for damages caused by AI systems. It lays down rules that ease the burden of proof in relation to two aspects: disclosures of evidence and rebuttable presumptions of causality. In particular, the AILD enables courts to order the disclosure of relevant evidence about specific high-risk AI systems suspected of having caused damage. In case of non-compliance with such an order, the AILD introduces a rebuttable presumption of non-compliance with a duty of care. Secondly, the AILD alleviates the burden for claimants to establish a causal link between non-compliance with a duty of care and the damage caused by introducing rebuttable presumptions of causality under very limited and complex conditions. These rules are a welcome attempt to address AI liability at the EU level. Their enactment has the potential to close some liability gaps of the product liability proposal (PLD), such as offering protection to both natural and legal persons harmed by AI systems and allowing for a broad scope of damages to be covered. However, as long as the AILD fails to provide for more legal clarity and the same level of protection across the EU, it will be insufficient to safeguard victims of AI systems".

[150] European Consumer Organisation (BEUC), Press Release, "EU liability rules to be modernised but contain AI services blind spot for consumers", 28.09.2022. Also, according to Ursula Pachl, Deputy Director General of the European Consumer Organisation (BEUC): "It is essential that liability rules catch up with the fact we are increasingly surrounded by digital and AI-driven products and services like home assistants or insurance policies based on personalised pricing. However, consumers are going to be less well protected when it comes to AI services, because they will have to prove the operator was at fault or negligent in order to claim compensation for damages. Asking consumers to do this is a real let down. In a world of highly complex and obscure 'black box' AI systems, it will be practically impossible for the consumer to use the new rules. As a result,

Also, according to Mozilla, the Commission's measures to alleviate the burden of proof on harmed people (i.e., enabling them to request evidence from providers or users if they can plausibly argue that a high-risk AI system may have caused harm and foreseeing a 'rebuttable presumption of causality') are positive measures towards the right direction. However, despite this approach, the path towards effective redress for individuals who have been harmed is still filled with major obstacles and is often lengthy.[151] An example used by Mozilla illustrates the time and resources that would likely be required for a case brought under the proposed AI Liability Directive, and the slim chances of success in demonstrating non-compliance with the requirements of the AI Act. This example refers to the case of a female job applicant whose application is rejected by an AI-powered resume-screening tool (which would be considered high-risk under the AI Act) used by the prospective employer due to biased data and discrimination against women. The applicant would have to go through a lengthy and costly series of steps to seek compensation for this violation of his right to non-discrimination. The process outlined by the proposed AI Liability Directive does not appear to provide genuine access to redress. On the contrary, as it stands, the current draft of the AI Liability Directive lacks the potential and falls short of being a powerful tool and robust mechanism for redress and justice.[152]

---

consumers will be better protected if a lawnmower shreds their shoes in the garden than if they are unfairly discriminated against through a credit scoring system".

[151] Mozilla's comments on the Commission proposal for an AI Liability Directive (AILD) – The long road to redress, November 2022, at p. 6: "the co-legislators should pay close attention to what the process of seeking remedy would actually look like to victims and design a process that works for all parties involved. Presenting victims with a bar that realistically will be too high to meet in most cases cannot be the desired outcome".

[152] Ibid., at pp. 2–3: "Given the process envisioned by the AILD, it appears unlikely that the directive will provide people with genuine access to redress. Take, as an example, the case of a female job applicant whose application is discarded by an AI-enabled resume-screening tool (which would be considered high-risk under the AI Act) used by the prospective employer because the tool has been trained on biased data and consequently discriminates against women. The rejected applicant now has to succeed in taking a long and cost-intensive series of steps in order to be compensated for this violation of her right to non-discrimination. First, even if the applicant suspected that she might have been discriminated against, it is not a given that she would even be aware of the fact that this was due to a biased AI system. Yet knowing that one was adversely affected by an AI system is a precondition for seeking redress under the AILD—and even with the transparency provisions foreseen under the AI Act, the fact that an AI system was used in the recruitment process may not be disclosed to her if it is used on the backend. Second, the rejected applicant would need to be aware of the possibility to seek redress under the AILD. Third, she would need to identify the actor against whom she wants to take action. But even this is not straightforward, given the complexity of the AI supply chain, in which different actors (most notably providers and users) will need to comply with different obligations. Determining where along the supply chain a harm originated at this stage—and who is legally liable—will be close to impossible. Fourth, the applicant will then need to request evidence and documentation from the prospective defendant, and they would need to know what evidence to request in the first place to support their case. However, given a lack of consequences for refusing such requests on the side of defendants, such requests can largely be expected to be futile. Fifth, this therefore means that the

This is why consumer, civil society, and other non-profit organisations as well as various academic/research institutes recommended the introduction of a strict liability regime applicable to users/operators of high-risk AI systems/applications (as well as for general purpose AI systems).[153] Furthermore, civil society and consumer associations as well as various academic/research institutes proposed that all other AI systems (i.e., non-high risk AI systems) should fall under a fault-based liability regime where the presumption of fault lies on the operator (i.e., they supported a complete reversal of the burden of proof for non-high risk AI systems). In other words, in relation to the non-high risk AI systems, they called for a rebuttable presumption of fault of the operator, in addition to a rebuttable presumption of a causal link between the damage and the fault (reversal of the burden of proof for fault and causation for non-high risk AI systems).[154]

---

rejected applicant will need to request a court to order the defendant to disclose all relevant information (and identify where to file such a request), but only after making a convincing case that the AI system in question can, in fact, be causally linked to the harm caused to the applicant. Sixth, only now can the applicant (together with her lawyer) assess the evidence and information she received for potential fault. However, the information in question, to be documented by defendants in accordance with the AI Act, was never meant to be inspected by people harmed by an AI system or their legal counsel. Instead, it is meant for notified bodies and regulators with specific expertise to assess an AI system's conformity with the AI Act, for example, compliance with regard to risk management, data governance, or accuracy and robustness requirements. In consequence, under the proposed AILD it would be extremely unlikely for a claimant to successfully demonstrate fault on the part of a provider or user, at least not without external expertise at presumably significant cost. In short, this example demonstrates how much time and resources a case brought under the AILD would be likely to take, and how slim the odds of success would be given the difficulty of showing non-conformity with the AI Act's requirements. It is further important to note that the above would be a rather straightforward example. The journey might be even more complex and difficult where it's unclear whether an AI system is considered high-risk under the AI Act or not. The European institutions should therefore explore ways of reducing the burden for claimants to demonstrate fault. At minimum, this should include, for example, broader public disclosure of information from providers and users to facilitate easier access to evidence for claimants as well as exploring mechanisms for sharing or shifting the costs of consulting relevant experts from claimants to defendants. If necessary, they should also consider shifting the burden of proof to defendants where claimants' cases are determined to be plausible and sufficiently substantiated given the information available to them".

[153] Amongst NGOs, academic/research institutions, and consumer organisations there was clear support for either full or minimum harmonization of strict liability for operating AI-enabled products and providing AI-enabled services, where these activities create serious injury risks (e.g. life, health, property) for the public. See, for instance, Commission, DG GROW and DG JUST, "Factual summary report of the open public consultation on Adapting Civil Liability Rules to the Digital Age and AI", Ref. Ares(2022)2620305, 06.04.2022, p. 10.

[154] It should be stressed that the Irish Council for Civil Liberties (ICCL) argued that a strict liability regime should apply for all (and not just for high-risk) AI systems across the EU: "The AILD relies on a fault-based liability regime, where the victim must prove that the harm from the AI system was caused by the fault of the defendant. In contrast, in a strict liability regime, the victim does not have to show causation. The victim only shows that the AI systems harmed them and the defendant is held liable regardless of the intent and fault. ... Victims will often not know if the damage they suffered involved an AI system. Even if they do, AI systems are complex and difficult to understand. This Directive provides no mechanism to correct this. The EU AI database5 set up

As it was stated by the Ada Lovelace Institute, the AI Liability Directive "should introduce a strict liability regime for high-risk AI systems, and a complete reversal of the burden of proof for other AI systems. This would clarify the scope and application by offering more legal certainty. It would also be much more practically navigable for harmed persons, as they would not have to prove fault and causation, which we underline would not be realistic for most people in regards to AI systems. Further, it would ensure harmed people have equal protection across the EU".[155] Similarly, the Future of Life Institute recommended "a strict liability regime for high-risk AI systems as defined by the AI Act, as well as for General Purpose AI Systems. Strict liability has been the solution for comparable risk situations in the past and accounts for the knowledge gap between the operator of a system and courts. In line with the thinking of the Expert Group on Liability and New Technologies and the European Parliament, strict liability appears to be the appropriate approach for dealing with risks stemming from high-risk and General Purpose AI Systems".[156]

---

under the AI Act does not aid here: it is limited to high-risk AI systems and it does not register users of AI systems. . . . Both users and providers of non-high-risk AI systems are hard to identify because the EU AI database is limited to high-risk AI systems. . . . The operators of non-high-risk AI systems may not even have created basic documentation for their AI systems. They are not required to fulfil the requirements in Title III Chapter 2 of the AI Act that applies to high-risk AI systems. Without access to such documentation, it will be nearly impossible for victims to prove causal link between the harm and the defendant. For such AI systems, it is even more necessary to apply strict liability". See the Irish Council for Civil Liberties (ICCL), Submission to the consultation on AI Liability, 28 November 2022, at pp. 1–3.

[155] The Ada Lovelace Institute, "Feedback to the European Commission on its proposal for a Directive on adapting non-contractual civil liability rules to artificial intelligence", November 2022, at p. 3.

[156] The Future of Life Institute (FLI), "FLI Position Paper on AI Liability – FLI position on the proposal for a Directive on adapting non-contractual civil liability rules to artificial intelligence (AI Liability Directive)", November 2022, at p. 4. See also at pp. 4–5: "Fault-based liability applies in scenarios when a duty of care is breached. For cases related to AI, the necessary level of care and acceptable level of risk may be difficult to determine in view of its capabilities and rapidly evolving nature. Both levels are ultimately determined by the judiciary, which is likely to have less technological and risk knowledge than developers and manufacturers, ultimately leading to a lack of legal certainty. Fault-based liability can be ineffective when risks are not well-understood based on the state of the scientific and technical knowledge. For instance, while a General Purpose AI System used as a chatbot in a healthcare context has great potential benefits in increasing access to relevant health information, it could equally become a source for potential damage by encouraging self-harm. In such cases, courts may lack the scientific and technical knowledge to establish the appropriate level of care, or to judge whether the damage was caused due to a negligent action or omission. As opposed to fault-based liability, a strict liability regime can be an instrument of technology risk control under uncertainty because there is no need for in-depth knowledge on the optimal level of care. This incentivises further development of technologies to make them safer and may increase acceptance by the public (at p. 4). . . . A strict liability regime should equally apply to General Purpose AI Systems given their emerging capabilities, surprising and unexpected outputs, instrumental autonomous goal development and low level of interpretability. Furthermore, their frequent use at the source of the value chain often leads to significant downstream risks if liability regimes do not create the right incentives for developers" (at p. 5).

With regard to non-high risk AI systems, the Future of Life Institute called for a rebuttable presumption of fault of the operator, in addition to a rebuttable presumption of a causal link between the damage and the fault. In particular, it repeated the Commission's acknowledgment that specific characteristics of AI could make it difficult and prohibitively expensive for injured parties to identify and prove the fault of a potentially liable entity (i.e., uncertainty as regards the allocation of responsibilities) as well as the causal link between that fault and the damage suffered. It stressed that tracing the victim's loss back to the defendant may be challenging, and the way the AI action is performed cannot be understood, mainly due to the opacity of certain forms of AI, since harmed individuals "are subject to significant information asymmetry with respect to the AI systems they interact with because they may not know which code or input caused a harm".[157] It also underlined that AI systems display certain levels of complexity due to the interdependency between different components. Combining different digital components in a complex ecosystem and the plurality of actors involved, in addition to the increasing autonomy of AI systems, can make it more complicated for victims to identify the liable person and thus prove fault. As a result, the Future of Life Institute stated that a fault-based liability regime with a reversed burden of proof for AI systems other than high-risk and General Purpose AI Systems is "a reasonable and balanced approach",[158] and recommended that "AI systems other than high-risk and General Purpose AI Systems fall under a fault-based liability regime where the presumption of fault lies on the operator. Pursuing this course of action would ease the burden for claimants and facilitate their access to justice by minimizing their information asymmetry and transaction costs. Operators can rebut this presumption of fault by proving their observance to the required level of care, and that the damage caused was not their fault".[159]

Therefore, according to the arguments received by consumer protection and civil liberties groups on the proposed AI Liability Directive during the public consultation process, it is proportionate to impose an EU strict liability regime on high-risk AI systems (especially since they are singled out in the proposed AI Act), while maintaining a regime of rebuttable presumptions for other (non-high risk) AI systems.

Besides, it is reminded that, in the recent past (2021), the Commission presented as a "possible policy option at EU level" the extension of harmonisation of strict liability based on a 'risk-based' approach, i.e. taking into consideration whether the AI-systems have a specific risk profile (such as those endangering the lives, health and property of members of the public). This option looks to harmonise the existing

[157] Ibid., at p. 6.

[158] Ibid.: "Following the risk-based approach of the AI Act, it seems sensible to have less stringent requirements for these AI systems as compared to high-risk and General Purpose AI Systems, which should be subject to a strict liability regime. This is also in line with the tradition to reserve strict liability for particularly dangerous activities or things".

[159] Ibid.

national strict liability schemes of operators/users that apply to AI-equipped products and providers of AI-based services (where injured parties only have to prove that the damage emanates from the sphere of the operator of the AI-system). This would be similar to what exists in almost all Member States' legal systems as regards motor vehicle liability, namely strict liability of the producer for defects under the Product Liability Directive as well as strict liability of the owner/operator. Accordingly, back in 2021 the Commission appeared willing to develop a separate and complementary (to the Product Liability Directive) instrument (the AI Liability Directive) on strict civil liability (for the owner/user/operator) for AI based on the risk profile of AI systems, i.e., depending on whether the AI system causing the harm has been classified as low or high risk. In other words, the Commission was considering reserving strict liability for AI systems presenting high risks, i.e., it was considering limiting strict liability to some specifically defined AI systems (possibly to the "high risk" AI systems defined as such under the proposed AI Act). Such an option is in line with the principle of proportionality, as products and services should not be subject to increased liability rules simply because they integrate AI (i.e., irrespective of whether the product or service presents a unique and severe risk of harm, or whether the AI component is a contributing factor to that risk). As the Commission put it, "strict liability means that a certain risk of damage is assigned to a person irrespective of fault. A possible policy option at EU level could be to harmonise strict liability (full or minimum), separately from the Product Liability Directive, for damage caused by the operation of certain AI-enabled products or the provision of certain AI-enabled services. This could notably be considered in cases where the use of AI (e.g. in autonomous vehicles and autonomous drones) exposes the public to the risk of damage to important values like life, health and property. Where strict liability rules already exist in a Member State, e.g. for cars, the EU harmonisation would not lead to an additional strict liability regime".[160]

This option (i.e., harmonisation of strict liability for high-risk AI-enabled products and services) would be also in line with the Report from the Expert Group on Liability and New Technologies, which stated that "emerging digital technologies make it difficult to apply fault-based liability rules, due to the lack of well-established models of proper functioning of these technologies and the possibility of their developing as a result of learning without direct human control".[161] Accordingly, the Report underlined that strict liability of the operator of some emerging digital technology may be justified: "a person operating a permissible technology that nevertheless carries an increased risk of harm to others, for example AI-driven

[160] Commission's Inception Impact Assessment "Adapting liability rules to the digital age and circular economy", Ref. Ares(2021)4266516, 30.06.2021, p. 4.

See also Commission's Public Consultation, "Adapting liability rules to the digital age and Artificial Intelligence", 18 October 2021, p. 36.

[161] Report from the Expert Group on Liability and New Technologies – New Technologies Formation "Liability for Artificial Intelligence and Other Emerging Digital Technologies", 21 November 2019, at p. 23.

robots in public spaces, should be subject to strict liability for damage resulting from its operation"; "strict liability is an appropriate response to the risks posed by emerging digital technologies, if, for example, they are operated in non-private environments and may typically cause significant harm".[162]

This is why, in 2020, based on the analysis of the Report from the Expert Group on Liability and New Technologies, the Commission stated that the application of strict liability should be limited to situations where the emerging technologies may create specific risks (which are likely to arise in circumstances where digital technologies move in public spaces, e.g., drones, autonomous cars, traffic management services), expose the public at large to risks, and cause significant harm to life, health, and property: "the operation of some autonomous AI devices and services could have a specific risk profile in terms of liability, because they may cause significant harm to important legal interests like life, health and property, and expose the public at large to risks. This could mainly concern AI devices that move in public spaces (e.g. fully autonomous vehicles, drones and package delivery robots) or AI-based services with similar risks (e.g. traffic management services guiding or controlling vehicles or management of power distribution). The challenges of autonomy and opacity to national tort laws could be addressed following a risk-based approach. Strict liability schemes could ensure that whenever that risk materialises, the victim is compensated regardless of fault. The impact of choosing who should be strictly liable for such operations on the development and uptake of AI would need to be carefully assessed and a risk-based approach be considered".[163]

It is also recalled that this option follows the recommendation put forward by the European Parliament's Resolution of 20 October 2020 on a civil liability regime for AI,[164] which stated that an AI-system that entails an inherent high risk and acts autonomously potentially endangers the user or the general public to a much higher degree and in a manner that is random and goes beyond what can reasonably be expected.[165] Therefore, different liability rules should apply for different risks, following a risk-based approach.[166] As a result, the Parliament stated that "the victims of harm or damage caused by AI-systems need to have a right to redress

[162] Ibid., at pp. 3, 39 and 40.

[163] Commission Communication "Report on the safety and liability implications of Artificial Intelligence, the Internet of Things and robotics", COM (2020) 64 final, Brussels, 19.2.2020, p. 16.

[164] European Parliament Resolution of 20 October 2020 with recommendations to the Commission on a civil liability regime for artificial intelligence (2020/2014(INL)) P9_TA(2020)0276 (European Parliament's Resolution of 20 October 2020 on a civil liability regime for AI). Also: Annex to the Resolution: detailed recommendations for drawing up a Regulation on liability for the operation of artificial intelligence-systems, A. Principles and Aims of the Proposal. B. Text of the Proposal Requested—Proposal for a Regulation on liability for the operation of Artificial Intelligence-systems (Annex to the European Parliament's Resolution of 20 October 2020 on a civil liability regime for AI – Text of the Proposal for a Regulation on liability for the operation of AI systems).

[165] European Parliament's Resolution of 20 October 2020 on a civil liability regime for AI, section "Liability of the operator", at points 14 and 15.

[166] Ibid., section "Liability of the operator", at point 14.

and to full compensation for the harm or damage that they have suffered"[167] and that "it seems reasonable to set up a common strict liability regime for those high-risk autonomous AI-systems".[168] So, the European Parliament's Resolution of 20 October 2020 on a civil liability regime for AI stressed that a strict liability regime for high-risk AI systems should apply, i.e. the operator of a high-risk AI-system should be strictly liable for any harm or damage that was caused by a physical or virtual activity, device or process driven by that AI-system.[169]

(ii) Business stakeholders on strict liability and alleviation of the burden of proof (evidence disclosure requirements, presumption of non-compliance and presumption of causality)

(a) Feedback on strict liability:

It is recalled that business stakeholders disagreed with the harmonisation of strict liability for AI systems.[170] They also argued that, if the co-legislators opt to proceed with the harmonisation of strict liability, this harmonisation should be limited to a few high-risk cases.[171]

For instance, as it was stated by BSA—The Software Alliance, "the consultation identifies a range of situations involving AI systems in which it might be appropriate to impose liability regardless of the producer's fault or whether a product is defective—e.g., products that continuously learn and adapt, malfunctioning products, or scenarios where the producer failed to comply with its obligations under the AI Act. This sort of strict liability, however, is generally reserved only for circumstances involving dangerous activities that pose substantial risks to third parties having no contractual relationship to the supplier (e.g., pedestrians harmed by autonomous driving). In effect, the "condition" of allowing the substantial risk is that the party carrying out activities that may lead to substantial risks to others takes responsibility for harms that result from it, irrespective of any fault or product defect.

---

[167] Annex to the European Parliament's Resolution of 20 October 2020 on a civil liability regime for AI – B. Text of the Proposal for a Regulation on liability for the operation of AI systems, at recital 5.

[168] European Parliament's Resolution of 20 October 2020 on a civil liability regime for AI, section "Liability of the operator", at point 14.

[169] Annex to the European Parliament's Resolution of 20 October 2020 on a civil liability regime for AI – B. Text of the Proposal for a Regulation on liability for the operation of AI systems, Article 4(1).

See also the Report of the Expert Group on Liability and New Technologies which stated that "strict liability should lie with the person who is in control of the risk connected with the operation of emerging digital technologies and who benefits from their operation (operator)". Report from the Expert Group on Liability and New Technologies – New Technologies Formation "Liability for Artificial Intelligence and Other Emerging Digital Technologies", 21 November 2019, Key Finding [10], at pp. 6, 39, 41.

[170] Commission, DG GROW and DG JUST, "Factual summary report of the open public consultation on Adapting Civil Liability Rules to the Digital Age and AI", Ref. Ares(2022)2620305, 06.04.2022, p. 10.

[171] Ibid.

Strict liability should only be imposed on AI-enabled products in similarly narrow circumstances. Given the burgeoning state of AI development and deployment in the EU, subjecting all AI systems that, for example, continuously learn and adapt, is unwarranted. If the Commission chooses to proceed, it might, for example, limit the application of strict liability to those high-risk AI systems that pose inherent and unavoidable risks to the public (e.g., AI systems used in critical infrastructure)".[172]

It should be stressed that some business stakeholders, such as MedTech Europe, questioned the need to create a separate Directive regulating key aspects of civil liability involving AI systems ("regulating fault-based civil liability cases involving AI in a separate piece of legislation can create confusion") and stated that "the provisions of this Directive could have been included in either the AI Act or in the Product Liability Directive to avoid potential inconsistencies, confusion, and repeating discussions".[173]

(b) General feedback on specific provisions of the proposed AI Liability Directive:

With regard to specific provisions (mainly Article 3 and 4) of the proposed AI Liability Directive, the vast majority of business stakeholders did not agree with the view that the existing framework places consumers at a disadvantage, and they

[172] BSA – The Software Alliance, "Response to the European Commission's consultation on civil liability – adapting liability rules to the digital age and artificial intelligence", 10.01.2022, p. 5: "Apply "strict liability" only to the highest risk AI: The consultation identifies a range of situations involving AI systems in which it might be appropriate to impose liability regardless of the producer's fault or whether a product is defective—e.g., products that continuously learn and adapt, malfunctioning products, or scenarios where the producer failed to comply with its obligations under the AI Act. This sort of strict liability, however, is generally reserved only for circumstances involving dangerous activities that pose substantial risks to third parties having no contractual relationship to the supplier (e.g., pedestrians harmed by autonomous driving). In effect, the "condition" of allowing the substantial risk is that the party carrying out activities that may lead to substantial risks to others takes responsibility for harms that result from it, irrespective of any fault or product defect. Strict liability should only be imposed on AI-enabled products in similarly narrow circumstances. Given the burgeoning state of AI development and deployment in the EU, subjecting all AI systems that, for example, continuously learn and adapt, is unwarranted. If the Commission chooses to proceed, it might, for example, limit the application of strict liability to those high-risk AI systems that pose inherent and unavoidable risks to the public (e.g., AI systems used in critical infrastructure). The need to consider which AI systems (if any) are sufficiently high-risk to merit strict liability is yet another reason to delay legislating for liability until the AI Act has been adopted and enters into force".

See also the Confederation of European Security Services (CoESS) ("Confederation of European Security Services (CoESS) - Position Paper on the European Commission Consultation on adapting liability rules to the digital age and AI", 20 December 2021, pp. 1–2): "Strict liability rules for AI should be reserved for a limited number of AI-enabled products and services which impose a high material risk (e.g. life, health, property) for the public, following a risk-based and use-case focused approach. All AI-systems with a high-risk, including their use-cases, should be exhaustively listed in an Annex of the liability regime. Systems that are not listed in the Annex should remain subject to fault-based liability. Due to the rapid technological developments in AI, such a list should be able to be amended by means of Delegated Acts".

[173] MedTech Europe, Feedback to the European Commission's proposal for a Directive on Liability rules for Artificial Intelligence, 24 November 2022, at p. 1.

expressed concerns that the Commission's proposal could hinder innovation and create instability for AI-based technology investment. As the U.S. Chamber of Commerce put it, "if adopted in its current form, the Proposal risks hindering the potential of AI as a powerful force for good. Indeed, it risks creating material – and unjustified – imbalances between the rights of claimants and defendants, tilting the playing field in the claimant's favour by introducing far-reaching evidence disclosure requirements and applying a set of ambiguous claimant-friendly presumptions. . . . As such, the impact of the Proposal could be material and may cause a substantial chilling effect on AI innovation in Europe, which would go squarely against the European AI Strategy and the Commission's goal to 'reap the economic and societal benefits of AI and promote the transition to the digital economy'".[174] Furthermore, the App Association argued that obliging AI developers to disclose confidential information and alleviating the burden of proof on consumers will hurt business and lead to extensive de facto liability claims and unnecessarily increased business and insurance costs (inviting frivolous legal action and causing disproportionate harm for small businesses that do not possess the resources to defend themselves, through prolonged court proceedings).[175] As a result, it urged the Commission "to reconsider

[174] U.S. Chamber of Commerce Institute of Legal Reform, Comments on the Proposed AI Liability Directive, November 2022, p. 1, points 4 and 6.

See also: eco – Association of the Internet Industry, Position Paper on the Commission's proposal for an AI Liability Directive, 28.11.2022, at pp. 5–6: "The reversal of the burden of proof provided for in the draft in Articles 3 and 4 is not purposeful in our view. For businesses, this could lead to more bureaucracy and unfounded claims for damages. In order to realise the aim of the Directive and to create legal certainty for providers and users of AI products throughout Europe, it is also important to define relevant terms in a uniform manner and not to leave them to national legal systems. This would lead to fragmentation of implementation and hinder the development of the Internal Market".

[175] ACT - The App Association, feedback to the proposed Artificial Intelligence Liability Directive, 28 November 2022, at p. 4: "Concerning the burden of proof, the App Association does not believe that the current framework places consumers at a disadvantage. Extending strict liability and alleviating the burden of proof on consumers, as the AILD proposes, will only hurt businesses and lead to extensive de facto liability claims and unnecessarily increased business and insurance costs. We, thus, oppose alleviating the claimant's burden of proof. Introducing a rebuttable presumption of causality where, for example, certain obligations have not been met under national or EU laws could invite frivolous legal action and cause disproportionate harm for small businesses that don't have the resources to defend themselves, even if they are fully in the right, through prolonged court proceedings. Making blanket assertions about AI liability is not appropriate given that each case of alleged defectiveness will be heavily fact dependent. As a result, SMEs would be increasingly prevented from developing new products to meet emerging market demands across consumer and enterprise use cases. . . . We strongly oppose the proposed requirements that would have AI developers disclose confidential information (including trade secrets and other intellectual property) in response to court orders and allegations of defectiveness, particularly if not disclosing such information would lead to an easing of the burden of proof for the claimant, as the AILD proposes. Blanket policies on such matters are inappropriate and liability frameworks should always allow for the protection of confidential information, subject to fact-specific determinations by relevant courts. The Commission's policy and law concerning AI liability must reflect that each allegation of defectiveness will be very fact-dependent, and this system should interoperate with other portions of EU law (e.g. intellectual property protections)".

the provisions of the AILD that would have AI developers disclose confidential information (Art.3), and that would lead to extensive liability claims and increased insurance costs (Art. 4), disproportionately harming small businesses".[176] Similarly, the European Organisation for Security (EOS) stated that the mandatory disclosure of information and the presumption of causality will discourage investments and hinder innovation,[177] whereas the alleviation of the burden of proof would lead to "misleading or abusive litigation".[178]

(c) Feedback on Article 3 of the proposed AI Liability Directive: Evidence disclosure requirements and presumption of non-compliance:

MedTech Europe argued that obliging AI developers to disclose confidential information will hinder innovation because the evidence disclosure requirements are 'excessive' and 'one sided' ("the current proposal lacks proper and clear limits to the type and scope of information that a defendant will be required to disclose"). Accordingly, it stressed that "considering the innovative nature of AI systems, it is critical to ensure that IP and trade secrets are more clearly protected from overreaching evidence disclosure requests".[179] Also, it pointed out that the Commission's proposal leads to a de-facto reversal of the burden of proof which could deter innovation by increasing the costs of launching AI systems due to extensive liability claims ("a constant threat of unnecessary litigation").[180]

Upwork is concerned that the proposed framework for disclosure is "too vague and open-ended" and that the evidence disclosure requirement, as it is drafted, would impose unreasonably high compliance burdens on providers and users of AI systems.[181] For instance, it argued that opening up the inner workings of an online platform would not only threaten the operation of the business, but would also lead to unfair or even illegal behaviour.[182] Also, it stated that the proposal's disclosure

---

[176] Ibid., at p. 5.

[177] European Organisation for Security (EOS), Feedback to the proposed Artificial Intelligence Liability Directive, November 2022, at p. 1: "EOS warns that the mandatory disclosure of information relative to high-risk AI systems threatens the security of information. Systems classified as 'high-risk' by the AIA include those used for law enforcement, management and operation of critical infrastructure, and management of migration, asylum, and border control, which may involve sensitive information. Failure of disclosure should therefore not imply the presumption of non-compliance with a duty of care but rather reflect the confidential nature of information linked to certain high-risk applications that providers may not be able to share".

[178] Ibid.

[179] MedTech Europe, Feedback to the European Commission's proposal for a Directive on Liability rules for Artificial Intelligence, 24 November 2022, at p. 2.

[180] Ibid., at pp. 1–2.

[181] Upwork, Feedback on the Proposal for a Directive on adapting non-contractual civil liability rules to artificial intelligence, 28 November 2022, at pp. 2 and 4.

[182] ibid., at p. 3: "For example, on an individual level, some parties may use the proposal's disclosure requirements to obtain detailed information about Upwork's search function that allows them to seek an unfair advantage over other users. On a more macro level, the machine learning techniques that platforms like ours use to help detect patterns of illegal or illegitimate behavior such

requirements would lead to an increase of frivolous legal action and could potentially encourage claimants to file a lawsuit simply for the purpose of seeking access to information ('fishing expeditions').[183]

This position was also supported by the U.S. Chamber of Commerce, which stated that "there is certainly a question to be considered relating to the circumstances in which a potentially liable party has not taken reasonable steps to log the data relevant for assessing liability or is unwilling to share it with an alleged victim when required to do so in a legal proceeding. ... A potentially liable party may simply not have access to the data it requires to rightfully absolve itself of liability. In that sense, difficulties in sharing data could be due to a lack of information altogether, or the disproportionately high cost or complexity of doing so, as opposed to an information imbalance caused by a reluctance to share. ... In setting aside well-established procedural guarantees, the Proposal will frustrate efforts to foster innovation. The increased threat of frivolous, excessive, and expensive litigation will ultimately hinder economic growth and reduce consumer choice. The proposed changes will be particularly burdensome for SMEs and start-ups, who may lack the capacity to prove that they had no responsibility for harm caused and who also may be least able to afford litigation costs".[184] This is why the U.S. Chamber of Commerce suggested that the requirement to disclose evidence, if implemented, should be accompanied by a reciprocal obligation on claimants to disclose any relevant evidence that could support the defense. For instance, it may be extremely difficult for a defendant to substantiate an alternative explanation for an alleged harm without access to all relevant details pertaining to that harm.[185]

Furthermore, Upwork pointed out that the risks associated with obtaining disclosure could be intensified by the fact that the threshold outlined in Article 3 of the proposed AI Liability Directive is set very low. It is reminded that, according to Article 3(1), a "potential claimant" only needs to provide evidence that is "plausible" in order to support a claim for damages. However, the term "plausibility" is not clearly defined, which raises concerns about potential broad interpretations by national courts. As a result, relying solely on a "plausibility" threshold may not

as international fraud rings, attempts at evading UN and other sanctions regimes, or money laundering, would be compromised by over-disclosure, allowing bad actors to evade detection. A requirement for platforms such as Upwork to disclose the inner workings of anti-fraud algorithms would effectively hand criminals a roadmap for evading detection".

[183] Ibid.: "At the same time, the disclosure obligation would also lead to an increase in frivolous claims being lodged. In addition to simply increasing the caseload of national courts dealing with such claims, there is a meaningful risk that claimants and "potential claimants" would be encouraged to bring early-stage cases for the sole purposes of seeking access to information ('fishing expeditions'). It is worth noting here that claimants could include actual and potential competitors of the defendant seeking access to information for anti-competitive purposes. This effect would run counter to the objectives of the proposal".

[184] U.S. Chamber of Commerce Institute of Legal Reform, Comments on the Proposed AI Liability Directive, November 2022, p. 4, points 21 and 22.

[185] Ibid., p. 5, point 24.

effectively guard against frivolous claims or those brought with the ulterior motive of gaining access to proprietary information.[186]

Also, it is stressed that having access to information about an AI system can be highly valuable to various stakeholders across different jurisdictions. If a national court in one Member State orders disclosure, it could set a precedent that could be relied upon by multiple claimants alleging similar harm. This could potentially result in an increased number of disclosure requests, possibly through representative actions as outlined in Article 2(6)(c) of the proposed AI Liability Directive. As a result, there is a risk that courts in some Member States may interpret the disclosure

[186] Upwork, Feedback on the Proposal for a Directive on adapting non-contractual civil liability rules to artificial intelligence, 28 November 2022, at p. 3.

See also the feedback provided by Siemens (Siemens, First assessment and recommendations – EU's AI Liability Directive proposal, 28 November 2022, at p. 2): "We support limiting the obligation to disclose only to minimum and proportionate evidence, however only as a last resort measure and with severe limitations to this rule and legal consequences of breaching proportionality. Otherwise, this obligation may heavily hinder uptake of AI in EU, since the proposal does not offer sufficient safeguards to intellectual property, trade secrets and confidential or personal information (e.g. no definition/restriction/limitation of what is "proportionate and limited to what is necessary to support a claim"). For instance, trained AI models currently enjoy limited intellectual property protection other than as a trade secret. Judicial safeguards applied in court proceedings are insufficient to protect this highly sensitive know-how of the market participants in Europe. The disclosure obligation should not apply here. • The respondent should not be obliged to disclose information belonging to third parties, including personal information. • To avoid abusive claims and "fishing expeditions" regarding the know-how of AI providers, there should be a threshold requirement for the plaintiff to fulfil before it can bring the disclosure request".

For an opposite view, see the argument put forward by academic/research institutions as well as civil society and consumer organisations. Specifically with regard to Article 3(2) of the proposed AI Liability Directive, national courts can only order the disclosure of relevant evidence only if the claimant "has undertaken all proportionate attempts" to obtain the evidence from the defendant. Accordingly, it was argued that there is a significant lack of legal clarity (and major barriers that claimants need to overcome) regarding the circumstances in which the national courts can order the disclosure of evidence. See, for instance:

The Ada Lovelace Institute, "Feedback to the European Commission on its proposal for a Directive on adapting non-contractual civil liability rules to artificial intelligence", November 2022, at pp. 1–2: "Article 3 is supposed to support affected people in pursuing their claims by allowing potential claimants to ask national courts to order disclosure, thus enabling them to see if they should file a lawsuit, which is not necessarily affordable to all. The hurdles the claimant would have to overcome just to get this evidence is prohibitive, however. Firstly, the claimant would have to know they were harmed by an AI system in the first place, which is not always clear. . . . Secondly, they would have to know which company is possibly liable, and then make all 'proportionate' attempts at gathering evidence from the defendant. Only after this, could they ask the court to order disclosure. The court's interpretation of the word 'proportionate' will therefore determine how feasible it will be for individuals to actually bring a claim, as evidence at the pre-trial stage is essential in building a case, or even figuring out against whom to bring the case, especially given the complexity of the AI value chain. These are hugely challenging hurdles to be placed on an affected person".

The Irish Council for Civil Liberties (ICCL), Submission to the consultation on AI Liability, 28 November 2022, at p. 2: "The victim has no opportunity to make 'proportionate attempts' to gather evidence because it is disproportionately difficult for them to even identify which providers and users of AI systems have caused harm".

obligation broadly, and claimants may exploit this by choosing to file claims primarily in jurisdictions perceived as 'more lenient' or 'sympathetic' towards document disclosure requests.[187]

Moreover, in the event that the disclosure obligation of Article 3 is maintained in the final text of the Directive, it is recognised that the proposed safeguards in the second and third subparagraphs of Article 3(4) of the proposed AI Liability Directive play a critical role. Indeed, it is crucial that national courts take into consideration the legitimate interests of all parties, particularly when it comes to trade secrets, confidential information, and even information pertaining to public or national security. This is why the Commission is encouraged by business stakeholders to include even stronger safeguards in the final text of the AI Liability Directive to ensure consistent interpretation of what constitutes "proportionate disclosure" across Member States and to prevent potential abuses. For instance, additional safeguards could entail limiting the disclosure obligation to documents that are under the control of the defendant and adversely affect their case, restricting disclosure to documents related to compliance with the AI Act or other relevant EU regulations, and imposing limits on the requirement to conduct proportionate searches for documents, among other measures.[188]

Furthermore, if the disclosure obligation is retained, the Commission is urged to remove the concept of "potential claimant" (defined in Article 2(7) of the proposed AI Liability Directive as "a natural or legal person who is considering but has not yet brought a claim for damages") from the proposal. Indeed, it is anticipated that the concept of 'potential claimant' will create a loophole that could allow individuals and companies with no clear connection to the AI system, and who may not have suffered any injury from the output of an AI system, to file claims solely for the purpose of gaining access to information. Such a mechanism could become 'a

[187] Upwork, Feedback on the Proposal for a Directive on adapting non-contractual civil liability rules to artificial intelligence, 28 November 2022, at p. 3.

[188] Ibid., at p. 4.

See also: eco – Association of the Internet Industry, Position Paper on the Commission's proposal for an AI Liability Directive, 28.11.2022, at p. 4: "[T]here is an expansion on the handling of the disclosed evidence, especially if they contain trade secrets. The protection of trade secrets is especially important since evidence will be most likely found in the algorithms of AI products, which also contain trade secrets. For many AI companies, the composition of their AI is the foundation of their business models; therefore, there should be resolute measures to secure the full protection of these trade secrets. It is therefore necessary to allow AI developers to decide what part of the disclosed evidence should be considered as a trade secret. According to Article 3(4) this is to be decided by the courts, which might lead to inaccurate decisions and could therefore endanger trade secrets of AI developers across Europe. Article 3 (4) should therefore be amended to allow the companies concerned to decide what they consider to be a trade secret".

For an opposite view, see the position of the Irish Council for Civil Liberties (ICCL), Submission to the consultation on AI Liability, 28 November 2022, at p. 3, which stated: "we are concerned that the provision for 'trade secret or alleged trade secret' will allow defendants to refuse disclosure of relevant documents to victims. We believe that a strict liability regime will benefit victims while not requiring defendants to share trade secrets".

powerful tool for harassment' without providing countervailing benefits to consumers.[189]

Also, it is reminded that Article 3(5) of the proposed AI Liability Directive establishes a presumption of non-compliance with a duty of care when a defendant fails to disclose documents or preserve evidence in accordance with a court order. This provision aims to compel defendants to make disclosures even if it may be detrimental to their company. However, it is argued that it may be practically unfeasible for defendants to comply with a preservation order, leading to "significant injustices and game-playing within litigation", where liability is presumed even if the defendant has fulfilled its duty of care obligations under the AI Act and other relevant EU laws.[190]

(d) Feedback on Article 4 of the proposed AI Liability Directive: Presumption of a causal link in the case of fault:

With regard to Article 4 of the proposed AI Liability Directive (presumption of a causal link in the case of fault), it was pointed out that there is no compelling reason to exempt claimants from establishing a causal link between the defendant's fault and the output generated by the AI system or the failure of the AI system to produce an output. The presumption of a causal link creates an unjustifiable "imbalance of rights between the claimant and the defendant", particularly considering that the proposal is intended to be a consumer protection measure. Even though theoretically it is possible, in practice it would be extremely challenging for a defendant to successfully rebut the presumption by providing evidence to the contrary (for instance, by providing evidence that another factor was responsible for the damage incurred).[191]

---

[189] Upwork, Feedback on the Proposal for a Directive on adapting non-contractual civil liability rules to artificial intelligence, 28 November 2022, at p. 4.

[190] Ibid., at p. 5.

See also: eco – Association of the Internet Industry, Position Paper on the Commission's proposal for an AI Liability Directive, 28.11.2022, at p. 4: "An automatic presumption of breach of the duty of care is not appropriate in eco's view, as there can be many reasons why a specific demand is not met in a given time. Especially in complex cases, providing the relevant information can be time and resource consuming. Moreover, it is not always clear as to whether the defendant itself has all the information that could be relevant".

[191] Upwork, Feedback on the Proposal for a Directive on adapting non-contractual civil liability rules to artificial intelligence, 28 November 2022, at pp. 5–6.

See also Siemens, First assessment and recommendations – EU's AI Liability Directive proposal, 28 November 2022, at p. 3: "The right to rebut the presumption overburdens providers or users as requiring them to prove the absence of causality is impossible given the specifics of AI (opacity, autonomy, complexity, algorithmic probability). A less prohibitive standard (than proving a negative fact) should apply, e.g., a showing that other elements than the provider's fault may have led to the damage. Otherwise, plaintiffs may abuse the leverage given to them by the presumption".

See also the response submitted by the U.S. Chamber of Commerce Institute of Legal Reform, Comments on the Proposed AI Liability Directive, November 2022, pp. 2–3, points 10 and 12: "If the Proposal is introduced in its current form, a claimant need only allege a hypothetical complaint in order to shift the burden to a defendant, who in turn will be required to prove a negative by

Furthermore, there is a significant lack of legal clarity regarding the circumstances in which the presumption of causality would be applicable in practice. For instance, it is reminded that, according to Article 4(4) of the proposed AI Liability Directive, in the case of a claim for damages concerning a high-risk AI system, if it is demonstrated by the defendant that the claimant can reasonably access sufficient evidence and expertise (e.g., through documentation and logging requirements)—and therefore the claimant's ability to prove a causal link is not excessively hindered—the national court should not apply the presumption of causality. However, it remains unclear how the national courts would assess what constitutes "reasonable access" to "sufficient evidence".[192]

---

submitting sufficient technical information to disprove the allegation. This would lead to a de facto reversal of the burden of proof from claimant to defendant. . . . A defendant will only be able to reverse the presumption of causality if it can demonstrate the lack of excessive evidential difficulties faced by the claimant, which may prove an impossible task: the defendant would have to demonstrate not only that a claim is not complex but will also have to seek to establish an effective defence. Providers may be more reluctant to invest where they face material risks of product liability pay-outs that are based on assumptions, rather than proof, of any harm".

On the other hand, academic/research institutions and civil society and consumer organisations stressed that Article 4 of the proposed AI Liability Directive is insufficient to safeguard victims of AI systems. See, for instance:

The Ada Lovelace Institute, "Feedback to the European Commission on its proposal for a Directive on adapting non-contractual civil liability rules to artificial intelligence", November 2022, at p. 2: "Even if a claimant succeeds in getting the court ordering the defendant to disclose information, huge barriers remain. While in theory, Article 4 offers an avenue towards a presumption of causality, to benefit from this presumption, a claimant would have to prove the following - (a) fault by non-compliance with a duty directly intended to protect against the damage that occurred; (b) likelihood that the fault has influenced the output produced by the AI system; and (c) that the output produced caused the damage. The first condition raises serious difficulties. Not only that a claimant would have to prove non-compliance with the AI Act, but they would also have to prove that the obligation imposed under the AI Act was directly intended to protect against the damage that occurred. That is a very challenging task, which could likely be overcome only where the Commission has imposed fines on AI providers/users for non-compliance, and even in that case, the "directly intended" scope of the obligation remains to be proven. Proving non-compliance with the AI Act to benefit from a presumption of causality under Art. 4(2) is a tall task for an affected person. They would have to build a case around highly complex documentation meant for use by certification bodies as part of the AI Act's conformity assessments. Without a very strong legal and technical knowledge, most people would struggle to build a case based on this evidence, thus again underlining that the AILD is not fit for use for harmed people".

See also the Irish Council for Civil Liberties (ICCL), Submission to the consultation on AI Liability, 28 November 2022, at p. 2: "The information asymmetry between the defendant and the victim is immense. Even when the victims have identified the relevant defendant and evidence has been disclosed, the victims will have difficulty interpreting the technical evidence. Should an average person be expected to assess whether an AI system was designed with "appropriate level of accuracy, robustness and cybersecurity"? [at Article 4(2)(d) of the proposed AI Liability Directive]. That assessment requires technical expertise, which is readily available to industry but not to victims. The Directive should be amended to remove this barrier to victims' claims".

[192] U.S. Chamber of Commerce Institute of Legal Reform, Comments on the Proposed AI Liability Directive, November 2022, p. 3, point 13.

Additionally, Article 4(5) of the proposed AI Liability Directive suggests that the presumption of causality could apply to AI systems that are not classified as high-risk, in situations where the claimant faces significant difficulties in providing proof. Nevertheless, the claimant "should neither be required to explain the characteristics of the AI system concerned nor how these characteristics make it harder to establish the causal link"[193] and, as a result, this lack of legal clarity regarding the circumstances in which the presumption of causality would apply in practice could lead to "costly legal test cases",[194] thus contradicting one of the main aims of the Commission's proposal, i.e., "saving time and costs for the parties involved and reducing the case load for courts".[195]

This is why it was argued that, in order to safeguard AI providers from unfounded and opportunistic claims while ensuring a fair allocation of product liability risk, a fair balance between the interests of both providers and consumers should be

---

See also: eco – Association of the Internet Industry, Position Paper on the Commission's proposal for an AI Liability Directive, 28.11.2022, at p. 5: "Article 4(4) creates a limitation to the presumption under Article 4 (1) for systems that fall under the definition of high-risk AI. Here, the rebuttable presumption under Article 4 (1) shall not apply if the defendant can prove that the claimant had sufficient access to information to establish a link. Providers of high-risk AI are to be obliged by the AI Act to comply with comprehensive transparency and information obligations, which could lead to less use of the presumption under paragraph 1, as a great deal of information should be available. Nevertheless, from eco's point of view, it is not comprehensible as to why the burden of proof here lies with the defendant. It would also be possible for the claimant to reasonably argue as to why the information available to him/her is not sufficient to prove a connection between damage and defective AI".

[193] Proposed AI Liability Directive, Recital 28.

[194] U.S. Chamber of Commerce Institute of Legal Reform, Comments on the Proposed AI Liability Directive, November 2022, p. 3, points 13 and 14.

See also: eco – Association of the Internet Industry, Position Paper on the Commission's proposal for an AI Liability Directive, 28.11.2022, at p. 5: "Article 4(5) also contains restrictions on this practice according to Article 4 (1). It should only apply to systems that do not fall under the definition of high-risk AI if 'the national court finds it excessively difficult for the claimants to prove the casual link'. eco welcomes the fact that this exists in order to relieve companies of this burden; however, the wording leaves a great degree of leeway for national courts, which could possibly weaken the protective effect of this clause".

For the opposite view, see Mozilla's comments on the Commission proposal for an AI Liability Directive (AILD) – The long road to redress, November 2022, at pp. 3–4: "The bar for claimants would be even higher to seek redress for harm caused by non-high-risk AI systems, as the rebuttable presumption of causality would only apply where a court concludes that a causal link is too difficult to prove for the claimant. However, not being designated as high-risk under the AI Act doesn't mean that such systems pose no risk, material or immaterial, to individuals. At the same time, without access to reasonably understandable evidence or evidence similar to that which providers of high-risk AI systems would have to keep to comply with the AI Act and make available to claimants under the AILD, it seems unlikely that claimants would be able to demonstrate a causal link in almost any case. If harmed by such systems, individuals should not be confronted with additional adversity. The AILD should therefore clarify and strengthen the position of individuals who have been harmed by non-high-risk AI systems and improve their access to relevant information that may prove fault".

[195] Proposed AI Liability Directive, Explanatory Memorandum, at p. 12.

achieved. To this end, if the presumption of causality is to be introduced, it was stressed that it is essential to establish clear and explicit rules to enhance legal certainty. For instance, the proposed AI Liability Directive should delineate specific standards for claimants to substantiate evidential issues related to proving causation. Moreover, in order to establish that the causal link is "likely" (see Article 4(1)(b): "... reasonably likely that the fault has influenced the output produced by the AI system or the failure of the AI system to produce an output"), claimants should be required to refer to objective criteria, such as an assessment of benefits and risks or other relevant information within their possession.[196] It was underlined that, in situations where a claimant encounters evidential challenges related to AI, the Commission's proposal should incorporate a "sliding scale" approach to the burden of proof, which would depend on the extent to which the AI is part of a human-driven decision-making process (in which case standard evidentiary processes should apply) or functions autonomously. In the latter case, liability should be determined based on factors such as the degree of transparency of the AI, the constraints imposed on it by its creators or users, and the level of vigilance exercised in monitoring its conduct.[197]

Finally, it was pointed out that liability should lie with the natural or legal person who is most in control over a risk connected with the operation and functioning of the AI-system and benefits from its operation.[198] Instead of a one-size-fits-all approach, the EU liability regime should acknowledge the differences in risk profiles among various AI applications and tailor the rules on a case-by-case basis. It is crucial to incorporate more nuance, considering factors such as the complexity of the AI system in question and distinguishing between sophisticated AI systems and less complex algorithms that have a long history of safe use by the general public.[199] This

[196] U.S. Chamber of Commerce Institute of Legal Reform, Comments on the Proposed AI Liability Directive, November 2022, p. 3, points 15 and 16.

[197] Ibid., p. 3, point 17.

[198] Ibid., p. 4, point 18.

See also the Annex to the European Parliament's Resolution of 20 October 2020 on a civil liability regime for AI – B. Text of the Proposal for a Regulation on liability for the operation of AI systems, at Article 3 (d)-(f): "(d)'operator' means both the frontend and the backend operator as long as the latter's liability is not already covered by Directive 85/374/EEC; (e) 'frontend operator' means any natural or legal person who exercises a degree of control over a risk connected with the operation and functioning of the AI-system and benefits from its operation; (f) 'backend operator' means any natural or legal person who, on a continuous basis, defines the features of the technology and provides data and an essential backend support service and therefore also exercises a degree of control over the risk connected with the operation and functioning of the AI-system".

[199] U.S. Chamber of Commerce Institute of Legal Reform, Comments on the Proposed AI Liability Directive, November 2022, p. 4, point 18.

See also the European Parliament's Resolution of 20 October 2020 on a civil liability regime for AI, section "Liability of the operator", points 14 and 15, which stated that an AI-system that entails an inherent high risk and acts autonomously potentially endangers the user or the general public to a much higher degree and in a manner that is random and goes beyond what can reasonably be expected. Therefore, different liability rules should apply for different risks, following a risk-based approach.

'risk-based' approach would enable AI developers and users to implement risk management practices that align with the specific use case and risk profile (i.e., taking into consideration whether the AI-systems have a specific risk profile in terms of liability, such as those endangering the lives, health and property of members of the public).

8.4.7.2 Calls for Adequately Addressing Immaterial Damages and Societal Harms

(i) Civil society, consumer organisations and academic/research institutions on including non-material and societal harms in the definition of damages

Determining the claimant's entitlement to compensation is heavily reliant on the interpretation of the concept of damage. The significance of immaterial (non-material)[200] damages resulting from AI systems was acknowledged in the Commission's 2020 White Paper on Artificial Intelligence.[201] These immaterial harms include infringement of fundamental rights[202] such as "loss of privacy,

[200] Commission Staff Working Document, "Impact Assessment Report – Accompanying the document Proposal for a Directive of the European Parliament and of the Council on adapting non-contractual civil liability rules to artificial intelligence", SWD(2022) 319 final, Brussels, 28.9.2022, at p. 163: "Immaterial or non-material damage refers to losses which do not relate to a person's assets, wealth or income and, as such, cannot be quantified in an objective manner by reference to a market price or value. Such losses are, for example, damage to reputation, discrimination, loss of confidentiality, psychological harm and mental suffering. This type of damage is different from the concept of pure economic loss".

See also the Opinion of Advocate General Wahl in case C-371/12, Petillo v Unipol, ECLI:EU:C:2013:652, at para. 38: "By 'non-material damage' I refer, generally speaking, to losses which do not relate to a person's assets, wealth or income and, as such, cannot be quantified in an objective manner by reference to a market price or value". This Opinion referred to Cf. Horton Rogers, W.V. (ed.), Damages for Non-Pecuniary Loss in a Comparative Perspective, European Centre of Tort and Insurance Law, Springer Verlag, Wien New York: 2001, p. 246.

On the other hand, "pure economic loss usually refers to financial loss suffered by a party, which is not the result of any damage to that party's own person or property. Instead, the damage arises from economic relationships in which the party is involved. This concept is distinct from the concept of consequential economic loss, i.e. loss that arises from physical injury or property damage. However, one should bear in mind that there is no universally accepted definition or description of pure economic loss in Member States' or EU law". Commission Staff Working Document, "Impact Assessment Report – Accompanying the document Proposal for a Directive of the European Parliament and of the Council on adapting non-contractual civil liability rules to artificial intelligence", SWD(2022) 319 final, Brussels, 28.9.2022, at p. 163.

[201] Commission Communication "White Paper On Artificial Intelligence - A European approach to excellence and trust", COM(2020) 65 final, Brussels, 19.2.2020.

[202] Proposed AI Liability Directive, Explanatory Memorandum, at pp. 9–10: "The proposal will enable effective private enforcement of fundamental rights and preserve the right to an effective remedy where AI-specific risks have materialised. In particular, the proposal will help protect fundamental rights, such as the right to life (Article 2 of the EU Charter of Fundamental Rights), the right to the physical and mental integrity (Article 3), and the right to property (Article 17). In

limitations to the right of freedom of expression, human dignity, discrimination for instance in access to employment".[203]

---

addition, depending on each Member State's civil law system and traditions, victims will be able to claim compensation for damage to other legal interests, such as violations of personal dignity (Articles 1 and 4 of the Charter), respect for private and family life (Article 7), the right to equality (Article 20) and non-discrimination (Article 21)".

[203]Commission Communication "White Paper On Artificial Intelligence - A European approach to excellence and trust", COM(2020) 65 final, Brussels, 19.2.2020, at pp. 10–11: "While AI can do much good, including by making products and processes safer, it can also do harm. This harm might be both material (safety and health of individuals, including loss of life, damage to property) and immaterial (loss of privacy, limitations to the right of freedom of expression, human dignity, discrimination for instance in access to employment), and can relate to a wide variety of risks. A regulatory framework should concentrate on how to minimise the various risks of potential harm, in particular the most significant ones. The main risks related to the use of AI concern the application of rules designed to protect fundamental rights (including personal data and privacy protection and non-discrimination), as well as safety [this includes issues of cybersecurity, issues associated with AI applications in critical infrastructures, or malicious use of AI] and liability-related issues. ... *Risks for fundamental rights, including personal data and privacy protection and non-discrimination*: The use of AI can affect the values on which the EU is founded and lead to breaches of fundamental rights, including the rights to freedom of expression, freedom of assembly, human dignity, non-discrimination based on sex, racial or ethnic origin, religion or belief, disability, age or sexual orientation, as applicable in certain domains, protection of personal data and private life, or the right to an effective judicial remedy and a fair trial, as well as consumer protection. These risks might result from flaws in the overall design of AI systems (including as regards human oversight) or from the use of data without correcting possible bias (e.g. the system is trained using only or mainly data from men leading to suboptimal results in relation to women). AI can perform many functions that previously could only be done by humans. As a result, citizens and legal entities will increasingly be subject to actions and decisions taken by or with the assistance of AI systems, which may sometimes be difficult to understand and to effectively challenge where necessary. Moreover, AI increases the possibilities to track and analyse the daily habits of people. For example, there is a potential risk that AI may be used, in breach of EU data protection and other rules, by state authorities or other entities for mass surveillance and by employers to observe how their employees behave. By analysing large amounts of data and identifying links among them, AI may also be used to retrace and de-anonymise data about persons, creating new personal data protection risks even in respect to datasets that per se do not include personal data. AI is also used by online intermediaries to prioritise information for their users and to perform content moderation. The processed data, the way applications are designed and the scope for human intervention can affect the rights to free expression, personal data protection, privacy, and political freedoms. Bias and discrimination are inherent risks of any societal or economic activity. Human decision-making is not immune to mistakes and biases. However, the same bias when present in AI could have a much larger effect, affecting and discriminating many people without the social control mechanisms that govern human behaviour. This can also happen when the AI system 'learns' while in operation".

The 2020 White Paper on AI also stressed (at p. 11) that certain AI algorithms, when utilised to predict criminal recidivism, may exhibit bias based on gender and race, resulting in varying prediction probabilities for women versus men, or for citizens versus foreigners (see: Tolan S., Miron M., Gomez E. and Castillo C. "Why Machine Learning May Lead to Unfairness: Evidence from Risk Assessment for Juvenile Justice in Catalonia", Best Paper Award, International Conference on AI and Law, 2019).

It also underlined that specific AI programs designed for facial analysis may demonstrate bias based on gender and race, with lower accuracy in determining the gender of darker-skinned women

Following the same approach, the proposed AI Liability Directive recognises the inclusion of non-material damages, such as discrimination, privacy violations, other breaches of fundamental rights (e.g., mental integrity, personal dignity, equality) and cybersecurity vulnerabilities.[204] Also, as the Commission stated, "this proposal covers national liability claims mainly based on the fault of any person with a view of compensating *any type of damage* …";[205] "the new AI Liability Directive … will apply to claims [for the compensation of] … any type of damage covered under national law (including resulting from discrimination or breach of fundamental rights like privacy)".[206] The recognition of non-material harm is also specifically outlined in Recital 2 of the proposed AI Liability Directive, which identifies the potential basis for damage claims as stemming from the violation of rights such as the right to equal treatment and non-discrimination.[207]

It should be stressed, however, that the proposed AI Liability Directive grants Member States the authority to define the specific types of damages (including non-material damages) covered through their national laws.[208] It relies on the civil law of Member States to protect people from fundamental rights infringements, including violation of personal dignity, right to equality and non-discrimination, and respect for private and family life. Thus, it leaves it up to Member States to define through their national laws the exact types of damages that could be covered, in contrast to the proposal for an amended Product Liability Directive which includes a harmonised definition of damages for defective products across the EU.[209] Accordingly, individuals harmed by defective products could have consistent protection throughout the EU under the amended Product Liability Directive, while the level of protection for those harmed by AI systems will solely rely on the legislation of each Member State.

---

compared to lighter-skinned men (see: Joy Buolamwini, Timnit Gebru; Proceedings of the 1st Conference on Fairness, Accountability and Transparency, PMLR 81:77–91, 2018).

[204] Proposed AI Liability Directive, Explanatory Memorandum, at p. 10.

[205] Ibid., Explanatory Memorandum, at p. 3.

[206] European Commission, Questions & Answers: AI Liability Directive, Brussels, 28 September 2022, pp. 1–2.

[207] Proposed AI Liability Directive, at Recital 2: "… the use of AI can adversely affect a number of fundamental rights, including life, physical integrity and in respect to non-discrimination and equal treatment".

[208] Ibid., Explanatory Memorandum, Recital 22: "this Directive does not harmonise the conditions related to the damage, for instance what damages are compensable, which are also regulated by applicable national and Union law". See also Article 2(9) of the proposed AI Liability Directive.

[209] Proposal for a Directive of the European Parliament and of the Council on liability for defective products, European Commission, COM(2022) 495 final, Brussels, 28.9.2022 [the 'proposal for a revised Product Liability Directive (PLD)'/the 'proposed new Product Liability Directive (PLD)], Article 4(6): "'damage' means material losses resulting from: (a) death or personal injury, including medically recognised harm to psychological health; (b) harm to, or destruction of, any property, except: (i) the defective product itself; (ii) a product damaged by a defective component of that product; (iii) property used exclusively for professional purposes; (c) loss or corruption of data that is not used exclusively for professional purposes".

As the proposed AI Liability Directive does not harmonise the criteria for determining damages, divergences between national systems of Member States can pose challenges. For example, in certain Member States, the Directive could be invoked to seek compensation for psychological harm caused by an AI system, whereas in other Member States, such harm may not be considered eligible for compensation. For instance, as it was put by the Future of Life Institute (FLI), "this could mean that a person discriminated against by a credit scoring AI system could claim damages for such discrimination in one Member State but not in another".[210]

This is why NGOs, civil society, and consumer organisations as well as academic/research institutes expressed concerns because immaterial damage is generally non-recoverable under civil law in many member states. Indeed, there seems to be a lack of consistency within the EU regarding the possibility of recovering non-material damages. As it was stressed by the comparative law study commissioned for the Commission's impact assessment, "there are important differences throughout Europe when it comes to recognizing which damage triggers tort claims in the first place (specifically evident in the case of pure economic loss). Furthermore, jurisdictions differ with regard to which consequences of an initial harm will be indemnified at all. The range and extent of remedies available are equally divergent, in particular (but clearly not limited to) the extent of compensation for immaterial harm".[211] One group of member states treats both material and immaterial damages as equally recoverable, without differentiation. This approach is followed by Belgium, France, Luxembourg, Spain, Hungary, and Slovenia: "The starting point is that all damage or damage in general is recoverable".[212] On the other hand, a second group of member states operates on the premise that non-material damages are generally not recoverable, unless specifically provided for by law. This category includes countries like Italy, Germany, Poland, Austria, the Netherlands, Estonia, Lithuania and the Nordic Countries: "these Member States depart from the opposite premise: immaterial damage is generally non-recoverable".[213]

---

[210] The Future of Life Institute (FLI), "FLI Position Paper on AI Liability – FLI position on the proposal for a Directive on adapting non-contractual civil liability rules to artificial intelligence (AI Liability Directive)", November 2022, at p. 6.

[211] Ernst Karner/Bernhard Koch/Mark Geistfeld, 'Comparative Law Study on Civil Liability for Artificial Intelligence', European Commission, Directorate-General for Justice and Consumers, 2021, at pp. 9 and 105.

[212] Commission Staff Working Document, "Impact Assessment Report – Accompanying the document Proposal for a Directive of the European Parliament and of the Council on adapting non-contractual civil liability rules to artificial intelligence", SWD(2022) 319 final, Brussels, 28.9.2022, at p. 164.

[213] Ibid., at pp. 164–165: "However, there are a number of "exceptions", in which the law expressly provides for the recovery of immaterial damage. One such situation is if the infringed rights deserve special protection. In this sense, most legal systems allow recovery if the tort infringes certain protected rights such as health and bodily integrity, liberty or the right to sexual self-determination. This is true, for instance, for Italy, Poland, Greece, the Czech Republic, Slovakia, Germany, the Netherlands, Estonia and the Nordic Countries. Similarly, Italy generally permits recovery if the tort also constitutes a crime or if the tort causes a permanent and negative detrimental effect on a

Furthermore, it could be argued that the proposed AI Liability Directive falls short in defining liability claims for societal damages, such as environmental harm and the dissemination of fake content that manipulates people. Indeed, one of the most noticeable accountability gaps in the proposed AI Liability Directive is the absence of safeguards against societal harms, such as manipulation and discrimination, which are inherent to the unique characteristics of AI systems, at least in comparison with traditional product safety risks (which are related to physical harm and covered by the Product Liability Directive).[214]

Based on the above, NGOs, civil society, and consumer organisations as well as academic/research institutes argued that the proposed AI Liability Directive should

person's life and social interaction with others. The Spanish legal system, which generally considers immaterial damage as recoverable, also expressly provides for compensation in case of criminal activity. Intention or gross negligence may also justify compensation for immaterial damage. This is the case in Austria and the Netherlands. In cases of intentional damage, the tort will often also constitute a crime. The Member States also frequently grant compensation for immaterial damage if recovery would otherwise be difficult or impossible. Poland, Estonia and the Nordic Countries allow recovery if the tort concerns incorporeal rights of personality. The Netherlands permit recovery if the harming party violates the reputation of the dead".

[214] See, for instance, the Irish Council for Civil Liberties (ICCL), Submission to the consultation on AI Liability, 28 November 2022, point 15, at p. 4: "the AILD lacks clarity on liability claims for societal harms including environmental harms, and manipulation of people through the generation of fake content. Recently an AI system was released to the public with the claim that it 'can store, combine and reason about scientific knowledge'. This AI system was soon withdrawn after it was observed to have 'made up fake papers (sometimes attributing them to real authors)'. Such AI systems could produce social harms including reducing trust in scientific information".

See also the Future of Life Institute (FLI), "FLI Position Paper on AI Liability – FLI position on the proposal for a Directive on adapting non-contractual civil liability rules to artificial intelligence (AI Liability Directive)", November 2022, at pp. 6–7: "It is also not clear whether the Directive would allow for broader societal harms caused by AI systems to be covered, such as manipulation at scale, election interference or environmental harms".

See also the Ada Lovelace Institute, "Feedback to the European Commission on its proposal for a Directive on adapting non-contractual civil liability rules to artificial intelligence", November 2022, at p. 2: "To take an example, imagine a situation in which a disabled person (or many disabled people) was less likely to be passed through an initial screening conducted by an AI system during a recruitment process. The harm suffered would be non-pecuniary in nature (i.e. it would not be possible to definitively calculate a sum for the award of damages) in the form of discrimination. How would the affected person/s be protected and offered a right to redress? The first step would be for those affected to even know they had been harmed: very difficult when they are just subject to an AI system's decision, but at no point are interacting with an AI system. Even if they did know, it is an open question if they would be protected against discrimination, as this would be dependent on the Member States national laws. Then, granted they are covered by their national courts, they would then have to build a case, which is hugely burdensome, starting by locating who is liable: is it the developer, or the company that deployed the AI system used for CV screening? If there was human oversight (as required in the AI Act's high-risk requirements) of the system, would that person become liable? On top of this, even if they could successfully prove fault and causation, how would the damages be decided? The AILD only provides for quantifiable (pecuniary) damages. In this case, how would one make this calculation? Would there be other forms of (non-material) damages which would be more fitting? The number of open questions show the difficulty in ensuring adequate protection from societal and non-material harms".

include a definition of damages that extends to immaterial and societal harms, i.e., they advocated for a harmonised regime for damages across the EU, encompassing both immaterial and societal harms.[215] This was also recommended by BEUC (the European Consumer Organisation), which argued that non-material damages should be included in the range of damages for which compensation can be claimed.[216] This

[215] See, for instance, the Irish Council for Civil Liberties (ICCL), Submission to the consultation on AI Liability, 28 November 2022, points 14 and 16, at pp. 3–4: "AILD should provide for immaterial damages in Article 2 and harmonise the compensation for these damages across the Union. Article 4 (6) of Product Liability Directive defines damages for that Directive. AILD should take a similar approach to provide legal certainty" (point 14). ... "Social harms should be explicitly addressed in this Directive. The compensation for such damages should not rely on member state liability rules, but should be uniform across the union" (point 16).

See also the Ada Lovelace Institute, "Feedback to the European Commission on its proposal for a Directive on adapting non-contractual civil liability rules to artificial intelligence", November 2022, at pp. 3–4: "a harmonised regime for damages, to ensure equal protection against non-material and social harms for all people in the EU, would help a great deal in making the AI liability regime more legally clear, and in offering protection against the most those risks more likely to arise from AI". ... "To truly meet its objectives, the AILD must go beyond evidence rules and presumptions and provide for non-pecuniary damages that AI systems can cause rather than leave this to individual Member States". ... "we suggest including non-material harms in the definition of damages. This would address the problem of the lack of coverage of the harms most likely to arise from AI systems (e.g. discrimination, manipulation), and mean that persons in the EU are protected to the same degree across Member States, as relying on national courts to employ their own regime to damages would see divergence and fragmentation in application".

Furthermore, the Future of Life Institute (FLI), "FLI Position Paper on AI Liability – FLI position on the proposal for a Directive on adapting non-contractual civil liability rules to artificial intelligence (AI Liability Directive)", November 2022, at p. 6, called "for a harmonisation of compensable damages across the EU that should include immaterial and societal harms. Covering immaterial harms is necessary to account for the particular nature of damages caused by AI systems. Furthermore, to ensure that victims harmed by AI systems are equally protected no matter which EU country they live in, the specific types of recoverable damages should be defined by EU law".

Interestingly, ACT – The App Association (a global trade association for small and medium-sized technology companies) follows the same approach. See ACT - The App Association feedback to the proposed Artificial Intelligence Liability Directive, 28 November 2022, at p. 3: "encourage the Commission to reconsider leaving matters such as the calculation of damages ... to the Member States. Especially concerning damages, it is essential to establish maximum uniformity, particularly for 'immaterial' damages and non-physical injury to ensure that such damage awards are based on demonstrated and quantifiable harms".

[216] Response submitted by BEUC (the European Consumer Organisation) to the European Commission's public consultation on Civil liability – adapting liability rules to the digital age and artificial intelligence, 23.12.2021, at p. 9: "All harm should be compensated: AI systems may cause a wide range of harm, including immaterial damage. It is essential that all type of harm be compensated. If not, this instrument will remain a limited relevance as a large part of consumer harm will not be compensated. While Member States follow different traditions in this field of law, we consider that harmonisation of the damages victims could be entitled to ask for is necessary to ensure a high-level of consumer protection across the Union. In this regard, material and immaterial damages (such as data loss) should be part of the upcoming rules".

See also BEUC (the European Consumer Organisation) "Position Paper on the Proposal for an AI Liability Directive", 02.05.2023, pp. 12–13, which stated that the AI Liability Directive should harmonise both material and non-material harm. According to BEUC, it is essential that all types of

has been a common position of NGOs, civil society, and consumer organisations, which favoured the extension of the range of damages for which compensation could be claimed (i.e., life, health, and consumer property) to non-material damages (e.g., loss of profit, loss of or damage to data, privacy infringements, reputational damage or psychological harm, environmental damage).[217]

(ii) Business stakeholders on immaterial damages and societal harms

On the other hand, business stakeholders acknowledged that it is understandable to include non-material damages, such as alleged discrimination, in the scope of protection of the proposed AI Liability Directive, since safeguarding universal fundamental rights, including protection against discrimination, is crucial. However, they opposed encompassing immaterial damages in the definition of damage under the AI Liability Directive. They argued that this would give rise to various problems

---

harm, including non-material harm (such as pain, loss of an opportunity or inconvenience), are compensated: "The European Commission did not propose to harmonise the types of damage covered by the AILD. As a result, it is up to each Member State to decide which types of damages, material and non-material, can be claimed by consumers. It is essential that all types of harm, including non-material harm (such as pain, loss of an opportunity or inconvenience), are compensated. For example, if a chess robot grabs and breaks the arm of a toddler and leaves him permanently disabled for life, this may cause non-material damage such as loss of quality of life. An injury caused by a defective lawnmower to a gardener may cause material damages (related to the physical injury) but also non-material damages (pain related to the injury). The denial of a loan based on discriminatory grounds can cause stress, anxiety or affect someone's reputation. Also, the harmonisation of non-material damages is particularly relevant for generative AI systems like ChatGPT. For example, recently, ChatGPT wrongly said that an US professor had touched a student inappropriately on a class trip to Alaska. Not only did the trip never take place but the chatbot even cited a non-existent article form the media. This type of outputs from generative AI systems can create significant non-material harm to the person (reputational damage, anxiety, etc.) and it's only fair that harmed consumers are compensated for it. While some Member States already cover non-material damages, only through a harmonisation of the damages covered will the AILD achieve a high-level of consumer protection across the EU. Importantly, there is a precedence of harmonisation of damages at EU level. For instance, the General Data Protection Regulation (GDPR), the Package Travel Directive, the Directive on the Enforcement of Intellectual Property and the Directive on the Protection of Trade Secrets35 all cover both material and non-material harm. There is no reason why victims of non-material harm should be entitled to claim compensation if harm was caused by a privacy infringement, by a breach of a package travel contract, by a violation of intellectual property or by a violation of trade secrets but may have to depend on Member States if non-material harm was caused by flawed AI system".

[217] See, for instance, Commission, DG GROW and DG JUST, "Factual summary report of the open public consultation on Adapting Civil Liability Rules to the Digital Age and AI", Ref. Ares(2022) 2620305, 06.04.2022, p. 10.

See also Commission Staff Working Document, "Impact Assessment Report – Accompanying the document Proposal for a Directive of the European Parliament and of the Council on adapting non-contractual civil liability rules to artificial intelligence", SWD(2022) 319 final, Brussels, 28.9.2022, at p. 83: "Amongst EU citizens, consumer associations, NGOs and research institutions there was clear support for EU rules prescribing the compensability of pure economic loss (e.g. loss of profit), loss of or damage to data (not covered by the GDPR) and immaterial harm (like pain and suffering, reputational damage or psychological harm)".

in practice. For instance, in certain cases, it may be extremely difficult (or, even impossible) to establish that a specific action or non-action of an AI system has resulted in unequal treatment or discrimination. Consequently, this could lead to unjustifiable allegations against AI product manufacturers, as many of these immaterial damages are challenging to prove due to their very nature. Additionally, it was argued that it can be problematic for manufacturers to entirely eliminate erroneous actions and non-actions owing to the complexity and adaptive nature of AI systems. Furthermore, it was pointed out that there are already legal provisions that address these concerns (e.g. anti-discrimination legislation).[218]

This is a standard position followed by business stakeholders, namely that liability should be limited to physical/material damage to consumers. They have consistently emphasised this stance in the past and urged the Commission and the co-legislators not to extend the scope of compensable harm. They have rejected an extension of liability to non-material damage as not necessary, arguing that damages for privacy infringements are difficult to quantify, that financial liability associated with non-material damages is less predictable, that environmental damages could raise complex issues of causation that would be difficult to address under a strict liability regime, and that existing EU legislation already provides redress mechanisms for consumers for many types of non-material damages (e.g., non-material damage can be compensated under data protection law, anti-discrimination law and tort law).[219]

---

[218] See, for instance, eco – Association of the Internet Industry, Position Paper on the Commission's proposal for an AI Liability Directive, 28.11.2022, at p. 2.

[219] Commission, DG GROW and DG JUST, "Factual summary report of the open public consultation on Adapting Civil Liability Rules to the Digital Age and AI", Ref. Ares(2022)2620305, 06.04.2022, p. 10. "... business stakeholders were mainly opposed to such rules. Their opposition was strongest regarding the compensability of immaterial harm (63% disagreement (52 out of 83) v. 23% support (19 out of 83) and of data loss/damage not resulting in a verifiable economic loss (75% opposition (63 out of 84) v. 12% support (10 out of 84)). The written contributions submitted by business stakeholders emphasised the very diverse approaches under existing national rules and the concern that harmonisation for AI-related damage would create inconsistent outcomes compared to cases not involving AI".

See also Commission Staff Working Document, "Impact Assessment Report – Accompanying the document Proposal for a Directive of the European Parliament and of the Council on adapting non-contractual civil liability rules to artificial intelligence", SWD(2022) 319 final, Brussels, 28.9.2022, at pp. 83–84.

See also the position taken by Google ("Google's comments - Public consultation: Civil liability – adapting liability rules to the digital age and artificial intelligence", 7 January 2022, p. 5): "many of the non-material damages referenced in the public consultation questionnaire are notoriously difficult to quantify. This is the case, for example, of damages for privacy infringements. Risks for consumers in this area are already covered by the GDPR, whose severe penalties are a powerful incentive for producers to protect their customers' privacy. Environmental damages, as another example, would raise particularly complex issues of causation and remoteness that would be difficult to address under a strict liability regime. It is also hard to imagine how environmental damage could be associated with an individual consumer in a way that would be appropriate to a consumer protection framework".

(iii) The Commission's position

It is reminded that, according to the European Parliament's Resolution of 20 October 2020 on a civil liability regime for AI, the proposed Regulation should cover violations (harm or damage) of the important legally protected rights to life, health, physical integrity, property as well as significant immaterial harm that results in a verifiable economic loss above a specific threshold.[220] In this respect, the Commission was tasked by the European Parliament to assess the legal traditions and national laws of all Member States that provide compensation for immaterial harm, in order to determine whether the inclusion of immaterial harm is essential and whether it conflicts with the current EU or national legal framework.[221]

Furthermore, see the response submitted by Siemens ("Siemens – Executive summary on EU (civil) tort liability framework", 07.01.2022, p. 5): "No additional types of harm due to use of technology (immaterial harm e.g. pain and suffering, reputational damage or psychological harm). Since infringements of data privacy and personal rights are already sanctioned in data privacy law, anti-discrimination law and tort liability, we see no gaps in legal protection. In addition, a risk-oriented approach to liability also means that there should not be multiple liability for any damage under the same conditions".

[220] European Parliament's Resolution of 20 October 2020 on a civil liability regime for AI, section "Different liability rules for different risks", point 19, p. 112: "... the proposed Regulation should cover violations of the important legally protected rights to life, health, physical integrity and property, and should set out the amounts and extent of compensation, as well as the limitation period; ... the proposed Regulation should also incorporate significant immaterial harm that results in a verifiable economic loss above a threshold harmonised in Union liability law, that balances the access to justice of affected persons and the interests of other involved persons".

See also the Annex to the European Parliament's Resolution of 20 October 2020 on a civil liability regime for AI – A. Principles and Aims of the Proposal, point 8, p. 115: "Both material and immaterial harm should be taken into account in the future proposal for a Regulation. ... Based on the currently available information, Parliament believes that significant immaterial harm should be included if the affected person suffers a noticeable, meaning a verifiable, economic loss".

Also, the Annex to the European Parliament's Resolution of 20 October 2020 on a civil liability regime for AI – B. Text of the Proposal for a Regulation on liability for the operation of AI systems, at recital 16: "This Regulation should cover harm or damage to life, health, physical integrity, property and significant immaterial harm that results in a verifiable economic loss above a threshold, harmonised in Union liability law, that balances the access to justice of affected persons with the interests of other involved persons. ... Significant immaterial harm should be understood as meaning harm as a result of which the affected person suffers considerable detriment, an objective and demonstrable impairment of his or her personal interests and an economic loss calculated having regard, for example, to annual average figures of past revenues and other relevant circumstances".

Furthermore, see the Annex to the European Parliament's Resolution of 20 October 2020 on a civil liability regime for AI – B. Text of the Proposal for a Regulation on liability for the operation of AI systems, Article 3(i): "'Harm or damage' means an adverse impact affecting the life, health, physical integrity of a natural person, the property of a natural or legal person or causing significant immaterial harm that results in a verifiable economic loss".

[221] European Parliament's Resolution of 20 October 2020 on a civil liability regime for AI (section "Different liability rules for different risks"), point 19, p. 112: "the Commission should analyse in depth the legal traditions in all Member States and their existing national laws that grant compensation for immaterial harm, in order to evaluate if the inclusion of immaterial harm in AI-specific

The Commission found that the legal situation regarding compensating for non-material harm and pure economic loss varies greatly among Member States, due to differing legal traditions. It acknowledged that existing national civil liability rules allow victims to seek compensation for various forms of harm, such as immaterial harm and damage to business property. Therefore, it is crucial to guarantee that victims have equal protection under these national laws: "The Commission's analysis has shown that the legal situation in Member States regarding the compensability of non-material harm, as well as pure economic loss, is fragmented. The matter is marked by differing long-standing legal traditions. It is not an AI-specific question but rather a horizontal one. Creating a situation whereby victims might be able to claim compensation for a certain type of harm, for instance immaterial harm, only if it was caused by AI would not be in line with the Parliament's and the Commission's common objective to ensure that victims have the same level of protection. Such an approach would give victims of harm caused by AI-systems a better protection compared to harm caused by other technologies".[222]

The Commission took into consideration the concerns expressed by business stakeholders who stressed that harmonising the types of compensable harm only with respect to cases where AI causes damage could create inconsistencies and fragmentation within national legal systems. As a result, the Commission concluded that the most reasonable and balanced approach is to ensure that victims are not less protected under existing national liability rules when AI causes harm, but avoid the harmonisation of the types of compensable harm in an AI-specific instrument: "It is therefore appropriate not to include a harmonisation of the compensable harm in the envisaged AI-specific instrument on civil liability. By ensuring the effectiveness of existing liability rules, the envisaged policy measures will nevertheless help victims to claim compensation also for other types of harm such as immaterial harm or pure economic loss, to the extent that such harm is compensable under national liability rules".[223]

legislative acts is necessary and if it contradicts the existing Union legal framework or undermines the national law of the Member States".

See also the Annex to the European Parliament's Resolution of 20 October 2020 on a civil liability regime for AI – A. Principles and Aims of the Proposal, principle 8, p. 115: "The European Commission is called upon to profoundly analyse the legal traditions in all Member States as well as the existing legislative provisions that grant compensation for immaterial harm in order to evaluate if the inclusion of immaterial harm in the future proposal for a Regulation is legally sound and necessary from the perspective of the affected person".

[222] Commission Staff Working Document, "Impact Assessment Report – Accompanying the document Proposal for a Directive of the European Parliament and of the Council on adapting non-contractual civil liability rules to artificial intelligence", SWD(2022) 319 final, Brussels, 28.9.2022, at pp. 41–42.

[223] Ibid., at pp. 42 and 84. See also at pp. 168–169, where the Commission stated that there are valid reasons for not including provisions on the types of compensable harm on the preferred policy option on AI liability. These reasons are: "First, the specific characteristics of AI (such as an increasing degree of autonomy, complexity, opacity, and a lack of transparency and predictability)

8.5 Conclusion

It is reminded that there are three AI-specific problems regarding liability, namely: (i) lack of compensation for victims contributing to the lack of societal trust in AI use; (ii) legal uncertainty, and (iii) increased legal fragmentation, which in their combination cause internal market obstacles.

These three problems are driven by the fact that, under existing liability rules, victims normally have to prove the necessary conditions for a successful claim, i.e., they have to identify the possibly liable person(s), the action/omission of that person which could be characterised as fault, and the causal link between that action/omission and the damage. However, there are neither targeted provisions for AI to ease the victim's burden of proof under fault-based claims, nor AI-specific strict liability regimes that would exempt the victim from making this proof. Therefore, these three major problems are primarily linked to the difficulty of the victim to prove the necessary facts due to the specific characteristics of certain AI systems, which make it very difficult to attribute directly the damaging output of the AI to an action/omission of a liable person.

Therefore, the objectives of the proposed AI Liability Directive are: (i) to prevent a lack of compensation, by ensuring that victims of AI-enabled products/services are equally protected as victims of traditional technologies (when persons suffer harm caused by AI systems, they should enjoy the same level of protection as those having suffered harm caused by other technologies, because lack of compensation could affect their trust in AI and ultimately the uptake of AI-enabled products/services); (ii) to reduce legal uncertainty regarding the liability exposure of businesses developing or using AI; and (iii) to prevent the emergence of fragmented AI-specific adaptations of national civil liability rules.

The purpose of the proposed AI Liability Directive is to harmonise in a targeted and proportionate manner certain aspects of fault-based liability rules at EU level in

---

do not alter the existing types or concepts of damage. The recoverability of immaterial harm therefore does not form part of the AI-specific issues to be addressed by the AI liability initiative. ... Second, Member States have developed varying concepts and approaches as regards the compensation for immaterial damage. Novel concepts such as "significant immaterial harm resulting in a verifiable economic loss" will not easily fit into the existing legal regimes. ... Third, treating AI-induced damage as a category apart when it comes to its recoverability could upset the coherence of the existing national rules concerning the types of compensable harm. The prevailing divergences between MS' approaches and legal traditions apply horizontally irrespective of whether immaterial damage was caused with the involvement of AI systems or not. Harmonising this aspect in the AI liability proposal would potentially lead to a situation where victims can claim compensation for certain types of harm, but only if AI was involved in causing it. ... Fourth, it is doubtful whether the current lack of harmonisation of the types of compensable harm amounts to an internal market barrier justifying harmonised measures. ... Fifth, recoverability of damage in tort law has implications for the recoverability of damage in contract law. Harmonising the recoverability in tort law could lead to wider gaps between contract and tort law. Countries that treat recoverability of immaterial damage in tort and contract law the same or at least similar might face difficulties implementing such EU measures into their national law".

order to increase legal certainty and create a level playing field for AI systems. The focus is on targeted proof-related measures and, therefore, the measures provided in the proposed AI Liability Directive were chosen as pragmatic and proportionate. Therefore, despite potential shortcomings in addressing complex liability questions, the introduction of these measures ensure that victims of AI-enabled products/ services suffering loss or damage can get compensation in the most straightforward cases. On the other hand, given the intrinsic complexity and opacity of AI systems, more ambitious action (in addition to the measures alleviating the burden of proof) could be justified for the introduction of a higher level of legal intervention, i.e., the need for harmonising strict liability for AI use cases with a particular risk profile.

In addition, the proposed AI Liability Directive follows a minimum harmonisation approach, thus allowing claimants in cases of damage caused by AI systems to invoke more favourable national rules. As already discussed, the objectives of the proposed AI Liability Directive, namely to ensure legal certainty and to prevent fragmentation, thus creating the right conditions for the rollout and development of AI-enabled products and services across the internal market, can be better achieved at EU level by ensuring a minimum level of harmonisation of the relevant liability rules to respond to the risks posed by AI systems.

Therefore, the proposed AI Liability Directive follows a minimum harmonisation approach, based on a minimum intervention at EU level, putting forward a balanced approach regarding liability for damage caused by AI. It focuses on the alleviation of the burden of proof, ensures that victims of AI-enabled products/services are not less (but also not more) protected victims of traditional technologies, and respects to the maximum extent possible Member States' well-established liability systems. The approach followed by the proposed AI Liability Directive does not go beyond what is necessary, since it takes into account the different levels of regulatory intervention of Member States as regards the tort liability for damages caused by AI systems. As a result, this minimum harmonisation approach—contrary to full harmonisation—ensures that the new rules can be integrated without frictions into the existing legal civil liability framework within each Member State.

The proposed AI Liability Directive introduces two key measures: First, the 'presumption of causality', which relieves victims from having to explain in detail how a specific fault or omission caused the damage. If victims can show that a party was at fault for not complying with a relevant obligation and that a causal link with the AI performance is reasonably likely, the court can presume that this non-compliance caused the damage. The liable party, however, can rebut this presumption by proving that another cause was responsible for the damage. Second, it assists victims in accessing relevant evidence from companies or suppliers when dealing with high-risk AI systems. Victims can request the court to order the disclosure of information about high-risk AI systems, facilitating the identification of the liable party and the understanding of the fault. This disclosure is subject to safeguards to protect sensitive information, including trade secrets.

The proposed AI Liability Directive is limited to the measures strictly necessary (proportional) to address the AI-specific problems identified. Thus its intervention is targeted because it will only alleviate the burden of proof for victims. Indeed, it focuses on targeted proof-related measures (disclosure of information and alleviation of the burden of proof through establishment of causality rebuttable presumptions subject to strict conditions). From the various tools available in national legal regimes for easing the burden of proof, the approach followed by the proposed AI Liability Directive is to use rebuttable presumptions (they are commonly found in national liability systems and they balance the interests of claimants and defendants) as the least interventionist tool. As a result, the AI Liability Directive does not lead to a reversal of the burden of proof, in order to avoid exposing providers, operators and users of AI systems to higher liability risks, which may hinder innovation and prevent the rollout of AI-enabled products and services.

Moreover, since the proposed AI Liability Directive follows an approach of a minimum intervention at EU level (minimum harmonisation), i.e., focuses on disclosure of information and alleviation of the burden of proof through establishment of causality presumption subject to strict conditions, victims of damage caused by AI systems are allowed to invoke more favourable rules of national law. Thus, Member States remain free to use in their national legal regimes more invasive tools/ extensive measures if they deem it appropriate, such as reversals of the burden of proof under fault-based regimes, irrebuttable presumptions, national no-fault liability (strict liability) regimes of which there are already a large variety in national laws, etc. The minimum harmonisation approach means that Member States could maintain or—outside of the scope of the Product Liability Directive—introduce national liability rules that are more favourable for victims (for instance, Member States could maintain general strict liability regimes, e.g. for 'dangerous things or activities', applicable also to damage caused by AI systems). On the other hand, however, it could be argued that the minimal harmonisation approach could lead to fragmented liability regimes in the EU.

Furthermore, the proposed AI Liability Directive will only harmonise elements of liability that are challenged by AI, leaving other elements like the determination of fault and causality to the existing national laws. It does not touch upon the substantive conditions of liability like fault or causality (which remain in the remit of national law). Instead, it focuses on targeted proof-related measures. Therefore, the proposed Directive builds on the substantive conditions of liability currently existing in national rules, such as fault or causality, but focuses on targeted proof-related measures, ensuring that victims receive the same level of protection as they would in cases not involving AI systems.

Finally, the assessment of the need to harmonise strict liability has been postponed to a later stage, when more information about the AI and its uses can be gathered. Indeed, under the review clause, the proposed Directive provides for re-assessing the need for more stringent or more extensive measures (including situations where strict liability would be more appropriate), at a later stage (five years later), without committing to specific outcomes of such review. Therefore, the proposed AI Liability Directive attempts to achieve the aforementioned objectives with a minimally invasive approach through a staged approach. In particular:

(a) In the first stage, the proposal introduces the following three measures to alleviate the victims' burden to prove their liability claim: (i) Harmonising how the information recorded/documented according to the product safety rules of the EU AI Act can be disclosed in court proceedings so that the victim can identify and prove which action/omission led to the damage suffered. (ii) If the victim shows that the liable person did not comply with the EU AI Act's safety requirements designed to prevent damage, the courts could presume that this non-compliance caused the damage. The potentially liable person would have the opportunity to rebut such a presumption, e.g. by proving than another cause led to the damage. (iii) In case the only way for the victim to prove the liability claim is to demonstrate what happened inside the AI, such burden on the victim would be alleviated. The potentially liable person would have the opportunity to prove that they did not act negligently.

(b) In the second stage, on the basis of a review clause, the proposed AI Liability Directive introduces a review mechanism (which takes a "forward-looking perspective") to re-assess (five years later, once a more robust evidence base that could justify more ambitious action is in place) the need (in addition to the measures alleviating the burden of proof) for a higher level of regulatory intervention, i.e., the need for harmonising strict liability for AI use cases with a particular risk profile, possibly coupled with a mandatory insurance. Under this scenario, instead of a one-size-fits-all approach, the EU liability regime would acknowledge the differences in risk profiles among various AI applications and tailor the (strict liability) rules on a case-by-case basis. Therefore, the application of strict liability would be limited to situations where the AI-enabled technologies may create specific risks (which are more likely to arise in circumstances where digital technologies move in public spaces, e.g., drones, autonomous cars, traffic management services), expose the public at large to risks, and cause significant harm to life, health, and property. This is in line with the approach recommended by the European Parliament's 2020 Resolution on a civil liability regime for artificial intelligence.[224]

Any type of victim (natural or legal person) can bring a claim for damages against any person for fault that influenced the AI system which caused the harm. The victim can be compensated if harmed by the fault or omission of a provider, developer or user of AI resulting in a damage covered by national law (e.g., health, property, including damage caused by safety issues or resulting from unlawful discrimination or breach of fundamental rights such as privacy). Once ratified, the AI Liability Directive is expected to strengthen the rights of victims who have suffered damage—as admissible under national law—due to the wrongful use of artificial intelligence. This will enable victims to file successful claims against any party whose fault influenced the AI system causing the damage/harm. Consequently, it

[224] European Parliament Resolution of 20 October 2020 with recommendations to the Commission on a civil liability regime for artificial intelligence (2020/2014(INL)) P9_TA(2020)0276 ('European Parliament's Resolution of 20 October 2020 on a civil liability regime for AI').

Also: Annex to the Resolution: detailed recommendations for drawing up a Regulation on liability for the operation of artificial intelligence-systems, A. Principles and Aims of the Proposal. B. Text of the Proposal Requested—Proposal for a Regulation on liability for the operation of Artificial Intelligence-systems ('Annex to the European Parliament's Resolution of 20 October 2020 on a civil liability regime for AI').

will facilitate compensation for victims, whether individuals or businesses, for damages resulting from an AI system's output.

Legal/Policy Documents, Studies, Reports and Other Sources

Proposal for a Directive of the European Parliament and of the Council on adapting non-contractual civil liability rules to artificial intelligence (AI Liability Directive), European Commission, COM (2022) 496 final, Brussels, 28.9.2022 (the 'proposed AI Liability Directive').

European Commission ('Commission') Staff Working Document, "AI Subsidiarity Grid – Accompanying the document Proposal for a Directive of the European Parliament and of the Council on adapting non contractual civil liability rules to artificial intelligence (AI Liability Directive)", SWD(2022) 318 final, Brussels, 28.9.2022.

Commission Staff Working Document, "Impact Assessment Report – Accompanying the document Proposal for a Directive of the European Parliament and of the Council on adapting non-contractual civil liability rules to artificial intelligence", SWD(2022) 319 final, Brussels, 28.9.2022.

Commission Staff Working Document, "Executive Summary of the Impact Assessment Report – Accompanying the document Proposal for a Directive of the European Parliament and of the Council on adapting non-contractual civil liability rules to artificial intelligence", SWD(2022) 320 final, Brussels, 28.9.2022.

Regulation (EU) 2024/1689 of the European Parliament and of the Council of 13 June 2024 laying down harmonised rules on artificial intelligence and amending Regulations (EC) No 300/2008, (EU) No 167/2013, (EU) No 168/2013, (EU) 2018/858, (EU) 2018/1139 and (EU) 2019/2144 and Directives 2014/90/EU, (EU) 2016/797 and (EU) 2020/1828 (*EU Artificial Intelligence Act*), OJ L, 12.07.2024.

Council Directive 85/374/EEC of 25 July 1985 on the approximation of the laws, regulations and administrative provisions of the Member States concerning liability for defective products, as modified by Directive 1999/34/EC of the European Parliament and of the Council of 10 May 1999 (OJ L 210/29, 7.8.1985, and OJ L 141/20, 4.6.1999) (the Product Liability Directive).

Proposal for a Directive of the European Parliament and of the Council on liability for defective products, European Commission, COM(2022) 495 final, Brussels, 28.9.2022 (the 'proposal for a revised Product Liability Directive (PLD)').

Directive 2014/104/EU of the European Parliament and of the Council of 26 November 2014 on certain rules governing actions for damages under national law for infringements of the competition law provisions of the Member States and of the European Union (the 'Damages Directive'), OJ L 349, 5.12.2014, pp. 1–19.

Directive 2004/48/EC of the European Parliament and of the Council of 29 April 2004 on the enforcement of intellectual property rights (the 'Enforcement Directive'), OJ L 157, 30.4.2004, pp. 45–86.

Commission Communication, "Artificial Intelligence for Europe", COM (2018) 237 final, Brussels, 25.4.2018.

Commission Staff Working Document on "Liability for emerging digital technologies" - Accompanying the document Commission Communication "Artificial intelligence for Europe", SWD(2018) 137 final, Brussels, 25.4.2018.

Commission Communication "Report on the safety and liability implications of Artificial Intelligence, the Internet of Things and robotics", COM (2020) 64 final, Brussels, 19.2.2020.

Commission Communication "White Paper On Artificial Intelligence - A European approach to excellence and trust", COM (2020) 65 final, Brussels, 19.2.2020.

Commission, DG GROW and DG JUST, "Factual summary report of the open public consultation on Adapting Civil Liability Rules to the Digital Age and AI", Ref. Ares(2022)2620305, 06.04.2022.

Commission's Inception Impact Assessment "Adapting liability rules to the digital age and circular economy", Ref. Ares(2021)4266516, 30.06.2021.

Commission's Public Consultation, "Adapting liability rules to the digital age and Artificial Intelligence", 18 October 2021.

European Parliament Resolution of 20 October 2020 with recommendations to the Commission on a civil liability regime for artificial intelligence (2020/2014 (INL)) P9_TA(2020)0276 ('European Parliament's Resolution of 20 October 2020 on a civil liability regime for AI').

Annex to the European Parliament Resolution of 20 October 2020 with recommendations to the Commission on a civil liability regime for artificial intelligence: detailed recommendations for drawing up a Regulation on liability for the operation of artificial intelligence systems, A. Principles and Aims of the Proposal. B. Text of the Proposal Requested—Proposal for a Regulation on liability for the operation of Artificial Intelligence-systems ('Annex to the European Parliament's Resolution of 20 October 2020 on a civil liability regime for AI').

Deloitte, Study to support the Commission's Impact Assessment on liability for artificial intelligence, 2021.

'European enterprise survey on the use of technologies based on artificial intelligence', Study prepared for the European Commission, DG Communications Networks, Content & Technology by Ipsos Belgium and iCite (International Centre for Innovation, Technology and Education), 2020, Final report.

Report from the Expert Group on Liability and New Technologies – New Technologies Formation "Liability for Artificial Intelligence and Other Emerging Digital Technologies", 21 November 2019.

Responses by Organisations, Associations and Corporations to Public Consultations

The Ada Lovelace Institute, "Feedback to the European Commission on its proposal for a Directive on adapting non-contractual civil liability rules to artificial intelligence", November 2022.

The Future of Life Institute (FLI), "FLI Position Paper on AI Liability – FLI position on the proposal for a Directive on adapting non-contractual civil liability rules to artificial intelligence (AI Liability Directive)", November 2022.

BEUC (the European Consumer Organisation), "Position Paper on the Proposal for an AI Liability Directive", 02.05.2023.

BEUC (the European Consumer Organisation), Press Release, "EU liability rules to be modernised but contain AI services blind spot for consumers", 28.09.2022.

BEUC (the European Consumer Organisation), Response to the European Commission's public consultation on Civil liability – adapting liability rules to the digital age and artificial intelligence, 23.12.2021.

Mozilla, Response to the Commission proposal for an AI Liability Directive (AILD) – The long road to redress, November 2022.

Irish Council for Civil Liberties (ICCL), Submission to the consultation on AI Liability, 28 November 2022.

BSA – The Software Alliance, "Response to the European Commission's consultation on civil liability – adapting liability rules to the digital age and artificial intelligence", 10.01.2022.

Confederation of European Security Services (CoESS) ("Confederation of European Security Services (CoESS) - Position Paper on the European Commission Consultation on adapting liability rules to the digital age and AI", 20 December 2021.

MedTech Europe, Feedback to the European Commission's proposal for a Directive on Liability rules for Artificial Intelligence, 24 November 2022.

U.S. Chamber of Commerce Institute of Legal Reform, Comments on the Proposed AI Liability Directive, November 2022.

eco – Association of the Internet Industry, Position Paper on the Commission's proposal for an AI Liability Directive, 28.11.2022.

ACT - The App Association feedback to the proposed Artificial Intelligence Liability Directive, 28 November 2022.

European Organisation for Security (EOS), Feedback to the proposed Artificial Intelligence Liability Directive, November 2022.

Upwork, Feedback on the Proposal for a Directive on adapting non-contractual civil liability rules to artificial intelligence, 28 November 2022.

Siemens, First assessment and recommendations – EU's AI Liability Directive proposal, 28 November 2022.

Siemens, "Executive summary on EU (civil) tort liability framework", 07.01.2022.

Google, "Comments - Public consultation: Civil liability – adapting liability rules to the digital age and artificial intelligence", 7 January 2022.

References

Adams-Prassl J (2019) What if your boss was an algorithm? The rise of artificial intelligence at work. Comp Lab Law Policy J 41(1):123

Akhtar N, Mian A (2018) Threat of adversarial attacks on deep learning in computer vision: a survey. IEEE Access 6:14410

Bathaee Y (2018) The artificial intelligence black box and the failure of intent and causation. Harv J Law Technol 31(2):889–938

Beck S (2016) The problem of ascribing legal responsibility in the case of robotics. AI Soc 31(4): 473–481

Beckers A, Teubner G (2021) Three liability regimes for artificial intelligence: algorithmic actants, hybrids, crowds. Bloomsbury Publishing

Bertolini A (2013) Robots as products: the case for a realistic analysis of robotic applications and liability rules. Law Innov Technol 5:214–247

Bertolini A (2018) Artificial intelligence and civil law - liability rules for drones, Study requested by the European Parliament's Committee on Legal Affairs, Policy Department for Citizens' Rights and Constitutional Affairs, November 2018

Bertolini A (2020) Artificial intelligence and civil liability, Study requested by the European Parliament's Committee on Legal Affairs, Policy Department for Citizens' Rights and Constitutional Affairs – Directorate-General for Internal Policies, PE 621.926, July 2020

Borges G (2019) New liability concepts: the potential of insurance and compensation funds. In: Lohsse S, Schulze R, Staudenmeyer D (eds) Liability for artificial intelligence and the internet of things. Nomos, Baden-Baden, pp 145–163

Borghetti J-S (2019) How can artificial intelligence be defective. In: Lohsse S, Schulze R, Staudenmayer D (eds) Liability for artificial intelligence and the internet of things. Nomos, Baden-Baden, pp 63–76

Bratu I (2023) A first critical analysis of the European approach to damage caused by artificial intelligence enabled by global navigation satellite systems. A bridge to nowhere or a cloud with a silver lining? Int Rev Law Comput Technol 37(2):147–165

Brown R (2021) Property ownership and the legal personhood of artificial intelligence. Inf Commun Technol Law 30(2):208–234

Buiten MC (2024) Product liability for defective AI. Eur J Law Econ 57:239–273

Buiten M, de Streel A, Peitz M (2021) EU liability rules for the age of artificial intelligence. Centre on Regulation in Europe (CERRE), March 2021

Buolamwini J, Gebru T (2018) Proceedings of the 1st Conference on Fairness, Accountability and Transparency. PMLR 81:77–91

Cabral TS (2020) Liability and artificial intelligence in the EU: assessing the adequacy of the current Product Liability Directive. Maastricht J Eur Comp Law 27(5):615–635

Chatzipanagiotis M, Leloudas G (2020) Automated vehicles and third-party liability: a European perspective. Univ Ill J Law Technol Policy 1:109–199

Christidis K, Devetsikiotis M (2016) Blockchains and smart contracts for the internet of things. IEEE Access 4:2292–2303

Cowls J, Tsamados A, Taddeo M, Floridi L (2023) The AI gambit: leveraging artificial intelligence to combat climate change—opportunities, challenges, and recommendations. AI Soc 38:283–307

Crootof R, Kaminski ME, Nicholson Price W II (2023) Humans in the loop. Vanderbilt Law Rev 76:429–510

Custers B, Fosch-Villaronga E (2022) Law and artificial intelligence – regulating AI and applying AI in legal practice. Information Technology and Law Series (ITLS), vol 35. Springer

de Bruin R (2016) Autonomous intelligent cars on the European intersection of liability and privacy: regulatory challenges and the road ahead. Eur J Risk Regul 7(3):485–501

De Bruyne J, Van Gool E, Gils T (2021) Tort law and damage caused by AI systems. In: De Bruyne J, Vanleenhove C (eds) Artificial intelligence and the law. Intersentia, pp 359–404

De Bruyne J, Dheu O, Ducuing C (2023) The European Commission's approach to extra-contractual liability and AI – an evaluation of the AI Liability Directive and the Revised Product Liability Directive. Comput Law Secur Rev 51:105894
De Luca S (2023) New Product Liability Directive. In: "A Europe Fit for the Digital Age", Legislative Train Schedule, European Parliamentary Research Service (EPRS), 15 December 2023
De Luca S (2024) New Product Liability Directive. In: "A Europe Fit for the Digital Age", Legislative Train Schedule, European Parliamentary Research Service (EPRS), 20 April 2024
de Meeus C (2019) The Product Liability Directive at the age of the digital industrial revolution: fit for innovation? J Eur Consum Market Law 8(4):149–154
del Castillo AP (2017) A law on robotics and artificial intelligence in the EU? (October 3, 2017). Foresight Brief, European Trade Union Institute (ETUI) Research Paper - Foresight Brief #02-September 2017
Del Monte M, Smialowski SB (2021) Understanding trilogue – informal tripartite meetings to reach provisional agreement on legislative files. European Parliamentary Research Service (EPRS), May 2021
Dheu O, De Bruyne J (2023) Artificial intelligence and tort law: a 'multi-faceted' reality. Eur Rev Priv Law 31(2):261–298
Dheu O, De Bruyne J, Ducuing C (2022) The European Commission's approach to extra contractual liability and AI – a first analysis and evaluation of the two proposals. CiTiP Working Paper Series, 6 October 2022
Duffourc MN, Gerke S (2023) The proposed EU Directives for AI liability leave worrying gaps likely to impact medical AI. npj Digit Med 6:77
Ebers M (2021) Liability for artificial intelligence and EU consumer law. JIPITEC 12:204–220
Eldakak A, Alremeithi A, Dahiyat E et al (2024) Civil liability for the actions of autonomous AI in healthcare: an invitation to further contemplation. Humanit Soc Sci Commun 11:305
Evas T (2018) A common EU approach to liability rules and insurance for connected and autonomous vehicles, Study. European Added Value Assessment - Accompanying the European Parliament's legislative own-initiative report (Rapporteur: Mady Delvaux). Study, European Parliamentary Research Service (EPRS), February 2018
Evas T (2020) Civil liability regime for artificial intelligence, Study, European Parliamentary Research Service (EPRS), September 2020
Fairgrieve D, Rajneri E (2019) Is software a product under the Product Liability Directive? Zeitschrift für Internationales Wirtschaftsrecht 1(2019):24–28
Fairgrieve D, Howells G, Møgelvang-Hansen P et al (2016) Product Liability Directive. In: Machnikowski P (ed) European Product Liability: an analysis of the state of the art in the era of new technologies. Principles of European tort law. Intersentia, pp 17–108
Frizberg D, Porubčanová P (2024) 'Adapting liability rules to artificial intelligence', Briefing, Initial Appraisal of a European Commission Impact Assessment, European Parliamentary Research Service (EPRS), March 2024
Froomkin AM, Kerr I, Pineau J (2019) When AIs outperform doctors: confronting the challenges of a tort-induced over-reliance on machine learning (February 20, 2019). Ariz Law Rev 61:33–99. University of Miami Legal Studies Research Paper No. 18-3
Geistfeld MA, Karner E, Koch BA, Wendehorst C (2023) Civil liability for artificial intelligence and software. De Gruyter, Berlin, Boston
Grundmann S, Hacker P (2017) Digital technology as a challenge to European contract law – from the existing to the future architecture. Eur Rev Contract Law 13:255–293
Hacker P (2023a) The European liability directives - critique of a half-hearted approach and lessons for the future. Comput Law Secur Rev 51:105871
Hacker P (2023b) Manipulation by algorithms. Exploring the triangle of unfair commercial practice, data protection, and privacy law. Eur Law J 29(1–2):142–175

Hacker P, Passoth J-H (2022) Varieties of AI explanations under the law. From the GDPR to the AIA, and beyond. In: Holzinger, Goebel, Fong, Moon, Müller, Samek (eds) Lecture Notes on Artificial Intelligence 13200: xxAI - beyond explainable AI. Springer
Hacker P, Krestel R, Grundmann S, Naumann F (2020) Explainable AI under contract and tort law: legal incentives and technical challenges. Artif Intell Law 28:415
Helberger N, Sax M, Strycharz J et al (2022) Choice architectures in the digital economy: towards a new understanding of digital vulnerability. J Consum Policy 45:175–200
Howells G, Twigg-Flesner C, Willett C (2017) Product liability and digital products. In: Synodinou T-E, Jougleux P, Markou C, Prastitou T (eds) EU internet law: regulation and enforcement. Springer Nature, pp 183–195
Karner E, Koch BA (2023) Comparative study on civil liability for artificial intelligence. In: Geistfeld MA, Karner E, Koch BA, Wendehorst C (eds) Civil liability for artificial intelligence
Karner E, Koch BA, Geistfeld MA (2021) Comparative law study on civil liability for artificial intelligence. European Commission, Directorate-General for Justice and Consumers
Koch BA, Borghetti J-S, Machnikowski P, Pichonnaz P, Rodríguez de las Heras Ballell T, Twigg-Flesner C, Wendehorst C (2022) Response of the European Law Institute to the public consultation on civil liability – adapting liability rules to the digital age and artificial intelligence. J Eur Tort Law 13(1):25–63
Kramer E, Cantarelli A (2023) Updating liability rules for defective products. Briefing, European Parliamentary Research Service (EPRS), January 2023
Kritikos M (2016) Legal and ethical reflections concerning robotics. Scientific Foresight Unit (STOA) Policy Briefing, European Parliament Research Service (EPRS), PE 563.501, June 2016
Kritikos M (2019) Artificial Intelligence ante portas: legal & ethical reflections. European Parliamentary Research Service (EPRS), Scientific Foresight Unit (STOA), March 2019
Leenes R, Palmerini E, Koops B-J, Bertolini A, Salvini P, Lucivero F (2017) Regulatory challenges of robotics: some guidelines for addressing legal and ethical issues. Law Innov Technol 9:1–44
Levy D (2020) Intelligent no-fault insurance for robots. J Future Robot Life 1:1–23
Li J-h (2018) Cyber security meets artificial intelligence: a survey. Front Inf Technol Electron Eng 19:1462–1474
Lodie A, Juarez SC, Karathanasis T (2022) Towards a new regime of civil liability for AI systems: Comment on the European Commission's Proposals. hal-04130851
Lohmann MF (2016) Liability issues concerning self-driving vehicles. Eur J Risk Regul 7(2): 335–340
Lohsse S, Schulze R, Staudenmayer D (2019) Liability for artificial intelligence. In: Lohsse S, Schulze R, Staudenmayer D (eds) Liability for artificial intelligence and the internet of things. Nomos, Baden-Baden, pp 99–116
Luzak J (2020) A broken notion: impact of modern technologies on product liability. Eur J Risk Regul 11(3):630–649
Machnikowski P (2016) Conclusions. In: Machnikowski P (ed) European product liability: an analysis of the state of the art in the era of new technologies. Principles of European tort law. Intersentia, pp 669–705
Madiega T (2020) Reform of the EU Liability Regime for Online Intermediaries: Background on the Forthcoming Digital Services Act: In Depth Analysis. European Parliamentary Research Service (EPRS), May 2020
Madiega T (2023) Artificial intelligence liability directive. Briefing, European Parliamentary Research Service (EPRS), February 2023
Marchisio E (2021) In support of "no-fault" civil liability rules for artificial intelligence. SN Soc Sci 1(1):54
Martín-Casals M (2019) Causation and scope of liability in the internet of things (IoT). In: Lohsse S, Schulze R, Staudenmayer D (eds) Liability for artificial intelligence and the internet of things. Nomos, Baden-Baden, pp 201–228

Maume P (2019) Reducing legal uncertainty and regulatory arbitrage for robo-advice. Eur Company Financ Law Rev:622–651
Mazzini G (2019) A system of governance for artificial intelligence through the lens of emerging intersections between AI and EU law. In: De Franceschi A, Schulze R (eds) Digital revolution – new challenges for law
Mezzanotte F (2019) Liability for digital products. In: A De Franceschi/R Schulze (eds) Digital revolution – new challenges for law, 169-188. Nomos
Mosoreanu M, Ulicna D, Paetz S, Podobea V, Schubert M, Stauf J, Renda A, Sipiczki A (2022) Behavioural Study on the link between challenges of artificial intelligence for Member States' civil liability rules and consumer attitudes towards AI-enabled products and services. Report, European Commission, Directorate-General for Justice and Consumers, Publications Office of the European Union
Navas S (2020) Robot machines and civil liability. In: Ebers M, Navas S (eds) Algorithms and law. Cambridge University Press, pp 157–173
Nawaz SA (2022) The proposed EU AI liability rules: ease or burden? European Law Blog
Nevejans N (2016) European civil law rules in robotics. Study requested by the European Parliament's Committee on Legal Affairs (JURI Committee)
Nikolinakos NT (2022) Adapting the EU Liability Regime to Artificial Intelligence (AI): The European Commission's Proposed Policy Options. Comput Telecommun Law Rev (C.T.L.R.) 28(3):66–83
Ntoutsi E, Fafalios P, Gadiraju U et al (2020) Bias in data-driven artificial intelligence systems—an introductory survey. Wiley Interdisciplinary Reviews: Data Mining and Knowledge Discovery 10:e1356
Pagallo U (2022) The way ahead on AI liability issues - will the developing EU liability framework for regulating AI prove sufficient? The Ada Lovelace Institute, 20 October 2022
Palmerini E, Bertolini A, Battaglia F, Koops B-J, Carnevale A, Salvini P (2016) RoboLaw: towards a European framework for robotics regulation. Robot Auton Syst 86:78–85
Patti FP (2019) The European road to autonomous vehicles. Fordham Int Law J 43:125
Rachum-Twaig O (2020) Whose robot is it anyway?: Liability for artificial intelligence-based products. Univ Ill Law Rev 2020(4):1141–1175
Rogers WVH (ed) (2001) Damages for non-pecuniary loss in a comparative perspective, European Centre of Tort and Insurance Law. Springer Verlag, Wien New York, p 246
Schellekens M (2018) No-fault compensation schemes for self-driving vehicles. Law Innov Technol 10(2):314–333
Schütte B, Majewski L, Havu K (2021) Damages liability for harm caused by artificial intelligence – EU law in flux. Helsinki Legal Studies Research Paper No. 69, August 2021
Shavell S (2020) On the redesign of accident liability for the world of autonomous vehicles. J Leg Stud 49:243–285
Soyer B, Tettenborn A (2023) Artificial intelligence and civil liability—do we need a new regime? Int J Law Inf Technol 30(4):385–397
Spindler G (2019) User liability and strict liability in the internet of things and for robots. In: Lohsse S, Schulze R, Staudenmayer D (eds) Liability for artificial intelligence and the internet of things. Nomos, Baden-Baden, pp 125–145
Strauß S (2021) Deep automation bias: how to tackle a wicked problem of AI? Big Data Cogn Comput 5:18
Tenhunen S (2022) Aligning the Product Liability Directive with the circular economy and emerging technologies: revision of Directive 85/374/EEC. Implementation Appraisal Briefing, European Parliamentary Research Service (EPRS), October 2022
Timan T, Snijders R, Kirova M, Suardi S, Lieshout MV, Chen M, Costenco P, Palmerini E, Bertolini A, Tejada A, Montfort SV, Bolchi M, Alberti S, Brouwer R, Karanilokova K, Episcopo F, Jansen S (2019) Study on safety of non-embedded software. Service, data access, and legal issues of advanced robots, autonomous, connected, and AI-based vehicles and

systems: final study report regarding CAD/CCAM and industrial robots. European Commission, Brussel
Tolan S, Miron M, Gomez E, Castillo C (2019) Why machine learning may lead to unfairness: evidence from risk assessment for juvenile justice in Catalonia. Best Paper Award, International Conference on AI and Law
Twigg-Flesner C (2021a) Guiding Principles for Updating the Product Liability Directive for the Digital Age (Pilot ELI Innovation Paper), European Law Institute (January 2021)
Twigg-Flesner C (2021b) Guiding principles for updating the Product Liability Directive for the digital age. European Law Institute (ELI) Innovation Paper Series
van Boom WH, Borghetti J-S, Ehlers AB, Karner E, Nolan D, Oliphant K, Scarso A, Ulfbeck V, Wagner G (2018) Product liability in Europe. In: Koziol H, Green MD, Lunney M, Oliphant K, Yang L (eds) Product liability: fundamental questions in a comparative perspective. De Gruyter, Berlin, Boston, pp 255–356
Van Uytsel S (2021) Different liability regimes for autonomous vehicles: one preferable above the other? In: Van Uytsel S, Vargas DV (eds) Autonomous vehicles – business, technology and law. Part of the book series: Perspectives in Law, Business and Innovation (PLBI), Springer 2021, pp 67–92
Vellinga NE (2024) Rethinking compensation in light of the development of AI. Int Rev Law Comput Technol, pp 1–22
Verheyen T (2018) Full harmonization, consumer protection and products liability: a fresh reading of the case law of the ECJ. Eur Rev Priv Law 26(1):119–140
Verheyen T (2021) On behavioural asymmetry in product liability law: how privatising nudging will get European product liability theory back on track. J Eur Tort Law 12(1):40–64
Wagner G (2019a) Robot liability. In: Lohsse S, Schulze R, Staudenmayer D (eds) Liability for artificial intelligence and the internet of things. Nomos, Baden-Baden, pp 27–62
Wagner G (2019b) Robot, Inc.: personhood for autonomous systems? Fordham Law Rev 88:591
Wagner G (2021) Liability for artificial intelligence: a proposal by the European Parliament. In: Eidenmüller H, Wagner G (eds) Law by algorithm, 127
Wagner G (2022a) Liability rules for the digital age – aiming for the Brussels effect. J Eur Tort Law (JETL) 13(3):191–243
Wagner G (2022b) Software as a product. In: Lohsse S, Schulze R, Staudenmayer D (eds) Smart Products, 157. Hart, Nomos
Watts K (2020) Potential of no-fault comprehensive compensation funds to deal with automation and other 21st century transport developments. Eur J Commer Contract Law 12:1–21
Wendehorst C (2020a) Strict liability for AI and other emerging technologies. J Eur Tort Law (JETL) 11(2):150–180
Wendehorst C (2020b) Liability for pure data loss. In: Karner E, Magnus U, Spier J, Widmer P (eds) Essays in honor of Helmut Koziol, pp 225–242
Wendehorst C (2021) Safety and liability related aspects of software. Study commissioned by the European Commission
Wendehorst C (2022) AI liability in Europe: anticipating the EU AI Liability Directive. Ada Lovelace Institute
Wuyts D (2014) The Product Liability Directive – more than two decades of defective products in Europe. J Eur Tort Law 5(1):1–34
Zech H (2019) Liability for autonomous systems: tackling specific risks of modern IT. In: Lohsse S, Schulze R, Staudenmeyer D (eds) Liability for artificial intelligence and the internet of things. Nomos, Baden-Baden, pp 187–200
Zech H (2021) Liability for AI: public policy considerations. Academy of European Law (ERA) Forum, vol 22. Springer, pp 147–158
Ziosi M, Mökander J, Novelli C, Casolari F, Taddeo M, Floridi L (2023) The EU AI Liability Directive (AILD): bridging information gaps. Eur J Law Technol 14(3)

Chapter 9
Reforming the EU Civil Liability Framework Applicable to Artificial Intelligence and Other Emerging Digital Technologies: Defective Products—the Revised Product Liability Directive

9.1 Introduction

This chapter discusses in detail the European Commission's proposal for a new Directive on liability of defective products, which will revise, repeal, and replace the existing Product Liability Directive (the 'proposal for a revised Product Liability Directive').[1] The chapter compares the Commission's proposal with the Council of the EU's "compromise" proposal (general approach) and thoroughly examines the position of the European Parliament. Additionally, it covers in detail the provisional (political) agreement reached on 14 December 2023 and the final text of the revised Product Liability Directive (March 2024).

The current Product Liability Directive (PLD)[2] harmonises no-fault based (i.e., strict) liability regimes for claims for damage caused to a consumer due to the defectiveness of a (movable) product at EU level (i.e., it establishes common rules at the EU level for the non-fault (strict) liability of producers for damage caused by defective products, regardless of fault or negligence). It harmonises the liability of the producer (i.e., deals with consumer claims against producers) of defective products, laying down common rules under which the producer is held liable for damage caused by a defect in his product. The actual cause of events that lead to damage or incident is decisive for the attribution of liability. It provides an avenue

[1]Proposal for a Directive of the European Parliament and of the Council on liability for defective products, European Commission, COM(2022) 495 final, Brussels, 28.9.2022 (the 'proposal for a revised Product Liability Directive (PLD)').

[2]Council Directive 85/374/EEC of 25 July 1985 on the approximation of the laws, regulations and administrative provisions of the Member States concerning liability for defective products, as modified by Directive 1999/34/EC of the European Parliament and of the Council of 10 May 1999 (OJ L 210/29, 7.8.1985, and OJ L 141/20, 4.6.1999) [the 'Product Liability Directive' – 'PLD'].

N. T. Nikolinakos, *Adapting the EU Civil Liability Regime to the Digital Age: Artificial Intelligence, Robotics, and Other Emerging Technologies*, Law, Governance and Technology Series 68, https://doi.org/10.1007/978-3-031-67969-8_9

for individuals (whether they are the owner or a bystander) who have suffered personal injuries, damage to consumer property, or death due to a defective product to claim financial compensation.

The current Product Liability Directive introduced the concept of strict liability of producers, according to which if a defective product causes death, personal injury or material damage (above EUR 500) to consumers or their private property, the producer is liable to provide compensation irrespectively of whether there is negligence or fault on the consumers' part. Therefore, producers are responsible for defective products, regardless of whether the defect of the product is their fault. A product is considered defective if it does not provide the safety a person is entitled to expect. To sustain their claim, those who have suffered injury (physical damage) or material damage must prove the defect in the product (i.e. that the product did not provide the safety that the public is entitled to expect), the damage, and the causal link between the defect and the damage.[3]

The evaluation of the Product Liability Directive concluded that the PLD had several shortcomings, such as the lack of legal clarity on how to apply the PLD's definitions to products in the digital and circular economy, difficulties related to the burden of proof in the case of complex products, and limitations on making claims. In particular, it was found that two are the main problems affecting the existing PLD, namely: (i) certain products, economic actors and damage in the digital and circular economy escape (are not covered under) no-fault (strict) liability; (ii) consumers face obstacles to getting compensation. Whereas victims do not have to prove fault (producers bear liability irrespective of fault), proving defectiveness and causal link with damage is very difficult and costly for complex products. Also, liability claims are subject to a number of restrictions (claimants face time limits and thresholds that might disproportionately restrict the number of claims).

In September 2022, in response to the shortcomings affecting the current PLD, the Commission published a proposal for a new Directive on liability of defective products, which would revise, repeal, and replace the existing Product Liability Directive (the 'proposal for a revised Product Liability Directive'/the 'proposed new Product Liability Directive').[4] The aim of the proposal for a revised Product Liability Directive (PLD) is to modernise the current EU's product liability regime, based on

---

[3]Commission Staff Working Document, "Impact Assessment Report – Accompanying the document Proposal for a Directive of the European Parliament and of the Council on adapting non-contractual civil liability rules to artificial intelligence", SWD(2022) 319 final, Brussels, 28.9.2022, at p. 4: "Victims may have, under the PLD, a claim against the producer of a defective product for a defect present when the product was put on the market. The victim must prove that the product was defective and the causal link between that defect and the damage. Under the PLD, the victim can claim compensation for personal injury or damage to consumer property. The PLD does not cover damage caused to property intended for professional use, damage caused during the provision of a service, damage to victims other than natural persons or claims based on the wrongful use of a product".

[4]Proposal for a Directive of the European Parliament and of the Council on liability for defective products, European Commission, COM(2022) 495 final, Brussels, 28.9.2022 (the 'proposal for a revised Product Liability Directive (PLD)'/the 'proposal for a revised PLD').

the strict liability of manufacturers, for the compensation of personal injury, damage to property or data loss caused by unsafe products.

The revised PLD is designed to accommodate the latest technological advancements, circular economy business models, and global value chains. This is achieved by ensuring the following: (i) businesses and consumers/victims are subject to fair and predictable rules; (ii) victims are adequately compensated for any harm caused by hazardous products, including digital products and AI systems; and (iii) a level playing field exists between EU and non-EU manufacturers. To this end, the revised PLD attempts to achieve the following four specific objectives. First, in order to adapt product liability rules to the digital age and circular economy: (i) ensuring liability rules reflect the nature and risks of products in the digital age and circular economy; (ii) ensuring there is always an EU-based business that can be held liable, i.e. it is possible to obtain compensation, when defective products are bought directly from manufacturers/producers outside the EU. Second, in order to reduce disproportionate obstacles to getting compensation: (iii) easing the burden of proof in complex cases (and clarifying liability for undiscoverable defects), while ensuring fair balance between producers/manufacturers and consumers; (iv) easing restrictions on making claims as well as ensuring legal certainty by better aligning the PLD with the new legislative framework created by Decision 768/2008/EC7 and with product safety rules.

The Commission's proposal for a revised PLD introduces provisions to address liability for products such as software (including AI systems) and digital services that affect the functioning of the product (e.g. navigation services in autonomous vehicles). Additionally, it clarifies the liability rules for companies that substantially modify products before reselling them. The Commission's proposal also ensures that consumers are compensated for defective products manufactured outside the EU. The Commission's proposed new PLD broadens the notion of "defect" and allows compensation for damage when products like robots, drones or IoT smart-home systems become unsafe by software updates, AI or digital services that are needed to operate the product, as well as in cases where manufacturers fail to address connectivity risks and cybersecurity vulnerabilities. Under certain circumstances, the Commission's proposal requires manufacturers to disclose information in cases where plausible claims for compensation are made, and alleviates the burden of proof for victims (consumers) seeking compensation for damages resulting from defective products.

The Commission's proposal for a revised Product Liability Directive must be reviewed and adopted by the European Parliament and Member States before it comes into effect and, to this end, the Commission's proposal was discussed by the co-legislators (the main decision-making bodies of the EU), i.e., the European Parliament ("the Parliament") and the Council of the European Union ("the Council").

On 14 June 2023, at the Committee of the Permanent Representatives (COREPER) meeting, the Council of the EU (the Council) adopted its negotiating mandate and formalised its position ("general approach") for a new EU Directive on liability for defective products,[5] extending product liability rules to software and Artificial Intelligence. In general, EU countries have largely maintained the Commission's proposal and have gone further in certain aspects, notably by giving national liability regimes the possibility to cover non-material damages and to hold manufacturers liable for defects that could not be known at the time of the market launch.

On the Parliamentary front, the discussions were led by the Committee on Internal Market and Consumer Protection (IMCO) and the Committee on Legal Affairs (JURI) under a joint committee procedure. On 5 April 2023 the European Parliament's co-leading Committees on the proposal for a revised PLD issued their draft Joint Report,[6] which constitutes a significant tone-down of the revised PLD. On 9 October 2023, following their draft Joint Report of 5 April 2023, the joint committees adopted the final Report[7] and decided to enter into trilogue (i.e. interinstitutional) negotiations with the Council of the EU (and the Commission),[8] with the aim of reaching a political agreement on the legislative text of the amended PLD in the coming months. The European Parliament confirmed the draft mandate at the Plenary session of 16 October 2023.

Following the Interinstitutional negotiations (trilogue), the co-legislators (Council of the EU and the European Parliament) reached a provisional (political) agreement on 14 December 2023. At its meeting on 24 January 2024, the Permanent Representatives Committee of the Council of the EU confirmed the agreement on the compromise text of the revised Product Liability Directive,[9] as it was reached between the negotiating parties on 14 December 2023, and authorised the Presidency to address the habitual offer letter to the European Parliament.

---

[5] Council of the European Union, Note: From: General Secretariat of the Council. To: Delegations. Subject: Proposal for a Directive of the European Parliament and of the Council on liability for defective products - Mandate for negotiations with the European Parliament, Brussels, 15 June 2023, Council doc. 10694/23 ("General Secretariat of the Council - General approach on the proposal for a revised PLD, 15 June 2023").

[6] Draft Report of the European Parliament's Committee on Internal Market and Consumer Protection and the Committee on Legal Affairs on the proposal for a directive of the European Parliament and of the Council on Liability for defective products (COM(2022)0495 – C9-0322/2022 – 2022/0302(COD)), 05.04.2023, ("Draft Joint Report of the European Parliament's co-leading IMCO and JURI Committees on the proposal for a revised PLD, 5 April 2023").

[7] Joint Report of the European Parliament's co-leading IMCO and JURI Committees on the proposal for a directive of the European Parliament and of the Council on liability for defective products, A9-0291/2023, 12 October 2023.

[8] On 16.10.2023, the joint committees' decision to enter into interinstitutional negotiations was announced in plenary. On 18.10.2023, the joint committees' decision to enter into interinstitutional negotiations was confirmed by the plenary.

[9] Council of the European Union, Information Note: From: General Secretariat of the Council. To: Delegations. Subject: Proposal for a Directive of the European Parliament and of the Council on liability for defective products – Letter sent to the European Parliament, Brussels, 24 January 2024, Council doc. 5809/24 ("General Secretariat of the Council – Proposal for a Directive on liability for defective products – Letter sent to the European Parliament, Council doc. 5809/24, 24 January 2024").

The text of the provisional agreement[10] was submitted to the Committee on the Internal Market and Consumer Protection (IMCO) and the Committee on Legal Affairs (JURI), which voted on 22 February 2024. The final text of the revised PLD was formally endorsed by the European Parliament at the Plenary of 12 March 2024, which adopted its position at first reading.[11] The revised Product Liability Directive will have to be formally approved by the Council of the EU, too. It will enter into force on the twentieth day following its publication in the EU Official Journal. The new rules will apply to products placed on the market or put into service 24 months after entry into force of the revised PLD.

This chapter argues that, although the revised PLD appears poised to tip the scales further in favor of claimants, particularly in complex cases, thus increasing the likelihood of manufacturers/producers facing considerable litigation risks, including the heightened risk of third-party litigation funding, it ultimately succeeds in establishing an EU product liability framework that: (i) ensures liability rules reflect the nature and risks of products in the digital age and circular economy, (ii) supports businesses bringing safe, AI-enabled and other innovative products to market, (iii) ensures that consumers' health and property are afforded a high level of protection, (iv) reduces disproportionate obstacles to obtaining compensation, and v) strikes an appropriate balance between the interests of claimants and defendants in Member State courts.[12]

---

[10]European Parliament, Committee on the Internal Market and Consumer Protection (IMCO) and Committee on Legal Affairs (JURI), "Provisional Agreement Resulting from Interinstitutional Negotiations", Subject: Proposal for a Directive of the European Parliament and of the Council on Liability for defective products (COM(2022)0495 – C9 0322/2022 – 2022/0302(COD)), 31 January 2024.

[11]European Parliament legislative resolution of 12 March 2024 on the proposal for a Directive of the European Parliament and of the Council on liability for defective products (COM(2022)0495 – C9-0322/2022 – 2022/0302(COD)), (Ordinary legislative procedure: first reading) – P9_TC1-COD (2022)0302, Position of the European Parliament adopted at first reading on 12 March 2024 with a view to the adoption of Directive (EU) 2024/... of the European Parliament and of the Council on liability for defective products and repealing Council Directive 85/374/EEC ["Position of the European Parliament of 12 March 2024 for the adoption of a Directive on liability for defective products (revised PLD)"].

[12]This chapter discusses the different approaches of the European Institutions (European Commission, Council of the EU, European Parliament), which led to the political agreement reached on 14 December 2023 and the final text of the revised Product Liability Directive in March 2024.

The chapter focuses on the perspectives of stakeholders/actors with varied and, sometimes, conflicting interests who have been actively involved in the relevant public consultations. These stakeholders include governmental organisations and national competent authorities, industry representatives (corporations, business associations, software developers, manufacturers/producers etc.), consumer associations, civil society and other non-profit organisations, and academic/research institutions.

For interesting reading, analysis, and useful academic commentary, see the following:

Miriam C. Buiten, 'Product liability for defective AI', European Journal of Law and Economics 57, 239–273 (2024).

Nynke E. Vellinga, (2024). 'Rethinking compensation in light of the development of AI'. International Review of Law, Computers & Technology, 1–22.

Dieter Frizberg with Petra Porubčanová, 'Adapting liability rules to artificial intelligence', Briefing, Initial Appraisal of a European Commission Impact Assessment, European Parliamentary Research Service (EPRS), March 2024.

Stefano De Luca, 'New Product Liability Directive', In "A Europe Fit for the Digital Age", Legislative Train Schedule, European Parliamentary Research Service (EPRS), 20 April 2024.

Eldakak, A., Alremeithi, A., Dahiyat, E. et al. Civil liability for the actions of autonomous AI in healthcare: an invitation to further contemplation. Humanit Soc Sci Commun 11, 305 (2024).

Jan De Bruyne, Orian Dheu, Charlotte Ducuing, 'The European Commission's approach to extra-contractual liability and AI – An evaluation of the AI Liability Directive and the Revised Product Liability Directive', Computer Law & Security Review, Volume 51, November 2023, 105894.

Orian Dheu and Jan De Bruyne, 'Artificial Intelligence and Tort Law: A 'Multi-faceted' Reality', (2023), European Review of Private Law, Volume 31, Issue 2, pp. 261–298.

Marta Ziosi, Jakob Mökander, Claudio Novelli, Federico Casolari, Mariarosaria Taddeo, Luciano Floridi, "The EU AI Liability Directive (AILD): Bridging Information Gaps", European Journal of Law and Technology, Vol. 14 No. 3 (2023).

Ioana Bratu, "A First Critical Analysis of the European Approach to Damage Caused by Artificial Intelligence Enabled by Global Navigation Satellite Systems. A Bridge to Nowhere or a Cloud with a Silver Lining?", 2023, International Review of Law, Computers & Technology, 37 (2): 147–165.

Mindy Nunez Duffourc and Sara Gerke, 'The proposed EU Directives for AI liability leave worrying gaps likely to impact medical AI', npj Digit. Med. 6, 77 (2023).

Geistfeld, Mark A., Karner, Ernst, Koch, Bernhard A. and Wendehorst, Christiane. Civil Liability for Artificial Intelligence and Software, Berlin, Boston: De Gruyter, 2023.

E. Karner, B. A. Koch, Comparative Study on Civil Liability for Artificial Intelligence, in: M. A. Geistfeld/E. Karner/B. A. Koch/C. Wendehorst, Civil Liability for Artificial Intelligence (2023).

Baris Soyer and Andrew Tettenborn, "Artificial intelligence and civil liability—do we need a new regime?", International Journal of Law and Information Technology, 30(4), pp. 385–397, February 2023.

Philipp Hacker, "The European liability directives - Critique of a half-hearted approach and lessons for the future", Computer Law & Security Review 51 (2023) 105871.

Philipp Hacker, "Manipulation by algorithms. Exploring the triangle of unfair commercial practice, data protection, and privacy law. European Law Journal, 29(1–2), 142–175, (2023).

Josh Cowls, Andreas Tsamados, Mariarosaria Taddeo & Luciano Floridi, "The AI gambit: leveraging artificial intelligence to combat climate change—opportunities, challenges, and recommendations", AI & Society 38, 283–307, (2023).

Rebecca Crootof, Margot E. Kaminski, W. Nicholson Price II, "Humans in the Loop" (2023) 76 Vanderbilt Law Review 429–510.

Stefano De Luca, 'New Product Liability Directive', In "A Europe Fit for the Digital Age", Legislative Train Schedule, European Parliamentary Research Service (EPRS), 15 December 2023.

Esther Kramer with Arianna Cantarelli, 'Updating liability rules for defective products', Briefing, European Parliamentary Research Service (EPRS), January 2023.

Tambiama Madiega, 'Artificial intelligence liability directive', Briefing, European Parliamentary Research Service (EPRS), February 2023.

Orian Dheu, Jan De Bruyne, Charlotte Ducuing, 'The European Commission's Approach To Extra Contractual Liability and AI – A First Analysis and Evaluation of the Two Proposals', CiTiP Working Paper Series, 6 October 2022.

Koch, Bernhard A, Borghetti, Jean-Sébastien, Machnikowski, Piotr, Pichonnaz, Pascal, Rodríguez de las Heras Ballell, Teresa, Twigg-Flesner, Christian and Wendehorst, Christiane, “Response of the European Law Institute to the Public Consultation on Civil Liability – Adapting Liability Rules to the Digital Age and Artificial Intelligence”, Journal of European Tort Law, vol. 13, no. 1, 2022, pp. 25–63.

Ugo Pagallo, ‘The way ahead on AI liability issues - Will the developing EU liability framework for regulating AI prove sufficient?’, The Ada Lovelace Institute, 20 October 2022.

Christiane Wendehorst, “AI liability in Europe: anticipating the EU AI Liability Directive”, Ada Lovelace Institute, 2022.

Alexandre Lodie, Stephanie Celis Juarez, Theodoros Karathanasis. Towards a New Regime of Civil Liability for AI Systems: Comment on the European Commission’s Proposals. 2022. hal-04130851.

Nikos Th. Nikolinakos, ‘Adapting the EU Liability Regime to Artificial Intelligence (AI): The European Commission’s Proposed Policy Options’, (2022) 28 Computer & Telecommunications Law Review (C.T.L.R.), Issue 3, pp. 66–83.

Philipp Hacker and Jan-Hendrik Passoth, “Varieties of AI Explanations under the Law. From the GDPR to the AIA, and Beyond”, in: Holzinger, Goebel, Fong, Moon, Müller and Samek (eds.), Lecture Notes on Artificial Intelligence 13200: xxAI - beyond explainable AI, Springer, 2022.

Susanna Tenhunen, ‘Aligning the Product Liability Directive with the circular economy and emerging technologies: Revision of Directive 85/374/EEC’, Implementation Appraisal Briefing, European Parliamentary Research Service (EPRS), October 2022.

Mosoreanu, Marius; Ulicna, Daniela; Paetz, Stephan; Podobea, Vlad; Schubert, Manuel; Stauf, Julia; Renda, Andrea; Sipiczki, Agnes, ‘Behavioural Study on the link between challenges of artificial intelligence for Member States’ civil liability rules and consumer attitudes towards AI-enabled products and services’, Report, European Commission, Directorate-General for Justice and Consumers, Publications Office of the European Union, 2022.

Gerhard Wagner, “Liability Rules for the Digital Age – Aiming for the Brussels Effect”, Journal of European Tort Law (JETL) 2022, vol. 13, no. 3, pp. 191–243.

Gerhard Wagner, ‘Software as a Product’ in: S. Lohsse/R. Schulze/D. Staudenmayer (eds.), Smart Products, 157, (2022), Hart, Nomos.

Samar Abbas Nawaz, The Proposed EU AI Liability Rules: Ease or Burden? (2022), European Law Blog.

Bart Custers and Eduard Fosch-Villaronga, ‘Law and Artificial Intelligence – Regulating AI and Applying AI in Legal Practice’, Information Technology and Law Series (ITLS), volume 35, 2022, Springer.

N. Helberger, M. Sax, J. Strycharz et al., “Choice Architectures in the Digital Economy: Towards a New Understanding of Digital Vulnerability”, Journal of Consumer Policy 45, 175–200 (2022).

Christian Twigg-Flesner, ‘Guiding Principles for Updating the Product Liability Directive for the Digital Age’ (Pilot ELI Innovation Paper), European Law Institute (January 2021).

Martin Ebers, “Liability For Artificial Intelligence And EU Consumer Law”, 12 (2021) JIPITEC 204–220.

Ernst Karner, Bernhard A. Koch, Mark A. Geistfeld, ‘Comparative Law Study on Civil Liability for Artificial Intelligence’, European Commission, Directorate-General for Justice and Consumers, 2021.

Herbert Zech, ‘Liability for AI: public policy considerations’, Academy of European Law (ERA) Forum, Volume 22, 147–158, Springer, 2021.

Christiane Wendehorst, ‘Safety and Liability Related Aspects of Software’, Study commissioned by the European Commission, 2021.

Gerhard Wagner, Liability for Artificial Intelligence: A Proposal by the European Parliament, in: H. Eidenmüller/G. Wagner, Law by Algorithm (2021) 127.

Anna Beckers, Gunther Teubner, "Three Liability Regimes for Artificial Intelligence: Algorithmic Actants, Hybrids, Crowds", Bloomsbury Publishing, 2021.

Miriam Buiten, Alexandre de Streel, Martin Peitz 'EU Liability Rules for the Age of Artificial Intelligence', Centre on Regulation in Europe (CERRE), March 2021.

Emiliano Marchisio, "In support of "no-fault" civil liability rules for artificial intelligence" (2021) 1 SN Social Sciences 1, 54 (2021).

Thomas Verheyen, "On Behavioural Asymmetry in Product Liability Law: How Privatising Nudging Will Get European Product Liability Theory Back on Track", Journal of European Tort Law, vol. 12, no. 1, 2021, pp. 40–64.

Stefan Strauß, "Deep Automation Bias: How to Tackle a Wicked Problem of AI?", Big Data and Cognitive Computing, 5, 18 (2021).

Christian Twigg-Flesner, 'Guiding Principles for Updating the Product Liability Directive for the Digital Age', European Law Institute (ELI) Innovation Paper Series, 2021.

Steven Van Uytsel, 'Different Liability Regimes for Autonomous Vehicles: One Preferable Above the Other?', in Steven Van Uytsel and Danilo Vasconcellos Vargas (eds), Autonomous Vehicles – Business, Technology and Law. Part of the book series: Perspectives in Law, Business and Innovation (PLBI), Springer 2021, pp. 67–92.

Jan De Bruyne, Elias Van Gool, Thomas Gils, 'Tort Law and Damage Caused by AI Systems', in J. De Bruyne and C. Vanleenhove, Artificial Intelligence and the Law, 359–404, Intersentia, 2021.

Beatrice Schütte, Lotta Majewski, Katri Havu, 'Damages Liability for Harm Caused by Artificial Intelligence – EU Law in Flux', Helsinki Legal Studies Research Paper No. 69, August 2021.

Micaela Del Monte and Stephanie Brenda Smialowski, "Understanding trilogue – Informal tripartite meetings to reach provisional agreement on legislative files", European Parliamentary Research Service (EPRS), May 2021.

Roger Brown, 'Property Ownership and the Legal Personhood of Artificial Intelligence', (2021) Information & Communications Technology Law, 30(2), 208–234.

Tiago Sérgio Cabral, "Liability and artificial intelligence in the EU: Assessing the adequacy of the current Product Liability Directive", Maastricht Journal of European and Comparative Law, 27(5), 615–635, (2020).

Tatjana Evas, Civil liability regime for artificial intelligence, Study, European Parliamentary Research Service (EPRS), September 2020.

Christiane Wendehorst, "Strict liability for AI and other emerging technologies", Journal of European Tort Law (JETL) 2020, 11(2): 150–180.

Christiane Wendehorst, Liability for Pure Data Loss, in: E Karner/U Magnus/J Spier/P Widmer (eds), Essays in Honor of Helmut Koziol (2020) 225–242.

Tambiama Madiega, 'Reform of the EU Liability Regime for Online Intermediaries: Background on the Forthcoming Digital Services Act: In Depth Analysis', European Parliamentary Research Service (EPRS), May 2020.

Philipp Hacker, Ralf Krestel, Stefan Grundmann, Felix Naumann, "Explainable AI under contract and tort law: legal incentives and technical challenges", 28 Artificial Intelligence and Law 415, (2020).

Andrea Bertolini, Artificial intelligence and civil liability, Study requested by the European Parliament's Committee on Legal Affairs, Policy Department for Citizens' Rights and Constitutional Affairs – Directorate-General for Internal Policies, PE 621.926, July 2020.

Joasia Luzak, "A Broken Notion: Impact of Modern Technologies on Product Liability", European Journal of Risk Regulation, 11(3):630–649, (2020).

Susanna Navas, 'Robot Machines and Civil Liability'. In M. Ebers & S. Navas (eds.), Algorithms and Law. Cambridge University Press, 2020, 157–173.

Eirini Ntoutsi, P. Fafalios, U. Gadiraju and others, 'Bias in data-driven artificial intelligence systems—An introductory survey' (2020) 10 Wiley Interdisciplinary Reviews: Data Mining and Knowledge Discovery e1356.

Steven Shavell, "On the Redesign of Accident Liability for the World of Autonomous Vehicles", (2020) 49 The Journal of Legal Studies, 243–285.

Kim Watts, 'Potential of No-Fault Comprehensive Compensation Funds to Deal with Automation and Other 21st Century Transport Developments', European Journal of Commercial Contract Law, 2020, vol. 12, 1–21.

David Levy, 'Intelligent No-Fault Insurance for Robots', Journal of Future Robot Life, 2020, vol. 1, 1–23.

Omri Rachum-Twaig, 'Whose robot is it anyway?: Liability for artificial intelligence-based products', University of Illinois Law Review, Vol. 2020, No. 4, p. 1141–1175.

Michael Chatzipanagiotis and George Leloudas, 'Automated Vehicles and Third-Party Liability: A European Perspective', University of Illinois Journal of Law, Technology & Policy 2020(1), pp. 109–199.

Francesco Paolo Patti, "The European Road to Autonomous Vehicles", 43 Fordham Int'l L.J. 125 (2019).

Herbert Zech: "Liability for autonomous systems: tackling specific risks of modern IT". In: Lohsse, S., Schulze, R., Staudenmeyer, D. (eds.), Liability for Artificial Intelligence and the Internet of Things. Nomos, Baden-Baden (2019), pp. 187–200.

Borges, G.: New Liability Concepts: the potential of insurance and compensation funds. In: Lohsse, S., Schulze, R., Staudenmeyer, D. (eds.) Liability for Artificial Intelligence and the Internet of Things. Nomos, Baden-Baden (2019), pp. 145–163.

Borghetti J-S, 'How can artificial intelligence be defective'. In: Lohsse S, Schulze R, Staudenmayer D (eds) Liability for artificial intelligence and the Internet of Things. Nomos, Baden-Baden (2019), pp. 63–76.

Gerald Spindler, 'User Liability and Strict Liability in the Internet of Things and for Robots' in Sebastian Lohsse, Reiner Schulze and Dirk Staudenmayer (eds), Liability for Artificial Intelligence and the Internet of Things. Nomos, Baden-Baden (2019), pp. 125–145.

Miquel Martín-Casals, 'Causation and Scope of Liability in the Internet of Things (IoT)' in Sebastian Lohsse/Reiner Schulze/Dirk Staudenmayer (ed), Liability for Artificial Intelligence and the Internet of Things. Nomos, Baden-Baden (2019), pp. 201–228.

Jeremias Adams-Prassl, "What if Your Boss Was an Algorithm? The Rise of Artificial Intelligence at Work", (2019) 41(1) Comparative Labor Law & Policy Journal 123.

A. Michael Froomkin, Ian Kerr and Joelle Pineau, "When AIs Outperform Doctors: Confronting the Challenges of a Tort-Induced Over-Reliance on Machine Learning (February 20, 2019). 61 Ariz. L. Rev. 33–99, (2019), University of Miami Legal Studies Research Paper No. 18-3.

Philipp Maume, "Reducing Legal Uncertainty and Regulatory Arbitrage for Robo-Advice", European Company and Financial Law Review 2019, 622–651.

Lohsse, S., Schulze, R., & Staudenmayer, D., 'Liability for Artificial Intelligence', In S. Lohsse, R. Schulze, & D. Staudenmayer (eds.), Liability for Artificial Intelligence and the Internet of Things. Nomos, Baden-Baden (2019), 99–116.

Gerhard Wagner, 'Robot Liability' in S.Lohsse/R.Schulze/D.Staudenmayer (eds), Liability for Artificial Intelligence and the Internet of Things. Nomos, Baden-Baden (2019), pp. 27–62.

Timan, T., R. Snijders, M. Kirova, S. Suardi, M. v. Lieshout, M. Chen, P. Costenco, E. Palmerini, A. Bertolini, A. Tejada, S. v. Montfort, M. Bolchi, S. Alberti, R. Brouwer, K. Karanilokova, F. Episcopo and S. Jansen (2019). Study on safety of non-embedded software. Service, data access, and legal issues of advanced robots, autonomous, connected, and AI-based vehicles and systems: final study report regarding CAD/CCAM and industrial robots. Brussel, European Commission.

Gabriele Mazzini, "A System of Governance for Artificial Intelligence through the Lens of Emerging Intersections between AI and EU Law" in A. De Franceschi/ R. Schulze (ed), Digital Revolution – New challenges for Law (2019)

Gerhard Wagner, "Robot, Inc.: Personhood for Autonomous Systems?", 88 Fordham Law Review, 591 (2019).

Charlotte de Meeus, 'The Product Liability Directive at the Age of the Digital Industrial Revolution: Fit for Innovation?', (2019), Vol. 8, Journal of European Consumer and Market Law, Issue 4, pp. 149–154.

Mihalis Kritikos, 'Artificial Intelligence ante portas: Legal & ethical reflections', European Parliamentary Research Service (EPRS), Scientific Foresight Unit (STOA), March 2019.

Francesco Mezzanotte, 'Liability for Digital Products', in: A De Franceschi/R Schulze (eds), Digital Revolution – New Challenges for Law, 169–188. Nomos, (2019).

D. Fairgrieve and Eleonora Rajneri, 'Is Software a Product under the Product Liability Directive?', Zeitschrift für Internationales Wirtschaftsrecht, January 2019, Volume 1/2019, pp. 24–28.

Tolan S., Miron M., Gomez E. and Castillo C. "Why Machine Learning May Lead to Unfairness: Evidence from Risk Assessment for Juvenile Justice in Catalonia". Best Paper Award, International Conference on AI and Law, 2019.

Tatjana Evas, A common EU approach to liability rules and insurance for connected and autonomous vehicles, Study. European Added Value Assessment - Accompanying the European Parliament's legislative own-initiative report (Rapporteur: Mady Delvaux). Study, European Parliamentary Research Service (EPRS), February 2018.

Andrea Bertolini, Artificial Intelligence and civil law - Liability rules for drones, Study requested by the European Parliament's Committee on Legal Affairs, Policy Department for Citizens' Rights and Constitutional Affairs, November 2018.

Maurice Schellekens, 'No-Fault Compensation Schemes for Self-Driving Vehicles', Law, Innovation and Technology, 2018, 10:2, 314–333.

Boom, Willem H van, Borghetti, Jean-Sébastien, Ehlers, Andreas Bloch, Karner, Ernst, Nolan, Donal, Oliphant, Ken, Scarso, Alessandro, Ulfbeck, Vibe and Wagner, Gerhard. "Product Liability in Europe". Product Liability: Fundamental Questions in a Comparative Perspective, edited by Helmut Koziol, Michael D. Green, Mark Lunney, Ken Oliphant and Lixin Yang, Berlin, Boston: De Gruyter, 2018, pp. 255–356.

Yavar Bathaee, "The artificial intelligence black box and the failure of intent and causation", Harvard Journal of Law & Technology, Volume 31, Number 2, 889–938, (2018).

Thomas Verheyen, "Full Harmonization, Consumer Protection and Products Liability: A Fresh Reading of the Case Law of the ECJ", 26 (1) European Review of Private Law, 119–140, (2018).

Jian-hua Li, "Cyber security meets artificial intelligence: a survey", Frontiers of Information Technology & Electronic Engineering 19, 1462–1474 (2018).

Naveed Akhtar and Ajmal Mian, "Threat of adversarial attacks on deep learning in computer vision: A survey" (2018) 6 IEEE Access 14410.

Joy Buolamwini, Timnit Gebru, 'Proceedings of the 1st Conference on Fairness, Accountability and Transparency', PMLR 81:77–91, 2018.

Howells, G., Twigg-Flesner, C., and Willett, C., Product Liability and Digital Products. In T-E. Synodinou, P. Jougleux, C. Markou, & T. Prastitou (eds.), EU Internet Law: Regulation and Enforcement. 2017, Springer Nature, 183–195.

Leenes, R., E. Palmerini, B.-J. Koops, A. Bertolini, P. Salvini and F. Lucivero (2017). "Regulatory challenges of robotics: Some guidelines for addressing legal and ethical issues." Law Innovation and Technology 9: 1–44.

Stefan Grundmann and Philipp Hacker, "Digital Technology as a Challenge to European Contract Law – From the Existing to the Future Architecture", 13 European Review of Contract Law, 255–293, 2017.

9.2 Identification of the Major Problems–Need to Adapt the PLD to the Digital Age–Objectives of the Proposal for a Revised Product Liability Directive

9.2.1 Identification of the Major Problems–Reasons for a Revised Product Liability Directive

The Product Liability Directive establishes common rules at the EU level for the non-fault (strict) liability of producers for damage caused by defective products, regardless of fault or negligence. It provides an avenue for individuals (whether they are the owner or a bystander) who have suffered personal injuries, damage to consumer property, or death due to a defective product to claim financial compensation.

Aída Ponce del Castillo, 'A Law on Robotics and Artificial Intelligence in the EU?', (October 3, 2017). Foresight Brief, European Trade Union Institute (ETUI) Research Paper - Foresight Brief #02-September 2017.

Nathalie Nevejans, 'European Civil Law Rules in Robotics', Study requested by the European Parliament's Committee on Legal Affairs (JURI Committee), 2016.

D. Fairgrieve, G. Howells, P. Møgelvang-Hansen et al., Product Liability Directive. In: P. Machnikowski (ed), European Product Liability: An Analysis of the State of the Art in the Era of New Technologies. Principles of European Tort Law. Intersentia; 2016:17–108.

Piotr Machnikowski, Conclusions, in: P Machnikowski (ed), European Product Liability: An Analysis of the State of the Art in the Era of New Technologies. Principles of European Tort Law. Intersentia; 2016:669–705.

Melinda Florina Lohmann, "Liability issues concerning self-driving vehicles", European Journal of Risk Regulation, 7(2), 335–340, (2016).

Roeland de Bruin, "Autonomous Intelligent Cars on the European Intersection of Liability and Privacy: Regulatory Challenges and the Road Ahead", European Journal of Risk Regulation, 2016, 7(3):485–501.

Susanne Beck, 'The problem of ascribing legal responsibility in the case of robotics', AI & Society, 2016, vol 31, n°4, pp. 473–481.

Konstantinos Christidis and Michael Devetsikiotis, "Blockchains and Smart Contracts for the Internet of Things", (2016) IEEE Access, vol. 4, pp. 2292–2303.

Mihalis Kritikos, 'Legal and ethical reflections concerning robotics', Scientific Foresight Unit (STOA) Policy Briefing, European Parliament Research Service (EPRS), PE 563.501, June 2016.

Palmerini, E., A. Bertolini, F. Battaglia, B.-J. Koops, A. Carnevale and P. Salvini (2016). "RoboLaw: Towards a European framework for robotics regulation." Robotics and Autonomous Systems 86: 78–85.

Daily Wuyts, "The Product Liability Directive – More than two Decades of Defective Products in Europe" Journal of European Tort Law, vol. 5, no. 1, 2014, pp. 1–34.

Andrea Bertolini, 'Robots as Products: The Case for a Realistic Analysis of Robotic Applications and Liability Rules', Law Innovation and Technology, 2013, vol. 5, p. 214–247.

The evaluation of the Product Liability Directive in 2018[13] concluded that the Directive was, on the whole, an effective and relevant instrument. However, the PLD also had several shortcomings. In particular, the 2018 evaluation pointed out specific deficiencies, such as the lack of legal clarity on how to apply the PLD's definitions to products in the digital and circular economy, difficulties related to the burden of proof in the case of complex products, and limitations on making claims (e.g. damage claims needed to exceed 500 EUR).[14]

---

[13] Commission Staff Working Document, Evaluation of Council Directive 85/374/EEC of 25 July 1985 on the approximation of the laws, regulations and administrative provisions of the Member States concerning liability for defective products – Accompanying the Evaluation Report – SWD (2018) 157 final, Brussels, 7.5.2018 ['Commission Staff Working Document, 'Evaluation of Product Liability Directive', SWD(2018) 157 final, Brussels, 07.05.2018'].

Report from the Commission on the Application of the Council Directive on the approximation of the laws, regulations, and administrative provisions of the Member States concerning liability for defective products (85/374/EEC) {SWD(2018) 157 final} - {SWD(2018) 158 final}, COM(2018) 246 final, Brussels, 7.5.2018, ['Commission Report on the Application of the Product Liability Directive, COM(2018) 246 final, Brussels, 07.05.2018'].

[14] Proposal for a Directive of the European Parliament and of the Council on liability for defective products, European Commission, COM(2022) 495 final, Brussels, 28.9.2022 ('proposal for a revised Product Liability Directive' - PLD), Explanatory Memorandum, p. 1: "However, the [Product Liability] Directive also had several shortcomings: - it was legally unclear how to apply the PLD's decades-old definitions and concepts to products in the modern digital economy and circular economy (e.g. software and products that need software or digital services to function, such as smart devices and autonomous vehicles); - the burden of proof (i.e. the need, in order to obtain compensation, to prove the product was defective and that this caused the damage suffered) was challenging for injured persons in complex cases (e.g. those involving pharmaceuticals, smart products or AI-enabled products); - the rules excessively limited the possibility of making compensation claims (e.g. property damage worth less than EUR 500 is simply not recoverable under the PLD)".

See also the proposal for a revised Product Liability Directive, at Recitals 3 and 4: "(3) Directive 85/374/EEC needs to be revised in light of developments related to new technologies, including artificial intelligence (AI), new circular economy business models and new global supply chains, which have led to inconsistences and legal uncertainty, in particular as regards the meaning of the term 'product'. Experience gained from applying Directive 85/374/EEC has also shown that injured persons face difficulties obtaining compensation due to restrictions on making compensation claims and due to challenges in gathering evidence to prove liability, especially in light of increasing technical and scientific complexity. This includes claims for damages related to new technologies, including AI. The revision will therefore encourage the roll-out and uptake of such new technologies, including AI, while ensuring that claimants can enjoy the same level of protection irrespective of the technology involved. (4) A revision of Directive 85/374/EEC is also needed in order to ensure coherence and consistency with product safety and market surveillance legislation at Union and national level. In addition, there is a need to clarify basic notions and concepts to ensure coherence and legal certainty and to reflect recent case law of the Court of Justice of the European Union".

See also Commission Staff Working Document, "Impact Assessment Report – Accompanying the document Proposal for a Directive of the European Parliament and of the Council on liability for defective products", SWD(2022) 316 final, Brussels, 28.9.2022, at p. 5. See also at p. 9: "The evaluation of the PLD found that, while the Directive was on the whole effective, its effectiveness was hampered by outdated concepts that are unclear when applied to the modern economy and by an unfair balance of interests between producers and consumers in some respects".

Building on the 2018 evaluation findings of the PLD, the Commission's proposal for a revised PLD aims at addressing specific shortcomings[15] and identifies the following two major problems (with the respective drivers and consequences):

The shortcomings of the Product Liability Directive in the area of emerging digital technologies were analytically described in the 2020 White Paper on AI [Commission "White Paper On Artificial Intelligence - A European approach to excellence and trust", Brussels, 19.2.2020, COM(2020) 65 final]; the accompanying report on liability for AI, the Internet of Things and robotics [Commission "Report on the safety and liability implications of Artificial Intelligence, the Internet of Things and robotics", COM (2020) 64 final, 19.2.2020]; the 2019 report of the Expert Group on Liability and New Technologies [Report from the Expert Group on Liability and New Technologies – New Technologies Formation "Liability for Artificial Intelligence and Other Emerging Digital Technologies", 21 November 2019]; and the European Parliament's 2020 Resolution on a civil liability regime for AI [European Parliament Resolution of 20 October 2020 with recommendations to the Commission on a civil liability regime for artificial intelligence (2020/2014(INL)) P9_TA(2020)0276 ('European Parliament's 2020 Resolution on a civil liability regime for AI')].

[15] As the Commission put it: "Why do product liability rules need to be updated? – For nearly 40 years, the Product Liability Directive (PLD) has provided a legal safety net for citizens to claim compensation when they suffer damage caused by defective products. However, the PLD dates back to 1985 and does not cover categories of products emerging from new digital technologies, like smart products and artificial intelligence (AI). Similarly, the current rules are unclear about how to determine who would be liable for defective software updates, defective machine learning algorithms or defective digital services that are essential for a product to operate. The current rules are silent on who is liable when a business substantially modifies a product that is already on the market or when a product has been directly imported from outside the Union by a consumer. This makes it difficult for businesses to assess the risks of marketing innovative products and leaves victims of damages without the possibility of compensation for an increasing number of products. The revision of the PLD will ensure that the new rules for product liability are adapted to new types of products to the benefit of both businesses and consumers". European Commission – Questions & Answers on the revision of the Product Liability Directive, Brussels, 28 September 2022, p. 1.

With regard to the reasons why there is urgent need to adapt the Product Liability Directive to the digital age, see also the comment submitted by the European Consumer Organisation (BEUC): "The products the EU legislator had in mind when adopting the PLD in 1985 were traditional tangible items. However, since then the world of products has drastically changed. Every-day items such as watches, toys, or household appliances have become equipped with sensors, are connected to the internet, and may increasingly be driven by self-learning Artificial Intelligence (AI) systems. In addition, more and more products have become in-tangible. Instead of buying CDs or books, consumers are downloading music files, software or e-books to their connected devices. Consequently, digitalisation is increasingly blurring the line between products and services. Defects may no longer only be caused by defective components but also by software bugs, integrated biased AI, loss of connectivity or cybersecurity vulnerabilities. Digital technology may cause a much broader range of damage than traditional products, such as damage to digital property or privacy. At the same time, the features of digital technology, such as its complexity and opacity, makes it almost impossible for consumers to prove a defect and a causal link with the damage as highlighted in the European Commission's expert report on "Liability for Artificial Intelligence and other emerging digital technologies". Furthermore, new economic operators, such as online marketplaces, have become an important part of the supply chain and should bear their share of responsibility for defective products. In light of these developments and new challenges, the PLD urgently needs to be up-dated to close loopholes and to provide consumers with the protection they need". See the European Consumer Organisation (BEUC), "Revision of the Product Liability Directive – Time to ensure effective and comprehensive protection for consumers damaged by defective products", 01.03.2023, p. 4.

9.2.1.1 Problem 1: Certain Products, Economic Actors and Damage in the Digital and Circular Economy Escape No-Fault (Strict) Liability

Some products, economic actors, and damage in the digital and circular economy are not covered under no-fault (strict) liability. This is because the Product Liability Directive (which dates back to 1985) was conceived long before the digital revolution and, accordingly, is not adapted to the digital age and circular economy.[16] In particular:

9.2.1.1.1 Driver—Regulatory Failure: Liability Rules Are Unclear and, Thus, Not Adapted for Products in the Digital Age

The PLD does not cover categories of products emerging from new digital technologies, like AI and smart products. Furthermore, it is unclear how the current PLD's provisions apply to software[17] (for instance, to determine who would be liable for defective software updates and defective machine learning algorithms) and products that need software or digital services in order to function (such as smart devices and autonomous vehicles).[18] In other words, it is unclear whether the PLD's provisions

[16]Proposal for a revised Product Liability Directive, Explanatory Memorandum, p. 1: "Since the adoption of the PLD in 1985, there have been significant changes in the way products are produced, distributed and operated, including the modernisation of product safety and market surveillance rules. The green and digital transitions are underway and bring with them enormous benefits for Europe's society and economy, be it by extending the life of materials and products, e.g. through remanufacturing, or by increasing productivity and convenience thanks to smart products and artificial intelligence".

See also Commission Staff Working Document, "Impact Assessment Report – Accompanying the document Proposal for a Directive of the European Parliament and of the Council on liability for defective products", SWD(2022) 316 final, Brussels, 28.9.2022, at p. 11: "No-fault liability of producers was introduced as a necessary response to the risks inherent in technological production in the 20th century. Products and technologies have continued to develop since the PLD was enacted in 1985 but the rules have not. The safety of products, be they robotic lawnmowers, connected or autonomous vehicles or smart home systems, is determined more and more by software and digital services that may be supplied once a product is already on the market. As the evaluation has shown, the PLD is no longer adapted for products in the digital age in a number of respects. In the digital age, the features of a product are not set in stone when it is put into circulation, but are determined by software and digital services after that moment, which may be provided by economic operators other than the producer of the 'finished product'".

[17]Commission Staff Working Document, "Subsidiarity Grid – Accompanying the document Proposal for a Directive of the European Parliament and of the Council on liability for defective products, SWD(2022) 315 final, Brussels, 28.9.2022, at p. 2: "National courts' role is to interpret the Directive, but because of unclear provisions (e.g. the extent to which software is covered as a product under the Directive), these interpretations are divergent, undermining the internal market".

[18]Commission Staff Working Document, "Impact Assessment Report – Accompanying the document Proposal for a Directive of the European Parliament and of the Council on liability for defective products", SWD(2022) 316 final, Brussels, 28.9.2022, at p. 11.

apply to software and ancillary digital services. The definition of product under the PLD appears to no longer be as clear-cut and, therefore, a clarification of its scope (e.g., whether software is covered by the legal concept of product or product component) is required. The crucial question is whether the PLD should be extended beyond physical products to encompass intangible items, i.e., software, digital services and digital content.

Furthermore, the current PLD does not cover liability for defects that emerge after a product is marketed, including defective updates and cybersecurity vulnerabilities. Indeed, Article 7(b) of the Product Liability Directive provides an exemption for producers from liability if they can demonstrate that a defect causing damage likely occurred after the product entered the market, also known as the "later-defect defense". This defense is based on the assumption that the producer no longer has control over the product once it was put into circulation. However, in the digital age, this assumption is no longer valid as producers often retain control over their products through updates and upgrades, which themselves can be defective.[19] This is the reason why the EU Agency for Cybersecurity has identified software updates as the main cause of non-malicious security threats to IT systems and applications.[20] Failing to provide updates can also jeopardize product safety, just like providing defective updates, particularly with the emergence of evolving cybersecurity threats.[21]

Also, new types of damages such as damage to digital property are not covered by the current PLD's provisions. It is reminded that the Product Liability Directive protects life and health as well as consumer property. However, it is not entirely clear, for instance, whether 'consumer property' covers damage to data, since data may not be an 'item of property' within the meaning of Article 9 (b) of the Product Liability Directive. Indeed, it is not universally accepted that damage to or the destruction of data constitutes a property loss, because, according to various legal systems, the notion of 'property' excludes intangibles and, therefore, tortious liability cannot be triggered. This is why the 2018 evaluation of the PLD highlighted that products using digital technologies are capable of causing a broader range of harm

[19] Ibid., at p. 13.

[20] European Union Agency for Cybersecurity (ENISA) – ENISA Threat Landscape (ETL) Report, ninth edition, 2021, p. 82.

[21] Commission Staff Working Document, "Impact Assessment Report – Accompanying the document Proposal for a Directive of the European Parliament and of the Council on liability for defective products", SWD(2022) 316 final, Brussels, 28.9.2022, at pp. 13–14: "For example, a cyber-attack may target a vulnerability in a machinery product's software that makes the machinery malfunction and injure the user. Lack of adequate cybersecurity is one of the barriers that limits the uptake of new technological developments. In recognition of this, economic operators are now required to provide software and security updates to ensure the ongoing safety of products after they are placed on the market. So software updates are not only necessary to keep products safe, they are also required by legislation, yet the later-defect defence exonerates producers from liability under the PLD. The digital security industry (Eurosmart) has argued that the "later-defect defence" makes the concept of no-fault liability meaningless when applied to smart/connected products and AI systems that could let vulnerabilities emerge only after the placement of a product on the market".

than traditional products, in particular (i) damage to a user's digital property, and (ii) infringement of personality rights such as privacy or discrimination.[22] This was also followed by the Commission's 2021 Inception Impact Assessment, which suggested extending the range of damages for which compensation could be claimed under the Product Liability Directive to non-material damages (i.e. data loss, privacy infringements or environmental damage).[23]

9.2.1.1.2 Driver—Regulatory Failure: Liability Rules Are Unclear for Refurbished/Remanufactured Products

In the circular economy (where the life of materials is extended through upgrading and repairing digital products and components), it is also uncertain who should be liable in cases where a product that has been (substantially) modified by a refurbisher or remanufacturer (and placed back on the market) is defective and causes harm. As a result, businesses are faced with a challenge to assess their liability exposure due to uncertainty and different interpretations in every Member State. Furthermore, consumers are less able to get compensation for defective products using digital technologies or "circular" products.[24]

9.2.1.1.3 Driver—Regulatory Failure: No Liable Person Under PLD When Consumer Purchases Product from a Third Country Directly

Also, the current rules of the PLD are silent on who should be liable when a product has been directly imported from outside the EU by a consumer. Indeed, due to new global supply chains, it is becoming increasingly common for people to purchase products from non-EU countries without any EU-based producer or importer. Online marketplaces have enabled consumers to buy products from outside the EU without there being an importer, leaving consumers with no liable person from whom to seek compensation under the Product Liability Directive if damage has occurred.[25] As no

[22] Commission Staff Working Document, 'Evaluation of Product Liability Directive', SWD(2018) 157 final, Brussels, 07.05.2018, at p. 55.

See also Commission Staff Working Document, "Impact Assessment Report – Accompanying the document Proposal for a Directive of the European Parliament and of the Council on liability for defective products", SWD(2022) 316 final, Brussels, 28.9.2022, at pp. 16–17.

[23] Commission's Inception Impact Assessment "Adapting liability rules to the digital age and circular economy", Ref. Ares(2021)4266516, 30.06.2021, Option 1.b, p. 4.

[24] Commission Staff Working Document, "Impact Assessment Report – Accompanying the document Proposal for a Directive of the European Parliament and of the Council on liability for defective products", SWD(2022) 316 final, Brussels, 28.9.2022, at pp. 12, 17–18.

[25] Commission, DG GROW and DG JUST, "Factual summary report of the open public consultation on Adapting Civil Liability Rules to the Digital Age and AI", Ref. Ares(2022)2620305, 06.04.2022, pp. 3–4.

EU-based economic operator is subject to no-fault liability, consumers are left without the possibility of compensation for an increasing number of products when purchasing from a third country directly: "In such cases, if a product is defective and causes harm, there is no EU-based liable person from whom to seek compensation under the PLD".[26] This also creates an uneven playing field between EU and non-EU producers, as EU businesses face unfair competition from third country producers who are beyond the reach of the Product Liability Directive.[27] According to the Commission, there are various consequences resulting from all the above economic operators escaping no-fault based (strict) liability.[28]

9.2.1.2 Problem 2: Consumers Face Obstacles to Getting Compensation

The Product Liability Directive seeks to achieve a fair balance of interests between consumers and producers. Whereas victims do not have to prove fault (producers bear liability irrespective of fault), claimants have to prove that a product is defective and, therefore, they shoulder the burden of proof and face time limits and thresholds. According to the 2018 evaluation, the balance struck in the current PLD is not always fair to consumers, mainly "due to the difficulties in proving liability when complex products cause harm, and due to the time limits and thresholds that disproportionately restrict the number of claims".[29] More analytically:

See also the Commission's Inception Impact Assessment "Adapting liability rules to the digital age and circular economy", Ref. Ares(2021)4266516, 30.06.2021, p. 2.

[26] Commission Staff Working Document, "Impact Assessment Report – Accompanying the document Proposal for a Directive of the European Parliament and of the Council on liability for defective products", SWD(2022) 316 final, Brussels, 28.9.2022, at p. 19.

[27] Ibid., at p. 12.

[28] Ibid. These consequences include: "the deterrence function of the PLD, designed to encourage producers to do their best to make products safe, is missing; no-fault liability is shouldered instead by other economic operators (principally hardware manufacturers) who may not be best placed to minimise software-related safety risks; competition between market operators is distorted, since producers of hardware products and components are subject to no-fault liability; levels of consumer protection across the EU are unequal, since some Member States do impose no-fault liability outside of the PLD regime for digital services necessary for products to operate; and consumers face uncertainty about how to get compensation for harm caused by digital and refurbished or remanufactured products and from whom".

[29] Commission Staff Working Document, "Impact Assessment Report – Accompanying the document Proposal for a Directive of the European Parliament and of the Council on liability for defective products", SWD(2022) 316 final, Brussels, 28.9.2022, at pp. 12–13.

See also Commission Staff Working Document, 'Evaluation of Product Liability Directive', SWD(2018) 157 final, Brussels, 07.05.2018, at p. 61.

9.2.1.2.1 Driver—Regulatory Failure: Proving Defectiveness and Causal Link with Damage Is Very Difficult and Costly for Complex Products

Under the Product Liability Directive the burden of proof is less onerous on victims than under national fault-based liability rules, mainly because the victim does not have to prove fault. Nevertheless, proving that a product is defective (i.e. that it does not provide the level of safety a person is entitled to expect) is still (extremely) challenging for complex products, such as AI-enabled products, even if the victim does not have to prove how the product became unsafe. In cases that involve complex products such as AI-enabled products, smart products, or pharmaceuticals, it can be very challenging for victims of harm to prove that the product was defective and caused the damage.[30]

The Evaluation of Product Liability Directive stressed that the most significant condition for an injured person to get compensation under the PLD is proving that the product was defective and that this defectiveness caused the damage suffered. Failure to discharge this burden of proof is the most frequent reason for a claim to be rejected (accounting for 53% of total rejections).[31] Also, in the course of the 2021–2022 public consultation, respondents argued that, due to the technical complexity of specific products, it could become difficult for the victim/injured party to obtain compensation, i.e. to identify the potentially liable person, to prove the defect in the product and the causal link between the defect and the damage. This difficulty becomes even higher as emerging digital technologies/products are becoming increasingly connected and complex.[32]

It is also reminded that the Product Liability Directive does not provide victims with a right to access technical information—held by a producer—that may be necessary to establish liability.[33] Additionally, even if a claimant gets the

[30] Commission Staff Working Document, "Impact Assessment Report – Accompanying the document Proposal for a Directive of the European Parliament and of the Council on liability for defective products", SWD(2022) 316 final, Brussels, 28.9.2022, at p. 19.

[31] Commission Staff Working Document, 'Evaluation of Product Liability Directive', SWD(2018) 157 final, Brussels, 07.05.2018, at p. 23.

[32] Commission, DG GROW and DG JUST, "Factual summary report of the open public consultation on Adapting Civil Liability Rules to the Digital Age and AI", Ref. Ares(2022)2620305, 06.04.2022, at p. 5: "Respondents point to difficulties in proving defectiveness and causality in the event of damage due to the technical complexity of certain products. In particular, they pointed to moderate, large and very large difficulties in case of: AI-enabled products (77%), technically complex products (77%), IoT products (72%) and pharmaceuticals (65%)". Amongst consumer organisations, non-governmental organisations and citizens, 95% underlined the difficulties/challenges for each of these items. On the other hand, only 38% amongst business respondents acknowledged such challenges in demonstrating defectiveness and causality.

[33] CJEU, Judgment of 20 November 2014, Case C-310/13, at ground 25: "As regards the consumer's right to obtain information on the adverse effects of a product, it should be noted that neither that right nor the scope of the information that the consumer could require the manufacturer of that product to provide are covered, as such, by Directive 85/374".

information, proving liability can still be challenging, since there is no explicit possibility to alleviate the burden of proof under the PLD when victims face disproportionate difficulties.[34] Furthermore, liability for undiscoverable defects is uncertain (e.g. machine learning). As a result, it is very difficult and costly to get compensation for harm caused by complex products, whereas individual victims may unfairly bear the risk of damage from undiscoverable defects.

Finally, according to the so-called development risk defence, the producer is allowed to avoid liability if the state of scientific and technical knowledge at the time when he put the product into circulation was not such as to enable the existence of the defect to be discovered (Article 7(e) of the Product Liability Directive). It should be noted that the PLD allows Member States to derogate from applying the defence.[35] The 2018 PLD evaluation found that the development risk defence was a crucial factor for guaranteeing the stability of product liability insurance costs within the EU market while avoiding substantial increases in litigation levels.[36] In

---

However, the ECJ underlined that access to information makes it easier for a claimant to produce the necessary evidence to prove the producer's liability, and has endorsed national rules that give claimants this right (at ground 27): "In that regard, it should be acknowledged that national legislation under which the victim has the right to obtain information on the adverse effects of the product concerned may make it easier for that person to produce the requisite evidence enabling him to establish liability on the part of the manufacturer".

[34]This is why "national courts make use of various mechanisms to make it easier for claimants to come up with the proof. National courts have, for example, held that products that do not comply with safety requirements can be presumed to be defective, and claimants do not need to show how a defect was caused or what specific defect led to the lack of safety. National courts have referred questions on how to apply the PLD's burden-of-proof rules three times in the last 10 years. In response, the ECJ has endorsed national rules that allow courts to presume the existence of a causal link even if there is no conclusive evidence, so long as the factual evidence available was sufficiently robust. It has also ruled that a pacemaker could be considered defective without proof of actual defect by virtue of being from the same production series as another pacemaker already proven to be defective. The ECJ has therefore endorsed efforts of national courts to make it easier for claimants to produce the evidence needed to prove the producer's liability". Commission Staff Working Document, "Impact Assessment Report – Accompanying the document Proposal for a Directive of the European Parliament and of the Council on liability for defective products", SWD (2022) 316 final, Brussels, 28.9.2022, at p. 20.

For relevant cases, see: CJEU, Judgment of 20 November 2014, Case C-310/13; CJEU, Judgment of 21 June 2017, Case C-621/15 (the case turned on whether a causal link between a vaccine and the onset of multiple sclerosis could be inferred from the fact that the disease manifested itself shortly after injection and there were no family antecedents related to the disease); CJEU, Judgment of 5 March 2015, Joined Cases C-503/13 and C-504/13.

[35]Commission Staff Working Document, "Impact Assessment Report – Accompanying the document Proposal for a Directive of the European Parliament and of the Council on liability for defective products", SWD(2022) 316 final, Brussels, 28.9.2022, at p. 21: "Finland and Luxembourg derogate entirely, while Spain, France and Hungary derogate in respect of certain categories of product".

[36]Commission Staff Working Document, 'Evaluation of Product Liability Directive', SWD(2018) 157 final, Brussels, 07.05.2018, at p. 31.

On the other hand, the Expert Group on liability stressed that assessing the state of scientific knowledge at the moment of putting into circulation fails to take account of the fact that producers

the course of the public consultation, industry stakeholders argued that the development risk defence should not be changed/removed, whereas consumer organisations and NGOs supported the possibility of removing the development risk defence from the PLD.[37]

---

retain control over digital products beyond that moment and therefore have the means to tackle defects that become discoverable. This is true of many digital products, including IoT and AI-enabled products. The development risk defence should not apply for AI products that continue to learn and adapt while in operation (at p. 6). . . . "The producer should be strictly liable for defects in emerging digital technologies even if said defects appear after the product was put into circulation, as long as the producer was still in control of updates to, or upgrades on, the technology. A development risk defence should not apply". See Report from the Expert Group on Liability and New Technologies – New Technologies Formation "Liability for Artificial Intelligence and Other Emerging Digital Technologies", 21 November 2019, Key Finding [14], at p. 42.

[37] Commission, DG GROW and DG JUST, "Factual summary report of the open public consultation on Adapting Civil Liability Rules to the Digital Age and AI", Ref. Ares(2022)2620305, 06.04.2022, p. 5.

On the one hand, see for instance the argument put forward by BusinessEurope, "Comments – Adapting liability rules to the digital age and Artificial Intelligence", 10.01.2022, at p. 4: "the use of the development risk defence should remain available without any change. . . . We should allow leeway for innovation and not impose a de facto indefinite liability for the producer in case of systems that operate with a degree of autonomy. Instead, the defences should be interpreted in such a way that they also apply for such systems, where it may be equally possible that the defect did not exist or could not be discovered when the product was put into circulation".

On the other hand:

According to the Irish Council for Civil Liberties (ICCL) ("ICCL - Submission to the consultation on adapting liability rules to the digital age and artificial intelligence", 7 January 2022, pp. 3–4): "The 'development risk defence' should be removed for all AI systems so that producers remain strictly liable for damage. Under Article 7(e) of PLD, 'development risk defence' exempts producers from liability if they can prove "that the state of scientific and technical knowledge at the time when he put the product into circulation was not such as to enable the existence of the defect to be discovered". This exemption is inappropriate for AI for the following reasons: a) PLD assumes "material objects placed on the market by a one-time action of the producer, after which the producer does not maintain control over the product". . . . This is not applicable to software that can be updated. b) In addition, the producers should be held liable if they do not update software when new information about a defect is known, in scientific literature or elsewhere. Whether the scientific and technical knowledge was available when the software was initially placed on the market should not be considered. c) 'Development risk defence' creates a perverse incentive for producers to deploy products without adequate safety research, or to delay safety related research and/or the publication of research results until the product is placed on the market".

See also BEUC (the European Consumer Organisation), "Product Liability 2.0 - How to make EU rules fit for consumers in the digital age", submitted on 07.05.2020, at pp. 2, 17, 19–20: "the time at which the product was placed on the market should no longer be relevant when assessing defects. . . . When it is established that a product is defective, the PLD provides the defendant with several defences to escape liability. Two are particularly controversial in the context of new technologies, namely the so-called 'development-risk defence' and the 'regulatory compliance' defence. The development risk defence (Art. 7e) provides that the producer shall not be liable if the state of scientific and technical knowledge at the time when the product was put into circulation was not such as to enable the existence of the defect to be discovered. . . . Many digital goods may change after they have been put onto the market. It is therefore essential that an injured person who

9.2.1.2.2 Driver—Regulatory Failures: Liability Claims Are Subject to a Number of Restrictions

The PLD imposes certain limitations on claims.[38] In particular, consumers can claim compensation only for damage to property intended and used for private purposes.[39]

---

suffers damage be always compensated regardless of whether the defect was detectable or not. ... BEUC recommendation: the development risk-defence should be abolished".

See also the response submitted by BEUC (the European Consumer Organisation) to the European Commission's public consultation on Civil liability – adapting liability rules to the digital age and artificial intelligence, 23.12.2021, at p. 7: "More and more digital products are dynamic in the sense that they evolve during their lifespan. In parallel, professionals also collect on an ongoing basis data from consumers about the use of their products. Professionals know how their tools are used and may detect problems quickly when they arise. In other words, producers keep a much higher degree of control over their products even after they have been placed on the market. Liability rules must follow and be adapted to this evolution. The risk-development defence or the late defect defence are clearly incompatible with the dynamic nature of digital goods".

Similarly, as it was stated by Eurosmart ("Eurosmart on the Product Liability Directive", 12.01.2022, p. 3), "Artificial intelligence challenges Article 7 of the Product Liability Directive, which states that a producer shall not be liable if he proves 'that having regard to the circumstances, it is probable that the defect which caused the damage did not exist at the time when the product was put into circulation by him or that this defect came into being afterwards'. Artificial intelligence systems evolve over time, and vulnerabilities might arise in the course of such an evolution. The concept of liability would be meaningless if producers were not liable for such vulnerabilities arising after placing on the market as they still designed the systems in the first place".

In line with this opinion, see also the argument put forward by the Confederation of European Security Services (CoESS) ("Confederation of European Security Services (CoESS) - Position Paper on the European Commission Consultation on adapting liability rules to the digital age and AI", 20 December 2021, p. 4): "As regards 'development risk defence' of providers, we believe that the concept should be evaluated in the face of emerging technologies. Notably, we believe that the defence should not be available for products designed to be influenced by other interconnected products or services (e.g. complex IoT systems), and for AI products that continue to learn and adapt while in operation".

[38] Commission Staff Working Document, "Impact Assessment Report – Accompanying the document Proposal for a Directive of the European Parliament and of the Council on liability for defective products", SWD(2022) 316 final, Brussels, 28.9.2022, at pp. 21–23.

See also Commission's Inception Impact Assessment "Adapting liability rules to the digital age and circular economy", Ref. Ares(2021)4266516, 30.06.2021, p. 3.

Furthermore, see the Report from the Commission on the Application of the Council Directive on the approximation of the laws, regulations, and administrative provisions of the Member States concerning liability for defective products (85/374/EEC) -{SWD(2018) 157 final} - {SWD(2018) 158 final}, COM(2018) 246 final, Brussels, 7.5.2018 ('Commission Report on the Application of the Product Liability Directive', COM(2018) 246 final, Brussels, 07.05.2018'), at p. 6, para. 5.1 ('Effectiveness'): "The EUR 500 threshold and time limitations for claims (especially for certain products such as pharmaceuticals) also limit the number of cases for which consumers can claim compensation".

[39] Commission Staff Working Document, 'Evaluation of Product Liability Directive', SWD(2018) 157 final, Brussels, 07.05.2018, at p. 31, para. 5.1.2.: "consumers believe that the Directive is not always effective in protecting consumers mainly because ... compensation of the damage only if the item of property was intended and used for private purpose and not when the defective product was used for professional purposes".

Also, consumers can claim compensation only for damage to property worth more than EUR 500. Therefore, claims for property damage valued at less than EUR 500 are not permitted and, as a result, consumers who suffer property damage less than EUR 500 receive no compensation.[40] On the other hand, it was argued that any

[40]The 2018 PLD evaluation found that the EUR 500 threshold overly limited claims for property damage, undermining the effectiveness of the PLD in protecting consumer property. See Commission Staff Working Document, 'Evaluation of Product Liability Directive', SWD(2018) 157 final, Brussels, 07.05.2018, at p. 25, para. 5.1.1.1.: "… concerning material damages, the effectiveness of the condition on the EUR 500 threshold seems to be questionable: Firstly, there are concerns as regards its national interpretation. Some Member States transposed Article 9 of the Directive interpreting the EUR 500 threshold as a threshold which, when reached, would allow for pursuing compensation for the entirety of the damage suffered, whereas others (e.g. France, Germany, Netherland and Spain) transposed it as a deductible, i.e. as a sum to be deducted from the compensation owed without regard to the scale of the damage. This divergence in the interpretation may create a different degree of protection of the injured party across Member States. Secondly, according to the information obtained, in four out of five cases a compensation is not claimed as the damage is below the threshold. This could explain why this is rarely cited as a reason for rejecting a claim in court and why most cases relate to physical well-being. Therefore, despite the fact that the Directive seems to be effective and particularly for damages to well-being, the EUR 500 threshold represent, according to consumer representatives, an obstacle for the full effectiveness of the Directive to cover claims for compensation in many cases of material damage since claims for lower material damages cannot be introduced". See also, at pp. 4 and 31: "consumer organisations asked for more protection at a lower cost, which would imply removing the threshold of EUR 500" (at p. 4, para. 1.2.). … "consumers believe that the Directive is not always effective in protecting consumers mainly because … the EUR 500 threshold aims to avoiding litigation for small claims" (at p. 31, para. 5.1.2.).

See also Commission Report on the Application of the Product Liability Directive, COM(2018) 246 final, Brussels, 07.05.2018, at p. 6, para. 5.1.

In the course of the 2021-2022 consultation, 55% of all respondents argued that the EUR 500 threshold for damage to property creates obstacles to consumers making compensation claims. Out of this 55%, 89% were consumer organisations and NGOs (i.e., non-business respondents), asking for more protection at a lower cost, while only 11% were business respondents (who argued that any relaxation on the threshold for property damages would lead to more claims for minor damages). See Commission, DG GROW and DG JUST, "Factual summary report of the open public consultation on Adapting Civil Liability Rules to the Digital Age and AI", Ref. Ares(2022) 2620305, 06.04.2022, p. 6.

With regard to consumer organisations and NGOs, see for instance the following responses:

Response submitted by BEUC (the European Consumer Organisation) to the European Commission's public consultation on Civil liability – adapting liability rules to the digital age and artificial intelligence, 23.12.2021, at p. 8: "Currently, the PLD only covers physical injuries and damage to property arising out in non-professional activities with a lower threshold of €500. This is problematic for several reasons. First, the PLD excludes immaterial damage although IoT products may cause a much wider range of harm than traditional products, including data destruction or losses. Second, the 500€ threshold is arbitrary and in practice has been impairing access to justice for consumers in too many cases. As the European Commission already noted in its 2018 report, 'in four out of five cases, a compensation is not claimed as the damage is below the threshold'. It is essential that all consumers have access to compensation regardless of the value and the type of their harm".

See also the response of BEUC (the European Consumer Organisation), "Product Liability 2.0 - How to make EU rules fit for consumers in the digital age", submitted on 07.05.2020: "Consumers have long indicated that the €500 threshold unduly restrains the number of cases for which consumers can claim compensation. First, the threshold was initially adopted to avoid a flood of small cases against producers. However, in practice, this concern has been more hypothetical than real. Conversely, this threshold has contributed to impairing consumers' access to justice and limiting their compensation. As the Commission noted in 2018, "according to the information obtained, in four out of five cases a compensation is not claimed as the damage is below the threshold". Second, the threshold has given rise to diverging national interpretations. In some Member States, the threshold is regarded as a deductible (i.e. the amount of damages awarded to the claimant is reduced by this amount in case of success) while in others this amount is a minimum, below which no damages can be recovered. Consumers may therefore suffer from different levels of protection across the EU, which is not acceptable from a Single Market perspective. Third, should a loss or destruction of data eventually be regarded as a compensable harm, quantifying such a loss may lead to different results in Member States. For example, some Member States may take the view that a loss of data is below the threshold. This would create the risk of unequal treatment between consumers. Fourth, there is a contradiction between, on the one hand, current EU efforts to facilitate law enforcement and compensation for small-value claims (see for example the proposal for a Directive on representative actions for consumers) and, on the other hand, the €500 threshold, which precisely hinders such claims from being brought" (at pp. 15–16). ... "BEUC recommendations: ... The €500 threshold should be removed" (at p. 16).

Furthermore, see The Future of Life Institute (FLI), "Comments on the Commission's Inception Impact Assessment on 'Civil liability – adapting liability rules to the digital age and artificial intelligence'", submitted on 28 July 2021: "we support easing the conditions for making liability claims (option 2.1.d.). We believe there are multiple reasons to lower the 500 euros threshold. Some of the non-material damages caused by digital products can be hard to quantify (e.g. data loss, environmental damage). In addition, a defective AI system could impose a small loss to all the individuals subject to its use, which would amount to a large loss for society at large" (at p. 4).

See also the contribution by The Future Society (TFS), "Liability rules for Trust in Excellence & Excellence in Trust - Inception Impact Assessment - Adapting liability rules to the digital age and circular economy", Belgium, 28 July 2021: "while material compensation is often assumed to be the primary driver, consumers also value non-material compensation such as the peace of mind associated with justice and fairness, whether at the individual level or in society at large. Focusing solely on a financial threshold to determine whether to pursue a case assumes a narrow view of society - especially if non-material damages are likely to occur. While the time limit can be justified by the fact that case-relevant information or evidence degrades over time and increases the cost of efficient adjudication, the financial threshold seems arbitrary. Even if focusing on quantifiable material damages out of practicality, it is unclear why a threshold would be needed at all: given the costs in time and energy to the consumers, a presumably injured consumer anyway has to decide for himself whether it is worthwhile to take action. That consumer surely knows best whether the damages suffered justify taking action, without having to quantify them financially and officially - and the consumer can even factor in non-material factors much more efficiently. The threshold therefore only adds burdensome quantification and fees to an already complex procedure to obtain fair compensation for damages due to defects. This extra step reduces the efficiency of the liability system and introduces inequality in access to non-material compensation such as justice - especially for the least wealthy citizens of the EU for whom <500€ is a significant share of yearly income. While we are concerned about frivolous civil liability claims or, in the longer term, a form of "trolling" (in a way similar to Intellectual Property trolls), we do not think the threshold prevents such behaviors and another, more nuanced legal test will very probably be more appropriate if these abuses do start to occur. Therefore, we would recommend withdrawing the financial threshold for damage to property" (at pp. 6–7).

relaxation on the threshold for property damages would lead to more claims for minor damages, thus contradicting one of the main purposes of the threshold, namely to avoid litigation for small claims.[41]

Furthermore, consumers have to start legal proceedings within three (3) years of becoming aware of the damage. In addition, producers are released from liability for property damage and death/personal injury ten (10) years after placing the product on the market. As a result, under the current PLD, victims of harm that emerges after ten (10) years receive no compensation, whereas victims of harm who miss the three (3) year deadline to start legal proceedings get no compensation as well.[42]

[41] Commission Staff Working Document, 'Evaluation of Product Liability Directive', SWD(2018) 157 final, Brussels, 07.05.2018, at p. 4, para. 1.2.: "On the side of the producers and insurers, however, the arguments raised focused on the risk that any relaxation of the rules on the burden of proof or on the threshold for property damages would lead to more claims for minor damages".

For comments supporting this option, see for instance: Response of the App Association (ACT) to the European Commission's inception impact assessment on civil liability - Adapting liability rules to the digital age and circular economy, 28.07.2021: "As for the impact on fundamental rights, we stress again that lightening the burden of proof and lowering the €500 threshold could lead to frivolous claims and put businesses at an unnecessary disadvantage" (at p. 6).

According to Google's response, "changing the conditions under which claims can be made under the [Product Liability] directive is unnecessary and carries substantial risks. The rationale for a minimum damage threshold in the Directive was to avoid overburdening the courts with frivolous litigation. This risk is arguably greater for software-related claims, given that a defect in a single line of code (out of millions) that was used in millions of devices could (under this proposal) be the basis for a strict liability claim from each individual user. It is also unnecessary, since nothing would prevent consumers from bringing actions in the national courts for lower value claims, they just cannot rely on strict liability under the Directive when doing so". See Google's views on the European Commission's inception impact assessment on civil liability - adapting liability rules to the digital age and AI, 28.07.2021, at pp. 4–5.

See also: Bitkom Bundesverband Informationswirtschaft, Telekommunikation und neue Medien e.V. (Federal Association for Information Technology, Telecommunications and New Media), "Position Paper - Inception Impact Assessment: Adapting liability rules to the digital age and artificial intelligence", 27.07.2021: "The minimum threshold for making claims for damage of property under the Product Liability Directive should remain at EUR 500 in order to avoid litigation in an excessive number of cases, as stated in Recital 9 of the Product Liability Directive. In accordance with the applicable fault-based law, an injured party can always pursue any claim for lesser damages under the applicable fault-based law, so that there is no gap in legal protection" (at p. 6).

[42] In the course of the 2021–2022 consultation, just more than half (51%) of all respondents indicated that the 10-year time limit for death/personal injury creates obstacles to consumers making compensation claims. Out of this 51%, while consumer organisations and NGOs accounted for 89%, corporations and business organisations/associations represented the remaining 11%. In contrast, there was greater disagreement among respondents who stated that the requirement to start legal proceedings within three (3) years of becoming aware of damage is the least significant obstacle to making claims (only 37% of the respondents argued that this constitutes an obstacle). See Commission, DG GROW and DG JUST, "Factual summary report of the open public consultation on Adapting Civil Liability Rules to the Digital Age and AI", Ref. Ares(2022) 2620305, 06.04.2022, p. 6.

See also Commission Staff Working Document, 'Evaluation of Product Liability Directive', SWD(2018) 157 final, Brussels, 07.05.2018, at pp. 26, 27 and 31: "During the consultation activities, the three-year period to lodge a claim has been challenged by stakeholders: on average, 41% of the businesses and around a third of the stakeholders declared this limitation should be updated in light of recent technical developments. Moreover, the majority of stakeholders expressed difficulties in observing the three-year period for making a claim to recover damages in case of complex products, such as pharmaceutical products, that need expertise and research to find the defect and the link to the damage" (at p. 26, para. 5.1.1.1.). ... "As for the 10-year period, the Study for the evaluation has identified issues mainly related to its relation with the concept of "put into circulation". ... The 10-year period starts from the moment a producer puts the product into circulation. For products that remain in the distribution chain for a long time or deploy their effects over a long time span, the protection of the consumer may be reduced in comparison with his or her possible expectations: this is particularly the case of pharmaceutical products" (at p. 27, para. 5.1.1.1.). ... "Consumers believe that the Directive is not always effective in protecting consumers mainly because ... the time limit of 3 and 10 years to obtain compensation is too short in cases of complex products that require more expertise" (at p. 31, para. 5.1.2.).

For comments supporting this option, see for instance: BEUC (the European Consumer Organisation), "Product Liability 2.0 - How to make EU rules fit for consumers in the digital age", submitted on 07.05.2020: "Review timelines and prescription periods: The 10-year limitation period should be extended to 20 years" (at p. 2). ... "Timelines and prescription periods: What is the situation? The PLD establishes two deadlines: the PLD no longer applies three years after the injured party knew or could have become aware of the relevant facts (i.e. the damage, the defect and the identity of the producer) (Art. 10), and it ends ten years after the date the product was put onto the market (Art. 11). Why this is problematic: The PLD introduced these time limits to counterbalance the strict liability regime and to avoid hindering innovations. However, these timelines are no longer appropriate. First, when it comes to digital goods, producers keep significant control over their products even after they have been put onto the market. When digital contents are provided on a continuous basis, it is essential that consumers be protected during the entire lifespan of the product. Second, the time limits are not appropriate for certain types of products such as foodstuffs or pharmaceutical products where damage is likely to occur long after the product has been put into circulation. ... Third, these time limits should be regarded as a violation of the right of access to justice. ... Fourth, BEUC calls for a more sustainable consumption where products have a longer lifespan. This preoccupation is in line with the European Green Deal, and goes hand-in-hand with the right to have products repaired. Therefore, liability rules must ensure that the time limits in which producers shall be held liable match consumer expectations on long-lasting products. Furthermore, spare parts can also have an impact on product safety, so it is important that in the event of harm stemming from the replacement of parts and components, consumers have a right to recourse against the parts producer. Ultimately, it is important that the PLD strikes a balance between the need for flexible prescription periods adapted to the dynamic features of digital goods and the need to provide legal certainty for all stakeholders. Moreover, the need for harmonisation is needed to avoid the risk of patchy national legislations that would set different timelines. ... BEUC recommendation: • The limitation period should be extended to 20 years" (at pp. 21–22).

For the opposite view, see for instance: BusinessEurope, "Comments – Adapting liability rules to the digital age and Artificial Intelligence", 10.01.2022, at p. 4, which argued that "the 10-year time limit also provides important certainty about producers' claims risk and is important for insurance purposes. It provides legal certainty for industry and other stakeholders as well (e.g., healthcare professionals). Additionally, providing an expiry period of 10 is five times as long as most warranties, which are typically around 2 years".

Similarly, according to Google, the PLD points out that "it is in the interests of both the injured person and of the producer to have a uniform period of limitation for bringing a claim. The limitation period provides an incentive to diligently pursue damages claims and provides legal certainty to all parties involved". See Google's views on the European Commission's inception

9.2.2 *Objectives of the Commission's Proposal for a Revised Product Liability Directive*

Facilitating investment and increasing users' trust and social acceptance in emerging technologies require legal certainty and trust. In order to fully unlock the digital economy, the current EU liability framework needs to keep up to date with emerging trends and take account of new technological developments. Indeed, enhancing legal clarity is a crucial objective of the proposal for a revised PLD. The current Product Liability Directive, which has been in place for almost four decades, lacks clear liability rules for defective products in the digital era and the circular economy.

The revision of the Product Liability Directive aims to achieve two primary goals in response to the aforementioned problems. These goals are built upon the existing PLD and include: (i) maintaining the proper functioning of the internal market, as well as promoting the free movement of goods and undistorted competition amongst market players; and (ii) ensuring that consumers' health and property are still afforded a high level of protection.[43]

Accordingly, the proposal for a revised PLD is designed to accommodate the latest technological advancements, circular economy business models, and global value chains. This is achieved by ensuring the following: (i) businesses and consumers/victims are subject to fair and predictable rules; (ii) victims are adequately compensated for any harm caused by hazardous products, including digital products and AI systems; and (iii) a level playing field exists between EU and non-EU manufacturers.

To this end, the Commission's initiative has set out to achieve the following four specific objectives. First, in order to adapt product liability rules to the digital age and circular economy: (i) ensuring liability rules reflect the nature and risks of products in the digital age and circular economy;[44] (ii) ensuring there is always an EU-based

impact assessment on civil liability - adapting liability rules to the digital age and AI, 28.07.2021, at p. 5.

[43] Commission Staff Working Document, "Impact Assessment Report – Accompanying the document Proposal for a Directive of the European Parliament and of the Council on liability for defective products", SWD(2022) 316 final, Brussels, 28.9.2022, at p. 26.

[44] Ibid.: "*SO 1: Ensure liability rules reflect nature and risks of products in the digital age*: The aim here is to ensure that not only traditional products that were commonplace in the 1980s are adequately covered by product liability rules, but that digital products are too. Adapting or clarifying definitions will bring product liability rules into line with EU safety legislation already adapted to digital technologies, and will help reduce uncertainties in the implementation of the PLD. The aim is also to reflect the reality that product safety is nowadays impacted after the formal production process, including through updates/upgrades or through evolving cybersecurity threats. The aim is also to ensure any new and relevant types of damage that products using digital technologies may cause are appropriately covered, with the goal of ensuring consistent interpretation (e.g. of digital property) and avoiding overlaps with other regimes (e.g. GDPR, non-discrimination legislation). ... *SO 2: Ensure liability rules reflect nature of products in the circular economy*: The aim here is to ensure that products produced according to circular business models and placed on the market are adequately covered".

business that can be held liable, i.e. it is possible to obtain compensation, when defective products are bought directly from manufacturers/producers outside the EU.[45] Second, in order to reduce disproportionate obstacles to getting compensation: (iii) easing the burden of proof in complex cases (and clarifying liability for undiscoverable defects), while ensuring fair balance between producers/manufacturers and consumers;[46] (iv) easing restrictions on making claims as well as ensuring legal certainty by better aligning the PLD with the new legislative framework created by Decision 768/2008/EC7 and with product safety rules, and by codifying PLD-related case law.[47]

9.3 Need for Action at EU Level—Choice of Instrument

The Commission stressed that there is need for action at EU level ("the revision of the Product Liability Directive can only be done at EU level"). In the absence of EU action, Member States could adopt/adjust their own (divergent) national liability rules for compensating people harmed by defective digital products or products in the circular economy, resulting in further fragmentation and increased costs for businesses active across borders. This in turn would increase legal uncertainty, creating obstacles to the rollout of digital products and services across the EU market. As the Commission stated, "the Product Liability Directive is a longstanding

---

[45] Ibid., at pp. 26–27: "*SO 3: Ensure there is always an EU-based liable person for defective products bought from producers outside the EU*: The aim here is to ensure that when a consumer purchases a product directly from a non-EU producer, there is an economic operator based in the EU from whom to seek compensation if the product is defective and causes harm. The aim is also to ensure consumer protection no matter how a product is purchased and to guarantee a level playing field for EU and non-EU businesses alike".

[46] Ibid., at p. 27: "*SO 4: Ease the burden of proof in the case of complex products and clarify liability for undiscoverable defects, while ensuring fair balance between producers and consumers*: The aim here is to alleviate difficulties that consumers face in proving producers' liability in the case of complex products, and so achieve a fairer balance of interests. The aim is also to provide legal certainty regarding defects that were undiscoverable when the product was put into circulation".

[47] Commission Staff Working Document, "Impact Assessment Report – Accompanying the document Proposal for a Directive of the European Parliament and of the Council on liability for defective products", SWD(2022) 316 final, Brussels, 28.9.2022, at p. 27: "*SO 5: Ease restrictions on making claims, while ensuring fair balance between producers and consumers*: The aim here is to ease restrictions that currently disproportionately limit consumers' ability to make claims".

For the initiative's five specific objectives, see also:

Commission Staff Working Document, "Subsidiarity Grid – Accompanying the document Proposal for a Directive of the European Parliament and of the Council on liability for defective products, SWD(2022) 315 final, Brussels, 28.9.2022, at p. 3.

Commission Staff Working Document, "Executive Summary of the Impact Assessment Report – Accompanying the document Proposal for a Directive of the European Parliament and of the Council on liability for defective products", SWD(2022) 317 final, Brussels, 28.9.2022, at p. 1.

See also the proposal for a revised Product Liability Directive, Explanatory Memorandum, at p. 2.

EU law from 1985. It works well on the whole, but is not adapted to the digital age and circular economy. Without a uniform set of rules for compensating people harmed by defective digital products or products in the circular economy, manufacturers would be faced with 27 different sets of rules. This would lead to different levels of consumer protection and distorted competition among businesses from different Member States. The revision of the Product Liability Directive can only be done at EU level".[48]

With regard to the issue of the choice of instrument, the Commission stated that several policy options were taken into consideration in the preparation of the proposed action. In particular, although a non-binding instrument, such as a recommendation, presents a less intrusive approach and allows Member States maximum flexibility in assessing how to adjust their national rules, it is not suitable to address the identified problems in an effective manner and to ensure a consistent implementation of the proposed measures. Soft law has been discarded since both the desired harmonisation effect and legal certainty are unlikely to be delivered by a non-binding instrument. On the contrary, a mandatory instrument is able to prevent protection gaps stemming from partial or no implementation and, among the binding instruments, the revision (and not the repeal) of the PLD seems to be the most appropriate legislative tool. A revised Product Liability Directive can achieve the set policy objectives and provide the desired harmonisation effect and legal certainty, while giving the Member States the needed flexibility (in contrast to a Regulation which would have been too stringent) to integrate the harmonised measures into their national liability regimes.

As the Commission put it, "the repeal of the Product Liability Directive or issuing only guidance would not have achieved the objectives of legal certainty and a level playing field between businesses. Converting the Directive into a regulation was considered disproportionate, given the close interaction of product liability rules with national legal systems. Equally, extending the scope of the regime to cover harm to fundamental rights was considered disproportionate. The revision of the Directive to clarify its scope, definitions and the way it operates for products in the digital age and circular economy was considered proportionate and not exceeding what was necessary to achieve the objectives. . . . The proposed action is limited to the essential aspects of the liability regime for defective products and the choice of instrument, a directive, will allow Member States the flexibility needed to embed the rules into their national legal systems. . . . Given that the Product Liability Directive's liability rules interact closely with national civil codes and are deeply embedded into diverse national legal systems, the option of converting the current Product Liability Directive into a regulation was discarded as disproportionate. A directive achieves

[48] Commission Staff Working Document, "Subsidiarity Grid – Accompanying the document Proposal for a Directive of the European Parliament and of the Council on liability for defective products, SWD(2022) 315 final, Brussels, 28.9.2022, at pp. 2 and 3.

See also the proposal for a revised Product Liability Directive, Explanatory Memorandum, p. 6.

the policy objectives effectively and allows flexibility to seamlessly embed the rules into national systems”.[49]

9.4 Subject Matter, Scope, Maximum Harmonisation Instrument, Definitions

The proposal for a revised Product Liability Directive seeks to tackle the implementation challenges that have emerged due to recent advancements in technologies, like AI and connected products, as well as the increased role software plays in products.

Articles 1 and 2 specify the subject matter and scope of the proposal for a revised Product Liability Directive, which harmonises the liability of economic operators for damage suffered by natural persons caused by defective products, i.e., it lays down common rules under which the economic operator is held liable for damage caused to a natural person due to the defectiveness of a product.[50]

The proposal for a revised PLD does not apply to damage resulting from nuclear accidents in so far as liability for such damage is covered by international conventions ratified by Member States.[51] The proposed Directive does also not affect the applicability of EU law on the protection of personal data[52] as well as certain

[49] Commission Staff Working Document, “Subsidiarity Grid – Accompanying the document Proposal for a Directive of the European Parliament and of the Council on liability for defective products, SWD(2022) 315 final, Brussels, 28.9.2022, at pp. 4 and 5.

See also the proposal for a revised Product Liability Directive, Explanatory Memorandum, p. 7: “The proposal takes the form of a directive, which gives Member States flexibility to seamlessly embed its rules into national systems. This is important, given that its rules interact closely with national civil codes and are deeply integrated into national legal systems. This proposal seeks to replace the PLD entirely. Changing the PLD by way of recast or amending act was deemed inappropriate in light of the need for changes in almost every article”.

[50] Proposal for a revised Product Liability Directive, Article 1.

With regard to the relationship between the proposal for a revised Product Liability and the proposed AI Liability Directive (the latter covered extensively in Chap. 8 of this book), the Commission stated that “the PLD makes manufacturers strictly liable for harm caused by their defective products – this covers the full range of products, including software and AI systems. However, the PLD does not exist in isolation and victims often have a choice on which legal basis they want to make a claim. All Member States have fault-based liability regimes that require injured people to prove somebody’s fault caused the harm they suffered. If a victim seeks compensation under such national fault-based liability rules (e.g. for harm not covered by the PLD such as infringements of fundamental rights or claims against users of products rather than against the manufacturer) and the claim concerns damage caused by an AI system, the proposed AI Liability Directive could, on certain conditions, help claimants overcome the difficulties they might otherwise face because of the opacity of the AI system involved”. See European Commission – Questions & Answers on the revision of the Product Liability Directive, Brussels, 28 September 2022, p. 2.

[51] Proposal for a revised Product Liability Directive, Article 2(2), and Recital 7.

[52] Ibid., Article 2(3)(a).

national rules, such as rules 'concerning the right of contribution or recourse between two or more economic operators that are jointly and severally liable' under the listed conditions.[53] Furthermore, the proposed Directive does not affect the rights that an injured person may have under existing national rules concerning contractual liability or concerning non-contractual liability on grounds other than the defectiveness of a product, including national rules implementing EU legislation such as the (proposed) AI Liability Directive.[54] It also does not affect any rights that an injured person may have under any special liability system that existed in national laws on 30 July 1985.[55]

The proposal for a revised Product Liability Directive aims to achieve the internal market objective and ensure that businesses have legal certainty. To this end, as a maximum harmonisation instrument,[56] the proposed Directive prohibits Member States from implementing provisions that are more or less stringent than those within the Directive's scope.[57] However, the Commission's proposal leaves intact alternative means of compensation available to individuals who have suffered harm, such

---

[53] Ibid., Article 2(3)(b).

[54] Ibid., Article 2(3)(c).

See also Recital 9: "Under the legal systems of Member States an injured person may have a claim for damages on the basis of contractual liability or on grounds of non-contractual liability that do not concern the defectiveness of a product, for example liability based on warranty or on fault. This includes the provisions of the [AI Liability Directive], which lays down common rules on the disclosure of information and the burden of proof in the context of fault-based claims for damages caused by an AI system. Such provisions, which also serve to attain inter alia the objective of effective protection of consumers, should remain unaffected by this Directive".

[55] Ibid., Article 2(3)(d).

See also Recital 10: "In certain Member States, injured persons may be entitled to make claims for damages caused by pharmaceutical products under a special national liability system, with the result that effective protection of consumers in the pharmaceutical sector is already attained. The right to make such claims should remain unaffected by this Directive".

[56] "Does the Union action leave as much scope for national decision as possible while achieving satisfactorily the objectives set? (e.g. is it possible to limit the European action to minimum standards or use a less stringent policy instrument or approach?): In order to achieve the internal market objective and give businesses legal certainty, the Product Liability Directive is a maximum harmonisation instrument and does not allow Member States to adopt more, or less, stringent provisions at national level if those provisions are within the scope of the Directive. However, the proposed action leaves intact other routes to compensation that injured people have at national level (such as compensation on the basis of contract, warranty or fault)". Commission Staff Working Document, "Subsidiarity Grid – Accompanying the document Proposal for a Directive of the European Parliament and of the Council on liability for defective products, SWD(2022) 315 final, Brussels, 28.9.2022, p. 5.

[57] Proposal for a revised Product Liability Directive, Article 3: "Member States shall not maintain or introduce, in their national law, provisions diverging from those laid down in this Directive, including more, or less, stringent provisions to achieve a different level of consumer protection, unless otherwise provided for in this Directive".

See also Recital 8: "In order to create a genuine internal market with a high and uniform level of consumer protection, and to reflect the case law of the Court of Justice, Member States should not be, in respect of matters within the scope of this Directive, maintain or introduce more, or less, stringent provisions than those laid down in this Directive".

as contract-based, warranty-based, or fault-based compensation at the national level.[58] Also, the proposed Directive does not affect national rules on calculating compensation, which should be laid down by Member States.[59]

9.4.1 Broader Definition of Product

The proposal for a revised Product Liability Directive applies to products placed on the market or put into service after 12 months upon the entry into force of the Directive.[60] In addition to products, the proposed Directive creates a new regime for 'defective components'.[61]

[58]Commission Staff Working Document, "Subsidiarity Grid – Accompanying the document Proposal for a Directive of the European Parliament and of the Council on liability for defective products, SWD(2022) 315 final, Brussels, 28.9.2022, at p. 4: "The Product Liability Directive leaves intact all other national rules concerning other types of liability, such as liability based on fault, warranty or contract".

See also the proposal for a revised Product Liability Directive, Recitals 9 and 21: "(9) - Under the legal systems of Member States an injured person may have a claim for damages on the basis of contractual liability or on grounds of non-contractual liability that do not concern the defectiveness of a product, for example liability based on warranty or on fault. This includes the provisions of the [AI Liability Directive], which lays down common rules on the disclosure of information and the burden of proof in the context of fault-based claims for damages caused by an AI system. Such provisions, which also serve to attain inter alia the objective of effective protection of consumers, should remain unaffected by this Directive". . . . "(21) - This Directive should not affect the various means of seeking redress at national level, whether through court proceedings, non-court solutions, alternative dispute resolution or representative actions under Directive (EU) 2020/182845 of the European Parliament and of the Council or under national collective redress schemes".

[59]Proposal for a revised Product Liability Directive, Recital 18.

[60]Ibid., Article 2(1).

See also Recital 20: "This Directive should apply to products placed on the market or, where relevant, put into service in the course of a commercial activity, whether in return for payment or free of charge, for example products supplied in the context of a sponsoring campaign or products manufactured for the provision of a service financed by public funds, since this mode of supply still has an economic or business character".

Article 4(8)-(10) of the Commission's proposal for a revised PLD provides definitions of the terms 'placing on the market', 'making available on the market', 'putting into service': "(8) 'placing on the market' means the first making available of a product on the Union market; (9) 'making available on the market' means any supply of a product for distribution, consumption or use on the Union market in the course of a commercial activity, whether in return for payment or free of charge; (10) 'putting into service' means the first use of a product in the Union in the course of a commercial activity, whether in return for payment or free of charge, in circumstances in which the product has not been placed on the market prior to its first use".

[61]As the Commission stated: "What products will be covered by the revised rules? – The revised product liability rules will apply to all products, from garden chairs to cancer medicines, from agricultural products to advanced machinery but also to software updates. Like other products, defective software and AI systems could also cause harm, for example if they are embedded in, a cleaning robot, or placed on the market as a digital product in its own right, like a medical health app

As already described, it was legally unclear how to apply the existing Product Liability Directive's definitions and concepts to products in the modern digital and circular economy (for instance, software and products that need software or digital services to function, such as smart devices and autonomous vehicles). This is why, according to the Commission's proposal, the term product is defined as "all movables, even if integrated into another movable or into an immovable".[62]

One of the most significant changes in the proposal for a revised PLD is the extension of the PLD's scope by widening the definition of 'product'. Indeed, in contrast to the current PLD, and in order to respond "to the reality of products in the digital age, in a technology-neutral manner",[63] the Commission's proposal explicitly includes (alongside electricity) software (whether embedded or standalone), including AI systems,[64] and digital manufacturing files[65] within the definition of product: "'Product' includes electricity, digital manufacturing files and software".[66] Also, the

for a smartphone. The new PLD makes explicit that injured people can claim compensation if software or AI systems cause damage. The new rules also consider products stemming from circular economy business, namely business models in which products are modified or upgraded. The proposal creates the legal clarity that industry needs in order to embrace circular business models. The rules of the PLD (including the possible presumptions) would apply to remanufacturers and other businesses that substantially modify products in case these products cause damage to a person, unless they show that the defect relates to an unmodified part of the product". European Commission – Questions & Answers on the revision of the Product Liability Directive, Brussels, 28 September 2022, p. 1.

[62] Proposal for a revised Product Liability Directive, Article 4(1).

[63] Ibid., Explanatory Memorandum, p. 11.

[64] Ibid., Recital 12: "Products in the digital age can be tangible or intangible. Software, such as operating systems, firmware, computer programs, applications or AI systems, is increasingly common on the market and plays an increasingly important role for product safety. Software is capable of being placed on the market as a standalone product and may subsequently be integrated into other products as a component, and is capable of causing damage through its execution. In the interest of legal certainty it should therefore be clarified that software is a product for the purposes of applying no-fault liability, irrespective of the mode of its supply or usage, and therefore irrespective of whether the software is stored on a device or accessed through cloud technologies". As a result, it could be argued that software is covered by the Commission's proposal as an intangible component of a tangible product, for example the operating system of a smart device, as standalone software, for instance a smartphone application, or as a service, for instance cloud computing.

[65] Ibid., Article 4(2): "'digital manufacturing file' means a digital version or a digital template of a movable".

See also Recital 14: "Digital manufacturing files, which contain the functional information necessary to produce a tangible item by enabling the automated control of machinery or tools, such as drills, lathes, mills and 3D printers, should be considered as products, in order to ensure consumer protection in cases where such files are defective".

[66]Ibid., Article 4(1).

The European Consumer Organisation (BEUC) welcomed the Commission's proposal to broaden the scope of the PLD by including software, such as AI systems. However, BEUC argued that the definition of product should explicitly state that software, including AI, is covered as component of a product, as standalone product and as a service: "BEUC suggests to explicitly state in the definition of product, not only in the recitals, that software, including AI, is covered as a component of a product, as a standalone product or as a service. Software is increasingly present in the daily lives of consumers, be it in the form of a pre-installed operating system on their smart devices, an app that they download or a service that they access via the internet. As such software may cause damage to consumers, for instance a battery saving app may cause a smartphone battery to overheat and ignite, thereby damaging other property or causing even physical damage. AI-driven products may come with particular risks for consumers, inter alia because of their autonomy and unpredictability. Therefore, software including AI should be covered by product liability rules". See: The European Consumer Organisation (BEUC), "Revision of the Product Liability Directive – Time to ensure effective and comprehensive protection for consumers damaged by defective products", 01.03.2023, pp. 1 and 5.

The Irish Council for Civil Liberties (ICCL) also favoured the inclusion of software as a product, stating that consumers could finally hold companies liable for damage caused by software, including third party software: "The old Product Liability Directive from 1985 did not include software as a product. Consequently, natural persons could not hold companies liable for damage caused by software. The Commission has now rectified this in the updated PLD. Companies would now be liable for software, including 3rd-party software, that cause harm". Irish Council for Civil Liberties (ICCL), "New liability rules on product and AI are encouraging but need improvement", 4 October 2022.

The European Consumer Organisation (BEUC) also welcomed the Commission's proposal to include "digital manufacturing files" in the definition of a product: "3D printers and similar tools allow consumers to generate movable items out of data and raw material. While raw material is already explicitly covered by the PLD, data for the manufacturing of products with 3D printers is currently not mentioned. However, data that is incorrect, incomplete or otherwise unfit for purpose may cause a defect of the produced item and should thus be covered by the PLD. Nevertheless, consumers who generate products with a 3D printer for their private use should not be liable as a manufacturer under the PLD in case these products damage another person. Therefore, BEUC also welcomes that the proposal clarifies that the PLD should only apply to products put on the market or into service in the course of a commercial activity". See: The European Consumer Organisation (BEUC), "Revision of the Product Liability Directive – Time to ensure effective and comprehensive protection for consumers damaged by defective products", 01.03.2023, pp. 1 and 6.

For the opposite view, see the following responses:

The response submitted by the Computer and Communications Industry Association (CCIA Europe), which stated that software should not be considered as a product, since software tends to evolve over time and has never caused any physical harm in itself. Software cannot have the same liability as tangible goods. This extension of the PLD's scope by widening the definition of 'product' could lead to legal uncertainty for businesses and hinder innovation: "Article 4(2) of the PLD revision broadens the definition of a "product" from tangible goods only to also include software (whether embedded or standalone), artificial intelligence (AI) systems, as well as digital services necessary for the product's functioning. A strict liability regime usually applies to products that pose a significant risk, such as severe physical injury or damage to property, for example in the case of explosives. While the purpose of the PLD is to be general, it is hard to imagine how software could physically act upon any person or physical property to provoke such injury or damage. Indeed, the nature and risk profile of software differ fundamentally from those of physical goods.

This is particularly true as software simply cannot be completely bug-free. Software continuously evolves, even after being put on the market, which means that it is constantly improved and fixed as developers identify new risks. For example, developers identify bugs encountered by users and will prepare a software update to fix them. As it stands, this extension of the PLD's scope is not fit for purpose and does not account for the properties of software and technological products. It should also be noted that the proposed revision does not provide any precise definition of "software". Embedded software is already covered by the current PLD, as underlined in the impact assessment conducted for this revision. Hence, we fail to see the added value of including 3 standalone software in the scope of the PLD as there are no liability gaps. Besides, if the software is defective, the EU's Sale of Goods Directive and the Digital Content and Digital Services Directive already offer a very high level of contractual protection to consumers. Consumers can also seek remedies under fault-based liability regimes of Member States. In fact, this extension of the product scope would discourage software developers from innovating, as they would be subject to a strict liability regime. Bringing non-embedded software within the scope of the PLD could thus have significant consequences. Developers may be discouraged from developing, or releasing, software in the EU, or may raise the price of software for consumers to cover potential liability costs. This could result in the roll-out and uptake of digital technologies in the EU lagging behind the rest of the world. It would also discourage the sharing of security-related information across the developer ecosystem and would discourage all players along the supply chain to assist in providing security fixes, as they would try to avoid future liability. This is clearly detrimental to end-users, who may be exposed to security risks for longer. This would even be damaging to product safety itself, as software components are used to improve physical goods. Software developed for cars, or apps monitoring energy systems, would be negatively impacted for example". Computer & Communications Industry Association (CCIA Europe), "Making EU product liability rules fit for the digital age – Position Paper on the Revision of the Product Liability Directive", December 2022, pp. 2–3.

See also the response submitted by BSA – The Software Alliance, which stated that traditional product liability rules should not be simply extended to standalone software that is more akin to a service. According to the BSA, strict liability regime for standalone software could have a detrimental impact on software development and innovation in the EU. Nonetheless, in the event that standalone software is included in the scope of the revised PLD, the Directive should restrict the application of strict liability to exceptional situations involving extraordinarily hazardous activities that impose significant risks on others. This limitation would be appropriate for cases where software could potentially pose substantial risks of severe harm: "The draft PLD seeks to classify standalone software as a product. However, modern software can have many attributes that are normally associated with a service and would therefore be ill-suited to the product-focused liability regime of the draft PLD. Introducing strict liability for standalone software could extend liability to developers that could not reasonably be expected to bear responsibility for situations beyond their control. Standalone software can be integrated and deployed in an almost unlimited number of scenarios and for a wide range of uses. The draft PLD provisions, which are designed for products, could result in considerable challenges for standalone software used inappropriately. The draft PLD should exclude standalone software, especially software supplied by so-called "as-a-service" models, from its scope, given its fundamentally different nature from physical products. Strict liability regime for standalone software could have a detrimental impact on software development and innovation in Europe. Software developers could be discouraged from innovating, leading to less innovative features, reduced performance, and trends towards more basic functionalities. However, if standalone software were to be included in the scope of product liability rules, the proposal should: - reserve strict liability regime to extreme circumstances involving abnormally dangerous activities that impose substantial risks to others, therefore for cases in which software may present material risks of severe harm; and - avoid overlapping and inconsistent standards especially for the artificial intelligence (AI) systems, therefore the AI systems should be excluded from the scope of the draft PLD altogether. Liability for AI systems should instead be regulated by the AI Liability Directive, which specifically anticipates a review of AI Liability five years after its entry into force and is directly linked to the AI Act". BSA – The Software Alliance, "Recommendations on the Draft EU Product Liability Directive", March 2023, pp. 2–3.

In addition, see the position of Developers Alliance, which opposed a generalised inclusion of standalone software in the definition of product': "Imposing a strict liability regime on software in a generalized way will have a significant impact on software development and availability in the EU. Developers with limited resources (e.g. startups) will be particularly discouraged by increased legal risks and costs associated with litigation and indemnity to platforms, device manufacturers and distributors. . . . The generalized inclusion of standalone software in the definition of 'product' is not justified. The vast range of software applications, with various features and functions, provide a multitude of situations with very different levels of risk, as well as control from software developers. In general, the nature of software makes it more akin to services. . . . The strict liability regime is intended for high risk situations like those directly affecting the life and physical integrity of persons. The nature of software and computer processing needs to be considered, in particular with regard to reliability. There is no 100% foolproof software, even for military and telecom grade systems. Software will always include flaws, bugs are inherent and subject to constant code review for fixes. Treating software defects as careless is inconsistent with how software development works. Software should only be implicated where negligence is involved. Strict liability is inappropriate because perfection is unachievable in software development. Software is covered by specific requirements in certain sectoral regulation, to address the high risk specificity of certain sectors (e.g. medical devices). Defective products, not compliant with relevant harmonized requirements can produce harm, but it's inevitably the case that software is embedded in or enabled through hardware. It is not the software itself that is considered a defective product, but the software-enabled product can be defective as a result of a malfunction of software. Contractual and national tort liability covers a broader range of damages, including from services. Consumers can rely on these regimes for situations involving standalone software as well". Developers Alliance, "Position on the European Commission's proposal for a Directive on liability for defective products", 14 December 2022, pp. 1–2.

Furthermore, see the response submitted by the American Chamber of Commerce to the European Union (AmCham EU), which disagreed with the Commission's proposal to expand the scope of products covered to all AI systems, irrespective of the degree of risk classification. In addition, the AmCham EU stressed that strict liability should not be expanded to cover standalone software: "The definition of a 'product' has been broadened from tangible goods to software – both embedded and standalone – and digital services necessary for the functioning of the product. The simplicity of the existing PLD ensures that rules apply to all physical products. It is generally recognised that the current definition of 'product' includes embedded software, which also encompasses Artificial Intelligence (AI) technology within that software. As with other products that operate in an automated fashion (eg microwave ovens, dryers), the allocation of liability is usually clear. Neither opacity nor complexity are specific to AI, rather, they also apply to many other products. AI is always linked to the software as part of a product and simply relates to techniques that can be used to develop, offer and improve products and services. Standalone AI does not exist, it is always linked to the software. Even in the case of an AI system that operates with a high degree of autonomy, there are always human actors involved – for example the developer, deployer or user – who could be held liable in case of defects that result in harm. Further, beyond EU level provisions, national tort and contract laws apply. In the 1985 PLD, there seems to be no significant uncertainties, gaps or difficulties as to how the legislation can be applied to damages caused by software and AI. Jurisdiction has been clear for damages caused by products, including AI-enabled products. In addition, the European Commission's proposal also expands the scope of products covered to all AI systems, irrespective of the degree of risk classification. Given that the objective of the revised PLD is compensation for damage caused by a lack of safety, there should be a clearer link to safety-specific uses/scenarios of software and AI (ie when software/AI is used). Changes to the EU's product liability rules that expressly target AI-powered products and services without distinction of the degree of risk could create disincentives and deter producers from offering new AI-powered products and services that may be safer and more effective than their non-AI counterparts. Strict liability should not be expanded to cover standalone software. Standalone software, inherently, does not represent the same level of risk to consumers as physical products, for which strict liability is justified. A defect in a physical product can lead to physical damage to consumers or property, and it cannot be repaired at a distance. This is not the case for standalone software, which can never be completely free of 'bugs', but said 'bugs' can be fixed through updates, and cannot physically act upon persons or property. It is also to be clarified whether any updates of standalone software would be considered as resetting the time-limitation period that the PLD provides for. Considering this risk excluding software developers from this important liability threshold. This fundamental difference in characteristics and risk to safety between physical products (containing embedded software or not) and standalone software has already been accepted in previous revisions of EU product safety laws, including the revision of the General Product Safety Directive. Therefore, the proposal should avoid including stand-alone software in the scope of the PLD and subjecting it to a strict liability regime. While introducing very limited benefits to consumers, these changes in the definition of a product represent a significant possibility of discouraging software developers from innovating as they would potentially be covered by a strict liability regime". The American Chamber of Commerce to the European Union (AmCham EU), "Our Position – Feedback on Product Liability Directive proposal", 11 December 2022, pp. 2–3.

According to DigitalEurope, "the proposal significantly broadens the definition of product, capturing not only tangible products but also all types of software (including all standalone software not linked to a tangible product) and all components, regardless of the intended purpose. This means that a whole host of large and small software providers, the majority with low-risk and benign uses, will need to cope with a framework they are today largely unfamiliar with. Recent estimates put the number of companies developing software in Europe at more than 370,000, employing almost 1.5 million people. Any expansion of scope beyond finished tangible products must be clear and proportionate. The greater legal exposure for software developers, in combination with the expanded definition of damage and the unclear concept of defectiveness, may not achieve the desired legal certainty and will likely result in higher prices for software. In addition, measures should be taken to prevent unintended consequences, including potentially holding software developers liable for damage caused by taking action to prevent exploits. For instance, an operating system removes a malicious app from users' devices, resulting in lost user data for which the operating system could be liable". DigitalEurope, "Creating a proportionate Product Liability Directive", 3 March 2023, p. 3.

See also the response submitted by Google, which strongly opposed the inclusion of stand-alone software in the revised PLD. Applying a strict liability regime directly to standalone software (i.e., expanding the scope of the revised PLD to cover standalone software) is not proportionate or consistent with the existing legislative framework, hinders innovation in the EU and risks significant adverse consequences for users: "• Strict liability deviates from the legal norm that liability should entail fault and is reserved for situations that bear a risk of severe damage to persons or property. • Strict liability for standalone software will in most cases not be justified given software's fundamentally different nature and risk profile from physical goods. Software can be readily fixed through wireless updates, bugs are generally accepted as inherent to software development, software developers often lack control over how their software is integrated along the supply chain, and standalone software cannot physically act upon any person or property. • This greater legal exposure for software developers could have a number of profound unintended consequences, such as: (i) a chilling effect on innovation and digitization in Europe; (ii) higher priced devices and software, to compensate the manufacturer/developer for higher potential costs; (iii) worsened software performance and a trend toward basic functionality for users (in light of the security-performance trade-off for software development); (iv) potentially holding developers liable for user

Commission's proposal covers digital services where they are essential for products to function as components of the product with which they are interconnected or integrated (e.g. navigation services in an autonomous vehicle), and clarifies when a related service is to be treated as a component of a product: a digital service will be considered as a component of a product if it is integrated into or connected with a

---

harm caused by taking action to prevent exploits (for example, where taking such action results in lost user data); (v) reduction in coverage of, or complete removal of, useful factual information made available by the software". Google, "Response to the new Product Liability Directive consultation", 9 December 2022, pp. 1 and 3–8.

Also, according to Google, there are numerous examples of (standalone) software that may not have been developed if strict liability had been in place at the time, including: • Temperature monitoring and controlling software, which has been crucial in prolonging shelf-life and advancements in food and drug safety (as well as other products sensitive to temperature changes). • Food traceability software, allowing users to track and store information about food products' composition and origins, facilitating health and safety requirements. • Exercise apps that offer access to health and fitness for many, where unclear instructions can cause physical injury. • Flood/fire prediction software, earthquake detection and early alerts. • Routing and direction apps, which help users find their way and navigate, could suggest inaccurate directions" (at p. 8).

Furthermore, according to the Information Technology Industry Council (ITI), the expansion of the definition of product fails to take into account the specific characteristics of software. Introducing strict liability for software and AI-based technologies would prevent innovation and investment and hinder the roll-out and uptake of AI-enabled technologies: "The proposals' main changes to the PLD framework in article 4(1) is the expansion of the definition of product to include software (embedded and standalone), components, AI systems, and 'related services.' ITI is concerned about this extension of the definition of product, which fails to take into account the specific characteristics of software. Unlike software, hardware cannot be fixed remotely, and that justifies a stricter treatment of physical products. At the same time, the tangibility of hardware also creates higher risk of physical harm compared to software, which cannot physically act upon any person or property. Finally, while bugs are inevitable in software development, hardware malfunctions can be a more infrequent consequence of a permanent design problem or an unforeseen event affecting individual products. If the EU were to become the first global player to apply strict liability to services and software, especially to the extent that current definitions are left excessively vague and could potentially contemplate a large number of cases which would be difficult to prove, the roll-out and uptake of AI-based technologies would also be hindered. This would impact businesses and start-ups operating in Europe and come into conflict with the stated goals of the Commission to encourage innovation and create an ecosystem of excellence in Europe. Strict liability is a powerful tool which should only be used for a very limited number of cases. Introducing strict liability for software and AI-based technologies would disproportionately spread liability throughout the supply chain, also exposing to liability actors that could not and should not reasonably be expected to bear responsibility for situations beyond their control". Information Technology Industry Council (ITI), "Comments to the Revision of the Product Liability Directive (PLD): Ensuring a Proportionate Framework for all Actors", December 2022, pp. 1–2.

product by the manufacturer or within the control of the manufacturer in such a way that the absence of the service would prevent the product from functioning.[67]

---

[67] Proposal for a revised Product Liability Directive, Article 4(4): "'related service' means a digital service that is integrated into, or inter-connected with, a product in such a way that its absence would prevent the product from performing one or more of its functions".

Proposal for a revised Product Liability Directive, Article 4(5): "'manufacturer's control' means that the manufacturer of a product authorises (a) the integration, inter-connection or supply by a third party of a component including software updates or upgrades, or (b) the modification of the product".

See also Recital 15: "It is becoming increasingly common for digital services to be integrated in or inter-connected with a product in such a way that the absence of the service would prevent the product from performing one of its functions, for example the continuous supply of traffic data in a navigation system. While this Directive should not apply to services as such, it is necessary to extend no-fault liability to such digital services as they determine the safety of the product just as much as physical or digital components. Such related services should be considered as components of the product to which they are inter-connected, when they are within the control of the manufacturer of that product, in the sense that they are supplied by the manufacturer itself or that the manufacturer recommends them or otherwise influences their supply by a third party".

The European Consumer Organisation (BEUC) welcomed the Commission's proposal to include "related digital services" in the definition of a product. However, it stressed that, in addition to "related digital services", "related digital content" should be covered by the scope of the PLD: "BEUC welcomes the proposal to include 'related digital services'. Digital technologies often blur the lines between products and services since some products are provided as a service or depend on a constant supply of certain services to function. However, while some digital services may be essential for the functioning of a product, some digital content may be so as well. For instance, the supply of traffic data for a navigation system may be considered as a related service. However, the supplied traffic data itself should also be covered as a product by the PLD as the data may be incomplete, incorrect, or otherwise unfit for purpose and may thus cause damage. Therefore, any kind of data that is essential for the functioning of a product should be covered by the scope of the PLD, for instance as "related digital content" to use a similar term as "related digital services" that is already part of the proposal. To include digital services as well as digital content that is essential for the functioning of a product in the scope of the PLD would ensure consistency with the Digital Content and Digital Services Directive that provides rules on the supply of these items". The European Consumer Organisation (BEUC), "Revision of the Product Liability Directive – Time to ensure effective and comprehensive protection for consumers damaged by defective products", 01.03.2023, pp. 1 and 5–6.

For the opposite view, see the following:

The response submitted by the Computer and Communications Industry Association (CCIA Europe), which stated that "covering software, AI, and digital services under the exact same, strict liability regime as traditional products raises more questions than it solves. At the very minimum, the PLD should use narrower and clearer definitions to avoid overly-broad interpretations and uncertain implementation. … While the proposal excludes services from the scope, "related services" are included to cover digital services without which a product would not function (Article 4(4)). The definition of related services should be further limited to avoid inadvertently covering a wide range of services under this strict liability regime. Indeed, including services in the scope of the PLD would be a shift in EU law and case law, both of which have recognised the separation of the liability regimes for goods and services. Recital 15 of the proposal should at least mention that only digital 5 services necessary to the core functionality of a product are in scope". Computer & Communications Industry Association (CCIA Europe), "Making EU product liability rules fit for the digital age – Position Paper on the Revision of the Product Liability Directive", December 2022, p. 3.

Therefore, in relation to AI in particular, the Commission's proposal confirms that AI systems and AI-enabled goods should be considered as 'products' and thus fall within the proposed Directive's scope, meaning that, just like for any other product, compensation is available when damage is caused by defective AI, without the injured person having to prove the manufacturer's/economic operator's fault (the latter are responsible for defective products, regardless of whether the defect of the product is their fault).

Also, according to the American Chamber of Commerce to the European Union (AmCham EU), "the proposal brings 'related services' in its scope, while it is widely understood and confirmed by Recital 15 that 'this Directive should not apply to services'. The current definition of related service is overly broad and could be understood to apply to almost all digital services that interact with the products. Further, the lack of a definition of software creates an additional uncertainty as to what extend the PLD would apply to digital services". The American Chamber of Commerce to the European Union (AmCham EU), "Our Position – Feedback on Product Liability Directive proposal", 11 December 2022, p. 4.

Furthermore, see the detailed response submitted by Google, which stressed that the definition of "related services" is very broad. The expansion of the scope of the PLD to cover certain services cuts across existing EU legislation and leaves the position on liability of services unclear. Including related services results in an inconsistent liability regime. This is why Google suggested to remove related services from the scope of the proposal: "The PLD regime has never sought to impose liability for services and the Commission's proposal acknowledges that "this Directive should not apply to services" (Recital 15). At the same time, the proposal seeks to distinguish "related services", which it proposes to bring in scope. The definition of "related services" is very broad ("a digital service that is integrated into, or inter-connected with, a product in such a way that its absence would prevent the product from performing one or more of its functions") and in practice could apply to many digital services that interact with technology products, including – for example – services delivered through apps. This is particularly the case as the proposal suggests that 3rd party services can be considered a "related service" for which a manufacturer can have liability (Recital 37). This approach risks making the PLD apply to many digital services (potentially even digital content), which is – in our understanding – not the intention of the Commission. Indeed, it is unclear why related services need to be included at all. In practice, it is extremely unlikely that a related service will pose a risk to the health or safety of users of digital services unless this manifests through a product, in which case users are already entitled to compensation under the PLD. Including related services also results in an inconsistent liability regime if the digital provision of a service (e.g. via an app) leads to a no-fault liability while the provision of the same service in non-digital form remains out of scope (cf. ECJ, Case C-65/20 – "Krone"). Moreover, EU law already provides strong protections to ensure legal protections – including under the Sale of Goods Directive 2019/771 and Digital Content Directive 2019/770 – which allow consumers to seek remedies for any lack of conformity under a contract. Taking account of these concerns, we would respectfully suggest to remove related services from the scope of the proposal". Google, "Response to the new Product Liability Directive consultation", 9 December 2022, pp. 8–9.

In addition, according to the Information Technology Industry Council (ITI), "the proposal brings "related services" in scope, although recital 15 expressly states that "this Directive should not apply to services". The definition of "related services" is very broad and could cover many digital services interacting with technology products (e.g., services delivered through apps). The inclusion of related services in the PLD scope also results in an inconsistent liability regime if providing a service digitally (e.g., on an app) leads to strict liability, whereas providing the same service in a non-digital manner is not in the scope of the PLD". Information Technology Industry Council (ITI), "Comments to the Revision of the Product Liability Directive (PLD): Ensuring a Proportionate Framework for all Actors", December 2022, p. 4.

With regard to software in particular, and with the aim of not hampering innovation or research, the Commission's proposal stressed that (i) free and open-source software developed or supplied outside the course of a commercial activity, as well as (ii) the source code of software (as this is pure information), should be excluded from the definition of products for the purposes of this proposed Directive.[68] Yet, where software is supplied in exchange for a price or personal data is provided in the course of a commercial activity (*i.e.* for other purposes than exclusively improving

---

[68] Proposal for a revised Product Liability Directive, Recitals 12 and 13.

According to the American Chamber of Commerce to the European Union (AmCham EU), "Open-source software and software code should be excluded from the scope, as they are crucial for software innovation in the single market, especially in AI research and development. This exclusion should be added directly into the article of the text in addition of the recital 13. Many services and software systems, including AI systems, are the result of numerous entities building on top of other efforts, leveraging open-source libraries, tools and frameworks created by thousands of contributors—often in volunteer capacities". The American Chamber of Commerce to the European Union (AmCham EU), "Our Position – Feedback on Product Liability Directive proposal", 11 December 2022, p. 3.

The same approach is followed by the Information Technology Industry Council (ITI): "We support the exclusion of open-source software in recital 13, and we call to specifically add this exclusion directly into the article of the text in addition to the recital. However, participants in the open-source ecosystem could still be exposed to strict liability in the event that a software is commercialised. While there are practical concerns on how the strict liability framework may apply to such ecosystem, it is also important to note that applying strict liability to every open-source contributor would create disincentives to open-source software development, severely undermine the open-source ecosystem that has been critical to AI development and especially disincentivise smaller developers from taking part in AI innovation. We therefore call to extend this exclusion to all open-source software". Information Technology Industry Council (ITI), "Comments to the Revision of the Product Liability Directive (PLD): Ensuring a Proportionate Framework for all Actors", December 2022, pp. 3–4.

This is also proposed by the Developers Alliance, which stated that "the exemptions for open source software mentioned in recital 13 should be included in the operative part of the directive. The exemptions should be strengthened, taking into consideration that the definitions of 'making available on the market', and respectively 'putting into service', include circumstances when products are placed on the market and distributed free of charge. It is worth noting that, given the prevalence of open source in software development, a strict liability regime for software in general will defeat any incentive to utilize open source resources for commercial applications. Software developers use open source code in building different applications, as reusing code is saving time and money. In the context of strict liability they would be forced to review in detail each piece of code and duplicate such efforts and relative costs for any application reusing the same snippets of open source code. Writing code from scratch and relying on proprietary software will be thus the obvious choice to limit liability risks". Developers Alliance, "Position on the European Commission's proposal for a Directive on liability for defective products", 14 December 2022, pp. 2–3.

Similarly, Google stressed that the open source exemption is unclear: "The exemptions for open source software are currently very narrow and only set out in the recitals, not the text of the proposal itself. It would be helpful to clarify within the text (for example, in Article 4(1) or 4(3)) that both OSS software and its use regardless of the purpose is not within the scope. According to the current text, manufacturers would be subject to liability under the PLD also for defects due to the (commercial) use of OSS components. This is likely to lead to widespread liability scenarios and also significantly impair the use and development of OSS software". Google, "Response to the new Product Liability Directive consultation", 9 December 2022, p. 11.

the security, compatibility or interoperability of the software), the proposed Directive should apply.[69]

9.4.2 *Broader Scope of Liable Parties*

The proposal for a revised PLD has a significantly wider range of application than the current PLD, as it applies to 'economic operators'. It sets a broader scope of liable parties compared to the existing Product Liability Directive. In particular, an economic operator is defined as "the manufacturer of a product or component, the provider of a related service, the authorised representative, the importer, the fulfilment service provider or the distributor".[70] Also, the developer or producer of software, including AI system providers, should be treated as a manufacturer. Therefore, not only hardware manufacturers but also software providers and providers of digital services that affect how the product works can be held liable. Furthermore, online platform providers could also be held liable as 'economic operators' for damage caused by defective products,[71] provided that the conditions of Article 6(3) of the Digital Services Act are fulfilled.

In addition, the notion of "economic operator" is much more extensive than that of "producer" in the current PLD, as this extended concept also covers manufacturers of components ("where a defective component has caused the product to be defective, the manufacturer of a defective component can also be held liable")[72] which include 'any related service'.[73] As it was stated, "by enlarging the scope of the EU's product liability regime to explicitly include software providers, businesses that make substantial modifications to products, authorised representatives and fulfilment service providers, injured persons will have a better chance of being compensated for damage suffered, and a level playing field will be established between businesses".[74]

[69] Proposal for a revised Product Liability Directive, Recital 13.

[70] Ibid., Article 4(16).

[71] Ibid., Article 7(5) and (6).

[72] Ibid., Article 7(1), paragraph 2.

[73] Ibid., Article 4(3) and (4): "(3) 'component' means any item, whether tangible or intangible, or any related service, that is integrated into, or inter-connected with, a product by the manufacturer of that product or within that manufacturer's control; (4) 'related service' means a digital service that is integrated into, or inter-connected with, a product in such a way that its absence would prevent the product from performing one or more of its functions".

[74] Ibid., Explanatory Memorandum, p. 6.

9.4.3 Removing the Lower and Upper Liability Limits

Unlike the current version of the PLD, the Commission's proposal does not contain any lower or upper liability limits. Therefore, it removes the threshold of €500 (under Article 9(b) of the current PLD, consumers may only seek compensation for damage to property if the worth of the damage surpasses an amount of €500) and the possibility for Member States to impose a financial ceiling of €70 million (under Article 16(1) of the current PLD, Member States are allowed to introduce upper limits of at least €70m for product liability claims).[75]

9.4.4 Expanding the Definition of Damage: Harm to Psychological Health and Loss or Corruption of Data—What About Non-Material Damage and Pure Economic Loss?

It is reminded that, under the existing Product Liability Directive, the producer is liable for defective products which have caused death, personal injury, or material damage.

The proposal for a revised PLD expands the notion of compensable damage by including material losses[76] resulting from: (a) death or personal injury, including

[75]This was welcomed by the European Consumer Organisation (BEUC). See BEUC, "Revision of the Product Liability Directive – Time to ensure effective and comprehensive protection for consumers damaged by defective products", 01.03.2023, pp. 2 and 10: "BEUC welcomes that the proposal does not contain any lower or upper liability limits" (at p. 2); . . . The threshold of €500 "is highly problematic for several reasons. First, it is incoherent with the Representative Actions Directive which lists the PLD in its annex and which aims at facilitating consumer claims regardless of their amount. Secondly, the provision has been interpreted differently across the EU. In some Member States, the amount of €500 is regarded as deductible, which means that in case of success, the amount of damages awarded to the claimant is reduced by €500, while in other Member States €500 represents a threshold, below which no damages can be claimed. Depending in which Member State they live, consumers may therefore not get full compensation or even no compensation at all, which is both completely arbitrary. As a result, the €500 threshold has impeded access to justice in four out of five cases because the damage was below €500. . . . In addition to the lower limit of €500, . . . the upper limits of at least €70m for product liability claims . . . may also impede consumers from getting full compensation and thus should not be included in the revised PLD" (at p. 10).

[76]The Commission's proposal stated that only material loss, which results from death, personal injury, harm to or destruction of property and the loss or corruption of data, is compensable under the revised PLD. Therefore, the proposal does not recognise pure economic loss as compensable damage. According to the Commission, "pure economic loss usually refers to financial loss suffered by a party, which is not the result of any damage to that party's own person or property. Instead, the damage arises from economic relationships in which the party is involved. This concept is distinct from the concept of consequential economic loss, i.e. loss that arises from physical injury or property damage. However, one should bear in mind that there is no universally accepted definition or description of pure economic loss in Member States' or EU law". Commission Staff Working

medically recognised harm to psychological health;[77] (b) property damage (with the exception of (i) the defective product itself; (ii) a product damaged by the defective

Document, "Impact Assessment Report – Accompanying the document Proposal for a Directive of the European Parliament and of the Council on adapting non-contractual civil liability rules to artificial intelligence", SWD(2022) 319 final, Brussels, 28.9.2022, at p. 163.

The European Consumer Organisation (BEUC) stated that "all kinds of material damage, including pure economic loss, should be compensable under the PLD. Material damage in the form of unwanted expenditures often is the consequence of another harm. For instance, a medical bill might be the consequence of a personal injury and repair costs may be the consequence of a damage to property. However, defective products may also cause pure economic loss. For instance, insufficient cybersecurity may allow malicious third parties to access a connected devices and to steal valuable data that cannot be restored. Defective smart devices, such as voice assistants or smart household applications, may order goods or services online without the consent of consumers thereby causing financial loss in case an order cannot be revoked. Therefore, pure economic loss should be included in the list of compensable damage". The European Consumer Organisation (BEUC), "Revision of the Product Liability Directive – Time to ensure effective and comprehensive protection for consumers damaged by defective products", 01.03.2023, p. 11.

[77]Proposal for a revised Product Liability Directive, Article 4(6)(a). See also Recital 17: "In the interests of legal certainty, it should be clarified that personal injury includes medically recognised damage to psychological health".

The European Consumer Organisation (BEUC) welcomed the Commission's clarification that harm to psychological health is covered by the notion of personal injury: "BEUC welcomes the proposal to clarify that medically recognised harm to psycho-logical health is recognised as personal injury under the PLD if it was caused by a defective product. Death or personal injuries are explicitly mentioned in the current version of the PLD. However, it is unclear whether psychological health is covered by the PLD as well. The proposal therefore increases the protection of consumers for instance in case they suffer from a post-traumatic stress disorder as a consequence of an accident caused by a defective product". The European Consumer Organisation (BEUC), "Revision of the Product Liability Directive – Time to ensure effective and comprehensive protection for consumers damaged by defective products", 01.03.2023, p. 9.

On the other hand, the Developers Alliance stated that "concerning psychological harm, even medically attested, this could lead to excessive litigation based on legal uncertainty. Psychological suffering is a subjective experience, and considering the proposed generalized qualification of software as a product, different categories of software developers would be under constant risk of litigation (e.g. mobile application developers, game developers)". Developers Alliance, "Position on the European Commission's proposal for a Directive on liability for defective products", 14 December 2022, p. 2.

See also the response submitted by the Computer and Communications Industry Association (CCIA Europe), which stressed that non-material damage such as loss of data or psychological harm should not be part of the revised PLD's liability regime. The scope of damages in the revised PLD should remain limited to material harm: "Article 4(6) of the proposal expands the list of damages to include both "psychological health" and "loss or corruption of data". While damages remain limited to material losses, this expansion creates uncertainty, especially in combination with the wide definition of "product" discussed above. That is why the proposal needs to better outline what is meant by material losses resulting from harm to psychological health. While recital 17 implies that this addition is merely a clarification, current case law proves that this understanding varies greatly from one Member State to another. This is even more important as non-embedded software is now within the scope of the revised PLD. It will be difficult to clearly establish and quantify software's impact on psychological health. For example, a wellness app might have warned its users of its indicative nature, but would still be held liable for a mental illness developed by one of its users. This type of damage is particularly unforeseeable. As psychological health is already tackled by

component of that product or iii) property exclusively used for professional purposes);[78] and (c) loss, destruction or corruption of data (such as content deleted from a hard drive) that is not used exclusively for professional purposes.[79]

---

standard liability regimes, including national liability rules, the appropriateness of this inclusion in the context of a strict liability regime should be reconsidered". Computer & Communications Industry Association (CCIA Europe), "Making EU product liability rules fit for the digital age – Position Paper on the Revision of the Product Liability Directive", December 2022, p. 3.

Furthermore, according to the American Chamber of Commerce to the European Union (AmCham EU), the definition of 'damage' has also been broadened to include the material losses resulting from personal injury, including medically recognised harm to psychological health. There is currently no clear definition of what 'medically recognized harm to psychological health' entails. While common definitions would refer to emotional health, wellbeing and behavioural change, these notions are difficult to quantify and will result in legal uncertainty for manufacturers and the industry at large. This lack of clear definitions also risks resulting in the notion of damage being interpreted and transposed differently throughout the EU, ultimately resulting in consumers not receiving the same level of protection depending on the jurisdiction they find themselves in". The American Chamber of Commerce to the European Union (AmCham EU), "Our Position – Feedback on Product Liability Directive proposal", 11 December 2022, p. 4.

According to BSA – The Software Alliance, "with regard to psychological harm, further clarity is needed on what could constitute material damages and what thresholds (e. g., financial) would need to be met to claim compensation for damage to psychological harm. "Medically recognized" should be defined to include what claimants must prove (i.e. diagnosis by any medical professional and/or defined categories of conditions or standards) to claim such damage". BSA – The Software Alliance, "Recommendations on the Draft EU Product Liability Directive", March 2023, p. 7.

See also the response submitted by Google, which stressed that "the proposal expands the scope of recoverable damage to include immaterial harms such as medically recognised harm to psychological health and data loss. We have significant reservations about this proposal, which stretches the ambit of damages under the PLD beyond that which the strict liability framework was designed to help injured persons recover. Strict liability was intended to help individuals recover damages for death, personal injury and damage to property above a certain threshold (which does not include the cost of the defective product itself). Strict liability is appropriate to protect interests in clear-cut cases of personal injury and damage to property that have direct, tangible and severe consequences for individuals. It is not appropriate for strict liability to be extended to psychological harm . . . due to the challenges caused by remoteness of loss, quantification of damages and causation. . . . These issues are compounded by the lack of clear definitions for these additional harms. In particular, "medically recognised harm to psychological health" is open to a wide range of different interpretations. For example, would it be sufficient to show a doctor's note that lists the symptoms the patient had reported? Or, would the claimant need to show evidence of a disease or disorder that has been recognised (and is diagnosable) according to the evidence of reliable, peer-reviewed medical literature? . . . The lack of definitions for these key concepts leads to legal uncertainty and complexity in the application, with the risk of Member States interpreting these definitions differently, meaning individuals across the EU may not receive the same level of protection. In particular, it is important that the proposal clarifies that "medically recognised harm to psychological health" does not include stress or anxiety – as recognised by the Impact Assessment Report (see Annex 5, which states that: "Medically diagnosed psychological damage is generally accepted as falling under the concept of "personal injury", while just stress or anxiety is not")". Google, "Response to the new Product Liability Directive consultation", 9 December 2022, pp. 11-12.

[78] Proposal for a revised Product Liability Directive, Article 4(6)(b).

Contrary to Article 9(b)(ii) of the current version of the PLD (which only covers property if it is mainly used for private purposes), the Commission's proposal stated that damage to any property item is recognised as compensable damage under the PLD, unless the item is exclusively used for professional purposes [Article 4(6)(b)(iii) – Damage to mixed used property items].

According to Recital 19 of the proposal for a revised PLD, damage to any property owned by a natural person should be compensated. It is stressed that, as property is increasingly used for both private and professional purposes, it is appropriate to provide for the compensation of damage to such mixed-use property. Therefore, in light of the Directive's aim to protect consumers, property that is used exclusively for professional purposes should not fall within the Directive's scope.

The European Consumer Organisation (BEUC) welcomed the Commission's proposal that all property items are covered (i.e., that damage to all property items is compensable under the PLD), unless they are exclusively used for professional purposes. As it stated, "nowadays property items are often used both for private and professional purposes, for instance laptops and mobile phones. It might thus be difficult to determine for which purpose a property item is mainly used. The proposal would thus ensure that consumers are not left unprotected in case they use products both for private and professional purposes". The European Consumer Organisation (BEUC), "Revision of the Product Liability Directive – Time to ensure effective and comprehensive protection for consumers damaged by defective products", 01.03.2023, p. 9.

[79] Proposal for a revised Product Liability Directive, Article 4(6)(c).

The European Consumer Organisation (BEUC) welcomed the Commission's proposal that material loss resulting from the loss or corruption of data that was caused by a defective product is also recognised as compensable damage. However, it stressed that theft and unauthorised copying of data should also be recognised as compensable damage: "BEUC welcomes the proposal to recognise loss and corruption of data as compensable damage. Defective connected devices may not only cause damage in the physical world but may also cause damage to data that is stored on a device. Loss and corruption of data should thus be recognised as compensable damage under the revised PLD. How-ever, insufficient cybersecurity, which in our view should be considered as a defect, may allow malicious third parties to access connected devices and steal or copy sensitive data. Stolen or copied credentials could be used to cause financial damage while stolen or copied personal data, such as private messages, could be used to cause non-material damage for instance in the form of reputational damage. Compensating only loss or corruption of data, but not theft or unauthorised copying of data would thus leave consumers partly unprotected. Therefore, theft and unauthorised copying of data should also be recognised as relevant damage". The European Consumer Organisation (BEUC), "Revision of the Product Liability Directive – Time to ensure effective and comprehensive protection for consumers damaged by defective products", 01.03.2023, pp. 9–10.

For the opposite view, see the written contributions submitted by business stakeholders and organisations. For instance:

The Developers Alliance stressed that, "with regard to loss or corruption of data, this significantly increases legal uncertainty, as the notion is extremely broad and risks being interpreted in very different ways across jurisdictions. Recital 16 offers insufficient clarifications and justifications. The legal frameworks for data protection, privacy and cybersecurity are highly relevant and more appropriate to respond to consumer issues related to data. Furthermore, the provisions on liability for data loss could be in conflict with the necessity to take cybersecurity measures or even comply with legal obligations regarding content curation". Developers Alliance, "Position on the European Commission's proposal for a Directive on liability for defective products", 14 December 2022, p. 2.

According to the American Chamber of Commerce to the European Union (AmCham EU), "the European Commission's proposal is also expanding the notion of 'damage' to the 'loss or corruption of data'. While this inclusion should first and foremost be linked to the product's safety, clarifying the threshold of data loss/corruption that makes the loss material is also essential. Without clear definitions and thresholds, this extension of the scope could lead to waves of compensation claims against economic operators on illegitimate grounds. Strict liability is only appropriate in the cases of personal injury and damage to property that have direct and severe consequences for individuals. The existing definition of damages in the existing PLD has been working effectively, and there is no evidence that the definition is incomplete. This extension of strict liability does therefore not seem appropriate, especially when considering the challenges caused by remoteness of loss, quantification of damages and causation. As serious claims could be expected under additional categories of harm, it first needs to be defined how these (additional) damages could be quantified before including them in the legislation". The American Chamber of Commerce to the European Union (AmCham EU), "Our Position – Feedback on Product Liability Directive proposal", 11 December 2022, p. 4.

Also, according to BSA – The Software Alliance, "the draft PLD introduces some new categories of damage which subjects manufacturers to liability for "loss or corruption of data that is not used exclusively for professional purposes", instead of relying on existing regulation and legal remedies available in other legislations such as the GDPR (i.e. data breaches and related obligations are already governed there for personal data). Inclusion of "loss or corruption of data" in the draft PLD creates a competing and overlapping liability system and risks confusion and, possibly, multiple claims for the same loss or, at the very least, it would make it more difficult for claimants and defendants to decide under which regime a claim should be made. If the intention is to cover non-personal data, then personal data should be excluded from the remit of compensable damage under the draft PLD. Creation of an overlapping liability regime for loss or corruption of data would decrease clarity for both, consumers and businesses. We would therefore oppose the inclusion of the loss or corruption of data into the scope of damage recognized by the draft PLD. Especially when there is not enough clarity as to what could constitute "material damages" linked to loss or corruption of data and what threshold would need to be triggered (e.g., financial) to claim compensation for damage". BSA – The Software Alliance, "Recommendations on the Draft EU Product Liability Directive", March 2023, p. 6.

See also the response submitted by Google, which stated that "the proposal expands the scope of recoverable damage to include immaterial harms such as . . . data loss. We have significant reservations about this proposal, which stretches the ambit of damages under the PLD beyond that which the strict liability framework was designed to help injured persons recover. Strict liability was intended to help individuals recover damages for death, personal injury and damage to property above a certain threshold (which does not include the cost of the defective product itself). Strict liability is appropriate to protect interests in clear-cut cases of personal injury and damage to property that have direct, tangible and severe consequences for individuals. It is not appropriate for strict liability to be extended to . . . data loss/corruption, due to the challenges caused by remoteness of loss, quantification of damages and causation. The procedural burdens for all parties involved in cases alleging these categories of damages would be disproportionate and complex, and would require a significant amount of time and resources from national court systems, as well as the parties involved. For example, if a student failed to submit a paper due to a software crash that caused loss or corruption of data, and failed their university studies as a result, these proposals would allow them to sue the software developer for compensation for all the consequential damages, including an additional year of studies and lost income. This is plainly disproportionate, as the damages suffered by the student in this scenario were not foreseeable at the time the software was developed, and are potentially unlimited. . . . These issues are compounded by the lack of clear definitions for these additional harms. In particular, . . . data loss and data corruption are concepts that need to be clearly defined. For instance, what is in scope of "data", and what would constitute its loss or corruption? . . . The inclusion of immaterial harms such as data loss creates a risk of potentially unlimited liability for EU businesses. Popular software is often used by huge numbers of users - potentially even billions of users worldwide. A strict liability regime for immaterial harms such as data loss, combined with the removal of the €500 threshold and the EU's new Representative Actions Directive 2020/1828, could lead to businesses facing potentially limitless damages claims for minor service issues (outages, bugs, crashes etc.). These risks will significantly drive up

By expanding the notion of compensable damage to include the loss, destruction or corruption of data, the Commission's proposal recognises the growing importance and value of data in the digital age.[80] However, the proposal "does not go beyond what is necessary" and, therefore, does not address other forms of harm (e.g., infringement of personality rights such as privacy or discrimination or environmental damage), which would be more appropriately dealt with under other legislation.[81]

While the proposal for a revised PLD stipulates that Member States should provide full compensation for all *material* losses resulting from death, or personal injury, or damage to or destruction of property and data loss or corruption, Member States should lay down the rules on calculating compensation for such damages.[82] In addition, the proposed Directive does not affect national rules relating to non-material damage, i.e., as under Article 9(2) of the current PLD, the Commission's proposal leaves it to Member States to decide whether compensation for *non-material* damage can be claimed.[83]

---

the cost of doing business, including through greater insurance and legal costs, which will ultimately be passed on to the users. It could also potentially create uninsurable losses, which would have a particular impact on start-ups and SMEs. In addition, extending the PLD to cover immaterial harms is likely to have a chilling effect on innovation and software development. We consider that there are numerous examples of software that may not have been developed with strict liability extended to data loss. For example: • Operating systems, given that operating system developers could be held liable in the event of lost data (e.g., media, messages, files) caused by a crash. • Social media apps distributing user-generated content (based on the lack of definition of software and broad definition of related services, content could also be in scope), which could cause emotional damage if content moderation mechanisms did not prevent the distribution of offensive user-generated content". Google, "Response to the new Product Liability Directive consultation", 9 December 2022, pp. 11–12.

[80] Proposal for a revised Product Liability Directive, Recital 16: "In recognition of the growing relevance and value of intangible assets, the loss or corruption of data, such as content deleted from a hard drive, should also be compensated, including the cost of recovering or restoring the data. As a result, the protection of consumers requires compensation for material losses resulting not only from death or personal injury, such as funeral or medical expenses or lost income, and from damage to property, but also for loss or corruption of data".

[81] Ibid., Explanatory Memorandum, p. 6.

See also European Commission – Questions & Answers on the revision of the Product Liability Directive, Brussels, 28 September 2022, pp. 1–2: "Can you use the PLD to get compensation for infringements of fundamental rights? – People will be able to bring a claim for damages against the manufacturer if the defective product has caused death, personal injury, including medically recognised psychological harm, damage to property or data loss. The new rules do not allow compensation for infringements of fundamental rights, for example if someone failed a job interview because of discriminatory AI recruitment software. The draft AI Act currently being negotiated aims to prevent such infringements from occurring. Where they nevertheless do occur, people can turn to national liability rules for compensation, and the proposed AI Liability Directive could assist people in such claims".

[82] Proposal for a revised Product Liability Directive, Recital 18.

[83] Ibid.

It is reminded that, according to the Commission, "immaterial or non-material damage refers to losses which do not relate to a person's assets, wealth or income and, as such, cannot be quantified in an objective manner by reference to a market price or value. Such losses are, for example, damage

9.5 Right to Compensation

The Commission's proposal for a revised PLD stipulated that Member States must ensure that any 'natural person' who suffers damage caused by a defective product ('the injured person') is entitled to compensation, in accordance with the provisions laid down in the proposed Directive.[84] The proposed Directive also refers to the 'claimant'[85] who is defined as 'an injured person claiming compensation for damage caused by a defective product'.[86] The proposed Directive, therefore, excludes non-natural persons (such as businesses and any other public or private entities) from bringing a claim for damages on this legal ground.

The proposal for a revised PLD stressed that claims for damages can be brought not only by the injured person but also by persons that have succeeded in or have

---

to reputation, discrimination, loss of confidentiality, psychological harm and mental suffering. This type of damage is different from the concept of pure economic loss". Commission Staff Working Document, "Impact Assessment Report – Accompanying the document Proposal for a Directive of the European Parliament and of the Council on adapting non-contractual civil liability rules to artificial intelligence", SWD(2022) 319 final, Brussels, 28.9.2022, at p. 163.

See also the Opinion of Advocate General Wahl in case C-371/12, Petillo v Unipol, ECLI:EU:C:2013:652, at para. 38: "By 'non-material damage' I refer, generally speaking, to losses which do not relate to a person's assets, wealth or income and, as such, cannot be quantified in an objective manner by reference to a market price or value". This Opinion referred to Cf. Horton Rogers, W.V. (ed.), Damages for Non-Pecuniary Loss in a Comparative Perspective, European Centre of Tort and Insurance Law, Springer Verlag, Wien New York: 2001, p. 246.

The European Consumer Organisation (BEUC) argued that the revised PLD should also cover non-material harm as it is already the case under the General Data Protection Regulation or the Package Travel Directive: "BEUC strongly regrets that the proposal does not cover compensation for non-material damage. In particular personal injuries may cause non-material damage such as a shock, temporary physical limitations, for instance as consequence of a fracture, or persistent pain. But defective products may also cause other types of non-material dam-age. For instance, the violation of privacy by a defective smart device may in itself present a non-material damage or may lead to reputational damage if personal data is accessible for third parties. However, as under the current PLD, the proposal leaves it to Member States to decide whether compensation for non-material damage can be claimed. To ensure a high protection of consumers across the EU, the revised PLD should cover both material and non-material damage. This is already the case under other pieces of EU legislation, for instance under the General Data Protection Regulation, the Package Travel Directive, the Directive on the enforcement of intellectual property, and the Directive on the protection of trade secrets. There is no reason why victims of non-material damage should be entitled under EU law to claim compensation if damage was caused by a privacy infringement, by a breach of a package travel contract, by a violation of intellectual property or by a violation of trade secrets, but should depend on the goodwill of Member States if non-material damage was caused by a defective product". The European Consumer Organisation (BEUC), "Revision of the Product Liability Directive – Time to ensure effective and comprehensive protection for consumers damaged by defective products", 01.03.2023, p. 11.

[84] Proposal for a revised Product Liability Directive, Article 5(1).

[85] Ibid., Articles 8(1), 9(1), 14(2), 7(5)(a).

[86] Ibid., Article 8(1).

been subrogated into the rights of the injured person.[87] Furthermore, it stated that an action for damages can also be brought by someone acting on behalf of one or more injured parties, in accordance with EU or national law.[88]

9.6 Defectiveness—Safety as Benchmark—Criteria for Determining Whether a Product Is Defective

According to the Commission, the evaluation of defectiveness should be conducted through an objective analysis that does not take into account the safety expectations of any specific individual. The defectiveness of a product should be determined by reference not to its fitness for use but to the lack of safety that the public at large is entitled to expect.[89] The Commission's proposal clarifies that the reference to 'safety' intends to protect "the health and property of consumers".[90] This is why, according to the proposal for a revised PLD, a product will be considered defective when it fails to provide the safety which the public at large is entitled to expect, taking all circumstances into account.[91]

---

[87] Ibid., Article 5(2)(a).

For a definition of the term 'subrogation', see the proposal for a Directive of the European Parliament and of the Council on adapting non-contractual civil liability rules to artificial intelligence (AI Liability Directive), European Commission, COM(2022) 496 final, Brussels, 28.9.2022 (the 'proposed AI Liability Directive'), Explanatory Memorandum, at p. 12: "Subrogation is the assumption by a third party (such as an insurance company) of another party's legal right to collect a debt or damages. Thus one person is entitled to enforce the rights of another for their own benefit. Subrogation would also cover heirs of a deceased victim".

[88] Proposal for a revised Product Liability Directive, Article 5(2)(b).

[89] Ibid., Explanatory Memorandum, p. 12 and Recital 22.

[90] Ibid., Explanatory Memorandum, Recital 22.

[91] Ibid., Article 6(1).

For a critique of this narrow definition of defect, see the response submitted by the European Consumer Organisation (BEUC), which stated that products should be considered defective whenever they are not in compliance with the law or deviate from the functioning consumers are entitled to expect: "BEUC believes that the current narrow definition of defect, which is limited to safety expectations, unduly restricts the potential of the PLD. Instead, the notion of defect should be understood in a broader way. EU and Member States have adopted a waste framework of provisions that apply to products and at the same time aim at protecting consumers, not only their safety, for instance the GDPR. The PLD should complement those provisions by allowing consumers who suffered damage from non-compliant products to claim compensation. Therefore, products should be considered defective under the PLD whenever they are not in compliance with such provisions that apply to products and aim at protecting consumers. However, since legal requirement do not necessarily cover all potential risks for consumers, products should also be considered defective if they deviate from the functioning consumers are entitled to expect. In particular, AI driven products may develop malfunctions that do not necessarily present non-compliance with applicable law. The revised PLD should cover such risks by establishing a broad understanding of the notion of defect". See the European Consumer Organisation (BEUC), "Revision of the Product Liability Directive –

This definition of 'defectiveness' (in other words, the test for determining whether a product is defective—i.e. whether the product provided the safety which the public at large is entitled to expect) is substantively the same as under the currently applicable Product Liability Directive. However, the non-exclusive list of those circumstances that allow to assess the product's defectiveness is expanded. Indeed, in order to respond to the changing nature of products in the digital age, and to reflect case law of the CJEU, more factors (such as the interconnectedness or self-learning functions of products) have been added to the non-exhaustive list of factors to be taken into account by courts when assessing defectiveness.[92]

In particular, the factors that should be taken into account in order to assess whether a product is defective are, *inter alia*, the following (in other words, the assessment of a product's safety—i.e., the safety that the public at large is entitled to expect—should take into account, amongst others, the following factors): (a) the presentation of the product, including the instructions for installation, use and maintenance;[93] (b) the reasonably foreseeable use and misuse of the product;[94]

Time to ensure effective and comprehensive protection for consumers damaged by defective products", 01.03.2023, pp. 6–7.

On the other hand, see the response submitted by the American Chamber of Commerce to the European Union (AmCham EU), which stated that "the European Commission's proposal also expands the criteria to assess the defectiveness of products. The PLD states that 'a product shall be considered defective when it does not provide the safety which the public at large is entitled to expect'. It is unclear, however, how the defectiveness characteristics will apply to intangible products, in particular to software and AI systems, and the loss or corruption of data. Defectiveness standards must be objective and clear to avoid overreaching into quality considerations. It should be clarified how this factor weighs for/against liability of the developer when changes happen outside of the developer's control". The American Chamber of Commerce to the European Union (AmCham EU), "Our Position – Feedback on Product Liability Directive proposal", 11 December 2022, p. 4.

[92] Proposal for a revised Product Liability Directive, Explanatory Memorandum, p.12.

The European Consumer Organisation (BEUC) welcomed the Commission's proposal that the general understanding of "defect" should be complemented by a non-exhaustive list of circumstances that must be taken into account when assessing whether a product is defective. In this regard BEUC fully agrees with the proposal to extend the existing non-exhaustive list of circumstances because it increases legal certainty for consumers and provides incentives for manufactures to consider these additional circumstances when developing products to reduce potential liability risks. See the European Consumer Organisation (BEUC), "Revision of the Product Liability Directive – Time to ensure effective and comprehensive protection for consumers damaged by defective products", 01.03.2023, pp. 1 and 7–8.

[93] Proposal for a revised Product Liability Directive, Article 6(1)(a). See also Recital 22.

According to the European Consumer Organisation (BEUC), "a product may become defective in case installation, use or maintenance are done incorrectly due to misleading instructions. For instance, a piece of furniture may become unstable, fall apart and thereby injure a consumer because of a faulty or unprecise assembly instructions". The European Consumer Organisation (BEUC), "Revision of the Product Liability Directive – Time to ensure effective and comprehensive protection for consumers damaged by defective products", 01.03.2023, p. 7.

[94] Proposal for a revised Product Liability Directive, Article 6(1)(b). See also Recital 22.

According to the European Consumer Organisation (BEUC), "consumers should not be deprived of the possibility to claim compensation in case they use a product incorrectly in a way that could

(c) the effect on the product of any ability to continue to learn after deployment;[95] (d) the effect on the product of other products that can reasonably be expected to be used together with the product;[96] (e) the moment in time when the product was

happen to anyone else or in case a product is misused by a malicious third party". The European Consumer Organisation (BEUC), "Revision of the Product Liability Directive – Time to ensure effective and comprehensive protection for consumers damaged by defective products", 01.03.2023, p. 7.

On the other hand, DigitalEurope stated that "the proposal refers to 'reasonably foreseeable use and misuse' in relation to defining the defectiveness of a product. The misuse of a product does not indicate defectiveness, and manufacturers should not be held liable for misuse under strict liability. The notion of 'foreseeable' already implies some degree of fault. National liability regimes already cover these kinds of scenarios as fault-based, e.g. breach of vigilance/monitoring duties. . . . The law must remove liability for manufacturers for all misuse that is reasonably foreseeable, but for which the manufacturer has included relevant warnings". DigitalEurope, "Creating a proportionate Product Liability Directive", 3 March 2023, pp. 4–5.

[95] Proposal for a revised Product Liability Directive, Article 6(1)(c). See also Recital 23: "The effect on a product's safety of its ability to learn after deployment should also be taken into account, to reflect the legitimate expectation that a product's software and underlying algorithms are designed in such a way as to prevent hazardous product behaviour".

According to the European Consumer Organisation (BEUC), "the self-learning ability of AI systems should be taken into account when assessing whether a product is defective because, contrary to the positive connotation of the concept of "learning" and due to the complexity and unpredictability of AI systems, the autonomous process of self-learning may not necessarily improve the performance of an AI system but may also lead to unwanted output, for instance a smart assistant whose recommendations increasingly deviate from the interests of its user". The European Consumer Organisation (BEUC), "Revision of the Product Liability Directive – Time to ensure effective and comprehensive protection for consumers damaged by defective products", 01.03.2023, p. 8.

On the other hand, the Information Technology Industry Council (ITI) stated that "'Article 6(1)(c) expands the notion of defectiveness to the "effect on the product of any ability to continue to learn after deployment". However, it should be clarified how this factor weighs for/against liability of the developer when that learning happens outside of their control". Information Technology Industry Council (ITI), "Comments to the Revision of the Product Liability Directive (PLD): Ensuring a Proportionate Framework for all Actors", December 2022, p. 5.

See also the response submitted by DigitalEurope, which stated that "the proposal expands the notion of defectiveness to the 'effect on the product of any ability to continue to learn after deployment,' directly targeting AI systems. In practice, such learning will likely happen outside the provider's control because the user deploying the AI system may have retrained the system according to their needs or be feeding their own input data to the system. The proposed AI Act recognises the complexity of allocating responsibilities across different actors, notably that users may exercise control over the input data. For this reason, this consideration of defectiveness should be deleted from Art. 6". DigitalEurope, "Creating a proportionate Product Liability Directive", 3 March 2023, p. 5.

[96] Proposal for a revised Product Liability Directive, Article 6(1)(d). See also Recital 23: "In order to reflect the increasing prevalence of inter-connected products, the assessment of a product's safety should also take into account the effects of other products on the product in question".

According to the European Consumer Organisation (BEUC), "the interactions between different products, for instance between two smart home devices such as a smart heating system and the app that allows the user to control the system, should be taken into account when assessing whether a product is defective because on the Internet of Things the misfunction of one connected device may

placed on the market or put into service or, where the manufacturer retains control over the product after that moment, the moment in time when the product left the control of the manufacturer;[97] (f) product safety requirements, including safety-relevant cybersecurity requirements;[98] (g) any intervention by a regulatory authority or by an economic operator referred to in Article 7 of the proposed Directive relating

easily cause a defect of another connected device". The European Consumer Organisation (BEUC), "Revision of the Product Liability Directive – Time to ensure effective and comprehensive protection for consumers damaged by defective products", 01.03.2023, p. 8.

[97] Proposal for a revised Product Liability Directive, Article 6(1)(e). See also Recital 23: "In order to reflect that in the digital age many products remain within the manufacturer's control beyond the moment at which they are placed on the market, the moment in time at which a product leaves the manufacturer's control should also be taken into account in the assessment of a product's safety. A product can also be found to be defective on account of its cybersecurity vulnerability".

[98] Ibid., Article 6(1)(f). See also Recitals 23 and 24: "(23) - A product can also be found to be defective on account of its cybersecurity vulnerability. . . . (24) - In order to reflect the relevance of product safety and market surveillance legislation for determining the level of safety that the public at large is entitled to expect, it should be clarified that safety requirements, including safety-relevant cybersecurity requirements, . . . should also be taken into account in that assessment".

According to the European Consumer Organisation (BEUC), "product safety requirements including cybersecurity requirements should be taken into account when assessing whether a product is defective to strengthen the link between product safety rules and the PLD. In view or digital technologies it is particularly necessary to consider cybersecurity requirements because connected devices are often lacking adequate cybersecurity features as illustrated by tests performed by BEUC's members. In this context BEUC welcomes that the proposal states that the liability of an economic operator should not be reduced if the damage is caused by the defectiveness, for instance the non-compliance with cyber security requirements, and an act of a third party, for instance the exploitation of this very cybersecurity vulnerability by a cyber-criminal". The European Consumer Organisation (BEUC), "Revision of the Product Liability Directive – Time to ensure effective and comprehensive protection for consumers damaged by defective products", 01.03.2023, p. 8.

On the other hand, the Information Technology Industry Council (ITI) stressed that "Article 6(1)(f) also includes safety-relevant cybersecurity requirements among the circumstances to take into account when assessing defectiveness. It is not clear here if cyber vulnerabilities would be considered as a defect. This should not be the case as these are dynamic risks that can in most instances be mitigated through responsible system configuration to enable remote updates and responsible cyber hygiene practices by consumers. Applying strict liability will stifle cybersecurity professionals and likely lead to delays in launching products out of concern that some unknown, and potentially unknowable, vulnerability exists. Discovered vulnerabilities in software products can be remedied after the products have been placed on the market via patches developed in a timely manner by the manufacturer. However, software producers do not fully control in all instances whether updates are installed – oftentimes, it falls to the user to install or accept these updates and in such cases vulnerabilities can either go unnoticed or are not fixed, with users maintaining some level of responsibility for mitigation. The imperative of user responsibility also underscores a particular challenge in the use of existing product testing and certification regimes - which are largely geared toward the assessment of static product safety risks - to fully assess dynamic risks such as cyber vulnerabilities. It is important to educate consumers regarding responsible cyber hygiene practices, so they are aware of the importance of updating systems in those instances where automated remote updates are unavailable or even not permissible. For example, remote updates are problematic under the Sale of Goods Directive EU 2019/771, since the user should be able to decide in every case whether they want to install updates or not (cf. recital 30: "The consumer should remain free to choose whether to install the updates provided".) Information Technology Industry Council (ITI),

to product safety;[99] (h) the specific expectations of the end-users for whom the product is intended.[100] Also, the Commission stated that specific products, "such as life-sustaining medical devices, entail an especially high risk of damage to people and therefore give rise to particularly high safety expectations".[101] As a result, in order to respond to those high safety expectations, the Commission argued that "it should be possible for a court to find a product defective without establishing its

---

"Comments to the Revision of the Product Liability Directive (PLD): Ensuring a Proportionate Framework for all Actors", December 2022, p. 5.

Similarly, Google stressed that references to product safety and cybersecurity requirements need further clarification: "The references to product safety and cybersecurity requirements as circumstances relevant to defectiveness in Article 6(1)(f) are currently very broad. At the very least, it should be clarified that it is applicable 'product safety requirements, including safety-relevant cybersecurity requirements' that are mandatory under Union or national law. This should be understood in a narrow sense to cover mandatory laws applicable to the product in question (e.g. covering violations of the Cyber Resilience Act). The scope of the provision would otherwise be extremely broad, potentially covering all legislation, as well as guidance and standards. In particular in combination with the foreseeable use in Article 6(1)(b), this would otherwise lead to an unforeseeable myriad of possible liability scenarios. These changes would track similar clarifications that are already in the proposal in Article 9(2)(b) which refers to 'mandatory safety requirements laid down in Union law or national law'". Google, "Response to the new Product Liability Directive consultation", 9 December 2022, pp. 10–11.

Furthermore, according to the American Chamber of Commerce to the European Union (AmCham EU), "a product should not be considered defective as a result of issues related to safety-relevant cybersecurity requirements. Cybersecurity is an ongoing struggle against existing and evolving threats and cybersecurity professionals constantly strive to stop malicious actors. The idea that a producer can be liable for an unknown vulnerability exploited by an evolving threat puts undue burden on those trying to stop malicious actors". The American Chamber of Commerce to the European Union (AmCham EU), "Our Position – Feedback on Product Liability Directive proposal", 11 December 2022, p. 4.

[99]Proposal for a revised Product Liability Directive, Article 6(1)(g). See also Recital 24: "Interventions by regulatory authorities, such as issuing product recalls, or by economic operators themselves, should also be taken into account in that assessment. Such interventions should, however, not of themselves create a presumption of defectiveness".

According to the European Consumer Organisation (BEUC), "interventions by regulatory authorities such as product recalls by market surveillance authorities should be taken into account to strengthen the link between market surveillance rules and the PLD. If a market surveillance authority identifies that a product presents a risk for consumers and recalls the product, this intervention should suffice to consider the product as defective if it has caused damage". The European Consumer Organisation (BEUC), "Revision of the Product Liability Directive – Time to ensure effective and comprehensive protection for consumers damaged by defective products", 01.03.2023, p. 8.

[100]Proposal for a revised Product Liability Directive, Article 6(1)(h). See also Recital 22: "... the specific requirements of the group of users for whom the product is intended".

According to the Information Technology Industry Council (ITI), "the 'specific expectations of the end-users for whom the product is intended' (Article 6 (1) (h)) remains an unclear and subjective element that does not present any reasonable standard of control and would need to be clarified as well". Information Technology Industry Council (ITI), "Comments to the Revision of the Product Liability Directive (PLD): Ensuring a Proportionate Framework for all Actors", December 2022, p. 5.

[101]Proposal for a revised Product Liability Directive, Recital 22.

actual defectiveness, where it belongs to the same production series as a product already proven to be defective".[102] This is why the European Consumer Organisation stated that "well-founded concerns that products from the same product series are defective, for instance presented by a consumer organisation, should be added to the list of circumstances that have to be taken into account when assessing whether a product is defective".[103]

Finally, it is underlined that, in order to promote innovation and allow consumers to have a wider range of choices, a product should not be considered defective for the sole reason that a better product, including updates or upgrades to a product, is already or subsequently placed on the market or put into service.[104]

9.7 Economic Operators Liable for Defective Products

Article 7 of the proposal for a revised PLD lists the types of 'economic operators' which can be held liable for defective products. It introduces a layered approach (liability cascade) to liability depending on the different qualification of the economic operator, and attempts to ensure—taking into account the increasing significance of products manufactured outside the EU that are placed on the EU market—that there is always an economic operator in the EU against whom a compensation claim can be made.[105]

---

[102] Ibid.

[103] The European Consumer Organisation (BEUC), "Revision of the Product Liability Directive – Time to ensure effective and comprehensive protection for consumers damaged by defective products", 01.03.2023, p. 8.

[104] Proposal for a revised Product Liability Directive, Article 6(2). See also Recital 25: "In the interests of consumer choice and in order to encourage innovation, the existence, or subsequent placing, on the market of a better product should not in itself lead to the conclusion that a product is defective. Equally, the supply of updates or upgrades to a product should not in itself lead to the conclusion that a previous version of the product is defective".

[105] Ibid., Explanatory Memorandum, at p. 12. Also, at p. 2: "This proposal ... aims to ensure there is always a business based in the EU that can be held liable for defective products bought directly from manufacturers outside the EU, in light of the increasing trend for consumers to purchase products directly from non-EU countries without there being a manufacturer or importer based in the EU".

See also Commission Staff Working Document, "Impact Assessment Report – Accompanying the document Proposal for a Directive of the European Parliament and of the Council on liability for defective products", SWD(2022) 316 final, Brussels, 28.9.2022, at pp. 26–27: "*SO 3: Ensure there is always an EU-based liable person for defective products bought from producers outside the EU*: The aim here is to ensure that when a consumer purchases a product directly from a non-EU producer, there is an economic operator based in the EU from whom to seek compensation if the product is defective and causes harm. The aim is also to ensure consumer protection no matter how a product is purchased and to guarantee a level playing field for EU and non-EU businesses alike".

See also European Commission – Questions & Answers on the revision of the Product Liability Directive, Brussels, 28 September 2022, p. 2: "Who is liable for defective products manufactured outside the EU? – The existing PLD makes importers liable for defective products manufactured

The list of economic operators comprises the following: (i) the manufacturer of a product or component; (ii) the provider of a related service; (iii) the authorised representative; (iv) the importer; (v) the fulfilment service provider; and (vi) the distributor.[106] Furthermore, substantial modifiers of products and online marketplaces are added to the list of liable economic operators.

---

outside the Union. This is because it would have been too difficult for consumers to seek compensation from companies outside the Union. Today's global value chains allow consumers to buy products from outside the Union directly, without an importer. That is why the new PLD will allow consumers to seek compensation from the non-EU manufacturer's representative. Thanks to the Market Surveillance Regulation and the upcoming revision of the General Product Safety Regulation, this will mean that, there will be an EU-based liable person from whom to seek compensation. Distributors (offline and online sellers) can also be held liable if they fail to give the name of the EU-based liable person to the injured person on request. This applies to online marketplaces too, but only if they present themselves to the consumer as a distributor".

[106] Proposal for a revised Product Liability Directive, Article 4(16).

The European Consumer Organisation (BEUC), although it welcomed that the Commission's proposal aims to ensure that there is always one economic operator based in the EU who can be held liable under the revised PLD, it expressed disappointment over the proposal's imposition of a rigid hierarchy for consumer liability towards economic operators. According to BEUC, this effectively limits consumers to seeking compensation exclusively from the economic operators mentioned in the predetermined order. Consequently, consumers might encounter challenges in obtaining compensation from a specific economic operator, for instance because the operator lacks the necessary financial resources to compensate for the damage. This is why it stated that, if the manufacturer is based outside the EU, or if the addressed economic operator fails to identify the manufacturer, consumers should have the ability to hold any economic operator involved in the supply chain jointly and severally liable:

"BEUC regrets that the proposal establishes a strict order in which consumers can hold economic operators liable. In practice, this means that consumers may seek compensation only from one of the listed economic operators. However, consumers may have difficulties in getting compensation from a particular economic operator, for instance because the economic operator does not have the financial means to compensate for the damage. This could easily happen in case a consumer would, according to the proposal, only be able to hold an authorised representative liable. Currently, there are no EU rules on financial or qualitative requirements for authorised representatives. It is not even necessary to establish a legal person, which in some Member States would require to have a certain share capital as security for clients or business partners. Therefore, literally anyone can become an authorised representative regardless of their ability to bear liability under the PLD. To avoid such difficulties consumers should be able to hold any economic operator that is involved in the supply chain jointly and severally liable, be it the importer, authorised representative, the fulfilment service provider or any distributor, if the manufacturer is based outside the EU, or if the addressed economic operator fails to identify the manufacturer". The European Consumer Organisation (BEUC), "Revision of the Product Liability Directive – Time to ensure effective and comprehensive protection for consumers damaged by defective products", 01.03.2023, pp. 14–15.

In particular, the proposed Directive refers to the manufacturer[107] of a defective product[108] or of a component.[109] It states that any manufacturer of a defective product can be held liable for damages caused by a defect in that product.[110] Also, if a defective component has caused the product to be defective (and without prejudice to the liability of the manufacturer of the defective product), the manufacturer of the integrated defective component can also be held liable for the same damage.[111]

When the manufacturer of the defective product is established outside the EU (and without prejudice to its own liability), the importer[112] of the defective product (or component) and the authorised representative[113] of the manufacturer can be held liable for damage caused by that product.[114]

As a last resort, when the manufacturer of the defective product is established outside the EU and neither of the importer or authorised representative are established in the EU, the 'fulfilment service provider'[115] (offering at least two of the following services: warehousing, packaging, addressing and dispatching of a

---

[107] Proposal for a revised Product Liability Directive, Article 4(11): "'manufacturer' means any natural or legal person who develops, manufactures or produces a product or has a product designed or manufactured, or who markets that product under its name or trademark or who develops, manufactures or produces a product for its own use".

[108] Ibid., Article 4(1): "'product' means all movables, even if integrated into another movable or into an immovable. 'Product' includes electricity, digital manufacturing files and software".

[109] Ibid., Article 4(3): 'component' means any item, whether tangible or intangible, or any related service, that is integrated into, or inter-connected with, a product by the manufacturer of that product or within that manufacturer's control".

[110] Ibid., Article 7(1), first subparagraph. See also Recital 26: "The protection of the consumer requires that any manufacturer involved in the production process can be made liable, in so far as their product or a component supplied by them is defective".

[111] Ibid., Article 7(1), second subparagraph. See also Recital 26: "Where a manufacturer integrates a defective component from another manufacturer into a product, an injured person should be able to seek compensation for the same damage from either the manufacturer of the product or from the manufacturer of the component".

[112] Ibid., Article 4(13): "'importer' means any natural or legal person established within the Union who places a product from a third country on the Union market".

[113] Ibid., Article 4(12): "'authorised representative' means any natural or legal person established within the Union who has received a written mandate from a manufacturer to act on its behalf in relation to specified tasks".

[114] Proposal for a revised Product Liability Directive, Article 7(2). See also Recital 27: "In order to ensure that injured persons have an enforceable claim for compensation where a manufacturer is established outside the Union, it should be possible to hold the importer of the product and the authorised representative of the manufacturer liable".

[115] Ibid., Article 4(14): "'fulfilment service provider' means any natural or legal person offering, in the course of commercial activity, at least two of the following services: warehousing, packaging, addressing and dispatching of a product, without having ownership of the product, with the exception of postal services as defined in Article 2, point (1), of Directive 97/67/EC of the European Parliament and of the Council, of parcel delivery services as defined in Article 2, point (2), of Regulation (EU) 2018/644 of the European Parliament and of the Council, and of any other postal services or freight transport services".

product, without having ownership of the product) can be held liable for damage caused by the defective product.[116]

An innovation introduced in the Commission's proposal clarifies when economic operators who make modifications to a product, such as in the context of circular economy business models,[117] can be held liable. In particular, the proposal deals with the cases where a product is modified substantially outside the control of the original manufacturer. In those cases, the substantially modified product is considered to be a new product and, therefore, it should be possible to hold the person that undertook the substantial modification liable as a manufacturer of the modified product. Therefore, as it was stated, any natural or legal person that modifies a product that has already been placed on the market or put into service will be considered a manufacturer of the product. However, the modification of the product must have been 'substantial' under EU or national rules on product safety, and must be undertaken outside the original manufacturer's control.[118]

---

[116] Ibid., Article 7(3). See also Recital 27: "Practical experience of market surveillance has shown that supply chains sometimes involve economic operators whose novel form means that they do not fit easily into the traditional supply chains under the existing legal framework. Such is the case, in particular, with fulfilment service providers, which perform many of the same functions as importers but which might not always correspond to the traditional definition of importer in Union law. In light of the role of fulfilment service providers as economic operators in the product safety and market surveillance framework, in particular in Regulation (EU) 2019/1020 of the European Parliament and of the Council, it should be possible to hold them liable, but given the subsidiary nature of that role, they should be liable only where no importer or authorised representative is based in the Union".

[117] Ibid., Recital 29: "In the transition from a linear to a circular economy, products are designed to be more durable, reusable, reparable and upgradable. The Union is also promoting innovative and sustainable ways of production and consumption that prolong the functionality of products and components, such as remanufacturing, refurbishment and repair. In addition, products allow for modifications through changes to software, including upgrades".

[118] Ibid., Article 7(4).

Recital 29 of the proposal states that, in order to assess whether a modification is substantial, specific criteria (set out in relevant EU and national safety legislation) should be taken into account, "such as modifications that change the original intended functions or affect the product's compliance with applicable safety requirements". It is also stressed that "in the interests of a fair apportionment of risks in the circular economy, an economic operator that makes a substantial modification should be exempted from liability if it can prove that the damage is related to a part of the product not affected by the modification. Economic operators that carry out repairs or other operations that do not involve substantial modifications should not be subject to liability under this Directive".

See also Article 4(5) of the proposal for a revised Product Liability Directive: "'manufacturer's control' means that the manufacturer of a product authorises a) the integration, inter-connection or supply by a third party of a component including software updates or upgrades, or b) the modification of the product".

The European Consumer Organisation (BEUC) stressed that, in the circular economy, the refurbishment or the remanufacturing of products becomes increasingly important but, at the same time, consumers damaged by refurbished or remanufactured products are not able to hold the original manufacturer liable since the latter may claim that the defect only occurred after the original product was placed on the market. Therefore, in order to avoid consumers being left

According to the Commission's proposal, distributors[119] of a defective product (offline and online sellers) can also be held liable.[120] In particular, if an EU-based economic operator cannot be identified (or is established outside the EU), each distributor of the product is liable where i) the claimant/injured person requests that distributor to identify an EU-based economic operator or its own distributor with the product; and ii) the distributor fails to identify such an economic operator or its own distributor with the product within 1 month of receiving the request.[121]

Furthermore, in this chain of liability established by Article 7 of the Commission's proposal, online marketplaces are involved when no economic operator or authorised representative has been identified. Thus any provider of online platforms that allows consumers to conclude distance contracts with traders and that is not a manufacturer, importer or distributor can, under certain conditions, also be held

uncompensated, BEUC stated that the PLD should establish the liability of economic operators who place substantially refurbished or remanufactured products on the market. See the European Consumer Organisation (BEUC), "Revision of the Product Liability Directive – Time to ensure effective and comprehensive protection for consumers damaged by defective products", 01.03.2023, p. 16.

For a similar view, see the ACEA (The European Automobile Manufacturers' Association) response to the European Commission's inception impact assessment on civil liability - Adapting liability rules to the digital age and circular economy, 28.07.2021: "Companies that remanufacture or refurbish products should be held liable for damages caused by defects resulting from these changes. To the extent that the remanufacture or refurbishment results in a substantial modification of the initial product, they should be considered producers for the purpose of this Directive and be subject to all obligations it imposes on producers" (at pp. 1–2).

[119] Proposal for a revised Product Liability Directive, Article 4(15): "'distributor' means any natural or legal person in the supply chain, other than the manufacturer or the importer, who makes a product available on the market".

[120] Ibid., Recital 27: "In the interests of channelling liability in an effective manner towards manufacturers, importers, authorised representatives and fulfilment service providers, it should be possible to hold distributors liable only where they fail to promptly identify a relevant economic operator based in the Union".

[121] Ibid., Article 7(5).

liable.[122] In sum, according to the Commission's proposal, online platforms can be held liable if all the following conditions are met: (i) the manufacturer cannot be identified or is established outside the EU; (ii) an importer, authorised representative or fulfilment service provider cannot be identified; (iii) the online platform fails to identify the supplier of the product; and, (iv) the conditions of Article 6(3) of the Digital Services Act are fulfilled, meaning that the online platforms presented the product in a manner that would give an average consumer the impression that this product is provided either by the online platform/marketplace itself or by a third party acting under its authority or control.[123]

---

[122] Ibid., Article 7(6): "Paragraph 5 shall also apply to any provider of an online platform that allows consumers to conclude distance contracts with traders and that is not a manufacturer, importer or distributor, provided that the conditions of Article 6(3) set out in Regulation (EU)…/… of the European Parliament and of the Council on a Single Market for Digital Services (Digital Services Act) are fulfilled".

See also Recital 28: "Online selling has grown consistently and steadily, creating new business models and new actors in the market such as online platforms. … The Digital Services Act and Regulation on General Product Safety regulate, inter alia, the responsibility and accountability of online platforms with regard to illegal content, including products. When online platforms perform the role of manufacturer, importer or distributor in respect of a defective product, they should be liable on the same terms as such economic operators. When online platforms play a mere intermediary role in the sale of products between traders and consumers, they are covered by a conditional liability exemption under the Digital Services Act. However, the Digital Services Act establishes that online platforms that allow consumers to conclude distance contracts with traders are not exempt from liability under consumer protection law where they present the product or otherwise enable the specific transaction in question in a way that would lead an average consumer to believe that the product is provided either by the online platform itself or by a trader acting under its authority or control. In keeping with this principle, when online platforms do so present the product or otherwise enable the specific transaction, it should be possible to hold them liable, in the same way as distributors under this Directive. That means that they would be liable only when they do so present the product or otherwise enable the specific transaction, and only where the online platform fails to promptly identify a relevant economic operator based in the Union".

[123]For a critique of the Commission's proposal, see the response submitted by the European Consumer Organisation (BEUC), which, although it welcomed that the Commission's proposal lists online marketplaces as one of the liable economic operators, it nevertheless argued that consumers should be able to hold online marketplaces liable if the manufacturer or third-party vendor is based outside the EU, or if the online marketplace fails to identify the EU based manufacturer or third party vendor. BEUC is concerned that the Commission's proposal to hold online platforms liable for defective or illegal products sold on them are subject to conditions limiting their effective application:

"The proposed conditions for the liability of online marketplaces are far too narrow. Online marketplaces would only be liable as last resort if no other economic operator listed in the liability cascade could be held liable. Nevertheless, online market-places would still be able to escape liability simply by identifying the third-party vendor, even if the third party vendor is based outside the EU, and by informing consumers that the third-party vendor is not acting under their authority or control. This is not acceptable, given that online marketplaces provide the infrastructure for the dissemination of millions of defective products. Mystery shopping by BEUC's members has shown that, out of 250 products sold at online marketplaces, 165 products did not meet EU product safety standards. At the same time, online marketplaces greatly benefit from growing only demand. Therefore, online marketplaces should carry their share of responsibility for damage caused by defective products, even if they only act as intermediaries. In this regard inspiration should be drawn from recent Louboutin ruling of the Court of Justice of the EU, which confirms that online marketplaces can be held liable. Consumers need to be able to hold online marketplaces liable to incentivise them to prevent the circulation of potentially dangerous products. To avoid loopholes in the revised PLD, consumers should be able to hold online market-places liable, like any other economic operator involved in the supply chain, if the manufacturer or third-party vendor is based outside the EU, or if the online marketplace fails to identify the manufacturer or third-party vendor. The European Consumer Organisation (BEUC), "Revision of the Product Liability Directive – Time to ensure effective and comprehensive protection for consumers damaged by defective products", 01.03.2023, p. 15.

In contrast, business stakeholders argued that online marketplaces have neither access nor control over products. Therefore, imposing liability for them would put marketplaces at a disadvantage compared to other sales channels in the EU. Online marketplaces should not be liable for defective products sold on their platforms when no other economic operator can be identified. Recent EU legislation confirmed that marketplaces do not have to vet all products listed by traders. Therefore, expanding liability to them means punishing them for products they have never seen (for instance, online marketplaces are not able to determine if a product is defective since they are simply providing a platform for sales). Indeed, online marketplaces do not take direct possession (and thus are not capable of managing the risk) of products sold via a marketplace (unlike fulfilment service providers). Besides, according to business stakeholders, the existing EU legal framework on product safety already ensures sufficient consumer protection for products bought online. Thus, extending the scope of the PLD to create liability for online marketplaces is not proportionate or consistent with the existing EU legislative framework.

See, for instance the response submitted by the American Chamber of Commerce to the European Union (AmCham EU), which stated that "business entities which have no power over the manufacturing process (e.g. online marketplaces, retailers) should not be considered as having liability in cases of damage caused by defective products unless no other party in the EU can be identified within one month. The reference to the Digital Services Act liability exemption ensures coherence and consistency with product safety regulations. This should also be the case for fulfilment service providers, who should not be placed in a worse position than retailers. The proposal should remove article 7.3 and instead refer to article 7.5 for fulfilment service providers, as the marketplace provision in article 7.6 does". The American Chamber of Commerce to the European Union (AmCham EU), "Our Position – Feedback on Product Liability Directive proposal", 11 December 2022, p. 6.

See also the position submitted by Google: "The expansion of the scope of the PLD to create liability for online marketplaces is not proportionate or consistent with the existing EU legislative framework. Currently, online marketplaces acting as retailers or importers are within the scope of the PLD. Extending the scope of the PLD, such that platforms can be found liable for damage caused by defective products sold via them where they do not act as retailer or importer (and never take possession of the physical product) would be an unfair and inappropriate extension of the concept of liability. Liability systems work most efficiently when liability rests with the person most capable of managing the risk. Online marketplaces are not well-placed to do this, as they do not take direct possession of products sold via a marketplace (unlike fulfilment service providers). It is not clear how online marketplaces would be able to determine if a product is defective where they are simply providing a platform for sales to take place. To the extent that the online marketplace sells software rather than physical products, the revised PLD scope is doubly burdensome as the marketplace could plausibly be held liable for any software it distributes that is defective. Consumers purchasing products via online marketplaces will be able to identify a relevant economic operator (the manufacturer or importer) from whom to seek redress under the provisions in the proposed Article 20 of the General Product Safety Regulation, which sets out mandatory information that online marketplaces must enable traders to display. In addition, the Digital Services Act includes obligations for online marketplaces to collect trader information and removes the safe harbour provisions in certain circumstances, including where they have received information about dangerous products through the notice and action mechanism, offering additional protection for consumers. Where online platforms fail to meet statutory duties to display information about the manufacturer or importer, it is appropriate that enforcement is carried out by EU market surveillance authorities. However, as such regulatory non-compliance is wholly separate and distinct from the question of defectiveness of the product advertised, it is disproportionate to impose liability on the online marketplace. In addition, the proposal to extend liability to online marketplaces has the potential to limit competition between online marketplaces sector, as small and medium-sized marketplaces will not be able to absorb the liability costs easily, putting them at a competitive disadvantage compared to the larger online marketplaces". Google, "Response to the new Product Liability Directive consultation", 9 December 2022, pp. 12–13.

Furthermore, the Information Technology Industry Council (ITI) agreed with the Commission's position that "economic operators which have no power over the manufacturing process (e.g., online marketplaces, retailers) should not be considered as having the primary liability in cases of damage caused by defective products unless no other party in the EU can be identified within 1 month. This should also be the case for fulfilment service providers, who should not be placed in a worse position than retailers. The proposal should remove article 7.3 and instead refer to article 7.5 as the marketplace provision in article 7.6 does. It would be disproportionate to hold marketplaces liable as they are often not in contact with the producers or the importers, and would negate the purpose of online marketplaces". Information Technology Industry Council (ITI), "Comments to the Revision of the Product Liability Directive (PLD): Ensuring a Proportionate Framework for all Actors", December 2022, pp. 8–9.

Similarly, with regard to online marketplaces and fulfilment service providers, DigitalEurope stressed that agrees with "the recognition that businesses with no power over the manufacturing process, such as online marketplaces and retailers, should not be considered liable for damage caused by defective products. It would be unfair and inadequate to expand the scope of the PLD to make online marketplaces liable for damages caused by defective products sold via them, although they do not act as a retailer or importer, and hence never take possession of the physical product. In this regard, Art. 20 of the General Product Safety Regulation or the DSA will enable consumers to identify traders (manufacturer or importer) from whom to seek redress. We also support the

9.8 Alleviating the Burden of Proof: New Disclosure Obligations—Disclosure of Evidence

Like the current version of the PLD, the Commission's proposal for a revised Product Liability Directive places the burden of proof for the damage, the defect and the causal link between the defect and the damage on the consumer/claimant.[124] To alleviate the burden of proof, the proposal contains several provisions concerning the disclosure of evidence in relation to defective products that have caused damage. In sum, it empowers courts to order the disclosure of evidence on the request of a claimant, but only to the extent that confidential information and trade secrets are not concerned.

In particular, it is stated that, at least in specific cases (involving technical or scientific complexity), victims/injured persons are often disadvantaged by the burden of proof in product liability claims, facing difficulties to investigate claims

---

reference to the DSA liability exemption to ensure coherence and consistency with product safety regulations. This should also be the case for fulfilment service providers, who should not be placed in a worse position than retailers. The proposal should remove Art. 7(3) and instead refer to Art. 7(5) for fulfilment service providers, as the marketplace provision in Art. 7(6) does". DigitalEurope, "Creating a proportionate Product Liability Directive", 3 March 2023, p. 6.

[124] Proposal for a revised Product Liability Directive, Article 9(1).

The European Consumer Organisation (BEUC) criticised the Commission's proposal to place the burden of proof for the damage, the defect, and the causal link between the defect and the damage on the consumer, since the burden of proof presents the main obstacle for consumers to receive compensation: "According to the 2018 report on the evaluation of the PLD, 32% of all product liability claims are rejected because consumers are not able to prove the defect while 21% of all product liability claims are rejected because consumers are not able to prove the link between the defect and the damage. This means that in total, consumers are refused compensation in 53% of all cases because of the burden of proof regarding the defect and the causal link. These figures clearly show how placing the burden of proof on consumers undermines their fundamental right of access to justice. And the situation is getting even worse, since in 2019, the European Commission Expert Group on liability and new technologies found that the features of new technologies such as autonomy, opacity and unpredictability widen the information asymmetry between consumers and manufacturers and may result in unreasonable difficulties and costs for consumers to establish the applicable safety requirements and the non-compliance with these requirements". The European Consumer Organisation (BEUC), "Revision of the Product Liability Directive – Time to ensure effective and comprehensive protection for consumers damaged by defective products", 01.03.2023, p. 12.

As it will be seen below, the European Consumer Organisation (BEUC) stated that, although the proposed disclosure of evidence and the rebuttable presumptions seem to be steps in the right direction, "they are not enough to counterbalance the information asymmetry between consumers and economic operators and thus will not ensure full access to justice for consumers". As a result, "BEUC continues to call for a full reversal of the burden of proof regarding the defect and the causal link. Consumers should only have to prove the damage. Economic operators should have to prove that the product was not defective and that it therefore could not have caused the damage in question". The European Consumer Organisation (BEUC), "Revision of the Product Liability Directive – Time to ensure effective and comprehensive protection for consumers damaged by defective products", 01.03.2023, pp. 13 and 14.

properly and to gain access to essential information. Plaintiffs need to gather specific information/evidence to be able to prove the conditions for a claim for damages, i.e., to prove the defect of a product and the causal link with the damage suffered. Therefore, in order to substantiate a damages claim and establish liability, it is essential to introduce rules on the disclosure of specific evidence by those that have it at their disposal.[125]

As the Commission put it, "in light of the imposition on economic operators of liability irrespective of fault, and with a view to achieving a fair apportionment of risk, the injured person claiming compensation for damage caused by a defective product should bear the burden of proving the damage, the defectiveness of a product and the causal link between the two. Injured persons, are, however, often at a significant disadvantage compared to manufacturers in terms of access to, and understanding of, information on how a product was produced and how it operates. This asymmetry of information can undermine the fair apportionment of risk, in particular in cases involving technical or scientific complexity. It is therefore necessary to facilitate claimants' access to evidence to be used in legal proceedings".[126]

To this end, Member States' courts are empowered, upon request of the claimant (an injured person claiming compensation for damage caused by a defective product), to order the defendant to disclose to the claimant relevant evidence/necessary information that is at the defendant's disposal, provided that the claimant has presented facts and evidence that are sufficient to support the plausibility of the claim for compensation.[127]

---

[125] Similar approaches have been successfully implemented at EU level e.g. in the 'Damages Directive' (2014/104/EU) facilitating the private enforcement of EU competition law, and the 'Enforcement Directive' (2004/48/EC) ensuring a homogeneous level of protection in the internal market and the effective civil enforcement of harmonised intellectual property rights (see e.g., Articles 5 and 6 of the 'Enforcement Directive').

[126] Proposal for a revised Product Liability Directive, at Recitals 30 and 31.

See also European Commission – Questions & Answers on the revision of the Product Liability Directive, Brussels, 28 September 2022, p. 2: "What are the changes for companies? – Already today, companies are obliged to compensate people injured by defective products. In addition, the new PLD will now require companies to disclose evidence that a claimant would need to prove their case in court. This is to address the asymmetry of information between the manufacturer and consumer: manufacturers know much more than consumers about how the product in question was produced and brought to market".

[127] Proposal for a revised Product Liability Directive, Article 8(1).

The European Consumer Organisation (BEUC) stated that, although the proposed disclosure of evidence and the rebuttable presumptions seem to be steps in the right direction, "they are not enough to counterbalance the information asymmetry between consumers and economic operators and thus will not ensure full access to justice for consumers". BEUC argued that consumers (at least in order to better assess the success chances of a lawsuit) should be allowed to request the disclosure of evidence *prior* to filing a lawsuit for compensation: "Since the proposed rules on disclosure of evidence speak of "claimant" and "defendant", they would only apply in case consumers had already filed a lawsuit. Therefore, consumers would not be able to request the disclosure of evidence, for instance whether and what kind of an AI system was involved, and to assess the disclosed information before deciding whether a lawsuit to claim compensation would have chances to succeed. Economic operators might refuse any disclosure of evidence by invoking confidential

The national courts may order the disclosure of evidence only to the extent necessary to support the claim, i.e., the disclosure of evidence must be necessary and proportionate in order to prevent blanket requests. In other words, national courts must limit the disclosure of evidence to what is necessary and proportionate for sustaining a claim for damages caused by a defective product.[128] As it was put by the Commission, "it is necessary to facilitate claimants' access to evidence to be used

information and trade secrets. The dispute about whether certain information is confidential, or a trade secret would increase the length and costs of the proceedings. Where economic operators would finally be ordered to disclose evidence, consumers would need to hire expensive experts to interpret the obtained information, in particular in view of AI driven products, because the proposal does not require economic operators to provide the information in a way that is understandable for consumers. But even if consumers had access to, and understood certain information, it is highly likely that they would still not be able to prove the defectiveness of a complex product such as a smart device. To enable consumers at least to better assess the success chances of a lawsuit, they should be allowed to request the disclosure of evidence *before* filing a lawsuit for compensation. Economic operators should be obliged to provide the disclosed information in a way that is understandable for consumers". The European Consumer Organisation (BEUC), "Revision of the Product Liability Directive – Time to ensure effective and comprehensive protection for consumers damaged by defective products", 01.03.2023, pp. 13 and 14.

[128] Proposal for a revised Product Liability Directive, Article 8(2).

Business stakeholders are concerned mainly because the threshold for ordering the disclosure of evidence (i.e., the conditions for obtaining documentation) is extremely low and, at the same time, the potential scope of information/documentation that can be disclosed (obtained by claimants) is very broad. As a result, these new disclosure obligations imposed on economic operators could be used widely by claimants to obtain information at an early stage in order to determine whether there are potential claims. Therefore, defendants (including software developers) could be exposed to 'fishing expeditions' and frivolous litigation.

For instance, the Computer & Communications Industry Association (CCIA Europe) stated that "the PLD revision would enable national courts to ask for the disclosure of evidence to defendants upon claimants' demand in Article 8. The threshold for ordering such disclosures is very low as the claimant only has to present facts and evidence sufficient to support the plausibility of the claim. Furthermore, the scope of information that can be disclosed is very broad as it covers "what is necessary and proportionate". This disclosure obligation should be better framed to avoid burdening defendants and prevent abusive demands early in the procedure". Computer & Communications Industry Association (CCIA Europe), "Making EU product liability rules fit for the digital age – Position Paper on the Revision of the Product Liability Directive", December 2022, p. 6.

Furthermore, the Developers Alliance stressed that software developers should be protected from excessive litigation: "The obligation to disclose evidence (art. 8) could prove very burdensome for software developers and expose them to fishing expeditions and frivolous litigation. The conditions for obtaining documentation are quite indulgent with the claimants, while the types of documentation that can be obtained are very broad. The obligation is to be considered in strict correlation with the presumption of defectiveness (art. 9.2.a)". Developers Alliance, "Position on the European Commission's proposal for a Directive on liability for defective products", 14 December 2022, p. 3.

Also, according to the Information Technology Industry Council (ITI), "the risk we see is that the practical application of the provisions under article 8 during the course of proceedings is subject to changes in different national courts and under different laws, which creates a significant degree of uncertainty as notionally high-level concepts such as proportionality and legitimate interest, as well as courts willingness to apply protective measures on their own initiative, are not especially well harmonised across Member States. In addition, we note that the threshold for obtaining documentation is very low, while the scope of documentation that can be obtained is wide" Information

in legal proceedings, while ensuring that such access is limited to that which is necessary and proportionate".[129]

In determining whether an order for the disclosure of evidence is proportionate, national courts will be required to achieve a balance between the claimant's rights and the need to ensure that such disclosure would be subject to specific safeguards to protect the legitimate interests of all parties (and third parties) concerned, such as the

---

Technology Industry Council (ITI), "Comments to the Revision of the Product Liability Directive (PLD): Ensuring a Proportionate Framework for all Actors", December 2022, p. 6.

In addition, according to the American Chamber of Commerce to the European Union (AmCham EU), "Article 8 (2-4) contains certain protections for confidential information and trade secrets from disclosure in liability proceedings by injured claimants. Paragraphs 2-3 in particular are rather vague and limit disclosure to what is 'necessary and proportionate', which must consider 'the legitimate interests of all parties'. Paragraph 4 provides for protective measures when confidential information/trade secrets are referred to in legal proceedings, which can either be invoked by the courts, or upon a reasoned request by a party. The practical application of the provisions under article 8 during the course of proceedings is subject to changes in different national courts and under different laws, which creates a significant degree of uncertainty as notionally high-level concepts such as proportionality and legitimate interest, as well as courts willingness to apply protective measures on their own initiative, are not well harmonised across Member States". The American Chamber of Commerce to the European Union (AmCham EU), "Our Position – Feedback on Product Liability Directive proposal", 11 December 2022, p. 5.

See also the response submitted by Google, which stated that "the proposal to create new powers to order disclosure increases the burden on producers to provide documentation to claimants. In practice, these powers are likely to be used widely by claimant groups to obtain information at an early stage in order to determine whether there are potential claims (in the worst cases, so-called "fishing expeditions"). These powers would place a significant burden on EU economic operators. They are likely to have the effect of disincentivising businesses to sell in the EU and encouraging economic operators to establish their operations outside the EU in order to place themselves outside the direct jurisdiction of the EU courts to seek to avoid the costs and burdens of meeting these obligations, particularly where information is particularly commercially sensitive. ... Moreover, the threshold for obtaining documentation is extremely low – a claimant only needs to show facts and evidence sufficient to support the plausibility of the claim – and the potential scope of documentation that can be obtained is wide. Whilst there are limited safeguards in place, such as restrictions on the disclosure of confidential information and trade secrets, these protections are not comparable to those found in other jurisdictions that have wide disclosure powers. ... Article 8, as drafted, does not include any requirement for the applicant to identify categories of documents, reasons for the categories of documents requested or show that such documents are not only relevant but also necessary to advance their case. We consider it important to include such controls. ... There is also a risk that the disclosure powers will be applied differently by different Member States, meaning certain markets will become higher risk for producers or may be used by claimants to forum shop for access to information where there are claims in different Member States - for example under the Representative Actions Directive (EU) 2020/1828. ... It is notable that the disclosure powers under Article 8 can only be used by the injured party – i.e. the claimant – and there is no reciprocal power for the defendant. We consider that this is manifestly unfair, and out of step with Member State disclosure regimes (e.g. in Ireland, where either party can apply for a court motion). It is clearly in the interests of justice that a defendant can also obtain relevant documentation, such as proof of purchase or evidence of financial loss, in order to assess the merits of a claim. We suggest that any disclosure powers under Article 8 should apply to both claimants and defendants". Google, "Response to the new Product Liability Directive consultation", 9 December 2022, pp. 15–17.

[129] Proposal for a revised Product Liability Directive, Recital 31.

protection of trade secrets and of confidential information (e.g., information in relation to public or national security).[130]

Furthermore, where the disclosure of a confidential trade secret is ordered, national courts may take specific measures necessary to preserve confidentiality of disclosed evidence when that evidence is used or referred to in legal proceedings.[131]

---

[130] Ibid., Article 8(3). See also Recital 31: "It is therefore necessary to facilitate claimants' access to evidence to be used in legal proceedings, while ensuring . . . that confidential information and trade secrets are protected. Such evidence should also include documents that have to be created ex novo by the defendant by compiling or classifying the available evidence".

According to BSA – The Software Alliance, "the threshold for ordering such disclosures remains very low. It should be clarified to better protect trade secrets and avoid diverging legal interpretations among Member States. It could be clarified to state that, when determining whether to order the defendant to disclose information which is protectable as confidential information and/or trade secrets under the Trade Secrets Directive, national courts must consider that the disclosure of such information is "relevant and necessary" for the claimant to demonstrate in the course of the legal proceedings that the product is defective. Access request should remain limited to information required to assess whether the product was defective, who was the liable actor (manufacturer, repairer, . . .) or the causal link". BSA – The Software Alliance, "Recommendations on the Draft EU Product Liability Directive", March 2023, p. 7.

See also the American Chamber of Commerce to the European Union (AmCham EU), which stated that "the drafting of the article should be tightened to better protect trade secrets in product liability proceedings. For example, the article could be clarified to state that, when determining whether to order the defendant to disclose information which is protectable as confidential information and/or trade secrets within the meaning of article 2, point 1, of Directive (EU) 2016/943, national courts must consider inter alia that the disclosure of such information is 'relevant and necessary' for the claimant to demonstrate, in the course of the legal proceedings, that the product is defective. This would ensure higher standards and more detailed consideration for disclosure than merely whether it is 'proportionate'. Disclosure should also be restricted to information required to assess whether the product was defective, who is liable or the causal link". The American Chamber of Commerce to the European Union (AmCham EU), "Our Position – Feedback on Product Liability Directive proposal", 11 December 2022, pp. 5–6.

[131] Proposal for a revised Product Liability Directive, Article 8(4).

See also Recital 32: "In respect of trade secrets within the meaning of Directive (EU) 2016/943 of the European Parliament and of the Council, national courts should be empowered to take specific measures to ensure the confidentiality of trade secrets during and after the proceedings, while achieving a fair and proportionate balance between the interest of the trade-secret holder to secrecy and the interest of the injured person. This should include at least measures to restrict access to documents containing trade secrets or alleged trade secrets and access to hearings to a limited number of people, or allowing access to redacted documents or transcripts of hearings. When deciding on such measures, national courts should take into account: (i) the need to ensure the right to an effective remedy and to a fair trial; (ii) the legitimate interests of the parties and, where appropriate, of third parties; and (iii) any potential harm for either of the parties, and, where appropriate, for third parties, resulting from the granting or rejection of such measures".

9.9 Alleviating the Burden of Proof: Rebuttable Legal Presumptions

As already stated, like the current version of the PLD, the proposal for a revised PLD provides the conditions under which the claimant may claim compensation: the claimant has the burden of proving the damage suffered, the defectiveness of the product and the causal link between the defectiveness and the damage.[132]

The Commission's proposal for a revised PLD attempts to alleviate the burden of proof (in the case of complex products) in a harmonised way by setting conditions for defectiveness/causality to be presumed.[133] Indeed, the Commission's proposal alleviates the burden of proof on victims of harm by harmonising: (i) conditions for national courts to presume that a product was indeed defective or that the defect did indeed cause the damage, especially in complex cases (including cases involving AI systems)[134] where proving liability is excessively difficult;[135] and (ii) as already

[132] Ibid., Article 9(1).

[133] Ibid., Recital 33: "It is also necessary to alleviate the claimant's burden of proof provided that certain conditions are fulfilled. Rebuttable presumptions of fact are a common mechanism for alleviating a claimant's evidential difficulties, and allow a court to base the existence of defectiveness or causal link on the presence of another fact that has been proven, while preserving the rights of the defendant".

[134] Ibid., Explanatory Memorandum, p. 5. According to the Commission, in doing so (alongside the proposed AI Liability Directive), the revised PLD "responds in large part to the calls of the European Parliament to ensure liability rules are adapted to AI".

[135] In the Commission Staff Working Document, "Impact Assessment Report – Accompanying the document Proposal for a Directive of the European Parliament and of the Council on liability for defective products", SWD(2022) 316 final, Brussels, 28.9.2022 (at pp. 53 and 55), it is admitted that opting for a reversal of the burden of proof "would alleviate the difficulties that consumers face. However, especially if taken together with the removal of the development risk defence, this measure would overly favour consumers, thus undermining a fair balance of interests between consumers and producers. Reversing the burden of proof and removing the development risk defence would also have negative impact on innovation". This is why the Commission opted for easing the burden of proof in the case of complex products, as this (option 2a) "would achieve a fairer balance of interests between injured parties and producers. Option 2a would create greater legal certainty and achieve a more equal level of consumer protection across the EU, while still preserving innovation that could be hampered by further-reaching measures, especially in innovative sectors like pharmaceuticals and AI, and could undermine the uptake of new technologies" (at p. 53). … "A reversal of the burden of proof would expose producers to significantly higher liability risks, by requiring them to prove their products were safe. This and removing the development risk defence could hinder innovation, to the detriment of both industry (in particular SMEs, which would less easily absorb additional costs) and consumers" (at p. 55).

See also: Proposal for a revised Product Liability Directive, Explanatory Memorandum, p. 6: "The burden of proof will be more fairly shared between injured persons and manufacturers in complex cases, increasing the chances of enforcing a successful compensation claim. However, there will be no reversal of the burden of proof, as this would expose manufacturers to significantly higher liability risks and could hamper innovation, leading also to potentially higher product prices and reduced access to innovative products".

described, rules on when producers are obliged to disclose necessary technical information to the victim in court.

In sum, as it will be shown below, the Commission's proposal introduces several rebuttable presumptions:[136] (i) The defect will be presumed if the defendant fails to disclose evidence, the product does not comply with relevant safety requirements or that the damage was caused by an obvious malfunction ('presumption of defectiveness'). (ii) The causal link between the defect and the damage will be presumed if the damage is of a kind that is typically consistent with the defect ('presumption of the causal link'). (iii) Courts are empowered to presume the defect and the causal link between the defect and the damage if consumers face excessive difficulties, due to technical or scientific complexity ('general presumption'). In particular:

9.9.1 *Presumption of Defectiveness*

The Commission's proposal eases the burden of proof for the injured person by establishing a presumption of defectiveness under certain conditions. In particular, the defectiveness of the product will be presumed when (i) the defendant has failed to disclose relevant evidence pursuant to Article 8(1) of the proposed Directive;[137] or (ii) the claimant establishes that the product does not comply with mandatory safety requirements set out in EU or national law that are intended to protect against the risk

[136] The European Consumer Organisation (BEUC) stated that the rebuttable presumptions are not enough to counterbalance the information asymmetry between consumers and economic operators and, therefore, they cannot ensure full access to justice for consumers: "The conditions for triggering some of the presumptions are so high, that consumers would have great difficulties meeting them. For instance, how should a consumer establish that a complex product with digital components "does not comply with mandatory safety requirements laid down in EU or national law" without engaging not only a product safety lawyer but also a highly specialised IT engineer? And would the burden of proof really be alleviated by a presumption that requires consumers to prove "excessive difficulties, due to technical or scientific complexity" to prove the defect or the causal link, and to present "sufficiently relevant evidence". The conditions for triggering other presumptions are so narrow that they would only apply to very few cases. For instance, the presumption that requires an "obvious malfunction" of a product may apply to a simple case like an exploding glass bottle, but would not help consumers in complex cases where help is needed the most. And finally, some key words in the presumptions are formulated so vaguely that consumers would not know what conditions they would actually have to fulfil to trigger the presumptions. For instance, how should consumers prove that a damage is 'of a kind typically consistent with the defect in question'?". The European Consumer Organisation (BEUC), "Revision of the Product Liability Directive – Time to ensure effective and comprehensive protection for consumers damaged by defective products", 01.03.2023, p. 13.

[137] Proposal for a revised Product Liability Directive, Article 9(2)(a). See also at Recital 33: "In order to provide an incentive to comply with the obligation to disclose information, national courts should presume the defectiveness of a product where a defendant fails to comply with such an obligation".

of the damage that has occurred;[138] or (iii) the claimant establishes that the damage was caused by an obvious product malfunction during normal use or under ordinary circumstances.[139]

9.9.2 *Presumption of the Causal Link*

Furthermore, the proposal for a revised PLD eases the burden of proof for the injured person by establishing a presumption of the causal link between the defectiveness of the product and the damage. The causal link will be presumed when (i) the claimant establishes that the product is defective and (ii) the damage caused is typically consistent with the defect in question.[140]

9.9.3 *General Presumption*

In addition, the Commission's proposal establishes a more general presumption, which is particularly relevant in the context of AI systems. In particular, national courts will presume the defectiveness of a product or the causal link between its defectiveness and the damage, or both, where (notwithstanding the defendant's disclosure of information): (a) they consider that the claimant faces excessive difficulties, in particular due to technical or scientific complexity,[141] to prove the defectiveness of the product or the causal link between its defectiveness and the

[138] Ibid., Article 9(2)(b). See also at Recital 33: "Many legislative and mandatory safety requirements have been adopted in order to protect consumers and the public from the risk of harm. In order to reinforce the close relationship between product safety rules and liability rules, non-compliance with such requirements should also result in a presumption of defectiveness. This includes cases in which a product is not equipped with the means to log information about the operation of the product as required under Union or national law".

[139] Ibid., Article 9(2)(c). See also at Recital 33: "The same should apply in the case of obvious malfunction, such as a glass bottle that explodes in the course of normal use, since it is unnecessarily burdensome to require a claimant to prove defectiveness when the circumstances are such that its existence is undisputed".

[140] Ibid., Article 9(3).

[141] Ibid., at Recital 34: "Technical or scientific complexity should be determined by national courts on a case-by-case basis, taking into account various factors. Those factors should include the complex nature of the product, such as an innovative medical device; the complex nature of the technology used, such as machine learning; the complex nature of the information and data to be analysed by the claimant; and the complex nature of the causal link, such as a link between a pharmaceutical or food product and the onset of a health condition, or a link that, in order to be proven, would require the claimant to explain the inner workings of an AI system. The assessment of excessive difficulties should also be made by national courts on a case-by-case basis. While a claimant should provide arguments to demonstrate excessive difficulties, proof of such difficulties should not be required. For example, in a claim concerning an AI system, the claimant should, for

damage, or both; and (b) the claimant demonstrates, on the basis of sufficiently relevant evidence, that (i) the product contributed to the damage, and (ii) it is likely that the product is defective or that there is a causal link between the defectiveness and the damage, or both.[142]

The defendant, however, retains the right 'to contest the existence of excessive difficulties' or the aforementioned likelihood.[143] In addition, the defendant is allowed to rebut any of the above mentioned presumptions.[144]

9.10 Exemption from Liability: Defences Available to the Economic Operators

The proposal for a revised PLD contains several defences that allow economic operators to escape liability. As under the current Product Liability Directive, economic operators are entitled to be exempted from liability on certain conditions for which they carry the burden of proof: "In the interest of a fair apportionment of risk, economic operators should be exempted from liability if they can prove the existence of specific exonerating circumstances".[145]

These exemptions are designed to address the dynamic nature of digital-age products, which can undergo modifications after being made available in the market. To ensure a level playing field for manufacturers throughout the EU as well as consistent consumer protection, the exemption granted to economic operators for defects that are scientifically and technically impossible to detect should be applicable in all Member States. The option to deviate from this exemption (as is the case under the current PLD) should not be maintained. Therefore, under the revised

---

the court to decide that excessive difficulties exist, neither be required to explain the AI system's specific characteristics nor how these characteristics make it harder to establish the causal link".

142 Ibid., Article 9(4). See also at Recitals 34 and 35: "National courts should also presume the defectiveness of a product or the causal link between the damage and the defectiveness, or both, where, notwithstanding the defendant's disclosure of information, it would be excessively difficult for the claimant, in light of the technical or scientific complexity of the case, to prove its defectiveness or the causal link, or both. In such cases, requiring proof would undermine the effectiveness of the right to compensation. Therefore, given that manufacturers have expert knowledge and are better informed than the injured person, it should be for them to rebut the presumption" (Recital 34). ... "In order to maintain a fair apportionment of risk, and to avoid a reversal of the burden of proof, a claimant should nevertheless, in order to benefit from the presumption, be required to demonstrate, on the basis of sufficiently relevant evidence, that it is likely that, where the claimant's difficulties relate to proving defectiveness, the product was defective, or that, where the claimant's difficulties relate to proving the causal link, its defectiveness is a likely cause of the damage" (Recital 35).

143 Ibid., Article 9(4), second paragraph.

144 Ibid., Article 9(5).

145 Proposal for a revised Product Liability Directive, at Recital 36.

Product Liability Directive, the 'development risk defence' will no longer be subject to Member State derogations.[146]

In general, economic operators should be exempted from liability if: they did not put the product into circulation; the defect did not exist when they placed the product on the market; or the state of scientific and technical knowledge at the time of placing the product on the market made it impossible to discover the defect (the 'development risk defence').

In particular, an economic operator will not be liable for damage caused by a defective product if that economic operator can prove any of the following: (a) in the case of a manufacturer or importer, that it did not place the product on the market or put it into service (for instance, economic operators should not be liable where they can prove that a person other than themselves has caused the product to leave the manufacturing process against their will);[147] (b) in the case of a distributor, that it did not make the product available on the market;[148] (c) that it is probable that the defectiveness that caused the damage did not exist when the product was placed on the market, put into service or, in respect of a distributor, made available on the market, or that this defectiveness came into being after that moment.[149] However, exemptions from liability will not apply in the case of product defects within the manufacturer's control, linked to: a related service; software including software updates or upgrades; or a lack of updates or upgrades necessary to maintain safety. Indeed, since digital technologies allow manufacturers to exercise control beyond the moment of placing the product on the market or putting into service, manufacturers/economic operators should remain liable for defectiveness that comes into being after that moment as a result of software or related services within their control, be it in the form of upgrades or updates or machine-learning algorithms, or when the defectiveness of a product consists in the lack of software updates or upgrades necessary to address cybersecurity vulnerabilities and maintain the

[146] Ibid., Explanatory Memorandum, p. 12.

According to the so-called 'development risk defence', the producer is allowed to avoid liability if the state of scientific and technical knowledge at the time when he put the product into circulation was not such as to enable the existence of the defect to be discovered (Article 7(e) of the current Product Liability Directive).

The current PLD allows Member States to derogate from applying the defence. For instance, "Finland and Luxembourg derogate entirely, while Spain, France and Hungary derogate in respect of certain categories of product". Commission Staff Working Document, "Impact Assessment Report – Accompanying the document Proposal for a Directive of the European Parliament and of the Council on liability for defective products", SWD(2022) 316 final, Brussels, 28.9.2022, p. 21.

[147] Proposal for a revised Product Liability Directive, Article 10(1)(a). See also Recital 36.

[148] Ibid., Article 10(1)(b).

[149] Ibid., Article 10(1)(c). See also Recital 37: "The moment of placing on the market or putting into service is normally the moment at which a product leaves the control of the manufacturer, while for distributors it is the moment when they make the product available on the market. Therefore manufacturers should be exempted from liability where they prove that it is probable that the defectiveness that caused the damage did not exist when they placed the product on the market or put it into service or that it came into being after that moment".

product's safety.[150] (d) that the defectiveness is due to compliance of the product with legal requirements ('mandatory regulations issued by public authorities'/'regulatory compliance defence');[151] (e) that the objective/general state of scientific and technical knowledge (which is determined with reference to the most advanced level of objective knowledge accessible and not to the actual knowledge of the manufacturer in question), at the time when the product was placed on the market, put into service or in the period in which the product was within the manufacturer's control was such that the existence of defectiveness could not be discovered;[152] (f) in the

---

[150] Ibid., Article 10(2). With regard to when a manufacturer is considered to exercise control, see at Recitals 37 and 38: "Such software or related services should be considered within the manufacturer's control where they are supplied by that manufacturer or where that manufacturer authorises them or otherwise influences their supply by a third party" (Recital 37). ... "Such liability [for instance, for damage caused by the manufacturer's failure to supply software security updates] should not apply where the supply or installation of such software is beyond the manufacturer's control, for example where the owner of the product does not install an update or upgrade supplied for the purpose of ensuring or maintaining the level of safety of the product" (Recital 38).

[151] Ibid., Article 10(1)(d). See also Recital 36: "compliance with mandatory regulations was the very reason for the product's defectiveness".

[152] Ibid., Article 10(1)(e). See also Recital 39.

It should be stressed that the Commission's proposal – in comparison with the current PLD – offers a slight enhancement to consumer protection concerning the development risk defense. Indeed, unlike the current PLD, the proposal extends liability beyond the product's initial placement on the market to include the period during which the manufacturer retains control over the product. As a result, a software provider would remain liable as long as it can provide updates for the software.

However, especially in the case of traditional products that cannot be updated, the European Consumer Organisation (BEUC) argued that consumers should not carry the risk of gaps in scientific and technical knowledge. According to BEUC, the development-risk defence is particularly problematic and should be abolished: "the development-risk defence would allow, for instance, a manufacturer of a toy to escape liability if the objective state of scientific knowledge at the time when the toy was placed on the market did not allow it to realise that the chemical composition of the toy could cause physical harm to babies. The development-risk defence, regardless of the improvement that the proposal would bring, thus burdens consumers with the risk of gaps in the available scientific and technical knowledge". The European Consumer Organisation (BEUC), "Revision of the Product Liability Directive – Time to ensure effective and comprehensive protection for consumers damaged by defective products", 01.03.2023, p. 17.

Also, according to the Irish Council for Civil Liberties (ICCL) ("ICCL - Submission to the consultation on adapting liability rules to the digital age and artificial intelligence", 7 January 2022, pp. 3–4): "The 'development risk defence' should be removed for all AI systems so that producers remain strictly liable for damage. Under Article 7(e) of PLD, 'development risk defence' exempts producers from liability if they can prove "that the state of scientific and technical knowledge at the time when he put the product into circulation was not such as to enable the existence of the defect to be discovered". This exemption is inappropriate for AI for the following reasons: a) PLD assumes "material objects placed on the market by a one-time action of the producer, after which the producer does not maintain control over the product". ... This is not applicable to software that can be updated. b) In addition, the producers should be held liable if they do not update software when new information about a defect is known, in scientific literature or elsewhere. Whether the scientific and technical knowledge was available when the software was initially placed on the market should not be considered. c) 'Development risk defence' creates a perverse incentive for

case of a manufacturer of a defective component, that the defectiveness of the product is attributable to the design of the product in which the component has been integrated or to the instructions given by the manufacturer of that product to the manufacturer of the component;[153] (g) in the case of a person that modifies a product, that the defectiveness that caused the damage is related to a part of the product not affected by the modification.[154]

9.11 General Provisions on Liability

The Commission's proposal for a revised PLD contains several liability provisions of a more general nature, which are closely based on those of the current Product Liability Directive. In particular:

9.11.1 Liability of Multiple Economic Operators

The Commission acknowledges the growing prevalence of inter-connected products (the interconnectedness of devices and their increased dependency on external input and data), since many products are designed to be influenced by other interconnected products or services (e.g. complex IoT systems).[155]

The proposal refers to situations where two or more parties are liable for the same damage, in particular where a defective component is integrated into a product that

---

producers to deploy products without adequate safety research, or to delay safety related research and/or the publication of research results until the product is placed on the market".

See also the Irish Council for Civil Liberties (ICCL), "New liability rules on product and AI are encouraging but need improvement", 4 October 2022.

It is reminded that, with regard to digital and AI products in particular, the 2019 Report of the Expert Group on liability and new technologies stressed that assessing the state of scientific knowledge at the moment of putting the product into circulation fails to take account of the fact that producers retain control over digital products beyond that moment and therefore have the means to tackle defects that become discoverable. This is true of many digital products, including IoT and AI-enabled products. The development risk defence should not apply for AI products that continue to learn and adapt while in operation (at p. 6). ... "The producer should be strictly liable for defects in emerging digital technologies even if said defects appear after the product was put into circulation, as long as the producer was still in control of updates to, or upgrades on, the technology. A development risk defence should not apply". See Report from the Expert Group on Liability and New Technologies – New Technologies Formation "Liability for Artificial Intelligence and Other Emerging Digital Technologies", 21 November 2019, Key Finding [14], at p. 42.

[153] Proposal for a revised Product Liability Directive, Article 10(1)(f).

[154] Ibid.

[155] Ibid., Recital 23.

causes damage.[156] It is stated that, without prejudice to national law concerning the right of contribution or recourse, if two or more economic operators are liable for the same damage pursuant to the proposed Directive, they are liable jointly and severally (e.g., the injured person should be able to seek compensation for damages both from the manufacturer that integrated the defective component into its product and from the manufacturer of the defective component itself).[157]

9.11.2 Reduction of Liability

The proposal for a revised PLD stipulates that if a defective product causes damage, the contributory actions of third parties do not reduce or disallow the liability of the manufacturer, whereas the contributory negligent actions of the injured person may do so.

In particular, it is pointed out that there may be instances where the acts and omissions of persons other than a potentially liable economic operator (third persons) contribute, in addition to the defectiveness of the product, to the cause of the damage suffered. For example, this could occur when a third party exploits a cybersecurity vulnerability of a product.[158] In order to ensure a high level of consumer protection, and without prejudice to national law concerning the right of contribution or recourse, the economic operator's liability should not be reduced or disallowed as a result of such acts or omissions even if the damage "is caused both by the defectiveness of a product and by an act or omission of a third party".[159] However, the Commission's proposal adds a contributory negligence provision according to which it should be possible to reduce or disallow the economic operator's liability where the injured person itself has negligently contributed to the cause of the damage, i.e., when the damage is caused both by the defectiveness of the product and by the fault of the injured person or any person for whom the injured person is responsible.[160]

[156] Ibid., Recital 26: "Where a manufacturer integrates a defective component from another manufacturer into a product, an injured person should be able to seek compensation for the same damage from either the manufacturer of the product or from the manufacturer of the component".

[157] Ibid., Article 11.

See also Recital 40: "Situations may arise in which two or more parties are liable for the same damage, in particular where a defective component is integrated into a product that causes damage. In such a case, the injured person should be able to seek compensation both from the manufacturer that integrated the defective component into its product and from the manufacturer of the defective component itself. In order to ensure consumer protection, all parties should be held liable jointly and severally in such situations".

See also Article 7(1), second paragraph: "Member States shall ensure that, where a defective component has caused the product to be defective, the manufacturer of a defective component can also be held liable for the same damage".

[158] Ibid., Recital 41.

[159] Proposal for a revised Product Liability Directive, Article 12(1).

[160] Ibid., Article 12(2).

9.11.3 *Mandatory Nature—Exclusion or Limitation of Liability*

The Commission's proposal states that the economic operator's liability should not be, in relation to the injured person, limited or excluded by contract.[161] Indeed, according to the Commission, "the objective of consumer protection would be undermined if it were possible to limit or exclude an economic operator's liability through contractual provisions. Therefore no contractual derogations should be permitted".[162] Also, the liability of an economic operator pursuant to this Directive should not be excluded or limited by other provisions of national law.[163] It is therefore not permitted to set either maximum or minimum financial ceilings for compensation on an economic operator's liability.[164]

9.11.4 *Limitation and Expiry Periods*

It is reminded that the current Product Liability Directive establishes two deadlines. *First*, a limitation period of three years applies to proceedings for the recovery of damages. Therefore, the PLD does not apply three (3) years after the injured party knew or could have become aware of the relevant facts (i.e. the damage, the defect and the identity of the producer) (Article 10 PLD). *Second*, the current PLD ends ten (10) years after the date the product was put onto the market and, therefore, victims of harm that emerges after ten (10) years receive no compensation. In other words, Article 11 of the current Product Liability Directive releases the producer from liability for property damage and death/personal injury ten (10) years after the product causing the damage was put into circulation (unless the injured person has in the meantime instituted proceedings against the producer).

Based on the argument that the requirement to start legal proceedings within three years of becoming aware of the damage is considered to be the least significant obstacle to making claims,[165] the Commission kept unchanged—compared to the current PLD—the 3 year time limit for initiating proceedings. Therefore, victims of harm who miss the three (3) year deadline to start legal proceedings receive no compensation: "a limitation period of 3 years applies to the initiating of proceedings for claiming compensation for damage".[166] This limitation period runs "from the day

[161] Ibid., Article 13.

[162] Ibid., Recital 42.

[163] Ibid., Article 13.

[164] Ibid., Recital 42.

[165] See, for instance, Commission, DG GROW and DG JUST, "Factual summary report of the open public consultation on Adapting Civil Liability Rules to the Digital Age and AI", Ref. Ares(2022) 2620305, 06.04.2022, p. 6.

[166] Proposal for a revised Product Liability Directive, Article 14(1), first paragraph.

on which the injured person became aware or should reasonably have become aware of" the following facts: "(a) the damage; (b) the defectiveness; (c) the identity of the relevant economic operator that can be held liable for the damage".[167] However, the laws of Member States regulating suspension or interruption of the limitation period are not affected by the proposed Directive.[168]

Furthermore, the Commission kept unchanged—compared to the current PLD—the 10 year time limit, i.e. producers are released from liability for property damage and death/personal injury 10 years after placing the product on the market. Therefore, as under the current PLD, victims of harm that emerges after ten (10) years are no longer entitled to compensation pursuant to this Directive. Member States should ensure that the rights of the injured person in accordance with the proposed Directive are extinguished upon the expiry of a limitation period of 10 years "from the date on which the actual defective product which caused the damage was placed on the market, put into service or substantially modified",[169] unless the claimant has, in the meantime, initiated proceedings before a national court against an economic operator that can be held liable.[170] However, by way of exemption, claimants can enjoy an additional 5-year period in cases where the symptoms of personal injury are slow to emerge, such as following ingestion of a defective chemical or food product (i.e., "where an injured person has not been able to initiate proceedings within 10 years due to the latency of a personal injury", the injured person will no longer be entitled to compensation pursuant to this Directive upon the expiry of a period of 15 years).[171]

---

[167] Ibid.

[168] Ibid., Article 14(1), second paragraph.

[169] Ibid., Article 14(2).

See also Recitals 43 and 44: "(43) Given that products age over time, and that higher safety standards are developed as the state of science and technology progresses, it would not be reasonable to make manufacturers liable for an unlimited period of time for the defectiveness of their products. Therefore, the liability should be subject to a reasonable length of time, that is 10 years following placing on the market, without prejudice to claims pending in legal proceedings". … (44) Since substantially modified products are essentially new products, the limitation period should restart after a product has been substantially modified, for example as a result of remanufacturing, that modify a product in such a way that its compliance with the applicable safety requirements may be affected".

[170] Ibid., Article 14(2).

[171] Ibid., Article 14(3), and Explanatory Memorandum, p. 13.

According to the European Consumer Organisation (BEUC), the maximum limitation period for claims based on the PLD should be abolished: "The proposal to extend the maximum limitation period from 10 to 15 years for certain personal injuries was certainly inspired by the "Howald Moor" ruling of the European Court of Human Rights that found that a limitation period of 10 years violates the fundamental right of access to justice. However, latent personal injuries may occur with a greater delay than 15 years. At the same time products may also have hidden defects that only occur long after they have been placed on the market. To avoid that consumers lose their right to claim compensation even before they know that they are affected by a latent personal injury or by a hidden defect the maximum limitation period should be abolished". The European Consumer

9.12 Final Provisions

9.12.1 Transparency

In order to facilitate a more harmonised interpretation of the revised PLD by national courts, Member States will be required to publish (without delay and in an easily accessible and electronic format) relevant court judgments on product liability, so that other national courts could take these judgments into account.[172] The Commission may ("shall", according to the European Parliament) establish a monitoring programme by setting up and maintaining an easily accessible and publicly available database containing the aforementioned final judgements delivered by national courts.[173]

The draft Joint Report makes this provision mandatory and requires the Commission (i.e., it is not at the discretion of the Commission)[174] to implement and keep up-to-date an easily accessible repository of such cases ("The Commission shall set up and maintain an easily accessible and publicly available database containing the judgments referred to in paragraph 1").

9.12.2 Review

The aforementioned transparency measures will also facilitate the review to be undertaken by the Commission 6 years after entry into force of this Directive (and every 5 years thereafter) and the subsequent report to be presented to the European Parliament, to the Council and to the European Economic and Social Committee.[175]

Organisation (BEUC), "Revision of the Product Liability Directive – Time to ensure effective and comprehensive protection for consumers damaged by defective products", 01.03.2023, p. 18.

[172] Proposal for a revised Product Liability Directive, Article 15(1).

[173] Ibid., Article 15(2).

The European Consumer Organisation (BEUC) argued that this provision should be mandatory, i.e., that the Commission should be obliged to set up and keep up-to-date an easily accessible data base on PLD related case law: "Such an EU data base should also contain rulings of the Court of Justice of the EU. The 2018 report on the evaluation of the PLD noted that it was 'very difficult' to obtain comprehensive data on the application of the PLD in national courts [SWD(2018) 157, p. 20]. As one of the reasons, the report mentioned that only some Member States had public databases on court decisions. . . . The European Commission should be obliged to set up a public data base with EU and national case law on the application of the PLD". The European Consumer Organisation (BEUC), "Revision of the Product Liability Directive – Time to ensure effective and comprehensive protection for consumers damaged by defective products", 01.03.2023, p. 19.

[174] Proposal for a revised Product Liability Directive, Article 15(2).

[175] Ibid., Article 16.

9.12.3 *Repeal and Transitional Provision*

Alongside standard provisions on transposition and entry into force,[176] the proposal for a revised PLD provides for the repeal of the current PLD and sets out transitional measures. For reasons of legal certainty, the revised Product Liability Directive should not apply to products placed or put into service on the EU market before the date of its transposition. Therefore, the current PLD (85/374/EEC) will continue to apply with regard to products placed on the market or put into service before that date.[177]

9.13 The Position of the Council of the EU ("General Approach"): 14 June 2023

On 14 June 2023, at the Committee of the Permanent Representatives (COREPER) meeting, the Council of the EU (the Council) adopted its negotiating mandate and formalised its position ("general approach") for a new EU Directive on liability for defective products,[178] extending product liability rules to software and Artificial Intelligence. Coreper also agreed that, on the basis of its 'general approach' text, negotiations could start with the European Parliament in the context of the ordinary legislative procedure.

In sum, the Council's proposed compromise text is broadly aligned with the Commission's consumer-friendly proposal. It upheld the Commission's proposal and even expanded upon it in specific aspects. Some of the major amendments proposed by the Council include: (i) adding, alongside software, raw materials (such as gas and water) within the definition of a product; (ii) granting national liability regimes the option to encompass non-material damages; (iii) clarifying the

[176] Ibid., Articles 18 and 19.

[177] Ibid., Article 17(1).

See also at Recital 46: "... For reasons of legal certainty, this Directive should not apply to products placed or put into service on the Union market before the date of its transposition. It is necessary to provide for transitional arrangements in order to ensure continued liability under Directive 85/374/EEC for damage that caused by defective products which have been placed on the market or put into service before that date".

For a critique, see the Irish Council for Civil Liberties (ICCL), which stated that "unfortunately, the PLD also does not apply to products already in circulation before this Directive is transposed. This means that software that is already on the market, which can be updated after the directive has been transposed will not be liable". Irish Council for Civil Liberties (ICCL), "New liability rules on product and AI are encouraging but need improvement", 4 October 2022.

[178] Council of the European Union, Note: From: General Secretariat of the Council. To: Delegations. Subject: Proposal for a Directive of the European Parliament and of the Council on liability for defective products - Mandate for negotiations with the European Parliament, Brussels, 15 June 2023, Council doc. 10694/23 ("General Secretariat of the Council - General approach on the proposal for a revised PLD, 15 June 2023").

presumption of defectiveness of a product by national courts when claimants are facing excessive difficulties in proving a defect, in particular due to the technical or scientific complexity of the case; (iv) leaving the exemption afforded to manufacturers for scientifically and technically undiscoverable defects subject to member state derogations as under the existing PLD; (v) extending the expiry period from 15 to 20 years for the compensation which the injured person is entitled to in cases where the symptoms of a personal injury are slow to emerge.[179] In particular:

9.13.1 Scope

The Council's approach defined the term 'product' broadly, including raw materials (such as gas and water) and software (including software supplied through a software-as-a-service model).[180] Free and open-source software was kept out of the new product liability rules ("in order not to hamper innovation or research, this Directive should not apply to free and open-source software developed or supplied outside the course of a commercial activity, since products so developed or supplied are by definition not placed on the market").[181] However, the text clarified that if a manufacturer integrates the open-source software as a component of its product and it consequently causes a defect, the liability will fall on the manufacturer rather than the software provider.[182]

---

[179] The Council's general approach is summarised as follows: "The Council proposes, inter alia to: • Scope of application - add raw materials (such as gas and water) within the definition of a product. • Damages - keep the Commission proposal for damages including loss or corruption of data. • Presumption of defectiveness - clarify that the defectiveness of a product is determined by reference to the safety that the 'public at large' is entitled to expect and that warnings or other information provided with a product cannot by themselves make an otherwise defective product safe (e.g. liability cannot be circumvented simply by listing all conceivable side effects of a product). • Cascade of attributable liability - further establish that manufacturer includes any person who presents themselves as the manufacturer by affixing, or authorising a third party to affix, their name, trademark or other distinguishing feature. • Development risk defence - leave the exemption afforded to manufacturers for scientifically and technically undiscoverable defects subject to Member State derogations as under the existing PLD. • Compensation period - extend the expiry period from 15 to 20 years for the compensation which the injured person is entitled to in cases where the symptoms of a personal injury are slow to emerge". See Stefano De Luca, Members' Research Service, European Parliament, EPRS, Legislative Train Schedule – A Europe Fit for the Digital Age, New Product Liability Directive, 20 October 2023.

[180] General Secretariat of the Council - General approach on the proposal for a revised PLD, 15 June 2023, Article 4, point (1), and recitals 12 and 14.

[181] Ibid., recital 13.

[182] Ibid.: "If, however, free and open-source software supplied outside the course of a commercial activity is subsequently integrated by a manufacturer as a component into a product that is placed on the market, it would be possible to hold that manufacturer liable for damage caused by the defectiveness of such software, while not the manufacturer of the software itself because they would have not fulfilled the conditions of placing a product or component on the market".

On the other hand, according to the Council, information is not to be considered a product and, therefore, the revised PLD should not apply to the content of digital files (such as e-books, media files, or the mere source of software).[183] However, although digital files as such are not products under the revised PLD, digital manufacturing files[184] (which are used to produce a tangible item like for 3D-printing) should be considered as products (for example, a defective computer-assisted-design (CAD) file used to create a 3D-printed good that causes harm should give rise to liability under this Directive).[185]

While the revised PLD should not apply to digital services as such, strict liability should be extended to such services as they allow the core functioning of a product (and determine the safety of a product just as much as physical or digital components): "It is becoming increasingly common for digital services to be integrated in or inter-connected with a product in such a way that the absence of the service would prevent the product from performing one of its functions. ... Such related services should be considered as components of the product to which they are inter-connected, when they are within the control of the manufacturer of that product".[186] The Council provided examples of such digital services, and clarified that failing to provide software updates, such as security patches for known vulnerabilities, might also result in liability.[187]

9.13.2 *Damage*

The Commission's proposal for a revised PLD does not cover other types of damages like discrimination, privacy infringement and economic loss. However, the Council's text specified that this does not preclude seeking compensation for non-material damages on other legal grounds. The Council's general approach

[183] Ibid., recital 12.

[184] Ibid., Article 4, point (2): "'digital manufacturing file' means a digital version or a digital template of a movable, which contains the functional information necessary to produce a tangible item by enabling the automated control of machinery or tools".

[185] Ibid., recital 14.

[186] Ibid., recital 15.

[187] Ibid., recital 15: "Examples of such related services include the continuous supply of traffic data in a navigation system, a health monitoring service that relies on sensors of a physical product to track the user's physical activity or health metrics, a temperature control service that monitors and regulates the temperature of a smart fridge, or a voice assistant service, which allows control of one or more products by using voice commands. However, internet access services should not be treated as related services, since they cannot be considered as part of the product and it would be unreasonable to make manufacturers liable for harm caused by shortcomings in such services. Nevertheless, a product that relies on such services and that fails to maintain safety in the event of a loss of connectivity could be found to be defective under this Directive".

granted national liability regimes the option to include non-material losses, resulting from the damages covered by the proposed Directive.[188]

9.13.3 *Defectiveness*

A product will be considered defective when it does not provide the safety which the public at large is entitled to expect, taking into account, *inter alia*, any failure of the product to fulfil its purpose of preventing damage.[189]

The Council’s general approach clarified that, although the defectiveness of a product should consider how the product was presented, the liability under the proposed Directive cannot be circumvented by simply putting warnings or other information “since defectiveness is determined only by reference to the safety that the public at large is entitled to expect”.[190] It was specified that, when assessing the defectiveness of a product, reasonable foreseeable misuses (e.g., by children or someone who temporarily lacks concentration)[191] as well as the reasonably

[188] General Secretariat of the Council - General approach on the proposal for a revised PLD, 15 June 2023, at recitals 18, 18a, 20a, and Articles 5a(1) and 5a(2): “compensation of non-material losses resulting from the damages covered by this Directive, such as pain and suffering, should be provided in so far as they are compensable under national law” (recital 18). . . . “Types of damage other than those provided for in this Directive, such as pure economic loss, privacy infringements or discrimination, should not by themselves trigger liability under this Directive. However, this Directive should not affect the right to compensation for any damages, including non-material, under other liability regimes” (recital 18a), . . . “In so far as national law provides, the right to compensation for injured persons should apply both to direct victims, who suffer damage directly caused by a defective product, and to indirect victims, who suffer damage as a result of the direct victim’s damage” (recital 20a). . . . “The right to compensation shall cover all material losses and, in so far as they are compensable under national law, non-material losses, resulting from the damage referred to in the first subparagraph” (Article 5a(1), second sub-paragraph). . . . “This Article does not affect national law relating to the compensation of damages under other liability regimes” (Article 5a(2)).

[189] Ibid., Article 6(1)(i).

[190] Ibid., recital 22a.

[191] Ibid., Article 6(1)(b). See also recital (22a): “The assessment of defectiveness should take into account the product’s presentation. However, warnings or other information provided with a product cannot by themselves make an otherwise defective product safe, since defectiveness is determined only by reference to the safety that the public at large is entitled to expect. Therefore, liability under this Directive cannot be circumvented simply by listing all conceivable side effects of a product. When determining the defectiveness of a product, its reasonably foreseeable use should also encompass misuse that is not unreasonable under the circumstances, such as the foreseeable behaviour of a user of machinery resulting from lack of concentration or the foreseeable behaviour of certain user groups such as children”.

foreseeable effects of other products on the product in question (e.g. within a smart home system) should also be taken into account.[192]

9.13.4 *Liable Operators—Manufacturer's Control—Substantial Modification*

According to the Council, the liability affects any manufacturer involved in the production process, in so far as their product or a component supplied by them is defective.[193] This includes the persons who affix their name, trademark or other distinguishing feature on the product, as it is implied that they are involved in the production process and/or that they assume the responsibility for it.[194]

In order to reflect (i) the increasing prevalence of inter-connected products, (ii) the effect on a product's safety of its ability to learn after it is placed on the market or put into service, (iii) the fact that many products remain within the manufacturer's control[195] beyond the moment at which they are placed on the market as well as (iv) the legitimate expectation that a product's software and algorithms are designed in such a way as to prevent hazardous product behaviour, the Council clarified that "a manufacturer that designs a product with the ability to develop unexpected behaviour remains responsible for behaviour that causes

[192] Ibid., Article 6(1)(d). See also recital 23: "In order to reflect the increasing prevalence of inter-connected products, the assessment of a product's safety should also take into account the reasonably foreseeable effects of other products on the product in question, for example within a smart home system. The effect on a product's safety of its ability to learn after it is placed on the market or put into service should also be taken into account, to reflect the legitimate expectation that a product's software and underlying algorithms are designed in such a way as to prevent hazardous product behaviour. As such, a manufacturer that designs a product with the ability to develop unexpected behaviour remains responsible for behaviour that causes harm".

[193] General Secretariat of the Council - General approach on the proposal for a revised PLD, 15 June 2023, Article 7(1) (a) and (b): "Member States shall ensure that the following economic operators are liable for damage covered by Article 5a caused by a defective product: (a) the manufacturer of the defective product; (b) where a defective component that has been integrated into, or inter-connected with, the product within the manufacturer's control has caused the product to be defective, and without prejudice to the liability of the manufacturer under point (a), the manufacturer of that component".

[194] Ibid., recital 26. See also Article 4, point 11: "'manufacturer' means any natural or legal person who develops, manufactures or produces a product or has a product designed or manufactured, or who, by putting its name, trademark or other distinguishing features on that product, presents itself as its manufacturer, or who develops, manufactures or produces a product for its own use".

[195] Ibid., Article 4, point 5: "'manufacturer's control' means that: (a) the manufacturer of a product performs or, with respect to actions of a third party, authorises or consents to: (i) the integration, inter-connection or supply of a component including software updates or upgrades; (ii) the modification of the product, including substantial modifications; (b) the manufacturer of a product has the ability to supply software updates or upgrades itself or via a third party".

harm".[196] It was also stressed that "once a product has been placed on the market, it should be considered to be within the manufacturer's control in so far as the manufacturer retains the technical ability to supply software updates or upgrades itself or via a third party".[197]

Manufacturers can also be liable for damage caused by a defective component if it was integrated into their product within their control.[198] Therefore, manufacturers are exempted from liability if a defective component is integrated into their product outside their control. If a manufacturer integrates a defective component from another manufacturer into a product, an individual who suffers harm should have the right to pursue compensation for the resulting damages from either the product manufacturer or the component manufacturer.[199] However, an injured person can seek compensation from the manufacturer of the defective component in so far as the component is considered a product under the proposed Directive and is integrated into a product outside of the control of the product manufacturer.[200]

Furthermore, liability shifts on economic actors introducing substantial modifications[201] that make the product defective outside the manufacturer's control. Therefore, in case a substantial modification of the product, done independently of the original manufacturer, causes the defect, the liability would shift to those who did the modification. Substantial changes include software updates or the continuous learning of an AI model.[202] However, if the substantial modification that makes the

[196] Ibid., recital 23.

[197] Ibid., recital 15b. See also recital 15a: "Related services and other components, including software updates and upgrades, should be considered to be within the manufacturer's control where they are integrated, inter-connected or supplied by the manufacturer itself or where the manufacturer authorises or consents to their supply by a third party, for example where the manufacturer of a smart home appliance consents to the provision by a third party of software updates for its appliance or where a manufacturer presents a related service or component as part of the product even though it is supplied by a third party".

[198] Ibid., Article 7(1), second subparagraph.

[199] General Secretariat of the Council - General approach on the proposal for a revised PLD, 15 June 2023, Recital 26. "Where a manufacturer integrates a defective component from another manufacturer into a product, an injured person should be able to seek compensation for the same damage from either the manufacturer of the product or from the manufacturer of the component".

[200] Ibid.

[201] Ibid., Article 4, point 10a: "'substantial modification' means a modification of a product after it has been placed on the market or put into service: (a) that is considered substantial under relevant Union or national rules on product safety; or (b) where relevant Union or national rules lay down no threshold on what should be considered a substantial modification, that: (i) changes the product's original performance, purpose or type, without this being foreseen in the manufacturer's initial risk assessment; and (ii) changes the nature of the hazard, creates a new hazard or increases the level of risk".

[202] Ibid., Article 7(2): "Any natural or legal person that substantially modifies a product outside the manufacturer's control and thereafter makes it available on the market or puts it into service shall be considered a manufacturer of the product". See also at recital 29: "When a product is modified substantially and is thereafter made available on the market or put into service, it is considered to be a new product. Where the modification is made outside the control of the original manufacturer, it

product defective is carried out by the original manufacturer or under its control, the manufacturer will still bear responsibility.[203]

The same principles apply to substantial modifications made through software updates or upgrades or due to the continuous machine learning techniques of an AI system. In these cases, the substantially modified product should be considered to be made available on the market or put into service at the time the modification is actually made.[204]

9.13.5 *Burden of Proof—Presumption*

Article 9(4) of the Commission's proposal for a revised PLD provides that national courts can presume the defectiveness of a product or/and a causal link between the damage and the defectiveness in specific cases where it could be excessively difficult for the claimant to prove, especially due to technical or scientific complexity of a case. This provision is particularly important as it might apply to complex technologies such as AI, where it might be near to impossible for a claimant to prove the defectiveness of an AI model.

The Council modified the Commission's text in order to further ease the burden of proof for the injured person by clarifying that national courts will presume the defectiveness of the product and/or the causal link between its defectiveness and the damage, where the claimant: (i) faces excessive difficulties, due to technical or scientific complexity, to prove the defectiveness of the product and/or the causal link between its defectiveness and the damage; and (ii) demonstrates that it is likely that the product is defective or that there is a causal link between the defectiveness and the damage, or both.[205]

---

should be possible to hold the person that made the substantial modification liable as a manufacturer of the modified product, since under relevant Union legislation they are responsible for the product's compliance with safety requirements".

[203] Ibid., at recital 29: "Where a substantial modification is carried out by the original manufacturer, or within its control, and where such a substantial modification makes the product defective, that manufacturer should not be able to avoid liability by arguing that the defect came into being after it originally placed the product on the market or put it into service".

[204] Ibid., at recital 29a.

[205] General Secretariat of the Council - General approach on the proposal for a revised PLD, 15 June 2023, Article 9(4). See also at recital 34: "National courts should . . . presume the defectiveness of a product or the causal link between the damage and the defectiveness, or both, . . .by taking into account all the circumstances of the case. In such [technical or scientific complex] cases, requiring the usual standard of proof as required under national law, which often calls for a high degree of probability, would undermine the effectiveness of the right to compensation. Therefore, given that manufacturers have expert knowledge and are better informed than the injured person, and in order to maintain a fair apportionment of risk while avoiding a reversal of the burden of proof, the claimant should be required to prove only that it is likely that, where the claimant's difficulties relate

9.13.6 *Technical or Scientific Complexity—Derogation from the Development Risk Defence*

It is reminded that, according to the current PLD, Member States have the flexibility to decide whether to include the development risk defence in their national law or not, leading to a lack of harmonisation across Europe. The Commission's proposal for a revised PLD sought to close this loophole and required the development risk defence to be implemented in all Member States. Indeed, Article 10(1)(e) of the Commission's proposal for a revised Product Liability Directive exempts manufacturers/economic operators from liability if the defect that caused the damage could not be known due to the objective state of scientific and technical knowledge at the time the product was placed on the market (or put into service or during the period in which the product was within the manufacturer's control). Therefore, an economic operator could be exempted from liability if he proves that the state of scientific and technical knowledge at the time did not allow for discovering the product's defectiveness. The important point, according to the Commission, is that the option to deviate from this exemption (as is the case under the current PLD) should not be maintained. Therefore, under the Commission's proposal for a revised Product Liability Directive, the 'development risk defence' will no longer be subject to Member State derogations.[206]

However, the Council stated that the possibility offered to an economic operator to free itself from liability could be deemed by certain Member States as limiting unduly the protection of natural persons[207] and, therefore, proposed to reintroduce the option/discretion for Member States to derogate from the development risks defence. In particular, the Council added a provision stating that EU Member States can maintain in their legal systems existing measures to the effect that economic operators are to be liable even if they prove that the state of scientific and technical knowledge at the time when the product was placed on the market, put into service or in the period in which the product was within the manufacturer's control was not such that the defectiveness could be discovered.[208] To ensure transparency and legal certainty for economic operators operating across the EU, the relevant national legislation would have to be notified to the Commission by the Member State wishing to keep such measures that maintain existing derogations from the development risk defence in its legal system.[209]

Also, according to the Council's proposed text, Member States can introduce new measures or modify existing ones in their legal systems in order to limit such a relief

---

to proving defectiveness, the product was defective, or that, where the claimant's difficulties relate to proving the causal link, its defectiveness is a likely cause of the damage".

[206] Proposal for a revised Product Liability Directive, Explanatory Memorandum, p. 12.

[207] General Secretariat of the Council - General approach on the proposal for a revised PLD, 15 June 2023, recital 44a.

[208] Ibid., Article -15(1), first subparagraph. See also recital 44a.

[209] Ibid., Article -15(1), second subparagraph. See also recital 44a.

of responsibility, i.e., to extend liability of manufacturers even when the state of scientific and technical knowledge at the critical time did not allow for discovering the product's defectiveness,[210] provided that those measures are limited to specific categories of products, justified by public interest objectives (such as public policy, public security and public health), and proportionate.[211] The relevant national legislation would have to be notified to the Commission (which should then inform the other Member States) and put on hold for six months to allow the Commission to issue its non-binding opinion (following close cooperation between the Member State concerned and the Commission) on the text of the proposed measure and the accompanying justification provided by the relevant Member State.[212]

9.13.7 Court Database: Transparency

The proposal for a revised PLD requires Member States to publish relevant national court rulings resulting from its provisions. In order to limit administrative burden, the Council's text limited this measure to the judgments delivered by national courts of appeal or of the highest instance.[213]

9.13.8 Time Limitation: Expiry Period

The Commission's proposal for a revised PLD allows complainants to bring the defendant to court within 10 years of the product's placement into the market. According to the Council, in cases of substantial modification, a new 10 years expiry period starts to run again.[214] It was also clarified that software updates or upgrades that do not amount to a substantial modification of the product do not affect the expiry period that applies to the original product.[215] Furthermore, a longer deadline was provided for cases where the symptoms of injury takes are slow to emerge,

---

[210] Ibid., Article -15(2). See also recital 44a.

[211] Ibid., Article -15(3). See also recital 44a.

[212] Ibid., Article -15(4) and (5). See also recital 44a.

[213] Ibid., Article 15. See also Recital 45: "... Member States should be required to publish final court judgments on product liability under this Directive, meaning those judgments that cannot be, or can no longer be, appealed. In order to limit administrative burden, Member States should be required only to publish judgments of national courts of appeal or of the highest instance".

[214] Ibid., Article 14a(1)(b): "in the case of substantially modified products, [the expiry period shall run from] the date the product was made available on the market or put into service subsequent to the substantial modification". See also recital 44.

[215] Ibid., recital 44.

extending this time period from 15 (according to the Commission's proposal) to 20 years.[216]

9.14 The Position of the European Parliament

This section outlines the European Parliament's approach to specific and controversial issues of the proposal for a revised PLD, revealing the position (which appears more industry-friendly) followed by the European Parliament in the negotiations with the Commission and the Council on the text of the revised Product Liability Directive. In Parliament, the file was assigned jointly to the Committee on Internal Market and Consumer Protection (IMCO) and the Legal Affairs Committee (JURI). Vlad Botoş (Renew, Romania) and Pascal Arimont (EPP, Belgium) were appointed as rapporteurs.

9.14.1 Draft Joint Report of the Parliament's Co-Leading IMCO and JURI Committees: April 2023

On 5 April 2023 the European Parliament's Committees on the Internal Market and Consumer Protection (IMCO) and on Legal Affairs (JURI), i.e., the co-leading Committees on the proposal for a revised PLD, issued their draft Joint Report.[217] The co-rapporteurs' amendments to the Commission's proposal constitute a significant tone-down of the revised PLD, based on the need "to strike the right balance between the interests of injured persons and those of economic operators liable for defective products. Ensuring a fair allocation of risk is essential in [the co-rapporteurs'] view for the revision of the rules of the PLD".[218]

As it was stated, "by aligning the rules in the Union to get a fair compensation when defective products cause harm, the Co-Rapporteurs want to strengthen the level of consumer protection across the EU. At the same time, the new legal framework should enhance legal certainty for economic operators in the internal market, without overburdening them, thereby preventing a decline of innovative products in Europe, higher consumer prices and less product variety. The Co-Rapporteurs therefore commit to striking the right balance and ensuring a

[216] Ibid., Article 14a(2). See also recital 43.

[217] Draft Report of the European Parliament's Committee on Internal Market and Consumer Protection and the Committee on Legal Affairs on the proposal for a directive of the European Parliament and of the Council on Liability for defective products (COM(2022)0495 – C9-0322/2022 – 2022/0302(COD)), 05.04.2023, ("Draft Joint Report of the European Parliament's co-leading IMCO and JURI Committees on the proposal for a revised PLD, 5 April 2023").

[218] Draft Joint Report of the European Parliament's co-leading IMCO and JURI Committees on the proposal for a revised PLD, 5 April 2023, Explanatory Statement, p. 37.

proportionate product liability framework for economic operators and consumers. In their vision, strengthening consumer rights through harmonisation and ensuring an innovation friendly liability regime, which is fair to economic operators go together".[219]

One of the most controversial issues—not explicitly dealt with by the draft Joint Report—remains as to whether standalone software, i.e., software which is not embedded in a physical product, should be covered by the revised PLD.[220]

In order to achieve the aforementioned balance between the interests of consumers and those of economic operators, the co-rapporteurs proceeded with the introduction of the following, *inter alia*, amendments:

9.14.1.1 Damages Recognised Under the Revised PLD

Regarding the notion of damage, the co-rapporteurs excluded data loss or corruption of data from the scope of the Directive as they argued that this is already covered by existing EU laws, such as the GDPR.[221] Likewise, the draft Joint Report deleted the "medically recognised harm to psychological health" from the definition of 'damage', and clarified that confirmation of medically recognised harm to psychological health should be obtained through a court-ordered medical expert.[222]

---

[219] Ibid.

[220] "This thorny question is at the very heart of the political differences between conservative and progressive MEPs". EURACTIV, "MEPs start to scratch the surface of new product liability rules", by Luca Bertuzzi, 06.06.2023.

[221] "The Co-Rapporteurs consider that loss or corruption of data are appropriately dealt with under Regulation (EU) 2016/679 of the European Parliament and of the Council, Directive 2002/58/EC of the European Parliament and of the Council, Directive (EU) 2016/680 of the European Parliament and of the Council, and Regulation (EU) 2018/1725 of the European Parliament and of the Council. They do therefore not see a need to include this type of harm in the framework of the PLD". Draft Joint Report of the European Parliament's co-leading IMCO and JURI Committees on the proposal for a revised PLD, 5 April 2023, Explanatory Statement, pp. 37–38.

This is why the co-rapporteurs proposed the deletion of the first paragraph of recital 16 of the Commission's proposal: "(16) In recognition of the growing relevance and value of intangible assets, the loss or corruption of data, such as content deleted from a hard drive, should also be compensated, including the cost of recovering or restoring the data".

Also, Article 4, point 6 ('definition of damage') was deleted and replaced by Article 5a(new): "Damage – 1. For the purpose of this Directive, 'damage' means material losses resulting from: (a) death or personal injury, (b) harm to, or destruction of, any property, except: (i) the defective product itself; (ii) a product damaged by a defective component of that product; (iii) property used exclusively for professional purposes. 2. This Article shall not affect national rules relating to non-material damage".

[222] The Co-Rapporteurs "recognise that Member States may consider that personal injury includes medically recognised damage to psychological health amounting to an effect on the victim's psychological health that affects the general state of health as confirmed by a court-ordered medical expert". Draft Joint Report of the European Parliament's co-leading IMCO and JURI Committees on the proposal for a revised PLD, 5 April 2023, Explanatory Statement, p. 37.

9.14.1.2 Defectiveness of a Product

The co-rapporteurs stressed that a product should be deemed defective if it fails to meet the expected level of safety that an average person (not '*the public at large*', as proposed by the Commission) would anticipate, considering the relevant safety standards for that specific product ("A product shall be considered defective when it does not provide the safety an *average person* is entitled to expect and that is also required under Union or national law").[223]

When evaluating the defectiveness of a product, all relevant circumstances should be considered (for instance, the characteristics that are directly related to the damage, such as labelling, design, technical features, composition, packaging, and instructions), including the potential impact of other interconnected products on the defective product. This is particularly relevant when it can be reasonably expected, at the time of its market introduction or use, that the product will be used in conjunction with other products.[224]

In assessing the defectiveness, the draft Joint Report moved away from the concept of 'reasonably foreseeable use and misuse'[225] in favour of a narrower notion of 'intended use of the product'.[226] As a result, in order to request damages, the product must have a clear malfunction while being used for the purpose intended by the manufacturer. In addition, the co-rapporteurs specified that cybersecurity vulnerabilities in a product should be considered defects only when the product fails to comply with mandatory safety-relevant cybersecurity requirements outlined in EU or national legislation.[227] Furthermore, the notion of "the specific expectations of the end users for whom the product is intended"[228] has been removed from the list of circumstances to be considered when assessing the defectiveness of a product.

According to the Commission's proposal, the provider remains responsible for software damages resulting from defectiveness that should have been solved via an update. The draft Joint Report limited this scenario to the expected product lifetime

Therefore, in contrast to the Commission's proposal, it is not explicitly stated that personal injury includes medically recognised damage to psychological health (on the contrary, this was deleted from the definition of 'damage'). The co-rapporteurs stressed that Member States *may* consider that personal injury includes medically recognised damage to psychological health, "that is to say an effect on the victim's psychological health that affects the victim's general state of health as confirmed by a court-ordered medical expert". Draft Joint Report of the European Parliament's co-leading IMCO and JURI Committees on the proposal for a revised PLD, 5 April 2023, Explanatory Statement, recital 17.

[223] Draft Joint Report of the European Parliament's co-leading IMCO and JURI Committees on the proposal for a revised PLD, 5 April 2023, Explanatory Statement, p. 38. See also recitals 22, 24 and Article 6(1) (new).

[224] Ibid., Explanatory Statement, p. 38. See also recitals 22, 24 and Article 6(1)(d).

[225] Proposal for a revised Product Liability Directive, Article 6(1)(b).

[226] Draft Joint Report of the European Parliament's co-leading IMCO and JURI Committees on the proposal for a revised PLD, 5 April 2023, Article 6(1)(b).

[227] Ibid., at recitals 23 and 24, and Article 6(1)(f).

[228] Proposal for a revised Product Liability Directive, Article 6(1)(h).

or five years, whichever is shorter. Therefore, the draft Joint Report aligned the liability for defects caused by lack of software updates with the proposed Cyber Resilience Act[229] (i.e., a product's expected lifetime or five years, whichever is shorter).[230]

9.14.1.3 Right to Compensation—Collection of Evidence

The co-rapporteurs explicitly stated that Member States are entitled to empower national consumer protection bodies to act on behalf of consumers (i.e., to represent them collectively) when gathering evidence to prove the defectiveness of a product, the resulting damage caused by the defective product and the causal link between the two.[231]

Regarding the collection of evidence, the co-rapporteurs narrowed down the conditions for court-ordered disclosure of evidence, by proposing specific safeguards on evidence disclosure procedure.[232] Also, it is reminded that, according to the Commission's proposal, if the defendant fails to comply with an obligation to disclose such information/evidence that is at his disposal, national courts should presume the defectiveness of the product.[233] This provision [Article 9(2)(a) and

[229] Commission's Proposal for a Regulation of the European Parliament and of the Council on horizontal cybersecurity requirements for products with digital elements and amending Regulation (EU) 2019/1020, COM(2022) 454 final, Brussels, 15.9.2022, especially Article 10(6) and (12), and Article 23(2). For instance, Article 10(6) reads: "When placing a product with digital elements on the market, and for the expected product lifetime or for a period of five years from the placing of the product on the market, whichever is shorter, manufacturers shall ensure that vulnerabilities of that product are handled effectively and in accordance with the essential requirements set out in Section 2 of Annex I".

[230] Draft Joint Report of the European Parliament's co-leading IMCO and JURI Committees on the proposal for a revised PLD, 5 April 2023, Article 10(2) (b) and (c).

[231] Ibid., recital 30 and Article 5(2)(b): ". . .a person acting on behalf of injured persons, in accordance with Directive (EU) 2020/1828 of the European Parliament and of the Council of 25 November 2020 on representative actions for the protection of the collective interests of consumers and repealing Directive 2009/22/EC (OJ L 409, 4.12.2020, p. 1)".

[232] Ibid., Article 8(1): "Member States shall ensure that in proceedings relating to an action for compensation for damage caused by a defective product, at the request of a claimant who has presented a reasoned justification containing reasonably available facts and evidence sufficient to support the plausibility of the claim for compensation, and [where] there are reasons to believe that strictly relevant additional evidence lies in the control of the defendant, without which the claimant is unable to prove the claim for compensation, national courts may order the defendant to disclose such strictly relevant evidence, in accordance with national procedural law". See also recital 31, and Explanatory Statement, p. 38: "the Co-Rapporteurs estimate that a court-ordered disclosure of evidence, without which the claimant is unable to prove the claim for compensation, should be made possible when it is necessary and proportionate. The interests of all parties should be taken into account for this assessment, and confidential information and trade secrets within the meaning of Directive (EU) 2016/943 of the European Parliament and of the Council, deserve special protection by ensuring their confidentiality".

[233] Proposal for a revised Product Liability Directive, Article 9(2)(a).

recital 33] was removed from the draft Joint Report. The draft Joint Report also granted defendants the option to ask the national judge for the claimant to disclose 'strictly relevant evidence' on the claim.[234]

When determining whether the disclosure requests are necessary and proportionate, national courts must take into account the available facts and evidence justifying the request, the scope and costs of the disclosure, as well as whether the request touches upon commercially sensitive information, especially concerning any third parties.[235] Furthermore, in line with the Commission's proposed AI Liability Directive,[236] the co-rapporteurs added that those who receive an evidence disclosure request should have the appropriate procedural remedies in response to such orders, i.e., the opportunity to be heard by a national court.[237]

9.14.1.4 Reversal/Alleviation of the Burden of Proof

Regarding the reversal/alleviation of the burden of proof, it is reminded that, according to the Commission's proposal, the defectiveness of the product or the causal link between the defectiveness of the product and the damage will be presumed when it is technically or scientifically too complex for the claimant to prove the defectiveness of the product or the causal link between the defectiveness and the damage, or both (provided that the claimant has demonstrated that the product contributed to the damage and it is likely that the product was defective or that its defectiveness is a likely cause of the damage, or both).[238] Therefore, for highly complex systems like AI-related systems, it would fall on the defendant to rebut this presumption.

However, despite "acknowledging that the burden of proof can be more fairly shared between injured persons and manufacturers, especially in technically or scientific complex cases", the draft Joint Report of the Parliament's co-leading IMCO and JURI Committees opposed a general reversal for highly complex

[234] Draft Joint Report of the European Parliament's co-leading IMCO and JURI Committees on the proposal for a revised PLD, 5 April 2023, Article 8(1a)(new): "Member States shall ensure that national courts are able, at the request of the defendant, to order the claimant to disclose strictly relevant evidence, in accordance with national procedural law". See also recital 31.

[235] Ibid., Article 8(3)(a-c)(new).

[236] Proposal for a Directive of the European Parliament and of the Council on adapting non-contractual civil liability rules to artificial intelligence (AI Liability Directive), European Commission, COM(2022) 496 final, Brussels, 28.9.2022 (the 'proposed AI Liability Directive'), at Article 3(4), forth subparagraph: "Member States shall also ensure that the person ordered to disclose or to preserve the evidence mentioned in paragraphs 1 or 2 has appropriate procedural remedies in response to such orders".

[237] Draft Joint Report of the European Parliament's co-leading IMCO and JURI Committees on the proposal for a revised PLD, 5 April 2023, Article 8(4)(a)(new).

[238] Proposal for a revised Product Liability Directive, Article 9(4).

products like AI systems.[239] As a result, the reference to a rebuttable presumption was removed[240] and, in turn, a requirement was added for the claimant to prove that it is *highly* likely that the product's defectiveness was the direct cause of the damage. In other words, the claimant would be required to prove that the product contributed to the damage and, where proving defectiveness is too complex, that it is *highly* likely that the product was defective or the defectiveness is *highly* likely the cause of the damage.[241] The draft Joint Report also requires that 'experts in the relevant field' should be consulted by the national courts when determining whether such technical or scientific complexity applies to a particular case.[242]

9.14.1.5 Limitation Period

According to the Commission's proposal—as under the current PLD—producers are released from liability for property damage and death/personal injury 10 years after placing the product on the market (unless a claimant has, in the meantime, initiated proceedings before a national court against an economic operator that can be held liable). Therefore, victims of harm (due to a defective product that allegedly caused them damage) that emerges after 10 years are no longer entitled to compensation.[243] According to the Commission, by way of exemption, claimants can enjoy an additional 5-year period in cases where the symptoms of personal injury are slow to emerge.[244] The draft Joint Report extended this limitation period from 15 to 20 years.[245]

[239] Draft Joint Report of the European Parliament's co-leading IMCO and JURI Committees on the proposal for a revised PLD, 5 April 2023, Explanatory Statement, p. 38.

[240] Ibid. The co-rapporteurs use the wording "alleviate the burden of proving the defectiveness of a product or the causal link" instead of "presume" (at recital 34). Thus, instead of the defendant having the burden to rebut the presumption, "the claimant should be required to prove only that the product contributed to the damage and, where the claimant's difficulties relate to proving defectiveness, that it is highly likely that the product was defective, or where the claimant's difficulties relate to proving the causal link, that its defectiveness is a highly likely cause of the damage" (recital 34). Also, this sentence at recital 33 was deleted: "In order to provide an incentive to comply with the obligation to disclose information, national courts should presume the defectiveness of a product where a defendant fails to comply with such an obligation". See also Article 9(2)(a).

[241] Ibid., recital 34 and Article 9(4), subparagraph 1, point b.

[242] Ibid., recital 34 and Article 9(4), subparagraph 1, introductory part.

[243] Proposal for a revised Product Liability Directive, Article 14(2).

[244] Ibid., Article 14(3).

[245] Draft Joint Report of the European Parliament's co-leading IMCO and JURI Committees on the proposal for a revised PLD, 5 April 2023, Article 14(3) and recital 43.

9.14.1.6 Transparency

According to the Commission's proposal, Member States will be required to publish (without delay and in an easily accessible and electronic format) relevant court judgments on product liability, so that other national courts could take these judgments into account.[246] The draft Joint Report makes this provision mandatory and requires the Commission (i.e., it is not at the discretion of the Commission)[247] to implement and keep up-to-date an easily accessible repository of such cases ("The Commission shall set up and maintain an easily accessible and publicly available database containing the judgments referred to in paragraph 1").[248]

9.14.2 The Negotiating Position of the Plenary of the European Parliament: The Parliament's Compromise Text—October 2023

In Parliament, as already mentioned, the file of the amended PLD was assigned jointly to the Committee on the Internal Market and Consumer Protection (IMCO) and the Committee on Legal Affairs (JURI), with Vlad Botoş (Renew, Romania) and Pascal Arimont (EPP, Belgium) appointed as rapporteurs. On 9 October 2023, following their draft Joint Report of 5 April 2023, the joint committees adopted the final Report[249] (with 33 votes in favour, 2 against and no abstention) and decided

[246] Proposal for a revised Product Liability Directive, Article 15(1).

[247] Ibid., Article 15(2).

[248] Draft Joint Report of the European Parliament's co-leading IMCO and JURI Committees on the proposal for a revised PLD, 5 April 2023, Article 15(2). See also at recital 45: "Those judgments should be compiled in an easily accessible and publicly available database, set up and maintained by the Commission".

[249] Joint Report of the European Parliament's co-leading IMCO and JURI Committees on the proposal for a directive of the European Parliament and of the Council on liability for defective products, A9-0291/2023, 12 October 2023.

The Parliament's position (already expressed in the draft Joint Report of the European Parliament's co-leading IMCO and JURI Committees on the proposal for a revised PLD, 5 April 2023) is summarised as follows: "• Scope of application – adding raw materials in the definition of a product similarly to the Council. • Damages – clarifying that medically recognised harm to psychological health should be confirmed 'by a court-ordered medical expert' and that the destruction or irreversible corruption of data that is not used for professional purposes should not be compensated if the economic value of the damage is below € 1000 (e.g. setting a threshold to limit the potential risk of excessive litigations). • Assessment of defectiveness – considering a product defective when it does not provide the safety that an average person (instead of the 'public at large') is entitled to expect, taking into consideration in particular the standard of safety applicable to the product in question. • Cascade of attributable liability – allowing Member States to compensate persons who suffered damage caused by defective products via national schemes (which should not be funded by public revenues) when victims fail to obtain compensation because no economic operator is held liable, is insolvent or have ceased to exist. • Micro or small enterprises producing software exemption –

to enter into trilogue (i.e. interinstitutional) negotiations with the Council of the EU (and the Commission),[250] with the aim of reaching a political agreement on the legislative text of the amended PLD in the coming months.[251] The European Parliament confirmed the draft mandate at the Plenary session of 16 October 2023.

9.15 Political Agreement on the Revised Product Liability Directive (December 2023) – Final Text (March 2024)

Following the Interinstitutional negotiations (trilogue),[252] the co-legislators (Council of the EU and the European Parliament) reached a provisional (political) agreement on 14 December 2023.[253] At its meeting on 24 January 2024, the Permanent

---

introducing a new exemption from liability in the case of a manufacturer of software that, at the time of the placing on the market of that software, was micro or small enterprise provided that another economic operator would be liable for damaged caused by that software". See Stefano De Luca, Members' Research Service, European Parliament, EPRS, Legislative Train Schedule – A Europe Fit for the Digital Age, New Product Liability Directive, 20 October 2023.

[250] On 16.10.2023, the joint committees' decision to enter into interinstitutional negotiations was announced in plenary. On 18.10.2023, the joint committees' decision to enter into interinstitutional negotiations was confirmed by the plenary.

[251] Following the committee vote, JURI Committee co-rapporteur Pascal Arimont stated: "Like its predecessor, the revised Product Liability Directive aims to strike a balance between remaining an effective instrument for victims of defective products, and the legal certainty economic operators deserve in a fast changing market characterised by digitalisation, the circular economy, and global value chains". In the same press release, IMCO Committee co-rapporteur Vlad-Marius Botoş stessed: "In the new Product Liability Directive, we have a balance between the interests of citizens and legal clarity for economic operators regarding software and the loss and corruption of data. In addition, people can get help from consumer protection agencies in building their case to obtain damages". European Parliament, Press Release (IMCO-JURI), "Better protection for consumers against damages by defective products", 09.10.2023.

[252] "In order to pass legislation, Parliament and Council have to agree on an identical text, which requires time and negotiations. The complexity of the EU legislative process has been sometimes criticised for being lengthy and subject to gridlock, thus the risk of not responding to societal problems in a timely manner. To overcome this criticism, the legislators have developed informal contacts to speed up the legislative process while ensuring representativeness and oversight. One of the tools commonly used today to ensure the effectiveness of the legislative process is trilogue, defined as 'informal tripartite meetings on legislative proposals between representatives of the Parliament, the Council and the Commission'". Micaela Del Monte and Stephanie Brenda Smialowski, "Understanding trilogue – Informal tripartite meetings to reach provisional agreement on legislative files", European Parliamentary Research Service (EPRS), May 2021, at p. 1.

"Interinstitutional negotiations have become standard practice for the adoption of EU legislation. They enable the co-legislators to reach agreement at any stage of the legislative procedure. The Parliament's mandate is based either on a report adopted in committee or the position adopted in Plenary. As soon as the lead committee has adopted its report, it may decide to enter into negotiations. At first reading such a decision is subject to a plenary "check". Plenary can either endorse the committee's decision to enter into negotiations with its report as mandate or it can modify the content of the report and refer it back as amended to the committee for negotiations.

Plenary can always decide to conclude the first reading of Parliament without negotiations. Negotiations between the institutions on legislative proposals generally take the form of tripartite meetings ('trilogues') between Parliament, the Council and the Commission. For a given file, each institution designates its negotiators and defines its negotiating mandate. Trilogues may be organised at any stage of the legislative procedure (first, second or third reading). Any provisional agreement reached in trilogues is informal and has therefore to be approved by the formal procedures applicable within each of the two institutions. In Parliament, the text of the provisional agreement has to be approved by a vote in committee after which it is confirmed in plenary. Trilogues are informal tripartite meetings on legislative proposals between representatives of the Parliament, the Council and the Commission. Their purpose is to reach a provisional agreement on a text acceptable to both the Council and the Parliament. They may be organised at any stage of the legislative procedure and can lead to what are known as 'first reading', 'early second reading' or 'second reading' agreements, or to a 'joint text' during conciliation. Trilogue negotiations involve, on the Parliament side, a negotiating team consisting of the Chair or a Vice-Chair of the responsible committee, the rapporteur and at least the shadow rapporteurs from each political group that wishes to participate and, on the Council side, representatives of the Presidency of the Council of Ministers. The Commission is equally present. During trilogue meetings, which are chaired by the co-legislator hosting the meeting (i.e. either Parliament or the Council), the two institutions explain their position and a debate develops. The Commission acts as a mediator with a view to facilitating an agreement between the co-legislators. The participants in the trilogues operate on the basis of negotiating mandates given to them by their respective institutions: by the responsible committee or plenary in Parliament, by Coreper or Council in the Council, and by the College in the Commission. The three delegations explore possible avenues of compromise in an informal manner and report back on a regular basis according to their respective institutions' internal rules, i.e. via the negotiating team to the committee for Parliament, in Coreper or the responsible working party for Council". See European Parliament, "Ordinary Legislative Procedure - Interinstitutional negotiations for the adoption of EU legislation", at https://www.europarl.europa.eu/olp/en/interinstitutional-negotiations#:~:text=Trilogues%20are%20informal%20tripartite%20meetings,the%20Council%20and%20the%20Parliament.

[253] Stefano De Luca, Members' Research Service, European Parliament, EPRS, Legislative Train Schedule – A Europe Fit for the Digital Age, New Product Liability Directive, 15.12.2023.

See also: European Parliament, Press Release, "Deal to better protect consumers from damages caused by defective products", 14.12.2023: "... *On Thursday, Parliament and Council negotiators informally agreed on easier access to compensation for individuals suffering damage because of a defective product.* – The provisional agreement on the liability of economic operators for damage caused by defective products aims to respond to the increase in online shopping (including from outside the EU) and the emergence of new technologies (such as AI) as well as to ensure the transition to a circular economic model. In order not to stifle innovation, the rules will not apply to open-source software developed or supplied outside of a commercial activity. New rules ensure that there is always an EU-based business, such as a manufacturer, importer or their authorised representative that can be held liable for a product that caused damage, even if the product was not bought in the EU. MEPs insisted that in cases when such a liable business cannot be identified, member states may provide compensation using national compensation schemes. *Easier access to compensation* – The negotiators agreed to simplify the burden of proof for the person requiring compensation, who would normally have to prove that the product was defective and that this caused the damage suffered. For example, the defectiveness may be presumed by a court in case the claimant faces excessive difficulties in particular due to technical or scientific complexity and the product is likely to be defective. To further help victims of damage with their compensation claim, they will be able to request that the court order the business to disclose the "necessary and proportionate" evidence. MEPs also insisted that competent consumer protection authorities or bodies should be encouraged to provide additional help with compensation claims to consumers.

Extended liability – MEPs ensured, during the talks, that it will be possible to get compensation not only for material damage, such as destruction of property, but also for non-material losses, including medically recognised damage to psychological health. It will also be possible to claim compensation following the destruction or corruption of data that are not used for professional purposes (e.g. deletion of files from a hard drive). Negotiators also agreed on an extended liability period of 25 years in exceptional cases when symptoms are slow to emerge. The injured person will still be able to get compensation after this period if the proceeding was initiated within the given period".

See also: Council of the EU, Press Release, "Agreement between the Council and the European Parliament makes EU liability rules fit for the digital age and circular economy", 14.12.2023: "Negotiators from the Spanish presidency and the European Parliament have reached a political agreement on a new EU law on liability for defective products. The law will update the current, decades-old, civil liability rulebook in order to better take into account that nowadays many products have digital features and that the economy is becoming increasingly circular. *Digital economy* – Under the new liability directive, the definition of 'product' will be extended to digital manufacturing files and software. Free and open-source software that is developed or supplied outside the course of a commercial activity is excluded from the scope of the directive. The digital economy has led to a lot of online sales. It has therefore been decided that online platforms can also be held liable for a defective product if they present the product or otherwise enable the transaction for the sale of the product in a way that would lead an average consumer to believe that the product is provided either by the online platform itself or by a trader acting under its authority or control. *Circular economy* – In a circular economy, products are designed to be more durable, reusable, reparable and upgradable. When a product is modified substantially, outside the original manufacturer's control, and is made available on the market or put into service again, the new directive stipulates that the company or person that made the substantial modification should be held liable as the manufacturer of the modified product. *Right to compensation* – The Council and Parliament also agreed that any natural person who suffers damage by a defective product is entitled to compensation. Such damages include death or personal injury, including medically recognised damage to psychological health, damage to or destruction of property, as well as destruction or irreversible corruption of data. The right to compensation will cover material losses resulting from the damage as well as non-material losses resulting from the damage, in so far as they are compensable under national law. Due to the increasing technical complexity of many products, member states must ensure that an injured person who claims compensation before a national court can request access to relevant evidence at the disposal of the manufacturer in order to be able to prove their claim. *Products bought from non-EU manufacturers* – Consumers are increasingly buying products from manufacturers based outside the EU. However, the level of protection they receive should remain the same when those products prove to be defective. The agreement provides that when a manufacturer of a product or a component is established outside the EU, the importer of the defective product or component, the authorised representative of the manufacturer or, as a last resort, the fulfilment service provider (a company that typically takes care of the warehousing, packaging and dispatching of a product) can be held liable for damages. *Burden of proof* – One of the directive's objectives is to ensure that consumers will have a fair chance of getting compensation in complex cases. When a claimant (e.g. the injured consumer) is faced with excessive difficulties, in particular due to the technical or scientific complexity of the case, to prove the defectiveness of the product or the causal link between its defectiveness and the damage, a court may decide that the claimant is only required to prove the likelihood that the product was defective or that its defectiveness is a likely cause of the damage".

Representatives Committee of the Council of the EU confirmed the agreement on the compromise text of the revised Product Liability Directive,[254] as it was reached between the negotiating parties on 14 December 2023, and authorised the Presidency to address the habitual offer letter to the European Parliament.

The text of the provisional agreement[255] was submitted to the Committee on the Internal Market and Consumer Protection (IMCO) and the Committee on Legal Affairs (JURI), which voted on 22 February 2024. The final text of the revised PLD was formally endorsed by the European Parliament at the Plenary of 12 March 2024, which adopted its position at first reading.[256]

The revised Product Liability Directive will have to be formally approved by the Council of the EU, too. It will enter into force on the twentieth day following its publication in the EU Official Journal. The new rules will apply to products placed on the market or put into service 24 months after entry into force of the revised PLD.

The following sections of this chapter cover the final text of the revised Product Liability Directive.

9.15.1 Subject Matter—Objective—Maximum Harmonisation Instrument—Right to Compensation

The final text of the revised PLD lays down common rules on the liability of economic operators for damage suffered by natural persons caused by defective products, and on compensation for such damage.[257] The objective of the revised

---

[254] Council of the European Union, Information Note: From: General Secretariat of the Council. To: Delegations. Subject: Proposal for a Directive of the European Parliament and of the Council on liability for defective products – Letter sent to the European Parliament, Brussels, 24 January 2024, Council doc. 5809/24 ("General Secretariat of the Council – Proposal for a Directive on liability for defective products – Letter sent to the European Parliament, Council doc. 5809/24, 24 January 2024").

[255] European Parliament, Committee on the Internal Market and Consumer Protection (IMCO) and Committee on Legal Affairs (JURI), "Provisional Agreement Resulting from Interinstitutional Negotiations", Subject: Proposal for a Directive of the European Parliament and of the Council on Liability for defective products (COM(2022)0495 – C9 0322/2022 – 2022/0302(COD)), 31 January 2024.

[256] European Parliament legislative resolution of 12 March 2024 on the proposal for a Directive of the European Parliament and of the Council on liability for defective products (COM(2022)0495 – C9-0322/2022 – 2022/0302(COD)), (Ordinary legislative procedure: first reading) – P9_TC1-COD (2022)0302, Position of the European Parliament adopted at first reading on 12 March 2024 with a view to the adoption of Directive (EU) 2024/... of the European Parliament and of the Council on liability for defective products and repealing Council Directive 85/374/EEC ["Position of the European Parliament of 12 March 2024 for the adoption of a Directive on liability for defective products (revised PLD)"]. See also: CORRIGENDUM to the position of the European Parliament adopted at first reading on 12 March 2024 with a view to the adoption of Directive (EU) 2024/... of the European Parliament and of the Council on liability for defective products and repealing Council Directive 85/374/EEC, European Parliament, Plenary sitting, 18 July 2024 ["CORRIGENDUM to the position of the European Parliament for a Directive on liability for defective products, 18 July 2024"]. It contains a very small number of minor amendments that do not bear mentioning.

[257] Position of the European Parliament of 12 March 2024 for the adoption of a Directive on liability for defective products (revised PLD), Article 1, first subparagraph.

PLD is to ensure the proper functioning of the internal market, undistorted competition, legal certainty for businesses and a high-level of protection for natural persons.[258] To this end, as a maximum harmonisation instrument,[259] the revised PLD prohibits Member States from implementing provisions that are more or less stringent than those within the Directive's scope.[260]

Member States must ensure that any natural person who suffers damage caused by a defective product (the 'injured person') is entitled to compensation in accordance with the provisions laid down in the revised Product Liability Directive.[261] The revised PLD refers to the 'claimant' who is defined as 'an injured person who is claiming compensation in proceedings before a national court for damage caused by a defective product'.[262] The revised PLD, therefore, excludes non-natural persons (such as businesses and any other public or private entities) from bringing a claim for damages on this legal ground.

The revised PLD stipulates that claims for damages can be brought not only by the injured person but also by persons that have succeeded in or have been subrogated into the rights of the injured person.[263] Furthermore, it states that a claim for compensation can also be brought by a person acting on behalf of one or more

---

[258] Ibid., Article 1, second subparagraph.

[259] "Does the Union action leave as much scope for national decision as possible while achieving satisfactorily the objectives set? (e.g. is it possible to limit the European action to minimum standards or use a less stringent policy instrument or approach?): In order to achieve the internal market objective and give businesses legal certainty, the Product Liability Directive is a maximum harmonisation instrument and does not allow Member States to adopt more, or less, stringent provisions at national level if those provisions are within the scope of the Directive. However, the proposed action leaves intact other routes to compensation that injured people have at national level (such as compensation on the basis of contract, warranty or fault)". Commission Staff Working Document, "Subsidiarity Grid – Accompanying the document Proposal for a Directive of the European Parliament and of the Council on liability for defective products, SWD(2022) 315 final, Brussels, 28.9.2022, p. 5.

[260] Position of the European Parliament of 12 March 2024 for the adoption of a Directive on liability for defective products (revised PLD), Article 3: "Member States shall not maintain or introduce, in their national law, provisions diverging from those laid down in this Directive, including more stringent or less stringent provisions, to achieve a different level of protection for consumers and other natural persons, unless otherwise provided for in this Directive". See also recital 8: "In order to create a genuine internal market with a high and uniform level of protection of consumers and other natural persons, and to reflect the case law of the Court of Justice of the European Union, Member States should not, in respect of matters within the scope of this Directive, maintain or introduce provisions that are more stringent or less stringent than those laid down in this Directive".

[261] Ibid., Article 5, para. 1.

[262] Ibid., Article 9, para. 1.

[263] Ibid., Article 5, para. 2, point (a).

For a definition of the term 'subrogation', see the proposal for a Directive of the European Parliament and of the Council on adapting non-contractual civil liability rules to artificial intelligence (AI Liability Directive), European Commission, COM(2022) 496 final, Brussels, 28.9.2022 (the 'proposed AI Liability Directive'), Explanatory Memorandum, at p. 12: "Subrogation is the assumption by a third party (such as an insurance company) of another party's legal right to collect a debt or damages. Thus one person is entitled to enforce the rights of another for their own benefit. Subrogation would also cover heirs of a deceased victim".

injured parties, in accordance with EU (e.g., Directive 2020/1828 of 25 November 2020 on representative actions for the protection of the collective interests of consumers) or national law.[264]

The revised PLD explicitly states that Member States must ensure that national consumer protection authorities/bodies can assist affected consumers to effectively exercise their right to compensation in accordance with this Directive when gathering evidence to prove the defectiveness of a product, the resulting damage caused by the defective product and the causal link between the two.[265]

To the extent permitted by national law, the right to compensation for individuals harmed by defective products should extend to both direct victims (those who suffer damage directly caused by a defective product), and to indirect victims (i.e., those who suffer damage as a result of the direct victim's damage).[266]

9.15.2 Product—Scope

The revised PLD extends the definition of 'product' to digital manufacturing files[267] and software[268] (including Artificial Intelligence) as well as to electricity and raw

---

[264] Position of the European Parliament of 12 March 2024 for the adoption of a Directive on liability for defective products (revised PLD), Article 5, para. 2, point (b). See also recital 29: "This Directive does not affect the various means of seeking redress at national level, whether through court proceedings, non-court solutions, alternative dispute resolution or representative actions under Directive (EU) 2020/1828 of the European Parliament and of the Council or under national collective redress schemes.

[265] Ibid., recital 28.

[266] Ibid., recital 27.

[267] Ibid., Article 4, point 2: "'digital manufacturing file' means a digital version of, or digital template for, a movable which contains the functional information necessary to produce a tangible item by enabling the automated control of machinery or tools". See also recital 16: "Whereas digital files as such are not products within the scope of this Directive, digital manufacturing files, which contain the functional information necessary to produce a tangible item by enabling the automated control of machinery or tools, such as drills, lathes, mills and 3D printers, should be considered to be products, in order to ensure the protection of natural persons in cases where such files are defective. For example, a defective computer-assisted-design file used to create a 3D-printed good that causes harm should give rise to liability under this Directive, where such a file is developed or supplied in the course of a commercial activity".

[268] Ibid., recital 13: "Products in the digital age can be tangible or intangible. Software, such as operating systems, firmware, computer programs, applications or AI systems, is increasingly common on the market and plays an increasingly important role for product safety. Software is capable of being placed on the market as a standalone product or can subsequently be integrated into other products as a component, and it is capable of causing damage through its execution. In the interest of legal certainty, it should be clarified in this Directive that software is a product for the purposes of applying no fault liability, irrespective of the mode of its supply or usage, and therefore irrespective of whether the software is stored on a device, accessed through a communication network or cloud technologies, or supplied through a software-as-a-service model. ... A developer or producer of software, including AI system providers ..., should be treated as a manufacturer".

materials (such as gas and water): "'product' means all movables, even if integrated into, or inter-connected with, another movable or an immovable; it includes electricity, digital manufacturing files, raw materials and software".[269] The revised PLD applies to products placed on the market or put into service in the course of a commercial activity, regardless of whether they are provided for payment or free of charge.[270] This includes products distributed within sponsorship campaigns or manufactured for the provision of a service funded by public resources, as such arrangements still carry an economic or business nature.[271]

Free and open-source software that is developed or supplied outside the course of a commercial activity is excluded from the scope of the revised PLD.[272] If a manufacturer integrates the open-source software as a component[273] of its product and it consequently causes a defect, the liability will fall on the manufacturer rather than the software provider.[274] The liability rules apply when the software is supplied in exchange for a price or personal data is used other than exclusively for improving

[269] Ibid., Article 4, point 1. See also recital 6: "In order to ensure that the Union's product liability regime is comprehensive, no-fault liability for defective products should apply to all movables, *including software*, including when they are integrated into other movables or installed in immovables".

[270] Ibid., Article 4, points 7 to 9: "(7) 'making available on the market' means any supply of a product for distribution, consumption or use on the Union market in the course of a commercial activity, whether in return for payment or free of charge; (8) 'placing on the market' means the first making available of a product on the Union market; (9) 'putting into service' means the first use of a product in the Union in the course of a commercial activity, whether in return for payment or free of charge, in circumstances in which that product has not been placed on the market prior to its first use". See also at recital 26: "The concept of 'putting into service' is relevant for products that are not placed on the market prior to their first use, as can be the case in the lifts, machinery or medical devices sectors".

[271] Position of the European Parliament of 12 March 2024 for the adoption of a Directive on liability for defective products (revised PLD), recital 26.

[272] Ibid., Article 2, para. 2. See also recital 14: "Free and open-source software, whereby the source code is openly shared and users can freely access, use, modify and redistribute the software or modified versions thereof, can contribute to research and innovation on the market. Such software is subject to licences that allow anyone the freedom to run, copy, distribute, study, change and improve the software. In order not to hamper innovation or research, this Directive should not apply to free and open-source software developed or supplied outside the course of a commercial activity, since products so developed or supplied are by definition not placed on the market. Developing or contributing to such software should not be understood as making it available on the market. Providing such software on open repositories should not be considered as making it available on the market, unless that occurs in the course of a commercial activity. In principle, the supply of free and open-source software by non-profit organisations should not be considered as taking place in a business-related context, unless such supply occurs in the course of a commercial activity".

[273] Ibid., Article 4, point 4: "'component' means any item, whether tangible or intangible, or raw material or any related service, that is integrated into, or inter-connected with, a product".

[274] Ibid., recital 15: "Where free and open-source software supplied outside the course of a commercial activity is subsequently integrated by a manufacturer as a component into a product in the course of a commercial activity and is thereby placed on the market, it should be possible to hold that manufacturer liable for damage caused by the defectiveness of such software but not the

the software's security, compatibility or interoperability (and is, therefore, supplied in the course of a commercial activity).[275]

Information is not to be considered a product and, therefore, the revised PLD should not apply to the content of digital files (such as e-books, media files, or the mere source code of software).[276] While the revised PLD should not apply to digital services as such, strict liability should be extended to integrated or inter-connected digital services ('related services')[277] as they allow the core functioning of a product (and determine the safety of a product just as much as physical or digital components): "It is becoming increasingly common for digital services to be integrated into, or inter-connected with, a product in such a way that the absence of the service would prevent the product from performing one of its functions. ... Those related services should be considered components of the product into which they are integrated or with which they are inter-connected where they are within the control of the manufacturer of that product".[278] The revised PLD provides examples of such related services, and clarifies that failing to provide software updates, such as security patches for known vulnerabilities, might also result in liability.[279]

The revised PLD does not apply to damage resulting from nuclear accidents in so far as liability for such damage is covered by international conventions ratified by Member States.[280] The revised PLD does not affect the applicability of EU law on the protection of personal data[281] as well as the rights that an injured person may have under existing national rules concerning contractual liability or concerning non-contractual liability on grounds other than the defectiveness of a product,

---

manufacturer of the software because they would not have fulfilled the conditions of placing a product or component on the market".

[275] Ibid., recital 14.

[276] Ibid., recital 13.

[277] Position of the European Parliament of 12 March 2024 for the adoption of a Directive on liability for defective products (revised PLD), Article 4, point 3: "'related service' means a digital service that is integrated into, or inter-connected with, a product in such a way that its absence would prevent the product from performing one or more of its functions".

[278] Ibid., recital 17.

[279] Ibid.: "Examples of related services include the continuous supply of traffic data in a navigation system, a health monitoring service that relies on a physical product's sensors to track the user's physical activity or health metrics, a temperature control service that monitors and regulates the temperature of a smart fridge, or a voice-assistant service that allows one or more products to be controlled by using voice commands. Internet access services should not be treated as related services, since they cannot be considered as part of a product within a manufacturer's control and it would be unreasonable to make manufacturers liable for damage caused by shortcomings in internet access services. Nevertheless, a product that relies on internet access services and fails to maintain safety in the event of a loss of connectivity could be found to be defective under this Directive".

See also recital 19: "Once a product has been placed on the market, it should be considered to remain within the manufacturer's control where the manufacturer retains the ability to supply software updates or upgrades itself or via a third party".

[280] Ibid., Article 2, para. 3. See also recital 7.

[281] Ibid., Article 2, para. 4, point (a).

including national rules implementing EU legislation such as the (proposed) AI Liability Directive.[282] Also, it does not affect any rights that an injured person may have under any special liability system that existed in national laws on 30 July 1985.[283]

Furthermore, the Directive leaves intact alternative means of compensation available to individuals who have suffered harm, such as contract-based, warranty-based, or fault-based compensation at the national level.[284] Also, the revised PLD does not affect national rules on calculating compensation, which should be laid down by Member States.[285]

---

[282] Ibid., Article 2, para. 4, point (b). See also recital 9: "Under the legal systems of Member States, an injured person could have a claim for damages on the basis of contractual liability or on grounds of non-contractual liability that do not concern the manufacturer's liability for defectiveness of a product as established in this Directive. This concerns for example liability based on a warranty or on fault or strict liability of operators for damage caused by the properties of an organism resulting from genetic engineering. Such provisions, which serve to attain, inter alia, the objective of effective protection of consumers and other natural persons, should remain unaffected by this Directive".

[283] Position of the European Parliament of 12 March 2024 for the adoption of a Directive on liability for defective products (revised PLD), Article 2, para. 4, point (c).

See also recital 10: "In certain Member States, injured persons are entitled to make claims for damages caused by pharmaceutical products under a special national liability system, with the result that effective protection of natural persons in the pharmaceutical sector is already achieved. The right to make such claims should remain unaffected by this Directive. Furthermore, amendments to such special liability systems should not be precluded as long as they do not undermine the effectiveness of the system of liability provided for in this Directive or its objectives". Also, according to recital 11, "compensation schemes outside the context of liability regimes, such as national health systems, social security schemes or insurance schemes, fall outside the scope of this Directive and should therefore not be precluded. For example, some Member States have schemes in place to provide compensation in respect of pharmaceutical products that cause harm without being defective".

[284] Commission Staff Working Document, "Subsidiarity Grid – Accompanying the document Proposal for a Directive of the European Parliament and of the Council on liability for defective products, SWD(2022) 315 final, Brussels, 28.9.2022, at p. 4: "The Product Liability Directive leaves intact all other national rules concerning other types of liability, such as liability based on fault, warranty or contract".

See also: Position of the European Parliament of 12 March 2024 for the adoption of a Directive on liability for defective products (revised PLD), recitals 9 and 29: "(9) - Under the legal systems of Member States, an injured person could have a claim for damages on the basis of contractual liability or on grounds of non-contractual liability that do not concern the manufacturer's liability for defectiveness of a product as established in this Directive. This concerns for example liability based on a warranty or on fault or strict liability of operators for damage caused by the properties of an organism resulting from genetic engineering. Such provisions, which serve to attain, inter alia, the objective of effective protection of consumers and other natural persons, should remain unaffected by this Directive". ... "(29) - This Directive does not affect the various means of seeking redress at national level, whether through court proceedings, non-court solutions, alternative dispute resolution or representative actions under Directive (EU) 2020/1828 of the European Parliament and of the Council or under national collective redress schemes".

[285] Position of the European Parliament of 12 March 2024 for the adoption of a Directive on liability for defective products (revised PLD), recital 23.

9.15.3 Damage

The right to compensation under the revised PLD will apply in respect of the following types of damage. In particular, the definition of damage[286] includes (apart from death, personal injury, and destruction of property[287]) medically recognised damage to psychological health[288] as well as destruction or irreversible[289] corruption of data that are not used for professional purposes[290] (e.g. deletion of digital files from a hard drive). It is reminded that the European Parliament had proposed a threshold for the value of such data to qualify as material loss of €1,000 but this was rejected in the talks with the Council of the EU.

The right to compensation will cover all material losses resulting from damage covered by the revised PLD. It will also cover non-material losses (such as pain and suffering), in so far as they are compensable under national law. Therefore, national liability regimes are granted the option to encompass non-material losses, resulting

[286] Ibid., Article 6, para. 1: "1. The right to compensation pursuant to Article 5 shall apply in respect of only the following types of damage: (a) death or personal injury, including medically recognised damage to psychological health; (b) damage to, or destruction of, any property, except: (i) the defective product itself; (ii) a product damaged by a defective component that is integrated into, or inter-connected with, that product by the manufacturer of that product or within that manufacturer's control; (iii) property used exclusively for professional purposes; (c) destruction or corruption of data that are not used for professional purposes".

[287] Ibid., recital 22: "In line with this Directive's objective of making compensation available only to natural persons, damage to property used exclusively for professional purposes should not be compensated under this Directive". See also recital 25: "In order to protect natural persons, damage to any property owned by a natural person should be compensated. Since property is increasingly used for both private and professional purposes, it is appropriate to provide for the compensation of damage to such mixed-use property. In light of this Directive's objective of protecting natural persons, property used exclusively for professional purposes should be excluded from its scope".

[288] Ibid., recital 21: "In the interest of legal certainty, this Directive should clarify that personal injury includes medically recognised and medically certified damage to psychological health that affects the victim's general state of health and could require therapy or medical treatment, taking into account, inter alia, the International Classification of Diseases by the World Health Organization".

[289] Ibid., recital 20: "Destruction or corruption of data does not automatically result in a material loss, if the victim is able to retrieve the data at no cost, such as where a back-up of the data exists or the data can be downloaded again, or an economic operator restores or recreates temporarily unavailable data, for example in a virtual environment. Destruction or corruption of data is distinct from data leaks or breaches of data protection rules".

[290] Ibid.: "In recognition of the growing relevance and value of intangible assets, the destruction or corruption of data, such as digital files deleted from a hard drive, should also be compensated for, including the cost of recovering or restoring those data. The protection of natural persons necessitates compensation being available for material losses resulting not only from death or personal injury, such as funeral or medical expenses or lost income, and from damage to property, but also for destruction or corruption of data". See also at recital 22: "In order to address a potential risk of litigation in an excessive number of cases, the destruction or corruption of data that are used for professional purposes, even if not exclusively so, should not be compensated under this Directive".

from the damages covered by the revised PLD.[291] It is recalled that immaterial or non-material damage refers to losses (such as damage to reputation, discrimination, loss of confidentiality, psychological harm, and mental suffering) which do not relate to a person's assets, wealth or income and, as such, cannot be quantified in an objective manner by reference to a market price or value.

9.15.4 Assessment of Defectiveness

A product is deemed defective when it does not provide the safety that a person (instead of the 'public at large') is entitled to expect or that is required under EU or national law.[292] When assessing the defectiveness of a product, all circumstances should be taken into consideration, including:

[291] Position of the European Parliament of 12 March 2024 for the adoption of a Directive on liability for defective products (revised PLD), Article 6, para. 2. See also at recital 23: "compensation for non-material losses resulting from damage covered by this Directive, such as pain and suffering, should be provided in so far as such losses can be compensated for under national law".

[292] Ibid., Article 7, para. 1.

See also recital 30: "In order to protect the health and property of natural persons, the defectiveness of a product should be determined by reference not to its fitness for use but to the lack of the safety that a person is entitled to expect or that is required under Union or national law. The assessment of defectiveness should involve an objective analysis of the safety that *the public at large is entitled to expect and not refer to the safety that any particular person is entitled to expect*. [– *I assume that this inconsistency will be amended in the final text of the revised PLD.* –]. The safety that the public at large is entitled to expect should be assessed by taking into account, inter alia, the intended purpose, reasonably foreseeable use, presentation, objective characteristics and properties of the product in question, including its expected lifespan, as well as the specific requirements of the group of users for whom the product is intended". Furthermore, according to recital 30, "some products, such as life-sustaining medical devices, entail an especially high risk of causing damage to people and therefore give rise to particularly high safety expectations. In order to take such expectations into account, it should be possible for a court to find that a product is defective without establishing its actual defectiveness, where it belongs to the same production series as a product already proven to be defective".

See also Commission Staff Working Document, "Impact Assessment Report – Accompanying the document Proposal for a Directive of the European Parliament and of the Council on liability for defective products", SWD(2022) 316 final, Brussels, 28.9.2022, at p. 20, where it is stressed that the ECJ ruled that a pacemaker could be considered defective without proof of actual defect by virtue of being from the same production series as another pacemaker already proven to be defective".

(i) The presentation[293] and the characteristics of the product, including its labelling, design, technical features, composition, packaging and the instructions for its assembly, installation, use and maintenance.[294]
(ii) The reasonably foreseeable use (and misuse) of the product as well as the specific needs of the group of users for whom the product is intended.[295]
(iii) An important factor to be taken into account is the effect on the product of its capacity to continue to learn or acquire new features after it is placed on the market or put into service. This criterion extends to encompass technologies such as Artificial Intelligence based on machine learning techniques. It reflects the expectation that a product's software and underlying algorithms are designed in such a way as to prevent hazardous product behaviour. Therefore, a manufacturer that designs a product with the ability to develop unforeseen behavior should remain liable for any behaviour that leads to harm.[296]
(iv) In order to reflect the increasing prevalence of inter-connected products, the assessment of a product's safety should also take into account the reasonably foreseeable effect on the product of other products that can be expected to be used together with the product, including by means of interconnection (i.e., the potential impact of other interconnected products on the defective product). This is particularly relevant when it can be reasonably expected, at the time of its market introduction or use, that the product will be used in conjunction with other products, e.g., within a smart home system.[297]
(v) The moment in time at which the product was placed on the market or put into service or, where the manufacturer retains control over the product after that moment, the moment in time at which the product leaves the manufacturer's control (in order to reflect that in the digital age many products remain within the manufacturer's control beyond the moment at which these products are placed on the market).[298]
(vi) In order to reflect the relevance of product safety and market surveillance legislation for determining the level of safety that a person is entitled to

[293] Position of the European Parliament of 12 March 2024 for the adoption of a Directive on liability for defective products (revised PLD), recital 31: "The assessment of defectiveness should take into account the presentation of the product. However, warnings or other information provided with a product cannot be considered sufficient to make an otherwise defective product safe, since defectiveness should be determined by reference to the safety that the public at large is entitled to expect. Therefore, liability under this Directive cannot be circumvented simply by listing all conceivable side effects of a product".

[294] Ibid., Article 7(2), point (a).

[295] Ibid., Article 7(2), points (b) and (h). See also recital 31: "When determining the defectiveness of a product, reasonably foreseeable use also encompasses misuse that is not unreasonable under the circumstances, such as the foreseeable behaviour of a user of machinery resulting from a lack of concentration or the foreseeable behaviour of certain user groups such as children".

[296] Ibid., Article 7(2), point (c). See also recital 32.

[297] Ibid., Article 7(2), point (d). See also recital 32.

[298] Ibid., Article 7(2), point (e). See also recital 32.

expect, relevant product safety requirements, including safety-relevant cybersecurity requirements, must be taken into account in the assessment of defectiveness. In those cases, a product can be found to be defective on account of its cybersecurity vulnerability, e.g., if it does not fulfil safety-relevant cybersecurity requirements.[299]

(vii) Any recall of the product or any other relevant intervention by competent authorities or by economic operators themselves relating to product safety (such interventions should, however, not of themselves create a presumption of defectiveness).[300]

(viii) In the case of a product whose very purpose is to prevent damage (e.g., a warning mechanism like a smoke alarm), the assessment of such a product's defectiveness should take into account any failure of the product to fulfil that purpose.[301]

Finally, it is stated that, in order to encourage innovation, research and easy access to new technologies, a product will not be considered defective for the sole reason that a better product is already or subsequently placed on the market or put into service. Equally, the supply of updates or upgrades to a product should not in itself lead to the conclusion that a previous version of the product is defective.[302]

9.15.5 Economic Operators Liable for Defective Products

According to the revised PLD, "'economic operator' means a manufacturer of a product or component, a provider of a related service, an authorised representative, an importer, a fulfilment service provider or a distributor".[303]

Any manufacturer[304] involved in the production process should be held liable, in so far as a product or a component supplied by that manufacturer is defective.[305]

[299] Position of the European Parliament of 12 March 2024 for the adoption of a Directive on liability for defective products (revised PLD), Article 7(2), point (f). See also recitals 32 and 34.

[300] Ibid., point (g). See also recital 34.

[301] Ibid., point (i). See also recital 33.

[302] Ibid., Article 7, para. 3, and recital 35.

[303] Position of the European Parliament of 12 March 2024 for the adoption of a Directive on liability for defective products (revised PLD), Article 4, point (15).

[304] Ibid., Article 4, point (10): "'manufacturer' means any natural or legal person who: (a) develops, manufactures or produces a product; (b) has a product designed or manufactured, or who, by putting their name, trademark or other distinguishing features on that product, presents themselves as its manufacturer; or (c) develops, manufactures or produces a product for that person's own use".

[305] Ibid., Article 8, para. 1, points (a) and (b): "1. Member States shall ensure that the following economic operators are liable for damage in accordance with this Directive: (a) the manufacturer of a defective product; (b) the manufacturer of a defective component, where that component was integrated into, or inter-connected with, a product within the manufacturer's control and caused that product to be defective, and without prejudice to the liability of the manufacturer referred to in point (a). …".

This includes the persons who present themselves as the manufacturer by affixing (or authorising a third party to affix) their name, trademark or other distinguishing feature on the product, as it is implied that they are involved in the production process and/or that they assume the responsibility for it.[306]

In order to reflect (i) the increasing prevalence of inter-connected products, (ii) the effect on a product's safety of its ability to learn after it is placed on the market or put into service, (iii) the fact that many products remain within the manufacturer's control[307] beyond the moment at which they are placed on the market as well as (iv) the legitimate expectation that a product's software and algorithms are designed in such a way as to prevent hazardous product behaviour, the revised PLD clarifies that "a manufacturer that designs a product with the ability to develop unexpected behaviour should remain liable for behaviour that causes harm".[308] It also underlines that once a product has been placed on the market, it should be considered to remain within the manufacturer's control in so far as the manufacturer retains the technical ability to supply software updates or upgrades itself or through a third party.[309]

The liability of the manufacturer of a defective product will also cover any damage caused by a defective component if it was integrated into, or inter-connected with, a product within that manufacturer's control.[310] This means that manufacturers can also be liable for damage caused by a defective component if the latter was integrated into their product within their control. On the other hand, manufacturers are exempted from liability if a defective component is integrated into their product outside their control. Thus, if a manufacturer integrates a defective component from another manufacturer into a product, an individual who suffers harm should have the right to pursue compensation for the resulting damages from either the product manufacturer or the component manufacturer, or from both. However, an injured person should seek compensation from the manufacturer of the defective component

[306] Ibid., recital 36.

[307] Ibid., Article 4, point (5): "'manufacturer's control' means that: (a) the manufacturer of a product performs or, with regard to actions of a third party, authorises or consents to: (i) the integration, inter-connection or supply of a component, including software updates or upgrades; or (ii) the modification of the product, including substantial modifications; (b) the manufacturer of a product has the ability to supply software updates or upgrades itself or via a third party".

[308] Ibid., at recital 32.

[309] Position of the European Parliament of 12 March 2024 for the adoption of a Directive on liability for defective products (revised PLD), Article 4, point (5), (b). See also recital 19.

See also at recital 18: "Related services and other components, including software updates and upgrades, should be considered to be within the manufacturer's control where they are integrated into, or inter-connected with, a product, or supplied, by the manufacturer or where the manufacturer authorises or consents to their integration, inter-connection or supply by a third party, for example where the manufacturer of a smart home appliance consents to the provision by a third party of software updates for the manufacturer's appliance or where a manufacturer presents a related service or component as part of the product even though it is supplied by a third party".

[310] Ibid., Article 8, para. 1, second sub-paragraph.

in so far as the component is considered a product under the revised PLD and is integrated into a product outside the control of the product manufacturer.[311]

The Directive seeks to ensure that there will always be an EU-based business which can be held liable for damages caused by a defective product, even if the product was not bought in the EU. The scope has therefore been broadened. Indeed, consumers are increasingly buying products from manufacturers based outside the EU. When a manufacturer of a product or a component is established outside the EU, the importer[312] of the defective product or component, the authorised representative[313] of the manufacturer or, as a last resort, the fulfilment service provider[314] (a company that typically takes care of the warehousing, packaging and dispatching of a product)[315] can be held liable for damages.[316]

Distributors[317] may also be held liable under certain circumstances, i.e., only where they fail to promptly identify a relevant economic operator established in the

---

[311] Ibid., recital 36.

[312] Ibid., Article 4, point (12): "'importer' means any natural or legal person that places a product from a third country on the Union market".

[313] Ibid., Article 4, point (11): "'authorised representative' means any natural or legal person established within the Union that has received a written mandate from a manufacturer to act on that manufacturer's behalf in relation to specified tasks".

[314] Ibid., Article 4, point (13): "'fulfilment service provider' means any natural or legal person offering, in the course of commercial activity, at least two of the following services: warehousing, packaging, addressing and dispatching of a product, without having ownership of that product, excluding postal services as defined in Article 2, point (1), of Directive 97/67/EC of the European Parliament and of the Council, parcel delivery services as defined in Article 2, point (2), of Regulation (EU) 2018/644 of the European Parliament and of the Council, and any other postal services or freight transport services".

[315] Position of the European Parliament of 12 March 2024 for the adoption of a Directive on liability for defective products (revised PLD), at recital 37: "Market surveillance has shown that supply chains sometimes involve economic operators whose novel form means that they do not fit easily into traditional supply chains under the existing legal framework. Such is the case, in particular, with fulfilment service providers, which perform many of the same functions as importers but which might not always correspond to the traditional definition of importer in Union law. Fulfilment service providers play an increasingly significant role as economic operators, enabling and facilitating access to the Union market for products from third countries. That shift in relevance is already reflected in the product safety and market surveillance framework, in particular Regulations (EU) 2019/1020 and (EU) 2023/988 of the European Parliament and of the Council. Therefore, it should be possible to hold fulfilment service providers liable, but given the subsidiary nature of their role, they should be liable only where no importer or authorised representative is established in the Union".

[316] Ibid., Article 8, para. 1, point (c): "Member States shall ensure that the following economic operators are liable for damage in accordance with this Directive: ... (c) in the case of a manufacturer of a product or a component established outside the Union, and without prejudice to the liability of that manufacturer: (i) the importer of the defective product or component; (ii) the authorised representative of the manufacturer; and (iii) where there is no importer established within the Union or authorized representative, the fulfilment service provider".

[317] Ibid., Article 4, point (14): "'distributor' means any natural or legal person in the supply chain that makes a product available on the market, other than the manufacturer or importer of that product".

EU.[318] Furthermore, when online platforms[319] perform the role of manufacturer, importer, authorised representative, fulfilment service provider or distributor in respect of a defective product, they should be liable on the same terms as such economic operators. In particular, unless online platforms play a mere intermediary role in the sale of products between traders and consumers, they can be held liable for a defective product if they present the product or otherwise enable the transaction for the sale of the product in a way that would lead an average consumer to believe that the product is provided either by the online platform itself or by a trader acting under its authority or control. Therefore, provisions of the revised PLD relating to distributors should apply, mutatis mutandis, to such online platforms.[320]

In addition, in order to accommodate the realities of the circular economy (where products are designed to be more durable, reusable, repairable and upgradable), when a product is substantially modified[321] and is thereafter made available on the

[318] Ibid., Article 8, para. 3: "Member States shall ensure that, where an economic operator from among those referred to in paragraph 1 and established in the Union cannot be identified, each distributor of the defective product is liable where: (a) the injured person requests that distributor to identify an economic operator from among those referred to in paragraph 1 and established in the Union, or its own distributor that supplied it with that product; and (b) that distributor fails to identify an economic operator or its own distributor, as referred to in point (a), within one month of receiving the request referred to in point (a)".

[319] Ibid., Article 4, point (16): "'online platform' means online platform as defined in Article 3, point (i), of Regulation (EU) 2022/2065 of the European Parliament and of the Council ('Digital Services Act')", i.e.,: "'online platform' means a hosting service that, at the request of a recipient of the service, stores and disseminates information to the public, unless that activity is a minor and purely ancillary feature of another service or a minor functionality of the principal service and, for objective and technical reasons, cannot be used without that other service, and the integration of the feature or functionality into the other service is not a means to circumvent the applicability of this Regulation".

[320] Ibid., Article 8, para. 4: "Paragraph 3 of this Article shall also apply, mutatis mutandis, to any provider of an online platform that allows consumers to conclude distance contracts with traders and that is not an economic operator, provided that the conditions set out in Article 6(3) of Regulation (EU) 2022/2065 are fulfilled".

See also at recital 38: "That means that such online platforms should be liable only when they present the product or otherwise enable the specific transaction in a way that would lead an average consumer to believe that the product is provided either by the online platform itself or by a trader acting under its authority or control, and only where the online platform fails to promptly identify a relevant economic operator established in the Union".

[321] Position of the European Parliament of 12 March 2024 for the adoption of a Directive on liability for defective products (revised PLD), Article 4, point (18): 'substantial modification' means a modification of a product after it has been placed on the market or put into service: (a) that is considered substantial under relevant Union or national rules on product safety; or (b) where relevant Union or national rules on product safety lay down no threshold on what is to be considered a substantial modification, that: (i) changes the product's original performance, purpose or type, without that change being foreseen in the manufacturer's initial risk assessment; and (ii) changes the nature of the hazard, creates a new hazard or increases the level of risk".

See also at recital 39: "Whether a modification is substantial should be determined on the basis of criteria set out in relevant Union and national product safety legislation, including Regulation (EU) 2023/988. Where no such criteria are laid down in respect of the product in question,

market or put into service, it is considered to be a new product. As a result, if a product is substantially modified, outside the original manufacturer's control, and is made available on the market or put into service again, the legal or natural person that made the substantial modification should be held liable as the manufacturer of the modified product, since under relevant EU legislation that person is responsible for the product's compliance with safety requirements.[322] However, an economic operator that makes a substantial modification, other than the original manufacturer, should be able to avoid liability if it can prove that the damage is related to a part of the product not affected by the modification.[323] Therefore, liability shifts on economic actors introducing substantial modifications that make the product defective outside the manufacturer's control. On the other hand, if the substantial modifications that make the product defective are carried out by the original manufacturer or within its control, the said manufacturer will still bear responsibility (i.e., it should not be able to be exempted from liability by arguing that the defectiveness came into being after it placed the product on the market or put it into service).[324]

It should be noted that, in the transition from a linear to a circular economy, products can be designed in a manner that allows modifications to be made through changes to software and thus substantial modifications could include software updates/upgrades or the continuous learning of an AI model. Therefore, the same principles should apply (as those principles that apply to modifications made in other ways) to substantial modifications made through software updates or upgrades or due to the continuous machine learning techniques of AI systems In these cases, the substantially modified product should be considered to be made available on the market or put into service at the time the modification was actually made.[325]

Where victims fail to obtain compensation because no economic operator can be held liable under the revised PLD or because the liable economic operators are insolvent or have ceased to exist, Member States may use existing national sectoral compensation schemes or establish new ones under national law, which should preferably not be funded by public revenues (although it remains at the Member States' discretion to decide whether such compensation schemes are funded in whole or in part from public or private revenues), to appropriately compensate injured persons who suffered damage caused by defective products.[326]

---

modifications that change the original intended functions of the product or affect its compliance with applicable safety requirements or change its risk profile should be considered to be substantial modifications".

[322] Ibid., Article 8, para. 2.

[323] Ibid., at recital 39.

[324] Ibid.

[325] Ibid., at recital 40.

[326] Ibid., Article 8, para. 5. See also recital 41.

9.15.6 Disclosure of Evidence

Under the current Product Liability Directive, whereas victims claiming compensation for damage caused by a defective product do not have to prove fault (manufacturers/producers bear liability irrespective of fault), they still bear the burden of proving the damage, the defectiveness of a product and the causal link between damage and defectiveness, in accordance with the standard of proof applicable under national law.

Especially in cases involving technical or scientific complexity, however, individuals who have suffered harm often face a substantial disadvantage compared to manufacturers in terms of access to, and understanding of, information on how a product operates. In particular, they face major difficulties to investigate claims properly and to gain access to essential information. Plaintiffs need to gather specific information/evidence to be able to prove the conditions for a claim for damages, i.e., to prove the defect of a product and the causal link with the damage suffered. This asymmetry of information may compromise the fair apportionment of risk. Thus, in order to substantiate a damages claim and establish liability, it is essential to introduce rules on the disclosure of specific evidence[327] by those that have it at their disposal. In other words, it is imperative to harmonise rules on disclosure of evidence in order to facilitate the access of claimants to evidence to be used in legal proceedings.

To this end, Member States must ensure that, upon request of an injured person (victim of damage) who claims compensation in proceedings before a national court for damage caused by a defective product ('the claimant') and who has presented facts and evidence sufficient to support the plausibility of the claim for compensation, the defendant is required to disclose relevant 'necessary and proportionate' evidence that is at its disposal.[328]

Similarly, considering that defendants might also need access to evidence held by the claimant in order to counter a compensation claim under the revised PLD, defendants should also have the opportunity to access such evidence. Just as in the case of a disclosure requested by the claimant, when assessing the defendant's request for disclosure of evidence it should be ensured that such access is restricted to what is necessary and proportionate, i.e., to prevent non-specific searches for information that is not relevant to the proceedings, and to protect confidential information. Therefore, Member States must ensure that, upon request of a defendant

---

[327] Position of the European Parliament of 12 March 2024 for the adoption of a Directive on liability for defective products (revised PLD), at recital 42: "Such evidence includes documents that have to be created ex novo by the defendant by compiling or classifying the available evidence".

[328] Ibid., Article 9, paras 1 and 3. See also at recital 42: "In assessing the request for disclosure of evidence, national courts should ensure that such access is limited to that which is necessary and proportionate, inter alia to avoid non-specific searches for information that is not relevant to the proceedings, and to protect confidential information, such as information falling within the scope of legal professional privilege and trade secrets in accordance with Union and national law, in particular Directive (EU) 2016/943 of the European Parliament and of the Council".

who has presented facts and evidence sufficient to demonstrate its need for evidence for the purposes of countering a claim for compensation, the claimant is required to disclose relevant evidence (which should be limited to what is necessary and proportionate) that is at its disposal.[329]

In determining whether the disclosure requested by a party (claimant or defendant) is necessary and proportionate, national courts should consider the legitimate interests of all parties concerned, including third parties, in particular in relation to the protection of confidential information and trade secrets.[330]

Where a defendant is required to disclose information that is a trade secret or an alleged trade secret, national courts (balancing the interest of the trade-secret holder to secrecy and the interest of the injured person) should be empowered (upon a duly reasoned request of a party or on their own initiative) to take specific measures to protect the confidentiality of trade secrets during and after the legal proceedings.[331]

Taking into consideration the complexity of certain types of evidence, for example evidence relating to digital products, Member States must ensure that, where a party is required to disclose evidence, it should be possible for national courts, upon a duly reasoned request of the counterpart or where the national court deems it pertinent and in accordance with national law, to require the evidence to be presented in an easily accessible and easily understandable manner, if such presentation is deemed proportionate by the national court in terms of costs and effort for the required party.[332]

Finally, it is stated that the revised PLD harmonises rules on disclosure of evidence only in so far as such matters are regulated by it and that article 9 of the Directive does not affect national rules regarding pre-trial procedures on disclosure of evidence.[333]

---

[329] Ibid., Article 9, paras 2 and 3. See also recital 44.

[330] Ibid., Article 9, para. 4.

[331] Ibid., Article 9, para. 5. See also at recital 45: "Such measures should include at least measures to restrict access to documents containing trade secrets or alleged trade secrets and to restrict access to hearings to a limited number of people, or allowing access only to redacted documents or transcripts of hearings. When deciding on such measures, it is appropriate that national courts take into account the need to ensure the right to an effective remedy and to a fair trial, the legitimate interests of the parties and, where appropriate, of third parties, and potential harm for either of the parties to a dispute, and, where appropriate, for third parties, which results from the granting or rejection of such measures".

[332] Ibid., Article 9, para. 6. See also at recital 42.

[333] Position of the European Parliament of 12 March 2024 for the adoption of a Directive on liability for defective products (revised PLD), Article 9, para. 7: "This Article does not affect national rules relating to the pre-trial disclosure of evidence, where such rules exist". See also recital 43: "This Directive harmonises rules on disclosure of evidence only in so far as such matters are regulated by it. Matters not regulated by this Directive include rules on disclosure of evidence with regard to: pre-trial procedures; how specific a request for evidence must be; third parties; cases of declaratory actions, and sanctions for non-compliance with the obligation to disclose evidence".

9.15.7 Alleviating the Burden of Proof: Rebuttable Presumptions of Defectiveness and Causal Link

Pursuant to Article 4 of the current PLD, "the injured person shall be required to prove the damage, the defect and the(ir) causal relationship" for the manufacturer to be held liable. The revised PLD reiterates this general principle and provides the conditions under which the claimant may claim compensation: the claimant has the burden of proving the damage suffered, the defectiveness of the product and the causal link between the defectiveness and the damage.[334]

However, the revised PLD attempts to alleviate the burden of proof (especially in the case of complex products) in a harmonised way by setting conditions for defectiveness/causality to be presumed.[335] Therefore, according to the revised PLD, it is necessary to alleviate the claimant's burden of proof (who would normally/initially have to prove that the product was defective and that this caused the damage suffered), provided that certain conditions are fulfilled. In a sense, the revised PLD contains a set of rebuttable presumptions that basically shift the burden of proof to the defendant in a number of circumstances.

Presumption of the Defectiveness of the Product:
In particular, the defectiveness of the product will be presumed, and it will be on the defendant to disprove it, where any of the following conditions are met:

(i) The defendant fails to disclose relevant evidence that is at its disposal, upon request of an injured person who claims compensation in proceedings before a national court for damage caused by a defective product.[336] This works as an incentive for defendants to comply with the obligation to disclose information/evidence, since national courts will presume the defectiveness of a product where a defendant fails to comply with such an obligation.

(ii) The claimant demonstrates that the product does not comply with mandatory product safety requirements that are intended to protect against the risk of the damage suffered by the injured person.[337] Therefore, in order to strengthen the relationship between product safety rules and liability rules, non-compliance with such safety requirements will result in a presumption of defectiveness.[338]

[334] Ibid., Article 10, para. 1: "Member States shall ensure that a claimant is required to prove the defectiveness of the product, the damage suffered and the causal link between that defectiveness and that damage".

[335] Ibid., at recital 46: "Rebuttable presumptions of fact are a common mechanism for alleviating a claimant's evidential difficulties and allowing a court to base the existence of defectiveness or of a causal link on the presence of another fact that has been proven while preserving the rights of the defendant".

[336] Ibid., Article 10, para. 2, point (a). See also at recital 46.

[337] Ibid., Article 10, para. 2, point (b).

[338] Position of the European Parliament of 12 March 2024 for the adoption of a Directive on liability for defective products (revised PLD), at recital 46: "Many mandatory safety requirements have been adopted in order to protect consumers and other natural persons from the risk of harm, including

(iii) The claimant demonstrates that an obvious malfunction of the product caused the damage during reasonably foreseeable use or under ordinary circumstances.[339]

***Presumption of the Causal Link*:**
Similarly, the causal link between the defectiveness of the product and the damage will be presumed by national courts (and, therefore, the claimant should not be required to prove the causal link), where it has been established by the claimant that the product is defective and that the kind of damage that occurred is, based primarily on other similar cases, typically consistent with the defect in question.[340]

General Presumption:
The defectiveness of the product and/or the causal link between its defectiveness and the damage will also be presumed by national courts in cases where, notwithstanding the defendant's disclosure of information (in accordance with Article 9 of the revised PLD) and taking into account all relevant circumstances of the case: (i) the claimant faces excessive difficulties (proof of such difficulties are not required)[341] due to technical or scientific complexity[342] to prove the defectiveness of the product and/or

under Regulation (EU) 2023/988. . . . Non-compliance with such requirements should also result in a presumption of defectiveness. This includes cases in which a product is not equipped with the means to log information about the operation of the product as required under Union or national law".

[339] Ibid., Article 10, para. 2, point (c). See also at recital 46: "The same should apply in the case of obvious malfunction, such as a glass bottle that explodes in the course of reasonably foreseeable use, since it is unnecessarily burdensome to require a claimant to prove defectiveness when the circumstances are such that its existence is undisputed. Reasonably foreseeable use covers the use for which a product is intended in accordance with the information provided by the manufacturer or economic operator placing it on the market, the ordinary use as determined by the design and construction of the product, and use which can be reasonably foreseen where such use could result from lawful and readily predictable human behaviour".

[340] Ibid., Article 10, para. 3. See also recital 47: "Where it has been established that a product is defective and the kind of damage that occurred is, based primarily on similar cases, typically caused by the defectiveness in question, the claimant should not be required to prove the causal link and its existence should be presumed".

[341] Ibid., recital 48: "The assessment of excessive difficulties should also be made by national courts on a case-by-case basis. While a claimant should provide arguments to demonstrate excessive difficulties, proof of such difficulties should not be required. For example, in a claim concerning an AI system, the claimant should, for the court to decide that excessive difficulties exist, neither be required to explain the AI system's specific characteristics nor how those characteristics make it harder to establish the causal link".

[342] Ibid., recital 48: "Technical or scientific complexity should be determined by national courts on a case-by-case basis, taking into account various factors. Those factors should include the complex nature of the product, such as an innovative medical device; the complex nature of the technology used, such as machine learning; the complex nature of the information and data to be analysed by the claimant; and the complex nature of the causal link, such as a link between a pharmaceutical or food product and the onset of a health condition or a link that, in order to be proven, would require the claimant to explain the inner workings of an AI system".

the causal link, and (ii) the claimant demonstrates that it is *likely*[343] that the product is defective and/or that there is a causal link between the defectiveness and the damage.[344]

Right to Rebut Any of the Above Mentioned Presumptions:
It is expressly stated that the defendants retain the right to rebut/contest all elements of the claim and any of the above mentioned presumptions (including the existence of excessive difficulties and the likelihood that the product is defective or that there is a causal link between the defectiveness and the damage, or both) by submitting evidence to the contrary.[345]

9.15.8 Exemption from Liability: Defences Available to the Economic Operators

The revised PLD contains several defences that allow economic operators to escape liability. As under the current Product Liability Directive, economic operators are entitled to be exempted from liability on certain conditions for which they carry the burden of proof: "In the interest of a fair apportionment of risk, economic operators should be exempted from liability if they can prove the existence of specific exonerating circumstances".[346]

These exemptions are designed to address, *inter alia*, the dynamic nature of digital-age products, which can undergo modifications after being made available in the market. In particular, economic operators will be exempted from liability for damage caused by a defective product if they can prove any of the following:

---

[343] Therefore, the claimant is required to demonstrate only the 'likelihood' (and not the 'possibility') that the product is defective or that there is a causal link between the defectiveness and the damage, or both. As it is stated, in such cases (i.e., where it would be excessively difficult for the claimant, in particular due to the technical or scientific complexity of the case, to prove the defectiveness or the causal link, or both), "... imposing the usual standard of proof as required under national law, which often calls for a high degree of probability, would undermine the effectiveness of the right to compensation. Therefore, given that manufacturers have expert knowledge and are better informed than the injured person, and in order to maintain a fair apportionment of risk while avoiding a reversal of the burden of proof, that claimant should be required to demonstrate, where the claimant's difficulties relate to proving defectiveness, only that it is likely that the product was defective, or, where the claimant's difficulties relate to proving the causal link, only that the defectiveness of the product is a likely cause of the damage". Position of the European Parliament of 12 March 2024 for the adoption of a Directive on liability for defective products (revised PLD), at recital 48.

[344] Position of the European Parliament of 12 March 2024 for the adoption of a Directive on liability for defective products (revised PLD), Article 10, para. 4.

[345] Ibid., Article 10, para. 5. See also at recital 48.

[346] Ibid., recital 49.

(i) in the case of a manufacturer or importer, that it did not place the product on the market or put it into service (for instance, economic operators should not be liable where they can prove that a person other than themselves has caused the product to leave the manufacturing process against their will);[347]
(ii) in the case of a distributor, that it did not make the product available on the market;[348]
(iii) that it is probable that the defectiveness that caused the damage did not exist when the product was placed on the market, put into service or, in respect of a distributor, made available on the market, or that this defectiveness came into being after that moment.[349] However, exemptions from liability (i.e., the possibility for economic operators to avoid liability by proving that the defectiveness came into being after they placed the product on the market or put it into service) will not apply if the defectiveness of a product is due to any of the following, provided that it is within the manufacturer's control: a related service; software, including software updates or upgrades; a lack of software updates or upgrades necessary to maintain safety; or a substantial modification of the product.[350] Since digital technologies enable manufacturers to exercise control beyond the moment of placing the product on the market or putting into service, manufacturers/economic operators should remain liable for defectiveness that comes into being after that moment as a result of software or related services within their control, be it in the form of upgrades or updates or machine-learning algorithms or a substantial modification, or when the defectiveness of the product consists in the lack of software updates or upgrades necessary to address cybersecurity vulnerabilities and maintain the product's safety.[351]

---

[347] Ibid., Article 11(1)(a). See also recital 49.

[348] Ibid., Article 11(1)(b).

[349] Ibid., Article 11(1)(c). See also recital 50: "The moment of placing on the market or putting into service is normally the moment when a product leaves the control of the manufacturer, while for distributors it is the moment when they make the product available on the market. Manufacturers should therefore be exempted from liability where they prove that it is probable that the defectiveness that caused the damage did not exist when they placed the product on the market or put it into service or that the defectiveness came into being after that moment".

[350] Position of the European Parliament of 12 March 2024 for the adoption of a Directive on liability for defective products (revised PLD), Article 11(2).

[351] Ibid., recitals 50 and 51.

With regard to when a manufacturer is considered to exercise control, see recitals 50 and 51: "Such software or related services should be considered to be within the manufacturer's control where they are supplied by that manufacturer or where that manufacturer authorises them or otherwise consents to their supply by a third party. For example, if a smart television is presented as including a video application, but the user is required to download the application from a third party's website after the purchase of the television, the television manufacturer should remain liable, alongside the manufacturer of the video application, for damage caused by any defectiveness of the video application, even though the defectiveness came into being only after the television was placed on the market" (recital 50). . . . "The possibility for economic operators to avoid liability by proving that the defectiveness came into being after they placed the product on the market or put it

(iv) that the defectiveness that caused the damage is due to compliance of the product with legal requirements ('mandatory regulations issued by public authorities'/'regulatory compliance defence');[352]
(v) in the case of a manufacturer of a defective component, that the defectiveness of the product is attributable to the design of the product in which the component has been integrated or to the instructions given by the manufacturer of that product to the manufacturer of the component;[353]
(vi) in the case of a person that modifies a product, that the defectiveness that caused the damage is related to a part of the product not affected by the modification;[354]
(vii) that the objective/general state of scientific and technical knowledge (which is determined with reference to the most advanced level of objective knowledge accessible and not to the actual knowledge of the economic operator in question) at the time when the product was placed on the market, put into service or in the period in which the product was within the manufacturer's

---

into service should be restricted when a product's defectiveness consists in the lack of software updates or upgrades necessary to address cybersecurity vulnerabilities and maintain the safety of the product. Such vulnerabilities can affect the product in such a way that it causes damage within the meaning of this Directive. In recognition of manufacturers' responsibilities under Union law for the safety of products throughout their lifecycle, such as under Regulation (EU) 2017/745 of the European Parliament and of the Council, manufacturers should also not be exempted from liability for damage caused by their defective products when the defectiveness results from their failure to supply the software security updates or upgrades that are necessary to address those products' vulnerabilities in response to evolving cybersecurity risks. Such liability should not apply where the supply or installation of such software is beyond the manufacturer's control, for example where the owner of the product does not install an update or upgrade supplied for the purpose of ensuring or maintaining the level of safety of the product" (recital 52).

[352] Ibid., Article 11(1)(d). See also at recital 49, where it is stated that economic operators should be exempted from liability if they can prove that compliance with legal requirements was the very reason for the product's defectiveness.

According to the European Consumer Organisation (BEUC), the regulatory-compliance defence is particularly problematic and should be abolished. Consumers should not carry the risks caused by the regulatory framework; the risks should be placed on economic operators: "Because of the regulatory-compliance defence consumers cannot claim compensation if a product was defective because the manufacturer followed the relevant product rules. This in turn means that the relevant product rules inadvertently do not reflect or deliberately ignore the risk that has materialised in the damage. The regulatory-compliance defence thereby burdens consumers with the risk of gaps in the regulatory framework. Consumers have no means to protect themselves from the risks emanating from unsafe products and should therefore not be left without compensation in case of damage". The European Consumer Organisation (BEUC), "Revision of the Product Liability Directive – Time to ensure effective and comprehensive protection for consumers damaged by defective products", 01.03.2023, p. 17.

[353] Position of the European Parliament of 12 March 2024 for the adoption of a Directive on liability for defective products (revised PLD), Article 11(1)(f).

[354] Ibid., Article 11(1)(g).

> control was such that the existence of defectiveness could not be discovered.[355] Therefore, the 'development risk defence'[356] remains in the updated PLD.

It is reminded that, according to the current PLD, Member States have the flexibility to decide whether to include the development risk defence in their national law or not, leading to a lack of harmonisation across Europe. The Commission's proposal for a revised PLD sought to close this loophole and required the development risk defence to be implemented in all Member States. In other words, according to the Commission, the option to deviate from this exemption (as is the case under the current PLD) should not be maintained: the 'development risk defence' should no longer be subject to Member State derogations.[357]

However, contrary to the Commission's proposal, the final text of the revised PLD underlines that the possibility offered (under the 'development risk defence') to an economic operator to free itself from liability could be deemed by certain Member States as limiting unduly the protection of natural persons[358] and, thus, it reintroduced the option/discretion for Member States to derogate from the development risks defence.

---

[355] Ibid., Article 11(1)(e). See also recital 52.

The revised PLD – in comparison with the current PLD – offers a slight enhancement to consumer protection concerning the development risk defense. Indeed, unlike the current PLD, the revised PLD extends liability beyond the product's initial placement on the market to include the period during which the manufacturer retains control over the product. As a result, a provider of software, for instance, would remain liable as long as it can provide updates for the software. It should be reminded that, with regard to digital and AI products in particular, the 2019 Report of the Expert Group on liability and new technologies stressed that assessing the state of scientific knowledge at the moment of putting the product into circulation fails to take account of the fact that producers retain control over digital products beyond that moment and therefore have the means to tackle defects that become discoverable. This is true of many digital products, including IoT and AI-enabled products. The development risk defence should not apply for AI products that continue to learn and adapt while in operation (at p. 6). ... "The producer should be strictly liable for defects in emerging digital technologies even if said defects appear after the product was put into circulation, as long as the producer was still in control of updates to, or upgrades on, the technology. A development risk defence should not apply". See Report from the Expert Group on Liability and New Technologies – New Technologies Formation "Liability for Artificial Intelligence and Other Emerging Digital Technologies", 21 November 2019, Key Finding [14], at p. 42.

[356] According to the so-called 'development risk defence', the producer is allowed to avoid liability if the state of scientific and technical knowledge at the time when he put the product into circulation was not such as to enable the existence of the defect to be discovered [Article 7(e) of the current Product Liability Directive].

The current PLD allows Member States to derogate from applying the defence. For instance, "Finland and Luxembourg derogate entirely, while Spain, France and Hungary derogate in respect of certain categories of product". Commission Staff Working Document, "Impact Assessment Report – Accompanying the document Proposal for a Directive of the European Parliament and of the Council on liability for defective products", SWD(2022) 316 final, Brussels, 28.9.2022, p. 21.

[357] Commission's proposal for a revised Product Liability Directive, Explanatory Memorandum, p. 12.

[358] Position of the European Parliament of 12 March 2024 for the adoption of a Directive on liability for defective products (revised PLD), at recital 59.

Therefore, Member States may, by way of derogation from Article 11(1), point (e) of the revised PLD, maintain in their legal systems existing measures to the effect that economic operators are to be liable even if they prove that the objective state of scientific and technical knowledge—at the time when the product was placed on the market, put into service or in the period in which the product was within the manufacturer's control—was not such that the defectiveness could be discovered.[359] To ensure transparency and legal certainty for economic operators operating across the EU, the text of the relevant national legislation would have to be notified (no later than 24 months after entry into force of the revised PLD) to the European Commission by the Member State wishing to keep such measures that maintain existing derogations from the development risk defence in its legal system (the Commission should also inform the other Member States).[360]

Also, Member States may introduce new measures or modify existing ones in their legal systems in order to limit such a relief of responsibility, i.e., they can extend the liability of economic operators even when the state of scientific and technical knowledge at the critical time (i.e., at the time when the product was placed on the market, put into service or in the period in which the product was within the manufacturer's control) did not allow for discovering the product's defectiveness,[361] provided that those measures are limited to specific categories of products, justified by public interest objectives (such as public policy, public security and public health), and proportionate (in the sense that those measures are suitable for achieving the objectives pursued and do not go beyond what is necessary to accomplish those objectives).[362]

The use of such a derogation from the development risk defence (concerning the introduction of new measures or the amendment of existing ones) and the text of the (objectively justified and proportionate) proposed measure must be notified by the Member State to the Commission, who should then inform the other Member States.[363] In order to facilitate a coherent approach across Member States, the Commission may, within six months of receiving the notification of the text of the proposed measure, issue a non-binding opinion on the text of the proposed measure and the accompanying justification provided by the relevant Member State, following close cooperation between the Member State concerned and the Commission and after taking into account any observations received from other Member States.[364] In order to allow time for such an opinion, the Member State concerned should hold the proposed measure in abeyance for six months following its notification to the Commission, unless the Commission issues an opinion earlier.[365]

[359] Ibid., Article 18(1), first subparagraph. See also at recital 59.

[360] Ibid., Article 18(1), second subparagraph. See also at recital 59.

[361] Ibid., Article 18(2). See also at recital 59.

[362] Ibid., Article 18(3). See also at recital 59.

[363] Ibid., Article 18(4). See also at recital 59.

[364] Ibid., Article 18(5). See also at recital 44a.

[365] Ibid.

9.15.9 *Liability of Multiple Economic Operators and Right of Resource*

The revised PLD acknowledges the growing prevalence of inter-connected products (the interconnectedness of devices and their increased dependency on external input and data), since many products are designed to be influenced by other interconnected products or services (e.g. complex IoT systems). In order to reflect this new reality, the revised PLD refers to situations where two or more parties are liable for the same damage, in particular where a defective component is integrated into a product that causes damage.[366]

The revised PLD states that, without prejudice to national law concerning the right of contribution or recourse, Member States must ensure that if two or more economic operators are liable for the same damage pursuant to this Directive, they can be held liable jointly and severally (e.g., the injured person should be able to seek compensation for damages both from the manufacturer that integrated the defective component into its product and from the manufacturer of the defective component itself).[367]

In situations where more than one economic operator is liable for the same damage, the economic operator that has compensated the injured person should be entitled to pursue remedies against the other economic operators liable under Article 8 of the revised PLD, in accordance with national law (right of recourse).[368]

In recognition of the fact that innovation plays a crucial role in the software industry and in order to foster the innovative capacity of microenterprises and small enterprises that manufacture software, the revised PLD stresses that it should be possible for such enterprises to contractually agree with manufacturers that integrate their software into a product that the latter will refrain from pursuing legal action against (i.e., to agree that they will not seek recourse from) the software manufacturer in the event of a defective software component causing harm. The justification given by the revised PLD is that such contractual agreements, already used in some Member States, should be allowed, since the overall manufacturer (i.e., the manufacturer of the product as a whole) is in any event liable for any defectiveness in the

---

[366] Position of the European Parliament of 12 March 2024 for the adoption of a Directive on liability for defective products (revised PLD), at recital 36: "Where a manufacturer integrates a defective component from another manufacturer into a product, an injured person should be able to seek compensation for the same damage from the manufacturer of the product or the manufacturer of the component, or from both".

[367] Ibid., Article 12, para. 1. See also recital 53: "Situations can arise in which two or more parties are liable for the same damage, in particular where a defective component is integrated into a product that causes damage. In such a case, the injured person should be able to seek compensation both from the manufacturer that integrated the defective component into its product and from the manufacturer of the defective component itself. In order to ensure the protection of natural persons, all parties should be held liable jointly and severally in such situations".

[368] Ibid., Article 14.

product, including in components.[369] As a result, it is stated that a manufacturer that integrates a defective software component in a product should not have a right of recourse against the manufacturer of that defective software component that causes damage where: (i) the manufacturer of the defective software component was, at the time of the placing on the market of that software component, a microenterprise or a small enterprise, and (ii) the manufacturer that integrated the defective software component in the product contractually agreed with the manufacturer of the defective software component to waive that right.[370]

9.15.10 Reduction of Liability

The revised PLD stipulates that if a defective product causes damage, the contributory actions of third parties do not reduce or disallow the liability of the manufacturer, whereas the contributory negligent actions of the injured person may do so.

In particular, it is pointed out that there may be instances where the acts and omissions of persons other than a potentially liable economic operator (i.e., third persons) could contribute, in addition to the defectiveness of the product, to the cause of the damage suffered. For example, this could occur when a third party exploits a cybersecurity vulnerability of a product.[371]

In order to guarantee a high level of consumer protection, and without prejudice to national law concerning the right of contribution or recourse, Member States must ensure that, where a product is defective (e.g., due to a vulnerability that makes the product less safe than the public at large is entitled to expect), the economic operator's liability is not reduced or disallowed as a result of such acts or omissions, i.e., where the damage is caused both by the defectiveness of the product and by an act or omission of a third party.[372]

However, the revised PLD adds a contributory negligence provision according to which it should be possible to reduce or disallow the economic operator's liability where the injured person itself has negligently contributed to the cause of the damage (e.g., where the injured person negligently failed to install updates or upgrades provided by the economic operator that would have mitigated or avoided the damage), i.e., when the damage is caused both by the defectiveness of the product and by the fault of the injured person or any person for whom the injured person is responsible.[373]

---

[369] Ibid., recital 54. It is explicitly stated, however, that "liability towards an injured person should never be limited or excluded by such a contractual agreement".

[370] Ibid., Article 12, para. 2.

[371] Position of the European Parliament of 12 March 2024 for the adoption of a Directive on liability for defective products (revised PLD), recital 55.

[372] Ibid., Article 13, para. 1, and recital 55.

[373] Ibid., Article 13, para. 2, and recital 55.

9.15.11 Exclusion or Limitation of Liability

According to the revised PLD, Member States must ensure that the economic operator's liability pursuant to this Directive is not, in relation to the injured person, limited or excluded by contract.[374] Indeed, as it is stated, "the objective of protecting natural persons would be undermined if it were possible to limit or exclude an economic operator's liability through contractual provisions. Therefore no contractual derogations should be permitted".[375] For the same reason, Member States must ensure that the liability of an economic operator pursuant to this Directive should not be excluded or limited by other provisions of national law.[376] It is, therefore, not permitted to set either maximum or minimum financial ceilings for compensation on an economic operator's liability.[377]

9.15.12 Limitation Period

It is reminded that, according to the current Product Liability Directive, a limitation period of three years applies to proceedings for the recovery of damages. Therefore, the current PLD does not apply three (3) years after the injured party knew or could have become aware of the relevant facts (i.e. the damage, the defect, and the identity of the producer) (Article 10 of the current PLD). Based on the argument that the requirement to start legal proceedings within three years of becoming aware of the damage is considered to be the least significant obstacle to making claims,[378] the three year time limit for initiating proceedings has been kept unchanged under the revised PLD.

Therefore, victims of harm who miss the three (3) year deadline to start legal proceedings receive no compensation: "a limitation period of three years applies to the initiation of proceedings to claim compensation for damage falling within the scope of this Directive".[379] This limitation period runs "from the day on which the injured person became aware, or should reasonably have become aware, of" the following facts: "(a) the damage; (b) the defectiveness; (c) the identity of the relevant economic operator that can be held liable for that damage under Article 8".[380]

[374] Ibid., Article 15.

[375] Ibid., recital 56.

[376] Ibid., Article 15.

[377] Ibid., recital 56.

[378] See, for instance, Commission, DG GROW and DG JUST, "Factual summary report of the open public consultation on Adapting Civil Liability Rules to the Digital Age and AI", Ref. Ares(2022) 2620305, 06.04.2022, p. 6.

[379] Position of the European Parliament of 12 March 2024 for the adoption of a Directive on liability for defective products (revised PLD), Article 16, para. 1.

[380] Ibid.

However, the laws of Member States regulating suspension or interruption of the limitation period are not affected by the revised PLD.[381]

9.15.13 *Expiry Period*

It is also reminded that the provisions of the current Product Liability Directive do not apply ten (10) years after the date the product was put onto the market and, therefore, victims of harm that emerges after ten (10) years receive no compensation. In other words, Article 11 of the current Product Liability Directive releases the producer from liability for property damage and death/personal injury ten (10) years after the product causing the damage was put into circulation (unless the injured person has in the meantime instituted proceedings against the producer).

The revised PLD kept unchanged the 10 year time limit, i.e., a victim of harm (due to a defective product that allegedly caused damage) that emerges after ten (10) years is no longer entitled to compensation pursuant to this Directive,[382] unless the injured person has, in the meantime, initiated proceedings before a national court against an economic operator that can be held liable.[383] This expiry period starts to run from the date on which the defective product which caused the damage was placed on the market or put into service.[384] Since substantially modified products are essentially new products, this expiry period should restart (new expiry period) after a product has been substantially modified and has subsequently been made available on the market or put into service, e.g., as a result of remanufacturing.[385] It is also clarified that those software updates or upgrades that do not amount to a substantial modification of the product should not affect the expiry period that applies to the original product.[386]

By way of exemption, in order to avoid unreasonably denying the possibility of compensation for damage caused by a defective product (which violates the fundamental right of access to justice), claimants can enjoy an additional 15-year liability period in cases where the symptoms of personal injury are, according to medical evidence, slow to emerge (due to the latency of a personal injury, such as following

---

[381] Ibid., Article 16, para. 2.

[382] Ibid., Article 17, para. 1.

See also recital 57: "Given that products age over time and that higher safety standards are developed as the state of science and technology progresses, it would not be reasonable to make manufacturers liable for an unlimited period of time for the defectiveness of their products. Therefore, liability should be subject to a reasonable length of time, namely 10 years from the placing of a product on the market (the 'expiry period'), without prejudice to claims pending in legal proceedings".

[383] Ibid., Article 17, para. 1.

[384] Ibid., Article 17, para. 1, point (a).

[385] Ibid., Article 17, para. 1, point (b).

[386] Ibid., recital 58.

ingestion of a defective chemical or food product), extending this limitation time period from 15 (according to the Commission's proposal) to a total of 25 years.[387] The injured person will still be able to get compensation after this period if the proceeding against an economic operator that can be held liable was initiated within the given period.[388] It appears that defendants may face unpredictable liability risks due to this extended expiry period, the implications of which depend on how it will be applied in practice. This extension of the claim period—which is specifically targeted at latent damage in medical device and pharma claims—could create a longer liability tail for medtech companies and increase the cost and complexity of insurance coverage. Indeed, defending a claim 25 years after a product's release could be exceedingly challenging for defendants. Relevant/essential documents may have been lost, and individuals with pertinent knowledge may have since left the defending company/organisation. Additionally, the insurability of product liability risks is significantly affected.

9.15.14 Transparency—Court Database

In order to facilitate the harmonised interpretation of the revised PLD by national courts and, at the same time, to limit administrative burden, Member States are required to publish (in an easily accessible and electronic format) any judgment on product liability delivered by their national courts of appeal or of the highest instance (i.e., final judgments that cannot be, or can no longer be, appealed), so that other national courts could take these judgments into account.[389] In order to increase the understanding of how the revised PLD is applied at national level, the Commission will establish a monitoring programme by setting up and maintaining an easily accessible and publicly available database containing the aforementioned final

---

[387] Ibid., Article 17, para. 2. See also recital 57.

It is recalled that, according to the European Consumer Organisation (BEUC), the maximum limitation period for claims based on the PLD should be abolished: "The proposal to extend the maximum limitation period from 10 to 15 years for certain personal injuries was certainly inspired by the "Howald Moor" ruling of the European Court of Human Rights that found that a limitation period of 10 years violates the fundamental right of access to justice. However, latent personal injuries may occur with a greater delay than 15 years. At the same time products may also have hidden defects that only occur long after they have been placed on the market. To avoid that consumers lose their right to claim compensation even before they know that they are affected by a latent personal injury or by a hidden defect the maximum limitation period should be abolished". The European Consumer Organisation (BEUC), "Revision of the Product Liability Directive – Time to ensure effective and comprehensive protection for consumers damaged by defective products", 01.03.2023, p. 18.

[388] Position of the European Parliament of 12 March 2024 for the adoption of a Directive on liability for defective products (revised PLD), Article 17, para. 2.

[389] Ibid., Article 19, para. 1. See also recital 60.

judgements delivered by national courts as well as references to relevant judgments delivered by the Court of Justice of the EU.[390]

9.15.15 *Evaluation*

The aforementioned transparency measures will also facilitate the review/evaluation[391] to be undertaken by the Commission six years after entry into force of the revised Product Liability Directive (and every five years thereafter) and the subsequent report(s)[392] to be presented to the European Parliament, to the Council of the EU and to the European Economic and Social Committee.

9.15.16 *Entry Into Force—Repeal and Transitional Provision—Transposition*

The revised PLD will enter into force on the twentieth day following that of its publication in the Official Journal of the EU.[393] The revised PLD will apply to all

---

[390] Ibid., Article 19, para. 2. See also recital 61.

It is stressed that, according to the European Consumer Organisation (BEUC), this provision should be mandatory, i.e., that the Commission should be obliged to set up and keep up-to-date an easily accessible data base on PLD related case law: "Such an EU data base should also contain rulings of the Court of Justice of the EU. The 2018 report on the evaluation of the PLD noted that it was 'very difficult' to obtain comprehensive data on the application of the PLD in national courts [SWD(2018) 157, p. 20]. As one of the reasons, the report mentioned that only some Member States had public databases on court decisions. . . . The European Commission should be obliged to set up a public data base with EU and national case law on the application of the PLD". The European Consumer Organisation (BEUC), "Revision of the Product Liability Directive – Time to ensure effective and comprehensive protection for consumers damaged by defective products", 01.03.2023, p. 19.

[391] Position of the European Parliament of 12 March 2024 for the adoption of a Directive on liability for defective products (revised PLD), Article 20. See also recital 62: "[The] evaluation should be based on the five criteria of efficiency, effectiveness, relevance, coherence and value added and should provide the basis for impact assessments of possible further measures".

[392] Ibid., Article 20. Those reports will include information about the cost and benefits of the transposition of the revised PLD, a comparison with OECD countries and the availability of product liability insurance.

See also recital 62: "In its evaluation report, the Commission should provide the methodology for the calculation used in its evaluation. It is important that the Commission gather all relevant information in a way that avoids overregulation and an administrative burden for Member States and economic operators, using information from all relevant and reliable sources, including Union institutions, bodies, offices and agencies, national competent authorities and internationally recognised bodies and organisations".

[393] Ibid., Article 23.

products placed on the EU market or put into service twenty-four months after it enters into force.[394] Member States are required to transpose the revised PLD into national legislation two years after the Directive enters into force.[395]

The revised PLD provides for the repeal of the current PLD Directive (85/374/EEC) twenty four months from the date of entry into force of the revised PLD.[396] For reasons of legal certainty, it is necessary to provide for transitional arrangements/measures in order to ensure continued liability under the current PLD (85/374/EEC) for damage caused by defective products which have been placed on the market or put into service before that date. Therefore, the current PLD (85/374/EEC) will continue to apply with regard to products placed on the market or put into service before the date of entry into force of the revised PLD (i.e., the 'old' PLD will continue to apply to products already on the market).[397]

The agreed text of the revised Product Liability Directive, following its formal approval by the Plenary of the European Parliament on March 12, 2024 (which adopted its position at first reading), will also need to be formally endorsed by the Council of the EU (Member States).

9.16 Conclusion

The current Product Liability Directive establishes common rules at the EU level for the non-fault (strict) liability of producers for damage caused by defective products, regardless of fault or negligence. It provides an avenue for individuals (whether they are the owner or a bystander) who have suffered personal injuries, damage to consumer property, or death due to a defective product to claim financial compensation.

However, the evaluation of the Product Liability Directive concluded that the PLD had several shortcomings, such as the lack of legal clarity on how to apply the PLD's definitions to products in the digital and circular economy, difficulties related to the burden of proof in the case of complex products, and limitations on making claims. In particular, it is true that under the Product Liability Directive the burden of proof is less onerous on victims than under national fault-based liability rules, mainly because the victim does not have to prove fault. Nevertheless, proving that a product is defective (i.e. that it does not provide the level of safety a person is entitled to expect) is still (occasionally, extremely) challenging for complex products, such as AI-enabled products, even if the victim does not have to prove how the product became unsafe. The PLD evaluation found that it was difficult to apply its rules to digital technologies in general, including AI-enabled products. It also found

[394] Ibid., Article 2.

[395] Ibid., Article 22.

[396] Ibid., Article 21.

[397] Ibid.

that the rules made it difficult to prove liability in the case of complex products, including AI-enabled products, but also others such as pharmaceuticals.

In particular, the main two problems affecting the existing PLD are the following:

(a) *Certain products, economic actors and damage in the digital and circular economy escape (are not covered under) no-fault (strict) liability*. This is because the Product Liability Directive was conceived long before the digital revolution and, accordingly, is not adapted to the digital age and circular economy.
(b) *Consumers face obstacles to getting compensation*. Whereas victims do not have to prove fault (producers bear liability irrespective of fault), proving defectiveness and causal link with damage is very difficult and costly for complex products. Also, liability claims are subject to a number of restrictions (claimants face time limits and thresholds that might disproportionately restrict the number of claims).

Therefore, due to the aforementioned shortcomings affecting the current PLD, it becomes clear that enhancing legal clarity is a crucial objective of the revised PLD. The aim of the revised PLD is to modernise the current EU's product liability regime, based on the strict liability of manufacturers, for the compensation of personal injury, damage to property or data loss caused by unsafe products. The revision of the Product Liability Directive aims to achieve two primary goals in response to the above-mentioned problems. These goals are built upon the existing PLD and include: (i) maintaining the proper functioning of the internal market, as well as promoting the free movement of goods and undistorted competition amongst market players; and (ii) ensuring that consumers' health and property are still afforded a high level of protection.

Accordingly, the revised PLD is designed to accommodate the latest technological advancements, circular economy business models, and global value chains. This is achieved by ensuring the following: (i) businesses and consumers/victims are subject to fair and predictable rules; (ii) victims are adequately compensated for any harm caused by hazardous products, including digital products and AI systems; and (iii) a level playing field exists between EU and non-EU manufacturers.

To this end, the revised PLD attempts to achieve the following four specific objectives. First, in order to adapt product liability rules to the digital age and circular economy: (i) ensuring liability rules reflect the nature and risks of products in the digital age and circular economy; (ii) ensuring there is always an EU-based business that can be held liable, i.e. it is possible to obtain compensation, when defective products are bought directly from manufacturers/producers outside the EU. Second, in order to reduce disproportionate obstacles to getting compensation: (iii) easing the burden of proof in complex cases (and clarifying liability for undiscoverable defects), while ensuring fair balance between producers/manufacturers and consumers; (iv) easing restrictions on making claims as well as ensuring legal certainty by better aligning the PLD with the new legislative framework created by Decision 768/2008/EC and with product safety rules, and by codifying PLD-related case law.

Scope – Damage – Compensation:
The revised PLD extends the definition of 'product' to digital manufacturing files, software (including AI systems) and digital services that affect the functioning of the product (e.g. navigation services in autonomous vehicles) as well as to electricity and raw materials (such as gas and water)—"'product' means all movables, even if integrated into, or inter-connected with, another movable or an immovable". The revised PLD applies to products placed on the market or put into service in the course of a commercial activity, regardless of whether they are provided for payment or free of charge. Free and open-source software that is developed or supplied outside the course of a commercial activity is excluded from the scope of the revised PLD. Additionally, the revised PLD clarifies the liability rules for companies that substantially modify products before reselling them. It also ensures that consumers are compensated for defective products manufactured outside the EU.

The revised PLD broadens the definition of damage, which includes (apart from death, personal injury, and destruction of property) medically recognised damage to psychological health as well as destruction or irreversible corruption of data that are not used for professional purposes. The right to compensation will cover all material losses resulting from damage covered by the revised PLD. It will also cover non-material losses (such as pain and suffering, damage to reputation, discrimination), in so far as they are compensable under national law. Therefore, national liability regimes are granted the option to encompass non-material losses, resulting from the damages covered by the revised PLD.

***Defectiveness*:**
The Directive expands the notion of defectiveness by taking into account the effect on the product of its capacity to continue to learn or acquire new features after it is placed on the market or put into service. Also, in order to reflect the increasing prevalence of inter-connected products, the assessment of a product's defectiveness will take into account the reasonably foreseeable effect on the product of other products that can be expected to be used together with the product, including by means of interconnection (i.e., the potential impact of other interconnected products on the defective product). Furthermore, manufacturers of products will also be liable as long as they have control over the product. Indeed, software and AI models are updateable and remain in control of the manufacturer after the product is placed on the market (in the digital age many products remain within the manufacturer's control beyond the moment at which these products are placed on the market). The revised PLD also allows compensation for damage when products like robots, drones or IoT smart-home systems become unsafe by software updates, AI or digital services that are needed to operate the product, as well as in cases where manufacturers fail to address connectivity risks and cybersecurity vulnerabilities. Compliance with mandatory product safety requirements becomes a critical factor in determining defectiveness. Any product failing to meet the safety standards mandated by EU or national laws (e.g., violating relevant product safety regulations) will be deemed defective.

Alleviating the Burden of Proof:
Proving that a product was defective (burden of proof) is a key obstacle for consumers when claiming compensation. This is especially true for complex products such as connected AI-driven products. Indeed, especially in cases involving technical or scientific complexity, individuals who have suffered harm often face a substantial disadvantage compared to manufacturers in terms of access to, and understanding of, information on how a product operates. This asymmetry of information may compromise the fair apportionment of risk. As a result, the EU has decided to ease (but not to reverse) the burden of proof for consumers. Indeed, under certain circumstances, the revised PLD requires manufacturers to disclose information in cases where plausible claims for compensation are made, and alleviates the burden of proof for victims seeking compensation for damages resulting from defective products. In particular:

Alleviating the Burden of Proof—Disclosure/Discovery Requirements:
Member States must ensure that, upon request of an injured person (victim of damage) who claims compensation in proceedings before a national court for damage caused by a defective product ('the claimant') and who has presented facts and evidence sufficient to support the plausibility of the claim for compensation, the defendant is required to disclose relevant 'necessary and proportionate' evidence that is at its disposal. At least, these disclosure/discovery requirements are reciprocal and, therefore, considering that defendants might also need access to evidence held by the claimant to counter a compensation claim under the revised PLD, defendants will have the opportunity to access such evidence as well. These new disclosure requirements are expected to be particularly challenging for defendants, especially in Member States that lack robust disclosure practices or have limited or non-existent disclosure mechanisms under their national laws.

Alleviating the Burden of Proof—Rebuttable Presumptions of Defectiveness of the Product and Causal Link:
The revised PLD alleviates the claimant's burden of proof (who would normally/initially have to prove that the product was defective and that this caused the damage suffered) in a harmonised way by setting conditions for defectiveness/causality to be presumed. In a sense, the revised PLD contains a set of rebuttable presumptions that basically shift the burden of proof to the defendant in a number of circumstances.

In particular, the defectiveness of the product will be presumed *(presumption of the defectiveness of the product)*, and it will be on the defendant to disprove it, where any of the following conditions are met: (i) the defendant fails to comply with its disclosure obligations, i.e., the defendant fails to disclose relevant evidence that is at its disposal, upon request of an injured person who claims compensation in proceedings before a national court for damage caused by a defective product); (ii) the claimant demonstrates that the product does not comply with mandatory product safety requirements intended to protect against the risk of the damage suffered by the injured person; (iii) the claimant demonstrates that an 'obvious malfunction' of the product caused the damage during 'reasonably foreseeable use' or under 'ordinary circumstances'.

Similarly, the causal link between the defectiveness of the product and the damage will be presumed (*presumption of the causal link)* by national courts (and, therefore, the claimant should not be required to prove the causal link), where it has been established by the claimant that the product is defective and that the kind of damage that occurred is, based primarily on other similar cases, 'typically consistent' with the defect in question.

Furthermore, the defectiveness of the product and/or the causal link between its defectiveness and the damage will also be presumed (*general presumption)* by national courts in cases where, notwithstanding the defendant's disclosure of information and taking into account all relevant circumstances of the case: (i) the claimant faces 'excessive difficulties' (proof of such difficulties are not required), in particular, 'due to technical or scientific complexity' to prove the defectiveness of the product and/or the causal link; and (ii) the claimant demonstrates that it is *likely* that the product is defective or/and that there is a causal link between the defectiveness and the damage.

Right to Rebut Any of the Above Mentioned Presumptions:
It is expressly stated that the defendants retain the right to rebut/contest all elements of the claim and any of the above mentioned presumptions (including the existence of excessive difficulties and the likelihood that the product is defective or that there is a causal link between the defectiveness and the damage, or both) by submitting evidence to the contrary.

The Development Risk Defence:
The revised PLD contains several defences that allow economic operators to escape liability. In particular, economic operators will be exempted from liability for damage caused by a defective product if they can prove, amongst others, that the objective/general state of scientific and technical knowledge at the time when the product was placed on the market, put into service or in the period in which the product was within the manufacturer's control was such that the existence of defectiveness could not be discovered. Therefore, the 'development risk defence' remains in the updated PLD.

However, contrary to the Commission's proposal (where the 'development risk defence' should no longer be subject to Member State derogations), the final text of the revised PLD underlined that the possibility offered (under the 'development risk defence') to an economic operator to free itself from liability could be deemed by certain Member States as limiting unduly the protection of natural persons and, thus, it reintroduced the option/discretion for Member States to derogate from the development risks defence. Therefore, Member States may maintain in their legal systems existing measures to the effect that economic operators are to be liable even if they prove that the objective state of scientific and technical knowledge—at the time when the product was placed on the market, put into service or in the period in which the product was within the manufacturer's control—was not such that the defectiveness could be discovered. Also, Member States may introduce new measures or modify existing ones in their legal systems in order to limit such a relief of responsibility, i.e., they can extend the liability of economic operators even when the state of scientific and technical knowledge at the critical time did not allow for discovering the product's defectiveness, provided that those measures are limited to specific categories of products, justified by public interest objectives, and proportionate.

Removal of Minimum Thresholds and Maximum Limits:
Unlike the current version of the PLD, the revised Product Liability Directive does not contain any lower/minimum or upper/maximum liability limits for compensation claims. In particular, it removes the threshold of € 500 (under Article 9(b) of the current PLD, consumers may only seek compensation for damage to property if the worth of the damage surpasses an amount of € 500) and the possibility for Member States to impose a financial ceiling of €70 million (under Article 16(1) of the current PLD, Member States are allowed to introduce upper limits of at least €70m for product liability claims). It is noted that, according to consumer organisations and NGOs, the €500 threshold unduly restricts the number of cases for which consumers can claim compensation and, as a result, it contributed to impairing consumers' access to justice, limiting their compensation, decreasing the efficiency of the liability system, and creating inequality in access to non-material compensation, particularly for the least wealthy citizens of the EU.[398] It is also reminded that the

[398] With regard to consumer organisations and NGOs, see for instance the following responses:

Response submitted by BEUC (the European Consumer Organisation) to the European Commission's public consultation on Civil liability – adapting liability rules to the digital age and artificial intelligence, 23.12.2021, at p. 8: "the 500€ threshold is arbitrary and in practice has been impairing access to justice for consumers in too many cases. As the European Commission already noted in its 2018 report, 'in four out of five cases, a compensation is not claimed as the damage is below the threshold'. It is essential that all consumers have access to compensation regardless of the value and the type of their harm".

See also the response of BEUC (the European Consumer Organisation), "Product Liability 2.0 - How to make EU rules fit for consumers in the digital age", submitted on 07.05.2020: "Consumers have long indicated that the €500 threshold unduly restrains the number of cases for which consumers can claim compensation. First, the threshold was initially adopted to avoid a flood of small cases against producers. However, in practice, this concern has been more hypothetical than real. Conversely, this threshold has contributed to impairing consumers' access to justice and limiting their compensation. As the Commission noted in 2018, "according to the information obtained, in four out of five cases a compensation is not claimed as the damage is below the threshold". Second, the threshold has given rise to diverging national interpretations. In some Member States, the threshold is regarded as a deductible (i.e. the amount of damages awarded to the claimant is reduced by this amount in case of success) while in others this amount is a minimum, below which no damages can be recovered. Consumers may therefore suffer from different levels of protection across the EU, which is not acceptable from a Single Market perspective. Third, should a loss or destruction of data eventually be regarded as a compensable harm, quantifying such a loss may lead to different results in Member States. For example, some Member States may take the view that a loss of data is below the threshold. This would create the risk of unequal treatment between consumers. Fourth, there is a contradiction between, on the one hand, current EU efforts to facilitate law enforcement and compensation for small-value claims (see for example the proposal for a Directive on representative actions for consumers) and, on the other hand, the €500 threshold, which precisely hinders such claims from being brought" (at pp. 15–16). ... "BEUC recommendations: ... The €500 threshold should be removed" (at p. 16).

2018 PLD evaluation found that the EUR 500 threshold overly limited claims for property damage, undermining the effectiveness of the PLD in protecting consumer property.[399] On the other hand, it was argued that the implications of these changes,

---

Furthermore, see The Future of Life Institute (FLI), "Comments on the Commission's Inception Impact Assessment on 'Civil liability – adapting liability rules to the digital age and artificial intelligence'", submitted on 28 July 2021: "we support easing the conditions for making liability claims (option 2.1.d.). We believe there are multiple reasons to lower the 500 euros threshold. Some of the non-material damages caused by digital products can be hard to quantify (e.g. data loss, environmental damage). In addition, a defective AI system could impose a small loss to all the individuals subject to its use, which would amount to a large loss for society at large" (at p. 4).

See also the contribution by The Future Society (TFS), "Liability rules for Trust in Excellence & Excellence in Trust - Inception Impact Assessment - Adapting liability rules to the digital age and circular economy", Belgium, 28 July 2021: "while material compensation is often assumed to be the primary driver, consumers also value non-material compensation such as the peace of mind associated with justice and fairness, whether at the individual level or in society at large. Focusing solely on a financial threshold to determine whether to pursue a case assumes a narrow view of society - especially if non-material damages are likely to occur. While the time limit can be justified by the fact that case-relevant information or evidence degrades over time and increases the cost of efficient adjudication, the financial threshold seems arbitrary. Even if focusing on quantifiable material damages out of practicality, it is unclear why a threshold would be needed at all: given the costs in time and energy to the consumers, a presumably injured consumer anyway has to decide for himself whether it is worthwhile to take action. That consumer surely knows best whether the damages suffered justify taking action, without having to quantify them financially and officially - and the consumer can even factor in non-material factors much more efficiently. The threshold therefore only adds burdensome quantification and fees to an already complex procedure to obtain fair compensation for damages due to defects. This extra step reduces the efficiency of the liability system and introduces inequality in access to non-material compensation such as justice - especially for the least wealthy citizens of the EU for whom <500€ is a significant share of yearly income. While we are concerned about frivolous civil liability claims or, in the longer term, a form of "trolling" (in a way similar to Intellectual Property trolls), we do not think the threshold prevents such behaviors and another, more nuanced legal test will very probably be more appropriate if these abuses do start to occur. Therefore, we would recommend withdrawing the financial threshold for damage to property" (at pp. 6–7).

399 See Commission Staff Working Document, 'Evaluation of Product Liability Directive', SWD (2018) 157 final, Brussels, 07.05.2018, at p. 25, para. 5.1.1.1.: "… concerning material damages, the effectiveness of the condition on the EUR 500 threshold seems to be questionable: Firstly, there are concerns as regards its national interpretation. Some Member States transposed Article 9 of the Directive interpreting the EUR 500 threshold as a threshold which, when reached, would allow for pursuing compensation for the entirety of the damage suffered, whereas others (e.g. France, Germany, Netherland and Spain) transposed it as a deductible, i.e. as a sum to be deducted from the compensation owed without regard to the scale of the damage. This divergence in the interpretation may create a different degree of protection of the injured party across Member States. Secondly, according to the information obtained, in four out of five cases a compensation is not claimed as the damage is below the threshold. This could explain why this is rarely cited as a reason for rejecting a claim in court and why most cases relate to physical well-being. Therefore, despite the fact that the Directive seems to be effective and particularly for damages to well-being, the EUR 500 threshold represent, according to consumer representatives, an obstacle for the full effectiveness of the Directive to cover claims for compensation in many cases of material damage since claims for lower material damages cannot be introduced". See also, at pp. 4 and 31: "consumer organisations asked for more protection at a lower cost, which would imply removing the threshold of EUR 500" (at p. 4, para. 1.2.). … "consumers believe that the Directive is not always effective in

i.e., the removal of minimum thresholds and maximum limits for compensation claims, especially when paired with the EU's new class actions mechanism,[400] include an elevated risk of mass product liability claims. Any relaxation on the threshold for property damages could lead to more claims for minor damages, thus contradicting one of the main purposes of the threshold, namely to avoid litigation for small claims.[401]

---

protecting consumers mainly because ... the EUR 500 threshold aims to avoiding litigation for small claims" (at p. 31, para. 5.1.2.).

See also Commission Report on the Application of the Product Liability Directive, COM(2018) 246 final, Brussels, 07.05.2018, at p. 6, para. 5.1.

In the course of the 2021–2022 consultation, 55% of all respondents argued that the EUR 500 threshold for damage to property creates obstacles to consumers making compensation claims. Out of this 55%, 89% were consumer organisations and NGOs (i.e., non-business respondents), asking for more protection at a lower cost. See Commission, DG GROW and DG JUST, "Factual summary report of the open public consultation on Adapting Civil Liability Rules to the Digital Age and AI", Ref. Ares(2022)2620305, 06.04.2022, p. 6.

[400] Directive (EU) 2020/1828 of the European Parliament and of the Council of 25 November 2020 on representative actions for the protection of the collective interests of consumers and repealing Directive 2009/22/EC, OJ L 409, 4.12.2020, pp. 1–27 ('The Representative Actions Directive').

The Representative Actions Directive sets out rules to ensure that a representative action mechanism for the protection of the collective interests of consumers is available in all Member States. Therefore, Member States are required to have in place a mechanism allowing consumers to bring class actions relating to various EU law infringements, covering a broad range of areas including telecommunications, energy, financial services, travel and tourism, data protection and product liability. Member States must ensure that representative actions can be brought by qualified entities designated by the Member States for this purpose. Also, Member States must ensure that entities, in particular consumer organisations (including consumer organisations that represent members from more than one Member State), are eligible to be designated as qualified entities for the purpose of bringing domestic representative actions, cross-border representative actions, or both. It is expected that the establishment of this common legal framework will drive a significant increase in the number of class actions launched in the EU.

[401] Commission Staff Working Document, 'Evaluation of Product Liability Directive', SWD(2018) 157 final, Brussels, 07.05.2018, at p. 4, para. 1.2.: "On the side of the producers and insurers, however, the arguments raised focused on the risk that any relaxation of the rules on the burden of proof or on the threshold for property damages would lead to more claims for minor damages".

See also Commission, DG GROW and DG JUST, "Factual summary report of the open public consultation on Adapting Civil Liability Rules to the Digital Age and AI", Ref. Ares(2022) 2620305, 06.04.2022, p. 6.

For comments supporting this option, see for instance:

Google's views on the European Commission's inception impact assessment on civil liability - adapting liability rules to the digital age and AI, 28.07.2021: "Changing the conditions under which claims can be made under the [Product Liability] directive is unnecessary and carries substantial risks. The rationale for a minimum damage threshold in the Directive was to avoid overburdening the courts with frivolous litigation. This risk is arguably greater for software-related claims, given that a defect in a single line of code (out of millions) that was used in millions of devices could (under this proposal) be the basis for a strict liability claim from each individual user. It is also unnecessary, since nothing would prevent consumers from bringing actions in the national courts for lower value claims, they just cannot rely on strict liability under the Directive when doing so" (at pp. 4–5).

Expiry Period—Extension of Longstop in Cases of Latent Harm:
The revised PLD kept unchanged the 10 year time limit, i.e., a victim of harm (due to a defective product that allegedly caused damage) that emerges after ten (10) years is no longer entitled to compensation pursuant to the Directive, unless the injured person has, in the meantime, initiated proceedings before a national court against an economic operator that can be held liable. By way of exemption, in order to avoid unreasonably denying the possibility of compensation for damage caused by a defective product (which violates the fundamental right of access to justice), claimants can enjoy an additional 15-year liability period in cases where the symptoms of personal injury are, according to medical evidence, slow to emerge (due to the latency of a personal injury, such as following ingestion of a defective chemical or food product), extending this limitation time period from 15 (according to the Commission's proposal) to a total of 25 years. Defendants may face unpredictable liability risks due to this extended expiry period, which is specifically targeted at latent damage in medical device and pharma claims.

Based on the above, it is fair to say that the new EU product liability regime becomes more claimant/consumer-friendly (pro-claimant). The revised PLD raises the likelihood of manufacturers and other economic operators (e.g., importers) operating within the EU facing considerable litigation risks (including the heightened risk of third-party litigation funding), abusive discovery of evidence, and overall higher insurance costs. For instance, the easing of the disclosure of evidence obligation (i.e., access to relevant evidence at the disposal of the manufacturer) and the alleviation/lightening of the burden of proof could lead to frivolous and/or fraudulent claims and put businesses at an unnecessary disadvantage, causing disproportionate harm for businesses, especially SMEs that do not have the required resources to defend themselves through prolonged court proceedings. Also, insurance costs are likely to rise imminently for software. It is also reminded that, apart from the presumption of defectiveness of a product and/or causality with the alleged damage and the introduction of new disclosure obligations (new requirements for discovery), the longstop limitation period is extended significantly for latent harm cases. Furthermore, the removal of minimum thresholds and maximum limits for

---

Response of the App Association (ACT) to the European Commission's inception impact assessment on civil liability - Adapting liability rules to the digital age and circular economy, 28.07.2021: "As for the impact on fundamental rights, we stress again that lightening the burden of proof and lowering the €500 threshold could lead to frivolous claims and put businesses at an unnecessary disadvantage" (at p. 6).

Bitkom Bundesverband Informationswirtschaft, Telekommunikation und neue Medien e.V. (Federal Association for Information Technology, Telecommunications and New Media), "Position Paper - Inception Impact Assessment: Adapting liability rules to the digital age and artificial intelligence", 27.07.2021: "The minimum threshold for making claims for damage of property under the Product Liability Directive should remain at EUR 500 in order to avoid litigation in an excessive number of cases, as stated in Recital 9 of the Product Liability Directive. In accordance with the applicable fault-based law, an injured party can always pursue any claim for lesser damages under the applicable fault-based law, so that there is no gap in legal protection" (at p. 6).

compensation claims, especially when combined with the EU's new class actions mechanism, could lead to more claims for minor damages. In addition, there is a risk that claimants and "potential claimants" could be encouraged to bring early-stage cases (lawsuits) simply with the ulterior motive of seeking access to proprietary information ('fishing expeditions'). As a result, we might see an increased volume of legal claims, leading to higher insurance costs, hindering innovation, and putting smaller companies at risk.

Therefore, the evidentiary framework undergoes significant transformation. It remains to be seen how the rather ambiguous alleviation of the plaintiff's burden of proof "in complex cases" and the defendant's obligation to disclose "relevant evidence" will be implemented by the Member States (especially since many EU countries currently have limited or non-existent disclosure mechanisms under their national laws). The interpretation and scope of several new provisions within the revised PLD are unclear, underscoring the importance of monitoring their adoption and implementation by Member States and subsequent scrutiny by national courts.

Thus, it could be argued that while the revised Product Liability Directive strengthens the EU product liability regime for consumers, it concurrently reduces legal certainty for businesses. Concerns regarding heightened litigation risks may ultimately deter the development and availability of innovative products in the EU. This could also result in significant financial burdens, including increased insurance premiums and settlement costs, being transferred to businesses operating within the EU, ultimately impacting consumers.

The revised PLD appears poised to tip the scales further in favor of claimants, especially in complex cases. This new, more claimant-oriented product liability regime has the potential to substantially reshape the business risk environment within the EU, representing a major shift in the European product liability risk landscape.

Overall, however, I believe that the revised PLD succeeds in striking a delicate balance between protecting citizens/consumers and supporting technological innovation. This is achieved by establishing an EU product liability framework that does not discourage businesses from bringing AI-enabled and other innovative products to market. In practice, the legal framework becomes much more demanding for the industry, but without becoming excessively burdensome—businesses are subject to fair and predictable rules. After all, the requirements mainly concern obligations related to product safety. Therefore, the new legal framework appears to "reward" companies that are willing to invest in even safer products for consumers. Thus, without overlooking the fact that the scope of several new provisions within the revised PLD are unclear and we must await their implementation by Member States and interpretation by national courts decisions, the revised PLD provides legal certainty to the industry regarding the risks they may encounter in the course of their business. This is achieved, *inter alia*, by increasing the emphasis on defendants to ensure full compliance with mandatory product safety requirements and to have appropriate documentation and internal procedures in place. At the same time, the revised PLD ensures that liability rules reflect the nature and risks of products in the digital age and circular economy, reduces disproportionate obstacles to obtaining compensation, ensures that consumers' health and property are afforded a high level of protection, instills confidence in the safety and reliability of AI-related products and services, and maintains an appropriate balance between the interests of claimants and defendants in Member State courts.

Legal/Policy Documents, Reports, and Other Sources

Council Directive 85/374/EEC of 25 July 1985 on the approximation of the laws, regulations and administrative provisions of the Member States concerning liability for defective products, as modified by Directive 1999/34/EC of the European Parliament and of the Council of 10 May 1999 (OJ L 210/29, 7.8.1985, and OJ L 141/20, 4.6.1999) [the Product Liability Directive].

Commission Communication, "Report from the Commission on the Application of the Council Directive on the approximation of the laws, regulations, and administrative provisions of the Member States concerning liability for defective products (85/374/EEC) -{SWD(2018) 157 final} - {SWD(2018) 158 final}, COM(2018) 246 final, Brussels, 7.5.2018 ['Commission Report on the Application of the Product Liability Directive, COM(2018) 246 final, Brussels, 07.05.2018'].

Commission Staff Working Document, "Evaluation of Council Directive 85/374/EEC of 25 July 1985 on the approximation of the laws, regulations and administrative provisions of the Member States concerning liability for defective products – Accompanying the document Report from the Commission to the European Parliament, the Council and the European Economic and Social Committee on the Application of the Council Directive on the approximation of the laws, regulations, and administrative provisions of the Member States concerning liability for defective products (85/374/EEC) {COM(2018) 246 final} - {SWD (2018) 158 final}", SWD(2018) 157 final, Brussels, 7.5.2018. ['Commission Staff Working Document, 'Evaluation of Product Liability Directive', SWD (2018) 157 final, Brussels, 07.05.2018].

Proposal for a Directive of the European Parliament and of the Council on liability for defective products, European Commission, COM(2022) 495 final, Brussels, 28.9.2022 (the 'proposal for a revised Product Liability Directive (PLD)').

Commission Staff Working Document, "Subsidiarity Grid – Accompanying the document Proposal for a Directive of the European Parliament and of the Council on liability for defective products, SWD(2022) 315 final, Brussels, 28.9.2022.

Commission Staff Working Document, "Impact Assessment Report – Accompanying the document Proposal for a Directive of the European Parliament and of the Council on liability for defective products", SWD(2022) 316 final, Brussels, 28.9.2022.

Commission Staff Working Document, "Executive Summary of the Impact Assessment Report – Accompanying the document Proposal for a Directive of the

European Parliament and of the Council on liability for defective products", SWD (2022) 317 final, Brussels, 28.9.2022.

Proposal for a Directive of the European Parliament and of the Council on adapting non-contractual civil liability rules to artificial intelligence (AI Liability Directive), European Commission, COM (2022) 496 final, Brussels, 28.9.2022 (the 'proposed AI Liability Directive').

Commission Staff Working Document, "Impact Assessment Report – Accompanying the document Proposal for a Directive of the European Parliament and of the Council on adapting non-contractual civil liability rules to artificial intelligence", SWD(2022) 319 final, Brussels, 28.9.2022.

Council of the European Union, Note: From: General Secretariat of the Council. To: Delegations. Subject: Proposal for a Directive of the European Parliament and of the Council on liability for defective products - Mandate for negotiations with the European Parliament, Brussels, 15 June 2023, Council doc. 10694/23 ("General Secretariat of the Council - General approach on the proposal for a revised PLD, 15 June 2023").

Draft Report of the European Parliament's Committee on Internal Market and Consumer Protection and the Committee on Legal Affairs on the proposal for a directive of the European Parliament and of the Council on Liability for defective products (COM(2022)0495 – C9-0322/2022 – 2022/0302(COD)), 05.04.2023, ("Draft Joint Report of the European Parliament's co-leading IMCO and JURI Committees on the proposal for a revised PLD, 5 April 2023").

Commission Communication "Report on the safety and liability implications of Artificial Intelligence, the Internet of Things and robotics", COM (2020) 64 final, Brussels, 19.2.2020.

Commission Communication "White Paper On Artificial Intelligence - A European approach to excellence and trust", COM (2020) 65 final, Brussels, 19.2.2020.

European Parliament Resolution of 20 October 2020 with recommendations to the Commission on a civil liability regime for artificial intelligence (2020/2014 (INL)) P9_TA(2020)0276 ('European Parliament's Resolution of 20 October 2020 on a civil liability regime for AI').

Annex to the European Parliament Resolution of 20 October 2020 with recommendations to the Commission on a civil liability regime for artificial intelligence: detailed recommendations for drawing up a Regulation on liability for the operation of artificial intelligence systems, A. Principles and Aims of the Proposal. B. Text of the Proposal Requested—Proposal for a Regulation on liability for the operation of Artificial Intelligence-systems ('Annex to the European Parliament's Resolution of 20 October 2020 on a civil liability regime for AI').

Report from the Expert Group on Liability and New Technologies – New Technologies Formation "Liability for Artificial Intelligence and Other Emerging Digital Technologies", 21 November 2019.

European Union Agency for Cybersecurity (ENISA) – ENISA Threat Landscape (ETL) Report, ninth edition, 2021.

Commission's Inception Impact Assessment "Adapting liability rules to the digital age and circular economy", Ref. Ares(2021)4266516, 30.06.2021.

Commission, DG GROW and DG JUST, "Factual summary report of the open public consultation on Adapting Civil Liability Rules to the Digital Age and AI", Ref. Ares(2022)2620305, 06.04.2022.

Directive 2014/104/EU of the European Parliament and of the Council of 26 November 2014 on certain rules governing actions for damages under national law for infringements of the competition law provisions of the Member States and of the European Union (the 'Damages Directive'), OJ L 349, 5.12.2014, pp. 1–19.

Draft Report of the European Parliament's Committee on Internal Market and Consumer Protection and the Committee on Legal Affairs on the proposal for a directive of the European Parliament and of the Council on Liability for defective products (COM(2022)0495 – C9-0322/2022 – 2022/0302(COD)), 05.04.2023, ("Draft Joint Report of the European Parliament's co-leading IMCO and JURI Committees on the proposal for a revised PLD, 5 April 2023").

Joint Report of the European Parliament's co-leading IMCO and JURI Committees on the proposal for a directive of the European Parliament and of the Council on liability for defective products, A9-0291/2023, 12 October 2023.

European Parliament, Press Release (IMCO-JURI), "Better protection for consumers against damages by defective products", 09.10.2023.

European Parliament, Press Release, "Deal to better protect consumers from damages caused by defective products", 14.12.2023.

Council of the EU, Press Release, "Agreement between the Council and the European Parliament makes EU liability rules fit for the digital age and circular economy", 14.12.2023.

Council of the European Union, Information Note: From: General Secretariat of the Council. To: Delegations. Subject: Proposal for a Directive of the European Parliament and of the Council on liability for defective products – Letter sent to the European Parliament, Brussels, 24 January 2024, Council doc. 5809/24 ("General Secretariat of the Council – Proposal for a Directive on liability for defective products – Letter sent to the European Parliament, Council doc. 5809/24, 24 January 2024").

European Parliament, Committee on the Internal Market and Consumer Protection (IMCO) and Committee on Legal Affairs (JURI), "Provisional Agreement Resulting from Interinstitutional Negotiations", Subject: Proposal for a Directive of the European Parliament and of the Council on Liability for defective products (COM(2022)0495 – C9 0322/2022 – 2022/0302(COD)), 31 January 2024.

European Parliament legislative resolution of 12 March 2024 on the proposal for a Directive of the European Parliament and of the Council on liability for defective products (COM(2022)0495 – C9-0322/2022 – 2022/0302(COD)), (Ordinary legislative procedure: first reading) – P9_TC1-COD(2022)0302, Position of the European Parliament adopted at first reading on 12 March 2024 with a view to the adoption of Directive (EU) 2024/... of the European Parliament and of the Council on liability for defective products and repealing Council Directive

85/374/EEC ["Position of the European Parliament of 12 March 2024 for the adoption of a Directive on liability for defective products (revised PLD)"].
CORRIGENDUM to the position of the European Parliament adopted at first reading on 12 March 2024 with a view to the adoption of Directive (EU) 2024/ ... of the European Parliament and of the Council on liability for defective products and repealing Council Directive 85/374/EEC, European Parliament, Plenary sitting, 18 July 2024 ["CORRIGENDUM to the position of the European Parliament for a Directive on liability for defective products, 18 July 2024"].
EURACTIV, "MEPs start to scratch the surface of new product liability rules", by Luca Bertuzzi, 06.06.2023.
European Parliament, Press Release, 'Defective products: revamped rules to better protect consumers from damages', 12 March 2024.

Responses by Organisations, Associations and Corporations to Public Consultations

BEUC (The European Consumer Organisation), "Revision of the Product Liability Directive – Time to ensure effective and comprehensive protection for consumers damaged by defective products", 01.03.2023.
BEUC (the European Consumer Organisation), "Comments to the European Commission's public consultation on Civil liability – adapting liability rules to the digital age and artificial intelligence", 23.12.2021.
BEUC (the European Consumer Organisation), "Product Liability 2.0 - How to make EU rules fit for consumers in the digital age", submitted on 07.05.2020.
Irish Council for Civil Liberties (ICCL), "New liability rules on product and AI are encouraging but need improvement", 4 October 2022.
Irish Council for Civil Liberties (ICCL) ("ICCL - Submission to the consultation on adapting liability rules to the digital age and artificial intelligence", 7 January 2022.
The Future of Life Institute (FLI), "Comments on the Commission's Inception Impact Assessment on 'Civil liability – adapting liability rules to the digital age and artificial intelligence'", submitted on 28 July 2021.
The Future Society (TFS), "Liability rules for Trust in Excellence & Excellence in Trust - Inception Impact Assessment - Adapting liability rules to the digital age and circular economy", Belgium, 28 July 2021.
The American Chamber of Commerce to the European Union (AmCham EU), "Our Position – Feedback on Product Liability Directive proposal", 11 December 2022.
BusinessEurope, "Comments – Adapting liability rules to the digital age and Artificial Intelligence", 10.01.2022.
Eurosmart, "Eurosmart on the Product Liability Directive", 12.01.2022.

Confederation of European Security Services (CoESS) – "Position Paper on the European Commission Consultation on adapting liability rules to the digital age and AI", 20 December 2021.

App Association (ACT), Response to the European Commission's inception impact assessment on civil liability - Adapting liability rules to the digital age and circular economy, 28.07.2021.

Google, Response to the European Commission's inception impact assessment on civil liability - adapting liability rules to the digital age and AI, 28.07.2021.

Google, "Response to the new Product Liability Directive consultation", 9 December 2022.

Bitkom Bundesverband Informationswirtschaft, Telekommunikation und neue Medien e.V. (Federal Association for Information Technology, Telecommunications and New Media), "Position Paper - Inception Impact Assessment: Adapting liability rules to the digital age and artificial intelligence", 27.07.2021.

Computer & Communications Industry Association (CCIA Europe), "Making EU product liability rules fit for the digital age – Position Paper on the Revision of the Product Liability Directive", December 2022.

BSA – The Software Alliance, "Recommendations on the Draft EU Product Liability Directive", March 2023.

Developers Alliance, "Position on the European Commission's proposal for a Directive on liability for defective products", 14 December 2022.

DigitalEurope, "Creating a proportionate Product Liability Directive", 3 March 2023.

Information Technology Industry Council (ITI), "Comments to the Revision of the Product Liability Directive (PLD): Ensuring a Proportionate Framework for all Actors", December 2022.

ACEA (The European Automobile Manufacturers' Association) response to the European Commission's inception impact assessment on civil liability - Adapting liability rules to the digital age and circular economy, 28.07.2021.

References

Adams-Prassl J (2019) What if your boss was an algorithm? The rise of artificial intelligence at work. Comp Labor Law Policy J 41(1):123

Akhtar N, Mian A (2018) Threat of adversarial attacks on deep learning in computer vision: a survey. IEEE Access 6:14410

Bathaee Y (2018) The artificial intelligence black box and the failure of intent and causation. Harv J Law Technol 31(2):889–938

Beck S (2016) The problem of ascribing legal responsibility in the case of robotics. AI Soc 31(4): 473–481

Beckers A, Teubner G (2021) Three liability regimes for artificial intelligence: algorithmic actants, hybrids, crowds. Bloomsbury Publishing

Bertolini A (2018) Artificial Intelligence and civil law - Liability rules for drones, Study requested by the European Parliament's Committee on Legal Affairs, Policy Department for Citizens' Rights and Constitutional Affairs, November 2018

Bertolini A (2020) Artificial intelligence and civil liability, Study requested by the European Parliament's Committee on Legal Affairs, Policy Department for Citizens' Rights and Constitutional Affairs – Directorate-General for Internal Policies, PE 621.926, July 2020
Bertolini A (2013) Robots as products: the case for a realistic analysis of robotic applications and liability rules. Law Innov Technol 5:214–247
Borges G (2019) New liability concepts: the potential of insurance and compensation funds. In: Lohsse S, Schulze R, Staudenmeyer D (eds) Liability for artificial intelligence and the internet of things. Nomos, Baden-Baden, pp 145–163
Borghetti J-S (2019) How can artificial intelligence be defective. In: Lohsse S, Schulze R, Staudenmayer D (eds) Liability for artificial intelligence and the internet of things. Nomos, Baden-Baden, pp 63–76
Bratu I (2023) A first critical analysis of the European approach to damage caused by artificial intelligence enabled by global navigation satellite systems. A bridge to nowhere or a cloud with a silver lining? Int Rev Law Comput Technol 37(2):147–165
Brown R (2021) Property ownership and the legal personhood of artificial intelligence. Inf Commun Technol Law 30(2):208–234
Buiten M, de Streel A, Peitz M (2021) EU liability rules for the age of artificial intelligence. Centre on Regulation in Europe (CERRE), March 2021
Buiten MC (2024) Product liability for defective AI. Eur J Law Econ 57:239–273
Buolamwini J, Gebru T (2018) Proceedings of the 1st conference on fairness, accountability and transparency. PMLR 81:77–91
Chatzipanagiotis M, Leloudas G (2020) Automated vehicles and third-party liability: a European perspective. Univ Ill J Law Technol Policy 1:109–199
Christidis K, Devetsikiotis M (2016) Blockchains and smart contracts for the internet of things. IEEE Access 4:2292–2303
Cowls J, Tsamados A, Taddeo M, Floridi L (2023) The AI gambit: leveraging artificial intelligence to combat climate change—opportunities, challenges, and recommendations. AI Soc 38:283–307
Crootof R, Margot E, Kaminski W (2023) Nicholson Price II, "Humans in the Loop". Vanderbilt Law Rev 76:429–510
Custers B, Fosch-Villaronga E (2022) Law and artificial intelligence – regulating AI and applying AI in legal practice. Information Technology and Law Series (ITLS), Vol. 35. Springer
de Bruin R (2016) Autonomous intelligent cars on the European intersection of liability and privacy: regulatory challenges and the road ahead. Eur J Risk Regul 7(3):485–501
De Bruyne J, Van Gool E, Gils T (2021) Tort law and damage caused by AI systems. In: De Bruyne J, Vanleenhove C (eds) Artificial intelligence and the law. Intersentia, pp 359–404
De Bruyne J, Dheu O, Ducuing C (2023) The European Commission's approach to extra-contractual liability and AI – an evaluation of the AI Liability Directive and the Revised Product Liability Directive. Comput Law Secur Rev 51:105894
De Luca S (2023) New product liability directive. In: "A Europe Fit for the Digital Age", Legislative Train Schedule. European Parliamentary Research Service (EPRS), 15 December 2023
de Meeus C (2019) The product liability directive at the age of the digital industrial revolution: fit for innovation? J Eur Consum Mark Law 8(4):149–154
Del Monte M, Brenda Smialowski S (2021) Understanding trilogue – Informal tripartite meetings to reach provisional agreement on legislative files. European Parliamentary Research Service (EPRS), May 2021
Dheu O, De Bruyne J, Ducuing C (2022) The European Commission's approach to extra contractual liability and AI – a first analysis and evaluation of the two proposals. CiTiP Working Paper Series, 6 October 2022
Dheu O, De Bruyne J (2023) Artificial intelligence and tort law: a 'multi-faceted' reality. Eur Rev Priv Law 31(2):261–298

Dieter Frizberg with Petra Porubčanová (2024) Adapting liability rules to artificial intelligence. Briefing, Initial Appraisal of a European Commission Impact Assessment, European Parliamentary Research Service (EPRS), March 2024

Duffourc MN, Gerke S (2023) The proposed EU Directives for AI liability leave worrying gaps likely to impact medical AI. npj Digit Med 6:77

Ebers M (2021) Liability for artificial intelligence and EU consumer law. JIPITEC 12:204–220

Eldakak A, Alremeithi A, Dahiyat E et al (2024) Civil liability for the actions of autonomous AI in healthcare: an invitation to further contemplation. Humanit Soc Sci Commun 11:305

Esther Kramer with Arianna Cantarelli (2023) Updating liability rules for defective products. Briefing, European Parliamentary Research Service (EPRS)

Evas T (2018) A common EU approach to liability rules and insurance for connected and autonomous vehicles, Study. European Added Value Assessment - Accompanying the European Parliament's legislative own-initiative report (Rapporteur: Mady Delvaux). Study, European Parliamentary Research Service (EPRS), February 2018

Evas T (2020) Civil liability regime for artificial intelligence, Study, European Parliamentary Research Service (EPRS), September 2020

Fairgrieve D, Rajneri E (2019) Is software a product under the product liability directive? Zeitschrift für Internationales Wirtschaftsrecht 1:24–28

Fairgrieve D, Howells G, Møgelvang-Hansen P et al (2016) Product liability directive. In: Machnikowski P (ed) European product liability: an analysis of the state of the art in the era of new technologies. Principles of European tort law. Intersentia, pp 17–108

Florina Lohmann M (2016) Liability issues concerning self-driving vehicles. Eur J Risk Regul 7(2): 335–340

Geistfeld MA, Karner E, Koch BA, Wendehorst C (2023) Civil liability for artificial intelligence and software. De Gruyter, Berlin, Boston

Grundmann S, Hacker P (2017) Digital technology as a challenge to European contract law – from the existing to the future architecture. Eur Rev Contr Law 13:255–293

Hacker P, Krestel R, Grundmann S, Naumann F (2020) Explainable AI under contract and tort law: legal incentives and technical challenges. Artif Intell Law 28:415

Hacker P (2023) The European liability directives - Critique of a half-hearted approach and lessons for the future. Comput Law Secur Rev 51:105871

Hacker P (2023) Manipulation by algorithms. Exploring the triangle of unfair commercial practice, data protection, and privacy law. Eur Law J 29(1–2):142–175

Hacker P, Passoth J-H (2022) Varieties of AI explanations under the law. From the GDPR to the AIA, and beyond. In: Holzinger A, Goebel R, Fong R, Moon T, Müller KR, Samek W (eds) Lecture notes on artificial intelligence 13200: xxAI - beyond explainable AI. Springer

Helberger N, Sax M, Strycharz J et al (2022) Choice architectures in the digital economy: towards a new understanding of digital vulnerability. J Consum Policy 45:175–200

Howells G, Twigg-Flesner C, Willett C (2017) Product liability and digital products. In: Synodinou T-E, Jougleux P, Markou C, Prastitou T (eds) EU internet law: regulation and enforcement. Springer Nature, pp 183–195

Karner E, Koch BA (2023) Comparative study on civil liability for artificial intelligence. In: Geistfeld MA, Karner E, Koch BA, Wendehorst C (eds) Civil liability for artificial intelligence

Karner E, Koch BA, Geistfeld MA (2021) Comparative law study on civil liability for artificial intelligence. European Commission, Directorate-General for Justice and Consumers

Koch BA, Borghetti J-S, Machnikowski P, Pichonnaz P, Rodríguez de las Heras Ballell T, Twigg-Flesner C, Wendehorst C (2022) Response of the European law institute to the public consultation on civil liability – adapting liability rules to the digital age and artificial intelligence. J Eur Tort Law 13(1):25–63

Kritikos M (2016) Legal and ethical reflections concerning robotics. Scientific Foresight Unit (STOA) Policy Briefing, European Parliament Research Service (EPRS), PE 563.501

Kritikos M (2019) Artificial intelligence ante Portas: legal & ethical reflections. European Parliamentary Research Service (EPRS), Scientific Foresight Unit (STOA), March 2019

Leenes R, Palmerini E, Koops B-J, Bertolini A, Salvini P, Lucivero F (2017) Regulatory challenges of robotics: some guidelines for addressing legal and ethical issues. Law Innov Technol 9:1–44
Levy D (2020) Intelligent no-fault insurance for robots. J Future Robot Life 1:1–23
Li J-h (2018) Cyber security meets artificial intelligence: a survey. Front Inf Technol Electr Eng 19: 1462–1474
Lodie A, Celis Juarez S, Karathanasis T (2022) Towards a new regime of civil liability for AI systems: comment on the European Commission's Proposals. 2022. hal-04130851
Lohsse S, Schulze R, Staudenmayer D (2019) Liability for artificial intelligence. In: Lohsse S, Schulze R, Staudenmayer D (eds) Liability for artificial intelligence and the internet of things. Nomos, Baden-Baden, pp 99–116
Luzak J (2020) A broken notion: impact of modern technologies on product liability. Eur J Risk Regul 11(3):630–649
Machnikowski P (2016) Conclusions. In: Machnikowski P (ed) European product liability: an Analysis of the state of the art in the era of new technologies. Principles of European Tort Law. Intersentia, pp 669–705
Madiega T (2020) Reform of the EU Liability Regime for Online Intermediaries: Background on the Forthcoming Digital Services Act: In Depth Analysis. European Parliamentary Research Service (EPRS), May 2020.
Madiega T (2023) Artificial intelligence liability directive. Briefing, European Parliamentary Research Service (EPRS)
Marchisio E (2021) In support of "no-fault" civil liability rules for artificial intelligence. SN Soc Sci 1:54
Martín-Casals M (2019) Causation and scope of liability in the internet of things (IoT). In: Lohsse S, Schulze R, Staudenmayer D (eds) Liability for artificial intelligence and the internet of things. Nomos, Baden-Baden, pp 201–228
Maume P (2019) Reducing legal uncertainty and regulatory arbitrage for Robo-Advice. Eur Comp Financ Law Rev:622–651
Mazzini G (2019) A system of governance for artificial intelligence through the lens of emerging intersections between AI and EU law. In: De Franceschi A, Schulze R (eds) Digital revolution – new challenges for law
Mezzanotte F (2019) Liability for digital products. In: De Franceschi A, Schulze R (eds) Digital revolution – new challenges for law. Nomos, pp 169–188
Michael Froomkin A, Kerr I, Pineau J (2019) When AIs outperform doctors: confronting the challenges of a tort-induced over-reliance on machine learning (February 20, 2019). Ariz Law Rev 61:33–99. University of Miami Legal Studies Research Paper No. 18-3
Mosoreanu M, Ulicna D, Paetz S, Podobea V, Schubert M, Stauf J; Renda A, Sipiczki A (2022) 'Behavioural Study on the link between challenges of artificial intelligence for Member States' civil liability rules and consumer attitudes towards AI-enabled products and services', Report, European Commission, Directorate-General for Justice and Consumers, Publications Office of the European Union
Navas S (2020) Robot machines and civil liability. In: Ebers M, Navas S (eds) Algorithms and law. Cambridge University Press, pp 157–173
Nawaz SA (2022) The proposed EU AI liability rules: ease or burden? European Law Blog
Nevejans N (2016) European Civil Law Rules in Robotics. Study requested by the European Parliament's Committee on Legal Affairs (JURI Committee)
Nikolinakos NT (2022) Adapting the EU liability regime to artificial intelligence (AI): the European Commission's proposed policy options. Comput Telecommun Law Rev (C.T.L.R.) 28(3):66–83
Ntoutsi E, Fafalios P, Gadiraju U et al (2020) Bias in data-driven artificial intelligence systems—an introductory survey. Wiley Interdiscipl Rev Data Mining Knowl Discov 10:e1356
Pagallo U (2022) The way ahead on AI liability issues - will the developing EU liability framework for regulating AI prove sufficient? The Ada Lovelace Institute, 20 October 2022
Palmerini E, Bertolini A, Battaglia F, Koops B-J, Carnevale A, Salvini P (2016) RoboLaw: towards a European framework for robotics regulation. Robot Autonom Syst 86:78–85

Paolo Patti F (2019) The European road to autonomous vehicles. Fordham Int Law J 43:125
Ponce del Castillo A (2017) A Law on Robotics and Artificial Intelligence in the EU? (October 3, 2017). Foresight Brief, European Trade Union Institute (ETUI) Research Paper - Foresight Brief #02-September 2017
Rachum-Twaig O (2020) Whose robot is it anyway?: Liability for artificial intelligence-based products. Univ Ill Law Rev 4:1141–1175
Schellekens M (2018) No-fault compensation schemes for self-driving vehicles. Law Innov Technol 10(2):314–333
Schütte B, Majewski L, Havu K (2021) Damages liability for harm caused by artificial intelligence – EU law in flux. Helsinki Legal Studies Research Paper No. 69, August 2021
Sérgio Cabral T (2020) Liability and artificial intelligence in the EU: assessing the adequacy of the current product liability directive. Maastricht J Eur Comp Law 27(5):615–635
Shavell S (2020) On the redesign of accident liability for the world of autonomous vehicles. J Legal Stud 49:243–285
Soyer B, Tettenborn A (2023) Artificial intelligence and civil liability—do we need a new regime? Int J Law Inform Technol 30(4):385–397
Spindler G (2019) User liability and strict liability in the internet of things and for robots. In: Lohsse S, Schulze R, Staudenmayer D (eds) Liability for Artificial intelligence and the internet of things. Nomos, Baden-Baden, pp 125–145
De Luca S (2024) New product liability directive. In: "A Europe Fit for the Digital Age", Legislative Train Schedule, European Parliamentary Research Service (EPRS), 20 April 2024
Strauß S (2021) Deep automation bias: how to tackle a wicked problem of AI? Big Data Cogn Comput 5:18
Tenhunen S (2022) Aligning the product liability directive with the circular economy and emerging technologies: Revision of Directive 85/374/EEC. Implementation Appraisal Briefing, European Parliamentary Research Service (EPRS), October 2022
Timan T, Snijders R, Kirova M, Suardi S, Lieshout MV, Chen M, Costenco P, Palmerini E, Bertolini A, Tejada A, Montfort SV, Bolchi M, Alberti S, Brouwer R, Karanilokova K, Episcopo F, Jansen S (2019) Study on safety of non-embedded software. Service, data access, and legal issues of advanced robots, autonomous, connected, and AI-based vehicles and systems: final study report regarding CAD/CCAM and industrial robots. European Commission, Brussel
Tolan S, Miron M, Gomez E, Castillo C (2019) Why machine learning may lead to unfairness: evidence from risk assessment for juvenile justice in Catalonia. Best Paper Award, International Conference on AI and Law
Twigg-Flesner C (2021) 'Guiding principles for updating the product liability directive for the digital age' (Pilot ELI Innovation Paper). European Law Institute
Twigg-Flesner C (2021) Guiding principles for updating the product liability directive for the digital age. European Law Institute (ELI) Innovation Paper Series
van Boom WH, Borghetti J-S, Ehlers AB, Karner E, Nolan D, Oliphant K, Scarso A, Ulfbeck V, Wagner G (2018) Product liability in Europe. In: Koziol H, Green MD, Lunney M, Oliphant K, Yang L (eds) Product liability: fundamental questions in a comparative perspective. De Gruyter, Berlin, Boston, pp 255–356
Van Uytsel S (2021) Different liability regimes for autonomous vehicles: one preferable above the other? In: Van Uytsel S, Vasconcellos Vargas D (eds) Autonomous vehicles – business, technology and law. Part of the book series: perspectives in law, business and innovation (PLBI). Springer, pp 67–92
Vellinga NE (2024) Rethinking compensation in light of the development of AI. Int Rev Law Comput Technol:1–22
Verheyen T (2021) On behavioural asymmetry in product liability law: how privatising nudging will get European product liability theory back on track. J Eur Tort Law 12(1):40–64
Verheyen T (2018) Full harmonization, consumer protection and products liability: a fresh reading of the case law of the ECJ. Eur Rev Priv Law 26(1):119–140

Wagner G (2019) Robot, Inc.: personhood for autonomous systems? Fordham Law Rev 88:591
Wagner G (2021) Liability for artificial intelligence: a proposal by the European Parliament. In: Eidenmüller H, Wagner G (eds) Law by Algorithm, p 127
Wagner G (2022) Liability rules for the digital age – aiming for the brussels effect. J Eur Tort Law (JETL) 13(3):191–243
Wagner G (2022) Software as a product. In: Lohsse S, Schulze R, Staudenmayer D (eds) Smart products. Hart, Nomos, p 157
Gerhard Wagner, 'Robot liability' in S.Lohsse/R.Schulze/D.Staudenmayer (eds), Liability for artificial intelligence and the internet of things, Nomos, Baden-Baden (2019), pp. 27–62.
Watts K (2020) Potential of no-fault comprehensive compensation funds to deal with automation and other 21st century transport developments. Eur J Commer Contr Law 12:1–21
Wendehorst C (2020) Strict liability for AI and other emerging technologies. J Eur Tort Law (JETL) 11(2):150–180
Wendehorst C (2020) Liability for pure data loss. In: Karner E, Magnus U, Spier J, Widmer P (eds) Essays in Honor of Helmut Koziol 225–242
Wendehorst C (2021) Safety and liability related aspects of software. Study Commissioned by the European Commission
Wendehorst C (2022) AI liability in Europe: anticipating the EU AI liability directive. Ada Lovelace Institute
Wuyts D (2014) The product liability directive – more than two decades of defective products in Europe. J Eur Tort Law 5(1):1–34
Zech H (2019) Liability for autonomous systems: tackling specific risks of modern IT. In: Lohsse S, Schulze R, Staudenmeyer D (eds) Liability for artificial intelligence and the internet of things. Nomos, Baden-Baden, pp 187–200
Zech H (2021) Liability for AI: public policy considerations. Acad Eur Law (ERA) Forum 22:147–158, Springer
Ziosi M, Mökander J, Novelli C, Casolari F, Taddeo M, Floridi L (2023) The EU AI liability directive (AILD): bridging information gaps. Eur J Law Technol 14(3)

Chapter 10
Conclusions

10.1 Identification of the Problem—Liability Rules Are Not Fit for the Digital Age—Shortcomings Brought by AI and Other Digital Emerging Technologies to the Product Liability Frameworks

Liability-related issues are counted amongst the major risks associated with the use of AI. Indeed, liability ranks amongst the top three barriers to the use of AI by European companies and constitutes a major external barrier/challenge for companies that are planning to, but have not yet adopted AI (major obstacles to AI adoption).[1] Therefore, the creation of a clear liability regime for AI and other emerging digital technologies plays a vital role in driving the industry forward, ensuring a level playing field, and reducing the uncertainties for companies considering investing in AI-powered products and services. Creating a stable liability policy and rules is indispensable in order to allow a sound basis for long term

[1] 'European enterprise survey on the use of technologies based on artificial intelligence', Study prepared for the European Commission, DG Communications Networks, Content & Technology by Ipsos Belgium and iCite (International Centre for Innovation, Technology and Education), 2020, Final report, at pp. 57–60, figures 18–21: "One specific challenge or barrier that seems to stand out is liability for damage caused by AI: while it seems to not be as universally relevant, this barrier seems to pose a major challenge when it is applicable to the business context in which enterprises operate" (at p. 58). . . . "enterprises in the human health sector are consistently in the top three most concerned for all three external barriers, with risks associated with liability for damage caused by AI being rated as a major obstacle by 43% of interviewed enterprises in this sector – the highest proportion across all sectors. Liability for damage caused by AI also stands out as a major obstacle in the transport (39%), accommodation (37%) and other technical and/or scientific (36%) sectors" (at p. 60).

N. T. Nikolinakos, *Adapting the EU Civil Liability Regime to the Digital Age: Artificial Intelligence, Robotics, and Other Emerging Technologies*, Law, Governance and Technology Series 68, https://doi.org/10.1007/978-3-031-67969-8_10

planning in the industry and set the environment for commercial initiative and massive investment.

AI can benefit the whole of society and the economy but, at the same time, brings with it new challenges and raises critical legal questions. Furthermore, specific characteristics of certain AI systems could create risks related to user safety and fundamental rights, leading to uncertainty for companies and potentially slower uptake of AI technologies by businesses and citizens. Those risks created by certain AI systems must be addressed in order to avoid undesirable outcomes. In order to respond to these challenges, the EU liability regime must ensure a well-functioning internal market for AI systems where risks are effectively addressed.

Investment in and societal acceptance of AI-related technologies require legal certainty and trust. A clear legal framework is essential to accelerate innovation by providing businesses with legal certainty for the development and innovation of AI-based technology, whilst protecting citizens and increasing their trust in AI technologies. Citizens and businesses alike need to be able to trust the technology they interact with and have a predictable legal framework. As technology progresses, algorithms are behind progressively more decisions that affect our everyday lives. Thus the objective of promoting the uptake of AI can be achieved by increasing users' trust which, in turn, will increase the demand for AI used by companies and public authorities alike. Furthermore, by increasing legal certainty and trust, AI providers will access bigger markets, with products that users and consumers desire and purchase.

It is stressed that the objective of the EU liability regime is to address the specific challenges brought about by artificial intelligence and other emerging digital technologies, provide legal certainty for all parties involved, instill confidence in the safety and reliability of AI-powered products and services, and create stability for AI-based technology investment. It is imperative to ensure that AI is developed and applied in an appropriate legal framework which promotes innovation and, at the same time, guarantees a high level of safety/security. The overall goal is to stimulate the uptake of trustworthy AI in the EU economy. In other words, the EU's twin objective of promoting the uptake of AI and of addressing the risks associated with certain uses of AI-related technologies and products remains.

It is understandable that whilst the EU wants to encourage companies which can provide innovative AI-related technologies to compete in as many services as possible, it does not wish this to lead to inefficiencies which would be harmful to the market and the society. Therefore, the EU must be cautious in drawing the right balance: to encourage and promote the rapid dissemination of AI-related technology and innovation while, at the same time, ensuring that high levels of protection and safety are not affected. Therefore, in order to make the most of the opportunities offered by AI it is necessary to establish a liability framework which ensures high levels of consumer protection/safety and promotes their trust in AI technologies, while efficiently providing remedies/compensation to affected parties. At the same time, this liability framework must provide businesses with legal certainty, be future-oriented and flexible enough to foster innovation and encourage investment. Furthermore, it is necessary to create a more integrated Single Market, i.e., to reach a common European approach in order to avoid any potential disparities, barriers and fragmentation in the European Single Market resulting from differences in national legislation.

The emergence of new digital technologies like AI, the IoT and robotics raise new challenges in terms of product safety like connectivity, autonomy, data dependency, opacity, complexity of products and systems, software updates and more complex safety management and value chains. In turn, these new safety challenges create challenges in terms of liability. These liability related challenges need to be addressed to ensure that persons having suffered harm caused by AI-enabled systems and services will enjoy equal level of protection as victims of traditional technologies (which operate without AI), while maintaining the balance with the needs of technological innovation. This will help create trust in these new emerging digital technologies and establish investment stability.

Although the primary objective is to prevent/mitigate risks to safety and fundamental rights, it is inevitable that humans will suffer harm caused by AI-enabled systems and services. In such cases, it becomes crucial for the liability rules to ascertain the responsible party for the harm caused and establish the circumstances under which the victim can receive compensation. Therefore, the EU liability framework should serve as a safety net, ensuring compensation in the event of harm. Indeed, although AI-enabled products/services are (and should be) expected to be safer than traditional ones, accidents/harm will still occur. If/when the risks materialise, the characteristics of AI technologies make it difficult to trace back potentially problematic decisions made with the involvement of AI systems. This in turn may make it extremely difficult for persons having suffered harm to obtain compensation under the current EU and national liability legislation.

It is recalled that the existing liability framework in the EU relies on both (a) the current Product Liability Directive[2] (which harmonised the liability of the producer of defective products) and (b) other non-harmonised national liability regimes that apply in parallel. Therefore, at the national level, the rules implementing the Product Liability Directive coexist with other extra-contractual liability rules that could also be invoked by victims of damages. As a result, in relation to liability claims in the EU, the victim currently has three avenues available for claiming compensation (complementary pillars of liability), i.e., it can seek compensation based on a fault-based liability claim, on a strict liability claim, or on a claim against the producer of a defective product.[3]

[2]Council Directive 85/374/EEC of 25 July 1985 on the approximation of the laws, regulations and administrative provisions of the Member States concerning liability for defective products, as modified by Directive 1999/34/EC of the European Parliament and of the Council of 10 May 1999 (OJ L 210/29, 7.8.1985, and OJ L 141/20, 4.6.1999) (the Product Liability Directive - PLD).

[3]Commission Staff Working Document, "Impact Assessment Report – Accompanying the document Proposal for a Directive of the European Parliament and of the Council on adapting non-contractual civil liability rules to artificial intelligence", SWD(2022) 319 final, Brussels, 28.9.2022, p. 3: "A victim currently relies on national liability rules and in certain cases on the Product Liability Directive (PLD) to claim compensation for damage arising from AI-enabled

However, existing national fault-based liability rules are not adapted to handle compensation claims for harm caused by AI-enabled products/services. Under such rules, victims need to prove a wrongful action/omission of a person that caused the damage. The specific characteristics of AI, including autonomy and opacity ("black box" effect) make it difficult or even prohibitively expensive to identify the liable person and prove the requirements for a successful liability claim. Therefore, victims of harm caused by AI could be less protected than victims of traditional technologies. This potential lack of compensation could affect the consumers' trust in AI and ultimately the uptake of AI-enabled products/services.

At the same time, the current Product Liability Directive (PLD) lays down common EU rules for the strict liability (i.e. liability irrespective of fault or negligence—no-fault liability) of producers for damage caused by defective products. However, certain products, economic actors, and damage in the digital and circular economy are not covered under no-fault (strict) liability. This is because the Product Liability Directive (which dates back to 1985) was conceived long before the digital revolution and, accordingly, has not adapted to the digital age and circular economy. As a result, liability rules are unclear and, thus, should be adapted for products in the digital age. Also, liability rules are unclear for refurbished/remanufactured products. Furthermore, the current rules of the PLD are silent on who should be liable when a product has been directly imported from outside the EU by a consumer. In addition, it is argued that consumers face obstacles to getting compensation, mainly because (i) proving defectiveness and causal link with damage could be very difficult and costly for complex products (such as certain cases involving AI-enabled products) and (ii) liability claims are subject to a number of restrictions.

The emerging digital technologies involve many different layers, e.g. software components, sensors, or data services. The Internet of Things and the advent of robotics can present legal obstacles when it comes to identifying and establishing the defect which caused the damage and in determining liability among the various market players. Legal uncertainty may have a detrimental impact on the development and uptake of AI and emerging digital technologies. Therefore, civil liability rules for AI should ensure that damage caused by AI-enabled products and services is remedied efficiently. To this end, alongside a high level of safety and protection for users, it is imperative to provide efficient redress mechanisms for victims in case of damages. An efficient liability framework helps to build user trust and acceptance of AI and other emerging digital technologies, which is a prerequisite for encouraging innovation and technological uptake. The objectives of the EU civil liability rules for AI should be to (i) provide legal certainty to industry's market players about the

products and services. Depending on each case, a victim has several avenues available for claiming compensation. Various persons could be held liable in parallel under different conditions and for different reasons. Neither of these rules contains specific provisions for AI. Example: A traffic accident victim may have in parallel a fault-based liability claim against the driver whose fault caused the accident, a 'PLD' claim against the producer if the vehicle had a defect, and a strict liability claim against the vehicle's owner".

risk they take in the course of their business, (ii) encourage the prevention of damage and (iii) ensure injured parties are compensated.

The overarching objective is to strike a balance between protecting citizens and supporting technological innovation. In other words, apart from the issue of safety, the aim of an effective liability framework is to address unnecessary obstacles to getting compensation for damage in order to ensure that injured parties are equally protected throughout the EU, thus leading to consumer uptake of AI and other emerging digital technologies as well as creating trust in innovative products/services and in justice systems. In particular:

10.2 With Regard to the Proposed AI Liability Directive

The proposed AI Liability Directive[4] harmonises targeted aspects of the Member States' existing civil liability rules applicable to AI-systems and its aim is to complement and modernise the EU liability framework by introducing new rules specific to damages caused by AI systems.

As already described, the specific characteristics of AI make it difficult to meet the burden of proof. Current fault-based national liability rules are not fit to deal with compensation claims for harm caused by AI-enabled products/services. Under such rules, victims need to prove a wrongful action/omission of a person that caused the damage. Thus, in the absence of targeted measures to ease the burden of proof, the specific characteristics of certain AI-systems could make it extremely difficult and/or prohibitively expensive for victims to identify and prove the fault of a potentially liable person (i.e., uncertainty as regards the allocation of responsibilities) as well as the causal link between that fault and the damage suffered. Tracing the victim's loss back to the defendant may be challenging if the suspected cause of that loss is related to the operation of an AI system, due to the increasingly autonomous nature of some AI systems and their peculiar characteristics. In other words, the specific characteristics of AI make it difficult to meet the burden of proof and causation and thus prove the requirements for a successful liability claim.

Furthermore, there are three AI-specific problems regarding liability: (i) lack of compensation for victims contributing to the lack of societal trust in AI use; (ii) legal uncertainty, and (iii) increased legal fragmentation, which in their combination cause internal market obstacles. These three problems are driven by the fact that, under existing liability rules, victims normally have to prove the necessary conditions for a successful claim, i.e., they have to identify the possibly liable person(s), the action/omission of that person which could be characterised as fault, and the causal link between that action/omission and the damage. However, there are neither targeted

[4]Proposal for a Directive of the European Parliament and of the Council on adapting non-contractual civil liability rules to artificial intelligence (AI Liability Directive), European Commission, COM(2022) 496 final, Brussels, 28.9.2022 (the 'proposed AI Liability Directive').

provisions for AI to ease the victim's burden of proof under fault-based claims, nor AI-specific strict liability regimes that would exempt the victim from making this proof. Therefore, these three major problems are primarily linked to the difficulty of the victim to prove the necessary facts due to the specific characteristics of certain AI systems, which make it very difficult to directly attribute the damaging output of the AI to an action/omission of a liable person.

The main objective of the proposed AI Liability Directive is to promote the rollout of trustworthy AI in Europe by reducing legal uncertainty, by preventing the emergence of fragmented AI-specific adaptations of national civil liability rules, and by ensuring victims (e.g., citizens and businesses) of damage caused by AI obtain equivalent protection to victims of damage caused by other products in general or traditional technologies. In other words, the objectives of the proposed AI Liability Directive are: (i) to prevent a lack of compensation, by ensuring that victims of AI-enabled products/services are equally protected as victims of traditional technologies (when persons suffer harm caused by AI systems, they should enjoy the same level of protection as those having suffered harm caused by other technologies, because lack of compensation could affect their trust in AI and ultimately the uptake of AI-enabled products/services); (ii) to reduce legal uncertainty regarding the liability exposure of businesses developing or using AI; and (iii) to prevent the emergence of fragmented AI-specific adaptations of national civil liability rules.

The proposed AI Liability Directive introduces two key measures: *First*, the 'presumption of causality', which relieves victims from having to explain in detail how a specific fault or omission caused the damage. If victims can show that a party was at fault for not complying with a relevant obligation and that a causal link with the AI performance is reasonably likely, the court can presume that this non-compliance caused the damage. The liable party, however, can rebut this presumption by proving that another cause was responsible for the damage. *Second*, it assists victims in accessing relevant evidence from companies or suppliers when dealing with high-risk AI systems. Victims can request the court to order the disclosure of information about high-risk AI systems, facilitating the identification of the liable party and the understanding of the fault. This disclosure is subject to safeguards to protect sensitive information, including trade secrets.

The proposed AI Liability Directive is limited to the measures strictly necessary (proportional) to address the AI-specific problems identified. Thus its intervention is targeted because it only alleviates the burden of proof for victims. Indeed, it focuses on targeted proof-related measures (disclosure of information and alleviation of the burden of proof through establishment of causality rebuttable presumptions subject to strict conditions). From the various tools available in national legal regimes for easing the burden of proof, the approach followed by the proposed AI Liability Directive is to use rebuttable presumptions as the least interventionist tool. As a result, the proposed Directive does not lead to a reversal of the burden of proof, in order to avoid exposing providers, operators and users of AI systems to higher liability risks, which may hinder innovation and prevent the rollout of AI-enabled products and services.

Moreover, since the proposed AI Liability Directive follows an approach of a minimum intervention at EU level (minimum harmonisation), victims of damage caused by AI systems are allowed to invoke more favourable rules of national law. Thus, Member States remain free to use in their national legal regimes more invasive tools/extensive measures if they deem it appropriate, such as reversals of the burden of proof under fault-based regimes, irrebuttable presumptions, national no-fault liability (strict liability) regimes of which there are already a large variety in national laws, etc. In other words, Member States could maintain or—outside of the scope of the Product Liability Directive—introduce national liability rules that are more favourable for victims (for instance, Member States could maintain general strict liability regimes, e.g. for 'dangerous things or activities', applicable also to damage caused by AI systems). On the other hand, however, it could be argued that this minimal harmonisation approach could lead to fragmented liability regimes in the EU.

Furthermore, the proposed AI Liability Directive does not touch upon the substantive conditions of liability like fault or causality (which remain in the remit of national law). Instead, it focuses on targeted proof-related measures, attempting to ensure that victims receive the same level of protection as they would in cases not involving AI systems.

Finally, as already described, the assessment of the need to harmonise strict liability has been postponed to a later stage, when more information about the AI and its uses can be gathered. Under the proposed review clause/mechanism (which takes a "forward-looking perspective"), the proposed AI Liability Directive provides for re-assessing the need for more stringent or more extensive measures (including situations where strict liability would be more appropriate), at a later stage (five years later). In that case, and in line with the approach followed by the European Parliaments' 2020 Resolution on a civil liability regime for artificial intelligence[5] (which proposed that different liability rules should apply for different risks, following a risk-based approach),[6] the view of the Report from the Expert Group on Liability

[5]European Parliament Resolution of 20 October 2020 with recommendations to the Commission on a civil liability regime for artificial intelligence (2020/2014(INL)) P9_TA(2020)0276 (hereafter: European Parliament's Resolution of 20 October 2020 on a civil liability regime for AI).

Also: Annex to the Resolution: detailed recommendations for drawing up a Regulation on liability for the operation of artificial intelligence-systems, A. Principles and Aims of the Proposal. B. Text of the Proposal Requested—Proposal for a Regulation on liability for the operation of Artificial Intelligence-systems (hereafter: Annex to the European Parliament's Resolution of 20 October 2020 on a civil liability regime for AI).

For analysis of the European Parliament's Resolution of 20 October 2020 on a civil liability regime for AI (i.e., the European Parliament's proposal for a Regulation on liability for the operation of Artificial Intelligence-systems), see Chap. 5 of this book.

[6]According to the European Parliament, a strict liability regime for high-risk AI systems should apply, i.e. the operator of a high-risk AI-system should be strictly liable for any harm or damage that was caused by a physical or virtual activity, device or process driven by that AI-system. Annex to the European Parliament's Resolution of 20 October 2020 on a civil liability regime for AI – Text of the Proposal for a Regulation on liability for the operation of AI systems, Article 4(1).

and New Technologies[7] and the Commission's initial (2020) thinking,[8] a more robust evidence base could justify the need for a higher level of regulatory intervention, i.e., the need for harmonising strict liability for AI use cases with a particular risk profile, possibly coupled with a mandatory insurance. Under this scenario, the EU liability regime would acknowledge the differences in risk profiles among various AI applications and tailor the (strict liability) rules on a case-by-case basis. Therefore, the application of strict liability could be limited to situations where the AI-enabled technologies may create specific risks (which are more likely to arise in circumstances where digital technologies move in public spaces, e.g., drones, autonomous cars, traffic management services), expose the public at large to risks, and cause significant harm to life, health, and property.

In sum, the proposed AI Liability Directive follows a minimally invasive strategy through a staged approach. Any type of victim (natural or legal person) can bring a

---

See also the Report of the Expert Group on Liability and New Technologies which stated that "strict liability should lie with the person who is in control of the risk connected with the operation of emerging digital technologies and who benefits from their operation (operator)". Report from the Expert Group on Liability and New Technologies – New Technologies Formation "Liability for Artificial Intelligence and Other Emerging Digital Technologies", 21 November 2019, Key Finding [10], at pp. 6, 39, 41.

[7] Report from the Expert Group on Liability and New Technologies – New Technologies Formation "Liability for Artificial Intelligence and Other Emerging Digital Technologies", 21 November 2019. For instance, the Report stated that "emerging digital technologies make it difficult to apply fault-based liability rules, due to the lack of well-established models of proper functioning of these technologies and the possibility of their developing as a result of learning without direct human control" (at p. 23). This is why the Report underlined that strict liability of the operator of some emerging digital technology may be justified: "a person operating a permissible technology that nevertheless carries an increased risk of harm to others, for example AI-driven robots in public spaces, should be subject to strict liability for damage resulting from its operation" (at p. 40); "strict liability is an appropriate response to the risks posed by emerging digital technologies, if, for example, they are operated in non-private environments and may typically cause significant harm" (at p. 39).

[8] According to the Commission's initial (2020) thinking—based on the analysis of the Report from the Expert Group on Liability and New Technologies—, the application of strict liability should be limited to situations where the emerging technologies may create specific risks (which are likely to arise in circumstances where digital technologies move in public spaces, e.g., drones, autonomous cars, traffic management services), expose the public at large to risks, and cause significant harm to life, health, and property. As the Commission stated, "the operation of some autonomous AI devices and services could have a specific risk profile in terms of liability, because they may cause significant harm to important legal interests like life, health and property, and expose the public at large to risks. This could mainly concern AI devices that move in public spaces (e.g. fully autonomous vehicles, drones and package delivery robots) or AI-based services with similar risks (e.g. traffic management services guiding or controlling vehicles or management of power distribution). The challenges of autonomy and opacity to national tort laws could be addressed following a risk-based approach. Strict liability schemes could ensure that whenever that risk materialises, the victim is compensated regardless of fault. The impact of choosing who should be strictly liable for such operations on the development and uptake of AI would need to be carefully assessed and a risk-based approach be considered". Commission Communication "Report on the safety and liability implications of Artificial Intelligence, the Internet of Things and robotics", COM (2020) 64 final, Brussels, 19.2.2020, p. 16.

claim for damages against any person for fault that influenced the AI system which caused the harm. The victim can be compensated if harmed by the fault or omission of a provider, developer or user of AI resulting in a damage covered by national law (e.g., health, property, including damage caused by safety issues or resulting from unlawful discrimination or breach of fundamental rights such as privacy). Once ratified, the AI Liability Directive is expected to strengthen the rights of victims who have suffered damage—as admissible under national law—due to the wrongful use of artificial intelligence. This will enable victims to file successful claims against any party whose fault influenced the AI system causing the damage/harm. Consequently, it will facilitate compensation for victims, whether individuals or businesses, for damages resulting from an AI system's output.

10.3 With Regard to the Revised Product Liability Directive

The current Product Liability Directive establishes common rules at the EU level for the non-fault (strict) liability of producers for damage caused by defective products, regardless of fault or negligence. It provides an avenue for individuals (whether they are the owner or a bystander) who have suffered personal injuries, damage to consumer property, or death due to a defective product to claim financial compensation.

However, the evaluation of the Product Liability Directive concluded that the PLD had several shortcomings, such as the lack of legal clarity on how to apply the PLD's definitions to products in the digital and circular economy, difficulties related to the burden of proof in the case of complex products, and limitations on making claims. In particular, under the Product Liability Directive the burden of proof is less onerous on victims than under national fault-based liability rules, mainly because the victim does not have to prove fault. Nevertheless, proving that a product is defective (i.e. that it does not provide the level of safety a person is entitled to expect) is still (occasionally, extremely) challenging for complex products, such as AI-enabled products, even if the victim does not have to prove how the product became unsafe. The PLD evaluation found that it was difficult to apply its rules to digital technologies in general, including AI-enabled products. It also found that the rules made it difficult to prove liability in the case of complex products, including AI-enabled products, but also others such as pharmaceuticals.

In particular, the main two problems affecting the existing PLD are the following:

(a) *Certain products, economic actors and damage in the digital and circular economy escape (are not covered under) no-fault (strict) liability.* This is because the Product Liability Directive was conceived long before the digital revolution and, accordingly, is not adapted to the digital age and circular economy. In more detail:

(a1) Liability rules are unclear and, thus, not adapted for products in the digital age. For instance, the current PLD does not cover categories of products emerging from new digital technologies, like smart products, software, and AI. The definition of product under the PLD appears to no longer be as clear-cut and, therefore, a clarification of its scope (e.g., whether software is covered by the legal concept of product or product component) is required. The crucial question is whether the PLD should be extended beyond physical products to encompass intangible items, i.e., software, digital services and digital content. Furthermore, the current PLD does not cover liability for defects that emerge after a product is marketed, including defective updates and cybersecurity vulnerabilities. Indeed, the current Product Liability Directive provides an exemption for producers from liability if they can demonstrate that a defect causing damage likely occurred after the product entered the market, also known as the "later-defect defense". This defense is based on the assumption that the producer no longer has control over the product once it was put into circulation. However, in the digital age, this assumption is no longer valid as producers often retain control over their products through updates and upgrades, which themselves can be defective. Also, new types of damages such as damage to digital property are not covered by the current PLD's provisions. It is not entirely clear, for instance, whether 'consumer property' covers damage to data, since data may not be an 'item of property' within the meaning of the current Product Liability Directive. It is not universally accepted that damage to or the destruction of data constitutes a property loss, because, according to various legal systems, the notion of 'property' excludes intangibles and, therefore, tortious liability cannot be triggered.

(a2) Liability rules are unclear for refurbished/remanufactured products. Indeed, in the circular economy (where the life of materials is extended through upgrading and repairing digital products and components), it is uncertain who should be liable in cases where a product that has been (substantially) modified by a refurbisher or remanufacturer (and placed back on the market) is defective and causes harm. As a result, businesses are faced with a challenge to assess their liability exposure due to uncertainty and different interpretations in every Member State. Furthermore, consumers are less able to get compensation for defective products using digital technologies or "circular" products.

(a3) The current rules of the PLD are silent on who should be liable when a product has been directly imported from outside the EU by a consumer. Due to new global supply chains, it is becoming increasingly common for people to purchase products from non-EU countries without any EU-based producer or importer. Online marketplaces have enabled consumers to buy products from outside the EU without there being an importer, leaving consumers with no liable person from whom to seek compensation under the Product Liability Directive if damage has occurred. As no EU-based economic operator is subject to no-fault liability, consumers are left without the possibility of compensation for an increasing number of products when purchasing from a third country directly. This also creates an uneven playing field between EU and non-EU producers, as EU businesses face unfair competition from third country producers who are beyond the reach of the Product Liability Directive.

(b) *Consumers face obstacles to getting compensation.* Indeed, whereas victims do not have to prove fault (producers bear liability irrespective of fault), proving defectiveness and causal link with damage is very difficult and costly for complex products. Also, liability claims are subject to a number of restrictions (claimants face time limits and thresholds that might disproportionately restrict the number of claims). In more detail:

(b1) Proving defectiveness and causal link with damage is very difficult and costly for complex products. It is true that under the current Product Liability Directive the burden of proof is less onerous on victims than under national fault-based liability rules, mainly because the victim does not have to prove fault. Nevertheless, proving that a product is defective (i.e. that it does not provide the level of safety a person is entitled to expect) is still (extremely) challenging for complex products, such as AI-enabled products, even if the victim does not have to prove how the product became unsafe. In cases that involve complex products such as AI-enabled products, smart products, or pharmaceuticals, it can be very challenging for victims of harm to prove that the product was defective and caused the damage. Due to the technical complexity of specific products, it could become difficult for the victim/injured party to obtain compensation, i.e. to identify the potentially liable person, to prove the defect in the product and the causal link between the defect and the damage. This difficulty becomes even higher as emerging digital technologies/products are becoming increasingly connected and complex. Furthermore, the current Product Liability Directive does not provide victims with a right to access technical information—held by a producer—that may be necessary to establish liability. Even if a claimant gets this technical information, proving liability can still be challenging, since there is no explicit possibility to alleviate the burden of proof under the PLD when victims face disproportionate difficulties. Furthermore, liability for undiscoverable defects is uncertain (e.g. machine learning). As a result, it is very difficult and costly to get compensation for harm caused by complex products, whereas individual victims may unfairly bear the risk of damage from undiscoverable defects. Moreover, according to the so-called development risk defence, the producer is allowed to avoid liability if the state of scientific and technical knowledge at the time when he put the product into circulation was not such as to enable the existence of the defect to be discovered. At the same time, however, the PLD allows Member States to derogate from applying the defence. It is reminded that, in the course of the public consultation, industry stakeholders argued that the development risk defence should not be changed/removed, whereas consumer organisations and NGOs argued that this exemption is inappropriate for AI (e.g., it is not applicable to software that can be updated; it creates a perverse incentive for producers to deploy products without adequate safety research) and, therefore, the development risk defence should be removed for all AI systems so that producers remain strictly liable for damage.

(b2) Liability claims are subject to a number of restrictions/limitations. In particular, consumers can claim compensation only for damage to property intended and used for private purposes. Also, consumers can claim compensation only for damage to property worth more than EUR 500. Therefore, claims for property damage valued at less than EUR 500 are not permitted and, as a result, consumers who suffer property damage less than EUR 500 receive no compensation. On the other hand, it was argued that any relaxation on the threshold for property damages would lead to more claims for minor damages, thus contradicting one of the main purposes of the threshold, namely to avoid litigation for small claims. Furthermore, consumers have to start legal proceedings within three (3) years of becoming aware of the damage. In addition, producers are released from liability for property damage and death/personal injury ten (10) years after placing the product on the market. As a result, under the current PLD, victims of harm that emerges after ten (10) years receive no compensation, whereas victims of harm who miss the three (3) year deadline to start legal proceedings get no compensation as well.

Therefore, due to the aforementioned shortcomings affecting the current PLD, it becomes clear that enhancing legal clarity is a crucial objective of the revised PLD. The aim of the revised Directive on liability of defective products ("the revised Product Liability Directive")[9] is to modernise the current EU's product liability regime, based on the strict liability of manufacturers/producers, for the compensation of personal injury, damage to property or data loss caused by unsafe products.

The revision of the Product Liability Directive aims to achieve two primary goals in response to the above-mentioned problems. These goals are built upon the existing PLD and include: (i) maintaining the proper functioning of the internal market, as well as promoting the free movement of goods and undistorted competition amongst market players; and (ii) ensuring that consumers' health and property are still afforded a high level of protection.

Accordingly, the revised PLD is designed to accommodate the latest technological advancements, circular economy business models, and global value chains. This is achieved by ensuring the following: (i) businesses and consumers/victims are subject to fair and predictable rules; (ii) victims are adequately compensated for any harm caused by hazardous products, including digital products and AI systems; and (iii) a level playing field exists between EU and non-EU manufacturers. To this end, the revised PLD attempts to achieve the following four specific objectives. First, in order to adapt product liability rules to the digital age and circular economy: (i) ensuring liability rules reflect the nature and risks of products in the digital age and circular economy; (ii) ensuring there is always an EU-based business that can be held liable, i.e. it is possible to obtain compensation, when defective products are bought directly from manufacturers/producers outside the EU. Second, in order to

---

[9] European Parliament legislative resolution of 12 March 2024 on the proposal for a Directive of the European Parliament and of the Council on liability for defective products (COM(2022)0495 – C9-0322/2022 – 2022/0302(COD)), (Ordinary legislative procedure: first reading) – P9_TC1-COD (2022)0302, Position of the European Parliament adopted at first reading on 12 March 2024 with a view to the adoption of Directive (EU) 2024/… of the European Parliament and of the Council on liability for defective products and repealing Council Directive 85/374/EEC ["Position of the European Parliament of 12 March 2024 for the adoption of a Directive on liability for defective products (revised PLD)"].

reduce disproportionate obstacles to getting compensation: (iii) easing the burden of proof in complex cases (and clarifying liability for undiscoverable defects), while ensuring fair balance between producers/manufacturers and consumers; (iv) easing restrictions on making claims as well as ensuring legal certainty by better aligning the PLD with the new legislative framework created by Decision 768/2008/EC7 and with product safety rules, and by codifying PLD-related case law.[10]

The revised PLD raises the likelihood of manufacturers/producers/economic operators operating within the EU facing considerable litigation risks (including the heightened risk of third-party litigation funding), abusive discovery of evidence, and overall higher insurance costs. For instance, the easing of the disclosure of evidence obligation (i.e., access to relevant evidence at the disposal of the manufacturer) and the alleviation/lightening of the burden of proof could lead to frivolous and/or fraudulent claims and put businesses at an unnecessary disadvantage, causing disproportionate harm for businesses, especially SMEs that do not have the required resources to defend themselves through prolonged court proceedings. It is also reminded that, apart from the presumption of defectiveness of a product and/or causality with the alleged damage and the introduction of new disclosure obligations (new requirements for discovery), the longstop limitation period is extended significantly for latent harm cases. Furthermore, the removal of minimum thresholds and maximum limits for compensation claims, especially when combined with the EU's new class actions mechanism, could lead to more claims for minor damages. Also, there is a risk that claimants and "potential claimants" could be encouraged to bring early-stage cases (lawsuits) simply with the ulterior motive of seeking access to proprietary information ('fishing expeditions'). As a result, we might see an increased volume of legal claims, leading to higher insurance costs, hindering innovation, and putting smaller companies at risk.

Therefore, the evidentiary framework undergoes significant transformation. It remains to be seen how the rather ambiguous alleviation of the plaintiff's burden of proof "in complex cases" and the defendant's obligation to disclose "relevant evidence" will be implemented by the Member States (especially since many EU countries currently have limited or non-existent disclosure mechanisms under their

---

[10] Commission Staff Working Document, "Impact Assessment Report – Accompanying the document Proposal for a Directive of the European Parliament and of the Council on liability for defective products", SWD(2022) 316 final, Brussels, 28.9.2022, at p. 27: "*SO 5: Ease restrictions on making claims, while ensuring fair balance between producers and consumers*: The aim here is to ease restrictions that currently disproportionately limit consumers' ability to make claims".

For the initiative's five specific objectives, see also:

Commission Staff Working Document, "Subsidiarity Grid – Accompanying the document Proposal for a Directive of the European Parliament and of the Council on liability for defective products, SWD(2022) 315 final, Brussels, 28.9.2022, at p. 3.

Commission Staff Working Document, "Executive Summary of the Impact Assessment Report – Accompanying the document Proposal for a Directive of the European Parliament and of the Council on liability for defective products", SWD(2022) 317 final, Brussels, 28.9.2022, at p. 1.

See also the Commission's proposal for a revised Product Liability Directive, Explanatory Memorandum, at p. 2.

national laws). The interpretation and scope of several new provisions within the revised PLD are unclear, underscoring the importance of monitoring their adoption and implementation by Member States and subsequent scrutiny by national courts. Thus, it could be argued that, while the revised Product Liability Directive strengthens the EU product liability regime for consumers, it concurrently reduces legal certainty for businesses. The revised PLD appears poised to tip the scales further in favor of claimants, especially in complex cases, thus increasing the likelihood of manufacturers/producers facing significant litigation risks, including the heightened risk of third-party litigation funding. This new, more claimant-oriented product liability regime has the potential to substantially reshape the business risk environment within the EU, representing a major shift in the European product liability risk landscape.

Overall, however, I believe that the revised PLD succeeds in striking a delicate balance between protecting citizens/consumers and supporting technological innovation. In practice, the liability framework becomes much more demanding for the industry, but without becoming excessively burdensome—businesses are subject to fair and predictable rules. After all, the requirements mainly concern obligations related to product safety. Therefore, the new legal framework appears to "reward" companies that are willing to invest in even safer products for consumers. Thus, without overlooking the fact that the scope of several new provisions within the revised PLD are unclear and we must await their implementation by Member States and interpretation by national courts decisions, the revised PLD provides legal certainty to the industry regarding the risks they may encounter in the course of their business. This is achieved, *inter alia*, by increasing the emphasis on defendants to ensure full compliance with mandatory product safety requirements and to have appropriate documentation and internal procedures in place. At the same time, the revised PLD ensures that consumers' health and property are afforded a high level of protection, instills confidence in the safety and reliability of AI-related products and services, reduces disproportionate obstacles to obtaining compensation, and maintains an appropriate balance between the interests of claimants and defendants in Member State courts.

10.4 Concluding Remarks

The forthcoming EU civil liability regime for AI and other innovative products becomes more claimant/consumer-friendly (pro-claimant). Both Directives (the revised PLD and the proposed AI Liability Directive) raise the likelihood of manufacturers/providers/economic operators operating within the EU facing considerable litigation risks (including the heightened risk of third-party litigation funding), abusive discovery of evidence, and overall higher insurance costs.

On the other hand, one of the main objectives of the forthcoming EU liability regime for AI and other emerging digital technologies is to ensure that consumers will have a fair chance of getting compensation, especially in complex cases.

Therefore, specific measures have been introduced to address unnecessary obstacles to getting compensation for damage, i.e., to ensure that injured/harmed parties are equally protected throughout the EU. It is anticipated that this could lead to consumer uptake of AI and other emerging digital technologies as well as creating trust in innovative products/services and in justice systems. It could also ensure that businesses and consumers are subject to fair and predictable rules, and victims are adequately compensated for any harm caused by hazardous products, including digital products and AI systems.

It is expected that the forthcoming EU liability framework for AI and other emerging digital technologies (designed to accommodate the latest technological developments, circular economy business models, and global value chains) will succeed in achieving the EU's overarching objective, namely to strike the right balance between protecting citizens and supporting technological innovation.

This could be achieved by ensuring that businesses and consumers/victims are subject to fair and predictable rules (legal certainty), and victims are adequately compensated for any harm caused by hazardous products, including digital products and AI systems. The forthcoming EU liability framework reduces disproportionate obstacles to getting compensation, tackles restrictions on making claims, eases the burden of proof in complex cases, while ensuring fair balance between producers/ manufacturers and consumers. By addressing unnecessary obstacles to getting compensation for damage, it is ensured that injured parties/victims are equally protected throughout the EU, leading to consumer uptake of AI and other emerging digital technologies as well as creating trust in innovative products/services and in justice systems. It also ensures that consumers' health and property are afforded a high level of protection and, at the same time, strikes an appropriate balance between the interests of claimants and defendants in Member State courts.

Therefore, the forthcoming EU liability framework for AI and other emerging digital technologies could succeed in promoting legal certainty and predictability, guaranteeing user safety and adequate/fair compensation for victims, while fostering innovation across the EU, without discouraging investment and innovation by producers/manufacturers and providers of AI-powered products and services. If the implementation and enforcement of the revised PLD and the proposed AI Liability Directive can be effectively monitored, this will strengthen the internal market, instill confidence in the safety and reliability of AI-enabled and other innovative products and services, encourage further investment, and stimulate the uptake of trustworthy AI. Therefore, under the current circumstances, the EU's approach appears pragmatic, well-balanced and, consequently, likely to be successful. Nonetheless, the ultimate assessment of the forthcoming EU civil liability framework for AI and other emerging digital technologies will depend on its impact on investment, innovation, safety, and its efficiency in providing remedies/compensation to affected parties. In short, it will have to be judged in practice by the outcome it delivers and the effectiveness it demonstrates.

MIX
Papier aus verantwortungsvollen Quellen
Paper from responsible sources
FSC® C105338

If you have any concerns about our products,
you can contact us on
ProductSafety@springernature.com

In case Publisher is established outside the EU,
the EU authorized representative is:
Springer Nature Customer Service Center GmbH
Europaplatz 3, 69115 Heidelberg, Germany

Printed by Libri Plureos GmbH
in Hamburg, Germany